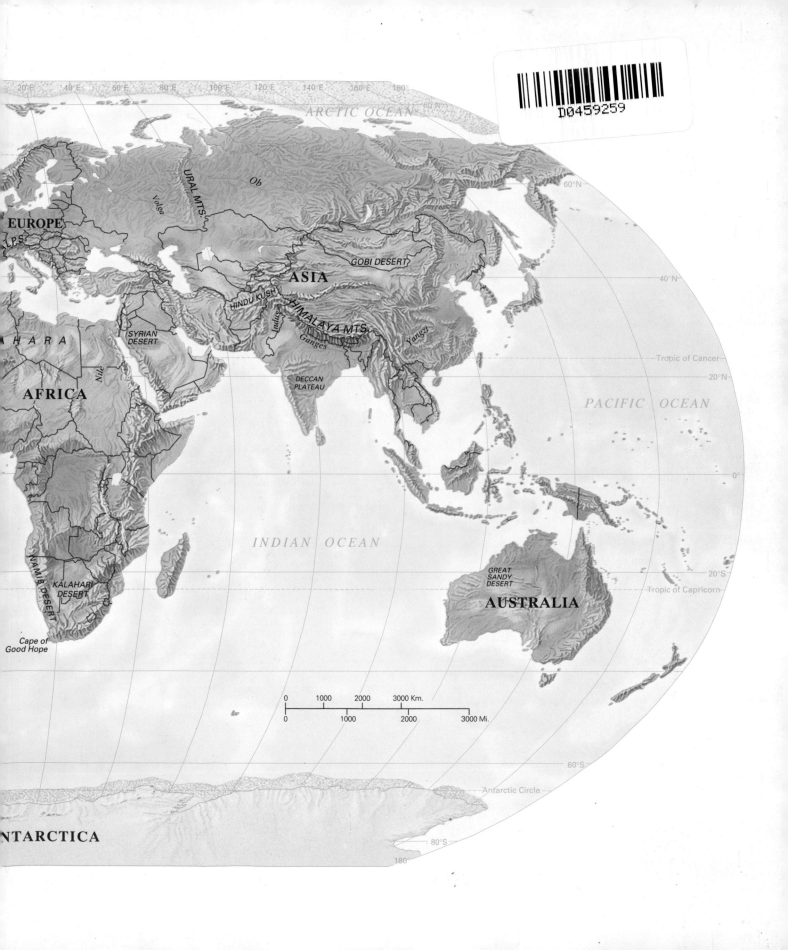

THE EARTH AND ITS PEOPLES
A GLOBAL HISTORY

SECOND EDITION

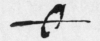

Richard W. Bulliet
Columbia University

Pamela Kyle Crossley
Dartmouth College

Daniel R. Headrick
Roosevelt University

Steven W. Hirsch
Tufts University

Lyman L. Johnson
University of North Carolina–Charlotte

David Northrup
Boston College

Houghton Mifflin Company   Boston   New York

Editor-in-chief for history and political science: Jean L. Woy
Sponsoring editor: Nancy Blaine
Senior development editor: Jennifer E. Sutherland
Associate editor: Julie Dunn
Editorial associate: Gillie Jones
Senior project editor: Carol Newman
Senior designer: Henry Rachlin
Senior production/design coordinator: Jill Haber
Senior manufacturing coordinator: Marie Barnes
Senior marketing manager: Sandra McGuire

Cover design: Anthony L. Saizon
Cover image: *Akbar's Journey to Agra by Water in 1562.* Painting from the Akbamama. Gouache on paper. Mughal.Victoria and Albert Museum, London, Great Britain.

Printed in the U.S.A.

Library of Congress Catalog Card Number: 00-132429

ISBN: 0-618-00073-9

1 2 3 4 5 6 7 8 9-VH-04 03 02 01 00

Brief Contents

CONTENTS

PART TWO

THE FORMATION OF NEW CULTURAL COMMUNITIES, 1000 B.C.E.–400 C.E.

81

4 NEW CIVILIZATIONS IN THE AMERICAS AND WESTERN EURASIA, 1200–250 B.C.E.   84

5 GREECE AND IRAN, 1000–30 B.C.E.   113

PART FIVE

THE GLOBE ENCOMPASSED, 1500–1750
441

PART EIGHT

THE PERILS AND PROMISES OF A GLOBAL COMMUNITY, 1945–2000

827

MAPS

ENVIRONMENT AND TECHNOLOGY

SOCIETY AND CULTURE

PREFACE

History is not easy. We met ten years ago in a conference room at Houghton Mifflin: six professional historians seated around a table hammering out our ideas on what a global history textbook at the start of a new millennium should be. Together we brought to the project a high level of knowledge about Africa, the Americas, Asia, Europe, the Middle East. We argued; we made up over dinner; we debated some more.

But there was no short cut. We were determined to write the best history we could. That meant testing ideas aloud; considering alternatives put forward by smart, articulate colleagues; and bargaining over what to include and what, with regret, to pass over. We believe the result was worth the sweat.

So began the Preface to the first edition of this book. Then came the wait for responses and a fresh wave of satisfaction as teachers and students from a wide variety of institutions reported positive results from the classroom. Unalloyed praise, however, was too much to hope for from a first edition. Users of the book spotted many possibilities for improvement, and these became our mandate for preparing the second edition.

Our overall goal remains the same: to produce a textbook that not only speaks for the past but speaks to today's student and today's teacher. Students and instructors alike should take away from this text a broad vision of human societies beginning as sparse and disconnected communities reacting creatively to local circumstances; experiencing ever more intensive stages of contact, interpenetration, and cultural expansion and amalgamation; and arriving at a twenty-first century world in which people increasingly visualize a single global community.

Along this trajectory, different parts of the world have moved or paused at different points in time, and each has followed its own path. Domestication of plants and animals in the Western Hemisphere developed independently of the analogous process in the Eastern Hemisphere, as did the growth of empires. Similarly, industrialization of western Europe and North America preceded by a century or two industrialization elsewhere. Yet the world all came together in the late twentieth century, a paradoxical period of global political and economic forces confronting intensified reassertions of particular national and cultural identities. People who speak today of an emerging global community are answered by others who insist on their own distinctive identities.

Process, not progress, is the keynote of this book: a steady process of change over time, at first differently experienced in various regions but eventually entangling peoples from all parts of the globe. Students should come away from this book with a sense that the problems and promises of their world are rooted in a past in which peoples of every sort, in every part of the world, confronted problems of a similar character and coped with them as best they could. We believe our efforts will help students see where their world has come from and learn thereby something useful for their own lives.

CENTRAL THEME

We subtitled *The Earth and Its Peoples* "A Global History" because the book explores the common challenges and experiences that unite the human past. Although the dispersal of early humans to every livable environment resulted in myriad different economic, social, political, and cultural systems, all societies displayed analogous patterns in meeting their needs and exploiting their environments. Our challenge was to select the particular data and episodes that would best illuminate these global patterns of human experience.

To meet this challenge, we adopted a central theme to serve as the spinal cord of our history. That theme is "technology and environment," the commonplace bases of all human societies at all times and a theme that grants no special favor to any cultural group even as it embraces subjects of the broadest topical, chronological, and geographical range.

It is vital for students to understand that technology, in the broad sense of experience-based knowledge of the physical world, underlies all human activity. Writing is a technology, but so is oral transmission from generation to generation of lore about medicinal or poisonous plants. The magnetic compass is a navigational technology, but so is Polynesian mariners' hard-won knowledge of winds, currents, and tides that made possible the settlement of the Pacific islands.

All technological development has come about in

interaction with environments, both physical and human, and has, in turn, affected those environments. The story of how humanity has changed the face of the globe is an integral part of our central theme.

Yet technology and the environment do not by themselves explain or underlie all important episodes of human change and experience. Discussions of politics, culture, and society constantly interweave with our central theme to reveal additional historical patterns. Most notable among these is the interplay of dominance—whether political, economic, social, religious, or gender—with human variety. When narrating the histories of empires, for example, we describe a range of human experiences within and beyond the imperial frontiers without assuming that the imperial institutions are a more fit topic for discussion than the economic and social organization of pastoral nomads or the life patterns of peasant women.

CHANGES IN THE SECOND EDITION

Our overriding concerns in conceiving the second edition were updating the scholarship, better unifying the presentation, and addressing issues raised by instructors and students who had used the first edition. The most obvious change is the adoption of a full-color format, which not only brightens the page but makes maps clearer and more effective. The opening pages of each part of the text were similarly reconceived to give students a geographic and chronological overview of what is to come. The timelines and world maps that now accompany the part-opening essays are designed to focus student's attention on broad themes and historical benchmarks. Consolidated timelines within each chapter enable students to see at a glance the sorts of comparisons being made in the text.

Guides to the pronunciation of uncommon words and foreign terms, previously at the back of the book, now appear at the bottom of each page. Key terms are bold-faced in the text, listed at the end of each chapter, and defined in the Glossary at the end of the book. In addition, focus questions at the end of the vignette opening each chapter call attention to the main themes of the chapter. We believe that these unobtrusive changes will improve students' understanding of the main narrative and make it easier for them to grasp the main points of each chapter, as well as to review for examinations.

We sifted through a mass of helpful suggestions on how to revise and reorganize the content itself. Along with hundreds of minor revisions and clarifications, we effected a number of major changes:

- To facilitate comparison among different regions of the globe, we moved discussion of the earliest periods of Western Hemisphere history from Chapter 12 to Chapter 4.
- We greatly increased the coverage of Russian history, including entirely new sections in Chapter 10 (Chapter 9 of the first edition) and Chapter 22.
- Intellectual history gained increased attention with expanded coverage of Confucianism and Legalism in China; scholasticism, the Renaissance, and the Enlightenment in Europe; and twentieth-century modernism.
- Chapters 9 and 10 in the first edition were reversed, so the discussion of the rise of Islam now precedes that of Christian Europe.
- Coverage of the Industrial Revolution was revised to take in a broader geographical purview.
- The organization of twentieth-century history (Chapters 30–35) was completely reconceived to strengthen the chronological narrative.
- Suggested Reading lists were updated with recent scholarship.

The full-color format favored substantial changes in the illustration program, and many of the feature essays also were changed. Topics for the eleven new "Environment and Technology" essays include water engineering in Rome and China, Inca roads, Vasco da Gama's fleet, biomedical technologies, and global warming. The primary-source document feature of the first edition has been renamed "Society and Culture" to emphasize its complementarity with "Environment and Technology." Topics for the thirteen essays new to this edition include the Babylonian New Year's festival, the status of women in Indian literature, everyday law in Ming China, Charles Babbage, Ada Lovelace, and the "Analytical Engine," self-government in Africa, and "Silent Spring."

ORGANIZATION

The Earth and Its Peoples uses eight broad chronological divisions to define its conceptual scheme of global historical development. In **Part One: The Emergence of Human Communities, to 500 B.C.E.,** we examine important patterns of human communal organization. Early human communities were small, and most parts of the world were populated sparsely, if at all. As the human species spread worldwide, it encountered and responded to enormously diverse environmental conditions. Humans' responses gave rise to many technologies, ranging from implements for meeting daily needs—such as acquiring and handling foods, fabricating clothing and shelter, and utilizing the natural forces of fire, wind, and animal power—to the compilation of exhaustive lore about plants, animals, the climate, and the heavens.

Part Two: The Formation of New Cultural Communities, 1000 B.C.E.–400 C.E., introduces the concept of a "cultural community," in the sense of a coherent pattern of activities and symbols pertaining to a specific human community. Although all human communities develop distinctive cultures, including those discussed in Part One, historical development in this stage of global history prolonged and magnified the impact of some cultures more than others. In the geographically contiguous African-Eurasian landmass, as well as in Mesoamerica and the Andean region of the Western Hemisphere, the cultures that proved to have the most enduring influence traced their roots to the second and first millennia B.C.E.

Part Three: Growth and Interaction of Cultural Communities, 300 B.C.E.–1200 C.E., deals with early episodes of technological, social, and cultural exchange and interaction on a continental scale both within and beyond the framework of imperial expansion. These are so different from earlier interactions arising from more limited conquests or extensions of political boundaries that they constitute a distinct era in world history—an era that set the world on the path of increasing global interaction and interdependence that it has been following ever since.

In **Part Four: Interregional Patterns of Culture and Contact, 1200–1550,** we take a look at the world during the three and a half centuries that saw both intensified cultural and commercial contact and increasingly confident self-definition of cultural communities in Europe, Asia, and Africa. The Mongol conquest of a vast empire extending from the Pacific Ocean to eastern Europe greatly stimulated trade and interaction. In the West, strengthened European kingdoms began maritime expansion in the Atlantic, forging direct ties with sub-Saharan Africa and beginning the conquest of the civilizations of the Western Hemisphere.

Part Five: The Globe Encompassed, 1500–1750, treats a period dominated by the global effects of European expansion and continued economic growth. European ships took over, expanded, and extended the maritime trade of the Indian Ocean, coastal Africa, and the Asian rim of the Pacific Ocean. This maritime commercial enterprise had its counterpart in European colonial empires in the Americas and a new Atlantic trading system. The contrasting capacities and fortunes of traditional land empires and new maritime empires, along with the exchange of domestic plants and animals between the hemispheres, underline the technological and environmental dimensions of this first era of complete global interaction.

In **Part Six: Revolutions Reshape the World, 1750–1870,** the word *revolution* is used in several senses: in the political sense of governmental overthrow, as in France and the Americas; in the metaphorical sense of radical transformative change, as in the Industrial Revolution; and in the broadest sense of a perception of a profound change in circumstances and world-view. Technology and environment lie at the core of these developments. With the rapid ascendancy of the Western belief that science and technology could overcome all challenges—environmental or otherwise—technology became not only an instrument of transformation but also an instrument of domination, to the point of threatening the integrity and autonomy of cultural traditions in non-industrial lands.

Part Seven: Global Dominance and Diversity, 1850–1945, examines the development of a world arena in which people conceived of events on a global scale. Imperialism, world war, international economic connections, and world-encompassing ideological tendencies, such as nationalism and socialism, present the picture of a globe becoming increasingly interconnected. European dominance took on a worldwide dimension, seeming at times to threaten the diversity of human cultural experience with permanent subordination to European values and philosophies, while at other times triggering strong political or cultural resistance.

For **Part Eight: The Perils and Promises of a Global Community, 1945–2000,** we divide the last half of the twentieth century into three time periods: 1945–1975, 1975–1991, and 1991–2000. The challenges of the Cold War and post-colonial nation building dominated the period as a whole and involved global economic, technological, and political forces that became increasingly important factors in all aspects of human life. Technology plays a central role in this part, because of its integral role in the growth of a global community and because its many benefits in improving the quality of life seem clouded by real and potential negative impacts on the environment.

FORMATS

To accommodate different academic calendars and approaches to the course, *The Earth and Its Peoples* is issued in three formats. There is a one-volume hardcover version containing all 35 chapters, along with a two-volume paperback edition: Volume I: *To 1550* (Chapters 1–17), and Volume II: *Since 1500* (Chapters 17–35). For readers at institutions with the quarter system, we offer a three-volume paperback version: Volume A: *To 1200* (Chapters 1–12); Volume B: *From 1200 to 1870* (Chapters 12–27); and Volume C: *Since 1750* (Chapters 23–35).

A new introduction to Volume II has been written for this edition to recapitulate themes contained in Volume I and lay a groundwork for students studying only the period since 1500.

SUPPLEMENTS

We have assembled with care an array of text supplements to aid students in learning and instructors in teaching. These supplements, including *@history* web site, *GeoQuest: World CD-ROM*, a *Study Guide*, an *Instructor's Resource Manual, Test Items, Computerized Test Items*, and *Map Transparencies*, provide a tightly integrated program of teaching and learning.

Houghton Mifflin's *@history* web site provides a wealth of text-based materials for students and instructors. For students, this site offers primary sources, text-specific self-tests, and gateways to relevant history sites. In addition, *History WIRED: Web Intensive Research Exercises and Documents*, prepared by Jonathan Lee of San Antonio College, offers text-specific links to visual and written sources on the World Wide Web, along with exercises to enhance learning. Additional resources are provided for instructors, including historical maps suitable for classroom presentation or assignments.

A New CD-ROM, *GeoQuest: World,* features thirty interactive maps that illuminate world history events from the days of the Persian Empire to the present. Each map is accompanied by exercises with answers and essay questions. The four different types of interactivity allow students to move at their own pace through each section. Four demo maps can be viewed on the Houghton Mifflin *@history* web site.

The *Study Guide,* authored by Michele G. Scott James of MiraCosta College, contains learning objectives, chapter outlines (with space for students' notes on particular sections), key-term identifications, multiple-choice questions, short-answer and essay questions, and map exercises. Included too are distinctive "comparison charts" to help students organize the range of information about different cultures and events discussed in each chapter. The *Study Guide* is published in two volumes, to correspond to Volumes I and II of the textbook: Volume I contains Chapters 1–17; Volume II, Chapters 17–35.

The *Instructor's Resource Manual,* prepared by Harold M. Tanner of the University of North Texas, provides useful teaching strategies for the global history course and tips for getting the most out of the textbook. Each chapter contains instructional objectives, a detailed chapter outline, lecture topics with pertinent suggested readings, discussion questions, paper topic suggestions, and audio-visual resources. The revised preface contains new information on journal writing, as well as contact information for organizations, multimedia distributors, and journals.

Each chapter of the *Test Items,* revised by Jane Scimeca of Brookdale Community College, offers 20 to 25 key-term identifications, 5 to 10 essay questions with answer guidelines, 35 to 40 multiple-choice questions, and 3 to 5 history and geography exercises. We also provide a computerized version of the *Test Items,* to enable instructors to alter, replace, or add questions. Each entry in the *Computerized Test Items* is numbered according to the printed test items to ease the creation of customized tests.

In addition, a set of *Transparencies* of all the maps in the textbook is available on adoption.

ACKNOWLEDGMENTS

In preparing the second edition, we benefited from the critical readings of many colleagues. Our sincere thanks go in particular to the following instructors: Henry Abramson, Florida Atlantic University; Paul V. Adams, Shippensburg University/University of San Carlos; Maria S. Arbelaez, University of Nebraska at Omaha; William J. Astore, United States Air Force Academy; Fritz Blackwell, Washington State University; Thomas Borstelmann, Cornell University; Byron Cannon, University of Utah; David A. Chappell, University of Hawaii; Nancy Clark, California Polytechnic State University at San Luis Obispo; Lee Congdon, James Madison University; James Coolsen, Shippensburg University; Bruce Cruikshank, Hastings College; Linda T. Darling, University of Arizona; Susan Deans-Smith, University of Texas at Austin; Gregory C. Ference, Salisbury State University; Alan Fisher, Michigan State University; Donald M. Fisher, Niagara County Community College; Cathy A. Frierson, University of New Hampshire; Rosanna Gatens, Belmont University; Lorne E. Glaim, Pacific Union College; Matthew S. Gordon, Miami University; Steve Gosch, University of Wisconsin at Eau Claire; Kolleen M. Guy, University of Texas at San Antonio; James R. Hansen, Auburn University; Randolph C. Head, University of California at Riverside; David Hertzel, Southwestern Oklahoma State University; Richard J. Hoffman, San Francisco State University; Catherine M. Jones, North Georgia College and State University; Joy Kammerling, Eastern Illinois University; Carol A. Keller, San Antonio College; Jonathan Lee, San Antonio College; Miriam R. Levin, Case Western Reserve University; Richard Lewis, St. Cloud State University; James E. Lindsay, Colorado State University; Charles W. McClellan, Radford University; Andrea McElderry, University of Louisville; Stephen L. McFarland, Auburn University; Gregory McMahon, University of New Hampshire; Mark McLeod, University of Delaware; Stephen S. Michot, Mississippi County Community College; Shawn W. Miller, Brigham Young University; Kalala Joseph Ngalamulume, Central Washington University; Patricia O'Neill, Central Oregon Community College; Chandrika Paul, Shippensburg University; John R. Pavia, Ithaca College; Thomas Earl Porter, North Carolina A&T State University; Jean H. Quataert, SUNY at Binghamton; William Reddy, Duke University; Thomas Reeves, Roxbury Community College; Dennis Reinhartz, University of Texas at Arlington; Richard Rice, University of Tennessee at Chattanooga; Jane Scimeca, Brookdale Community College; Alyssa Goldstein Sepinwall, California State University at San Marcos; Deborah Shackleton, United States Air Force Academy; Anita Shelton, Eastern Illinois University; David R. Smith, California State Polytechnic University at Pomona; Mary Frances Smith, Ohio University; George E. Snow, Shippensburg University; Charlotte D. Staelin, Washington College; Paul D. Steeves, Stetson University; Yi Sun, University of San Diego; Willard Sunderland, University of Cincinnati; Thaddeus Sunseri, Colorado State University; Sara W. Tucker, Washburn University; John M. VanderLippe, SUNY at New Paltz; Mary A. Watrous-Schlesinger, Washington State University; Eric Van Young, University of California at San Diego; and Alex Zukas, National University, San Diego.

We also want to extend our collective thanks to Lynda Schaffer for her early conceptual contributions as well as to the history departments of Shippensburg University, the United States Air Force Academy, and the State University of New York at New Paltz for arranging reviewer conferences that provided crucial feedback for our revision of the book. Individually, Richard W. Bulliet thanks Jack Garraty and Isser Woloch for first involving him in world history; Pamela Kyle Crossley wishes to thank Gene Garthwaite, Charles Wood, and David Morgan; Steven W. Hirsch extends his gratitude to Dennis Trout and Peter L. D. Reid; Lyman L. Johnson extends his to Kenneth J. Andrien, Richard Boyer, Grant D. Hones, William M. Ringle, Hendrik Kraay, Daniel Dupre, and Steven W. Usselman; and David Northrup thanks Allen Howard and Prasanan Parthasarathi. Lyman Johnson also thanks the members of the Department of History of North Carolina A&T University for their many helpful and pertinent suggestions.

The three people who kept us on course in preparing the second edition deserve our special thanks: Jean L. Woy, Editor-in-Chief for History and Political Science; Nancy Blaine, Sponsoring Editor; and Jennifer E. Sutherland, Senior Development Editor. In carrying out our task, we got to know and value the work of several new staff at Houghton Mifflin: Carol Newman, Senior Project Editor; Julie Dunn, Associate Editor; Gillie Jones, Editorial Associate; Jennifer O'Neill, Editorial Assistant; and Henry Rachlin, Senior Designer. We also had the pleasure of working again with several people who helped so much with the first edition, including Charlotte Miller, Map Editor; Carole Frolich, Photo Researcher; Anthony L. Saizon, Design Director; Jill Haber, Senior Production/Design Coordinator; and Marie Barnes, Senior Manufacturing Coordinator.

We thank also the many students whose questions and concerns, expressed directly or through their instructors, shaped much of this revision. We continue to welcome all our readers' suggestions, queries, and criticisms. Please contact us at our respective institutions or at this e-mail address: college. hmco. com/history.

ABOUT THE AUTHORS

Richard W. Bulliet   Professor of Middle Eastern History at Columbia University and Director of its Middle East Institute, Richard W. Bulliet received his Ph.D. from Harvard University. He has written scholarly works on a number of topics: the social history of medieval Iran (*The Patricians of Nishapur*), the historical competition between pack camels and wheeled transport (*The Camel and the Wheel*), the process of conversion to Islam (*Conversion to Islam in the Medieval Period*), and the overall course of Islamic social history (*Islam: The View from the Edge*). He is the editor of the *Columbia History of the Twentieth Century*. He has published four novels, co-edited *The Encyclopedia of the Modern Middle East*, and hosted an educational television series on the Middle East. He was awarded a fellowship by the John Simon Guggenheim Memorial Foundation.

Pamela Kyle Crossley   Pamela Kyle Crossley received her Ph.D. in Modern Chinese History from Yale University. She is Professor of History, Rosenwald Research Professor in the Arts and Sciences, and Chair of Asian and Middle Eastern Studies at Dartmouth College. Her books include *A Translucent Mirror: History and Identity in Qing Imperial Ideology*, *The Manchus*, and *Orphan Warriors: Three Manchu Generations and the End of the Qing World*. Her research, which concentrates on the cultural history of China, Inner Asia, and Central Asia, has most recently been supported by the John Simon Guggenheim Memorial Foundation and the National Endowment for the Humanities.

Daniel R. Headrick   Daniel R. Headrick received his Ph.D. in History from Princeton University. Professor of History and Social Science at Roosevelt University in Chicago, he is the author of several books on the history of technology, imperialism, and international relations, including *The Tools of Empire: Technology and European Imperialism in the Nineteenth Century*, *The Tentacles of Progress: Technology Transfer in the Age of Imperialism*, *The Invisible Weapon: Telecommunications and International Politics*, and *When Information Came of Age: Technologies of Knowledge in the Age of Reason and Revolution, 1700–1850*. His articles have appeared in the *Journal of World History* and the *Journal of Modern History*, and he has been awarded fellowships by the National Endowment for the Humanities, the John Simon Guggenheim Memorial Foundation, and the Alfred P. Sloan Foundation.

Steven W. Hirsch   Steven W. Hirsch holds a Ph.D. in Classics from Stanford University and is currently Associate Professor of Classics and History at Tufts University. He has received grants from the National Endowment for the Humanities and the Massachusetts Foundation for Humanities and Public Policy. His research and publications include *The Friendship of the Barbarians: Xenophon and the Persian Empire*, as well as articles and reviews in the *Classical Journal*, the *American Journal of Philology*, and the *Journal of Interdisciplinary History*.

Lyman L. Johnson   Professor of History at the University of North Carolina at Charlotte, Lyman L. Johnson earned his Ph.D. in Latin American History from the University of Connecticut. A two-time Senior Fulbright-Hays Lecturer, he also has received fellowships from the Tinker Foundation, the Social Science Research Council, the National Endowment for the Humanities, and the American Philosophical Society. His recent books include *The Faces of Honor* (with Sonya Lipsett-Rivera), *The Problem of Order in Changing Societies*, *Essays on the Price History of Eighteenth-Century Latin America* (with Enrique Tandeter), and *Colonial Latin America* (with Mark A. Burkholder). He also has published in journals, including the *Hispanic American Historical Review*, the *Journal of Latin American Studies*, the *International Review of Social History*, *Social History*, and *Desarrollo Económico*. He recently served as president of the Conference on Latin American History.

David Northrup   Professor of History at Boston College, David Northrup earned his Ph.D. in African and European History from the University of California at Los Angeles. He has published scholarly volumes on precolonial Nigeria, on precolonial and colonial Congo, on the Atlantic slave trade, and on Asian, African, and Pacific Islander indentured labor in the nineteenth century. His recent work appeared in the *Oxford History of the British Empire*, *Revue française d'histoire d'outremer*, *Slavery and Abolition*, and the *Journal of World History*. He currently serves on the Executive Council of the World History Association and has received research support from the Fulbright-Hays Commission, the National Endowment for the Humanities, and the Social Science Research Council.

NOTE ON SPELLING AND USAGE

Where necessary for clarity, dates are followed by the letters C.E. or B.C.E. The abbreviation C.E. stands for "Common Era" and is equivalent to A.D. (*anno Domini*, Latin for "in the year of the Lord"). The abbreviation B.C.E stands for "before the Common Era" and means the same as B.C. ("before Christ"). In keeping with our goal of approaching world history without special concentration on one culture or another, we chose these neutral abbreviations as appropriate to our enterprise. Because many readers will be more familiar with English than with metric measurements, however, units of measure are generally given in the English system, with metric equivalents following in parentheses.

In general, Chinese has been romanized according to the *pinyin* method. Exceptions include proper names well established in English (e.g., Canton, Chiang Kai-shek) and a few English words borrowed from Chinese (e.g., kowtow). Spellings of Arabic, Ottoman Turkish, Persian, Mongolian, Manchu, Japanese, and Korean names and terms avoid special diacritical marks for letters that are pronounced only slightly differently in English. An apostrophe is used to indicate when two Chinese syllables are pronounced separately (e.g., Chang'an).

For words transliterated from languages that use the Arabic script—Arabic, Ottoman Turkish, Perisan, Urdu—the apostrophe indicating separately pronounced syllables may represent either of two special consonants, the *hamza* or the *ain*. Because most English-speakers do not hear the distinction between these two, they have not been distinguished in transliteration and are not indicated when they occur at the beginning or end of a word. As with Chinese, some words and commonly used place-names from these languages are given familiar English spellings (e.g., Quran instead of Qur'an, Cairo instead of al-Qahira). Arabic romanization has normally been used for terms relating to Islam, even where the context justifies slightly different Turkish or Persian forms, again for ease of comprehension.

There is an ongoing debate about how best to render Amerindian words in English. It has been common for authors writing in English to follow Mexican usage for Nahuatl and Yucatec Maya words and place-names. In this style, for example, the capital of the Aztec state is spelled Tenochtitlán, and the important late Maya city-state is spelled Chichén Itzá. Although these forms are still common even in the specialist literature, we have chosen to follow the scholarship that sees these accents as unnecessary. The exceptions are modern place-names, such as Mérida and Yucatán, which are accented. A similar problem exists for the spelling of Quechua and Aymara words from the Andean region of South America. Although there is significant disagreement among scholars, we follow the emerging consensus and use the spellings khipu (not quipu), Tiwanaku (not Tiahuanaco), and Wari (not Huari). However, we keep Inca (not Inka) and Cuzco (not Cusco), since these spellings are expected by most of our potential readers and we hope to avoid confusion.

Note on Spelling and Usage

THE EARTH AND ITS PEOPLES

A GLOBAL HISTORY

PART ONE

THE EMERGENCE OF HUMAN COMMUNITIES,

TO 500 B.C.E.

*M*ost of the long evolutionary history of the human species occurred before the advent of writing and thus lies beyond the conventional bounds of history. Nevertheless, these remote events are fundamental for understanding the origins of human nature and culture.

Human beings evolved over several million years from primates in Africa. Differing from other primates in their ability to walk upright on two legs and their possession of large brains, hands with opposable thumbs, and the capacity for speech, early humans used teamwork and created tools that enabled them to survive in diverse environments. Relatively rapidly they spread to almost every habitable area of the world, sustaining themselves by hunting and by gathering wild plant products. Then, around 10,000 years ago, some human groups began to cultivate plants, domesticate animals, and make pottery vessels for storage. One consequence of this shift to agriculture was the emergence of permanent settlements—at first small villages but eventually larger towns as well.

The earliest complex societies arose in the great river valleys of Asia and Africa: around 3100 B.C.E. in the valley between the Tigris and Euphrates Rivers in Mesopotamia and along the Nile River in Egypt, somewhat later in the valley of the Indus River in Pakistan and on the floodplain of the Yellow River in China. In these arid regions, agriculture depended on irrigation with river water, and centers of political power arose to organize the massive human labor required to dig and maintain channels to carry water to the fields and dikes to protect lives and property from river floodings.

1

Kings and priests dominated these early societies. Kings controlled the military forces; priests managed the temples and the wealth of the gods. Within the urban centers—in the midst of palaces, temples, fortification walls, and other monumental buildings—lived administrators, soldiers, priests, merchants, craftsmen, and others with specialized skills. The production of surplus food grown on rural estates by a dependent peasantry sustained the activities of these groups. Professional scribes kept administrative and financial records and preserved their civilization's religious and scientific knowledge.

Over time, certain centers extended their influence and came to dominate broad expanses of territory. The rulers of these early empires were motivated primarily by the need to secure access to vital raw materials—especially tin and copper, from which to make bronze. A similar motive accounts for the development of long-distance trade and diplomatic relations between major powers. Fueling long-distance trade was the desire for bronze, which had both practical and symbolic importance. From bronze, artisans made weapons, tools and utensils, and ritual objects. Ownership of bronze items was a sign of wealth and power. Trade and diplomacy contributed to the spread of culture and technology from the core river-valley areas to neighboring regions, such as Nubia and the Aegean.

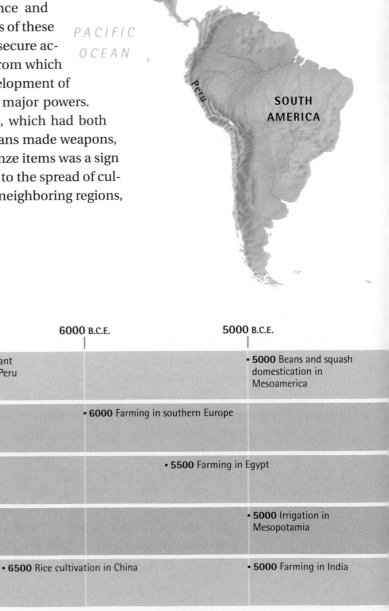

	8000 B.C.E.	7000 B.C.E.	6000 B.C.E.	5000 B.C.E.
Americas		• **7000** Incipient plant domestication in Peru		• **5000** Beans and squash domestication in Mesoamerica
Europe	Spread of Indo-European languages		• **6000** Farming in southern Europe	
Africa	• **8000** Farming in eastern Sahara			• **5500** Farming in Egypt
Middle East	• **8000** Domestication of plants and animals in Fertile Crescent			• **5000** Irrigation in Mesopotamia
Asia and Oceania			• **6500** Rice cultivation in China	• **5000** Farming in India

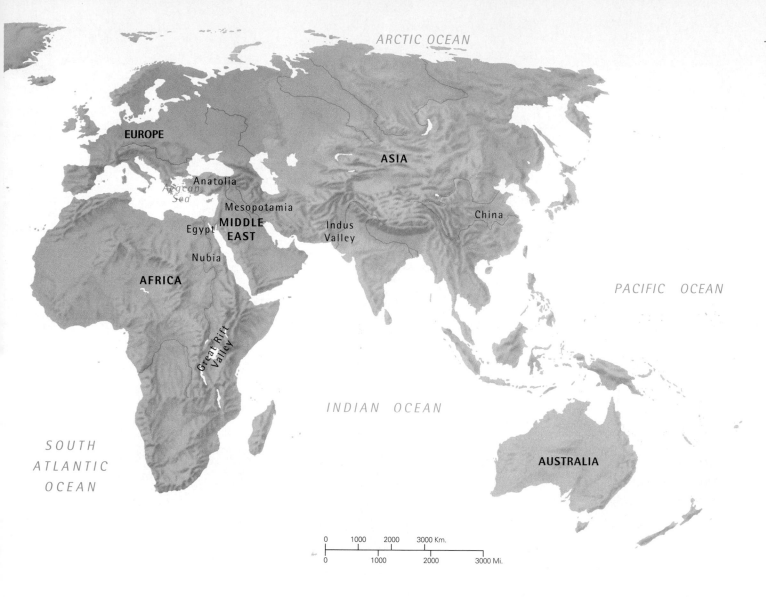

ARCTIC OCEAN

EUROPE

ASIA

Anatolia

Aegean Sea

Mesopotamia

MIDDLE EAST

Egypt

China

Indus Valley

Nubia

AFRICA

PACIFIC OCEAN

Great Rift Valley

INDIAN OCEAN

SOUTH ATLANTIC OCEAN

AUSTRALIA

| 0 | 1000 | 2000 | 3000 Km. |
| 0 | 1000 | 2000 | 3000 Mi. |

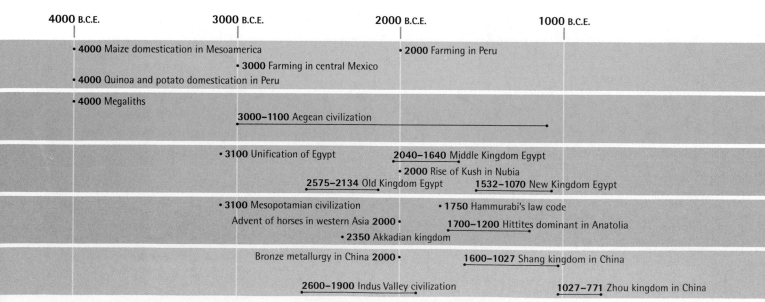

4000 B.C.E.	3000 B.C.E.	2000 B.C.E.	1000 B.C.E.

• **4000** Maize domestication in Mesoamerica

• **2000** Farming in Peru

• **3000** Farming in central Mexico

• **4000** Quinoa and potato domestication in Peru

• **4000** Megaliths

3000–1100 Aegean civilization

• **3100** Unification of Egypt

2040–1640 Middle Kingdom Egypt

• **2000** Rise of Kush in Nubia

2575–2134 Old Kingdom Egypt

1532–1070 New Kingdom Egypt

• **3100** Mesopotamian civilization

• **1750** Hammurabi's law code

Advent of horses in western Asia **2000** •

1700–1200 Hittites dominant in Anatolia

• **2350** Akkadian kingdom

Bronze metallurgy in China **2000** •

1600–1027 Shang kingdom in China

2600–1900 Indus Valley civilization

1027–771 Zhou kingdom in China

1

NATURE, HUMANITY, AND HISTORY: THE FIRST FOUR MILLION YEARS

c

African Genesis • **History and Culture in the Ice Age** • **The Agricultural Revolutions** • **Life in Neolithic Communities**
ENVIRONMENT AND TECHNOLOGY: **The Iceman**
SOCIETY AND CULTURE: **Interpreting Rock Art**

Giraffe in the Sahara, ca. 5000 B.C.E.   Millennia ago an unknown artist painted on a rock this scene from a rainy era when hunters could view majestic herds of game in what is now desert.

ccording to a story handed down by the Yoruba° people of West Africa, at one time there was only water below the sky. Then the divine Owner of the Sky let down a chain by which his son Oduduwa° descended along with sixteen male companions. Oduduwa scattered a handful of soil across the water and set down a chicken that scratched the soil into the shape of the land. A palm nut that he planted in the soil grew to become the bountiful forest that is the home of the Yoruba people. Oduduwa was their first king.

At some point in their history most human societies began telling similar stories about their origins. Some related that the first humans came down from the sky, others that they emerged out of a hole in the ground. Historical accuracy was not the point of such creation myths. Like the story of Adam and Eve in the Hebrew Bible, their primary purpose was to define the moral principles that people thought should govern their dealings with the supernatural world, with each other, and with the rest of nature. In addition, they provided an explanation of how a people's way of life, social divisions, and cultural system arose.

In the nineteenth century evidence started to accumulate that human beings had quite different origins. Natural scientists were finding remains of early humans who resembled apes rather than gods. Other evidence suggested that the familiar ways of life based on farming and herding did not arise within a generation or two of creation, as the myths suggested, but tens of thousands of years after humans first appeared. Although such evidence has long stirred controversy, a careful questioning of it reveals insights into human identity that may be as meaningful as those propounded by the creation myths.

As you read this chapter, ask yourself the following questions:

- What is the significance of the fact that humans evolved as part of the natural world, subject to its laws?

Yoruba (yoh-roo-bah)   **Oduduwa** (oh-DOO-doo-wah)

- How did the physical and mental abilities that humans gradually evolved give them a unique capacity to adapt to new environments by altering their way of life rather than by evolving physically as other species did?
- After nearly 2 million years of physical and cultural development, how did human communities in different parts of the world learn how to manipulate the natural world, domesticating plants and animals for their food and use? In short, how did people's relationship with their environments change?

AFRICAN GENESIS

The discovery in the mid-nineteenth century of the remains of ancient creatures that were at once human-like and apelike generated both excitement and controversy. The evidence upset many people because it challenged accepted beliefs about human origins. Others welcomed the new evidence as proof of what some researchers had long suspected: the physical characteristics of modern humans, like those of all other creatures, had evolved over incredibly long periods of time. Until recently, the evidence was too fragmentary to be convincing.

Interpreting the Evidence

In 1856 in the Neander Valley of what is now Germany workmen discovered fossilized bones of a creature with a body much like that of modern humans but with a face that, like the faces of apes, had heavy brow ridges and a low forehead. Although we now know these "Neanderthals" were a type of human common in Europe some 40,000 years ago, in the mid-nineteenth century the idea that earlier forms of humans could have existed was so novel that some of the scholars who first examined them thought they were deformed individuals from recent times.

Another perspective on human links to the distant past was already gaining ground. Three years after the Neanderthal finds, Charles Darwin, a young English naturalist (student of natural history), published *On the Origin of Species*. In this work he argued that the time frame for all biological life was far longer than most persons had supposed. Darwin based his conclusion on pioneering naturalists' research and on his own investigations of

Fossilized Footprints Archaeologist Mary Leakey (shown at top) found these remarkable footprints of a hominid adult and child at Laetoli, Tanzania. The pair had walked through fresh volcanic ash that solidified after being buried by a new volcanic eruption. Dated to 3.5 million years ago, the footprints are the oldest evidence of bipedalism yet found. (John Reader/Photo Researchers, Inc.)

fossils and living plant and animal species in Latin America. He proposed that the great diversity of living species and the profound changes in them over time could be explained by **natural selection**, the process by which biological variations that enhance a population's ability to survive became dominant in that species. He theorized that, over very long periods of time, accumulating changes in a group of organisms, mainly due to natural selection and genetic mutation, led to the **evolution** of distinct new species.

Turning to the sensitive subject of human evolution in *The Descent of Man* (1871), Darwin summarized the growing consensus among naturalists that, by the same process of natural selection, humans were "descended from a hairy, tailed quadruped" (four-footed animal). Because humans shared so many physical similarities with African apes, he proposed that Africa must have

been the home of the first humans, even though no evidence then existed to substantiate this hypothesis.

As it happened, the next major discoveries pointed to Asia, rather than Africa, as the original human home. On the Southeast Asian island of Java in 1891 Eugene Dubois uncovered an ancient skullcap of what was soon called "Java man," a find that has since been dated to between 1 million and 1.8 million years ago. In 1929 W. C. Pei discovered near Peking (Beijing°), China, a similar skullcap that became known as "Peking man."

By then, even older fossils had been found in southern Africa. In 1924, while examining fossils from a lime quarry, Raymond Dart found the skull of an ancient creature that he named *Australopithecus africanus°* (African southern ape), which he argued was transitional between apes and early humans. For many years most specialists disputed Dart's idea, because, although *Australopithecus africanus* walked upright like a human, its brain was ape-size. Such an idea went against their expectations that large brains would have evolved first and that Asia, not Africa, was the first home of humans.

Since 1950, Louis and Mary Leakey and their son Richard, along with many others, have discovered a wealth of other fossils in the exposed sediments of the Great Rift Valley of eastern Africa. These finds are strong evidence for Dart's hypothesis and for Darwin's guess that the tropical habitat of the African apes was the cradle of humanity.

The development of precise archaeological techniques has enhanced the quantity of evidence currently available. Rather than collect isolated bones, modern researchers literally sift the neighboring soils to extract the remains of other creatures existing at the time, locating fossilized seeds and even pollen by which to document the environment in which the humans lived. They can also measure the age of most finds by the rate of molecular change in potassium, in minerals in lava flows, or in carbon from wood and bone.

By combining that evidence with the growing understanding of how other species adapt to their natural environments, scientists can describe with some precision when, where, and how human beings evolved and how they lived. As the result of this new work, it is now possible to trace the evolutionary changes that produced modern humans during a period of 4 million years. As Darwin suspected, the earliest transitional creatures have been found only in Africa; the later human species (including Java man and Peking man) had wider global distribution.

Beijing (bay-jeeng) *Australopithecus africanus* (aw-strah-loh-PITH-uh-kuhs ah-frih-KAH-nuhs)

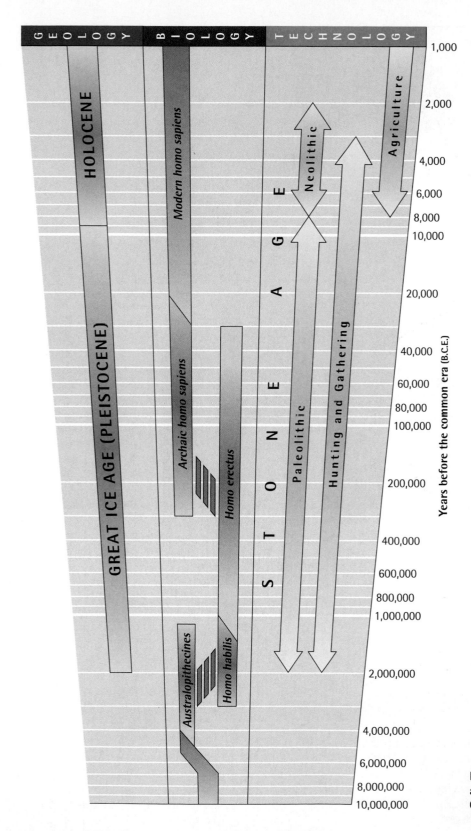

Figure 1.1   Human Biological Evolution and Technological Development in Geological and Historical Context

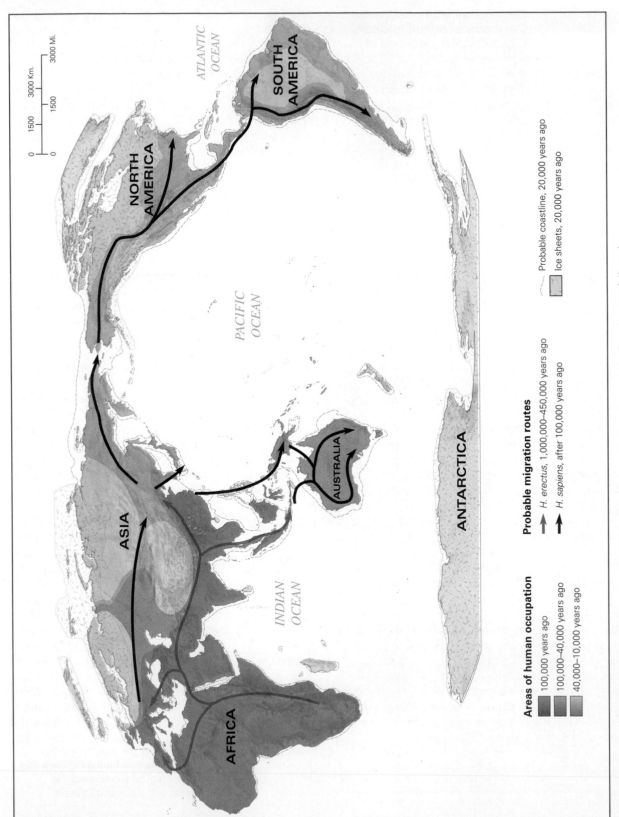

Areas of human occupation

- 100,000 years ago
- 100,000–40,000 years ago
- 40,000–10,000 years ago

Probable migration routes

- *H. erectus,* 1,000,000–450,000 years ago
- *H. sapiens,* after 100,000 years ago

⎯⎯ Probable coastline, 20,000 years ago

Ice sheets, 20,000 years ago

Map 1.1 **Human Dispersal to 10,000 Years Ago** Early migrations from Africa into southern Eurasia were followed by treks across land bridges during cold spells when giant ice sheets had lowered ocean levels.

Human Evolution

The accumulating evidence that humans evolved gradually over millions of years has led to much debate about how our species should be defined. Biologists classify **australopithecines°** and humans as members of a family of primates known as **hominids°**. Primates are members of a family of warm-blooded, four-limbed, social animals known as mammals that first appeared about 65 million years ago.

Within the primate kingdom modern humans are most closely related to the African apes—chimpanzees and gorillas. Since Darwin's time it has been popular (and controversial) to say that we are descended from apes. Modern research has found that over 98 percent of human DNA, the basic genetic blueprint, is identical to that of the great apes.

But three traits distinguish humans from apes and other primates. As Dart's australopithecines demonstrated, the earliest of these traits to appear was **bipedalism** (walking upright on two legs). This frees the forelimbs from any necessary role in locomotion and enhances an older primate trait: a hand that has a long thumb that can work with the fingers to manipulate objects skillfully. Modern humans' second trait, a very large brain, distinguishes us more profoundly from the australopithecines than does our somewhat more upright posture. Besides enabling humans to think abstractly, experience profound emotions, and construct complex social relations, this larger brain controls the fine motor movements of the hand and of the tongue, increasing humans' tool-using capacity and facilitating the development of speech. The physical possibility of language, however, depends on a third distinctive human trait: the location of the human larynx (voice box). It lies much lower in the neck than does the larynx of any other primate. This trait is associated with many other changes in the face and neck.

How and why did these immensely important biological changes take place? Scientists still employ Darwin's concept of natural selection, attributing the development of distinctive human traits to the preservation of genetic changes that enhanced survivability. Although the details have not been fully worked out, it is widely accepted that major shifts in the world's climate led to evolutionary changes in human ancestors and other species. About 10 million years ago falling temperatures in temperate regions culminated in the **Great Ice Age,** or Pleistocene° epoch, extending from about 2 million to about 11,000 years ago (see Figure 1.1 on page 7). The Pleistocene included more than a dozen very cold periods, each spanning several thousand years, separated by warmer periods. The changes that these climate shifts produced in rainfall, vegetation, and temperature imposed great strains on existing plant and animal species. As a result, large numbers of new species evolved during the Pleistocene.

During the Pleistocene, massive glaciers of frozen water spread out from the poles and mountains. At their peak such glaciers covered a third of the earth's surface and contained so much frozen water that ocean levels were lowered by over 450 feet (140 meters), exposing land bridges between many places now isolated by water (see Map 1.1).

Unlike the frozen lands to the north and south, the equatorial regions of the world were not touched by the glaciers, but during the Pleistocene they probably experienced altered climates. Between 3 million and 4 million years ago several new species of bipedal australopithecines evolved in southern and eastern Africa. In a remarkable find in northern Ethiopia in 1974, Donald Johanson unearthed a remarkably well preserved skeleton of a twenty-five-year-old female, whom he nicknamed "Lucy." In northern Tanzania in 1977, Mary Leakey discovered fossilized footprints that provide spectacular visual evidence of how australopithecines walked.

Bipedalism evolved because it provided australopithecines with some advantage for survival. Some studies suggest that a decisive advantage of bipedalism may have come from its energy efficiency in walking and running. Another theory is that bipeds survived better because they could fill their arms with food to carry back to mates and children. Whatever its decisive advantage, bipedalism led to other changes.

Climate changes between 2 million and 3 million years ago led to the evolution of a new species, the first to be classified in the same genus (*Homo*) with modern humans. At Olduvai° Gorge in northern Tanzania in the early 1960s Louis Leakey discovered the first fossilized remains of this creature, which he named ***Homo habilis°*** (handy human). What most distinguished *Homo habilis* from the australopithecines was a brain that was nearly 50 percent larger. A larger brain would have added to the new species' intelligence. What was happening in this period that favored greater mental capacity? Some scientists believe that the answer had to do with food. Greater intelligence enabled *Homo habilis* to locate a vast number of different kinds of things to eat throughout the seasons of the year. They point to seeds and other fossilized remains in ancient *Homo habilis* camps that indicate the new species ate a greater variety of more nutritious seasonal foods than the australopithecines ate.

Australopithecine (aw-strah-loh-PITH-uh-seen)
hominid (HOM-uh-nid) **Pleistocene** (PLY-stuh-seen)

Olduvai (ol-DOO-vy) *Homo habilis* (HOH-moh HAB-uh-luhs)

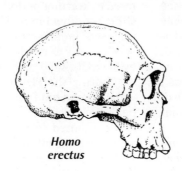

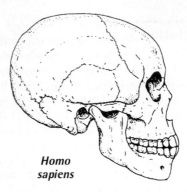

Homo habilis

Homo erectus

Homo sapiens

Evolution of the Human Brain   These drawings of skulls show the extensive cranial changes associated with the increase in brain size during the 3 million years from *Homo habilis* to *Homo sapiens sapiens*.

By 1 million years ago *Homo habilis* and all the australopithecines had become extinct. In their habitat lived a new hominid, **Homo erectus°** (upright human), which had first appeared in eastern Africa about 1.8 million years ago. These creatures possessed brains a third larger than those of *Homo habilis*, which presumably accounted for their better survivability. A nearly complete skeleton of a twelve-year-old male of the species discovered by Richard Leakey in 1984 on the shores of Lake Turkana in Kenya shows that *Homo erectus* closely resembled modern people from the neck down. *Homo erectus* was very successful in dealing with different environments and underwent hardly any biological changes during a million years.

However, by a long, imperfectly understood evolutionary process between 400,000 and 100,000 years ago, a new human species emerged: **Homo sapiens°** (wise human). The brains of *Homo sapiens* were a third larger than those of *Homo erectus*, whom they gradually superseded. *Homo sapiens* also had greater speech capacity.

This slow but remarkable process of physical evolution that distinguished humans by a small but significant degree from other primates was one part of what was happening. Equally remarkable was the way in which humans were extending their habitat.

Migrations from Africa

Early humans gradually expanded their range in eastern and southern Africa. Then they ventured out of Africa, perhaps following migrating herds of animals or searching for more abundant food supplies in time of drought. The details are unsettled, but the end result is vividly clear: humans learned to survive in every part of the globe—

from the arctic to the equator, from deserts to tropical rain forests. This dispersal demonstrates early humans' talent for adaptation (see Map 1.1).

Homo erectus was the first human species to inhabit all parts of Africa and the first to be found outside Africa. By migrating overland from Africa across southern Asia, *Homo erectus* reached Java as early as 1.8 million years ago. At that time, because of the great volume of water trapped in ice-age glaciers, sea levels were so low that Java was not an island but was part of the Southeast Asian mainland. New evidence suggests that members of this species continued to live on Java until about 50,000 years ago. Java's climate would have been no colder than East Africa's. Posing a greater challenge for early humans were the harsh winters of northern Europe and northern China, where *Homo erectus* settled between 700,000 and 300,000 years ago.

DNA and fossil evidence suggest that *Homo sapiens* also spread outward from an African homeland. Their migrations to the rest of the world would have been made easier by a wet period that transformed the normally arid Sahara and Middle East into fertile grasslands until about 40,000 years ago. The abundance of plant and animal food during this wet period would have promoted an increase in human populations.

By the end of that wet period further evolutionary changes had produced fully modern humans (*Homo sapiens sapiens*), which some evidence suggests may have originated in Africa. This new species displaced older human populations, such as the Neanderthals in Europe, and penetrated for the first time into the Americas, Australia, and the Arctic.

During the last glacial period, between 32,000 and 13,000 years ago, when the sea levels were low, hunters were able to cross a land bridge from northeastern Asia into North America. As these pioneers and later migrants moved southward (penetrating southern South America by at least 12,500 years ago), they passed through lands

---

Homo erectus (HOH-moh ee-REK-tuhs)
Homo sapiens (HOH-moh SAY-pee-enz)

teeming with life, including easily hunted large animal species. Meanwhile, traveling by boat from Java, other modern humans colonized New Guinea and Australia when both were part of a single landmass, and they crossed the land bridge then existing between the Asian mainland and Japan. Despite the generally cool climate of this period, human bands also followed reindeer even into northern arctic environments during the summer months.

As populations migrated, they may have undergone some minor evolutionary changes that helped them adapt to extreme environments. One such change was in skin color. The deeply pigmented skin of today's indigenous inhabitants of the tropics (and presumably of all early humans who evolved there) is an adaptation that reduces the harmful effects of the harsh tropical sun. At some point, possibly as recent as 5,000 years ago, especially pale skin became characteristic of Europeans living in northern latitudes with far less sunshine especially during winter months. The loss of pigment enabled their skins to produce more vitamin D from sunshine, though it exposed Europeans to a greater risk of sunburn and skin cancer when they migrated to sunnier climates. This was not the only possible way to adapt to the arctic. Eskimos who began moving into northern latitudes of North America no more than 5,000 years ago retain the deeper pigmentation of their Asian ancestors but are able to gain sufficient vitamin D from eating fish and sea mammals.

As distinctive as skin color is, it represents a very minor biological variation. What is far more remarkable about the widely dispersed populations of modern humans is that we vary so little. Although widely dispersed and adapted to diverse environments, all modern humans are members of the same species. Instead of needing to evolve physically like other species in order to adapt to new environments, modern humans have been able to change their eating habits and devise new forms of clothing and shelter. As a result, human communities have become culturally diverse while remaining physically homogeneous.

HISTORY AND CULTURE IN THE ICE AGE

Evidence of early humans' splendid creative abilities first came to light in 1940 near Lascaux in southern France. Examining a newly uprooted tree, youths discovered the entrance to a vast underground cavern. Once inside, they found that its walls were covered with paintings of animals, including many that had been extinct for thousands of years. Other cave paintings have been found in Spain and elsewhere in southern France.

Modern observers have been struck by the artistic quality of these ancient cave paintings. To even the most skeptical person, such rich finds are awesome demonstrations of richly developed imaginations and skill. Though ancient people's specialized tools and complex social relations are less striking visually, they also exhibit uniquely human talents.

The fact that similar art and tools were produced over wide areas and long periods of time demonstrates that skills and ideas were not simply individual but were deliberately passed along within societies. These learned patterns of action and expression constitute **culture.** Culture includes material objects, such as dwellings, clothing, tools, and crafts, along with nonmaterial values, beliefs, and languages. Although it is true that some animals also learn new ways, their activities are determined primarily by inherited instincts. Among humans the proportions are reversed: instincts are less important than the cultural traditions that each new generation learns. All living creatures are part of natural history, which traces biological development, but only human communities trace profound cultural developments over time. The development, transmission, and transformation of cultural practices and events are the subject of **history.**

Food Gathering and Stone Technology

When archaeologists examine the remains of ancient human sites, the first thing that jumps out at them is the abundant evidence of human toolmaking—the first recognizable cultural activity. Because the tools that survive are made of stone, the extensive period of history from the appearance of the first fabricated stone tools around 2 million years ago until the appearance of metal tools around 4 thousand years ago has been called the **Stone Age.**

The name can be misleading. In the first place, not all tools were made of stone. Early humans would also have made useful objects and tools out of bone, skin, wood, and other natural materials less likely than stone to survive the ravages of time. In the second place, this period of nearly 2 million years contains many distinct periods and cultures. Early students recognized two distinct periods in the Stone Age: the **Paleolithic°** (Old Stone Age) down to 10,000 years ago and the **Neolithic°** (New Stone Age) associated with agriculture. Modern research scientists recognize many more divisions.

Paleolithic (pay-lee-oh-LITH-ik)   **Neolithic** (nee-oh-LITH-ik)

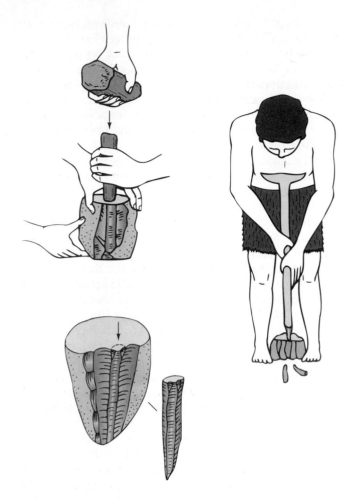

Making Stone Tools About 35,000 years ago the manufacture of stone tools became highly specialized. Small blades chipped from a rock core were mounted in a bone or wooden handle. Not only were such composite tools more varied than earlier all-purpose hand axes, but the small blades required fewer rock cores—an important consideration in areas where suitable rocks were scarce. (From Jacques Bordaz, *Tools of the Old and New Stone Age.* Copyright 1970 by Jacques Bordaz. Redrawn by the permission of Addison-Wesley Educational Publishers, Inc.)

Most early human activity centered on gathering food. Like the australopithecines, early humans depended heavily on vegetable foods such as leaves, seeds, and grasses, but one of the changes evident in the Ice Age is the growing consumption of highly nutritious animal flesh. Moreover, unlike australopithecines, humans regularly made tools. These two changes—increased meat eating and toolmaking—appear to be closely linked.

The first crude tools made their appearance with *Homo habilis.* Most stone tools made by *Homo habilis* have been found in the Great Rift Valley of eastern Africa, whose sides expose sediments laid down over millions of years. One branch of this valley, the Olduvai Gorge in Tanzania, explored by Louis and Mary Leakey, has been a particularly important source. *Homo habilis* made tools by chipping flakes off the edges of volcanic stones. Modern experiments show that the razor-sharp edges of such flakes are highly effective for skinning and butchering wild animals. Later human species made much more sophisticated tools.

Small-brained *Homo habilis* probably lacked the skill to hunt and kill large animals and probably obtained animal protein by scavenging meat from kills made by animal predators or resulting from accidents. There is evidence that they used large stone "choppers" for cracking open bones to get at the nutritious marrow. The fact that many such tools are found together far from the outcrops of volcanic rock suggests that people carried them long distances for use at kill sites and camps.

Homo erectus were also scavengers, but their larger brains would have made them cleverer at it—capable, for example, of finding and stealing the kills that leopards and other large predators dragged up into trees. They also made more effective tools for butchering large animals, although the stone flakes and choppers of earlier eras continued to be made. The stone tool most associated with *Homo erectus* was a hand ax formed by removing chips from both sides of a stone to produce a sharp outer edge.

Modern experiments show the hand ax to be an efficient multipurpose tool, suitable for skinning and butchering animals, for scraping skins clean for use as clothing and mats, for sharpening wooden tools, and for digging up edible roots. Since a hand ax can also be hurled accurately for nearly 100 feet (30 meters), it might also have been used as a projectile to fell animals. From sites in Spain there is evidence that *Homo erectus* even butchered elephants, which then ranged across southern Europe, by driving them into swamps where they became trapped and died.

Homo sapiens were far more skillful hunters. They tracked and killed large animals (such as mastodons, mammoths, and bisons) throughout the world. Their success reflected their superior intelligence and use of an array of finely made tools. Sharp stone flakes chipped from carefully prepared rock cores were often used in combination with other materials. A spear could be made by attaching a stone point to a wooden shaft. Embedding several sharp stone flakes in a bone handle produced a sawing tool.

Indeed, *Homo sapiens* were so skillful and successful as hunters that they may have caused or contributed to a series of ecological crises. Between 40,000 and 13,000 years ago the giant mastodons and mammoths gradually disappeared, first from Africa and Southeast Asia and then from northern Europe. In North America the sudden disappearance around 11,000 years ago of highly successful large-animal hunters known as the Clovis people was almost simultaneous with the extinction of three-fourths of the large mammals in the Americas, including giant bisons, camels, ground sloths, stag-moose, giant cats, mastodons, and mammoths. In Australia there was a similar event. Since these extinctions occurred during the last series of severe cold spells at the end of the Ice Age, it is difficult to measure which effects were the work of global and regional climate changes and which resulted from the excesses of human predators.

Finds of fossilized animal bones bearing the marks of butchering tools clearly attest to the scavenging and hunting activities of Stone Age peoples, but anthropologists do not believe that early humans depended primarily on meat for their food. Modern **foragers** (hunting and food-gathering peoples) in the Kalahari Desert of southern Africa and Ituri Forest of central Africa derive the bulk of their day-to-day nourishment from wild vegetable foods; meat is the food of feasts. It is likely that Stone Age peoples did the same, even though the tools and equipment for gathering and processing vegetable foods have left few traces because they were made of materials unable to survive for thousands of years.

Like modern foragers, ancient humans would have used skins and mats woven from leaves for collecting fruits, berries, and wild seeds. They would have dug edible roots out of the ground with wooden sticks. Archaeologists believe that the donut-shaped stones often found at Stone Age sites may have been weights placed on wooden digging sticks to increase their effectiveness.

Both meat and vegetables become tastier and easier to digest when they are cooked. The first cooked foods were probably found by accident after wildfires, but there is new evidence from East and South Africa that humans were setting fires deliberately between 1 million and 1.5 million years ago. The wooden spits and hot rocks that they would have used for roasting, frying, or baking are not distinctive enough to stand out in an archaeological site. Only with the appearance of clay cooking pots some 12,500 years ago in East Asia is there hard evidence of cooking.

Gender Divisions and Social Life

Some researchers have studied the organization of nonhuman primates for clues about very early human society. Gorillas and chimpanzees live in groups consisting of several adult males and females and their offspring. Status varies with age and sex, and a dominant male usually heads the group. Sexual unions between males and females generally do not result in long-term pairing. Instead, the strongest ties are those between a female and her children and among siblings. Adult males are often recruited from neighboring bands.

Very early human groups likely shared some of these primate traits, but by the time of modern *Homo sapiens* the two-parent family would have been characteristic. How this change from a mother-centered family to a two-parent family developed over the intervening millennia can only be guessed at, but it is likely that physical and social evolution were linked. Larger brain size was a contributing factor. Big-headed humans have to be born in a less mature state than other mammals so they can pass through the narrow birth canal. Other large mammals are mature at two or three years of age; humans are not able to care for themselves until the age of twelve to fifteen. Human infants' and children's need for much longer nurturing makes care by mothers, fathers, and other family members a biological imperative.

The human reproductive cycle also became unique at some point. In other species sexual contact is biologically restricted to a special mating season of the year or to the fertile part of the female's menstrual cycle. As well, among other primates the choice of mate is usually not a matter for long deliberation. To a female baboon in heat (estrus) any male will do, and to a male baboon any receptive female is a suitable sexual partner. In contrast, adult humans can mate at any time and are much choosier about their partners. Once they mate, frequent sexual contact promotes deep emotional ties and long-term bonding.

An enduring bond between human parents made it much easier for vulnerable offspring to receive the care they needed during the long period of their childhood. Working together, mothers and fathers could nurture dependent children of different ages at the same time, unlike other large mammals whose females must raise their offspring nearly to maturity before beginning another reproductive cycle. Spacing births close together also ensured offspring a high rate of survival and would have enabled humans to multiply more rapidly than other large mammals.

Other researchers have studied the few surviving present-day foragers for models of what such early societies could have been like. They infer that Ice Age women would have done most of the gathering and cooking (which they could do while caring for small children). Older women, past child-bearing age, would have been the most knowledgeable and productive food gatherers. Men, with stronger arms and shoulders, would have been more suited than women to hunting, particularly for large animals. Some early cave art shows males in hunting activities.

Other aspects of social life in the Ice Age are suggested by studies of modern peoples. All recent hunter-gatherers have lived in small groups or bands. The community had to have enough members to defend itself from predators and to divide responsibility for the collection and preparation of animal and vegetable foods. However, if it had too many members, it risked exhausting the food available in its immediate vicinity. Even a band of optimal size had to move at regular intervals to follow migrating animals and take advantage of seasonally ripening plants in different places. Archaeological evidence from Ice Age campsites suggests early humans, too, lived in highly mobile bands.

Hearths and Cultural Expressions

Because frequent moves were necessary to keep close to migrating herds and ripening plants, early hunting and gathering peoples usually did not lavish much time on housing. Natural shelters under overhanging rocks or in caves in southern Africa and southern France are known to have been favorite camping places to which bands returned at regular intervals. Where the climate was severe or where natural shelters did not exist, people erected huts of branches, stones, bones, skins, and leaves as seasonal camps. More elaborate dwellings were common in areas where protection against harsh weather was necessary.

An interesting camp dating to 15,000 years ago has been excavated in the Ukraine southeast of Kiev. Its communal dwellings were framed with the bones of elephant-like mammoths, then covered with hides. Each oblong structure, measuring 15 to 20 feet (4.5 to 6 meters) by 40 to 50 feet (12 to 15 meters), was capable of holding fifty people and would have taken several days to construct. The camp had five such dwellings, making

Interior of a Neolithic House   This stone structure from the Orkney Islands off Scotland shows a double hearth for cooking and a small window in the center, along with stone partitions. Elsewhere, few Neolithic houses were made of stone, but wood was scarce in the Orkneys.   (Ronald Sheridan/Ancient Art & Architecture)

ENVIRONMENT + TECHNOLOGY

The Iceman

Unusually detailed information about everyday technologies of the fourth millennium B.C.E. comes from the well-preserved remains of a man of about fifty years of age. The Iceman was discovered at the edge of a melting glacier in the European Alps in 1991. Not only his body was preserved but so too were his clothing and tools.

From head to toe he was dressed for the cold weather of the mountains. He was wearing a fur hat fastened under the chin with a strap, a tailored vest of different colored deer-skins, leather leggings and loincloth, and a padded cloak made of grasses. On his feet he wore calfskin shoes also padded with grass for warmth and comfort. The articles of clothing had been sewn together with fiber and leather cords. He also carried a birch-bark drinking cup.

Most of his tools were those of the late Stone Age. In a sort of leather fanny pack he carried small flint tools for cutting, scraping, and punching holes, as well as some tinder for making a fire. He also carried a leather quiver with flint-tipped arrows, but his 6-foot (1.8-meter) bow was unfinished, lacking a bowstring. In addition he had a flint knife and a tool for sharpening flints. His most sophisticated tool was of the age of metals just dawning: a copper-bladed ax with a wooden handle.

The Iceman This is an artist's rendition of what the Iceman might have looked like. Notice his tools, remarkable evidence of the technology of his day.
(Weislav Smetzk/STERN)

it a large settlement for a foraging community. Large, solid structures were common in fishing villages that grew up along rivers and lake shores where the abundance of fish permitted people to occupy the same site year-round.

Making clothing was another necessary technology in the Stone Age. Animal skins were an early form of clothing, and the oldest evidence of fibers woven into cloth dates from about 26,000 years ago. An "Iceman" from 5,300 years ago, whose frozen remains were found in the European Alps in 1991, was wearing many different garments made of animal skins sewn together with cord fashioned from vegetable fibers and rawhide (see Environment and Technology: The Iceman).

Although accidents, erratic weather, and disease took a heavy toll on a foraging band, there is no reason to believe that day-to-day existence was particularly hard or unpleasant. Some studies suggest that under the conditions operating on the African savannas and in other game-rich areas, securing the necessities of food,

Interpreting Rock Art

Drawings of animals and people found in caves and rock shelters in many parts of the world are visually spectacular but hard to interpret. Some of them seem to record hunting and other common activities. Others are puzzling mixtures of realistic and fantastic shapes in odd configurations. Archaeologist David Lewis-Williams has extracted rich meaning from one school of cave art by connecting it with the beliefs and rituals of a southern African hunting and gathering people now known as the San.

The last San groups to create such paintings died out a century ago, but Lewis-Williams believes the records of their beliefs, customs, and symbols provide a way to interpret a tradition of rock art that extends back thousands of years. He thinks that the artists were shamans—men and women in San society who acquired the power to cure sickness, control antelope herds, and make rain while they were in trances. Their drawings depict scenes of shamans shaking, sweating, and falling into a deep sleeps during which they have out-of-body experiences.

Lewis-Williams reads the scene reproduced here as representing a shaman's efforts to control the rain by leading a mystical animal across a parched landscape. The figure marked 1 is a shaman entering a trance, characteristically bending forward at the waist and throwing his arms behind

him. Figure 2 is a shaman fully in a trance, lying down; the lines represent his spirit leaving his body. The partially obscured figure marked 3, above the animal, has his hand to his nose in a depiction of "snoring," which the San associated with curing illness. The line of small dots above the animal, marked 4, are bees, whose swarming the San believed marked a particularly potent time for trance medicine.

Unfortunately, nowhere else in the world has a recorded system of beliefs been connected to rock art. However, Lewis-Williams's reconstructions do hint at the symbolic belief and mystical lore that may lie behind the cave art of early periods.

If you had only the drawing to go by, how would you interpret it? Why is it important to understand the cultural context in which a work of art is made? What do you know about the San that helps explain why they attached such importance to animals? Why might the San prize personal mystical experiences?

Source: Adapted from Martin Hall, *Farmers, Kings, and Traders: The People of Southern Africa, 200–1860* (Chicago: University of Chicago Press, 1990), 62. The illustration is reproduced by permission of David Lewis-Williams, "Introductory Essay: Science and Rock Art," *South African Archaeological Society, Goodwin Series* 4 (1983): 3–13.

clothing, and shelter would have occupied only from three to five hours a day. This would have left a great deal of time for artistic endeavors as well as for tool-making and social life.

The foundations of what later ages called science, art, and religion were also built during the Stone Age. Basic to human survival was extensive and precise knowledge about the natural environment. Gatherers needed to know which local plants were best for food and the seasons when they were available. Successful hunting required intimate knowledge of the habits of game animals. People learned how to use plant and animal parts for clothing, twine, and building materials, as well as which natural substances were effective for medicine, consciousness altering, dyeing, and other purposes. Knowledge of the natural world included identifying minerals suitable for paints, stones for making the best tools, and so forth. Given humans' physical capacity for speech, it is likely that the transmission of such prescientific knowledge involved verbal communication, even though direct evidence for language appears only in later periods.

Early music and dance have left no traces, but there is abundant evidence of painting and drawing. The oldest known cave paintings in Europe and North Africa date to 32,000 years ago, and there are many others from later times in other parts of the world. Because many cave paintings feature wild animals such as oxen, reindeer, and horses that were hunted for food, some believe that the art was meant to record hunting scenes or that it formed part of some magical and religious rites to ensure successful hunting. However, a newly discovered cave at Vallon Pont-d'Arc° in southern France features rhinoceros, panthers, bears, owls, and a hyena, which probably were not the objects of hunting. Still other drawings include people dressed in animal skins and smeared with paint. In many caves there are large numbers of stencils of human hands. Are these the signatures of the artists or the world's oldest graffiti? Some scholars suspect that other marks in cave paintings and on bones from this period may represent efforts at counting or writing.

Newer theories suggest that cave and rock art represent concerns with fertility, efforts to educate the young, or elaborate mechanisms for time reckoning. Another approach to understanding such art draws on the traditions of peoples like the San—hunters, gatherers, and

Vallon Pont-d'Arc (vah-LON pon-DAHRK)

artists in southern Africa since time immemorial (see Society and Culture: Interpreting Rock Art).

Some cave art suggests that Stone Age people had well-developed religions, but without written religious texts it is difficult to know exactly what they believed. Sites of deliberate human burials from about 100,000 years ago give some hints. The fact that an adult was often buried with stone implements, food, clothing, and red-ochre powder suggests that early people revered their leaders enough to honor them after death and may imply a belief in an afterlife.

Today we recognize that the Stone Age, whose existence was scarcely dreamed of two centuries ago, was a formative period. Important in its own right, it also laid the basis for major changes ahead as human communities passed from being food gatherers to being food producers. Future discoveries are likely to add substantially to our understanding of these events.

THE AGRICULTURAL REVOLUTIONS

Early humans depended on wild plants and animals for their food. But around 10,000 years ago some humans began to meet their food needs by raising domesticated plants and animals. Gradually over the next millennium most people became food producers, although hunting and gathering continued to exist in some places. This transition to food production was a major milestone in humans' manipulation of nature and had myriad implications for the human species and their planet (see Map 1.2).

The change from food gathering to food production at the end of the Stone Age has been called the "Neolithic Revolution." The name can be misleading, for two reasons: stone tools were not its essential component, and it was not a single event but a series of separate transformations in different parts of the world. The term **Agricultural Revolutions** is more precise because it emphasizes that the central change was in food production, and it indicates that agriculture arose independently in many different places. In most cases agriculture included the domestication of animals for food as well as the cultivation of new food crops. Changes in global climate appear to have caused this transformation.

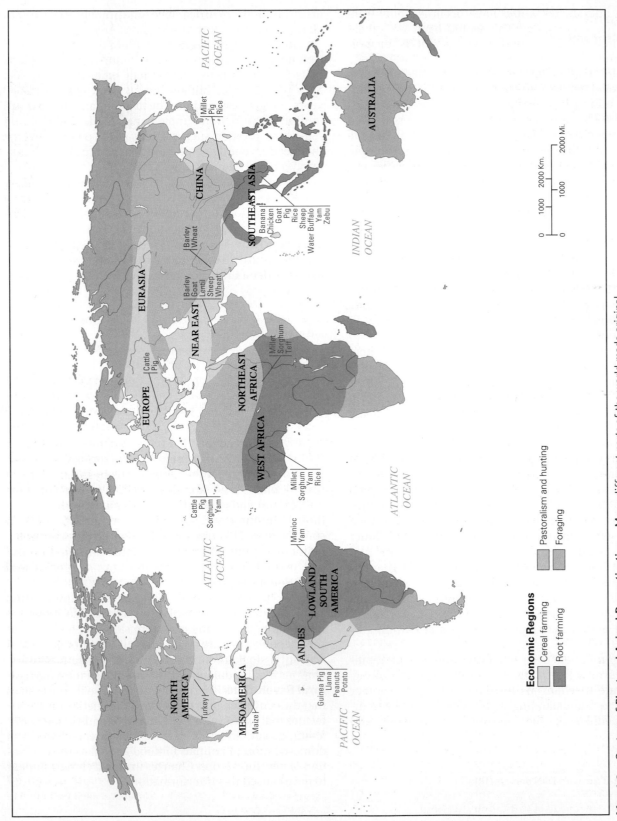

Map 1.2   Centers of Plant and Animal Domestication   Many different parts of the world made original contributions to domestication during the Agricultural Revolutions that began about 10,000 years ago. Later interactions helped spread these domesticated animals and plants to new locations. In lands less suitable for crop cultivation, pastoralism and hunting predominated.

The Transition to Plant Cultivation

Food gathering gave way to food production in stages spread over hundreds of generations. The process may have begun when forager bands returning year after year to the same seasonal camps took measures to encourage the nearby growth of the foods they liked. They deliberately scattered the seeds of desirable plants in locations where they would thrive, and they discouraged the growth of competing plants by clearing them away. Such techniques of semicultivation could have supplemented food gathering for many generations. Families willing to devote their energies principally to food production, however, would have had to settle permanently in a camp.

Settled agriculture required new, specialized tools. Indeed, it was the presence of new tools that first alerted archaeologists to the beginning of a food production revolution. Many specialized stone tools were developed or improved for agricultural use, including polished or ground stone heads to work the soil, sharp stone chips imbedded in bone or wooden handles to cut grain, and stone mortars to pulverize grain. However, stone axes were not very efficient for clearing away shrubs and trees. To do that, farmers used a much older technology: fire. Fires got rid of unwanted undergrowth, and the ashes were a natural fertilizer. After the burn-off farmers could use blades and axes to cut away the regrowth.

Also fundamental to the success of agriculture was selecting the highest-yielding strains of wild plants, which over time led to the development of valuable new domesticated varieties. Because women were the principal gatherers of wild plant foods, they are likely to have played a major role in this transition to plant cultivation. The success of a farming community also would have required extensive male labor, especially to clear fields.

The transition to agriculture has been traced in greatest detail in the Middle East. By 8000 B.C.E. human selection had transformed certain wild grasses into higher-yielding domesticated grains now known as emmer wheat and barley. Communities there also discovered that alternating the cultivation of grains and pulses (plants yielding edible seeds such as lentils and peas) helped to maintain soil fertility.

Crops that were first domesticated in the Middle East were later grown elsewhere, but the spread of agriculture was not essentially a process of diffusion. Agriculture arose independently in many parts of the world. Over time much borrowing occurred, but it was societies that already had begun to practice agriculture on their own that were most likely to borrow new plants, animals, and farming techniques from their neighbors.

Domestication of Wheat   Through selection of the largest seeds of this wild grass, early farmers in the Middle East were able to develop varieties with larger edible kernels. Bread wheat was grown in the Nile Valley by 5000 B.C.E.   (From Iris Barn, *Discovering Archaeology*, © 1981)

The oldest traces of food production in northern Africa are in the eastern Sahara, which was able to support farming during a particularly wet period after 8000 B.C.E. As in the Middle East, emmer wheat and barley became the principal crops and sheep, goats, and cattle the main domesticated animals. The return of drier conditions about 5000 B.C.E. led many Saharan farmers to move to the Nile Valley, where the annual flooding of the Nile River provided moisture for cereal farming.

In Europe cultivation of wheat and barley began as early as 6000 B.C.E. in Greece, combining local experiments and Middle Eastern borrowings. Shortly after 4000 B.C.E. farming developed in the light-soiled plains of Central Europe and along the Danube River. As forests receded because of climate changes and human clearing efforts, agriculture spread to other parts of Europe over the next millennium.

Early farmers in Europe and elsewhere practiced shifting cultivation, also known as swidden agriculture. After a few growing seasons, the fields were left fallow (abandoned to natural vegetation), and new fields were cleared nearby. Between 4000 and 3000 B.C.E., for example, communities of from 40 to 60 people in the Danube Valley of Central Europe supported themselves on about 500 acres (200 hectares) of farmland, cultivating a third or less each year while leaving the rest fallow to restore its fertility. From around 2600 B.C.E. people in Central Europe began using ox-drawn wooden plows to till heavier and richer soils.

Although the lands around the Mediterranean seem to have shared a complex of crops and farming techniques, there were major geographical barriers to the spread of this complex elsewhere. Wheat and barley were unsuited to the rainfall patterns south of the Sahara. Instead, farming in sub-Saharan Africa came to be based on a wide variety of locally domesticated grains, including sorghums, millets, and (in Ethiopia) teff. Middle Eastern grains could not be grown at all in the very humid regions of equatorial West Africa, where there is early evidence of indigenous domestication of yams.

Eastern and southern Asia were also major centers of plant domestication, although the details are not so clearly documented as in the Middle East. Rice was first domesticated in southern China, the northern half of Southeast Asia, or northern India, possibly as early as 10,000 B.C.E. but more likely closer to 5000 B.C.E. Rice cultivation thrived in the warm and wet conditions of southern China. In India several pulses (including hyacinth beans, green grams, and black grams) domesticated about 2000 B.C.E. were cultivated along with rice.

While food production was spreading in Eurasia and Africa, the inhabitants of the isolated American continents were creating other major centers of crop domestication. As game animals declined in the Tehuacán° Valley of Mexico after 8000 B.C.E., people had to eat more wild vegetable foods. Agriculture based on maize° (corn) developed there about 3000 B.C.E. and gradually spread to other parts of the Americas. At about the same time, the inhabitants of Peru were developing a food production system based on potatoes and quinoa°, a protein-rich seed grain. People in the more tropical parts of Mesoamerica cultivated tomatoes, peppers, squash, and potatoes. In South American tropical forests, the root crop manioc became the staple crop after 1500 B.C.E. Manioc and maize then spread to the Caribbean.

The fact that Asia, the Americas, and tropical Africa developed their own domesticated plants in isolation from outside influences added to the variety of cultivated plants. After 1500 C.E. many of these crops became important foods throughout the world.

Animal Domestication and Pastoralism

The revolution in food production was not confined to plants. The domestication of animals also expanded rapidly during these same millennia. The first domesticated animal was probably the dog, tamed to help early hunters track game. Later animals were domesticated to provide meat, milk, and energy. Like the domestication of plants, this process is best known in the Middle East.

By studying the refuse dumped outside some Middle East villages during the centuries after 7000 B.C.E., archaeologists have been able to document a gradual decline in the quantity of wild gazelle bones. This finding probably reflects the depletion of such wild animals through overhunting by the local farming communities. Meat eating, however, did not decline; the deposits show sheep and goat bones gradually replacing gazelle bones. It seems likely that wild sheep and goats had learned to scavenge for food scraps around agricultural villages and that people began to feed the tamer sheep and goats and protect them from wild predators in order to provide themselves with a ready supply of food. At first the biological differences between tame and wild species are too slight to date domestication precisely. Distinct domesticated species evolved as people controlled the breeding of their sheep and goats to produce desirable characteristics such as high milk production and long wool.

Elsewhere in the world other animal species were being domesticated during the centuries before 3000 B.C.E. Wild cattle were domesticated in northern Africa; pigs and water buffalo in China; and humped-back Zebu° cattle, buffalo, and pigs in India. As in the case of food plants, varieties of domesticated animals from abroad sometimes replaced the species initially domesticated. For example, the Zebu cattle originally domesticated in India first became important in sub-Saharan Africa about 2,000 years ago.

In most parts of the world, farming populations depended on domesticated plants and animals for food and also used domesticated oxen, cattle, or (in China) water buffalo as draft animals. Animal droppings were important for fertilizing the soil; their wool and hides were used for clothing. However, there were two notable deviations from this pattern of mixed agriculture and animal husbandry.

One variation was in the Americas. There, comparatively few species of wild animals were suitable for domestication, other than llamas (for transport and wool) and guinea pigs and some fowl (for meat). No species could be borrowed from elsewhere because the Americas' land bridge to Asia had submerged as melting glaciers raised sea levels. Hunting remained an important source of meat for Amerindians, but perhaps their exceptional contributions to the world's domesticated plant crops were partly in compensation for the shortage of domesticated meat animals (see Chapter 12).

Tehuacán (teh-wah-KAHN)   **maize** (mayz)   **quinoa** (kee-NOH-uh)   **Zebu** (ZEE-boo)

The other notable variation from mixed farming occurred in more arid parts of Africa and Central Asia. There, pastoralism, a way of life dependent on large herds of small and large stock, predominated. For example, pastoralists had replaced farmers in the Sahara as it became drier, up until about 2500 B.C.E.; then desert conditions forced them to migrate southward. The necessity of moving their herds to new pastures and watering places throughout the year meant that pastoralists needed to be almost as mobile as foragers and thus could accumulate little in the way of bulky possessions and substantial dwellings. Like modern pastoralists, early cattle-keeping people were probably not great meat-eaters but relied heavily on the milk from their animals for their diet. During seasons when grasses for grazing and water were plentiful, they also could have done some hasty crop cultivation or bartered meat and skins for plant foods with nearby farming communities.

Agriculture and Ecological Crisis

Why in the Neolithic period did societies in so many parts of the world gradually abandon a way of life based on food gathering? Some theories assume that people were drawn to food production by its obvious advantages. For example, it has recently been suggested that people settled down in the Middle East so they could grow enough grains to ensure themselves a ready supply of beer. Beer drinking is frequently depicted in ancient Middle Eastern art and can be dated to as early as 3500 B.C.E.

However, most researchers today believe that climate change drove people to abandon hunting and gathering in favor of pastoralism and agriculture. So great was the global warming that ended the Great Ice Age that geologists give the era since about 9000 B.C.E. a new name: the **Holocene°**. Scientists have also found evidence that temperate lands were exceptionally warm between 6000 and 2000 B.C.E., the era when people in so many parts of the world adopted agriculture. The precise nature of the crisis probably varied. In the Middle East taking up food production may have been a response to shortages of wild food caused by a dry spell or population growth. Elsewhere a warmer, wetter climate could have promoted rapid forest growth in former grasslands, reducing the supplies of game and wild grains.

Additional support for an ecological explanation comes from the fact that in many drier parts of the world, where wild food remained abundant, agriculture was not adopted. The inhabitants of Australia continued

Holocene (HAWL-oh-seen)

to rely exclusively on foraging until recent centuries, as did some peoples in all the other continents. Many Amerindians in the arid grasslands from Alaska to the Gulf of Mexico hunted bison, while in the Pacific Northwest others took up salmon-fishing. Abundant supplies of fish, shellfish, and aquatic animals permitted food gatherers east of the Mississippi River in North America to become increasingly sedentary. In the equatorial rain forest and in the southern part of Africa conditions favored retention of the older ways. The reindeer-based societies of northern Eurasia were also unaffected by the spread of farming.

Whatever the causes, the effects of the gradual adoption of food production in most parts of the world were momentous. A hundred thousand years ago there were fewer than 2 million people, and their range was largely confined to the temperate and tropical regions of Africa and Eurasia. During the last glacial epoch, between 32,000 and 13,000 years ago, human population may have fallen even lower. Then, as the glaciers retreated, people moved into new land and adopted agriculture. Their numbers gradually rose to 10 million by 5000 B.C.E. and mushroomed to between 50 million and 100 million by 1000 B.C.E.[1] This increase brought important changes to social and cultural life.

LIFE IN NEOLITHIC COMMUNITIES

The evidence that an ecological crisis may have driven people to food production has led researchers to reexamine the assumption that people in agricultural societies were better off than foragers. Modern studies demonstrate that food producers have to work much harder and for much longer periods than do food gatherers. In return for modest harvests, early farmers needed to put in long days of arduous labor clearing and cultivating the land. Pastoralists had to guard their herds from wild predators, guide them to fresh pastures, and tend to their many needs.

There also is evidence that even though the food supply of early farmers was more secure than that of food-gathering peoples and pastoralists, the farmers' diet was less varied and nutritious. Skeletal remains show that on average Neolithic farmers were shorter than earlier food-gathering peoples and more likely to die at an earlier age from contagious diseases. People in permanent settlements were more exposed to diseases from water contaminated by human waste, to disease-bearing vermin and insects that infested their bodies and homes, and to new diseases that migrated from their domesticated animals (especially pigs and cattle).

The great benefit that agriculture provided was a dependable supply of food that could be stored between harvests to tide people over seasonal changes and short-term climate fluctuations such as droughts. Over several millennia, farmers came to outnumber nonfarmers, permanent settlements experienced profound changes in culture, and towns and craft specialization began to emerge.

Rural Population and Settlement

Researchers have long wondered exactly how farmers displaced foragers. Some have envisioned a violent struggle between practitioners of the two ways of life; others believe there was a more peaceful transition. Some violence was likely, especially as the amount of cleared land reduced the wild foods available to foragers. Probable too were conflicts among farmers for control of the best land. A growing body of evidence, however, suggests that in most cases farmers displaced foragers by a process of gradual infiltration rather than by rapid conquest.

The key to the food producers' expansion may have been the simple fact that their small surpluses gave them a long-term advantage in population growth, by ensuring slightly higher survival rates during times of drought or other crisis. The respected archaeologist Colin Renfrew argues, for example, that over a few centuries farming-population densities in Europe could have increased by from fifty to one hundred fold. According to his scenario, as population densities rose, those individuals who had to farm at a great distance from their native village eventually formed a new farming settlement.

Renfrew finds it consistent with the archaeological evidence for a steady nonviolent expansion of agricultural peoples—moving only 12 to 19 miles (20 to 30 kilometers) a generation—to have repopulated the whole of Europe from Greece to Britain between 6500 and 3500 B.C.E.[2] The process would have been so gradual that it need not have provoked any sharp conflicts with existing foragers, who simply could have stayed clear of the agricultural frontier or gradually adopted agriculture themselves and been absorbed by the advancing farming communities. This hypothesis of a gradual spread of agricultural people across Europe from southeast to northwest is also supported by new studies that map similar genetic changes in the population.[3]

Like forager bands, the expanding farming communities were organized around kinship and marriage.

Nuclear families (parents and their children) probably did not become larger, but people traced kinship relations back over more generations so that distant cousins were clearly aware of their membership in the same kin network. This was important because landholding was likely to be vested in large kinship units known as lineages° and clans.

Even if one assumes stable marriage patterns, tracing descent is a complex matter. Because each person has two parents, four grandparents, eight great-grandparents, and so on, each individual has a bewildering number of ancestors. Some societies trace descent equally through both parents, but most give greater importance to descent through either the mother (matrilineal° societies) or the father (patrilineal° societies).

Some scholars have argued that very ancient peoples traced descent through women and may have been ruled by women. For example, the traditions of Kikuyu° farmers on Mount Kenya in East Africa relate that women ruled until the Kikuyu men conspired to get all the women pregnant at once and then overthrew them while the women were unable to fight back. No specific evidence can prove or disprove legends such as this, but it is important not to confuse tracing descent through women (matrilineality) with the rule of women (matriarchy°).

Cultural Expressions

Kinship systems influenced early agricultural people's outlook on the world. Reverence for departed ancestors fostered group solidarity, and the deaths of old persons tended to be marked by elaborate burials. The existence of a plastered skull from Jericho° in the Jordan Valley of modern Israel may be evidence of an early ancestor cult (religious rituals expressing reverence for or worship of ancestors).

The religion of food producers also reflected their awareness of their relationship to nature. The religions of food gatherers tended to center on sacred groves, springs, and wild animals. In contrast, the religions activities of many farming communities centered on the Earth Mother, a female deity believed to be the source of all new life, and on other gods and goddesses representing fire, wind, and rain. Belief in an all-powerful (and usually male) Sky God was also common.

The story in an ancient Hindu text about the burning of a large forest near modern India's capital, New

---

lineage (LIN-ee-ij)   **matrilineal** (mat-ruh-LIN-ee-uhl)
patrilineal (pat-ruh-LIN-ee-uhl)   **Kikuyi** (ki-KOO-yoo)
matriarchy (MAY-tree-ahr-key)   **Jericho** (JER-ih-koh)

Stonehenge, in Southern England   This view from the center of the megalithic circle looks through an arch to the Heel Stone, which marks the precise place where the sun rises on the horizon on the summer solstice, the beginning of summer. The changing of the seasons was an important part of religion in Neolithic Europe. (© Mick Sharp)

Delhi°, may preserve a memory of the conflict between old and new beliefs. In the story the gods Krishna° and Arjuna° are picnicking in the forest when Agni, the fire-god, appears in disguise and asks them to satisfy his hunger by burning the forest and every creature in it. As interpreted by some scholars, this story portrays both the clearing of the land for cultivation and the destruction of the wildlife on which food gatherers depended.[4]

Religions placed different emphasis on the role of ancestors, the Sky God, and the Earth Mother, but most seem to have included all three in their religious practices, along with older rituals and deities. Striking evidence comes from **megaliths** (meaning "big stones"). A recently discovered complex in the Egyptian desert in use by 5000 B.C.E. includes stone burial chambers, a calendar circle, and pairs of upright stones that frame the rising sun on the summer solstice. Observation and worship of the sun is also evident at the famous Stonehenge monolithic site in England constructed about 2000 B.C.E. Megalithic burial chambers dating from 4000 B.C.E. provide some evidence of an ancestor cult in western and southern Europe. The early ones appear to have been communal burial chambers, which descent groups may have erected to mark their claims to farmland. In the Middle East, the Americas, and other parts of the world, giant earth burial mounds may have served similar functions.

Another fundamental cultural contribution of the Neolithic period was the dissemination of the large language families that form the basis of most languages spoken today. Renfrew has suggested that the spread of the western half of the giant Indo-European language family (from which Germanic, Romance, and Celtic languages are derived) was the work of the pioneering agriculturalists who gradually moved across Europe. The differentiation of the language family into many related languages is indeed more consistent with a pattern of gradual infiltration than with rapid conquest. Similarly, the Afro-Asiatic language family that spans the Middle East and northern Africa might have been the result of the food producers' expansion, as might the spread of the Sino-Tibetan family in East and Southeast Asia.

Early Towns and Specialists

Most early farmers lived in small villages, but in some geographically favored parts of the world a few villages grew into towns, which were centers of trade and craft specialization. Towns had elaborate dwellings and ceremonial buildings made of mud brick, stone, and wood, as well as many large structures for storing surplus food until the next harvest. Baskets and other woven containers held dry foods; pottery jugs, jars, and pots stored liquids. Agriculturalists could make most of these structures and

Delhi (DEL-ee)   **Krishna** (KRISH-nuh)   **Arjuna** (AHR-joo-nuh)

objects in their spare time, but in large communities craft specialists devoted their full energies to making products of unusual complexity or beauty. Such specialization was possible because farmers produced a surplus of food and other necessities.

Two towns in the Middle East that have been extensively excavated are Jericho on the west bank of the Jordan River and Çatal Hüyük° in central Anatolia (modern Turkey). (Map 2.1 shows their location.) The excavations at Jericho revealed an unusually large and elaborate early agricultural settlement. Around 8000 B.C.E. dwellings at Jericho were round, mud-brick structures, perhaps imitating the shape of the tents of hunters who once had camped near Jericho's natural spring. A millennium later there were rectangular rooms with finely plastered walls and floors and wide doorways that opened on a central courtyard. Around the 10-acre (4-hectare) settlement extended a massive stone wall—probably for defense against invasion by local pastoralists.

The ruins of Çatal Hüyük, an even larger Neolithic town, date to between 7000 and 5000 B.C.E. and cover 32 acres (13 hectares). Its residents also occupied plastered mud-brick rooms that were elaborately decorated. Unlike Jericho, Çatal Hüyük had no defensive fortifications. But the outer walls of its houses formed a continuous barrier without doors or large windows, so invaders would have found it difficult to break in. Residents entered their house by climbing down a ladder through a hole in the roof.

Çatal Hüyük was a bustling town that prospered from long-distance trade in obsidian, a hard volcanic rock that craftspeople skillfully chipped, ground, and polished into tools, weapons, mirrors, and ornaments. Other residents made fine pottery and practiced many other crafts, including weaving baskets and woolen cloth, making stone and shell beads, and working leather and wood. House sizes varied, but there is no evidence that Çatal Hüyük had a dominant class or a centralized political structure.

Although the amount and importance of craftwork in Jericho and Çatal Hüyük were quite new in history, the two towns displayed many close links with older ways of living. Representational art at Çatal Hüyük makes it clear that hunting retained a powerful hold on people's minds. Elaborate wall paintings of hunting scenes are remarkably similar to those of earlier cave paintings. Many of them depict persons, both males and females, adorned with the skins of wild leopards. Also, men were buried with weapons of war and hunting, not with the tools of farming, and discarded bones are proof that wild game featured prominently in the diet of the town's residents.

Neolithic Goddess   Many versions of a well-nourished and pregnant female figure were found at Çatal Hüyük. Here she is supported by twin leopards whose tails curve over her shoulders. To those who inhabited the city some 8,000 years ago the figure likely represented fertility and power over nature.   (C. M. Dixon)

However neglected in the art of Çatal Hüyük, agriculture was the basis of the town's existence. Fields around Çatal Hüyük produced crops of barley and emmer wheat, as well as legumes° and other vegetables. Pigs were kept along with goats and sheep. Yet wild foods still featured prominently in the diet of the town's residents. Archaelogists have dug up remains of acorns, wild grains, and wild game animals.

Perhaps the most striking finds at Çatal Hüyük are those that reveal religious practices. There is a religious shrine for every two houses. At least forty rooms contained shrines with depictions of horned wild bulls, female breasts, goddesses, leopards, and handprints. There are dishes in which grains, legumes, and meat were burned as offerings; there is no evidence of live animal sacrifice. The fact that statues of plump female deities far outnumber statues of male deities persuaded

---

Çatal Hüyük (cha-TAHL hoo-YOOK)

legume (LEG-yoom)

the principal excavator of Çatal Hüyük that a cult of the goddess was central to the town's religion. He further concluded that the large number of females who had received elaborate burials in the shrine rooms were priestesses of this cult. In his view, although male priests were also present, "It seems extremely likely that the cult of the goddess was administered mainly by women."[5]

Metalworking was another important specialized occupation in the late Neolithic period. At Çatal Hüyük objects of copper and lead—metals that occur naturally in a fairly pure form—can be dated to about 6400 B.C.E. In many parts of the world silver and gold were also worked at an early date. Because of their rarity and their softness those metals did not replace stone tools and weapons but instead were used primarily to make decorative or ceremonial objects. The discovery of many such objects in graves suggests they were symbols of status and power.

The growth of towns, specialized crafts, and elaborate religious shrines added to the workload of agriculturalists, who already had to work hard to till the soil. Extra food had to be produced to feed the nonfarming full-time priests and craft specialists. In addition, the towns' permanent houses needed much labor to build, as did Jericho's defensive walls and towers. Building religious monuments in stone must have occupied much time during the less busy season of the agricultural year. It is estimated, for example, that even a fairly small structure like Stonehenge took 30,000 person-hours to build. No evidence from this period indicates whether these tasks were performed freely or coerced.

CONCLUSION

The period of time that this chapter covers is immense, far longer than the combined time span of all the rest of the chapters in this book. Compressing so long a period into a single chapter highlights the fundamental and gradually evolving relationships between humans and their natural environment—relationships that underlie all human history.

In the first stage the struggle to survive in the changing environments of the early Ice Age gave rise to the physical evolution of human beings. Next, early humans' distinctive physical and mental abilities enabled them to adapt to many different natural environments. The cultures, consisting of tools, techniques, and specialized technical knowledge that societies passed down from one generation to the next, enabled humans to exploit many natural environments.

Technology enabled cultural change to become the alternative to biological change. By the late Paleolithic period all hominid species had become extinct except one: *Homo sapiens sapiens*. They were the least varied biologically of any living organism, yet they were the earth's most widely dispersed mammals. Our ancestors had learned how to thrive in all the habitable continents, where they had developed many diverse cultures.

Then the transition from food collection to food production brought the greatest modification of the natural environment and the greatest cultural changes since people first walked on earth. Indeed, the agricultural revolutions were among the most momentous changes in all of human history. Agriculture brought many toils and hardships, but it enabled people to exercise over the natural environment a degree of control that no other species had ever attained. The transition to farming and settled life opened the way to still greater changes in technology and population size as well as in social and cultural diversity. The patterns of language and belief, of diet, dress, and dwelling, that emerged in the Neolithic period shaped the next several millennia. As Chapters 2 and 3 detail, specialization made possible by settled life gave rise to significant advances in architecture and metallurgy, to artistic achievements, and to the growth of complex religious and political systems.

■ Key Terms

natural selection	culture
evolution	history
australopithecine	Stone Age
hominid	Paleolithic
bipedalism	Neolithic
Great Ice Age	forager
Homo habilis	Agricultural Revolutions
Homo erectus	Holocene
Homo sapiens	megalith

■ Suggested Reading

Useful reference works for this period are the *Encyclopedia of Human Evolution and Prehistory* (1988) and the *Cambridge Encyclopedia of Human Evolution* (1992). Reliable textbooks are Brian Fagan's *People of the Earth: An Introduction to World Prehistory*, 9th ed. (1997), and Bernard G. Campbell, *Humankind Emerging*, 6th ed. (1992). Fagan also has written *World Prehistory: A Brief Introduction*, 4th ed. (1998).

Accounts of the discoveries of early human remains, written for the nonspecialist by eminent researchers, include Donald Johanson, Leorna Johanson, and Blake Edgar, *In Search of Human Origins* (1994), based on the *Nova* television series of the same name; Richard Leakey and Roger Lewin, *Origins Reconsidered: In Search of What Makes Us Human* (1992); and Donald C. Johanson and Maitland A. Edey, *Lucy: The Beginnings of Mankind* (1981). Other useful books that deal with this subject include George D. Brown, Jr., *Human Evolution* (1995), for a precise biological and geological perspective; Adam Kuper, *The Chosen Primate: Human Nature and Cultural Diversity* (1994), for an anthropological analysis; Glyn Daniel and Colin Renfrew, *The Idea of Prehistory*, 2d ed. (1988), detailing the development of the discipline and relying primarily on European examples; and Robert Foley, *Another Unique Species: Patterns in Human Evolutionary Ecology* (1987), a thoughtful and readable attempt to bring together archaeological evidence and biological processes.

More analytical overviews of the evolutionary evidence are James L. Newman, *The Peopling of Africa: A Geographical Interpretation* (1995); L. Luca Cavalli-Sforza and Francesco Cavalli-Sforza, *The Great Human Diasporas: The History of Diversity and Evolution* (1995), for genetic evidence; Richard G. Klein, *The Human Career: Human Biological and Cultural Origins* (1989); and Paul Mellars, ed., *The Emergence of Modern Humans* (1991). Thoughtful explorations of key issues are Colin Renfrew, *Archaeology and Language: The Puzzle of Indo-European Origins* (1988); and Marija Gimbutas, *The Civilization of the Goddess: The World of Old Europe* (1991). Margaret Ehrenberg, *Women in Prehistory* (1989), and M. Kay Martin and Barbara Voorhies, *Female of the Species* (1975), provide interesting, though necessarily speculative, discussions of women's history.

Cave and rock art and their implications are the subject of many works. A broad, global introduction is Hans-Georg Bandi, *The Art of the Stone Age: Forty Thousand Years of Rock Art* (1961).

Ann Sieveking, *The Cave Artists* (1979), provides a brief overview of the major European finds. Other specialized studies are Robert R. R. Brooks and Vishnu S. Wakankar, *Stone Age Painting in India* (1976); R. Townley Johnson, *Major Rock Paintings of Southern Africa* (1979); J. D. Lewis-Williams, *Believing and Seeing* (1981) and *Discovering Southern African Rock Art* (1990); Mario Ruspoli, *The Cave Art of Lascaux* (1986); and N. K. Sanders, *Prehistoric Art in Europe* (1968).

For the transition to food production see Jared Diamond, *Guns, Germs, and Steel: The Fates of Human Societies* (1997), and Allen W. Johnson and Timothy Earle, *The Evolution of Human Societies: From Foraging Group to Agrarian State* (1987). Jean-Pierre Mohen, *The World of Megaliths* (1990), analyzes early monumental architecture. James Mellaart, the principal excavator of Çatal Hüyük, has written an account of the town for the general reader: *Çatal Hüyük: A Neolithic Town in Anatolia* (1967). A pioneering work on human ecology, whose early sections are about this period, is Madhav Gadgil and Ramachandra Guha, *This Fissured Land: An Ecological History of India* (1992).

■ Notes

1. Colin McEvedy and Richard Jones, *Atlas of World Population History* (New York: Penguin Books, 1978), 13–15.
2. Colin Renfrew, *Archaeology and Language: The Puzzle of Indo-European Origins* (New York: Cambridge University Press, 1988), 125, 150.
3. Luigi Cavalli-Sforza, L. Luca, Paolo Menozzi, and Alberto Piazza, *The History and Geography of Human Genes* (Princeton, NJ: Princeton University Press, 1994).
4. Madhav Gadgil and Ramachandra Guha, *This Fissured Land: An Ecological History of India* (Berkeley: University of California Press, 1992), 79.
5. James Mellaart, *Çatal Hüyük: A Neolithic Town in Anatolia* (New York: McGraw-Hill, 1967), 202.

2

THE FIRST RIVER-VALLEY CIVILIZATIONS,
3500–1500 B.C.E.

Mesopotamia • Egypt • The Indus Valley Civilization
ENVIRONMENT AND TECHNOLOGY: Environmental Stress in the Indus Valley
SOCIETY AND CULTURE: The Babylonian New Year's Festival

Painted Wooden Models from the Tomb of an Egyptian Nobleman, ca. 2000 B.C.E.
Meketre, seated at right, oversees inspection of his cattle with the help of herdsmen and other servants.

he *Epic of Gilgamesh*, whose roots date to some time before 2000 B.C.E., making it one of the oldest surviving works of literature, provides a definition of *civilization* as the people of ancient Mesopotamia (present-day Iraq) understood it. Gilgamesh, an early king, sends a temple-prostitute to tame Enkidu°, a wild man who lives like an animal in the grasslands. After using her sexual charms to win Enkidu's trust, she says to him:

> Come with me to the city, to Uruk°,
> to the temple of Anu and the goddess Ishtar . . .
> to Uruk, where the processions are and music,
> let us go together through the dancing
> to the palace hall where Gilgamesh presides.[1]

She then clothes Enkidu and teaches him to eat cooked food, drink brewed beer, and bathe and oil his body. By her words and actions she indicates some of the behavior that ancient Mesopotamians associated with civilized life.

The tendency of the Mesopotamians, like other peoples throughout history, to equate civilization with their own way of life should serve as a caution for us. What assumptions are hiding behind the frequently made claim that the "first" civilizations, or the first "advanced" or "high" civilizations, arose in western Asia and northeastern Africa sometime before 3000 B.C.E.? Given that *civilization* is a loaded and ambiguous concept, the idea that the first civilizations emerged in ancient Mesopotamia and Egypt needs to be explained carefully.

Scholars agree that certain political, social, economic, and technological phenomena are indicators of **civilization:** (1) cities that served as administrative centers, (2) a political system based on control of a defined territory rather than on connections of kinship, (3) a significant number of people engaged in specialized, non-food-producing activities, (4) status distinctions, usually linked to the accumulation of substantial wealth by some groups, (5) monumental building, (6) a system for keeping permanent records, (7) long-distance trade, and (8) major advances in science and the arts. The earliest societies in which those features are apparent developed in the floodplains of great rivers in Asia and Africa: the Tigris° and Euphrates° in Iraq, the Indus in Pakistan, the Yellow (Huang He°) in China, and the Nile in Egypt (see Map 2.1). The periodic flooding of the rivers brought benefits—deposits of fertile silt and water for agriculture—but also threatened lives and property. To protect themselves and channel these powerful forces of nature, people living near the rivers created new technologies and forms of political and social organization.

In this chapter we trace the rise of complex societies in Mesopotamia, Egypt, and the Indus River Valley from approximately 3500 to 1500 B.C.E. Our starting point roughly coincides with the origins of writing, so we can observe aspects of human experience that scholars cannot deduce from archaeological evidence alone. Because the independent emergence of civilization based on river floods and irrigation occurred somewhat later in China than in Mesopotamia, Egypt, and the Indus Valley, early China is taken up in the next chapter.

As you read this chapter, ask yourself the following questions:

- Why did the earliest civilizations rise in such challenging environments?
- How did the need to organize labor resources shape the political and social structures of these societies?
- To what degree did new technologies, such as metallurgy, writing, and monumental construction, contribute to the power and wealth of elite groups?
- How is the interaction of these societies with the environment reflected in their religious beliefs and world-views?

Enkidu (EN-kee-doo)   Uruk (OO-rook)

Tigris (TIE-gris)   Euphrates (you-FRAY-teez)
Huang He (hwang huh)

CHRONOLOGY

	Mesopotamia	Egypt	Indus Valley
3500 B.C.E.			
3000 B.C.E.	**3000–2350** B.C.E. Early Dynastic (Sumerian)	**3100–2575** B.C.E. Early Dynastic	
2500 B.C.E.	**2350–2230** B.C.E. Akkadian (Semitic)	**2575–2134** B.C.E. Old Kingdom	**2600** B.C.E. Beginning of Indus Valley civilization
2000 B.C.E.	**2112–2004** B.C.E. Third Dynasty of Ur (Sumerian) **1900–1600** B.C.E. Old Babylonian (Semitic)	**2134–2040** B.C.E. First Intermediate Period **2040–1640** B.C.E. Middle Kingdom	**1900** B.C.E. End of Indus Valley civilization
1500 B.C.E.	**1500–1150** B.C.E. Kassite	**1640–1532** B.C.E. Second Intermediate Period **1532–1070** B.C.E. New Kingdom	

MESOPOTAMIA

Because of the unpredictable nature of the Tigris and Euphrates Rivers and the weather, the peoples of ancient Mesopotamia saw the world as a hazardous place where human beings were at the mercy of gods who embodied the forces of nature. One of their explanations for the origins and characteristics of their world is what we know as the Babylonian Creation Myth (**Babylon** was the most important city in southern Mesopotamia in the second and first millennia B.C.E.). The high point of the myth is a cosmic battle between Marduk, the chief god of Babylon, and Tiamat°, a female figure who personifies the salt sea. Marduk cuts up Tiamat and from her body fashions the earth and sky. He then creates the divisions of time, the celestial bodies, rivers, and weather phenomena, and from the blood of a defeated rebel god he creates human beings. Creation myths of this sort provided the ancient inhabitants of Mesopotamia with a satisfactory explanation for the environment in which they were living.

Settled Agriculture in an Unstable Landscape

Mesopotamia is a Greek word meaning "land between the rivers." It reflects the centrality of the Euphrates and Tigris Rivers to the way of life in this region (see Map 2.2). Mesopotamian civilization developed in the plain alongside and between the Tigris and Euphrates, which originate in the mountains of eastern Anatolia (modern Turkey) and empty into the Persian Gulf. This is an alluvial plain—a flat, fertile expanse built up over many millennia by silt that the rivers deposited.

Mesopotamia lies mostly within modern Iraq. Certain natural features establish its boundaries. To the north and east, an arc of mountains extends from northern Syria and southeastern Anatolia to the Zagros°

Tiamat (TIE-ah-mat)

Zagros (ZAG-ruhs)

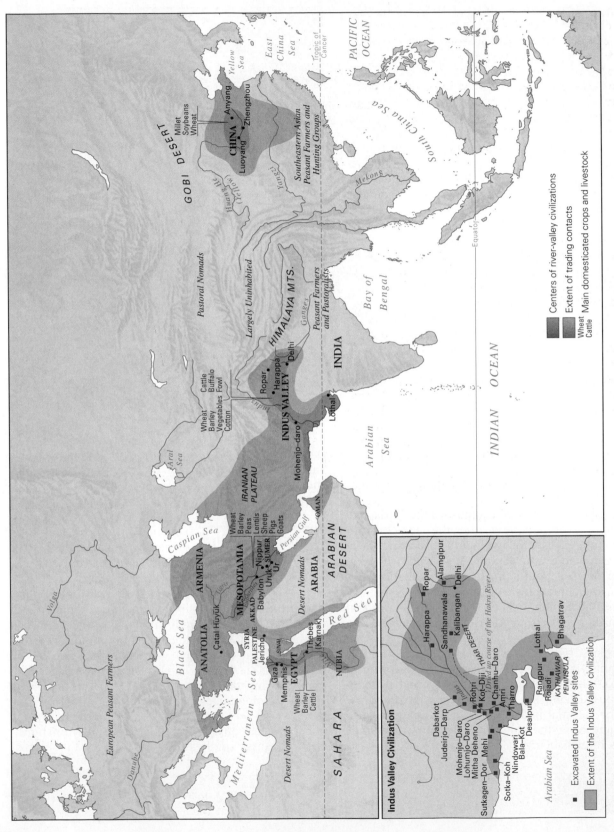

Map 2.1   River-Valley Civilizations, 3500–1500 B.C.E.   The earliest complex societies arose in the flood plains of large rivers: in the fourth millennium B.C.E. in the valley of the Tigris and Euphrates Rivers in Mesopotamia and the Nile River in Egypt, in the third millennium B.C.E. in the valley of the Indus River in Pakistan, and in the second millennium B.C.E. in the valley of the Yellow River in China.

Mountains, which cut off the plain of the Tigris and Euphrates from the Iranian Plateau. To the west and southwest lie the Syrian and Arabian deserts. To the southeast lies the Persian Gulf. This region is subject to unpredictable extremes of weather. Floods can be sudden and violent and tend to come at the wrong time for grain agriculture—in the spring when the crop is ripening in the field. Also ever present is the danger of the rivers changing course, suddenly cutting off fields and population centers from supplies of water and avenues of communication.

The first domestication of plants and animals took place not far away, in the "Fertile Crescent" region of northern Syria and southeastern Anatolia, around 8000 B.C.E. Agriculture did not come to Mesopotamia until approximately 5000 B.C.E. Agriculture that depends on rain requires annual rainfall of at least 8 inches (20 centimeters). In hot, dry southern Mesopotamia, agriculture depended on irrigation—the artificial provision of water to growing crops. At first, people probably took advantage of the occasional flooding of the rivers into the nearby fields, but shortly after 3000 B.C.E. they learned to construct canals to supply water as needed and to carry water to more distant parcels of land.

By 4000 B.C.E. farmers were using plows pulled by cattle to turn over the earth. A funnel attached to the plow dropped a carefully measured amount of seed. Barley was the main cereal crop in southern Mesopotamia because it was able to tolerate the hot, dry conditions and to withstand the effects of the salt drawn to the surface of the soil when the fields were flooded. Fields were left fallow (unplanted) every other year, to replenish the nutrients in the soil. Date palms provided food, fibers, and some wood. Small garden plots produced vegeta-

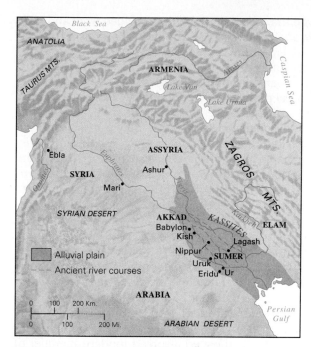

Map 2.2   Mesopotamia   The Sumerians of southern Mesopotamia developed new technologies, complex political and social institutions, and distinctive cultural practices, responding to the need to organize labor resources to create and maintain an irrigation network in the Tigris-Euphrates Valley, a land of little rain.

bles. Reed plants, which grew on the river banks and in the marshy southern delta, could be woven into mats, baskets, huts, and boats. Fish from the rivers and marshes were an important part of people's diet. Herds of sheep and goats, which grazed on the fallow land and

Reed Huts in the Marshes of Southern Iraq   Reeds growing along the riverbanks or in the swampy lands at the head of the Persian Gulf were used in antiquity—and continue to be used today—for a variety of purposes, including baskets and small watercraft as well as dwellings. (Courtesy, Dominique Collon)

beyond the zone of cultivation, provided wool and milk. Cattle and donkeys carried or pulled burdens; in the second millennium B.C.E. they were joined by newly introduced camels and horses.

The earliest people living in Mesopotamia in the "historical period"—the period for which we have some written evidence—are the **Sumerians.** There is mounting archaeological evidence that they were in southern Mesopotamia at least by 5000 B.C.E. and perhaps even before then. The Sumerians created the main framework of civilization in Mesopotamia, and the third millennium B.C.E. was primarily a Sumerian epoch, although even in this period the Sumerians were not the only ethnic and linguistic group inhabiting the Tigris-Euphrates Valley. From as early as 2900 B.C.E. the names of individuals recorded in inscriptions from northerly cities in the plain suggest the presence of Semites, people who spoke a **Semitic°** language. (The term *Semitic* refers to a family of related languages that have long been spoken across parts of western Asia and northern Africa. In antiquity these languages included Hebrew, Aramaic°, and Phoenician°; the most widespread modern member of the Semitic family is Arabic.) Historians believe that these Semites descended from nomadic peoples who had migrated into the Mesopotamian plain from the western desert. There is little indication of ethnic conflict between Sumerians and Semites. The Semites assimilated to Sumerian culture and sometimes gained positions of wealth and power.

By 2000 B.C.E. the Semitic peoples had become politically dominant, and from this time forward Akkadian°, a Semitic language, was the primary language in Mesopotamia. Much of the Sumerian cultural legacy, however, was preserved. Sumerian-Akkadian dictionaries were compiled, Sumerian literature was translated, and the characteristics and adventures of the Semitic gods indicated borrowing from Sumerian religion. This cultural synthesis parallels a biological merging of Sumerian and Semitic stocks through intermarriage. Other ethnic groups, including mountain peoples such as the Kassites° as well as Elamites° and Persians from Iran, played a part in Mesopotamian history. But not until the arrival of Greeks in the Middle East in the late fourth century B.C.E. was the Sumerian/Semitic cultural heritage of Mesopotamia fundamentally altered.

Cities, Kings, and Trade

Mesopotamia was a land of villages and cities. Villages—groups of families that live close to one another—are common in agricultural societies. By banding together, farming families can protect each other, share tools and facilities such as barns and threshing floors, and help each other at key times in the agricultural cycle. Villages also serve human social needs by providing companionship as well as a pool of potential marriage partners.

Most cities evolved from villages. As a successful village grew, small satellite villages developed nearby, and eventually the main village and its satellites coalesced into an urban center. Cities and villages were linked in a relationship of mutual dependence. Cities depended on agriculture. The earliest known urban centers in the Middle East, such as Jericho° and Çatal Hüyük°, sprang up shortly after the first appearance of agriculture (see Chapter 1), and many early Mesopotamian city dwellers went out each day to labor in nearby fields. In nonurban societies almost everyone engaged in the basic tasks of subsistence, gathering or growing enough food to feed themselves and their families. Cities, however, depended on villagers to produce surplus food to feed urban residents who did not engage in food production but, instead, specialized in activities such as metallurgy (creating useful objects from metal), crafts, administration, and serving the gods. In Mesopotamia, a city controlled the agricultural land and villages in its vicinity, requiring surplus foodstuffs to feed its population of specialists. In return, the city provided rural districts with military protection against bandits and raiders and a market where villagers could trade surplus products for manufactured goods produced by urban specialists.

We use the term **city-state** to refer to independent ancient urban centers and the agricultural territories they controlled. Early Mesopotamia was a land of many small city-states. Stretches of open and uncultivated land, whether desert or swamp, lay between the territories controlled by the various communities and served as buffers. However, disputes over land, water rights, and movable property often sparked hostilities between neighboring cities and prompted most to build protective walls of sun-dried mud bricks. But cities also cooperated in various ways, sharing water and allowing safe passage of trade goods through their territories.

To produce adequate food surpluses in the Tigris-Euphrates Valley, the Mesopotamians opened new land

---

Semitic (suh-MIT-ik)   **Aramaic** (ar-uh-MAY-ik)
Phoenician (fi-NEE-shuhn)   **Akkadian** (uh-KAY-dee-uhn)
Kassite (KAS-ite)   **Elamite** (EE-luh-mite)

Jericho (JER-ih-koe)   **Çatal Hüyük** (cha-TAHL hoo-YOOK)

to agriculture by building and maintaining an extensive irrigation network. Canals brought water to fields far away from the rivers. Drainage ditches carried water away from flooded fields before salt and minerals harmful to crops were drawn to the surface of the soil. Dikes protected young plants emerging in fields near the riverbanks from being destroyed by floods. Gravity moved water through the network. Dams raised the water level of the river so that water could flow into irrigation channels. A machine with counterweights was invented to lift heavy buckets of water—for example, up from the river and over the dike to the land beyond. Because the rivers carried so much silt, channels got clogged and needed constant dredging.

The successful operation of such a sophisticated irrigation infrastructure depended on the emergence of individuals or groups capable of compelling and organizing large numbers of people to work together. Other projects also relied on the cooperation of many people: the harvest, sheep shearing, the erection of fortification walls, the construction of large public buildings, and warfare. Little is known about the political institutions of early Mesopotamian city-states, although there are traces of some sort of citizens' assembly that may have evolved from the traditional village council. The two centers of power for which there are written records are the temple and the palace of the king.

Each Mesopotamian city contained one or more temples, centrally located, housing the cult (a set of religious practices) of the deity or deities who watched over the community. The temples owned extensive tracts of agricultural land and stored the gifts that worshipers donated. The importance of cults is confirmed by the central location of the temple buildings. The leading members of the priesthood, who controlled the shrine and managed the deity's considerable wealth, appear to have been the most prominent political and economic force in early Mesopotamian communities.

In the third millennium B.C.E. another kind of leadership developed in the Sumerian cities. A figure referred to in Sumerian documents as *lugal°*, or "big man"—we would call him a king—emerged. How this position evolved is not clear, but it may have been related to an increase in the frequency and scale of warfare as ever-larger communities quarreled over land, water, and raw materials. According to one plausible theory, certain men chosen by the community to lead the armies in time of war found ways to extend their authority in

lugal (LOO-guhl)

Stone Wall Plaque Depicting the Sumerian Ruler of Lagash, Twenty-Fifth Century, B.C.E. In the upper register the king, Ur-Nanshe, carries on his head a basket containing mud bricks, symbolizing his role as a builder. The figures to the right may be his wife and sons. In the lower register subjects or members of court approach the king, seated on his throne. The king's superior status is indicated by his size. (Louvre © R.M.N.)

peacetime and to assume key judicial and ritual functions. The position of lugal was not automatically hereditary, but capable sons could succeed their fathers.

The later development of this secular authority may be reflected in the position of the palace, the seat of the king's power. The palace tends not to be as centrally located as the temple, having emerged after the heart of the city was established. The overall trend, however, favored the king, presumably because the army backed him. Though remaining influential because of their wealth and religious mystique, the priests and temples gradually became dependent on the palace. By the late third millennium B.C.E. royal officials were supervising the temples. Some Mesopotamian kings claimed to be gods on earth, but this concept did not take root, and the normal pattern was for the king to portray himself as the earthly representative of the god.

Accordingly, the king assumed responsibility for the upkeep and building of temples and the proper performance of ritual. Other key royal responsibilities included maintenance of the city walls and defenses, upkeep and extension of the irrigation channels, preservation of property rights, and protection of the people from outside attackers and from perversions of justice at home.

In the *Epic of Gilgamesh* we catch glimpses of both the restless ambition and the value to the community of this new breed of rulers. The story is probably based on a historical figure who was king of Uruk. Gilgamesh is depicted as the strongest man in his community. His subjects resent his prerogative to demand sexual favors from new brides, but they depend on his wisdom and courage to protect them. In his quest for everlasting glory, Gilgamesh builds magnificent walls around the city and stamps his name on all the bricks. His journey to the far-away Cedar Mountains reflects the king's role in bringing valuable resources to the community.

Over time certain political centers became powerful enough to extend their control over other city-states. Sargon°, ruler of the city of Akkad° around 2350 B.C.E., was the first to unite many cities under the control of one king and capital. His title, "King of Sumer and Akkad," became symbolic of this claim to universal dominion. Sargon and the four members of his family who succeeded him over a period of 120 years secured their power in a number of ways. They razed the walls of conquered cities and installed governors backed by garrisons of Akkadian troops. Soldiers were given land to ensure their loyalty. Because Sargon and his people were of Semitic stock, the cuneiform° system of writing used for Sumerian (discussed later in the chapter) was adapted to express their language. A uniform system of weights and measures and standardized formats for official documents facilitated tasks of administration such as the assessment and collection of taxes, recruitment of soldiers, and organization of large labor projects.

For reasons that are not completely clear to modern scholars, the Akkadian state fell around 2230 B.C.E. A last resurgence of Sumerian language and culture in the cities of the southern plain was seen under the Third Dynasty of Ur (2112–2004 B.C.E.). Based on a combination of campaigns of conquest and alliances cemented by marriage, the dynasty encompassed five kings who ruled for a century. This state did not control territories as extensive as those of its Akkadian predecessor, but a rapidly expanding bureaucracy of administrators led to tight government control of a wide range of activities and an obsessive degree of recordkeeping. A corps of messengers and well-maintained road stations facilitated rapid communication, and an official calendar, standardized weights and measures, and uniform writing practices enhanced the effectiveness of the central administra-

tion. As the southern plain came under increasing pressure from Semitic Amorites° in the northwest, the kings erected a great wall 125 miles (201 kilometers) in length to keep out the nomadic invaders. In the end, though, the Third Dynasty of Ur succumbed to the combined pressure of nomadic incursions and an attack of Elamites coming from the southeast.

The Amorites founded a new city at Babylon, not far from Akkad. Toward the end of a long reign, **Hammurabi°** (r. 1792–1750 B.C.E.) initiated a series of aggressive military campaigns, and Babylon became the capital of what historians have named the "Old Babylonian" state, which eventually extended its control not only over Sumer and Akkad but also far to the north and northwest from 1800 to 1600 B.C.E. Hammurabi is best known for his Law Code, inscribed on a polished black stone pillar. Though probably not a comprehensive list of all the laws of the time, Hammurabi's Code provided judges with a lengthy set of examples illustrating the principles they were to employ when deciding cases. Some of its formulations call for severe physical punishments to be inflicted on the body of an offender to compensate for a crime. When we compare them to the monetary penalties in the earlier codes from Ur, we see that the Amorites introduced their own principles of justice.

The far-reaching conquests of some Mesopotamian states were motivated, at least in part, by the need to obtain vital resources. The alternative was to trade for raw materials, and long-distance commerce did flourish in most periods. Evidence of boats used in sea trade goes back as far as the fifth millennium B.C.E. Wood, metals, and stone had to be imported from afar. In exchange, wool, cloth, barley, and oil were exported. Wood was acquired from cedar forests in Lebanon and Syria. Silver came from Anatolia, gold from Egypt, copper from the eastern Mediterranean and Oman (on the Arabian peninsula), tin from Afghanistan (in south-central Asia). Chlorite, a greenish stone from which bowls were carved, came from the Iranian Plateau. For jewelry and carved figurines, black diorite was imported from the Persian Gulf, blue lapis lazuli° from eastern Iran and Afghanistan, and reddish carnelian° from Pakistan.

In the third millennium B.C.E. merchants were primarily in the employ of the palace or temple. Those were the only two institutions with the financial resources and long-distance connections to organize the collection, transport, and protection of goods. Merchants exchanged the surplus from the agricultural estates of

---

Sargon (SAHR-gone)   **Akkad** (AH-kahd)
cuneiform (kyoo-NEE-uh-form)

Amorite (AM-uh-rite)   **Hammurabi** (HAM-uh-rah-bee)
lapis lazuli (LAP-is LAZ-uh-lee)   **carnelian** (kahr-NEEL-yuhn)

kings or priests for vital raw materials and luxury goods. In the second millennium B.C.E. commerce came more and more into the hands of independent merchants, and merchant guilds became powerful forces in the community.

Modern scholars do not know where in the Mesopotamian city the most important commercial activities took place. Two possible locations are the area just inside the city gates and in the vicinity of the docks. Wherever it occurred, commercial activity was accomplished without the benefit of money. Coins—pieces of metal whose value the state guarantees—were not invented until the sixth century B.C.E. and did not reach Mesopotamia until several centuries later. For most of Mesopotamian history, items could be bartered—traded for one another—or valued in relation to fixed weights of precious metal, primarily silver, or measures of grain.

Mesopotamian Society

A persistent feature of urbanized civilizations is the development of social divisions—that is, obvious variations in the status and privileges of different groups of people due to differences in wealth, social functions, and legal and political rights. The rise of cities, specialization of function, centralization of power, and use of written records enabled certain groups of people to amass wealth on an unprecedented scale. In Mesopotamia temple leaders and the kings controlled large agricultural estates, and the palace administration collected various taxes from subjects. It is less apparent how the Mesopotamians who made up what we might call an elite class acquired large holdings of land, for the sale of land was rare. Debtors who could not pay what they owed forfeited their land, and soldiers and religious officials received plots of land in return for their services.

Social divisions in Mesopotamian society must have varied considerably over time and place, but the situation that historians can infer from the Law Code of Hammurabi for Babylon in the eighteenth century B.C.E. may reveal fundamental distinctions valid for other places and times. Society was divided into three classes: (1) the free, landowning class, which included royalty, high-ranking officials, warriors, priests, merchants, and some artisans and shopkeepers; (2) the class of dependent farmers and artisans, who were legally attached to land that belonged to king, temple, or elite families and thus provided the bulk of the work force for the rural estates and temple complexes; and (3) the class of slaves, primarily employed in domestic service. Penalties for crimes prescribed in the Law Code depended on the class of the offender. The most severe punishments were reserved for the lower orders.

Slavery existed but was not as prevalent and fundamental to the economy as it would be in the later societies of Greece and Rome (see Chapters 5 and 6). Many of the slaves came from mountain tribes and had been either captured in war or sold by slave traders. There was a separate category of slavery for those who were unable to pay off a debt. Under normal circumstances slaves were not chained or otherwise constrained, but they had to wear a distinctive hair style. If they were given their freedom, a barber shaved off the telltale mark. In the surviving documents it is often hard to distinguish slaves or dependent workers from free laborers, because all were compensated with commodities such as food and oil in quantities proportional to a person's age, gender, and task. In the Old Babylonian period, as the class of people who were not dependent on the great institutions of temple or palace grew in numbers and importance, the amount of land and other property in private hands increased, and there was a greater tendency to hire free laborers.

It is difficult to reconstruct the life experiences of ordinary Mesopotamians, especially those who lived in villages or on large estates in the countryside, because they left little trace in the archaeological or literary record. Rural peasants built their houses out of materials such as mud brick and reed, which quickly disintegrate, and they possessed little in the way of metals. Being illiterate, they were not able to write about their lives.

It is particularly difficult to discover very much about the experiences of women in ancient Mesopotamia. The written sources are the product of male **scribes**—trained professionals who applied their skills in reading and writing to tasks of administration—and for the most part reflect elite male activities. Archaeological remains provide only limited insight into attitudes toward women, their status, and activities.

Anthropologists theorize that women lost social standing and freedom in societies where agriculture superseded hunting and gathering (see Chapter 1). In hunting and gathering societies women provided most of the community's food from their gathering activities, and this work was highly valued. But in a place like Mesopotamia the provision of food for the community depended on the hard physical work of dragging around a plow and digging irrigation channels, and that sort of labor usually was done by men. Food surpluses permitted families to have more children, and bearing and raising children became the primary occupation of many women. The amount of time that women gave to the care of children prevented most of them from acquiring the specialized skills of the scribe or artisan.

Women had no political role, but they were able to own property, maintain control of their dowry, and even engage in trade. Some women worked outside the household, in textile factories and breweries or as prostitutes, tavern keepers, bakers, or fortunetellers. Non-elite women who stayed at home must have engaged in other tasks as well as child care, such as helping with the harvest, planting vegetable gardens, cooking and baking, cleaning the house, fetching water, tending the household fire, and weaving baskets and textiles.

The standing of women seems to have declined further in the second millennium B.C.E. Perhaps this development was linked to the rise of an urbanized middle class and an increase in private wealth. The husband became more dominant in the household and received greater latitude in laws relating to marriage and divorce. Although Mesopotamian society was generally monogamous, a man could obtain a second wife if the first gave him no children, and in the later stages of Mesopotamian history kings and others who could afford to do so had several wives. A woman could be used by her family to preserve and increase the family's wealth through an arranged marriage, which created an alliance between families. Or a family could decide to avoid the marriage of a daughter—and the resulting loss of a dowry—by dedicating a girl to the service of a deity as "god's bride." Some scholars believe that from the second millennium B.C.E. may originate the constraints on women that eventually became part of the Islamic tradition, such as the expectation that they confine themselves to the household and wear veils in public (see Chapter 9).

Gods, Priests, and Temples

The ancient Mesopotamians believed in a multitude of gods who embodied the forces of nature. For the Sumerians the god Anu was the sky, Enlil the air, Enki the water, Utu the sun, Nanna the moon. The emotional impulses of sexual attraction and violence were the domain of the goddess Inanna. When the Semitic peoples became dominant, they equated their deities with those of the Sumerians. For example, the Sumerian gods Nanna and Utu became the Semitic Sin and Shamash, and the goddess Inanna became Ishtar. The myths of the Sumerian deities were transferred to their Semitic counterparts, and many of the same rituals continued to be practiced.

Mesopotamian Cylinder Seal   Seals indicated the identity of an individual and were impressed into wet clay or wax to "sign" legal documents or to mark ownership of an object. This seal, produced in the period of the Akkadian Empire, depicts Ea (second from right), the god of underground waters, symbolized by the stream with fish emanating from his shoulders; Ishtar, whose attributes of fertility and war are indicated by the date cluster in her hand and the pointed weapons showing above her wings; and the sun-god Shamash, cutting his way out of the mountains with a jagged knife, an evocation of sunrise.   (Courtesy of the Trustees of the British Museum)

People believed the gods were anthropomorphic°—like humans in form and conduct. They thought the gods had bodies and senses, sought nourishment from sacrifice, enjoyed the worship and obedience of humanity, and were driven by lust, love, hate, anger, and all the other emotions that motivated human beings. The Mesopotamians feared their gods. They believed the gods were responsible for the changes that occurred without warning in the landscape in which they lived, and they sought to appease the deities by any means.

Most visible in the archaeological record is the public, state-organized religion. Each city built temples to one or more patron divinities who protected the community and were given special devotion. Nippur (see Map 2.2), with its temple of the air-god Enlil, was especially venerated as a religious center for all the peoples of Sumer. The temple was regarded as the residence of the god, and the cult statue, in a special interior shrine, was believed to embody the life-force of the deity. Priests literally waited on this physical image of the divinity, trying to anticipate and meet its every need in a daily cycle of waking, bathing, dressing, feeding, moving around, entertaining, soothing, and revering. These efforts reflected the emphatic claim of the Babylonian Creation Myth that humankind had been created to be the servants of the gods. Several thousand priests may have staffed a large temple such as the temple at Babylon of the chief god Marduk.

The office of priest was hereditary; fathers passed along sacred lore to their sons. Priests were paid in food taken from the crops raised on the deity's estates. The amount an individual received depended on his rank. Within the priesthood there was a complicated hierarchy of status and specialized function. The high priest performed the central acts in the great rituals. Certain priests made music to please the gods. Others knew the appropriate incantations for exorcising evil spirits. Still others were seers who interpreted dreams and divined the future by methods such as examining the organs of sacrificed animals, reading patterns in the rising incense smoke, or casting dice.

A high wall surrounded the temple precinct. Within the enclosed area were the shrine of the chief deity, as well as open-air plazas, chapels for lesser gods, housing, dining facilities, and offices for the priests and other members of the temple staff, and craft shops, storerooms, and service buildings to meet the needs of a large and busy organization. The most visible part of the temple compound was the **ziggurat**°, a multistory, mud-brick, pyramid-shaped tower approached by ramps and stairs. Modern scholars are not certain of the ziggurat's function and symbolic meaning.

Even harder to determine are the everyday beliefs and religious practices of the common people. Modern scholars do not know how accessible the temple buildings were to the general public. Individuals placed votive statues in the sanctuaries. They believed that these miniature replicas of themselves could continually beseech and seek the favor of the deity. The survival of many **amulets** (small charms meant to protect the bearer from evil) and representations of a host of demons suggest widespread belief in the value of magic—the use of special words and rituals to manipulate and control the forces of nature. A headache, for example, was believed to be caused by a demon that could be driven out of the ailing body. Lamashtu, who was held responsible for miscarriages, could be frightened off if a pregnant woman wore an amulet with the likeness of the hideous but beneficent demon Pazuzu. Or, in return for an appropriate gift or sacrifice, a god or goddess might be persuaded to reveal information about the future. The religion of the elite and the religion of ordinary people came together in great festivals such as the twelve-day New Year's Festival held each spring in Babylon to mark the beginning of a new agricultural cycle (see Society and Culture: The Babylonian New Year's Festival).

Technology and Science

The ancient Mesopotamians, like all complex societies, developed technologies that allowed them to exert some control over their environment. The term *technology* comes from the Greek word *techne*, meaning "skill" or "specialized knowledge." It normally refers to tools and machinery that humans use to manipulate the physical world. Many scholars are now using the term more broadly to encompass any specialized knowledge that is used to transform the natural environment and human society. Thus, for the ancient Mesopotamians, irrigation was used to expand agricultural production. But they also believed that the priests' sacred knowledge of prayers and rituals to win the favor of the gods led to greater prosperity.

A particularly important example of the latter type of technology is writing, which first appeared in Mesopotamia before 3300 B.C.E. The earliest inscribed tablets, found in the chief temple at Uruk, date from a time when the temple was the most important economic institution in the community. According to a plausible recent theory, writing originated from a system of tokens

---

anthropomorphic (an-thruh-puh-MORE-fik)
ziggurat (ZIG-uh-rat)

SOCIETY & CULTURE

The Babylonian New Year's Festival

The Babylonian New Year's Festival was one of the grandest and most important religious celebrations in ancient Mesopotamia. During the twelve-day festival, complex rituals, both private and public, were performed in accordance with the detailed prescriptions of the priests. Our primary evidence comes from fragmentary Babylonian documents of the third century B.C.E. (fifteen hundred years after Hammurabi). But because of the continuity of culture over several millennia in ancient Mesopotamia, our reconstruction of the later Babylonian New Year's Festival is likely to contain some elements of the beliefs and practices of earlier epochs.

In the first days of the festival, most of the activity took place within the temple of Marduk, patron deity of Babylon, in inner chambers off limits to all but ranking members of the priesthood. A particularly interesting ceremony was a ritualized humiliation of the king, followed by a renewal of the institution of divinely sanctioned kingship:

On the fifth day of the month Nisannu . . . they shall bring water for washing the king's hands and then shall accompany him to the temple Esagil. The *urigallu*-priest shall leave the sanctuary and take away the scepter, the circle, and the sword from the king. He shall bring them before the god Bel [Marduk] and place them on a chair. He shall leave the sanctuary and strike the king's cheek. He shall accompany the king into the presence of the god Bel. He shall drag him by the ears and make him bow to the ground. The king shall speak the following only once: "I did not sin, lord of the countries. I was not neglectful of the requirements of your godship. I did not destroy Babylon. The temple Esagil, I did not forget its rites. I did not rain blows on the cheek of a subordinate." . . . [The *urigallu*-priest responds:] "The god Bel will listen to your prayer. He will exalt your kingship. The god Bel will bless you forever. He will destroy your enemy, fell your adversary." After the *urigallu*-priest says this, the king shall regain his composure. The scepter, circle, and sword shall be restored to the king.

Also in the early days of the festival, in conjunction with rituals of purification and invocations to Marduk, a priest recited the entire text of the Babylonian Creation Epic to the image of the god.

On the fourth day of the month Nisannu, three and one-third hours of the night remaining, the *urigallu*-priest shall arise and wash with river water . . . He shall then go out to the Exalted Courtyard, turn to the north and bless the temple Esagil three times with the blessing: "Esagil, image of heaven and earth." He shall then open the doors. All the *eribitti*-priests shall enter and perform their rites in the traditional manner. The *kalu*-priests and the singers shall do likewise . . . After the second meal of the late afternoon, the *urigallu*-priest shall recite to the god Bel the composition entitled *Enuma Elish* [the Babylonian Creation Myth]. While he recites, the front of the tiara [crown] of the god Anu and the resting place of the god Enlil shall be covered.

Much of the subsequent festival activity, which took place in the temple courtyard and streets, was a kind of reenactment of the events of the Creation Myth. The festival occurred at the beginning of spring, when the grain shoots were beginning to emerge above ground. Indeed, the essential symbolism of the event concerns the return of natural life to the world. The Babylonians believed that time moved in a circular path and the natural world had a life cycle consisting of birth, growth, maturity, and death. Winter was the time when the cycle drew to a close, and there was no guarantee that the cycle would repeat itself and life would return to the world. Babylonians hoped that the New Year's Festival would encourage the gods to grant a renewal of time and life.

How did the symbolism of the New Year's Festival validate such concepts as kingship, the primacy of Babylon, and mankind's relationship to the gods? What would have been the mood of the inhabitants of Babylon during the period of the festival?

Source: Translations adapted from James B. Pritchard, ed., *Ancient Near Eastern Texts Relating to the Old Testament*, 3d ed. (Princeton, NJ: Princeton University Press, 1969), 332–334. Copyright © 1969 by Princeton University Press. Reprinted by permission of Princeton University Press.

used to keep track of property—such as sheep, cattle, or wagon wheels—as increases in the amount of accumulated wealth and the volume and complexity of commercial transactions strained the capacity of people's memory to preserve an accurate record. The tokens were made in the shape of the commodity and were inserted and sealed in clay envelopes. Pictures of the tokens were incised on the outside of an envelope as a reminder of what was inside.

Eventually people realized that the incised pictures provided an adequate record of the transaction and made the tokens inside the clay envelope redundant. These pictures were the first written symbols. These earliest symbols not only represented various objects; they also could stand for the sound of that word for an object if the sound was part of a longer word. For example, the symbols *shu* for "hand" and *mu* for "water" could be combined to form *shumu*, the word for "name."

The most common method of writing was to use a sharpened reed to incise a moist clay tablet. Because the reed made wedge-shaped impressions, the early pictures were increasingly stylized into a combination of strokes and wedges that evolved into **cuneiform** (Latin for "wedge-shaped") writing. Mastering this system required years of training and practice. Several hundred signs were in use at any one time, as compared to the twenty-five or so signs required for an alphabetic system. In the "tablet-house," which may have been attached to a temple or palace, students were taught writing and mathematics by a stern headmaster and were tutored by bullying older students called "big brothers." Members of the scribal class had prestige and regular employment because of their skill and thus may have been reluctant to simplify the cuneiform system. In the Old Babylonian period, the growth of the private commercial sector was accompanied by an increase in the number of people who could read and write. Nevertheless, only a small percentage of the population was literate.

Cuneiform is not a language but a system of writing. Developed originally for the Sumerian language, it was later adapted to express the Akkadian language of the Mesopotamian Semites as well as other languages of western Asia such as Hittite, Elamite, and Persian. The influence of Mesopotamia on other parts of western Asia became especially clear after archaeologists unearthed the ancient city of Ebla° in northern Syria (see Map 2.2). Besides the remains of buildings and artifacts inspired by Mesopotamian models, they found thousands of tablets, inscribed with cuneiform symbols in both

---

Ebla (EH-bluh)

Sumerian and the local Semitic dialect. The high point of Ebla's wealth and power occurred from 2400 to 2250 B.C.E., roughly contemporary with the Akkadian Empire, when Ebla controlled extensive territory and derived wealth from agriculture, manufacture of woolen cloth, and trade with Mesopotamia and the Mediterranean.

The earliest Mesopotamian documents are economic, but cuneiform is an outstanding example of a technology that came to have wide-ranging uses beyond the purpose for which it was originally conceived. In the early period, legal acts had been validated by the recitation of oral formulas and the performance of symbolic actions. After the development of cuneiform, written documents marked with the seal of the participants became the primary proof of legitimacy. In similar fashion cuneiform also came to be used for political, literary, religious, and scientific purposes.

Other technologies enabled the Mesopotamians to meet the challenges of their physical environment. Irrigation, indispensable to agriculture, called for the construction and maintenance of canals, dams, and dikes. Appropriate means of transportation were developed for different terrains. Carts and sledges drawn by cattle were common in some locations. In the south, where numerous water channels cut up the landscape, boats and barges were more effective. In northern Mesopotamia, donkeys were the chief pack animals for overland caravans in the centuries before the advent of the camel (see Chapter 8).

The Mesopotamians had to import raw metal ore, but they became skilled in metallurgy, mixing copper with arsenic or tin to make bronze. Bronze has the advantage of being more malleable than stone. Liquid bronze can be poured into molds, and hardened bronze takes a sharper edge than stone, is less likely to break, and is more easily repaired. Stone implements, however, continued to be produced, for the poorest members of the population usually could not afford bronze.

Resource-poor Mesopotamians possessed one commodity in abundance: clay. Mud bricks, dried in the sun or baked in an oven for greater durability, were their primary building material. Construction on a monumental scale, such as city walls, temples, and palaces, required practical knowledge of architecture and engineering. For example, the reed mats that Mesopotamian builders laid between the mud-brick layers of ziggurats served the same stabilizing purpose as girders in modern high-rise construction. Because of the abundance of good clay, pottery was the most common form of dishware and storage vessel. The potter's wheel, a revolving platform that made possible the rapid production of vessels with precise and complex shapes, was in use by 4000 B.C.E.

In the military sphere, there were innovative developments in organization, tactics, and weapons and other machinery of warfare. Early military forces were militias made up of able-bodied members of the community called up for short periods when needed. The powerful states of the later third and second millennia B.C.E. built up armies of well-trained and well-paid full-time soldiers. In the early second millennium B.C.E. horses appeared in western Asia, and the horse-drawn chariot came into vogue. Infantry men found themselves at the mercy of swift chariots carrying a driver and an archer who could ride up close and unleash a volley of arrows. Using increasingly effective siege machinery, Mesopotamian soldiers could climb over, undermine, or knock down the walls protecting the cities of their enemies.

In other ways, too, the Mesopotamians sought to gain control of their physical environment. They used a base-60 number system (the origin of the seconds and minutes we use today) in which numbers were expressed as fractions or multiples of 60 (in contrast to our base-10 system). Advances in mathematics and careful observation of the skies made the Mesopotamians sophisticated practitioners of astronomy. Mesopotamian priests compiled lists of omens or unusual sightings on earth and in the heavens, together with a record of the events that coincided with them. They consulted these texts at critical times, for they believed that the recurrence of such phenomena could provide clues to future developments. The underlying premise was that the elements of the material universe, from the microscopic to the macrocosmic, were interconnected in mysterious but undeniable ways.

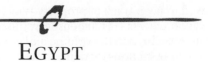

EGYPT

Nowhere is it more apparent how profoundly natural environment shapes the history and culture of a society than in ancient Egypt. Located at the intersection of Asia and Africa, Egypt was protected by surrounding barriers of desert and a harborless, marshy seacoast. Mesopotamia was open to migration or invasion and was dependent on imported resources. In contrast, natural isolation and essential self-sufficiency allowed Egypt to develop a unique culture that for long periods had relatively little to do with other civilizations.

The Land of Egypt: "Gift of the Nile"

The fundamental geographical feature of Egypt, ancient and modern, is the Nile River. The world's longest river, the Nile originates from Lake Victoria and from several large tributaries in the highlands of tropical Africa and flows northward, carving a narrow valley between the chain of hills on either side, until it reaches the Mediterranean Sea (see Map 2.3). The land through which it flows is mostly desert, but the river makes green a narrow strip on either side of its banks. About 100 miles (160 kilometers) from the Mediterranean the river divides into channels to form a triangular delta. Nearly the entire population of the region lives in that twisting, green ribbon alongside the river or in the Nile Delta. The rest

Limestone Relief of an Egyptian Cargo Boat, from a Tomb at Saqqara, ca. 2300 B.C.E. The large sail, used for going upstream, is rolled up as the vessel floats downstream (northward) with the current. The helmsman holds the tiller to steer the boat while men with long poles watch out for shallow water. The helmsman is kneeling on a large block of stone from one of the quarries upriver for use in a monumental construction project. (Egyptian Museum, Cairo)

of the country, 90 percent or more, is a bleak and inhospitable desert of mountains, rocks, and dunes. The ancient Egyptians recognized this stark dichotomy between the low-lying, life-sustaining "Black Land" with its dark soil alongside the river and the elevated, deadly "Red Land" of the desert. With justification and insight did the fifth-century B.C.E. Greek traveler Herodotus° call Egypt the "gift of the Nile."

The river was the main means of travel and communication. The orientation of the country was along the axis of the river, with the most important cities located considerably upstream. Because the river flows from south to north, the Egyptians called the southern part of the country "Upper Egypt" and the northern delta "Lower Egypt." The southern boundary of Egypt in most periods was the First Cataract of the Nile, the northernmost of a series of impassable rocks and rapids below Aswan° (about 500 miles [800 kilometers] south of the Mediterranean). At times Egyptian control extended farther south into what was called "Kush" (later Nubia, the southern part of the modern state of Egypt and northern Sudan). The Egyptians also settled a number of large oases, green and habitable "islands" in the midst of the desert, which lay some distance west of the river.

The hot climate with plenty of sunshine was favorable for agriculture, but south of the delta there is practically no rainfall. Thus agriculture was entirely dependent on river water. Throughout Egyptian history irrigation channels were dug to carry water out into the desert and increase the amount of land suitable for planting. And in the basin of Lake Faiyum°, a large depression west of the Nile, drainage techniques reduced the size of the lake and allowed more land to be reclaimed for agriculture.

Each September, with considerable regularity, the river overflowed its banks, spreading water out into the bordering depressed basins. Unlike the Mesopotamians, the Egyptians did not need to construct dams to lift river water to channels and fields. And unlike the Tigris and Euphrates, whose flood came at a disadvantageous time, the Nile flooded at exactly the right time for grain agriculture. When the waters receded, they left behind a fertile layer of mineral-rich silt, and farmers could easily plant their crops in the moist soil. The Egyptians had many versions of the Creation Myth, but it often involved the emergence of a life-supporting mound of earth from a primeval swamp.

The height of the river when it crested was crucial to the prosperity of the country. "Nilometers," stone stair-

---

Herodotus (he-ROD-uh-tuhs)   Aswan (AS-wahn)
Faiyum (fie-YOOM)

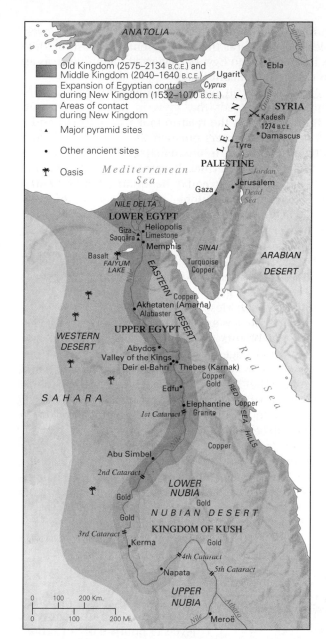

Map 2.3   Ancient Egypt The Nile River, flowing south to north, carved out of the surrounding desert a narrow green valley that became heavily settled in antiquity.

cases with incised units of measure, were placed along the river's edge to gauge the flood surge. When the flood was too high, dikes protecting inhabited areas were washed out and much damage resulted. When the flood was too low for a series of years, less land could be cultivated and the country was plunged into famine and decline. Indeed, the ebb and flow of successful and failed regimes seems to be linked to the cycle of floods. Nevertheless, in most eras there was a remarkable stability to this landscape, and Egyptians viewed the universe as an orderly and beneficent place.

Egypt was well endowed with natural resources. Egyptians used reeds that grew in marshy areas and along the banks of the river to make sails, ropes, and a kind of paper. Hunters pursued the wild animals and birds that abounded in the marshes and on the edge of the desert, and fishermen lowered their nets into the river. Building stone could be quarried and floated downstream from a number of locations in southern Egypt. Clay for mud bricks and pottery could be found almost everywhere. Copper and turquoise deposits in the Sinai desert to the east and gold from Nubia to the south were within reach, and the state organized armed expeditions and mustered forced labor to exploit these resources. Thus Egypt was self-sufficient to a much larger degree than Mesopotamia.

Farming villages appeared in Egypt as early as 5500 B.C.E. as inhabitants of the Nile Valley borrowed and adapted knowledge of how to domesticate various species of plants and animals that had emerged several millennia earlier in western Asia. However, the circumstances that led to Egypt becoming a focal point of civilization were due, at least in part, to a change in climate that took place gradually from the fifth to the third millennium B.C.E. Until that time, the Sahara, the vast region that is now the world's largest desert, had a relatively mild and wet climate and lakes and grasslands that supported a variety of plant and animal species as well as populations of hunter-gatherers (see Chapter 8). As the climate changed and the Sahara began to dry up and become a desert, displaced groups migrated into the Nile Valley, where they developed a sedentary way of life.

Divine Kingship

The increase in population produced new, more complex levels of political organization, including a form of local kingship. The pivotal event, in the view of later generations of Egyptians, was the conquest of these smaller units and the unification of all Egypt by Menes°, a ruler from the south, around 3100 B.C.E. Although some scholars question whether Menes was a historical or mythical figure, many authorities equate him with Narmer, a historical ruler who is represented on a decorated slate palette that shows a king exulting over defeated enemies. Later kings of Egypt were referred to as "Rulers of the Two Lands"—Upper and Lower Egypt—and were depicted with two crowns and implements symbolizing the unification of the country. In contrast to Mesopotamia, Egypt was unified early in its history.

The system that historians use to organize Egyptian history is based on thirty dynasties (sequences of kings from the same family) identified by Manetho, an Egyptian from the third century B.C.E. The rise and fall of dynasties often reflects the dominance of different parts of the country. At a broader level of generalization, scholars refer to the "Old," "Middle," and "New Kingdoms," each a period of centralized political power and brilliant cultural achievement, punctuated by "Intermediate Periods" of political fragmentation and cultural decline. Although experts disagree about specific dates for these periods, the chronology (on page 29) is representative of current opinion.

The central figure in the Egyptian state was the king (often known by the term **pharaoh,** from an Egyptian phrase meaning "palace," that began to be used in the New Kingdom). From the period of the Old Kingdom if not earlier, the principle was established that the king was a god come to earth, the incarnation of Horus and the son of the sun-god Re°. Egyptians believed that their king had been placed on earth by the gods to maintain **ma'at°**, the divinely authorized order of the universe. He was the indispensable link between his people and the gods, and through his benevolent rule he ensured the welfare and prosperity of the country. The Egyptians' conception of a divine king who was the source of law and justice may explain the apparent lack of effort to publish in Egypt an impersonal code of law comparable to Hammurabi's Code in Mesopotamia.

The death of the king was a critical moment in the life of the country because so much depended on him. Every effort was made to ensure the well-being of his spirit on its perilous journey to rejoin the the gods. Massive resources were poured into the construction of royal tombs, the celebration of elaborate funerary rites, and the sustenance of kings' spirits in the afterlife by perpetual offerings in funerary chapels attached to the royal tombs. Early rulers were buried in flat-topped, rectangular tombs made of mud brick. But around 2630 B.C.E., Djoser°, a Third Dynasty king, ordered the construction for himself at Saqqara°, near Memphis, of a spectacular stepped **pyramid** consisting of a series of stone platforms laid one on top of the other. Rulers in the Fourth Dynasty filled in the steps to create the smooth-sided, limestone pyramids that have become the most memorable symbol of ancient Egypt. Between 2550 and 2490 B.C.E., the pharaohs Khufu° and Khefren° erected huge

---

Menes (MEH-neez)

Re (ray)   ma'at (muh-AHT)   Djoser (JO-sur)
Saqqara (suh-KAHR-uh)   Khufu (KOO-foo)   Khefren (KEF-ren)

Pyramids of Menkaure, Khafre, and Khufu at Giza, ca. 2500 B.C.E.   With a width of 755 feet (230 meters) and a height of 480 feet (146 meters), the Great Pyramid of Khufu is the largest stone structure ever built. The construction of these massive edifices depended on relatively simple techniques of stonecutting, transport (the stones were floated downriver on boats and rolled to the site on sledges), and lifting (the stones were dragged up the face of the pyramid on mud-brick ramps). However, the surveying and engineering skills required to level the platform, lay out the measurements, and securely position the blocks were very sophisticated and have withstood the test of time.   (Carolyn Clarke/Spectrum Colour Library)

pyramids at Giza, several miles to the north of Saqqara, the largest stone structures ever built by human hands. Khufu's pyramid originally reached a height of 480 feet (146 meters).

Egyptians accomplished all this construction with stone tools (bronze was still expensive and rare) and no machinery other than simple levers, pulleys, and rollers. What really made it possible was almost unlimited human muscle power. Calculations of the human resources needed to build a pyramid within the lifetime of the ruler suggest that large numbers of people must have been pressed into service for part of each year, probably during the flood season, when no agricultural work could be done. Although this labor was compulsory, the Egyptian masses probably regarded it as a kind of religious service that helped to ensure the prosperity of their environment. Most of the surplus resources of the country went into the construction of these artificial mountains of stone. The age of the great pyramids lasted only about a century, although pyramids continued to be built on a smaller scale for two millennia afterward.

Administration and Communication

Various cities served as the royal capital at different times, for the capital was usually the original power base of the dynasty that occupied the throne. **Memphis,** on the Lower Nile near the apex of the delta (close to Cairo, the modern capital), held this central position during the Old Kingdom. **Thebes,** far to the south, came to prominence during much of the Middle and New Kingdom periods (see Map 2.3).

The need for detailed records of the resources of the country led to the creation of a complex bureaucracy. An extensive administrative apparatus began at the village level and progressed to the districts into which the country was divided and, finally, to the central government based in the capital city. Bureaucrats in the central administration kept track of land, labor, products, and people, extracting as taxes a substantial portion of the annual revenues of the country—at times as much as 50 percent. The income was used to subsidize the palace, bureaucracy, and army, to build and maintain temples, and to raise great monuments celebrating the ruler's reign. The government maintained a monopoly over key sectors of the economy and controlled long-distance trade. This was quite different from Mesopotamia, where commerce increasingly fell into the hands of an acquisitive urban middle class.

The hallmark of the administrative class was literacy. A system of writing had been developed by the beginning of the Early Dynastic period. **Hieroglyphics°,** the earliest form of this writing system, were picture symbols standing for words, syllables, or individual sounds. Our ability to read ancient Egyptian writing is due to the decipherment, in the early nineteenth century C.E., of the Rosetta Stone, a document from the second century B.C.E. that gave hieroglyphic and Greek versions of the same text.

Hieroglyphic writing long continued in use on monuments and ornamental inscriptions. By 2500 B.C.E., however, a cursive script, in which the original pictorial nature of the symbol was less readily apparent, had been developed for the everyday needs of administrators and copyists working with ink on a writing material called **papyrus°,** after the reed from which it was made. The stems of the papyrus reed were laid out in a vertical and horizontal grid pattern and then pounded with a soft mallet until the moist fibers merged to form a sheet of writing material. The plant grew only in Egypt but was in demand throughout the ancient world and was exported in large quantities. Indeed, the word *paper* is derived from Greek and Roman words for papyrus.

The Egyptians used writing for many purposes other than administrative recordkeeping. Their written literature included tales of adventure and magic, love poetry, religious hymns, and manuals of instruction on technical subjects. Scribes in workshops attached to the temples made copies of traditional texts.

When the monarchy was strong, officials were appointed and promoted on the basis of merit and accomplishment. Officials received grants of land from the king and were supported by dependent peasants who worked the land. Low-level officials were assigned to work in villages and district capitals; high-ranking officials served in the royal capital. When Old Kingdom officials died, they were buried in tombs laid out around the monumental tomb of the king so that they could serve him in death as they had done in life.

Throughout Egyptian history there is an underlying tension between the centralizing power of the monarchy and the decentralizing forces created by the Egyptian bureaucracy. One sign of the breakdown of centralized power in the late Old Kingdom and First Intermediate Period was the presence of officials' tombs not near the royal tomb but in their home districts, where they spent much of their time and exercised power more or less independently. Another sign of the ebb of centralization was the tendency of administrative posts to become hereditary. The early monarchs of the Middle Kingdom responded to the fragmentation of the preceding period by reducing the power and prerogatives of the old elite and creating a new middle class of administrators.

It has often been said that Egypt was a land of villages and did not have any real cities, because the political capitals were primarily extensions of the palace and central administration. It is true that, in comparison with Mesopotamia, a far larger percentage of the Egyptian population lived in rural villages and engaged in agriculture, and that the essential wealth of Egypt resided to a higher degree in the land and its products. But there were towns and cities in ancient Egypt, although they were less crucial than Mesopotamian urban centers to the economic and cultural dynamism of the country. Unfortunately, archaeologists have been unable to excavate many ancient urban sites in Egypt because they have been continuously inhabited and lie beneath modern communities.

During the Old and Middle Kingdoms, Egypt was essentially isolationist in its foreign policy. Technically, all foreigners were regarded as enemies. When necessary, local militia units backed up a small standing army of professional soldiers. Nomadic tribes living in the eastern and western deserts and Libyans living in the northwest were a nuisance rather than a real danger to the Nile Valley and were readily handled by the Egyptian military. The king maintained limited contact with the other advanced civilizations of the region. Egypt's interests abroad focused primarily on maintaining access to valuable resources rather than on acquiring territory. Trade with the coastal towns of the Levant° (modern Israel, Lebanon, and Syria) brought in cedar wood. In return, Egypt exported grain, papyrus, and gold.

In all periods the Egyptians had a particularly strong interest in goods that came from the south. Nubia contained rich sources of gold (in Chapter 3 we examine the rise of a civilization in Nubia that, though considerably influenced by Egypt, created a vital and original culture that lasted for more than two thousand years), and the southern course of the Nile offered the only easily passable corridor to sub-Saharan Africa.

In the Old Kingdom, Egyptian noblemen living at Aswan on the southern border led donkey caravans south to trade for gold, incense, and products of tropical

---

hieroglyphics (high-ruh-GLIF-iks)   **papyrus** (puh-PIE-ruhs)   **Levant** (luh-VANT)

Africa such as ivory, dark ebony-wood, and exotic jungle animals. A line of forts along the southern border protected Egypt from attack. In the early second millennium B.C.E. Egyptian forces struck south into Nubia, extending the Egyptian border as far as the Third Cataract of the Nile and taking possession of the gold fields. Still farther to the south, perhaps in the northern coastal region of present-day Somalia, lay the fabled land of Punt°, source of the fragrant myrrh resin that priests burned on the altars of the Egyptian gods.

The People of Egypt

The population of ancient Egypt is estimated at between 1 million and 1.5 million people. It was physically heterogeneous, ranging from dark-skinned people related to the populations of sub-Saharan Africa to lighter-skinned people akin to the Berber and Arab populations of North Africa and western Asia. Although Egypt was not subject to the large-scale migrations and invasions that Mesopotamia experienced, throughout the historical period settlers trickled into the Nile Valley and assimilated with the people already living there.

Social stratification clearly existed in Egypt: some people possessed more status, wealth, and power than others. But, in contrast to Mesopotamia, no formal class structure emerged. At the top of the social hierarchy were the king and high-ranking officials. In the middle were lower-level officials, local leaders, priests and other professionals, artisans, and well-to-do farmers. At the bottom were peasants, constituting the vast majority of the population.

Peasants lived in rural villages. Their lives were filled with the seasonally changing tasks of agriculture: plowing, sowing, tending emerging shoots, reaping, threshing, and storing grain or other products of the soil. The irrigation network of channels, basins, and dikes had to be maintained, improved, and extended. Domesticated animals—cattle, sheep, goats, and fowl—and fish supplemented a diet based on wheat or barley, beer, and garden vegetables. Inhabitants of the same village must have shared implements, work animals, and storage facilities, as well as helped one another at peak times in the agricultural cycle and in the construction of houses and other buildings. They also prayed and feasted together at festivals to the local gods and other public celebrations. Villagers periodically were required to contribute labor to state projects, such as construction of the pyramids. If the burden of taxation or compulsory service proved too great, few avenues of resistance were available to villagers other than fleeing into the desert.

This account of the lives of ordinary Egyptians is largely conjectural because the villages of ancient Egypt, like those of Mesopotamia, left few traces in the archaeological or literary record. Tomb paintings of the elite sometimes depict the lives of common folk. The artists employed pictorial conventions to indicate status, such as obesity for the possessors of wealth and comfort, baldness and deformity for members of the working classes. Egyptian poets frequently used metaphors of farming and hunting, and legal documents on papyrus preserved in the hot, dry sands tell of property transactions and the disputes of ordinary people.

Slavery existed on a limited scale but was of little significance for the economy. Prisoners of war, condemned criminals, and debtors could be found on the country estates or in the households of the king and wealthy families. Treatment of slaves was relatively humane, and they could be given their freedom.

It is also difficult to recover the experiences of women in ancient Egypt. Some information is available about the lives of women of the upper classes, but it is filtered through the brushes and pens of male artists and scribes. Tomb paintings show women of the royal family and elite classes accompanying their husbands and engaging in typical domestic activities. They are depicted with dignity and affection, though clearly they are subordinate to the men. The artistic convention of depicting men with a dark red and women with a yellow flesh tone implies that the elite woman's proper sphere was indoors, away from the searing sun. In the beautiful love poetry of the New Kingdom, lovers address each other in terms of apparent equality and express emotions akin to our own ideal of romantic love. We cannot be sure how accurately this poetry represents the prevalent attitude in other periods of Egyptian history or among groups other than the educated elite.

Legal documents show that Egyptian women could own property, inherit from their parents, and will their property to whomever they wished. Marriage, usually monogamous, was not confirmed by any legal or religious ceremony and essentially constituted a decision by a man and woman to establish a household together. Either party could dissolve the relationship, and the woman retained rights over her dowry in case of divorce. At certain times queens and queen-mothers played significant behind-the-scenes roles in the politics of the royal court, and priestesses sometimes supervised the cults of female deities. In general, the limited evidence suggests that women in ancient Egypt were treated more respectfully and had more legal rights and social freedom than women in Mesopotamia and other ancient societies.

Punt (poont)

Belief and Knowledge

The religion of the Egyptians was rooted in the landscape of the Nile Valley and in the vision of cosmic order that this environment evoked. The consistency of their environment—the sun rose every day into a clear and cloudless sky, and the river flooded on schedule every year, ensuring a bounteous harvest—persuaded the Egyptians that the natural world was a place of recurrent cycles and periodic renewal. The sky was imagined to be a great ocean surrounding the inhabited world. The sun-god Re traversed this blue waterway in a boat by day, then returned through the Underworld at night, fighting off the attacks of demonic serpents so that he could be born anew each morning. The story of Osiris°, a god who once ruled the land of Egypt, was especially popular. Osiris was slain by his jealous brother Seth, who then scattered the dismembered pieces. Isis, Osiris's devoted sister and wife, found and reconstructed the remnants and Horus, his son, took revenge on Seth. Osiris was restored to life and installed as king of the Underworld, and his example gave people hope of a new life in a world beyond this one.

The king, who was seen as Horus (son of Osiris) and as the son of Re, was thus associated with both the return of the dead to life and the life-giving and self-renewing symbolism of the sun-god. He was the chief priest of Egypt, intervening with the gods on behalf of his land and people. When a particular town attained special significance as the capital of a ruling dynasty, the chief god of that town became prominent across the land. Thus did Ptah° of Memphis, Re of Heliopolis°, and Amon° of Thebes become gods of all Egypt, serving to unify the country and strengthen the monarchy.

Egyptian rulers took a special interest in building new temples, refurbishing old ones, and making lavish gifts to the gods, as well as overseeing the construction of their own monumental tombs. Thus a considerable portion of the wealth of Egypt was used for religious purposes as part of a ceaseless effort to win the gods' favor, maintain the continuity of divine kingship, and ensure the renewal of the life-giving forces that sustained the world.

The many gods of ancient Egypt were diverse in origin and nature. Some deities were normally depicted with animal heads; others were always given human form. Few myths about the origins and adventures of the gods have survived, but there must have been a rich oral tradition. Many towns had temples in which locally prominent deities were thought to reside. The fluidity of the metaphysical realm allowed for local deities to be viewed as manifestations of the great gods, and gods could be merged to form hybrids such as Amon-Re. Cult activities were carried out in the private inner reaches of the temples, off limits to all but the priests who daily served the needs of the deity by attending to his or her statue. Food offered to the image was later distributed to temple staff. As in Mesopotamia, some temples came to possess extensive landholdings worked by dependent peasants, and the priests who administered the deity's wealth played an influential role locally and sometimes even throughout the land.

During great festivals, a boat-shaped litter carrying the shrouded statue and cult items of the deity was paraded around the town. Such occasions allowed large numbers of people to have contact with the deity and to participate in a mass outpouring of devotion and celebration. Little is known about the day-to-day beliefs and practices of the common people, however. In the household family members revered and made small offerings to Bes, the grotesque god of marriage and domestic happiness, to local deities, and to the family's ancestors. Amulets and depictions of demonic figures were supposed to protect the bearer and ward off evil forces. In later times Greeks and Romans regarded Egypt as a place where the devotion to magic was especially strong.

Egyptians believed in the reality of the afterlife and made extensive preparations for a safe passage to the next world and a comfortable existence once they arrived there. One common belief was that death was a journey beset with hazards. The Egyptian Book of the Dead, present in many excavated tombs, contained rituals and spells to protect the spirit of the deceased at each point of the trip. The final and most important challenge was the weighing of the deceased's heart (believed to be the source of an individual's personality, intellect, and emotion) in the presence of the judges of the Underworld to determine whether the deceased had led a good life and deserved to reach the ultimate blessed destination.

The Egyptians' obsession with the afterlife produced great concern about the physical condition of the cadaver. They perfected techniques of mummification to preserve the dead body. The idea probably derived from the early practice of burying the dead in the hot, dry sand on the edge of the desert, where bodies decomposed slowly. The elite classes utilized the most expensive kind of mummification. Vital organs were removed, preserved, and stored in stone jars laid out around the corpse. Body cavities were filled with various packing materials. The cadaver was immersed for long periods in dehydrating and preserving chemicals and eventually was wrapped in linen. The **mummy** was then placed in

---

Osiris (oh-SIGH-ris)   Ptah (puh-TAH)
Heliopolis (he-lee-OP-uh-lis)   Amon (AH-muhn)

Scene from the Egyptian Book of the Dead, ca. 1300 B.C.E.   The mummy of a royal scribe named Hunefar is approached by members of his household before being placed in the tomb. Behind Hunefar is jackel-headed Anubis, the god who will conduct the spirit of the deceased to the afterlife. The Book of the Dead provided Egyptians with the instructions they needed to complete this arduous journey and gain a blessed existence in the afterlife.   (Courtesy of the Trustees of the British Museum)

one or more decorated wooden caskets and was deposited in a tomb.

Tombs usually were built at the edge of the desert so as not to tie up valuable farmland. They were filled with pictures and samples of food and the objects of everyday life so that the deceased would have whatever he or she might need in the next life. Archaeologists and historians have gleaned much of what is now known about ancient Egyptian life from this practice of stocking the tomb with utilitarian and luxury household objects. Small figurines called shawabtis° were included to play the part of servants and to take the place of the deceased in case the regimen of the afterlife included periodic calls for compulsory labor. The elite classes ordered chapels attached to their tombs and left endowments to subsidize the daily attendance of a priest and offerings of foodstuffs to sustain their spirits for all eternity.

The form of the tomb also reflected the wealth and status of the deceased. Common people had to make do with simple pit graves or small mud-brick chambers. Members of the privileged classes built larger tombs and covered the walls with pictures and inscriptions. Kings erected pyramids and other grand edifices, employing

---

shawabtis (shuh-WAB-tees)

subterfuge to hide the sealed chamber containing the body and treasures, as well as curses and other magical precautions to foil tomb robbers. Rarely did they succeed, however. Nearly all the royal tombs that archaeologists have discovered were plundered.

The ancient Egyptians made remarkable advances in many areas of knowledge and developed an array of advantageous technologies. They learned about chemistry through their experiments to find methods for preserving the dead body. The process of mummification also provided opportunities to learn about human anatomy, and Egyptian doctors were in demand in the courts of western Asia because of their relatively advanced medical knowledge and techniques.

The centrality of the Nile flood to their lives spurred the Egyptians to find ways to control and profit from this critical event. They devoted much effort to constructing, maintaining, and expanding the network of irrigation channels and holding basins. They needed mathematics to survey and measure the dimensions of fields and calculate the quantity of agricultural produce owed to the state. By careful observation of the stars they constructed the most accurate calendar in the world, and they knew that when the star Sirius appeared on the horizon shortly before sunrise, the Nile flood surge was imminent.

Pyramids, temple complexes, and other monumental building projects called for great skill in engineering and architecture. Vast quantities of earth had to be moved and the construction site made level. Large stones had to be quarried, dragged on rollers, floated downstream on barges, lifted into place along ramps of packed earth, then carved to the exact size needed and made smooth. Long underground passageways were excavated to connect mortuary temples by the river with tombs near the desert's edge, and on several occasions Egyptian kings dredged out a canal more than 50 miles (80 kilometers) long in order to join the Nile Valley to the Red Sea and expedite the transport of goods.

Relatively simple technologies facilitated the transportation of goods and people. River barges were used to carry stones from quarries to construction sites. Lightweight ships equipped with sails and oars were well suited for travel on the peaceful Nile and sometimes were used for voyages on the Mediterranean and Red Seas. Carts and sledges pulled by draft animals were of limited use in a landscape interrupted by canals and flooded basins. Archaeologists recently discovered an 8-mile (13-kilometer) road made of slabs of sandstone and limestone connecting a rock quarry with Faiyum Lake. Dating to the second half of the third millennium B.C.E., it is the oldest known paved road in the world.

THE INDUS VALLEY CIVILIZATION

Civilization arose almost as early in South Asia as in Mesopotamia and Egypt. Just as each of the Middle Eastern civilizations was centered on a great river valley, civilization in the Indian subcontinent originated on a fertile floodplain. In the valley of the Indus River, settled farming created the agricultural surplus essential to urbanized society.

Natural Environment

In the central portion of the Indus Valley, in the Sind° region of modern Pakistan, a plain of more than 1 million acres (400,000 hectares) lies between the mountains to the west and the Thar° Desert to the east (see Map 2.1). Because the Indus River carries a great load of silt, over the

ages the riverbed and its containing banks have risen above the plain. Twice a year the river overflows its banks and spreads for as much as 10 miles (16 kilometers). In March and April melting snow feeds the river's sources in the Pamir° and Himalaya° mountain ranges. Then in August, the great monsoon (seasonal wind) blowing off the ocean to the southwest brings rains that swell the streams flowing into the Indus. As a result, farmers in this region of little rainfall are able to plant and harvest two crops a year. In ancient times, the Hakra° River (sometimes referred to as the Saraswati), which has since dried up, ran parallel to the Indus about 25 miles (40 kilometers) to the east and provided a second area suitable for intensive cultivation.

Several adjacent regions shared many cultural attributes with this core area. To the northeast is the Punjab, where five rivers converge to form the main course of the Indus. Lying beneath the shelter of the towering Himalaya range, the Punjab receives considerably more rainfall than the central plain but is less prone to flooding. From this region settlements spread as far as Delhi° in northwest India. Another zone of settlement extended south into the great delta where the Indus empties into the Arabian Sea, and southeast into India's hook-shaped Kathiawar° Peninsula, an area of alluvial plains and coastal marshes. The territory covered by the Indus Valley civilization is roughly equivalent in size to modern France—much larger than the zone of Mesopotamian civilization.

Material Culture

The Indus Valley civilization flourished from approximately 2600 to 1900 B.C.E. Although archaeologists have located several hundred sites, the culture is best known from the archaeological remains of two great cities first discovered eighty years ago. The ancient names of these cities are unknown, so they are referred to by modern names: **Harappa** and **Mohenjo-Daro°**. Unfortunately, a rise in the water table at these sites has made excavation of the lowest and earliest levels of settlement nearly impossible.

The identity, origins, and fate of the people who created and maintained this advanced civilization are in dispute. Until recently, scholars assumed that they were related to speakers of the Dravidian° languages whose descendants were later pushed out of the north into central and southern India by invading Indo-European

---

Sind (sinned)   Thar (tahr)

Pamir (pah-MEER)   Himalaya (him-uh-LAY-uh)   Hakra (HAK-ruh)
Delhi (DEL-ee)   Kathiawar (kah-tee-uh-WAHR)
Mohenjo-Daro (moe-hen-joe–DAHR-oh)
Dravidian (druh-VID-ee-uhn)

herders around 1500 B.C.E. Skeletal evidence, however, indicates that the population of the Indus Valley remained stable from ancient times to the present. Scholars now think that settled agriculture in this part of the world dates back to at least 5000 B.C.E. The precise relationship between the Indus Valley civilization and several earlier cultural complexes in the Indus Valley and in the hilly lands to the west is unclear. Also unclear are the forces giving rise to the urbanization, population increase, and technological advances that occurred in the mid-third millennium B.C.E. Nevertheless, the case for continuity with the earlier cultures seems stronger than the case for a sudden transformation due to the movement of new peoples into the valley.

Like the Mesopotamians and Egyptians, the people of the Indus Valley had a system of writing. They used more than four hundred signs to represent syllables and words. Archaeologists have recovered thousands of inscribed seal stones and copper tablets. Unfortunately, these documents do not yet provide us with a picture of the society, because no one has been able to decipher them.

This society produced major urban centers. Harappa was 3½ miles (5.6 kilometers) in circumference and may have housed a population of 35,000. Mohenjo-Daro was several times larger. In planning and construction, these cities show marked similarities. High, thick brick walls surrounded each. The streets were laid out in a rectangular grid pattern. Covered drainpipes carried away waste. The regular size of the streets and length of the city blocks, and the uniformity of the mud bricks used in construction, have been taken as evidence of a strong central authority. The seat of this authority may have been located in the citadel—an elevated, enclosed compound containing large buildings. Nearby stood well-ventilated structures that scholars think were storehouses of grain for feeding the urban population and for export. The presence of barracks may point to some regimentation of the skilled artisans.

A common assumption has been that these urban centers controlled the rural farmlands around them, though there is no proof that they did. Various factors may account for the location of the chief centers, and different centers may have had different functions. Mohenjo-Daro seems to dominate the great floodplain of the Indus. Harappa, which is nearly 500 miles (805 kilometers) from Mohenjo-Daro, is on a frontier between farmland and herding land; no other settlements have been found west of its location. Harappa may have served as a "gateway" to the natural resources of the northwest, such as copper, tin, and precious stones. Coastal towns to the south also would have had commercial functions, gathering fish and highly prized seashells and expediting seaborne trade with the Persian Gulf.

Mohenjo-Daro and Harappa have received the most attention from archaeologists, and published accounts of the Indus Valley civilization tend to treat those urban centers as the norm. Most people, however, lived in smaller settlements. The considerable standardization of styles and shapes for many kinds of artifacts and the presence of the full range of artifacts, not only in large cities but also in smaller settlements, is striking. Some scholars suggest that this standardization may be due to extensive exchange and trading of goods within the zone of Indus Valley civilization, rather than to a strong and authoritarian central government.

There is a greater abundance of metal in the Indus Valley than in Mesopotamia or Egypt, and most of the metal objects that archaeologists have found in the Indus Valley are utilitarian—tools and other useful objects. In contrast, metal objects unearthed in Mesopotamia

Bronze Statue from the Indus Valley   Found in a house in Mohenjo-Daro, this small statue represents a young woman whose only apparel is a necklace and an armful of bracelets. Appearing relaxed and confident, she has been identified by some scholars as a dancer.   (National Museum, New Delhi)

Environmental Stress in the Indus Valley

The three river-valley civilizations discussed in this chapter were located in arid or semiarid regions. Such regions are particularly vulnerable to changes in the environment. Scholars' debates about the existence and impact of changes in the climate and landscape of the Indus Valley illuminate some of the potential factors at work, as well as the difficulties of verifying and interpreting such long-ago changes.

One of the points at issue is climatic change. An earlier generation of scholars believed that the climate of the Indus Valley was considerably wetter during the height of that civilization than it is now. As evidence, they cited the enormous quantities of timber, cut from extensive forests, that would have been needed to bake the millions of mud bricks used to construct the cities (see photo), the distribution of human settlements on land that is now unfavorable for agriculture, and the representation of jungle and marsh animals on decorated seals. This approach assumes that the growth of population, prosperity, and complexity in the Indus Valley in the third millennium B.C.E. required wet conditions, and it concludes that the change to a drier climate in the early second millennium B.C.E. pushed this civilization into decline.

Other experts, skeptical about a radical climatic change, countered with alternative calculations of the amount of timber needed and evidence of plant remains—particularly barley, a grain that is tolerant of dry conditions. However, recent studies of the stabilization of sand dunes, which occurs in periods of heavy rainfall, and analysis of the sediment deposited by rivers and winds have been used to strengthen the claim that the Indus Valley used to be wetter and in the early-to-mid second millennium B.C.E. entered a period of relatively dry conditions that have persisted to the present.

A much clearer case can be made for changes in the landscape caused by shifts in the courses of rivers. These shifts are due, in many cases, to tectonic forces such as earthquakes. Dry channels, whether detected in satellite photographs or by on-the-ground inspection, reveal the location of old riverbeds, and it appears that a second major river system, the Hakra, once ran parallel to the Indus some distance to the east. The Hakra, with teeming towns and fertile fields along its banks, appears to have been a second axis of this civilization. Either the Sutlej, which now feeds into the Indus, or the Yamuna, which now pours into the Ganges, may have been the main source of water for this long-gone system before undergoing a change of course. The consequences of the drying-up of this major waterway must have been immense—

Mud-Brick Fortification Wall of the Citadel at Harappa Built upon a high platform, this massive and towering construction required large numbers of bricks and extensive labor resources. *The Cambridge History of India: The Indus Civilization*, 3d ed. (1968), by Sir Mortimer Wheeler. With permission of the Syndics of the Cambridge University Press.

the loss of huge amounts of arable land and the food that it produced, the abandonment of cities and villages and consequent migration of their populations, shifts in the trade routes, and desperate competition for shrinking resources.

As for the Indus itself, the present-day course of the lower reaches of the river has shifted 100 miles (161 kilometers) to the west since the arrival of the Greek conqueror Alexander the Great in the late fourth century B.C.E., and the deposit of massive volumes of silt has pushed the mouth of the river 50 miles (80 kilometers) farther south. Such a shift of the river bed and buildup of alluvial deposits also may have occurred in the third and second millennia B.C.E.

A recent study concludes: "It is obvious that ecological stresses, caused both climatically and technically, played an important role in the life and decay" of the Indus civilization.

Source: Quotation from D. P. Agarwal and R. K. Sood in Gregory L. Possehl, ed., *Harappan Civilization: A Contemporary Perspective* (Warminster, England: Aris and Phillips, 1982), 229.

and Egypt tend to be decorative—jewelry and the like. Moreover, in the Indus Valley metal objects were available to a large cross-section of the population, but in the Middle East they were primarily reserved for the elite.

The civilization of the Indus Valley possessed impressive technological capabilities. These people were adept in the technology of irrigation. They used the potter's wheel. They laid the foundations of large public buildings with mud bricks baked in a kiln (sun-dried bricks exposed to floodwaters would have dissolved quickly). Smiths worked with various metals—gold, silver, copper, and tin. The varying ratios of tin to copper in their bronze objects suggest that they were acutely aware of the hardness of different mixtures and conserved the relatively rare tin by using the smallest amount necessary, since, for example, knives need not be as hard as axes.

Archaeological evidence proves the people of the Indus Valley had widespread trading contacts. Utilizing passes through the mountains in the northwest, they had ready access to the valuable resources found in eastern Iran and Afghanistan, as well as to ore deposits in western India. These resources included metals (such as copper and tin), precious stones (lapis lazuli, jade, and turquoise), building stone, and timber. Rivers served as major thoroughfares for the movement of goods within the zone of Indus Valley culture. It has been suggested that the undeciphered writing on the many seal stones that have been found may convey the names of merchants who stamped their wares.

The inhabitants of the Indus Valley and of Mesopotamia obtained raw materials from some of the same sources. Because Indus Valley seal stones have been found in the Tigris-Euphrates Valley, some scholars believe that Indus Valley merchants served as middlemen in the long-distance trade, obtaining raw materials from the lands of west-central Asia and shipping them to the Persian Gulf.

We know little about the political, social, economic, and religious structures of Indus Valley society. Attempts have been made to demonstrate the presence at this early date of many cultural features that are characteristic of later periods of Indian history (see Chapter 7), including sociopolitical institutions (a system of hereditary occupational groups, the predominant role of priests), architectural forms (bathing tanks like those later found in Hindu temples, private interior courtyards in houses), and religious beliefs and practices (depictions of gods and sacred animals on the seal stones, a cult of the mother-goddess). Much of this work is highly speculative, however, and further knowledge about this society can come only from additional archaeological finds and decipherment of the Indus Valley script.

Transformation of the Indus Valley Civilization

The Indus Valley cities were abandoned sometime after 1900 B.C.E. Archaeologists once thought that invaders destroyed them, but now they believe that this civilization suffered "systems failure"—the breakdown of the fragile interrelationship of the political, social, and economic systems that sustained order and prosperity. The precipitating cause may have been one or more natural disasters, such as an earthquake or massive flooding. Gradual ecological changes may also have played a role.

The Hakra river system dried up, and salinization (an increase in the amount of salt in the soil, inhibiting plant growth) and erosion may have taken their toll (see Environment and Technology: Environmental Stress in the Indus Valley). Towns no longer on the river, ports no longer by the sea, and regions suffering a loss of fertile soil and water would have necessitated the relocation of large numbers of people and a change in the livelihood of those who remained. The causes, patterns, and pace of change probably varied in different areas. Urbanization is likely to have persisted longer in some regions than in others. But in the end, the urban centers could not be sustained, and village-based farming and herding took their place. As the interaction between regions lessened, distinct regional variations replaced the standardization of technology and style of the previous era.

Historians can do little more than speculate about the causes behind the changes and the experiences of the people who lived in the Indus Valley around 1900 B.C.E. But it is important to keep two tendencies in mind. In most cases like this, the majority of the population adjusts to the new circumstances. But members of the political and social elite, who depended on the urban centers and complex political and economic structures, lose the source of their authority and are merged with the population as a whole.

CONCLUSION

It is surely no accident that the first civilizations to develop high levels of political centralization, urbanization, and technology were situated in river valleys where rainfall was insufficient for dependable agriculture. Dependent as they were on river water to irrigate the cultivated land that fed their populations, Mesopotamia, Egypt, and the Indus Valley civilization channeled significant human resources into the construction and maintenance of canals, dams, and dikes. This work required expertise in engineering, mathematics, and metallurgy, as well as the formation of political centers that could organize the necessary labor force.

The unpredictable and violent floods in the Tigris-Euphrates Basin were a constant source of alarm for the people of Mesopotamia. In contrast, the predictable, opportune, and gradual Nile floods were eagerly anticipated events in Egypt. The relationship with nature stamped the world-view of both peoples. Mesopotamians nervously tried to appease their harsh deities so as to survive in a perverse world. Egyptians largely trusted in, and nurtured, the supernatural powers that they believed guaranteed orderliness and prosperity.

In both Egypt and Mesopotamia, kingship emerged as the dominant political form. The Egyptian king's divine origins and symbolic association with the forces of renewal made him central to the welfare of the entire country and gave him a religious monopoly superseding the authority of the temples and priests. Egyptian monarchs lavished much of the country's wealth on their tombs, believing that a proper burial would ensure the continuity of kingship and the attendant blessings that it brought to the land and people. Mesopotamian rulers, who were not normally regarded as divine, built new cities, towering walls, splendid palaces, and religious edifices as lasting testaments to their power.

The religious outlook of both cultures included a hierarchy of gods, ranging from protective demons and local deities to the gods of the state, whose importance rose or fell with the power of the political centers with which they were associated. Cheered by the essential stability of their environment, the Egyptians tended to have a more positive conception of the gods' designs for humankind. The Egyptians believed that although the journey to the next world was beset with hazards, the righteous spirit that overcame them could look forward to a blessed existence. In contrast, Gilgamesh, the hero of the Mesopotamian epic, is tormented by terrifying visions of the afterlife: disembodied spirits of the dead stumbling around in the darkness of the Underworld for all eternity, eating dust and clay, and slaving for the heartless gods of that realm.

The populations of Egypt and Mesopotamia were ethnically heterogeneous, yet both regions experienced a remarkable degree of cultural continuity. New immigrants readily assimilated to the dominant language, belief system, and lifestyles of the civilization. Culture, not physical appearance, was the criterion by which people were identified. Mesopotamian women's apparent loss of freedom and legal privilege in the second millenium B.C.E. may have been related to the higher degree of urbanization and class stratification in this society. In contrast, Egyptian pictorial documents, love poems, and legal records indicate an attitude of respect and a higher degree of equality for women in the valley of the Nile.

In the second millenium B.C.E., as the societies of Mesopotamia and Egypt consolidated their cultural achievements and entered new phases of political expansion, and as the Indus Valley centers went into irreversible decline, a new and distinctive civilization, based likewise on the exploitation of the agricultural potential of a floodplain, was emerging in the valley of the Yellow River in eastern China. It is to that area that we turn our attention in Chapter 3.

■ Key Terms

civilization	pharaoh
Babylon	ma'at
Sumerians	pyramid
Semitic	Memphis
city-state	Thebes
Hammurabi	hieroglyphics
scribe	papyrus
ziggurat	mummy
amulet	Harappa
cuneiform	Mohenjo-Daro

■ Suggested Reading

Jack M. Sasson, ed., *Civilizations of the Ancient Near East*, 4 vols. (1993), contains up-to-date articles and bibliography on a wide range of topics. An excellent starting point for geography, chronology, and basic institutions and cultural concepts in ancient western Asia is Michael Roaf, *Cultural Atlas of Mesopotamia and the Ancient Near East* (1990). Amelie Kuhrt, *The Ancient Near East, c. 3000–330 B.C.*, 2 vols. (1995), is the best and most up-to-date introduction to the historical development of western Asia and Egypt, offering a clear and concise historical outline and a balanced presentation of continuing controversies. Other general historical introductions can be found in A. Bernard Knapp, *The History and Culture of Ancient Western Asia and Egypt* (1988); Hans J. Nissen, *The Early History of the Ancient Near East, 9000–2000 B.C.* (1988); H. W. F. Saggs, *Civilization Before Greece and Rome* (1989); and Georges Roux, *Ancient Iraq*, 3d ed. (1992). Joan Oates, *Babylon* (1979), focuses on the most important of all the Mesopotamian cities. J. N. Postgate, *Early Mesopotamia: Society and Economy at the Dawn of History* (1992), offers deep insights into the political, social, and economic dynamics of Mesopotamian society. Daniel C. Snell, *Life in the Ancient Near East 3100–322 B.C.E.* (1997), emphasizes social and economic matters for those already familiar with the main outlines of ancient Near Eastern history. Stephanie Dalley, ed., *The Legacy of Mesopotamia* (1998), explores the interactions of the Mesopotamians with other peoples of the ancient world.

The most direct and exciting introduction to the world of early Mesopotamians is through the *Epic of Gilgamesh,* in the attractive translation of David Ferry, *Gilgamesh: A New Rendering in English Verse* (1992). Thorkild Jacobsen, *The Treasures of Darkness: A History of Mesopotamian Religion* (1976), is a classic study of the evolving mentality of Mesopotamian religion. Stephanie Dalley, *Myths from Mesopotamia* (1989), and Henrietta McCall, *Mesopotamian Myths* (1990), deal with the mythical literature. Jeremy Black and Anthony Green, *Gods, Demons and Symbols of Ancient Mesopotamia* (1992), is a handy illustrated encyclopedia of myth, religion, and religious symbolism. Pierre Amiet, *Art of the Ancient Near East* (1980), offers a richly illustrated introduction to a wide spectrum of artistic media. Dominique Collon, *First Impressions: Cylinder Seals in the Ancient Near East* (1988), explores a class of common objects that reveal much about art and daily life.

C. B. F. Walker, *Cuneiform* (1987), is a concise guide to the Mesopotamian system of writing. James B. Pritchard, *Ancient Near Eastern Texts Relating to the Old Testament,* 3d ed. (1969), contains an extensive collection of translated documents and texts from western Asia and Egypt. Attitudes, roles, and the treatment of women are taken up by Barbara Lesko, "Women of Egypt and the Ancient Near East," in *Becoming Visible: Women in European History,* 2d ed., ed. Renata Bridenthal, Claudia Koonz, and Susan Stuard (1994), and by Guity Nashat, "Women in the Ancient Middle East," in *Restoring Women to History* (1988). The significance of ancient Syria as a region with its own cultural vitality as well as indebtedness to Mesopotamia is taken up in Harvey Weiss, ed., *Ebla to Damascus: Art and Archaeology of Ancient Syria* (1985), and Giovanni Pettinato, *Ebla: A New Look at History* (1991).

A fine and lavishly illustrated introduction to the many facets of ancient Egyptian civilization is David P. Silverman, ed., *Ancient Egypt* (1997). John Baines and Jaromir Malek, *Atlas of Ancient Egypt* (1980), and T. G. H. James, *Ancient Egypt: The Land and Its Legacy* (1988), are primarily organized around the sites of ancient Egypt and provide general introductions to Egyptian civilization. Historical treatments include B. G. Trigger, B. J. Kemp, D. O'Connor, and A. B. Lloyd, *Ancient Egypt: A Social History* (1983); Barry J. Kemp, *Ancient Egypt: Anatomy of a Civilization* (1989); and Nicholas-Cristophe Grimal, *A History of Ancient Egypt* (1992). John Romer, *People of the Nile: Everyday Life in Ancient Egypt* (1982); Miriam Stead, *Egyptian Life* (1986); and Eugen Strouhal, *Life of the Ancient Egyptians* (1992), emphasize social history. For women see the article by Lesko cited above; Barbara Watterson, *Women in Ancient Egypt* (1991); Gay Robins, *Women in Ancient Egypt* (1993); and the articles and museum exhibition catalogue in Anne K. Capel and Glenn E. Markoe, eds., *Mistress of the House, Mistress of Heaven: Women in Ancient Egypt* (1996).

Stephen Quirke, *Ancient Egyptian Religion* (1990), is a highly regarded treatment of a complex subject. George Hart, *Egyptian Myths* (1990), gathers the limited written evidence for what must have been a thriving oral tradition. Pritchard's collection, cited above, and Miriam Lichtheim, *Ancient Egyptian Literature: A Book of Readings, vol. 1, The Old and Middle Kingdoms* (1973), provide translated original texts and documents. William Stevenson Smith, *The Art and Architecture of Ancient Egypt* (1998), and Gay Robins, *The Art of Ancient Egypt* (1997), are introductions to the visual record.

For the Indus Valley civilization there is a brief treatment in Stanley Wolpert, *A New History of India,* 3d ed. (1989). Mortimer Wheeler's *Civilizations of the Indus Valley and Beyond* (1966) and *The Indus Civilization,* 3d ed. (1968), though still useful, are now largely superseded by Jonathan Mark Kenoyer, *Ancient Cities of the Indus Valley Civilization* (1998). Gregory L. Poschl has edited two collections of articles by Indus Valley scholars: *Ancient Cities of the Indus* (1979) and *Harappan Civilization: A Contemporary Perspective* (1982).

■ Note

1. David Ferry, *Gilgamesh: A New Rendering in English Verse* (New York: Noonday Press, 1992).

3

THE LATE BRONZE AGE IN THE EASTERN HEMISPHERE, 2200–500 B.C.E.

Early China • The Cosmopolitan Middle East • Nubia • The Aegean World •
The Fall of Late Bronze Age Civilizations

ENVIRONMENT AND TECHNOLOGY: Chinese and Mesopotamian Divination
SOCIETY AND CULTURE: The Amarna Letters

Wall Painting of Nubians Arriving in Egypt with Rings and Bags of Gold, Fourteenth Century B.C.E.
This image decorated the tomb of an Egyptian administrator in Nubia.

round 1460 B.C.E. Queen Hatshepsut° of Egypt sent a naval expedition down the Red Sea to the fabled land that the Egyptians called "Punt°." Historians believe Punt was in the northern coastal region of modern Somalia. Myrrh° (a reddish-brown resin obtained from the hardened sap of a local tree) exported from Punt usually passed through the hands of several intermediaries, increasing in price with each transaction, before reaching Egypt. Hatshepsut hoped to bypass the middlemen and establish direct trade between Punt and Egypt.

A fascinating written and pictorial record of this expedition and its aftermath is preserved in the mortuary temple of Hatshepsut at Deir el-Bahri°, near Thebes. Besides bringing back myrrh and various sub-Saharan luxury goods—ebony and other rare woods, ivory, cosmetics, live monkeys, panther skins—the ships also carried young myrrh trees, probably to create a home-grown source of this precious substance, which the Egyptians burned on the altars of their gods. These items are represented in the royal Egyptian tomb as tribute given by the people of Punt to their Egyptian overlord. Egyptian power, however, did not reach that far, so the Egyptian emissaries must have traded for these treasures from southern lands. Hatshepsut staged public displays of them and emphasized that she had accomplished what none of her predecessors had been able to do.

Hatshepsut's highly touted expedition to Punt reveals much that is important about the ancient world in the second millennium B.C.E. The major centers pursued access to important resources, by trade or conquest, because their power, wealth, and legitimacy depended on the acquisition of these commodities. A conspicuous feature of this period in northeastern Africa, the eastern Mediterranean, western Asia, and East Asia was the interconnectedness of regions and states, large and small, in complex webs of political relationships and economic activities. Embassies, treaties, trade agreements, political marriages, and scribes utilizing widely recognized languages and writing systems were some of the links connecting the heterogeneous peoples of these regions. Commerce over long distances, centering on the trade in metals, was vital to the power and prosperity of the ruling classes.

The movement of goods across long distances promoted the flow of ideas and technologies. These included concepts of kingship, methods of administration, systems of writing, religious beliefs and rituals, artistic tastes, metallurgical skills, and new forms of transportation. By the standards of the ancient world, the Late Bronze Age was a cosmopolitan and comfortable era, a time of stability and prosperity, technological progress, and cultural accomplishment.

The spread of ideas and technologies sparked important political changes across the Eastern Hemisphere (the vast landmass comprising the continents of Asia, Africa, and Europe). This period witnessed the last flourishing of the ancient centers of civilization in Egypt and southern Mesopotamia (introduced in Chapter 2) and also saw the formation of new centers of power and the first stirrings of the peoples who took center stage in the first millennium B.C.E.—Assyrians in northern Mesopotamia, Nubians in northeastern Africa, Greeks in the eastern Mediterranean, and the Shang and Zhou in northeastern China.

As you read in this chapter, ask yourself the following questions:

- Why was access to raw materials so important to the ruling elites?

- What were the primary means by which the civilizations of the Late Bronze Age communicated, exchanged goods, and settled their differences?

- How did the technological and cultural influences of the ancient centers affect the formation of new civilizations?

EARLY CHINA

On the eastern edge of the great Eurasian landmass, Neolithic cultures developed as early as as 8000 B.C.E. In the second millenium B.C.E., a more complex civilization evolved. Under the political domination of the Shang

---

Hatshepsut (hat-SHEP-soot) **Punt** (poont) **myrrh** (murr)
Deir el-Bahri (DIRE uhl–BAH-ree)

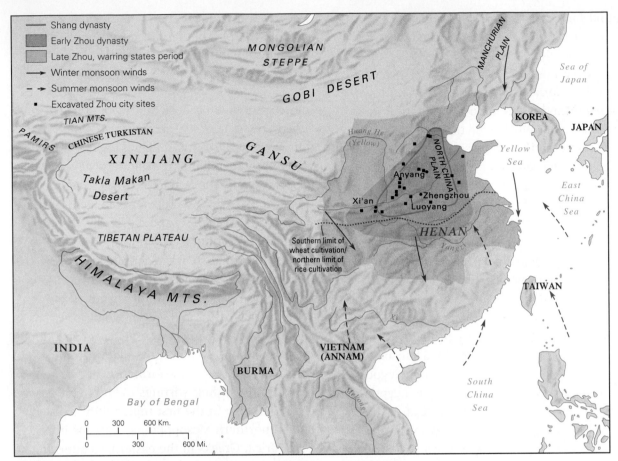

Map 3.1 China in the Shang and Zhou Periods, 1750–221 B.C.E. The Shang dynasty arose in the second millennium B.C.E. in the floodplain of the Yellow River. While southern China benefits from the monsoon rains, northern China depends on irrigation. As population increased, the Han Chinese migrated from their eastern homeland to other parts of China, carrying their technologies and cultural practices. Other ethnic groups predominated in more outlying regions, and the nomadic peoples of the northwest constantly challenged Chinese authority.

and Zhou monarchs many of the institutions, patterns, and values of classical Chinese civilization emerged and spread south and west. As in Mesopotamia, Egypt, and the Indus Valley, the rise of a complex society possessing cities, specialization of labor, bureaucratic government, writing, and other advanced technologies depended on the marshaling of human labor and exploitation of the waters of a great river system—the Yellow River (Huang He) and its tributaries—to support intensive agriculture in the plains. Although there is archaeological evidence of some movement of goods and ideas between western and eastern Asia, these developments were largely independent of the rise of complex societies in the Middle East and the Indus Valley.

Geography and Resources

China is isolated from the rest of the Eastern Hemisphere by formidable natural barriers: to the southwest the Himalayas°, the highest mountains on the planet; to the west the Pamir° and Tian° Mountains and the Takla Makan° Desert; to the northwest the Gobi° Desert and the treeless and grassy hills and plains of the Mongolian Steppe (see Map 3.1). To the east lies the vastness of the Pacific Ocean. Although China's separation was not total—trade goods, people, and ideas moved back and forth between

Himalayas (HIM-uh-LAY-uhz)   Pamir (pah-MEER)   Tian (tee-en)
Takla Makan (TAH-kluh muh-KAHN)   Gobi (GO-bee)

CHRONOLOGY

	China	Western Asia and Southeastern Europe	Northeastern Africa
2500 B.C.E.	**8000–2000 B.C.E.** Neolithic cultures	**2500 B.C.E.** Bronze metallurgy	
			2040–1640 B.C.E. Middle Kingdom in Egypt
2000 B.C.E.	**2000 B.C.E.** Bronze metallurgy **1750–1027 B.C.E.** Shang dynasty	**ca. 2000 B.C.E.** Early Minoan civilization on Crete **2000 B.C.E.** Horses in use in western Asia **1700–1200 B.C.E.** Hittites dominant in Anatolia **1600 B.C.E.** Rise of Mycenaean civilization in Greece	**1750 B.C.E.** Rise of kingdom of Kush
1500 B.C.E.		**1460 B.C.E.** Kassites assume control of southern Mesopotamia **1450 B.C.E.** Destruction of Minoan palaces in Crete	**1532 B.C.E.** Beginning of New Kingdom in Egypt **1500 B.C.E.** Egyptian conquest of Nubia; bronze metallurgy **1470 B.C.E.** Queen Hatshepsut of Egypt dispatches expedition to Punt **1353 B.C.E.** Akhenaten launches reforms in Egypt **1285 B.C.E.** Pharoah Ramesses II battles Hittites at Kadesh
		1200–1150 B.C.E. Destruction of Late Bronze Age centers in Anatolia, Syria, and Greece	**1200–1150 B.C.E.** Peoples of the Sea attack **1070 B.C.E.** End of New Kingdom in Egypt
1000 B.C.E.	**1027–221 B.C.E.** Zhou dynasty **600 B.C.E.** Iron metallurgy	**1000 B.C.E.** Iron metallurgy	**1000 B.C.E.** Iron metallurgy

China, India, and Central Asia—its development in many respects was distinctive.

Most of the East Asian subcontinent is covered with mountains, making overland travel, transport, and communications difficult and slow. The great river systems of eastern China, however—the Yellow River, the Yangzi° River, and their tributaries—facilitate east-west movement. It is useful to distinguish between the eastern river valleys, where intensive agriculture was practiced and the population clustered, and the steppe

Yangzi (yang-zuh)

lands of Mongolia, the deserts and oases of Xinjiang°, and the high plateau of Tibet, where sparser populations practiced quite different forms of livelihood. The topographical diversity of East Asia is matched by climate zones ranging from the dry, subarctic reaches of Manchuria in the north to the lush, subtropical forests of the south, and by rich variation in the plant and animal life adapted to these zones.

Even within the eastern zone there is a fundamental distinction between north and south. The same forces that create the great monsoon of India and Southeast Asia (see Chapter 2) also drench southern China with substantial amounts of rainfall in the summer months, the most beneficial time for agriculture. Northern China, in contrast, receives a much more erratic and restricted amount of moisture. As a result, in north and south there are different patterns for the use of land, the kinds of crops that can flourish, and the organization of agricultural labor. As in Mesopotamia, the Indus Valley, and southern Greece (see below), technological and social developments in China unfolded in relatively adverse conditions. The early history of China centers on the demanding environment of the northern plains. In that region arose important technologies, political traditions, and a set of philosophical and religious views that are hallmarks of Chinese civilization. In the third century C.E., the gradual flow of population toward the warmer southern lands caused the political and intellectual center to move south.

The eastern river valleys and North China Plain contained timber, stone, and scattered deposits of metals. Above all, this region offered potentially productive land. Since prehistoric times, winds rising over the vast expanse of Central Asia have deposited a yellowish-brown silt called **loess°** (silt in suspension in the water gives the Yellow River its distinctive hue and name). Over the ages this annual sprinkling has accumulated into a thick mantle of soil that is extremely fertile and soft enough to be worked with wooden digging sticks. The lack of compactness of this soil accounts for the severity of the damage that earthquakes cause in this region.

In this landscape, agriculture demanded immense human labor. In parts of northern China forests had to be cleared to open land for planting. The Yellow River was prone to devastating floods, necessitating the construction of earthen dikes and channels to carry off the overflow. The region was equally vulnerable to prolonged droughts, for which the best defense was the digging of catch basins (reservoirs) to store river water and rainfall. As the population of ancient China expanded, people claimed more land for cultivation by building retaining walls to partition the hillsides into tiers of flat terraces. In both northern and southern China, agriculture required the coordinated efforts of large groups of people.

The staple crops in the northern region were millet, a grain indigenous to China, and wheat, which spread to East Asia from the Middle East. Rice prospered in the south because it requires a relatively high air temperature. The cultivation of rice in the Yangzi River Valley and the south required great outlay of labor, but the effort was worthwhile since rice can feed a larger number of people per cultivated acre than any other grain.

Rice paddies must be absolutely flat and surrounded by water channels to bring and lead away water according to a precise schedule. Seedlings sprout in a nursery and then are transplanted one by one into the paddy and are flooded for a time. The flooding eliminates weeds and other rival plants and supports microscopic organisms that keep the soil fertile. When the crop is ripe, the paddy must be drained, the rice stalks harvested with a sickle, and the edible kernels separated out. The reward for this effort is a spectacular yield.

The Shang Period

Archaeologists have identified several Neolithic cultural complexes in China, primarily on the basis of styles of pottery and forms of burial. These early populations grew millet and raised pigs and chickens. They used stone tools. They made pottery on a wheel and fired it in high-temperature kilns. They mastered techniques for manufacturing silk cloth: first raising silkworms (which spin cocoons after gorging themselves with the leaves of mulberry trees) and then carefully unraveling silkworm cocoons to produce silk thread. The early Chinese built walls of pounded earth by hammering the soil inside temporary wooden frames until it became hard as cement. By 2000 B.C.E. they had acquired bronze metallurgy (roughly one millennium after the beginnings of bronzeworking in the Middle East).

Later generations of Chinese told stories about the ancient dynasty of the Xia, who are said to have ruled the core region of the Yellow River Valley. The validity of those stories is difficult to gauge, though some archaeologists identify the Xia with the Neolithic Longshan cultural complex in the centuries before and after 2000 B.C.E. For all practical purposes Chinese history begins with the rise to power of the Shang° clans, coinciding

---

Xinjiang (shin-jyahng)   **loess** (less)

Shang (shahng)

with the earliest written records in the early second millennium B.C.E.

The prominent class among the Shang was a warrior aristocracy whose greatest pleasures in life were warfare, hunting (for recreation and to fine-tune the skills required for war), exchanging gifts, feasting, and wine-filled revelry. The **Shang** originated in the part of the Yellow River Valley that lies in the present-day province of Henan°. Between approximately 1750 and 1027 B.C.E. they extended their control across a large swath of territory extending north into Mongolia, west as far as Gansu°, and south into the Yangzi River Valley. Various cities served as the capital of the Shang Empire. The last and most important of them was near modern Anyang° (see Map 3.1).

The king and his administrators ruled the core area of the Shang state directly. Aristocrats served, as needed, as generals, ambassadors, and supervisors of public projects. Members of the royal family and high-ranking nobility managed provinces farther out. The most distant regions were governed by native rulers bound by ties of allegiance to the Shang king. The king was often on the road, traveling to the courts of his subordinates to reinforce their ties of loyalty.

Frequent military campaigns provided the warrior aristocracy with a theater for brave achievements and yielded considerable plunder. The "barbarians," as the Chinese called the nomadic peoples who occupied the steppe and desert regions to the north and west, periodically were rolled back and given a demonstration of Shang power. (The word *barbarian* reflects the language and view of Chinese sources. Modern readers should be wary of the Chinese claim that these nomads were culturally backward and morally inferior to the Chinese.) The campaigns against peoples in the north and west produced large numbers of prisoners of war who were carried off to the Shang capital and used as slaves.

Far-reaching networks of trade sprang up across China, bringing to the core area of the Shang domain valued commodities such as jade, ivory, and mother of pearl (a hard, shiny substance from the interior of mollusk shells) used for jewelry, carved figurines, and decorative inlays. There are even faint indications that Shang China was in contact with the distant civilization of Mesopotamia and that these centers exchanged goods and ideas with one another.

The Shang kings devised an ideology of kingship that reinforced their power. They presented themselves as indispensable intermediaries between their people and the gods. The Shang royal family and aristocracy worshiped the spirits of their male ancestors. They believed that these ancestors were intensely interested in the fortunes of their descendants and had special influence with the gods. Before taking any action, the Shang used **divination** to ascertain the will of the gods (see Environment and Technology: Chinese and Mesopotamian Divination). Court ritual called for sacrifices to gods and to ancestors in order to win divine favor. Burials of kings also entailed sacrifices, not only of animals but also of humans, including noble officials of the court, women, servants, soldiers, and prisoners of war.

Possession of bronze objects was a sign of authority and nobility. Bronze was used in warfare and ritual, which, according to ancient sources, were the primary purposes of the state. Bronze weapons allowed the state to assert its authority, and the use of bronze ritual vessels was the best way to gain the support of ancestors and gods. The sheer quantity of bronze objects found in tombs of the Shang ruling class is impressive. The relatively modest tomb of one queen contained 450 bronze articles (ritual vessels, bells, weapons, and mirrors) —remarkable because copper and tin, the principal ingredients of bronze, were not plentiful in northern China. (Also found in the queen's tomb were numerous objects in jade, bone, ivory, and stone; 7,000 cowrie shells; 16 sacrificed men, women, and children; and 6 dogs!)

Bronze Food and Wine Vessels from the Shang Period
Such vessels were used in rituals that allowed members of the Shang ruling class to make contact with their ancestors. Signifying both the source and the proof of this elite's authority, these vessels were often buried in Shang tombs. The complex shapes and elaborate decorations testify to the artisans' skill.   (Courtesy of the Trustees of the British Museum)

Henan (heh-nahn)   Gansu (gahn-soo)   Anyang (ahn-yahng)

Chinese and Mesopotamian Divination

The inhabitants of China and Mesopotamia and many other peoples of the ancient world believed that the gods controlled the forces of nature and shaped destinies. Starting from this premise, they practiced various techniques of divination—the effort to interpret certain phenomena in the natural world as signs of the gods' will and intentions. Through divination the ancients sought to communicate with the gods and thereby anticipate, and even influence, the future.

The Shang ruling class in China frequently sought information from shamans, individuals who claimed the ability to make direct contact with ancestors and other higher powers. The Shang monarch himself often functioned as a shaman. Chief among the tools of divination used by a shaman were oracle bones. The shaman took a tortoise shell or the shoulder bone of an animal (sometimes holes had been drilled in it ahead of time) and touched it with the heated point of a stick. The shell or bone would crack, and the cracks were "read" as a message from the spirit world.

Tens of thousands of oracle bones survive. They are a major source of information about Shang life, because usually the question that was being posed and the resulting answer were inscribed on the back side of the shell or bone. The rulers asked about the proper performance of ritual, the likely outcome of wars or hunting expeditions, the prospects for rainfall and the harvest, and the meaning of strange occurrences.

In Mesopotamia in the third and second millennia B.C.E. the most important divination involved the close inspection of the form, size, and markings of the organs of sacrificed animals. Archaeologists have found models of sheep's livers accompanied by written explanations of the meaning of various features. Two other techniques of divination were following the trail of smoke from burning incense and examining the patterns that resulted when oil was thrown on water.

From about 2000 B.C.E. Mesopotamian diviners also foretold the future from their observation of the movements of the sun, moon, planets, stars, and constellations. In the centuries after 1000 B.C.E. celestial omens were the most important source of predictions about the future, and specialists maintained precise records of astronomical events. Mesopotamian mathematics, essential for calculations of the movements of celestial bodies, was the most sophisticated math in the ancient Middle East. A place-value system, in which a number stands for its value multiplied by the value of the particular column in which it appears (such as our ones, tens, and hundreds columns, moving from right to left), made possible complex operations with large numbers and small fractions.

Astrology, with its division of the sky into the twelve segments of the zodiac and its use of the position of the stars and planets to predict an individual's destiny, developed out of long-standing Mesopotamian attention to the movements of celestial objects. Horoscopes—charts with calculations and predictions based on an individual's date of birth—have been found from shortly before 400 B.C.E. In the Hellenistic period (323–30 B.C.E.), Greek settlers flooding into western Asia built on this Mesopotamian foundation and greatly advanced the study of astrology.

Chinese Divination Shell After inscribing questions on a bone or shell, the diviner applied a red-hot point and interpreted the resulting cracks as a divine response.
(Institute of History and Philology, Academia Sinica)

Clearly the Shang elite expended a huge effort on finding and mining deposits of copper and tin, refining the mixed ores into pure metal, transporting the precious cargo to the capital, and commissioning the creation of skillfully made and beautifully decorated objects.

The artisans, who worked in foundries outside the walls of the main cities, were sufficiently well rewarded to enjoy a comfortable lifestyle. After mixing the copper and tin in the right proportions, they poured the molten bronze into clay molds. Separate hardened pieces were later joined together as necessary. Shang artisans made weapons, chariot fittings, musical instruments, and, most important of all, the ritual vessels that held the liquids and solids used in religious ceremonies. Many of these elegant bronze vessels were vividly decorated with the stylized forms of real and imaginary animals.

The Shang period was a time of other significant technological advances as well. The horse-drawn chariot, which the Shang may have adopted from the contemporary Middle East, was a formidable instrument of war. Domestication of the water buffalo provided additional muscle power. Growing knowledge of the principles of engineering and an effective administrative organization for mobilizing human labor led to the construction of cities, massive defensive walls of pounded earth, and monumental royal tombs.

A key to effective administration was the form of writing developed in this era. Pictograms (pictures representing objects and concepts) and phonetic symbols representing the sounds of syllables were combined to form a complex system requiring scribes to memorize hundreds of signs. Because of the time needed to master this system, the ability to write was a skill exercised by the elite class. Despite substantial changes through the ages, the fundamental principles of the Chinese system have endured for thousands of years. In contrast, other ancient systems of writing that also were difficult to learn and brought special status and opportunities to those who did so—such as the cuneiform of Mesopotamia and the hieroglyphics of Egypt—eventually were replaced by simpler alphabetic approaches.

The Zhou Period

Shang domination of central and northern China lasted more than six centuries. In the eleventh century B.C.E. the last Shang king was defeated by Wu, the ruler of **Zhou°**, a dependent state in the valley of the Wei° River. The Zhou line of kings (ca. 1027–221 B.C.E.) was the longest lasting and most revered of all dynasties in Chinese history. As the Semitic peoples in Mesopotamia had adopted and adapted the Sumerian legacy (see Chapter 2), the Zhou preserved the foundations of culture created by their predecessors, adding important new elements of ideology and technology.

The positive image of Zhou rule, in many respects accurate, was skillfully constructed by propagandists for the new regime. The early Zhou monarchs had to formulate a new ideology of kingship to justify their seizure of power to the restive remnants of the Shang clans, as well as to their other subjects. The chief deity was now referred to as "Heaven," the monarch was called the "Son of Heaven," and his rule was called the **"Mandate of Heaven."** According to the new theory, the ruler was chosen and favored by the supreme deity and would retain this backing as long as he served as a wise, principled, and energetic guardian of his people. The proof of divine favor was prosperity and the stability of the kingdom. If the ruler misbehaved, as the last Shang ruler had done, his right to rule could be withdrawn. Corruption, violence, arrogance, and insurrection were signs of divine displeasure and validated the replacement of the failed Shang regime by a new dynasty that knew the moral order of the universe and was committed to just rule.

Although elements of Shang ritual were allowed to continue, there was a marked decline in the practice of divination and in the extravagant and bloody sacrifices and burials used in Shang court ceremonial. The priestly power of the ruling class, which alone during the Shang period had been able to make contact with the powerful spirits of ancestors, was largely removed. The resulting separation of religion from political activity allowed China to develop important secular philosophies in the Zhou period. The beautifully crafted bronze vessels that had been sacred implements in the Shang period became family treasures.

The early period of Zhou rule, the eleventh through ninth centuries B.C.E., is sometimes called the Western Zhou era. These centuries saw the development of a sophisticated administrative apparatus. The Zhou built a series of capital cities with pounded-earth foundations and walls. The major buildings all faced south, in keeping with an already ancient concern to orient structures so that they would be in a harmonious relationship with the terrain, the forces of wind, water, and sunlight, and the invisible energy perceived to be flowing through the natural world. All imperial officials, including the king, were supposed to be models of morality, fairness, and concern for the welfare of the people.

Like the Shang, the Zhou regime was highly decentralized. More than a hundred subject territories were ruled with considerable autonomy by members and allies of the royal family. The court was the scene of elaborate ceremonials, embellished by music and dance, that

Zhou (joe)   **Wei** (way)

Women Beating Chimes   This scene, from a bronze vessel of the Zhou era, illustrates the important role of music in festivals, religious rituals, and court ceremonials. During the politically fragmented later (Eastern) Zhou era, many small states marked their independence by having their own musical scales and distinctive arrangements of orchestral instruments.   (Courtesy, Imperial Palace Museum, Beijing)

impressed on observers the glory of Zhou rule and reinforced the bonds of obligation between rulers and ruled.

Around 800 B.C.E. Zhou power began to wane. Proud and ambitious local rulers operated ever more independently and waged war on one another, and nomadic peoples began to press on the borders from the northwest (see Map 3.1). The subsequent epoch of Chinese history is sometimes called the Eastern Zhou era. Members of the Zhou lineage, who in 771 B.C.E. had relocated to a new, more secure, eastern capital near Luoyang°, continued to hold the imperial title and to receive at least nominal homage from the real power brokers of the age. This was a time of political fragmentation, rapidly shifting centers of power, and fierce competition and warfare among numerous small and independent states. The Eastern Zhou is also conventionally subdivided. The years between 771 and 481 B.C.E. are called the "Spring and Autumn Period," after a collection of chronicles that give annual entries for those two seasons. The period from 480 B.C.E. to the unification of China in 221 B.C.E. is called the "Warring States Period."

The many states of the Eastern Zhou era, when not paralyzed by internal power struggles, contended with one another for leadership. Cities, some of them quite large, spread across the Chinese landscape. Long walls of pounded earth, the ancestors of the Great Wall of China, protected the kingdoms from suspect neighbors and northern nomads. By 600 B.C.E. iron began to replace bronze as the primary metal for tools and weapons.

Luoyang (LWOE-yahng)

There is mounting evidence that the earliest knowledge of ironworking came to China from the nomadic peoples of the northwest. Subsequently, metalworkers in the states of southern China, which had limited access to bronze, pioneered new techniques, such as the introduction of carbon into the smelting process to produce hard-edged steel. The Chinese also learned from the steppe nomads to put fighters on horseback.

In many of the states bureaucrats expanded in number and function. Codes of law were written down. The government collected taxes from the peasants directly, imposed standardized money, and managed large-scale public works projects. The wealth and power of the state and its demands for obedience were justified by an authoritarian political philosophy that came to be called **Legalism.** Legalist thinkers maintained that human nature is essentially wicked and people behave in an orderly fashion only if compelled by strict laws and harsh punishments administered by a powerful ruler. Legalists believed that every aspect of human society ought to be controlled and personal freedom sacrificed to the needs and demands of the state.

By expanding the range of government actions, the government and administrators in the major Zhou states were taking over many of the traditional functions of the aristocracy. Hoping to maintain their influence, aristocrats sought for themselves a new role in government as political advisers to the rulers. One of those who lived through the political flux and social change of this anxious time was Kongzi (551–479 B.C.E.)— known in the West by the Latin form of his name, **Confucius.** Coming from one of the small states in Shandong, he had not been particularly successful in obtaining administrative posts. The doctrine of duty and public service that he developed, initially aimed at aristocrats in a position similar to his own, was to become one of the most influential strains in Chinese thought.

Many elements in Confucius's teaching had roots in earlier Chinese belief, borrowing from folk religion and rites of the Zhou royal family. Confucius incorporated veneration of ancestors and elders and worship of the Zhou deity Heaven. He started from the assumption that hierarchy is innate in the order of the universe and that the patterns of human society should echo and harmonize with the cycles of the natural world. It followed, Confucius taught, that each person has a particular role to play, with prescribed rules of conduct and proper ceremonial behavior, in order to maintain the social order. He drew a parallel between the family and the state. As the family is a hierarchy with the father at its top, sons next, then wives and daughters in order of age, so the state is a hierarchy, with the ruler at the top, the public officials as the sons, and the common people as the women.

Confucius tended to transform specific social ideas into broad moral abstractions. He took a traditional term for the feelings between family members (*ren*) and expanded it into a universal ideal of benevolence, which he believed was the foundation of moral government: government exists, he said, to serve the people, and the administrator or ruler gains respect and authority by displaying fairness and integrity. Confucian teachings emphasized benevolence, avoidance of violence, justice, rationalism, loyalty, and dignity. They sought to affirm and maintain the political and social order by improving it.

Confucius apparently made little impact in his own time. His later follower Mencius (Mengzi, 371–289 B.C.E.), who opposed despotism and argued against the authoritarian political ideology of the Legalists, made Confucius's teachings much better known. And in the era of the early emperors, Confucianism became the dominant political philosophy (see Chapter 6).

The "Warring States Period" also saw the rise of the school of thought known as **Daoism.** According to tradition, Laozi sought to stop the warfare of the age by urging humanity to follow the *Dao*, or "path." Daoists° accept the world as they find it, avoiding futile struggles and deviating as little as possible from the "path" of nature. When they must act, they avoid violence if at all possible, and take the minimal action necessary for a

task. According to Daoism, rather than fight the current of a stream, a wise man allows the onrushing waters to pass around him. This passivity arises from the Daoist's awareness that the world is always changing and lacks any absolute morality or meaning. In the end, Daoists believe, all that really matters is the individual's own fundamental understanding of the "path."

The original Daoist philosophy was greatly elaborated in subsequent centuries and embraced a mixture of popular beliefs, magic, and mysticism. Daoism represents an important stream of thought throughout Chinese history. With its idealization of the individual who finds his or her own "path" to right conduct, it offered an alternative both to the Confucian emphasis on hierarchy and duty and to the Legalist approval of force.

This period also saw changes in social organization. The clan-based kinship structures prominent in the Shang and early Zhou periods went into decline. Taking their place was the three-generation family—grandparents, parents, and children—which became the fundamental social unit. Related to this development was the emergence of the concept of private property. Land was considered to belong to the men of the family and was divided equally among the sons when the father died.

Very little is known about the conditions of life for women in early China. Some scholars believe that women may have had an important role as shamans, entering into trance states to communicate with supernatural forces, making requests on behalf of their communities, and receiving predictions of the future. By the time written records begin to illuminate our knowledge of women's experiences, women were in a subordinate position in the strongly patriarchal family.

Confucian thought codified this male/female hierarchy. Only men were allowed to conduct the all-important rituals and make offerings to the ancestors, though women helped to maintain the ancestral shrines in the household. Fathers held authority over the women and children, arranged marriages for their offspring, and were free to sell the labor of family members. A man was supposed to have only one wife but was permitted additional sexual partners, who had the lower status of concubines. The elite classes used marriage to create political alliances, and it was common for the groom's family to offer a substantial "bride-gift" to the family of the prospective bride. A man whose wife died had a duty to remarry in order to produce male heirs to keep alive the cult of the ancestors.

Differences in male and female activities were rationalized by the concept of **yin** and **yang,** which represented the complementary nature of male and female roles in the natural order. The male principle (yin) was

---

Daoist (DOW-ist)

equated with the sun, active, bright, and shining; the female principle (yang) echoed the moon, passive, shaded, and reflective. Male toughness was to be balanced by female gentleness, male action and initiation by female endurance and need for completion, male leadership by female supportiveness. In its earliest form, the theory considered yin and yang as equal and alternatingly dominant, like day and night, creating balance in the world. Later, however, that viewpoint changed.

The classical Chinese patterns of family, property, and bureaucracy took shape during the long centuries of Zhou rule and the rise of competitive and quarreling smaller states. All that remained was for a strong central power to unify the Chinese lands. This outcome was achieved by the state of Qin°, whose aggressive tendencies and disciplined way of life made it the premier power among the warring states by the third century B.C.E. (see Chapter 6).

THE COSMOPOLITAN MIDDLE EAST

Both Mesopotamia and Egypt succumbed to outside invaders in the seventeenth century B.C.E. (see Chapter 2). Eventually the outsiders were either ejected or assimilated, and a new political equilibrium was achieved. Between 1500 and 1200 B.C.E. a number of large territorial states dominated the Middle East (see Map 3.2). Those centers of power controlled the smaller city-states, kingdoms, and kinship groups as they competed with, and sometimes fought against, one another for control of valuable commodities and trade routes.

Historians have called the Late Bronze Age in the Middle East a "cosmopolitan" era, meaning one in which elements of culture and lifestyle were widely shared among different groups. Extensive diplomatic relations and commercial contacts between states fostered the flow of goods and ideas, and throughout the region one could find among the elite groups a relatively high standard of living and similar possessions and values. The majority of the population—peasants in the countryside—may have seen some improvement in their standard of living, but they reaped far fewer of the benefits deriving from increased contacts and trade among different societies.

Qin (chin)

Western Asia

By 1500 B.C.E. Mesopotamia was divided into two distinct political zones: Babylonia in the south and Assyria in the north (see Map 3.2). The city of Babylon had gained political and cultural ascendancy over the southern plain under the dynasty of Hammurabi in the eighteenth and seventeenth centuries B.C.E. Subsequently there was a persistent inflow of Kassites°, peoples from the Zagros Mountains to the east who spoke a non-Semitic language, and by 1460 B.C.E a Kassite dynasty had come to power in Babylon. The Kassites retained names in their native language but otherwise embraced Babylonian language and culture and intermarried with the native population. During their 250 years in power, the Kassite lords of Babylonia did not actively pursue territorial conquest and were content to defend their core area and trade for vital raw materials.

The Assyrians of the north had more expansionist designs. Back in the twentieth century B.C.E. the city of Ashur, the most important early urban center on the northern Tigris, had become one pole of a busy trade route that crossed the northern Mesopotamian plain and ascended the Anatolian Plateau, where representatives of Assyrian merchant families maintained trade settlements outside the walls of important Anatolian cities. This commerce brought tin (bronze metallurgy developed in western Asia around 2500 B.C.E.) and textiles to Anatolia in exchange for silver. In the eighteenth century B.C.E. an Assyrian dynasty gained control of Mari°, a key city-state on the upper Euphrates River near the present-day border of Syria and Iraq. Although this "Old Assyrian" kingdom, as it is now called, was short-lived, it illustrates the importance of the cities that lay astride the trade routes connecting Mesopotamia to Anatolia and the Syria-Palestine coast. After 1400 B.C.E. a resurgent "Middle Assyrian" kingdom was once again engaged in campaigns of conquest and expansion of its economic interests.

Other ambitious states emerged on the periphery of the Mesopotamian heartland, including Elam in southwest Iran and Mitanni° in the broad plain lying between the upper Euphrates and Tigris Rivers. Most formidable of all were the **Hittites°**, speakers of an Indo-European language, who became the foremost power in Anatolia from around 1700 to 1200 B.C.E. From their capital at Hattusha°, near present-day Ankara° in central Turkey, they exploited the fearsome new technology of horse-drawn war chariots. The hills of Anatolia contained rich

Kassite (KAS-ite)   Mari (MAH-ree)   Mitanni (mih-TAH-nee)
Hittite (HIT-ite)   Hattusha (haht-tush-SHAH)
Ankara (ANG-kuh-ruh)

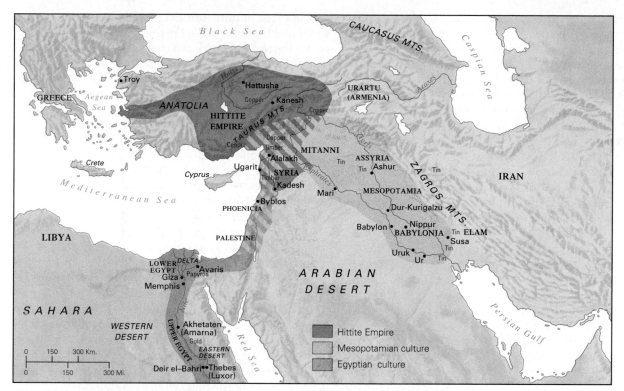

Map 3.2   The Middle East in the Second Millennium B.C.E.   Although warfare was not uncommon, treaties, diplomatic missions, and correspondence in Akkadian cuneiform fostered cooperative relationships between states. All were tied together by extensive networks of exchange centering on the trade in metals, and peripheral regions, such as Nubia and the Aegean Sea, were drawn into the web of commerce.

deposits of metals that were prized in this age—copper, silver, and iron—and the Hittites came to play an indispensable role in international commerce. The Hittite king laid down a standardized code of law, demanded military service and labor in exchange for grants of land, and supported artists and craftsmen engaged in the construction and decoration of palaces and temples.

A distinctive feature of western Asia during the second millennium B.C.E. was the diffusion of Mesopotamian political and cultural concepts from the original Sumerian core area in southern Mesopotamia across much of the region. Akkadian° was the language of international diplomacy and correspondence between governments (see Society and Culture: The Amarna Letters). The cuneiform system of writing also was employed to communicate in Elamite°, Hittite, and other languages. Mesopotamian myths and legends were taken over by other peoples, and Mesopotamian styles of art and archi-

tecture were imitated. In this new regional order the old core area was often hard-pressed by newcomers who had learned well and improved on the lessons of Mesopotamian civilization. The small, fractious, Mesopotamian city-states of the third millennium B.C.E. had been concerned with their immediate neighbors in the southern plain. In contrast, the larger states of the second millennium B.C.E. interacted politically, militarily, and economically in a geopolitical sphere extending across western Asia.

New Kingdom Egypt

The Middle Kingdom declined in the seventeenth century B.C.E. Because of the increased independence of high-level officials and the pressure of new groups migrating into the Nile Valley, Egypt entered a period of political fragmentation, economic decline, and cultural disruption. Around 1640 B.C.E. it came under foreign rule for the first

---

Akkadian (uh-KAY-dee-uhn)   **Elamite** (ee-luh-mite)

time, at the hands of the Hyksos°, or "Princes of Foreign Lands."

Historians are uncertain about the precise identity of the Hyksos and how they came to power. Semitic peoples from the Syria-Palestine region to the northeast (today the countries of Israel, Palestine, Jordan, Lebanon, and Syria) had been migrating into the eastern Nile Delta for centuries. In the chaotic conditions of this time other peoples may have joined them and established control, first in the delta and then throughout the middle portion of the country (see Map 3.2). This process may not have been far different from that by which the Amorites and Kassites first settled in and gained control in Babylonia. The Hyksos intermarried with the Egyptian population and largely assimilated to native ways. They used the Egyptian language and maintained Egyptian institutions and culture. Nevertheless, in contrast to the relative ease with which outsiders were assimilated in Mesopotamia, the Egyptians, with their strong sense of ethnic identity and long tradition of political unity, continued to regard the Hyksos as "foreigners."

As with the formation of the Middle Kingdom approximately five hundred years earlier, the reunification of Egypt under a native dynasty again came from the princes of Thebes. Through three decades of unrelenting fighting, Kamose° and Ahmose° were able to expel the Hyksos from Egypt, thereby inaugurating the New Kingdom, which lasted from about 1532 to 1070 B.C.E.

A century of foreign domination was a blow to Egyptian pride and shook the new leaders of Egypt out of the isolationist mindset of earlier eras. New Kingdom Egypt was an aggressive and expansionist state, engaging in frequent campaigns of conquest and extending its territorial control north into Syria-Palestine and south into Nubia. In this way Egypt won access to valuable commodities such as timber, copper (bronze metallurgy took hold in Egypt around 1500 B.C.E.), and gold, and to a constant infusion of wealth in the form of taxes and tribute (compulsory payments from a subject state to a conqueror). A buffer zone of occupied territory protected Egypt against foreign attack. The mechanisms of Egyptian control in the Syria-Palestine region included strategically placed forts and garrisons of Egyptian soldiers and support for local rulers who were willing to collaborate (see Society and Culture: The Amarna Letters). In contrast, Egypt imposed direct control over Nubia and pressed the native population to adopt Egyptian language and culture.

New Kingdom Egypt became a full participant in the network of diplomatic and commercial relations that linked the large and small states of western Asia. Egyp-

tian soldiers, administrators, diplomats, and merchants spent much time outside Egypt. Their travels abroad exposed Egypt to new fruits and vegetables, new musical instruments, and new technologies, such as improved potter's wheels and weaver's looms, and the war chariot. In sum, the New Kingdom was a period of innovation.

At least one woman held the throne of New Kingdom Egypt. **Hatshepsut** was the queen of Pharaoh Tuthmosis° II. When he died, she served at first as regent for her young stepson but soon claimed the royal title for herself (r. 1473–1458 B.C.E.). In the inscriptions that she commissioned for her mortuary temple at Deir el-Bahri, she often used the male pronoun to refer to herself, and drawings show her wearing the long, conical beard symbolic of the ruler of Egypt. It was Hatshepsut who dispatched the naval expedition to Punt described at the beginning of this chapter, to open direct trade between Egypt and the source of the prized myrrh resin. She may have used the success of this expedition to bolster her claim to the throne. After her death, in a reaction that reflected opposition in some official quarters to having a woman as ruler, her picture was defaced and her name blotted out wherever it appeared.

The reign of another ruler also saw sharp departures from the ways of the past. Originally called Amenhotep° IV, this ruler began to refer to himself as **Akhenaten°** (r. 1353–1335 B.C.E.), which means "beneficial to the Aten°" (the disk of the sun). Changing his name was just one of the ways in which he spread his belief in Aten as the supreme deity. He closed the temples of the other gods, thus challenging the long-standing supremacy of Amon° among the gods and the temporal power and influence of the priests of Amon.

Scholars have drawn various conclusions about the spiritual impulses behind these changes. Some have even credited Akhenaten with the invention of monotheism—the belief in one exclusive god. It is likely that Akhenaten's motives were at least partly political and that he was attempting to reassert the superiority of the king over the priests and to renew belief in the divinity of the king. The worship of Aten was actually confined to the royal family in the palace. The people of Egypt were pressed to revere the divine ruler.

Akhenaten built a new capital at modern-day Amarna°, halfway between Memphis and Thebes. He transplanted thousands of Egyptians to the new site to work in construction and to serve the elite members of his government. Akhenaten and his artists created a new style of realism: the king, his wife Nefertiti°, and their

---

Hyksos (HICK-soes) Kamose (KAH-mose) Ahmose (AH-mose)

Tuthmosis (tuth-MOE-sis) Amenhotep (ah-muhn-HOE-tep)
Aten (AHT-n) Amon (AH-muhn) Amarna (uh-MAHR-nuh)
Nefertiti (nef-uhr-TEE-tee)

SOCIETY & CULTURE

The Amarna Letters

The Amarna Letters are nearly four hundred documents discovered in 1887 C.E. at modern Tell el-Amarna (ancient Akhetaten), the capital of the Egyptian pharaoh Akhenaten. The documents date from approximately 1355 to 1335 B.C.E.—from the last years of Akhenaten's father, Amenhotep III, through the reign of Akhenaten. Primarily they are correspondence between the Egyptian monarch and various subordinate local rulers within the territory of modern Israel, Palestine, Lebanon, and Syria. Using Akkadian cuneiform, the medium for international communication at the time, the scribes sometimes betray their origins as Canaanites (the indigenous Semitic people of Syria-Palestine) by linguistic slips.

This archive reveals the complex and shifting political dynamics of the Egyptian empire, as can be seen in this letter from Lab'ayu, (luh-BAH-you) the Canaanite ruler of Shechem (shuh-KEM) in central Israel, to Amenhotep III:

To the king, my lord and my Sun-god: Thus Lab'ayu thy servant, and the dirt on which thou dost tread. At the feet of the king, my lord, and my Sun-god, seven times and seven times I fall. I have heard the words which the king wrote to me, and who am I that the king should lose his land because of me? Behold, I am a faithful servant of the king, and I have not rebelled and I have not sinned, and I do not withhold my tribute, and I do not refuse the requests of my commissioner. Now they wickedly slander me, but let the king, my lord, not impute rebellion to me!

The opening language of abject subordination to the divine king is a formula that appears in almost every document. Apparently Lab'ayu had been accused of disobedience by some of his neighbors and was writing to protest his innocence. In fact, Lab'ayu is frequently accused in the Amarna Letters of attacking the territory and robbing the caravans of other Egyptian subjects. This document lists the Egyptian government's general expectations of a subordinate local ruler: loyalty, payment of tribute, and obedience to Egyptian officials assigned to the region. It also may be the case that the Egyptians tolerated, and perhaps even encouraged, quarreling and competition among subject-rulers, as a way of keeping them weak and disunited.

Other documents in the archive provide glimpses of the goods (including human beings) traded through this region—a crossroads between Egypt, Syria, the Mediterranean, and Mesopotamia:

To Milkilu, prince of Gezer. Thus the king. Now I have sent thee this tablet to say to thee: Behold, I am sending to thee Hanya, the commissioner of the archers, together with goods, in order to procure fine concubines (i.e.) weaving women: silver, gold, linen garments, turquoise, all sorts of precious stones, chairs of ebony, as well as every good thing, totalling 160 deben. . . . So send very fine concubines in whom there is no blemish.

The appearance of Canaanite, Egyptian, and Indo-European names in the letters reveals the diverse mix of ethnic groups living in this region. There are also frequent references to the troubles caused by the Apiru (uh-PEE-roo), wandering peoples who preyed on the farmlands and towns, as in this appeal to Akhenaten from Shuwardata (shoo-wuhr-DUH-tuh), a local ruler from the Hebron region:

Let the king, my lord, learn that the chief of the Apiru has risen in arms against the lands which the god of the king, my lord, gave me; but I have smitten him. . . . So let it be agreeable to the king, my lord, and let him send Yanhamu, and let us make war in earnest, and let the lands of the king, my lord, be restored to their former limits!

As far as we can tell, the Apiru were not a specific ethnic group but rather a class of people who existed on the fringes of the settled and cultivated regions of Egypt and Syria-Palestine. They may have included truly nomadic groups as well as exiles, criminals, and other outcasts from cities and villages. They were looked down upon as backward, dishonest, and violent by townsmen and farmers (as Gypsies have been scorned throughout Europe and the Middle East in more recent times). It is evident from these documents that threats of raids and banditry created bonds of shared self-interest between local rulers and their Egyptian overlord. While Shuwardata can take the initiative and lead local troops against the raiders, he must turn to the Pharaoh for additional forces.

Why might the Egyptian government have chosen to exercise a lesser control in Syria-Palestine than in Nubia? Why did local elites cooperate with and serve the Egyptian empire?

Source: Translated by W.F. Albright in James B. Pritchard, ed., *Ancient Near Eastern Texts Relating to the Old Testament* (3rd, ed., Princeton, 1969.)

Colossal Statues of Ramesses II at Abu Simbel   Strategically placed at a bend in the Nile River so as to face the southern frontier, this monument was an advertisement of Egyptian power. A temple was carved into the cliff behind the gigantic statues of the pharaoh. Within the temple, a corridor decorated with reliefs of military victories leads to an inner shrine containing images of the divine ruler seated alongside three of the major gods. In a modern marvel of engineering, the monument was moved to higher ground in the 1960s C.E. to protect it from rising waters when a dam was constructed upriver.   (Susan Lapides/Woodfin Camp & Associates)

daughters were depicted in fluid, natural poses. The discovery at Amarna of an archive containing correspondence between the Egyptian government and various rival powers as well as local rulers in the Syria-Palestine dependencies illuminates the diplomatic currents of this so-called Amarna period (see Society and Culture: The Amarna Letters).

The reforms of Akhenaten stirred resistance from government officials, the priesthood, and other groups whose privileges and wealth were linked to the traditional system. After his death the old ways were restored with a vengeance: the temples were reopened, Amon was returned to his position of primacy in the pantheon, and the institution of kingship was weakened to the advantage of the priests. The boy-king Tutankhamun° (r. 1333–1323), one of the immediate successors of Akhenaten and famous solely because his is the only royal tomb found by archaeologists that had not been pillaged

by tomb robbers, reveals both in his name (meaning "beautiful in life is Amon") and in his insignificant reign the ultimate failure of Akhenaten's revolution.

Shortly thereafter the general Haremhab took possession of the throne for his family, the Ramessides, and this dynasty renewed the policy of conquest and expansion that had been neglected in the Amarna period. The greatest monarch of this line, **Ramesses° II**—Ramesses the Great, as he is sometimes called—ruled for sixty-six years (r. 1290–1224 B.C.E.) and dominated his age. Ramesses looms large in the archaeological record because he undertook monumental building projects all over Egypt. Living into his nineties, he had 200 wives and fathered 160 children. Archaeologists recently discovered a sprawling network of more than a hundred corridors and chambers carved deep into a hillside in the Valley of the Kings, where many sons of Ramesses were buried.

Tutankhamun (toot-ahng-KAH-muhn)

Ramesses (ram-ih-SEEZ)

Commerce and Diplomacy

Early in his reign Ramesses II commanded Egyptian forces in a major battle against the Hittites at Kadesh in northern Syria (1285 B.C.E.). Although Egyptian scribes presented this encounter as a great victory for their side, other evidence suggests that it was essentially a draw. In subsequent years Egyptian and Hittite diplomats negotiated a series of territorial agreements, which were strengthened by the marriage of Ramesses to a Hittite princess. At issue was control of the region lying between them, Syria-Palestine, the pivot in the trade routes that bound together this part of the globe. Lying at a crossroads between the great powers of the Middle East and at the end of the east-west land route across Asia, the inland cities of Syria-Palestine—such as Mari on the upper Euphrates and Alalakh° in western Syria—were meeting places where merchants from different lands could exchange goods. The coastal port towns—particularly Ugarit° on the Syrian coast and the up-and-coming Phoenician towns of the Lebanese seaboard—served as transshipment points for products going to or coming from the lands ringing the Mediterranean Sea.

In the eastern Mediterranean, northeastern Africa, and western Asia in the Late Bronze Age, access to metal resources was vital for any state with pretensions to power. Indeed, commerce in metals energized the long-distance trade that bound together the economies of the various states of the time. We have seen the Assyrian traffic in silver from Anatolia, and later in this chapter we discuss the Egyptian passion for Nubian gold. The sources of the most important *utilitarian* metals—copper and tin to make bronze—lay in different directions. Copper came from Anatolia and Cyprus; tin came from Afghanistan and possibly the British Isles. Both ores had to be carried long distances and pass through a number of hands before arriving in the political centers where they were melded and shaped.

New modes of transportation expedited communications and commerce across great distances and inhospitable landscapes. Horses arrived in western Asia around 2000 B.C.E. Domesticated by nomadic peoples in Central Asia, they were brought into Mesopotamia from the northeastern mountains. They reached Egypt by about 1500 B.C.E. The speed of travel and communication made possible by the horse opened new opportunities for the creation of large territorial states and empires, because soldiers and government agents on horseback could cover great distances in a relatively short time. Swift and maneuverable horse-drawn chari-

ots became the premier instrument of war. The team of driver and archer could ride forward and unleash a volley of arrows or trample terrified foot soldiers.

Sometime after 1500 B.C.E in western Asia, but not for another thousand years in Egypt, people began to make common use of camels, though the animal may have been domesticated a millennium earlier in southern Arabia. Thanks to their strength and capacity to go long distances without water, camels were able to travel across barren terrain. Their fortitude led, eventually, to the emergence of a new kind of desert nomad and to the creation of cross-desert trade routes (see Chapter 8).

NUBIA

The long-distance commerce in precious goods that flourished in the second millennium B.C.E. in western Asia and the eastern Mediterranean had repercussions to the south. Of even greater importance to Egypt than myrrh and other products from southern lands was the gold of Nubia.

Since the first century B.C.E. the name "Nubia" has been applied to a thousand mile (1,600-kilometer) stretch of the Nile Valley lying between Aswan° and Khartoum° (see Map 3.3). The ancient Egyptians called it "Ta-sety," meaning "Land of the Bow," after the favorite weapon of its warriors. This region straddles the southern part of the modern nation of Egypt and the northern part of Sudan. Nubia is the only continuously inhabited stretch of territory connecting sub-Saharan Africa (the lands south of the vast Sahara Desert) with North Africa. For thousands of years it has served as a corridor for trade between tropical Africa and the Mediterranean. It also was richly endowed with coveted natural resources such as gold, copper, and semiprecious stones like diorite, which it exported.

Nubia's vital intermediary position and natural wealth explain the early rise there of a civilization with a complex political organization, social stratification, metallurgy, monumental building, and writing. Egyptian efforts to secure control of Nubian gold sparked the emergence of this vital and long-lived civilization. Nubia traditionally was considered a periphery, or outermost region, of Egypt, and its culture was regarded as derivative. Now, however, most scholars emphasize the interactions between Egypt and Nubia and the mutually beneficial borrowings and syntheses that took place.

Alalakh (UH-luh-luhk)   **Ugarit** (OO-guh-reet)

Aswan (AS-wahn)   **Khartoum** (kahr-TOOM)

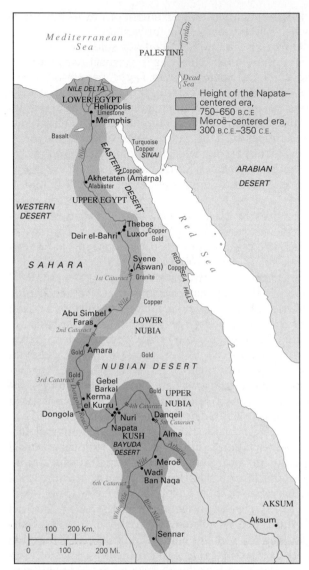

Map 3.3   Ancient Nubia   The land route alongside the Nile River as it flows through Nubia has long served as a corridor connecting sub-Saharan Africa with North Africa. The centuries of Egyptian occupation, as well as time spent in Egypt by Nubian hostages, mercenaries, and merchants, led to a marked Egyptian cultural influence in Nubia.   (Based on Map 15 from *The Historical Atlas of Africa*, ed. by J. F. Ajyi and Michael Crowder. Reprinted by permission of Addison Wesley Longman Ltd.)

Early Cultures and Egyptian Domination

The central geographical feature of Nubia, as of Egypt, is the Nile River. In this part of its course the Nile flows through a landscape of rocky desert, grassland, and fertile plain. Water from the river was essential for agriculture in a climate that was severely hot and nearly without rainfall. Six cataracts, barriers formed by large boulders and threatening rapids, made it impossible for boats to follow the river continuously. Nevertheless, commerce and travel were achieved by boats operating over shorter distances between the cataracts and by tracks for walking and riding alongside the river or across the desert.

In the fourth millennium B.C.E. bands of people in northern Nubia made the transition from seminomadic hunting and gathering to a settled life based on grain agriculture and cattle herding. Even before 3000 B.C.E., Nubia was serving as a corridor for long-distance commerce. Egyptian craftsmen of that period were working in ivory and in ebony wood—products of tropical Africa that had to come through Nubia.

Nubia first enters the historical record around 2300 B.C.E., in Old Kingdom Egyptian accounts of trade missions dispatched to southern lands. At that time Aswan, just north of the First Cataract, was the southern limit of Egyptian control. Egyptian noblemen stationed there led donkey caravans south in search of gold, incense, ebony, ivory, slaves, and exotic animals from tropical Africa. This was dangerous work, requiring delicate negotiations with local Nubian chiefs in order to secure protection, but it brought substantial rewards to those who succeeded.

During the Middle Kingdom (ca. 2040–1640 B.C.E.) Egypt adopted a more aggressive stance toward Nubia. Egyptian rulers were eager to secure direct control of the gold mines located in the desert east of the Nile and to cut out the Nubian middlemen who drove up the cost of luxury goods from the tropics. The Egyptians erected a string of mud-brick forts on islands and riverbanks south of the Second Cataract. These forts and the garrisons residing within them protected the southern frontier of Egypt against Nubians and desert raiders and regulated the flow of commerce. There seem to have been peaceable relations but little interaction between the occupying Egyptian forces and the native population of northern Nubia, which continued to practice its age-old farming and herding ways.

Farther south, where the Nile makes a great U-shaped turn in the fertile plain of the Dongola Reach (see Map 3.3), a more complex political entity was evolving from the chiefdoms of the third millennium B.C.E. The Egyptians gave the name **Kush** to the kingdom whose capital was located at Kerma, one of the earliest urbanized centers in tropical Africa. Beginning around 1750 B.C.E., the kings of Kush assembled and organized the labor to build monumental walls and structures of mud brick, and they were accompanied to the grave by dozens or even hundreds of servants and wives. These human sacrifices as well as the rich objects found in the tombs prove the wealth and power of the kings and suggest a belief in some sort of afterlife where attendants and possessions would be useful. Kushite craftsmen were skilled in metalworking, whether for weapons or jewelry, and their pottery surpassed in skill and beauty anything produced in Egypt.

During the expansionist New Kingdom (ca. 1532–1070 B.C.E.) the Egyptians penetrated even more deeply into Nubia. They destroyed the kingdom of Kush and its capital at Kerma, and they extended their frontier to the Fourth Cataract. The Egyptians built a new administrative center at Napata°, near Gebel Barkal°, the "Holy Mountain," believed to be the abode of a local god. A high-ranking Egyptian official called "Overseer of Southern Lands" or "King's Son of Kush" ruled Nubia. In an era of intense commerce among the states of the Middle East, when everyone was looking to Egypt as the prime source of gold, Egypt extensively exploited the mines of Nubia at considerable human cost. Fatalities were high among native workers in the brutal desert climate, and the army had to ward off attacks from desert dwellers.

Five hundred years of Egyptian domination in Nubia left many marks. The Egyptian government imposed Egyptian culture on the native population. The children of high-ranking natives were brought to the Egyptian royal court, simultaneously serving as hostages to ensure the good behavior of their families back in Nubia and absorbing Egyptian language, culture, and religion, which they later carried home with them. Many Nubians went north to serve as archers in the Egyptian armed forces. The manufactured goods that they brought back to Nubia have been found in their graves. The Nubians built towns on the Egyptian model and erected stone temples to Egyptian gods, particularly Amon. The frequent depiction of Amon with the head of a ram, however, may reflect a blending of the chief Egyptian god with a Nubian ram deity.

The Kingdom of Meroë

Egyptian weakness after 1200 B.C.E. led to the collapse of Egypt's authority in Nubia (see page 78). In the eighth century B.C.E. a powerful new native kingdom emerged in southern Nubia. The story of this civilization, which lasted for over a thousand years, can be divided into two parts. During the early period, between the eighth and fourth centuries B.C.E., Napata, the former Egyptian headquarters, was the primary center. During the later period, from the fourth century B.C.E. to the fourth century C.E.,

the center of gravity shifted farther south to the site of **Meroë°,** near the Sixth Cataract.

For half a century, from around 712 to 660 B.C.E., the kings of Nubia ruled all of Egypt as the Twenty-fifth Dynasty. They conducted themselves in the age-old manner of Egyptian rulers. They were addressed by the royal titles, depicted in traditional costume, and buried according to Egyptian custom. However, they kept their Nubian names and were depicted with Nubian physical features. They inaugurated an artistic and cultural renaissance, building on a monumental scale for the first time in centuries and reinvigorating Egyptian art, architecture, and religion by drawing selectively on practices and motifs of various periods. In this period each Nubian king resided at Memphis, the Old Kingdom capital. Thebes, the capital of the New Kingdom, was the residence of a female member of the king's family who remained celibate and was titled "God's Wife of Amon."

The Nubian dynasty overextended itself beginning in 701 B.C.E. by assisting local rulers in Palestine in their resistance to the Assyrian Empire. The Assyrians retaliated by invading Egypt and driving the Nubian monarchs back to their southern domain by 660 B.C.E. Napata again became the chief royal residence and the religious center of the kingdom, and Egyptian cultural influences remained strong. Egyptian hieroglyphs were the medium of written communication. Pyramids of modest size made of sandstone blocks were erected over the subterranean burial chambers of royalty. Royal bodies were mummified and the tombs filled with shawabtis°, human figurines intended to play the role of servants in the next life.

By the fourth century B.C.E. the center of gravity had shifted south to Meroë, perhaps because Meroë was better situated for both agriculture and trade, the economic mainstays of the Nubian kingdom. One consequence was a movement in cultural patterns away from Egypt and toward sub-Saharan Africa. A clear sign is the abandonment of Egyptian hieroglyphs and the adoption of a new set of symbols to write the Meroitic language. This form of writing is still essentially undeciphered. People continued to worship Amon as well as Isis, an Egyptian goddess connected to fertility and sexuality. But those deities had to share the stage with Nubian deities like the lion-god Apedemak, and elephants had some religious significance. Meroitic art was an eclectic mixture of Egyptian, Greco-Roman, and indigenous traditions.

Women of the royal family played an important role in the Meroitic era, another reflection, perhaps, of the influence of cultural concepts from sub-Saharan Africa. The Nubians employed a matrilineal system in which

---

Napata (na-PAY-tuh)   **Gebel Barkal** (JEB-uhl BAHR-kahl)

Meroë (MER-oh-ee)   **shawabti** (shuh-WAB-tee)

Shawabtis of King Taharka The Nubians adopted the Egyptian practice of placing in their tombs these miniature figures to perform required tasks in the afterlife. Taharka (r. 690–664), who ruled all of Egypt for a time, was buried in a large pyramid in Nubia with more than a thousand stone shawabtis. (Courtesy of the Trustees of the British Museum)

Temple of the Lion-Headed God Apedemak at Naqa in Nubia, First Century C.E. Queen Amanitore (right) and her husband, Natakamani, are shown here slaying their enemies. The architectural forms are Egyptian, but the deity is Nubian. The costumes of the monarchs and the important role of the queen also reflect the trend in the Meroitic era to draw upon sub-Saharan cultural practices. (P.L. Shinnie)

the king was succeeded by the son of his sister. In a number of cases Nubia was ruled by queens, either by themselves or in partnership with their husbands. Greek, Roman, and biblical sources refer to a queen of Nubia named Candace. However, these sources relate to different times, so *Candace* was most likely a title borne by a succession of rulers rather than a proper name. At least seven of these queens can be dated to the period between 284 B.C.E. and 115 C.E. Few details of their reigns are known, but they played a part in warfare, diplomacy, and the building of great temples and pyramid tombs.

Meroë itself was a huge city for its time, more than a square mile in area, overlooking a fertile stretch of grasslands and dominating a converging set of trade routes. Great reservoirs were dug to catch precious rainfall. The city was a major center for iron smelting (after 1000 B.C.E.

iron had replaced bronze as the primary metal for tools and weapons). The Temple of Amon was approached by an avenue of stone rams, and the enclosed "Royal City" was filled with palaces, temples, and administrative buildings. The ruler, who may have been regarded as divine, was assisted by a professional class of officials, priests, and army officers.

Weakened by shifts in the trade routes when profitable commerce with the Roman Empire was diverted to the Red Sea and to the rising kingdom of Aksum° (in present-day Ethiopia), Meroë collapsed in the early fourth century C.E. Nomadic groups from the western desert who had become more mobile because of the arrival of the camel in North Africa may have overrun Meroë. In any case, the end of the Meroitic kingdom, and of this phase of civilization in Nubia, was as closely linked to Nubia's role in long-distance commerce as had been its beginning.

THE AEGEAN WORLD

Parallels between the rise of Nubian civilization in the second millennium B.C.E.—catalyzed by contact with the already ancient civilization of Egypt but striking out on its own unique path of cultural evolution—and concurrent developments in the lands of the Aegean Sea, a gulf of the eastern Mediterranean, are intriguing. The emergence of the Minoan° civilization on the island of Crete and the Mycenaean° civilization of Greece is another manifestation of the fertilizing influence of older centers on outlying lands and peoples.

The landscape of southern Greece and the Aegean islands is mostly rocky and arid, with small plains lying between the ranges of hills. The limited arable land is suitable for grains, grapevines, and olive trees. Flocks of sheep and goats graze the slopes. Sharply indented coastlines, natural harbors, and small islands lying practically within sight of one another made sea travel the fastest and least costly mode of travel and transport. This region is resource-poor, having few deposits of metals and little timber. Those vital commodities, as well as surplus food for a large population, had to be imported from abroad. Indeed, because of their deficiency in important raw materials, the rise, success, and eventual fall of these societies was closely connected to their commercial and political relations with other peoples in the region.

The Minoan Civilization of Crete

By 2000 B.C.E. the island of Crete, which forms the southern boundary of the Aegean Sea (see Map 3.4), was the home of the first civilization in Europe to have complex political and social structures and advanced technologies such as those found in western Asia and northeastern Africa. These features include centralized government, monumental building, bronze metallurgy, writing, and recordkeeping. Archaeologists labeled this civilization **Minoan** after Greek legends about King Minos. Tradition claimed that the king ruled a vast naval empire and kept the monstrous Minotaur° (half-man, half-bull) beneath his palace in a mazelike labyrinth built by the ingenious inventor Daedalus°. Thus later Greeks recollected a time when Crete was home to many ships and sophisticated technologies.

Little is known about the ethnicity of the Cretans of this period, and their writings still cannot be translated. But archaeology has revealed sprawling palace complexes at the sites of Cnossus°, Phaistos°, and Mallia°, and the distribution of Cretan pottery and other artifacts around the Mediterranean and Middle East testifies to widespread trading connections. The layout and architectural forms of the Minoan palaces, the methods of centralized government, and the system of writing all seem to owe much to the influence of the older civilizations of Egypt, Syria, and Mesopotamia. The absence of identifiable representations of the Cretan ruler, however, contrasts sharply with the grandiose depictions of the king in the Middle East and suggests a different conception of authority.

Small statues of women with elaborate headdresses and serpents coiling around their limbs have been interpreted as female deities embodying the forces of fertility. Colorful **frescoes** (paintings done on a moist plaster surface) on the walls of Cretan palaces portray groups of women in frilly, layered skirts enjoying themselves in conversation and observation of rituals or entertainments. We do not know whether pictures of young acrobats vaulting over the horns and back of an onrushing bull show a religious activity or mere sport. Scenes of servants briskly carrying jars and fishermen throwing nets and hooks from their boats suggest a joyful attitude toward work, though this portrayal may say more about the sentimental tastes of the elite classes than about the reality of daily toil for the masses. The stylized depictions of flora and fauna on painted vases—plants with sway-

---

Aksum (Ahk-soom)   Minoan (mih-NO-uhn)
Mycenaean (my-suh-NEE-uhn)

Minotaur (MIN-uh-tor)   Daedalus (DED-ih-luhs)
Cnossus (NOSS-suhs)   Phaistos (FIE-stuhs)   Mallia (mahl-YAH)

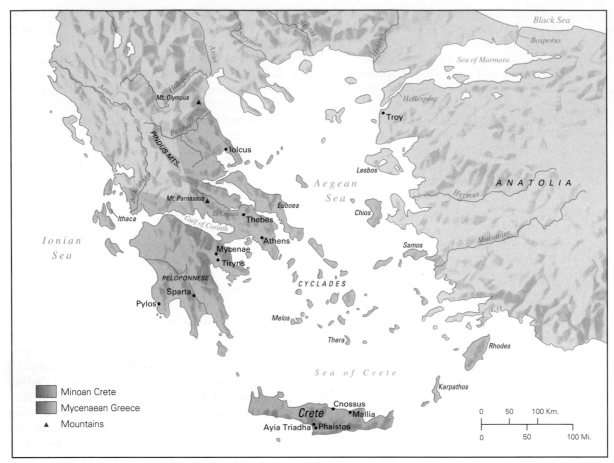

Map 3.4   Minoan and Mycenaean Civilizations of the Aegean   The earliest complex civilizations in Europe arose in the Aegean Sea. The Minoan civilization on the island of Crete evolved in the later third millennium B.C.E. and had a major cultural influence on the Mycenaean Greeks. Palaces decorated with fresco paintings, a centrally controlled economy, and the use of a system of writing for record keeping are some of the most conspicuous features of these societies.

ing leaves and playful octopuses whose tentacles wind around the surface of the vase—reflect delight in the beauty and order of the natural world.

Other than Cnossus, all the Cretan palaces, and even houses of the elite and peasant villages in the country-side, were deliberately destroyed round 1450 B.C.E. Because Mycenaean Greeks took over at Cnossus, most historians regard them as the likely culprits.

The Rise of Mycenaean Civilization

The standard view of Greek origins is that speakers of an Indo-European language ancestral to Greek migrated into the Greek peninsula around 2000 B.C.E., although some scholars argue for a much earlier date. A synthesis—through intermarriage, blending of languages, and melding of cultural practices and religious concepts—must have taken place between the indigenous population and the newcomers. Out of this mix emerged the first Greek culture. For centuries this society remained simple and static. Farmers and shepherds lived in essentially Stone Age conditions, wringing a bare living from the land. Then, sometime around 1600 B.C.E., life on the Greek mainland changed relatively suddenly.

More than a century ago a German businessman, Heinrich Schliemann, set out to prove the historical veracity of the *Iliad* and the *Odyssey*, two great epics attributed to a poet named Homer, who probably lived shortly before 700 B.C.E. Homer's Greeks were led by Agamemnon°, the king of **Mycenae**° in southern Greece. In 1876 Schliemann stunned a skeptical scholarly world by his

---

Agamemnon (ag-uh-MEM-non)   **Mycenae** (my-SEE-nee)

Minoan Vase Depicting an Octopus Produced around 1500 B.C.E., this vase shows the Minoan use of decorative motifs drawn from nature. Members of the Minoan elite seem to have enjoyed playful and idealized depictions of sea and plant life. The prosperity of the island civilization of Crete depended on exploitation of marine resources and on seaborne trade throughout the Mediterranean. (Josephine Powell, Rome)

discovery at Mycenae of a circle of graves at the base of deep, rectangular shafts. These **shaft graves,** containing the bodies of men, women, and children, were filled with gold jewelry and ornaments, weapons, and utensils. Clearly, some people in this society had acquired a new level of wealth, authority, and the capacity to mobilize human labor. Subsequent excavation at Mycenae uncovered a large palace complex, massive fortification walls, another circle of shaft graves, and other components of a rich and technologically advanced civilization that lasted from around 1600 to 1150 B.C.E.

How is the sudden rise of Mycenae and other centers in mainland Greece to be explained? Greek legends later spoke of the arrival of immigrants from Phoenicia (modern Lebanon) and Egypt, but archaeology provides no confirmation. Another legend recalled the power of King Minos of Crete, who demanded from the Greek city of Athens an annual tribute of ten maidens and ten young men. The Athenian hero Theseus° went to Crete, entered the labyrinth, and slew the Minotaur, thereby liberating his people.

Theseus (THEE-see-uhs)

Although there is no archaeological evidence for Cretan political control of the Greek mainland, there is much evidence of the powerful cultural influence exerted by Crete. The Mycenaeans borrowed from the Minoans the idea of the palace, the centralized economy, and the administrative bureaucracy, as well as the Minoan writing system. Also from the Minoans they learned styles and techniques of architecture, pottery making, and fresco and vase painting. This explains where the Mycenaean Greeks got their technology. But how did they suddenly accumulate power and wealth? Most historians look to the profits from trade and piracy and perhaps also to the pay and booty brought back by mercenaries (soldiers who served for pay in foreign lands).

This first advanced civilization in Greece is called "Mycenaean" largely because Mycenae was the first site excavated. Other centers have been excavated since Schliemann's day, including Tiryns°, about 10 miles (16 kilometers) from Mycenae; Pylos°, in the southwest; Athens and Thebes in central Greece; and Iolcus° in northern Greece. Mycenae exemplifies the common pattern of these citadels: a commanding location on a hilltop surrounded by high, thick fortification walls made of stones so large that later Greeks believed the giant, one-eyed Cyclopes° of legend lifted them into place. Within the fortified enclosure were the palace and administrative complex. The large central hall with an open hearth and columned porch was surrounded by courtyards, by living quarters for the royal family, courtiers, and servants, and by offices, storerooms, and workshops. The palace walls were covered with brightly painted frescoes depicting scenes of war, the hunt, and daily life, as well as decorative motifs from nature. The fortified enclosure also provided a place of refuge for the entire community in time of danger.

Nearby lay the tombs of the rulers and other leading families: shaft graves and later, much grander, beehive-shaped tombs made of rings of stone and covered with a mound of earth. Large houses, probably belonging to the aristocracy, lay just outside the walls. The peasants lived on the lower slopes and in the plain below, close to the land that they worked.

Additional information about Mycenaean life is provided by over four thousand baked clay tablets. The writing found on the tablets, today known as **Linear B,** uses pictorial signs to represent syllables, like the earlier, still undeciphered system employed on Crete, but it is recognizably an early form of Greek. An unwieldy system of writing, it was probably known only to the palace administrators. These tablets are essentially lists: of chariot

---

Tiryns (TEER-inz) **Pylos** (PIE-lohs) **Iolcus** (YOL-kuhs)
Cyclopes (sigh-KLOE-pees)

wheels piled up in palace storerooms, of rations paid to textile workers, of gifts dedicated to a particular deity, of ships stationed along the coasts. An extensive palace bureaucracy kept track of people, animals, and objects in exhaustive detail and exercised a high degree of control over the economy of the kingdom. Well-organized grain production supported large populations in certain regions, such as the territory controlled by Pylos in the southwest. (Archaeologists can make a rough estimate of population through surface surveys in which they tabulate the number of pieces of broken pottery from a given period that are visible on the ground.)

Certain industries seem to have been state monopolies. For instance, the state controlled the wool industry from raw material to finished product. Scribes kept track of the flocks in the field, the sheared wool, the distribution of raw wool to spinners and weavers, and the production, storage, and disbursal of cloth articles.

The view of this society that modern researchers can extract from the archaeological evidence and from the texts of the tablets is very limited. We know almost nothing about individual personalities—not even the name of a single Mycenaean king—very little about the political and legal systems, social structures, gender relations, and religious beliefs, and nothing about particular historical events and relations with other Mycenaean centers or peoples overseas.

The limited evidence for the overall political organization of Greece in this period is contradictory. In Homer's *Iliad* Agamemnon, the king of Mycenae, is in charge of a great expedition of Greeks from different regions against the city of **Troy** in northwest Anatolia. To this can be added the cultural uniformity to be found in all the Mycenaean centers: a remarkable similarity in the shapes, decorative styles, and production techniques of buildings, tombs, utensils, tools, clothing, and works of art. Some scholars argue that such cultural uniformity can be understood only within a context of political unity. The plot of the *Iliad*, however, revolves around the difficulties Agamemnon has in asserting control over other Greek leaders, such as the indomitable warrior Achilles°. And the archaeological remains and contents of the Linear B tablets give strong indications of independent centers of power at Mycenae, Pylos, and elsewhere. Given this evidence, cultural uniformity might best be explained by extensive contacts and commerce between the various Greek kingdoms.

Achilles (uh-KIL-eez)

Overseas Commerce, Settlement, and Aggression

Long-distance contact and trade were made possible by the seafaring skill of Minoans and Mycenaeans. Two sources provide evidence of the appearance and functioning of Aegean vessels: (1) wall paintings from Egypt and from Thera, an Aegean island, and (2) the excavation of vessels that sank and were preserved in sand at the bottom of the Mediterranean. Freighters depended entirely on wind and sail. The crews of warships could take down the mast and use oars when necessary. In general ancient sailors preferred to keep the land in sight and sail in daylight hours. Their sleek, light, wooden vessels had little decking and storage area, so the crew had to go ashore for food and sleep every night. With their low keels the ships could run up onto the beach.

The wide dispersal of Cretan and Greek pottery and crafted goods indicates that Cretans and Greeks engaged in trade not only within the Aegean but with other parts of the Mediterranean and Middle East. At certain sites, where the quantity and range of artifacts suggest a settlement of Aegean peoples, an interesting pattern is evident. The oldest artifacts are Minoan; then Minoan and Mycenaean objects are found side by side; and eventually Greek wares replace Cretan goods altogether. The physical evidence seems to indicate that Cretan merchants opened up commercial routes and established trading posts in the Mediterranean, then admitted Mycenaean traders to these locations, and were supplanted by the Greeks in the fifteenth century B.C.E.

What commodities formed the basis of this widespread commercial activity? The numerous Aegean pots found throughout the Mediterranean and Middle East must once have contained products such as wine or olive oil. Other possible exports include weapons and other crafted goods, as well as slaves and mercenary soldiers. Minoan and Mycenaean sailors may also have served as middlemen along long-distance trading networks, making a tidy profit by carrying goods to and from other places.

As for imports, amber (a hard, translucent, yellowish-brown fossil resin used for jewelry) from northern Europe and ivory carved in Syria have been discovered at Aegean sites, and it seems likely that the large population of southwest Greece and other regions necessitated imports of grain. Above all, the Aegean lands needed metals, both the gold so highly prized by the rulers and the copper and tin needed to make bronze. A number of sunken ships carrying copper ingots have been excavated recently on the floor of the Mediterranean. Scholars believe these ships probably carried metals from the

Fresco from the Aegean Island of Thera, ca. 1600 B.C.E. This picture, originally painted on wet plaster, depicts the arrival of a fleet in a harbor as people watch from the walls of the town. The Minoan civilization of Crete was famous in later legend for its naval power. The fresco reveals the appearance and design of ships in the Bronze Age Aegean. In the seventeenth century B.C.E., the island of Thera was devastated by a massive volcanic explosion, thought by many to be the origin of the myth of Atlantis sinking beneath the sea. (Archaeological Receipts Fund, Athens)

island of Cyprus, in the northeast corner of the Mediterranean, to the Aegean (see Map 3.2). As in early China, members of the elite classes were practically the only people who possessed things made of metal, and their near monopoly of metals may have had symbolic significance, working to legitimate their power. The bronze tripods piled up in the storerooms of the Greek heroes in Homer's epic poems bring to mind the bronze vessels buried in Shang tombs.

In an unsettled world, trade and piracy can be closely linked. Mycenaeans were tough, warlike, and acquisitive. They traded with those who were strong enough to hold their own and took from those who were too weak to resist. There is reason to believe that they became a thorn in the side of the Hittite kings of Anatolia in the fourteenth and thirteenth centuries B.C.E. A number of documents found in the archives at Hattusha, the Hit-

tite capital, refer to the king and land of Ahhijawa°, most likely a Hittite rendering of *Achaeans*°, the term used most frequently by Homer for the Greeks. The documents indicate that relations were sometimes friendly, sometimes strained, and they give the impression that the people of Ahhijawa were aggressive and taking advantage of Hittite preoccupation or weakness. Homer's tale of the ten-year Greek siege and eventual destruction of Troy, a city located on the fringes of Hittite territory and controlling an important commercial route connecting the Mediterranean and Black Seas, should be seen against this backdrop of Mycenaean belligerence and opportunism. Archaeology has confirmed a destruction at Troy around 1200 B.C.E.

Ahhijawa (uh-key-YAW-wuh)   **Achaeans** (uh-KEY-uhns)

C

THE FALL OF LATE BRONZE AGE CIVILIZATIONS

Hittite difficulties with Ahhijawa and the Greek attack on Troy foreshadow the troubles that culminated in the destruction of many of the old centers of the Middle East and Mediterranean around 1200 B.C.E. In this period, for reasons that historians do not completely understand, large numbers of people were on the move. As migrants or invaders swarmed into one region, they displaced other peoples, who then became part of the tide of refugees.

Around 1200 B.C.E. unidentified invaders destroyed Hattusha, and the Hittite kingdom in Anatolia came crashing down (see Map 3.3). The tide of destruction moved south into Syria, and the great coastal city of Ugarit was swept away. Egypt managed to beat back two attacks. Around 1220 B.C.E., Pharaoh Merneptah, the son and successor of Ramesses II, repulsed an assault on the Nile Delta. His official account identified the attackers as "Libyans and Northerners coming from all lands." About thirty years later Ramesses III checked a major invasion of "Peoples of the Sea" in Palestine. The Egyptian pharaoh claimed to have won a great victory, but one group of invaders, the Philistines, occupied the coast of Palestine. Egypt survived, barely, but gave up its territories in Syria-Palestine and lost contact with the rest of western Asia. The Egyptians also lost their foothold in Nubia, opening the way for the emergence of the native kingdom centered on Napata (see page 71).

Among the invaders listed in the Egyptian inscriptions are the Ekwesh°, a group that could be Achaeans—that is, Greeks. In this time of troubles it is easy to imagine opportunistic Mycenaeans taking a prominent role. Whether or not the Mycenaeans participated in the destructions elsewhere, in the first half of the twelfth century B.C.E. their own centers collapsed. The rulers apparently had seen trouble coming, for at some sites they began to build more extensive fortifications and took steps to guarantee the water supply of the citadels. But their efforts were in vain, and nearly all the palaces were destroyed. The Linear B tablets survive only because they were baked hard like pottery in the fires that consumed the palaces.

Scholars used to attribute the Mycenaean destruction to foreign invaders, but the archaeological record contains no trace of outsiders, and later Greek legends portrayed this as a time of internal dynastic struggles and wars between rival Greek kingdoms. A compelling explanation has been advanced that combines external and internal factors, since it is likely to be more than coincidence that the collapse of Mycenaean civilization occurred at roughly the same time as the fall of other great civilizations in the region. If members of the ruling class in the Mycenaean centers depended for their wealth and power on the import of vital commodities and the profits from trade, then the annihilation of major trading partners and disruption of trade routes would have weakened their position. Competition for limited resources may have led to the growth of internal unrest and, ultimately, political collapse.

The end of Mycenaean civilization illustrates the degree to which the major centers of the Late Bronze Age were interdependent. It also serves as a case study of the consequences of political and economic collapse. The destruction of the palaces meant the end of the political and economic domination of the ruling class. The massive administrative apparatus revealed in the Linear B tablets disappeared, and the technique of writing was forgotten, having no function outside the context of palace administration. People were displaced and on the move. Surface studies in various parts of Greece indicate depopulation in some regions and an inflow of people to other regions that had escaped the destruction. The Greek language, however, persisted, and a thousand years later people were still worshiping certain gods mentioned in the Linear B tablets. There was also continuity in material culture: people continued to make and use the vessels and implements that they were familiar with. But this society was much poorer, and there was a marked decline in artistic and technical skill. Different regions developed local shapes, styles, and techniques. This change from the uniformity of the Mycenaean Age was a consequence of the isolation of different parts of Greece from one another in this period of limited travel and communication.

Thus perished the cosmopolitan world of the Late Bronze Age in the Mediterranean and Middle East. The fragile infrastructure of civilization was shattered by a combination of external violence and internal weaknesses. Societies that had long prospered together through complex links of trade, diplomacy, and shared technologies, now fell together into a "Dark Age," a period of poverty, isolation, and loss of knowledge that lasted for several centuries.

Ekwesh (ECK-wesh)

CONCLUSION

This chapter traces the development of a number of civilizations in Africa, Europe, and Asia in the second and first millennia B.C.E. In all these societies, access to metals—above all, copper and tin alloyed into bronze—and the production of bronze tools, weapons, and luxury and ceremonial implements were vital to the success of elite groups.

Bronze metallurgy began at different times in different parts of the Eastern Hemisphere—in western Asia around 2500 B.C.E., in East Asia around 2000, in northeastern Africa around 1500. The Bronze Age also ended at different times in different parts of the world. The transition to iron as the primary metal came around 1000 B.C.E. in the eastern Mediterranean, northeastern Africa, and western Asia, and about five hundred years later in East Asia.

The acquisition of copper and tin to make bronze was a priority of Bronze Age elite classes. To a significant degree, political, military, and economic strategies reflected the demand for this commodity. Bronze was acquired in various ways in different parts of the hemisphere. In early China the state largely controlled the prospecting, mining, refining, alloying, and manufacturing processes. In western Asia long-distance networks of exchange were built up to facilitate the trade in metals. Cities sprang up and achieved great prosperity as a result of their location on trade routes. Commercial crossroads became targets of military and diplomatic activity for the major powers of the time, as, for instance, the Syria-Palestine region was for the Egyptian and Hittite states.

The uses to which bronze was put also varied in different societies. Normally this costly metal was available only to the elite classes. Possession of bronze weapons with their hard, sharp edges enabled the warriors of the Mycenaean and Shang ruling classes, as well as the royal armies of Egypt and Mesopotamia, to dominate the peasant masses. In the poems of Homer, Greek aristocrats hoard bronze weapons and utensils in their heavygated storerooms and give them to one another in rituals of gift exchange that create bonds of friendship and obligation. In Shang China the most important use of bronze was to craft the bronze vessels that played a vital role in the rituals of contact with the spirits of ancestors.

The period from 2200 to 500 B.C.E. saw the rise of complex societies in China, Iran, Syria-Palestine, Anatolia, Nubia, and the Aegean. Many of these new civilizations learned much from the already ancient centers in Mesopotamia and Egypt. At the same time, the old centers could hardly afford to remain static. In the competitive circumstances of this increasingly interconnected world, new means had to be found to expedite travel, transport, and communication. So, for instance, Akkadian cuneiform writing was used throughout western Asia, and the use of horses speeded up communication between central governments and their outlying areas.

The interdependence of the societies of the eastern Mediterranean and western Asia promoted prosperity, development, and the spread of ideas and technologies in the Late Bronze Age. Ironically, that interdependence became a source of weakness at the end of the era, during the time of migrations and invasions around 1200 B.C.E. The disruption of trading networks weakened ruling classes accustomed to easy access to metals and other valuable commodities, and the attacks of invaders and the wanderings of displaced peoples brought down unwieldy bureaucracies.

In East Asia at roughly the same time there was no "fall," because China was far away and not tightly linked by trade relations to the eastern Mediterranean and western Asia. The Zhou replaced the Shang, but there was much continuity in political, religious, and cultural traditions. In contrast, in the eastern Mediterranean and western Asia the destruction was so great that the old centers did not survive or were severely weakened. Within a few centuries new peoples would come to the fore, in particular the Assyrians, Phoenicians, and Israelites, whose story unfolds in the next chapter.

■ Key Terms

loess	Akhenaten
Shang	Ramesses II
divination	Kush
Zhou	Meroë
Mandate of Heaven	Minoan
yin/yang	shaft grave
Legalism	fresco
Confucius	Linear B
Daoism	Mycenae
Hittites	Troy
Hatshepsut	

■ Suggested Reading

Caroline Blunden and Mark Elvin, *Cultural Atlas of China* (1983), contains general geographic, ethnographic, and historical information about China through the ages, as well as many maps and illustrations. Conrad Schirokauer, *A Brief History of Chinese Civilization* (1991), and John King Fairbank, *China: A New History* (1992), offer useful chapters on early China. Edward L. Shaughnessy and Michael Loewe, eds., *The Cambridge History of Ancient China* (1998), approaches the subject in far greater depth. Jessica Rawson, *Ancient China: Art and Archaeology* (1980), and Kwang-chih Chang, *The Archaeology of Ancient China*, 4th ed. (1986), emphasize archaeological evidence. W. Thomas Chase, *Ancient Chinese Bronze Art: Casting the Precious Sacral Vessel* (1991), contains a brief but useful discussion of the importance of bronzes in ancient China, as well as a detailed discussion of bronze-casting techniques. Robert Temple, *The Genius of China: 3,000 Years of Science, Discovery, and Invention* (1986), explores many aspects of Chinese technology, using a division into general topics such as agriculture, engineering, and medicine. Sharon L. Sievers, in *Restoring Women to History* (1988), and Patricia Ebrey, "Women, Marriage, and the Family in Chinese History," in *Heritage of China: Contemporary Perspectives on Chinese Civilization*, ed. Paul S. Ropp (1990), address the very limited evidence for women in early China. Michael Loewe and Carmen Blacker, *Oracles and Divination* (1981), addresses practices in China and other ancient civilizations. Simon Leys, *The Analects of Confucius* (1997), provides a translation of and a commentary on this fundamental text. Benjamin I. Schwartz, *The World of Thought in Ancient China* (1985), is a broad introduction to early Chinese ethical and spiritual concepts.

Many of the books recommended in the Suggested Reading list for Chapter 2 are useful for Mesopotamia, Syria, and Egypt in the Late Bronze Age. In addition see Miriam Lichtheim, *Ancient Egyptian Literature: A Book of Readings, vol. 2, The New Kingdom* (1973); Donald B. Redford, *Egypt, Canaan, and Israel in Ancient Times* (1992), which explores the relations of Egypt with the Syria-Palestine region in this period; and H. W. F. Saggs, *Babylonians* (1995), which devotes several chapters to this more thinly documented epoch in the history of southern Mesopotamia. On the Hittites see O. R. Gurney, *The Hittites*, 2d ed., rev. (1990), and J. G. Macqueen, *The Hittites and Their Contemporaries in Asia Minor* (1975). Tamsyn Barton, *Ancient Astrology* (1994), devotes her first chapter to early manifestations of astrology in Mesopotamia and Egypt.

After a long period of scholarly neglect, with an occasional exception such as Bruce G. Trigger, *Nubia Under the Pharaohs* (1976), the study of ancient Nubia is beginning to receive considerable attention. David O'Connor, *Ancient Nubia: Egypt's Rival in Africa* (1993); Joyce L. Haynes, *Nubia: Ancient Kingdoms of Africa* (1992); Karl-Heinz Priese, *The Gold of Meroë* (1993); P. L. Shinnie, *Ancient Nubia* (1996); and Derek A. Welsby, *The Kingdom of Kush: The Napatan and Meroitic Empires* (1996), all reflect the new interest of major museums in the art and artifacts of this society. John H. Taylor, *Egypt and Nubia* (1991), also emphasizes the fruitful interaction of the Egyptian and Nubian cultures.

R. A. Higgins, *The Archaeology of Minoan Crete* (1973) and *Minoan and Mycenaean Art*, new rev. ed. (1997); J. Walter Graham, *The Palaces of Crete* (1987); O. Krzyszkowska and L. Nixon, *Minoan Society* (1983); and N. Marinatos, *Minoan Religion* (1993), examine the archaeological evidence for the Minoan civilization. The brief discussion of M. I. Finley, *Early Greece: The Bronze and Archaic Ages* (1970), and the much fuller accounts of Emily Vermeule, *Greece in the Bronze Age* (1972), and J. T. Hooker, *Mycenaean Greece* (1976), are still useful treatments of Mycenaean Greece, based primarily on archaeological evidence. For the evidence of the Linear B tablets see John Chadwick, *Linear B and Related Scripts* (1987) and *The Mycenaean World* (1976). J. V. Luce, *Homer and the Heroic Age* (1975), and Carol G. Thomas, *Myth Becomes History: Pre-Classical Greece* (1993), examine the usefulness of the Homeric poems for reconstructing the Greek past. For the disruptions and destructions of the Late Bronze Age in the eastern Mediterranean, see N. K. Sandars, *The Sea Peoples: Warriors of the Ancient Mediterranean* (1978), and Trude Dothan and Moshe Dothan, *People of the Sea: The Search for the Philistines* (1992).

THE FORMATION OF
NEW CULTURAL COMMUNITIES,
1000 B.C.E.–400 C.E.

The fourteen centuries from 1000 B.C.E. to 400 C.E. mark a new chapter in the story of humanity. Important changes in the ways of life established in the river-valley civilizations in the two previous millennia occurred, and the scale of human institutions and activities increased.

The political and social structure of the earliest river-valley centers reflected the importance of irrigation for agriculture. Powerful kings, hereditary priesthoods, dependent laborers, limited availability of metals, and very restricted literacy are hallmarks of the complex societies described in Part One. In the first millennium B.C.E. new centers arose, in lands watered by rainfall and worked by a free peasantry, on the shores of the Mediterranean, in Iran, India, South-

east Asia, and in Central and South America. Shaped by the natural environments in which they arose, they developed new patterns of political and social organization and economic activity, and moved in new intellectual, artistic, and spiritual directions, though under the influence of the older centers.

The rulers of the empires of this era took steps intended to control and tax their subjects: they constructed extensive networks of roads and promoted urbanization. These measures brought incidental benefits: more rapid communication, the transport of trade goods over greater distances, and the broad diffusion of religious ideas, artistic styles, and technologies. Large cultural zones unified by common traditions emerged. A number of these cultural traditions—

Hellenistic, Roman, Chavín, Olmec—were to exercise substantial influence on subsequent ages. The influence of some—Hindu and Chinese—persists into our own time.

The expansion of agriculture and trade and improvements in technology led to population increases, the spread of cities, and the growth of a comfortable middle class. In many parts of the world iron replaced bronze as the preferred metal for weapons, tools, and utensils. People using iron tools cleared extensive forests around the Mediterranean, in India, and in eastern China. Iron weapons gave an advantage to the armies of Assyria, Greece, Rome, and imperial China. Metal, still an important item of long-distance trade, was available to more people than it had been in the preceding age. Metal coinage, which originated in Anatolia, was adopted by many peoples. Metal coins facilitated commercial transactions and the acquisition of wealth.

New systems of writing also developed. Because they were more easily and rapidly learned, writing moved out of the control of specialists. The vast majority of people remained illiterate, but writing became an increasingly important medium for preserving and transmitting cultural knowledge. The spread of literacy gave birth to new ways of thinking, new genres of literature, and new types of scientific endeavor.

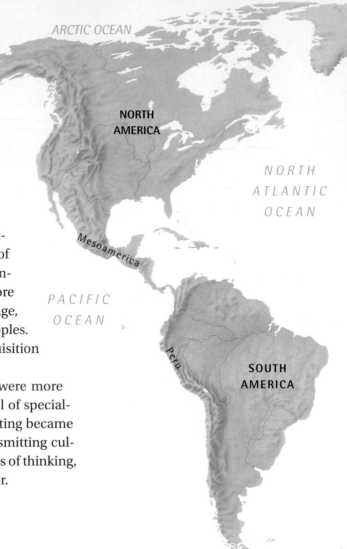

	1000 B.C.E.	800 B.C.E.	600 B.C.E.	
Americas	1200–400 Olmec civilization in Mesoamerica		Gold metallurgy in Chavin 500 •	
		900–250 Chavin civilization in Peru		
Europe	• 1000 Iron metallurgy	Hoplite warfare 700 •	Celts spread across Europe 500 •	477–404 Athenian Empire and democracy
		800–500 Archaic period in Greece	Roman Republic 507 •	
Africa		• 814 Carthage founded	Hanno of Carthage explores West African coast 465 •	
	Rise of Nubian kingdom at Napata 800 •		712–660 Nubian domination of Egypt	
Middle East	• 1000 David establishes Jerusalem as capital of Israel	Assyrian attack on Phoenician Tyre 701 •	Babylonian conquest of Jerusalem 587 •	522–486 Darius I rules Persian Empire
		911–612 Neo-Assyrian Empire		
Asia and Oceania	• 1000 Aryans settle Ganges Plain	Iron metallurgy in China 600 •	563–483 Life of the Buddha	
	1027–771 Zhou kingdom in China		551–479 Life of Confucius	

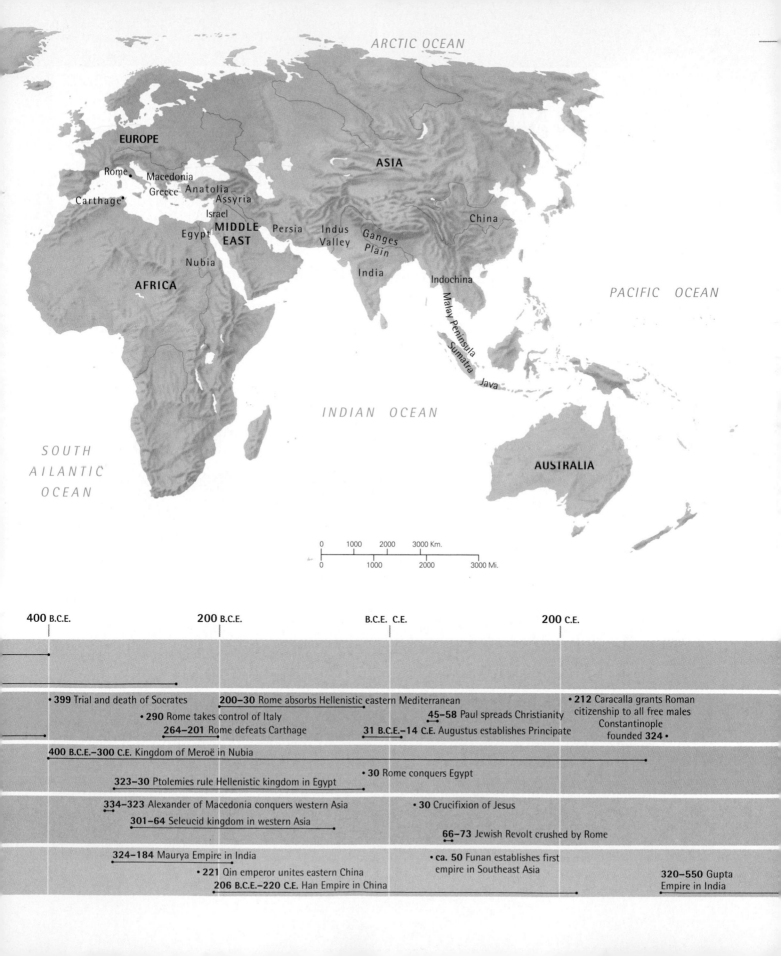

ARCTIC OCEAN

EUROPE

ASIA

Rome
Macedonia
Greece
Anatolia
Carthage
Assyria
Israel
Egypt
MIDDLE
EAST
Persia
Indus
Valley
Ganges
Plain
China

Nubia

India

Indochina

AFRICA

Malay Peninsula
Sumatra
Java

PACIFIC OCEAN

INDIAN OCEAN

SOUTH
ATLANTIC
OCEAN

AUSTRALIA

| 0 | 1000 | 2000 | 3000 Km. |
| 0 | 1000 | 2000 | 3000 Mi. |

400 B.C.E.   **200** B.C.E.   B.C.E. C.E.   **200** C.E.

• **399** Trial and death of Socrates   **200–30** Rome absorbs Hellenistic eastern Mediterranean   • **212** Caracalla grants Roman citizenship to all free males

• **290** Rome takes control of Italy   **45–58** Paul spreads Christianity

264–201 Rome defeats Carthage   **31** B.C.E.–**14** C.E. Augustus establishes Principate   Constantinople founded **324** •

400 B.C.E.–**300** C.E. Kingdom of Meroë in Nubia

323–30 Ptolemies rule Hellenistic kingdom in Egypt   • **30** Rome conquers Egypt

334–323 Alexander of Macedonia conquers western Asia   • **30** Crucifixion of Jesus

301–64 Seleucid kingdom in western Asia   **66–73** Jewish Revolt crushed by Rome

324–184 Maurya Empire in India   • ca. **50** Funan establishes first empire in Southeast Asia

• **221** Qin emperor unites eastern China   **320–550** Gupta Empire in India

206 B.C.E.–**220** C.E. Han Empire in China

4

NEW CIVILIZATIONS IN THE AMERICAS AND WESTERN EURASIA, 1200–250 B.C.E.

First Civilizations of the Americas • Celtic Europe • The Assyrian Empire • Israel • Phoenicia and the Mediterranean • Failure and Transformation

ENVIRONMENT AND TECHNOLOGY: Ancient Textiles and Dyes

SOCIETY AND CULTURE: Mass Deportation in the Neo-Assyrian Empire

Section of Balawat Gates   Bronze bands with images of military campaigns were affixed to the gates of the palace of the Assyrian king Shalmaneser III (r. 858–824 B.C.E.)

*A*ncient peoples were very interested in the origins of their communities. Even if the stories they told are not always historically accurate, they provide valuable insights into how people thought about their origins and identity. One famous story concerned the great city of Carthage in present-day Tunisia, which for centuries dominated the waters and commerce of the western Mediterranean. Tradition held that Dido, a member of the royal family of the Phoenician city-state of Tyre° in southern Lebanon, fled in 814 B.C.E. with her supporters to the western Mediterranean after her husband had been viciously murdered by her brother, the king of Tyre. Setting ashore on the North African coast, these refugees made friendly contact with the local population, who agreed to give them as much land as a cow's hide could cover. By cleverly cutting the hide into narrow strips, they were able to mark out a substantial piece of territory for their new foundation: Kart Khadasht, the "New City" (*Carthago* on the tongues of their Roman enemies). At a later time, faithful to the memory of her dead husband, Dido committed suicide rather than marry a local chieftain.

This story evokes an important phenomenon of the Early Iron Age in the Mediterranean lands and western Asia: the migration and resettlement of peoples. For a variety of reasons, large numbers of people relocated during the first millennium B.C.E. Some populations fled when conquerors occupied their territories. Other conquered peoples were forcibly removed from their ancestral homes. Still others chose to settle in distant lands in response to political and military pressures or in the hope of improving their lot in life.

In this same period, the earliest complex societies arose in the Western Hemisphere. The Olmec° people in east-central Mexico and the Chavín° civilization in western Peru laid the foundations of vibrant cultural and technological traditions that would have a decisive influence on the subsequent history of the Americas. In many respects these developments were analogous to what had taken place in the original centers of the Eastern Hemisphere at an earlier date. As we shall see, however, the cultural and technological evolution of the Western Hemisphere did not necessarily parallel the sequence in the Eastern Hemisphere.

The first part of this chapter traces the story of the first complex societies in the Americas. The remainder of the chapter examines the history of Europe north of the Alps, western Asia, and North Africa in the late second and early first millennia B.C.E. but carries the story farther forward when necessary. The focus is on four societies: the Celtic peoples of Europe; the Assyrians of northern Mesopotamia; the Israelites of Israel; and the Phoenicians of Lebanon and Syria and their colonies in the western Mediterranean, mainly Carthage. After the decline or demise of the ancient centers dominant throughout the third and second millennia B.C.E., these four societies evolved into new political, cultural, and commercial centers.

By the end of the second millennium B.C.E. many of the societies of the Eastern Hemisphere had entered the **Iron Age:** they had begun to use iron for tools and weapons. Iron offered several advantages over bronze, the primary metal of the preceding period. It was a single metal rather than an alloy and thus was simpler to obtain; there were many potential sources of iron ore. Once the technology of iron making had been mastered, iron tools had a harder, sharper edge than bronze. These advantages were not discovered all at once. Some scholars believe that, in the disrupted period after 1200 B.C.E., metalworkers who could not obtain copper and tin turned to dumps of slag—the byproduct of bronze production—containing iron residue and found that they could create useful objects from it. Iron has to be heated to a higher temperature than bronze, and its hardness depends on the amount of carbon present during the forging process. As its usefulness became recognized and techniques were perfected, it came to be used on an ever wider scale, though bronze continued to be used alongside it.

Tyre (tire)   **Olmec** (OHL-meck)   **Chavín** (cha-BEAN)

As you read this chapter, ask yourself the following questions:

- What environmental, technological, political, and cultural factors led these contemporary societies to develop such distinctive institutions and values?
- What were the causes and consequences of large-scale movements of peoples to new homes during this era?
- Why were certain cultures destroyed or assimilated while others survived long after this period?
- Why did societies in the Eastern and Western Hemispheres acquire complex organizations and potent technologies at different times and in different sequences?

FIRST CIVILIZATIONS OF THE AMERICAS

The Western Hemisphere was populated through a series of migrations from the Asian mainland (see Chapter 1). Although some scholars believe the first migrations occurred as early as the period 35,000–25,000 B.C.E., others argue for the period 20,000–13,000 B.C.E. For at least fifteen thousand years peoples in the Western Hemisphere lived in virtual isolation from the rest of the world. The duration and comprehensiveness of their isolation distinguishes the Americas from the world's other major cultural regions. While technological innovations passed back and forth among the civilizations of Asia, Africa, and Europe, the peoples of the Americas faced the challenges of the natural environment on their own.

Over thousands of years the descendants of these immigrants increased in number and dispersed across the hemisphere's landscape, responding to environments as different as the frozen regions of the polar extremes, tropical rain forests, deserts, high mountain ranges, woodlands, and prairies. Two of the hemisphere's most impressive cultural traditions developed in Mesoamerica (Mexico and northern Central America) and in the Andean region of South America. Well before 1000 B.C.E. the domestication of new plant varieties, the introduction of new technologies, and a limited development of trade led to greater social stratification and urbanization in both regions. Cultural elites used their increased political and religious authority to organize great numbers of laborers to dig large-scale irrigation and drainage works, to clear forests, and to develop terraced fields on hillsides. These transformed environments provided the economic platform for the construction of urban centers dominated by monumental structures devoted to religious purposes and housing for members of the elite. By 1000 B.C.E. the major urban centers of Mesoamerica and the Andes had begun to project their political and cultural power over broad territories: they had become civilizations. The cultural legacies of the two most important of these early civilizations, the Olmec and Chavín, would persist in Mesoamerica and the Andes respectively for more than a thousand years.

The Mesoamerican Olmecs, 1200–400 B.C.E.

Mesoamerica is a region of great geographic and climatic diversity. Within the ecological niches created by this diversity, Amerindian peoples developed specialized technologies that exploited indigenous plants and animals, as well as minerals like obsidian, quartz, and jade. Contacts across these environmental boundaries led to trade and cultural exchange. Enhanced trade, increasing agricultural productivity, and rising population led, in turn, to urbanization and the appearance of powerful political and religious elites. Although a number of militarily powerful civilizations developed in Mesoamerica, the region was never unified politically. All the civilizations that appeared in Mesoamerica, however, did share fundamental elements of material culture, technology, religion, political organization, art, architecture, and sport.

The most influential early Mesoamerican civilization was the **Olmec,** flourishing between 1200 and 400 B.C.E. (see Map 4.1). The center of Olmec civilization was located near the tropical Atlantic coast of what are now the Mexican states of Veracruz and Tabasco. In recent years archaeologists have excavated smaller sites that indicate that Olmec cultural influence reached to the Pacific coast of Central America and the Central Plateau of Mexico.

The cultural core of the early Olmec civilization was located at San Lorenzo but included smaller centers nearby (1200–900 B.C.E.). La Venta°, which developed at about the same time, became the most important Olmec center after 900 B.C.E. when San Lorenzo was abandoned or destroyed. Tres Zapotes° was the last dominant center after La Venta collapsed or was destroyed around 600 B.C.E. In each case, the defacing and burying of monu-

---

La Venta (LA BEN-tah)   **Tres Zapotes** (TRACE zah-POE-tace)

CHRONOLOGY

	Israel	Phoenicia/Carthage	Mesopotamia	Americas
1200 B.C.E.	**1250–1200 B.C.E.** Israelite occupation of Canaan			**1200–900 B.C.E.** Rise of Olmec civilization, centered on San Lorenzo
1000 B.C.E.	**1000 B.C.E.** David establishes Jerusalem as capital	**969 B.C.E.** Hiram of Tyre comes to power		
	960 B.C.E. Solomon builds First Temple			
	920 B.C.E. Division into two kingdoms			
900 B.C.E.			**911 B.C.E.** Rise of Neo-Assyrian Empire	**900–600 B.C.E.** La Venta, the dominant Olmec center
				900–250 B.C.E. Chavín civilization in the Andes
800 B.C.E.		**814 B.C.E.** Foundation of Carthage		
	721 B.C.E. Assyrian conquest of northern kingdom	**744–727 B.C.E.** Reforms of Tiglath-pileser		
		701 B.C.E. Assyrian humiliation of Tyre		
700 B.C.E.			**668–627 B.C.E.** Reign of Ashurbanipal	
			626–539 B.C.E. Neo-Babylonian kingdom	
600 B.C.E.			**612 B.C.E.** Fall of Assyria	**600–400 B.C.E.** Ascendancy of Tres Zapotes and Olmec decline
	587 B.C.E. Neo-Babylonian capture of Jerusalem	**ca. 550–300 B.C.E.** Rivalry of Carthaginians and Greeks in western Mediterranean		

ments and the destruction of buildings prior to the abandonment of Olmec centers are commonly interpreted by archaeologists as evidence of internal upheavals or invasion by neighboring peoples.

Olmec urban development was made possible by earlier advances in agriculture. The staples of the Mesoamerican diet—corn, beans, and squash—were domesticated by 3500 B.C.E. The ability of farmers to produce dependable surpluses of these products permitted the first stages of craft specialization and social stratification. As religious and political elites emerged, they found ways to organize the population to dig irrigation and drainage canals, develop raised fields that could be farmed more intensively, and construct the large-scale

Map 4.1 Olmec and Chavín Civilizations The regions of Mesoamerica (most of modern Mexico and Central America) and the Andean highlands of South America have hosted impressive civilizations since early times. The civilizations of the Olmec and Chavín were the originating civilizations of these two regions, providing the foundations of architecture, city planning, and religion.

religious and civic buildings that became the cultural signature of Olmec civilization.

Large artificial platforms and mounds of packed earth dominated Olmec urban centers and served to frame the collective ritual and political activities that attracted the rural population at special times in the year. Although most of these constructions served a religious purpose, some of the raised platforms also served as foundations for elite residences. These urban complexes were aligned with the paths of certain stars, reflecting a strong belief in the significance of astronomical events. Since these centers had small permanent populations, the scale of construction suggests the ability of the Olmec elite to direct the labor of thousands of men and women recruited from a broad region. Their labor sup-

plemented the work of skilled artisans who lived in the urban core and produced high-quality crafts, such as exquisite carved jade figurines, necklaces, and ceremonial knives and axes. Archaeological evidence also suggests the existence of a class of merchants who maintained exchanges with distant peoples and imported obsidian, jade, and pottery.

Little is known about the political structure of Olmec civilization, but it seems likely that the appearance of a form of kingship that combined religious and secular roles coincided with the rise of urban centers.

There is little evidence for the existence of an Olmec empire. However, the discovery of Olmec products and images, such as jade carvings decorated with the jaguar-god, as far away as central Mexico provides evidence that

Olmec Head   Giant heads sculpted from basalt are a widely recognized legacy of Olmec culture. Sixteen heads have been found, the largest approximately 11 feet (3.4 meters) tall. Experts in Olmec archaeology believe the heads are portraits of individual rulers, warriors, or ballplayers.   (Georg Gerster/Photo Researchers, Inc.)

the Olmec exercised influence over a wide area. The best-known monuments of Olmec culture are colossal carved stone heads as large as 11 feet (3.4 meters) high. Since each head is unique and suggestive of individual personality, most archaeologists believe they were carved to memorialize individual rulers. The ability of the Olmec elite to control this complex society was based on their control of religious ritual, possession of finely crafted objects, and association with awe-inspiring architecture.

The Olmec were polytheistic, and most of their deities had dual (male and female) natures. Human and animal characteristics also were blended. For example, images of jaguars or men being transformed into jaguars were common decorative motifs. An important class of shamans and healers organized religious life and was responsible for developing an early form of writing. From close observation of the movement of the stars these religious figures were able to produce a calendar that charted the cycle of the year. The Olmec were the likely originators of a ritual ball game that became an enduring part of Mesoamerican ceremonial life.

Early South American Civilization: Chavín, 900–250 B.C.E.

Geography played an important role in directing the development of human society in the Andes. The region's diverse environment—a mountainous core, arid coastal plain, and dense interior jungles—challenged human populations. These same conditions also encouraged the development of specialized regional production, as well as complex social institutions and cultural values that facilitated interregional exchanges and shared labor responsibilities. These adaptations to environmental challenge became enduring features of Andean civilization.

Chavín was the first major urban civilization in South America (see Map 4.1). Its capital, Chavín de Huántar°, was located at 10,300 feet (3,139 meters) in the eastern range of the Andes north of the modern city of Lima. Between 900 and 250 B.C.E., a period roughly coinciding with Olmec civilization, Chavín became politically and economically dominant in a densely populated region that included large areas of the Peruvian coastal plain and Andean foothills. Chavín de Huántar's location at the intersection of trade routes connecting the coast with populous mountain valleys allowed the city's rulers to control trade between two important ecological zones and gain an important economic advantage over regional rivals.

The enormous scale of the capital and the dispersal of this culture's pottery styles, religious motifs, and architectural forms over a wide area suggest that Chavín imposed on its neighbors some form of political integration and trade dependency that may have relied on military force. Most modern scholars, however, believe that, as in the case of the Olmec, Chavín's regional influence depended more on the development of an attractive and convincing religious belief system and related rituals. Certainly the dispersal of Chavín's most potent religious symbol, a jaguar deity, over a broad area seems to confirm this explanation.

Chavín's role as a ceremonial and commercial center depended on earlier developments in agriculture and trade. The abundance of fish and mollusks along the coast of Peru had provided a dependable supply of food that made the development of cities possible in the centuries before the rise of Chavín. The introduction of maize cultivation from the north dramatically altered agricultural production. As Chavín grew, its trade linked the coastal economy with the producers of quinoa (a

Chavín de Huántar (cha-BEAN day WAHN-tar)

local grain), potatoes, and llamas in the high mountain valleys and, to a lesser extent, with Amazonian producers of coca and fruits.

These developments were accompanied by the evolution of reciprocal labor obligations that permitted the construction and maintenance of roads, bridges, temples, palaces, and large irrigation and drainage projects as well as textiles. Although the exact nature of these reciprocal labor obligations at Chavín is unknown, the clan later served this purpose. Members of a clan claimed descent from a common ancestor and held land communally. Clan members thought of each other as brothers and sisters and were obligated to aid each other, providing a model for the organization of labor and the distribution of goods at every level of Andean society.

These changes in Andean society coincided with the increased use of **llamas** to move goods from one ecological zone to another, thus promoting specialization of production and trade. Llamas were the only domesticated beasts of burden in the Americas and played an important role in the integration of the Andean region. They were first domesticated in the mountainous interior of Peru and were crucial to Chavín's development, not unlike the importance of the camel in the evolution of trans-Saharan trade (see Chapter 8). Llamas not only provided meat and wool, they also multiplied the scale of commercial exchange by decreasing the labor needed to transport goods. A single driver could control from 10 to 30 animals, each carrying up to 70 pounds (32 kilograms); a human porter could carry only about 50 pounds (22.5 kilograms).

The architectural signature of Chavín was a large complex of multilevel platforms made of packed earth or rubble faced with cut stone or adobe (sun-dried brick made of clay and straw). Small buildings used for ritual purposes or as elite residences were built on these platforms. Nearly all these buildings were decorated with relief carvings of serpents, condors, jaguars, or human forms. The largest of the buildings at Chavín de Huántar measured 250 feet (76 meters) on each side and rose to a height of 50 feet (15 meters). About one third of its interior is hollow, containing narrow galleries and small rooms that may have housed the remains of important royal ancestors.

American metallurgy was first developed in the Andean region and later transferred to Mesoamerica. Archaeological investigations of Chavín de Huántar and smaller centers have revealed remarkable three-dimensional gold and gold alloy ornaments that represent a clear advance over earlier technologies. Improvements in both the manufacture and the decoration of textiles are also associated with the rise of Chavín. The quality of these products, probably used only by the elite or in religious rituals, added to the reputation and prestige of the culture and aided in the projection of its power and influence. The most common decorative motif in sculpture, pottery, and textiles was a jaguar-man similar in conception to a common Olmec symbol.

Archaeological evidence strongly suggests that class distinctions increased during this period of expansion. A class of priests directed religious life. Modern scholars also see evidence that both local chiefs and a more powerful chief or king dominated Chavín's politics. Excavations of graves reveal that superior-quality textiles as well as gold crowns, breastplates, and jewelry distinguished rulers from commoners. These rich objects, the quality and abundance of pottery, and the skills needed to build and decorate the monumental architecture of the major centers all suggest the presence of highly skilled artisans as well.

There is no convincing evidence that the eclipse of Chavín (unlike the Olmec centers) was associated with conquest or rebellion. However, recent investigations have suggested that increased warfare throughout the region around 200 B.C.E. disrupted Chavín's trade and undermined the authority of the governing elite. Regardless of what caused the collapse of this powerful culture, the technologies, material culture, statecraft, architecture, and urban planning associated with Chavín influenced the Andean region for centuries.

CELTIC EUROPE

To this point we have taken little note of Europe except for the emergence on its southeast fringe of the Late Bronze Age cultures of Crete and Greece (see Chapter 3). Humans had been living in Europe for a very long time (see Chapter 1), but their lack of any system of writing severely limits our knowledge of the earliest Europeans.

Around 500 B.C.E. Celtic peoples spread across a substantial portion of Europe and, by coming into contact with the literate societies of the Mediterranean, entered the historical record. Information about the early **Celts°** can be found in the archaeological record, in the accounts of Greek and Roman travelers and conquerors, and in the Celtic literature from Wales and Ireland—literature that originated in the oral traditions preserved by bards and was written down centuries later during the European Middle Ages.

Celts (kelts)

The Spread of the Celts

The term *Celtic* is a linguistic designation referring to a branch of the Indo-European family of languages. Archaeologists link this language group to a cultural complex that originated in Central Europe—in parts of present-day Germany, Austria, and the Czech Republic—in the early first millennium B.C.E. (see Map 4.2). The early Celts lived in or near hill-forts—lofty natural locations made even more defensible by earthwork fortifications. By 500 B.C.E. Celtic elites were trading with the Mediterranean lands, seeking crafted goods and wine. This contact may have stimulated the new styles of manufacture and art that appeared at this time.

The development of those new cultural features coincided with a rapid expansion of Celtic groups in several directions. Moving to the west, Celtic groups occupied nearly all of France, much of Britain, and Ireland, and Celts and indigenous peoples merged to create the Celtiberian culture of northern Spain. Celts also migrated east and south. They overran northern Italy in the fifth century B.C.E. They made destructive raids into central Greece, and one group—Galatians—settled in central Anatolia (modern Turkey). By 300 B.C.E. Celtic peoples were spread across Europe north of the Alps, from present-day Hungary to Spain and Ireland. Their traces remain in the names of many places: rivers (Danube, Rhine, Seine, Thames, and Shannon); countries (Belgium); regions (Bohemia, Aquitaine); and towns (Paris, Bologna, Leiden). They shared elements of language and culture, but there was no Celtic "state," for they were grouped into hundreds of small, loosely organized kinship groups.

Map 4.2   The Celtic Peoples   Celtic civilization originated in Central Europe in the early part of the first millennium B.C.E. Around 500 B.C.E. Celtic peoples began to migrate, making Celtic civilization the dominant cultural style in Europe north of the Alps. The Celts' interactions with the peoples of the Mediterranean, including Greeks and Romans, encompassed both warfare and trade.   (From *Atlas of Classical History*, Fifth Edition, by Michael Grant. Copyright © 1994 by Michael Grant. Used by permission of Oxford University Press, Inc.)

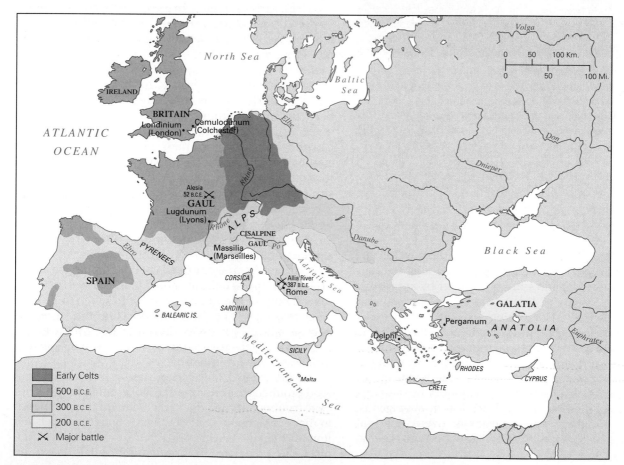

Celtic Hill-Fort in England Hundreds of these fortresses have been found across Europe. They served as centers of administration, gathering points for Celtic armies, manufacturing centers, storage depots for food and trade goods, and places of refuge. The natural defense offered by a hill could be improved, as here, by the construction of ditches and earthwork walls. Particularly effective was the so-called Gallic Wall, made of a combination of earth, stone, and timber to create both strength and enough flexiblility to absorb the pounding from siege engines. (Royal Commission for Historic Monuments)

Greeks and Romans were struck by the physical appearance of male Celts—their burly size, long red hair (which they often made stiff and upright by applying a cementlike solution of lime), shaggy mustaches, and loud, deep voices. Also striking was their strange apparel: pants (usually an indication of horse-riding peoples) and twisted gold collars around their necks. Particularly terrifying were the warriors who fought naked and eagerly made trophies of the heads of defeated enemies. Mediterranean neighbors of the Celts characterized them as wildly fond of war, courageous, childishly impulsive and emotional, overly fond of boasting and exaggeration, yet quick-witted and eager to learn.

Celtic Society

Our greatest source of information about Celtic social and political organization is the Roman military commander Gaius Julius Caesar, who composed a detailed account of his eight-year conquest of Gaul (present-day France) between 58 and 51 B.C.E. Many of the Celtic groups in Gaul had been ruled by kings at an earlier time, but by about 60 B.C.E. they periodically chose public officials, perhaps under Greek and Roman influence.

Celtic society was divided into an elite class of warriors, professional groups of priests and bards, and commoners (the largest group of all). The warriors owned land and flocks of cattle and sheep and monopolized both wealth and power. The common people labored on their land. The warriors of Welsh and Irish legend reflect a stage of political and social development less complex than that of the Celts whom the Romans encountered in France. They would raid one another's flocks, revel in drunken feasts, and engage in impromptu contests of strength and wit. At banquets warriors would fight to the death just to claim the choicest part of the animal, the "hero's portion."

Celtic priests, called **Druids**, belonged to a highly respected and well-organized fraternity with religious, judicial, and educational functions. Trainees learned secret lore—prayers, rituals, legal precedents, and other traditions—through long years of memorization. The priesthood was the one Celtic institution that crossed tribal lines. The Druids sometimes headed off warfare between feuding groups and served as judges in cases involving Celts from different groups. In the first century C.E. the Roman government methodically set about stamping out the Druids, probably because of concern that they might serve as a rallying point for Celtic opposition to Roman rule, as well as because of their alleged involvement in bloody human sacrifices repugnant to Roman sensibilities.

The Celts were successful agriculturalists, able to support large populations by tilling the heavy but fertile soils of continental Europe. Their metallurgical skills probably surpassed those of the Mediterranean peoples. Celts living on the Atlantic shore of France built solid ships that braved ocean conditions, and they used the large, navigable rivers as thoroughfares for extensive commerce. By the first century B.C.E. some of the old hill-forts were evolving into urban centers.

Celtic women engaged primarily in child rearing, food production, and some crafts. Although they did not have true equality with men, their situation was superior to that of women in the Middle East or in the Greek and Roman Mediterranean. Greek and Roman sources depict Celtic women as strong and proud, and in Welsh and

Irish tales the portrayal of self-assured women who sit at banquet with their husbands, engage in witty conversation, and often provide ingenious solutions to vexing problems supports that depiction. Marriage was a partnership to which both parties contributed property. Each party had the right to inherit the estate if the other died. Celtic women also had greater freedom in their sexual relations than did their southern counterparts.

Some of the Celtic burial chambers that archaeologists have excavated contain rich collections of clothing, jewelry, and furniture for use in the next world, identifying them as the tombs of elite women. Daughters of the elite were married to leading members of other tribes to create alliances. When the Romans invaded Celtic Britain in the first century C.E., they sometimes were opposed by Celtic tribes headed by queens (although some experts see this as an abnormal circumstance created by the Roman invasion itself).

Belief and Knowledge	

Historians know the names of more than four hundred Celtic gods and goddesses. Most of them are associated with particular localities and kinship groups, although certain deities have wider currency. Lug°, for example, is the god of light, crafts, and inventions. Some are associated with animals or even depicted with animal features, such as the horse-goddess Epona° or the horned god Cernunnos°. "The Mothers," three goddesses depicted together holding symbols of abundance, are generally thought to have played a part in some kind of fertility cult. Modern traditions of Halloween and May Day preserve the ancient Celtic holidays of Samhain and Beltaine, which took place at key moments in the growing cycle.

The early Celts did not build temples, preferring instead to worship wherever they felt the presence of divinity, such as at springs, groves, and hilltops. At the sources of the Seine and Marne Rivers, archaeologists have found huge caches of wooden statues thrown into the water by hopeful devotees.

The burial of elite members of early Celtic society in wagons filled with extensive grave goods suggests belief in some sort of afterlife. In Irish and Welsh legends the barriers between the natural and supernatural worlds are far more permeable than they are in the mythology of other cultures. Celtic heroes and divinities pass back and forth from one to the other with relative ease, and magical occurrences are commonplace. Celtic priests set forth a doctrine of reincarnation—the rebirth of the soul

in a new body. In contrast, other ancient peoples in Europe and western Asia believed the barrier separating life from death could not be crossed.

The Roman conquest from the second century B.C.E. to the first century C.E. of the Celtic lands of Spain, southern Britain, France, and parts of Central Europe curtailed the evolution of Celtic society. The peoples in these lands were largely assimilated to Roman ways (see Chapter 6). That is why the inhabitants of modern Spain and France speak languages that are descended from Latin. Germanic invaders from the third century C.E. on all but finished the job, and the English language spoken by present-day inhabitants of Britain has a Germanic base. Only on the western fringes of the European continent—in Brittany (northwest France), Wales, Scotland, and Ireland—did Celtic peoples maintain their language, art, and culture into modern times.

THE ASSYRIAN EMPIRE

Far to the south and east of the Celtic lands of continental Europe, the peoples of western Asia also were experiencing momentous changes in the first millennium B.C.E. The chief force for change was the rise of the powerful and aggressive **Neo-Assyrian Empire.** Although historians sometimes apply the term *empire* to earlier regional powers, the Assyrians of the early first millennium B.C.E. were the first to rule over far-flung lands and diverse peoples (see Map 4.3).

As we saw in Chapter 3, the Assyrian homeland in northern Mesopotamia differs in essential respects from the flat expanse of Sumer and Akkad to the south. It is hillier and more temperate in climate, has greater rainfall, and is more exposed to raiders from the mountains to the east and north and from the arid plain to the west. Sturdy peasant farmers, accustomed to defending themselves against marauders, provided the military base for a revival of Assyrian power in the ninth century B.C.E. The rulers of the Neo-Assyrian Empire (911–612 B.C.E.) struck out in a ceaseless series of campaigns: westward across the steppe and desert as far as the Mediterranean, north into mountainous Urartu° (modern Armenia), east across the Zagros range onto the Iranian Plateau, and south along the Tigris River to Babylonia.

It is no accident that these tracks largely coincided with the most important long-distance trade routes in western Asia. These campaigns provided immediate booty and the prospect of tribute and taxes. They also

---

Lug (loog)   **Epona** (eh-POH-nuh)
Cernunnos (KURN-you-nuhs)

Urartu (ur-RAHR-too)

Map 4.3 The Assyrian Empire From the tenth to the seventh century B.C.E. the Assyrians of northern Mesopotamia created the largest empire the world had yet seen, extending from the Iranian Plateau to the eastern shore of the Mediterranean and containing a diverse array of peoples.

Stone Statue of Ashurnasirpal II, Ninth Century B.C.E. This statue of the Assyrian king was found in a temple at Kalhu, the new royal capital that Ashurnasirpal built to advertise his greatness to contemporaries and posterity. Assyrian kings had themselves depicted in various guises. The scepter and flail in the king's hands are symbols of royal power; the shawl indicates his role as a high priest. (Courtesy of the Trustees of the British Museum)

guaranteed access to vital resources such as iron and silver and brought the Assyrians control of profitable international commerce. Indeed, Assyria had a long tradition of commercial and political interests in Syria and Anatolia. A thousand years earlier Assyrian merchants had established trading settlements alongside major cities, and in the eighteenth century B.C.E. their kings had extended direct control over the upper Euphrates region (see Chapter 3).

What started out as an aggressive program of self-defense and reestablishment of old claims soon became far more ambitious. Driven by pride, greed, and religious conviction, the Assyrians defeated all the rival great kingdoms of the day—Elam (southwest Iran), Urartu, Babylon, and Egypt. At its peak their empire stretched from Anatolia, Syria-Palestine, and Egypt in the west, across Armenia and Mesopotamia, as far as western Iran. In the end the Assyrians created a new kind of empire, larger in extent than anything seen before and dedicated to the enrichment of the imperial center at the expense of the subjugated periphery.

God and King

The king was both literally and symbolically at the center of the Assyrian universe. All the land belonged to him, and all the people, even the highest-ranking officials, were his "servants." Assyrians believed that the gods chose the king to rule as their earthly representative and instrument. Normally the sitting king chose one of his sons to be his successor, and the choice was confirmed both by divine oracles and by the Assyrian elite. In the revered ancient city of **Ashur** the high priest anointed the new king by sprinkling his head with oil and gave him insignia of kingship: a crown and scepter. The kings were buried in Ashur.

The duties of the king were enormous. Every day he received information carried by messengers and spies from all corners of the empire. He made decisions, appointed officials, heard complaints, corresponded with subordinates by dictating his wishes to an army of scribes, and received and entertained foreign envoys and high-ranking government figures. He was the military leader, responsible for the strategic planning of campaigns, and often was on tour inspecting the troops and commanding important operations.

Among the king's chief responsibilities was supervision of the state religion. He devoted much of his time to elaborate public and private rituals as well as to overseeing the upkeep of the temples. The king made no decisions of state without first consulting and gaining the approval of the gods through elaborate rituals of divination. All the decisions made by the king and central government were carried out under the banner of Ashur, the chief god, and were justified as being in accordance with Ashur's wishes. All victories were cited as proof of Ashur's superiority over the gods of the conquered peoples.

A relentless tide of government propaganda secured the acquiescence and participation of the Assyrian people in military campaigns that mostly benefited and enriched the king and nobility. On public display throughout the empire were royal inscriptions cataloging recent military victories, the charisma and relentless will of the king, and the ruthless punishments that would be given to anyone who resisted. Even art served the Assyrian state. Relief sculptures depicting hunts, battles, sieges, executions, and deportations covered the walls of the royal palaces at Kalhu° and Nineveh°. Looming over most scenes was the king, larger than anyone else, muscular and fierce, having the very visage of the gods. The purpose of these images was to overawe visitors to the court.

Conquest and Control

What made possible the Assyrians' conquest of their extensive and heterogeneous empire? A fundamental factor was their superior military organization and technology. Early Assyrian armies were put together one campaign at a time. They consisted of men from two groups: (1) men who were obligated to give military service as part of the terms by which they held grants of land and (2) peasants and slaves whose service was contributed by large landowners. Later, Tiglathpileser° (r. 744–727 B.C.E.) added a core army of professional soldiers drawn from both Assyrians and the most formidable subject peoples. At its peak the Assyrian state could mobilize a half-million troops, divided into contingents of light-armed bowmen and slingers who launched stone projectiles, spearmen with body armor, cavalry equipped with bow or spear, and four-man chariots.

Kalhu (KAL-oo)   Nineveh (NIN-uh-vuh)
Tiglathpileser (TIG-lath-pih-LEE-zuhr)

Iron weapons gave Assyrian soldiers an advantage over many opponents, and cavalry provided unprecedented speed and mobility. Assyrian engineers developed machinery and tactics for besieging fortified towns. They dug tunnels under the walls, built mobile towers to position their archers above defending forces, and brought up rams to batter weak points. The Assyrians destroyed some of the most ancient and best-fortified cities of the Middle East—Egyptian Thebes, Phoenician Tyre, Elamite Susa, and Babylon (see Map 4.2). Couriers and signal fires made communication across vast distances possible, and a network of spies gathered intelligence.

The Assyrians also used terror tactics to discourage resistance and rebellion, inflicting swift and harsh retribution and offering an occasional brutal example. The Assyrian state found in the practice of **mass deportation**—the forcible uprooting of large numbers of people or even entire communities from their homes in order to transport and resettle them—a means to accomplish a number of objectives simultaneously (see Society and Culture: Mass Deportation in the Neo-Assyrian Empire). The abrupt removal of a community was an effective way to break the spirit of the rebellious and served as a conspicuous warning to others who might be contemplating resistance. The deployment of deportees was also part of a grand economic strategy to shift human resources from the periphery to the center, where the deportees were employed as mass labor on the estates of king and nobility, to open additional lands for agriculture, and to build the new palaces and cities. Skilled craftsmen and soldiers among the deportees could be assigned to units of the Assyrian army.

The need to control their empire posed enormous problems of organization and communication for the Assyrians. They had to contend with vast distances and diverse landscapes within which lived an array of peoples who differed in language, customs, religion, and political organization. Nomadic and sedentary kinship groups, temple-states, city-states, and, in a few instances, kingdoms composed the Assyrian domain. The Assyrians never found a single, enduring solution to the problem of how to govern such an empire. Control tended to be tight and effective at the center and in lands closest to the core area, less so as one moved outward. The Assyrian kings waged many campaigns to reimpose control on territories subdued in a previous campaign or reign.

The primary duties of Assyrian provincial officials were to ensure payment of tribute and taxes, to maintain law and order, to raise troops, to undertake necessary public works, and to provision armies and administrators passing through their territory. The central government intervened directly in provincial affairs, and local

SOCIETY & CULTURE

Mass Deportation in the Neo-Assyrian Empire

We can gain some insight about the mentality of Assyrian rule by examining a standard practice of Assyrian imperial policy: mass deportation. This tactic already had a long history in the ancient Middle East—in Sumer, Babylon, Urartu, Egypt, and the Hittite Empire. But the Neo-Assyrian monarchs used it on an unprecedented scale. Surviving documents record the relocation of over 1 million people, and historians estimate the true figure exceeds 4 million.

The following entries from a set of inscriptions recording the year-by-year achievements of King Sargon II (r. 721–705 B.C.E.) reveal the fate of the people and territory of the northern Israelite kingdom and of several coastal cities.

[First Year] I besieged and conquered Samaria [the capital of the northern Israelite kingdom], led away as booty 27,290 inhabitants of it. I formed from among them a contingent of 50 chariots and made the remaining inhabitants resume their social positions. I installed over them an officer of mine and imposed upon them the tribute of the former king.... [Seventh Year] Upon a trust-inspiring oracle given by my lord Ashur, I crushed the tribes of Tamud, Ibadidi, Marsimanu, and Haiapa, the Arabs who live, far away, in the desert [and] who know neither overseers nor officials and who had not yet brought their tribute to any. I deported their survivors and settled them in Samaria.... [Eleventh Year] I besieged and conquered the cities Ashdod, Gath, Asdudimmu; I declared his [the ruler of Ashdod's] images, his wife, his children, all the possessions and treasures of his palace as well as the inhabitants of his country as booty. I reorganized the administration of these cities and settled therein people from the regions of the East which I had conquered personally. I installed an officer of mine over them and declared them Assyrian citizens and they pulled the straps of my yoke.

Notice the variety of uses to which deportees were put. Some were drafted into the Assyrian military. Others were employed in construction and agriculture. The specific number of prisoners given suggests careful recordkeeping, though it may be an exaggeration. We don't always know why some people were designated for deportation and others were permitted to stay in their homeland. The Assyrians may have chosen to remove members of the elite classes who provided leadership and individuls with useful skills. Though technically regarded as "booty," the conquered people were subject to the same obligations as other Assyrian citizens.

In both cases mentioned in this document, the king orchestrates an exchange of populations. Both groups in such exchanges were immediately rendered docile and even loyal to the interests of the very state that had removed them, because submission was their only protection in an often hostile new environment. What these documents, for all their numerical and geographical precision, do not reveal is the human experience of the deportees.

What would have been the psychological and emotional impacts of being forcibly removed from the familiar landscape, monuments, climate, and people of one's homeland, and of being resettled in an alien environment? How might the deportees' culture have changed to adapt to the new circumstances?

Source: Transcriptions recording the year-by-year achievements of King Sargon II: James B. Pritchard, ed., The Ancient Near East: An Anthology of Texts and Pictures (Princeton, NJ: Princeton University Press, 1958), 195–197. Copyright © 1958 by Princeton University Press. Reprinted with permission of Princeton University Press.

ruling classes and Assyrian provincial governors were subject to frequent inspections by royal overseers.

Courtiers, supervisors, scribes, and servants maintained the palace and the various offices of the central government. High-ranking officials had their own courts and estates worked by peasants tied to the land. This elite class was bound to the monarchy by oaths of obedience, by fear of punishment for misbehavior, and by the expectation of rewards, such as grants of land and a share in booty and taxes, for loyalty and good performance. The support of the class of professionals—priests, diviners, scribes, doctors, and artisans—was also vital to the functioning of the state, and they too were bound to the monarchy by oaths and rewards.

Wall Relief from the Palace of Sennacherib at Nineveh   Against a backdrop of wooded hills representing the landscape of Assyria, workers are hauling a huge stone sculpture from the riverbank to the palace under the watchful eyes of officials and soldiers. They accomplish this task with simple equipment—a lever, a sledge, and thick ropes—and a lot of human muscle power.   (Courtesy of the Trustees of the British Museum)

The Assyrians exploited to the maximum the wealth and resources of their subjects. The cost of military campaigns and administration had to be covered by the plunder the victors captured and the tribute they imposed. Much of the wealth of the periphery was funneled to the center, where the king and nobility grew rich. Proud kings used their riches to expand the ancestral capital and religious center at Ashur and build magnificent new royal cities adorned with walls, palaces, and temples. Dur Sharrukin, the "Fortress of Sargon," was completed in a mere ten years, proof of the enormous human resources dedicated to the task. The labor force for these projects was drawn from prisoners of war transferred to the core zone, as well as from Assyrian citizens who owed periodic service to the state.

Nevertheless, the Assyrian Empire was not simply parasitic. There is some evidence of royal investment in provincial infrastructure. The cities and merchant classes thrived on expanded long-distance commerce, and elements of the subject populations were surprisingly loyal to their Assyrian rulers.

Assyrian Society and Culture

The extant sources shed light primarily on the deeds of kings, victories of armies, and workings of government. Nevertheless, a certain amount is known about the lives and activities of the millions of subjects of the Assyrian Empire. In the core area people were assigned to the same three classes that had existed in Hammurabi's Babylon a millennium before (see Chapter 2): (1) free, landowning citizens, (2) farmers and artisans attached to the estates of the king or other rich landholders, and (3) slaves. Slaves—drawn from debtors who had failed to make good and from prisoners of war—had legal rights and, if sufficiently talented, could rise to positions of influence.

The government normally did not distinguish between native Assyrians and the increasingly large number of subjects and deportees residing in the Assyrian homeland. All were referred to as "human beings," entitled to the same legal protections and liable for the same obligations of labor and military service. Over time this inflow of outsiders led to changes in the ethnic makeup of the population of Assyria.

Agriculture constituted the economic foundation of the Assyrian Empire. The vast majority of subjects worked on the land, and the agricultural surpluses that they produced allowed substantial numbers of people—the standing army, government officials, religious experts, merchants, artisans, and all manner of professionals in the towns and cities—to engage in specialized activities.

Individual artisans and small workshops in the towns manufactured goods. Most trade took place at the local level and involved foodstuffs and simple crafted goods such as pottery, tools, and clothing. The state fostered long-distance trade, for imported luxury goods—such as metals, fine textiles, dyes, gems, and ivory—brought in substantial customs revenues and ultimately found their way into the possession of the royal family and elite classes. Silver was the basic medium of exchange, weighed out for each transaction in a time before the invention of coins.

The Assyrian era saw both the preservation of old knowledge and the acquisition of new knowledge. Assyrian scholars devoted much effort to the creation and preservation of lists covering all manner of subjects, such as plant and animal names, geographic terms, and astronomical occurrences. Building on the achievements of their Mesopotamian ancestors (see Environment and Technology: Chinese and Mesopotamian Divination, in Chapter 3), the Assyrians continued to make original contributions in mathematics and astronomy. Their assumption that gods or demons caused disease obstructed the investigation of natural causes, but in addition to the specialists whose job was to exorcise the demons thought to be possessing a sick person, another type of physician experimented with medicinal and surgical treatments to relieve symptoms.

Libraries may have been attached to temples in various Assyrian cities. When archaeologists excavated the palace of Ashurbanipal° (r. 668–627 B.C.E.), one of the last Assyrian kings, at Nineveh, they discovered more than twenty-five thousand tablets or fragments of tablets. This **Library of Ashurbanipal** contained official documents and an array of literary and scientific texts. Some were originals that had been brought to the capital; others were copies made at the king's request. Ashurbanipal was clearly an avid collector of the literary and scientific heritage of Mesopotamia, and the "House of Knowledge" referred to in some of the documents may have been an academy that attracted learned men to the imperial center. The Assyrians preserved many of the achievements of Mesopotamian art, literature, and science, and much of what we know about earlier eras in Mesopotamian history comes to us through discoveries at Assyrian sites.

Ashurbanipal (ah-shur-BAH-nuh-pahl)

ISRAEL

On the western edge of the Assyrian Empire, in a land bordering the "Upper Sea" as the Assyrians called the Mediterranean, lived a people who probably seemed of no great significance to the masters of western Asia but were destined to play an important role in world history. The history of ancient Israel is marked by two grand and interconnected dramas that played out over more than fifteen hundred years, from around 2000 to 500 B.C.E.: (1) a loose collection of kinship groups of nomadic herders and caravan drivers became a sedentary, agricultural people, developed complex political and social institutions, and became integrated into the commercial and diplomatic networks of the Middle East; and (2) the austere cult of a desert god evolved into a unique concept of deity and generated the rich ethical and intellectual traditions and the distinctive way of life of the Jewish people.

Both the land and the people at the heart of this story have gone by various names: Canaan, Israel, Palestine; Hebrews, Israelites, Jews. For the sake of consistency, the people are referred to here as *Israelites*, the land they occupied in antiquity as **Israel.**

Israel is a crossroads, linking Anatolia, Egypt, Arabia, and Mesopotamia (see Map 4.4). This accident of geography has given the place an importance in history, both ancient and modern, out of all proportion to its size and economic or political potential. Its natural resources are few. The Negev Desert and the vaster wasteland of the Sinai lie to the south. The Mediterranean coastal plain was usually in the hands of others, particularly the Philistines throughout much of the biblical period. At the center are the rock-strewn hills of the Shephelah°. Galilee to the north, with its sea of the same name, was a relatively fertile land of grassy hills and small plains. The narrow ribbon of the Jordan River runs down the eastern side of the region into the Dead Sea, so named because of its high salt content.

Origins, Exodus, and Settlement

Information about the history of ancient Israel comes from several sources, including archaeological excavation and references in documents from other Middle Eastern societies, particularly Egyptian and Assyrian royal annals. However, the fundamental source is the extraordinarily

Shephelah (sheh-FEH-luh)

rich yet problematic collection of writings preserved in the **Hebrew Bible** (called the Old Testament by Christians). The text of the Hebrew Bible is a compilation of several collections of materials that originated with different groups, employed distinctive vocabularies, and advocated particular interpretations of past events. Traditions about the Israelites' early days were long transmitted orally. Not until the tenth century did they begin to be written down, by means of an alphabet borrowed from the nearby Phoenicians. The canonical text that we have today was primarily compiled in the fifth century B.C.E., with a few later additions, and reflects the point of view of the priests who controlled the Temple in Jerusalem. Historians disagree about the degree to which this document accurately represents Israelite history; but, given the absence of alternative written sources, it continues to provide a foundation, to be used critically and modified in light of archaeological discoveries.

The Hebrew language of the Bible reflects the speech of the Israelites until about 500 B.C.E. It is a Semitic language, most closely related to Phoenician and to Aramaic (the language that later supplanted Hebrew in Israel), more distantly related to the Akkadian language of Mesopotamia and to Arabic. This linguistic affinity probably parallels the Israelites' ethnic relationship to the neighboring peoples.

In some respects the history of the ancient Israelites is unique, the primary source of the Judaeo-Christian tradition so central to Western civilization. But in another sense that history reflects a familiar pattern in the ancient Middle East. It is the story of nomadic pastoralists who occupied marginal land between the inhospitable desert and settled agricultural areas. Early on, these nomads periodically raided the farms and villages of settled peoples, but eventually they settled down to an agricultural way of life and at a somewhat later stage developed a state apparatus.

The Hebrew Bible preserves vivid traditions about Abraham, Isaac, and Jacob, the male leaders of the early Israelite groups. Abraham was born in the city of Ur in southern Mesopotamia, probably in the twentieth century B.C.E. He left the city of his birth, disgusted by the idol worship that predominated there, and moved with his herd animals (sheep, cattle, donkeys) and his extended family through the Syrian desert. Eventually he arrived in the land of Israel, which, according to the biblical account, had been promised to him and his descendants as part of a "covenant," or pact, with the Israelite god, Yahweh.

These "recollections" of the journey of Abraham may compress the experiences of generations of pastoralists who moved through the grazing lands between the upper reaches of the Tigris and Euphrates Rivers and

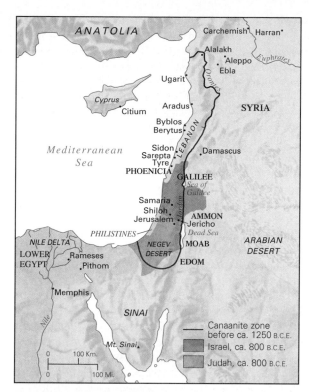

Map 4.4 Phoenicia and Israel The lands along the eastern shore of the Mediterranean Sea—sometimes called the Levant or Syria-Palestine—have always been a crossroads, traversed by migrants, nomads, merchants, and armies moving between Egypt, Arabia, Mesopotamia, and Anatolia.

the Mediterranean coastal plain. Abraham, his family, and companions were following the usual pattern in this part of the world. They camped by a permanent water source in the dry season, then drove herds of domesticated animals to a well-established sequence of grazing areas during the rest of the year. The animals provided them with the basic necessities of milk, cheese, meat, and cloth.

The early Israelites and the settled peoples of the region were suspicious of one another. This friction between nomadic herders and settled farmers, as well as the Israelites' view of their ancestors as being on the nomadic side of the equation, comes through in the story of the innocent shepherd Abel, who was killed by his farmer brother Cain, and in the story of Sodom and Gomorrah°, two cities that Yaweh destroyed because of their wickedness.

Abraham's son and grandson, Isaac and Jacob, succeeded him as leaders of this wandering group of

Gomorrah (guh-MORE-uh)

herders. In the next generation the story of Jacob's son Joseph, who was sold as a slave to passing merchants by his brothers, reveals the tensions that could arise within a leading family between children of different mothers. Through luck and ability Joseph became a high official at the court of the Egyptian pharaoh. Thus he was in a position to help his people when drought swept the land of Israel and the Israelites and their flocks migrated to Egypt. The sophisticated Egyptians, however, both feared and looked down on these rough herders and eventually reduced the Israelites to the status of slaves and put them to work on the grand building projects of the pharaoh.

That is the version of events given in the Hebrew Bible. Several points need to be made about it. First, the biblical account glosses over the very centuries (1700–1500 B.C.E.) during which Egypt was dominated by the Hyksos, who generally are identified as Semitic groups that infiltrated the Nile Delta from the northeast (see Chapter 3). The Israelites' migration to Egypt and their later enslavement may have been connected to the rise and fall of the Hyksos. Second, although extant Egyptian sources do not refer to Israelite slaves, they do complain about Apiru°, a derogatory term applied to caravan drivers, outcasts, bandits, and other marginal and stateless groups. The word seems to designate a class of people rather than a particular ethnic group, but some scholars have suggested an etymological connection between *Apiru* and *Hebrew* (see Society and Culture: The Amarna Letters, in Chapter 3). Third, the period of Israelite slavery coincided with the era of Egyptian history (1400 to 1200 B.C.E) during which pharaohs Sethos I and Ramesses II engaged in ambitious building programs (see Chapter 3).

According to the Hebrew Bible, the Israelite slaves were led out of captivity by Moses, an Israelite with connections to the Egyptian royal family. The narrative of this departure, the Exodus, is overlaid with folktale motifs—for example, ten plagues that were inflicted on Egypt before the pharaoh agreed to allow the Israelites to leave and a miraculous parting of the waters of the Red Sea, which enabled the refugees to escape the Egyptian army. Still, oral tradition may have preserved memories of an emigration from Egypt and years of wandering in the wilderness of Sinai.

During their forty-year sojourn in the desert the Israelites became devoted to a stern and warlike god. According to the Hebrew Bible, Yahweh made a covenant with the Israelites: they would be his "Chosen People" if they promised to worship him exclusively. This pact was confirmed by tablets that Moses brought down from the top of Mount Sinai. Written on the tablets were Ten Commandments, which laid down the basic tenets of Jewish belief and practice. This document prohibited murder, adultery, theft, lying, and envy, and it demanded that the Israelites respect their parents and refrain from work on the Sabbath, the seventh day of the week.

The biblical account claims that the Israelites came from the east into the land of Canaan (modern Israel and Palestine). Led by Joshua, Moses's successor, they attacked and destroyed Jericho and other Canaanite cities (see Map 4.4). The evidence of archaeology shows the destruction of Canaanite towns between 1250 and 1200 B.C.E. (though not necessarily the towns mentioned in the biblical account). Shortly thereafter, lowland sites were resettled and new sites were established in the hills, thanks to the development of cisterns carved into nonporous rock to hold rainwater and the construction of leveled terraces on the slopes to expand the cultivable area. The new settlers were a population with a material culture that is cruder but still related to that of the Canaanites.

Most scholars doubt the biblical depiction of the conquest of Canaan by a unified army of Israelite invaders. In a time of disruption and the decline of cities throughout the region, it is more likely that the Israelites migrating into the hill country took advantage of the disorder and were joined by other loosely organized groups and even refugees from the Canaanites cities.

In a pattern common throughout history, the new coalition of peoples invented a common ancestry. The "Children of Israel," as they called themselves, were divided into twelve tribes supposedly descended from the sons of Jacob and Joseph. Each tribe installed itself in a different part of the country, and each tribe looked for guidance to one or more chiefs. Such leaders usually had limited coercive authority and were primarily responsible for mediating disputes and seeing to the welfare and protection of the group. Certain charismatic figures, famed for their daring in war or their genius in arbitration, were called "Judges" and (like the Celtic Druids) had a special standing that transcended tribal boundaries. The tribes were also bound together by their common access to a shrine in the hill country at Shiloh. The shrine housed the holy Ark of the Covenant, a chest containing the tablets of commandments that Yahweh had given to Moses.

Rise of the Monarchy

The Israelites were not the only newcomers in this region. The years around 1200 B.C.E. were a time of troubles throughout the eastern Mediterranean (see Chapter 3). In the early twelfth century B.C.E. the Philistines, who may be

---

Apiru (uh-PEE-roo)

connected to the pre-Greek population of the Aegean Sea region and had participated in the "Sea People's" attack on Egypt, occupied the coastal plain of Israel. Israelites and Philistines fought frequently in this period. Their wars were memorialized in the biblical traditions about the long-haired strongman Samson, who pulled down the walls of a Philistine temple, and the bravery of young David, whose slingshot felled the towering warrior Goliath.

An influential religious leader named Samuel, recognizing the need for a stronger central authority if the Israelites were to contend successfully against the Philistine city-states, anointed Saul as first king of Israel around 1020 B.C.E. Saul had mixed success, and when he perished in battle, the throne passed to David (r. ca. 1000–960 B.C.E.).

Gifted musician, brave warrior, and adroit politician, David completed the transition from tribal confederacy to unified monarchy. He strengthened royal authority by making the recently captured hill city of Jerusalem, which lay outside tribal boundaries, his new capital. Soon after, the Ark was brought to Jerusalem, making that city the religious as well as political center of the kingdom. To curtail the disorder caused by blood feuds, David designated "cities of refuge"—places to which those guilty of certain crimes could flee and escape retribution. A census was taken to facilitate the collection of taxes by the central government, and a standing army, with soldiers paid by and loyal to the king, was instituted. These innovations gave David the resources to win a string of military victories and substantially expand Israel's borders.

The reign of David's son Solomon (r. ca. 960–920 B.C.E.) marked the high point of the Israelite monarchy. Alliances and trade linked Israel with near and distant lands. Solomon and Hiram, the king of Phoenician Tyre, together commissioned a fleet that sailed south into the Red Sea and brought back gold, ivory, jewels, sandal-

Artist's Rendering of Solomon's Jerusalem Strategically located in the middle of lands occupied by the Israelite tribes and on a high plateau overlooking the central hills and the Judaean desert, Jerusalem was captured around 1000 B.C.E. by King David, who made it his capital (the City of David is at left, the citadel and palace complex at center). The next king, Solomon, built the First Temple to serve as the center of worship of the Israelite god, Yahweh. Solomon's Temple (at upper right) was destroyed during the Neo-Babylonian sack of the city in 587 B.C.E. The modest structure soon built to take its place was replaced by the magnificent Second Temple, erected by King Herod in the last decades of the first century B.C.E. and destroyed by the Romans in 70 C.E. (Ritmeyer Archaeological Design, London)

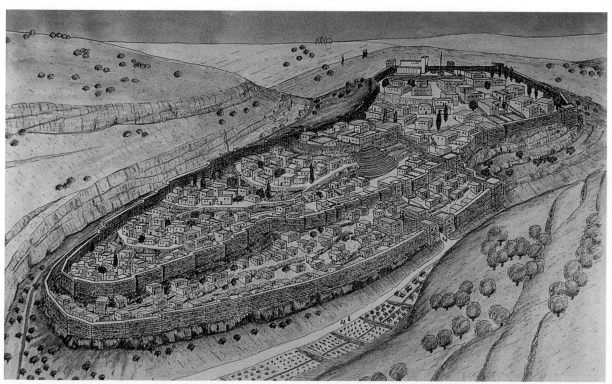

wood, and exotic animals from distant Ophir. The story of the fabulous visit to Solomon by the queen of Sheba, who brought gold, precious stones, and spices, may be mythical, but it reflects the reality of trade with Saba (biblical Sheba) in south Arabia (present-day Yemen) or the Horn of Africa (present-day Somalia). Considerable wealth flowed into the royal coffers, subsidizing the lavish lifestyle of Solomon's court, the expanding administrative bureaucracy, and a standing chariot army that made Israel into a regional power. Solomon undertook an ambitious building program employing slaves and the compulsory labor of citizens. To further link religious and secular authority, he built the **First Temple** in Jerusalem. Henceforth, the Israelites had a central shrine and an impressive set of rituals that could compete with the attractions of pagan cults.

The Temple priesthood, which carried out animal sacrifices to Yahweh on behalf of the community, received a percentage of the annual agricultural yield and evolved into a powerful and wealthy class. The expansion of Jerusalem, new commercial opportunities, and the increasing prestige of the Temple hierarchy began to change the social composition of Israelite society. A gap emerged between urban and rural, rich and poor, polarizing a people that previously had been relatively homogeneous.

The Israelites lived in extended families. Several generations lived together in the "house of the father," as it was called—under the authority of the eldest male. Marriages, usually arranged between families, were an important economic as well as social institution. The groom gave a substantial gift to the father of the bride. Her entire family participated in the ceremonial weighing out of silver or gold. The wife brought into the marriage a dowry that often included a slave girl who attended her for life.

Monogamy was the norm. Male heirs were of paramount importance, and firstborn sons received a double share of the inheritance. If no son was forthcoming from the marriage, the couple could adopt a son, or the husband could have a child by the wife's slave attendant. If a man died childless, his brother was expected to marry the widow and provide an heir.

In early Israel women provided a vital portion of the goods and services that sustained the family. As a result, women were regarded with respect and had relative equality with their husbands in family and village life. Women did suffer from certain legal disadvantages, however. They could not inherit, nor could they initiate divorce. Men were permitted extramarital relations, but equivalent behavior by wives was punishable by death. Women of the working classes labored with other family members in agriculture or herding, in addition to maintaining the household and raising the children. As the society became more urbanized, some women worked outside the home as cooks, bakers, perfumers, wet nurses (usually recent mothers, still producing milk, who were hired to provide nourishment to another person's child), prostitutes, and singers of laments at funerals. On occasion women reached positions of influence, such as Deborah the Judge, who led troops in battle against the Canaanites. Women known collectively as "wise women" appear to have been educated and composed sacred texts in poetry and prose. This reality has been obscured, in part by the male bias of the Hebrew Bible, in part because the status of women was diminished as Israelite society became more urbanized in the period of the monarchy.

Fragmentation and Dispersal

After the death of Solomon around 920 B.C.E., resentment over the demands of the crown and royal neglect of tribal prerogatives led to the split of the monarchy into two kingdoms: Israel in the north, with its capital at Samaria; and Judah in the southern territory around Jerusalem (see Map 4.4). The two kingdoms were sometimes at war, sometimes in alliance with one another.

This period saw the crystallization of **monotheism,** the absolute belief in Yahweh as the one and only god. Nevertheless, religious leaders had to contend with the appeal of polytheistic (involving belief in multiple gods) cults. Many Israelites were attracted to the ecstatic rituals of the Canaanite storm-god Baal and the fertility goddess Astarte°. Fiery prophets claiming to convey messages from Yahweh rose up to oppose the adoption of foreign ritual and to castigate the monarchs and aristocracy for their corruption, impiety, and neglect of the poor.

In response to the rise of the aggressive Neo-Assyrian Empire, the small states of Syria and Israel lay aside their rivalries and resisted together, but to no avail. In 721 B.C.E. the Assyrians destroyed the northern kingdom of Israel and deported a substantial portion of its population to the east (see Society and Culture: Mass Deportation in the Neo-Assyrian Empire). New settlers were brought in, altering the ethnic composition, culture, and religious practices of this land and removing it from the mainstream of Jewish history. The southern kingdom of Judah survived for over a century, at times

---

Astarte (uh-STAHR-tee)

paying tribute to the Neo-Assyrian Empire and then to the Neo-Babylonian kingdom (626–539 B.C.E.) that succeeded it, at other times breaking into rebellion. When the Neo-Babylonian monarch Nebuchadnezzar° captured Jerusalem in 587 B.C.E., he destroyed the Temple and deported to Babylon the royal family, aristocracy, and workers with useful skills such as blacksmiths and scribes.

The deportees adapted quickly and prospered in their new home "by the waters of Babylon," and half a century later most of their descendants refused the offer of the Persian monarch Cyrus (see Chapter 5) to return to their homeland. This was the origin of the Jewish **Diaspora**—a Greek word meaning "dispersal" or "scattering"—which continues to this day. The communities of the Diaspora began to develop institutions that allowed them to maintain their religion and culture outside the homeland. One such institution was the synagogue (a Greek term meaning "bringing together"), a communal meeting place that came to serve religious, educational, and social functions.

Several groups of Babylonian *Jews*—as we may now begin to call these people, since an independent Israel no longer existed—did make the long trek back to Judah, where they met a cold reception from the local population. Nevertheless, the Temple was rebuilt in modest form and a new set of regulations, the Deuteronomic° Code (*deuteronomic* is Greek for "second code of laws"), became the basis of law and conduct for the Jewish community. The fifth century B.C.E. also saw the compilation of much of the Hebrew Bible in roughly its present form.

The loss of political autonomy and the experience of exile had sharpened the Jewish identity and put an unyielding monotheism at the core of that identity. Jews lived by a rigid set of rules. Dietary restrictions forbade the eating of pork and shellfish and mandated that meat and dairy products not be consumed together. Rules of purity required women to take ritual baths to remove the taint of menstruation. The requirement to venerate the Sabbath (Saturday, the seventh day of the week) meant refraining from work and from fighting, in imitation of their god, who, according to the biblical story of the creation of the world, rested on the seventh day (this is the origin of the concept of the weekend). There also was a ban on marrying non-Jews. These strictures tended to isolate the Jews from other peoples, but they also yielded a powerful sense of community and belief in the protection of a watchful and beneficent deity.

PHOENICIA AND THE MEDITERRANEAN

While the Assyrians were recovering from the disorders at the end of the Bronze Age and laying the foundation for future expansion, and the Israelite tribes were being forged into a united kingdom, important transformations also were taking place among another people who occupied the eastern shore of the Mediterranean. The ancient inhabitants of present-day Syria, Lebanon, and Israel (sometimes called the Levant or Syria-Palestine) are commonly designated **Phoenicians°**, though they referred to themselves by the ethnic designation "Can'ani"—Canaanites. Their story is complicated by sparse written evidence and the disturbance of the archaeological record by frequent migrations and invasions, yet we can draw some insights into the history of this ethnic group.

When western Asia and the eastern Mediterranean entered a period of violent upheaval and mass movement of population around 1200 B.C.E. (see Chapter 3), many settlements in Syria-Palestine were destroyed. Aramaeans—nomadic pastoralists similar to the early Israelites—migrated into the interior portions of Syria. Farther south, Israelites wandered into Canaan, perhaps participating in the destruction of Canaanite cities, and settled as herders and farmers. At the same time, the Philistines occupied the coast of much of present-day Israel and introduced iron-based metallurgy to this part of the world.

The Phoenician City-States

As a result of those invasions and migrations, by 1100 B.C.E. the zone that the Canaanites occupied was no more than a narrow strip of land lying between the mountains and the sea in present-day Lebanon (see Map 4.4). The inhabitants of this densely populated area adopted new political forms and sources of livelihood, particularly in manufacture and seaborne commerce. This region was the homeland of the Phoenicians, as the Canaanites came to be called by Greeks who encountered them in the early first millennium B.C.E. The Greek term *Phoinikes°* may mean "red men" and have something to

---

Nebuchadnezzar (NAB-oo-kuhd-nez-uhr)
Deuteronomic (doo-tuhr-uh-NAHM-ik)

Phoenician (fi-NEE-shunn) **Phoinikes** (FOY-nee-kes)

Ancient Textiles and Dyes

Throughout human history the production of textiles—cloth for clothing, blankets, carpets, and coverings of various sorts—may have required an expenditure of human labor second only to the amount of work necessary to provide food. Nevertheless, little is known about textile production in antiquity because it leaves so few traces in the archaeological record. The plant fibers and animal hair used for cloth are organic and quickly decompose except in rare and special circumstances. Some textile remains have been found in the hot, dry conditions of Egypt, the cool, arid Andes of South America, and the peat bogs of northern Europe. But most of our knowledge of ancient textiles depends on the discovery of equipment used in textile production—such as spindles, loom weights, and dyeing vats—and on pictorial representations and descriptions in texts.

The production of cloth usually has been the work of women, for a simple but important reason. Responsibility for child rearing limits women's ability to participate in other activities but does not consume all their time and energy. In many societies textile production has been complementary to child-rearing activities, for it can be done in the home, is relatively safe, does not require great concentration, and can be interrupted without consequence. For many thousands of years cloth production has been one of the great common experiences of women around the globe. The growing and harvesting of plants such as cotton or flax (from which linen is made) and the shearing of wool from sheep and, in the Andes, llamas are outdoor activities, but the subsequent stages of production can be carried out indoors in the household environment. The basic methods of textile production did not change much from early antiquity until the mid-eighteenth century C.E., when the fabrication of textiles was transferred to mills and mass production began.

When textile production has been considered "women's work," most of the output has been for household consumption.

Ancient Peruvian Textiles   The weaving of Chavín was famous for its color and symbolic imagery. Artisans both wove designs into the fabric and used paint or dyes to decorate plain fabric. This early Chavín painted fabric was used in a burial. Notice how the face suggests a jaguar and the headress includes the image of a serpent.   (Private collection)

The early civilizations of Peru provide an exception to this general rule. Around 3,000 years ago, the region's women weavers developed new raw materials, new techniques, and new decorative motifs. They began to use the wool of llamas and alpacas in addition to cotton. Limitations to the width of woven fabric imposed by the back-strap loom were overcome by having three women work side by side and pass the weft from hand to hand. Women weavers also introduced embroidery, and they decorated garments with new religious motifs, such as the jaguar-god of Chavín. Their high-quality textiles were given as tribute to the elite and were used in trade to acquire luxury goods as well as dyes and metals.

More typically men dominated commercial production. In ancient Phoenicia, fine textiles with bright, permanent colors became a major export product. These striking colors were produced by dyes derived from several species of snail. Most prized was the red-purple known as Tyrian purple because Tyre was the major source. Persian and Hellenistic kings wore robes dyed this color, and a white toga with a purple border was the sign of a Roman senator.

The production of Tyrian purple was an exceedingly laborious process. The spiny dye-murex snail lives on the sandy Mediterranean bottom at depths ranging from 30 to 500 feet (10 to 150 meters). Nine thousand snails were needed to produce 1 gram (0.035 ounce) of dye. The dye was made from a colorless liquid in the snail's hypobranchial gland. The gland sacs were removed, crushed, soaked with salt, and exposed to sunlight and air for some days; then they were subject to controlled boiling and heating.

Huge mounds of broken shells on the Phoenician coast are testimony to the ancient industry. It is likely that the snail was rendered nearly extinct at many locations, and some scholars have speculated that Phoenician colonization in the Mediterranean may have been motivated in part by the search for new sources of snails.

do with the color of the Canaanites' skin, or it may refer to the purple pigment that they produced from the murex snail and used to dye expensive garments (see Environment and Technology: Ancient Textiles and Dyes).

Rivers and rocky spurs of Mount Lebanon sliced the coastal plain into a series of small city-states. The most important were Aradus, Byblos°, Berytus°, Sidon, Sarepta°, and Tyre. Thriving commerce brought in considerable wealth and gave the Phoenician city-states an important role in international politics. This commercial activity centered on raw materials, foodstuffs, and crafted luxury products: cedar and pine, metals, papyrus, wine, spices, salted fish, incense, textiles, carved ivory, and glass.

The Phoenicians developed earlier Canaanite models into the first alphabetic system of writing. In such a system each symbol stands for a sound, and only about two dozen symbols are needed. This technology was a considerable advance over cuneiform and hieroglyphics, which required hundreds of signs to represent syllables and words. Little indigenous written material survives from this period, however. Whatever "historical" records the Phoenicians may have had are lost, probably because they were written on perishable papyrus, though some information in Greek and Roman sources may be based on them.

In the second millennium B.C.E. Byblos was the most important Phoenician city-state. It was a distribution center for cedar timber from the slopes of Mount Lebanon and for Egyptian papyrus, the precious writing medium of the age (the Greek word *biblion*, meaning "book written on papyrus from Byblos," comes down as our word *bible*). In the early centuries of the first millennium B.C.E. Tyre, in southern Lebanon, came to play an ever more dominant role. King Hiram, who came to power in 969 B.C.E., was responsible for Tyre's initial rise to prominence. According to the Hebrew Bible, he formed a close friendship and alliance with the Israelite king Solomon. When Solomon built the Temple at Jerusalem, he used cedar from Lebanon and drew upon the skills of Phoenician craftsmen. In return, Tyre gained access to silver, surplus food, and trade routes to the east and south. In the ninth century B.C.E. Tyre extended its territorial control over nearby Sidon and monopolized the Mediterranean coastal trade.

Tyre was practically impregnable because of its location on an island directly off-shore. It had both a northern- and a southern-facing harbor connected by a canal. It also had a large marketplace, a magnificent palace complex with treasury and archives, temples to the gods Melqart° and Astarte, suburbs spilling onto the adjacent mainland, and a population of 30,000 or more. Its one weakness was its dependence on the mainland for food and fresh water.

Little is known about the internal affairs of Tyre and the other Phoenician cities. The names of a series of kings are preserved, and the scant evidence suggests that leading merchant families dominated the political arena. Between the ninth and seventh centuries B.C.E. the Phoenician city-states had to contend with Assyrian aggression, followed in the sixth century B.C.E. by the expansion of the Neo-Babylonian kingdom and later the Persian Empire (see Chapter 5). Just as in the previous millennium, these small states of the Levantine coast had to be adept at diplomacy, preserving their autonomy by playing the great powers off against one another when possible, accepting a subordinate relationship to a distant master when necessary.

Expansion into the Mediterranean

In the ninth century B.C.E. Tyre began to turn its attention westward into the Mediterranean. Colonies were established on Cyprus, a large island 100 miles (161 kilometers) west of the Syrian coast (see Map 4.5), which was a major source of copper and strategically located on the routes taken by trading vessels. Phoenician merchants sailing into the Aegean Sea are mentioned in the *Iliad* and *Odyssey* of the Greek poet Homer (ca. 700 B.C.E.). In the ninth and eighth centuries B.C.E. a string of settlements in the western Mediterranean gradually formed a "Phoenician triangle" composed of (1) the stretch of North African coast that today lies in western Libya, Tunisia, and Morocco, (2) the south and southeast coast of Spain (including Gades—modern Cadiz—located astride the Strait of Gibraltar and controlling access between the Mediterranean and the Atlantic Ocean), and the (3) major islands of Sardinia, Sicily, and Malta off the coast of Italy. Many of these new settlements were situated on promontories or offshore islands in imitation of Tyre. The result was a Phoenician trading network that spanned the entire Mediterranean.

A combination of state enterprise and private initiative made Tyrian expansion westward in the Mediterranean possible. It probably was a response both to the frequent and destructive invasions of the Syria-Palestine region by the Neo-Assyrian Empire and to the shortage of arable land to feed Tyre's swelling population. Overseas settlement provided an outlet for excess population,

---

Byblos (BIB-loss)   **Berytus** (buh-RIE-tuhs)
Sarepta (suh-REP-tuh)

Melqart (MEL-kahrt)

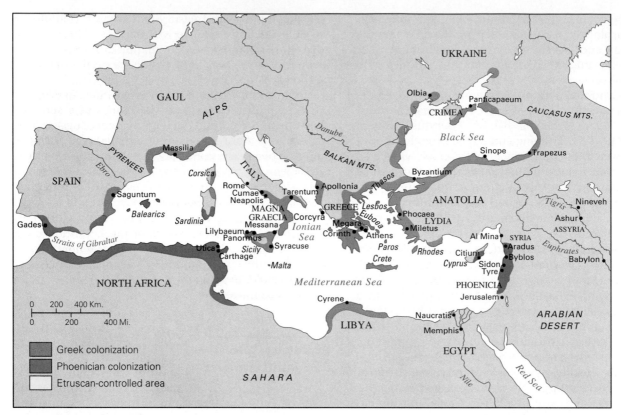

Map 4.5   Colonization of the Mediterranean   In the ninth century B.C.E., the Phoenicians of Lebanon began to explore and colonize parts of the western Mediterranean, including the coast of North Africa, southern and eastern Spain, and the islands of Sicily and Sardinia. The Phoenicians were primarily interested in access to valuable raw materials and trading opportunities.

new sources of valuable trade commodities, and new trading partners. For a time Tyre maintained its autonomy by providing the considerable sums of money and goods that the Assyrian kings demanded as tribute. By 701 B.C.E., however, the Assyrians conquered Tyre and stripped it of much of its territory and population, and in the sixth and fifth centuries B.C.E. Sidon became the leading city in Phoenicia.

The Phoenicians' activities in the western Mediterranean often brought them into conflict with the Greeks, who at this time were also seeking out valuable resources in the western Mediterranean and colonizing southern Italy and Sicily. The focal point of this rivalry was Sicily. Phoenicians occupied the western end of the island, and Greeks colonized the eastern and central sectors. For centuries Greeks and Phoenicians fought for control of Sicily in some of the most savage wars in the history of the ancient Mediterranean. The sources contain many stories of atrocities, massacres, wholesale enslavements, and removals of populations. The unusual level of bru-

tality must reflect the fact that each side felt its very existence to be at stake. In the end both communities survived, but the Carthaginians, who led the coalition of Phoenician communities in the western Mediterranean, gained the upper hand and by the mid-third century B.C.E. controlled all of Sicily.

Carthage's Commercial Empire

Historians know far more about the new settlements in the western Mediterranean—particularly Carthage—than they know about the cities in the Phoenician homeland. Much of this knowledge comes from the Greeks' and Romans' reports of their wars with the western Phoenician communities.

This chapter opens with an account of the origins of Carthage—an account preserved by Roman sources but probably derived from a Carthaginian original. However much truth may lie behind the legend of Dido, archaeological excavation has roughly confirmed the traditional foundation date of 814 B.C.E. **Carthage** was established at a strategic location, very near the present-day city of Tunis in Tunisia, at that point in the middle portion of the Mediterranean where the sea crossing from Europe to Africa is narrowest. The new settlement prospered and grew rapidly, soon coming to dominate other Phoenician colonies in the west.

The city of Carthage was located on a narrow promontory jutting out into the Mediterranean from the North African mainland. The crowded heart of the city stretched between Byrsa°, the original fortified hilltop citadel of the community, and a double harbor. The inner harbor could accommodate up to 220 warships. Naval command headquarters were situated on an island in the middle of it. A watchtower allowed surveillance of the surrounding area, and high walls made it impossible to see in from the outside. The outer commercial harbor was filled with docks for merchant ships and with sheds and yards for shipbuilding and refitting. In case of attack, the mouth of the harbor could be closed off by a huge iron chain.

Around the perimeter of a large central square lay government office buildings. Open space in the square itself was used by magistrates to hear legal cases outdoors. The inner city was a maze of narrow, winding streets, multistory apartment buildings, and sacred enclosures of the gods. Out from the center was Megara, a sprawling suburban district where fields and vegetable gardens separated the spacious houses of the well-to-do. This entire urban complex was enclosed by a wall 22 miles (35 kilometers) in length. At the most critical point—the 2½-mile-wide (4-kilometer-wide) isthmus connecting the promontory to the mainland—the wall was over 40 feet high (13 meters) and 30 feet thick (10 meters) and had high watchtowers at intervals.

With a population of roughly 400,000, Carthage was one of the largest cities in the world in the mid-first millennium B.C.E. Given the limitations of ancient technology, the provision of food, water, and sanitation must have posed substantial challenges. The city housed an ethnically diverse population, including people of Phoenician stock, indigenous people likely to have been the ancestors of modern-day Berbers, and immigrants from all over the Mediterranean and sub-Saharan Africa who had come to Carthage to make their fortunes. Despite the reluctance of Dido in the foundation legend, the Phoenicians quite readily intermarried with other peoples.

Each year two "judges" (a word having the same Semitic root as the Israelites' word for their early leaders)

were elected from the upper-class families. They served as heads of state and carried out administrative and judicial functions. The real seat of power was the Senate, made up of members of the leading merchant families, who sat for life, formulating policy and directing the affairs of the state. Within the Senate, an inner circle of the heads of the thirty or so most influential families made the crucial decisions. Occasionally an Assembly of the people was called together to elect public officials and vote on important issues. Normally the Senate and officials made decisions, but if the leaders were divided or wanted to stir up popular enthusiasm for some venture, they would turn to the people as a whole.

There is little evidence at Carthage of the kind of social and political unrest that later plagued Greece and Rome (see Chapters 5 and 6). This perception may be due in part to the limited information in our sources about internal affairs at Carthage. However, a merchant aristocracy (unlike an aristocracy of birth) was not a closed circle, and in a climate of economic and social mobility ambitious and successful new families and individuals could push their way into the circle of politically influential citizens. The ruling class also saw to it that everyone benefited from the riches of empire, and the masses usually were ready to defer to those who made that prosperity possible.

The most important arm of Carthaginian power was the navy. With citizens of Carthage playing important roles as rowers and navigators, the Carthaginian navy ruled the seas of the western Mediterranean for centuries. The many Phoenician towns along the shores of the western Mediterranean provided a chain of friendly ports.

Expert in the design and construction of ships and highly proficient as sailors, the Carthaginians had a fleet of fast and maneuverable warships. These vessels were outfitted with a sturdy pointed ram in front that could be driven into an enemy vessel to poke a deadly hole at the water line. A deck allowed marines (soldiers aboard a ship) to fire weapons at the enemy. Innovations in the placement of benches and oars made room for 30, 50, and eventually as many as 170 rowers to propel a ship at high speed. The Phoenicians of the eastern and western Mediterranean and their rivals the Greeks contributed to these technological advances and used similar vessels.

The foreign policy of the Carthaginian state reflected its economic interests. Protection of the sea lanes, access to raw materials, and fostering of trade opportunities mattered most to the dominant merchant class. Indeed, Carthage claimed the waters of the western Mediterranean as its own. Merchant vessels of other peoples were free to sail to Carthage to market their goods, but if they tried to operate on their own, they

---

Byrsa (BURR-suh)

risked being sunk by the Carthaginian navy. Treaties between Carthage and other states included formal recognition of this maritime commercial monopoly.

Carthaginian merchants were active all around the Mediterranean, but the archaeological record provides little evidence of which commodities they traded. This commerce may have included perishable goods—for example, foodstuffs, textiles, and animal skins, as well as slaves, which would not survive in the archaeological record—and raw metals (silver, lead, iron, and tin) whose Carthaginian origin would not be evident. Goods manufactured elsewhere were carried by Carthaginian ships, and products brought to Carthage by foreign traders were reexported for a profit.

There is also evidence for some form of trade with sub-Saharan Africans. Hanno, an eminent Carthaginian of the fifth century B.C.E., claimed to have sailed through the Strait of Gibraltar into the Atlantic Ocean, stopping at various points to found small settlements and explore the West African coast (see Map 4.5). A surviving version of his adventure-filled official report includes descriptions of ferocious savages, drums in the night, and rivers of fire. Scholars have had difficulty matching up Hanno's topographic descriptions and distances with the actual geography of the Atlantic coast of Africa. Some regard the document as an outright fiction. Others surmise that Hanno purposely altered distances and exaggerated the dangers so that other explorers would not dare to follow in his tracks and compete in this new commercial sphere. Other Carthaginian commanders explored the Atlantic coast of Spain and France and secured control of an important source of tin (a component of bronze, still important in the Iron Age) in the "Tin Islands," probably Cornwall in the British Isles.

War and Religion

It is important to be precise about the goals and methods of the Carthaginian "empire" in the western Mediterranean between the sixth and third centuries B.C.E. Unlike Assyria, Carthage did not seek direct rule of a large amount of territory. A belt of fertile land in northeastern Tunisia, owned by Carthaginians but worked by native peasants and imported slaves, provided a secure food supply. Beyond this core area Carthaginian domination was usually indirect. Other Phoenician communities in the western Mediterranean were essentially independent. However, because of Carthage's superior economic and military resources and the shared interests of all the Phoenician communities of the west, they normally looked to Carthage for military protection, and they followed Carthage's lead in foreign policy. Sardinia and southern Spain were

provinces under the direct control of a Carthaginian governor and garrison, probably because they contained vital agricultural, metal, and manpower resources.

Carthage's overarching emphasis on commerce may explain an unusual feature of the state: citizens were not required to serve in the military, because they were of more value in a civilian capacity. Carthage had little to fear from potential enemies close to home. The indigenous North African population was not well organized politically or militarily and thus was easily controlled. Carthage did need armies for military operations overseas, and it engaged in a series of fierce and destructive wars with Greeks and Romans from the fifth through third centuries B.C.E. For these conflicts it came to rely on mercenaries, soldiers whom the Carthaginians hired from the most warlike peoples in their dominions or in neighboring areas—such as Numidians from North Africa, Iberians from Spain, Gauls from France, and various Italian peoples. These well-paid mercenaries were under the command of professional Carthaginian officers.

Another sign that the conduct of war was not seen as the primary business of the state was the separation of military command from civilian government. From time to time, generals were chosen by the Senate and kept in office for as long as they were needed. This practice led to the rise of a professional class of military experts, men who studied the art of war and gained experience and a high level of skill over the course of long commands. In contrast, the kings of Assyria and the other major states of the ancient Middle East normally led military campaigns.

Carthaginian religion fascinated Greek and Roman writers. Like the deities of Mesopotamia (see Chapter 2), the gods of the Carthaginians—chief among them Baal Hammon, a male storm-god, and Tanit°, a female fertility figure—were powerful and capricious entities whose worshipers sought to appease them at any price. It was reported, for example, that members of the Carthaginian elite sacrificed their own male children at times of crisis. Excavations at Carthage and other Phoenician towns in the west have turned up **tophets**°—walled enclosures in which were buried thousands of small, sealed urns containing the burned bones of children. Some scholars see these compounds as the final resting place of infants born prematurely or taken by childhood illnesses. Most experts, however, maintain that the western Phoenicians practiced child sacrifice on a more or less regular basis.

The motivation behind this activity and the meanings that it held for its practitioners are not well understood. Presumably it was intended to win the favor of the

Tanit (TAH-nit)   **tophet** (TOE-fet)

The Tophet of Carthage   Here, from the seventh to second centuries B.C.E., the cremated bodies of sacrificed children were buried. Archaeological excavation has confirmed the claim in ancient sources that the Carthaginians sacrificed children to their gods at times of crisis. Stone markers, decorated with magical signs and symbols of divinities as well as family names, were placed over ceramic urns containing the ashes and charred bones of one or more infants or, occasionally, older children.   (Martha Cooper/Peter Arnold, Inc.)

gods at critical moments, such as the eve of decisive battles with Greek and Roman foes. Originally practiced by the upper classes, child sacrifice was later taken over by broader elements of the population and became increasingly common in the fourth and third centuries B.C.E.

Plutarch, a Greek who lived around 100 C.E., long after the demise of Carthage, but who had access to earlier sources, wrote the following about the Carthaginians:

> The Carthaginians are a hard and gloomy people, submissive to their rulers and harsh to their subjects, running to extremes of cowardice in times of fear and of cruelty in times of anger; they keep obstinately to their decisions, are austere, and care little for amusement or the graces of life.[1]

We should not take at face value what was said about the Carthaginians by their Greek and Roman enemies, but it is important to recognize that the Carthaginians were perceived as different and that cultural barriers, leading to misunderstanding and prejudice, played a significant role in the encounters of these peoples of the ancient Mediterranean. In Chapter 6 we follow the protracted and bloody struggle between Rome and Carthage for control of the western Mediterranean.

FAILURE AND TRANSFORMATION

The extension of Assyrian power over the entire Middle East had enormous consequences for all the peoples of this region and caused the stories of Mesopotamia, Israel, and Phoenicia to converge. As we have seen, in 721 B.C.E. the Assyrians destroyed the northern kingdom of Israel and deported a substantial portion of the population, and for over a century the southern kingdom of Judah was exposed to relentless pressure (see Society and Culture: Mass Deportation in the Neo-Assyrian Empire). Assyrian threats and demands for tribute spurred the Phoenicians to explore, colonize, and commercially exploit the western Mediterranean. The humiliation of Tyre, the leading Phoenician state, by the Assyrians in 701 B.C.E. accelerated the decline of the Phoenician homeland, but the western colonies, especially Carthage, lying far beyond Assyrian reach, flourished for centuries.

Even Egypt, for so long impregnable behind its desert barriers, was conquered and occupied for a time by Assyrian forces in the mid-seventh century B.C.E. Thebes, its ancient capital, was damaged beyond recovery. The southern plains of Sumer and Akkad, the birthplace of Mesopotamian civilization, were reduced to a protectorate. The venerable old metropolis at Babylon was alternately razed and rebuilt by Assyrian kings of differing dispositions. Urartu and Elam, Assyria's great-power rivals close to home, were ultimately destroyed.

By the mid-seventh century B.C.E. Assyria stood seemingly unchallenged in western Asia. But the cost had been high. The arms race with Urartu, the frequent expensive campaigns, and protection of lengthy borders had overextended Assyrian resources. The brutality of Assyrian conduct and the exploitation of the conquered peoples had aroused the hatred of many subjects and neighbors. And changes in the ethnic composition of the army and in the population of the homeland had rendered both soldiers and civilians less committed to the interests of the Assyrian state.

Two dynamic new political entities spearheaded resistance to Assyria: (1) a resurgent Babylonia under the Neo-Babylonian, or Chaldaean, dynasty (the Chaldaeans had infiltrated southern Mesopotamia around 1000 B.C.E.) and (2) the kingdom of the Medes, an Iranian people who by the seventh century B.C.E. were extending their control eastward across the Iranian Plateau. These two powers launched a series of attacks on the Assyrian homeland, and by 612 B.C.E. the chief Assyrian cities had been destroyed. The rapidity of the Assyrian decline and fall is stunning. The destruction systematically carried out by the victorious attackers led to the depopulation of northern Mesopotamia. Two centuries later, when a corps of Greek mercenaries passed by mounds that concealed the ruins of the Assyrian capitals, the Athenian chronicler Xenophon° had no inkling of the existence of the Assyrians and their once-mighty empire.

The Medes took over the Assyrian homeland and the northern steppe as far as eastern Anatolia, but most of the immediate benefits went to the **Neo-Babylonian kingdom** (626–539 B.C.E.) Kings Nabopolassar° (r. 625–605 B.C.E.) and Nebuchadnezzar (r. 604–562 B.C.E.), both energetic campaigners, took over much of the territory of

the old empire. Babylonia underwent a cultural renaissance. The city of Babylon was enlarged and adorned, becoming the greatest urban complex in the world in the sixth century B.C.E. Old cults were reactivated, temples rebuilt, festivals resurrected. The related pursuits of mathematics, astronomy, and astrology reached new heights.

CONCLUSION

This chapter traces the rise of new societies on five continents in the first millennium B.C.E. In the Eastern Hemisphere, Assyria represents a continuation of the Mesopotamian tradition, and Israel and Phoenicia reflect the cultural influence of Mesopotamia and Egypt but also evolve distinctive cultural traditions. In this same era, new societies arose in lands more distant from the ancient river-valley centers. The Celts of continental Europe received trade goods and some cultural influences from the Mediterranean, but they developed along an essentially independent track, responding to the terrain, resources, and climate of temperate Europe. The Olmec and Chavín civilizations of Mexico and the Andes developed without any contact with, or influences from, Eastern Hemisphere societies.

The rise of powerful civilizations in the Western Hemisphere centuries later than in the Eastern Hemisphere raises fundamental questions about why political, technological, and cultural developments occur when and where they do. Recent scholarly efforts to understand these phenomena have focused on environmental differences between the hemispheres.

The Eastern Hemisphere possessed certain fundamental advantages. It was home to a far larger number of wild plant and animal species that were particularly well suited for domestication. In addition, the natural east-west axis of the huge landmass of Europe and Asia allowed for the relatively rapid spread of domesticated plants and animals to climatically similar zones lying along the same latitudes. Settled agriculture then led to population growth, more complex political and social organization, specialization of function for certain members of society, and increased technological sophistication.

In contrast, in the Americas there were fewer wild plant and animal species that could be domesticated, the north-south axis of the continents and greater variation in climate made it more difficult for domesticated species to spread, and the processes that foster the development of complex societies evolved somewhat more slowly. In addition, the geography of the Western Hemi-

---

Xenophon (ZEN-uh-fuhn)
Nabopolassar (NAB-oh-poe-lass-uhr)

sphere, with its physical barriers of mountains, deserts, and dense forests, retarded development by preventing the exchange of useful technologies such as metallurgy between cultural regions.

The comparison of the two hemispheres leads to another important conclusion. The complex societies of the Western Hemisphere did not necessarily develop technologies in the same sequence as their Eastern Hemisphere counterparts. The Olmec and Chavín peoples did not possess large draft animals (such as the cattle and horses of the Eastern Hemisphere, though llamas did play an important part in the development of Chavín), wheeled vehicles, or metal weapons and tools. Nevertheless, they created sophisticated political, social, and economic institutions that rivaled those developed in the Eastern Hemisphere in the third and second millennia B.C.E.

A thread running through this chapter is population movement and the relocation of large numbers of people to new homes. The population movements of the first millennium B.C.E. sparked profound changes in the lands of Europe, North Africa, and western Asia. The Assyrians exemplify a pattern of coerced population movement. They deported large numbers of prisoners of war from outlying subject territories to the core area in northern Mesopotamia. Phoenician colonization of nearby Cyprus and the more distant shores of North Africa, Spain, and the islands off Italy was a response to Assyrian aggression but also exemplifies a different pattern: citizens voluntarily leaving their overpopulated homeland to make better lives for themselves in new settlements. In their new homes Phoenician colonists tried to duplicate familiar ways of life from the old country. In contrast, the Israelites who settled in Canaan and the Celts who spread from Central Europe across a wide swath of Europe north of the Alps underwent significant political, social, and cultural transformations as they adapted to new zones of settlement.

It is no accident that several of the peoples featured in this chapter who settled in large numbers outside their places of origin had long and glorious destinies ahead of them. In the first millennium B.C.E., as in later historical eras, diasporas proved to be fertile sources of innovation and safety valves for the preservation of culture. The Carthaginian enterprise eventually was cut short by the Romans, but Jews and Celts survive into our own time. Ironically the Assyrians, for a time the most powerful of all these societies, suffered the most complete termination of their way of life. Because Assyrians did not settle outside their homeland in significant numbers, when their state was toppled in the late seventh century B.C.E. their culture also fell victim.

The Neo-Babylonian kingdom that arose on the ashes of the Neo-Assyrian Empire would prove to be the last revival of the ancient Sumerian and Semitic cultural legacy in western Asia. The next chapter relates how the destiny of the peoples of the Middle East became enmeshed in the stories of Iran and Greece.

■ Key Terms

Olmec
Chavín
llama
Celts
Druids
Neo-Assyrian Empire
Ashur
mass deportation
Library of Ashurbanipal
Israel
Hebrew Bible
First Temple
monotheism
Diaspora
Phoenicians
Carthage
tophet
Neo-Babylonian kingdom

■ Suggested Reading

Jared Diamond, *Guns, Germs, and Steel: The Fates of Human Societies* (1997), tackles the difficult question of why technological development occured at different times and took different paths of development in the Eastern and Western Hemispheres.

A number of useful books provide an introduction to the early Americas. In *Prehistory of the Americas* (1987) Stuart Fiedel provides an excellent summary of the early history of the Western Hemisphere. *Early Man in the New World*, ed. Richard Shutler, Jr. (1983), is also a useful general work. *Atlas of Ancient America* (1986), by Michael Coe, Elizabeth P. Benson, and Dean R. Snow, offers a compendium of maps and information. George Kubler, *The Art and Architecture of Ancient America: The Mexican, Maya, and Andean Peoples* (1984), is an essential tool, though dated.

For the Olmecs see Jacques Soustelle, *The Olmecs: The Oldest Civilization in Mexico* (1984). More reliable is Michael Coe, *The Olmec World* (1996). Richard W. Keatinge, ed., *Peruvian Prehistory* (1988), provides a helpful introduction to the scholarship on Andean societies. The most useful summary of recent research on Chavín is Richard L. Burger, *Chavín and the Origins of Andean Civilization* (1992).

The best concise introduction to Celtic civilization is Simon James, *The World of the Celts* (1993). Also of use are Peter Ellis, *The Celtic Empire: The First Millennium of Celtic History, c. 1000 B.C.–51 A.D.* (1990); T. G. E. Powell, *The Celts* (1980); and Barry Cunliffe, *The Celtic World* (1979). Miranda J. Green, *The Celtic World* (1995), is a large and comprehensive collection of articles on many aspects of Celtic civilization. On Celtic religion and mythology see James MacKillop, *Dictionary of Celtic Mythology* (1998); Proinsias Mac Cana, *Celtic Mythology* (1983); and two books by Miranda Green: *The Gods of the Celts* (1986) and *Celtic Myths* (1993). Peter Ellis, *Celtic Women: Women in Celtic Society and Literature* (1996), collects and evaluates the evidence for women's roles. Celtic art is covered by Ruth and Vincent Megaw, *Celtic Art: From Its Beginnings to the Book of Kells* (1989), and I. M. Stead, *Celtic Art* (1985). For translations and brief discussion of Celtic legends see Patrick K. Ford, *The Mabinogi and Other Medieval Welsh Tales* (1977), and Jeffrey Gantz, *Early Irish Myths and Sagas* (1981).

Fundamental for all periods in the ancient Middle East is Jack M. Sasson, ed., *Civilizations of the Ancient Near East*, 4 vols. (1995), containing nearly two hundred articles by contemporary experts and bibliography on a wide range of topics. Barbara Lesko, ed., *Women's Earliest Records: From Ancient Egypt and Western Asia* (1989), is a collection of papers on the experiences of women in the ancient Middle East. John Boardman, I. E. S. Edwards, N. G. L. Hammond, and E. Sollberger, *The Cambridge Ancient History*, 2d ed., vols. 3.1–3.3 (1982–1991), provides extremely detailed historical coverage of the entire Mediterranean and western Asia.

For general history and cultural information about the Neo-Assyrian Empire and Mesopotamia and western Asia in the first half of the first millennium B.C.E. see Michael Roaf, *Cultural Atlas of Mesopotamia and the Ancient Near East* (1990); Amelie Kuhrt, *The Ancient Near East, c. 3000–300 B.C.* (1995); H. W. F. Saggs, *Civilization Before Greece and Rome* (1989); and A. Bernard Knapp, *The History and Culture of Ancient Western Asia and Egypt* (1988). H. W. F. Saggs, *Babylonians* (1995), has coverage of the fate of the old centers in southern Mesopotamia during this era in which the north attained dominance. Primary texts in translation for Assyria and other parts of western Asia can be found in James B. Pritchard, ed., *Ancient Near Eastern Texts Relating to the Old Testament*, 3d ed. (1969).

Jeremy Black and Anthony Green, *Gods, Demons and Symbols of Ancient Mesopotamia: An Illustrated Dictionary* (1992), is valuable for religious concepts, institutions, and mythology. Julian Reade, *Assyrian Sculpture* (1983), provides a succinct introduction to the informative relief sculptures from the Assyrian palaces. J. E. Curtis and J. E. Reade, eds., *Art and Empire: Treasures from Assyria in the British Museum* (1995), relates the art to many facets of Assyrian life. Andre Parrot, *The Arts of Assyria* (1961), provides full coverage of all artistic media.

For general historical introductions to ancient Israel see Michael Grant, *The History of Israel* (1984); J. Maxwell Miller and John H. Hayes, *A History of Ancient Israel and Judah* (1986);

and J. Alberto Soggin, *A History of Israel: From the Beginnings to the Bar Kochba Revolt*, A.D. *135* (1984). Amnon Ben-Tor, *The Archaeology of Ancient Israel* (1991), and Amihai Mazar, *Archaeology of the Land of the Bible, 10,000–586 B.C.E.* (1990), provide overviews of the discoveries of archaeological excavation in Israel. Hershel Shanks, *Jerusalem, an Archaeological Biography* (1995), explores the long and colorful history of the city. For social and economic issues see Shunya Bendor, *The Social Structure of Ancient Israel: The Institution of the Family (beit 'ab) from the Settlement to the End of the Monarchy* (1996), and Moses Aberbach, *Labor, Crafts and Commerce in Ancient Israel* (1994). Carol Meyers, *Discovering Eve: Ancient Israelite Women in Context* (1998), carefully sifts through literary and archaeological evidence to reach a balanced assessment of the position of women in the period before the monarchy. For the Philistines see Trude Dothan, *The Philistines and Their Material Culture* (1982).

Donald Harden, *The Phoenicians* (1962), and Gerhard Herm, *The Phoenicians: The Purple Empire of the Ancient World* (1975), are general introductions to the Phoenicians in their homeland. Maria Eugenia Aubet, *The Phoenicians and the West: Politics, Colonies and Trade* (1993), is an insightful investigation of the dynamics of Phoenician expansion into the western Mediterranean. Lionel Casson, *The Ancient Mariners: Seafarers and Sea Fighters of the Mediterranean in Ancient Times*, 2d ed. (1991), 75–79, discusses the design of warships and merchant vessels. For Carthage see Serge Lancel, *Carthage: A History* (1995), and David Soren, Aicha Ben Abed Ben Khader, and Hedi Slim, *Carthage: Uncovering the Mysteries and Splendors of Ancient Tunisia* (1990). Aicha Ben Abed Ben Khader and David Soren, *Carthage: A Mosaic of Ancient Tunisia* (1987), includes articles by American and Tunisian scholars as well as the catalog of a museum exhibition. R. C. C. Law, "North Africa in the Period of Phoenician and Greek Colonization, c. 800 to 323 B.C.," Chapter 2 in *The Cambridge History of Africa*, vol. 2 (1978), places the history of Carthage in an African perspective.

Elizabeth Wayland Barber, *Women's Work: The First 20,000 Years: Women, Cloth, and Society in Early Times* (1994), is an intriguing account of textile manufacture in antiquity, with emphasis on the social implications and primary role of women. I. Irving Ziderman, "Seashells and Ancient Purple Dyeing," *Biblical Archaeologist* 53 (June 1990): 98–101, is a convenient summary of Phoenician purple-dyeing technology.

◼ Note

1. Plutarch, *Moralia*, 799 D, trans. B. H. Warmington *Carthage* (Harmondsworth, England: Penguin 1960), 163.

5

GREECE AND IRAN,

1000–30 B.C.E.

Ancient Iran • The Rise of the Greeks • The Struggle of Persia and Greece •
The Hellenistic Synthesis
ENVIRONMENT AND TECHNOLOGY: The Farmer's Year
SOCIETY AND CULTURE: Greeks and Egyptians in Hellenistic Egypt

Painted Cup of Arcesilas of Cyrene The ruler of this Greek community in North Africa
supervises the weighing and export of silphium, a valuable medicinal plant.

he Greek historian Herodotus° (ca. 485–425 B.C.E.), chronicler of the struggles of the city-states of Greece with the Persian Empire in the sixth and fifth centuries B.C.E., tells a revealing story about cultural differences. The Persian king Darius° I, who ruled a vast empire stretching from eastern Europe to northwest India, summoned the Greek and Indian wise men who served him at court. He first asked the Greeks whether under any circumstances they would be willing to eat the bodies of their deceased fathers. The Greeks, who cremated their dead, recoiled at the impiety of such an act. Darius then asked the Indians whether they would be prepared to burn the bodies of their dead parents. The Indians were repulsed, because their practice was to ritually partake of the bodies of the dead. The point, as Herodotus wryly pointed out, was that different peoples have very different practices but each regards its own way as "natural" and superior.

The effort of some thinkers to distinguish between what was natural and what was mere cultural convention was creating much discomfort among Greeks in Herodotus's lifetime, for it called into question the validity of their fundamental beliefs. Herodotus's story also reminds us that the Persian Empire (and the Hellenistic Greek kingdoms that succeeded it) brought together, in Europe and in Asia, peoples and cultural systems that previously had known little direct contact, and that this new cross-cultural interaction had the potential to be alarming as well as to stimulate new and exciting cultural syntheses.

In this chapter we look at the eastern Mediterranean and western Asia in the first millennium B.C.E., emphasizing the experiences of the Persians and Greeks. The rivalry and wars of Greeks and Persians from the sixth to fourth centuries B.C.E. are traditionally seen as the first act of a drama that has continued intermittently ever since: the clash of the civilizations of East and West, of two peoples and two ways of life that were fundamentally different and thus almost certain to come into conflict. Some would see recent tensions between the United States and Middle Eastern states such as Iran and Iraq as the latest manifestation of this age-old conflict.

Ironically, Greeks and Persians had far more in common than they realized. They both spoke in tongues belonging to the same Indo-European family of languages found throughout Europe and western and southern Asia. Many scholars believe that all the ancient peoples who spoke languages belonging to this family inherited fundamental cultural traits, forms of social organization, and religious outlooks from their shared past.

As you read this chapter, ask yourself the following questions:

- How did geography, environment, and contacts with other peoples shape the institutions and values of Persians and Greeks?

- What brought the Greek city-states and the Persian Empire into conflict, and which factors dictated the outcome of their rivalry?

- In what ways were the lands and peoples of the eastern Mediterranean and western Asia influenced—culturally, economically, and politically—by the domination of the Persian Empire and the Greek kingdoms that succeeded it?

Ancient Iran

The location of Iran, "land of the Aryans," makes it a link between western Asia and southern and Central Asia, and its history has been marked by this mediating position (see Map 5.1). In the sixth century B.C.E. the vigorous Persians of southwest Iran created the largest empire the world had yet seen. Heirs to the long legacy of Mesopotamian history and culture, they introduced distinctly Iranian elements and developed new forms of political and economic organization in western Asia.

Relatively little written material from within the Persian Empire has survived, so we are forced to view it mostly through the eyes of the ancient Greeks—

Herodotus (heh-ROD-uh tuhs)   Darius (duh-RIE-uhs)

CHRONOLOGY

	Greece and the Hellenistic World	Persian Empire
1000 B.C.E.	**1150–800 B.C.E.** Greece's "Dark Age"	**ca. 1000 B.C.E.** Persians settle in southwest Iran
800 B.C.E.	**ca. 800 B.C.E.** Resumption of Greek contact with eastern Mediterranean **800–480 B.C.E.** Greece's Archaic Period **ca. 750–550 B.C.E.** Era of colonization **ca. 700 B.C.E.** Beginning of hoplite warfare **ca. 650–500 B.C.E.** Era of tyrants	
600 B.C.E.	**594 B.C.E.** Solon reforms laws at Athens	
	546–510 B.C.E. Pisistratus and sons hold tyranny at Athens	**550 B.C.E.** Cyrus overthrows Medes **550–530 B.C.E.** Reign of Cyrus **546 B.C.E.** Cyrus conquers Lydia **539 B.C.E.** Cyrus takes control of Babylonia **522–486 B.C.E.** Reign of Darius **530–522 B.C.E.** Reign of Cambyses; Conquest of Egypt
500 B.C.E.	**499–494 B.C.E.** Ionian Greeks rebel against Persia **490 B.C.E.** Athenians check Persian punitive expedition at Marathon **477 B.C.E.** Athens becomes leader of Delian League **461–429 B.C.E.** Pericles dominant at Athens; Athens completes evolution to democracy **431–404 B.C.E.** Peloponnesian War	**480–479 B.C.E.** Xerxes' invasion of Greece
400 B.C.E.	**399 B.C.E.** Trial and execution of Socrates **359 B.C.E.** Philip II becomes king of Macedonia **338 B.C.E.** Philip takes control of Greece	**387 B.C.E.** King's Peace makes Persia arbiter of Greek affairs **334–323 B.C.E.** Alexander the Great defeats Persia and creates huge empire **323–30 B.C.E.** Hellenistic period
300 B.C.E.	**317 B.C.E.** End of democracy in Athens **ca. 300 B.C.E.** Foundation of the Museum and start of lighthouse construction **200 B.C.E.** First Roman intervention in the Hellenistic East	
100 B.C.E.	**30 B.C.E.** Roman annexation of Egypt, the last Hellenistic kingdom	

outsiders who were ignorant at best, usually hostile, and interested primarily in events that affected themselves. This Greek perspective leaves us unaware of developments in the central and eastern portions of the Persian Empire. Nevertheless, recent archaeological discoveries and close analysis of the limited written material from within the empire can supplement and correct the perspective of the Greek sources.

Geography and Resources

Iran is bounded by the Zagros Mountains to the west, the Caucasus° Mountains and Caspian Sea to the northwest and north, the mountains of Afghanistan and the desert of Baluchistan° to the east and southeast, and the Persian

---

Caucasus (KAW-kuh-suhs)   Baluchistan (buh-loo-chi-STAN)

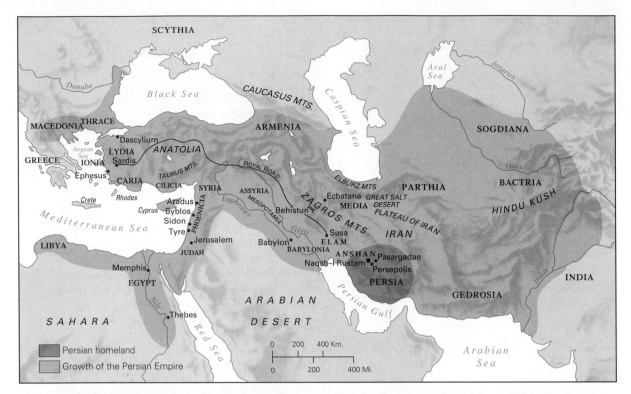

Map 5.1   The Persian Empire   Between 550 and 522 B.C.E., the Persians of southwest Iran, under their first two kings, Cyrus and Cambyses, conquered each of the major states of western Asia—Media, Babylonia, Lydia, and Egypt. The third king, Darius I, extended the boundaries as far as the Indus Valley to the east and the European shore of the Black Sea to the west. The first major setback came when the fourth king, Xerxes, failed in his invasion of Greece in 480 B.C.E. The Persian Empire was considerably larger than its recent predecessor, the Assyrian Empire. For their empire, the Persian rulers developed a system of provinces, governors, regular tribute, and communication by means of royal roads and couriers that allowed for efficient operations for almost two centuries.

Gulf to the southwest. The northeast is less protected by natural boundaries, and from that direction Iran was open to attacks by the nomads of Central Asia.

The fundamental topographical features of Iran are high mountains at the edges, salt deserts in the interior depressions, and mountain streams crossing a sloping plateau and draining into seas or interior salt lakes and marshes. Humans trying to survive in these harsh lands had to find ways to exploit limited water resources. Unlike the valleys of the Nile, Tigris-Euphrates, Ganges, and Yellow Rivers, ancient Iran never had a dense population. The best-watered and most populous parts of the country lie to the north and west; aridity increases and population decreases as one moves south and east. On the interior plateau, oasis settlements sprang up beside streams or springs. The Great Salt Desert, which covers most of eastern Iran, and Baluchistan in the southeast corner were extremely inhospitable. Scattered settle-

ments in the narrow plains beside the Persian Gulf were cut off from the interior plateau by mountain barriers.

In the first millennium B.C.E. irrigation enabled people to move down from the mountain valleys and open the plains to agriculture. To prevent evaporation of precious water in the hot, dry climate, they devised underground irrigation channels. Constructing and maintaining these subterranean channels and the vertical shafts that provided access to them was labor-intensive work. Normally, local leaders oversaw the expansion of the network in each district. Activity accelerated during periods when a strong central authority was able to organize large numbers of laborers. The connection between royal authority and prosperity is evident in the ideology of the first Persian Empire (see below). Even so, human survival depended on a delicate ecological balance, and a buildup of salt in the soil or a falling water table sometimes forced the abandonment of settlements.

Iran's mineral resources—copper, tin, iron, gold, and silver—were exploited on a limited scale in antiquity. Mountain slopes, more heavily wooded than they are now, provided fuel and materials for building and crafts. Because this austere land could not generate much of an agricultural surplus, objects of trade tended to be minerals and crafted goods such as textiles and carpets.

The Rise of the Persian Empire

In antiquity many groups of people, whom historians refer to collectively as "Iranians" because they spoke related languages and shared certain cultural features, spread out across western and Central Asia—an area comprising not only the modern state of Iran but also Turkmenistan, Afghanistan, and Pakistan. Several of these groups arrived in western Iran near the end of the second millennium B.C.E. The first to achieve a complex level of political organization was the Medes (Mada in Iranian).* They settled in the northwest and came under the influence of the ancient centers in Mesopotamia and Urartu (modern Armenia and northeast Turkey). The Medes played a major role in the destruction of the Assyrian Empire in the late seventh century B.C.E. and extended their control westward across Assyria into Anatolia (modern Turkey). They also projected their power southeast toward the Persian Gulf, a region occupied by another Iranian people, the Persians (Parsa).

The Persian rulers—now called Achaemenids° because they traced their lineage back to an ancestor named Achaemenes—cemented their relationship with the Median court through marriage. **Cyrus** (Kurush), the son of a Persian chieftain and a Median princess, united the various Persian tribes and overthrew the Median monarch sometime around 550 B.C.E. His victory should perhaps be seen less as a conquest than as an alteration of the relations between groups, for Cyrus placed both Medes and Persians in positions of responsibility and retained the framework of Median rule. The differences between these two Iranian peoples were not great—principally differences in the dialects they spoke and variations in the way they dressed. The Greeks could not readily tell the two apart.

Like most Indo-European peoples, the early inhabitants of western Iran had a patriarchal family organization: the male head of the household had nearly absolute

Stone Relief of Two Persian Magi This relief from Dascylium, headquarters of the Persian governor in northwest Anatolia, shows two magi wearing veils over their mouths and holding bundles of sticks used in the ceremony of sacrifice. The Persian kings and their subordinates were Zoroastrians, and it is likely that Zoroastrianism spread to the provinces, where significant numbers of Persians lived, and influenced the beliefs of other peoples. (Courtesy, Archaeological Museums of Istanbul)

authority over family members. Society was divided into three social and occupational classes: warriors, priests, and peasants. Warriors were the dominant element. A landowning aristocracy, they took pleasure in hunting, fighting, and gardening. The king was the most illustrious member of this group. The priests, or Magi (*magush*), were ritual specialists who supervised the proper performance of sacrifices. The common people—peasants—were primarily village-based farmers and shepherds.

Over the course of two decades the energetic Cyrus (r. 550–530 B.C.E.) redrew the map of western Asia. In 546 B.C.E. he prevailed in a cavalry battle outside the gates of Sardis, the capital of the kingdom of Lydia in western Anatolia, reportedly because the smell of his camels

---

* Iranian groups and individuals are known in the Western world by Greek approximations of their names; thus these familiar forms are used here. The original Iranian names are given in parentheses.

Achaemenid (a-KEY-muh-nid)

caused a panic among his opponents' horses. All Anatolia, including the Greek city-states on the western coast, came under Persian control. In 539 B.C.E. he swept into Mesopotamia, where the Neo-Babylonian dynasty had ruled since the collapse of Assyrian power (see Chapter 4). Cyrus made a deal with disaffected elements within Babylon, and when he and his army approached, the gates of the city were thrown open to him without a struggle. A skillful propagandist, Cyrus showed respect to the Babylonian priesthood and had his son crowned king in accordance with native traditions.

After Cyrus lost his life in 530 B.C.E. while campaigning against a coalition of nomadic Iranians in the northeast, his son Cambyses° (Kambujiya, r. 530–522 B.C.E.) set his sights on Egypt, the last of the great ancient kingdoms of the Middle East. The Persians prevailed over the Egyptians in a series of bloody battles; then they sent exploratory expeditions south to Nubia and west to Libya. Greek sources depict Cambyses as a cruel and impious madman, but contemporary documents from Egypt show him operating in the same practical vein as his father, cultivating local priests and notables and respecting native traditions.

When Cambyses died in 522 B.C.E., **Darius I** (Darayavaush) seized the throne. His success in crushing many early challenges to his rule was a testimony to his skill, energy, and ruthlessness. From this reign forward, Medes played a lesser role, and the most important posts went to members of leading Persian families. Darius (r. 522–486 B.C.E.) extended Persian control eastward as far as the Indus Valley and westward into Europe, where he bridged the Danube River and chased the nomadic Scythian° peoples north of the Black Sea. The Persians erected a string of forts in Thrace (modern-day northeast Greece and Bulgaria) and by 500 B.C.E. were on the doorstep of Greece. Darius also promoted the development of maritime routes. He dispatched a fleet to explore the waters from the Indus Delta to the Red Sea, and he completed a canal linking the Red Sea with the Nile.

Imperial Organization and Ideology

The empire of Darius I was the largest the world had yet seen (see Map 5.1). Stretching from eastern Europe to Pakistan, from southern Russia to Sudan, it encompassed a multitude of ethnic groups and every form of social and political organization, from nomadic kinship group to subordinate kingdom to city-state. Darius can rightly be considered a second founder of the Persian Empire, after Cyrus, because he created a new organizational structure that was maintained throughout the remaining two centuries of the empire's existence.

Darius divided the empire into twenty provinces. Each one was under the supervision of a Persian **satrap**°, or governor, likely to be related or connected by marriage to the royal family. The satrap's court was a miniature version of the royal court. The tendency for the position of satrap to become hereditary meant that satraps' families lived in the province governed by their head, acquired a fund of knowledge about local conditions, and formed connections with the local native elite. The farther a province was from the center of the empire, the more autonomy the satrap had, because slow communications made it impractical to refer most matters to the central administration.

One of the satrap's most important duties was to collect and send tribute to the king. Darius prescribed how much precious metal each province was to contribute annually. This amount was forwarded to the central treasury. Some of it was disbursed for necessary expenditures, but most of it was hoarded. As more and more precious metal was taken out of circulation, the price of gold and silver rose, and provinces found it increasingly difficult to meet their quotas. Evidence from Babylonia indicates a gradual economic decline setting in by the fourth century B.C.E. The increasing burden of taxation and official corruption inadvertently may have caused the economic downturn.

Royal roads, well maintained and patrolled, connected the outlying provinces to the heart of the empire. Way stations were built at intervals to receive important travelers and couriers carrying official correspondence. At strategic points, such as mountain passes, river crossings, and important urban centers, garrisons controlled people's movements. The administrative center of the empire was Susa, the ancient capital of Elam, in southwest Iran near the present-day border with Iraq. It was to Susa that Greeks and others went with requests and messages for the king. It took a party of Greek ambassadors at least three months to make the journey to Susa. Altogether, travel time, time spent waiting for an audience with the Persian king, delays due to weather, and the duration of the return trip probably kept the ambassadors away from home a year or more.

The king lived and traveled with his numerous wives and children. The little information that we have about the lives of Persian royal women comes from foreign sources and is thus suspect. The Book of Esther in the

---

Cambyses (kam-BIE-sees)   **Scythian** (SITH-ee-uhn)

satrap (SAY-trap)

Hebrew Bible tells a romantic story of how King Ahasuerus° (Xerxes) picked the Jewish woman Esther to be one of his wives and how the beautiful, courageous, clever queen later saved the Jewish people from a plot to massacre them. Greek sources make clear that women of the royal family could become pawns in the struggle for power. Darius strengthened his claim to the throne by marrying a daughter of Cyrus, and later the Greek conquerer Alexander the Great married a daughter of the last Persian king. Greek sources portray Persian queens as vicious intriguers, poisoning rival wives in the king's large harem and plotting to win the throne for their sons.

Besides the royal family, the king's large entourage included several other groups: (1) the sons of Persian aristocrats, who were educated at court and also served as hostages for their parents' good behavior; (2) many noblemen, who were expected to attend the king when they were not otherwise engaged; (3) the central administration, including officials and employees of the treasury, secretariat, and archives; (4) the royal bodyguard; and (5) countless courtiers and slaves. Long gone was the simplicity of the days when the king hunted and caroused with his warrior companions. Inspired by Mesopotamian conceptions of monarchy, the king of Persia had become an aloof figure of majesty and splendor: "The Great King, King of Kings, King in Persia, King of countries." He referred to everyone, even the Persian nobility, as "my slaves," and anyone who approached him had to bow down before him.

The king owned vast tracts of land throughout the empire. Some of this land he gave to his supporters. Donations called "bow land," "horse land," and "chariot land" in Babylonian documents obliged the recipient to provide military service. Scattered around the empire were gardens, orchards, and hunting preserves belonging to the king and the high nobility. The *paradayadam* (meaning "walled enclosure"—the term has come into English as *paradise*), a green oasis in an arid landscape, advertised the prosperity that the king and empire could bring to those who loyally served them.

Surviving administrative records from the Persian homeland give us a glimpse of how the complex tasks of administration were managed. The Persepolis Treasury and Fortification Texts, inscribed in Elamite cuneiform on baked clay tablets, show that government officials distributed food and other essential commodities to large numbers of workers of many different nationalities. Some of these workers may have been prisoners of war brought to the center of the empire to work on construction projects, maintain and expand the irrigation network, and farm on the royal estates. Workers were divided into groups of men, women, and children. Women received less than men of equivalent status, but pregnant women and women with babies received more. Men and women performing skilled jobs received more than their unskilled counterparts.

Tradition remembered Darius as a lawgiver who created a body of "laws of the King" and a system of royal judges operating throughout the empire, as well as encouraging the codification and publication of the laws of the various subject peoples. In a manner that typifies the decentralized character of the Persian Empire, he allowed each people to live in accordance with its own traditions and ordinances.

The central administration was based not in the Persian homeland (present-day Fars, directly north of the Persian Gulf) but farther west in Elam and Mesopotamia. Closer to the geographical center of the empire, this location allowed the kings to employ the trained administrators and scribes of those ancient civilizations. However, on certain occasions the kings returned to one special place back in the homeland. Darius began construction of a ceremonial capital at **Persepolis** (Parsa). An artificial platform was erected, and on it were built a series of palaces, audience halls, treasury buildings, and barracks. Here, too, Darius (and his son Xerxes°, who completed the project) was inspired by Mesopotamian traditions, for each of the great Assyrian kings had created a fortress-city as an advertisement of his wealth and power.

Darius's approach to governing can be seen in the luxuriant relief sculpture that covers the foundations, walls, and stairwells of the buildings at Persepolis. Representatives of all the peoples of the empire—recognizable by their distinctive hair, beards, dress, hats, and footwear—are depicted in the act of of bringing gifts to the king. Historians used to think that the sculpture represented a real event that transpired each year at Persepolis, but now they see it as an exercise in what today we would call public relations or propaganda. It is Darius's carefully crafted vision of an empire of vast extent and abundant resources in which all the subject peoples willingly cooperate. In one telling sculptural example, Darius subtly contrasted the character of his rule with that of the Assyrian Empire, the Persians' predecessors in these lands (see Chapter 4). Where Assyrian kings had gloried in their power and depicted subjects staggering under the weight of a giant platform that supported the throne, Darius's artists showed erect subjects shouldering the burden willingly and without strain.

Ahasuerus (uh-HAZZ-yoo-ear-uhs)

Xerxes (ZERK-sees)

View of the East Front of the Apadana (Audience Hall) at Persepolis, ca. 500 B.C.E. To the right lies the Gateway of Xerxes. Persepolis, in the Persian homeland, was built by Darius I and his son Xerxes, and it was used for ceremonies of special importance to the Persian king and people—coronations, royal weddings, funerals, and the New Year's festival. The stone foundations, walls, and stairways of Persepolis are filled with sculpted images of members of the court and embassies bringing gifts, offering a vision of the grandeur and harmony of the Persian Empire. (Courtesy of the Oriental Institute, University of Chicago)

What actually took place at Persepolis? This opulent retreat in the homeland probably was the scene of events of special significance for the king and his people: the New Year's Festival, coronation, marriage, death and burial. The kings, from Darius on, were buried in elaborate tombs cut into the cliffs at nearby Naqsh-i Rustam°.

Another perspective on what the Persian monarchy claimed to stand for is provided by the several dozen inscriptions that have survived. At Naqsh-i Rustam, Darius makes the following claim:

> Ahuramazda° [a Persian deity], when he saw this earth in commotion, thereafter bestowed it upon me, made me king. . . . By the favor of Ahuramazda I put it down in its place. . . . I am of such a sort that I am a friend to right, I am not a friend to wrong. It is not my desire that the weak man should have wrong done to him by the mighty; nor is that my desire, that the mighty man should have wrong done to him by the weak.[1]

As this inscription makes clear, behind Darius and the empire lies the will of god. Ahuramazda made Darius king and gave him a mandate to bring order to a world in turmoil, and, despite his reasonable and just disposition, the king will brook no opposition. Ahuramazda is the great god of a religion called **Zoroastrianism°,** and it is nearly certain that Darius and his successors were Zoroastrians.

The origins of this religion are shrouded in uncertainty. The Gathas, hymns in an archaic Iranian dialect, are said to be the work of Zoroaster (Zarathushtra). The dialect and physical setting of the hymns indicate that Zoroaster lived in eastern Iran. Scholarly guesses about when he lived range from 1700 to 500 B.C.E. He revealed that the world had been created by Ahuramazda, "the wise lord," and was threatened by Angra Mainyu°, "the hostile spirit," backed by a host of demons. In this dualist universe the struggle between good and evil plays out over twelve thousand years. At the end of this period,

Naqsh-i Rustam (NUHK-shee ROOS-tuhm)
Ahuramazda (ah-HOOR-uh-MAZZ-duh)

Zoroastrianism (zo-ro-ASS-tree-uh-niz-uhm)
Angra Mainyu (ANG-ruh MINE-yoo)

good is destined to prevail, and the world will return to the pure state of creation. In the meantime, humanity is a participant in this cosmic struggle, and individuals are rewarded or punished in the afterlife for their actions.

In addition to Zoroastrianism, the Persians drew on moral and metaphysical conceptions with deep roots in the Iranian past. They were sensitive to the beauties of nature and venerated beneficent elements, such as water, which was not to be sullied, and fire, which was worshiped at fire altars. They were greatly concerned about the purity of the body. Corpses were exposed to wild beasts and the elements to prevent them from putrifying in the earth or tainting the sanctity of fire. The Persians still revered major deities from the pagan past, such as Mithra, associated with the sun and defender of oaths and compacts. They were expected to keep promises and tell the truth. In his inscriptions at Persepolis, Darius castigated evildoers as followers of "the Lie."

Zoroastrianism was one of the great religions of the ancient world. It preached belief in one supreme deity, held humans to a high ethical standard, and promised salvation. It traveled across western Asia with the advance of the Persian Empire, and it may have exerted a major influence on Judaism and thus, indirectly, on Christianity. God and the Devil, Heaven and Hell, reward and punishment, the Messiah and the End of Time, all appear to be legacies of this profound belief system, which, because of the accidents of history—the fall of the Achaemenid Persian Empire in the later fourth century B.C.E. and the Islamic conquest of Iran in the seventh century C.E. (see Chapter 9)—has all but disappeared (except for a relatively small number of Parsees, as Zoroastrians are now called, in Iran and India).

THE RISE OF THE GREEKS

Because Greece was a relatively resource-poor region, the cultural features that emerged there in the first millennium B.C.E. came into being only because the Greeks had access to foreign sources of raw materials and to markets abroad. Greeks were in contact with other peoples, and Greek merchants and mercenaries brought home not only raw materials and crafted goods but also ideas. Under the pressure of population, poverty, war, or political crisis, Greeks moved to other parts of the Mediterranean and western Asia, carrying with them their language and culture and exerting a powerful influence on other societies. Awareness of the different practices and beliefs of other peoples stimulated the formation of a Greek identity and sparked interest in geography, ethnog-

raphy, and history. A two-century-long rivalry with the Persian Empire also played a large part in shaping the destinies of the Greek city-states.

Geography and Resources

Greece is part of a large ecological zone that encompasses the Mediterranean Sea and the lands surrounding it (see Map 4.4). This zone is bounded by the Atlantic Ocean to the west, the several ranges of the Alps to the north, the Syrian desert to the east, and the Sahara to the south. The lands lying within this zone have a roughly uniform climate, experience a similar sequence of seasons, and are home to similar plants and animals. In the summer a weather front stalls near the entrance of the Mediterranean, impeding the passage of storms from the Atlantic and allowing hot, dry air from the Sahara to creep up over the region. In winter the front dissolves and the ocean storms roll in, bringing waves, wind, and cold. It was relatively easy for people to migrate to new homes within this ecological zone without having to alter familiar cultural practices and means of livelihood.

Greek civilization arose in the lands bordering the Aegean Sea: the Greek mainland, the islands of the Aegean, and the western coast of Anatolia (see Map 5.2). As we saw in Chapter 3, southern Greece is a dry and rocky land with small plains carved up by low mountain ranges. No navigable rivers ease travel or the transport of commodities across this difficult terrain. The small islands dotting the Aegean were inhabited from early times. People could cross the water from Greece to Anatolia almost without losing sight of land. From about 1000 B.C.E. Greeks began to settle on the western edge of Anatolia. Rivers that formed broad and fertile plains near the coast made Ionia, as the ancient Greeks called this region, a comfortable place. The interior of Anatolia is rugged plateau, and the Greeks of the coast were in much closer contact with their fellows across the Aegean than with the native peoples of the interior. The sea was always a connector, not a barrier.

Without large rivers, Greek farmers on the mainland depended entirely on rainfall to water their crops (see Environment and Technology: The Farmer's Year, on page 124). The limited arable land, thin topsoil, and sparse rainfall in the south could not sustain large populations. In the historical period farmers usually planted grain (mostly barley, which was hardier than wheat) in the flat plain, olive trees at the edge of the plain, and grapevines on the terraced lower slopes of the foothills. Sheep and goats grazed in the hills during the growing season. In northern Greece, where the rainfall is greater and the land opens out into broad plains, cattle and horses were

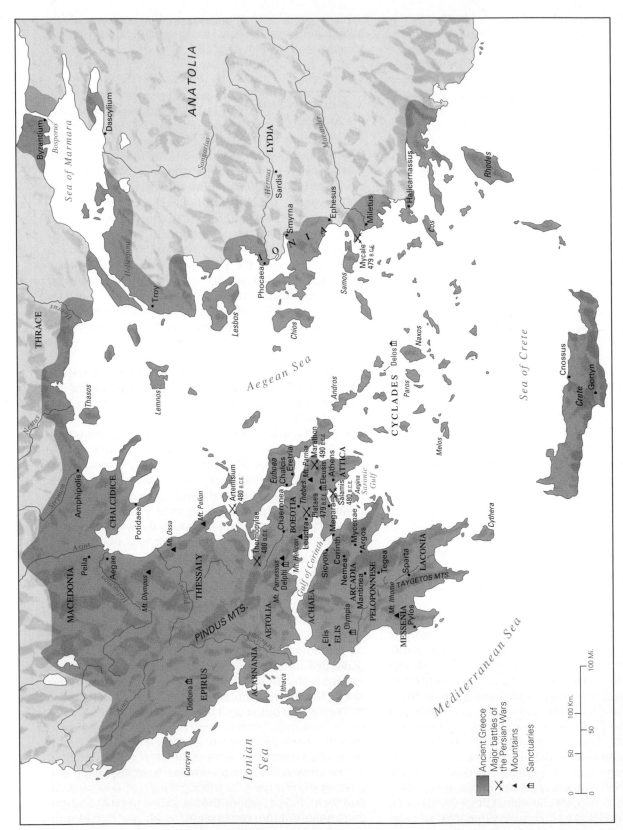

Map 5.2 Ancient Greece By the early first millennium B.C.E. Greek-speaking peoples were dispersed throughout the Aegean region, occupying the Greek mainland, most of the islands, and the western coast of Anatolia. The rough landscape of central and southern Greece, with small plains separated by ranges of mountains, and the many islands in the Aegean favored the rise of hundreds of small, independent communities. The presence of adequate rainfall meant that agriculture was organized on the basis of self-sufficient family farms. As a result of the limited natural resources of this region, the Greeks had to resort to sea travel and trade with other lands in the Mediterranean to acquire metals and other vital raw materials.

more abundant. These Greek lands had few metal deposits and little timber, although both building stone, including some fine marble, and clay for the potter were abundant.

A glance at a map of Greece reveals a deeply pitted coastline with many natural harbors. A combination of circumstances—the difficulty of overland transport, the availability of good anchorages, and the need to import metals, timber, and grain—drew the Greeks to the sea. They obtained timber from the northern Aegean, gold and iron from Anatolia, copper from Cyprus, tin from the western Mediterranean, and grain from the Black Sea, Egypt, and Sicily. Sea transport was much cheaper and faster than overland transport. Thus, though never comfortable with "the wine-dark sea," as Homer called it, the Greeks had no choice but to embark upon it in their small, frail ships, hugging the coastline or island-hopping where possible.

The Emergence of the Polis

The first flowering of Greek culture in the Mycenaean civilization of the second millennium B.C.E. is described in Chapter 3. For several centuries after the destruction of the Mycenaean palace-states, Greece lapsed into a "Dark Age" (ca. 1150–800 B.C.E.): for those who lived through it, dark because of depopulation, poverty, and backwardness; for us, dark because it left few traces in the archaeological record. During the Dark Age, Greece and the whole Aegean region were isolated from the rest of the world. The importation of raw materials, especially metals, had been the chief source of Mycenaean prosperity. Lack of access to vital resources lay behind the poverty of the Dark Age. Within Greece, regions that had little contact with one another developed distinctive styles in pottery and other crafts.

The isolation of Greece ended around 800 B.C.E. when Phoenician sailors arrived in the Aegean (see Chapter 4). The Phoenician city-states were dominated by a merchant class that was making ever more distant voyages west in search of valuable commodities and trading partners. By reestablishing contact between the Aegean and the Middle East, the Phoenicians gave Greek civilization an important push and inaugurated what scholars now term the "Archaic" period of Greek history (ca. 800–480 B.C.E.). Soon Greek ships were also plying the waters of the Mediterranean in search of raw materials, trade opportunities, and fertile farmland.

Various evidence reveals the influx of new ideas from the east, such as the appearance of lifelike human and animal figures and imaginative mythical beasts on painted Greek pottery. The most auspicious of all the gifts of the Phoenicians was a writing system. The Phoenicians used a set of twenty-two symbols to represent the consonants in their language, leaving the vowel sounds to be inferred by the reader. To represent Greek vowel sounds, the Greeks utilized some of the Phoenician symbols for which there was no equivalent sound in the Greek language, thus producing the first true alphabet. An alphabet offers tremendous advantages over systems of writing such as cuneiform and hieroglyphics, whose signs represent entire words or syllables. Because cuneiform and hieroglyphics required years of training and the memorization of several hundred signs, they remained the preserve of a scribal class whose elevated social position stemmed from their mastery of this technology. An alphabet opens the door for more widespread literacy. Because only a few dozen signs are required to represent all the possible statements in a language, people can learn an alphabet in a relatively short period of time.

There is controversy over the earliest uses of the Greek alphabet. Some scholars maintain that the Greeks first used it for economic purposes, such as to keep inventories. Others propose that it originated as a vehicle for preserving the oral poetic tradition. Whatever its first use was, the Greeks were quick to use the new technology to produce new forms of literature, law codes, religious dedications, and epitaphs on gravestones. This does not mean, however, that Greek society immediately became literate in the modern sense. For many centuries, Greece remained a primarily oral culture: people used storytelling, rituals, and performances to preserve and transmit information. Many of the distinctive intellectual and artistic creations of Greek civilization, such as theatrical drama, philosophical dialogues, and political and courtroom oratory, are products of the dynamic interaction of speaking and writing.

One indicator of the powerful new forces at work in the Archaic period was a veritable explosion of population. Studies of cemeteries in the vicinity of Athens show that there was a dramatic increase (perhaps as much as five- or sevenfold) during the eighth century B.C.E. The reasons for it are not fully understood but probably include a more intensive use of land as farming replaced herding and small, independent farmers and their families began to work previously unused land on the margins of the plains. The accompanying shift to a diet based on bread rather than meat may have increased both fertility and life span. A second factor was increasing prosperity based on the importation of food and raw materials. Rising population density led to the merging of villages into urban centers. It also created the potential for specialization of labor: freed from agricultural tasks, some members of the society were able to

The Farmer's Year

Perhaps the first Greek whom we can get to know as an individual is Hesiod. Hesiod lived near a village in Boeotia, in central Greece, around 700 B.C.E. In his poem *Works and Days*, we learn about his work as a farmer and about his relationships with family members and neighbors. The poem is presented as advice to his good-for-nothing brother, stressing the necessity of hard and perpetual work in order to survive. Much of the poem is a kind of farmer's almanac, describing the annual cycle of tasks on a Greek farm.

As Hesiod makes clear, it was very important for farmers to perform work at the right time. How did Greeks of the Archaic period, with no clocks, calendars, or newspapers, know where they were in the cycle of the year? They oriented themselves by acute observation of natural phenomena such as the flowering of plants and trees and the behavior of animals, the migration of birds and changes in the weather, and the movements of planets, stars, and constellations in the night sky.

Hesiod gives the following advice for determining the proper times for planting and harvesting grain:

> Pleiades rising in the dawning sky,
>   Harvest is nigh.
> Pleiades setting in the waning night,
>   Plowing is right.

The Pleiades is a cluster of seven stars visible to the naked eye. In Greek mythology, the Pleiades were seven sisters whom the gods placed in the sky to help them escape from the hunter Orion. The ancient Greeks observed that individual stars and constellations (groups of stars perceived by the human eye to form images in the sky) moved from east to west during the night and appeared in different parts of the sky at different times of the year. (In fact, the apparent movement of the stars is due to the the earth rotating on its axis and moving in its orbit around the sun against a background of unmoving stars. To earthly observers, however,

the stars appear to move.) Hesiod is telling his audience that, when the Pleiades appear above the eastern horizon just before the light of the rising sun makes all the other stars invisible (in May on the modern calendar), a sensible farmer will cut down his grain crop. Some months later (in our September), when the Pleiades dip below the western horizon just before sunrise, it is time to plow the fields and plant seeds for the next year's harvest.

Other events in nature provide similar indicators:

> Mind now, when you hear the call of the crane
> Coming from the clouds, as it does year by year:
> That's the sign for plowing . . .

And even the stern Hesiod allows himself a break at the height of summer:

> But when the thistle's in bloom, and the cicada
> Chirps from its perch in a branch, pouring down
> Shrill song from its wings in the withering heat,
> Then goats are plumpest, wine at its best, women
> Most lustful, but men at their feeblest, since Sirius
> Scorches head and knees, and skin shrivels up. . . .
>   Time to drink sparkling wine
> Sitting in the shade, heart satisfied with food,
> Face turned toward the cooling West Wind . . .

Sirius, the brightest star in the sky, rose with the sun in late July. The ancients believed that the addition of its heat to the heat already provided by the sun accounted for the sizzling temperature at this time of year. The ancient Egyptians connected the rising of Sirius with the beginning of the Nile flood.

It is clear to any reader of Hesiod's poem that he and his fellow Greek farmers were intimately attuned to their environment and their extensive knowledge of the natural world provided them with information vital for survival.

Source: Translations from Stanley Lombardo, *Hesiod: Works and Days and Theogony*, Indianapolis/Cambridge: Hackett Publishing, 1993, pp. 33, 37, 41.

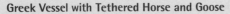

Greek Vessel with Tethered Horse and Goose
This vessel, used for mixing wine with water, may have been made in Boeotia in Hesiod's lifetime. It represents a farm scene. (Courtesy of the Trustees of the British Museum)

The Acropolis at Athens   This steep, defensible plateau jutting up from the Attic Plain served as a Mycenaean fortress in the second millennium B.C.E., and the site of Athens has been continuously occupied since that time. In the mid-sixth century B.C.E. the tyrant Pisistratus built a temple to Athena, the patron goddess of the community. It was destroyed by the Persians when they invaded Greece in 480 B.C.E. The Acropolis was left in ruins for three decades as a reminder of what the Athenians sacrificed in defense of Greek freedom, but in the 440s B.C.E. Pericles initiated a building program, using funds from the naval empire that Athens then headed. These construction projects, including a new temple to Athena—the Parthenon—brought glory to the city and popularity to Pericles and to the new democracy that he championed.   (Robert Harding Picture Library)

develop skills in other areas, such as crafts, commerce, and religion.

Greece at this time consisted of hundreds of independent political entities, reflecting the facts of Greek geography—small plains separated from each other by mountain barriers. The Greek **polis**° (usually translated "city-state") consisted of an urban center and the rural territory that it controlled. City-states came in various sizes, having populations as small as several thousand or as large as several hundred thousand in the case of Athens.

Most urban centers had certain characteristic features. A hilltop *acropolis* ("top of the city") offered a place of refuge in an emergency. The town spread out around the base of this fortified high point. An *agora* ("gathering place") was an open area where citizens came together to ratify the decisions of their leaders or to line up with

their weapons before military ventures. Government buildings were located there, but the agora soon developed into a marketplace as well (vendors everywhere are eager to set out their wares wherever crowds gather). Fortified walls surrounded the urban center; but as the population expanded, new buildings went up beyond the perimeter.

City and country were not so sharply distinguished as they are today. The urban center depended on its agricultural hinterland to provide food, and many of the people living within the walls of the city went out to work nearby farms during the day. Unlike the dependent workers on the estates of early Mesopotamia, the rural populations of the Greek city-states were free and members of the community.

Each polis was fiercely jealous of its independence and suspicious of its neighbors, and this state of mind led to frequent conflict. By the early seventh century B.C.E. the Greeks had developed a new kind of warfare,

---

polis (POE-lis)

waged by **hoplites**—heavily armored infantrymen who fought in close formation. Protected by a helmet, a breastplate, and leg guards, each hoplite held a round shield over his own left side and the right side of the man next to him and brandished a thrusting spear, keeping a sword in reserve. In this style of combat the key to victory was maintaining the cohesion of one's own formation while breaking open the enemy's line. Most of the casualties were suffered by the defeated army in flight.

Recent studies have emphasized the close relationship of hoplite warfare to the agricultural basis of Greek society. Greek states were defended by armies of private citizens—mostly farmers—called up for brief periods of crisis, rather than by a professional class of soldiers. Although this kind of fighting called for strength to bear the weapons and armor, and courage to stand one's ground in battle, no special training was required of the citizen-soldiers. When a hoplite army marched into the fields of another community, the enraged farmers of that community, who had expended a lot of hard labor on their land and buildings, could not fail to meet the challenge. And, though brutal and terrifying, the clash of two hoplite lines did offer a quick decision. Battles rarely lasted more than a few hours, and the survivors could promptly return home to tend their farms.

The expanding population soon surpassed the capacity of the small plains, and many communities sent excess population abroad to establish independent "colonies" in distant lands. Not every colonist left willingly. Sources tell of people being chosen by lot and forbidden to return on pain of death. Others, seeing an opportunity to escape from poverty, avoid the constraints of family, or find adventure, voluntarily set out to seek their fortunes on the frontier. After obtaining the approval of the god Apollo from his sanctuary at Delphi, the colonists departed, carrying with them fire from the communal hearth of the "mother-city," a symbol of the kinship and religious ties that would connect the two communities. They settled by the sea in the vicinity of a hill or other natural refuge. The "founder," a prominent member of the mother-city, allotted parcels of land and drafted laws for the new community. In some cases the indigenous population was driven away or reduced to a semiservile status; in other cases there was some intermarriage and mixing between colonists and natives.

A wave of colonization from the mid-eighth through mid-sixth centuries B.C.E. spread Greek culture far beyond the land of its origins. New settlements sprang up in the northern Aegean area, around the Black Sea, and on the Libyan coast of North Africa. In southern Italy and on the island of Sicily (see Map 4.4) another Greek core area was established. Although the creation of new homes, farms, and communities undoubtedly posed many challenges for the Greek settlers, they were able to transplant their entire way of life, mostly because of the general similarity in climate and ecology in the Mediterranean lands.

Greeks began to use the term *Hellenes°* (*Graeci* is what the Romans later called them) to distinguish themselves from *barbaroi* (the root of the English word "barbarian"). Interaction with new peoples and exposure to their different practices made the Greeks aware of the factors that bound them together: their language, religion, and lifestyle. It also introduced them to new ideas and technologies. Developments first appearing in the colonial world traveled back to the Greek homeland—urban planning, new forms of political organization, and, as we shall see shortly, new intellectual currents.

Another significant new development was the invention of coins in the early sixth century B.C.E., probably in Lydia (western Anatolia). They soon spread throughout the Greek world and beyond. In the ancient world a coin was a piece of metal whose weight and purity, and thus value, were guaranteed by the state. Silver, gold, bronze, and other metals were an attractive choice for a medium of exchange: sufficiently rare to be valuable, relatively lightweight and portable (at least in the quantities available to most individuals), seemingly indestructible and therefore permanent, yet easily divided. (Other items with similar qualities have been used as money in various historical societies, including beads, hard-shelled beans, and cowrie shells.) Prior to the invention of coinage, people in the lands of the eastern Mediterranean and western Asia weighed out quantities of gold, silver, or bronze in exchange for the items they wanted to buy. Coinage allowed for more rapid exchanges of goods as well as for more efficient record-keeping and storage of wealth. It stimulated trade and increased the total wealth of the society. Even so, international commerce could still be confusing because different states used different weight standards that had to be reconciled, just as people have to exchange currencies when traveling today.

By reducing surplus population, colonization helped to relieve pressures within the Archaic Greek world. Nevertheless, it was an era of political instability. Kings ruled the Dark Age societies depicted in Homer's *Iliad* and *Odyssey*, but at some point councils composed of the heads of noble families superseded the kings. This aristocracy derived its wealth and power from ownership of large tracts of land. Peasant families worked this land. They were allowed to occupy a plot and keep a portion of what they grew. Debt-slaves, too, worked the land. They were people who had borrowed money or seed from the

---

Hellenes (HELL-leans)

Vase Painting Depicting a Sacrifice to the God Apollo, ca. 440 B.C.E. For the Greeks, who believed in a multitude of gods who looked and behaved like humans, the central act of worship was the sacrifice, the ritualized offering of a gift. Sacrifice created a relationship between the human worshiper and the deity and raised expectations that the god would bestow favors in return. Here we see a number of male devotees, wearing their finest clothing and garlands in their hair, near a sacred outdoor altar and statue of Apollo. The god is shown at the far right, standing on a pedestal and holding his characteristic bow and laurel branch. The first worshiper offers the god bones wrapped in fat. All of the worshipers will feast on the meat carried by the boy. (Museum für Vor-und. Frühgeschichte, Frankfurt)

lord and lost their freedom when they were unable to repay the loan. Also living in a typical community were free peasants, who owned small farms, and urban-based craftsmen and merchants, who began to constitute a "middle class."

In the mid-seventh and sixth centuries B.C.E. in one city-state after another, an individual **tyrant**—a person who seized and held power in violation of the normal political institutions and traditions of the community—gained control. Greek tyrants were often disgruntled or ambitious members of the aristocracy, backed by the emerging middle class. New opportunities for economic advancement and the declining cost of metals meant more and more men could acquire arms. These individuals, already playing an important role as hoplite soldiers in the local militias, must have demanded some political rights as the price of their support for their local tyrant.

Ultimately, the tyrants of this age were unwitting catalysts in an evolving political process. Some were able to pass their position on to their sons, but eventually the tyrant-family was ejected and authority in the community developed along one of two lines: toward oligarchy°, the exercise of political privilege by only the wealthiest members of society, or toward **democracy,** the exercise of political power by all free, adult males. In any case, the absence of a professional military class in the early Greek states was essential to this broadening of the base of political participation.

Greek religion encompassed a wide range of cults and beliefs. The ancestors of the Greeks brought a collection of sky-gods with them when they entered the Greek peninsula at the end of the third millennium B.C.E. Male gods predominated, but several female deities had important roles. Some of the gods represented forces in nature: for example, Zeus sent storms and lightning, and Poseidon was master of the sea and earthquakes. The *Iliad* and *Odyssey*, which Greek schoolboys memorized and professional performers recited, put a distinctive stamp on the personality and character of these deities. The gods that Homer portrayed were anthropomorphic°—that is, conceived as humanlike in appearance (though they were taller, more beautiful, and more powerful than mere mortals and had a supernatural radiance) and humanlike in their displays of emotion (love, anger, jealousy, and other recognizably human feelings stirred them to act). Indeed, the chief difference between them and human beings was humans' mortality.

The worship of these gods at state-sponsored festivals was as much an expression of civic identity as of personal piety. **Sacrifice,** the central ritual of Greek religion, was performed at altars in front of the temples that the Greeks built to be the gods' places of residence. Greeks gave their gods gifts, often as humble as a small cake or a cup of wine poured on the ground, in the hope that the gods would favor and protect the donor. In more spectacular forms of sacrifice, a group of people would kill one or more animals, spray the altar with the victim's blood, and burn parts of its body so that the aroma would ascend to the gods on high. In this way the Greeks created a sense of community out of shared participation in the taking of life.

---

oligarchy (OLL-ih-gahr-key)

anthropomorphic (an-thruh-puh-MORE-fik)

Greek individuals and communities sought information, advice, or predictions about the future from oracles—sacred sites where they believed the gods communicated with humans. Especially prestigious was the oracle of Apollo at Delphi in central Greece. The god responded at Delphi through his priestess, the Pythia°, whose obscure, ecstatic utterances were interpreted by the male priests who administered the sanctuary. Because most Greeks were farmers, fertility cults, whose members worshiped and sought to enhance the productive forces in nature (usually conceived as female), were popular though often hidden from modern view because of our dependence on literary texts expressing the values of an educated, urban elite.

New Intellectual Currents

The material changes taking place in Greece in the Archaic period—new technologies, increasing prosperity, and social and political development—led to innovations in the intellectual and artistic outlook of the Greeks. One distinctive feature of the Archaic period was a growing emphasis on the individual. In early Greek communities the family enveloped the individual, and land belonged collectively to the family, including ancestors and descendants. Ripped out of this communal network and forced to establish a new life on a distant frontier, the colonist became a model of rugged individualism, as did the tyrant who seized power for himself alone. These new patterns led toward the concept of humanism—a valuing of the uniqueness, talents, and rights of the individual—which remains a central tenet of Western civilization.

We see clear signs of individualism in the new lyric poetry—short verses in which the subject matter is intensely personal, drawn from the experience of the poet and expressing his or her feelings and views. Archilochus°, a soldier and poet living in the first half of the seventh century B.C.E., made a surprising admission:

> Some barbarian is waving my shield, since I was
>   obliged to
> leave that perfectly good piece of equipment behind
> under a bush. But I got away, so what does it matter?
> Let the shield go; I can buy another one equally good.[2]

Here Archilochus is poking fun at the heroic ideal that scorned a soldier who ran away from the enemy. In challenging traditional values and exploiting the medium to express personal feeling and opinion, lyric poets paved the way for the modern Western conception of poetry.

There were also challenges to traditional religion. Thinkers now known as pre-Socratic philosophers called into question the kind of gods that Homer had popularized. Xenophanes°, living in the sixth century B.C.E., protested:

> But if cattle and horses or lions had hands, or were
> able to draw with their hands and do the works that
> men can do, horses would draw the forms of the gods
> like horses, and cattle like cattle, and they would make
> their bodies such as they each had themselves.[3]

The pre-Socratic philosophers rejected traditional religious explanations of the origins and nature of the world and sought rational explanations for things. They were primarily concerned with learning how the world was created, what it is made of, and why changes occur. (The term *pre-Socratic* refers to philosophers before Socrates, who in the later fifth century B.C.E. shifted the focus of philosophy to ethical questions.) Some pre-Socratic thinkers postulated various combinations of earth, air, fire, and water as the primal elements that combine or dissolve to form the numerous substances found in nature. One advanced the theory that the world is composed of microscopic atoms (from a Greek word meaning "indivisible") that move through the void of space, colliding randomly and combining in various ways to form the many substances of the natural world. In some respects startlingly similar to modern atomic theory, this model was merely a lucky intuition, but it is a testament to the sophistication of these thinkers. It is probably no coincidence that most of them came from Ionia and southern Italy, two zones in which Greeks were in close contact with non-Greek peoples. The shock of encountering people with very different ideas may have stimulated new lines of inquiry.

Another important intellectual development also took place in Ionia in the sixth century B.C.E. A group of men later referred to as logographers ("writers of prose accounts") began gathering information on a wide range of topics, including ethnography (description of a people's physical characteristics and cultural practices), the geography of Mediterranean lands, the foundation of important cities, and the origins of famous Greek families. *Historia*, "investigation/research," was the name they gave to the method they used to collect, sort, and select information In the mid-fifth century B.C.E. **Herodotus** (ca. 485–425 B.C.E.), from Halicarnassus in southwest Anatolia, published his *Histories*. Early parts of the work are filled with the geographic and ethnographic reports, legends, folktales, and marvels dear to

---

Pythia (PITH-ee-uh)   Archilochus (ahr-KIL-uh-kuhs)

Xenophanes (zeh-NOFF-eh-nees)

the logographers, but in later sections Herodotus focuses on the great event of the previous generation: the wars between the Greeks and the Persian Empire.

Herodotus declared his new conception of his mission in the first lines of the book:

> I, Herodotus of Halicarnassus, am here setting forth my history, that time may not draw the color from what man has brought into being, nor those great and wonderful deeds, manifested by both Greeks and barbarians, fail of their report, and, together with all this, the reason why they fought one another.[4]

In stating that he wants to find out *why* Greeks and Persians came to blows, he reveals that he has become a historian seeking the causes behind historical events. Herodotus directed the all-purpose techniques of *historia* to the service of *history* in the modern sense of the term, thereby narrowing the meaning of the word. For this achievement he is known as the "father of history."

Athens and Sparta

The two preeminent Greek city-states of the late Archaic and Classical periods were Athens and Sparta. The different character of these two communities underscores the potential for diversity in the evolution of human societies, even those arising in similar environmental and cultural contexts.

The ancestors of the Spartans migrated into the Peloponnese, the southernmost part of the Greek mainland, around 1000 B.C.E. For a time Sparta followed a typical path of development, participating in trade and fostering the arts. Then in the seventh century B.C.E. something happened to alter the destiny of the Spartan state. Like many other parts of Greece, the Spartan community was feeling the effects of rising population and a shortage of arable land. However, instead of sending out colonies, the Spartans crossed their mountainous western frontier and invaded the fertile plain of Messenia (see Map 5.2). Hoplite tactics may have given the Spartans the edge they needed to prevail over fierce Messenian resistance. The result was the takeover of Messenia and the domination of the native population, who descended to the status of helots°, the most abused and exploited population on the Greek mainland.

Fear of a helot uprising led to the evolution of the unique Spartan way of life. The Spartan state became a military camp in a permanent state of preparedness. Territory in Messenia and Laconia (the Spartan homeland) was divided into several thousand lots, which were assigned to Spartan citizens. Helots worked the land and turned over a portion of what they grew to their Spartan masters, who were thereby freed from food production and able to spend their lives in military training and service.

The professional Spartan soldier was the best in Greece, and the Spartan army was superior to all others; the other Greek states relied on citizen militias called out only in time of crisis. The Spartans, however, paid a huge personal price for their military readiness. At age seven, boys were taken from their families and put into barracks, where they were toughened by a severe regimen of discipline, beatings, and deprivation. A Spartan male's whole life was subordinated to the demands of the state.

Sparta essentially stopped the clock, declining to participate in the economic, political, and cultural renaissance taking place in the Archaic Greek world. There were no longer any poets or artists at Sparta. In an attempt to maintain equality among citizens, precious metals and coinage were banned, and Spartans were forbidden to engage in commerce. The fifth-century B.C.E. historian Thucydides°, a native of Athens, remarked that in his day Sparta appeared to be little more than a large village and that no future observer of the ruins of the site would be able to guess its power.

Other Greeks admired the Spartans for their courage, commitment, and martial skills but were put off by the Spartans' arrogance, ignorance, and cruelty. The Spartans purposefully cultivated a mystique by rarely putting their reputation to the test. Under the leadership of a Council of Elders and two kings who commanded troops in the field, Sparta practiced a foreign policy that was cautious and isolationist. Reluctant to march far from home for fear of a helot uprising, the Spartans sought to maintain peace in the Peloponnese° through the Peloponnesian League, a system of alliances between Sparta and its neighbors.

Athens followed a different path. In comparison with other Greek city-states it possessed an unusually large and populous territory: the entire region of Attica. By the fifth century B.C.E. it had a population of approximately 300,000 people. Attica contained a number of moderately fertile plains and was ideally suited for cultivation of olive trees. In addition to the urban center of Athens, located some 5 miles (8 kilometers) from the sea where the sheer-sided Acropolis towered above the Attic Plain, the peninsula was dotted with villages and a few larger towns.

helot (HELL-ut)

Thucydides (thoo-SID-ih-dees)
Peloponnese (PELL-eh-puh-neze)

Attica's large land area provided a buffer against the initial stresses of the Archaic period, but by the early sixth century B.C.E. things had reached a critical point. In 594 B.C.E., to avert a civil war, Solon, a member of the aristocracy with ties to the merchant community, was appointed lawgiver and given extraordinary powers. He divided Athenian citizens into four classes based on the annual yield of their farms. Those in the top three classes could hold state offices. Members of the lowest class, who had little or no property, could not hold office but were allowed to participate in meetings of the Assembly. This arrangement, which made rights and privileges a function of wealth, was a far cry from democracy. But it broke the absolute monopoly on power of a small circle of aristocratic families, and it allowed for social and political mobility. And by abolishing the practice of enslaving individuals for failure to repay their debts, Solon guaranteed the freedom of Athenian citizens.

Despite Solon's efforts to defuse the crisis, political turmoil continued until 546 B.C.E., when an aristocrat named Pisistratus° seized power. At this time most Athenians still lived in villages in the Attic countryside, identified primarily with their district, and were under the thumb of local lords who lived in strongly constructed manor houses. To strengthen his position and weaken the aristocracy, the tyrant Pisistratus tried to shift the allegiance of the rural population to the urban center of Athens, where he was the dominant figure. He undertook a number of monumental building projects, including a Temple of Athena on the Acropolis. He also instituted or expanded several major festivals: the City Dionysia°, which was to become the setting for dramatic performances, and the Panathenaea°, which drew people to Athens for a religious procession and athletic and poetic competitions.

Pisistratus passed the tyranny on to his sons, but with Spartan assistance the Athenians turned the tyrant-family out in the last decade of the sixth century B.C.E. In the 460s and 450s B.C.E. Pericles° and his political allies took the last steps in the evolution of Athenian democracy, transferring all power to popular organs of government: the Assembly, Council of 500, and People's Courts. From that time on, it was possible in Athens for men of moderate or little means to hold office and participate in the political process. Men were selected by lot to fill even the highest offices in the state, and they were paid for public service so they could afford to take time off from their work. Offices with responsibility in sensitive areas, such as managing public money and commanding military forces, were filled by means of election to guarantee the ability of those chosen.

The focal point of Athenian political life became the Assembly of all citizens. Several times a month proposals were debated there, decisions were openly made, and anyone could speak to the issues of the day. There was no strong executive office; members of the Council of 500 took turns presiding and representing the Athenian state. **Pericles** (ca. 495–429 B.C.E.), who dominated Athenian politics from 461 B.C.E. until his death, must have created an effective political organization that got out the vote on every important occasion.

In tandem with this century and a half of internal political evolution, Athens's economic clout and international reputation rose steadily. From the time of Pisistratus, Athenian pottery is increasingly prominent in the archaeological record at sites all around the Mediterranean, crowding out the products of former Greek commercial powerhouses such as Corinth and Aegina (see Map 5.2). These pots often contained olive oil, Athens's chief export, but elegant painted vases were desirable luxury commodities in their own right. Extensive trade increased the numbers and wealth of the middle class and helps to explain why Athens took the path of increasing democratization.

THE STRUGGLE OF PERSIA AND GREECE

For the Greeks of the fifth and fourth centuries B.C.E., Persia was the great enemy and the wars with Persia were the decisive historical event. Probably the Persians viewed these events differently, were more concerned about developments farther east, and did not regard the wars with the Greeks in the early fifth century B.C.E. as being so consequential. Nevertheless, in the end, the encounter with the Greeks over a period of two centuries was of profound importance for the history of the eastern Mediterranean and western Asia.

Early Encounters

Cyrus's conquest of Lydia in 546 B.C.E. led to the subjugation of the Greek cities on the Anatolian seacoast. In the years that followed, these cities were ruled by local groups or individuals who collaborated with the Persian government so as to maintain themselves in power and allow their city to operate

---

Pisistratus (pie-SIS-truh-tuhs)   Dionysia (die-uh-NIZ-ee-uh)
Panathenaea (pan-ath-uh-NEE-uh)   Pericles (PER-eh-kleez)

with minimal Persian interference. All this changed when the Ionian Revolt, a great uprising of Greeks and other subject peoples on the western frontier, broke out in 499 B.C.E. The Persians needed five years and a massive infusion of troops and resources to stamp out the insurrection.

This failed revolt in western Anatolia led to the **Persian Wars**—two Persian attacks on Greece in the early fifth century B.C.E. In 490 B.C.E. Darius dispatched a naval fleet to punish Eretria° and Athens, two states on the Greek mainland that had given assistance to the Ionian rebels, and to warn others about the foolhardiness of crossing the Persian king. Eretria was betrayed to the Persians by several of its own citizens, and the survivors were marched off to permanent exile in southwest Iran. In this, as in many things, the Persians took over the practices of their Assyrian predecessors, although they resorted to mass deportation less often and were more reticent to advertise it. Next on the Persians' list were the Athenians, who probably would have suffered a similar fate if their hoplites had not defeated the lighter-armed Persian troops in a short, sharp engagement at Marathon, 26 miles (42 kilometers) from Athens.

Xerxes (Khshayarsha, r. 486–465 B.C.E.) succeeded his father on the Persian throne in 486 B.C.E. and soon turned his attention to the troublesome Greeks. In 480 B.C.E. he set out with a huge invasionary force consisting of the Persian army, contingents summoned from all the peoples of the Persian Empire, and a large fleet of ships drawn from maritime subjects. Crossing the Hellespont (the narrow strait at the edge of the Aegean separating Europe and Asia) and journeying across Thrace, the Persian throng descended into central and southern Greece (see Map 5.2). Xerxes sent messengers ahead to most of the Greek states, bidding them to offer up "earth and water"—tokens of submission.

Many Greek communities acknowledged Persian overlordship. But in southern Greece an alliance of states bent on resistance was formed under the leadership of the Spartans. This Hellenic League, as modern historians call it, initially failed to halt the Persian advance. At the pass of Thermopylae° in central Greece, three hundred Spartans and their king gave their lives to buy time for their fellows to escape. However, after seizing and sacking the city of Athens in 480 B.C.E., the Persians allowed their navy to be lured into the narrow straits of nearby Salamis°, where they lost their advantage in numbers and maneuverability and suffered a devastating defeat. The following spring (479 B.C.E.), the Persian land army

Eretria (er-EH-tree-uh)   Thermopylae (thuhr-MOP-uh-lee)
Salamis (SAH-lah-miss)

was routed at Plataea and the immediate threat to Greece receded. A number of factors account for the outcome: the Persians' difficulty in supplying their very large army in a distant land; the Persian high command's tactical error in allowing naval forces to be drawn into the narrow waters off Salamis; and the superiority of heavily armed Greek hoplite soldiers over lighter-armed Asiatic infantry.

The collapse of the threat to the Greek mainland, however, did not mean the end of the war. The Greeks went on the offensive. Athens's stubborn refusal to submit to the Persian king, even after the city was sacked twice in two successive years, and the vital role played by the Athenian navy, which made up fully half of the allied Greek fleet, earned the city a large measure of respect. The next phase of the war, designed to drive the Persians away from the Aegean and liberate Greek states still under Persian control, was naval. Thus Athens replaced land-based, isolationist Sparta as leader of the campaign against Persia.

In 477 B.C.E. the Delian League was formed. It was a voluntary alliance of Greek states eager to prosecute the war against Persia. In less than twenty years, League forces led by Athenian generals swept the Persians from the waters of the eastern Mediterranean and freed all Greek communities except those in distant Cyprus (see Map 4.4).

The Height of Athenian Power

By scholarly convention, the Classical period of Greek history (480–323 B.C.E.) begins with the successful defense of the Greek homeland against the forces of the Persian Empire. Ironically the Athenians, who had played such a crucial role, exploited these events to become an imperial power. Success and the passage of time led many of their Greek allies to contribute money instead of military forces. The Athenians used the money to build up and man their navy. Eventually they saw the other members of the Delian League as their subjects and demanded annual contributions and other signs of submission from them. States that tried to leave the League were brought back by force, stripped of their defenses, and rendered subordinate to Athens.

Athens's mastery of naval technology transformed Greek warfare and politics and brought power and wealth to Athens itself. Unlike commercial ships, whose stable, round-bodied hulls were propelled by a single, square sail, military vessels, which could not risk depending on the wind, relied on large numbers of rowers. Having little deck room or storage space, these ships

Replica of Ancient Greek Trireme   Greek warships had a metal-tipped ram in front to pierce the hulls of enemy vessels and a pair of steering rudders in the rear. Though equipped with masts and sails, in battle these warships were propelled by 170 rowers. This modern, full-size replica represents one solution to the puzzle of how three tiers of oars could operate simultaneously without becoming entangled. Volunteer crews are helping scholars to determine attainable speeds and maneuvering techniques.   (Courtesy, The Trireme Trust)

needed to hug the coastline and put ashore nightly to replenish food supplies and to give the crew a chance to sleep. For centuries the primary warship in Greek waters had been the pentekonter, a sturdy vessel powered by fifty oars. Naval battles fought in pentekonters were crude engagements in which warriors launched spears and arrows to clear the decks of the enemy ship before boarding and fighting hand to hand. By the late sixth century B.C.E. experimentation had begun with the **trireme°**, a sleeker, faster vessel powered by 170 rowers.

The design of the trireme has long been a puzzle, but the unearthing at Athens of the slips where these vessels were moored, and recent experiments with a full-scale replica manned by international volunteers, have revealed much about the design of the trireme and the battle tactics that it made possible. The Greek trireme measured approximately 115 by 15 feet (35 by 6 meters) and was fragile. Rowers using oars of different lengths

and carefully positioned on three levels so as not to run afoul of one another were able to achieve short bursts of speed of up to 7 knots. Athenian crews, by constant practice, became the best in the eastern Mediterranean. They could disable enemy vessels by sheering off their oars, smashing their hulls below the water line with an iron-tipped ram, or forcing them to collide with one another by running around them in ever-tighter circles.

The effectiveness of the new Athenian navy had significant consequences both at home and abroad. The emergence at Athens of a democratic system in which each male citizen had, at least in principle, an equal voice is connected to the new primacy of the fleet. Hoplites were members of the middle and upper classes (they had to provide their own protective gear and weapons). Rowers, in contrast, came from the lower classes, but because they were providing the chief protection for the community and were the source of its power, they could insist on full rights.

Possession of a navy allowed Athens to project its power farther than it could have done with a citizen mili-

---

trireme (TRY-reem)

tia (which could be kept in arms for only short periods of time). In previous Greek wars, the victorious state had little capability to occupy a defeated neighbor permanently (with the exception, as we have seen, of Sparta's takeover of Messenia). Usually the victor satisfied itself with booty and, perhaps, minor adjustments to boundary lines. Athens was able to continually dominate and exploit other, weaker communities in an unprecedented way.

Athens did not hesitate to use political power to promote its commercial interests. Athens's port, Piraeus°, grew into the most important commercial center in the eastern Mediterranean. The money collected each year from the subject states helped to subsidize the increasingly expensive Athenian democracy as well as underwrite the construction costs of the beautiful buildings on the Acropolis, including the majestic new temple of Athena, the Parthenon. Many Athenians worked on the construction and decoration of these monuments. Indeed, the building program was a means by which the Athenian leader Pericles redistributed the profits of empire to the Athenian people and gained extraordinary popularity. When his political enemies protested against the use of Delian League funds for the building program, Pericles replied: "They [Athens's subjects] do not give us a single horse, nor a soldier, nor a ship. All they supply is money. . . . It is no more than fair that after Athens has been equipped with all she needs to carry on the war, she should apply the surplus to public works, which, once completed, will bring her glory for all time."[5]

In other ways as well Athens's cultural achievements were dependent on the profits of empire. The economic advantages that empire brought to Athens subsidized indirectly the festivals at which the great dramatic tragedies of Aeschylus, Sophocles, and Euripides, and the comedies of Aristophanes°, were performed. Money and power are a prerequisite for support of the arts and sciences, and the brightest and most creative artists and thinkers in the Greek world were drawn to Athens. Traveling teachers called Sophists ("wise men") provided instruction in logic and public speaking to pupils who could afford their fees. The new discipline of rhetoric—the construction of attractive and persuasive arguments—gave those with training and quick wits a great advantage in politics and the courts. The Greek masses became connoisseurs of oratory, eagerly listening for each innovation yet so aware of the power of words that *sophist* came to mean one who uses cleverness to distort and manipulate reality.

Piraeus (pih-RAY-uhs) Aristophanes (ar-uh-STOFF-uh-neze)

These new intellectual currents came together in 399 B.C.E. when the philosopher **Socrates** (ca. 470–399 B.C.E.) was brought to trial on charges of corrupting the youth of Athens and not believing in the gods of the city. A sculptor by trade, Socrates spent most of his time in the company of young men who enjoyed conversing with him and observing him deflate the pretensions of those who thought themselves wise. He wryly commented that he knew one more thing than everyone else: that he knew nothing.

At his trial, Socrates was easily able to dispose of the actual charges, because he was a deeply religious man and had the support of the families of the young men who had associated with him. He argued that the real basis of the hostility he faced was twofold: (1) He was being held responsible for the actions of several of his aristocratic students who had tried to overthrow the Athenian democracy. (2) He was being blamed unfairly for the controversial teachings of the Sophists and other intellectuals, which were widely believed to be contrary to traditional religious beliefs and to undermine morality. In Athenian trials juries of hundreds of citizens decided guilt and punishment, often motivated more by emotion than by legal principles. The vote that found Socrates guilty was fairly close. But his lack of contrition in the penalty phase—he proposed that he be rewarded for his services to the state—led the jury to condemn him to death by drinking hemlock. Socrates' disciples regarded his execution as a martyrdom, and smart young men such as Plato withdrew from public life and dedicated themselves to the philosophical pursuit of knowledge and truth.

This period also encompasses the last stage in Greece of the transition from orality to literacy. Socrates himself wrote nothing, preferring to converse with people he met in the street. His disciple Plato (ca. 428–347 B.C.E.) may represent the first generation to be truly literate. He gained much of his knowledge from books and habitually wrote down his thoughts. On the outskirts of Athens, Plato founded the Academy, a school where young men could pursue a course of higher education. Yet even Plato retained traces of the orality of the world in which he had grown up. He wrote dialogues—an oral form—in which his protagonist, Socrates, uses the "Socratic method" of question and answer to reach a deeper understanding of the meaning of values such as justice, excellence, and wisdom. Plato refused to write down the most advanced stages of the philosophical and spiritual training that took place at his Academy. He believed that full apprehension of a higher reality, of which our own sensible world is but a pale reflection, could be entrusted only to "initiates" who had completed the earlier stages.

Inequality in Classical Greece

It is important to keep in mind that Athenian democracy, the inspiration for the concept of democracy in the Western tradition, was a democracy only for the relatively small percentage of the inhabitants of Attica who were truly citizens—free, adult males of pure Athenian ancestry. Excluding women, children, slaves, and foreigners, this group amounted to 30,000 or 40,000 people out of a total population of approximately 300,000—only 10 or 15 percent. Other democratic Greek city-states, less well known to us than Athens, probably were equally exclusive.

Slaves, mostly of foreign origin, constituted perhaps one-third of the population of Attica in the fifth and fourth centuries B.C.E., and the average Athenian family owned one or more. Slaves were needed to run the shop or work on the farm while the master was attending meetings of the Assembly or serving on one of the boards that oversaw the day-to-day activities of the state. The slave was a "living piece of property," required to do any work, submit to any sexual acts, and receive any punishments that the owner ordained. Some communities prohibited the arbitrary killing of a slave, and, for the most part, slaves in Greece were not subjected to the extremes of cruelty and abuse suffered by slaves in other places and times.

In the absence of huge estates there were no rural slave gangs, and most Greek slaves were treated like favored domestic servants, often working together with the master or mistress on the same tasks. Close daily contact between owners and slaves meant, in many cases, that a relationship developed, making it hard for Greek slave owners to deny the essential humanity of their slaves. Still, Greek thinkers rationalized the institution of slavery by arguing that barbaroi (non-Greeks) lacked the capacity to reason and thus were better off under the direction of rational Greek owners. The social stigma attached to slavery was so great that most Athenians refused to work as wage laborers for another individual because following the orders of an employer was akin to being his slave.

Equally essential to providing Athenian men with the leisure time to engage in political and social life were women. The position of women varied across Greek communities. The women of Sparta, who were expected to bear and raise strong children, were encouraged to exercise, and they enjoyed a level of public visibility and outspokenness that shocked other Greeks. Athens—the case historians know best because of the abundance of written sources and vase paintings—may have been at the opposite extreme as regards the confinement and oppression of women. Ironically, the exploitation of women in Athens is linked to the high degree of freedom enjoyed by Athenian men in the democratic state.

Athenian marriages were unequal affairs. The man might be thirty, reasonably well educated, a veteran of war, experienced in business and politics. Under law he had nearly absolute authority over the members of his household. He arranged his marriage with the parents of his prospective wife, who was likely to be a teenager brought up with no formal education and only minimal training in weaving, cooking, and household management. Coming into the home of a husband she hardly knew, she had no political rights and limited legal protection. Given the differences in age, social experience,

Vase Painting Depicting Women at an Athenian Fountain House, ca. 520 B.C.E.   Paintings on Greek vases provide the most vivid pictorial record of ancient Greek life. The subject matter usually reflects the interests of the aristocratic males who purchased the vases—warfare, athletics, mythology, drinking parties—but sometimes we are given glimpses into the lives of women and the working classes. These women are presumably domestic servants sent to fetch water for the household from a public fountain. The large water jars they are filling are like the one on which this scene is depicted.   (William Francis Warden Fund. Courtesy, Museum of Fine Arts, Boston)

and authority, the relationship between husband and wife was in many ways similar to that of father and daughter.

The primary function of marriage was to produce children, preferably male. It is impossible to prove the extent of infanticide—the killing through exposure of unwanted children—because the ancients were sufficiently ashamed to say little about it. But it is likely that more girls than boys were abandoned.

Husbands and wives had limited daily contact. The man spent the day outdoors attending to work or political responsibilities; he dined with male friends at night; and usually he slept alone in the men's quarters. The woman stayed home to cook, clean, raise the children, and supervise the servants. The closest relationship in the family was likely to be between the wife and her slave attendant. These women were of roughly the same age and spent enormous amounts of time together. The servant could be sent into town on errands. The wife stayed in the house, except to attend funerals and certain festivals and to make discreet visits to the houses of female relatives. Greek men justified the confinement of women by claiming that they were naturally promiscuous and likely to introduce other men's children into the household—an action that would threaten the family property and violate the strict regulation of citizenship rights. Athenian law allowed a husband to kill an adulterer caught in the act with his wife.

Without any documents written by women in this period, we cannot tell the extent to which Athenian women resented their situation or accepted it because they knew little else. Women's festivals, such as the Thesmophoria°, provided a rare opportunity for women to get out. During this three-day festival the women of Athens lived together and managed their own affairs in a great encampment, carrying out mysterious rituals meant to enhance the fertility of the land. The appearance of bold and self-assertive women on the Athenian stage is also suggestive: the defiant Antigone° of Sophocles' play, who buried her brother despite the prohibition of the king; and the wives in Aristophanes' comedy *Lysistrata*°, who refused to have sex with their husbands until the men ended a war. Although these plays were written by men and probably reflect a male fear of strong women, the playwrights must have had models in their mothers, sisters, and wives.

The inequality of men and women posed obstacles to creating a meaningful relationship between the sexes.

Thesmophoria (thes-moe-FOE-ree-uh)   **Antigone** (ar-TIG-uh-nee)
Lysistrata (lis-uh-STRAH-tuh)

To find his intellectual and emotional "equal," a man often looked to other men. Bisexuality was common in ancient Greece, as much a product of the social structure as of biological inclinations. A common pattern was that of an older man serving as admirer, pursuer, and mentor of a youth. Bisexuality became part of a system by which young men were educated and initiated into the community of adult males. At least this was true of the elite intellectual groups that loom large in the written sources. It is hard to say how prevalent bisexuality and the confinement of women were among the Athenian masses.

Failure of the City-State and Triumph of the Macedonians

The emergence of Athens as an imperial power in the half-century after the Persian invasion aroused the suspicions of other Greek states and led to open hostilities between former allies. In the year 431 B.C.E. the **Peloponnesian War** broke out. This nightmarish struggle for survival between the Athenian and Spartan alliance systems encompassed most of the Greek world. It was a war unlike any previous Greek war because the Athenians used their naval power to insulate themselves from the dangers of an attack by land. In midcentury they had built three long walls connecting the city with the port of Piraeus and the adjacent shoreline. As long as Athens controlled the sea lanes and was able to provision itself, it could not be starved into submission by a land-based siege.

At the start of the war, Pericles formulated an unprecedented strategy, refusing to engage the Spartan-led armies that invaded Attica each year. Pericles knew that the enemy hoplites must soon return to their farms. Thus, instead of culminating in a short, decisive battle like most Greek hoplite warfare, the Peloponnesian War dragged on for nearly three decades with great loss of life and squandering of resources. It sapped the morale of all of Greece, and ended only with the defeat of Athens in a naval battle in 404 B.C.E. The Persian Empire had bankrolled the construction of ships by the Spartan alliance, so Sparta was able to take the conflict into Athens's own element, the sea.

The victorious Spartans, who had entered the war championing "the freedom of the Greeks," took over Athens's overseas empire until their own increasingly highhanded behavior aroused the opposition of other city-states. Indeed, the fourth century B.C.E. was a time of nearly continuous skirmishing among Greek states. One can make the case that the independent polis, from one point of view the glory of Greek culture, was also the fundamental structural flaw, because it fostered rivalry, fear, and mistrust among neighboring communities.

Internal conflict in the Greek world allowed the Persians to recoup old losses. By the terms of the King's Peace of 387 B.C.E., to which most of the states of war-weary Greece subscribed, all of western Asia, including the Greek communities of the Anatolian seacoast, were conceded to Persia. The Persian king became the guarantor of a status quo that kept the Greeks divided and weak. Luckily for the Greeks, rebellions in Egypt, Cyprus, and Phoenicia as well as trouble with some of the satraps in the western provinces diverted Persian attention from thoughts of another Greek invasion.

Meanwhile, in northern Greece developments were taking place that would irrevocably alter the balance of power in the eastern Mediterranean and western Asia. Philip II (r. 359–336 B.C.E.) was transforming his previously backward kingdom of Macedonia into the premier military power in the Greek world. (Although southern Greeks had long doubted the "Greekness" of the rough and rowdy Macedonians, modern scholarship is inclined to regard their language and culture as Greek at base, though much influenced by contact with non-Greek neighbors.) Philip had made a number of improvements to the traditional hoplite formation. He increased the striking power and mobility of his force by equipping his soldiers with longer thrusting spears and less armor. And, because horses thrived in the broad, grassy plains of the north, he experimented with the coordinated use of infantry and cavalry. His engineers had also developed new kinds of siege equipment, including the first catapults—machines using the power of twisted cords that, when relaxed, hurled arrows or stones great distances.

In 338 B.C.E. Philip defeated a coalition of southern states and established the Confederacy of Corinth as an instrument for controlling the Greek city-states. Philip had himself appointed military commander for a planned all-Greek campaign against Persia, and his generals established a bridgehead on the Asiatic side of the Hellespont. It appears that Philip was following the advice of Greek thinkers who had pondered the lessons of the Persian Wars of the fifth century B.C.E. and urged a crusade against the national enemy as a means of unifying their quarrelsome countrymen.

We will never know how far Philip's ambitions extended, for an assassin killed him in 336 B.C.E. When **Alexander** (356–323 B.C.E.), his son and heir, crossed over into Asia in 334 B.C.E., his avowed purpose was to exact revenge for Xerxes' invasion a century and half before. Alexander defeated the Persian forces in three pitched battles—against the satraps of the western provinces at the Granicus River in northwest Anatolia and against King Darius III (r. 336–330 B.C.E.) himself at Issus in southeast Anatolia and at Gaugamela°, north of Babylon (see Map 5.3).

Alexander the Great, as he came to be called, maintained the framework of Persian administration in the lands he conquered. He realized that it was well adapted to local circumstances and reassuringly familiar to the subject peoples. At first, however, he replaced Persian officials with his own Macedonian and Greek comrades. To control strategic points in his expanding empire, he established a series of Greek-style cities, beginning with Alexandria in Egypt, and he settled wounded and aged ex-soldiers in them. After his victory at Gaugamela (331 B.C.E.), he began to experiment with leaving cooperative Persian officials in place. He also admitted some Persians and other Iranians into his army and into the circle of his courtiers, and he adopted elements of Persian dress and court ceremonial. Finally, he married several Iranian women who had useful royal or aristocratic connections, and he pressed his leading subordinates to do the same.

Scholars have reached widely varying conclusions about why Alexander adopted policies that were so unexpected and so fiercely resented by the Macedonian nobility. It is probably wisest to see Alexander as operating from a combination of motives, both pragmatic and idealistic. He set off on his Asian campaign with visions of glory, booty, and revenge. But the farther east he traveled, the more he began to see himself as the legitimate successor of the Persian king (a claim facilitated by the death of Darius III at the hands of subordinates). Alexander may have recognized that he had responsibilities to all the diverse peoples who fell under his control. He also may have realized the difficulty of holding down so vast an empire by brute force and without the cooperation of important elements among the conquered peoples. In this, he was following the example of the Achaemenids.

THE HELLENISTIC SYNTHESIS

At the time of his sudden death in 323 B.C.E. at the age of thirty-two, Alexander apparently had made no plans for the succession. Thus his death ushered in a half-century of chaos as the most ambitious and ruthless of his officers struggled for control of the vast empire. When the dust cleared, the empire had been broken up

Gaugamela (GAW-guh-mee-luh)

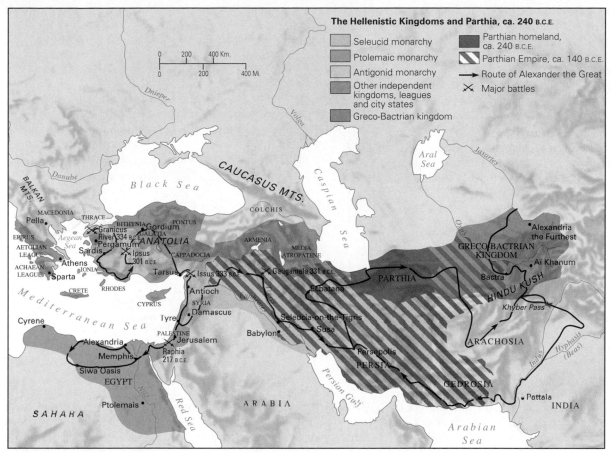

The Hellenistic Kingdoms and Parthia, ca. 240 B.C.E.

- Seleucid monarchy
- Ptolemaic monarchy
- Antigonid monarchy
- Other independent kingdoms, leagues and city states
- Greco-Bactrian kingdom
- Parthian homeland, ca. 240 B.C.E.
- Parthian Empire, ca. 140 B.C.E.
- → Route of Alexander the Great
- ✕ Major battles

Map 5.3   Hellenistic Civilization   After the death of Alexander the Great in 323 B.C.E., his vast empire soon split apart into a number of large and small political entities. A Macedonian dynasty was established on each continent: the Antigonids ruled the Macedonian homeland and tried with varying success to extend their control over southern Greece; the Ptolemies ruled Egypt; and the Seleucids inherited the majority of Alexander's conquests in Asia, though they lost control of the eastern portions because of the rise of the Parthians of Iran in the second century B.C.E. This period saw Greeks migrating in large numbers from their overcrowded homeland to serve as a privileged class of soldiers and administrators on the new frontiers, where they replicated the lifestyle of the city-state.

into three major kingdoms, each ruled by a Macedonian dynasty—the Seleucid°, Ptolemaic°, and Antigonid° kingdoms (see Map 5.3). Each major kingdom faced a unique set of problems, and although the three frequently were at odds with one another, a rough balance of power prevented any one of them from gaining the upper hand and enabled smaller states to survive by playing off the great powers.

Historians call the epoch ushered in by the conquests of Alexander the **"Hellenistic Age"** (323–30 B.C.E.), because the lands in northeastern Africa and western Asia that came under Greek rule tended to be "Hellenized"—that is, powerfully influenced by Greek culture. This was a period of large kingdoms with heterogeneous populations, great cities, powerful rulers, pervasive bureaucracies, and vast disparities in wealth between rich and poor—a far cry from the small, homogeneous, independent city-states of Archaic and Classical Greece. It was a cosmopolitan age of long-distance trade and communications, which saw the rise of new institutions like libraries and universities, new kinds of scholarship and science, and the cultivation of sophisticated tastes in art and literature. In many respects, in comparison with the preceding Classical era, it was a world much more like our own.

Seleucid (sih-LOO-sid)   **Ptolemaic** (tawl-uh-MAY-ik)
Antigonid (an-TIG-uh-nid)

Hellenistic Cameo, Second Century B.C.E.
This sardonyx cameo is an allegory of the
prosperity of Ptolemaic Egypt. At left, the
bearded river-god Nile holds a horn of plenty
while his wife, seated on a sphinx and dressed
like the Egyptian goddess Isis, raises a stalk of
grain. Their son, at center, carries a seed bag
and the shaft of a plow. The Seasons are
seated at right. Two wind-gods float overhead. The style is entirely Greek, but the
motifs are a blending of Greek and Egyptian
elements.   (G. Dagli-Orti, Paris)

Of all the successor states, the kingdom of the Seleucids, who took over the bulk of Alexander's conquests,
faced the greatest challenges. The Indus Valley and
Afghanistan soon split off, and over the course of the
third and second centuries B.C.E. Iran was lost to the
Parthians. What remained for the Seleucids was a core in
Mesopotamia, Syria, and parts of Anatolia, which the Seleucid monarchs ruled from their capital at Syrian Antioch. Their sprawling territories were open to attack from
many directions, and, like the Persians before them, they
had to administer lands inhabited by many different ethnic groups organized under various political and social
forms. In the countryside, where most of the native
peoples resided, the Seleucids maintained an administrative structure modeled on the Persian system. They
also continued Alexander's policy of founding Greek-
style cities throughout their domains. These cities served
as administrative centers and were also the lure that the
Seleucids used to attract colonists from Greece. The Seleucids desperately needed Greek soldiers, engineers,
administrators, and other professionals.

The dynasty of the **Ptolemies**° ruled Egypt and
sometimes laid claim to adjacent Palestine. The people

of Egypt belonged to only one ethnic group and were
fairly easily controlled because the vast majority of them
were farmers living in villages alongside the Nile. The
Ptolemies were able to take over much of the administrative structure of the pharaohs and to extract the surplus
wealth of this populous and productive land. The Egyptian economy was centrally planned and highly controlled. Vast revenues poured into the royal treasury
from rents (the king owned most of the land), taxes of all
sorts, and royal monopolies on olive oil, salt, papyrus,
and other key commodities.

The Ptolemies ruled from **Alexandria,** the first of the
new cities laid out by Alexander himself. The orientation
and status of this city says much about Ptolemaic policies and attitudes. Memphis and Thebes, the capitals of
ancient Egypt, had been located upriver. Alexandria was
situated near to where the westernmost branch of the
Nile runs into the Mediterranean Sea and clearly was
meant to be a link between Egypt and the Mediterranean
world. In the language of the Ptolemaic bureaucracy,
Alexandria was technically "beside Egypt" rather than in
it, as if to emphasize the gulf between rulers and subjects.

Like the Seleucids, the Ptolemies actively encouraged the immigration of Greeks from the homeland and,
in return for their skills and collaboration in the military

Ptolemies (TAWL-uh-meze)

or civil administration, gave them land and a privileged position in the new society. But the Ptolemies did not seek to plant Greek-style cities throughout the Egyptian countryside, and they made no effort to encourage the native population to adopt the Greek language or ways. In fact, so separate was the Greek ruling class from the subject population that only the last Ptolemy, Queen Cleopatra (r. 51–30 B.C.E.), even bothered to learn the language of the Egyptians. For the Egyptian peasant population laboring on the land, life was little changed by the advent of new masters. Yet from the early second century B.C.E., periodic native insurrections in the countryside, which government forces in cooperation with Greek and Hellenized settlers quickly stamped out, were signs of Egyptians' growing resentment of the Greeks' exploitation and arrogance.

In Europe, the Antigonid dynasty ruled the Macedonian homeland and adjacent parts of northern Greece. This was a compact and ethnically homogeneous kingdom, so there was little of the hostility and occasional resistance that the Seleucid and Ptolemaic ruling classes faced. Macedonian garrisons at strongpoints gave the Antigonids a toehold in central and southern Greece, and the shadow of Macedonian intervention always hung over the south. The southern states met the threat by banding together into confederations, such as the Achaean° League in the Peloponnese, in which the member-states maintained local autonomy but pooled resources and military power.

Athens and Sparta, the two leading cities of the Classical period, stood out from these confederations. The Spartans never quite abandoned the myth of their own invincibility and made a number of heroic but futile stands against Macedonian armies. Athens, which held a special place in the hearts of all Greeks because of the artistic and literary accomplishments of the fifth century B.C.E., pursued a foreign policy of neutrality. The city became a large museum, filled with the relics and memories of a glorious past, as well as a university town that attracted the children of the well-to-do from all over the Mediterranean and western Asia.

In an age of cities, the greatest city of all was Alexandria, with a population of nearly half a million. At the heart of this city was the royal compound, containing the palace and administrative buildings for the ruling dynasty and its massive bureaucracy. The centerpiece was the magnificent Mausoleum of Alexander. The first Ptolemy had stolen the body of Alexander while it was being brought back to Macedonia for burial. The theft

was a move aimed at gaining legitimacy for Ptolemaic rule by claiming the blessing of the great conqueror, who was declared to be a god.

Alexandria gained further luster from its famous Library, which had several hundred thousand volumes, and from its Museum, or "House of the Muses" (divinities who presided over the arts and sciences), a research institution that supported the work of the greatest poets, philosophers, doctors, and scientists of the day. Two harbors served the needs of the many trading ventures that linked the commerce of the Mediterranean with the Red Sea and Indian Ocean. A great lighthouse—the first of its kind, a multistory tower with a fiery beacon visible at a distance of 30 miles (48 kilometers)—was one of the wonders of the ancient world.

Greek residents of Alexandria enjoyed citizenship in a Greek-style polis with Assembly, Council, and officials who dealt with purely local affairs, and they took advantage of public works and institutions that signified the Greek way of life. Public baths and shaded arcades were places to relax and socialize with friends. Ancient plays were revived in the theaters, and musical performances and demonstrations of oratory took place in the concert halls. Gymnasiums offered facilities for exercise and fitness and were places where young men of the privileged classes were schooled in athletics, music, and literature. Jews had their own civic corporation, officials, and courts and predominated in two of the five main residential districts. Other quarters were filled with the sights, sounds, and smells of ethnic groups from Syria, Anatolia, and the Egyptian countryside.

In all the Hellenistic states, ambitious members of the indigenous populations learned the Greek language and adopted elements of the Greek way of life, because doing so put them in a position to become part of the privileged and wealthy ruling class. For the ancient Greeks, to be Greek was primarily a matter of language and lifestyle rather than physical traits. In the Hellenistic Age there was a spontaneous synthesis of Greek and indigenous ways. Egyptians migrated to Alexandria, and Greeks and Egyptians intermarried in the villages of the countryside. Greeks living amid the monuments and descendants of the ancient civilizations of Egypt and western Asia were exposed to the mathematical and astronomical wisdom of Mesopotamia, the elaborate mortuary rituals of Egypt, and the many attractions of foreign religious cults. With little official planning or blessing, stemming for the most part from the day-to-day experiences and actions of ordinary people, a great multicultural experiment unfolded as Greek and Middle Eastern cultural traits clashed and merged (see Society and Culture: Greeks and Egyptians in Hellenistic Egypt).

Achaean (uh-KEY-uhn)

Greeks and Egyptians in Hellenistic Egypt

Whatever may have been the intentions of Alexander the Great regarding his Greek and barbarian subjects, the Hellenistic rulers of Egypt had no policy of cultural and biological fusion. The city of Alexandria was essentially Greek in both architectual forms and civic institutions, though some ancient Egyptian monuments were recycled to ornament public spaces. Egyptians and other non-Greeks living there were expected to conform to Greek language and culture.

In the fields and villages of the countryside, however, the frequent interactions of Greek administrators, soldiers, and settlers with the indigenous Egyptian population led to unintended mixing of peoples and cultures. Thanks to the preservation of some papyrus documents in the hot, dry sands of Egypt, we have illustrations of such cross-cultural encounters. The following document is a legal petition to the king, dated in both the Macedonian and the Egyptian calendars.

To King Ptolemy, greeting from Philista daughter of Lysias, resident in Trikomia. I am wronged by Petechon. For as I was bathing in the baths of the aforesaid village on Tybi 7 of year 1, and had stepped out to soap myself, he being bathman in the women's rotunda and having brought in the jugs of hot water, emptied one over me and scalded my belly and my left thigh down to the knee, so that my life was in danger. On finding him, I gave him into the custody of Nechthosiris the chief policeman of the village in the presence of Simon the *epistates*. I beg you, therefore, O king, if it please you, as a suppliant who has sought your protection, not to suffer me, who am a working woman, to be thus lawlessly treated, but to order Diophanes to write to Simon the *epistates* and Nechthosiris the policeman that they are to bring Petechon before him in order that Diophanes may inquire into the case, hoping that having sought the protection of you, O king, the common benefactor of all, I may obtain justice. Farewell.

We can often identify who is Greek and who is Egyptian from the form of their names (although Greeks sometimes bear Egyptian names and vice versa). In this case, Philista is a Greek woman living in a rural village who was scalded (accidentally?) in the public bath house by Petechon, an Egyptian attendant. The village policeman, Nechthosiris, who arrests Petechon, is also an Egyptian, but he is subordinate to Greek officials—the local supervisor Simon and the judicial officer Diophanes. Although it is not clear what punishment or compensation Philista is seeking from the court, she has petitioned the king to make sure that her case is

---

CONCLUSION

Profound changes took place in the lands of the eastern Mediterranean and western Asia in the first millennium B.C.E. Persians and Greeks played pivotal roles. Let us compare the impacts of these two peoples and assess the broad significance of these centuries.

The empire of the Achaemenid Persians was the largest empire yet to appear in the world. It was also a new kind of empire because it encompassed such a wide variety of landscapes, peoples, and social, political, and economic systems. How did the Persians manage to hold together this diverse collection of lands for more than two centuries?

The answer did not lie entirely in brute force. The Persians lacked the manpower to install garrisons everywhere, and communication between the central administration and provincial officials was sporadic and slow. They managed to co-opt leaders among the subject peoples, who were willing to collaborate in return for being allowed to retain their power and influence. The Persian government demonstrated flexibility and tolerance in its handling of the laws, customs, and beliefs of subject peoples. Persian administration, superimposed on top of local structures, left a considerable role for local institutions.

The Persians also displayed a flair for public relations. The Zoroastrian religion underlined the authority of the king as the appointee of god and upholder of world order. In their art and inscriptions, the Persian kings broadcast an image of a benevolent empire in *dealt with. We see that Greeks are politically and socially superior to Egyptians, but it is interesting to note Philista's fear that her case will be ignored. We cannot tell whether her anxiety was prompted by the weakness of her case, the concern that a woman might not be taken seriously, or the general inefficiency of the judicial process.*

The following document is a letter from a wife to her husband.

Isias to her brother Hephaistion greeting. If you are well and other things are going right, it would accord with the prayer which I make continually to the gods. I myself and the child and all the household are in good health and think of you always. When I received your letter from Horos, in which you announce that you are in *katoche* in the Serapeum at Memphis, for the news that you are well I straightaway thanked the gods, but about your not coming home, when all the others who had been secluded there have come, I am ill-pleased, because after having piloted myself and your child through such bad times and been driven to every extremity owing to the price of wheat, I thought that now at least, with you at home, I should enjoy some respite, whereas you have not even thought of coming home nor given any regard to our circumstances, remembering how I was in want of everything while you were still here, not to mention this long lapse of time and these critical days, during which you have sent us nothing. As, moreover, Horos who delivered the letter has brought news of your having been released from detention, I am thoroughly ill-pleased. Notwithstanding, as your mother is also annoyed, for her sake as well as for mine please return to the city, if

nothing more pressing holds you back. You will do me a favor by taking care of your bodily health. Farewell.

Isias and her husband Hephaistion are probably Greeks and live in the city, but their lives also reflect the influence of Egyptian culture. Isias may be using Egyptian custom in referring to her husband as "her brother," though it is also possible that brother and sister have married, also an Egyptian practice. Hephaistion has voluntarily confined himself for a time in the sanctuary of the god Serapis at the ancient Egyptian capital of Memphis. Serapis was a creation of the Ptolemies, combining Greek practices with elements of the cult of the Egyptian god of death and rebirth, Osiris. Beyond that, we hear echoes of the timeless complaints of women who have been neglected or abandoned by irresponsible mates.

Here, as so often in the papyruses of Hellenistic Egypt, we have a rare opportunity to view everyday events in the lives of ordinary people. What do these two documents suggest about the freedoms and limitations of women in Hellenistic society? In what ways was the lifestyle of Greeks in Ptolemaic Egypt influenced by contact with the indigenous Egyptian population?

Source: Translations from Roger S. Bagnall and Peter Derow, *Greek Historical Documents: The Hellenistic Period* (Chico, CA: Scholar's Press, 1981), 195, 235. Adapted and reprinted from *Greek Historical Documents: The Hellenistic Period,* trans. by Roger S. Ragnall and Peter Derow. Sources for Biblical Studies Series #16. Copyright 1981 by the Society of Biblical Literature.

which the dependent peoples contributed to the welfare of the realm. Certain peoples with long and proud traditions, such as the Egyptians and Babylonians, revolted from time to time. But most subjects found the Persians to be decent enough masters and a great improvement over earlier Middle Eastern empires such as that of the Assyrians.

Western Asia underwent significant changes in the period of Persian supremacy. First, the early Persian kings put an end to the ancient centers of power in Mesopotamia, Anatolia, and Egypt. Then, by imposing a uniform system of law and administration and by providing security and stability, the Persian government fostered commerce and prosperity, at least for some. Some historians have argued that this period was a turning point in the economic history of western Asia. The Achaemenid government possessed an unprecedented

capacity to organize labor on a large scale, for the purposes of constructing an expanded water distribution network and working the extensive estates of the Persian royal family and nobility. The Persian "paradise" was not only the symbol but also the proof of the connection between political authority and the productivity of the earth.

Most difficult to assess is the cultural impact of Persian rule. The long-dominant culture of Mesopotamia fused with some Iranian elements. The resulting new synthesis is most visible in the art, architecture, and inscriptions of the Persian monarchs. The lands east of the Zagros Mountains as far as northwest India were brought within this cultural sphere. It has been suggested that the Zoroastrian religion spread across the empire and influenced other religious traditions, such as Judaism, but it does not appear that Zoroastrianism had broad, popular appeal. The Persian administration relied heavily on the scribes and written languages of its Mesopotamian, Syrian, and Egyptian subjects, and literacy remained the preserve of a small, professional class. Thus the Persian language does not seem to have been widely adopted by inhabitants of the empire. And even if there was a greater degree of Persianization in the provinces than is suggested by the extant evidence, it was so thoroughly swamped by Hellenism in the succeeding era that few traces are left.

Nearly two centuries of trouble with the Greeks on their western frontier were a vexation for the Persians but probably not their first priority. It appears that Persian kings were always more concerned about the security of their eastern and northeastern frontiers, where they were vulnerable to attack by the nomads of Central Asia. The technological differences between Greece and Persia were not great. The only difference that seems to have been of much significance was a set of arms and a military formation used by the Greeks that often allowed them to prevail over the Persians. The Persian king's response in the later fifth and fourth centuries B.C.E. was to hire Greek mercenaries to use hoplite tactics for his benefit. The claim is sometimes made that the Persian Empire was weak and crumbling by the time Alexander invaded, but there is little evidence for this, and no one could have anticipated the charismatic leadership and boundless ambition of Alexander of Macedonia.

The shadow of Persia loomed large over the affairs of the Greek city-states for more than two centuries, and even after the repulse of Xerxes' great expeditionary force there was a perpetual fear of another Persian invasion. The victories in 480 and 479 B.C.E. did allow the Greek city-states to continue to evolve politically and culturally at a critical time. Athens, in particular, vaulted into power, wealth, and intense cultural creativity as a result of its role in the Greek victory. It evolved into a new kind of Greek state, upsetting the rough equilibrium of the Archaic period by threatening the autonomy of other city-states and changing the rules of war. The result was the Peloponnesian War, which squandered lives and resources for a generation, raised serious doubts about the viability of the city-state, and diminished many people's allegiance to it.

Alexander's conquests brought to the Greek world changes almost as radical as those suffered by the Persians. Greeks spilled out into the sprawling new frontiers in northeastern Africa and western Asia, and the independent city-state became inconsequential in a world of large kingdoms. The centuries of Greek domination had a far more pervasive cultural impact on the Middle East than did the Persian period. Alexander had been in-

clined to preserve the Persian administrative apparatus, leaving native institutions and personnel in place. His successors relied almost exclusively on a privileged class of Greek soldiers, officers, and administrators.

Equally significant were the foundation of Greek-style cities, which exerted a powerful cultural influence on important elements of the native populations, and a system of easily learned alphabetic Greek writing, which led to more widespread literacy and far more effective dissemination of information. The end result of all this was that the Greeks had a profound impact on the peoples and lands of the Middle East, and Hellenism persisted as a cultural force for a thousand years. As we shall see in the next chapter, the Romans who arrived in the eastern Mediterranean in the second century B.C.E. were greatly influenced by the cultural and political practices of the Hellenistic kingdoms.

■ Key Terms

Cyrus	Herodotus
Darius I	Pericles
satrap	Persian Wars
Persepolis	trireme
Zoroastrianism	Socrates
polis	Peloponnesian War
hoplite	Alexander
tyrant	Hellenistic Age
democracy	Ptolemies
sacrifice	Alexandria

■ Suggested Reading

The most accessible treatment of the Persian Empire is J. M. Cook, *The Persian Empire* (1983). Josef Wiesehofer, *Ancient Persia: From 550 B.C. to 650 A.D.* (1996); Richard N. Frye, *The History of Ancient Iran* (1984); and volume 2 of *The Cambridge History of Iran*, ed. Ilya Gershevitch (1985), are written by Iranian specialists and have abundant bibliography. John Curtis, *Ancient Persia* (1989), emphasizes the archaeological record. Roland G. Kent, *Old Persian: Grammar, Texts, Lexicon*, 2d ed. (1953), contains translations of the royal inscriptions.

Maria Brosius, *Women in Ancient Persia, 559–331 B.C.* (1996), gathers and evaluates the scattered evidence. William W. Malandra, *An Introduction to Ancient Iranian Religion: Readings from the Avesta and Achaemenid Inscriptions* (1983), contains documents in translation pertaining to religious subjects. Vesta Sarkhosh Curtis, *Persian Myths* (1993), is a concise, illustrated introduction to Iranian myths and legends.

The fullest treatment of Greek history and civilization in this period is in *The Cambridge Ancient History*, 3d ed., vols. 3–7 (1970–). Sarah B. Pomeroy, Stanley M. Burstein, Walter Donlan, and Jennifer Tolbert Roberts, *Ancient Greece: A Political, Social, and Cultural History* (1999), is a fine one-volume treatment of Greek civilization. Others include J. B. Bury and Russell Meiggs, *A History of Greece* (1975), and Nancy Demand, *A History of Ancient Greece* (1996*)*. For the Archaic period see Oswyn Murray, *Early Greece,* 2d ed. (1993), and Robin Osborne, *Greece in the Making, 1200–479 B.C.* (1996).

Social history is emphasized by Frank J. Frost, *Greek Society,* 3d ed. (1987). Peter Levi, *Atlas of the Greek World* (1980), is filled with maps and pictures. Michael Grant and Rachel Kitzinger, eds., *Civilization of the Ancient Mediterranean* (1987), is a three-volume collection of essays by contemporary experts on nearly every aspect of ancient Greco-Roman civilization and includes up-to-date bibliographies.

We are fortunate to have an abundant written literature from ancient Greece, and the testimony of the ancients themselves should be the starting point for any inquiry. Herodotus, Thucydides, and Xenophon chronicled the history of the Greeks and their Middle Eastern neighbors from the sixth through fourth centuries B.C.E. Arrian, who lived in the second century C.E., provides the most useful account of the career of Alexander the Great. Among the many collections of documents in translation, see Michael Crawford and David Whitehead, eds., *Archaic and Classical Greece: A Selection of Ancient Sources in Translation* (1983). David G. Rice and John E. Stambaugh, eds., *Sources for the Study of Greek Religion* (1979); Mary R. Lefkowitz and Maureen B. Fant, eds., *Women's Life in Greece and Rome: A Source Book in Translation* (1982); Thomas Wiedemann, ed., *Greek and Roman Slavery* (1981); and Michael Gagarin and Paul Woodruff, *Early Greek Political Thought from Homer to the Sophists* (1995), are specialized collections.

Victor Davis Hanson, *The Other Greeks: The Family Farm and the Agrarian Roots of Western Civilization* (1995), emphasizes the centrality of farming to the development of Greek institutions and values. Eric A. Havelock, *The Muse Learns to Write: Reflections on Orality and Literacy from Antiquity to the Present* (1986), explores the profound impacts of alphabetic literacy on the Greek mind.

Valuable treatments of other key topics include Elaine Fantham, Helene Peet Foley, Natalie Boymel Kampen, Sarah B. Pomeroy, and H. Alan Shapiro, *Women in the Classical World* (1994); Cynthia Patterson, *The Family in Greek History* (1998); Yvon Garlan, *Slavery in Ancient Greece* (1988); Walter Burkert, *Greek Religion* (1985); Victor Davis Hanson, *The Western Way of War: Infantry Battle in Classical Greece* (1989); Lionel Casson, *The Ancient Mariners: Seafarers and Sea Fighters of the Mediterranean in Ancient Times,* 2d ed. (1991); Michail Yu Treister, *The Role of Metals in Ancient Greek History* (1996); Joint Association of Classical Teachers, *The World of Athens: An Introduction to Classical Athenian Culture* (1984); N. G. L. Hammond, *The Macedonian State: The Origins, Institutions and History* (1989); Joseph Roisman, ed., *Alexander the Great: Ancient and Modern Perspectives* (1995); and William R. Biers, *The Archaeology of Greece: An Introduction* (1990). Mary R. Lefkowitz and Guy MacLean Rogers, *Black Athena Revisited* (1996), explores the controversies surrounding the Greek cultural obligation to Egypt and western Asia. Jack Martin Balcer, *Sparda by the Bitter Sea: Imperial Interaction in Western Anatolia* (1984), is a study of the interaction of Greeks and Persians.

For the Hellenistic world see F. W. Walbank, *The Hellenistic World,* rev. ed. (1993), and Michael Grant, *From Alexander to Cleopatra: The Hellenistic World* (1982). M. M. Austin, ed., *The Hellenistic World from Alexander to the Roman Conquest: A Selection of Ancient Sources in Translation* (1981), provides sources in translation. Jean-Yves Empereur, *Alexandria Rediscovered* (1998), summarizes exciting new finds from the palace precinct in the waters off Alexandria.

■ Notes

1. Quoted in Roland G. Kent, *Old Persian: Grammar, Texts, Lexicon,* 2d ed. (New Haven, CT: American Oriental Society, 1953), 138, 140.
2. Richmond Lattimore, *Greek Lyrics,* 2d ed. (Chicago: University of Chicago Press, 1960), 2.
3. G. S. Kirk and J. E. Raven, *The Presocratic Philosophers: A Critical History with a Selection of Texts* (Cambridge, England: Cambridge University Press, 1957), 169.
4. Herodotus, *The History,* trans. David Grene (Chicago: University of Chicago Press, 1988), 33. (Herodotus 1.1)
5. Plutarch, *Pericles* 12, trans. Ian Scott-Kilvert, *The Rise and Fall of Athens: Nine Greek Lives by Plutarch* (Harmondsworth: Penguin Books, 1960), 178.

AN AGE OF EMPIRES: ROME AND HAN CHINA,

753 B.C.E.–330 C.E.

Rome's Creation of a Mediterranean Empire, 753 B.C.E.–330 C.E. • **The Origins of Imperial China, 221 B.C.E.–220 C.E.** • **Imperial Parallels**

ENVIRONMENT AND TECHNOLOGY: Water Engineering in Rome and China

SOCIETY AND CULTURE: Slavery in Rome and China

Terracotta Soldiers from the Tomb of Shi Huangdi, "First Emperor" of China
Thousands of these life-size, baked-clay figures—each with distinctive features—have been unearthed.

According to Chinese sources, in the year 166 C.E. a group of travelers identifying themselves as delegates from Andun, the king of distant Da Qin, arrived at the court of the Chinese emperor Huan, one of the Han rulers. Andun was Marcus Aurelius Antoninus, the emperor of Rome.

As far as we know, these travelers were the first "Romans" to reach China, although they probably were not natives of the Italian peninsula but residents of one of the eastern provinces of the Roman Empire, perhaps Egypt or Syria. They may have stretched the truth in claiming to be official representatives of the Roman emperor. More likely they were merchants hoping to set up a profitable trading arrangement at the source of the silk so highly prized in the West. Chinese officials, however, were in no position to disprove their claim, since there was no direct contact between the Roman and Chinese Empires.

We do not know what became of these travelers, and their mission apparently did not lead to any more direct or regular contact between the empires at opposite ends of the vast Eurasian landmass. Even so, the episode raises some interesting points. First, it is clear that in the early centuries C.E. Rome and China were linked by far-flung international trading networks encompassing the entire Eastern Hemisphere, and were dimly aware of each other's existence. Second, the period of the last centuries B.C.E. and the first centuries C.E. saw the emergence of two manifestations of a new kind of empire.

The Roman and Han Chinese Empires were both quantitatively and qualitatively different from earlier empires. The Roman Empire encompassed all the lands surrounding the Mediterranean Sea as well as substantial portions of continental Europe and the Middle East. The Han Empire stretched from the Pacific Ocean to the oases of Central Asia. They were the largest empires the world had yet seen, extending over a greater diversity of lands and peoples than the Assyrian and Persian Empires in the Middle East and the Mauryan Empire in India. Yet they were able to centralize control to a greater degree than the earlier empires, their cultural impact on the lands and peoples they dominated was more pervasive, and they were remarkably stable and lasted for many centuries.

Thousands of miles separated the empires of Rome and Han China; neither one influenced the other. Why did two such unprecedented political entities flourish at the same time? Historians have put forth theories stressing supposedly common factors operating in both places—such as climate change or the pressure of nomadic peoples from Central Asia on the Roman and Chinese frontiers—but no theory has won the support of most scholars.

As you read this chapter, ask yourself the following questions:

- How did the Roman and Han Empires come into being?
- What were the sources of their stability or instability?
- What benefits and liabilities did these empires bring to the rulers and their subjects?

ROME'S CREATION OF A MEDITERRANEAN EMPIRE, 753 B.C.E.–330 C.E.

Rome's central location contributed to its success in unifying first Italy and then all the lands ringing the Mediterranean Sea (see Map 6.1). The middle of three peninsulas that jut from the European landmass into the Mediterranean, the boot-shaped Italian peninsula and the large island of Sicily constitute a natural bridge almost linking Europe and North Africa. Italy was a crossroads in the Mediterranean, and the site of Rome was a crossroads within Italy. Rome lay at the midpoint of the peninsula, about 15 miles (24 kilometers) from the western coast, where a north-south road intersected an east-west river route. The Tiber River on one side and a double ring of seven hills on the other afforded natural protection to the site.

The developing Roman state drew on the considerable natural resources of the peninsula. Italy is a land of

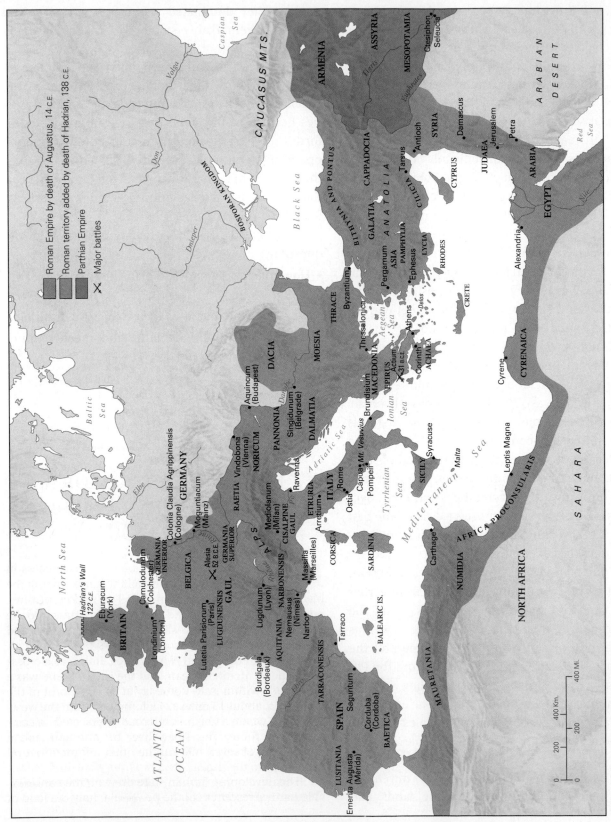

Map 6.1 The Roman Empire The Roman Empire came to encompass all the lands surrounding the Mediterranean Sea, as well as parts of continental Europe. When Augustus died in 14 C.E., he left instructions to his successors not to expand beyond the limits he had set, but Claudius invaded southern Britain in the mid-first century and the soldier-emperor Trajan added Romania early in the second century. Deserts and seas provided solid natural boundaries, but the long and vulnerable river border in central and eastern Europe would eventually prove expensive to defend and vulnerable to invasion by Germanic and Central Asian peoples.

CHRONOLOGY

	Rome	China
1000 B.C.E.	**1000 B.C.E.** First settlement on site of Rome	
500 B.C.E.	**507 B.C.E.** Establishment of the Republic	
		480–221 B.C.E. Warring States Period
300 B.C.E.	**290 B.C.E.** Defeat of tribes of Samnium gives Romans control of Italy	
	264–202 B.C.E. Wars against Carthage guarantee Roman control of western Mediterranean	**221 B.C.E.** Qin emperor unites eastern China
200 B.C.E.	**200–146 B.C.E.** Wars against Hellenistic kingdoms lead to control of eastern Mediterranean	**206 B.C.E.** Han dynasty succeeds Qin
		140–87 B.C.E. Emperor Wu expands the Han Empire
100 B.C.E.	**88–31 B.C.E.** Civil wars and failure of the Republic	
	31 B.C.E.–14 C.E. Augustus establishes the Principate	**23 C.E.** Han capital transfered from Chang'an to Luoyang
50 C.E.	**45–58 C.E.** Paul spreads Christianity in the eastern Mediterranean	
200 C.E.		
		220 C.E. Fall of Han Empire
	235–284 C.E. Third-century crisis	
300 C.E.	**324 C.E.** Constantine moves capital to Constantinople	

hills and mountains. The Apennine range runs along its length like a spine, separating the eastern and western coastal plains, while the arc of the Alps shields it on the north. Many of the rivers of Italy are navigable, and passes through the Apennines and even through the snowcapped Alps allowed merchants and armies to travel overland. The mild Mediterranean climate affords a long growing season and conditions suitable for a wide variety of crops. The hillsides, largely denuded of cover today, were well forested in ancient times, providing tim-

ber for construction and fuel. The region of Etruria in the northwest was rich in iron and other metals.

Even though as much as 75 percent of the total area of the Italian peninsula is hilly, there is still ample arable land in the coastal plains and river valleys. Much of this land has extremely fertile volcanic soil and sustained a much larger population than was possible in Greece. While expanding within Italy, the Roman state created effective mechanisms for tapping the human resources of the countryside.

A Republic of Farmers

According to popular legend, the city of Rome was founded in 753 B.C.E. by Romulus, who, as a baby, was cast adrift on the Tiber River and nursed by a she-wolf. Archaeological research, however, shows that the earliest occupation of the Palatine Hill—one of the seven hills on the site of Rome—took place as early as 1000 B.C.E. The merging of several hilltop communities to form an urban nucleus, made possible by the draining of a swamp on the site of the future Roman Forum (civic center), took place shortly before 600 B.C.E.

The original inhabitants of the site, with their Latin speech and cultural patterns, were typical of the indigenous population of most of the peninsula. Tradition remembered the arrival of Etruscan immigrants in the seventh century B.C.E and proudly acknowledged the early community as a destination for exiles and outcasts of various nationalities.

Agriculture was the essential economic activity in the early Roman state, and land was the basis of wealth. As a consequence, social status, political privilege, and fundamental values were related to landownership. The vast majority of early Romans were self-sufficient independent farmers owning small plots of land. A relatively small number of families managed to acquire large tracts of land. The heads of these wealthy families were members of the Senate—a "Council of Elders"—that played a dominant role in the politics of the Roman state. These wealthy families constituted the senatorial class.

According to tradition, between 753 and 507 B.C.E. there were seven kings of Rome. The first was Romulus; the last was the tyrannical Tarquinius Superbus. In 507 B.C.E. members of the senatorial class, led by Brutus "the Liberator," deposed Tarquinius Superbus and instituted a *res publica*, a "public possession," or republic.

The **Roman Republic,** which lasted from 507 to 31 B.C.E., was hardly a democracy. Sovereign power resided in several assemblies that male citizens were eligible to attend, but the votes of the wealthy classes counted for more than the votes of poor citizens. A slate of civic officials was elected each year, and a hierarchy of state offices evolved. The culmination of a political career was to be selected as one of the two consuls. The consuls presided over meetings of the Senate and assemblies and commanded the army on military campaigns.

The real center of power was the **Roman Senate.** Technically an advisory council, first to the kings and later to the annually changing Republican officials, the Senate increasingly made policy and governed. Senators nominated their sons for public offices and filled vacancies in the Senate from the ranks of former officials. This

Statue of a Roman Carrying Busts of his Ancestors, First Century B.C.E.   Roman society was extremely conscious of status, and the status of an elite Roman family was determined in large part by the public achievements of ancestors and living members. A visitor to a Roman home found portraits of distinguished ancestors in the entry hall, along with labels listing the offices they held. Portrait heads were carried in funeral processions. (Alinari/Art Resource, NY)

self-selected body, whose members served for life, was the repository of the wealth, influence, and political and military experience in the state.

The basic unit of Roman society was the family, consisting of several generations as well as the domestic slaves. Every member of the family was under the absolute authority of the oldest living male, the *paterfamil-*

ias. The head of the family and the most important male members of society as a whole were invested with _auctoritas_, the quality that enabled a man to inspire and demand obedience from his inferiors.

Roman society was unashamedly hierarchical. Individuals and families were connected by complex ties of obligation, such as the **patron/client relationship.** This fundamental social relationship existed between a _patron_, a man of wealth and influence, and a _client_, a man who sought a patron's help and protection. A senator might be the patron of dozens or even hundreds of men. He could provide his clients with legal advice and representation, physical protection, and loans of money in tough times. In turn, the client was expected to follow his patron out to battle, to support him in the political arena, to work on his land, and even to contribute toward the dowry of his daughter. A throng of clients awaited their patron in the morning and accompanied him from his house to the Forum for the day's business. A man with an especially large retinue enjoyed great prestige. Middle-class clients of the aristocracy might be patrons of poorer men. In sum, at Rome inequality was accepted, institutionalized, and turned into a system of mutual benefits and obligations.

Our sources do not often permit us to observe the activities of Roman women, largely because they played no public role. Nearly all our information about Roman women pertains to those in the upper classes. In early Rome, a woman never ceased to be a child in the eyes of the law. She started out under the absolute authority of her paterfamilias. When she married, she came under the jurisdiction of the paterfamilias of her husband's family. Unable to own property or represent herself in legal proceedings, she had to depend on a male guardian to advocate her interests.

However, despite the limitations put on them, Roman women seem less constrained than their counterparts in the Greek world (see Chapter 5). Over time they gained greater personal protection and economic freedom: for instance, some took advantage of a new form of marriage that left a woman under the jurisdiction of her father and independent after his death. There are many stories of strong women who had great influence on their husbands or sons and thereby helped to shape Roman history. Roman poets confess their love for women who appear to us to be educated and outspoken, and the accounts of the careers of the early emperors are filled with tales of self-assured and assertive queen-mothers and consorts.

How did the early Romans view the natural world and their place in it? Like other Italian peoples, they believed the world was filled with invisible, shapeless forces known as _numina_. Vesta, the living, pulsating energy of fire, dwelled in the hearth. Janus guarded the door. The Penates watched over food stored in the cupboard. Other deities resided in nearby hills, caves, grottoes, and springs. Small offerings of cakes and liquids were made to win the favor of these spirits. Certain gods had a larger sphere of operation—for example, Jupiter, the god of the sky, and Mars, initially a god of agriculture as well as war.

The Romans were especially concerned to maintain the _pax deorum_ ("peace of the gods"), a covenant between the gods and the Roman state. Boards of priests drawn from the aristocracy performed sacrifices and other rituals to win the gods' favor. In return, the gods were expected to bring success to the undertakings of the Roman state. When the Romans came into contact with the Greeks of southern Italy (see Chapter 5), they equated their major deities with gods from the Greek pantheon, such as Zeus (Jupiter) and Ares (Mars), and they took over the myths attached to the Greek gods.

Expansion in Italy and the Mediterranean

At the dawn of the Roman Republic, around 500 B.C.E., Rome was a relatively insignificant city-state among many in the region of central Italy called Latium. Three-and-a-half centuries later Rome was the center of a huge empire encompassing virtually all the lands surrounding the Mediterranean Sea. Expansion began slowly but picked up momentum, reaching a peak in the third and second centuries B.C.E.

Scholars have long debated the forces that propelled this expansion. Some credit the greed and aggressiveness of a people fond of war. Others observe that the structure of the Roman state encouraged recourse to war, because the two consuls had only one year in office in which to gain glory through a military command. The Romans invariably claimed that they were only defending themselves. A case can be made that fear drove the Romans to expand the territory under their control in order to provide a buffer against attack: each new conquest became vulnerable, and a sense of insecurity led to further expansion. In any event, the Romans were quick to seize any opportunities that presented themselves.

Rome's conquest of Italy was sparked by ongoing friction between the pastoral hill tribes of the Apennines, whose livelihood depended on their ability to drive their herds to seasonal grazing grounds, and the agriculturalists of the coastal plains. In the fifth century B.C.E. Rome rose to a position of leadership within a league of central Italian cities organized for defense against the hill tribes.

In the fourth century B.C.E. the Romans were called in on several occasions to defend the wealthy and sophisticated cities of Campania, the region on the Bay of Naples possessing the richest farmland in the peninsula. By 290 B.C.E., in the course of three wars with the tribes of Samnium, in central Italy, the Romans had extended their "protection" over nearly the entire peninsula.

One key to the Romans' success in consolidating their hold over Italy was their willingness to grant the political, legal, and economic privileges of Roman citizenship to conquered populations. In this they contrasted sharply with the Greeks, who were reluctant to share the privileges of citizenship with outsiders (see Chapter 5). In essence, the Romans co-opted the most influential elements within the conquered communities and made Rome's interests their interests. Rome demanded that its Italian subjects provide soldiers for the Roman military. A seemingly inexhaustible reservoir of manpower was a key element of Rome's military success. In a number of crucial wars Rome was able to endure higher casualties than the enemy and to prevail by sheer numbers.

Between 264 and 202 B.C.E. Rome fought two protracted and bloody wars against the Carthaginians, those energetic descendants of Phoenicians from Lebanon who had settled in present-day Tunisia and dominated the waters and commerce of the western Mediterranean (see Chapter 4). In the end, the Roman state emerged as the unchallenged master of the western Mediterranean and acquired its first overseas provinces in Sicily, Sardinia, and Spain (see Map 6.1). Between 200 and 146 B.C.E. a series of wars pitted the Roman state against the major Hellenistic kingdoms in the eastern Mediterranean. The Romans were at first reluctant to occupy such distant territories and withdrew their troops at the conclusion of several wars. But when the settlements that they imposed failed to take root, a frustrated Roman government took over direct administration of these turbulent lands.

To this point Rome's territorial acquisitions were all in the Mediterranean. However, the conquest of the Celtic peoples of Gaul (modern France; see Chapter 4) by Rome's most brilliant general, Gaius Julius Caesar, between 59 and 51 B.C.E., led to the first occupation of land in the continental heartland of Europe and presented new challenges of administration and defense.

At first the Romans did not find it feasible to extend to the distant provinces the system of governance and the privileges of citizenship rights that they employed in Italy. But considerable autonomy, including responsibility for local administration and tax collection, was given to indigenous elite groups willing to collaborate with the Roman authorities. In addition, every year a member of the Senate, usually someone who recently had held a high public post, was dispatched to each province to serve as governor. The governor took with him a surprisingly small retinue of friends and relations to serve as advisers and deputies. His primary responsibilities were to defend the province against outside attack and internal disruption, to oversee the collection of taxes and other revenues due Rome, and to decide legal cases.

Over time this system of provincial administration proved inadequate. Officials were chosen because of their political connections at Rome and often lacked competence or experience. Yearly changes of governor meant that the incumbent had little time to gain experience or make local contacts. Although many governors were honest, some were notoriously unscrupulous and extorted huge sums of money from the provincial populace. While governing an ever-larger Mediterranean empire, the Romans were still relying on the institutions and attitudes that had developed when Rome was merely a city-state.

The Failure of the Republic

The spectacular achievement of Rome in creating an empire of unprecedented proportions unleashed powerful forces that eventually brought down the Republican system of government. As a result of the frequent wars and territorial expansion of the third and second centuries B.C.E., profound changes were taking place in the Italian landscape. Two factors were driving this complex process: (1) Italian peasant farmers were away from home on military service for long periods of time, and (2) most of the wealth generated by the conquest and control of new provinces ended up in the hands of the upper classes, who were eager to funnel the profits of empire into the purchase of Italian land. While the soldier-farmers were away, it was easy for investors to take possession of their farms by purchase, deception, or intimidation. As a result, the small, self-sufficient peasant farms of the Italian countryside, from which had come the soldiers who were the backbone of the Roman legions (units of 6,000 soldiers), were replaced by *latifundia*, literally "broad estates," or ranches.

The owners of these large estates found it more lucrative to graze herds of cattle or to grow crops—such as grapes for wine—that brought in a big profit than to grow wheat, the staple food of ancient Italy. Thus large segments of the population of Italy, especially in the burgeoning cities, became dependent on expensive imported grain. Meanwhile, peasants who had lost their farms and could not find work in the countryside because of the cheapness of slave labor (a result of large numbers of prisoners captured in Rome's wars—see Society and Culture: Slavery in Rome and China) moved to Rome and other cities. But they found no work in the cities either and ended up living in dire poverty. The growing urban masses, idle and prone to riot, would play a major role in the political struggles of the late Republic.

A critical factor contributing to the Senate's loss of authority was a change in the composition of the Roman army. One consequence of the decline of peasant farmers in Italy was a shortage of men who owned the minimum amount of property required for eligibility to serve in the military. This shortage was felt acutely during a war that the Romans fought in North Africa at the end of the second century B.C.E. Gaius Marius—a "new man" as the Romans labeled politically active individuals who did not belong to the traditional ruling class—achieved political prominence by accepting into the Roman legions poor, propertyless men and promising to give them farms when they retired from military service. These troops became devoted to the man who guaranteed their future, and they helped him get elected to an unprecedented (and illegal) six consulships.

Between 88 and 31 B.C.E., a series of ambitious individuals—Sulla, Pompey, Julius Caesar, Mark Antony, and Octavian—commanded armies whose primary loyalties were to their generals rather than to the state. These men did not hesitate to use Roman troops to increase their personal power and influence. A number of bloody civil wars pitted Roman army against Roman army. The city of Rome itself was taken by force on several occasions, and victorious commanders executed their political opponents and exercised dictatorial control of the state.

Julius Caesar's grandnephew and heir, Octavian (63 B.C.E.–14 C.E.), eliminated all rivals by 31 B.C.E. and painstakingly set about refashioning the Roman system of government. He fundamentally altered the realities of power but was careful to maintain the forms of the Republic—the offices, honors, and social prerogatives of the senatorial class. A military dictator in fact, he never called himself king or emperor, claiming merely to be *princeps*, "first among equals" in a restored Republic. For this reason it is conventional to refer to the period following the Roman Republic as the **Roman Principate.** *Augustus,* one of the many honorific titles that the Roman Senate gave Octavian, combines connotations of prosperity and piety and became the name by which he is best known to posterity. Augustus succeeded thanks to a combination of ruthlessness, patience, and his intuitive grasp of the psychology of all elements of Roman society, which enabled him to manipulate each group in turn. He also had the good sense to live a long time.

Base and Lower Registers of Trajan's Column   The Roman emperor Trajan erected this soaring (125-foot, 38-meter) marble column in Rome in the early second century C.E. to commemorate his triumphant campaign in Dacia (modern Romania). The relief carving, which snakes around the column for 656 feet (200 meters), illustrates numerous episodes of the conquest and provides a detailed pictorial record of the uniforms, weaponry, equipment, procedures, rituals, and conduct of the Roman army in the field. (Scala/Art Resource, NY)

When he died in 14 C.E., after forty-five years of carefully veiled rule, almost no one was still alive who could remember the Republic. During his reign Egypt and parts of the Middle East and Central Europe were added to the empire (the only significant later additions were the southern half of Britain and modern Romania).

So popular was Augustus when he died that four members of his family succeeded to the position of "emperor" (as we may call it) despite their serious personal and political shortcomings. The emperorship was never automatically regarded as a hereditary privilege, and

SOCIETY & CULTURE

Slavery in Rome and China

Although slaves were to be found in most ancient societies, Rome was one of the few historical societies in which slave labor became the indispensable foundation of the economy. In the course of the frequent wars of the second century B.C.E., *large numbers of prisoners were carried into slavery. The cost of purchasing such slaves was low, and landowners and manufacturers found they could compel slaves to work longer and harder than hired laborers. Periodically, the harsh working and living conditions resulted in slave revolts.*

The following excerpt, from one of several surviving manuals on agriculture, gives advice about controlling and efficiently exploiting slaves:

When the head of a household arrives at his estate, after he has prayed to the family god, he must go round his farm on a tour of inspection on the very same day, if that is possible.

. . . On the next day after that he must call in his manager. . . . If the work doesn't seem to him to be sufficient, and the manager starts to say how hard he tried, but the slaves weren't any good, and the weather was awful, and the slaves ran away, and he was required to carry out some public works, then when he has finished mentioning these and all sorts of other excuses, you must draw his attention to your calculation of the labor employed and time taken. . . . There are all sorts of jobs that can be done in rainy weather—washing wine-jars, coating them with pitch, cleaning the house, storing grain, shifting muck, digging a manure pit, cleaning seed, mending ropes or making new ones. . . . The head of the household . . . should sell any old oxen, cattle or sheep that are not up to standard, wool and hides, an old cart or old tools, an old slave, a sick slave—anything else that is surplus to requirements. (Cato the Elder, *Concerning Agriculture*, bk. 2, second century B.C.E.)

Cato, the Roman author of that excerpt, equated slaves with other property such as animals and tools, and in his calculations of productivity he did not take into account the slaves' feelings. Cato was notorious among his contemporaries for his stern manner and hard-edged traditionalism, and he expresses a point of view that Roman society found acceptable. In reality, the treatment of slaves by Roman masters varied as widely as does the treatment of employees by bosses in our society. Cato also indicates some of the passive-resistance tactics that slaves resorted to—feigning ignorance and stupidity, claiming to be ill, and running away.

---

after the mid-first century C.E. other families obtained the post. In theory the early emperors were affirmed by the Senate. In reality they were chosen by the armies. By the second century C.E. a new mechanism of succession had been worked out by the so-called Good Emperors of that era: each designated as his successor a mature man of proven ability whom he adopted as his son and with whom he shared offices and privileges.

Augustus had allied himself with the *equites,* the class of well-to-do Italian merchants and landowners second in wealth and social status only to the senatorial class. This body of competent and self-assured individuals became the core of a new civil service that helped to run the Roman Empire. At last Rome had an administrative bureaucracy up to the task of managing a large empire with considerable honesty, consistency, and efficiency.

An Urban Empire

The Roman Empire of the first three centuries C.E. was an "urban" empire. This term does not mean that most people were living in cities and towns. Perhaps 80 percent of the 50 million to 60 million people living within the borders of the empire engaged in agriculture and lived in villages or on isolated farms in the countryside. The empire, however, was administered through a network of towns and cities and brought the greatest benefits to the urban populace.

The number of people living in urban centers varied widely. Numerous towns had perhaps several thousand inhabitants. A handful of major cities—Alexandria in Egypt, Antioch in Syria, and Carthage—had populations of several hundred thousand. Rome itself had approximately a million residents. The largest cities put a huge strain on the limited technological capabilities of the

Slavery was far less prominent in ancient China. During the Warring States Period, dependent peasants as well as slaves worked the large holdings of the landowning aristocracy. The Qin government sought to abolish slavery, but the institution persisted into the Han period, although it involved only a small fraction of the population and was not a central component of the economy. The relatives of criminals could be seized and enslaved, and poor families sometimes sold unwanted children into slavery. In China, slaves generally performed domestic tasks, whether they belonged to the state or to individuals.

Wang Ziyuan of Shu Commandery went to the Jian River on business, and went up to the home of the widow Yang Hui, who had a male slave named Bianliao. Wang Ziyuan requested him to go and buy some wine. Picking up a big stick, Bianliao climbed to the top of the grave mound and said: "When my master bought me, Bianliao, he only contracted for me to care for the grave and did not contract for me to buy wine for some other gentleman."

Wang Ziyuan was furious and said to the widow: "Wouldn't you prefer to sell this slave?". . . Wang Ziyuan immediately settled on the sale contract. . . .

The slave again said: "Enter in the contract everything you wish to order me to do. I, Bianliao, will not do anything not in the contract."

Wang Ziyuan said: "Agreed."

The text of the contract said: . . . The slave shall obey orders about all kinds of work and may not argue. He shall rise at dawn and do an early sweeping. After eating he shall wash up. Ordinarily he should pound the grain mortar, tie up broom straws, carve bowls and bore wells, scoop out ditches, tie up fallen fences, hoe the garden, trim up paths and dike up plots of land, cut big flails, bend bamboos to make rakes, and scrape and fix the well pulley . . . [the list of tasks continues for two-and-a-half pages]. . . .

The reading of the text of the contract came to an end. The slave was speechless and his lips were tied. Wildly he beat his head on the ground, and beat himself with his hands. He said: "If it is to be exactly as master Wang says, I would rather return soon along the yellow-soil road, with the grave worms boring through my head. Had I known before I would have bought the wine for master Wang." (Wang Bao, first century B.C.E.)

This story shows that Chinese slaves could be forced to work hard and engaged in many of the same menial tasks as their Roman counterparts. However, it is hard to imagine a Roman slave daring to refuse a request and argue publicly with a nobleman, for fear of severe physical punishment. It also appears that slaves in China had some legal protections provided by contracts specifying and limiting what could be demanded of them.

Why might slavery have been less important in Han China than in the Roman Empire? Why would the treatment of slaves have been less harsh in China than in Rome?

Source: Thomas Wiedemann, *Greek and Roman Slavery,* (Baltimore: John Hopkin's University Press (1981), 139–141, 183–184; C. Martin Wilbur, *Slavery in China During the Former Han Dynasty, 206 B.C.–A.D. 25* (Chicago: Field Museum of Natural History, 1943), 383, 388.

---

ancients. Providing adequate supplies of food and water and removing sewage were always problems.

At Rome the upper classes lived in elegant townhouses on one or another of the seven hills. The house was centered around an *atrium*, a rectangular courtyard. In the ceiling of the atrium an open skylight let in light and rainwater, which fell into a basin for later use. Surrounding the atrium were a large dining room for dinner and drinking parties, an interior garden, a kitchen, and, perhaps, a private bath. Bedrooms were on the upper level. The floors were decorated with pebble mosaics. The walls and ceilings were covered with frescoes (paintings done directly on wet plaster) representing mythological scenes or outdoor vistas and giving a sense of openness in the absence of windows. The typical aristocrat also owned a number of villas in the Italian countryside, a retreat from the pressures of city life.

The poor of Rome lived in crowded slums in the low-lying parts of the city. Their wooden tenements were subject to frequent fires and must have been damp, dark, and smelly, with few furnishings. Fortunately, for much of the year Romans could spend the day outdoors.

The cities, towns, and even the ramshackle settlements that sprang up on the edge of frontier forts were miniature replicas of the capital city in political organization, physical layout, and appearance. A town council and two annually elected officials drawn from prosperous members of the community maintained law and order and collected the imperial taxes from both the urban center and its agricultural hinterland. In return for the privilege of running local affairs with considerable autonomy and in appreciation for how the Roman state protected their wealth and position, this "municipal aristocracy" loyally served the interests of Rome. In their drive to imitate the manners and values of Roman senators, they made lavish gifts to their communities. They endowed cities and towns, which had very little revenue of their own, with attractive elements of Roman urban life—a forum (an open plaza that served as a civic center), government buildings, temples, gardens, baths, theaters, amphitheaters, and games and public entertainments of all sorts. Because of these amenities, the situation of the urban poor was superior to that of the rural poor. Poor people living in a city could pass time at the baths, seek refuge from the elements amid the colonnades, and attend the games.

Life in the countryside was much as it always had been. Hard work and drudgery were relieved by an occasional holiday or village festival and by the everyday pleasures of sex, family, and social exchange. Most of the time the rural population had to fend for itself in dealing with bandits, wild animals, and other hazards of country life. People living away from urban centers had little direct contact with the Roman government other than an occasional run-in with bullying soldiers and the dreaded arrival of the tax collector.

The process by which ownership of the land tended to become concentrated in ever fewer hands was temporarily reversed during the civil wars that brought an end to the Roman Republic. In the era of the emperors it resumed. However, after the era of conquest ended in the early second century C.E., slaves were no longer plentiful or inexpensive, and landowners had to find a new source of labor. Over time the numbers of the independent farmers decreased, and they were replaced by "tenant farmers" who were allowed to live on and cultivate plots of land as long as they turned over a portion of their crop to the landlord. In the early centuries C.E. the landowners still lived in the cities and hired foremen to manage their estates. Thus wealth was concentrated in the cities but was based on the productivity of rural agricultural laborers.

Another source of prosperity for some urban dwellers was manufacture and trade. Commerce was greatly enhanced by the ***pax romana*** ("Roman peace"), the safety and stability guaranteed by Roman might. Grain, meat, vegetables, and other bulk foodstuffs usually could be exchanged only locally, because transporting them very far was not economical and many products spoiled quickly without refrigeration. However, the city of Rome was dependent on the import of massive quantities of grain from Sicily and Egypt to feed its huge population, and special naval squadrons were assigned this vital task.

Sign for a Roman Shop The woman behind the counter is selling fruit to one customer while two men are taking game hanging from a rack. The snail and two monkeys to the right of the shopkeeper may represent the name of the establishment. Towns served as markets where farmers exchanged their surplus products for crafted goods made by urban artisans. Local commerce in agricultural products must have been a major component of the economy of the Roman Empire, but it is hard to trace in the archaeological record. (Archivo Fotografico della Soprintendenza Archeologica di Ostia)

Glass, metalwork, delicate pottery, and other fine manufactured products were exported throughout the empire. Over time the centers of production, at first located in Italy, moved outward into the provinces as knowledge of the necessary skills spread. Roman armies stationed on the frontiers were a large market of consumers, and their presence promoted the prosperity of border provinces. There also was trade in luxury items coming from far beyond the boundaries of the empire, especially silk from China and spices from India and Arabia.

Trade was of vital importance to the imperial system. The surplus revenues of rich interior provinces like Gaul (France) and Egypt were transferred to Rome to support the emperor and the central government, and to the frontier provinces to subsidize the armies. This transfer of wealth was made possible by the taxes demanded by the central government and the networks of trade that enabled troops to purchase necessary supplies on the distant frontiers where they were stationed.

One of the most enduring consequences of this empire, which encompassed such a wide diversity of ethnic and linguistic groups and forms of political and social organization, was **Romanization,** the spread of the Latin language and Roman way of life. This phenomenon was confined primarily to the western half of the empire, because the eastern Mediterranean already had Greek as a common idiom, a legacy of the Hellenistic kingdoms (see Chapter 5). The evolution of modern Portuguese, Spanish, French, Italian, and Romanian from the Latin language proves that the language of the conquerors eventually was taken over not only by elite groups in the provinces but also by the common people.

There is little evidence that the Roman government pursued a policy of forcibly Romanizing the provinces. The switch to Latin and adoption of the cultural habits that went with it were choices that the inhabitants of the provinces made for themselves. However, those who made this choice were responding to the very significant advantages available to individuals who spoke Latin and wore a *toga* (the traditional cloak worn by Roman male citizens), just as today in developing nations there often are advantages to moving to the city, learning English, and putting on a suit and tie. The use of Latin facilitated dealings with the Roman administration, and a merchant who spoke Latin could get contracts to supply the military and be understood anywhere he went in the empire. Many also must have been drawn to the aura of success surrounding the language and culture of a people who had created so vast an empire.

As towns sprang up and acquired the features of Roman urban life, they served as magnets for ambitious members of the indigenous populations. At first reluc-

tant to grant Roman citizenship, with its attendant privileges, legal protections, and exemptions from some types of taxation, to people living outside Italy, the Romans gradually extended it. Men who completed a twenty-six-year term of service in the native military units that backed up the Roman legions were granted citizenship and could pass this coveted status on to their descendants. Emperors made grants of citizenship to individuals or entire communities as rewards for good service. Then in 212 C.E. the emperor Caracalla granted citizenship to all free, adult, male inhabitants of the empire.

The gradual diffusion of citizenship epitomizes the process by which the empire was transformed from an Italian dominion over the Mediterranean lands into a commonwealth of peoples. As early as the first century C.E. some of the leading literary and intellectual figures came from the provinces. By the second century even the emperors hailed from Spain, Gaul, and North Africa.

The Rise of Christianity

During this same period of general peace and prosperity, at the eastern end of the Mediterranean events were taking place that, though little noted at the moment, would prove to be of great historical significance. The Jewish homeland of Judaea (see Chapter 4), roughly equivalent to present-day Israel, was put under direct Roman rule in 6 C.E. Over the next half-century a series of Roman governors insensitive to the Jewish belief in one god managed to increase tensions. Among the Jews various kinds of opposition to Roman rule sprang up. Many waited for the arrival of the Messiah, the "Anointed One," presumed to be a military leader who would liberate the Jewish people and drive the Romans out of the land.

It is in this context that we must see the career of **Jesus,** a young carpenter from the Galilee region in northern Israel. Offended by what he perceived as Jewish religious and political leaders' excessive concern with money and power and by the perfunctory nature of mainstream Jewish religious practice in his time, Jesus prescribed a return to the personal faith and spirituality of an earlier age. He eventually attracted the attention of the Jewish authorities in Jerusalem, who regarded popular reformers as potential troublemakers. They turned him over to the Roman governor, Pontius Pilate. Jesus was imprisoned, condemned, and executed by crucifixion, a punishment usually reserved for common criminals. His followers, the Apostles, carried on after his death and sought to spread his teachings and their belief that he had been resurrected (returned from death to life) among their fellow Jews.

In the 40s C.E. **Paul,** a Jew from the Greek city of Tarsus in southeast Anatolia, became converted to the new creed and between 45 and 58 C.E. threw his enormous talent and energy into spreading the word. Traveling throughout Syria-Palestine, Anatolia, and Greece, he became increasingly frustrated with the refusal of most Jews to accept his claim that Jesus was the Messiah and had ushered in a new age. Discovering a spiritual hunger among many non-Jews, Paul redirected his efforts toward this population (sometimes called "gentiles") and set up a string of Christian (from the Greek term *christos,* meaning "anointed one," given to Jesus by his followers) communities in the eastern Mediterranean.

The career of Paul exemplifies the cosmopolitan nature of the Roman Empire in this era. Speaking both Greek and Aramaic, he moved comfortably between the Greco-Roman and Jewish worlds. He used Roman roads, depended on the peace guaranteed by Roman arms, called on his Roman citizenship to protect him from the arbitrary action of local authorities, and moved from city to city in his quest for converts.

In 66 C.E. long-building tensions in Roman Judaea erupted into a full-scale revolt that lasted until 73. One of the casualties of the Roman reconquest of Judaea was the Jerusalem-based Christian community, which saw its primary mission among the Jews. This left the field clear for Paul's non-Jewish converts, and Christianity began to diverge more and more from its Jewish roots.

For more than two centuries, the sect grew slowly but steadily. Many of the first converts were from disenfranchised groups—women, slaves, the urban poor. They hoped to receive respect not accorded them in the larger society and to obtain positions of responsibility when the members of early Christian communities assembled to democratically elect their leaders. However, as the religious movement grew and prospered, it developed a hierarchy of priests and bishops and became subject to bitter disputes over theological doctrine (see Chapter 10).

As monotheists forbidden to worship other gods, early Christians were vulnerable to persecution by Roman officials who regarded their refusal to worship the emperor as a sign of disloyalty. Nevertheless, despite occasional government-sponsored attempts at suppression and spontaneous mob attacks, or perhaps because of them, the young Christian movement continued to gain strength and attract converts. By the late third century C.E. adherents to Christianity were a sizable minority within the Roman Empire, and membership in the sect had spread up the social ranks to include many educated and prosperous people holding posts in the local and imperial governments.

The expansion of Christianity should be seen as part of a broader religious tendency of the age. Already in the Greek Classical period a number of "mystery" cults had gained popularity by claiming to provide secret information about the nature of life and death and promising a blessed afterlife to their adherents (see the discussion of the mysteries of Eleusis in Chapter 5). In the Hellenistic and Roman periods, a number of belief systems making similar promises arose in the eastern Mediterranean and spread throughout the Greco-Roman lands, presumably in response to a growing spiritual and intellectual hunger not satisfied by traditional pagan practices. These included the cults of the mother-goddess Cybele in Anatolia, the Egyptian goddess Isis, and the Iranian sun-god Mithra. As we shall see, the ultimate victory of Christianity over these rivals had as much to do with historical circumstances as with its spiritual appeal.

Technology and Transformation

We have seen how the early Christians took advantage of the relative ease and safety of travel brought by Roman arms and engineering to spread their faith. Remnants of roads, fortification walls, aqueducts, and buildings still visible today testify to the engineering expertise of the ancient Romans. Some of the best engineers served with the army, building bridges, siege works, and ballistic weapons that hurled stones and shafts. In peacetime the soldiers were often put to work on construction projects. **Aqueducts**—long elevated or underground conduits—carried water from a source to an urban center, using only the force of gravity (see Environment and Technology: Water Engineering in Rome and China). The Romans were pioneers in the use of arches, which allow the even distribution of great weights without thick supporting walls. The invention of concrete—a mixture of lime powder, sand, and water that could be poured into molds set on scaffolding—allowed the Romans to create vast vaulted and domed interior spaces and to move away from the rectilinear pillar-and-post construction methods employed by the Greeks.

One of the greatest challenges for Roman imperial administration was the defense of borders stretching for thousands of miles. Augustus recommended to his successors, in a document released after his death, that they not expand the empire, because the costs of administering and defending any subsequent acquisition would be greater than the revenues it brought in. Thus, after Augustus's death, the Roman army was reorganized and redeployed to reflect the shift from an offensive to a defensive strategy. At most points the empire was pro-

Roman Aqueduct Near Tarragona, Spain   How to provide an adequate supply of water was a problem posed by the growth of Roman towns and cities. Aqueducts channeled water from a source, sometimes many miles away, to an urban complex, using only the force of gravity. To bring an aqueduct from high ground into the city, Roman engineers designed long, continuous rows of arches that maintained a steady downhill slope. Roman troops were often used in such large-scale construction projects. Scholars sometimes can roughly estimate the population of an ancient city by calculating the amount of water that was available to it.   (Robert Frerck/Woodfin Camp & Associates)

tected by mountains, deserts, and seas. But the Rhine/Danube frontier in Germany and Central Europe was a vulnerable area. A string of forts with relatively small garrisons adequate for dealing with raiders guarded this lengthy frontier. On particularly desolate frontiers, such as in Britain and North Africa, the Romans built long walls to keep out the peoples who lived beyond.

Fortunately for Rome, its neighbors, with one exception, were less technologically advanced and more loosely organized peoples who did not pose a serious threat to the security of the empire as a whole. That one exception was on the eastern frontier, where the Parthian kingdom, heir to earlier Mesopotamian and Persian Empires, controlled the lands that are today Iran and Iraq. For centuries Rome and Parthia engaged in a rivalry that sapped both sides without leading to any significant territorial gain for either party.

The Roman state prospered for two-and-a-half centuries after Augustus stabilized the internal political situation and addressed the needs of the empire with an ambitious program of reforms. Then in the third century C.E. cracks in the edifice became visible. Historians use the expression **"third-century crisis"** to refer to the period from 235 to 284 C.E., in which political, military, and economic problems beset and nearly destroyed the Roman Empire. The most visible symptom of the crisis was the frequent change of rulers. It has been estimated that twenty or more men claimed the office of emperor during this period. Most reigned for only a few months or years before being overthrown by a rival or killed by their own troops. Germanic tribesmen on the Rhine/Danube frontier took advantage of the frequent civil wars and periods of anarchy to raid deep into the empire. For the first time in centuries, Roman cities began to erect walls

Water Engineering in Rome and China

People needed water to drink, it was vital for agriculture, and it provided a rapid and economical means for transporting people and goods. Some of the most impressive technological achievements of ancient Rome and China involved hydraulic (water) engineering.

Roman cities, with their large populations, required abundant and reliable sources of water. One way to obtain it was to build aqueducts—stone channels to bring water from distant lakes and streams to the cities. The water flowing in these conduits was moved only by the force of gravity. Surveyors measured the land's elevation and for each aqueduct plotted a course that very gradually moved downhill.

Some conduits were elevated high aboveground on walls or bridges, which made it difficult for unauthorized parties to tap the water line for their own use. Portions of some aqueducts were built underground. Still-standing, aboveground segments indicate that the Roman aqueducts were well-built structures made of large cut stones closely fitted and held together by a cement-like mortar. Construction of the aqueducts was labor-intensive, and often both design and construction were carried out by military personnel. This was one of the ways in which the Roman government could keep large numbers of soldiers busy in peacetime.

Sections of aqueduct that crossed rivers presented the same construction challenges as bridges. Roman engineers lowered prefabricated wooden cofferdams—large, hollow cylinders—into the riverbed and pumped out the water so workers could descend and construct cement piers to support the arched segments of the bridge and the water channel itself. This technique is still used for construction in water.

When an aqueduct reached the outskirts of a city, the water flowed into a reservoir, where it was stored. Pipes connected the reservoir to different parts of the city. Even within the city, gravity provided the motive force until the water reached the public fountains used by the poor and the private storage tanks of individuals wealthy enough to have plumbing in their houses.

In ancient China, rivers running generally in an east-west direction were the main thoroughfares. The earliest development of complex societies centered on the Yellow River Valley, but by the beginning of the Qin Empire the Yangzi River Valley and regions farther south were becoming increasingly important to China's political and economic vitality. In this era the Chinese began to build canals connecting the northern and southern zones, at first for military purposes but eventually for transporting commercial goods as well. In later periods, with the acquisition of more advanced engineering skills, an extensive network of canals was built, including the 1,100-mile-long (1,771-kilometer-long) Grand Canal.

One of the earliest efforts was the construction of the Magic Canal. A Chinese historian tells us that the Qin emperor Shi Huangdi ordered his engineers to join two rivers by a 20-mile-long (32.2-kilometer-long) canal so that he could more easily supply his armies of conquest in the south. Construction of the canal posed a difficult engineering challenge, because the rivers Hsiang and Li, though coming within 3 miles (4.8 kilometers) of one another, flowed in opposite directions and with a strong current.

The engineers took advantage of a low point in the chain of hills between the rivers to maintain a relatively level grade. The final element of the solution was to build a snout-shaped mound to divide the waters of the Hsiang, funneling part of that river into an artificial channel. Several spillways further reduced the volume of water flowing into the canal, which was 15 feet wide and 3 feet deep (about 4.5 meters wide and 1 meter deep). The joining of the two rivers completed a network of waterways that permitted continuous inland water transport of goods between the latitudes of Beijing and Guangzhou, a distance of 1,250 miles (2,012 kilometers). Modifications were made in later centuries, but the Magic Canal is still in use.

The Magic Canal Engineers of Shi Huangdi, "First Emperor" of China, exploited the contours of the landscape to connect the river systems of northern and southern China. (From Robert Temple, *The Genius of China* (1986). Photographer: Robert Temple)

for protection. Several regions, feeling that the central government in Rome was not adequately protecting them, turned power over to a man on the spot who promised to put their interests first.

These political and military emergencies had a devastating impact on the empire's economy. The cost of paying large rewards to the troops to win their support and of subsidizing the defense of the increasingly permeable frontiers drained the imperial treasury. In turn, the unending demands of the central government for more tax revenues from the provinces, as well as the interruption of commerce by fighting, eroded the towns' prosperity. Shortsighted emperors, desperate for cash, secretly cut back the amount of precious metal in Roman coins and pocketed the excess. But the public quickly caught on, and the devalued coinage became less and less acceptable as a medium for exchange. Indeed, the empire reverted to a barter economy, a far less efficient system that further curtailed large-scale and long-distance commerce.

The municipal aristocracy, once the most vital and public-spirited class in the empire, was slowly crushed out of existence. As town councilors, its members were personally liable to make up any shortfall in the tax revenues owed to the state. But the decline in trade eroded their wealth, which often was based on manufacture and commerce. Many began to evade their civic duties and even go into hiding.

There was an overall shift of population out of the cities and into the countryside. Many people sought employment and protection—from raiders and from government officials—on the estates of wealthy and powerful country landowners. In the shrinking of cities and the movement of the population to the country estates, we can see the roots of the social and economic structures of the European Middle Ages—a roughly seven-hundred-year period in which wealthy rural lords dominated a peasant population tied to the land (see Chapter 10).

Just when things looked bleakest, a man arose who pulled the empire back from the brink of self-destruction. Like many of the rulers of that age, Diocletian was from one of the eastern European provinces most vulnerable to invasion. A commoner by birth, he had risen through the ranks of the army and gained power in 284. The measure of his success is indicated by the fact that he ruled for more than twenty years and died in bed.

Diocletian implemented a series of radical solutions that saved the Roman state by transforming it. To halt inflation (the process by which prices rise as money becomes worth less), he issued an edict that specified the maximum prices that could be charged for various commodities and services. To ensure an adequate supply of workers in vital services, many people were frozen into their professions and were required to train their sons to succeed them. This kind of government regulation of prices and vocations was completely new in Roman history and had unforeseen consequences. One was the creation of a "black market" among buyers and sellers who chose to ignore the government's price controls and establish their own prices for goods and services. Another was a growing tendency among the inhabitants of the empire to consider the government an oppressive entity that no longer deserved their loyalty.

When Diocletian resigned in 305, the old divisiveness reemerged as various claimants battled for the throne. The eventual winner was **Constantine** (r. 306–337), who by 324 was able to reunite the entire empire under his sole rule.

In 312 Constantine won a key battle at the Milvian Bridge over the Tiber River near Rome. He later claimed that before this battle he had seen in the sky a cross (the sign of the Christian God) superimposed on the sun. Believing that the Christian God had helped him achieve the victory, the new emperor converted to Christianity. Throughout his reign he supported the Christian church, although he tolerated other beliefs as well. Historians disagree about whether Constantine was motivated by primarily spiritual motives or was pragmatically seeking to unify the peoples of the empire under a single religion. In either case his conversion was of tremendous historical significance. Large numbers of people began to convert, because they saw that Christians seeking political office or favors from the government had clear advantages over non-Christians.

Another decisive step taken by Constantine was the transfer of the imperial capital from Rome to Byzantium, an ancient Greek city on the Bosporus° strait leading from the Mediterranean into the Black Sea. The city was renamed Constantinople°, "City of Constantine." This move, in 324, both reflected and accelerated changes already taking place. Constantinople was closer than Rome to the most-threatened borders of the empire, in eastern Europe (see Map 6.1). The urban centers and prosperous middle class in the eastern half of the empire had better withstood the third-century crisis than had those in the western half. In addition, more educated people and more Christians were living in the eastern provinces (see Chapter 10).

Bosporus (BAHS-puhr-uhs)
Constantinople (cahn-stan-tih-NO-pul)

The conversion of Constantine and the transfer of the imperial capital away from Rome often have been considered events marking the end of Roman history. This conventional view, however, is open to question for at least two reasons: (1) Many of the important changes that culminated during Constantine's reign had their roots in events of the previous two centuries. (2) The Roman Empire as a whole survived for at least another century, and the eastern, or Byzantine, portion of it (discussed in Chapter 10), survived Constantine by more than a thousand years. It is true, however, that the Roman Empire of the fourth century was fundamentally different from what had existed before, and for that reason it is convenient to see in Constantine's reign the beginning of a new epoch in the West.

THE ORIGINS OF IMPERIAL CHINA, 221 B.C.E.–220 C.E.

The early history of China (described in Chapter 3) was marked by the fragmentation that geography seemed to dictate. The authority of the first dynasties, Shang (ca. 1750–1027 B.C.E.) and Zhou (1027–221 B.C.E.), was confined to a relatively compact zone in northeastern China. The last few centuries of nominal Zhou rule—the Warring States Period—was an age of rivalry and belligerence among a group of small states. They differed to some extent in language and culture and in many ways bring to mind the contemporary Greek city-states (see Chapter 5). As in Greece, so also in China: an era of competition and conflict saw the formation of many of the distinctive elements of a national culture.

In the second half of the third century B.C.E. one of the warring states—the Qin° state of the Wei° Valley—rapidly conquered its rivals and created China's first empire (221–206 B.C.E.). But the Qin Empire, itself built at a great cost in human lives and labor, barely survived the death of its founder, Shi Huangdi. Power soon passed to a new dynasty, the Han, which ruled China for the next four centuries (206 B.C.E.–220 C.E.) (see Map 6.2). Thus began the long history of imperial China—a tradition of political and cultural unity and continuity that lasted into the early twentieth century C.E. and still resonates in the very different China of our own time.

Qin (chin) **Wei** (way)

Resources and Population

That achievement was especially remarkable for a region that not only was vast in extent but also marked by great diversity in its topography, climate, plant and animal life, and human population. An imperial state controlling these lands faced greater obstacles to long-distance communications and to a uniform way of life than did the Roman Empire. The Roman state encompassed lands whose climates and agricultural potentials were, for the most part, roughly similar. The Roman Empire also had the benefit of an internal sea—the Mediterranean—which facilitated relatively rapid and inexpensive travel and transport of commodities. What resources, technologies, institutions, and values made possible the creation and maintenance of a Chinese empire?

Agricultural production was the primary source of the wealth and taxes that supported the institutions of imperial China. The main tax, a percentage of the annual yield of the fields, was used to support the government in its many manifestations, from the luxurious lifestyle enjoyed by members of the royal court to the many levels of officials and the military units stationed throughout the country and on the frontiers. China's capital cities, first Chang'an° and later Luoyang°, had large populations that had to be fed. As intensive agriculture spread in the Yangzi River Valley, transporting southern crops to the north became important, and the first steps were taken toward construction of canals to connect the two great river systems, the Yangzi and the Yellow (see Environment and Technology: Water Engineering in Rome and China). The government also exercised foresight in collecting and storing, in prosperous times, surplus grain that could be distributed at reasonable prices in times of shortage.

Human labor was the other fundamental commodity. The government periodically carried out a census of inhabitants. The results for the years 2 C.E. and 140 C.E. are preserved in extant historical writings. The earlier survey indicates totals of approximately 12 million households and 60 million people; the later, not quite 10 million households and 49 million people. Thus the average household contained 5 persons. Then, as now, the vast majority of the population lived in the eastern portion of the country, the river-valley regions where intensive agriculture could support a dense population. At first the largest concentration was in the Yellow River Valley and North China Plain, but by early Han times the demographic center had begun to shift to the Yangzi River Valley.

Chang'an (chahng-ahn) **Luoyang** (LWOE-yahng)

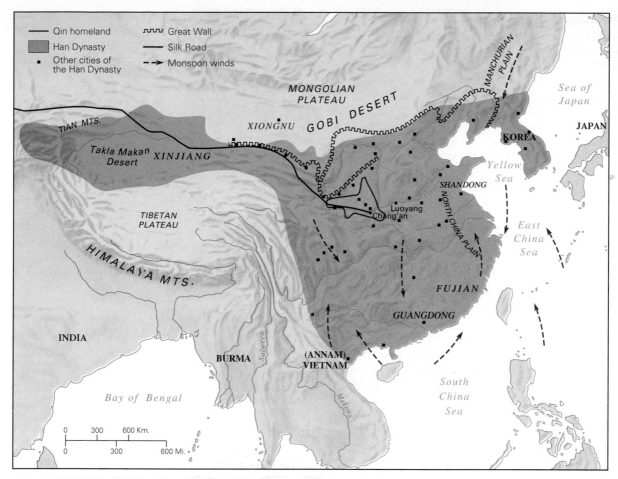

Map 6.2   Han China   The Qin and Han rulers of northeast China extended their control over all of eastern China and extensive territories to the west. A series of walls in the north and northwest, built to check the incursions of nomadic peoples from the steppes, were joined together to form the ancestor of the present-day Great Wall of China. An extensive network of roads connecting towns, cities, and frontier forts promoted rapid communication and facilitated trade. The Silk Road carried China's most treasured product to Central, South, and West Asia and the Mediterranean lands.

How did the Qin and Han governments take advantage of an expanding population? In the intervals between seasonal agricultural tasks, every able-bodied man was expected to donate one month of labor a year to public works projects—work on the construction of palaces, temples, fortifications, and roads; transporting goods; excavating and maintaining canal channels; labor on imperial estates; or service in the mines. Another obligation was two years of military service. Young Chinese men were marched to the frontiers. There they built walls and forts, kept an eye on barbarian neighbors, fought when necessary, and grew crops to support themselves. Annually updated registers of land and households enabled imperial officials to keep track of money

and services due. We again see strong parallels between the Roman and Chinese governments in their dependence on a large population of free peasants who contributed both taxes and services to the state.

Throughout the Han period the Han Chinese gradually but persistently expanded at the expense of other ethnic groups. The growth of population in the core regions and a shortage of good, arable land spurred pioneers to push into new areas. Sometimes the government organized the opening of new areas, as when it resettled people in colonies at militarily strategic sites and on the frontiers. Neighboring kingdoms also invited in Chinese settlers in order to exploit their skills and learn their technologies.

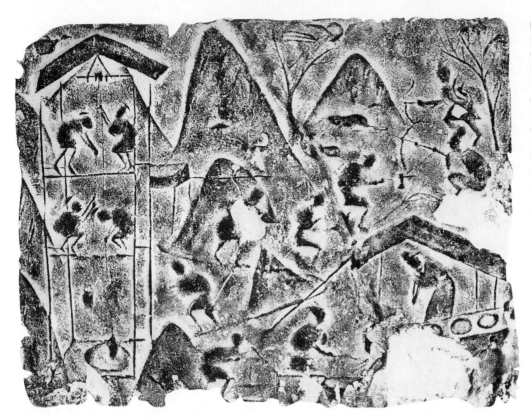

Rubbing of Salt Mining
Found in a Chinese tomb of the first century C.E., this rubbing illustrates a procedure for mining salt. The tower on the left originally served as a derrick for drilling a deep hole through dirt and rock. In this scene workers are hauling up buckets full of brine (saltwater) from underground deposits. In the background are hunters in the mountains. (Courtesy of the Trustees of the British Museum)

The pattern of expansion is significant. Han people tended to move into regions suitable for the kind of agriculture they had practiced in the eastern river valleys. They took over land on the northern frontier, pushing back nomadic populations. They also expanded into the tropical forests of southern China and settled in the western oases. In places not suitable for their preferred kind of agriculture, particularly the steppe and the desert, Han Chinese were not able to displace other groups.

Hierarchy, Obedience, and Belief

As the Han Chinese expanded into new regions, they brought with them their social organization, values, language, and other elements of their culture. The basic unit of Chinese society was the family. The Chinese family included not only the living generations but also all the previous generations—the ancestors. The Chinese believed their ancestors maintained an ongoing interest in the fortunes of living family members. Thus people were careful to consult, appease, and venerate their ancestors in order to maintain their favor. The family was viewed as a living, self-renewing organism, and it

was absolutely necessary for each generation to have sons to perpetuate the family and ensure the immortality offered by the ancestor cult.

A fundamental source of values was the doctrine of Confucius (Kongzi), which had its origins in the sixth century B.C.E. (see Chapter 3) but became very influential in the imperial period. Confucianism regarded hierarchy as a natural aspect of human society and assigned specific tasks to each person and laid down rules of appropriate conduct. Within the family absolute authority rested with the father. He served as an intermediary between the living members and the ancestors, presiding over the rituals of ancestor worship. Every member of the family saw himself or herself as part of an interdependent unit rather than as an individual agent. Each person had a place and responsibilities within the domestic hierarchy, based on his or her gender, age, and relationship to other family members. The same concepts operated in society as a whole. Peasants, soldiers, administrators, and rulers all made their distinctive and necessary contributions to the welfare of society. Confucianism optimistically maintained that people could be guided to the right path through education, imitation of proper role models, and self-improvement. The family inculcated the basic values of Chinese society: loyalty, obedience to authority, respect for elders and ancestors, and concern for honor and appropriate conduct. Because the hierarchy in the state mirrored the hierarchy in the family, these same attitudes carried over into the relationship between individuals and the state.

The experiences of women in ancient Chinese society are hard to pinpoint because, as elsewhere, contemporary written sources are largely silent on the subject. Confucian ethics stressed the impropriety of women participating in public life. Traditional wisdom about the conduct appropriate for women is preserved in an account of the life of the mother of the Confucian philosopher Mencius (Mengzi). According to this account:

> A woman's duties are to cook the five grains, heat the wine, look after her parents-in-law, make clothes, and that is all! . . . [She] has no ambition to manage affairs outside the house. . . . She must follow the "three submissions." When she is young, she must submit to her parents. After her marriage, she must submit to her husband. When she is widowed, she must submit to her son.[1]

That is an ideal perpetuated by males of the upper classes, the social stratum about which we are best informed because it is the source of most of the written texts. Female members of this group probably were under considerable pressure to conform to those expectations. In contrast, women of the lower classes, less affected by Confucian ways of thinking, may have been less constrained than their more "privileged" counterparts.

Marriages were arranged by parents. A young bride left home to reside with her husband's family. To them she was a stranger who had to prove herself. In such circumstances ability and force of personality (as well as the capacity to produce sons) could make a difference. Dissension between the wife and her mother-in-law and sisters-in-law was frequent as they competed for influence with husbands, sons, and brothers and a larger share of the economic resources held in common by the family.

Like the early Romans, the ancient Chinese believed that divinity resided within nature rather than being outside and above it, and they worshiped and tried to appease the forces of nature. The state erected and maintained shrines to the lords of rain and winds as well as to certain great rivers and high mountains. Gathering at mounds or altars where the local spirit of the soil was thought to reside, people sacrificed sheep and pigs and beat drums loudly to promote the fertility of the earth. Strange or disastrous natural phenomena, such as eclipses or heavy rains, called for symbolic restraint of the deity by tying a red cord around the sacred spot. Because it was believed that supernatural forces, bringing good and evil fortune, flowed through the landscape, experts in *feng shui*, meaning "earth divination," were consulted to determine the most favorable location and orientation for buildings and graves. The faithful learned to adapt their lives to the complex rhythms they perceived in nature.

There was widespread interest in ways of cheating death, whether by making the body immortal with life-enhancing drugs or providing for a blessed afterlife. The rich built ostentatious tombs, flanked by towers or covered by mounds of earth, and filled them with the equipment they believed they would need to maintain the quality of life they had enjoyed on earth. The objects in these tombs have provided archaeologists with a wealth of knowledge about Han society.

The First Chinese Empire

For centuries eastern China was divided among rival states whose frequent hostilities gave rise to the label "Warring States Period" (480–221 B.C.E.). In the second half of the third century B.C.E. the state of the **Qin** suddenly burst forth and took over the other states one by one. By 221 B.C.E., the first emperor had united for the first time the northern plain and the Yangzi River Valley under one rule, marking the creation of China and the inauguration of the imperial age. Many scholars maintain that the very name "China," by which this land has been known in the Western world, is derived from "Qin."

Several factors account for the meteoric rise of the Qin. The Qin ruler, who took the title ***Shi Huangdi*** ("First Emperor"), and his adviser and prime minister Li Si, were able and ruthless men who exploited the exhaustion resulting from the long centuries of interstate rivalry. The Qin homeland in the valley of the Wei, a tributary of the Yellow River, was less urbanized and commercialized than the kingdoms farther east, and the leadership could draw from a large pool of sturdy peasants to serve in the army. Moreover, long experience of mobilizing manpower for the construction of irrigation and flood-control works had strengthened the authority of the Qin king at the expense of the nobles and endowed his government with superior organizational skills.

Shi Huangdi and Li Si created a totalitarian structure that subordinated the individual to the needs of the state. They cracked down on Confucianism, regarding its demands for benevolent and nonviolent conduct from rulers as a check on the absolute power that they claimed to hold. They drew, instead, from a stream of political thought known as Legalism (see Chapter 3) to justify the actions of the Qin government. According to this philosophy, whose major exponent was Li Si himself, the will of the ruler was supreme, and his subjects were to be trained in discipline and obedience through the rigid application of rewards and punishments.

The new regime was determined to eliminate any rival centers of authority. Its first target was the landowning aristocracy of the conquered rival states and the system on which aristocratic wealth and power had been based. The Qin government abolished primogeniture—the right of the eldest son to inherit all the landed property—because primogeniture allowed a small number of individuals to accumulate vast tracts of land. The Qin required estates to be broken up and passed on to several heirs.

The large estates of the aristocracy had been worked by slaves (see Society and Culture: Slavery in Rome and China) and by a serf class of peasants who turned over to the landlord a substantial portion of what they grew. The Qin abolished slavery and took steps to bring into being a free peasantry. The members of this group were numerous small landholders who could not evade the government's demands for taxes and who would serve in the army and devote a portion of their labor each year to state projects.

The Qin government's commitment to standardization in many areas of life helped to create a unified Chinese civilization. During the Warring States Period, the small states had emphasized their independence through a wide array of symbolic practices. For example, each state had its own particular forms of music, with different scales, systems of notation, and instruments. The Qin imposed standard weights, measures, and coinage, a uniform law code, a common system of writing, and even regulations governing the axle length of carts so as to leave just one set of ruts on the roads.

The Qin built thousands of miles of roads—comparable in scale to the roads of the Roman Empire—to connect the parts of the empire and to facilitate the rapid movement of Qin armies. They also built canals to connect the river systems of northern and southern China (see Environment and Technology: Water Engineering in Rome and China). The various frontier walls of the old states began to be linked into a continuous barricade, the precursor of the Great Wall (see Chapter 11), to protect cultivated lands from incursions by nomads from the north. To build these walls and roads, large numbers of subjects were forced to donate their labor and often their lives. So oppressive were the financial exploitation and the demands for forced labor that when Shi Huangdi died in 210 B.C.E., a series of rebellions broke out and brought down the Qin dynasty.

The Long Reign of the Han

When the dust cleared, Liu Bang, who may have been from a peasant background, had outlasted his rivals and established a new dynasty, the **Han** (206 B.C.E.–220 C.E.). The new emperor claimed to reject the excesses and mistakes of the Qin and to restore the institutions of a venerable past. To sustain and protect so large an empire, however, the Han system of administration maintained much of the structure and Legalist ideology put in place by the Qin, though with less fanatical zeal. The Han tempered Legalist methods of government with a form of Confucianism revised to address the new circumstances of a large, centralized political entity. This version of Confucianism emphasized the benevolence of government and the appropriateness of particular rituals and behaviors in a manifestly hierarchical society. The Han system of administration became the standard for later ages, and the Chinese people today refer to themselves ethnically as "Han."

The first eighty years of the Han dynasty was a time of consolidation. Then, in the later second century B.C.E., Emperor Wu (r. 140–87 B.C.E.) launched a period of military expansion, south into Fujian, Guangdong, and present-day north Vietnam and north into Manchuria and present-day North Korea. Han armies were also sent west, to inner Mongolia and Xinjiang°, to secure the lucrative Silk Road (see Chapter 8). However, controlling the newly acquired territories proved expensive, so Wu's successors curtailed further expansion.

The Han Empire endured, with a brief interruption between 9 and 23 C.E., for more than four hundred years. From 202 B.C.E. to 8 C.E.—the period of the Early, or Western, Han—the capital was at **Chang'an,** in the Wei Valley, an ancient seat of power from which the Zhou and Qin dynasties had emerged. From 23 to 220 C.E. the Later, or Eastern, Han established its base farther east, in the more centrally located Luoyang.

Chang'an, well protected by a ring of hills but having ready access to the fertile plain, was surrounded by a wall of pounded earth and brick 15 miles (24 kilometers) in circumference. We know from contemporary descriptions that Chang'an was a bustling place, filled with courtiers, officials, soldiers, merchants, craftsmen, and foreign visitors. A population of 246,000 is recorded for 2 C.E. Part of the city was carefully planned. Broad thoroughfares running north and south intersected with those running east and west. High walls protected the palaces, administrative offices, barracks, and storehouses of the imperial compound, and access was

---

Xinjiang (SHIN-jyahng)

restricted. Temples and marketplaces were scattered about the civic center. Chang'an became a model of urban planning. Its main features were imitated in the cities and towns that sprang up throughout the Han Empire.

The complaints of moralists provide glimpses of the private lives of well-to-do officials and merchants in the capital. Living in multistory houses, wearing fine silks, traveling about the city in ornate horse-drawn carriages, they devoted their leisure time to art and literature, occult religious practices, elegant banquets, and various entertainments—music and dance, juggling and acrobatics, dog and horse races, cock and tiger fights. Far different were the lives of the common people of the capital. They inhabited a sprawling warren of alleys, living in dwellings packed "as closely as the teeth of a comb," as one poet put it.

As in the Zhou monarchy (see Chapter 3), the emperor was the "Son of Heaven," chosen to rule in accordance with the Mandate of Heaven. The emperor stood at the center of government and society. As the father held authority in the family and was a link between the living generations and the ancestors, so the emperor was supreme in the state. He brought the support of powerful imperial ancestors and guaranteed the harmonious interaction of heaven and earth. To a much greater degree than his Roman counterpart, he was regarded as a divinity on earth, and his word was law. If he failed to govern well, however, he could lose the backing of Heaven. Since the Chinese believed there was a strong correspondence between events in heaven, in the natural world, and in human society, they regarded natural disasters such as floods, droughts, and earthquakes as both the consequence and the evidence of the emperor's ethical failure and mismanagement. Successful revolutions were viewed as proof that Heaven had withdrawn its support from an unworthy ruler.

The emperor lived in seclusion within the walled palace compound, surrounded by his many wives and children, servants, courtiers, and officials. Life in the palace compound was an unceasing round of pomp and ritual emphasizing the worship of Heaven and imperial ancestors as well as the practical business of government. The royal compound was also a hive of intrigue, particularly when the emperor died. His chief widow had the prerogative of choosing his heir from among the male members of the ruling clan.

The central government was run by a prime minister and a civil service director and included nine ministers who had military, economic, legal, and religious responsibilities. Like the imperial Roman government, the Han government depended on local officials to carry out the day-to-day business of administering the vast empire. Local people were responsible for collecting taxes and dispatching revenues to the central government, for regulating the system of conscription for the army and for labor projects, for protection of the area, and for settling disputes. The central government was a remote entity that rarely impinged on the lives of most citizens; their only experience of government was their contact with local officials. Who, then, made up the large bureaucracy of local officials in the Han Empire?

Tax Collection in the Han Empire This stamped brick, found in a tomb in western China, depicts, at center, a stooped peasant pouring into a basket the grain demanded by the government. The tax collector, seated and wearing fine clothing, clutches bamboo slips on which he keeps his records. A number of pictorial elements—positioning in the composition, posture, clothing, and vehicles—contrast the wealth, comfort, and superior social status of the government official with the poverty, toil, and low status of the peasant. (Chinese Cultural Center of San Francisco)

A significant development during the Han period was the rise of a class that scholars refer to as the **gentry.** As part of their strategy to weaken the rural aristocrats and to exclude them from political posts, the Qin and Han emperors allied themselves with the class next in wealth below the aristocrats. The members of this class were moderately prosperous landowners and men with education and valued expertise. Like the Roman equites favored by Augustus and his successors, the gentry class was the source of the local officials that the central government required. These officials were a privileged and respected group within Chinese society, and they made the government more efficient and responsive than it had been in the past.

The new gentry class of officials, with imperial support, adopted as its guiding philosophy a version of Confucianism that (1) provided a system for training officials to be intellectually capable and morally worthy of their role in administration and (2) set forth a code of conduct for measuring their performance. According to Chinese tradition, an imperial university, located outside Chang'an and said to have as many as thirty thousand students, and provincial centers of learning were established. (Some scholars doubt that such a complex institution existed this early.) From these centers, students were chosen to enter various levels of government service.

As civil servants advanced in the bureaucracy, they received distinctive emblems and privileges of rank, including preferential treatment in the legal system and exemption from military service. In theory, young men from any class could rise in the state hierarchy. In practice, sons of the gentry had an advantage, because they were in the best position to receive the necessary training in the Confucian classics. Over time, members of the gentry became a new aristocracy of sorts, banding together in cliques and family alliances that had considerable clout and worked to advance the careers of members of their group.

In the Han period Daoism, which also had its origins in the Warring States Period (see Chapter 3), took deeper root, becoming popular with the common people. As we have seen, Daoism emphasized the search for the *Dao*, or "path," of nature and the value of harmonizing with the cycles and patterns of the natural world. Enlightenment was to be achieved not so much by education as by solitary contemplation and physical and mental discipline. Daoism was skeptical, calling into question age-old beliefs and values and rejecting the hierarchy, rules, and rituals of the Confucianism of the elite classes. It urged passive acceptance of the disorder of the world, denial of ambition, contentment with simple pleasures, and following one's own instincts about what was right.

Technology and Trade

China was the home of many important inventions, and what the Chinese did not invent they improved. Tradition seems to have recognized the importance of technology for the success and spread of Chinese civilization. The legendary first five emperors were all culture heroes whom the Chinese credited with the introduction of major new technologies.

The advent of bronze tools around 1500 B.C.E. had given a powerful push to the effort to clear the forests of the North China Plain and open more land for agriculture. Almost a thousand years later, iron arrived, and the Qin may have been among the first to take full advantage of the new iron technology. Chinese metallurgists employed more advanced techniques than their counterparts elsewhere in the hemisphere. Whereas Roman blacksmiths produced wrought-iron tools and weapons by hammering heated iron, the Chinese mastered the technique of liquefying iron and pouring it into molds. The resulting cast-iron or steel tools and weapons had a higher carbon content and were harder and more durable.

In the succeeding centuries, the crossbow and use of cavalry helped the Chinese military to beat off the attacks of nomads from the steppe regions. The watermill, which harnessed the power of running water to turn a grindstone, was in use in China long before it appeared in Europe. The development of a horse collar that did not constrict the animal's breathing allowed horses in China to pull loads much heavier than the loads pulled by horses in Europe at the same time.

The Qin had undertaken an extensive program of road building, and Han rulers continued this project. Roads were necessary to enable rapid movement of military forces and supplies. The imperial government also depended on a network of couriers carrying messages to and from the central administration, using horses, boats, and even footpaths, and finding food and shelter at relay stations. The existing network of navigable rivers was improved and connected by construction of canals (see Environment and Technology: Water Engineering in Rome and China).

The roads and waterways connected an expanding network of urban centers. Growth in population and increasing trade resulted in the development of local market centers. The importance of these thriving towns grew as they became county seats from which imperial officials operated. Estimates of the proportion of the population living in Han towns and cities range from 10 to 30 percent.

Along with the growth of local and regional trade networks came the development of long-distance com-

Han-era (first century B.C.E.) Stone Rubbing of a Horse-Drawn Carriage   The "trace harness," a strap running across the horse's chest, was a Chinese invention that allowed horses to pull far heavier loads than were possible with the constricting throat harness used in Europe. In the Han period, officials, professionals, and soldiers who served the regime enjoyed a lifestyle made pleasant by fine clothing, comfortable transportation, servants, and delightful pastimes, but at the same time they were guided by a Confucian emphasis on duty, honesty, and appropriate behavior.   (From Wu family shrine, Jiaxiang, Shantung. From *Chin-shih-so* [Jinshisuo])

merce. China's most important export commodity was silk. Silk cocoons are secreted onto the leaves of mulberry trees by silkworms. For a long time this simple fact was a closely guarded secret that gave the Chinese a monopoly on the manufacture of silk. Carried on a perilous journey westward through the Central Asian oases to the Middle East, India, and the Mediterranean, and passing through the hands of many middlemen, each of whom raised the price in order to make a profit, this beautiful textile may have increased in value a hundredfold by the time it reached its destination. The Chinese government sought to control the Silk Road and the profits that it carried by launching periodic campaigns into Central Asia. Garrisons were installed and colonies of Chinese settlers were sent out to occupy the oases.

Decline of the Han Empire

For the Han government, as for the Romans, maintaining the security of the frontiers—particularly the north and northwest frontiers—was a primary concern. Yet, in the end, the pressure of non-Chinese peoples raiding from across the frontier or moving into the prosperous lands of the empire led to the decline of Han authority.

In general, the Han Empire was able to consolidate its hold over lands occupied by sedentary farming peoples, but nearby were nomadic tribes whose livelihood depended on their horses and herds. The very different ways of life of farmers and herders gave rise to suspicions and insulting stereotypes on both sides. The settled Chinese tended to think of nomads as "barbarians"—rough, uncivilized peoples—much as the inhabitants of the Roman Empire looked down on the Germanic tribes living beyond their frontier.

Along the boundary between settled agriculturalists and nomadic pastoralists there was frequent contact. Often the closeness of the two populations led to significant commercial activity. The nomads sought the food commodities and crafted goods produced by the farmers and townsfolk, and the settled peoples depended on the nomads for horses and other herd animals and products. Sometimes, however, contact took the form of raids on the settled lands by nomad bands, which seized what they needed or wanted. Tough and warlike because of the demands of their way of life, mounted nomads could strike swiftly and just as swiftly disappear.

Although nomadic groups tended to be relatively small and to fight often with each other, from time to time circumstances and a charismatic leader could create a large coalition of tribes. The major external threat to Chinese civilization in the Han period came from the **Xiongnu°**, a great confederacy of Turkic peoples. For centuries Chinese policy had succeeded in containing the Xiongnu. In order to mount periodic campaigns onto the steppe, the Chinese had developed cavalry forces that could match the mobility of the nomads, and access to good stocks of horses and pasturing of herds on northern grasslands became a state priority. Other strategies included maintenance of colonies of soldier-farmers and garrisons on the frontier; the settlement of compliant nomadic groups within the borders of the empire to serve as a buffer against warlike groups; bribes to promote dissension within the nomad leadership; and payment of protection money. One frequently successful approach was a "tributary system" in which nomad rulers accepted Chinese supremacy and sent in payments of tribute for which they were rewarded with marriages to Chinese princesses, dazzling receptions at court, and gifts from the Han emperor that exceeded the value of the tribute.

In the end, the cost of continuous military vigilance along the frontier imposed a crushing burden on Han finances and worsened the economic troubles of later Han times. And, despite the earnest efforts of Qin and Early Han emperors to reduce the power and wealth of the aristocracy and to turn land over to a free peasantry, by the end of the first century B.C.E. nobles and successful merchants again were beginning to acquire control of huge tracts of land, and many peasants were seeking their protection against the exactions of the imperial government. This trend became widespread in the next two centuries. Strongmen largely independent of imperial control emerged, and the central government was deprived of tax revenues and manpower. The system of military conscription broke down, forcing the government to hire more and more foreign soldiers and officers. These men were willing to serve for pay, but their loyalty to the Han state was weak.

Several factors combined to weaken and eventually bring down the Han dynasty in 220 C.E.: factional intrigues within the ruling clan, official corruption and inefficiency, uprisings of desperate and hungry peasants, the spread of banditry, unsuccessful reform movements, attacks by nomadic groups on the northwest frontier, and the ambitions of rural warlords. After 220 C.E. China entered a period of political fragmentation and economic and cultural regression that lasted until the rise of the Sui° and Tang° dynasties in the late sixth and early seventh centuries C.E., a story that we take up in Chapter 11.

Xiongnu (SHE-OONG-noo) **Sui** (sway) **Tang** (tahng)

IMPERIAL PARALLELS

It remains to analyze the similarities and differences between the Roman and Han Empires and to determine the historical implications. The similarities begin at the level of the family. In both cultures the family comprised the living generations and was headed by an all-powerful patriarch. It was a tightly knit unit to which individual members were bound by strong loyalties and obligations. The family inculcated obedience, respect for superiors, piety, and a strong sense of duty and honor—values that individuals carried with them into the wider social and political world, creating a pervasive social cohesion.

For each civilization, agriculture was the fundamental economic activity and source of wealth. The revenues of both imperial governments derived primarily from a percentage of the annual agricultural yield. Each empire depended on a free peasantry—sturdy farmers who could be pressed into military service or other forms of compulsory labor. Conflicts over who owned the land and how the land was to be used were at the heart of the political and social turmoil that occurred in both places. The autocratic rulers of the Roman and Chinese states secured their positions by breaking the power of the old aristocratic families, seizing the excess land that they had amassed, and giving land back to small farmers (as well as keeping extensive tracts for themselves). They veiled the revolutionary nature of these changes by claiming to restore the institutions of a venerable past. The later reversal of this process, as wealthy noblemen once again gained control of vast tracts of land and reduced the peasants to dependent tenant farmers, signaled the erosion of the authority of the state.

Both empires spread out from an ethnically homogeneous core to encompass widespread territories containing diverse ecosystems, populations, and ways of life. Both brought to those regions a cultural unity that has persisted, at least in part, to the present day. This development involved far more than military conquest and political domination. The skill of Roman and Chinese farmers and the high yields that they produced led to a dynamic expansion of population. As the population of the core areas outstripped the available resources, Italian and Han settlers moved into new regions, bringing their languages, beliefs, customs, and technologies with them. Many people in the conquered lands were attracted to the culture of the ruler nation and chose to adopt these practices and to attach themselves to a "winning cause."

Both empires found similar solutions to the problems of administering far-flung territories and large populations in an age when a message could not be transmitted faster than a man on horseback or on foot could carry it. The central government had to delegate considerable autonomy to officials at the local level. These local elites came to identify their own interests with those of the central government that they loyally served. In both empires a kind of civil service developed, staffed by educated and capable members of a prosperous middle class.

Technologies that facilitated imperial control also fostered cultural unification and improvements in the general standard of living. Roads built to expedite the movement of troops became the highways of commerce and the thoroughfares by which imperial culture spread. A network of cities and towns served as the nerve center of each empire, providing local administrative bases, further promoting commerce, and radiating imperial culture out into the surrounding countryside.

Cities and towns modeled themselves on the capital cities—Rome and Chang'an. Travelers throughout each empire could find in outlying regions the same types and styles of buildings and public spaces, as well as other attractive features of urban life, that they had seen in the capital, though on a smaller scale. The majority of the population still resided in the countryside, but most of the advantages of empire were enjoyed by people living in urban centers.

The empires of Rome and Han China faced similar problems of defense: long borders located far from the administrative center and aggressive neighbors who coveted the prosperity of the empire. Both empires had to build walls and maintain a chain of forts and garrisons to protect against incursions. The cost of frontier defense was staggering and eventually eroded the economic prosperity of the two empires. Rough neighbors gradually learned the skills that had given the empires an initial advantage and were able to close the "technology gap." As governments under pressure became ever more beholden to the military and demanded more taxes and services from the hard-pressed civilian population, they lost the loyalty of their own people, many of whom sought protection on the estates of powerful rural landowners. Eventually, both empires were so weakened that their borders were overrun and their central governments collapsed. Ironically, the new peoples who migrated in and took over political control had been so deeply influenced by imperial culture that they maintained it to the best of their abilities.

However, in referring to the eventual failure of these two empires, we are brought up against the different long-term consequences of their respective demises. In China the imperial model was revived in subsequent eras, but the lands of the Roman Empire never again achieved such a level of unification. Several interrelated factors help to account for the different outcomes.

First, these cultures had different attitudes toward the importance of the individual and the obligations of individuals to the state. In China the individual was deeply embedded in the larger social group. The Chinese family, with its emphasis on a precisely defined hierarchy, unquestioning obedience, and solemn rituals of deference to elders and ancestors, served as the model for society and the state. Thus in China respect for authority was (and remains) a deep-seated habit. The architects of Qin Legalism largely got their way, and the emperor's word was regarded as law. Moreover, Confucianism, which sanctified hierarchy and provided a code of conduct for professionals and public officials, had arisen long before the imperial system and could be revived and tailored to fit subsequent political circumstances. Although the Roman family had its own hierarchy and traditions of obedience, the cult of ancestors was not as strong among the Romans as it was among the Chinese, and the family did not serve as the model for the organization of Roman society and the Roman state. Also, there was no Roman equivalent of Confucianism—no ideology of political organization and social conduct that could survive the dissolution of the Roman state.

It is probably also fair to say that economic and social mobility, which make it possible for some people to rise dramatically in wealth and status, tends to enhance a society's sense of the significance of the individual. In ancient China opportunities for individuals to improve their economic status were more limited than they were in the Roman Empire, and the merchant class in China was frequently disparaged and constrained by the government. The more important role played by commerce in the Roman Empire, and the resulting economic mobility, heightened Roman awareness of the rights of individuals. To a much greater extent than the Chinese emperor, the Roman emperor had to resort to persuasion, threats, and promises in order to forge a consensus for his initiatives.

Another factor differentiating the empires of Han China and Rome is political and religious ideology. Although Roman emperors tried to create an ideology to bolster their position, they were hampered by the persistence of Republican traditions and the ambiguities about the position of emperor deliberately cultivated by Augustus. As a result, Roman rulers were likely to be chosen either by the army or by the Senate, the dynastic principle never took deep root, and the cult of the emperor had little spiritual content. This stands in sharp contrast to the clear-cut Chinese belief in the emperor as the divine Son of Heaven with privileged access to the beneficent power of the royal ancestors. Thus, in the West, there was no compelling basis for reviving the position of emperor and the territorial claims of empire in later ages.

Finally, weight also must be given to differences in the new belief systems that took root in each empire. Christianity, with its insistence on monotheism and one doctrine of truth, negated the Roman emperor's pretensions to divinity and was essentially unwilling to come to terms with pagan beliefs. The spread of Christianity through the provinces during the Late Roman Empire, and the decline of the western half of the empire in the fifth century C.E. (see Chapter 10), constituted an irreversible break with the past. However, Buddhism, which came to China in the early centuries C.E. and flourished in the post-Han era (see Chapter 11), was more easily reconciled with traditional Chinese values and beliefs.

CONCLUSION

Both the Roman Empire and the first Chinese empire arose from relatively small states that, because of their discipline and military toughness, initially were able to subdue other small and quarreling neighbors. Ultimately they unified widespread territories under strong central governments.

In China the Qin Empire emerged rapidly, in the reign of a single ruler, because many of the elements for unification were already in place. The "First Emperor" looked back to the precedents of the Shang and Zhou states, which had controlled large core areas in the North China Plain. He drew upon the preexisting concept of the Mandate of Heaven, a claim to divine backing for the ruler who was himself the Son of Heaven; and the Legalist political philosophy justified authoritarian measures. The harshness of the new order generated discontent and resistance that soon brought down the Qin dynasty, but Han successors were able to moderate and build on Qin structures to create a durable imperial regime.

The early Roman state had no such precedents to draw upon. The creation of the Roman Empire was a much slower process, in which solutions were discovered by trial and error. The Republican form of government, developed to meet the needs of an Italian city-state, proved inadequate to the demands of empire, and Rome's military success led to social and economic disruption and an acute political struggle. Out of this crisis emerged the institutions of the Principate, which persevered for several centuries. Even so, the Roman emperors were never able to develop an effective ideology of rule.

In both empires, large and efficient professional armies maintained social order and defended the frontiers. An administrative bureaucracy staffed by educated civil servants kept records and collected taxes for the support of the military and government. Roads, cities, standardized systems of money and measurement, and widely understood languages facilitated travel, commerce, and communication. The culture of the imperial center spread throughout the lands under its control, and this shared culture, as well as shared self-interest, bonded local elites to the ruling class of the empire.

For long periods these stabilizing forces, bringing peace, prosperity, and an improved standard of living to many, were stronger than the weaknesses inherent in these two great empires. Over time, however, the costs of defending lengthy frontiers drained imperial treasuries and imposed greater burdens of taxation on the subjects. As hard-pressed subjects sought the protection of rural landowners, cities became depopulated, commerce was disrupted, and the central government was less able to compel payment of taxes and to find recruits for the armed forces.

In the end, both empires succumbed to a combination of external pressures and internal divisions. However, their legacies were quite different. In China the imperial tradition and the class structure and value system that maintained it were eventually revived (see Chapters 11 and 14), and they survived with remarkable continuity into the twentieth century C.E. In Europe, North Africa, and the Middle East, in contrast, there was no restoration of the Roman Empire, and the later history of those lands was marked by great political changes and cultural diversity.

In the next chapter we turn to the homeland of Buddhism and Hinduism in South Asia and trace the development of Indian civilization.

■ Key Terms

Roman Republic	aqueduct
Roman Senate	third-century crisis
patron/client relationship	Constantine
Roman Principate	Qin
Augustus	Shi Huangdi
equites	Han
pax romana	Chang'an
Romanization	gentry
Jesus	Xiongnu
Paul	

■ Suggested Reading

Tim Cornell and John Matthews, *Atlas of the Roman World* (1982), offers a general introduction, pictures, and maps to illustrate many aspects of Roman civilization. Michael Grant and Rachel Kitzinger, eds., *Civilization of the Ancient Mediterranean*, 3 vols. (1988), is an invaluable collection of essays with bibliographies by specialists on every major facet of life in the Greek and Roman worlds. Among the many good surveys of Roman history is Michael Grant, *History of Rome* (1978). Naphtali Lewis and Meyer Reinhold, eds., *Roman Civilization*, 2 vols. (1951), contains extensive ancient sources in translation.

For Roman political and legal institutions, attitudes, and values see J. A. Crook, *Law and Life of Rome: 90 B.C.–A.D. 212* (1967). Michael Crawford, *The Roman Republic*, 2d ed. (1993), and Chester G. Starr, *The Roman Empire, 27 B.C.–A.D. 476: A Study in Survival* (1982), assess the evolution of the Roman state during the Republic and Principate. Fergus Millar, *The Emperor in the Roman World (31 B.C.–A.D. 337)* (1977), is a comprehensive study of the position of the princeps.

For Roman military expansion and defense of the frontiers see W. V. Harris, *War and Imperialism in Republican Rome* (1979), and Stephen L. Dyson, *The Creation of the Roman Frontier* (1985). For military technology see M. C. Bishop, *Roman Military Equipment: From the Punic Wars to the Fall of Rome* (1993). David Macaulay, *City: A Story of Roman Planning and Construction* (1974), uses copious illustrations to reveal the wonders of Roman engineering; more depth and detail are found in K. D. White, *Greek and Roman Technology* (1984). The characteristics of Roman urban centers are highlighted in John E. Stambaugh, *The Ancient Roman City* (1988).

Kevin Greene, *The Archaeology of the Roman Economy* (1986), showcases new approaches to social and economic history. Suzanne Dickson, *The Roman Family* (1992) explores this most basic social group. Lionel Casson, *Everyday Life in Ancient Rome* (1998), and U. E. Paoli, *Rome: Its People, Life and Customs* (1983), look at the features that typified daily life. Jo-Ann Shelton, ed., *As the Romans Did: A Sourcebook in Roman Social History* (1998), offers a selection of translated ancient sources. Elaine Fantham, Helene Peet Foley, Natalie Boymel Kampen, Sarah B. Pomeroy, and H. Alan Shapiro, *Women in the Classical World: Image and Text* (1994), provides an up-to-date discussion of women in the Roman world. Many of the ancient sources on Roman women can be found in Mary R. Lefkowitz and Maureen B. Fant, eds., *Women's Life in Greece and Rome: A Source Book in Translation* (1982). Thomas Wiedemann, ed., *Greek and Roman Slavery* (1981), contains the ancient sources in translation.

A number of the chapters in John Boardman, Jasper Griffin, and Oswyn Murray, eds., *The Roman World* (1988), survey the intellectual and literary achievements of the Romans. Ronald Mellor, ed., *The Historians of Ancient Rome* (1998), provides context for reading the historical sources. Michael von Albrecht, *History of Roman Literature: From Livius Andronicus to Boethius: With Special Regard to Its Influence on World Liberature* (1997), and Nancy H. Ramage and Andrew Ramage, *The Cambridge Illustrated History of Roman Art* (1991) are surveys of Roman creative arts. R. M. Ogilvie, *The Romans and Their Gods in the Age of Augustus* (1969), is an introduction to religion in its public and private manifestations. R. A. Markus, *Christianity in the Roman World* (1974), investigates the rise of Christianity.

For the geography and demography of China see the well-illustrated *Cultural Atlas of China* (1983) by Caroline Blunden and Mark Elvin. Basic surveys of Chinese history include Jacques Gernet, *A History of Chinese Civilization* (1982), and John K. Fairbank, *China: A New History* (1992). In greater depth for the ancient period is Edward L. Shaughnessy and Michael Loewe, eds., *The Cambridge History of Ancient China* (1998); Denis Twitchett and Michael Loewe, eds., *The Cambridge History of China*, vol. 1, *The Ch'in and Han Empires, 221 B.C.–A.D. 220* (1986); and Michele Pirazzoli-t'Serstevens, *The Han Dynasty* (1982). Kwang-chih Chang, *The Archaeology of Ancient China*, 4th ed. (1986), emphasizes the archaeological record. W. de Bary, W. Chan, and B. Watson, eds., have assembled sources in translation in *Sources of Chinese Tradition* (1960). Sima Qian, *Historical Records* (1994), translated by Raymond Dawson, provides a very readable selection of varied material pertaining to the Qin dynasty compiled by the premier historian of the Han period.

For social history see Michael Loewe, *Everyday Life in Early Imperial China During the Han Period, 202 B.C.–A.D. 220* (1988), and the chapter by Sharon L. Sievers in *Restoring Women to History* (1988). For economic history and foreign relations see Hsin-ju Liu, *Ancient India and Ancient China: Trade and Religious Exchanges, A.D. 1–600* (1994), and Ying-shih Yu, *Trade and Expansion in Han China* (1967). For scientific and technological achievements see Robert Temple, *The Genius of China: 3,000 Years of Science, Discovery, and Invention* (1986).

Benjamin I. Schwartz addresses intellectual history in *The World of Thought in Ancient China* (1985). Spiritual matters are taken up by Laurence G. Thompson, *Chinese Religion: An Introduction*, 3d ed. (1979). For art see Michael Sullivan, *A Short History of Chinese Art*, rev. ed. (1970), and Jessica Rawson, *Ancient China: Art and Archaeology* (1980).

For a stimulating comparison of the Roman and Han Empires that emphasizes the differences, see the first chapter of S. A. M. Adshead, *China in World History*, 2d ed. (1995).

■ Note

1. Patricia Buckley Ebrey, ed., *Chinese Civilization and Society: A Sourcebook* (New York: Free Press, 1981), 33–34.

7

INDIA AND SOUTHEAST ASIA,
1500 B.C.E.–1100 C.E.

Foundations of Indian Civilization • **Imperial Expansion and Collapse** • **Southeast Asia**

ENVIRONMENT AND TECHNOLOGY: **Indian Mathematics**

SOCIETY AND CULTURE: **Reflections of the Status of Women in Indian Literature**

Cave Temples at Ajanta   During and after the Gupta period, natural caves in the Deccan were turned into complexes of shrines decorated with sculpture and painting.

n the *Bhagavad-Gita,* the most renowned of all Indian sacred texts, Arjuna°, the greatest warrior of Indian legend, rides out in his chariot between two armies preparing for battle. Torn between his social duty to fight for his family's claim to the throne and his conscience, which balks at the prospect of killing the relatives, friends, and former teachers who are in the enemy camp, Arjuna slumps down in his chariot and refuses to fight. But his chariot driver, the god Krishna° in disguise, persuades him, in a carefully structured dialogue, both of the necessity to fulfill his duty as a warrior and of the proper frame of mind for performing these acts. In the climactic moment of the dialogue Krishna endows Arjuna with a "divine eye" and permits him to see the true appearance of god:

> It was a multiform, wondrous vision,
> with countless mouths and eyes
> and celestial ornaments,
> Everywhere was boundless divinity
> containing all astonishing things,
> wearing divine garlands and garments,
> anointed with divine perfume.
> If the light of a thousand suns
> were to rise in the sky at once,
> it would be like the light
> of that great spirit.
> Arjuna saw all the universe
> in its many ways and parts,
> standing as one in the body
> of the god of gods.[1]

In all of world literature, this is one of the most compelling attempts to depict the nature of deity. Graphic images emphasize the vastness, diversity, and multiplicity of the god, but in the end we learn that Krishna is the organizing principle behind all creation, that behind diversity and multiplicity lies a higher unity.

This is an apt metaphor for Indian civilization. If there is one word that might be used to characterize India in both ancient and modern times, it is *diversity.* The enormous variety of the Indian landscape is mirrored in the patchwork of ethnic and linguistic groups that occupy it, the political fragmentation that has marked most of Indian history, the elaborate hierarchy of social groups into which the Indian population is divided, and the thousands of deities who are worshiped at the innumerable holy places that dot the subcontinent. Yet, in the end, one can speak of an Indian civilization that is united by a set of shared views and values.

In this chapter we survey the history of South and Southeast Asia from approximately 1500 B.C.E. to 1100 C.E., focusing on the evolution of defining features of Indian civilization. Considerable attention is given to Indian religious conceptions. This coverage is due, in part, to religion's profound role in shaping Indian society. It is also a consequence of the sources of information available to historians. Lengthy epic poems, such as the *Mahabharata* and *Ramayana,* preserve useful information about early Indian society, but most of the earliest texts are religious documents—such as the *Vedas°, Upanishads°,* and Buddhist dialogues and stories—that were preserved and transmitted orally long before they were written down. In addition, Indian civilization held a conception of vast expanses of time during which creatures are repeatedly reincarnated and live many lives. This belief may account for why ancient Indians did not develop a historical consciousness like that of their Israelite and Greek contemporaries but instead took little interest in recording specific historical events: such events seemed relatively insignificant when set against the long cycles of time and lives.

As you read this chapter, ask yourself the following questions:

- What historical forces led to the development of the complex social groupings in ancient India?

- Why did Indian civilization develop religious traditions with such distinctive conceptions of space, time, gods, and the life cycle, and how did these beliefs shape nearly every aspect of South Asian culture?

Arjuna (AHR-joo-nuh)   Krishna (KRISH-nuh)

Vedas (VAY-duhs)   *Upanishads* (oo-PAHN-ih-shahds)

- How, in the face of powerful forces that tended to keep India fragmented, did two great empires—the Mauryan° Empire of the fourth to second centuries B.C.E., and the Gupta Empire of the fourth to six centuries C.E.—succeed in unifying much of India?

- How did a number of states in Southeast Asia become wealthy and powerful by exploiting their position on the trade routes between China and India?

FOUNDATIONS OF INDIAN CIVILIZATION

India is called a *subcontinent* because it is a large—roughly 2,000 miles (3,200 kilometers) in both length and breadth—and physically isolated landmass within the continent of Asia. It is set off from the rest of Asia by the Himalayas°, the highest mountains on the planet, to the north, and by the Indian Ocean on its eastern, southern, and western sides (see Map 7.1, page 176). The most permeable frontier, and the one used by a long series of invaders and migrating peoples, lies to the northwest. But people using even this corridor must cross over the mountain barrier of the Hindu Kush (via the Khyber Pass) and the Thar° Desert east of the Indus River.

The Indian Subcontinent

This region—which encompasses the modern nations of Pakistan, Nepal, Bhutan, Bangladesh, India, and the adjacent island of Sri Lanka—can be divided into three distinct topographical zones. The mountainous northern zone takes in the heavily forested foothills and high meadows on the edge of the Hindu Kush and Himalaya ranges. Next come the great basins of the Indus and Ganges Rivers. Originating in the ice of the Tibetan mountains to the north, through the millennia these rivers have repeatedly overflowed their banks and deposited layer on layer of silt, creating large alluvial plains. Northern India is divided from the third zone, the peninsula proper, by the Vindhya range and the Deccan°, an arid, rocky plateau that brings to mind parts of the American south-

---

Mauryan (MORE-yuhn)   Himalayas (him-uh-LAY-uhs)
Thar (tahr)   Deccan (de-KAN)

west. The tropical coastal strip of Kerala (Malabar) in the west, the Coromandel Coast in the east with its web of rivers descending from the central plateau, the flatlands of Tamil Nadu on the southern tip of the peninsula, and the island of Sri Lanka often have followed paths of political and cultural development separate from those of northern India.

The rim of mountains looming above India's northern frontier shelters the subcontinent from cold Arctic winds and gives it a subtropical climate. The most dramatic source of moisture is the **monsoon** (seasonal wind). The Indian Ocean is slow to warm or cool, and the vast landmass of Asia swings rapidly between seasonal extremes of heat and cold. The temperature difference between the water and the land acts like a bellows, producing a great wind in this and adjoining parts of the globe. The southwest monsoon begins in June. It picks up huge amounts of moisture from the Indian Ocean and drops it over a swath of India that encompasses the rain-forest belt on the western coast and the Ganges Basin. Three harvests a year are possible in some places. Rice is grown in the moist, flat Ganges Delta (the modern region of Bengal). Elsewhere the staples are wheat, barley, and millet. The Indus Valley, in contrast, gets little precipitation (see Chapter 2). In this arid region the successful practice of agriculture depends on extensive irrigation. Moreover, the volume of water in the Indus is irregular, and the river has changed course from time to time.

Although invasions and migrations usually came by land through the northwest corridor, the ocean surrounding the peninsula has not been a barrier to travel and trade. Indian Ocean mariners learned to ride the monsoon winds across open waters from northeast to southwest in January and to make the return voyage in July. Ships made their way west across the Arabian Sea to the Persian Gulf, the southern coast of Arabia, and East Africa, and east across the Bay of Bengal to Indochina and Indonesia (see Chapter 8).

The Vedic Age, 1500–500 B.C.E.

It is tempting to trace many of the characteristic features of later Indian civilization back to the Indus Valley civilization of the third and early second millennia B.C.E., but proof is hard to come by because the writing from that period has not yet been deciphered. That society, which responded to the challenge of an arid terrain by developing high levels of social organization and technology, seems to have succumbed around 1900 B.C.E. to some kind of environmental crisis (see Chapter 2).

CHRONOLOGY

	India	Southeast Asia
2000 B.C.E.		**ca. 2000** B.C.E. Swidden agriculture
		ca. 1600 B.C.E. Beginning of migrations from mainland Southeast Asia to islands in Pacific and Indian Oceans
1500 B.C.E.	**ca. 1500** B.C.E. Migration of Indo-European peoples into northwest India	
1000 B.C.E.	**ca. 1000** B.C.E. Indo-European groups move into the Ganges Plain	
500 B.C.E.	**ca. 500** B.C.E. Siddhartha Gautama founds Buddhism; Mahavira founds Jainism	
	324 B.C.E. Chandragupta Maurya becomes king of Magadha and lays foundation for Mauryan Empire	
1 C.E.	**184** B.C.E. Fall of Mauryan Empire	
		ca. 50–560 C.E. Funan dominates southern Indochina and the Isthmus of Kra
	320 C.E. Chandra Gupta establishes Gupta Empire	
500 C.E.		**ca. 500** C.E. Trade route develops through Strait of Malacca
	550 C.E. Collapse of Gupta Empire	
	606–647 C.E. Reign of Harsha Vardhana	
		683 C.E. Rise of Srivijaya in Sumatra
		770–825 C.E. Construction of Borobodur in Java
1000 C.E.		**1025** C.E. Chola attack on Palembang and decline of Srivijaya

Historians call the period from 1500 to 500 B.C.E. the "Vedic Age," after the *Vedas,* religious texts that are our main source of information about the period. The foundations for Indian civilization were laid in the Vedic Age. Most historians believe that new groups of people—nomadic warriors speaking Indo-European languages—migrated into northwest India around 1500 B.C.E. Some argue for a much earlier Indo-European presence in this region in conjunction with the spread of agriculture. In any case, in the mid-second millennium B.C.E. northern

India entered a new historical period associated with the dominance of Indo-European groups.

In the arid northwest, large-scale agriculture depends on irrigation. After the collapse of the Indus Valley civilization there was no central authority to direct these efforts, and the region became home to kinship groups that depended mostly on their herds of cattle for sustenance and perhaps also on some gardening to supplement their diet. These societies, like those of other Indo-European peoples—Celts, Greeks, Iranians, Romans—

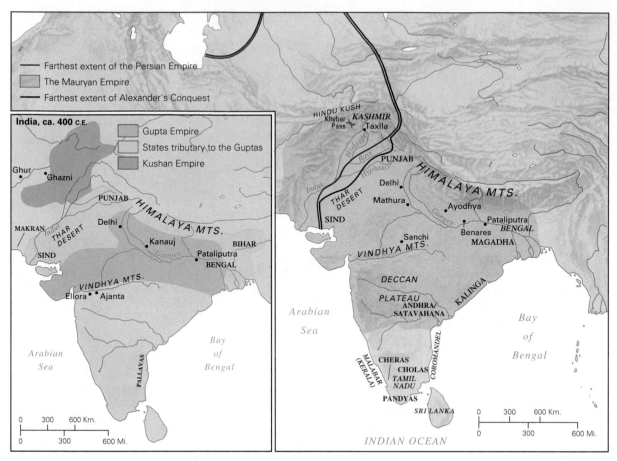

Map. 7.1 Ancient India Mountains and ocean largely separate the Indian subcontinent from the rest of Asia. Migrations and invasions usually came through the Khyber Pass, in the northwest. Seaborne commerce with western Asia, Southeast Asia, and East Asia often flourished. Peoples speaking Indo-European languages migrated into the broad valleys of the Indus and Ganges Rivers in the north. Dravidian-speaking peoples remained the dominant population in the south. The diversity of the Indian landscape, the multiplicity of ethnic groups, and the primary identification of people with their class and caste lie behind the division into many small states that has characterized much of Indian political history.

were patriarchal. The father dominated the family as the king ruled the tribe. Members of the warrior class boasted of their martial skill and courage, relished combat, celebrated with lavish feasts of beef and rounds of heavy drinking, and filled their leisure time with chariot racing and gambling.

After 1000 B.C.E. some of these groups began to push east into the Ganges Plain. New technologies made this advance possible. Iron tools—harder than bronze and able to hold a sharper edge—allowed settlers to fell trees and to work the newly cleared land with plows pulled by oxen. The soil of the Ganges Plain was fertile, well watered by the annual monsoon, and able to sustain two or

three crops a year. As in Greece at roughly the same time (see Chapter 5), in India the use of iron tools to open new land for agriculture must have led to a significant increase in population.

Stories about this era, not written down until much later but long preserved by memorization and oral recitation, speak of bitter rivalry and warfare between two groups of people: the Aryas, relatively light-skinned speakers of Indo-European languages, and the Dasas, dark-skinned speakers of Dravidian languages. Some scholars argue that the real process by which Arya groups became dominant in the north was more complicated, involving the absorption of some Dasas into Arya populations and a merging of elites from both groups. For the most part, however, Aryas pushed the Dasas south into central and southern India, where their descendants still live. A sign of the ultimate success of the Aryas is the languages spoken in northern India today: they are primarily members of the Indo-European language family. Dravidian speech prevails in the south.

Skin color has been a persistent concern of Indian society and is one of the bases for its historically sharp internal divisions. Over time there evolved a system of **varna**—literally "color," though the word came to indicate something akin to "class." Individuals were born into one of four classes: *Brahmin*, the group comprising priests and scholars; *Kshatriya°*, warriors and officials; *Vaishya°*, merchants, artisans, and landowners; or *Shudra°*, peasants and laborers. The designation *Shudra* originally may have been reserved for Dasas, who were given the menial jobs in society. Indeed, the very term *dasa* came to mean "slave." Eventually a fifth group was marked off: the Untouchables. They were excluded from the class system, and members of the other groups literally avoided them because of the demeaning or polluting work to which they were relegated—such as leather tanning, which involved touching dead animals, and sweeping away ashes after cremations.

People at the top of the social pyramid in ancient India could explain why this hierarchy existed. According to one creation myth, a primordial creature named Purusha allowed himself to be sacrificed. From its mouth sprang the class of Brahmin priests, the embodiment of intellect and knowledge. From his arms came the Kshatriya warrior class, from his thighs the Vaishya landowners and merchants, and from his feet the Shudra workers.

The varna system was just one of the mechanisms that Indian society developed to regulate relations between different groups. Within the broad class divisions, the population was further subdivided into numerous **jati,** or birth groups (sometimes called *castes* from a Portuguese term meaning "breed"). Each jati had its proper occupation, duties, and rituals. The individuals who belonged to a given jati lived with members of their group, married within the group, and ate only with members of the group. Elaborate rules governed their interactions with members of other groups. Members of higher-status groups feared pollution from contact with lower-caste individuals and had to undergo elaborate rituals of purification to remove any taint.

The class and caste systems came to be connected to

Kshatriya (kshuh-TREE-yuh)   *Vaishya* (VIESH-yuh)
Shudra (SHOOD-ra)

a widespread belief in reincarnation. The Brahmin priests taught that every living creature had an immortal essence: the *atman*, or "breath." Separated from the body at death, at a later time the atman was reborn in another body. Whether the new body was that of an insect, an animal, or a human depended on the **karma,** or deeds, of the atman in its previous incarnations. People who lived exemplary lives would be reborn into the higher classes. Those who misbehaved would be punished in the next life by being relegated to a lower class or even a lower life form. The underlying message was: You are where you deserve to be, and the only way to improve your lot in the next cycle of existence is to accept your current station and its attendant duties.

The dominant deities in Vedic religion were male and were associated with the heavens. To release the dawn, Indra, god of war and master of the thunderbolt, daily slew the demon encasing the universe. Varuna, lord of the sky, maintained universal order and dispensed justice. Agni, the force of fire, consumed the sacrifice and bridged the spheres of gods and humans.

Sacrifice—the dedication to a god of a valued possession, often a living creature—was the essential ritual. The purpose of these offerings was to invigorate the gods and thereby sustain their creative powers and promote stability in the world.

Brahmin priests controlled the technology of sacrifice, for only they knew the rituals and prayers. The *Rig Veda*, a collection of more than a thousand poetic hymns to various deities, and the *Brahmanas,* detailed prose descriptions of procedures for ritual and sacrifice, were collections of priestly lore couched in the Sanskrit language of the Arya upper classes. This information was handed down orally from one generation of priests to the next. Some scholars have hypothesized that the Brahmins opposed the introduction of writing. Such opposition would explain why this technology did not come into widespread use in India until the Gupta period (320–550 C.E.), long after it had begun to play a conspicuous role in other societies of equivalent complexity. The priests' "knowledge" (the term *veda* means just that) was the basis of their economic well-being. They were amply rewarded for officiating at sacrifices, and their knowledge gave them social and political power because they were the indispensable intermediaries between gods and humans.

As in nearly all ancient societies, it is difficult to uncover the experiences of women in ancient India. Limited evidence indicates that in the Vedic period women studied sacred lore, composed religious hymns, and participated in the sacrificial ritual. They had the opportunity to own property and usually were not married until

Reflections of the Status of Women In Indian Literature

Literature does not necessarily depict life exactly as it is, but it does reflect the values of the culture that produces it. Thus we may turn to the literature of ancient India for clues about the status, treatment, and roles of women.

One episode in the great Indian epic, the Mahabharata, concerns a female heroine named Shakuntala who resolutely pursues a king who has forgotten his promise that the child resulting from their brief love affair in the forest will inherit his throne. Their initial meeting is described as follows.

The king . . . looked at the girl who had addressed him and saw that she had beautiful hips, a lustrous appearance, and a charming smile. She was radiant with beauty, with the sheen of austerities, and the calm of self restraint. The king now said to the maiden, as perfect of shape as of age, "Who are you? Whose are you? Why, fair-waisted girl, have you come to this wilderness? . . . For one look at you, lovely, has carried my heart away! I want to know about you, tell me, my pretty."

[Shakuntala explains how she has come to live, as the adopted daughter of an ascetic, in a remote forest hermitage.]

[The king then says:] Be my wife, buxom woman! Tell me, what can I do for you? Today I shall bring you golden necklaces, clothes, earrings wrought of gold, and sparkling gems from many countries, my pretty, and breast plates and hides. Today all my kingdom will be yours.

[When Shakuntala urges the king to wait until her father returns, so that he might agree to the marriage, the king tells her that there is a form of marriage in which she may decide for herself:] Oneself is one's own best friend, oneself is one's only recourse. You yourself can lawfully make the gift of yourself. . . .

Shakuntala said: If this is the course of the Law, and if I am my own mistress, then . . . this is my condition in giving myself in marriage, my lord. Give your own true promise to the secret covenant I make between us: the son that may be born from me shall be Young King to succeed you, great king, declare this to me as the truth! If it is to be thus, . . . you may lie with me.

Both here and later in the Mahabharata *story, Shakuntala is clearly an intelligent, confident, and resourceful young woman, reflecting the relatively favorable position of women in the Vedic period. When we encounter her in the literature of a later age, we confront the significant changes that have taken place for women in Indian society.*

---

they reached their middle or late teens. A number of strong and resourceful women appear in the epic poem *Mahabharata* (see Society and Culture: Reflections of the Status of Women in Indian Literature). One of them, the beautiful and educated Draupadi, married by her own choice the five royal Pandava brothers. This accomplishment probably should not be taken as evidence for the regular practice of polyandry (having more than one husband). In India, as in Greece, legendary figures played by their own rules.

The sharp internal divisions of Indian society, the complex hierarchy of groups, and the claims of some to superior virtue and purity served important social functions in Indian culture. They provided each individual with a clear identity and role and offered the benefits of group solidarity and support. There is evidence that groups sometimes were able to upgrade their status. Thus the elaborate system of divisions was not static and provided a mechanism for working out social tensions. Many of these features persisted into modern times.

Challenges to the Old Order: Jainism and Buddhism

After 700 B.C.E. various forms of reaction against Brahmin power and privilege emerged. People who objected to the rigid hierarchy of classes and castes or the community's demands on the individual could always retreat to the forest. Despite the clearing of extensive tracts of land for agriculture, much of ancient India was covered with forest. Never very far from civilized areas, these wild places served as a refuge and symbolized freedom from societal constraints.

A number of the works of drama of the Gupta period were love stories, providing us glimpses of the lifestyle and manners of high society. The greatest of all ancient Indian dramatists, Kalidasa, was active in the reign of Chandra Gupta II (r. 375–415 C.E.). Seven of his plays survive. As the Athenian dramatists of the fifth century B.C.E. had drawn their plots from the legendary tradition preserved in Homer but altered details and reworked the characters to comment on the values and issues of their own times, so Kalidasa refashioned elements drawn from the great Indian epics. In Shakuntala or the Ring of Recollection, *he reworked that ancient tale:*

Shakuntala (to her attendants): Don't leave me alone.
King: You have nothing to worry about as long as I'm here. Shall I fan you with the lotus leaf? Would you rather I pressed your tired feet?
Shakuntala: I am giving you unnecessary trouble. (She tries to leave.)
King: It's blazing hot, Shakuntala, and you're in no condition to walk alone. You won't be able to stand the sun after your bed of lotus leaves. (He catches her by the arm.)
Shakuntala: Please, sire. I am a woman. It's not my fault I'm in love. What will the others think?

[He is about to kiss her when the woman who takes care of her calls her to bed. The king hides behind a bush.]

Shakuntala: (aside) When I had my chance, I was coy. Now I have only regret. (Aloud) I will return, ivy bower: you were my best doctor.

Apparently the conventions of the stage or the prudishness of the age required that the liaison of Shakuntala and the king be treated with considerable delicacy. More significantly, for our purposes, we see that Kalidasa turned Shakuntala into a docile figure animated more by forlorn love than by confident self-assertion. In this way he validated the prevailing conception of women, emphasizing the importance of female passivity, chastity, and devotion to the husband.

Language itself provides another clue to the status of women in the Gupta period. In the plays, Sanskrit, the ancient language of sacred texts, is spoken by Brahmins and other men of the upper classes. Prakrit, the form of speech used in everyday life, is spoken by women, low-class men, and servants, as if to equate the status of women with the lowest social groups. This and other evidence seem to indicate that women's situations worsened after the Vedic period.

Why is it problematic to reconstruct the roles, conduct, and treatment of women from the testimony of male authors? How does the situation of women in ancient India compare to that in ancient China, the Middle East, and the Mediterranean?

Source: Translations from J. A. B. van Buitenen, *The Mahabharata*, vol. 1 (Chicago: University of Chicago Press, 1973); and P. Lal, *Great Sanskrit Plays in Modern Translation* (New York: New Directions Books, 1957).

Certain charismatic individuals who abandoned their town or village and moved to the forest attracted bands of followers. Calling into question the priests' exclusive claims to wisdom and the necessity of Vedic chants and sacrifices, these persons offered an alternate path to salvation: the individual pursuit of insight into the nature of the self and the universe through physical and mental discipline (*yoga*), special dietary practices, and meditation. They taught that by distancing oneself from desire for the things of this world, one could achieve **moksha,** or "liberation." This release from the cycle of reincarnations and union with the divine force that animates the universe sometimes was likened to "a deep, dreamless sleep." The Upanishads—a collection of more than one hundred mystical dialogues between teachers and disciples—reflect this questioning of the foundations of Vedic religion.

The most serious threat to Vedic religion and to the prerogatives of the Brahmin priestly class came from two new religions that emerged around this time: Jainism° and Buddhism. Mahavira (540–468 B.C.E.) was known to his followers as Jina, "the Conqueror," from which is derived *Jainism*, the name of the belief system that he established. Emphasizing the holiness of the life force that animates all living creatures, Mahavira and his followers practiced strict nonviolence. They wore masks to prevent themselves from accidentally inhaling small insects, and before sitting down they carefully brushed off the surface of the seat. Those who gave themselves over completely to Jainism practiced extreme asceticism and nudity, ate only what they were given by others, and eventually starved themselves to death. Less zealous

Jainism (JINE-iz-uhm)

Jainists, restricted from agricultural work by the injunction against killing, tended to be city dwellers engaged in commerce and banking.

Of far greater significance for Indian and world history was the rise of Buddhism. So many stories have been told about Siddhartha Gautama (563–483 B.C.E.), known as the **Buddha**, "the Enlightened One," that it is difficult to separate fact from legend. He came from a Kshatriya family of the Sakyas, a people in the foothills of the Himalayas. As a young man he enjoyed the princely lifestyle to which he had been born, but at some point he experienced a change of heart and gave up family and privilege to become a wandering ascetic. After six years of self-deprivation, he came to regard asceticism as being no more likely to produce spiritual insight than the luxury of his previous life, and he decided to adhere to a "Middle Path" of moderation. Sitting under a tree in a deer park near Benares on the Ganges River, he gained a sudden and profound insight into the true nature of reality, which he set forth as "Four Noble Truths": (1) life is suffering; (2) suffering arises from desire; (3) the solution to suffering lies in curbing desire; and (4) desire can be curbed if a person follows the "Eightfold Path" of right views, aspirations, speech, conduct, livelihood, effort, mindfulness, and meditation. Rising up, the Buddha preached his First Sermon, a central text of Buddhism, and set into motion the "Wheel of the Law." He soon attracted followers, some of whom took vows of celibacy, nonviolence, and poverty.

In its original form Buddhism centered on the individual. Although it did not quite reject the existence of gods, it denied their usefulness to a person seeking enlightenment. What mattered was living one's life with moderation, in order to minimize desire and suffering, and searching for spiritual truth through self-discipline and meditation. The ultimate reward was *nirvana*, literally "snuffing out the flame." With nirvana came release from the cycle of reincarnations and achievement of a state of perpetual tranquility. The Vedic tradition emphasized the eternal survival of the atman, the "breath" or nonmaterial essence of the individal. In contrast, Buddhism regarded the individual as a composite without any soul-like component that survived upon entering nirvana.

When the Buddha died, he left no final instructions, instead urging his disciples to "be their own lamp." As the Buddha's message—contained in philosophical discourses memorized by his followers—spread throughout India and beyond into Central, Southeast, and East Asia, its very success began to subvert the individualistic and essentially atheistic tenets of the founder. Buddhist monasteries were established, and a hierarchy of Buddhist monks and nuns came into being. Worshipers

Gateway Leading into the Precinct of the Great Stupa at Sanchi Pilgrims traveled long distances to visit these mounds containing relics of the Buddha (one is depicted, surrounded by elephants, in the center of the lowest horizontal post). The complex at Sanchi, in central India, was begun by Ashoka in the third century B.C.E., though the gates probably date to the first century C.E. The elaborate relief sculpture includes Buddhist symbols, scenes from the lives of the Buddha, and voluptuous female tree spirits. (Jean-Louis Nou)

erected *stupas* (large earthen mounds that symbolized the universe) over relics of the cremated founder and walked around them in a clockwise direction. Believers began to worship the Buddha himself as a god. Many Buddhists also revered *bodhisattvas*°, men and women who had achieved enlightenment and were on the threshold of nirvana but chose to be reborn into mortal bodies to help others along the path to salvation.

The makers of early pictorial images had refused to show the Buddha as a living person and represented him only indirectly, through symbols such as his footprints,

---

bodhisattva (boe-dih-SUT-vuh)

Sculpture of the Buddha, Second or Third Century C.E.
This depiction of the Buddha, showing the effects of a protracted fast, is from Gandhara in the northwest. It displays the influence of Greek artistic styles emanating from Greek settlements established in that region by Alexander the Great in the late fourth century B.C.E. (Robert Fisher)

begging bowl, or the tree under which he achieved enlightenment, as if to emphasize his achievement of a state of nonexistence. From the second century C.E., however, statues of the Buddha and bodhisattvas began to proliferate, done in native sculptural styles and in a style that showed the influence of the Greek settlements established in Bactria (modern Afghanistan) by Alexander the Great (see Chapter 5). A schism emerged within Buddhism. Devotees of **Mahayana**° ("Great Vehicle") **Buddhism** embraced the popular new features. In contrast, practitioners of **Theravada**° ("Teachings of the Elders") **Buddhism** followed most of the original teachings of the founder.

Mahayana (mah-huh-YAH-nuh)
Theravada (there-eh-VAH-duh)

The Rise of Hinduism

Challenged by new, spiritually satisfying, and egalitarian movements, Vedic religion made important adjustments, evolving into **Hinduism,** the religion of hundreds of millions of people in South Asia today. (The term *Hinduism,* however, was imposed from outside. Islamic invaders who reached India in the eleventh century C.E. labeled the diverse range of practices they saw there as Hinduism: "what the Indians do.") The foundation of Hinduism is the Vedic religion of the Arya tribes of northern India. But Hinduism also incorporated elements drawn from the Dravidian cultures of the south, such as an emphasis on intense devotion to the deity and the prominence of fertility rituals and symbolism. Also present are elements of Buddhism.

The process by which Vedic religion was transformed into Hinduism by the fourth century C.E. is largely hidden from us. The Brahmin priests emerged with their high social status and influence essentially intact. But sacrifice, though still part of traditional worship, was less central, and there was much more opportunity for direct contact between gods and individual worshipers.

The gods were altered, both in identity and in their relationships with humanity. Two formerly minor deities, Vishnu and Shiva, assumed a preeminent position in the Hindu pantheon. Hinduism emphasized the worshiper's personal devotion to a particular deity, usually Vishnu, Shiva, or Devi ("the Goddess"). Both Shiva and Devi appear to be derived from the Dravidian tradition, in which a fertility cult and female deities played a prominent role. Their Dravidian origin is a telling example of how Arya and non-Arya cultures fused to form classic Hindu civilization. It is interesting to note that Vishnu, who has a clear Arya pedigree, remains more popular in northern India, while Shiva is dominant in the Dravidian south. These gods can appear in many guises. They are identified by various cult names and are represented by a complex symbolism of stories, companion animals, birds, and objects.

Vishnu, the preserver, is a benevolent deity who helps his devotees in time of need. Hindus believe that whenever demonic forces threaten the cosmic order, Vishnu appears on earth in one of a series of *avataras,* or incarnations. Among his incarnations are the legendary hero Rama, the popular cowherd-god Krishna, and the Buddha (a clear attempt to co-opt the rival religion's founder). Shiva, who lives in ascetic isolation on Mount Kailasa in the Himalayas, is a more ambivalent figure. He represents both creation and destruction, for both are part of a single, cyclical process. He often is represented performing dance steps that symbolize the acts of creation and destruction. Devi manifests herself in various ways—as a full-bodied mother-goddess who promotes fertility and procreation, as the docile and loving wife Parvati, and as the frightening deity who, under the name Kali or Durga, lets loose a torrent of violence and destruction.

The multiplicity of gods (330 million according to one tradition), sects, and local practices within Hinduism is dazzling, reflecting the ethnic, linguistic, and cultural diversity of India. Yet within this variety there is unity. A worshiper's devotion to one god or goddess does not entail denial of the other main deities or the host of lesser divinities and spirits. Ultimately, all are seen as manifestations of a single divine force that pervades the universe. This sense of underlying unity is expressed in many ways: in texts such as the passage from the Bhagavad-Gita quoted at the beginning of this chapter; in the different potentials of women represented in the various manifestations of Devi; in composite statues that are split down the middle—half Shiva, half Vishnu—as if to say that they are complementary aspects of one cosmic principle.

Hinduism offers the worshiper a variety of ways to approach god and obtain divine favor—through special knowledge of sacred truths, mental and physical discipline, or extraordinary devotion to the deity. The activity of worship centers on the temples, which range from humble village shrines to magnificent, richly decorated stone edifices built under royal patronage. Beautifully proportioned statues beckon the deity to take up temporary residence within the image, where he or she can be reached and beseeched by eager worshipers. A common form of worship is *puja*, service to the deity, which can take the form of bathing, clothing, or feeding the statue. Potent blessings are conferred on the man or woman who glimpses the divine image.

Pilgrimage to famous shrines and attendance at festivals offer worshipers additional opportunities to show devotion. The entire Indian subcontinent is dotted with sacred places where a worshiper can directly sense and benefit from the inherent power of divinity. Mountains, caves, and certain trees, plants, and rocks are enveloped in an aura of mystery and sanctity. The literal meaning of *tirthayatra*, the term for a pilgrimage site, is "journey to a

Hindu Temple at Khajuraho   This sandstone temple of the Hindu deity Shiva, representing the celestial mountain of the gods, was erected at Khajuraho, in central India, around 1000 C.E., but it reflects the architectural symbolism of Hindu temples developed in the Gupta period. Worshipers made their way through several rooms to the image of the deity, located in the innermost "womb-chamber" directly beneath the tallest tower.   (Jean-Louis Nou)

Stone Relief Depicting Vishnu Asleep and Dreaming on the Ocean Floor, Fifth Century C.E. In this relief from a temple at Deogarh, in central India, Vishnu reclines on the coiled body of a giant multiheaded serpent that he subdued. The beneficent god of preservation, Vishnu appears in a new incarnation whenever demonic forces threaten the world. The Indian view of the vastness of time is embodied in this mythic image, which conceives of Vishnu as creating and destroying universes as he exhales and inhales. (John C. Huntington)

comes a student and studies the sacred texts; (2) he then becomes a householder, marries, has children, and acquires material wealth; (3) when his grandchildren are born, he gives up home and family and becomes a forest dweller, meditating on the nature and meaning of existence; (4) he abandons his personal identity altogether and becomes a wandering ascetic awaiting death. In the course of a virtuous life he has fulfilled first his duties to society and then his duties to himself, so that by the end of his life he is so disconnected from the world that he can achieve moksha (liberation).

The successful transformation of a religion based on Vedic antecedents and the ultimate victory of Hinduism over Buddhism—Buddhism was driven from the land of its birth, though it maintains deep roots in Central, East, and Southeast Asia (see Chapters 8 and 11)—are remarkable phenomena. Hinduism responded to the needs of people for personal deities with whom they could establish direct connections. The austerity of Buddhism in its most authentic form, its denial of the importance of gods, and its expectation that individuals find their own path to enlightenment may have demanded too much of ordinary individuals. And the very features that made Mahayana Buddhism more accessible to the populace—gods, saints, and myths—also made it more easily absorbed into the vast social and cultural fabric of Hinduism.

IMPERIAL EXPANSION AND COLLAPSE

Political unity in India, on those rare occasions when it has been achieved, has not lasted long. A number of factors have contributed to India's habitual political fragmentation. The landscape—mountains, foothills, plains, forests, steppes, deserts—is extremely varied. Different terrains called forth different forms of organization and economic activity, and peoples occupying topographically diverse zones differed from one another in language and cultural practices. Perhaps the most significant barrier to political unity lay in the complex social hierarchy. Individuals identified themselves primarily in terms of their class and caste (birth group); allegiance to a higher political authority was of secondary concern.

Despite these divisive factors, two empires arose in the Ganges Plain: the Mauryan Empire of the fourth to second centuries B.C.E. and the Gupta Empire of the fourth to sixth centuries C.E. Each extended political control over a substantial portion of the subcontinent and fostered the formation of a common Indian civilization.

river-crossing," pointing up the frequent association of Hindu sacred places with flowing water. Hindus consider the Ganges River to be especially sacred, and each year millions of devoted worshipers travel to its banks to bathe and receive the restorative and purifying power of its waters. The habit of pilgrimage to the major shrines has promoted contact and the exchange of ideas among people from different parts of India and has helped to create a broad Hindu identity and the concept of India as a single civilization, despite enduring political fragmentation.

Religious duties may vary, depending not only on the worshiper's social standing and gender but also on his or her stage of life. A young man from one of the three highest classes (Brahmin, Kshatriya, or Vaishya) undergoes a ritual rebirth through the ceremony of the sacred thread, marking the attainment of manhood and readiness to receive religious knowledge. From this point, the ideal life cycle passes through four stages: (1) the young man be-

The Mauryan Empire, 324–184 B.C.E.

Around 600 B.C.E. separate kinship groups and independent states dotted the landscape of north India. The kingdom of Magadha, in eastern India south of the Ganges (see Map 7.1), began to play an increasingly influential role, however, thanks to wealth based on agriculture, iron mines, and its strategic location astride the trade routes of the eastern Ganges Basin. In the late fourth century B.C.E. Chandragupta Maurya°, a young man who may have belonged to the Vaishya or Shudra class, gained control of the kingdom of Magadha and expanded it into the **Mauryan Empire**—India's first centralized empire. He may have been inspired by the example of Alexander the Great, who had followed up his conquest of the Persian Empire with a foray into the Punjab (northern Pakistan) in 326 B.C.E. (see Chapter 5). Indeed, Greek tradition claimed that Alexander met a young Indian native by the name of "Sandracottus," an apparent corruption of "Chandragupta."

The collapse of Greek rule in the Punjab after the death of Alexander created a power vacuum in the northwest. Chandragupta (r. 324–301 B.C.E.) and his successors Bindusara (r. 301–269 B.C.E.) and Ashoka (r. 269–232 B.C.E.) extended Mauryan control over the entire subcontinent except for the southern tip of the peninsula. Not until the height of the Mughal Empire of the seventeenth century C.E. or the advent of British rule in the nineteenth century was so much of India again under the control of a single government.

Tradition holds that Kautilya, a crafty elderly Brahmin, guided Chandragupta in his conquests and consolidation of power. Kautilya is said to have written a surviving treatise on government, the *Arthashastra*. Although recent studies have shown that the *Arthashastra* in its present form is a product of the third century C.E., its core text may well go back to Kautilya. This coldly pragmatic guide to political success and survival advocates the so-called *mandala* (circle) theory of foreign policy: "My enemy's enemy is my friend." It also relates a long list of schemes for enforcing and increasing the collection of tax revenues, and it prescribes the use of spies to keep watch on everyone in the kingdom.

A tax equivalent to one-fourth of the value of the agricultural crop supported the Mauryan kings and government. Close relatives and associates of the king governed administrative districts based on traditional ethnic boundaries. A large imperial army—with infantry, cavalry, chariot, and elephant divisions—and royal control of mines, shipbuilding, and the manufacture of armaments further secured the power of the central government. Standard coinage issued throughout the empire fostered support for the government and military and promoted trade.

The Mauryan capital was at Pataliputra (modern Patna), where five tributaries join the Ganges. Several extant descriptions of the city composed by foreign visitors provide valuable information and testify to the international connections of the Indian monarchs. Surrounded by a timber wall and moat, the city extended along the river for 8 miles (13 kilometers). It was governed by six committees with responsibility for features of urban life such as manufacturing, trade, sales, taxes, the welfare of foreigners, and the registration of births and deaths.

Ashoka, Chandragupta's grandson, is a towering figure in Indian history. At the beginning of his reign he engaged in military campaigns that extended the boundaries of the empire. During his conquest of Kalinga (modern Orissa, a coastal region southeast of Magadha), hundreds of thousands of people were killed, wounded, or deported. Overwhelmed by the brutality of this victory, the young monarch became a convert to Buddhism and preached nonviolence, morality, moderation, and religious tolerance in both government and private life.

Ashoka publicized this program by inscribing edicts on great rocks and polished pillars of sandstone scattered throughout his enormous empire. Among the inscriptions that have survived—they constitute the earliest decipherable Indian writing—is the following:

> For a long time in the past, for many hundreds of years have increased the sacrificial slaughter of animals, violence toward creatures, unfilial conduct toward kinsmen, improper conduct toward Brahmins and ascetics. Now with the practice of morality by King [Ashoka], the sound of war drums has become the call to morality. . . . You [government officials] are appointed to rule over thousands of human beings in the expectation that you will win the affection of all men. All men are my children. Just as I desire that my children will fare well and be happy in this world and the next, I desire the same for all men. . . . King [Ashoka] . . . desires that there should be the growth of the essential spirit of morality or holiness among all sects. . . . There should not be glorification of one's own sect and denunciation of the sect of others for little or no reason. For all the sects are worthy of reverence for one reason or another.[2]

Ashoka, however, was not naive. Despite his commitment to employ peaceful means whenever possible, he hastened to remind potential transgressors that "the king, remorseful as he is, has the strength to punish the wrongdoers who do not repent."

Maurya (MORE-yuh)

Commerce and Culture in an Era of Political Fragmentation

The Mauryan Empire prospered for a time after Ashoka's death in 232 B.C.E. Then, weakened by dynastic disputes, it collapsed from the pressure of attacks in the northwest in 184 B.C.E. Five hundred years passed before another indigenous state was able to extend its control over northern India.

In the meantime, a series of foreign powers dominated the Indus Valley and extended their influence east and south. The first was the Greco-Bactrian kingdom (180–50 B.C.E.), descended from troops and settlers that Alexander the Great had left behind in Afghanistan. Domination by two nomadic peoples from Central Asia followed: the Shakas (known as Scythians in the Mediterranean world) from 50 B.C.E. to 50 C.E. and the Kushans from 50 to 240 C.E. Several foreign kings—most notably the Greco-Bactrian Milinda (Menander in Greek) and the Kushan Kanishka—were converts to Buddhism, a logical choice because Hinduism had no easy mechanism for working foreigners into its system of class and caste. The eastern Ganges region reverted to a patchwork of small principalities, as it had been before the Mauryan era.

Indeed, despite the political fragmentation of India in the five centuries after the collapse of the Mauryan Empire, there were many signs of economic, cultural, and intellectual development. The network of roads and towns that had sprung up under the Mauryans fostered lively commerce within the subcontinent, and India was at the heart of international land and sea trade routes that linked China, Southeast Asia, Central Asia, the Middle East, East Africa, and the lands of the Mediterranean. In the absence of a strong central authority, guilds of merchants and artisans in the Indian towns became politically powerful, regulating the lives of their members and having an important say in local affairs. Their economic clout enabled them to serve as patrons of culture and to endow the religious sects to which they adhered—particularly Buddhism and Jainism—with richly decorated temples and monuments.

During the last centuries B.C.E. and first centuries C.E. the two greatest Indian epics, the *Ramayana* and the *Mahabharata*, based on oral predecessors dating back many centuries, achieved their final form. The events that both epics describe are said to have occurred several million years in the past, but the political forms, social organization, and other elements of cultural context—proud kings, beautiful queens, wars among kinship groups, heroic conduct, chivalric values—seem to reflect the conditions of the early Vedic period, when Arya warrior societies were moving onto the Ganges Plain.

The *Ramayana* relates the exploits of Rama, a heroic prince, who is an incarnation of the god Vishnu. When his beautiful wife is kidnapped, aided by his loyal brother and the king of the monkeys, he defeats and destroys the chief of the demons and his evil horde. The vast pageant of the **Mahabharata** (it is eight times the length of the Greek *Iliad* and *Odyssey* combined) tells the story of two sets of cousins, the Pandavas and Kauravas, whose quarrel over succession to the throne leads them to a cataclysmic battle at the field of Kurukshetra. The battle is so destructive on all sides that the eventual winner, Yudhishthira, is reluctant to accept the fruits of so tragic a victory.

The **Bhagavad-Gita,** quoted at the beginning of this chapter, is a self-contained (and perhaps originally separate) episode set in the midst of those events. The great hero Arjuna, at first reluctant to fight his own kinsmen, is tutored by the god Krishna and learns the necessity of fulfilling his duty as a warrior. Death means nothing in a universe in which souls will be reborn again and again. The climactic moment comes when Krishna reveals his true appearance—awesome and overwhelmingly powerful—and his identity as time itself, the force behind all creation and destruction. The Bhagavad-Gita offers an attractive resolution to the tension in Indian civilization between duty to society and duty to one's own soul. Disciplined action—that is, action taken without regard for any personal benefits that might derive from it—is a form of service to the gods and will be rewarded by release from the cycle of rebirths.

This era also saw significant advances in science and technology. Indian doctors had a wide knowledge of herbal remedies and were in demand in the courts of western and southern Asia. Indian scholars made impressive strides in linguistics. Panini (late fourth century B.C.E.) undertook a detailed analysis of Sanskrit word forms and grammar. The work of Panini and later linguists led to the standardization of Sanskrit, which arrested its natural development and turned it into a formal, literary language. Prakrits—popular dialects—emerged to become the ancestors of the modern Indo-European languages of northern and central India.

This period of political fragmentation in the north also saw the rise of important states in central India, particularly the Andhra dynasty in the Deccan Plateau (from the second century B.C.E. to the second century C.E.), and the three **Tamil kingdoms** of Cholas, Pandyas, and Cheras in southern India (see Map 7.1). The three Tamil kingdoms were in frequent conflict with one another and experienced periods of ascendancy and decline, but they persisted in one form or another for over two thousand years. Historians regard the period from the third century B.C.E. to the third century C.E. as a "classical" period of great literary and artistic productivity in Tamil society. Under the patronage of the Pandya kings and the intellectual leadership of an academy of five hundred authors, works of literature on a wide range of topics— grammatical treatises, collections of ethical proverbs, epics, short poems about love, war, wealth, and the beauty of nature—were produced and performances of music, dance, and drama were given.

The Gupta Empire, 320–550 C.E.

In the early fourth century C.E. a new imperial entity took shape in northern India. Like its Mauryan predecessor, the **Gupta Empire** grew out of the kingdom of Magadha on the Ganges Plain and had its capital at Pataliputra. Clear proof that the founder of this empire consciously modeled himself on the Mauryans is the fact that he called himself Chandra Gupta (r. 320–335), borrowing the very name of the Mauryan founder. A claim to wide dominion was embodied in the title that the monarchs of this dynasty assumed—"Great King of Kings"—although they never controlled territories as extensive as those of the Mauryans. Nevertheless, over the fifteen-year reign of Chandra Gupta and the forty-year reigns of his three successors—Samudra Gupta, Chandra Gupta II, and Kumara Gupta—Gupta power and influence reached across northern and central India, west to Punjab and east to Bengal, north to Kashmir and south into the Deccan Plateau (see Map 7.1).

This new empire enjoyed the same strategic advantages as its Mauryan predecessor, sitting astride important trade routes, exploiting the agricultural productivity of the Ganges Plain, and controlling nearby iron deposits. It adopted similar methods for raising revenue and administering broad territories. The chief source of revenue was a 25 percent tax on agriculture. Those who used the irrigation network also had to pay for the service, and there were special taxes on particular commodities. The state maintained monopolies in key areas such as the mining of metals and salt. The state also owned extensive tracts of farmland and demanded a specified number of days of labor annually from the subjects for the construction and upkeep of roads, wells, and the irrigation network.

Gupta control, however, was never as effectively centralized as Mauryan authority. The Gupta administrative bureaucracy and intelligence network were smaller and less pervasive. A powerful army maintained tight control and taxation in the core of the empire, but outlying areas were left to their governors to organize. The position of governor offered tempting opportunities

to exploit the populace. It often was hereditary, passed on from father to son in families of high-ranking members of the civil and military administrations. Distant subordinate kingdoms and areas inhabited by kinship groups were expected to make annual donations of tribute, and garrisons were stationed at certain key frontier points to keep open the lines of trade and expedite the collection of customs duties.

Limited in its ability to enforce its will on outlying areas, the empire found ways to "persuade" others to follow its lead. One medium of persuasion was the splendor, beauty, and orderliness of life at the capital and royal court. A constant round of solemn rituals, dramatic ceremonies, and exciting cultural events were such a potent advertisement for the benefits of association with the empire that modern historians point to the Gupta Empire as a good example of a **"theater-state."** The relationship of ruler and subjects in a theater-state also has an economic base. The center collects luxury goods and profits from trade and redistributes these accumulated resources to its dependents through the exchange of gifts and other means. Subordinate princes gained prestige by emulating the Gupta center on whatever scale they could manage, and maintained close ties through visits, gifts, and marriages to the Gupta royal family.

Astronomers, mathematicians, and other scientists received royal Gupta support. Indian mathematicians invented the concept of zero and developed the "Arabic" numerals and system of place-value notation that are in use in most parts of the world today (see Environment and Technology: Indian Mathematics).

Because the moist climate of the Ganges Plain does not favor the preservation of buildings and artifacts, there is for the Gupta era, as for earlier eras in Indian history, relatively little archaeological data. An eyewitness account, however, provides valuable information about the Gupta kingdom and Pataliputra, its capital city. A Chinese Buddhist monk named Faxian° made a pilgrimage to the homeland of his faith around 400 C.E. and left a record of his journey:

> The royal palace and halls in the midst of the city, which exist now as of old, were all made by spirits which [King Ashoka] employed, and which piled up the stones, reared the walls and gates, and executed the elegant carving and inlaid sculpture-work—in a way which no human hands of this world could accomplish. . . . By the side of the stupa of Ashoka, there has been made a Mahayana [Buddhist] monastery, very grand and beautiful; there is also a Hinayana

---

Faxian (fah-shee-en)

[Theravada] one; the two together containing six hundred or seven hundred monks. The rules of demeanor and the scholastic arrangements in them are worthy of observation. . . . The cities and towns of this country are the greatest of all in the Middle Kingdom. The inhabitants are rich and prosperous, and vie with one another in the practice of benevolence and righteousness. . . . The heads of the Vaishya families in them establish in the cities houses for dispensing charity and medicines. All the poor and destitute in the country, orphans, widowers, and childless men, maimed people and cripples, and all who are diseased, go to those houses, and are provided with every kind of help.[3]

Various kinds of evidence point to a decline in the status of women in this period (see Society and Culture: Reflections of the Status of Women in Indian Literature). In all likelihood, this development was similar to developments in Mesopotamia from the second millennium B.C.E., in Archaic and Classical Greece, and in China from the first millennium B.C.E. In those civilizations, several factors—urbanization, the formation of increasingly complex political and social structures, and the emergence of a nonagricultural middle class that placed high value on the acquisition and inheritance of property—led to a loss of women's rights and an increase in male control over women's behavior.

Over time, women in India lost the right to own or inherit property. They were barred from studying sacred texts and participating in the sacrificial ritual. In many respects they were treated as equivalent to the lowest class, the Shudra. As in Confucian China, a woman was expected to obey first her father, then her husband, and finally her sons (see Chapter 6). Indian girls were married at an increasingly early age, sometimes as young as six or seven. This practice meant that the prospective husband could be sure of his wife's virginity and, by bringing her up in his own household, could train and shape her to suit his purposes. The most extreme form of control of women's conduct took place in certain parts of India where a widow was expected to cremate herself on her husband's funeral pyre. This ritual, called *sati*°, was seen as a way of keeping a woman "pure." Women who declined to make this ultimate gesture of devotion were forbidden to remarry, shunned socially, and given little opportunity to earn a living.

Some women escaped these instruments of male control. One way to do so was by entering a Jainist or Buddhist religious community. Status also gave women more freedom. Women who belonged to powerful families and courtesans who were trained in poetry and music as well as in ways of providing sexual pleasure had high social standing and sometimes gave money for the erection of Buddhist stupas and other shrines.

The Mauryans had been Buddhists, but the Gupta monarchs were Hindus. They revived ancient Vedic practices to bring an aura of sanctity to their position. This period also saw a reassertion of the importance of class and caste and the influence of Brahmin priests. Nevertheless, it was an era of religious tolerance. The Gupta kings were patrons for Hindu, Buddhist, and Jain endeavors. Buddhist monasteries with hundreds or even thousands of monks and nuns in residence flourished in the cities. Northern India was the destination of Buddhist pilgrims from Southeast and East Asia, traveling to visit the birthplace of their faith.

The classic form of the Hindu temple evolved during the Gupta era. Sitting atop a raised platform surmounted by high towers, the temple was patterned on the sacred mountain or palace in which the gods of mythology resided, and it represented the inherent order of the universe. From an exterior courtyard worshipers approached the central shrine, where the statue of the deity stood. Paintings or sculptured depictions of gods and mythical events covered the walls of the best-endowed sanctuaries. Cave-temples carved out of rock were also richly adorned with frescoes or with sculpture.

During the period of political fragmentation between the eclipse of the Mauryan Empire and the rise of the Guptas, extensive networks of trade within India, as well as land and sea routes to foreign lands, developed. This vibrant commerce continued into the Gupta period. Coined money served as the medium of exchange, and artisan guilds played an influential role in the economic, political, and religious life of the towns. The Guptas sought control of the ports on the Arabian Sea but saw a decline in trade with the weakened Roman Empire. In compensation, trade with Southeast and East Asia was on the rise. Adventurous merchants from the ports of eastern and southern India made the sea voyage to the Malay° Peninsula and islands of Indonesia in order to exchange Indian cotton cloth, ivory, metalwork, and exotic animals for Chinese silk or Indonesian spices. The overland Silk Road from China was also in operation but was vulnerable to disruption by Central Asian nomads (see Chapter 8).

By the later fifth century C.E. the Gupta Empire was coming under pressure from the Huns. These nomadic invaders from the steppes of Central Asia poured into

---

sati (suh-TEE)

Malay (muh-LAY)

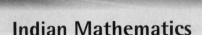

Indian Mathematics

The so-called Arabic numerals used in most parts of the world today were developed in India. The Indian system of place-value notation was far more efficient than the unwieldy numerical systems of Egyptians, Greeks, and Romans, and the invention of zero was a profound intellectual achievement. Indeed, it has to be ranked as one of the most important and influential discoveries in human history. This system is used even more widely than the alphabet derived from the Phoenicians (see Chapter 4) and is, in one sense, the only truly global language.

In its fully developed form the Indian method of arithmetic notation employed a base-10 system. It had separate columns for ones, tens, hundreds, and so forth, as well as a zero sign to indicate the absence of units in a given column. This system makes possible the economical expression of even very large numbers. And it allows for the performance of calculations not possible in a system like the numerals of the Romans, where any real calculation had to be done mentally or on a counting board.

A series of early Indian inscriptions using the numerals from 1 to 9 are deeds of property given to religious institutions by kings or other wealthy individuals. They were incised in the Sanskrit language on copper plates (see below). The earliest known example has a date equivalent to 595 C.E. A sign for zero is attested by the eighth century. Other textual evidence leads to the inference that a place-value system and the zero concept were already known in the fifth century.

This Indian system spread to the Middle East, Southeast Asia, and East Asia by the seventh century. Other peoples quickly recognized its capabilities and adopted it, sometimes using indigenous symbols. Europe received the new technology somewhat later. Gerbert of Aurillac, a French Christian monk, spent time in Spain between 967 and 970, where he was exposed to the mathematics of the Arabs. A great scholar and teacher who eventually became Pope Sylvester II (r. 999–1003), he spread word of the "Arabic" system in the Christian West.

Knowledge of the Indian system of mathematical notation seems to have spread throughout Europe primarily through the use of a mechanical calculating device—an improved version of the Roman counting board, with counters inscribed with variants of the Indian numeral forms. Because the counters could be turned sideways or upside down, at first there was considerable variation in the forms. But by the twelfth century they had become standardized into forms close to those in use today. As the capabilities of the place-value system for written calculations became clear, the counting board fell into disuse. The abandonment of this device led to the adoption of the zero sign—not necessary on the counting board, where a column could be left empty—by the twelfth century.

Why was this marvelous system of mathematical notation invented in ancient India? The answer may lie in the way in which the range and versatility of this number system correspond to elements of Indian cosmology. The Indians conceived of immense spans of time—trillions of years (far exceeding current scientific estimates of the age of the universe as between 15 billion and 20 billion years old)—during which innumerable universes like our own were created, existed for a finite time, then were destroyed. In one popular creation myth, Vishnu is slumbering on the coils of a giant serpent at the bottom of the ocean, and worlds are being created and destroyed as he exhales and inhales. In Indian thought our world, like others, has existed for a series of epochs lasting more than 4 million years, yet the period of its existence is but a brief and insignificant moment in the vast sweep of time. The Indians developed a number system that allowed them to express concepts of this magnitude.

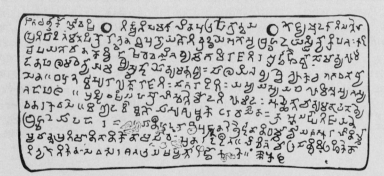

Copper Plate with Indian Numerals
This property deed from western India shows an early form of the symbol system for numbers that spread to the Middle East and Europe, and today is used all over the world. (Facsimile by Georges Ifrah. Reproduced by permission of Georges Ifrah.)

Wall Painting from the Caves at Ajanta, Fifth or Sixth Century C.E.   Kings and other wealthy patrons donated lavishly for the construction and decoration of Buddhist, Hindu, and Jain religious shrines, including elaborate complexes of caves. At Ajanta, in central India, twenty-nine caves are filled with paintings and relief sculptures illustrating religious and secular scenes. This segment depicts, at left, a princess and her attendants in a garden and, at right, a royal couple in the harem. While representing scenes from the earlier lives of the Buddha, the artists also give us a glimpse of life at the royal court in their own times.   (Jean-Louis Nou)

the northwest corridor. Defense of this distant frontier region eventually exhausted the imperial treasury, and the empire collapsed by 550.

The early seventh century saw a brief but glorious revival of imperial unity. Harsha Vardhana (r. 606–647), ruler of the region around Delhi, extended his power over the northern plain and moved his capital to Kanauj on the Ganges River. We have an account of the life and long reign of this fervent Buddhist, poet, patron of artists, and dynamic warrior, written by the courtier Bana. In addition, the Chinese Buddhist pilgrim Xuanzang° (600–664) left an account of his travels in India during Harsha's reign. After Harsha's death, northern India reverted to its customary state of political fragmentation and remained

divided until the Islamic invasions of the eleventh and twelfth centuries (see Chapter 15).

During the centuries of Gupta ascendancy and decline in the north, the Deccan Plateau and the southern part of the peninsula followed an independent path. In this region, where the landscape is segmented by mountains, rocky plateaus, tropical forests, and sharply cut river courses, there were many small centers of power. Later, from the seventh to twelfth centuries, the Pallavas, Cholas, and other warrior dynasties collected tribute and plundered as far as their strength permitted, storing their wealth in urban fortresses. These rulers sought legitimacy and fame as patrons of religion and culture, and much of the distinguished art and architecture of the period was produced in the kingdoms of the south. These kingdoms served as the conduit through which Indian religion and culture reached Southeast Asia.

Xuanzang (shoo-wen-zahng)

SOUTHEAST ASIA

Southeast Asia consists of three geographical zones: the Indochina mainland, the Malay Peninsula, and thousands of islands extending on an east-west axis far out into the Pacific Ocean (see Map 7.2). Encompassing a vast area of land and water, today this region is occupied by the countries of Myanmar° (Burma), Thailand°, Laos°, Cambodia, Vietnam, Malaysia, Singapore, Indonesia, Brunei°, and the Philippines. Poised between the ancient centers of China and India, Southeast Asia has been influenced by the cultures of both civilizations. The region first rose to prominence and prosperity because of its intermediate role in the trade exchanges between southern and eastern Asia.

The strategic importance of Southeast Asia is enhanced by the region's natural resources. This is a geologically active zone; the islands are the tops of a chain of volcanoes. Lying along the equator, Southeast Asia has a tropical climate. The temperature hovers around 80 degrees Fahrenheit (30 degrees Celsius), and the monsoon winds provide dependable rainfall throughout the year. Thanks to several growing cycles each year, the region is capable of supporting a large human population. The most fertile agricultural lands lie along the floodplains of the largest silt-bearing rivers or contain rich volcanic soil deposited by ancient eruptions.

Early Civilization Rain forest covers much of Southeast Asia. Rain-forest ecosystems are particularly fragile because of the great local variation of plant forms within them and because of the vulnerability of their soil to loss of fertility if the protective forest canopy is removed. As early as 2000 B.C.E. people in this region were practicing swidden agriculture—clearing a patch of land for farming by cutting and burning the vegetation growing on it. The cleared land, known as swidden, was farmed for several growing seasons. When the soil was exhausted, the farmers abandoned the patch to the forest, allowing it to regenerate before they cleared it again for agriculture. In the meantime, they cleared and cultivated other nearby fields in similar fashion.

A number of plant and animal species spread from Southeast Asia to other regions. Among them were wet rice (rice cultivated in deliberately flooded fields), soybeans, sugar cane, yams, bananas, coconuts, cocoyams, chickens, and pigs. Rice was the staple food product, for even though rice cultivation is labor-intensive (see Chapter 3), it can support a large population.

Historians believe that the **Malay peoples** who became the dominant population in this region were the product of several waves of migration from southern China beginning around 3000 B.C.E. In some cases the indigenous peoples merged with the Malay newcomers; in other cases they retreated to remote mountain and forest zones. Subsequently, rising population and disputes within communities prompted streams of people to leave the Southeast Asian mainland in the longest-lasting colonization movement in human history. By the first millennium B.C.E. the inhabitants of Southeast Asia had developed impressive navigational skills. They knew how to ride the monsoon winds and to interpret the patterns of swells, winds, clouds, and bird and sea life. Over a period of several thousand years groups of Malay peoples in large, double outrigger canoes spread out across the Pacific and Indian Oceans—half the circumference of the earth—to settle thousands of islands.

The inhabitants of Southeast Asia tended to cluster along riverbanks or in fertile volcanic plains. Their fields and villages were never far from the rain forest, with its wild animals and numerous plant species. Forest trees provided fruit, wood, and spices. The shallow waters surrounding the islands teemed with fish. This region was also an early center of metallurgy, particularly bronze. Metalsmiths heated bronze to the right temperature for shaping by using hollow bamboo tubes to funnel a stream of oxygen to the furnace.

The first political units were small. The size of the fundamental unit reflected the number of people who drew water from the same source. Water resource "boards," whose members were representatives from the leading families of the different villages involved, met periodically to allocate and schedule the use of this critical resource.

Larger states emerged in the early centuries C.E. in response to two powerful forces: commerce and Hindu/Buddhist culture. Southeast Asia was strategically situated along a new trade route that merchants used to carry Chinese silk westward to India and the Mediterranean. The movements of nomadic peoples had disrupted the old land route across Central Asia. But in India demand for silk was increasing—silk both for domestic use and for transshipment to the Arabian Gulf and Red Sea to satisfy the fast-growing luxury market in the Roman Empire. At first a route developed across the South China Sea, by land over the Isthmus of Kra on the

Myanmar (myahn-MAH) Thailand (TIE-land)
Laos (louse) Brunei (broo-NIE)

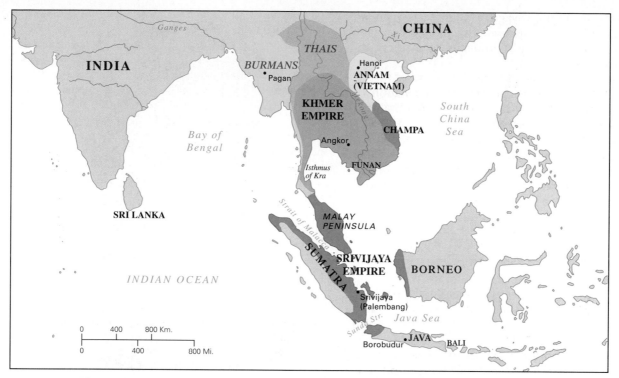

Map. 7.2   Southeast Asia   Southeast Asia's position between the ancient centers of civilization in India and China had a major impact on its history. In the first millennium C.E. a series of powerful and wealthy states arose in the region by gaining control of major trade routes: first Funan, based in southern Vietnam and the Malay Peninsula, then Srivijaya on the island of Sumatra, then smaller states on the island of Java. Shifting trade routes led to the demise of one and the rise of others.

Malay peninsula, and across the Bay of Bengal to India (see Map 7.2). Over time merchants extended this exchange network to include not only silk but goods from Southeast Asia, such as aromatic woods, resins, and cinnamon, pepper, cloves, nutmeg, and other spices. By serving this trade network and controlling key points, Southeast Asian centers rose to prominence.

The other force leading to the rise of larger political entities was the influence of Hindu/Buddhist culture, imported from India. Commerce brought Indian merchants and sailors into the ports of Southeast Asia. As Buddhism spread, Southeast Asia became a way station for Indian missionaries and East Asian pilgrims going to and coming from the birthplace of their faith. Indian cosmology, rituals, art, and statecraft constituted a rich treasury of knowledge and a source of prestige and legitimacy for local rulers who adopted them. The use of Sanskrit terms such as *maharaja*° (great king), the adaptation of Indian ceremonial practices and forms of

artistic representation, and the employment of scribes skilled in writing all proved invaluable to the most ambitious and capable Southeast Asian rulers.

The first major Southeast Asian center, called **"Funan"** by Chinese visitors, flourished between the first and sixth centuries C.E. (see Map 7.2). Its capital was at the modern site of Oc-Eo in southern Vietnam. Funan occupied the delta of the Mekong River, a "rice bowl" capable of supporting a large population. By extending its control over most of southern Indochina and the Malay Peninsula, Funan was able to dominate the Isthmus of Kra—a key point on the trade route from India to China. Seaborne merchants from the ports of northeast India found that offloading their goods from ships and carrying them across the narrow strip of land was safer than making the thousand-mile (sixteen-hundred-kilometer) voyage around the Malay Peninsula—a dangerous trip marked by treacherous currents, rocky shoals, and pirates. Once the portage across the isthmus was finished, the merchants needed food and lodging while they waited for the monsoon winds to shift so that they could

---

maharaja (mah-huh-RAH-juh)

make the last leg of the voyage to China by sea. Funan stockpiled food and provided security for those engaged in this trade—in return, most probably, for customs duties and other fees.

According to one legend (a sure indicator of the influence of Indian culture in this region), the kingdom of Funan arose out of the marriage of an Indian Brahmin and a local princess. Chinese observers have left reports of the prosperity and sophistication of Funan, emphasizing the presence of walled cities, palaces, archives, systems of taxation, and state-organized agriculture. Nevertheless, for reasons not yet clear to modern historians, Funan declined in the sixth century. The most likely explanation is that international trade routes changed, bypassing Funan.

The Srivijayan Kingdom

By the sixth century, a new, all-sea route had developed. Merchants and travelers from south India and Sri Lanka sailed through the Strait of Malacca (lying between the west side of the Malay Peninsula and the northeast coast of the large island of Sumatra) and into the South China Sea. This route presented both human and navigational hazards, but it significantly shortened the journey. Another factor promoting the use of this route was a decline in the demand of the Eastern Roman (Byzantine) Empire for imported Chinese silk. Christian monks had hidden silkworms in bamboo stalks, smuggled them out of China, and brought them to Constantinople, thereby exposing the secret of silk production and breaking the Chinese monopoly.

A new center of power, **Srivijaya°**—Sanskrit for "Great Conquest"—was dominating the new southerly route by 683 C.E. The capital of the Srivijayan kingdom was at modern-day Palembang, 50 miles (80 kilometers) up the Musi River from the southeastern coast of Sumatra. Srivijaya had a good natural harbor on a broad and navigable river and a productive agricultural hinterland. The kingdom was well situated to control the southern part of the Malay Peninsula, Sumatra, parts of Java and Borneo, and the Malacca and Sunda straits—vital passageways for shipping (see Map 7.2).

The Srivijayan capital, one of several thriving Sumatran river ports, gained ascendancy over its rivals and assumed control of the international trade route by fusing four distinct ecological zones into an interdependent network. The core area was the productive agricultural plain along the Musi River. The king and administrative specialists—clerks, scribes, judges, and tax collectors—

Srivijava (sree-vih-JUH-yuh)

Stone Image of Durga, a Fierce Manifestation of the Goddess, Slaying the Buffalo-Demon, from Java, Thirteenth Century C.E. The Goddess, one of the three major Hindu divinities, appeared in a number of complementary manifestations. The most dramatic is Durga, a murderous warrior equipped with multiple divine weapons. That the same divine figure could, in its other manifestations, represent life-bringing fertility and docile wifely duties in the household shows how attuned Indian thought was to the interconnectedness of different aspects of life. (Eliot Elisofon Collection, Harry Ransom Humanities Center, University of Texas, Austin)

whom he employed controlled this zone directly. Less direct was the king's control of the second zone, the upland regions of Sumatra's interior, which were the source of commercially valuable forest products. The local rulers of this area were bound to the center in a dependent relationship held together by oaths of loyalty, elaborate court ceremonies, and the sharing of profits from trade. The third zone consisted of river ports that had been Srivijaya's main rivals. They were conquered and controlled thanks to an alliance between Srivijaya and neighboring sea nomads, pirates who served as a Srivijayan navy as long as the king guaranteed them a steady income.

The fourth zone was a fertile "rice bowl" on the central plain of the nearby island of Java—a region so productive, because of its volcanic soil, that it houses and feeds the majority of the population of present-day

View of the Buddhist Monument at Borobodur, Java   The great monument was more than 300 feet (90 meters) in length and over 100 feet (30 meters) high. Pilgrims made a three-mile-long (nearly 5-kilometer-long) winding ascent through ten levels intended to represent the ideal Buddhist journey from ignorance to enlightenment. (Josephine Powell, Rome)

Indonesia. Srivijayan monarchs maintained alliances with several ruling dynasties that controlled this region. The alliances were cemented by intermarriage, and the Srivijayan kings even claimed descent from the main Javanese dynasty. These arrangements gave Srivijaya easy access to the large quantities of foodstuffs that people living in the capital and merchants and sailors visiting the various ports needed.

The kings of Srivijaya who constructed and maintained this complex network of social, political, and economic relationships were men of extraordinary energy and skill. Although their authority depended in part on force, it owed more to diplomatic and even theatrical talents. Like the Gupta monarchy, Srivijaya should be seen as a theater-state, securing its position of prominence and binding dependents to it by its sheer splendor and its ability to attract labor resources, talent, and luxury products. According to one tradition, the Srivijayan monarch was so wealthy that he deposited bricks of gold in the river estuary to appease the local gods, and a hillside near town was said to be covered with silver and gold images of the Buddha to which devotees brought lotus-shaped vessels of gold. The gold originated in West Africa and came to Southeast Asia through trade with the Muslim world (see Chapter 8).

The Srivijayan king was believed to have great magical powers. He mediated between the spiritually potent realms of the mountains and the sea, and he embodied powerful forces of fertility associated with the rivers in flood. His capital and court were the scene of ceremonies designed to dazzle observers and reinforce the image of wealth, power, and sanctity surrounding the king. Subjects and visitors recognized the king as a "winner" and wanted to be associated with his success. Subordinate rulers took oaths of loyalty that carried dire threats of punishment for violations, and in their own home locales they imitated the splendid ceremonials of the capital.

The kings built and patronized Buddhist monasteries and schools. In central Java local dynasties allied with Srivijaya built magnificent temple complexes to advertise their glory. **Borobodur**, built between 770 C.E. and 825 C.E., the most famous of these, was the largest human construction in the Southern Hemisphere. The winding ascent through the ten tiers of this mountain of volcanic stone is a Buddhist allegory for the progressive stages of enlightenment. Numerous sculptured reliefs depicting Buddhist legends provide modern viewers with glimpses of daily life in early Java.

In all of this, the cultural influence of India was paramount. Shrewd Malay rulers looked to Indian traditions to supply conceptual rationales for kingship and social order. They utilized Indian models of bureaucracy and the Sanskrit system of writing to expedite government business. Their special connection to powerful gods and higher knowledge raised them above their rivals. Southeast Asia's central position on long-distance trade routes and pilgrimage routes guaranteed the presence of foreigners with useful skills to serve as priests, scribes, and administrators. Hindu beliefs and social structures have survived to this day on the island of Bali, east of Java. Even more influential was Buddhism because of the flow of Buddhist pilgrims and missionaries between East Asia and India. (Islam, the dominant religion in modern-day Indonesia, was not introduced until the thirteenth century.)

The Southeast Asian kingdoms, however, were not just passive recipients of Indian culture. They took what was useful to them and synthesized it with indigenous beliefs, values, and institutions—for example, local concepts of chiefship, ancestor worship, and forms of oaths. Moreover, they trained their own people in the new ways, so that the bureaucracy contained both foreign experts and native disciples. The whole process amounted to a cultural dialogue between India and Southeast Asia, one in which both partners were active participants.

The kings of Srivijaya carried out this marvelous balancing act for centuries. But the system they erected was vulnerable to shifts in the pattern of international trade. Some such change must have contributed to the decline of Srivijaya in the eleventh century, even though the immediate cause was a destructive raid in 1025 C.E. on the Srivijayan capital by forces of the Chola kingdom of southeast India.

After the decline of Srivijaya, the leading role passed to new, vigorous kingdoms on the eastern end of of Java, and the maritime realm of Southeast Asia remained prosperous and connected to the international network of trade. A few Europeans were aware of this region as a source of spices and other luxury items. Some four centuries after the decline of Srivijaya, an Italian navigator serving under the flag of Spain—Christopher Columbus—embarked on a westward course across the Atlantic Ocean, seeking to establish a direct route to the fabled "Indies" from which the spices came.

CONCLUSION

This chapter traces the emergence of complex societies in India and Southeast Asia between the second millennium B.C.E. and the first millennium C.E. Because of migrations, trade, and the spread of belief systems, an Indian style of civilization spread throughout the subcontinent and adjoining regions and eventually made its way to the mainland and island chains of Southeast Asia. In this period were laid cultural foundations that in large measure still endure.

The development and spread of belief systems—Vedism, Buddhism, Jainism, and Hinduism—has a central place in this chapter, because nearly all the sources from which scholars can reconstruct the story of antiquity in this part of the world are religious. A visitor to a museum who examines artifacts from ancient Mesopotamia, Egypt, the Greco-Roman Mediterranean, China, and India will find that a prominent part of the collection consists of objects from religious shrines or with cultic function. Only the Indian artifacts, however, will be almost exclusively from the religious sphere.

The prolific use of writing came later to India than to other parts of the Eastern Hemisphere, for reasons particular to the Indian situation. Like Indian artifacts, most of the ancient Indian texts are of a religious nature. Ancient Indians did not generate historiographic texts of the kind written elsewhere in the ancient world, primarily because they held a strikingly different view of time. Mesopotamian scribes compiled lists of political and military events and the strange celestial and earthly phenomena that coincided with them. They were inspired by a cyclical conception of time and believed that the recurrence of an omen at some future date potentially signaled a repetition of the historical event associated with it. Greek and Roman historians described and analyzed the progress of wars and the character of rulers. They believed that these accounts would prove useful because of the essential constancy of human nature and the value for future leaders and planners of understanding the past as a sequence of causally linked events. Chinese annalists set down the deeds and conduct of rulers as inspirational models of right conduct and cautionary tales of the consequences of impropriety. In contrast, the distinctive Indian view of time—as vast epochs in which universes are created and destroyed again and again and the essential spirit of living creatures is reincarnated repeatedly—made the particulars of any brief moment seem relatively unilluminating.

The tension between divisive and unifying forces can be seen in many aspects of Indian life. Political and social division has been the norm throughout much of the history of India. It is a consequence of the topographical and environmental diversity of the subcontinent and the complex mix of ethnic and linguistic groups inhabiting it. The elaborate structure of classes and castes was a response to this diversity—an attempt to organize the population and position individuals within an accepted hierarchy, as well as to regulate group interactions. Strong central governments, such as those of the Mauryan and Gupta kings, gained ascendancy for a time and promoted prosperity and development. They rose to dominance by gaining control of metal resources and important trade routes, developing effective military and administrative institutions, and creating cultural forms that inspired admiration and emulation. However, as in Archaic Greece and Warring States China, the periods of fragmentation and multiple small centers of power seemed as economically and intellectually fertile and dynamic as the periods of unity.

India possessed many of the advanced technologies available elsewhere in the ancient world—agriculture, irrigation, metallurgy, textile manufacture, monumental construction, military technology, writing, and systems of administration. But of all the ancient societies, India made the most profound contribution to mathematics, devising the so-called Arabic numerals and place-value notations.

Many distinctive social and intellectual features of Indian civilization—the class and caste system, models of kingship and statecraft, and Vedic, Jainist, and Buddhist belief systems—originated in the great river valleys of the north, where descendants of Indo-European immigrants came to dominate. Hinduism embraced elements drawn from the Dravidian cultures of the south as well as from Buddhism. Hindu beliefs and practices are less fixed and circumscribed than the beliefs and practices of Judaism, Christianity, and Islam, which rely on clearly defined textual and organizational sources of authority. The capacity of the Hindu tradition to assimilate a wide range of popular beliefs facilitated the spread of elements of a common Indian civilization across the subcontinent, although there was, and is, considerable variation from one region to another.

This same malleable quality also came into play as the pace of international commerce quickened in the first millennium C.E. and Indian merchants embarking by sea for East Asia passed through Funan, Srivijaya, and other commercial centers in Southeast Asia. Indigenous elites in Southeast Asia came into contact with Indian merchants, sailors, and pilgrims. Involvement in the lucrative long-distance commerce and adoption of Indian political and religious ideas and methods brought wealth, power, and prestige to able and ambitious leaders. Finding elements of Indian civilization attractive and useful, they fused it with their own traditions to create a culture unique to Southeast Asia. Chapter 8 describes how the networks of long-distance trade and communication established in the Eastern Hemisphere in antiquity continued to expand and foster technological and cultural development in the subsequent era.

■ Key Terms

monsoon	Ashoka
Vedas	*Mahabharata*
varna	*Bhagavad-Gita*
jati	Tamil kingdoms
karma	Gupta Empire
moksha	theater-state
Buddha	Malay peoples
Mahayana Buddhism	Funan
Theravada Buddhism	Srivijaya
Hinduism	Borobodur
Mauryan Empire	

■ Suggested Reading

A useful starting point for the Indian subcontinent is Karl J. Schmidt, *An Atlas and Survey of South Asian History* (1995), with maps and facing text illustrating geographic, environmental, cultural, and historical features of South Asian civilization. Concise discussions of the history of ancient India can be found in Stanley Wolpert, *A New History of India,* 3d ed. (1989), and Romila Thapar, *A History of India,* vol. 1 (1966). D. D. Kosambi, *Ancient India: A History of Its Culture and Civilization* (1965), and Paul Masson-Oursel, *Ancient India and Indian Civilization* (1998), are fuller presentations.

Ainslie T. Embree, *Sources of Indian Tradition,* vol. 1, 2d ed. (1988), contains translations of primary texts, with the emphasis almost entirely on religion and few materials from southern India. Barbara Stoler Miller, *The Bhagavad-Gita: Krishna's Counsel in Time of War* (1986), is a readable translation of this ancient classic with a useful introduction and notes. An abbreviated version of the greatest Indian epic can be found in R. K. Narayan, *The Mahabharata: A Shortened Modern Prose Version of the Indian Epic* (1978). The filmed version of Peter Brook's stage production of *The Mahabharata* (3 videos, 1989) generated much controversy because of its British director and multicultural cast, but it is a painless introduction to the plot and main characters. To sample the fascinating document on state building supposedly composed by the adviser to the founder of the Mauryan Empire, see T. N. Ramaswamy, *Essentials of Indian Statecraft: Kautilya's Arthasastra for Contemporary Readers* (1962). James Legge, *The Travels of Fa-hien [Faxian]: Fa-hien's Record of Buddhistic Kingdoms* (1971), and John W. McCrindle, *Ancient India as Described by Megasthenes and Arrian* (1877), provide translations of reports of foreign visitors to ancient India.

A number of works explore political institutions and ideas in ancient India: Charles Drekmeier, *Kingship and Community in Early India* (1962); John W. Spellman, *Political Theory of Ancient India: A Study of Kingship from the Earliest Times to Circa A.D. 300* (1964); and R. S. Sharma, *Aspects of Political Ideas and Institutions in Ancient India,* 2d ed. (1968). Romila Thapar, *Asoka and the Decline of the Mauryas* (1963), is a detailed study of the most interesting and important Maurya king.

For fundamental Indian social and religious conceptions see David R. Kinsley, *Hinduism: A Cultural Perspective* (1982). See also David G. Mandelbaum, *Society in India,* 2 vols. (1970), who provides essential insights into the complex relationship of class and caste. Jacob Pandian, *The Making of India and Indian Tradition* (1995), contains much revealing historical material, with particular attention to often neglected regions such as southern India, in its effort to explain the diversity of contemporary India. The chapter on ancient India by Karen Lang in Bella Vivante, ed., *Women's Roles in Ancient Civilizations: A Reference Guide* (1999), provides an up-to-date overview and bibliography. Stephanie W. Jamison, *Sacrificed Wife/Sacrificer's Wife: Women, Ritual, and Hospitality in Ancient India* (1996), deals with the roles early Indian women filled in ritual practices and the creation and maintenance of social relations, including several forms of marriage. Stella Kramrisch, *The Hindu Temple,* 2 vols. (1946), and Surinder M. Bhardwaj, *Hindu Places of Pilgrimage in India: A Study in Cultural Geography* (1973), examine important elements of worship in the Hindu tradition.

Roy C. Craven, *Indian Art* (1976), is a clear, historically organized treatment of its subject. Mario Bussagli and Calembus Sivaramamurti, *5000 Years of the Art of India* (1971), is lavishly illustrated.

For the uniqueness and decisive historical impact of Indian mathematics see Georges Ifrah, *From One to Zero: A Universal History of Numbers* (1985).

Jean W. Sedlar, *India and the Greek World: A Study in the Transmission of Culture* (1980), relates the interaction of Greek and Indian civilizations. Lionel Casson, *The Periplus Maris Erythraei: Text with Introduction, Translation and Commentary* (1989), explicates a fascinating mariner's guide to the ports, trade goods, and human and navigational hazards of Indian Ocean commerce in the Roman era. Liu, Hsin-ju, *Ancient India and Ancient China: Trade and Religious Exchanges, A.D. 1–600* (1994), covers interactions with East Asia.

Richard Ulack and Gyula Pauer, *Atlas of Southeast Asia* (1989), provides a very brief introduction and maps for the environment and early history of Southeast Asia. Nicholas Tarling, ed., *The Cambridge History of Southeast Asia,* vol. 1 (1992); D. R. SarDeSai, *Southeast Asia: Past and Present,* 3d ed. (1994); and Milton E. Osborne, *Southeast Asia: An Introductory History* (1995), provide general accounts of Southeast Asian history. Lynda Shaffer, *Maritime Southeast Asia to 1500* (1996), focuses on early Southeast Asian history in a world historical context. Also useful is Kenneth R. Hall, *Maritime Trade and State Development in Early Southeast Asia* (1985).

The art of Southeast Asia is taken up by M. C. S. Diskul, *The Art of Srivijaya* (1980); Maud Girard-Geslan et al., *Art of Southeast Asia* (1998); and Daigoro Chihara, *Hindu-Buddhist Architecture in Southeast Asia* (1996).

■ Notes

1. Barbara Stoler Miller, *The Bhagavad-Gita: Krishna's Counsel in Time of War* (New York: Bantam, 1986), 98–99.
2. B. G. Gokhale, *Asoka Maurya* (New York: Twayne, 1966), 152–153, 156–157, 160.
3. James Legge, *The Travels of Fa-hien: Fa-hien's Record of Buddhistic Kingdoms* (Delhi: Oriental Publishers, 1971), 77–79.

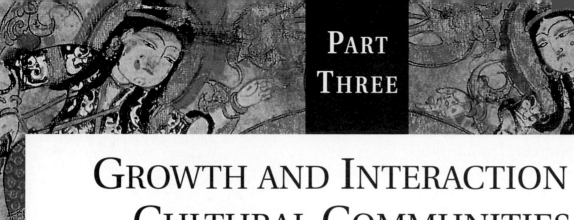

GROWTH AND INTERACTION OF CULTURAL COMMUNITIES,
300 B.C.E.–1200 C.E.

n 300 B.C.E., societies still had only limited contacts beyond their frontiers. Fifteen centuries later, by 1200 C.E., this situation had changed dramatically. Trade, folk migrations, and religious missionary work had created a world of pervasive interconnections among peoples. Three long-distance trade routes fostered the exchange of products and technologies: the Silk Road across Central Asia, trans-Saharan caravan routes linking northern and sub-Saharan Africa, and a variety of maritime routes connecting the coastal lands of the Indian Ocean.

In Africa, the spread of the Bantu peoples from West Africa brought iron implements and new techniques of food production to most of sub-Saharan Africa and helped foster a distinctive African cultural pattern. In the Middle East, the Arabs of the Arabian peninsula, under the inspiration of the Prophet Muhammad, conquered an empire that stretched from Spain to India, implanting their faith, their cultural values, and an urban-based style of life.

In Asia, Buddhism drew on the energies of missionaries and pilgrims as it spread by land and sea from India to Sri Lanka, Tibet, Southeast Asia, China, Korea, and Japan. In each of these lands, the new faith interacted with older philosophies and religious outlooks to produce distinctive patterns of social interaction. At about the same time, the expansion of the Tang Empire resulted in the dissemination of Chinese culture and technologies throughout Central and East Asia.

In Europe, monks and missionaries labored to convert the Celtic, Germanic, and Slavic peoples to Christianity. Christian beliefs became wedded to new political and social structures: a struggle between royal and church authority in western Europe; a combining of religious and imperial authority in the Byzantine East; and distinctive Christian kingdoms in Armenia, Kievan Russia, and Ethiopia. The Crusades opened new contacts between western Europe and lands to the east after centuries of near isolation.

Unexplored seas still separated the Eastern and Western Hemispheres, but the development of urban, agricultural civilizations in the Andes, the Yucatán lowlands, and the central plateau of Mexico climaxed during this period in the Aztec and Inca Empires and, somewhat earlier, in the flourishing of the Maya. All of the aspects of long-distance cultural exchange and interaction that mark this era in Eurasia and Africa have their counterparts in the Western Hemisphere.

	300 B.C.E.	B.C.E. C.E.	300 C.E.
Americas	• **300** Migrants from Mesoamerica bring irrigation farming to Arizona	• **100** Teotihuacan founded	**250–900** Classic period of Maya civilization **200–700** Moche culture in coastal Peru
Europe		• **146** Rome destroys Carthage, begins direct control of territories ouside Europe	Council of Nicaea **325** • Fall of Roman Empire in West **476** • Reign of Roman emperor Diocletian **284–305**
Africa	Bananas and yams reach Africa from Southeast Asia **ca. 100** • **500 B.C.E.–1000 C.E.** Bantu migrations	First Christian bishop in Ethiopia **ca. 330** • • **ca. 300** Camel use spreads in southern Sahara	
Middle East	• **300** Petra flourishes as caravan city in Jordan **248 B.C.E–226 C.E** Kingdom of Parthia in Iran	• **276** Prophet Mani martyred **226–650** Sasanid Empire in Iraq and Iran	
Asia and Oceania	• **128** Chinese general Zhang Jian explores Silk Road **206 B.C.E–220 C.E** Han Empire in China	• **ca. 100** Stirrup developed in Afghanistan **200–400** Rice introduced to Japan from Korea	

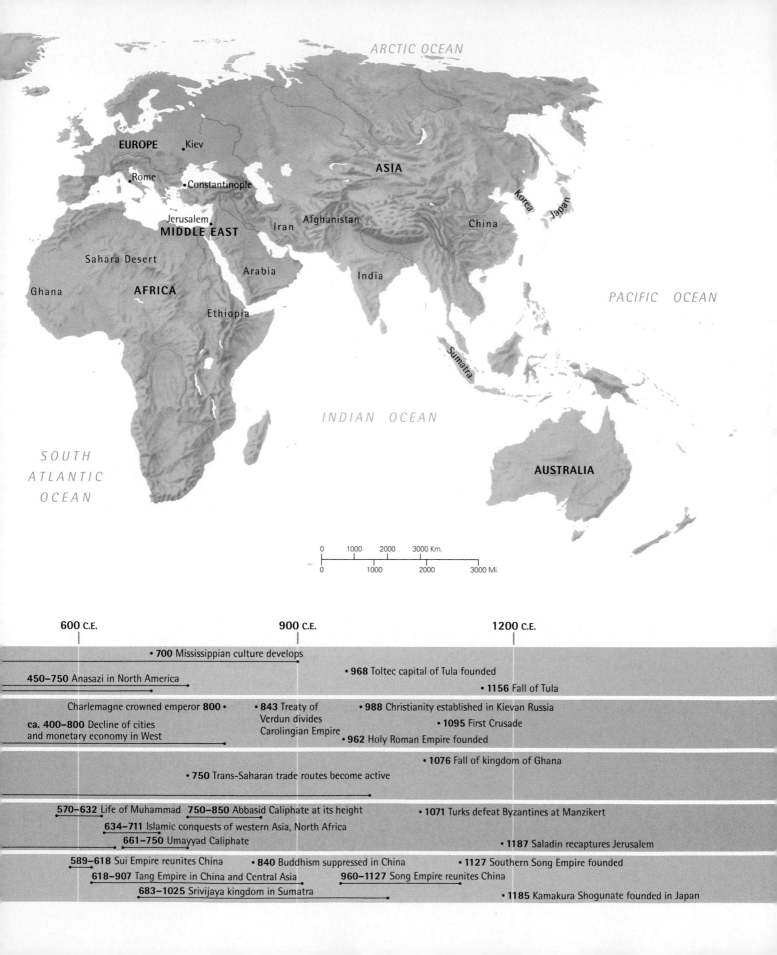

ARCTIC OCEAN

EUROPE
• Kiev

ASIA

• Rome
• Constantinople

Korea
Japan

Jerusalem •
MIDDLE EAST

Iran
Afghanistan
China

Sahara Desert

Arabia

India

Ghana
AFRICA

PACIFIC OCEAN

Ethiopia

Sumatra

INDIAN OCEAN

SOUTH
ATLANTIC
OCEAN

AUSTRALIA

| 0 | 1000 | 2000 | 3000 Km. |
| 0 | 1000 | 2000 | 3000 Mi. |

600 C.E.

900 C.E.

1200 C.E.

• **700** Mississippian culture develops

• **968** Toltec capital of Tula founded

450–750 Anasazi in North America

• **1156** Fall of Tula

Charlemagne crowned emperor **800** •

• **843** Treaty of
Verdun divides
Carolingian Empire

• **988** Christianity established in Kievan Russia

ca. 400–800 Decline of cities
and monetary economy in West

• **1095** First Crusade

• **962** Holy Roman Empire founded

• **1076** Fall of kingdom of Ghana

• **750** Trans-Saharan trade routes become active

570–632 Life of Muhammad **750–850** Abbasid Caliphate at its height

• **1071** Turks defeat Byzantines at Manzikert

634–711 Islamic conquests of western Asia, North Africa

661–750 Umayyad Caliphate

• **1187** Saladin recaptures Jerusalem

589–618 Sui Empire reunites China   • **840** Buddhism suppressed in China

• **1127** Southern Song Empire founded

618–907 Tang Empire in China and Central Asia   **960–1127** Song Empire reunites China

683–1025 Srivijaya kingdom in Sumatra

• **1185** Kamakura Shogunate founded in Japan

8

NETWORKS OF COMMUNICATION AND EXCHANGE,

300 B.C.E.–1100 C.E.

The Silk Road • The Indian Ocean • Routes Across the Sahara • Sub-Saharan Africa • The Spread of Ideas
ENVIRONMENT AND TECHNOLOGY: Camel Saddles
SOCIETY AND CULTURE: Caravan Cities

Indian Ocean Sailing Vessel   Ships like this one, in a rock carving in the Buddhist temple of Borobodur in Java, probably carried colonists from Indonesia to Madagascar.

round the year 800 C.E., a Chinese poet named Po Zhuyi° nostalgically wrote:

Iranian whirling girl, Iranian whirling girl—
Her heart answers to the strings,
Her hands answer to the drums.
At the sound of the strings and drums, she raises
    her arms,
Like whirling snowflakes tossed about, she turns
    in her twirling dance.

Iranian whirling girl,
You came from Sogdiana°.
In vain did you labor to come east more than ten
    thousand tricents.
For in the central plains there were already some
    who could do the Iranian whirl,
And in a contest of wonderful abilities, you would
    not be their equal.[1]

The western part of Central Asia, the region around Samarkand° and Bukhara° known in the eighth century C.E. as Sogdiana, was 2,500 miles (4,000 kilometers) from the Chinese capital of Chang'an°. Caravans took more than four months to trek across the mostly unsettled deserts, mountains, and grasslands. How many Iranian dancing girls reached China? Enough to make their style of dance legendary and the object of local imitation. Indeed, contemporary pottery figurines excavated from Chinese graves show troupes of Iranian performers.

The Silk Road connecting China and the Middle East across Central Asia fostered the exchange of agricultural goods, manufactured products, and ideas. But musicians and dancing girls traveled, too—as did camel pullers, merchants, monks, and pilgrims. The Silk Road was not just a means of bringing peoples and parts of the world into contact; it was a social system. However, it was a social system that neither lay within a state or empire nor gave rise to one. Consequently, this and similar trading networks that have had a deep impact on world history deserve special scrutiny.

As we have seen, political units in ancient times grew only slowly into kingdoms, and a few developed further into empires. With every expansion of territory,

the accumulation of wealth by temples, kings, and emperors enticed traders to venture ever farther afield for precious goods. For the most part, their customers were wealthy elites. But the knowledge of new products, agricultural and industrial processes, and foreign ideas and customs these long-distance traders brought with them sometimes affected an entire society.

Nevertheless, travelers and traders were not always admired or respected. They seldom owned much land or wielded political power. Moreover, they were often socially isolated (sometimes by law) and secretive because any talk about markets, products, routes, and travel conditions could help their competitors. Yet their mostly anonymous efforts contributed more to drawing the world together than did all but a few kings and emperors.

This chapter examines the social systems and historical impact of exchange networks that developed between 300 B.C.E. and 1100 C.E. in Europe, Asia, and Africa. The Silk Road, the Indian Ocean maritime system, and the trans-Saharan caravan routes in Africa illustrate the nature of long-distance trade in this era.

Trading networks were not the only medium for the spread of new ideas, products, and customs, however. Chapter 6 discussed the migration into the Roman Empire of peoples speaking Germanic languages and the beginning of Christian missionary activity in Europe. This chapter compares the development of the Saharan trading system of northern Africa with the simultaneous folk migrations of Bantu-speaking peoples within sub-Saharan Africa. It also discusses the spread of Buddhism in Asia and Christianity in Africa. The politically and militarily more consequential expansion of Islam is the subject of Chapter 9.

As you read this chapter, ask yourself the following questions:

- What is the role of technology in long-distance trade?
- How does geography affect trade patterns?
- How do human groups affect communication between regions?
- Why do some goods and ideas travel more easily than others?

Po Zhuyi (boh joo-yee) Sogdiana (sog-dee-A-nuh)
Samarkand (SAM-mar-kand) Bukhara (boo-CAR-ruh)
Chang'an (chahng-ahn)

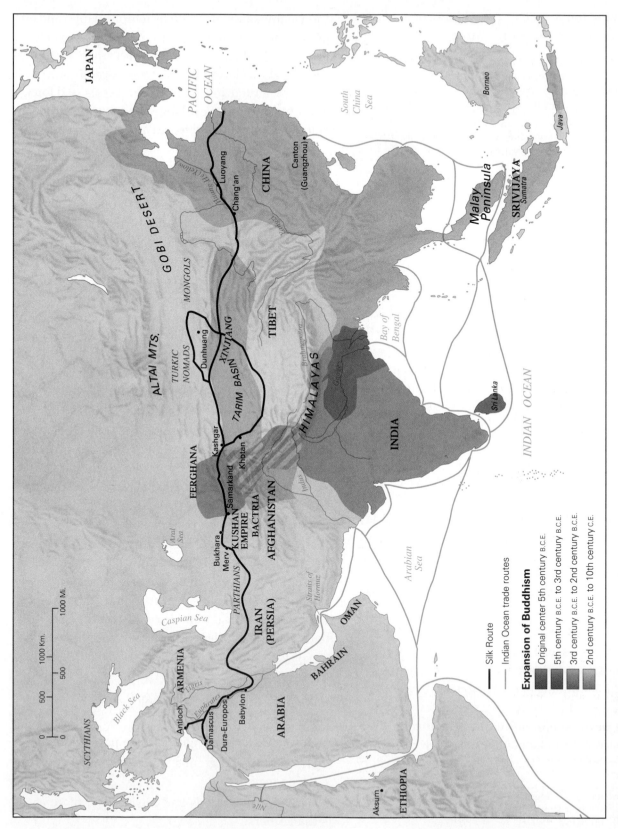

Map. 8.1 Asian Trade and Communication Routes The overland Silk Road was vulnerable to political disruption, but was much shorter than the maritime route from the South China Sea to the Red Sea, and ships were more expensive than pack animals. Moreover, China's political centers were in the north. Historians remain puzzled by the lack of Buddhist expansion westward from Afghanistan.

Chronology

	Silk Road	Indian Ocean Trade	Saharan Trade
			500 B.C.E.–ca. 1000 C.E. Bantu migrations
300 B.C.E.	**247 B.C.E.** Parthian rule begins in Iran **128 B.C.E.** General Zhang Jian reaches Ferghana		**ca. 200 B.C.E.** Camel nomads in southern Sahara
1 C.E.	**100 B.C.E.–300 C.E.** Kushans rule northern Afghanistan and Sogdiana	**1st cent. C.E.** *Periplus of the Erythraean Sea*; Indonesian migration to Madagascar	**46 B.C.E.** First mention of camels in northern Sahara
300 C.E.	**ca. 400** Buddhist pilgrim Faxian travels Silk Road		**ca. 300** Beginning of camel nomadism in northern Sahara
600 C.E.	**ca. 630** Buddhist pilgrim Xuanzang travels Silk Road	**683–1025** Srivijaya trading kingdom in Southeast Asia **711** Arabs conquer lower Indus Valley partially by sea	**6th cent.** Kingdom of Ghana begins **639–42** Arabs conquer Egypt **711** Berbers and Arabs conquer Spain **740** Berber revolts; independent states in North Africa; trade develops across Sahara
900 C.E.	**907** Collapse of Tang Empire	**ca. 900** Arab and Persian merchants in Canton	**1076** Almoravids defeat ruler of Ghana

THE SILK ROAD

Archaeology and linguistic studies show that the peoples of Central Asia engaged in long-distance movement and exchange from at least 1500 B.C.E. In Roman times the imagination of Europeans became captivated by the idea of the **Silk Road.** A trade route linking the lands of the Mediterranean with China by way of Mesopotamia, Iran, and Central Asia, the Silk Road experienced several periods of heavy use. The first extended from approximately 100 B.C.E. to 907 C.E., when the collapse of the Tang° Empire in China led to disruption at its eastern end (see Chapter 11). Another period of heavy use began in the thirteenth century C.E. and lasted until the seventeenth century. During that period, much of the Silk Road's traffic skirted the northern shore of the Caspian Sea and ended at ports on the Black Sea instead of in Mesopotamia (see Map 8.1). The operation of that segment of the route is considered in Chapter 13. This chapter examines the origins of trade along the Silk Road and the importance of the Silk Road in drawing together different parts of the Eurasian landmass during its first centuries of use.

Tang (tahng)

Origins and Operations

The Seleucid kings who succeeded to the eastern parts of Alexander the Great's empire in the third century B.C.E. focused their energies on Mesopotamia and Syria, allowing an Iranian nomadic leader to establish an independent kingdom in northeastern Iran. Historians disagree about the stages by which the **Parthians,** named after their homeland east of the Caspian Sea, took over Iran and then Mesopotamia, but they were certainly a major force by 247 B.C.E. They left few written sources, and recurring wars between the Parthians and the Seleucids, and later between the Parthians and the Romans, prevented travelers from the Mediterranean region from gaining firm knowledge of the Parthian kingdom. It seems likely, however, that their place of origin on the threshold of Central Asia and the lifestyle they had in common with nomadic pastoral groups farther to the east were key to their encouragement of trade along what became known as the Silk Road.

In 128 B.C.E. a Chinese general named Zhang Jian° made his first exploratory journey westward across the dangerous deserts of Central Asia on behalf of Emperor Wu of the Han dynasty. After crossing the broad and desolate Tarim Basin north of Tibet, he reached the fertile valley of Ferghana° and for the first time encountered westward-flowing rivers. There he found horse breeders whose animals far outclassed any horses he had seen. In China these noble animals were deemed descendants of a heavenly horse.

Later Chinese historians looked on General Zhang as the originator of overland trade with the western lands, and they credited him with personally introducing into China a whole garden of new plants and trees. Zhang's own account, however, proves that the people of Ferghana were already receiving goods from China, though probably by way of India. Specifically, he saw them using canes made from a square type of bamboo that grows only in western China. But this does not diminish the fact that Zhang, as leader of some eighteen imperial expeditions, was an important pioneer.

Long-distance travel was much more familiar to the Central Asians than to the Chinese. Kin to the trouser-wearing, horse-riding Parthians in language and customs, the populations of Ferghana and neighboring regions included many nomads. For more than a thousand years they had lived by following their herds of horses, cattle, and sheep across the Asian deserts, steppes, and mountains from the Black Sea to the Chinese frontier. But their migrations had had little to do with trade, despite the occasional piece of silk or Chinese manufactured item that found its way into their animals' packs.

We need to distinguish between (1) trips made by occasional travelers and the movements of migrating pastoralists and (2) the deliberate fostering of trading connections. The keys to the opening of the Silk Road were, on the eastern end, Chinese eagerness for western products, especially horses, and on the western end, the organized Parthian state controlling the flourishing markets of Mesopotamia and culturally linked to the pastoralists of Central Asia. In between were caravan cities to support the traders and camel- and horse-breeding nomads to supply them with livestock. All of these factors were necessary to justify the high cost in human hardship and pack-animal mortality that the Silk Road exacted.

Historians put great emphasis on the long distances traveled: once the route was fully functioning, around 100 B.C.E., for example, Greeks could buy Chinese silk from Parthian traders in Mesopotamian border entrepôts. Yet caravans also bought and sold goods along the way in prosperous Central Asian trading cities like Samarkand and Bukhara. These cities grew and flourished, often under the rule of local princes who cultivated good relations with the nomads who provided the caravans with camels, guides, and animal handlers.

One industry that developed along with the caravan trade was the breeding of hybrid camels. Figurines, graffiti, and other pictorial sources show that the two-humped Bactrian camel (named for Bactria° in northern Afghanistan) was initially the mainstay of the Central Asian caravan trade. Closely related to the one-humped camel, or dromedary, of torrid Arabia, the Bactrian camel has a heavy coat of hair and is able to withstand the frigid winters of Central Asia.

Hybrid camels began to appear early in the Silk Road's operations. The historian Diodorus of Sicily wrote in the first century B.C.E. about an area that seems to be Parthian-controlled southern Mesopotamia, where Arabs bred different types of camels, including "both the hairless and the shaggy, and those which have two humps, one behind the other, along their spines." Diodorus's "shaggy" camel is the first evidence of the hybrid camel, which combined the merits of Bactrian camels and dromedaries: it was larger and stronger than either parent and had a heavy coat that suited it to the Central Asian climate. The hybrid was so perfectly adapted for work on the Silk Road that the eventual decline of the route after 1600 C.E. led to its almost total disappearance.

Zhang Jian (jahng jee-en)   **Ferghana** (fer-GAH-nuh)

Bactria (BAK-tree-uh)

Camel Caravan Crossing the Pamir Mountains   Silk Road caravans often traveled during the winter to avoid torrid summer temperatures that added to the hardship of humans and animals. These two-humped camels have heavy coats of wool that they shed in the spring. The ratio of one camel-puller for every two or three camels indicates how much human labor, exclusive of merchants, pilgrims, and other passengers, was involved in Silk Road trading. (R. & S. Michaud/Woodfin Camp & Associates)

The breeding of hybrid camels called for careful herd management and is an example of how the caravan trade itself generated new economic activities. Of greater importance, however, was the exchange of products between East and West. Chinese sources abound in references to products imported across the Silk Road.

General Zhang seems to have brought to China two plants from one of his many trips west: alfalfa and domestic grapes. The former provided the best fodder for the growing Chinese herds of Ferghana horses. The latter were integral to the famous trio of "wine, women, and song" that Chinese explorers noted as prominent in Central Asian life, and later images of Iranian musicians and whirling dancing girls confirm their allure. In addition, Chinese farmers adopted pistachios, walnuts, pomegranates, sesame, coriander, spinach, and other new crops. Chinese artisans and physicians used other trade products, such as jasmine oil, oak galls (used in tanning animal hides, dyeing, and ink making), sal ammoniac (for medicines), copper oxides, zinc, and precious stones.

Caravan traders going from east to west carried from China new fruits such as peaches and apricots, which the Romans attributed mistakenly to the eastern lands of Persia and Armenia, respectively. They also carried cinnamon, ginger, and other spices that could not be grown in the West. China was best known for its manufactured goods—particularly silk, pottery, and paper—all of which were eventually adopted or imitated in western lands, starting with Iran.

Chinese pottery figurines of pack camels and figurines from the Parthian period found in Mesopotamia usually show them with almost hemispherical loads hanging on either side of the animal. If we assume that the potters depicted items of special distinction, we can say that these loads most likely contained silk. Thus, despite the great diversity of goods exchanged by caravan across Central Asia, the traditional name of the Silk Road seems well justified.

The Impact of Silk Road Trade

As trade became a more important part of Central Asian life, the Iranian-speaking peoples settled increasingly in trading cities and surrounding farm villages. This allowed nomads originally from the Altai Mountains farther east to spread across the steppes and become the dominant pastoral group. These peoples spoke Turkic languages unrelated to the Iranian tongues and are well in evidence by the sixth century C.E. The prosperity that trade created affected not only the ethnic mix of the region but also cultural values. The nomads continued to live in the round, portable felt huts called yurts that can still be seen occasionally in Central Asia, but prosperous merchants and landholders built stately homes decorated with brightly colored wall paintings. The paintings show these merchants and landholders wearing Chinese silks and Iranian brocades and riding on richly outfitted horses and camels. They also give evidence of an avid interest in Buddhism, which competed with Christianity, Manichaeism, Zoroastrianism, and—eventually—Islam in a lively and inquiring intellectual milieu.

Religion (discussed later in this chapter) exemplifies the impact of foreign customs and beliefs on the Central Asian peoples, but Central Asian practices also affected surrounding areas. For example, Central Asian military techniques had a profound impact on both East and West. Chariot warfare and the use of mounted bowmen originated in Central Asia and spread eastward and westward through military campaigns and folk migrations that began in the second millennium B.C.E. and recurred throughout the period of the Silk Road.

Evidence of the **stirrup,** one of the most important inventions, comes first from the Kushan people who ruled northern Afghanistan in approximately the first century C.E. At first a solid bar, then a loop of leather to support the rider's big toe, and finally a device of leather and metal or wood supporting the instep, the stirrup gave riders far greater stability in the saddle—which in all likelihood was an earlier Central Asian invention.

Using stirrups, a mounted warrior could supplement his bow and arrow with a long lance, and charge

Iranian Musicians from Silk Road   This three-color glazed pottery figurine, 23 inches (58.4 centimeters) high, is one of hundreds of Silk Road camels and horses found in northern Chinese tombs from the sixth to ninth centuries C.E. The musicians playing Iranian instruments testify to the migration of Iranian culture across the Silk Road. At the same time, dishes decorated by the Chinese three-color glaze technique were in vogue in northern Iran. (The National Museum of Chinese History)

his enemy at a gallop without fear that the impact of his attack would push him off his mount. Far to the west, the stirrup made possible the armored knights who dominated the battlefields of Europe (see Chapter 10), and it contributed to the superiority of the Tang cavalry in China (see Chapter 11).

The prosperity of the Silk Road sowed the seeds of eventual change. From Parthian times until well after the Arab invasions of the seventh century C.E. (see Chapter 9), each Central Asian caravan city and mountain valley seems to have had its own ruling family. These many small states enjoyed various sorts of relations, presumably centered on their common interest in trade. Fear of disrupting the trade may be why none seems to have tried to conquer the others. Yet the Turkic-speaking pastoral nomads who initially provided traders with animals and animal handlers gradually came to grasp the potential for political activity on a larger scale. A short-lived but geographically extensive Turkic kingdom was established by the Uigur people in the mid-eighth century C.E. (see Chapter 11).

THE INDIAN OCEAN

Some Chinese and western products were exchanged by sea rather than by land. A multilingual, multiethnic society of seafarers established the **Indian Ocean Maritime System,** a trade network across the Indian Ocean and the South China Sea. These people left few records and seldom played a visible part in the rise and fall of kingdoms and empires, but they forged increasingly strong economic and social ties between the coastal lands of East Africa, southern Arabia, the Persian Gulf, India, Southeast Asia, and southern China.

This trade took place in three distinct regions: (1) In the South China Sea, Chinese and Malays (including Indonesians) dominated trade. (2) From the east coast of India to the islands of Southeast Asia, Indians and Malays were the main traders. (3) From the west coast of India to the Persian Gulf and the east coast of Africa, merchants and sailors were predominantly Persians and Arabs. These divisions were customary rather than politically formalized. Chinese and Malay sailors could and did voyage to East Africa, and Arab and Persian traders reached southern China.

The Indian Ocean Maritime System

From the time of Herodotus in the fifth century B.C.E., Greek writers regaled their readers with stories of marvelous voyages down the Red Sea into the Indian Ocean and around Africa from the west. Most often, they attributed such trips to the Phoenicians, the most fearless of Mediterranean seafarers. But occasionally a Greek appears. One such was Hippalus, a Greek ship's pilot who was said to have discovered the seasonal monsoon winds that facilitate sailing across the Indian Ocean. Though this story is questionable (see Chapter 7), it highlights the importance of the monsoon.

The regular, seasonal alternation of steady winds could not have remained unnoticed for thousands of years, waiting for an alert Greek to happen along. The great voyages and discoveries made before written records became common should surely be attributed to the peoples who lived around the Indian Ocean—Africans, Arabs, Persians, Indians, Malays—rather than to interlopers from the Mediterranean Sea. The story of Hippalus resembles the Chinese story of General Zhang Jian, whose role in opening trade with Central Asia so strongly overshadows the anonymous contributions made by the indigenous peoples.

The sailing traditions and techniques of the Indian Ocean differed markedly from those of the Mediterranean. Mediterranean sailors of the time of Alexander used square sails and long banks of oars to maneuver among the sea's many islands and small harbors. Indian Ocean vessels relied on lateen sails and normally did without oars in running before the wind on long ocean stretches. The lateen sail, a four-sided sail with a very short leading edge and a tall peak, could sail more directly into the wind than could a square sail, and it may have had greater stability, since the pressure of the wind was strongest on its lower portion. Mediterranean shipbuilders nailed their vessels together. The planks of Indian Ocean ships were pierced, tied together with palm fiber, and caulked with bitumen. Mediterranean sailors rarely ventured out of sight of land. Indian Ocean sailors, thanks to the monsoon winds, could cover the long reaches between southern Arabia and India entirely at sea.

The world of the Indian Ocean developed differently from the world of the Mediterranean Sea. The Phoenicians and Greeks fostered trade around the Mediterranean by establishing colonies that maintained contact with their home cities, thus giving rise to the maritime empires of Carthage and Athens (see Chapters 4 and 5). The traders of the Indian Ocean, where distances were greater and contacts less frequent, seldom retained political ties with their homelands. The colonies they established were sometimes socially distinctive but rarely independent of the local political powers. The Mediterranean region was smaller than the Indian Ocean basin and more competitive with respect to a small number of exchangeable goods—copper, tin, wine, olive oil, pottery. These political and environmental factors contributed to the recurrent warfare and intense rivalry that marked the Mediterranean world, a political situation favoring rowed warships that remained easily maneuverable even in windless conditions. By contrast, war seldom beset the Indian Ocean maritime system prior to the arrival of European explorers at the end of the fifteenth century C.E. Its early history is primarily concerned with population movements and the exchange of goods and ideas.

Burial Mounds on the Island of Bahrain   Trade around the Persian Gulf and through it into the Indian Ocean occurred at least as early as 3000 B.C.E. Thousands of ancient burial mounds attest to Bahrain's lively participation in this trade. The island was not only a fertile site well provided with fresh water but also a prime location for pearl fishing. (Christine Osborne Pictures)

Origins of Contact and Trade

As early as 2000 B.C.E. Sumerian records spoke of regular trading contacts between Mesopotamia, the islands of the Persian Gulf, Oman, and the Indus Valley. However, this early trading contact eastward broke off, and later Mesopotamian trade references mention East Africa more often than India.

A similarly early chapter in Indian Ocean history concerns migrations from Southeast Asia to Madagascar, the world's fourth largest island, situated off the southeastern coast of Africa. Some two thousand years ago, people from one of the many Indonesian islands of Southeast Asia established themselves in that forested, mountainous land some 6,000 miles (9,500 kilometers) from home. They could not possibly have carried enough supplies for a direct voyage across the Indian Ocean, so their route must have touched the coasts of India and southern Arabia. No remains of their journeys have been discovered, however.

Apparently, the sailing canoes of these people plied the seas along the increasingly familiar route for several hundred years. Settlers farmed the new land and entered into relations with Africans, who found their way across the 250-mile-wide (400-kilometer-wide) Mozambique° Channel around the fifth century C.E. Descendants of the seafarers preserved the language of their homeland and some of its culture, such as the cultivation of bananas, yams, and other native Southeast Asian plants. These food crops spread to mainland Africa. But gradually the

memory of their distant origins faded, not to be recovered until modern times, when scholars established the linguistic link between the two lands.

The examples of Hippalus and of Southeast Asians in Madagascar illustrate the difficulty historians encounter in writing the history of the Indian Ocean maritime system. Written sources are extremely rare, and archaeological finds are often hard to interpret. Yet the historical importance of communication across the Indian Ocean is unquestionable.

The Impact of Indian Ocean Trade

The only extensive written account of trade in the Indian Ocean before the rise of Islam in the seventh century C.E. is an anonymous work by a Greco-Egyptian of the first century C.E. *The Periplus of the Erythraean° Sea* (that is, the Red Sea) describes ports of call along the Red Sea and down the East African coast to somewhere south of the island of Zanzibar. Then it describes the ports of southern Arabia and the Persian Gulf before continuing eastward to India, mentioning ports all the way around the subcontinent to the mouth of the Ganges River. Though the geographer Ptolemy, who lived slightly later, had heard of ports as far away as Southeast Asia, the author of the *Periplus* had obviously voyaged to the places he mentions and was not merely an armchair traveler. What he describes is unquestionably a trading *system* and is clear evidence of the steady

---

Mozambique (moe-zam-BEEK)

Erythraean (eh-RITH-ree-an)

Caravan Cities

Archaeology reveals a lot about daily life in caravan cities, but travelers' descriptions give a better indication of the impact that such cities made at the time. Two geographer-historians from the first century B.C.E., Diodorus of Sicily and Strabo, provide valuable descriptions of the terminal cities of the Arabian caravan route that linked the incense-producing region of southern Arabia with Jordan and Syria. At the southern end was Saba, in Yemen. At the northern end was Petra, in Jordan.

Saba

And a natural sweet odor pervades the entire land because practically all the things which excel in fragrance grow there unceasingly. Along the coast, for instance, grow balsam . . . and cassia. . . . And throughout the interior of the land there are thick forests, in which are great trees which yield frankincense and myrrh, as well as palms and reeds, cinnamon trees and every other kind which possesses a sweet odor such as these have. . . .

This people surpassed not only the neighboring Arabs but also all other men in wealth and in their several extravagances besides. For in the exchange and sale of their wares they, of all men who carry on trade for the sake of the silver they receive in exchange, obtain the highest price in return for things of the smallest weight. Consequently, since they have never for ages suffered the ravages of war because of their secluded position, and since an abundance of both gold and silver abounds in the country, especially in Saba, where the royal palace is situated, they have embossed goblets of every description, made of silver and gold, couches and tripods with silver feet, and every other furnishing of incredible costliness, and halls encircled by large columns, some of them gilded, and others having silver figures on the capitals. . . . For the fact is that these people have enjoyed their felicity unshaken since ages past because they have been entire strangers to those whose own covetousness leads them to feel that another man's wealth is their own godsend. . . . And there are prosperous islands nearby, containing unwalled cities. . . . These islands are visited by sailors from every part and especially from Potana, the city which Alexander founded on the Indus River.

Petra

The Nabataeans are a sensible people, and are so much inclined to acquire possessions that they publicly fine anyone who has diminished his possessions and also confer honors on anyone who has increased them. Since they have but few slaves, they are served by their kinsfolk for the most part, or by one another, or by themselves; so that the custom extends even to their kings. They prepare common meals together in groups of thirteen persons; and they have two girl-singers for each banquet. The king holds many drinking bouts in magnificent style, but no one drinks more than eleven cupfuls, each time using a different golden cup. The king is so democratic that, in addition to serving himself, he sometimes even serves the rest himself in his turn. He often renders an account of his kingship in the popular assembly; and sometimes his mode of life is examined. Their homes, through the use of stone, are costly; but, on account of peace, the cities are not walled. . . . The sheep are white-fleeced and the oxen are large, but the country produces no horses. Camels afford the service they require instead of horses. Some things are imported wholly from other countries, but others not altogether so, especially in the case of those that are native products, as, for example, gold and silver and most of the aromatics, whereas brass and iron, as also purple garb [for the kings], styrax, crocus, costaria, embossed works, paintings, and molded works are not produced in their country.

What role do imported goods play in the economies of Saba and Petra? To what degree is monarchy associated with trade?

Source: For Saba, Diodorus of Sicily, Book III, (Cambridge, MA: Harvard University Press) 46–47. Translated by C. H. Oldfather. For Petra, Strabo, Book 16, (Cambridge, MA: Harvard University Press) 4.26. Translated by H. L. Jones.

---

growth of interconnections in the region during the preceding centuries. An impression of the prosperity that trade could produce can be gained from reading contemporary accounts of caravan cities connected to the Red Sea and Persian Gulf (see Society and Culture: Caravan Cities).

The demand for products from the coastal lands inspired mariners to persist in their long ocean voyages.

Africa produced exotic animals, wood, and ivory. However, since ivory also came from India, Mesopotamia, and North Africa, the extent of African ivory exports cannot be determined. The highlands of northern Somalia and southern Arabia grew the scrubby trees whose aromatic resins were valued as frankincense and myrrh. Trees on the island of Socotra near the entrance of the Red Sea produced "dragon's blood," a scarlet resin that Roman artists valued highly as a pigment. Pearls abounded in the Persian Gulf, and evidence of ancient copper mines has been found in Oman in southeastern Arabia. India shipped spices and manufactured goods, and more spices came from Southeast Asia, along with manufactured items, particularly pottery, obtained in trade with China. In sum, the Indian Ocean trading region was one with a great variety of highly valued products. Given the long distances and the comparative lack of islands, however, the volume of trade there was undoubtedly much lower than in the Mediterranean Sea.

Furthermore, the culture of the Indian Ocean ports was often isolated from the hinterlands, particularly in the west. The coasts of the Arabian peninsula, the African side of the Red Sea, southern Iran, and northern India (today Pakistan) were mostly barren desert. Ports in all these areas tended to be small, and many suffered from meager supplies of fresh water. Farther south in India, the monsoon provided ample water, but steep mountains cut off the coastal plain from the interior of the country. Thus few ports between Zanzibar and Sri Lanka had substantial inland populations within easy reach. The head of the Persian Gulf was one exception: shipborne trade was possible as far north as Babylon and, from the eighth century C.E., nearby Baghdad.

By contrast, eastern India, the Malay Peninsula, and Indonesia afforded more hospitable and densely populated shores with easier access to inland populations. Though the fishers, sailors, and traders of the western Indian Ocean system supplied a long series of kingdoms and empires, none of these consumer societies became primarily maritime in orientation, as the Greeks and Phoenicians did in the Mediterranean. In the east, in contrast, seaborne trade and influence seem to have been important even to the earliest states, such as that of Srivijaya (see Chapter 7). The inland forest dwellers of the Malay Peninsula were far less potent politically than the citizens of the port cities.

In coastal areas throughout the Indian Ocean system, small groups of seafarers sometimes had a significant social impact despite their usual lack of political power. Women seldom accompanied their menfolk on long sea voyages, so sailors and merchants often married local women in port cities. The families thus established were bilingual and bicultural. As in many other situations in world history, women played a crucial though not well-documented role as mediators between cultures. Not only did they raise their children to be more cosmopolitan than children from inland regions, but they introduced their menfolk to customs and attitudes that they carried with them when they returned to sea. As a consequence, the designation of specific seafarers as Persian, Arab, Indian, or Malay often conceals mixed heritages and a rich cultural diversity.

The pace of communication across the Indian Ocean increased over time. By the early Islamic era of the eighth century C.E., eastern products were well known in the Middle East, Javanese and Indian communities had been established in Mesopotamia, and a partially seaborne Arab expedition had conquered the lower Indus Valley (711 C.E.). Around 900, a large colony of Arab and Persian traders was growing up in Canton, in southern China. Evidence of the worship of Hindu gods by Indian traders can be found in caves in southwestern Iran, and close relations exist to this day between Arab families long settled in Singapore and Jakarta and the land of their ancestors in southern Yemen.

ROUTES ACROSS THE SAHARA

The windswept Sahara, a desert stretching from the Red Sea to the Atlantic Ocean and broken only by the Nile River, isolates sub-Saharan Africa from the Mediterranean world (see Map 8.2). The current dryness of the Sahara dates only to about 2500 B.C.E., however. The period of drying out that preceded that date was twenty-five centuries long and encompassed several cultural changes. During that time, travel between a slowly shrinking number of grassy areas was comparatively easy. However, by 300 B.C.E., scarcity of water was restricting travel to a few difficult routes initially known only to desert nomads. Trade over **trans-Saharan caravan routes** was at first only a trickle, but it eventually expanded into a significant stream. By 1100 C.E., the riches in gold, slaves, and tropical goods flowing northward had begun to excite the envy of the Europeans, whose

Map. 8.2 Africa and the Trans–Saharan Trade Routes
The Sahara and the surrounding oceans isolated most of Africa from foreign contact before 1000 C.E. The Nile Valley, a few trading points on the east coast, and limited transdesert trade provided exceptions to this rule; but the dominant forms of sub-Saharan African culture originated far to the west, north of the Gulf of Guinea.

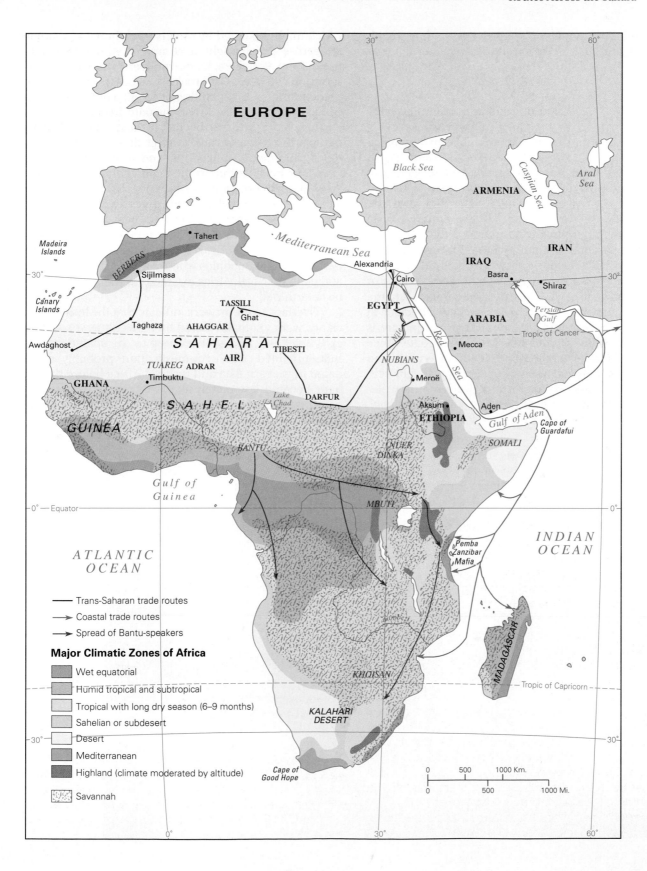

EUROPE

Black Sea

Madeira Islands

Caspian Sea

Aral Sea

ARMENIA

Mediterranean Sea

•Tahert

Alexandria

IRAN

IRAQ

Basra•

•Shiraz

BERBERS

•Sijilmasa

30°

30°

30°

Canary Islands

EGYPT

Persian Gulf

TASSILI

Taghaza•

AHAGGAR   •Ghat

ARABIA

Tropic of Cancer

Awdaghost•

S A H A R A   •TIBESTI

AIR

•Mecca

TUAREG ADRAR

Nile

NUBIANS

Red Sea

GHANA   •Timbuktu

S A H E L

•Meroë

Lake Chad

DARFUR

Aden

Gulf of Aden

Capo of Guardafui

GUINEA

Aksum•

ETHIOPIA

SOMALI

BANTU

NUER
DINKA

Gulf of Guinea

Congo

MBUTI

0° — Equator

0°

INDIAN OCEAN

ATLANTIC OCEAN

Pemba
Zanzibar
Mafia

Zambezi

MADAGASCAR

KHOISAN

Tropic of Capricorn

— Trans-Saharan trade routes

→ Coastal trade routes

→ Spread of Bantu-speakers

Major Climatic Zones of Africa

- Wet equatorial
- Humid tropical and subtropical
- Tropical with long dry season (6–9 months)
- Sahelian or subdesert
- Desert
- Mediterranean
- Highland (climate moderated by altitude)
- Savannah

KALAHARI
DESERT

30°

30°

Cape of Good Hope

| 0 | 500 | 1000 Km. |

| 0 | 500 | 1000 Mi. |

0°

30°

60°

desire to find the source of the Saharan trading wealth helped trigger their farflung explorations after the year 1400 C.E.

Early Saharan Cultures

Sprawling sand dunes, sandy plains, and vast expanses of exposed rock make up most of the great desert. Stark and rugged mountain and highland areas separate its northern and southern portions. The cliffs and caves of these highlands, which were the last spots where water and grassland could be found as the climate changed, preserve a vast treasury of rock paintings and engravings that constitute the primary evidence for early Saharan history.

Scholars have never discovered a method of dating these pictures. Some are darker than others because of longer exposure to the sun, which draws minerals to the surface of the rock to form a hard film. This difference in brightness, however, indicates only that one picture is older than another; it does not yield a fixed date. Since artists sometimes used the same flat surfaces again and again, relative dating can also be accomplished by seeing which paintings or engravings overlap others. Regrettably, no archaeological remains such as charcoal,

which might be dated by means of carbon-14, or stone projectiles, which might be compared with datable materials from elsewhere, have ever been found in clear association with any of this rock art. Ashes from a campfire at the foot of a rock painting, after all, could date from centuries earlier or later than the painting itself.

In what appear to be the earliest images, left by hunters in obviously much wetter times, elephants, giraffes, rhinoceros, crocodiles, and other animals that have long been extinct in the region come vividly alive. Presumably these early hunting peoples followed their game animals southward or northward as the rivers and luxuriant grasslands disappeared because of climate change. But whether they were more closely related to the later peoples of Africa south of the Sahara or to the Berber-speaking peoples who inhabited the mountains and plains of North Africa in Greco-Roman times cannot be determined.

Overlaps in the artwork indicate that the hunting societies were gradually joined by new cultures based on cattle breeding and well adapted to the sparse grazing that remained. Cattle domestication probably originated in western Asia and reached Africa before the Sahara became completely dry. However, the beautiful paintings of cattle and detailed scenes of daily life found

Cattle Herders in Saharan Rock Art   These paintings, the most artistically accomplished type of Saharan art, succeeded the depictions of hunters characteristic of the earliest art. Herding societies of modern times living in the Sahel region south of the Sahara strongly resemble the society depicted here. This suggests that as the Sahara became completely arid, the cattle herders moved south and played a role in the formation of sub-Saharan African culture.   (Henri Lhote)

in the Sahara depict pastoral societies that bear little similarity to any in Asia. Rather, the people seem physically akin to today's West Africans, and the customs depicted, such as dancing and wearing masks, as well as the breeds of cattle, strongly suggest later societies to the south of the Sahara. These factors support the hypothesis that some southern cultural patterns originated in the Sahara and migrated southward. In the Sahara itself, however, the cattle herders seem little related to the peoples who followed them.

Overlaps in artwork also clearly indicate that horse herders succeeded the cattle herders. The rock art changes dramatically in style. The superb realism of the cattle pictures is replaced by sketchier images that are often strongly geometric. Moreover, the horses are frequently shown drawing light chariots. This phase of Saharan rock art has provoked numerous theories. According to the most common theory, the charioteers were intrepid travelers from the Mediterranean shore who drove their flimsy vehicles across the desert and established societies in the few remaining green areas of the central Saharan highlands. The characteristic "flying gallop" posture of the horses—all four legs extended in a dramatic though unrealistic fashion—has been compared with similar representations in early Greek art. Some scholars have suggested possible chariot routes that refugees from the collapse of the Mycenaean and Minoan civilizations of Greece and Crete might have followed deep into the desert around the twelfth century B.C.E.

However, no archaeological evidence of actual chariot use in the Sahara has ever been discovered, much less any convincing indication of extensive migration along chariot routes. Moreover, though rock art in the mountainous areas of North Africa is rare compared with the abundant images from the central Saharan highlands, images of chariots are notably absent. Given the extreme aridity of the Sahara by the twelfth century B.C.E. and the absence of indications that charioteers penetrated the more hospitable lands north of the desert, it is difficult to imagine large numbers of refugees from the politically chaotic Mediterranean region trekking and driving chariots into the trackless desert in search of a new homeland somewhere to the south.

As in the case of the cattle herders, therefore, the identity of the Saharan horse breeders, and the source of their passion for drawing chariots, remain a mystery. Only with the coming of the camel is it possible to make firm connections with the Saharan nomads of today through the depiction of objects and geometric patterns still used by the veiled, blue-robed Tuareg° people of the highlands in southern Algeria, Niger, and Mali.

The Coming of the Camel

Taking note of two Roman military expeditions into central Libya in the first century B.C.E., some historians maintain that the Romans inaugurated an important trans-Saharan trade; but only scanty archaeological evidence supports this theory. More plausible is the idea that Saharan trade is related to the spread of camel domestication. Supporting evidence is visible in the highland rock art, where overlaps of paintings and engravings imply that camel riders in desert costume constitute the latest Saharan population. As in the transition from cattle to horses, artistic styles again change. The camel-oriented images are decidedly the crudest and most elementary to be found in the region.

Latin texts from 46 B.C.E. first mention camels in North Africa. The camel is not native to Africa, so it must have reached the Sahara from Arabia. Scholars do not know exactly when, but scattered sources hint that camels probably came into use in Egypt in the first millennium B.C.E. and from there became known to the people who lived in the deserts bordering the Nile Valley. From the upper Nile region in the Sudan they could have been adopted by peoples farther and farther to the west, from one central Saharan highland to the next, only much later spreading northward and coming to the attention of the Romans.

Evidence for this south-to-north diffusion of camels comes not from written sources but from the design of camel saddles and patterns of camel use (see Environment and Technology: Camel Saddles). In North Africa, including the northern Sahara, pack saddles of obvious Middle Eastern design predominate, and Greco-Roman sources stress the fact that the camel-using Berber groups native to the region did not fight on camelback but dismounted and used their animals as shields. In contrast, the peoples in the central and southern Sahara used riding saddles of a unique design and are regularly depicted, both in art and in later historical texts, as fighting with sword and spear while on camelback.

Once camel herding was established in the south, it became easier for people to move away from the highlands and roam the deep desert. Through contacts made by the new society of far-ranging camel herders, the people north of the Sahara finally gained access to the camel, though they exploited it primarily as a work animal, even developing harnesses for attaching camels to plows and carts. These practices, entirely unknown in the southern Sahara, are still in evidence in Tunisia° today.

Tuareg (TWAH-reg)

Tunisia (too-NEE-zhee-uh)

Camel Saddles

As seemingly simple a technology as saddle design can be an indicator of a society's economic structure. The South Arabian saddle was good for riding, and baggage could easily be tied to the wooden arches that attached it to the animal in the front. It was comparatively inefficient militarily, however, because the rider knelt on the cushion behind the camel's hump and so was poorly positioned to control his mount and use his weapons.

The North Arabian saddle was a significant improvement that came into use in the first centuries B.C.E. Its wooden framework made tying on cargo easy, and its prominent front and back arches and placement over the camel's hump gave warriors a decent perch from which to wield their swords and spears. Arabs in northern Arabia took control of the caravan trade in that region by using these saddles.

The best riding saddles were developed by the peoples south of the Sahara. The saddles of the Tuareg seated the rider on the camel's shoulders, giving him complete freedom to use his sword and allowing him to control his mount by pressure from his toes on the animal's neck. These excellent war saddles could not be used for baggage, however, because they did not offer a convenient place to tie bundles.

Camel Saddles The militarily inefficient south Arabian saddle (above) seats the rider behind the animal's hump atop its hindquarters. The rider controls his mount by tapping its neck with a long camelstick. The saddle of the Tuaregs (below) from the southern Sahara seats the rider over the animal's withers, allowing the rider's feet to rest on the camel's neck. Controlling his mount with his toes, the rider has his hands free to wield a sword. (above: Private collection; below: Fred Bavendam/Peter Arnold, Inc.)

Trade Across the Sahara

The coming of the camel did not automatically stimulate the beginning of trade across the Sahara. People on both sides of the desert used camels, but in different ways, and they seem to have had little influence on each other even though most of them spoke Berber languages. Linkage between two different trading systems, one in the south, the other in the north, developed slowly.

Southern traders concentrated on supplying salt from large deposits in the southern desert to the peoples of sub-Saharan Africa. Salt is a physiological necessity in torrid climates, and natural deposits are rare outside the desert. Traders from the equatorial forest zone brought forest products, such as kola nuts and palm oil, to trading centers near the desert's southern fringe. Each received from the other, or from the farming peoples of the Sahel°—literally "the coast" in Arabic, the southern borderlands of the Sahara (see Map 8.2)—the products they needed in their homelands. Middlemen who were native to the Sahel played an important role in this trade, but precise historical details are lacking.

In the north, the main trade of Roman North Africa consisted of supplying Italy with agricultural products, primarily wheat and olives, and with wild animals from the Atlas Mountains for the arena in Rome. Cities near the coast, such as Carthage (rebuilt as a Roman city after its destruction in the Punic Wars), Hippo in Tunisia, and Leptis Magna in Libya, were centers of exchange. Surviving mosaic pavements depicting scenes from daily life show that people living on the farms and in the towns of the interior consumed Roman manufactured goods and shared Roman styles.

This northern pattern began to change in the third century C.E. with the decline of the Roman Empire, which saw the abandonment of many Roman farms, the growth of nomadism, and a lessening of trade across the Mediterranean. After the Arabs invaded North Africa in the middle of the seventh century C.E., the direction of trade shifted to the Middle East, the center of Arab rule. Since the Arab conquests were inspired by the new religion of Islam (see Chapter 9), and the Christian lands of Europe constituted enemy territory, trans-Mediterranean trade diminished still further. Meanwhile, an east-west overland trade grew to compete with the coastal sea route, which was limited in effectiveness in Algeria and Morocco because high mountains separated most seaports from the interior. Many of the Arabs were members of camel-breeding tribes back in their Arabian homeland. Thus they felt a cultural kinship with those Berbers who had taken up camel pastoralism during the preceding few centuries, and they related better to the peoples of the interior than any previous conquerors had done.

A series of Berber revolts against Arab rule from 740 onward led to the appearance of several small principalities in what are today Morocco and Algeria. The rulers of these city-states on the northern fringe of the Sahara held Islamic beliefs somewhat different from those of the Arab rulers to the east. Their religious differences may have interfered with their east-west overland trade and led them to look for new possibilities elsewhere. From the fragmentary records that survive, it appears that these city-states, Sijilmasa° and Tahert°, were the first places to develop significant and regular trading contact with the south in the ninth century. Most of their populations were Berbers, so it is reasonable to assume that they already knew that nomads speaking closely related languages were roaming the central and southern reaches of the great desert. But prior to 740, they had little reason to explore the possibilities of trade with the south.

Once they did look south, however, they discovered that gold dust was one of the products the southern nomads received in exchange for salt. The gold came from deposits along the Niger and other West African rivers (see Map 8.2). The people who panned for the gold seem not to have used it extensively, and they did not value it nearly as highly as did the traders from Sijilmasa. For the latter, trading salt for gold was a dream come true. They were able to provide the nomads of the southern desert, who controlled the salt sources but had little use for gold, with products not available from the south, such as copper and certain manufactured goods. Thus everyone benefited from the creation of the new trade link. Sijilmasa and Tahert became wealthy cities, the former minting gold coins that circulated as far away as Egypt and Syria. The high value placed on gold in the Mediterranean lands greatly increased the profitability of the trade at every stage.

The Kingdom of Ghana

The earliest know sub-Saharan beneficiary of the new exchange system was the kingdom of Ghana°. First mentioned in an Arabic text of the late eighth century as the "land of gold," but presumed to date back to the sixth century, Ghana inaugurates the documentable political history of West Africa. Yet until the mid-eleventh century, few details are available about this realm, established by the

Sahel (SAH-hel)

Sijilmasa (sih-jil-MAS-suh)   Tahert (TAH-hert)
Ghana (GAH-nuh)

Soninke° people and covering parts of Mali, Mauritania, and Senegal. Then the Arab geographer al-Bakri (d. 1094) described it as follows:

> The city of Ghana consists of two towns situated on a plain. One of these towns is inhabited by Muslims. It is large and possesses a dozen mosques, one being for the Friday prayer, and each having imams [prayer leaders], muezzins [people to make the call to prayer], and salaried reciters of the Quran. There are jurisconsults [legal specialists] and scholars. Around the town are sweet wells, which they use for drinking and for cultivating vegetables. The royal city, called al-Ghaba ["the grove"], is six miles away, and the area between the two towns is covered with habitations. Their houses are constructed of stone and acacia wood. The king has a palace with conical huts, surrounded by a fence like a wall. In the king's town, not far from the royal court, is a mosque for the use of Muslims who visit the king on missions. . . . The interpreters of the king are Muslims, as are his treasurer and the majority of his ministers.
>
> Their religion is paganism, and the worship of idols. . . . Around the royal town are domed dwellings, woods and copses where live their sorcerers, those in charge of their religious cults. There are also their idols and their kings' tombs.[2]

Typical of monarchs with imperial powers, the king of Ghana required the sons of vassal kings to attend his court. He meted out justice and controlled trade, collecting taxes on the salt and copper coming from the north. His large army of bowmen and cavalry made Ghana the dominant power in the entire region. By the end of the tenth century, the king's sway extended even to Awdaghost°, the trade entrepôt that had grown up in the desert at the southern end of the track to Sijilmasa. Awdaghost was populated by Arabs and Berbers.

After 1076, Ghana fell prey to a new state formed by desert nomads who had been drawn into the trade in the region of Awdaghost. These conquerors, the Muslim Almoravids°, ruled both sides of the desert from their newly built capital city of Marrakesh° in Morocco. After little more than a decade, during which later Muslim historians assert many people in Ghana converted to Islam, Almoravid strength in the south dwindled because of demands for military manpower in the north. Although Ghana thereby regained its independence, many of its former provinces had been permanently

lost, and it never recovered its former greatness. Ghana's strength had clearly derived from its dominance of the new trading system. But with the Almoravids still powerful in Morocco, the old system could not easily be recreated.

Prior to the arrival of the religiously zealous Almoravids, the traders who had reached Ghana from the north had not been overly insistent on propagating Islam. Over the three centuries separating al-Bakri's account in the eleventh century from the earliest mention of Ghana, Muslims had come to hold high economic positions in Ghana, and the kings tolerated their religious practices. But, in general, the people of Ghana had not been stirred to convert to Islam. General adoption of the Islamic religion, with consequent impact on the way of life of the Sahel peoples, came under later kingdoms.

♫

SUB-SAHARAN AFRICA

The Indian Ocean network and, somewhat later, trade across the Sahara provided the vast region of **sub-Saharan Africa,** the portion of Africa south of the Sahara, with a few external contacts. The most important African network of cultural exchange from 300 B.C.E. to 1100 C.E., however, was within sub-Saharan Africa. These exchanges led to the formation of enduring characteristics of African culture.

A Challenging Geography

That a significant degree of cultural unity developed in sub-Saharan Africa, is especially remarkable because of the many geographic obstacles to movement (see Map 8.2). The Sahara, the Atlantic and Indian Oceans, and the Red Sea form the boundaries of the region. With the exception of the Nile, a ribbon of green traversing the Sahara from south to north, the major river systems empty either into the Atlantic, in the case of the Senegal, Niger, and Zaire°, or into the Mozambique Channel of the Indian Ocean, in the case of the Zambezi. Moreover, rapids limit the use of these rivers for navigation.

Stretching over 50 degrees of latitude, sub-Saharan Africa encompasses a large number of dramatically different environments. A 4,000-mile (6,500-kilometer) trek

---

Soninke (soh-NIN-kay)   Awdaghost (OW-duh-gost)
Almoravid (al-moe-RAH-vid)   Marrakesh (MAH-rah-kesh)

Zaire (zah-EER)

from the southern edge of the Sahara to the Cape of Good Hope would take a traveler from the flat, semiarid **steppes** of the Sahel region to tropical **savanna** covered by long grasses and scattered forest, next to **tropical rain forest** on the lower Niger and in the Zaire Basin. The rain forest then gives way to another broad expanse of savanna, followed by more steppe and desert, and finally a region of temperate highlands at the southern extremity, located as far south of the equator as Greece and Sicily are to its north. East-west travel is comparatively easy in the steppe and savanna regions but difficult in the equatorial rain-forest belt and across the mountains and deep rift valleys that abut the rain forest to the east and separate East from West Africa.

The Development of Cultural Unity

As we learned in Part Two, by the year 1 C.E., distinctive cultural regions had come into existence from China to the Mediterranean as the result of political expansion and conquest. More enduring than the political units, however, were cultural heritages shared by the educated elites within each region—heritages that some anthropologists call **"great traditions."** They typically included a written language, common legal and belief systems, ethical codes, and other intellectual traditions. They loom large in surviving written records as traditions that rise above the diversity of local customs and beliefs commonly distinguished as **"small traditions."**

By the year 1 C.E., sub-Saharan Africa, too, had become a distinct cultural region, but one that was not shaped by imperial conquest and not characterized by a shared elite culture, a "great tradition." The cultural unity of sub-Saharan Africa was especially complex because it rested on similar characteristics shared to varying degrees by many popular cultures, or "small traditions." These popular cultures had developed during sub-Saharan Africa's long period of isolation from the rest of the world and had been refined, renewed, and interwoven by repeated episodes of migration and social interaction. Unfortunately, historians know very little about this complex prehistory. Thus, to a greater degree than in other regions, they call on anthropological descriptions, oral history, and comparatively late records of various "small traditions" to reconstruct the broad outlines of prehistoric cultural formation.

Sub-Saharan Africa's cultural unity is less immediately apparent than its diversity. Indeed, both students and scholars find the number and variety of the continent's social and cultural forms bewildering. By one estimate, two thousand distinct languages are spoken on the continent, many of them corresponding to social and belief systems endowed with distinctive rituals and cosmologies. There are likewise numerous food production systems, ranging from hunting and gathering—very differently carried out by the Mbuti° Pygmies of the equatorial rain forest and the Khoisan° peoples of the southwestern deserts—to the cultivation of bananas, yams, and other root crops in forest clearings and of sorghum and other grains in the savanna lands. Pastoral societies display a similar diversity.

Such diversity is not surprising. Sub-Saharan Africa covers an area much larger than any of the other cultural regions of the first millennium C.E., and the diversity of its climate, terrain, and vegetation is more pronounced. Africans adapted to these many environments in distinctive ways. Moreover, the overall density of population was in most areas lower than in the temperate lands to the north. Thus societies and polities had abundant room to form and reform, and a substantial amount of space separated different groups. The contacts that did occur were neither so frequent nor so long lasting as to produce rigid cultural uniformity.

Another factor accounts for the persistent diversity of sub-Saharan Africa—the inability for centuries of external conquerors to penetrate the region's natural barriers and impose any sort of uniform culture. The Egyptians occupied Nubia for long periods but were blocked from going farther south by the Nile cataracts and the vast swampland in the Nile's upper reaches. The Romans sent expeditions against people living in the Libyan Sahara but could not incorporate them into the Roman world. Arabic sources tell of military expeditions reaching the southern parts of the Sahara in the seventh century C.E., but these accounts are tinged with legend and had little, if any, effect. Indeed, not until the nineteenth century did outsiders gain control of the continent and begin the process of establishing an elite culture—that of western Europe.

African Cultural Characteristics

Despite the great cultural variations, outside visitors who got to know the sub-Saharan region well in the nineteenth and twentieth centuries were always struck by the broad commonalities that underlay African life and culture. Though there were many varieties of African kingdom, kingship displayed common features, most notably the ritual isolation of the king himself (see Society and

---

Mbuti (m-BOO-tee)   **Khoisan** (KOI-sahn)

Culture: Personal Styles of Rule in India and Mali in Chapter 15). Even societies too small to organize themselves into kingdoms had social categories—age groupings, fixed kinship divisions, distinct gender roles and relations, and occupational groupings. Though not hierarchical, these filled a role similar to the divisions between noble, commoner, and slave prevalent where kings ruled. In agriculture, the common technique was cultivation by hoe and digging stick.

Commonalities are also evident in music. Africans played many musical instruments, yet there were underlying traditions, particularly in rhythm, that made African music as a whole distinctive. Music played an important role in social rituals, as did dancing and wearing masks.

These and other indications of underlying cultural unity have led modern observers to identify a common African quality throughout most of the region, even though most sub-Saharan Africans themselves did not perceive it—just as Greeks and Persians, though both part of a broad Indo-European linguistic and cultural grouping, did not recognize the shared features of their pantheons, social structures, and languages. An eminent Belgian anthropologist, Jacques Maquet, has called this quality "Africanity."

Some historians hypothesize that this cultural unity emanated originally from the peoples who once occupied the southern Sahara. In Paleolithic times, periods of dryness alternated with periods of wetness as the ice ages that locked up much of the world's fresh water in glaciers and icecaps came and went. As European glaciers receded with the waning of the last ice age, a storm belt brought increased wetness to the Saharan region. Rushing rivers scoured deep canyons. Now filled with fine sand, those canyons are easily visible on flights over the southern parts of the desert, which long ago were among the most habitable parts of the continent and perhaps the most densely populated. As the glaciers receded still farther, the storm belt moved northward to Europe, and a dry belt that had been farther south moved northward between 5000 and 2500 B.C.E. As a consequence, runs the hypothesis, the region's population migrated south, where it became increasingly concentrated in what is now the Sahel. That region may have been the initial incubation center for what were to become Pan-African cultural patterns.

Eventually, however, the dryness of the land and the pressures of population concentration drove some people out of this cultural core into more sparsely settled lands to the east, west, and south. A parallel process may have occurred in the northern Sahara, but the evidence

there is much more limited. As for the Nile Valley, migration away from the desert was surely one of the triggers for settling of the Nile Valley and the emergence of the Old Kingdom of Egypt around 2500 B.C.E.

The Advent of Iron and the Bantu Migrations

Although some aspects of this reconstruction are speculative, archaeological investigation has shown that sub-Saharan agriculture first became common north of the equator by the early second millennium B.C.E. and then spread southward, displacing hunting and gathering as a way of life. Moreover, there is botanical evidence that banana trees, probably introduced to southeastern Africa from Southeast Asia, made their way north and west, retracing the presumed migrations of the first agriculturists.

A second dispersal involved metallurgy. Archaeology has revealed traces of copper mining in the Sahara from the early first millennium B.C.E., in the Niger Valley somewhat later, and in the Central African copper belt between 400 and 900 C.E. Gold was mined in Zimbabwe by the eighth and ninth centuries C.E. Most important of all, iron smelting began in northern sub-Saharan Africa in the early first millennium C.E., and from there it spread southward to the rest of the continent, becoming firmly established in southern Africa by the year 800.

Iron does not naturally occur in metallic form, except in meteorites, and a very high temperature is necessary to extract it from ores. Thus many historians believe that the secret of smelting iron was discovered only once, by the Hittites of Anatolia (modern Turkey) around 1500 B.C.E. (see Chapter 3). But while its spread from this presumed point of origin can generally be traced in Europe and Asia, how iron smelting reached sub-Saharan Africa is not clear. By way of the Nile Valley is one possibility, but the earliest evidence of ironworking from the kingdom of Meroë, on the upper Nile, is no earlier than the evidence from West Africa (northern Nigeria). Even less plausible is the idea of a spread southward from Phoenician settlements in North Africa, since archaeological evidence has not substantiated vague Greek and Latin accounts of Phoenician contacts with the south by land.

Some historians suggest that Africans discovered for themselves how to smelt iron. They might have done so while firing pottery in kilns. No firm evidence exists to prove or disprove this theory.

Linguistic analysis provides the strongest evidence of extensive contacts among sub-Saharan Africans in the first millennium C.E.—and offers suggestions about the spread of iron. Linguists recognize that the more than three hundred languages spoken south of the equator belong to the branch of the Niger-Congo family known as **Bantu,** after the word meaning "people" in most of the languages.

The distribution of the Bantu languages both north and south of the equator is consistent with a divergence beginning in the first millennium B.C.E. By comparing core words common to most of the languages, linguists have drawn some conclusions about the original Bantu-speakers, whom they call "proto-Bantu." The proto-Bantu engaged in fishing, using canoes, nets, lines, and hooks. They lived in permanent villages on the edge of the rain forest, where they grew yams and grains and harvested wild palms from which they pressed oil. They possessed domesticated goats, dogs, and perhaps other animals. They made pottery and cloth. Linguists surmise that the proto-Bantu homeland was near the modern boundary of Nigeria and Cameroon, from which they trace western and eastern routes of linguistic dispersal into the equatorial rain forests to the south. Although dates for this long process are scarce, Bantu-speaking people are evident in East Africa by the eighth century C.E.

Because the presumed home of the proto-Bantu lies near the known sites of early iron smelting, migration by Bantu-speakers seems a likely mechanism for the southward spread of iron. Supplied with iron axes and iron hoes, the migrating Bantus are presumed to have hacked out forest clearings and planted crops. According to this scenario, they established an economic basis for new societies that were able to sustain much denser populations than could earlier societies dependent on hunting and gathering. Thus the period from 500 B.C.E. to 1000 C.E. saw a massive transfer of Bantu traditions and practices southward, eastward, and westward and their transformation into Pan-African traditions and practices.

THE SPREAD OF IDEAS

Ideas, like social customs, religious attitudes, and artistic styles, can spread along trade routes and through folk migrations. In both cases, documenting the dissemination of ideas, particularly in preliterate societies, poses a difficult historical problem.

Ideas and Things

Some ideas leave archaeological remains. Others depend on the survival of written sources. Customs surrounding the eating of pork are a case in point. Scholars disagree about whether the idea of domesticating pigs occurred only once and spread or whether several different peoples hit on the same idea at different times.

Southeast Asia was an important and early center of pig domestication. There the eating of pork became highly ritualized, sometimes being prohibited except on ceremonial occasions. On the other side of the Indian Ocean, in ancient Egypt, wild swine were common in the Nile swamps, pigs were considered sacred to the underworld-god Set, and eating them was prohibited. The biblical prohibition on the Israelites eating pork, echoed later by the Muslims, probably came from Egypt in the second millennium B.C.E.

In eastern Iran, an archaeological site dating from the third millennium B.C.E. provides evidence of another religious taboo on eating pork. Although the area around the site was swampy and home to many wild pigs, not a single pig bone has been found. Yet small pig figurines seem to have been used as symbolic religious offerings.

What accounts for the apparent connection between the domestication of pigs and religion in these widespread areas? There is no way of knowing. It has been hypothesized that pigs were first domesticated in Southeast Asia by people who had no herd animals—sheep, goats, cattle, horses—and relied on fish for most of their animal protein. The pig was thus a special animal to them. From Southeast Asia, pig domestication and the religious beliefs and rituals associated with the consumption of pork could have spread along the maritime routes of the Indian Ocean, eventually reaching Iran and Egypt.

A more certain example of objects indicating the spread of an idea is the practice of hammering a carved die onto a piece of precious metal and using the resulting coin as a medium of exchange. From its origin in Anatolia in the first millennium B.C.E., the idea of trading by means of struck coinage spread rapidly to Europe, North Africa, and India. Was the low-value copper coinage of China, made by pouring molten metal into a mold, also inspired by this practice from far away? It may have been, but it might also derive from indigenous Chinese metalworking. There is no way to be sure. Theoretically, all that is needed for an idea to spread is a single returning traveler telling about some wonder that he or she saw abroad.

The Spread of Buddhism

The spread of ideas in an organized way emerges as a new phenomenon in the first millennium B.C.E. From its original home in northern India in the fifth century B.C.E., Buddhism grew to become, with Christianity and Islam, one of the three most popular and widespread religions in the world (see Chapter 7). In all three cases, the religious ideas being spread were distinctive because of *not* being associated with specific ethnic or kinship groups.

King Ashoka, the Maurya ruler of India, and Kanishka, the greatest king of the Kushans of northern Afghanistan, were powerful royal advocates of Buddhism between the third century B.C.E. and the second century C.E. However, monks, missionaries, and pilgrims were the people who crisscrossed India, followed the Silk Road, or took ship in the Indian Ocean to bring the Buddha's teachings to Southeast Asia, China, Korea, and ultimately Japan (see Map 8.1).

The Chinese pilgrims Faxian° (died between 418 and 423 C.E.) and Xuanzang° (600–664 C.E.) left written accounts of their travels. Both followed the Silk Road, from which Buddhism had arrived in China. Along the way they encountered Buddhist communities and monasteries that previous generations of missionaries and pilgrims had established.

Faxian began his trip in the company of a Chinese envoy to an unspecified ruler or people in Central Asia. After traveling from one Buddhist site to another across Afghanistan and India, he reached Sri Lanka, a Buddhist land where he lived for two years. Then he embarked for China on a merchant ship with two hundred men aboard. A storm drove the ship to Java, which he did not describe because its religion was Hindu rather than Buddhist (the presence of Hinduism is an indication of earlier seaborne influences from India on Southeast Asia). After five months ashore, Faxian finally reached China on another ship. The narrative of Xuanzang's journey two centuries later is quite similar, though he returned to China the way he had come, along the Silk Road.

Less reliable accounts make reference to missionaries traveling to Syria, Egypt, and Macedonia, as well as to Southeast Asia. One of Ashoka's sons allegedly led a band of missionaries to Sri Lanka. Later his sister brought a company of nuns along with a branch of the sacred Bo tree under which the Buddha received enlightenment. According to Buddhist tradition, she accomplished her journey by air. At the same time, there are reports of other monks traveling to Burma, Thailand, and Sumatra. Ashoka's missionaries may also have reached Tibet by

Faxian (fah-shee-en)   Xuanzang (shoo-wen-zahng)

Statue of a Bodhisattva at Bamian   Carved into the side of a cliff, this is one of two monumental Buddhist sculptures near the top of a high mountain pass connecting Kabul, Afghanistan, with the northern parts of the country. Carved in the sixth or seventh century, C.E., the sculptures are surrounded by cave dwellings of monks and rock sanctuaries, some dating to the first century B.C.E. (Ian Griffiths/Robert Harding Picture Library)

way of trade routes across the Himalayas. A firmer tradition maintains that in 622 C.E. a minister of the Tibetan king traveled to India to study Buddhism and on his return introduced writing to his homeland.

The different lands that received the story and teachings of the Buddha preserved or adapted them in different ways. Theravada Buddhism, "Teachings of the Elder," centered in Sri Lanka. Holding closely to the Buddha's earliest teachings, it maintained that the goal of religion, available only to monks, is *nirvana*, the total absence of suffering and the end of the cycle of rebirth (see Chapter 7). This teaching contrasted with Mahayana, or "Great Vehicle" Buddhism, which stressed the goal of becoming a *bodhisattva,* a person who attains nirvana but chooses to remain in human company to help and guide others.

An offshoot of Mahayana Buddhism stressing ritual prayer and personal guidance by "perfected ones" became dominant in Tibet after the eighth century C.E. In China, another offshoot, Chan (called Zen in its Japanese form), focused on meditation and sudden enlightenment. It became one of the dominant sects in China, Korea, and Japan (see Chapter 11).

The Spread of Christianity

The post-Roman development of Christianity in Europe is discussed in Chapter 10. The Christian faith enjoyed an earlier spread in Asia and Africa before its confrontation with Islam (described in Chapter 9). Jerusalem in Palestine, Antioch in Syria, and Alexandria in Egypt became centers of Christian authority soon after the crucifixion, but the spread of Christianity to Armenia and Ethiopia illustrates the connections between religion, trade, and imperial politics.

Situated in eastern Anatolia (modern Turkey), **Armenia** served recurrently as a battleground between Iranian states to the south and east and Mediterranean states to the west. Each imperial power wanted to control this region so close to the frontier where Silk Road traders met their Mediterranean counterparts. In Parthian times, Armenia's kings favored Zoroastrianism. Armenian was not yet a written language so Christianity was known to "only those who were to some degree acquainted with Greek or Syriac learning" and thus able to obtain "some partial inkling of it."[3]

The invention of an Armenian alphabet in the early fifth century opened the way to a wider spread of Christianity and Greek culture in general. The Iranians did not give up domination easily, but within a century the Armenian Apostolic Church had become the center of Armenian cultural life.

Far to the south, Christians similarly sought to outflank Iran. The Christian emperors in Constantinople (see Chapter 10) sent missionaries along the Red Sea trade route to seek converts in Yemen and **Ethiopia.** In the fourth century C.E., a Syrian philosopher, traveling with two young relatives, sailed to India. On the way back the ship docked at a Red Sea port occupied by Ethiopians from the prosperous kingdom of Aksum. Being then at odds with the Romans, the Ethiopians killed everyone on board except the two boys, Aedisius—who later narrated this story—and Frumentius. Impressed by

their learning, the king made the former his cupbearer and the latter his treasurer and secretary.

When the king died, his wife urged Frumentius to govern Aksum on behalf of her and her infant son, Ezana. As regent, Frumentius sought out Roman Christians among the merchants who visited the country and helped them establish Christian communities. When he became king, Ezana, who may have become a Christian, permitted Aedisius and Frumentius to return to Syria.

Stele of Aksum   This 70-foot (21-meter) stone is the tallest remnant of a field of stelae, or standing stones, marking the tombs of Aksumite kings. The carvings of doors, windows, and beam ends imitate common features of Aksumite architecture, suggesting that each stele symbolized a multistory royal palace. The largest stelae date from the fourth century C.E.   (J. Allan Cash)

After reporting to the patriarch of Alexandria on the progress of Christianity in Aksum, Frumentius was elevated to the rank of bishop, though he had not previously been a clergyman, and he was sent back to Ethiopia as the first leader of its church.

The patriarch of Alexandria continues today to appoint the head of the Ethiopian Church, but the spread of Christianity into Nubia, the land south of Egypt along the Nile River, proceeded from Ethiopia rather than Egypt. Politically and economically Ethiopia became a power at the western end of the Indian Ocean trading system, occasionally even extending its influence across the Red Sea and asserting itself in Yemen (see Map 8.2). In the later competition with Islam, both Ethiopia and Armenia became important Christian outposts.

Like Armenian Christianity, Ethiopian Christianity developed its own unique features. One popular belief, perhaps deriving from the Ethiopian Jewish community, was that the Ark of the Covenant, the most sacred object of the ancient Hebrews (see Chapter 4), had been transferred from Jerusalem to the Ethiopian church of Our Lady of Zion. Another tradition maintains that Christ miraculously dried up a lake to serve as the site for this church, which became the place of coronation for Ethiopia's rulers.

CONCLUSION

Exchange within early long-distance trading systems differed in many ways from the ebb and flow of culture, language, and custom that folk migrations brought about. New technologies and agricultural products worked great changes on the landscape and in people's lives, but nothing akin to the Africanity observed south of the Sahara can be attributed to the societies involved in the Silk Road, Indian Ocean, or trans-Saharan exchanges. The peoples directly involved in these complex social systems of travel and trade were not very numerous in comparison with the populations their routes brought into contact, and their lifestyles as pastoral nomads or seafarers isolated them still further. The Bantu, however, if current theories are correct, brought with them metallurgical skills and agricultural practices that permitted much denser habitation in the lands they spread to. Moreover, they settled among and merged with the previous inhabitants, becoming not just the bearers of new technologies but their primary beneficiaries as well.

The most obvious exception to this generalization lies in the intangible area of ideas. Christianity, Buddhism, and Islam all developed local customs and understandings as they spread, despite the overall doctrinal unity of each. As "great traditions," these religions linked priests, monks, nuns, and religious scholars across the vast distances. The masses of believers, however, seldom considered their faith in such broad contexts. Missionary religions imported through long-distance trading networks merged with myriad "small traditions" to provide for the social and spiritual needs of peoples living in many lands under widely varying circumstances.

■ Key Terms

Silk Road	steppes
Parthians	savanna
stirrup	tropical rain forest
Indian Ocean Maritime System	great traditions
trans-Saharan caravan routes	small traditions
Sahel	Bantu
Ghana	Armenia
sub-Saharan Africa	Ethiopia

■ Suggested Reading

Broad and suggestive overviews on issues of cross-cultural exchange in this era may be found in Philip D. Curtin, *Cross-Cultural Trade in World History* (1985), and C. G. F. Simkin, *The Traditional Trade of Asia* (1968).

For readable overviews of the Silk Road see Luce Boulnois, *The Silk Road* (1966), and Irene M. Franck and David M. Brownstone, *The Silk Road: A History* (1986). A more detailed examination of products traded across Central Asia in the eighth century based on a famous Japanese collection is provided by Ryoichi Hayashi, *The Silk Road and the Shoso-in* (1975). Silk in Buddhism, Islam, and Christianity is the topic of Xinru Liu, *Silk and Religion* (1996). Owen Lattimore gives a superb first-person account of traveling by camel caravan in the region in *The Desert Road to Turkestan* (1928). More generally on peoples and historical developments in Central Asia see Denis Sinor, *Inner Asia, History-Civilization-Languages: A Syllabus* (1987), and Karl Jettmar, *Art of the Steppes*, rev. ed. (1967). Richard Foltz, *Religions of the Silk Road* (1999), is an excellent brief introduction.

For a readable but rather sketchy historical overview of the history of connections across the Indian Ocean see August Toussaint, *History of the Indian Ocean* (1966). Alan Villiers provides a stimulating account of what it was like to sail dhows between East Africa and the Persian Gulf in *Sons of Sinbad* (1940).

On a more scholarly plane, K. N. Chaudhuri's *Trade and Civilization in the Indian Ocean: An Economic History from the Rise of Islam to 1750* (1985), stresses the economic aspect of trading relations. Pierre Vérin gives an archaeologist's perspective on the special problem of Madagascar in *The History of Civilisation in North Madagascar* (1986). The question of Roman contact with India is the topic of E. H. Warmington's *The Commerce Between the Roman Empire and India* (1974); J. Innes Miller's *The Spice Trade of the Roman Empire, 29 B.C. to A.D. 641* (1969); and Vimala Begley and Richard Daniel De Puma's edited collection of articles, *Rome and India: The Ancient Sea Trade* (1991). The indispensable primary source for early Indian Ocean history is Lionel Casson, ed. and trans., *The Periplus Maris Arythraei: Text with Introduction, Translation, and Commentary* (1989). Seafaring as revealed in Arabic texts is the topic of George F. Hourani's brief book *Arab Seafaring in the Indian Ocean in Ancient and Early Medieval Times* (1975).

Richard W. Bulliet's *The Camel and the Wheel* (1975) deals with the development of camel use in the Middle East, along the Silk Road, and in North Africa and the Sahara. For an entertaining and well-illustrated account of the discovery of Saharan rock art see Henri Lhote, *The Search for the Tassili Frescoes: The Story of the Prehistoric Rock-Paintings of the Sahara* (1959). Additional views on the history and impact of Saharan trade may be found in E. Ann McDougall, "The Sahara Reconsidered: Pastoralism, Politics and Salt from the Ninth Through the Twelfth Centuries," *History in Africa* 12 (1983): 263–286, and Nehemia Levtzion, *Ancient Ghana and Mali,* 2d ed. (1980). The latter work is also essential to the broader topic of early West African history. For translated texts relating to both the Sahara and West Africa see J. F. P. Hopkins and Nehemia Levtzion, eds., *Corpus of Early Arabic Sources for West African History* (1981).

Two general works on the early history of sub-Saharan Africa containing many articles by numerous authors are J. F. A. Ajayi and Michael Crowder, *A History of West Africa,* vol. 1 (1976), and G. Mokhtar, ed., *General History of Africa II: Ancient Civilizations of Africa* (1981). The latter work contains extensive treatments of the issues of ironworking and the Bantu migrations. On African cultural unity see Jacques Maquet, *Africanity: The Cultural Unity of Black Africa* (1972).

The spread of Christianity and the spread of Buddhism are enormous topics. Of special importance on Christianity is Garth Fowden, *Empire to Commonwealth: Consequences of Monotheism in Late Antiquity* (1993). To follow up the particular aspects treated in this chapter see Stuart Munro-Hay, *Aksum: An African Civilisation of Late Antiquity* (1991); Xinru Liu, *Ancient India and Ancient China: Trade and Religious Exchanges, A.D. 1–600* (1998); Rolf A. Stein, *Tibetan Civilization* (1972); Tilak Hettiarachchy, *History of Kingship in Ceylon up to the Fourth Century A.D.* (1972); and Yoneo Ishii, *Sangha, State, and Society: Thai Buddhism in History* (1986). The Chinese travelers' accounts cited are Fa-hsien [Faxian], *The Travels of Fa-hsien (399–414 A.D.), or, Record of the Buddhistic Kingdoms,* trans. H. A. Giles (1923; reprint, 1981), and Hiuen Tsiang [Xuanzang], *Si-Yu-Ki: Buddhist Records of the Western World,* trans. Samuel Beal (1884; reprint, 1981).

■ Notes

1. Victor H. Mair, ed., *The Columbia Anthology of Traditional Chinese Literature* (New York: Columbia University Press, 1994) p. 485; translated by Victor H. Mair.
2. J. F. A. Ajayi and Michael Crowder, eds., *History of West Africa,* vol. 1 (New York: Columbia University Press, 1976), 120–121.
3. Pawstos Busand, *Epic Histories* (late fifth century), quoted in Garth Fowden, *Empire to Commonwealth* Princeton NJ: Princeton University Press, (1993), 105.

9

THE SASANID EMPIRE AND THE RISE OF ISLAM,

200–1200

The Sasanid Empire, 224–651 • The Origins of Islam • The Rise and Fall
of the Caliphate, 632–1258 • Islamic Civilization

ENVIRONMENT AND TECHNOLOGY: Automata

SOCIETY AND CULTURE: The Fraternity of Beggars

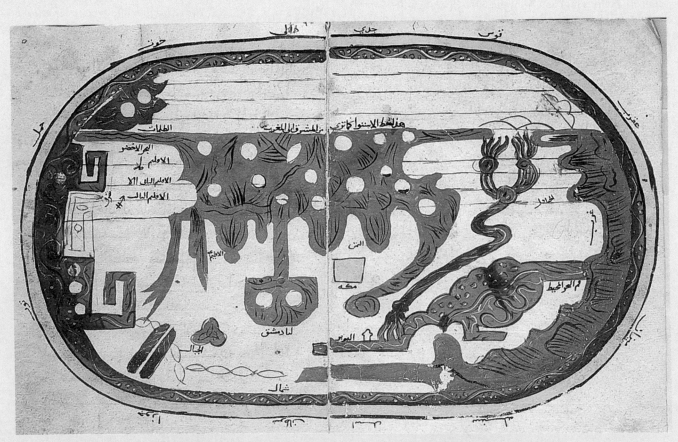

Islamic World Map   Oriented with south at the top, this copy
of a tenth-century original was probably made in the fourteenth century.

he story is told that in the early days of Islam, at the time of the Prophet Muhammad's last pilgrimage to Mecca in 630, a dispute over distribution of booty arose between his daughter's husband, Ali, who was also Muhammad's first cousin, and some troops Ali commanded. Muhammad quelled the grumbling and later on the same journey, at a place named Ghadir al-Khumm°, drew his followers together, took Ali's hand, and declared: "Am I not nearer to the believers than their own selves? Whomever I am nearest to, so likewise is Ali. O God, be the friend of him who is his friend, and the foe of him who is his foe."

Written narrations of Muhammad's praise of Ali date to well over a century after the event. By that time, Ali had served as leader of Muhammad's community for a brief time and then been defeated in a civil war and assassinated. Subsequently, his son Husain was killed with his family while trying to claim leadership as the Prophet's grandson.

Out of these events grew a severe division in the Islamic community: some believers thought that religious leadership rightfully belonged to Ali and his descendants; others felt that the community should choose its leaders more broadly. The members of the former group were called **Shi'ites**°, from the Arabic term *Shi'at Ali,* meaning "Party of Ali." The members of the latter eventually were called **Sunnis**°, followers of the sunna, or "tradition" of the community. Sunnis and Shi'ites agreed that Muhammad commended Ali at Ghadir al-Khumm. But the Sunnis thought that his remarks related only to the distribution of the booty, and the Shi'ites understood them to be Muhammad's formal and public declaration of Ali's special and elevated position and hence of his right to rule.

Shi'ite rulers rarely achieved power, but those who ruled from Cairo between 969 and 1171 made the commemoration of Ghadir al-Khumm a major festival. At the beginning of every year, Shi'ites also engaged in public mourning over the deaths of Husain and his family. Sunni rulers, in contrast, sometimes ordered that Ali be cursed in public prayers.

Muhammad's Arab followers conquered an enormous territory in the seventh century and created a mighty empire in the name of the Islamic religion. Like the empires of Alexander's Macedonians and Cyrus's Persians (see Chapter 5), the empire of Islam encompassed many peoples speaking many languages and worshiping in many ways. But its immediate forerunners were the realms of the Byzantine emperors (see Chapter 10) and Iran's Sasanid° shahs, who had linked religion with imperial politics.

Though urbanism, science, manufacturing, trade, and architecture flourished in the lands of Islam while medieval Europe was enduring hardship and economic contraction, religion shaped both societies. Just as the medieval Christian calendar revolved around Easter and Christmas, Islamic fasts and pilgrimages and political religious observances like Ghadir al-Khumm marked the yearly cycle in the territory populated by Muhammad's followers.

As you read this chapter, ask yourself the following questions:

- How did social and political developments under the Sasanid Empire pave the way for the spread of Islam?
- How did the Arab conquests grow out of the career of Muhammad?
- Why did the caliphate break up?
- What was the relationship between urbanization and the development of Islamic culture?

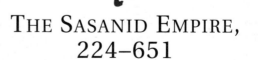

THE SASANID EMPIRE, 224–651

The rise in the third century of a new Iranian state— the **Sasanid Empire**—as guardian of the Silk Road and foe of the Byzantine Empire, as the eastern Roman provinces were called after 330 C.E., continued the old rivalry between Rome and the Parthians along the Euphrates frontier. However, behind this façade of

---

Ghadir al-Khumm (ga-DEER al-KUM)   Shi'ite (SHE-ite)
Sunni (SUN-nee)

Sasanid (suh-SAH-nid)

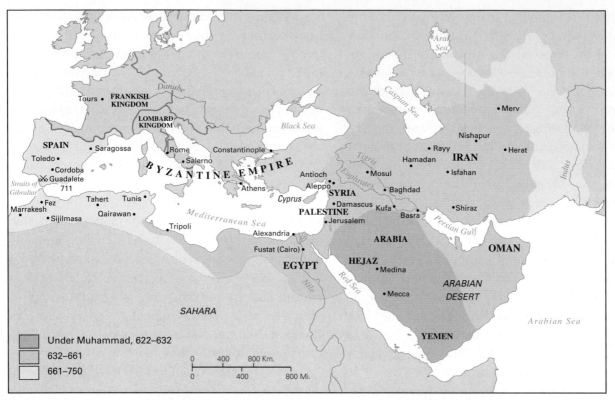

Map. 9.1   Early Expansion of Muslim Rule   The territory brought under Muslim rule during the Arab conquests of the first Islamic century was vast. However, the expansion of Islam as the religion of the majority of the population was much slower. In most areas outside the Arabian peninsula, the only region where Arabic was then spoken, conversion was uncommon during the first century but accelerated during the second.

continuity, a social and economic transformation was underway in the Middle East. The outcome of this transformation was not a return to a simpler, more fragmented, and less urbanized pattern of life, of the sort that developed in western Europe as Rome declined. Rather, together the Sasanid Empire and the Byzantine Empire set the stage for a new and powerful religio-political movement: Islam.

Politics and Society

Ardashir, a descendant of Sasan, defeated the Parthians around 224 and established the Sasanid kingdom. Unlike the Parthians, their nomadic predecessors from the northeast, the Sasanids hailed from Fars province (Persis in Greek) in southwestern Iran. The Sasanids were urbane and sophisticated with a cosmopolitan capital on the Tigris River at Ctesiphon, near the later site of Baghdad. Thus Mesopotamia, a land populated mostly by speakers of Semitic rather than Iranian languages, flourished as the capital province of the new Iranian dynasty.

To their west, the new rulers confronted the Romans, who became, after 330, the Byzantines. Along their desert Euphrates frontier, the Sasanids subsidized the chieftains of nomadic Arab groups to protect their empire from invasion (the Byzantines did the same with Arabs on their desert Jordanian frontier). This practice served to bring some Arab pastoralists into the orbit of imperial politics and culture, though others farther to the south remained isolated and independent. In the north, the international frontier ran down the upper Euphrates River in Mesopotamia. The rival Sasanid and Byzantine Empires launched numerous attacks on each other across that frontier between the 340s and 628. In times of peace, however, exchange between the empires flourished, allowing goods transported over the Silk Road to enter the zone of Mediterranean trade. Byzantine cities like Antioch, Damascus, and Aleppo—all in Syria—were thriving cultural, commercial, and manufacturing centers and benefited greatly from contacts with the Sasanids (see Map 9.1).

The Arab pastoralists who populated the desert between Syria and Mesopotamia also benefited from the

CHRONOLOGY

	Spain (al-Andalus) and North Africa	The Arab East	Iran and Central Asia
200			**224–651** Sasanid Empire
600	**639–42** Conquest of Egypt by Arabs	**570–632** Life of the Prophet Muhammad **634** Conquests of Iraq and Syria commence **656–61** Ali caliph; first civil war **661–750** Umayyad Caliphate rules from Damascus	
700	**711** Berbers and Arabs invade Spain from North Africa **740** Berber revolts in North Africa; Kharijite states founded **755** Umayyad state established in Spain	**750** Beginning of Abbasid Caliphate **776–809** Caliphate of Harun al-Rashid	**711** Arabs capture Sind in India **747** Abbasid revolt begins in Khurasan
800		**835–92** Abbasid capital moved from Baghdad to Samarra	
900	**909** Fatimids seize North Africa, found Shi'ite Caliphate **929** Abd al-Rahman III declares himself caliph in Cordoba **969** Fatimids conquer Egypt	**945** Shi'ite Buyids take control in Baghdad	**875** Independent Samanid state founded in Bukhara **945** Buyids from northern Iran take control of Abbasid Caliphate
1000	**ca. 1050** Hilali Arabs migrate into North Africa **1171** Fall of Fatimid Egypt	**1055** Seljuk Turks take control in Baghdad **1099** First Crusade captures Jerusalem **1187** Saladin recaptures Jerusalem **1250** Mamluks control Egypt **1258** Mongols sack Baghdad and end Abbasid Caliphate **1260** Mamluks defeat Mongols at Ain Jalut	**1036** Beginning of Turkish Seljuk rule in Khurasan

trade between the empires. They supplied camels and guides and played a significant role as merchants and organizers of caravans, especially during the mid-third century flourishing of the Arab kingdom of Palmyra° in the middle of the Syrian desert. Roman conquerors destroyed Palmyra's temples and colonaded avenues in 273, but depictions of the Palmyrene caravan-god leading his camel are still visible in the ruins.

Another key to Arab prosperity was the spread of a militarily efficient camel saddle first used around the

Palmyra (pal-MY-ruh)

Silver Plate Depicting Sasanid Shah Shapur II (309–379) Hunting Wild Boar The ruler hunting or banqueting was a common symbol of royalty in pre-Islamic Iran. Sasanid aristocrats favored silver plates like this. After the Muslim Arabs conquered Iran in the seventh century, the landed aristocracy gradually disappeared, and prosperous city dwellers made do with elegant but cheaper glazed pottery plates. (Smithsonian Institution, Courtesy of the Freer Gallery of Art, Washington, DC. Neg. #34.23)

third century B.C.E. The Arabs used it to take control of the caravan trade in their territories and became so important as suppliers of animal power even in agricultural districts that wheeled vehicles—mostly ox carts and horse-drawn chariots—entirely disappeared by the sixth century C.E.

The mountains and plateaus of Iran proper formed the Sasanids' political hinterland, often ruled by the cousins of the shah (king) or by powerful nobles. Cities there were small walled communities that served more as military strongpoints than as centers of population and production. Society revolved around a local aristocracy who lived on rural estates and cultivated the arts of hunting and war just like the noble warriors described in the sagas of ancient kings and heroes sung at their banquets. The small principalities along the Silk Road in Central Asia, mostly beyond Sasanid control, were home to a more developed urban culture in which Buddhism, Zoroastrianism, Judaism, and Christianity mixed (see Chapter 8).

Despite the dominance of powerful aristocratic families on the Iranian plateau, long-lasting political fragmentation of the medieval European variety did not develop. Also, although Arabs and other nomadic or seminomadic peoples were numerous in mountain and desert regions, no folk migration arose comparable to that of the Germanic peoples of the Late Roman Empire. The Sasanid and Byzantine Empires successfully maintained central control of imperial finances and military power and found effective ways of integrating frontier peoples as mercenaries or caravaneers.

The silver coins of the Sasanid rulers and the gold coins of the Byzantine emperors were plentiful, and trade with the East remained robust. The Silk Road brought new products to Mesopotamia, some of which became part of the agricultural landscape. Sasanid farmers pioneered in planting cotton, sugar cane, rice, citrus trees, eggplants, and other crops adopted from India and China. Although the acreage devoted to new crops increased slowly, these products were to become important consumption and trade items during the Islamic period following the fall of the Sasanid Empire in 651.

Religion and Empire

The Sasanids were Zoroastrians (see Chapter 5) and established their faith, which the Parthians before them had not particularly stressed, as a state religion similar to Christianity in the Byzantine Empire (see Chapter 6). The Zoroastrian equivalent of the patriarch of Constantinople was the *Mobadan-mobad*, "Priest of Priests," appointed by the Sasanid *Shahan-shah°*, "King of Kings."

The Hellenistic kingdoms that arose from Alexander's empire and, after them, the Early Roman Empire, had sponsored official cults focusing on the deified ruler, but they also had recognized the great variety of religious beliefs among their diverse populations. Moreover, their rulers and urban upper class were often more interested in varieties of Greek philosophy than in a specific religious sect. Thus the proclamation of Christianity and Zoroastrianism as official faiths marked the fresh emergence of religion as an instrument of politics both within and between the empires, setting a precedent for the subsequent rise of Islam as the focus of a political empire.

Both Zoroastrianism and Christianity practiced intolerance. A late-third-century inscription in Iran boasts of the persecutions of Christians, Jews, and Buddhists

Shahan-shah (SHAH-han–SHAH)

carried out by the Zoroastrian high priest. Yet sizable Christian and Jewish communities remained, especially in Mesopotamia. From the fourth century onward councils of Christian bishops declared many theological beliefs heretical—so unacceptable that they were un-Christian.

Christians became pawns in the political rivalry with the Byzantines, sometimes persecuted and sometimes patronized by the Sasanid kings. In 421 war broke out with Byzantium because of Sasanid persecution of Christians. Armenia, whose Christian population had cultural links with Iran, was another bone of contention between the empires. The Armenian Apostolic Church used the Armenian language in its services and hewed to Monophysite doctrine, considered heretical by the Byzantine emperors because of its too strong emphasis on Christ's divine nature (see Chapter 10). In 431 a council of bishops called by the Byzantine emperor declared the Nestorian Christians heretics for overemphasizing the humanness of Christ. The Nestorians believed that human characteristics and divinity coexisted in Jesus and that Mary was not the mother of God, as many other Christians maintained, but the mother of the human Jesus. After the bishops' ruling, the Nestorians sought refuge under the Sasanid shah and eventually spread their missionary activities across Central Asia.

In the third century a preacher named Mani had founded a new religion in Mesopotamia: Manichaeism. He preached a dualist faith—a struggle between Good and Evil—theologically derived from Zoroastrianism. Although at first Mani enjoyed the favor of the shah, he was martyred in 276 with many of his followers. Yet his religion survived and spread widely. Nestorian missionaries in Central Asia competed with Manichaean missionaries for converts. In later centuries, the term *Manichaean* was applied to all sorts of beliefs in a cosmic struggle between Good and Evil.

The Arabs, too, became enmeshed in this web of religious conflict. The border protectors subsidized by the Byzantines adopted the Monophysite faith; the allies of the Sasanids, the Nestorian. Thus both Arab groups retained a measure of religious independence from their patrons. Through them, knowledge of Christianity penetrated deeper into the Arabian peninsula during the fifth and sixth centuries.

The politicizing of religion contrasts sharply with earlier periods of East-West rivalry along the Euphrates frontier during the time of the Greek city-states (see Chapter 5) and the Roman-Parthian rivalry (see Chapter 8) when language, ethnic identity, or citizenship in a particular city-state defined political allegiances. Now, religion penetrated all aspects of community life. Most subjects of the Byzantine emperors and Sasanid shahs identified themselves first and foremost as members of a religious community. Their schools and law courts were religious. They looked on priests, monks, rabbis, and mobads as moral guides in daily life. Most books were on religious subjects. And in some areas, religious leaders represented their flocks even in secular matters such as tax collection.

THE ORIGINS OF ISLAM

The Arabs who lived beyond the frontiers of the Sasanid Empire seldom interested the Sasanid rulers. They did involve themselves in the Arab side of the Persian Gulf and Yemen, which were along their maritime trade routes. As for the interior of the Arabian peninsula, however, the Sasanid view, evident in a phrase attributed in later centuries to Muhammad, was that the Arabs were "monkeys on the backs of camels." But it was precisely in the interior of Arabia, far from the gaze and political reach of the Sasanid and Byzantine Empires, that the religion of Islam took form and inspired a movement that would humble the proud emperors.

The Arabian Peninsula Before Muhammad

Throughout history most of the people living on the Arabian peninsula have lived in settled communities rather than as pastoral nomads. The highlands of Yemen are fertile and abundantly watered by the spring monsoon blowing northward along the East African coast. The interior mountains farther east in southern Arabia are much more arid but in some places receive enough water to support farming and village life. And small inlets along the coast favored an occasional fishing or trading community. These southern regions have been largely cut off from the Arabian interior by the enormous sea of sand known as the "Empty Quarter." In the seventh century, most people in southern Arabia knew more about Africa, India, and the Persian Gulf than about the forbidding interior of the great peninsula and the scattered camel- and sheep-herding nomads who lived there.

Exceptions to this pattern were mostly associated with caravan trading. Several kingdoms rose and fell in Yemen, leaving stone ruins and enigmatic inscriptions to testify to their bygone prosperity. From these commercial entrepôts came the aromatic resins frankincense and myrrh. Nomads derived income from providing camels, guides, and safe passage to merchants wanting to transport incense northward, where the fragrant substances had long been burned in religious rituals. Return caravans brought manufactured products from Mesopotamia and the Mediterranean.

Just as the Silk Road enabled small towns in Central Asia to become major trading centers, so the trans-Arabian trade gave rise to desert caravan cities (see Society and Culture: Caravan Cities, in Chapter 8). The earliest and most prosperous, Petra in southern Jordan and Palmyra in northern Syria, were swallowed up by Rome. This, coupled with early Christian distaste for incense, which seemed too much a feature of pagan worship, contributed to a slackening of trade in high-value goods in Sasanid times. Nevertheless, trade across the Arabian desert did not lapse altogether. Camels, leather, and gold and other minerals mined in the mountains of western Arabia took the place of frankincense and myrrh as exports, and grain and manufactured goods were imported. This reduced trade kept alive the relations between the Arabs and the settled farming regions to the north forged in earlier centuries, and it familiarized the Arabs who accompanied the caravans with the cultures and lifestyles of the Sasanid and Byzantine Empires.

In the desert, Semitic polytheism, with its worship of natural forces and celestial bodies, still thrived but was affected by other religions. Christianity, as practiced by Arabs in Jordan and southern Mesopotamia, and Judaism, possibly carried by refugees from the Roman expulsion of the Jews from their homeland in the first century C.E., made inroads on polytheism.

Mecca, a late-blooming caravan city, lies in a barren mountain valley halfway between Yemen and Syria along the Red Sea coast of Arabia (see Map 9.1). The torrid coastal plain was ill suited to caravan travel, giving Mecca a good position in the trade from Yemen to the north and east. A nomadic kin group known as the Quraysh° settled in Mecca in the fifth century and assumed control of this trade. Mecca rapidly achieved a measure of prosperity, partly because it was too far from Byzantine Syria, Sasanid Iraq, and Ethiopian-controlled Yemen for them to attack it.

Mecca was also a cult center. A cubical shrine called the Ka'ba°, containing idols, a holy well called Zamzam, and a sacred precinct surrounding the two wherein killing was prohibited contributed to the emergence of Mecca as a pilgrimage site. Some Meccans associated the shrine with stories known to Jews and Christians. They regarded Abraham (Ibrahim in Arabic) as the builder of the Ka'ba, and they identified a site outside Mecca as the location where God asked Abraham to sacrifice his son. The son was not Isaac (Ishaq in Arabic), the son of Sarah, but Ishmael (Isma'il in Arabic), the son of Hagar, cited in the Bible as the forefather of the Arabs.

Muhammad in Mecca

Muhammad was born in Mecca in 570 and grew up an orphan in the house of his uncle. He engaged in trade and married a Quraysh widow named Khadija°, whose caravan interests he superintended. They had several children, but their one son died in childhood. Around the year 610, Muhammad began meditating at night in the mountainous terrain around Mecca. During one night vigil, known to later religious tradition as the "Night of Power and Excellence," a being whom Muhammad later understood to be the angel Gabriel (Jibra'il in Arabic) spoke to him:

> Proclaim! In the name of your Lord who created.
> Created man from a clot of congealed blood.
> Proclaim! And your Lord is the Most Bountiful.
> He who has taught by the pen.
> Taught man that which he knew not.[1]

Over the next three years he shared this and subsequent revelations only with his closest friends and family members. This period culminated in Muhammad's conviction that the words he was hearing were from God (Allah° in Arabic). Khadija, his uncle's son Ali, his friend Abu Bakr°, and others close to him shared this conviction. The revelations continued until Muhammad's death in 632.

Like most people in the ancient world, including Christians and Jews, the Arabs believed in unseen spirits: gods, desert spirits called *jinns*, demons known as *shaitans*, and so forth. They further believed, just as most ancient peoples did, that certain individuals had contact with the spirit world. Some were oracles or seers; others poets, who were thought to be possessed by a jinn. Therefore, when Muhammad began to recite his rhymed revelations in public, many people believed that he was inspired by an unseen spirit even as they questioned whether that spirit was, as Muhammad asserted, the one true god.

Quraysh (koo-RYYSH)   Ka'ba (KAH-buh)

Khadija (kah-DEE-juh)   **Allah** (AH-luh)
Abu Bakr (ah-boo BAK-uhr)

The content of Muhammad's earliest revelations called on people to witness that one god had created the universe and everything in it, including themselves. At the end of time, their souls would be judged, their sins balanced against their good deeds. The blameless would go to paradise; the sinful would taste hellfire:

> By the night as it conceals the light;
> By the day as it appears in glory;
> By the mystery of the creation of male and female;
> Verily, the ends ye strive for are diverse.
> So he who gives in charity and fears God,
> And in all sincerity testifies to the best,
> We will indeed make smooth for him the path to
>   Bliss.
> But he who is a greedy miser and thinks himself
>   self-sufficient,
> And gives the lie to the best,
> We will indeed make smooth for him the path to
>   misery.[2]

All people were called to submit themselves to God and accept Muhammad as the last of his messengers. Those who did so were called **muslim,** meaning one who makes "submission," **Islam,** to the will of God.

Because earlier messengers mentioned in the revelations included Noah, Moses, and Jesus, it seemed to Muhammad's hearers that what he was saying was in agreement with the Judaism and Christianity they were already somewhat familiar with. Yet his revelations were distinctly different. They charged the Jews and Christians with being negligent in preserving God's revealed word. Thus, even though the Ka'ba, which superseded Jerusalem as the focus of Muslim prayer in 624, was founded by Abraham/Ibrahim, whom Muslims consider the first Muslim, and even though many revelations narrated stories also found in the Bible, Muhammad's followers considered his revelation more perfect than the Bible because it had not gone through an editing process.

Some non-Muslim scholars maintain that Muhammad's revelations appealed especially to Meccans who were distressed that wealth was replacing kinship as the most important aspect of social relations. They see verses criticizing taking pride in money and neglecting obligations to orphans and other powerless people as conveying a message of social reform. Other scholars, along with most Muslims, put less emphasis on a social message and stress the enormous power and beauty of Muhammad's revelations. This forceful rhetoric and poetic vision, coming in the Muslim view directly from God, go far to explain Muhammad's early success.

The Formation of the Umma

Most Meccan leaders felt that their power and prosperity would be threatened by acceptance of Muhammad as the sole agent of the one true God. They put pressure on his kin to disavow him and persecuted the weakest of his followers. Stymied by this hostility, Muhammad and his followers fled Mecca in 622 to take up residence in the agricultural community of **Medina** 215 miles (346 kilometers) to the north. This carefully planned flight, the hijra°, marks the beginning of the Muslim calendar.

Prior to the hijra, representatives of the major kin groups of Medina had met with Muhammad and agreed to accept and protect him and his community of Muslims because they saw him as an inspired leader who could calm their perpetual feuding. Together, the Meccan migrants and major groups in Medina bound themselves into a single **umma°,** a community defined solely by acceptance of Islam and of Muhammad as the "Messenger of God," his most common title. Three Jewish kin groups chose to retain their own faith. Their decision is one reason why Muslims changed the direction of their prayer away from Jerusalem and toward the Ka'ba, now thought of as the "House of God," in 624.

During the last decade of his life, Muhammad took active responsibility for his umma. Without the support of their Meccan kinsmen, the Meccan immigrants in Medina were terribly vulnerable. Fresh revelations provided a framework for regulating social and legal affairs and stirred the Muslims to fight against the still-unbelieving city of Mecca. Sporadic war, much of it conducted by raiding and negotiation with desert nomads, sapped Mecca's strength and convinced many Meccans that God was on Muhammad's side. In 630 Mecca surrendered, and Muhammad and his followers made the pilgrimage to the Ka'ba unhindered.

Muhammad did not return to Mecca again. Medina had grown into a bustling Muslim city-state. The Jews, whom he had accused of disloyalty during the war, had been expelled or eliminated. Delegations from all over Arabia came to meet Muhammad, and he sent emissaries back with them to teach them about Islam and collect their alms. Whether he planned or desired it or not, Muhammad's mission to bring God's message to humanity had resulted in a political conflict that gave him unchallenged control of a state that was coming to dominate the Arabian peninsula. But the supremacy of the Medinan state, unlike preceding short-lived nomadic kingdoms, was based not on kinship but on a common faith in a single god.

---

hijra (HIJ-ruh)   **umma** (UM-muh)

In 632, after a brief illness, Muhammad died. Within twenty-four hours a group of Medinan leaders, along with three of Muhammad's close friends, determined that Abu Bakr, one of the earliest believers and the father of Muhammad's favorite wife A'isha°, should succeed him. They called him the *khalifa*°, or "successor," the English version of which is *caliph*. But calling Abu Bakr a successor did not clarify the capacity in which he was succeeding the Prophet. Everyone knew that neither Abu Bakr nor anyone else could receive revelations, and they likewise knew that Muhammad's revelations had made no provision for succession or for any government purpose beyond maintaining the Muslim community, the umma. Indeed, some people thought the world would soon end because God's last messenger was dead.

Abu Bakr's immediate tasks were two. First, he continued and confirmed Muhammad's religious practices, notably the so-called Five Pillars of Islam: (1) avowal that there is only one god and Muhammad is his messenger, (2) prayer five times a day, (3) fasting during the lunar month of Ramadan, (4) paying alms, and (5) making the pilgrimage to Mecca at least once during one's lifetime. Second, he reestablished and expanded Muslim authority over Arabia's nomadic and settled communities. After Muhammad's death, some had abandoned their allegiance to Medina or even switched allegiance to would-be prophets of their own. Muslim armies fought hard to confirm the authority of the newborn **caliphate.** In the process, some fighting spilled over into non-Arab areas in Iraq.

Abu Bakr summoned those who had acted as secretaries for Muhammad and ordered them to organize the Prophet's revelations into a book. Hitherto written haphazardly on pieces of leather or bone, the verses of revelation were written as a single document on parchment and gathered into chapters. The resulting book, which acquired its final form around the year 650, was called the **Quran**°, or the Recitation. Muslims regard it not as the words of Muhammad but as the unalterable word of God. As such, it is comparable not so much to the Bible, a book written by many hands over a long period of time, as to the person of Jesus Christ, who, according to Christian belief, is a human manifestation of God.

Though theoretically united in its acceptance of God's will, the umma soon fell prey to human disagreement over the succession to the caliphate. The first civil war in Islam followed the assassination of the third caliph, Uthman°, in 656. His assassins, rebels from the army, nominated to succeed him Ali, Muhammad's first cousin and the husband of his daughter Fatima. Ali had been passed over three times previously even though many people considered him to be the natural heir to the Prophet's mantle. Indeed, he and his supporters felt that Muhammad had indicated as much at Ghadir al-Khumm, as mentioned previously.

When Ali accepted the nomination to be caliph, two of Muhammad's close companions and his favorite wife A'isha challenged him. Ali defeated them in the Battle of the Camel (656), so called because the fighting raged around the camel on which A'isha was seated in an enclosed woman's saddle. But blood had been spilled within the umma.

After the battle, the governor of Syria, Mu'awiya°, a kinsman of the slain Uthman from the Umayya subgroup of the Quraysh, renewed the challenge. Inconclusive battle gave way to arbitration. The arbitrators decided that Uthman had been killed unjustly and that Ali had been at fault in accepting the nomination. Ali rejected the arbitrators' findings, but before he could resume fighting, one of his own supporters killed him for agreeing to arbitration in the first place. Mu'awiya then offered Ali's son Hasan a dignified retirement in the holy cities and thus emerged as caliph in 661.

Mu'awiya chose his own son, Yazid, to succeed him and thereby instituted the **Umayyad° Caliphate.** When Hasan's brother Husayn revolted to reestablish the right of Ali's family to rule, Yazid ordered Husayn and his family killed, in 680. Sympathy for Husayn's martyrdom was pivotal in the transformation of the Shi'ites from a political movement into a religious sect.

Several variations in Shi'ite belief developed, but Shi'ites have always agreed that Ali was the rightful successor to Muhammad and that God's choice as Imam, leader of the Muslim community, at any given time is one or another of Ali's descendants. They see the office of caliph as more secular than religious. Because the Shi'ites were seldom strong enough to establish their Imams in power, their religious feelings came to focus on outpourings of sympathy for Husayn and other martyrs and on messianic dreams of one of their Imams someday triumphing.

Those Muslims who thought the first three caliphs had been properly selected gradually came to be called "People of Tradition and Community"—in Arabic, *Ahl al-Sunna wa'l-Jama'a,* or Sunnis for short. Sunnis consider the caliphs to be the Imam. As for Ali's militant followers, who had abhorred his acceptance of arbitration in a matter they regarded as already determined by God, they evolved into small and rebellious Kharijite sects (from *kharaja* meaning "to secede or rebel"). These three main divisions of Islam, the last one now quite minor, still survive. Today the umma has grown to over 800 million people.

A'isha (AH-ee-shah)   **khalifa** (kah-LEE-fuh)   **Quran** (kuh-RAHN)
Uthman (ooth-MAHN)

Mu'awiya (moo-AH-we-yuh)   **Umayyad** (oo-MY-ad)

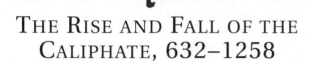

THE RISE AND FALL OF THE CALIPHATE, 632–1258

The Islamic caliphate was transformed into a mighty empire by the conquests the Arabs carried out after Muhammad's death. Although they fostered the growth of a dynamic and creative religious society, by the late 800s the caliphs already were losing control as one piece after another of their huge realm broke away. Yet they always retained the respect of the Sunni community, and the idea of a caliphate, however unrealistic it became, remained a touchstone of Sunni belief in the unity of the umma.

The residual religious authority of the declining caliphate cannot be compared with the authority of the Christian popes in Rome. Islam never recognized a single person as the absolute arbiter of true belief with the power to expel heretics and discipline clergy. Thus the caliphs had little theoretical basis for reestablishing their originally universal authority over the umma once they began to lose political and military power.

The Islamic Conquests, 634–711

Arab conquests outside Arabia began under the second caliph, Umar (r. 634–644), possibly prompted by forays into Iraq under his predecessor, Abu Bakr. Within fifteen years Arab armies, organized in kin groups, had wrenched Syria (636) and Egypt (639–642) away from the Byzantine Empire and defeated the last Sasanid shah, Yazdigird III (r. 632–651) (see Map. 9.1). After a decade-long lull, expansion began again. Tunisia fell and became the governing center from which was organized, in 711, the conquest of Spain by an Arab-led army mostly composed of Algerian and Moroccan Berbers. In the same year, Sind—the southern Indus Valley and westernmost region of India—succumbed to partially seaborne invaders from Iraq. Although a few pieces of territory were added later, such as Sicily in the ninth century, the extent of Muslim dominion remained roughly stable for the next three centuries. In the eleventh century, conquest began anew in India, Anatolia, and sub-Saharan Africa even as Islam was expanding peacefully by trade in these and other areas (see Chapter 15).

Muslim chroniclers portray the Arab conquests as manifestations of God's will. Non-Muslim historians have had a more difficult time explaining them. The speed and political cohesiveness of the campaigns of these warriors from Arabia set them apart from the piecemeal incursions of the Germanic peoples into the Roman Empire. Lust for booty, a frequently offered explanation, relies on the idea that pastoral Arab society was naturally warlike. But a majority of the Arabs lived in settled communities, and many of the nomadic groups had long experience in servicing the caravan trade. Greed also fails to explain the persistence of the campaigns in regions where terrain was difficult and booty was scarce. Yet the alternative theory—fanatical religious fervor—ignores the fact that most of the warriors had no firsthand experience of life in Medina and knew comparatively little about Islam. Moreover, non-Arab converts to Islam had a marginal role in the fighting, while certain Christian Arab groups were allowed to participate without converting, as if Arab ethnicity rather than religion defined the movement.

Nor were the Arabs' adversaries powerless or fatally divided by religious quarrels as some historians have suggested. Although the Byzantine and Sasanid Empires had pummeled each other in a war that shortly preceded the Arab conquests, they still resisted the initial Muslim onslaught. Indeed, the Byzantines successfully defended their Anatolian heartland, despite recurrent Muslim attacks, for four centuries after their loss of Syria, Egypt, and Tunisia.

The best explanation for this watershed in world history, the establishment of the caliphal empire through conquest, is that the close Meccan companions of the Prophet were men of political and economic sophistication who were truly inspired by their experience of his charisma. They guided the conquests. The social structure and hardy nature of Arab society lent itself to flexible military operations, and the authority of Medina, reconfirmed during the caliphate of Abu Bakr, ensured obedience.

More important than any specific military quality, however, was the decision made during Umar's caliphate to prohibit the Arab pastoral groups from taking over conquered territory for their own use. Umar tied army service, with its regular pay and occasional windfalls of booty, to residence in large military camps—two in Iraq, one in Egypt, and one in Tunisia. East of Iraq, Arabs were assigned to small garrison towns at strategically crucial locations, though one large garrison was established at Marv in present-day Turkmenistan. Down to the early eighth century, this policy kept the armies together and ready for action and preserved life in the countryside, where at least three-fourths of the population lived, virtually unchanged. Most people who became subjects of the caliphate by conquest probably never saw an Arab, and only a tiny proportion—in Syria and Iraq, where desert fringe areas seem to have been more open to Arab occupation—understood the Arabic language.

Spread over the largest territorial empire achieved to that time, the million or so Arabs who participated in the conquests constituted a small, self-isolated ruling minority living on the taxes paid by a vastly larger non-Arab, non-Muslim subject population. Far from requiring their conquered subjects to convert, the Arabs had little material incentive to encourage conversion; and there is no evidence of a coherent missionary effort to spread Islam during the conquest period. All of these factors contradict the common assumption that the Arabs sought to force their faith on the peoples they conquered.

The Umayyad and Early Abbasid Caliphates, 661–850

The Umayyad caliphs who came to power in 661 presided over an ethnically defined Arab realm rather than over a religious empire. Ruling from Damascus, they stemmed from a wealthy Meccan family that initially had opposed Muhammad. Their military forces were composed almost entirely of Muslim Arabs. They adopted and adapted the administrative practices of their Sasanid and Byzantine predecessors, as had the four caliphs who preceded them. Only gradually did they replace non-Muslim secretaries and tax officials with Muslims and introduce Arabic as the language of government. A major symbolic step was the introduction of distinctively Muslim silver and gold coins early in the eighth century. From that time on, silver dirhams and gold dinars bearing Arabic religious phrases held pride of place in monetary exchanges from Morocco to the frontiers of China. Islamic coins were even imitated occasionally in England and France.

The Umayyad dynasty fell in 750 after a decade of growing unrest from many quarters. Converts to Islam by that date were no more than 10 percent of the indigenous population, but they were numerically significant because of the comparatively small number of Arab warriors, and they resented not achieving equal status with the Arabs. The Arabs of Iraq and elsewhere felt the Syrian Arabs were too powerful in caliphal affairs. Pious Muslims looked askance at the secular and even irreligious behavior of the caliphs. And Shi'ites and Kharijites attacked the Umayyad family's religious legitimacy as rulers, giving rise to a number of rebellions.

In 747, one rebellion, in the region of Khurasan° in northeastern Iran, Afghanistan, and Central Asia, overthrew the last Umayyad caliph, though one family member escaped to Spain and set up an Umayyad state there in 755. Even with triumph at hand, however, it was un-

certain on whose behalf the fight had been fought. Many supporters of the rebellion were Shi'ites who thought they were fighting for the family of Ali. As it turned out, the secret organization that coordinated the revolt was loyal to the family of Abbas, one of Muhammad's uncles. The state they established is therefore called the **Abbasid° Caliphate**. Some of the Abbasid caliphs who ruled after 750 were lenient toward their relatives in Ali's family, and one even flirted with transferring the caliphate to them. The Abbasid family, however, held on to the caliphate until 1258, when Mongol invaders killed the last of them in Baghdad (see Chapter 13).

At the outset the Abbasid dynasty made a fine show of leadership and concern for Islam. Theology and religious law became preoccupations at court and among a growing community of scholars, along with interpretation of the Quran, collecting the sayings of the Prophet, and Arabic grammar. Some caliphs fought on the Byzantine frontier to extend Islam. Others sponsored ambitious projects to translate the great works of Greek, Persian, and Indian thought into Arabic.

At the same time, the new dynasty, with its roots among the semi-Persianized Arabs of Khurasan, gradually adopted many of the ceremonials and customs of the Sasanid shahs. Government grew increasingly complex in Baghdad, the newly built capital city on the Tigris River. As more and more non-Arabs converted to Islam, the ruling elite became more cosmopolitan. Greek, Iranian, Central Asian, and African cultural currents met in the capital and gave rise to an abundance of literary works, a process greatly facilitated by the introduction of papermaking from China. Arab poets neglected the traditional odes extolling life in the desert and wrote instead in praise of their patrons, the drinking of wine (despite its prohibition in Islam), and other diversions of the vibrant urban scene.

The translation of Aristotle into Arabic, the founding of the main currents of theology and law, and the splendor of the Abbasid court—reflected in stories of *The Arabian Nights* set in the time of the caliph Harun al-Rashid° (r. 776–809)—in some respects warrant the designation of the early Abbasid period as a "golden age." Yet the refinement of Baghdad culture only slowly made its way into the provinces. Egypt was still predominantly Christian and Coptic-speaking in the early Abbasid period. Iran never did adopt the Arabic language as a spoken tongue. And Berber-speaking North Africa freed itself almost entirely of caliphal rule: Morocco and Algeria through Kharijite revolts in 740, Tunisia after 800 by agreeing to pay a regular tribute to Baghdad.

Khurasan (kor-uh-SAHN)

Abbasid (ah-BASS-id)
Harun al-Rashid (hah-ROON al–rah-SHEED)

The gradual conversion to Islam of the conquered population did not accelerate until the second quarter of the ninth century. By that time most social discrimination against non-Arab converts had faded away, and the Arabs themselves—at least those living in cosmopolitan urban settings—had abandoned their previously strong attachment to kinship and ethnic identity. If the expression "golden age of Islam" implies a mass, multilingual, multiethnic society of Muslims with only minority non-Muslim elements, it finally came into existence around the end of the tenth century. By then, however, the Abbasid Caliphate had lost most of its power.

Political Fragmentation, 850–1050

The decline of Abbasid power became evident in the second half of the ninth century when the pace of conversion to Islam was at its peak (see Map 9.2). A single government ruling an empire stretching almost a quarter of the way around the world would be hard to hold together even under modern conditions. But the Abbasids had to reckon with the fact that caravans traveled only 20 miles (32 kilometers) a day and dispatches through the official post system usually did not exceed a hundred miles (160 kilometers) a day. News of revolts on the frontier took weeks to reach Baghdad. Military responses might take months. It was hard to centralize tax payments, which were often made in grain or other produce rather than in cash, and to ensure that provincial governors forwarded the proper amounts to Baghdad. The minting of coins in many locations also provided opportunities for local strongmen to profit from seizing power.

The first Arab garrisons had been strung like beads across territory populated mostly by non-Muslims, and revolts against Arab rule had been a concern. Members of the Muslim community, the umma, had had every reason to cling together, despite the long distances. But with the massive conversion of the population to Islam, the idea that Islam could be destroyed faded as Muslims became the overwhelming majority. It also became

Map. 9.2 Rise and Fall of the Abbasid Caliphate Though Abbasid rulers occupied the caliphal seat in Iraq from 750 to 1258, when Mongol armies destroyed Baghdad, real political power waned sharply and steadily after 850. Nevertheless, the idea of the caliphate remained central to Sunni Muslim political theory. The rival caliphates of the Fatimids (909–1171) and Spanish Umayyads (929–976) were comparatively short-lived.

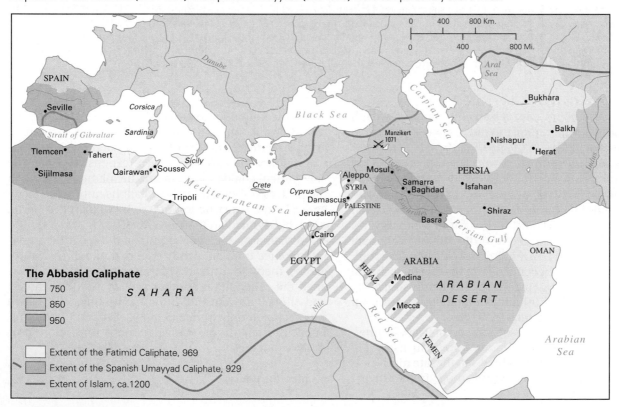

Mosque and Minaret at Samarra A unique spiral minaret 171 feet (52 meters) high is the most imposing remnant of the imperial city of Samarra, located on the east bank of the Tigris River 65 miles (104 kilometers) north of Baghdad. Begun in 835, this spacious Abbasid capital was a model of urban planning. It was abandoned in 892 when the caliph returned to Baghdad after the outbreak of severe friction between the people of Baghdad and Turkic military forces that the caliphs had quartered in Samarra. (Creswell Photographic Archive, Ashmolean Museum, Oxford, neg. C270)

apparent that a highly centralized empire meant wealth and splendor for the capital but did not necessarily serve the interests of people in the provinces.

Many eighth-century revolts had been directed against Arab or Muslim domination. By the middle of the ninth century, this type of rebellion gave way to movements within the Islamic community that concentrated on seizure of territory and formation of a principality. None of the states carved out of the Abbasid Caliphate after 850 repudiated or even threatened Islam. They did, however, prevent tax revenues from flowing to Baghdad, thereby increasing local prosperity. It is hardly surprising that local Muslim communities either supported such rebels or remained neutral.

Increasingly starved for funds by breakaway provinces and by a fall in revenues from Iraq itself, the caliphate entered a period of crisis in the late ninth century. Distrusting the generals and troops from outlying

areas, the caliphs purchased Turkic slaves, **mamluks°**, from Central Asia and established them as a standing army. Well trained and hardy, the Turks proved an effective military force, but they were expensive. When the government could not pay them, the mamluks took it on themselves to seat and unseat caliphs, a process made easier by the construction of a new capital at Samarra, north of Baghdad on the Tigris River.

At Samarra, the Turks dominated the court without interference from an unruly Baghdad populace that regarded them as rude and highhanded. Samarra weakened the caliphate in another way as well. The money and effort that went into building the huge city, which was occupied only from 835 to 892, sapped the caliphs' financial strength and deflected labor from more productive pursuits.

mamluk (MAM-luke)

In 945, after several attempts at finding a strongman who would reform government administration and restore military power, the Abbasid Caliphate itself fell under the control of rude mountain warriors from the province of Daylam in northern Iran. Led by the Shi'ite Buyid° family, they conquered western Iran as well as Iraq. Each Buyid commander ruled his own principality. After almost two centuries of glory, the sun began to set on Baghdad. The Abbasid caliph remained, but he was subject to the control of a Buyid prince or his lieutenant. Being Shi'ites, the Buyids had no special reverence for the Sunni caliph. But, according to their particular Shi'ite sect, the twelfth and last divinely appointed Imam had disappeared around 873 and would return as a messiah only at the end of the world. Thus they had no Shi'ite Imam to defer to and retained the caliph only to help control their predominantly Sunni subjects, who regarded him as the rightful ruler.

Dynamic growth in outlying provinces paralleled the caliphate's gradual loss of temporal power. In the east, in 875, the dynasty of the Samanids°, one of several Iranian families to achieve independent rule, established a glittering court in Bukhara, a major city on the Silk Road (see Map 9.2). Samanid princes patronized literature and learning much as the early Abbasids had done, but the language they favored was Persian written in Arabic letters. For the first time, a non-Arabic literature rose to challenge the eminence of Arabic within the Islamic world. The new Persian poetry and prose foreshadowed the world of today, in which Iran sharply distinguishes itself from the Arab world.

In Egypt a Shi'ite ruler established himself as a rival caliph in 969, culminating a sixty-year struggle by his family, the Fatimids°, to extend their power beyond an initial base in Tunisia. His governing complex outside Fustat° was named Cairo. For the first time Egypt became a major cultural, intellectual, and political center of Islam (see Map 9.2). The al-Azhar Mosque built at this time remains a paramount religious and educational center to this day. Although the Fatimid family was Shi'ite, their religious influence on Egypt was rather slight during the two centuries of Fatimid rule. Most of the population remained Sunni. Nevertheless, the abundance of Fatimid gold coinage, derived from West African sources, made them an economic power in the Mediterranean.

Cut off from the rest of the Islamic world by the Strait of Gibraltar and, from 740 onward, by independent city-states in Morocco and Algeria, Umayyad Spain developed a distinctive Islamic culture blending Roman, Germanic, and Jewish traditions with those of the Arabs and Berbers (see Map 9.1). Historians disagree on how rapidly and completely the Spanish population converted to Islam. If we assume that the process was similar to that in the eastern regions, it seems likely that the most rapid surge in Islamization occurred in the mid-tenth century.

Just as in the east, governing cities were at the core of the Islamic presence in al-Andalus, as the Muslims called the regions they ruled in Spain. Cordoba, Seville, Toledo, and other cities grew substantially, becoming much larger and richer than comparable cities in neighboring France. Converts to Islam and their descendants, unconverted Arabic-speaking Christians, and Jews joined with the comparatively few descendants of the Arab invaders to create new architectural and literary styles. In the countryside, where the Berbers preferred to settle, a fusion of preexisting agricultural technologies with new crops, notably citrus fruits, and irrigation techniques from the east gave Spain the most diverse and sophisticated agricultural economy in Europe.

Tomb of the Samanids in Bukhara   This early-tenth-century structure has the basic layout of a Zoroastrian fire temple: a dome on top of a cube. However, geometic ornamentation in baked brick marks it as an early masterpiece of Islamic architecture. The Samanid family achieved independence as rulers of northeastern Iran and western Central Asia in the tenth century. (Private collection)

Buyid (BOO-yid)   **Samanid** (sah-MAN-id)
Fatimid (FAT-uh-mid)   **Fustat** (fuss-TAHT)

Spanish Muslim Textile of the Twelfth Century This fragment of woven silk, featuring peacocks and Arabic writing, is one of the finest examples of Islamic weaving. The cotton industry flourished in the early Islamic centuries, but silk remained a highly valued product. Some fabrics were treasured in Christian Europe. (Victoria & Albert Museum)

writings of Ibn Rushd° (known in Latin as Averroës°) and Ibn Tufayl°, and the mystic speculations of Ibn al-Arabi.°

The Samanids, Fatimids, and Spanish Umayyads are representative of the political diversity and awakening of local awareness that characterized the period of Abbasid decline. Yet drawing and redrawing political boundaries did not result in the rigid division of the Islamic world into kingdoms, as was then occurring in Europe. Religious and cultural developments, particularly the rise in cities throughout the Islamic world of a social group of religious scholars known as the **ulama**°—Arabic for "people with (religious) knowledge"—worked against any permanent division of the Islamic umma.

Assault from Within and Without, 1050–1258

Outside the urban milieu, political fragmentation enabled nomadic groups to assert themselves. In the west, trade across the Sahara had brought prosperity to northern city-states—Sijilmasa in Morocco and Tahert in Algeria—and to the kingdom of Ghana in Senegal and Mali (see Chapter 8). In the mid-eleventh century, however, recently converted Berber nomads from the western Sahara overpowered these trading centers and established a kingdom that stretched from Morocco to Mali (see Chapter 15) and even penetrated into Spain. These Almoravid rulers, established in their new capital of Marrakesh, in Morocco, wore blue veils over their faces and retained other traits from their Saharan past. A century later, such practices offended Ibn Tumart°, a zealous Muslim preacher. He recruited a Berber army in the Atlas Mountains and launched a movement that, after his death in 1130, supplanted the Almoravids and established an Almohad° Empire that ruled from Tunisia to Spain from Fez, its capital, located in Morocco. In both instances, the rulers were sometimes sophisticated and urbane, but they depended on unruly rural warrior peoples and often resorted to harsh and intolerant measures.

The rulers of al-Andalus did not take the title *caliph* until 929, when Abd al-Rahman° III (r. 912–961) did so in Cordoba, in response to a similar declaration by the newly established Fatimid ruler in Tunisia. Toward the end of the tenth century, this caliphate encountered challenges from breakaway movements that eventually splintered al-Andalus into a number of small states. But political decay did not stand in the way of cultural growth. Some of the greatest writers and thinkers in Jewish history worked in Muslim Spain in the eleventh and twelfth centuries, sometimes writing in Arabic, sometimes in Hebrew. At the same time, Islamic thought in Spain was attaining its loftiest peaks in Ibn Hazm's treatises on love and other subjects, the philosophical

More gradually, Arabs from southern Egypt slowly made their way across North Africa. Contemporary historians portray these invaders as locusts bent on destroying the agrarian-based prosperity of the region. Though that may be exaggerated, the so-called Hilali incursions around 1050 coincided with a shift of the North African economy toward the Mediterranean Sea. Ports and cities situated between the mountains and the coast

---

Abd al-Rahman (AHB-d al–ruh-MAHN)

Ibn Rushd (IB-uhn RUSHED)   Averroës (uh-VERR-oh-eez)
Ibn Tufayl (IB-uhn too-FILE)
Ibn al-Arabi (IB-uhn ahl-AH-rah-bee)   ulama (oo-leh-MAH)
Ibn Tumart (IB-uhn TOO-mahrt)   Almohad (AL-moe-had)

flourished while cities connected with the desert dwindled. Trading contact across the Mediterranean grew, and Andalusian culture influenced urban styles throughout the region. Meanwhile, agriculture languished. The interior plains and habitable parts of the northern Sahara became mostly Arabic-speaking, with Berber remaining the language of the mountains and of the Tuareg tribes in the southern Sahara. Trans-Saharan trade continued, but new Muslim societies south of the desert developed in substantial isolation from the urban culture of the Mediterranean.

Syria and Iraq experienced nomadic upsurges as well. Nomad-based Arab kingdoms came and went, subjecting cities like Damascus, Aleppo, and Jerusalem to an ever-shifting array of political forces. Here, too, coastal cities like Acre and Tripoli began to grow as Mediterranean trade revived. In the Tigris and Euphrates valley Shi'ite Arabs from the desert and Sunni Kurds from the mountains competed in building small principalities.

But a powerful new Turkish presence overshadowed both Arabs and Kurds. Nomadic groups speaking one or another Turkic language had been known as allies or enemies ever since the Arab conquests. After 1000, these horse-breeding pastoralists from the steppes and deserts north and east of the Black, Caspian, and Aral Seas filtered into more central Islamic lands.

The role played by Turkish mamluks in the decline of Abbasid power had established an enduring stereotype of the Turk as a ferocious warrior little interested in religion or the sophistication of urban life. This image was reinforced in the 1030s when the Seljuk° family established the first Turkish Muslim state based on nomadic power. Taking the Arabic title *Sultan,* meaning "power," and the revived Persian title *Shahan-shah,* the Seljuk ruler Tughril° Beg created a kingdom that stretched from northern Afghanistan to Baghdad, which he occupied in 1055. After a century under the thumb of the Shi'ite Buyids, the Abbasid caliph breathed a bit easier under the slightly lighter thumb of the Sunni Turks. The Seljuks pressed on into Syria and Anatolia, administering a lethal blow to Byzantine power at the Battle of Manzikert° in 1071. The Byzantine army fell back on Constantinople, leaving Anatolia open to the entry of the Turks.

Under Turkish rule, cities shrank as their agricultural hinterlands, already short on labor because of migration to the cities, were overrun by pastoralists. Irrigation works suffered from lack of maintenance in the unsettled countryside. Tax revenues fell. Cities were fought over as Seljuk princes contested for power in the twelfth century. But few Turks participated in urban cultural and religious life. Thus the gulf that had arisen between the religiously based urban society and the culture and personnel of the government deepened. When factional riots broke out between Sunnis and Shi'ites, or between rival schools of Sunni law, the government remained aloof even when destruction and loss of life were extensive. Similarly, when princes fought for the title *sultan,* religious leaders advised citizens to remain neutral.

By the early twelfth century, unrepaired damage from floods, fires, and civil disorder had reduced old Baghdad on the west side of the Tigris to ruins. The caliphs took advantage of fighting among the Seljuks to regain some power locally and built a wall around the palace precinct on the east side of the river. Nevertheless, the heart of the city died, not to be restored to prosperity until the twentieth century. The withering of Baghdad was symptomatic of even broader change in the environment: the collapse of the canal system on which agriculture in the Tigris and Euphrates valley depended. For millennia a center of world civilization, Mesopotamia suffered substantial population loss.

The Turks alone cannot be blamed for the demographic and economic misfortunes of Iran and Iraq. Too-robust urbanization had strained food resources, and political fragmentation had resulted in reduced revenues. The growing practice of using land grants to pay soldiers and courtiers also played a role. When absentee grant holders used agents to collect taxes, the inevitable result was a tendency to gouge villagers and take little interest in improving production, all of which weakened the agricultural base of the regime.

Just as the Seljuk Empire was beset by internal quarreling, the first crusading armies of Christians reached the Holy Land. The First Crusade captured Jerusalem in 1099. Chapter 10 recounts the expeditions of Christian soldiers who trekked through the Balkans or sailed the Mediterranean to fight for the cross. Though charged with the stuff of romance, the Crusades had little lasting impact on the Islamic lands. The crusader principalities of Edessa, Anitoch, Tripoli, and Jerusalem simply became pawns in the shifting pattern of politics already in place. Newly arrived knights were eager to attack the Muslim enemy, whom they called "Saracens°." But those who stayed in the region, including the religious orders of the Knights of the Temple (Templars) and the Knights of the Hospital of St. John (Hospitallers), recognized that diplomacy and seeking partners of convenience among the rival Muslim princes was a sounder strategy.

The Muslims finally unified to face the European enemy in the mid-twelfth century. Nur al-Din ibn Zangi°

Seljuk (sel-JOOK)   **Tughril** (TUUG-ruhl)
Manzikert (MANZ-ih-kuhrt)

Saracen (SAR-uh-suhn)
Nur al-Din ibn Zangi (NOOR-al-DEEN ib-uhn ZAN-gee)

Scholarly Life in Medieval Islam
Books were scarce and expensive, so teachers often dictated to their students, as shown on the right. Notice that the student is writing on a single sheet of paper and the scholar in the center holds an entire book. On the left, an author is presenting his work to a wealthy patron.   (Bibliothèque nationale de France)

established a strong state based in Damascus and sent an army to terminate the Fatimid Caliphate in Egypt. A nephew of the Kurdish commander of that expedition was Salah-al-Din, known in the West as Saladin. Saladin took advantage of Nur al-Din's timely death to seize power and unify Egypt and Syria, bringing the Fatimid dynasty to an end in 1171. In 1187 he recaptured Jerusalem from the Europeans.

Saladin's descendants fought off all subsequent Crusades to the Holy Land. However, after one such battle, in 1250, Turkish mamluk troops seized control of the government, ending Saladin's dynasty. In 1260 these mamluks rode east to confront a new invading force. At the Battle of Ain Jalut° (Spring of Goliath), in Syria, they met and defeated an army of Mongols from Central Asia, thus stemming an invasion that had begun several decades before and legitimizing their claim to dominion over Egypt and Syria.

The Mongol invasions shocked the world of Islam. The full story of the Mongols' conquests is told in Chapters 13 and 14, but the impact of their destruction of the Abbasid Caliphate in Baghdad in 1258 and their imposition of non-Muslim rule from Iraq eastward for most of the thirteenth century bears mention here. Although the Mongols left few ethnic or linguistic traces in these lands, their initial destruction of cities, their subsequent promotion of trans-Asian trade along routes to the north of the

---
Ain Jalut (ine jah-LOOT)

traditional Silk Road, and their casual disregard for urban and religious life, even after they themselves converted to Islam, hastened currents of change already under way.

ISLAMIC CIVILIZATION

Though complex and unsettled in its political dimension, life in the ever-expanding Islamic world underwent a creative fruitful evolution in law, social structure, and religious expression. Religious conversion and urbanization reinforced each other to create a distinct Islamic civilization. Because of the immense geographical and human diversity of the Muslim lands, many "small traditions" coexisted with the developing "great tradition" of Islam—a "large tradition" that was more an urban than a rural phenomenon.

Law and Dogma   The foundation of Islamic civilization is the Shari'a, the law of Islam. Yet aside from certain parts of the Quran that conveyed specific divine ordinances—most pertaining to personal and family matters—no legal system was in place in the time of Muhammad. Only Arab custom and the Prophet's own authority offered guidance. After Muhammad died, the umma tried to conduct itself according to his example. This became harder and harder to do, however, as those who knew Muhammad best passed away and many Arabs found themselves living in far-off parts of the conquered territories. Living in accordance with the Prophet's tradition was even harder for non-Arab converts to Islam, who at first were also expected to follow Arab customs they had little familiarity with.

Islam slowly developed laws to shape social and religious life. The full sense of Islamic civilization, however, goes well beyond the basic Five Pillars mentioned earlier. Some Muslim thinkers felt that the reasoned consideration of a mature and intelligent man—women were only rarely heard in religious matters—provided the best way of resolving issues not covered by Quranic revelation. Others argued that the best guide was the sunna, or tradition, of the Prophet and that the best way to understand that sunna was to collect and study the many reports in circulation purporting to describe the precise words or deeds of Muhammad. These reports were called **hadith°**, and it gradually became customary to precede each hadith with a statement indicating whom the speaker had heard it from, whom that person had heard it from, and so on, back to the Prophet personally.

Some hadith dealt with ritual matters, such as how to perform ablutions before prayer; others were simply anecdotes. A significant number provided answers to legal questions not covered by Quranic revelation, or they suggested principles for resolving such matters. By the eleventh century, most specialists on Islamic legal thought had accepted the idea that Muhammad's personal behavior was the best model for society in general, and that the hadith were therefore the most authoritative basis for Islamic law after the Quran itself.

Yet the hadith themselves posed a problem. This body of lore, numbering tens of thousands of anecdotes, included not only genuine reports about the Prophet but also invented ones, politically motivated ones, and stories derived from non-Muslim religious traditions. Only a specialist could hope to separate a sound from a weak tradition. As the importance of hadith grew, so did the branch of learning devoted to their analysis. Thousands of hadith were deemed weak and discarded. The most reliable ones were collected into books that gradually were accorded an authoritative status. Sunnis placed six books in this category; Shi'ites, four.

The Shari'a was built up over centuries. It incorporated the ideas of many legal scholars as well as the implications of thousands of hadith, a body of material whose origin in the very mouth of the Prophet is sometimes disputed by modern scholars.

The Shari'a embodies a vision of an umma in which all Muslims are brothers and sisters and subscribe to the same moral values. From this perspective, political or ethnic divisions are not important, for the Shari'a assumes that a Muslim ruler will abide by and enforce the religious law. In practice, this vision was often lost in the hurly-burly of political life. Even so, it was an important basis for an urban lifestyle that varied surprisingly little from Morocco to India.

Converts and Cities

The early caliphs' determination that Arab warriors should live in garrisons at governing centers led to a significant change in the conquered lands by encouraging urbanization. The early political history of Islam concentrates on Mecca and Medina; Damascus and Baghdad, which became capitals in 661 and 762 respectively; and a few military encampments that grew into major cities: Kufa and Basra in Iraq, Fustat in Egypt, and Qayrawan° in Tunisia.

A major cause of urbanization was conversion to Islam. Conversion was more an outcome of the gradual communication of knowledge about the new rulers' religion than it was a step that people took to escape the tax on non-Muslims, as some scholars have suggested. Conversion was fairly simple. No extensive knowledge of the faith was required. To become a Muslim, a person recited, in the presence of a Muslim, the profession of faith in Arabic: "There is no God but God, and Muhammad is the Messenger of God."

Few converts knew Arabic, and most people were illiterate and hence unable to read the Quran. Indeed, many converts knew no more of the Quran than the few verses necessary for their daily prayers. Muhammad had established no priesthood to define and spread the faith. Thus new converts, whether Arab or non-Arab, faced the problem of finding out for themselves what Islam was about and how they should act as Muslims.

The best way to solve this problem was to spend time with other Muslims, learn their language, imitate their behavior, and gradually acquire a Muslim social identity. In many areas, the only way to do this was to migrate to an Arab governing center. The alternative, to convert to Islam but remain in one's home community, posed an additional problem. Even before the emergence of Islam, religion had become the main component of social identity in the Middle East. Converts to Islam thus encountered discrimination if they went on living within their Christian, Jewish, or Zoroastrian

---

hadith (hah-DEETH)

Qayrawan (kire-ah-WAHN)

The Fraternity of Beggars

Beggars, tricksters, and street performers were considered members of a single loose fraternity: Banu Sasan, or Tribe of Sasan. Tales of their tricks and exploits amused staid, pious Muslims, who often encountered them in cities and on their scholarly travels. Beggars and scholars were among the most mobile elements of the population. These descriptive verses come from a tenth-century poet who studied beggars' jargon and way of life.

> For we are the lads, the only lads who really matter, on land or on sea.
> We exact a tax from all mankind, from China to Egypt,
> And to Tangier; indeed, our steeds range over every land of the world.
> When one region gets too hot for us, we simply leave it for another one.
> The whole world is ours, and whatever is in it, the lands of Islam and the lands of unbelief alike.
> Hence we spend the summers in snowy lands, whilst in winter we migrate to the lands where the dates grow.
> We are the beggars' brotherhood, and no one can deny us our lofty pride . . .
> And of our number if the feigned madman and mad woman, with metal charms strung from their [sic] necks.
> And the ones with ornaments drooping from their ears, and with collars of leather or brass round their necks . . .
> And the one who simulates a festering internal wound, and the people with false bandages round their heads and sickly, jaundiced faces.
> And the one who slashes himself, alleging that he has been mutilated by assailants, or the one who darkens his skin artificially pretending that he has been beaten up and wounded . . .
> And the one who practices as a manipulator and quack dentist, or who escapes from chains wound round his body, or the one who uses almost invisible silk thread mysteriously to draw off rings . . .
> And of our number are those who claim to be refugees from the Byzantine frontier regions, those who go round begging on pretext of having left behind captive families . . .
> And the one who feigns an internal discharge, or who showers the passers-by with his urine, or who farts in the mosque and makes a nuisance of himself, thus wheedling money out of people . . .
> And of our number are the ones who purvey objects of veneration made from clay, and those who have their beards smeared with red dye.
> And the one who brings up secret writing by immersing it in what looks like water, and the one who similarly brings up the writing by exposing it to burning embers.

How do the beggars' practices reflect social values? How is the cosmopolitanism of Islamic society visible in these verses?

Source: Excerpts from Clifford Edmund Bosworth, *The Mediaeval Islamic Underworld: The Banu Sasan in Arabic Society and Literature* (Leiden: E. I. Brill, 1976), 191–199. Copyright © 1976. With kind permission of Koninklijke Brill N.V. Leiden, the Netherlands.

communities. Again, one solution was migration, an option made attractive by the fact that tax revenues from the conquered lands flowed into the Arab governing centers, providing many economic opportunities for converts.

Kufa and Basra in Iraq were the first new Arab settlements to blossom as cities. Both became important centers for Muslim cultural activities. But as conversion rapidly spread in the mid-ninth century, urbanization increased in other regions as well. It was particularly noticeable in Iran, where most cities previously had been quite small. Nishapur in the northeast grew from less than 10,000 at the time of conquest to between 100,000 and 200,000 by the year 1000. Other Iranian cities experienced similar growth. In Iraq, Baghdad and Mosul joined Kufa and Basra as major cities. In Syria, Aleppo and Damascus flourished under Muslim rule. New districts were added to Fustat—the final one in 969 was named Cairo—to create one of the largest and greatest of the Islamic cities. The primarily Christian patriarchal cities of

Jerusalem, Antioch, and Alexandria were not Muslim governing centers, did not benefit from this wave of migration, and consequently shrank and stagnated.

Cities were the centers of Islam; the countryside was slower to convert. Muhammad and his first followers had lived in a commercial city, and Islam acquired a peculiarly urban character very different from that of medieval European Christianity. Mosques in large cities were not only ritual centers but places for learning and social activities.

Urban social life was colored by Islam (see Society and Culture: The Fraternity of Beggars). Without religious officials to instruct them, the new Muslims imitated Arab dress and customs and sought out for guidance individual Muslims whom they regarded as particularly pious. Inevitably, in the absence of a central religious authority comparable to a pope, there was great local variation in the way people practiced Islam and in the collection of hadith attributed to the Prophet. That same absence of a centralized organization gave to the rapidly growing religion a flexibility that accommodated many different social situations. Since the profession of Islamic faith called only for the acknowledgment of God's unity and Muhammad's prophethood, Islam escaped most of the severe conflicts over heresy that beset the Christians at a comparable stage of development.

By the tenth century, the growth of cities was affecting the countryside by producing an expanding market of consumers. Citrus fruits, rice, and sugar cane increased in acreage and were introduced to new areas. Cotton became a major crop in Iran and elsewhere and gave rise to a diverse and profitable textile industry. Irrigation works expanded in certain areas. Diet diversified. Abundant Islamic coinage made for a lively economy. Intercity and long-distance trade flourished, providing regular links between isolated districts and integrating the pastoral nomads who provided pack animals into the region's economy. Manufacturing expanded as well, particularly the production of cloth, metal goods, and pottery. The market economy grew under the strong influence of Islamic ethics and law. Indeed, one of the few officials specified by the Shari'a was the market inspector.

Science and medicine also flourished (see Environment and Technology: Automata on page 244). Building on Hellenistic traditions and their own observations and experience, Muslim doctors and astronomers developed skills and theories far in advance of their European counterparts. The mathematician and physicist Ibn al-Haytham°, working in Egypt in the eleventh century, wrote more than a hundred works. Among other things,

---

Ibn al-Haytham (IB-uhn al–HY-tham)

he determined that the Milky Way is situated far beyond earth's atmosphere, he proved that light travels from a seen object to the eye and not the reverse, and he explained why the sun and moon appear larger on the horizon than overhead.

Islam, Women, and Slaves

Women rarely traveled. Those living in rural areas worked in the fields and tended animals. Urban women, particularly members of the elite, lived in seclusion and did not leave their homes without covering themselves completely. The practice of secluding women in their houses and veiling them in public already existed in Byzantine and Sasanid urban society. Through interpretation of specific verses from the Quran, these practices now became fixtures of Muslim social life. Although women sometimes studied and became literate, they did so away from the gaze of men who were not related to them. Although women played an influential role within the family, any public role had to be indirect, through their husbands. Slave women were an exception. They alone were permitted to perform before men as musicians and dancers. A man could have sexual relations with as many slave concubines as he pleased, in addition to having as many as four wives.

In some ways Muslim women fared better legally under the developing practices of Islamic law than did Christian and Jewish women under the practices of Christianity and Judaism. Muslim women could own property and retain it in marriage. They could remarry if their husbands divorced them, and they were entitled to a cash payment upon divorce. Although a man could divorce his wife without stating a cause, a woman was able to initiate divorce under specified conditions. Women could practice birth control. They could testify in court, although their testimony was weighed as half that of a man. And they could go on pilgrimage. Nevertheless, a misogynistic tone is sometimes evident in Islamic writings. One saying attributed to the Prophet observed: "I was raised up to heaven and saw that most of its denizens were poor people; I was raised into the hellfire and saw that most of its denizens were women."[3]

Because writings by women about women are almost unknown from this period, the status of women must be deduced from the writings of men. The Prophet's wife A'isha, the daughter of Abu Bakr, provides an example of how Muslim men appraised the role of women in society. A'isha was only eighteen when Muhammad died. She lived for another fifty years. The earliest reports stress her status as Muhammad's favorite and the only virgin he married. She was the only wife to

Automata

Muslim scientists made discoveries and advances in almost every field, from mathematics and astronomy to chemistry and optics. Many worked under the patronage of rulers who paid for translations from Greek and other languages into Arabic and built libraries and observatories to facilitate their work. In return, some engineers designed elaborate mechanical devices—automata—for the entertainment of the rulers. In this example, a conventional-looking *saqiya* (suh-KEY-yuh) of a type in use from Morocco to Afghanistan to raise water appears to be powered by a wooden cow.

A saqiya is a chain of buckets descending to a water source from a spoked drum attached to interlocking gears. An animal walks in a circle turning the first gear and setting the rest in motion. The real power comes from a water wheel and gears hidden underground. These turn the platform the animal stands on, causing the gears above to operate the chain of buckets lifting water to the outlet trough on the upper left.

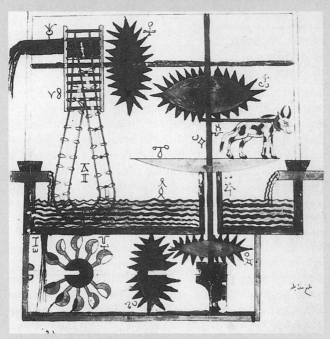

Model of a Water-Lifting Device   The artist's effort to render a three-dimensional construction in two dimensions shows a talent for schematic drawing.   (Widener Library Photographic Services)

see the angel Gabriel. These reports emanate from A'isha herself, who was an abundant source of hadith.

A'isha was especially known, however, for two episodes. As a fourteen-year-old she became separated from a caravan and rejoined it only after traveling through the night with a man who found her alone in the desert. Gossips accused her of being untrue to the Prophet, but a revelation from God proved her innocence. The other event was her participation in the Battle of the Camel, fought to prevent Ali from becoming the fourth caliph. These two episodes came to epitomize what Muslim men feared most about women: sexual infidelity and meddling in politics. As a result, even though the earliest literature dealing with A'isha stresses her position as Muhammad's favorite, his first wife, Khadija, and his daughter, Fatima, who was married to Ali, eventually surpassed A'isha as ideal women. Both were portrayed as model wives and

mothers, and neither aroused suspicions of sexual irregularity or political manipulation.

As the seclusion of women became commonplace in urban Muslim society, some writers recommended that men cultivate homosexual relationships, partly because a male lover was presentable in public or on a journey. Although Islam frowned on homosexuality, one ruler wrote a book in which he advised his son to follow moderation in all things and thus to share his affections equally between men and women. Another ruler and his slaveboy became models of perfect love extolled in the verses of mystic poets.

Islam allowed slavery but forbade Muslims from enslaving other Muslims or so-called People of the Book—Jews, Christians, and Zoroastrians, who revered holy books respected by the Muslims—living under Muslim protection. An exception was made when slavery re-

Women Playing Chess in Muslim Spain   Chess was a popular pastime in Islamic lands. As shown in this thirteenth-century miniature, women in their own quarters, without men present, wore whatever clothes and jewels they liked. Notice the henna decorating the hands of the woman in the middle. The woman on the left, probably a slave, is playing an oud. (Institute Amatller d'Art Hispanic. © Patrimonio Nacional, Madrid)

sulted from becoming a prisoner of war. In later centuries there was a constant flow of slaves into Islamic territory from Africa and Central Asia. A hereditary slave society, however, did not develop. Usually slaves converted to Islam, and many masters then freed them as an act of piety. The offspring of slave women and Muslim men were born free.

The Recentering of Islam

The caliphate was the original center of Islam, the concrete political expression of the unity of the umma. No formal organization or hierarchy, however, directed the process of conversion. Thus there emerged a multitude of local Islamic communities that were so disconnected from each other that numerous competing interpretations of the developing religion arose. Inevitably, the centrality of the caliphate diminished (see Map 9.2). The appearance of rival caliphates in Tunisia and Cordoba accentuated the problem of decentralization just when the Abbasids were losing the last of their temporal power.

The rise of the ulama as the leaders of Muslim communities did not prevent the growing fragmentation because the ulama themselves were often divided into contentious factions. During the twelfth century, however, factionalism began to abate, and new socioreligious institutions emerged to provide the umma with a differ-

ent sort of religious center. These new developments stemmed in part from an exodus of religious scholars from Iran in response to the economic and political disintegration of the late eleventh and twelfth centuries.

The flow of Iranians to the Arab countries and to newly conquered territories in India and Anatolia became a flood after the Mongol invasion. Scholars fully versed in Arabic as well as in their native Persian were well received wherever they went. They brought with them a view of religion developed in the urban centers of Iran. A type of higher religious college, the madrasa°, gained sudden popularity outside Iran, where madrasas had been known since the tenth century. Scores of madrasas, many under the patronage of local rulers, were established throughout the Islamic world.

Also in the twelfth and thirteenth centuries, and with a strong input from Iranians, mystic fraternities known as *Sufi* brotherhoods developed. The spread of the doctrines and rituals of certain Sufis from city to city gave rise to the first geographically extensive Islamic religious organizations. Sufi doctrines varied enormously, but the common denominator was the quest for a sense of union with God through rituals and training. This type of spiritual endeavor had begun in early Islamic times and had doubtless benefited from the ideas and beliefs of converts to Islam from religions with mystic traditions.

madrasa (MAH-dras-uh)

Quran Page Printed from a Woodblock   Printing from woodblocks and from tin plates was practiced in Islamic lands between approximately 800 and 1400. Most of the prints were narrow amulets designed to be rolled and worn around the neck in a cylindrical case. Less valued than handwritten amulets, many of the prints were made by Banu Sasan conmen. Why blockprinting had so little effect on society in general and eventually disappeared is unknown.   (Cambridge University Library)

The early Sufis had been saintly individuals given to ecstatic and poetic utterances and wonderworking. They attracted disciples but did not try to organize them. The growth of brotherhoods, a less ecstatic form of Sufism, set a tone for society in general. It soon became common for most Muslim men, particularly in the cities, to belong to at least one brotherhood.

A sense of the social climate the Sufi brotherhoods fostered can be gained from a twelfth-century manual:

> Every limb has its own special ethics. . . . The ethics of the tongue. The tongue should always be busy in reciting God's names (*dhikr*) and in saying good things of the brethren, praying for them, and giving them counsel. . . . The ethics of hearing. One should not listen to indecencies and slander. . . . The ethics of sight. One

should lower one's eyes in order not to see forbidden things. . . . The ethics of the hands: to give charity and serve the brethren and not use them in acts of disobedience.[4]

Special dispensations allowed people who merely wanted to emulate the Sufis and enjoy their company to follow less demanding rules:

> It is allowed by way of dispensation to possess an estate or to rely on a regular income. The Sufis' rule in this matter is that one should not use all of it for himself, but should dedicate this to public charities and should take from it only enough for one year for himself and his family. . . .
>
> There is a dispensation allowing one to be occupied in business; this dispensation is granted to him who has to support a family. But this should not keep him away from the regular performance of prayers. . . .
>
> There is a dispensation allowing one to watch all kinds of amusement. This is, however, limited by the rule: What you are forbidden from doing, you are also forbidden from watching.[5]

Some Sufi brotherhoods spread in the countryside. Local shrines and pilgrimages to the tombs of Muhammad's descendants and saintly Sufis became popular. The pilgrimage to Mecca, too, received new prominence as a religious duty. The end of the Abbasid Caliphate enhanced the religious centrality of Mecca, which eventually became an important center of madrasa education.

Altogether, the twelfth and thirteenth centuries saw a transition from the politically volatile and socially and religiously effervescent earliest centuries of Islamic history. The later centuries would see the weight of the fully developed Shari'a, of madrasa education, and of the Sufi brotherhoods create a more regimented, though more organized and supportive, society. The Islamic civilization that spread into Asia, Africa, and Europe after the period of the Mongols was of this later form.

CONCLUSION

With the way paved by the establishment of official state religions in the Sasanid and Byzantine Empires, Islam culminated the transition in the ancient world from identity based on ethnicity and localism to identity based on religion. The concept of the umma, originating in Mecca and Medina, united all Muslims in a universal community embracing enormous diversity of language, appearance, and social custom. Though

Muslim communities adapted to local "small traditions" in different regions, by the twelfth century a religious scholar could travel anywhere in the Islamic world and blend easily into the local Muslim community.

The political and economic forces contributing to this phenomenal growth changed over time. In the beginning, Arab armies led by people who had known and been inspired by Muhammad played an essential role in bringing an immense geographical area under the control of the caliphate. By the ninth century, however, the forces of conversion and urbanization were more important than military conquest in spreading the new faith and fostering social and religious experimentation in urban settings. From the eleventh century onward, political disruption and the spread of pastoral nomadism helped slow this early economic and technological dynamism. The Muslim community then turned to new religious institutions, such as the madrasas and Sufi brotherhoods, to create a flexible and durable community structure that carried Islam forward into new regions and protected the ordinary believer from capricious political rule.

Some of these developments are distinctive to Islamic history while others have parallels in the contemporary history of medieval Europe, as we shall see in the next chapter.

■ Key Terms

Shi'ites	umma
Sunnis	caliphate
Sasanid Empire	Quran
Mecca	Umayyad Caliphate
Muhammad	Abbasid Caliphate
muslim	mamluks
Islam	ulama
Medina	hadith

■ Suggested Reading

There is no convenient survey of Sasanid history in English though Richard N. Frye's *The Heritage of Persia* (1963; reprint, 1993) is helpful. Up-to-date articles on aspects of Iranian history in the centuries just prior to Islam are provided in Ehsan Yarshater, ed., *The Cambridge History of Iran*, vol. 3 (pts. 1–2), *The Seleucid, Parthian and Sasanian Periods* (1983).

Two comprehensive surveys of Islamic history devote substantial space to the period covered in this chapter and set it in broader contexts. Ira M. Lapidus, *A History of Islamic Societies* (1988), focuses on social developments and includes the histo-

ries of Islam in India, Southeast Asia, sub-Saharan Africa, and other parts of the world. Marshall G. S. Hodgson, *The Venture of Islam*, 3 vols. (1974), presents a critique of traditional ways of studying the Islamic Middle East while offering an interpretation based on the contributions of major intellectual and religious figures. Bernard Lewis's *The Middle East: A Brief History of the Last 2,000 Years* (1995) provides a lively narration that begins in the time of Christ.

For a shorter but eminently readable survey see J. J. Saunders, *History of Medieval Islam* (1965; reprint, 1990). Richard W. Bulliet, *Islam: The View from the Edge* (1993), offers, in brief form, an approach that minimizes discussion of political events and concentrates on the lives of converts to Islam and the local religious notables who guided their lives.

R. Stephen Humphreys, *Islamic History: A Framework for Inquiry*, rev. ed. (1991), provides the best introduction to issues of historiography and some of the major issues in recent scholarship. Thorny issues arising from new approaches to the sources of the earliest history of Islam are well reviewed by Fred Donner, *Narratives of Islamic Origins: The Beginnings of Islamic Historical Writing*, (1998). Bernard Lewis, ed. and trans., *Islam: From the Prophet Muhammad to the Capture of Constantinople* (1974; reprint, 1987), is an excellent selection of brief, well-introduced, translations from primary sources.

Muslims believe that the Quran is untranslatable because they consider the Arabic in which it is couched to be an inseparable part of God's message. There are numerous "Interpretations" in English, however. Most of these adhere reasonably closely to the Arabic text. There is no agreement on which is the best. Arthur J. Arberry, *The Koran Interpreted* (1955; reprint, 1986), represents an effort to capture the poetic quality of Quranic language.

Muslims prefer biographies of Muhammad that accept the basic story as contained in the earliest Muslim sources. Non-Muslims display skepticism about those sources. Martin Lings, *Muhammad: His Life Based on the Earliest Sources*, rev. ed. (1991), is a readable biography reflecting the Muslim point of view. The standard Western treatments have long been W. Montgomery Watt's *Muhammad at Mecca* (1953) and *Muhammad at Medina* (1956; reprint, 1981); there is a one-volume abbreviated version of those two works: *Muhammad, Prophet and Statesman* (1974). Michael A. Cook, *Muhammad* (1983), is a brief, intelligent discussion of the historiographical problems and source difficulties inherent in the subject. Karen Armstrong's *Muhammad: A Biography of the Prophet* (1993) achieves a sympathetic balance of views.

Wilfred Madelung's *The Succession to Muhammad: A Study of the Early Caliphate* (1997) gives an interpretation unusually sympathetic to Shi'ite viewpoints. G. R. Hawting, *The First Dynasty of Islam: The Umayyad Caliphate, A.D. 661–750* (1987), offers a more conventional and easily readable history of a crucial century.

Western historians have much debated the beginnings of the Abbasid Caliphate. Moshe Sharon, *Black Banners from the East:*

The Establishment of the 'Abbasid State—Incubation of a Revolt (1983), and Jacob Lassner, *Islamic Revolution and Historical Memory: An Inquiry into the Art of Abbasid Apologetics* (1987), give differing accounts based on newly utilized sources. For a broader history that puts the first three centuries of Abbasid rule into the context of the earlier periods see Hugh N. Kennedy, *The Prophet and the Age of the Caliphates: The Islamic Near East from the Sixth to the Eleventh Century* (1986). Harold Bowen, *The Life and Times of Ali ibn Isa "The Good Vizier"* (1928; reprint, 1975), supplements Kennedy's narrative superbly with a detailed study of corrupt caliphal politics in the tumultuous early tenth century.

Articles in Michael Gervers and Ramzi Jibran Bikhazi, eds., *Conversion and Continuity: Indigenous Christian Communities in Islamic Lands, Eighth to Eighteenth Centuries,* (1990) detail Christian responses to Islam. For a Zoroastrian perspective see Jamsheed K. Choksy, *Conflict and Cooperation: Zoroastrian Subalterns and Muslim Elites in Medieval Iranian Society* (1997). Jacob Lassner summarizes S. D. Goitein's definitive multivolume study of the Jews of medieval Egypt in *A Mediterranean Society: An Abridgement in One Volume* (1999). On the process of conversion see the work in quantitative history of Richard W. Bulliet, *Conversion to Islam in the Medieval Period* (1979).

With the fragmentation of the Abbasid Caliphate beginning in the ninth century, studies of separate areas become more useful than general histories. Richard N. Frye, *The Golden Age of Persia: The Arabs in the East* (1975), skillfully evokes the complicated world of early Islamic Iran and the survival and revival of Persian national identity. Thomas F. Glick, *Islamic and Christian Spain in the Early Middle Ages* (1979) and *From Muslim Fortress to Christian Castle: Social and Cultural Change in Medieval Spain* (1995), questions standard ideas about Christians and Muslims in Spain from a geographical and technological standpoint. For North Africa, Charles-André Julien, *History of North Africa: Tunisia, Algeria, Morocco, from the Arab Conquest to 1830* (1970), summarizes a literature primarily written in French. This same French historiographical tradition is challenged and revised by Abdallah Laroui, *The History of the Maghrib: An Interpretive Essay* (1977).

An English translation of the most important chronicle of early Islamic history, *The History of al-Tabari,* is now complete in thirty-eight volumes, under the general editorship of Ehsan Yarshater. Two later primary sources available in excellent translations are Usamah ibn Munqidh, *An Arab-Syrian Gentleman and Warrior in the Period of the Crusades,* trans. Philip Hitti (1929; reprint, 1987), and Ibn Battuta, *Travels in Asia and Africa, 1325–1354,* trans. H. A. R. Gibb (1929; reprint, 1983). The latter, by one of the greatest travelers in history, has been well studied by Ross E. Dunn, *The Adventures of Ibn Battuta: A Muslim Traveler of the Fourteenth Century* (1986; reprint, 1989).

Studies of particular aspects of Islamic history are useful for comparison with other regions. Roy P. Mottahedeh, *Loyalty and Leadership in an Early Islamic Society* (1980); Richard W. Bulliet, *The Patricians of Nishapur* (1972); and Ira Marvin Lapidus,

Muslim Cities in the Later Middle Ages (1984), discuss social history in tenth-century Iran, eleventh-century Iran, and fourteenth-century Syria, respectively. Jonathan Berkey, *The Transmission of Knowledge in Medieval Cairo: A Social History of Islamic Education* (1992), and Michael Chamberlain, *Knowledge and Social Practice in Medieval Damascus, 1190–1350* (1994), put forward competing assessments of education and the role of the ulama in Islamic society.

Ahmad Y. al-Hassan and Donald R. Hill, *Islamic Technology: An Illustrated History* (1986), is a well-illustrated introduction to this little-studied field. For a more crafts-oriented look at the subject see Hans E. Wulff, *The Traditional Crafts of Persia: Their Development, Technology, and Influence on Eastern and Western Civilizations* (1966).

Women's lives are difficult to study in Islamic contexts because of lack of sources. Denise Spellberg, *Politics, Gender, and the Islamic Past: The Legacy of A'isha bint Abi Bakr* (1994), provides pathbreaking guidance. Basim Musallam, *Sex and Society in Islamic Civilization* (1983), is an excellent treatment of the social, medical, and legal history of birth control in medieval Islam. On the subject of race and slavery see Bernard Lewis, *Race and Slavery in the Middle East: A Historical Enquiry* (1992).

Among the numerous introductory books on Islam as a religion, a reliable starting point is H. A. R. Gibb, *Mohammedanism: An Historical Survey,* 2d ed. (1969). For more advanced work, Fazlur Rahman, *Islam,* 2d ed. (1979), skillfully discusses some of the subject's difficulties.

Islamic law, one of the most important specialized fields of Islamic studies, is well covered in Noel J. Coulson *A History of Islamic Law* (1979). For Sufism, the mystic tradition in Islam, see Annemarie Schimmel, *Mystical Dimensions of Islam* (1975).

Two particularly valuable religious texts available in translation are Abu Hamid al-Ghazali, *The Faith and Practice of al-Ghazali,* trans. W. Montgomery Watt (1967; reprint, 1982), and Abu al-Najib al-Suhrawardi, *A Sufi Rule for Novices,* trans. Menahem Milson (1975). Both date from the twelfth and thirteenth-century transition period of Islamic history and show the variety of religious perspectives then common.

For detailed and abundant maps see William C. Brice, ed., *An Historical Atlas of Islam* (1981). The most complete reference work for people working in Islamic studies is *The Encyclopedia of Islam,* new ed. (Leiden: E. J. Brill, 1960–), now available in CD-ROM format.

■ Notes

1. Quran. Sura 96, verses 1–5.
2. Quran. Sura 92, verses 1–10.
3. Richard W. Bulliet, *Islam: The View from the Edge* (New York: Columbia University Press, 1994), 87.
4. Abu Najib al-Suhrawardi, *A Sufi Rule for Novices,* trans. Menahem Milson (Cambridge, MA: Harvard University Press, 1975), 45–58.
5. Ibid., 73–82.

10

CHRISTIAN EUROPE EMERGES,
300–1200

Early Medieval Europe, 300–1000 • The Western Church • The Byzantine Empire, 300–1200 • Kievan Russia, 900–1200 • Western Europe Revives, 1000–1200

ENVIRONMENT AND TECHNOLOGY: Castles and Fortifications

SOCIETY AND CULTURE: The Penitentials of Saint Patrick

Boatbuilding Scene from the Bayeux Tapestry   Eleventh-century shipwrights prepare vessels for William of Normandy's invasion of England.

Christmas Day in the year 800 found Charles, king of the Franks, in Rome instead of at his palace in northeastern France. At six-foot-three, Charles was a foot taller than the average man of his time, and his royal career had been equally gargantuan. Crowned king in his mid-twenties in 768, he had crisscrossed Europe for three decades, waging war on Muslim invaders from Spain, Avar invaders from Hungary, and myriad German princes.

Charles had subdued many enemies and become protector of the papacy. So it is hard to believe the eyewitness report of his secretary and biographer that Charles was surprised when Pope Leo III stepped forward as the king rose from his prayers and placed a new crown on his head. "Life and victory to Charles the August, crowned by God the great and pacific Emperor of the Romans," proclaimed the pope.[1] Then, amid the cheers of the crowd, he humbly knelt before the new emperor.

Charlemagne° (from Latin *Carolus magnus,* "Charles the Great") was the first to bear the title *emperor* in western Europe for over three hundred years. Rome's decline and Charlemagne's rise marked a shift of focus for Europe—away from the Mediterranean and toward the north and west. The world of Charlemagne, dominated by the Germanic peoples of the north, opened an era in European history in which German custom and Christian piety transformed the Roman heritage to create a new civilization. Irish monks replaced Greek philosophers as the leading intellectuals. Roads were neglected, and trade languished. The sumptuous villas of the Romans gave way to cold, stone castles. One of Charlemagne's consisted of a simple stone building with three large and eleven small rooms, surrounded by a wooden stockade also enclosing stables, kitchen, and bakery, and stocked with 355 pigs, 22 peacocks, one set of bedding, and one tablecloth. This era is commonly called early "**medieval**," literally "middle age," because it comes between the era of Greco-Roman civilization and the intellectual, artistic, and economic changes of the Renaissance in the fourteenth century.

Charlemagne (SHAHR-leh-mane)

The imperial title did not long survive Charlemagne. The unity of his realm fell apart under his less able successors; and during his lifetime even he had acknowledged a rival emperor in the East, where the political and legal heritage of Rome continued in the Eastern Roman, or **Byzantine Empire.** After Charlemagne, Western Europeans lived amid the ruins of an empire that haunted their dreams but was never rebuilt. In contrast, the Byzantines maintained and reinterpreted Roman traditions for centuries. The authority of the Byzantine emperors blended with the influence of the Christian church to form a new and creative synthesis that helped shape the emerging kingdom of Kievan Russia still farther to the east. The western area of the old Roman Empire, despite the respite of Charlemagne's reign, experienced generations of chaos with scores of competing regional powers. In the West the growing authority of the church was the only unifying force.

As you read this chapter ask yourself the following questions:

- What role did Christianity play in reshaping European society in east and west?
- What were the main features of the economy and social structure of medieval western Europe?
- Did Kievan Russia more closely resemble western Europe or the Byzantine Empire?
- How did Mediterranean trade and the Crusades help in the revival of western Europe?

EARLY MEDIEVAL EUROPE, 300–1000

The emperor Constantine (r. 306–337) reunited the Roman Empire under his sole rule (see Chapter 6). But the union did not last, and in 395 the empire was permanently divided into an eastern and a western half. Both halves came under pressure from the westward migrations of Germanic peoples fleeing a new invader from Asia, the Huns. Byzantine armies were able to defend the comparatively short Danube River frontier. But the Roman legions in the West could not hold their far-flung

CHRONOLOGY

	Western Europe	Eastern Europe
300		
		325 Constantine convenes Council of Nicaea; Arian heresy condemned
		392 Emperor Theodosius bans paganism in Byzantine Empire
	432 Saint Patrick begins missionary work in Ireland	
	476 Deposing of the last Roman emperor in the West	
500		
		527–565 Justinian and Theodora rule Byzantine Empire; imperial edicts collected in single law code
	ca. 547 Death of Saint Benedict	
		634–650 Muslims conquer Byzantine provinces of Syria, Egypt, and Tunisia
	711 Muslim conquest of Spain	
	732 Battle of Tours	
800	**800** Coronation of Charlemagne	
	843 Treaty of Verdun divides Carolingian Empire among Charlemagne's grandsons	
		882 Varangians take control of Kiev
	910 Monastery of Cluny founded	
	962 Beginning of Holy Roman Empire	
		980 Vladimir becomes grand prince of Kievan Russia
1000		
	1054 Formal schism between Latin and Orthodox Churches	
	1066 Normans under William the Conqueror invade England	
	1077 Climax of investiture controversy	
	1095 Pope Urban II preaches First Crusade	**1081–1118** Alexius Comnenus rules Byzantine Empire, calls for western military aid against Muslims
1200		**1204** Western knights sack Constantinople in Fourth Crusade
		1237–1240 Mongol invasion of Kievan Russia

territories. Gaul, Britain, Spain, North Africa—all fell to various Germanic peoples in the early fifth century. Rome itself was sacked by the Visigoths in 410, and the last Roman emperor was deposed in 476. The total number of Germans was not great in comparison with the indigenous population of western Europe, but their strong organization under warlike chiefs overwhelmed Roman forces.

The disappearance of the legal framework of unity and order that had persisted to the final days of the West-ern Roman Empire and the fragmentation of allegiance among kings, nobles, and chieftains dramatically changed the political landscape of western Europe. In region after region, the traditional, family-based law of the Germanic peoples supplanted the edicts of the Roman emperors.

Roman order broke down in other ways as well. Fear and physical insecurity led communities to seek the protection of local strongmen. In places where looters and pillagers were likely to appear at any moment, a local lord with a castle where peasants could take refuge was more important than a distant king. Dependency of weak people on strong people became a hallmark of the post-Roman period in western Europe.

From Roman Empire to Germanic Kingdoms

Rome's decline marked more than the end of the mighty empire. It signaled the end of the long era in which the eastern Mediterranean Sea was the center of a group of interrelated societies and economies in Egypt, Syria, Anatolia, and Tunisia. Roman political institutions and military prowess had united the Mediterranean lands, but Rome itself was on the western fringe of the empire, far from the great Eastern cities, such as Athens, Antioch, Damascus, Jerusalem, and Alexandria. The emperors Diocletian and Constantine concerned themselves most with preserving power in the East where population was greatest and the economy strongest.

Left on its own, the Western Roman Empire fragmented in the fifth century into a handful of kingdoms under Germanic rulers. The Franks held much of Gaul; the Visigoths ruled in Spain; Saxons and Angles took over Britain (see Map 10.1). In the sixth century a strong Lombard kingdom ruled northern Italy, and the Byzantines kept footholds in the south and around Ravenna along the east coast. Rome proper lost political importance even though it retained prominence as the seat of the most influential Western churchman, the bishop of Rome. Local noble families competed for control of this position, which acquired over several centuries the title of *pope* along with supreme power in the Western church.

The educated few, more and more to be found among Christian priests and monks, retained a somewhat simplified form of Latin. But the vulgar Latin of the uneducated masses rapidly evolved into Romance dialects—Portuguese, Spanish, French, Italian—except in northern and northeastern Europe, where Latin was too poorly established to stand in the way of Germanic and Scandinavian dialects. Thus Europe divided roughly into three linguistic zones: (1) countries in the west and south speaking Romance languages, (2) countries in the north and center speaking Germanic and Scandinavian languages, and (3) countries in the east speaking the Slavic languages of peoples who moved westward on the heels of the Germanic folk migrations.

New invasions continued to disrupt western Europe. In 711 a frontier raiding party of Arabs and Berbers, acting under the authority of the Muslim ruler in

Visigothic Crown of King Recceswinth from Seventh–Century Spain   Jewelry was one of the best-developed Germanic arts. Set with thirty pearls and thirty sapphires, this gold crown features pendant letters spelling "Reccesvinthus Rex Offerata" ("King Recceswinth Offers It").   (Museo Archeologico, Madrid)

Damascus, in Syria, crossed the Strait of Gibraltar and overturned the kingdom of the Visigoths in Spain (see Chapter 9). The Europeans were too disunited to stop them from consolidating their hold on the Iberian Peninsula. After pushing the remaining Christian chieftains into the Pyrenees Mountains, the Muslims moved on to France. There they conquered much of the southern coast and penetrated as far north as Tours, less than 150 miles (240 kilometers) from the English Channel, before Charlemagne's grandfather, Charles Martel, stopped their most advanced raiding party in 732.

Military effectiveness was key to the rapid emergence of the Carolingian° family (from Latin *Carolus*, "Charles") as chief protectors of the Frankish kings, then as kings themselves, and finally, under Charlemagne, as emperors. At the peak of Charlemagne's power, the Carolingian Empire encompassed all of Gaul and parts of Germany and Italy, part of the latter territory being assigned to the pope to rule. On the death of Charlemagne's son, Louis the Pious, the empire was divided by the Treaty of Verdun (843) into eastern, middle, and western portions, each to be ruled by one of Louis's sons. The three regions were never reunited, but the Carolingian economic system based on landed wealth and a brief intellectual revival sponsored personally by

Carolingian (kah-roe-LIN-gee-uhn)

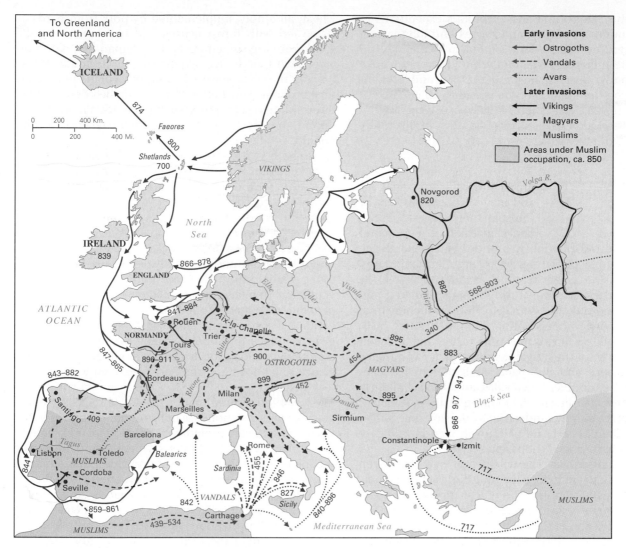

Map. 10.1   Raids and Invasions in the Era of Political Disruption   Early invasions focused on the primary care centers of Roman imperial authority: Rome, Milan, Carthage, and Constantinople. Later invasions reflect the shift of power to northern Europe. In contrast to raids in the northwest, extensive Viking activity along the rivers of eastern Europe consisted partly of establishing authority over Slavic peoples and partly of opening up trade routes to Byzantium and Iran.

Charlemagne—though he was illiterate—provided a common heritage to all three.

A new threat appeared in 793, when the Vikings, sea raiders from Scandinavia, attacked and plundered a monastery on the English coast. Local sources from France, the British Isles, and Muslim Spain attest to widespread dread of Viking warriors descending from multi-oared dragon-prowed boats to pillage monasteries, villages, and towns. In the ninth century, raiders from Denmark and Norway harried the British and

French coasts while Swedish Varangians° pursued raiding and trading interests, and eventually the building of kingdoms, along the rivers of eastern Europe and Russia (see pages 266–268). Although many Viking attacks were private pirate raids for booty and slaves, in the 800s and 900s Viking captains organized the settlement of Iceland, Greenland, and around the year 1000, Vinland on the eastern coast of Canada.

Varangians (va-RAN-gee-anz)

The most important and ambitious expeditions in terms of numbers of men and horses and long-lasting impact were by Vikings long settled in Normandy (in northwestern France). William the Conqueror, the duke of Normandy, invaded England in 1066 and brought Anglo-Saxon domination of the island to an end. Other Normans (from "North men") attacked Muslim Sicily in the 1060s and, after thirty years of fighting, permanently severed it from the Muslim world.

A Self-Sufficient Economy

Archaeological investigations and analyses of records kept by Christian monasteries and nunneries reveal that a profound economic transformation was under way beneath the political jumble of the newly arising Germanic kingdoms. With the ascent of the Germanic peoples, the urban-based civilization of the Romans withered and shrank. Cities built according to Roman architectural and institutional models lost population, in some cases becoming villages. Roads the Romans had built to facilitate the march of their legions and to foster commerce fell into disuse and disrepair. Small thatched houses sprang up beside abandoned villas, and public buildings made of marble became dilapidated in the absence of the laborers, money, and civic leadership needed to maintain them. Purchases paid for in coin largely gave way to the bartering of goods and services.

Trade languished. The wheat that had once been shipped from Egypt to feed the multitudes of Rome now went to Constantinople°. The wheat-growing lands of Tunisia, another of Rome's breadbaskets, were cut off in 439 by an invasion of Germanic Vandals from Spain. Although occasional shipments of goods from Egypt and Syria continued to reach Western ports, for the most part western Europe had to become self-sufficient and rely on its own meager resources. These resources, however, underwent a redistribution.

Roman centralization had long diverted the wealth and production of the empire toward the capital, from which Roman culture radiated outward to the provinces. As Germanic and other territorial lords replaced Roman governors, local self-sufficiency became ever more important, and the general disappearance of literacy and other aspects of Roman civilized life made room for new trends to flourish. These trends were based on local folk cultures, the "small traditions" of the various Germanic and Celtic peoples.

The diet in the northern countries was based on beer, lard or butter, and bread made of barley, rye, or wheat, all amply supplemented by pork from herds of swine fed with forest acorns and beechnuts, and by game from the same forests. The Roman diet based on wheat, wine, and olive oil persisted in the south. Nutritionally, the average western European of the ninth century probably did better than his or her descendants three hundred years later, when population was increasing and the forests were more and more reserved for the nobility.

In both north and south, self-sufficient farming estates known as **manors** became the primary centers of agricultural production. Wealthy Romans had commonly owned country houses situated on their lands. From the fourth century onward, political insecurity prompted common farmers to give their lands to large landowners in return for political and physical protection. The warfare and instability of the post-Roman centuries made unprotected country houses especially vulnerable to pillaging and encouraged the fortification of manors. Isolated by poor communications and lack of organized government, landowners depended on their own resources for survival. Many became warriors or maintained a force of armed men. Others swore allegiance to landowners who had the armed force to protect them.

A well-appointed manor possessed fields, gardens, grazing lands, fish ponds, a mill, a church, workshops for making whatever implements or goods were needed, and a village where the farmers dependent on the lord of the manor lived. The degree of protection that a manor required, ranging from a ditch and wooden stockade to a stone wall surrounding a fortified keep (a stone building), varied with local conditions. The trend was toward ever-greater fortification down to the twelfth century (see Environment and Technology: Castles and Fortifications).

Life on the manor reflected one's personal status. The lord and his family exercised almost unlimited power over their **serfs**—agricultural workers who belonged to the manor. Serfs were obligated to till their lord's fields and were subject to other dues and obligations. They were prohibited from leaving the manor where they were born and attaching themselves to another lord. Particular conditions varied from region to region. The majority of peasants in England, France, and western Germany were unfree serfs in the tenth and eleventh centuries. In Bordeaux°, Saxony, and a few other regions a tradition of free peasantry stemming from the egalitarian social structure of the Germanic peoples during their period of migration still survived. Outright slavery, the mainstay of the Roman economy

---

Constantinople (cahn-stan-tih-NO-pul)

Bordeaux (bore-DOE)

Castles and Fortifications

The word *castle* most often brings to mind great stone fortresses like Krak des Chevalliers, a crusader castle in Syria. These came as the climax of a long evolution, however. The Romans had built square army camps surrounded by stockades to protect their frontiers. Once those frontiers were breached, the new rulers of Europe, each with far fewer men than a Roman legion, turned to smaller fortifications: either a ringwork (a circular wooden stockade surrounding a group of wooden buildings) or, more often, a motte-and-bailey. The motte was an artificial mound with a trench around it and a wooden tower of some sort on top. The bailey was a courtyard or enclosed area with a wooden stockade at the foot of the mound. Archaeologists have identified the remains of over 200 ringworks and 1,050 mottes in Britain, Wales, and Scotland alone, but wood construction has caused most of their buildings to perish.

As security needs increased, some lords and rulers built a keep within the bailey or atop the motte. A keep was a fortified stone building. Castle Acre in England began as a country house surrounded by a fairly weak ringwork. In the mid-twelfth century the mound was raised and the house redesigned as a keep within a smaller, more imposing ringwork. The builders doubled the thickness of the house walls and buried much of the first floor to strengthen the house's foundation. The final twelfth-century version of the keep, looking more like today's image of a castle, was taller, smaller, and surrounded by a still more formidable wall.

Stone walls steadily replaced wooden stockades. Most interior buildings, except for the keep, were of wood, as were drawbridges, stairways, and other essential parts of the fortification. Further advances in castle design featured towers along the walls from which archers shooting through arrow slits could flank enemies attacking the walls; heavily fortified gateways; and a barbican, or fortified gateway, on the far side of the bridge over a moat.

Source: John R. Kenyon, *Medieval Fortifications* (Leicester, England: Leicester University Press, 1990). Used with permission of Girando/Art Resource, NY.

Remains of a Motte and Bailey Castle The immense stone castles of the Crusader era originated in this simple combination of an artificial hill and surrounding earthen rampart. (Aerofilms Limited)

(see Chapter 6), diminished as more and more peasants became serfs in return for a lord's protection.

Early Medieval Society

Europe's reversion to a self-sufficient economy limited the freedom and potential for personal achievement of most of the population. But an emerging class of nobles reaped great personal benefits. During the Germanic migrations, and continuing much later among the Vikings of Scandinavia, men regularly answered the call to arms issued by war chiefs, to whom they swore allegiance. All warriors shared in the booty gained from raiding. But as settlement enhanced the importance of agricultural tasks, laying down the plow and picking up the sword at the chieftain's call became harder to do.

Those who, out of loyalty or desire for adventure, continued to join the war parties included a growing number of horsemen. The mounted warrior was the mainstay of the Carolingian army. At first, fighting from horseback did not make a person either a nobleman or a landowner. By the tenth century, however, nearly constant warfare to protect rights to land or to support the claims of a superior lord brought about the gradual transformation of the mounted warrior into the noble knight—a transformation that led to landholding becoming almost inseparable from military service.

In trying to understand long-standing traditions of landholding and obligation, lawyers in the sixteenth century and later simplified the thousands of individual agreements on the subject into a neat system they called "feudalism." It thus became common to refer to medieval European society as a "feudal society" in which kings and lords gave land to "vassals" in return for sworn military support. By analyzing original records, more recent historians have discovered that this was an oversimplification. Relations between landholders and serfs or between lords and vassals varied a good deal from region to region and over the course of time. Yet military security was a constant concern in most parts of Europe.

The German foes of the Roman legions had equipped themselves with a helmet, a shield, and a sword, spear, or throwing ax. They did not wear body armor. Some rode horses, but most fought on foot. The rise of the mounted warrior as the paramount force on the battlefield is associated with the use of stirrups. Before the invention of the stirrup by Central Asian pastoralists in approximately the first century C.E., horsemen had gripped their mounts with their legs and fought with bow and arrow, throwing javelin, stabbing spear, and sword. Stirrups allowed the rider to stand in the saddle and absorb the impact of his lance striking his enemy at full gallop. This type of warfare required heavy, grain-fed horses rather than the small, grass-fed animals of the Central Asian pastoralists. Thus it was in predominantly agricultural Europe rather than among the nomads of the steppe that charges of mounted knights came to dominate the battlefield.

By the eleventh century, the knight had emerged as the central figure in medieval warfare. He wore an open-faced helmet and a long linen shirt, or hauberk°, studded with small metal disks. A century later, knightly equipment commonly included a visored helmet that covered the head and neck and a hauberk of chain mail. Armor was made for the knight's horse, too.

Each increase in armor for knight and horse entailed a greater financial outlay. Since land was the basis of all wealth, it rapidly became impossible for anyone to serve as a knight who did not have financial support from land revenues. Accordingly, kings began to reward meritorious armed service with grants of land from their own property. Nobles with extensive properties did the same to build up their own military retinues.

A grant of land in return for a sworn oath to provide specified military service was often called a **fief.** At first, kings granted fiefs only on a temporary basis, but by the tenth century, most fiefs could be inherited—by sons from their fathers, for example—as long as the specified military service continued to be provided. Though patterns varied greatly from one part of Europe to another, the association of landholding with military service lent a distinctive cast to medieval European history.

Kings tended to be weak and dependent on their **vassals,** noble followers whose services a king or some other noble might be able to command for only part of the year depending on the agreement between them. Vassals who held land from several different lords were likely to swear loyalty to each one. Moreover, the allegiance that a vassal owed to one lord was likely to entail military service to that lord's master in time of need.

A "typical" medieval realm—actual practices varied between and within realms—consisted of some lands directly owned by a king or a count and administered by his royal officers. Other lands, often the greater portion, were held and administered by the king's or count's major vassals in return for military service. These vassals, in turn, granted land to their own vassals. Instead of taxes, the lands of kings and other nobles yielded primarily military service.

A lord's manor was the effective source of governance and justice in most areas. Direct royal government was quite limited. The king had few financial resources at his disposal and seldom exercised legal jurisdiction at

---

hauberk (HAW-berk)

Noblewoman Directing Construction of a Church   This picture of Berthe, wife of Girat de Rouissillion, acting as mistress of the works is from a tenth-century manuscript but shows a scene from the ninth century. Wheelbarrows rarely appear in medieval building scenes.   (Copyright Bibliothèque royale Albert Ier, Bruxelles, Ms. 6, fol. 554 verso)

a local level. The fact that all members of the clergy, as well as the extensive agricultural lands owned by monasteries and nunneries, fell under the supervision and legal jurisdiction of the church further limited the reach and authority of the monarch.

Noblewomen became enmeshed in the tangle of obligations as heiresses and as candidates for marriage. A man who married the widow or daughter of a lord with no sons could gain for himself control of that lord's property. Entire kingdoms were put together or taken apart through marriage alliances. Noble daughters and sons had little say in marriage matters, for the important issues were land, power, and military service, not the feelings or preferences of individuals. Noblemen guarded the women in their families as closely as their other valuables.

This does not mean that all women lived powerless, sheltered lives. Women could own land. Some noblewomen exercised real power, administering their husband's lands when they were away at war. Women of the manor who were not of the noble class usually worked alongside their menfolk, performing agricultural tasks such as raking and stacking hay, shearing sheep, and picking vegetables. As artisans, women spun, wove, and sewed clothing. One of the greatest works of craft and art surviving from medieval Europe is the Bayeux° Tapestry, a piece of embroidery 230 feet (70 meters) long and 20 inches (51 centimeters) wide designed and executed entirely by women. It depicts in cartoon form the story of the invasion of England in 1066 by William the Conqueror.

Dhuoda°, a ninth-century Frankish noblewoman, reflected the social distinctions of early medieval society in the counsel she gave her son on how to direct his prayers. She urged young William to pray for "kings and all those of the highest ranks" at the pinnacle of society, then, in descending order, for his lord, his father, his enemies, and a final group consisting of the wayfarer, the infirm, the poor and suffering, and "all sorts of others whom I have omitted here." Among the omitted were the serfs of the manor. Notably, Dhuoda placed one category above even the king. "Pray first," she writes, "for the bishops and all the priests, that they may pour forth to God pure and worthy prayers for you and for all the people."[2] Already by her time the Christian church was showing promise of being the one institution capable of combating the political fragmentation, social stratification, and warfare of post-Roman Europe.

Bayeux (bay-YUH)   **Dhuoda** (do-OH-dah)

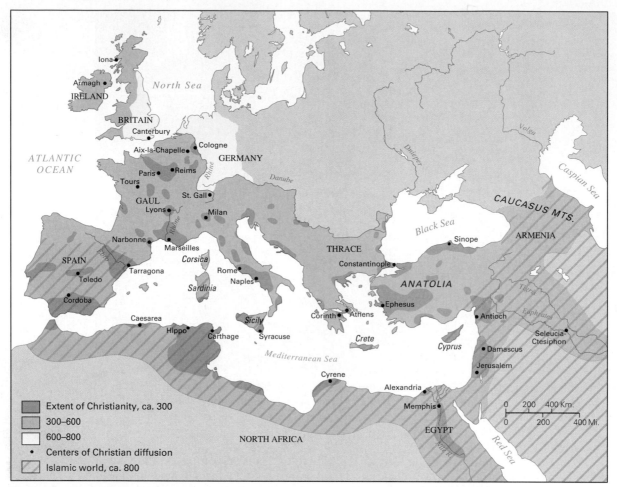

Map. 10.2   The Spread of Christianity   By the early eighth century, Christian areas around the southern Mediterranean from northern Syria to northern Spain, accounting for most of the Christian population, had fallen under Muslim rule; the slow process of conversion to Islam had begun. This accentuated the importance of the patriarchs of Constantinople, the popes in Rome, and the later converting regions of northern and eastern Europe.

THE WESTERN CHURCH

The Christian church was the sole institution claiming jurisdiction over, and the loyalty of, large segments of Europe's population. The growing Christian populations in eastern Europe recognized the authority of the patriarch of Constantinople, even in Slavic lands beyond the control of the Byzantine emperor (see Map 10.2). The pope commanded similar authority over church affairs in western Europe. There, missionaries added territory to Christendom with forays into the British Isles and the lands of the Germans.

Regional disagreements over church regulations, shortages of educated and trained clergy, difficult communications, political disorder, and the general insecurity of the period were formidable obstacles to unifying church standards and practices. By the eleventh century, clerics in some parts of western Europe were still issuing prohibitions against the worship of rivers, trees, and mountains and other superstitions. Problems confronting the church included lingering paganism and lax enforcement of prohibitions against practices such as clergy marrying, nepotism (giving preferment to one's close kin), and simony (selling ecclesiastical appointments, often to people who were not members of the clergy). The persistence of the **papacy**—the office of the pope—in asserting

The Penitentials of Saint Patrick

The medieval church believed that Christians could be absolved of their sins by performing public or private penalties, or acts of humiliation. Priests listened to the believers confess their sins and then set the nature and duration of the penance. Books called penitentials *guided the priests by stipulating the appropriate penance for specific sins. These books varied over time and from region to region and tended to reflect local conditions. One of the earliest is attributed to Saint Patrick, who began his missionary work in Ireland in 432. The selections below deal not just with penalties for sin but also with efforts to impose church discipline on priests.*

§ There shall be no wandering cleric in a parish.

§ If any cleric, from sexton [church caretaker] to priest, is seen without a tunic, and does not cover the shame and nakedness of his body; and if his hair is not shaven according to the Roman custom, and if his wife goes about with her head unveiled, he shall be alike despised by laymen and separated from the Church.

§ A monk and a virgin, the one from one place, the other from another, shall not dwell together in the same inn, nor travel in the same carriage from village to village, nor continually hold conversation with each other.

§ It is not permitted to the Church to accept alms from pagans.

§ A Christian who believes that there is a vampire in the world, that is to say, a witch, is to be anathematized [condemned by the Church]; whoever lays that reputation upon a living being, shall not be received into the Church until he revokes with his own voice the crime that he has committed and accordingly does penance with all diligence.

§ A Christian who defrauds anyone with respect to a debt in the manner of the pagans, shall be excommunicated [barred from Christian society] until he pays the debt.

How do these rules reflect a mixed Christian-pagan society? What do they indicate about the moral character and discipline of Christian clergy at that time?

Source: John T. McNeill and Helena M. Gamer, *Medieval Handbooks of Penance* (New York: Columbia University Press, 1938), 77–78.

---

its legal jurisdiction over clergy, combating heretical beliefs, and calling on secular rulers to recognize the pope's authority constituted a rare force for unity and order in a time of disunity and chaos.

The Structure of Christian Faith

From the fourth century onward, divisions on matters of doctrine endangered the Christian church. Jesus' disciples had established Christian communities, or patriarchates°, in Jerusalem, Antioch, Alexandria, and Rome. Most Christians recognized the heads of these early communities, called patriarchs, as the paramount leaders of the church. In the fourth century the emperor Constantine made his capital city, Constantinople, a fifth patriarchate. The patriarchs appointed bishops throughout the regions that recognized their authority, and each bishop consecrated

patriarchate (PAY-tree-ar-kayt)

priests within his area of jurisdiction, called a diocese. Church rules could be set by the patriarch or by councils of bishops, and priests were expected to follow these rules in serving the needs of ordinary believers (see Society and Culture: The Penitentials of Saint Patrick).

Commemoration of Christ's sacrifice on the cross in the consumption of bread and wine in the Mass, or church service, along with rituals related to birth, marriage, and death were central priestly duties. But church leaders did not always agree on the precise form of rituals or which rituals should be considered sacred mysteries, or sacraments. Before baptism became standardized as a ritual for newborns, for example, it was sometimes postponed until late in life so that the person baptized could benefit from the forgiveness of sin that it conveyed.

The church hierarchy was intended to ensure consistency in Christian belief throughout the Christian community. But church leaders sometimes disagreed on important matters of belief as well as on rituals. One area of disagreement centered on Jesus' relationship to God the Father and to the Holy Spirit. Christians generally agreed that these together formed a divine Trinity in which three aspects or manifestations of God were somehow united. But they did not all understand the Trinity in the same way. They also disagreed on such matters as whether Mary was the mother of God, or the mother of a man named Jesus; and on whether images of God or Jesus or Mary, called icons, were proper objects to pray before because they stimulated pious thoughts, or whether praying before them was too much like praying to pagan statues.

Disagreements like these could lead to charges and countercharges of heresy, beliefs or practices that were so unacceptable as to be un-Christian. Charges of heresy were important to ordinary people, even when they involved hard-to-understand theological issues, because they involved the ultimate issue of salvation. They also threatened the unity of the Christian church at a time when political fragmentation was rapidly increasing.

The most severe challenges to ecclesiastical authority arose in North Africa and the lands of the eastern Mediterranean and resulted in **schism**°—a formal division resulting from disagreements about doctrine. Monophysite° doctrine, for example, emphasized the divinity of Jesus Christ and minimized his human characteristics. It persists to this day: the Coptic Church of Egypt, the Ethiopian Church, and the Armenian Apostolic Church all accept it.

The common way of dealing with challenges to Christian unity was for a council of bishops to deliberate and declare a particular doctrine true or false. In the East, the Byzantine emperor claimed the authority to call such conferences. In the West, the pope took the lead after the tenth century, when Roman nobles lost control of the papacy and it became a more powerful international office. Schismatics—believers in heretical ideas—could call conferences of their own. Councils of bishops set rules, called canons, to regulate the priests and lay people (men and women who were not members of the clergy) under their jurisdiction.

The doctrine that most endangered church unity in western Europe was Arianism°, which was widespread among the Germanic peoples. Although the teaching of the Alexandrian bishop Arius that Jesus was a creation of God the Father and a lesser sort of divinity was declared heretical in 325 at the Council of Nicaea° called by the emperor Constantine (see Chapter 6), it did not quickly disappear.

Charges of heresy focused on matters of doctrine but often reflected underlying social or political issues, such as the desire of Monophysite Egyptians to resist the authority of Constantinople. In some cases, practices as ordinary as the wearing of beards—permitted in the Byzantine East but forbidden in the Latin West—or the way of shaving a priest's head stirred local desires for ecclesiastical independence. The overriding issue in such cases was *orthopraxy*, "correct practices," rather than *orthodoxy*, "correct beliefs." Ireland, in particular, challenged Rome in the eighth and ninth centuries by extolling its own church practices and exporting them to Scotland, Britain, France, and Switzerland by means of missionaries who established important monasteries like Iona, off the Scottish coast, and Saint Gall in Switzerland.

Politics and the Church

In politically fragmented western Europe, the pope needed allies. He found them in rulers like Charlemagne, who upheld papal rights in return for religious legitimization of his rule. Charlemagne's descendants, however, did not maintain his empire intact, and not until 962, with the papal coronation of a "Holy Roman Emperor" (Charlemagne never held this title), did a secular political authority come into being that claimed to represent general Christian interests. Essentially a loose confederation of German princes who named one of their own to the highest office, the **Holy Roman Empire** had little influence west of the Rhine River.

Although the pope crowned the early Holy Roman Emperors, he was not necessarily their political superior. The law of the church (known as canon law) accorded the pope exclusive legal jurisdiction over all clergy and church property wherever located. But bishops who held land as vassals owed military support or other services and dues to kings and princes. The secular rulers argued that they should have the power to appoint those bishops because that was the only way to ensure that they would fulfill their duties as vassals. The popes disagreed.

In the eleventh century, this conflict over the control of ecclesiastical appointments came to a head. Hildebrand°, an Italian monk, capped a career of reforming and reorganizing church finances by being named Pope Gregory VII in 1073. His personal notion of the papacy (preserved among his letters) represented an extreme position, stating among other claims, that

§   The pope can be judged by no one;

---

schism (SKIZ-uhm)   **Monophysite** (muh-NAH-fi-site)
Arianism (AIR-ree-uh-niz-uhm)   **Nicaea** (neye-SEE-uh)

Hildebrand (HILL-de-brand)

§   The Roman church has never erred and never will err till the end of time;
§   The pope alone can depose and restore bishops;
§   He alone can call general councils and authorize canon law;
§   He can depose emperors;
§   He can absolve subjects from their allegiance;
§   All princes should kiss his feet.[3]

Such claims antagonized lords and monarchs, who had become accustomed to *investing,* that is, conferring such things as a ring and a staff as symbols of authority on bishops and abbots in their domains. Historians use the term **investiture controversy** to refer to the struggle to control ecclesiastical appointments; the term also refers to the broader conflict of popes versus emperors and kings. When Holy Roman Emperor Henry IV defied Gregory's reforms, Gregory excommunicated him in 1076, thereby cutting him off from church rituals. Stung by the resulting decline in his influence, Henry stood barefoot in the snow for three days outside a castle in northern Italy waiting for Gregory, a guest there, to receive him. Henry's formal act of penance induced Gregory to forgive him and restore him to the church, but the reconciliation, an apparent victory for the pope, did not last. In 1078, Gregory declared Henry deposed. The emperor then forced the pope to flee from Rome to Salerno, where two years later, Gregory died, supported only by Sicily's Norman rulers.

Yet the reforming legacy of Gregory VII survived. The struggle between the popes and emperors continued until 1122, when a compromise was reached at Worms, a town in Germany. In the Concordat of Worms, Emperor Henry V renounced his right to choose bishops and abbots or bestow upon them spiritual symbols such as a staff and a ring. In return, Pope Calixtus II permitted the emperor to invest papal appointees for the position of bishop or abbot with any lay rights or obligations before their spiritual consecration. This was essentially a victory for the church, though not a complete or lasting one.

Assertions of royal authority triggered conflicts in other areas as well. Though barely twenty when he became king of England in 1154, Henry II, a great-grandson of William the Conqueror, instituted reforms designed to strengthen the power of the Crown and weaken the nobility. He appointed traveling justices to enforce his laws. He made juries, a holdover from traditional Germanic law, into powerful legal instruments. He established the principle that criminal acts violated the "king's peace" and should be tried and punished in accordance with charges brought by the Crown instead of in response to charges brought by victims.

Henry had a harder time controlling the church. His closest friend, the chancellor, or chief administrator, of England, was Thomas à Becket (ca. 1118–1170). A supporter of the king, Becket was a typical courtier who lived in a grand and luxurious manner. In 1162 Henry persuaded Becket to become a priest in order to assume the position of archbishop of Canterbury, the highest church office in England. Becket agreed but warned Henry that if he became an official of the church, he would act solely in the interest of the church when it came into conflict with the Crown. Accordingly, when Henry sought to try clerics accused of crimes in royal instead of ecclesiastical courts, Archbishop Becket, now leading an austere and pious life, resisted.

In 1170 four of Henry's knights, knowing that the king desired Becket's death, murdered the archbishop in Canterbury Cathedral. Their crime backfired, however. An outpouring of sympathy caused Canterbury to become a major pilgrimage center, and in 1173 the pope declared the martyred Becket a saint. Henry allowed himself twice to be publicly whipped in penance for the crime, but his authority had been badly damaged.

Although the Latin Church repeatedly and effectively defended its claim as the sole arbiter of doctrinal religious truth, the investiture controversy and Henry II's conflict with Thomas à Becket yielded no clear victor. Western Europe was heir to three legal traditions: (1) feudal law, with roots in Germanic custom; (2) canon, or church, law based on Roman precedent in its visualization of a single hierarchical legal institution with jurisdiction over all of Western Christendom; and (3) Roman law, a great compilation of Roman imperial decrees that after centuries of disregard began to be studied anew at the fledgling University of Bologna°, in Italy, around 1088. This pattern of conflicting legal theories and jurisdictions became a noteworthy feature of western European civilization and one that set the region apart from the Byzantine Empire, Russia, and the Muslim states that succeeded the Byzantines in Syria, Egypt, and Tunisia (see Chapter 9).

Monasticism

Another distinctive feature of Western Christendom in the medieval period was **monasticism.** The origins of monasticism lay in the eastern lands of the Roman Empire. Practices such as celibacy, continual devotion to prayer, and living apart from society (alone or in small groups) were not new, but they came together in Christian form in Egypt. A fourth-century

Bologna (boe-LOAN-yuh)

account portrays Anthony, perhaps the most important hermit monk, as a pious desert dweller continually tempted by Satan. On one occasion, "when he was weaving palm leaves . . . that he might make baskets to give as gifts to people who were continually coming to visit him . . . he saw an animal which had the following form: from its head to its side it was like a man, and its legs and feet were those of an ass."[4] As was his custom, Anthony prayed to God upon seeing this sight, and Satan left him alone.

In western Europe holy hermits given to mystic visions were comparatively few, though not unknown in Ireland. The most important form of monasticism involved groups of monks or nuns living together in a single community. Benedict of Nursia (ca. 480–547), in Italy, began his pious career as a hermit in a cave but eventually organized several monasteries, each headed by an abbot. The Rule he wrote to govern the monks' behavior emphasizes celibacy, poverty, and obedience to the abbot. Those who lived by this or any other rule were called *regular clergy*, in contrast with *secular clergy*, who followed no code of regulations.

The Rule of Benedict was the starting point for most forms of western European monastic life and remains in force today in Benedictine monasteries. It discusses both ritual activities and everyday life in passages like the following:

> §   Since the spirit of silence is so important, permission to speak should rarely be granted even to perfect disciples, even though it be for good, holy, edifying conversation. . . . If anything has to be asked of the Superior, it should be asked with all the humility and submission inspired by reverence. But as for coarse jests and idle words or words that move to laughter, these we condemn everywhere with a perpetual ban. . . .
>
> §   Let clothing be given to the brethren according to the nature of the place in which they dwell and its climate. . . . In ordinary places the following dress is sufficient for each monk: a tunic, a cowl (thick and woolly for winter, thin or worn for summer), a scapular [sleeveless cloak] for work, stockings and shoes to cover the feet. The monks should not complain about the color or the coarseness of any of these things, but be content with what can be found in the district where they live and can be purchased cheaply.[5]

Monastic life removed thousands of pious men and women from towns and villages and thus reinforced the tendency toward separation of religious affairs from ordinary politics and economics. Jesus' axiom that one should "render unto Caesar what is Caesar's and unto God what is God's" was taken seriously in the monastery

despite the fact that many bishops who were based in towns controlled vast properties and numerous retainers and behaved like lords.

Monasteries were the primary centers of literacy and learning in the centuries following the decline of the Western Empire, although a few rulers, like Charlemagne, encouraged scholarship at court. Many lay nobles were illiterate and interested only in warfare and hunting. Monks (but seldom nuns) saw copying manuscripts and even writing books as part of their religious calling. Were it not for monks of the ninth century, most ancient works in Latin would have disappeared.

Monasteries and nunneries served other functions as well. A few planted Christianity in new lands, as Irish monks did in parts of Germany. Most serviced the needs of travelers, organized agricultural production on their lands, and took in infants abandoned by their parents. Nunneries provided refuge for widows and other women who lacked male protection in the harsh medieval world or who desired a spiritual life. All such religious houses, however, presented problems of oversight to the church. A bishop might have authority over an abbot or abbess (head of a nunnery), but there was no way to exercise constant vigilance over what went on behind monastery walls.

An influential movement of reform arose within the monastic establishment itself at the Benedictine abbey of Cluny° in eastern France. Cluny was founded in 910 by William the Pious, the first duke of Aquitaine, who completely freed it of lay authority. A century later Cluny gained similar freedom from the local bishop. Its abbots then embarked on a vigorous campaign, in alliance with reforming popes like Gregory VII, to improve the discipline and administration of European monasteries. A magnificent new abbey church, designed in the Romanesque° style with small arched windows and heavy stone walls, symbolized Cluny's claims to eminence. With later additions, it became the largest church in the world.

At the peak of Cluny's influence, nearly a thousand Benedictine abbeys and priories (lower-level monastic houses) in various countries accepted the authority of the abbot of Cluny. The Benedictine Rule had presumed that each monastery would be independent; the Cluniac reformers stipulated that every abbot and every prior (head of a priory) be appointed by the abbot of Cluny and have had personal experience of the religious life of Cluny. The Cluniac movement set the pattern for the organizations of the monasteries, cathedral clergy, and preaching friars that would dominate ecclesiastical life in the thirteenth century.

Cluny (KLOO-nee)   **Romanesque** (roe-man-ESK)

Illuminated Manuscript from Monastic Library   This page from the Book of Kells, written around 800 in Ireland, contains the Greek letters chi and rho, or CR, a monogram for Jesus Christ. The intricate interwoven forms that fill the background derive from pagan design traditions that featured intertangled dragons, snakes, and other beasts.   (Trinity College Library, Dublin, Ms. 58, fol. 84v)

Shaping European Society

Christianity profoundly shaped European society. Roman society in Jesus' time had felt comfortable with slavery, religious pluralism, and overt sexuality. Christian society demanded a celibate clergy and discouraged all sex outside marriage, frowned on slavery, and looked on non-Christians as morally dangerous, to be feared and hated.

The fragile legal status of the Jews led them into money changing, goldsmithing, and other trades that they could take with them if forced to move. Rulers and popes protected or expelled Jews to suit their own political and economic ends and whims. When crusading enthusiasm overtook Europe in the early eleventh century (see below), some Christian zealots decided to murder and loot local Jewish communities rather than trek to the Holy Land. Despite these disadvantages, Jewish commu-

nity and intellectual life could be vibrant. Rashi, a commentator on the Bible in eleventh-century France, reached a level of scholarship equal to that of the Jews of Muslim Spain.

Roman society had been based on extended kinship lineages (see Chapter 6). Christian Europe conceived the family in a narrower sense. Christianity provided a framework for social life at all levels. Festivals and rituals, monumental building programs, artistic endeavor of all kinds—everything that conveyed a sense of civilization—manifested itself in Christian form rather than in the worldly trappings of Rome. In the fourth and fifth centuries, Germanic customs and tastes had been seen as overriding and destroying the more sophisticated traditions of Rome. By the year 1200, Christianity had forged in western Europe a new civilization that preserved selected features of the Roman and German past while evolving its own distinctive features.

THE BYZANTINE EMPIRE, 300–1200

European Christian civilization in the eastern region of the old Roman Empire was very different from its counterpart in the West. The Byzantine emperors represented the continuation of Roman imperial rule and tradition and brought to political, social, and religious life a continuity that was almost entirely absent in the West. The Eastern emperors inherited Roman law intact and, exercising an authority known as *caesaropapism,* combining both the imperial ("Caesar") and the papal, made a comfortable transition into the role of all-powerful Christian monarchs. The Byzantine drama, however, played on a smaller and steadily shrinking stage. Territorial losses and almost constant military pressure from north and south deprived the empire of long periods of peace.

Church and State

The Roman emperors who ruled in the East retained many imperial traditions and outlooks that disappeared in the West. In 324, in the nineteenth year of his reign, Constantine led a procession marking out the expanded limits of the city he had selected as his new capital: the millennium-old Greek city of Byzantium, located on a long, narrow inlet at the entrance to the Bosporus strait. In the forum of the new

Constantinople, he erected a 120-foot-tall (36-meter) column topped with a statue of Apollo, and he retained the old Roman title *pontifex maximus*° (chief priest). Nevertheless, he was sympathetic to Christianity, if not at that time a Christian himself, and he studded the city with churches.

The pope in Rome was chosen by ecclesiastical election and eventually claimed complete independence and authority over Western Christendom. In contrast, the Byzantine emperor appointed the patriarch of Constantinople and involved himself in doctrinal disputes over which beliefs constituted heresy. In 325 Constantine called hundreds of bishops to a council at the city of Nicaea (modern Iznik in northwestern Turkey) and persuaded them to reject the Arian doctrine that Jesus was of lesser importance than God the Father. Nevertheless, the Byzantine Empire was torn for centuries by new disputes over theology and by quarrels among the patriarchs of Constantinople, Alexandria, and Antioch. Much of the surviving literature of the Byzantine period is devoted to religious affairs, and it is apparent that religious differences permeated society. As a fourth-century bishop reported: "Everything is full of those who are speaking of unintelligible things. . . . I wish to know the price of bread; one answers, 'The Father is greater than the Son.' I inquire whether my bath is ready; one says, 'The Son has been made out of nothing.'"[6]

In the Byzantine world, in contrast with the West, polytheism died fairly quickly, surviving longest among the country folk (Latin *pagani,* whence the word *pagan* for people who believe in strange gods). The emperor Julian (r. 361–363) tried in vain to restore the old polytheistic faith. When a blind Christian called Julian an apostate (a renegade from Christianity), the emperor said, "You are blind, and your God will not cure you," to which the Christian replied, "I thank God for my blindness, since it prevents me from beholding your impiety." In 392 the emperor Theodosius banned all pagan ceremonies. The following year he terminated the Olympic Games.

Having a single ruler endowed with supreme legal and religious authority prevented the breakup of the Eastern Empire into a mosaic of petty principalities, but it did not guarantee peace or prosperity. In the fourth century the empire was threatened from the east, along its Euphrates River frontier, by a new Iranian empire ruled by the Sasanid family (see Chapter 9), and from the north by Germanic Goths and the nomadic Huns from Central Asia. Bribes, diplomacy, and occasional military victories persuaded the Goths and Huns either to settle

peacefully or move on toward targets in western Europe. War with the Sasanids, however, recurred for almost three hundred years. Finally, a new enemy appeared from the Arabian peninsula: followers of the Arab prophet Muhammad, who between 634 and 650 destroyed the Sasanid Empire and captured Egypt, Syria, and Tunisia. By the end of the twelfth century, at least two-thirds of the Christians in the former Byzantine territories had adopted the Muslim faith.

The loss of these populous and prosperous provinces permanently reduced the power of the Byzantine Empire, and its political path was generally downward. Although it survived until 1453, its later emperors were continually threatened by the Muslims to the south and by newly arriving Slavic and Turkic peoples to the north. At the same time, relations with the popes and princes of western Europe steadily worsened. In the mid-ninth century the patriarchs of Constantinople had challenged the territorial jurisdiction of the popes of Rome and some of the practices of the Latin Church. These arguments worsened over time and in 1054 culminated in a formal schism between the Latin Church and the Orthodox Church—a break that has been only partially mended. This ill will did not prevent Eastern and Western Christians from cooperating in some measure during the crusading era of the twelfth century. But it contributed to the decision by the leaders of the Fourth Crusade (see below) to sack Constantinople in 1204 and establish Latin principalities on Byzantine territory.

Society and Urban Life

The maintenance of imperial authority and the accompanying urban prosperity in the eastern provinces of the old Roman Empire buffered Byzantium against the population losses and severe economic decline suffered in the West from the third century on. Nevertheless, a similar though less pronounced transformation set in around the seventh century, possibly sparked by the loss of Egypt and Syria to the Muslims. Narrative histories give scant coverage to this period, but saints' lives show a transition from stories about educated saints hailing from cities to stories about saints originating as peasants. In many areas, barter replaced money transactions, cities declined in population and prosperity, and the traditional class of local urban notables nearly disappeared.

The disappearance of that class left a social gap between the high-ranking aristocrats at the imperial court and the rural landowners and peasants. By the end of the eleventh century, a family-based military aristocracy

---

pontifex maximus (PAHN-tih-fex MAX-ih-muhs)

somewhat similar to the landed nobility of western Europe had emerged. Of Byzantine emperor Alexius Comnenus° (r. 1081–1118) it was said: "He considered himself not a ruler, but a lord, conceiving and calling the empire his own house."

The situation of women changed, too. Earlier Roman family structure had been loose, and women had been comparatively active in public life. Now the family became a more rigid unit, and women increasingly found themselves confined to the home by their husbands and social custom. When they went out in public, they concealed their faces behind veils. The only men they socialized with were family members. Paradoxically, however, from 1028 to 1056 women ruled the Byzantine Empire with their husbands.

To what extent these changes were related to the social conditions that brought about a parallel seclusion of women in the neighboring Islamic countries has not been established. It is likely, however, that the two developments were linked despite the differences in religion. By comparison with Christianity in western Europe, Byzantine Christianity manifested less interest in, or felt less need for, the provision of refuge for women in nunneries. This, too, finds its parallel in the development of Islam.

Economically, the Byzantine emperors continued a Late Roman inclination to set prices, control the provision of grain to the capital city, and monopolize trade in certain goods, like Tyrian purple cloth. Whether government intervention slowed technological development and economic innovation in Byzantium is difficult to determine. As long as merchants and pilgrims hastened to the metropolis of Constantinople from all points of the compass, rare and costly goods were readily available for aristocratic consumption. Yet Constantinople was an exception. Other Byzantine cities suffered declines. And in the countryside, Byzantine farmers continued to use light scratch plows and creaky oxcarts long after farmers in western Europe had adopted heavy plows and efficiently harnessed horses.

Because Byzantium's inheritance from the earlier Roman Empire was so much richer than western Europe's, there was little recognition of the slow deterioration that began in the seventh century. Gradually, however, pilgrims and visitors from the West saw the reality beyond the awe-inspiring, incense-filled domes of cathedrals and beneath the glitter and silken garments of the royal court. An eleventh-century French visitor wrote:

The city itself [Constantinople] is squalid and fetid and in many places harmed by permanent darkness, for the wealthy overshadow the streets with buildings and leave these dirty, dark places to the poor and to travelers; there murders and robberies and other crimes which love the darkness are committed. Moreover, since people live lawlessly in this city, which has as many lords as rich men and almost as many thieves as poor men, a criminal knows neither fear nor shame, because crime is not punished by law and never entirely comes to light. In every respect she exceeds moderation; for, just as she surpasses other cities in wealth, so too, does she surpass them in vice.[7]

The view from the other side was expressed by Anna Comnena, the brilliant daughter of Emperor Alexius Comnenus. She described the Western knights of the First Crusade (1096–1099) as uncouth barbarians, albeit sometimes gifted with an impressive manliness. She even turned her scorn on a prominent churchman and

Byzantine Church from a Twelfth-Century Manuscript   The upper portion shows the church façade and domes. The lower portion shows the interior with a picture or mosaic of Christ enthroned at the altar end.   (Bibliothèque nationale de France)

Alexius Comnenus (uh-LEX-see-uhs kom-NAY-nuhs)

philosopher who happened to be from Italy: "Italos . . . was unable with his barbaric, stupid temperament to grasp the profound truths of philosophy; even in the act of learning he utterly rejected the teacher's guiding hand, and full of temerity and barbaric folly, [believed] even before study that he excelled all others."[8]

By the time of the Crusades, however, the Byzantines knew they were being surpassed by the western Europeans. They had lost their most valuable provinces. Their army played only a supporting role in the conquest of the Holy Land. And most of their maritime commerce was carried in ships from Genoa, Venice, and Pisa. From the sack of Constantinople during the Fourth Crusade in 1204 to its fall in 1453, vestiges of the legendary Byzantine pomp and political intrigue remained. But this heir to the Roman Empire amounted to little more than a small, weak principality centered on a shrunken, looted, and dilapidated Constantinople and a few outlying cities.

Cultural Achievements

Just as the maintenance of imperial authority facilitated the emergence of the Byzantine emperor as the ultimate arbiter of religious disputes, so his power persisted in secular legal affairs. Several emperors ordered collections of laws and edicts to be made. The most famous and complete collection was the *Corpus Juris Civilis (Body of Civil Law)* compiled in Latin by seventeen legal scholars at the behest of the emperor Justinian (r. 527–565). In the late eleventh century, it began to be studied at the University of Bologna and became the basis for *civil* law (as opposed to *canon* and *feudal* law) in western Europe as well. Many modern principles of law were thereby handed on from Roman models, a fact that accounts for the use of some Latin expressions in the legal profession today.

Also of lasting importance from the time of Justinian and his influential wife the empress Theodora is the architectural tradition represented by Hagia Sophia°, the great domed cathedral of Constantinople. Domed buildings, which required careful calculation of the stress of the stone dome's weight, were comparatively rare in the western lands of the Roman Empire. But they evolved splendidly in Byzantium, creating enormous spaces with an aesthetic appeal completely different from that of the long, lofty naves of Western cathedrals. The great architects of the Italian Renaissance (fifteenth and sixteenth centuries) had Byzantine models in mind when they turned their hand to designing domes for Catholic churches.

Other important Byzantine achievements date to the empire's long period of political decline. In the ninth century, two brothers named Cyril and Methodius embarked on a highly successful mission to the Slavs of Moravia (part of the modern Czech Republic). They preached in the local language, and their followers perfected a writing system, called Cyrillic°, that came to be used by Slavic Christians adhering to the Orthodox—that is, Byzantine—rite.

KIEVAN RUSSIA, 900–1200

After the fall of Byzantium, Russia became the paramount center of Orthodox Christianity and heir to the Byzantine imperial tradition. Russia, however, was a land unlike any ruled directly by the Byzantine emperors and quite unlike western Europe. The territory between the Black and Caspian Seas in the south and the Baltic and White Seas in the north divides into a series of zones running from east to west. Frozen tundra in the far north gives way to a cold forest zone, then a more temperate forest, then a mix of forest and steppe grasslands, and finally just grassland. Several navigable rivers running from north to south cross these zones.

Early historical sources refer to peoples in this region speaking widely varying languages and shifting territorially from century to century, seemingly under pressure from various poorly understood population migrations. Most of the Germanic peoples, along with some Iranian and west Slavic peoples, migrated westward in Roman times. Most of those who remained were eastern Slavs, except in the far north and south: Finns and related peoples lived in the former region, Turkic-speakers in the latter.

The societies that emerged in this broad territory varied widely. Forest dwellers, farmers, and steppe nomads complemented each other economically. Nomads exchanged animals for the farmers' grain, and honey, wax, and furs from the forest also were important trade items. Traders could travel east and west by steppe caravan, as they did in periods when the Silk Road passed north of the Caspian and Black Seas, or they could move north and south on the Volga, Dnieper°, and Don Rivers.

The most active river traders were Scandinavians, relatives of the Vikings who are called Varangians in early sources. They exchanged forest products and slaves for manufactured goods and Muslim silver coins at markets controlled by the Khazar Turks, whose powerful kingdom centered around the mouth of the Volga River.

Hagia Sophia (AH-yah SOH-fee-uh)

Cyrillic (sih-RIL-ik)   **Dnieper** (d-NYEP-er)

Cathedral of Saint Dmitry in Vladimir
Built between 1193 and 1197, this Russian Orthodox cathedral shows Byzantine influence. The three-arch façade, small dome, and symmetrical Greek-cross floor plan strongly resemble features of the Byzantine church shown on page 265.   (Sovfoto)

The Rise of the Kievan State

Historians have debated the early meaning of the word *Rus* (from which *Russia* is derived), but at some point it began to refer to societies of western Slavs ruled by Varangians. Most of the Slavs were farmers. The Varangian princes and their *druzhina* (military retainers), unlike western European lords, lived in cities. The princes were interested primarily in trade and fending off enemies. Their most important cities were Kiev°, which controlled trade on the Dnieper River, and Novgorod°, which played the same role on the Volga. The Dnieper flows into the Black Sea, so the Kievan Rus traded more with Byzantium than with the Muslim world. The semilegendary account of their conversion to Christianity must be seen against this background.

In 980, Vladimir° I, a former ruler of Novgorod, returned from exile to Kiev with a band of Varangians and made himself the grand prince of **Kievan Russia**. Though his grandmother Olga had been a Christian, Vladimir built a temple on Kiev's heights and placed there the statues of six gods, the deities of his Slavic subjects. Vladimir, however, seems to have wanted to use religion to strengthen Kiev's relations with surrounding territories. The earliest Russian chronicle reports that he and his advisers decided against Islam as the official religion because of its ban on alcohol, rejected Judaism (the religion to which the Khazars had converted) because

Kiev (KEE-yev)   **Novgorod** (NOHV-goh-rod)

Vladimir (VLAD-ih-mir)

they thought that a truly powerful god would not have let the ancient Jewish kingdom be destroyed, and even spoke with German emissaries advocating Latin Christianity. Eventually Vladimir chose Orthodox Christianity to be the religion of the Kievan state because of the magnificence of Constantinople. After visiting Byzantine churches, his agents reported: "We knew not whether we were in heaven or on earth, for on earth there is no such splendor of [sic] such beauty, and we are at a loss how to describe it. We know only that God dwells there among men, and their service is finer than the ceremonies of other nations."[9]

After choosing a reluctant bride from the Byzantine imperial family, Vladimir converted to Orthodox Christianity, probably in the year 988, and opened his lands to the influence of Orthodox clerics and missionaries. The patriarch of Constantinople appointed a metropolitan (chief bishop) at Kiev to govern ecclesiastical affairs. Churches were built in Kiev, one of them atop the ruins of Vladimir's earlier pagan temple. Writing was introduced, using the Cyrillic alphabet devised earlier for the western Slavs. The steady progression of Orthodox Christendom northward provided a barrier against the eastward expansion of Latin Christianity. Kiev also became firmly oriented toward trade with Byzantium and turned its back on the Muslim world, though the Volga trade continued through Novgorod.

Struggles within the ruling family and with other enemies, most notably the steppe peoples of the south, marked the later political history of Kievan Russia. But down to the time of the Mongols in the thirteenth century (see Chapter 12), the state retained its identity and served as an instrument for the Christianization of the eastern Slavs.

Society and Culture

In Kievan Russia, political power was more closely linked with trade than with landholding, so the manorial agricultural system of western Europe never developed there. Farmers practiced shifting cultivation of their own lands. They would burn a section of forest and then lightly scratch the ash-strewn surface with a plow. When fertility waned, they would move to another section of forest. Because the land was poor and the growing season short in the most northern latitudes, food was not always abundant. Living on their own estates, the druzhina were making the transition from infantry to cavalry warfare and focused more on horse breeding than on agriculture.

The population of large cities like Kiev and Novgorod may have reached 30,000 or 50,000—roughly the size of contemporary London or Paris but far smaller than Constantinople or major Muslim metropolises such as Baghdad or Nishapur. Many cities in Kievan Russia were scarcely more than fortified trading posts. Yet they served as centers for the development of crafts, some, such as glassmaking, based on skills imported from Byzantium. Artisans enjoyed a higher status in society than peasant farmers. Construction was mainly of wood, although Christianity brought with it the building of stone cathedrals and churches on the Byzantine model.

Christianity penetrated the general population slowly. Several pagan uprisings occurred in the eleventh century, particularly in times of famine. Most of the resistance to the official religion was passive. Some groups rejected Christian burial and persisted in cremating the dead and keeping the bones of the deceased in urns. Women were slow to stop using pagan designs on their clothing and bracelets, and as late as the twelfth century they turned to pagan priests for charms to cure sick children. Most scandalous to some of the clergy were traditional Slavic marriage practices. Monogamy did not easily displace more casual and polygamous relations.

Eventually, Christianity was triumphant, however, and with success came increasing church engagement in political and economic affairs. In the twelfth century, Christian clergy became involved in government administration, some of them collecting fees and taxes related to trade. Direct and indirect revenue from trade provided the rulers with the money they needed to pay their soldiers. The rule of law also spread as Kievan Russia experienced its peak of culture and prosperity in the century before the Mongol onslaught.

WESTERN EUROPE REVIVES, 1000–1200

Between 1000 and 1200, western Europe slowly emerged from nearly seven centuries of subsistence economy—an economy in which most people who worked on the land could meet only their basic needs for food, clothing, and shelter. Population and agricultural production climbed, and a growing food surplus found its way to town markets, enhancing the return of a money-based exchange economy and providing support for larger numbers of craftspeople, construction workers, traders, and artisans engaged in cloth making.

Historians have attributed western Europe's revival to population growth spurred by new technologies and to the appearance in Italy and Flanders (modern Belgium and Holland) of self-governing cities devoted primarily to trade and seafaring. Among the beneficiaries of these changes were kings, who began the long process of improving central administration, gaining greater control over their vassals, and consolidating realms that eventually became strong national kingdoms.

The Role of Technology

A lack of concrete evidence indicating how widespread various technological innovations were and exactly when they appeared frustrates efforts to relate the exact course of Europe's revival to technological change. Nevertheless, most historians agree that technology played a significant role in the near doubling of the population of western Europe between 1000 and 1200. The population of England, for example, seems to have risen from 1.1 million in 1086 to 1.9 million in 1200, and the population of the territory of modern France seems to have risen from 5.2 million to 9.2 million over the same period.

Some innovations that seem to have become increasingly widespread after the year 1000 are credited with launching the economy of western Europe into a robust and productive stage. An example that illustrates the difficulty of drawing historical conclusions from scattered evidence of technological change concerns the use of efficient draft harnesses for pulling wagons and a new type of plow. The Roman plow, which farmers in southern Europe continued to use, merely scratched the soil. The new plow had a coulter (blade), which made a vertical cut in the soil, and a moldboard, which lifted and turned the layer of soil cut loose by the plowshare. It was well suited to bite through the heavy, wet soil of the northern river valleys. Over time, the new harness and new plow contributed to the emergence of the horse as western Europe's primary work animal, replacing the ox in many areas. In no other part of the world did the draft horse become so important.

A mystery surrounds the adoption of harnesses that did not strangle a horse pulling a heavy load, as the old-style harnesses derived from the yoke tended to do. The **horse collar,** which lowers the point of traction from the animal's neck to its shoulders, first appears around 800 in a miniature painting, and it is shown clearly as a harness for plow horses in the Bayeux Tapestry, embroidered after 1066. The breast-strap harness, which is less well adapted for the heaviest work but was preferred in southern Europe, seems to have appeared around the year 500. In both cases, linguists have tried to trace key technical terms to Chinese or Turko-Mongol words and have argued for technological diffusion across Eurasia.

Yet third-century Roman farmers in Tunisia and Libya used both types of efficient harness to hitch horses and camels to plows and carts. This technology, which is still employed in Tunisia, is clearly depicted on Roman bas-reliefs and lamps, but there is no more evidence of its movement northward into Europe than there is of efficient harnessing moving across Asia. Thus the question of whether efficient harnessing began in 500 or in 800, or was known even earlier but not extensively used, cannot easily be resolved.

Hinging on this problem is the question of when and why landowners in northern Europe began to use teams of horses to pull plows through the moist, fertile river-valley soils that were too heavy for teams of oxen. Stronger and faster than oxen, horses increased the productivity of these and other lands by reducing the number of hours needed for plowing. This development undoubtedly contributed to a greater agricultural surplus, but the breeding of larger horses for knightly warfare may have been as important a factor as the new technology in starting the move away from oxen.

Cities and the Rebirth of Trade

Associated with the growth of population was the appearance, first in Italy and Flanders and then elsewhere, of independent cities governed and defended by communes of leading citizens. Lacking the extensive farmlands that had been nearly the sole basis of wealth in western Europe since the decline of Rome, these cities turned to manufacturing and trade. Equally important, they won for themselves a legally independent position between the jurisdiction of the church and that of the secular lord and therefore could frame their laws specifically to favor manufacturing and trade. These laws made serfs free, so these cities attracted many migrants from the countryside. Cities in Italy that had shrunk within walls built by the Romans now pressed against those walls, forcing the construction of new ones. Pisa built a new wall in 1000 and expanded it in 1156. Other twelfth-century cities that built new walls include Florence, Brescia°, Pavia, and Siena°.

Venice was a new city situated on a group of islands at the northern end of the Adriatic Sea that had been largely uninhabited in Roman times. In the eleventh century it rose to become the dominant seapower in the Adriatic. With its rivals Pisa and Genoa on the western side of Italy, Venice competed for leadership in the trade of goods from Muslim ports in North Africa and the eastern Mediterranean. A somewhat later merchant's list

Brescia (BREH-shee-uh)   **Siena** (see-EN-uh)

Vertical Two-Beam Loom   These women weavers set up their loom out-of-doors. The vertical strands are the warp threads around which the weft is interwoven. The pole across the bottom of the loom holds the warp threads taut. The kneeling weaver holds a beater to compact the weft at the loom's bottom. In Europe, horizontal looms were more common and paved the way for the mechanization of weaving.   (Trinity College, Cambridge, Ms. R17, 1, f. 263.1)

mentions some 3000 "spices" (including dyestuffs, textile fibers, and raw materials) being traded, among them alum (for dyeing), 11 types; wax, 11 types; cotton, 8 types; indigo, 4 types; ginger, 5 types; paper, 4 types; and sugar, 15 types; along with cloves, caraway, tamarind, dragon's blood (a scarlet pigment), and fresh oranges.

Ghent, Bruges°, and Ypres° in Flanders were the only northern cities that could rival the Italian cities in prosperity, trade, and industry. Enjoying comparable independence based on privileges gained by their communes from the counts of Flanders, these cities centralized the wool trade of the North Sea, transforming raw wool from England into woolen cloth that enjoyed a very wide market.

An additional sign of the upturn in economic activity was more abundant circulation of coinage. In the ninth and tenth centuries, most gold coins had come from Muslim lands and Byzantium. They were rarely seen in Germany, France, and England because they were worth too much for most trading purposes. In western Europe the standard coin for centuries was the widely imitated Carolingian silver penny. With the economic revival of the twelfth century, silver coins began to be minted locally in Scandinavia, Poland, and other outlying regions. In the following century the reinvigoration of Mediterranean trade made possible a new and abundant gold coinage.

Bruges (broozh)   **Ypres** (EEP-r)

The Crusades

The **Crusades,** a series of Christian military campaigns against Muslims in the eastern Mediterranean, dominated the politics of Europe from 1100 to 1200 (see Map 10.3). Though touted as a series of religiously inspired military campaigns designed to recapture the Holy Land, on the eastern shore of the Mediterranean, from the Muslims, they actually were a culmination of the social and economic currents of the eleventh century: First, reforming leaders of the Latin Church interested in softening the warlike tone of society popularized the Truce of God. This was a movement to limit fighting between Christian lords by specifying times of truce, such as during Lent (the 40 days before Easter) and on the Sunday sabbath. Knights were attracted by the idea of warfare approved by the church. Second, ambitious rulers were looking for new lands to conquer, an objective best represented by the Norman invasions of England and Sicily. Knights, particularly younger sons in areas where the oldest son inherited everything, were increasingly anxious about lacking the land they needed to maintain their noble status. Third, Italian merchants were eager to increase trade in the eastern Mediterranean and to acquire trading posts in Muslim territory.

Several factors focused attention on the Holy Land, which had been under Muslim rule for four centuries. Pilgrimages were particularly important. **Pilgrimage** was an important aspect of religious life in western

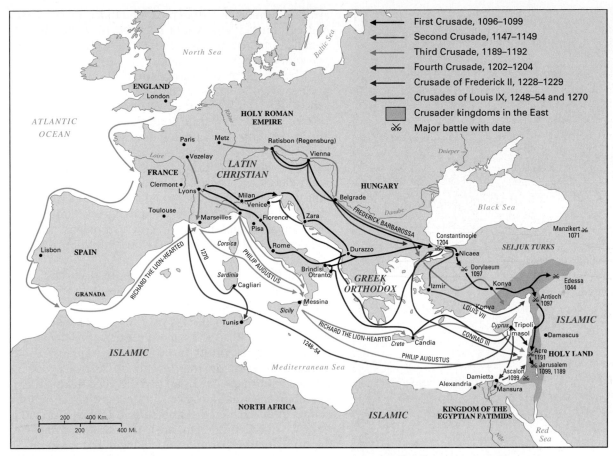

Map. 10.3   The Crusades   The first two Crusades proceeded overland through Byzantine territory. The Third Crusade included contingents under the French and English kings, Philip Augustus and Richard the Lion-Hearted, that traveled by sea, and a contingent under the Holy Roman Emperor Frederick Barbarossa that took the overland route. Frederick died in southern Anatolia. Later Crusades were mostly seaborne, with Sicily, Crete, and Cyprus playing important roles.

Europe. Pilgrims traveled in special costume under royal protection. Some were actually tramps, thieves, beggars, peddlers, and merchants using pilgrimage as a safe way of traveling. Others were deeply affected by the old churches and sacred relics preserved in Rome, Constantinople, and Jerusalem. Genuinely pious pilgrims often journeyed to fulfill a vow or to atone for a sin.

Knights who followed a popular pilgrimage route across northern Spain to pray at the shrine of Santiago de Compostela learned of the expanding campaigns of the Christian kings to dislodge the Muslims. Others heard of the war conducted by seafaring Normans against the Muslims in Sicily, whom they finally defeated in the 1090s after thirty years of fighting.

The tales of pilgrims returning from the East further induced both churchmen and nobles to consider the

Muslims a proper target for Christian militancy. Muslim rulers, who had controlled Jerusalem, Antioch, and Alexandria ever since the seventh century, generally tolerated and protected Christian pilgrims. But after 1071 that changed when a Turkish army defeated the Byzantine emperor at the Battle of Manzikert and opened the way for Turkish nomads to spread throughout Anatolia (see Chapter 9). Ancient centers of Christianity previously under Byzantine control were now threatened with absorption into the growing Muslim political realm, and this peril was duly reported back to western Europe.

From time to time the Byzantine emperor Alexius Comnenus suggested to the pope and western European rulers that they help him confront the Muslim threat. In 1095, at the Council of Clermont, Pope Urban II responded. He addressed a huge crowd of people gathered

Armored Knights in Battle This painting made around 1135 shows the armament of knights at the time of the Crusades. Chain mail, a helmet, and a shield carried on the left side are the rider's primary defenses. The lance carried underarm and the sword are the primary weapons. Notice that riders about to make contact with lances have their legs straight and braced in the stirrups and riders with swords and in flight have bent legs. (Pierpont Morgan Library/Art Resource, NY)

in a field and called on them, as Christians, to stop fighting one another and go to the Holy Land to fight Muslims.

"God wills it!" exclaimed voices in the crowd. People cut cloth into crosses and sewed them on their shirts to symbolize their willingness to march on Jerusalem. Thus began the holy war now known as the "First Crusade," a word taken from Latin *crux* for "cross." People at the time, however, spoke not of a "crusade" but of *peregrinatio,* a "pilgrimage." Indeed, the Crusades were basically

armed pilgrimages. Urban promised that crusaders who had committed sins would be freed from the normal penance, or acts of atonement, the usual reward for peaceful pilgrims to Jerusalem.

The impact of the Crusades on the Islamic world was not nearly so great as on Europe, even though the invaders did establish four small principalities along the eastern Mediterranean at Jerusalem, Edessa°, Antioch, and Tripoli, the last surviving until 1289. Knights of the higher nobility who became the rulers of these new principalities instituted European-style laws and granted Latin clergy ecclesiastical jurisdiction despite the fact that most local Christians owed allegiance to Constantinople. Later Crusades saw western Europe's most powerful kings embarking on lengthy campaigns to show their might and prove their piety, but they seldom stayed long in the Holy Land.

The three Crusades of the eleventh and twelfth centuries signaled the end of western Europe's centuries of intellectual isolation. Sicily, seized from the Muslims, yielded treasures in the form of Arabic translations of Greek philosophical and scientific works and equally important original works by Arabs and Iranians. Spain yielded an even greater bounty to translators who worked in both the Christian and the Muslim kingdoms. Later, Greece was ransacked for ancient Greek manuscripts after the Venetians persuaded the leaders of the Fourth Crusade in 1204 to satisfy their financial debts by capturing Constantinople and taking over, for a century, most of the shrunken Byzantine Empire. Generations passed before all these works were translated into Latin and studied, but they eventually transformed the thought of the western Europeans, who previously had had little familiarity with Greek writings except through Latin intermediaries.

CONCLUSION

The collapse of imperial Rome was not a unique phenomenon in world history. China's Han dynasty (see Chapter 6) and the Abbasid Caliphate (Chapter 9) both dissolved into successor states, as had Alexander the Great's short-lived empire in the fourth century B.C.E. (Chapter 5). Although the chaos, disunity, and economic regression that post-Roman western Europe experienced were particularly severe, the cultural vitality that emerged from the centuries of disorder bears comparison with

Edessa (ih-DESS-suh)

other instances. The Hellenistic Age, which followed the death of Alexander in 323 B.C.E., was a remarkable period of intellectual, religious, and scientific ferment and creativity. The Tang Empire, which emerged in China in the seventh century C.E. (Chapter 11), was a powerful new state with a distinctive and lively culture based only in part on survivals from the Han era. And in the Middle East the emergence of a mass society based on the Islamic religion was largely a phenomenon of the period following the collapse of the central Islamic state in the tenth century (Chapter 9). The dynamic development of Islam after this political collapse is remarkably parallel to the overwhelming influence gained by Christianity in western Europe by the end of the twelfth century.

In contrast, the Byzantine Empire continued and built on Roman practices in an economic and political environment that was both more prosperous and more peaceful than that of western Europe. Furthermore, Byzantine society became deeply Christian well before a comparable degree of Christianization had been reached in western Europe. Yet despite their success in transmitting their own version both of Christianity and of the imperial tradition to Russia and to the peoples of the Balkans, the Byzantines largely failed to demonstrate the dynamism and ferment that characterized both the Europeans to their west and the Muslims to their south. The Slavic-Varangian frontier society of Kievan Russia, bears greater comparison with the West though with its own distinctive economy and institutions.

The intermediate periods between empires seem to be unusually creative and culturally dynamic times, as these examples show. Perhaps one reason for this flowering is the opportunity that imperial dissolution affords different localities and peoples to follow their own particular lines of social, economic, and cultural development.

■ Key Terms

Charlemagne	investiture controversy
medieval	monasticism
Byzantine Empire	Kievan Russia
manor	horse collar
serf	Crusades
fief	pilgrimage
vassal	
papacy	
schism	
Holy Roman Empire	

■ Suggested Reading

Of the many general histories of Europe during this period, Roger Collins's *Early Medieval Europe, 300–1000* (1991) is the best survey stressing institutional and political developments. For a focus on the later part of the period see Susan Reynolds, *Kingdoms and Communities in Western Europe, 900–1300*, 2d ed. (1997). Georges Duby, *The Early Growth of the European Economy* (1974), provides an outstanding overview of economic and social history reflecting up-to-date historical methods. Jacques Le Goff, *Medieval Civilization, 400–1500* (1989), puts more stress on questions of social structure. Richard W. Southern, *Western Society and the Church in the Middle Ages* (1970), offers a survey concentrating on the all-important history of the church. The same author's *The Making of the Middle Ages* (1953) is a classic that gives a memorable impression of the period based on specific lives and events. Archibald R. Lewis, *Naval Power and Trade in the Mediterranean, A.D. 500–1100* (1951), offers an unusual focus on war and trade in the Mediterranean Sea and the ebb and flow of power between Christians and Muslims. Susan Reynolds makes the case for not using the term *feudalism* in medieval Europe in *Fiefs and Vassals* (1994).

More specialized studies of economic and technological issues include Lynn White, Jr., *Medieval Technology and Social Change* (1962), a pathbreaking work on technological history; C. M. Cipolla, *Money, Prices and Civilization in the Mediterranean World, Fifth to Seventeenth Century* (1956), an insightful and easily understood explanation of important economic matters, and Cipolla's more general history, *Before the Industrial Revolution: European Society and Economy, 1000–1700* (1980); J. C. Russell, *The Control of Late Ancient and Medieval Population* (1985), a thorough analysis of demographic history and the problems of interpreting medieval European data; and Georges Duby, *Rural Economy and Country Life in the Medieval West* (1990), a detailed portrayal of rural life accompanied by translated documents.

Good works focusing on specific countries include, on France, Pierre Riché, *Daily Life in the World of Charlemagne* (1978), and Georges Duby, *The Chivalrous Society* (1977); on England, Dorothy Whitelock, *The Beginnings of English Society* (1952), and Doris Mary Stenton, *English Society in the Early Middle Ages (1066–1307)* (1951); on Italy, Edward Burman, *Emperor to Emperor: Italy Before the Renaissance* (1991); on Germany and the Holy Roman Empire, Timothy Reuter, *Germany in the Early Middle Ages, c. 800–1056* (1991); on Spain, Bernard F. Reilly, *The Medieval Spains* (1993); and on Viking Scandinavia, Gwyn Jones, *A History of the Vikings* (1984).

Amy Keller, *Eleanor of Aquitaine and the Four Kings* (1950), is an extraordinary biography of an extraordinary medieval woman. Dhuoda, *Handbook for William: A Carolingian Woman's Counsel for Her Son*, trans. Carol Neel (1991), offers a firsthand look at the life of a noblewoman of the Carolingian era. More general works on women include Margaret Wade's classic popular history, *A Small Sound of the Trumpet: Women in Medieval Life* (1986), and Bonnie S. Anderson and Judith

P. Zinsser's *A History of Their Own: Women in Europe from Prehistory to the Present* (1989). In the area of religion, Caroline Bynum's *Jesus as Mother: Studies in the Spirituality of the High Middle Ages* (1982) illustrates new trends in the study of women in this period.

Hans Eberhard Mayer's *The Crusades* (1988) and Jonathan Riley-Smith's *The Crusades: A Short History* (1987) are excellent brief histories of the crusading era. For a longer masterful account, stressing particularly the Byzantine standpoint, see Steven Runciman, *A History of the Crusades,* 3 vols. (1987). Benjamin Z. Kedar, *Crusade and Mission: European Approaches Toward the Muslims* (1988), explains the religious issues underlying the conflict.

The classic account of the revival of trade and urban life is Henri Pirenne's *Medieval Cities: Their Origins and the Revival of Trade* (1952). A similarly influential work is Robert S. Lopez, *The Commercial Revolution of the Middle Ages, 950–1350* (1971). Lopez and Irving W. Raymond have compiled and translated an excellent collection of primary documents dealing with trade and urban life: *Medieval Trade in the Mediterranean World: Illustrative Documents with Introductions and Notes* (1990).

The standard histories of the Byzantine Empire are Georgij A. Ostrogorsky, *History of the Byzantine State* (1969); Alexander Aleksandrovich Vasiliev, *History of the Byzantine Empire,* 2 vols. (1952) and Warren Treadgold, *A History of Byzantine State and Society* (1997). Volume 1 of Vasiliev's work takes the history down to 1081. Cyril Mango's *Byzantium: The Empire of New Rome* (1980) provides a synthesis with a strong emphasis on cultural matters. Later Byzantine history, for which conventional narratives are scarce, is unusually well covered by A. P. Kazhdan and Ann Wharton Epstein in *Change in Byzantine Culture in the Eleventh and Twelfth Centuries* (1985). This book stresses social and economic issues instead of religion and politics and covers broader topics than its title indicates. Kievan Russia is well treated in Janet Martin's *Medieval Russia, 980–1584* (1995).

■ Notes

1. Lewis G. M. Thorpe, *Two Lives of Charlemagne* (Harmondsworth: Penguin, 1969).
2. Dhuoda, *Handbook for William: A Carolingian Woman's Counsel for Her Son,* trans. Carol Neel (Lincoln: University of Nebraska Press, 1991), 83–89.
3. R. W. Southern, *Western Society and the Church in the Middle Ages* (Harmondsworth: Penguin, 1970), 102.
4. Anne Fremantle, *A Treasury of Early Christianity* (New York: New American Library of World Literature, 1960), 400–401.
5. *St. Benedict's Rule for Monasteries,* trans. Leonard J. Doyle (Collegeville, MN: Liturgical Press, 1948), 20–21, 75–76.
6. A. A. Vasiliev, *History of the Byzantine Empire, 324–1453,* vol. 1 (Madison: University of Wisconsin Press, 1978), 79–80.
7. A. P. Kazhdan and Ann Wharton Epstein, *Change in Byzantine Culture in the Eleventh and Twelfth Centuries* (Berkeley: University of California Press, 1985), 255.
8. Ibid., 248.
9. S. A. Zenkovsky, ed., *Medieval Russia's Epics, Chronicles, and Tales* (New York: New American Library, 1974), 67.

11

CENTRAL AND EASTERN ASIA,
400–1200

The Sui and Tang Empires, 589–755 • Fractured Power in Central Asia and
China, to 907 • The Emergence of East Asia, to 1200
ENVIRONMENT AND TECHNOLOGY: Writing in East Asia, 400–1200
SOCIETY AND CULTURE: Poverty on the Land

Buddhism at a Distance   The Buddhist monk Xuanzang returns to the Tang capital Chang'an
from Tibet in 645, his ponies laden with Sanskrit texts.

After the fall of the Han Empire in 220 C.E., its former Han territories were divided among smaller kingdoms often at war with one another. In the warfare that resulted from Han disintegration and competition among the quarreling states, infectious diseases were transmitted from one army to another and spread rapidly to civilians. The scholar Ge Hong° (281–361 C.E.) described epidemics—probably smallpox—afflicting populations in north China and commented sharply on the chaotic circumstances in which the disease spread from Central Asia to northern China: "Because the epidemic was introduced . . . when Chinese armies attacked the barbarians . . . it was given the name of 'Barbarian pox.'"[1] As refugees from the fighting fled south of the Yellow River, they carried the deadly infection with them.

The third to sixth centuries produced not only social dislocation and disease but also remarkable discoveries and inventions. Ge Hong was a Daoist with a strong interest in alchemy, particularly in discovering the elixir of life (a formula for immortality). Though alchemists did not succeed in archieving immortality, their investigations increased knowledge of physiology and permitted refinement and use of stimulants such as ephedrine. Daoists of the time also made significant advances in metallurgy, pharmacology, and mathematics. Ge Hong himself passed to later ages his knowledge of such diverse topics as hallucinogenic drugs, the prevention of rabies, and magnetism.

After China was reunified in the late sixth century, knowledge gained during the centuries of political fragmentation spread over the recentralized networks of trade, travel, and education. Under the Sui° and then the Tang° rulers, scientific and cultural influences were rapidly transmitted not only through China but also throughout Central Asia and East Asia.

After the Tang Empire ended in 907, China, Central Asia, and East Asia dissolved into a number of smaller empires. Many of these societies preserved something of the cultural, scientific, and political heritage of the Tang. Often they were able to advance knowledge gained from the Tang. Song° China, in particular, became famous for its achievements in science, mathematics, and engineering. Korea excelled in printing and textiles, Japan in metallurgy and ceramics. This specialization and diversification of knowledge in turn created new technologies as well as brilliant achievements in economic growth, philosophy, and the arts.

As you read this chapter, ask yourself the following questions:

- What were the bases for the new relationships among the East Asian societies after the fall of the Tang?
- What accounts for the differences in the political roles of Buddhism in Tang China, Tibet, Korea, and Japan after the ninth century?
- What major factor accounts for the scientific and economic advancement of Song China?

THE SUI AND TANG EMPIRES, 581–755

The brief Sui Empire and its long-lived successor, the Tang, sprang from the political diversity of the period of disunion. The fall of the Han Empire had left a power vacuum. It was filled by many small kingdoms with various political styles. Some were run in the Chinese style, with an emperor, a bureaucracy using the Chinese language exclusively, and a Confucian state philosophy (see Chapter 3). Others were affected by the Tibetan, Turkic, and other regional cultures that had dominated in some parts of the former Han Empire, and they depended on Buddhism to legitimate their rule.

Reunification Under the Sui and Tang

In less than forty years the Sui rulers reunified China. They reestablished Confucianism as the central philosophy of government and passed it on to the Tang. But the Sui period is distinctive for the strong political influence of Buddhism, too, and the presence in society of a variety of religious and philosophical beliefs, including Daoism, Nestorian Christianity, and Islam.

Ge Hong (guh hoong)   Sui (sway)   Tang (tahng)

Song (soong)

CHRONOLOGY

	Central Asia	China	Northeast Asia	Japan
200		220–589 China disunited		
	552 Turkic Empire founded			
600		581–618 Sui unification		
	620–640 Tibetan Empire emerges under Songsam Gyampo	618 Tang Empire founded		
		627–649 Li Shimin reign		645–655 Taika era
		690–705 Wu Zhao reign	668 Silla victory in Korea	710–784 Nara as capital
	744 Uigur empire founded			752 "Eye-Opening" ceremony
	751 Battle of Talas River	755–757 An Lushan rebellion		794–1185 Heian era
800		840 Suppression of Buddhism		
	ca. 850 Buddhist political power secured in Tibet	879–881 Huang Chao rebellion		
		907 End of Tang		
			916 Liao Empire founded	
		938 Liao capital at Beijing	918 Koryo founded	
		960 Song Empire founded		ca. 950–1180 Fujiwara influence
1000				ca. 1000 *The Tale of Genji*
		1127–1279 Southern Song period	1115 Jin Empire founded	1185 Kamakura shogunate founded

The Sui rulers built a new capital city near the old Han capital in the Wei° River Valley (modern Shaanxi province). They called this city Chang'an° in honor of the Han capital. To facilitate communication and trade with growing population centers to the south, they built the 1,100-mile **Grand Canal**, linking the Yellow River in northern China with the Yangzi° River in southern China. The Sui also made improvements to the Great Wall, constructed irrigation systems in the increasingly populated regions of the Yangzi River Valley, and waged massive military campaigns against Korea and Vietnam.

Possibly the speed and scale of those undertakings led to the Sui downfall. Such intense military expansion and public works required levels of organization and resources—people, livestock, wood, iron, staple crops—that the Sui could not sustain. Overextension weakened Sui authority and prompted the transition to the Tang.

In 618 the powerful Li family ended Sui rule and created the **Tang Empire** (Map 11.1). Tang rulers maintained the eastern borders established by the Sui and expanded primarily westward into Central Asia, under the brilliant emperor **Li Shimin°** (r. 627–649). The Tang

Wei (way)   **Chang'an** (chahng-ahn)   **Yangzi** (yahng-zeh)

Li Shimin (lee shir-meen)

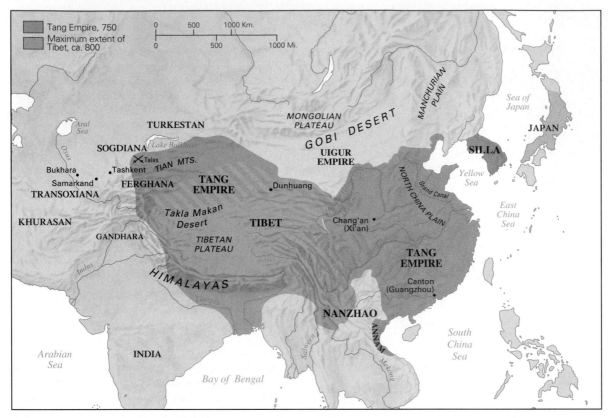

Map 11.1   The Tang Empire in Central and Eastern Asia, 750   For over a century the Tang Empire controlled China and a very large part of Central Asia. The defeat of Tang armies in 751 by a force of Arabs, Turks, and Tibetans at the Talas River near Tashkent ended Tang westward expansion. To the east, the Tang dominated Annam, and Japan and the Silla kingdom in Korea were leading tributary states of the Tang.

avoided overcentralization by allowing local nobles, gentry, officials, and religious establishments to exercise significant power.

The Tang emperors were descendants both of the Turkic elites of the small kingdoms that had existed in northern China after the Han, and of Chinese officials and settlers who had intermarried with the Turks. The Tang nobility was heavily influenced by Central Asian culture but also had knowledge of Chinese traditions. In warfare, for instance, the Tang combined Chinese weapons—the crossbow and armored infantrymen—with Central Asian expertise in horsemanship and the use of iron stirrups. As a result, from about 650 to about 750, the Tang armies were the most formidable on earth.

Buddhism and the Tang Empire

The Central Asian heritage of the Tang rulers was evident in their political use of Buddhism. The religion prescribed a spiritual function for kings and emperors—to bring

humankind into the Buddhist realm. According to this belief, protecting spirits would aid the ruler in the governing of the state and prevent harm from coming to the people living under him. State cults based on this idea were important in the kingdoms of Central Asia and north China after the fall of the Han Empire and were inherited from them by the Sui and the Tang.

In Central Asia, China, and other societies of East Asia, the most important Buddhist school of teaching was Mahayana°, or "Great Vehicle" Buddhism. Mahayana fostered faith in enlightened beings—bodhisattvas—who postpone nirvana (see Chapter 3) to help others achieve enlightenment. Faith in bodhisattvas permitted the absorption of many local gods and goddesses into Mahayana sainthood. Mahayana also encouraged the translation of Buddhist scripture into local languages, and it accepted religious practices that had little or no connection with the written texts. Being open to local deities and local languages and prac-

---

Mahayana (mah-HAH-YAH-nah)

Iron Stirrups This bas-relief from the tomb of Li Shimin depicts the type of horse on which the Tang armies conquered China and Central Asia. The horses were equipped with saddles having high supports in front and back, breastplates, and cruppers, all indicating the importance of high speeds and quick maneuvering on the field of battle. Most significant were the iron stirrups, which were in general use in Central Asia from the time of the Huns (fifth century). The stirrups could support the weight of fully shielded and well-armed soldiers who rose in the saddle to shoot arrows, use lances, or simply urge the horse to greater speeds. (University of Pennsylvania Museum, neg. #S8-62844)

tices made Mahayana Buddhism adaptable to many different societies and appealing to all classes of people. The tremendous reach of the Mahayana communities invigorated travel, language learning, and cultural exchange throughout Central and East Asia.

Because of its social, cultural, and political influence, Buddhism was an important ally of the early Tang imperial family. Princes competing for political influence enlisted monastic leaders to pray for them, to preach openly for them, to counsel aristocrats to support them, and—perhaps most important—to contribute part of their monasteries' considerable wealth to the princes' war chests. In return, the monasteries received tax exemptions, land privileges, and gifts from a prince who might become emperor.

The spread of Buddhism in Central Asia (see Chapter 8) and East Asia was fostered by the growth of empires and trade. As the Tang Empire expanded westward, Tang contacts with Central Asia and India increased and so did the complexity of Buddhist influence throughout China. Chang'an, the Tang capital, became the center of a continent-wide system of communication. Central Asians, Tibetans, Vietnamese, Japanese, and Koreans regularly visited the capital, and when they left they took away with them the most recent ideas and styles in Tang religion, philosophy, and the arts. In this way, the Mahayana network connecting Central Asia and China intersected with a vigorous commercial world where material goods and cultural influences mixed. Regional variety coexisted with shared knowledge of Buddhism, Confucianism, and other philosophies. Familiarity with written Chinese coexisted with regional commitments to other languages and writing systems. Textiles in Persian, Korean, and Vietnamese styles mixed with the colorful and changing attire of the period, while influences from every part of Asia were apparent in sports, music, and painting. Many historians characterize the Tang Empire as "cosmopolitan" because of its breadth and diversity.

To Chang'an by Land and Sea

The hub of Tang communications was Chang'an. Well-maintained roads and water transport, including the Grand Canal, connected the capital, in the Wei River Valley, to the coastal towns of south China, of which Canton (Guangzhou°) was most important. Chang'an was the destination of ambassadors and students sent to the Tang rulers as part of what is often called the **tributary system.** This was a practice, begun in Han times, in which independent countries acknowledged the supremacy of the emperor based in China by sending regular embassies to the capital to pay tribute. Thus Chang'an functioned as the cultural and economic capital of eastern Asia.

The Wei River Valley had been heavily populated since Han times. During the Tang period, Chang'an had something over a million people, of whom only a minority lived in the central city. Most people lived in the suburbs that extended out from each of the main gates. Many dwelt in specialized towns in the countryside—

Guangzhou (gwahng-jo)

such as the towns responsible for maintaining the imperial tombs or operating the nearby imperial resort, where aristocrats relaxed in sunken tile tubs while the steamy waters of the natural springs swirled around them.

The market networks of Chang'an kept the city's economy vibrating. Roads connected the capital city and its suburbs to the smaller cities, towns, and villages lying to the south and east along the Yellow River. Special compounds in Chang'an, including living accommodations and general stores, were established for foreign merchants, students, and ambassadors. Restaurants, inns, temples, mosques, and street stalls along the main streets kept busy every evening. At curfew, generally between eight and ten o'clock, commoners had to return to their neighborhoods, which were enclosed by brick walls and wooden gates that guards locked until dawn to control crime.

Market roads, major long-distance roads, caravan routes (including the Silk Road), sea routes, and canals all brought people and commerce toward Chang'an. The Grand Canal was especially important. Special armies patrolled the canal, special boats were designed for travel on it, special towns were built along it, and a special budget for its maintenance was established. The Grand Canal contributed to the economic and cultural development of eastern China. After the fall of the Tang Empire, rulers of China founded their capitals in the eastern part of the country largely because of the economic and political effects of the Grand Canal.

During the Tang period, Chinese control of what is now coastal southern China was consolidated. This increased Chinese access to the Indian Ocean, a factor in the spread of Islamic and Jewish influence to East Asia. The uncle of Muhammad is credited with erecting the Red Mosque at Canton in the mid-seventh century. By the end of the Tang period, the combined Western Asian population in Chang'an alone was probably well over 100,000 people.

At this time Chinese seamen were famous for their skills in compass design and shipbuilding. Tang ocean-going craft were renowned for their size. Government shipbuilding was limited to the construction of grain transport vessels, which plied the Chinese coastal cities and the Grand Canal. But commercial ships, built to connect the southern Chinese port cities to the Philippines and Southeast Asia, had twice the carrying volume of ships of the Byzantine and Abbasid Empires. Their purpose was to move large amounts of goods over increasing distances, quite different from the basic warship design of West Asian vessels.

The sea route between West Asia and Canton was also the means of transmitting **bubonic plague** to East Asia. In the fifth century, bubonic plague had moved from North Africa into West Asia. From there, it was transmitted to East Asia. Evidence of plague is found in references to Canton and south China in the early 600s. The pestilence found a hospitable environment in parts of southwestern China, and it lingered long after the near eradication of the disease in West Asia and Europe.

The trade and embassy routes of the Tang Empire quickly became channels for transmission of plague to Korea, Japan, and Tibet. All three experienced their first outbreaks after the establishment of diplomatic ties with Chang'an in the seventh century. Unlike their contemporaries in Europe and West Asia, city dwellers in East Asia soon learned to control the spread of plague, but the disease persisted in isolated rural areas.

Tang Integration

During the Tang period, influences from Central Asia and the Islamic world vividly affected the material culture of China. Lively new animal motifs from Iran and Central Asia brightened ceramics, painting, and silk designs, and life-size sculpture became common. In north China, clothing styles changed. Working people stopped wearing robes and adopted pants, introduced by horse-riding Turks from Central Asia. Cotton, which the Central Asian trade conveyed in large and affordable quantities, gradually replaced hemp in clothes worn by commoners. New pastimes included polo, also introduced from Central Asia and strongly promoted by the Tang court (which, following with Central Asian tradition, allowed noblewomen to compete). Music changed as various stringed instruments were imported across the Silk Road, along with the folk melodies of the Central Asian peoples. Food, too, was transformed, by the introduction of grape wine, tea, sugar, and spices.

These influences were signs of changes in China's economy and trade relationships with South Asia, West Asia, and northeastern Africa. In Han times, China's major export had been silk, most of it transported by caravan across Central Asia. During the Tang period, China's monopoly on silk disappeared, and several centers in West Asia became competitive in the production and distribution of basic silk. At the same time, western Asia lost its monopoly in cotton: by the end of the Tang period China had begun to grow and spin its own. This process of "import substitution"—the domestic production and sale of goods that had previously been imported—was also evident in China for tea and sugar.

Tang infrastructure of roads, dredged rivers, and canals facilitated the movement of goods across enormous distances and enhanced the ability of the Chinese economy to increase the quantity and quality of its out-

Tang Women at Polo The Tang Empire, like the Sui, was strongly influenced by Central Asian as well as Chinese traditions. As in many Central Asian cultures, women in Tang China were likely to exercise greater influence in the management of property, in the arts, and in politics than women in Chinese society at later times. They were not excluded from public view, and noblewomen could even compete at polo. The game, widely known in various forms in Central Asia from a very early date, combined the Tang love of riding, military arts, and festive spectacles.   (The Nelson-Atkins Museum of Art)

put. By about the year 1000, the magnitude of exports from Tang territories dwarfed the burgeoning trade between Europe, West Asia, and South Asia. Anecdotal accounts claimed that ships taking on Chinese exports outnumbered ships carrying South Asian, West Asian, European, or African goods by a hundred to one. Whatever the exact figures may have been, the Tang export trade unbalanced the commerce both in Central Asia and in the Indian Ocean.

China remained the source of superior silks. In the Tang period, factories began to create more and more complex styles, partly to counter the modest competition from abroad. China became the sole supplier of porcelain—a very fine kind of ceramic made from unusual clay—to West Asia. As a result, travel across Central Asia, Southeast Asia, and the Indian Ocean increased, and the economies of ports and oases involved in the trade—even those located in very distant places—became increasingly commercialized. The dramatic growth of long-distance trade also created special needs for new instruments of credit and finance.

FRACTURED POWER IN CENTRAL ASIA AND CHINA, TO 907

Between 600 and 750, Central Asia and East Asia saw the creation and expansion of not only the Tang Empire, but also of its rivals, the Uigurs° and Tibet. By about 750, the three had reached some degree of political accommodation. A hundred years after that, in the mid-800s, all three empires were experiencing political decay and military decline. Each one aggravated the problems of the other two, since the collapse of their governments meant that their soldiers, criminals, and freebooters were able to roam without hindrance into neighboring territories to rob, rape, and murder.

In Tang China the effects were felt most strongly because the impact of centralization and integration had been deepest there. All but the pretense to centralized power by the Tang emperors was gone by the early 800s. In the provinces, military governors suppressed the rebellion of the Sogdian general An Lushan°, which raged from 755 to 757, and then seized power for themselves. Farmers were nearly helpless before the demands of local bosses and their private armies. Chang'an and the Tang court were under the control of eunuchs, who publicly tried and executed bureaucrats who opposed them.

The nomadic and partially nomadic economies of parts of Central Asia cushioned the economic blows of social disorder and agricultural losses. But the cities along the caravan routes, which had gloried in the overland trade, had as much to lose as China in the massive political decentralization. In the course of things, the economies of Central Asia and East Asia actually proved resilient. The strongest backlashes were cultural, particularly in China, where disillusionment with Central Asian neighbors and social anxieties combined to fuel a powerful reaction against "foreign" cultures.

Reaction and Repression

After two centuries of widespread Buddhist influence in Tang society, members of the imperial family began to distrust the Buddhist monasteries and blame the Buddhist clergy for political upheavals. In 840 (a year in which Tang society was disintegrating on many fronts) the government moved to crush the economic power and

Uigur (WEE-ger)   **An Lushan** (ahn loo-shahn)

influence of the Buddhist monasteries. This action was followed by a strong reassertion of Confucian ideology by the Tang elites. In the aftermath of the rejection of Buddhism, the rationalist school of "neo-Confucianism" predominated.

Even Chinese gentry living in relatively safe and prosperous localities associated Buddhism with various social ills. Buddhism, with strong historical roots in Central Asia and India, had become a major influence in China when Turkic, Sogdian, and Tibetan influence was at its height. Chinese who worried that "barbarians" were ruining their society could point to Buddhism as evidence of the foreign evil.

Chinese elites claimed that the eradication of Buddhist influence would restore the ancient values of hierarchy and social harmony. Because of Buddhism's disapproval of earthly ties, men and women had to sever relations with the secular world in order to begin the road to enlightenment. They were exempt from taxes and military service. They deprived their families of the advantages that might have been realized from their marriages. And they denied descendants to their ancestors, which was strictly contrary to Confucian teaching. The Confusian elites feared that Buddhism was encouraging the dissolution of the family. Great family estates were fundamental to the economic and political structure of the Tang Empire. Consequently the government and the elites eventually regarded with suspicion anything that endangered the stability of these estates or, by extension, endangered the values of family cohesiveness on which they were founded.

Monasteries, where prayers were continually said for the preservation of the state and the salvation of souls, were exempt from taxes. This economic edge allowed them to purchase land and precious objects and to employ large numbers of serfs. Many wealthy believers gave the monasteries large tracts of land.

Poor people flocked to the monasteries and nunneries to work as artisans, field workers, cooks, housekeepers, and guards. Some were eventually converted to Buddhism and took up the monastic life. Other people came as beggars and then began study of the religion. By the ninth century, hundreds of thousands of people had entered monasteries and nunneries.

Equally worrisome to the Tang elites was the subversive influence of Buddhism with respect to women's roles in politics. Buddhism seemed to undermine the Confucian idea of the family as the model for the state. This was vividly demonstrated when Wu Zhao°, a woman who had married into the imperial family, seized control of the government in 690, declared herself

emperor, and reigned until 705. She tried to establish her legitimacy by claiming that she was a bodhisattva, and she favored Buddhists and Daoists over Confucianists.

In the later Tang era, Confucian writers expressed contempt for Emperor Wu and other powerful women, such as the concubine Yang Guifei°. Bo Zhuyi°, in his poem "Everlasting Remorse," lamented the influence of women at the Tang court, which he wrote had caused "the hearts of fathers and mothers everywhere not to value the birth of boys, but the birth of girls."[2] Confucian elites heaped every possible charge on prominent women who offended them. Yang Guifei was blamed for the An Lushan rebellion. Emperor Wu was accused of grotesque tortures, murders, and other mayhem, including the tossing of dismembered but still living bodies of her enemies into wine vats and cauldrons.

Such characterization of "evil" rulers by Confucian writers was stereotypical, and no serious historian credits the stories about Wu Zhao. In fact she seems to have been a reasonably effective and accepted ruler, who was not deposed until she was incapacitated by extreme old age (she was well over eighty in 705). But, because of the tendency of Confucian historians to describe unorthodox rulers and all powerful women as evil, Wu is among the many people in Chinese history about whom we will never know the facts.

When the Tang dissolved the monasteries, the result was an incalculable loss in cultural artifacts. Many of the great sculptures and grottoes that survived were permanently defaced. Most of the temples and the façades built to shelter the great stone carvings from the weather were made of wood and disappeared in the conflagrations that accompanied suppression of the Buddhist religion. In later times monasteries were legalized again, but Buddhism in China was never afterward the profound social, political, and cultural force it had been in early Tang times.

The End of the Tang Empire

The Tang order was destroyed by the very forces that were essential to its creation and maintenance. The campaigns of expansion in the seventh century left the empire large and powerful but dependent on local military commanders and a complex tax collection system. The Tang drive westward across Central Asia was stopped by a combined army of Arabs, Turks, and Tibetans in 751, at the battle of Talas River near Tashkent (see Map 11.1). The reverses led to demoralization and underfunding of the Tang armies. Suppression of the An Lushan rebellion a

Wu Zhao (woo jow)

Yang Guifei (yahng gway-fay)   Bo Zhuyi (baw joo-ee)

Poverty on the Land

In the Tang period, wealthy landowning families increasingly used their profits on townhouses and conspicuous consumption. Farmers, whose high rents and low pay were contributing to the growing wealth of the gentry, enjoyed fewer direct benefits from the landowners' profits. As the following account by a scholar living during the late 700s makes clear, thoughtful observers feared not only the consequences of extreme imbalances in distribution of wealth between social classes, but also the imbalances between the private incomes of powerful gentry and the income of the government.

When a farmer falls on bad times, he has to sell his field and his hut. If it is a good year, he might be able to pay his debts by selling out. But no sooner will the harvest be in than his storage bins will be empty again, and he will have to try to contract a new debt promising his labor for the next year. Each time he indentures himself he incurs higher interest rates, and soon will be destitute again.

If it is a bad year, and there is a famine, then the situation is hopeless. Families break up, parents separate, and all try to sell themselves into slavery. But in a bad year nobody will buy them.

In these circumstances land prices fall low enough that the rich buy up tens of thousands of acres, or simply seize the land of defaulted farmers. The poor then have no land, and try for places as servants, bodyguards, or enforcers for the rich families. If they manage to attach themselves to the organization of a gentry family, they can borrow seed and grain, and rent land as tenants. Then they will work themselves to death, all year round, without a day off. If they should manage to clear their debts, they live in constant anxiety about when the next bad patch will leave them destitute again.

The gentry, however, live off their rents, with no troubles and no cares. Wealth and poverty are very clearly divided.

This is how we have reached the situation where the rents from private land are much higher, and collected more ruthlessly, than the government's taxes. In areas around the capital, rents are twenty times higher than taxes. Even rents in more remote areas are ten times what the government collects in tax.

How do you interpret the increasing discrepancies in wealth in this period? How do you connect the differences in conditions between the cities and the countryside? What relationship do you see between the economic stratification in the countryside and the economic stratification in the cities? Why would the income of the government relative to the income of the large landowners be a cause for concern?

Source: Adapted from Etienne Balazs, *Chinese Civilization and Bureaucracy: Variations on a Theme*, trans. by H. M. Wright, ed. by Arthur F. Wright. Copyright © 1964. Reprinted by permission of Yale University Press.

few years later required new powers and independence for provincial military governors.

Despite the continuing prosperity of Chinese society, the disintegration of the political system and the elite's sense of cultural decay created an unsettled environment in which many aspiring dictators decided to chance a conquest. The most devastating uprising was the Huang Chao rebellion of 879–881, begun by a disgruntled member of the gentry. The rebellion, which imposed ruthless and violent control over every village it gained, attracted hundreds of thousands of poor farmers and tenants who could not protect themselves from the local bosses, who sought escape from oppressive landlords or taxes, or who simply did not know what else to do in the deepening chaos. (see Society and Culture: Poverty on the Land) The new hatred of "barbarians" was obvious among the rebels, who murdered thousands of foreign residents in Canton and Peking.

Finally a group of local bosses wiped out the rebels, using fully as much violence as the rebels themselves had used. But Tang society did not find peace. Refugees, the urban homeless, and migrant workers became permanent fixtures. Residents of northern China were driven toward the frontier regions of southern China as groups from Central Asia moved into the north.

The Tang Empire ended in 907 and was succeeded by a set of smaller states. Each of them controlled considerable territory, and some of them had lasting historical influence. But none had the Tang's capacity for integrating the economic and cultural interests of vastly disparate territories, or for transmitting goods and knowledge across huge distances. In ensuing centuries, East Asia was fragmented, and its communication with Europe and the Islamic world was obstructed. Important artistic styles, technical advances, and philosophical developments emerged in East Asia, but the particular brilliance that had resulted from the cosmopolitanism of the Tang was not seen again for centuries. Instead, the regional states refined Tang cultural influences and applied Tang technological knowledge.

The Uigur and Tibetan Empires in Central Asia

The fortunes of the Tang Empire were intertwined with the development of Turkic power in Central Asia. The original homeland of the Turks was in the northern part of modern Mongolia. After the fall of the Han Empire, Turkic peoples began moving south and west, through Mongolia, then on to Central Asia, on the long migration that eventually brought them to Anatolia. During most of the period of disunion in East Asia between the Han and Tang Empires, Central Asia was controlled by various Turkic groups, and in 552 a unified Turkic Empire was created. But after the Sui reunited China in 589, internal warfare among the Turks weakened their control of Central Asia. In the mid-600s the Turkic Empire was split in two. This fissure in the power of the Turks was one factor that allowed the Tang Empire under Li Shimin to establish control over Central Asia. Within about a century, however, much of Central Asia was under the control of a new Turkic group, the **Uigurs**.

Under the Uigurs, Central Asia's great cities of Bukhara, Samarkand and Tashkent (see Map 11.1)—all critical to the caravan trade—enjoyed a literate culture with strong ties to both the Islamic world and China. The Uigurs were famous as merchants and as professional scribes able to transact business in the many languages of the region. They had adapted the Sogdians' syllabic script, related to the Syriac script used in West Asia, to the writing of Turkic. This new script made possible several innovations in Uigur government, such as the change from a tax paid in kind (with products or services) to a money tax and, later, the minting of coins. An urban culture embracing the Buddhist classics, religious art based on the styles of northern India, and clothing, tools, and architecture revealing the mixture of East Asian and Islamic styles flourished in the Uigur Empire.

Unified Uigur power lasted only about half a century, and afterward only Tibet remained as a rival to the Tang Empire for influence in Central Asia. Tibet at this time was a large and stable empire in its own right, critically positioned at the meeting point of China, Southeast Asia, South Asia, and Central Asia. Because of this location, the variety of cultural influences in Tibet was extraordinary. In the seventh century, Chinese Buddhists began to route their pilgrimages to India through Tibet, so contacts between India and Tibet also flourished. It was from India that Tibetans took their alphabet, and from India also came a variety of artistic and architectural influences. From both India and China the Tibetans learned of mathematics, astronomy, and divination, as well as the cultivation of grains and the use of millstones. From Central Asia and the Middle East came knowledge of Islam and of the monarchical traditions of Iran and Rome. From Iran came knowledge of the medical science of the Greeks, which the Tibetan royal family favored over all other forms of healing.

In the time of Li Shimin, the rulers of Tang and Tibet were cautiously friendly to each other. They declared an alliance when a Tang princess, called Kongjo by the Tibetans, was sent to Tibet to be the Tibetan king's wife in 634. The arrival of Kongjo was also the arrival in Tibet of Mahayana Buddhism, which combined with the native religion to create a distinctive local religious style. In recognition of the close relationship between the empires, Tibet sent ambassadors to join Koreans, Japanese,

Monument to an Early Turk   The Turks originated in the northern part of what is now Mongolia. The flat expanses of the steppes, shown here in present-day Tuva, in Asiatic Southern Russia, suited the Turks and their herds. Steppe geography allowed constant communication between eastern Iran and western China. This monument to an unknown Turkic leader, probably of the late 500s, looks out over lands similar to those through which the Silk Road passed.   (Sergei I. Vainshtein, Institute of Ethnography, Moscow)

Women of Turfan Grinding Flour Women throughout Central Asia and East Asia were critical to all facets of economic life. In the Turkic areas of Central Asia, women commonly headed households, owned property, and managed businesses. These small figurines, made to be placed in tombs, portray women of Turfan—a Central Asian area crossed by the Silk Road—performing tasks in the preparation of wheat flour. (Xinjiang Uighur Autonomous District Museum)

and other peoples as students in the Tang imperial capital at Chang'an.

This regular contact, together with the influence of Buddhism, consolidated the relationship between the Tang and Tibetan Empires for a time. The Tibetan kings, like the early emperors of the Tang, encouraged the growth of Buddhist religious establishments and prided themselves on their role as cultural intermediaries between India and China. But Tibet also excelled at war. Horses and armor, both of which were introduced through contacts with the Turks, were used and improved by the Tibetans to a level that startled even the Tang. By the late 600s, the Tang emperor and the Tibetan king were rivals for religious leadership and political dominance in Central Asia, and Tibet was extending its sway not only into Central Asia but also through what are now Qinghai°, Sichuan° and Xinjiang° provinces in China. The small independent kingdom of Nanzhao°—ruled by a people related to the modern Miao people of southwestern China—allied itself with Tibet in the struggle against Tang. This alliance threatened the critical Tang extension across Turkestan into Central Asia. Peace between Tibet and Tang was restored only after the allied armies ended Tang expansion at Talas in 751.

But peace did not create political similarities between the two societies. At about the time of the suppression of Buddhism in China in the 800s, a new king in Tibet decided to follow the Tang lead and eradicate the political and social influence of the monasteries. The result in Tibet was very different. Monks assassinated the king, and control of the Tibetan royal family passed into the hands of religious leaders. In ensuing years the system of monastic domination isolated Tibet from surrounding regions and drew around Tibet a veil of timeless mysticism.

THE EMERGENCE OF EAST ASIA, TO 1200

Just as in the aftermath of the Han period, so in the aftermath of the Tang new states emerged and competed to inherit the legacy of the dissolved empire. Earliest and in some ways most distinctive was the Liao° Empire of the Kitan° people, who established their rule in the north, at what is now Beijing°, immediately after the overthrow of the last Tang emperor. Soon after, the Minyak people (closely related to the Tibetans) established a large empire in what is now western China and called themselves "Tangguts°" to show their connection with the former empire. In 960 the **Song Empire** was established in central China.

During the complex time in which these competing empires dominated East Asia, the ongoing relationship between East Asia and Central Asia characteristic of earlier times ended. Sea connections among East Asia, West Asia, and Southeast Asia continued, and the Song in particular distinguished themselves for seafaring and sailing technologies. The Song state struggled under enormous military demands, and members of Song elite society, like the elite of the late Tang, rejected what they considered "barbaric" or "foreign" influences. At the same time, Korea and Japan were strengthening their political and cultural ties with China, and some states of Southeast Asia, relieved that Tang military power no longer threatened them, entered into new, friendly relations with the Song court. The allied societies of East Asia formed a Confucian region in which goods, resources, and knowledge were vigorously exchanged.

Qinghai (CHING-hie) **Sichuan** (SUH-chwahn)
Xinjiang (shin-jee-yahng) **Nan Zhao** (nan-jow)

Liao (lee-OW) **Kitan** (kee-tan) **Beijing** (bay-jeeng)
Tanggut (TAHNG-gut)

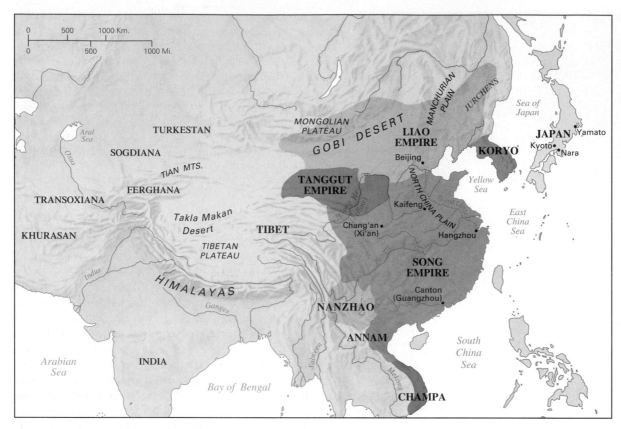

Map 11.2   Liao and Song Empires, c. 1100   The states of Liao in the north and Song in the south generally ceased open hostilities after a treaty in 1005 stabilized the border and imposed an annual payment on Song China.

The Liao and Jin Challenge

In the Liao and other northern empires, significant numbers of people were nomadic or moved from place to place as the seasons changed. The rulers of these empires acknowledged the various economies and social structures of diverse peoples and made no attempt to create a single elite culture. Instead, they encouraged Chinese elites to use their own language, study their own classics, and see the emperor through Confucian eyes, and they encouraged other peoples to use their own languages and see the emperor as a champion of Buddhism or as a nomadic leader. As a consequence, Buddhism was far more powerful than Confucianism in the northern states, where rulers depended on their roles as bodhisattvas or as Buddhist kings to legitimate their power.

The earliest of the states to emerge from the ruins of the Tang was the Liao Empire of the Kitan people, who ruled an expanse from Siberia to Central Asia and thus were intermediaries between the Chinese territories and

all societies to the north and west (Map 11.2). Variations on the name of the Kitans became the name for China in these regions of the world: "Kitai" for the Mongols, "Khitai" for the Russians, and "Cathay" for those, like the contemporaries of Marco Polo, who reached China from the medieval Europe.

The Liao Empire of the Kitans was both large and long-lived, lasting from 916 to 1121. It was the first empire to make the city we now know as Beijing one of its capitals, and relics of the Liao period can still be seen there today. In ceramics, painting, horsemanship, religion, and some forms of architecture, Liao made a lasting contribution to Asian civilization.

The Kitans not only were superb horsemen and archers but quickly adapted siege machines from both China and Central Asia. They were an insuperable military competitor for the Song Empire, which in 1005 agreed to a truce that included enormous payments in cash and silk each year to the Liao Empire in order to forestall further war. Liao and Song worked out an effi-

Silk Painting Depicting Kitan Hunters Resting Their Horses
The artist shows the Kitans' soft riding boots, leggings, and robes (much like those later used by the Mongols) and the Kitans' patterned hairstyle, with part of the skull shaved and some of the hair worn long. Men in Central and North Asia (including Japan) used patterned hairstyles to indicate their political allegiance. The custom was documented in the 400s (but is certainly much older) and continued up to the twentieth century.
(National Palace Museum, Taipei, Taiwan, Republic of China)

cient and sophisticated diplomatic system. But resentment of the economic burdens resulting from the Liao presence eventually led the Song into a secret alliance with the Jurchens of northeastern Asia, also chafing under Liao rule. In 1125 the Jurchens destroyed the Liao capital in Mongolia, announced their own empire—the Jin—and turned against the Song (Map 11.3).

The Jurchens were not nomads. They were hunters and fishers, and were semi-agricultural. But they had imbibed Kitan influence in military arts and political organization. They became formidable enemies of the Song Empire. In 1127 they mounted an all-out campaign that shortly brought the Song capital at Kaifeng° under siege, led to the capture of the Song emperor, and within a few years forced the Song to withdraw south of the Yellow River, leaving central as well as northern China in Jurchen control. The Song, forced to make annual payments to the Jin Empire to avoid open warfare, were confined to southern China, and historians generally refer to this period as the "Southern Song" (1127–1279).

Kaifeng (kie-fuhng)

Song Industries

Though the Song Empire enjoyed a number of complex political and economic relationships with neighboring societies, China in this period did not have access to the far-flung networks of communication that had existed in Tang times. Many of the advances in technology, medicine, astronomy, and mathematics for which Song is famous were based on information that had come to China in Tang times, sometimes from very distant places. Song had the motivation and resources to adapt Tang information and technology to meet practical, sometimes urgent Song requirements, particularly in warfare and colonization and in the development of new methods for managing changes in economy and society.

Like Indian, Uigur, and Middle Eastern scholars of the time, Chinese scholars were absorbed in the arts of measurement and observation. The similarities were not entirely accidental. Chinese knowledge of these things was partly a consequence of the migration of Indian and West Asian mathematicians and astronomers to the Tang Empire. Song mathematicians are the first known to have used fractions, which they originally employed to describe the phases of the moon. From lunar observations, Song astronomers constructed a very precise calendar. They were persistent and methodical observational astronomers—only they, for instance, noted the explosion of the Crab Nebula in 1054. As an outgrowth of their work in astronomy and mathematics, Chinese scholars made significant contributions to timekeeping and development of the compass.

In timekeeping, the most spectacular achievement was construction of the gigantic mechanical celestial clock by the engineer Su Song in 1088. Escapement mechanisms for the control of revolving wheels in clocks had been developed for a water-powered clock under the Tang, as had the application of water wheels to weaving and threshing machines. But this knowledge had not been widely applied. Su Song adapted the escapement and water wheel to his chain-driven clock, the earliest known chain-drive mechanism in history. The clock told the time of the day and the day of the month, and it indicated the movement of the moon and certain stars and planets across the night sky. At the top of the 80-foot (24-meter) structure were an observation deck and a mechanically rotated armillary sphere. The clock was a monument to the Song ability to integrate observational astronomy, applied mathematics, and engineering.

Familiarity with celestial coordinates, particularly the Pole Star, refined the production of compasses in the Song era. Long known in China, in Song times the magnetic compass was reduced in size and attached to a fixed stem

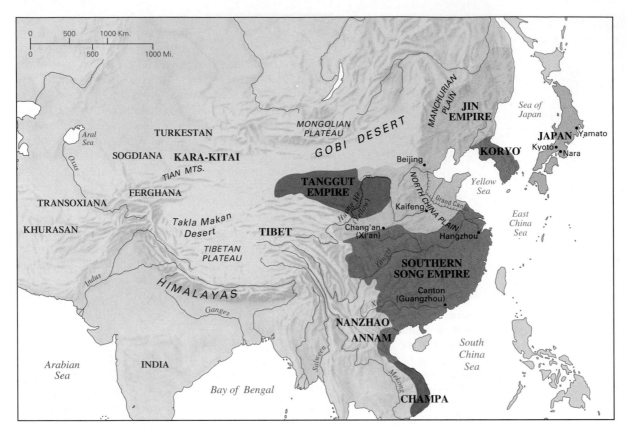

Map 11.3   Jin and Southern Song Empires, c. 1200   After 1127 Song was forced to abandon its northern territories to Jin. In the ensuing century Southern Song had to continue the policy of annual payments—to Jin rather than Liao—and maintain high military preparedness to prevent further invasions. (From John King Fairbank, et al., *East Asia: Tradition and Transformation*, rev. ed., p. 165. Copyright © 1989 by Houghton Mifflin Company.)

and in some instances was put into a small protective case that had a glass covering for the needle. These changes made the compass suitable for seafaring; the first attested naval application was in 1090. The Chinese compass and the Greek astrolabe, introduced later, improved navigation throughout Southeast Asia and the Indian Ocean.

Development of the seaworthy compass coincided with the improvement of techniques in the building of **junks.** A stern-mounted rudder improved the steering of the large ships in uneasy seas, and watertight bulkheads helped keep them afloat in emergencies. The merchants of the Persian Gulf quickly adopted these features.

The Song technological explosion was stimulated not only by a vibrant and expanding economy but also by military pressure from the Liao and Jin Empires. The Song Empire was less than half the size of the Tang, but its army was four times as large—about 1.25 million men (roughly the size of the present-day army of the United States of America). For military leadership, the Song employed men educated specially for the task, examined on military subjects, and paid regular salaries.

Because of the importance of iron and steel to warfare, the iron ore and coal regions of north China were constant sites of military confrontation between the Song and their northern rivals. The volume of Song mining and iron production (which once again became a government monopoly in the eleventh century) was huge. By the end of the eleventh century, Song production of cast iron was about 125,000 tons (113,700 metric tons), which in absolute terms would have rivaled the output of eighteenth-century Britain. Engineers became skilled at high-temperature metallurgy. They produced steel weapons of unprecedented strength through the use of enormous bellows, often driven by water wheels, to superheat the molten ore. Song defensive works also incorporated iron, which was impervious to fire or concussion. Bridges and small buildings were made of iron, as was mass-produced body armor for soldiers (in small, medium, and large sizes). Casting and assembly were made more efficient by the refinement of mass-production techniques that had been used in China for nearly two thousand years with bronze and ceramics.

To counter devastating cavalry assaults by the Kitans and Jurchens, the Song experimented with projectiles that could destroy groups of men and horses. **Gunpowder** was used to propel a cluster of flaming arrows into oncoming cavalry. During the wars against the Jurchens in the 1100s the Song introduced a new and terrifying weapon. Shells launched from Song fortifications exploded in the midst of the enemy, blowing out shards of iron. The horrifying result was the dismemberment of men and horses. But the short range of the shells limited them to defensive uses, and they made no major impact on the overall conduct of war.

Economy and Society

Given the continuous military peril and the vigor of Song responses to military challenges, it is remarkable that Chinese elite culture in the Song period idealized civil pursuits. In the social hierarchy the civil man outranked the military man. Private academies, designed both to train men for the official examinations and to develop their intellectual interests, became influential in culture and politics. The neo-Confucianism that had emerged at the end of the Tang became more sophisticated, more idealistic, and much more pervasive during the Song. But popular sects of Buddhism persisted, and elites elaborated on and adopted some folk practices established during the Tang period of close contact with India and Tibet. Best known of these was Chan Buddhism (in Japan known as **Zen,** in Korea as Son), which asserted that salvation was possible through mental discipline alone.

For many scholars, meditation offered relief from preparation for the civil service examinations. The written examination system for officials in China had been introduced during the Tang period. It was a dramatic departure from the tradition of the Han Empire, when officials were hired and promoted on the basis of recommendations. Under the Song, the examination system assumed the form it retained for nearly a thousand years. A large bureaucracy oversaw the design and administration of the examinations. Test questions, which changed each time the examinations were given, often related to economic management or foreign policy.

The social implications of the examinations were strong, for Song society was less bound by hereditary class distinctions than Tang society had been. The new examinations were intended to recruit the most talented men for government service, whether their backgrounds were prestigious or humble. Men from wealthy families, however, were most likely to succeed. The tests required memorization of classics believed to date from the time of Confucius. Preparation was so time-consuming that peasant boys, who had to spend their days working in the fields, could rarely compete.

Success in the examinations brought good marriage prospects, the chance for a high salary, and enormous prestige. Failure could bankrupt a family and ruin a man both socially and psychologically. These were not comforting thoughts for candidates who had to endure days at a time in tiny, airless, almost lightless examination cells, attempting to produce—in beautiful calligraphy—their answers to that year's examination questions.

Test materials were only one type of publication that became much more in demand. Changes in printing, from woodblock to an early form of movable type, allowed cheaper printing of many kinds of informative books. The Song government, like the Tang before it, realized that with its control of the standards for success in the examinations came the ability to indoctrinate millions of ambitious young men—many times the number who eventually would pass the tests. The advancement of printing aided both the ideological goals of the government and the personal goals of the candidates. By the year 1000 the Song state was mass-producing authorized preparation books. Though the examination system did not become egalitarian (a man had to be literate to buy even the cheap preparation books, and basic education was still not common), opportunities for those of limited means to take the examinations did increase, and a moderate number of bureaucrats with no noble, gentry, or elite background entered government service.

The versatility of printing literally changed the Chinese terrain. Printed material explained planting and irrigation techniques, harvesting, tree cultivation, threshing, and weaving. Landlords frequently gathered their tenants and workers together to show them the illustrated texts and explain their meaning. In combination with technological advances, this dissemination of knowledge helped to make possible the development of new agricultural land south of the Yangzi River. Iron agricultural implements such as plows and rakes, which had been introduced in the Tang, were adapted during the Song to wet-rice cultivation as the population moved south. Landowners and village leaders were able to gain information from books on how to fight the mosquitos that carried malaria. Control of the disease allowed more immigration by northerners and a sharp increase in the local population.

Printed material related to farming existed because farming was profitable enough to stimulate the demand for books. Commercial agriculture was among the pursuits that interested the sons of the gentry. Patterns of landholding in central and south China promoted the concentration of landownership in the hands of a few, very wealthy, families. This was partly a consequence of the fact that in

Going up the River Song cities hummed with commercial and industrial activity, much of it concentrated on the rivers and canals linking the capital Kaifeng to the provinces. This detail from the scroll painting *Going Upriver at the Qingming [Spring] Festival* shows only a tiny portion of the panorama that the great scroll represents. Zhang Zeduan, who completed the painting some time before 1125, was a master at the depiction of daily life, and this scroll is one of the most important sources of information on the activities of working people. Here, the open shop fronts and tea houses are clearly displayed, a camel caravan departs, goods are offloaded from donkey carts, a scholar rides loftily (if gingerly) on horseback above the crowd, and sedan-chair carriers transport shaded women of wealth. (The Palace Museum, Beijing)

Tang times what is now south China was still a frontier for Chinese settlers, who could claim extensive tracts of land for themselves before later colonists arrived. In the settlement process, the indigenous inhabitants of the region, who were related to modern-day populations of Malaysia, Thailand, and Laos, were driven into the mountains and southward toward Vietnam.

The prosperity and the vibrant trade of the Song era stimulated population growth. During the 1100s the total population of the Chinese territories rose above 100 million. An increasing proportion of that population was living in large towns and cities. It is not likely that any of the leading Song cities exceeded a million people. But they were still among the largest cities in the world during a period when the great cities of earlier times had declined and the gigantic cities of the modern era had not arisen.

In the Song capitals, multistory wooden apartment houses were common. Often the narrow streets—sometimes little more than 4 or 5 feet (1.2 to 1.5 meters) wide—were so clogged by pedlars or families spending time outdoors that they were impassable. The crush of population demanded expertise in the management of waste and the water supply and in firefighting. Song cities also were adept at controlling urban rodent and insect infestations and thus kept the bubonic plague isolated in a few rural areas for most of the period.

Hangzhou°, in particular, was engineered in such a way that the currents of the nearby river produced a steady flow of water and air through the city, flushing away waste and disease. Turkic, Arab, and European travelers—sensitive to the urban crowding that troubled their own societies—recorded their amazement at the way in which the dangers of Hangzhou's tremendous population density had been managed, while restaurants, parks, bookstores, wine shops, tea houses, and theaters gave beauty and pleasure to the inhabitants.

The idea of credit had been introduced in the Tang period, stimulated by the robust long-distance overland trade, but like many other innovations it was not widely applied until the Song. Intercity or interregional credit—what the Song called "flying money"—depended on the acceptance of guarantees that the paper could be redeemed for coinage at another location. The public accepted the practice because credit networks tended to be managed by families, so that usually brothers and cousins were honoring each other's certificates.

"Flying money" certificates were different from government-issued paper money, which the Song pioneered. In some years, military expenditures consumed as much as 80 percent of the government budget. In dan-

Hangzhou (hahng-jo)

ger of being smothered by this burden, the state attempted to respond to the financial pressure by distributing paper money. But the result was inflation so severe that by the beginning of the 1100s paper money traded for only 1 percent of its face value. Eventually the government withdrew the paper money and tried to meet its expenses by imposing new taxes, selling monopolies, and offering financial incentives to merchants.

The Song economy grew so rapidly that the government could not maintain the huge monopolies and strict regulation that had been traditional in China. As a consequence the Song empire was hard-pressed to gain the revenue it needed to maintain the army, canals, roads, waterworks, and other state functions. Some government functions, such as tax collection, were sold off to privateers, who made their profit by collecting the maximum amount and sending an agreed amount to the government. The result was exorbitant rates for services and much heavier tax burdens on the common people. But the privatization of the economy also created new opportunities for individuals with capital to engage in businesses that previously had been state monopolies.

Now merchants and artisans as well as gentry and officials could make fortunes. Urban life was transformed by the elite's growing taste for fine cloth, porcelain, exotic foods, large houses, and exquisite paintings and books. No longer was land the only source of wealth, and the traditional social hierarchy common to an agricultural economy was weakened by the rise of cities, commerce, consumption, and the use of money and credit. Because many of the new commercial and industrial activities of this period were not under the control of the government or of traditional elites, historians often describe Song China as "modern."

Not everyone's lot in life improved, and for women in China the Song era marked the beginning of a long period of cultural subordination, legal disenfranchisement, and social restriction. This outcome was consistent with the backlash against Buddhism and revival of Confucianism that began under the Tang and intensified under the Song. It also was closely tied to the economic and status concerns of the gentry and the rising merchant classes in China.

Merchants were away from home for long periods of time, and many maintained more than one household. Frequently they depended on their wives to manage their homes and even their businesses in their absence. As women were obliged to assume some responsibility for the management of their husbands' property, they were systematically deprived of the right to control property of their own. Laws were changed in the Song period, so that a woman's property automatically passed

The Players   Women—often enslaved—were used as entertainers at the courts of China from very early times. While Tang art often depicts women with slender figures, among the Tang there was clearly also great tolerance for, even admiration of, more robust physiques. By Song times, pale women with willowy figures were favored. In a more dramatic change, these women clearly have bound feet. Though footbinding appears to have been first practiced in Tang times, it was not widespread until the Song. Then, the image of weak, housebound women who were unable to work became a powerful status symbol and pushed aside the earlier enthusiasm for healthy women who participated in the business of their families.   (The Palace Museum, Beijing)

to her husband, and women were forbidden to remarry if their husbands divorced them or died.

Confucianism could be interpreted to require the absolute subordination of women to men, and it became fashionable to educate girls just enough so they could read simple versions of Confucian philosophy, edited to emphasize the lowly role that women were expected to play. Modest education made these young women more marketable as companions for the sons of other gentry or noble families and more desirable as mothers to the sons of aspiring families. In only a very few cases, such as the poet Li Qingzhao (1083–1141), were women of extremely high station and unusual personal determination permitted extensive education and freedom to pursue the literary arts.

The most dramatic change in the condition of Chinese women, however, resulted from footbinding, which first appeared among dancing slave women of the Tang court and was not widespread before the Song period. When the foot was bound, the toes were forced under and toward the heel, so that the bones eventually broke and the woman could not walk on her own. In families of the nobles and gentry, footbinding typically began when a girl was between five and seven years old. In many less wealthy families, girls had to work until they were older, so footbinding began later, perhaps even in a girl's teens.

Many literate men condemned the maiming of innocent girls and the general uselessness of footbinding. Nevertheless, bound feet became a powerful status symbol in rapidly changing Song society, and by 1200 the practice was firmly entrenched among the elites. A woman with unbound feet was undesirable in these circles, and mothers of elite position, or aspiring to it, almost without exception bound the feet of their daughters. They knew that without bound feet the girls would be rejected by society, by prospective husbands, and ultimately by their own families. Among working women and among the native peoples of what is now southern China, footbinding was unknown. Women in these classes and cultures enjoyed considerably more economic independence than did elite women.

Essential Partners: Korea, Japan, and Vietnam

In Korea, Japan, and Vietnam, Song China found societies that, like itself, were overwhelmingly agricultural. Many crops were important in East Asia, but rice was being widely disseminated. The cultivation of rice fit well with Confucian social ideas. Tending the young rice plants, irrigating the rice paddies, and managing the harvest required the coordination of considerable numbers of village and kin groups and reinforced the Confucian emphasis on hierarchy, obedience, and self-discipline. Confucianism also justified the use of agricultural profits to support the education, safety, and comfort of the literate elite.

Though there were similarities among these societies and governments, there also were differences. The countries of East Asia found niches for themselves in economic, technological and cultural specializations of their own.

Political ideologies in Korea, Japan, and Vietnam varied somewhat from the ideology of the Song, which asserted the predominance of Confucianism over all other philosophies, particularly Buddhism. These three East Asian neighbors had first centralized power under a ruling house in the early Tang period, and their state ideologies continued to resemble the ideology of the early Tang, when Buddhism and Confucianism were compatible political philosophies.

An examination system of the sort that reached elaborate form in Song China was not part of elite life elsewhere in East Asia. Government service in Korea, Japan, and Vietnam never called for the esoteric knowledge of Confucian texts that Song China demanded. In these countries, landowning and agriculture remained the major sources of income, and the traditional elites were not challenged by the growth of huge cities or rise of a large merchant class. There was little upward mobility, and examinations would not have been welcome in the selection of men for the bureaucracies.

Nevertheless, literacy in classical Chinese and a good knowledge of Confucian texts were highly prized for men in Korea, Japan, and Vietnam. The Confucian emphasis on hierarchy and harmony was increasingly instilled into the minds of ordinary people through popular education and indoctrination by the elite. Since Han times, the spread of Confucianism through East Asia had been strongly associated with the spread of the Chinese writing system. In all these countries, the elite learned to read Chinese and the Confucian classics. In Korea, a method of using Chinese characters to write the Korean language was in use before China was reunited under the Tang Empire, and Vietnam was not far behind in using a similar method for Vietnamese. A similar technique also emerged in Japan (see Environment and Technology: Writing in East Asia, 400–1200).

Those developments did not come soon enough for the East Asian societies to record their own earliest histories. Our first knowledge of Korea, Japan, and Vietnam comes from glimpses given by early Chinese officials and travelers. Korean history was first documented by Chinese bureaucrats of the third century B.C.E., when the Qin Empire established its first colony in Korea. During the Han Empire, the small kingdoms of Korea were distinguished for their knowledge of the horse, their strong hereditary elites, and their **shamanism** (belief in the ability of certain individuals to make direct contact with ancestors and the invisible spirit world). But they quickly absorbed Confucianism and Buddhism, both of which they transmitted to Japan.

The hereditary elites in Korea remained strong and in the early 500s made the system of inherited status—the "bone ranks"—permanent in Silla,° the leading Korean state. In 668, with the encouragement of the Tang Empire, Silla conquered its neighbors and brought much of the Korean peninsula under its control. But Silla, one of the most honored tributaries of the Tang Empire, proved unable to maintain its position without Tang support. After the fall of the Tang in the early 900s, the peninsula was united under the ruling house of **Koryo**°, from which the modern name "Korea" is taken. At con-

---

Silla (SILL-ah or SHILL-ah)   **Koryo** (KAW-ree-oh)

Writing in East Asia, 400–1200

An ideographic writing system that originated in China is the most distinctive communications tool of East Asia. Variations on this system, which is based on the depiction of meanings more than the representation of sounds, were widespread throughout East Asia by the time of the Sui and Tang Empires. Many of the peoples of East Asia adapted ideographic techniques to the writing of their own languages, which were not related to Chinese in grammar or in sound.

In Vietnam, Korea, and Japan, Chinese characters often were simplified and associated with the sounds of the local languages. For instance, the Chinese character *an,* meaning "peace" (Fig. 1), was pronounced "an" in Japanese and was familiar as a Chinese character to Confucian scholars in Japan's Heian (hay-ahn) period. But others besides scholars simplified the character and began to use it to write the Japanese sound "a" (Fig. 2). A set of more than thirty of these syllabic symbols adapted from Chinese characters permitted the writing of all the inflected forms of any Japanese word. Murasaki Shikibu used a syllabic system of this sort when she wrote *The Tale of Genji.*

In Vietnam and later in northern Asia, phonetic and ideographic elements were combined into new writing elements. The apparent circles in some *chu nom* writing from Vietnam (Fig. 3) are derived from the Chinese character for "mouth" and indicate a primary sound association for the word. The Kitans, who spoke a language related to Mongolian, developed an ideographic system of their own, inspired by Chinese characters. For instance, the Chinese character *wang* (Fig. 4), meaning "king, prince, ruler," was changed slightly to represent the Kitan word for an emperor: an upward stroke representing a "superior" ruler was added (Fig. 5). Because the system was ideographic, we do not know how this Kitan word was pronounced. The Kitan character for "God" or "Heaven" demonstrates the same ideographic logic: a top stroke representing the "supreme" ruler or power was added to the character meaning "ruler" (Fig. 6). Though inspired by Chinese characters, the Kitan characters could not be read by anyone who was not specifically educated in them.

The Kitans also developed a method of writing that was intended to represent the sounds and grammar of their language. They used small, simplified elements arranged within an imaginary frame, to indicate the sounds in any word. This practice might have been inspired by their knowledge of the phonetic script used by the Uigurs. Here (Fig. 7) we see the word for horse in a Kitan inscription. This method of fitting sound elements within a frame also occurred later in *hangul,* the Korean phonetic system introduced in the 1400s. Here (Fig. 8) we see the two words making up the country name "Korea."

The Chinese writing system was powerful and served well the needs of the Chinese elite to nearly the present day. But peoples speaking unrelated languages continually experimented with the Chinese invention to produce new ways of expressing themselves. The result was the emergence of several sound-based writing systems in East Asia, some in common use and some still being deciphered.

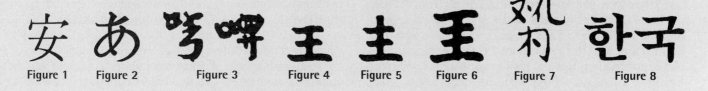

Figure 1 Figure 2 Figure 3 Figure 4 Figure 5 Figure 6 Figure 7 Figure 8

stant risk of attack by the Liao and then the Jin empires, Koryo pursued amicable relations with Song China. The Koryo kings were great patrons of Buddhism, and among their outstanding achievements are superb printed editions of Buddhist texts.

Of the many forms of technological exchange that Korea enjoyed with China, woodblock printing is the most remarkable. The oldest surviving example of woodblock printing of Chinese characters comes from Korea and is dated to the middle 700s. Commonly used during the Tang period, woodblock printing required time-consuming work by skilled artisans who carved hundreds of characters to produce a single page of type. Koreans rapidly made their own advances in printing techniques. By Song times China was benefiting from Korean experiments with **movable type,** and Song China in turn improved the technology, producing in metal or porcelain even more stable type from which texts could be cheaply and accurately printed.

Japan's earliest history, like Korea's, is also known from Chinese records. The first description, dating from the fourth century, tells of an island at the eastern edge of the world, divided into hundreds of small countries and ruled over by a shamaness named Himiko or Pimiko. This account suggests the ways in which the Japanese terrain, mountainous with small pockets and stretches of land suitable for agriculture, influenced the social and political structures of the early period. The unification of central Japan appears to have occurred some time in the fourth or fifth century C.E. How unification occurred remains a question, but there is evidence that horse-riding warriors from Korea may have united the small countries of Japan under a central government at Yamato, on the central plain of Honshu island.

In the mid-600s the rulers based at Yamato implemented the Taika° and other reforms, giving the Yamato regime many features of the Tang Chinese government, with which they were in direct contact through embassies to Chang'an. There was a legal code, an official variety of Confucianism, and a strong state interest in Buddhism. Within a century, a complex system of law stipulating a centralized government, and a massive history in the Confucian style were created. The Japanese mastered Chinese architectural science and styles so well that Japan's early capitals of Nara° and Kyoto have been invaluable for the study of wooden architecture that vanished from China. During the eighth century, Japan in some ways surpassed China as a center of Buddhist study. In 752 the "Great Buddha" statue was unveiled in an "eye-opening" ceremony. Dignitaries from all over Mahayana Buddhist Asia gathered at the enormous Todaiji temple, near the capital at Nara, to celebrate the event.

There were also significant departures from Chinese practice. Chinese buildings and some street plans were reproduced in Japan, but Chinese city walls were not. Central Japan of the seventh and eighth centuries (unlike central China) was not a site of constant warfare, so Japanese cities were built without fortifications. Also, Chinese Confucianism emphasized the importance of the Mandate of Heaven for legitimating the government, but there was no need for the Mandate of Heaven in Japan. The *tenno*, or hereditary head of state—often called "emperor" in English—was a member of the family that was believed to have ruled Japan since the beginning of its known history. Because there never had been a dynastic change in Japan, there was no need of the Mandate of Heaven to justify such change.

The royal line continued in Japan because only in exceptional cases did the emperors wield any real political power. Control was in the hands of a prime minister and the leaders of the native religion, which in later times was called Shinto, the "way of the gods."

In 794 the central government moved to Kyoto, usually called by its ancient name, Heian. This period of legally centralized government lasted until 1185, but in its later period real power was decentralized. Members of the Fujiwara° family—an ancient family of priests, bureaucrats and warriors—controlled power and assumed responsibility for protecting the emperor. The Fujiwara elevated men of Confucian learning over warriors, who generally were illiterate. Japanese noblemen of the Fujiwara period spent their time reading the Chinese classics, appreciating painting and poetry, and refining their sense of wardrobe and interior decoration.

To engage in their highly aesthetic way of life, Fujiwara nobles had to entrust responsibility for local government, policing, and tax collection to the warriors in their employ. Many of the warrior clans had humble beginnings, but by the late 1000s a small number of warriors had become wealthy and very powerful. The nobility was powerless to rein in these ambitious and violent groups, and by the middle 1100s the capital was engulfed in a civil war.

A literary epic, the *Tale of the Heike*, later celebrated the rise of a new elite culture based on military values. As nobles hurried to accommodate the new warlords, the standing of the Fujiwara family at court was destroyed. The emperor, too, had to acknowledge the warriors as his protectors. The new warrior class (in later times called *samurai*) in coming years absorbed some of the values of the Fujiwara aristocracy, but the age of the civil elite in Japan was ending. In 1185 the **Kamakura° Shogunate,** the first of three decentralized military regimes of Japan, was established in eastern Honshu, far from the old religious and political center at Kyoto.

Vietnam had had contact with empires based in China since the third century B.C.E., but not until Tang times did the relationship become close enough for economic and cultural assimilation. The rice-based agriculture of Vietnam made the region well suited for integration with southern China. As in southern China, the wet climate and hilly terrain of Vietnam demanded expertise in irrigation.

The ancestors of the Vietnamese were perhaps in advance of the Chinese in their use of draft animals in farming, in their metalworking, and in their mastery of certain forms of ceramics. But in Tang and Song times the elites of "Annam°"—as the Chinese called early Viet-

---

Taika (TIE-kah) **Nara** (NAH-rah)

Fujiwara (foo-jee-WAH-rah) **Kamakura** (kah-mah-KOO-rah)
Annam (ahn-nahm)

nam—modeled their culture on the culture of Chinese elites. Confucian bureaucratic training was strengthened, and Mahayana Buddhism was given pride of place among the religious influences in the region. When the Tang Empire was destroyed, Annamese elites decided to continue a government resembling the early Tang. Annam assumed the name Dai Viet° in 936 and it maintained good relations with Song China, but as an independent country.

Dai Viet's rival in Southeast Asia was Champa (located largely in what is now southern Vietnam). The impact on Champa of the cultures of India and Malaya was particularly strong, and Champa was part of the networks of trade and cultural influence that encompassed the Indian Ocean. During the period of Tang domination of Annam, Champa was hostile toward its northern neighbor. But during the Song period, when Dai Viet was independent, Champa voluntarily engaged itself as a tributary state of Song China. Indeed **Champa rice** (originally from India), a fast-maturing rice of the region, was sent to the Song by Champa as a tribute gift and became important in the advancement and specialization of Song agriculture.

Though a Confucian interest in heirarchy was shared by all the East Asian societies, specific practices relating to gender could differ from place to place. Footbinding was not practiced in strongly Confucian societies outside China. In Korea strong family alliances that functioned like political and economic organizations allowed women to retain a role in the negotiation and disposition of property. In Annam, before the arrival of Confucianism from China, it appears that women enjoyed higher status than women in China, perhaps because of the need for the whole community—both women and men—to participate in wet-rice cultivation. This suggests that women in south and southeastern China also may have enjoyed relatively high status before the growth of northern Chinese influence. The Trung sisters of Vietnam, who lived in the second century C.E. and led local farmers in resistance against the invading forces of the Han Empire, have been revered for almost two thousand years as national symbols in Vietnam and as local heroes in southern China. They represent a memory of a time when women were visible and active in community and political life.

Confucianism prescribed limited education for women, and that value was shared by all the East Asian neighbors. The hero of a Japanese novel, *The Tale of Genji*, written around the year 1000, remarks: "Women should have a general knowledge of several subjects, but it gives a bad impression if they show themselves to be

Dai Viet (die vee-yet)

attached to a particular branch of learning."[3] The author of the novel, the noblewoman Murasaki Shikibu, was both accurate and ironic in her observation. Fujiwara noblewomen were expected to live in near-total isolation. Generally they spent their leisure time studying Buddhism. To communicate with their families or among themselves they depended on writing. The simplified syllabic script that they used permitted them to write the Japanese language in its fully inflected form (Fujiwara men using the Chinese classical script that they had been taught could not do so). The combination of loneliness, free time, and a ready instrument for expression produced an outpouring of poetry, diaries, and story-telling by women of the Fujiwara era. Their best-known achievement, however, remains Murasaki's stunning portrait of Fujiwara court culture.

CONCLUSION

The Tang Empire put into place a solid system of travel, trade, and communications that allowed cultural and economic influences to move quickly from central Asia to Japan. The diversity within the empire produced great wealth and new ideas. But tensions among rival groups also weakened the political structure and led to great violence and misery.

The fragmentation of eastern Asia that followed the fall of the Tang Empire allowed the emergence of regional cultures that experimented with and in many cases improved the military, architectural, and scientific technologies whose transmission Tang rule had facilitated. In northern and Central Asia, these refinements included state ideologies based on Buddhism, bureaucratic practices based on Chinese traditions, and military techniques combining nomadic horsemanship and strategies with Chinese armaments and weapons. In Song China, the implementation of technological knowledge introduced during the Tang years transformed society. The results were privatization of commerce, major advances in technology and industry, increased productivity in agriculture, and deeper exploration of ideas relating to time, cosmology, and mathematics. China, however, was not self-reliant. Like its East Asian neighbors—Korea, Japan, and Vietnam—China was enriched by the sharing of technological advances.

The brilliant achievements of the Song period were due to mutually reinforcing developments in economy and technology. The Song economy, though only a fraction the size of the Tang economy, was intensely productive. Instead of distorting trade relations and inhibiting innovation and competition, the Song economy circulated goods and money throughout East Asia and stimulated the economies of its East Asian neighbors. All the East Asian societies made advances in agricultural technology and productivity, and all raised their literacy rates after the improvement of printing. They also developed a degree of industrial specialization: Song China dominated military technology and engineering, Japan developed advanced techniques in steel making, and Korea excelled in textiles and agriculture. In the long run Song China was not able to maintain the equilibrium necessary to sustain its own prosperity and that of the region. Constant military challenges from the north eventually overwhelmed Song finances, and the need for steel from Japan caused a drain of copper coinage.

The potential of any of the East Asian societies to adjust their mutual relationships and deepen their involvement in Pacific trade will never be known. In the thirteenth century the societies of continental eastern Asia were destroyed—and the region was united again—by the forces of the Mongol Empire.

■ Key Terms

Grand Canal	gunpowder
Tang Empire	Zen
Li Shimin	shamanism
tributary system	Koryo
bubonic plague	movable type
Uigurs	Kamakura shogunate
Song Empire	Champa rice
junk	

■ Suggested Reading

There are many excellent books on the history and culture of Central Asia, though some are now outdated and others are extremely detailed. Rene Grousset's *The Empire of the Steppes: A History of Central Asia* (1988) is a classic text. It can be very profitably supplemented by selected chapters from Denis Sinor, ed., *The Cambridge History of Early Inner Asia* (1990). On the transport technologies of early Central Asia see Richard Bulliet, *The Camel and the Wheel* (1975). For an important discussion of comparative economy, technology, and society see Francesca Bray, *The Rice Economies: Technology and Development in Asian Societies* (1994).

Arthur Wright, *The Sui Dynasty* (1978), is a very readable narrative of the reunification of China in the sixth century. The Tang Empire is the topic of a huge literature, but for a variety of enduring essays see Arthur F. Wright and David Twitchett, eds.,

Perspectives on the T'ang (1973). On Tang contacts with the cultures of Central, South, and Southeast Asia see Edward Schaeffer, *The Golden Peaches of Samarkand* (1963), *The Vermilion Bird* (1967), and *Pacing the Void* (1977). For an introduction to medieval Tibet see Christopher I. Beckwith, *The Tibetan Empire in Central Asia* (1987), and Rolf Stein, *Tibetan Civilization* (1972). On the Uigers see Colin MacKarras, *The Uighur Empire* (1968).

There is comparatively little secondary work in English on the Central and northern Asian empires that succeeded the Tang. But for a classic text see Karl Wittfogel and Chia-sheng Feng, *History of Chinese Society: Liao* (1949). On the Jurchen Jin, see Jin-sheng Tao, *The Jurchens in Twelfth Century China:* and on the Tangguts see Ruth Dunnell, *The State of High and White: Buddhism and the State in Eleventh-Century Xia* (1996).

On the Song, there is a large volume of material, particularly relating to technological achievements. For an introduction to the monumental work of Joseph Needham see *Science in Traditional China* (1981). A classic thesis on Song advancement (and Ming backwardness) is Mark Elvin, *The Pattern of the Chinese Past* (1973), particularly Part II. Joel Mokyr, *The Lever of Riches* (1990), is a more recent, comparative treatment. On the poet Li Qingzhao, see Hu Pin-ch'ing, *Li Ch'ing-chao* (1966). For neo-Confucianism and Buddhism see W. T. de Bary, W-T Chan, and B. Watson, compilers, *Sources of Chinese Tradition*, vol. 1 (1964). On social and economic history see Miyazaki Ichisada, *China's Examination Hell* (1971); Richard von Glahn, *The Land of Streams and Grottoes* (1987); and Patricia Ebery, *The Inner Quarters: Marriage and the Lives of Chinese Women in the Sung Period* (1993).

On the history of Korea see Andrew C. Nahm, *Introduction to Korean History and Culture* (1993); and Ki-Baik Kim, *A New History of Korea* (1984). An excellent introduction to Japanese history is Paul H. Varley, *Japanese Culture* (1984). Selections of relevant documents may be found in David John Lu, *Sources of Japanese History,* vol. 1 (1974), and R. Tsunoda, W. T. de Bary and D. Keene, compilers, *Sources of Japanese Tradition*, vol. 1 (1964). Ivan Morris, *The World of the Shining Prince: Court Life in Ancient Japan* (1979), is a classic introduction to the literature and culture of Fujiwara Japan at the time of the composition of Murasaki Shikibu's *The Tale of Genji.* For Vietnam see Keith Weller Taylor, *The Birth of Vietnam* (1983).

■ Notes

1. The edited quotation is from William H. McNeill, *Plagues and Peoples* (Garden City, NY: Anchor Press, 1976), 118. McNeill, following his translator, mistakes Ge Hong as "Ho Kung" (pinyin romanization "He Gong").
2. Quoted in David Lattimore, "Allusion in T'ang Poetry," in *Perspectives on the T'ang*, ed. Arthur F. Wright and David Twitchett (New Haven, CT: Yale University Press, 1973), 436.
3. Quoted in Ivan Morris, *The World of the Shining Prince: Court Life in Ancient Japan* (New York: Penguin Books, 1979), 221–222.

12

PEOPLES AND CIVILIZATIONS OF THE AMERICAS,

200–1500 C.E.

Classic-Era Culture and Society in Mesoamerica, 200–900 •
The Postclassic Period in Mesoamerica, 900–1500 • Northern Peoples •
Andean Civilizations, 200–1500

ENVIRONMENT AND TECHNOLOGY: Inca Roads

SOCIETY AND CULTURE: Acllas

Maya Scribe Maya scribes used a complex writing system to record religious concepts
and the actions of their kings. This picture of a scribe was painted on a ceramic plate.

I n late August 682 C.E., the Maya° princess Lady Wac-Chanil-Ahau° walked down the steep steps from her family's residence and mounted a sedan chair decorated with rich textiles and animal skins. As the procession exited from the urban center of Dos Pilas°, her military escort spread out through the fields and woods along her path to prevent ambush by enemies. Lady Wac-Chanil-Ahau's destination was the Maya city of Naranjo°, where she was to marry a powerful nobleman. Her marriage had been arranged to reestablish the royal dynasty that had been eliminated when Caracol, the region's major military power, had defeated Naranjo. Lady Wac-Chanil-Ahau's passage to Naranjo symbolized her father's desire to forge a military alliance that could resist Caracol. For us, the story of Lady Wac-Chanil-Ahau illustrates the importance of marriage and lineage in the politics of the classic-period Maya.

Smoking Squirrel, the son of Lady Wac-Chanil-Ahau, ascended the throne of Naranjo as a five-year-old in 693 C.E. During his long reign he proved to be a careful diplomat and formidable warrior. He was also a prodigious builder, leaving behind an expanded and beautified capital as part of his legacy. Mindful of the importance of his mother and her lineage from Dos Pilas, he erected numerous stelae (carved stone monuments) that celebrated her life.[1]

When population increased and competition for resources grew more violent, warfare and dynastic crisis convulsed the world of Wac-Chanil-Ahau. The defeat of the city-states of Tikal and Naranjo by Caracol undermined long-standing commercial and political relations in much of southern Mesoamerica and led to more than a century of conflict. Caracol, in turn, was challenged by the dynasty created at Dos Pilas by the heirs of Lady Wac-Chanil-Ahau. Despite a shared culture and religion, the great Maya cities remained divided by the dynastic ambitions of their rulers and by the competition for resources.

As the story of Lady Wac-Chanil-Ahau's marriage and her role in the development of a Maya dynasty suggests, the peoples of the Americas were in constant competition for resources. Members of hereditary elites organized their societies to meet these challenges, even as their ambition for greater power predictably ignited new conflicts. No single set of political institutions or technologies worked in every environment, and enormous cultural diversity existed in the ancient Americas. In Mesoamerica (Mexico and northern Central America) and in the Andean region of South America, Amerindian peoples developed an extraordinarily productive and diversified agriculture.[2] They also built great cities that rivaled the capitals of the Chinese and Roman Empires in size and beauty. The Olmecs of Mesoamerica and Chavín° of the Andes were the first great civilizations of the Americas (see Chapter 4). In the rest of the hemisphere, indigenous peoples adapted combinations of hunting and agriculture to maintain a wide variety of settlement patterns, political forms, and cultural traditions. All the cultures and civilizations of the Americas experienced cycles of expansion and contraction as they struggled with the challenges of environmental changes, population growth, social conflict, and war.

As you read this chapter, ask yourself the following questions:

- How did differing environments influence the development of Mesoamerican, Andean, and northern peoples?
- What technologies were developed to meet the challenges of these environments?
- How were the civilizations of Mesoamerica and the Andean region similar? How did they differ?
- How did religious belief and practice influence political life in the ancient Americas?

Maya (MY-ah)
Wac-Chanil-Ahau (wac-cha-NEEL-ah-HOW)
Dos Pilas (dohs PEE-las)   **Naranjo** (na-ROHN-hoe)

Chavín (cha-VEEN)

CHRONOLOGY

	Mesoamerica	Northern peoples	Andes
100	100 Teotihuacan founded	100–400 Hopewell culture in Ohio River Valley	
400	250 Maya early classic period begins		200–700 Moche culture of Peruvian coast
			500–1000 Tiwanaku and Wari control Peruvian highlands
700		700–1200 Anasazi culture	
1000	ca. 750 Teotihuacan destroyed 800–900 Maya centers abandoned, end of classic period 968 Toltec capital of Tula founded	919 Pueblo Bonito founded	
	1156 Tula destroyed	1050–1250 Cahokia reaches peak power 1150 Collapse of Anasazi centers begins	1200 Chimú begins military expansion
1300	1325 Aztec capital Tenochtitlan founded		
			1438 Inca expansion begins 1465 Inca conquer Chimú
1500	1502 Moctezuma II crowned Aztec ruler	1500 Mississippian culture declines	1500–1525 Inca conquer Ecuador

CLASSIC-ERA CULTURE AND SOCIETY IN MESOAMERICA, 200–900

Between 200 and 900 C.E. the peoples of Mesoamerica created a remarkable civilization. Despite enduring differences in language and the absence of regional political integration, Mesoamericans were unified by similarities in material culture, religious beliefs and practices, and social structures. Building on the earlier achievements of the Olmecs and others, the peoples of what is now Central America and south and central Mexico developed new forms of political organization, made great strides in astronomy and mathematics, and improved the productivity of their agriculture. During the classic period, population grew, a greater variety of products were traded over longer distances, and social hierarchies became more complex. Great cities were constructed, serving as centers of political life and as arenas of religious ritual and spiritual experience.

Classic-period civilizations built on the religious and political foundations established earlier in Olmec centers. The cities of the classic period continued to be dominated by platforms and pyramids devoted to religious functions, but they were more impressive and diversified architecturally. They had large full-time pop-

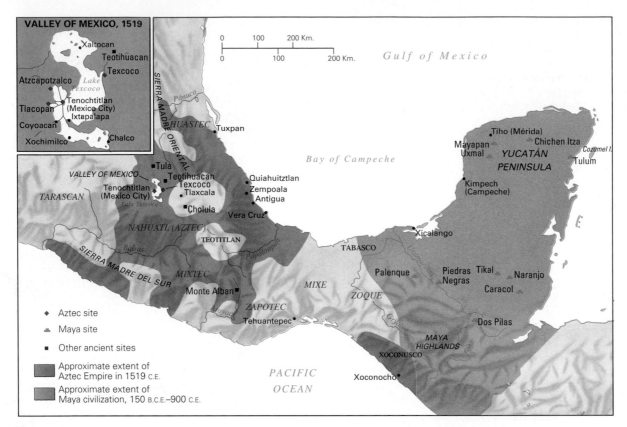

Map 12.1   Major Mesoamerican Civilizations, 1000 B.C.E.–1519 C.E.   From their island capital of Tenochtitlan, the Aztecs militarily and commercially dominated a large region. Aztec achievements were built on the legacy of earlier civilizations such as the Olmecs and Maya.

ulations divided into classes and dominated by hereditary political and religious elites who controlled nearby towns and villages and imposed their will on the rural peasantry.

The political and cultural innovations of this period did not depend on the introduction of new technologies. The agricultural foundation of Mesoamerican civilization had been developed centuries earlier. The major innovations in agriculture such as irrigation, the draining of wetlands, and the terracing of hillsides had all been in place for more than a thousand years when great cities were developed after 200 C.E. Instead, the achievements of the classic era depended on the ability of increasingly powerful elites to organize and command growing numbers of laborers and soldiers. What had changed was the reach and power of religious and political leaders. The scale and impressive architecture found at Teotihuacan°

or at the great Maya cities illustrate both Mesoamerican aesthetic achievements and the development of powerful political institutions.

Teotihuacan

Located about 30 miles (48 kilometers) northeast of modern Mexico City, **Teotihuacan** (100 B.C.E.–750 C.E.) was one of Mesoamerica's most important classic-period civilizations (see Map 12.1). At the height of its power, from 450 to 600 C.E., Teotihuacan was the largest city in the Americas. With between 125,000 and 200,000 inhabitants, it was larger than all but a small number of contemporary European and Asian cities.

Religious architecture rose above the city center. Enormous pyramids dedicated to the Sun and Moon and more than twenty smaller temples devoted to other gods were arranged along a central avenue. The people recognized and worshiped many gods and lesser spirits. Among the gods were the Sun, the Moon, a storm-god,

---

Teotihuacan (teh-o-tee-WAH-kahn)

and Quetzalcoatl°, the feathered serpent. Quetzalcoatl was a culture-god believed to be the originator of agriculture and the arts. Like the earlier Olmecs, people living at Teotihuacan practiced human sacrifice. More than sixty sacrificial victims were found during the excavation of the temple of Quetzalcoatl at Teotihuacan. Sacrifice was viewed as a sacred duty toward the gods and as essential to the well-being of human society.

The rapid growth in urban population was the result of the forced relocation of farm families from small villages in the region. More than two-thirds of the city's residents continued to work in agriculture, walking out from urban residences to their fields. The elite of Teotihuacan used the city's growing labor resources to bring marginal lands into production. Swamps were drained, irrigation works were constructed, terraces were built into hillsides, and the use of chinampas was expanded. **Chinampas°**, sometimes called "floating gardens," were narrow artificial islands anchored by trees and created by heaping lake muck and waste material on beds of reeds. Chinampas permitted year-round agriculture—because of subsurface irrigation and resistance to frost—and thus played a crucial role in sustaining the region's growing population. The productivity of the city's agriculture made possible its accomplishments in art, architecture, and trade.

As population grew, the housing of commoners underwent dramatic change. Apartment like stone buildings were constructed for the first time. Among the residents of these early apartment blocks were the craftsmen who produced the pottery and obsidian tools that were the most important articles of long-distance trade. Teotihuacan pottery has been found throughout central Mexico and even in the Maya region of Guatemala. More than 2 percent of the urban population was engaged in making obsidian tools and weapons.

The city's role as a religious center and commercial power provided both divine approval of and a material basis for the elite's increased wealth and status. Members of this elite controlled the state bureaucracy, tax collection, and commerce. Their prestige and wealth were reflected in their style of dress and diet and in the separate residence compounds built for aristocratic families. The central position and great prestige of the priestly class were evident in temple and palace murals. Teotihuacan's religious influence drew pilgrims from as far away as Oaxaca and Veracruz. Some of them became permanent residents.

Unlike the other classic-period civilizations, the people of Teotihuacan did not concentrate power in the

Quetzalcoatl (kate-zahl-CO-ah-tal)
chinampas (chee-NAM-pahs)

Teotihuacan Polychrome Mask   Masks made from many different materials, including semiprecious stones and clay, were an important part of ritual life at Teotihuacan. Some were attached to burial shrouds. This mask shows the large earspools and nose ornament worn by members of the elite.   (Enrique Franco-Torrijos)

hands of a single ruler. Although the ruins of their impressive housing compounds demonstrate the wealth and influence of the city's aristocracy, there is no clear evidence that individual rulers or a ruling dynasty gained overarching political power. In Teotihuacan the deeds of the rulers were not featured in public art, nor were their images represented by statues as in other Mesoamerican civilizations. In fact, some scholars suggest that Teotihuacan was ruled by alliances forged among elite families or by weak kings who were the puppets of these powerful families. Regardless of what form political decision making took, we do know that this powerful classic-period civilization achieved regional preeminence without subordinating its political life to the personality of a powerful individual ruler or lineage.

Historians debate the role of the military in the development of Teotihuacan. The absence of walls or other defensive structures before 500 C.E. suggests that Teotihuacan enjoyed relative peace during its early development. Archaeological evidence, however, reveals that the city created a powerful military to protect long-distance trade and to compel peasant agriculturalists to transfer their surplus production to the city. The discovery of representations of soldiers in typical Teotihuacan dress in the Maya region of Guatemala suggests to some that Teotihuacan used its military to expand trade relations. Unlike later postclassic civilizations, however, Teotihuacan was not an imperial state controlled by a military elite.

It is unclear what forces brought about the collapse of Teotihuacan about 650 C.E. Weakness was evident as early as 500 C.E., when the urban population declined to about 40,000 and the city began to build defensive walls. These fortifications and pictorial evidence from murals suggest that the city's final decades were violent. Early scholars suggested that the city was overwhelmed militarily by a rival city located nearby or by nomadic warrior peoples from the northern frontier. More recently, investigators have uncovered evidence of conflict within the ruling elite and the mismanagement of resources. This, they argue, led to class conflict and the breakdown of public order. As a result, most important temples in the city center were pulled down and religious images defaced. Elite palaces were also systematically burned and many of the residents killed. Regardless of the causes, the eclipse of Teotihuacan was felt throughout Mexico and into Central America.

The Maya

During Teotihuacan's ascendancy in the north, the **Maya** developed an impressive civilization in the region that today includes Guatemala, Honduras, Belize, and southern Mexico (see Map 12.1). Given the difficulties imposed by a tropical climate and fragile soils, the cultural and architectural achievements of the Maya were remarkable. Although they shared a single culture, they were never unified politically. Instead, rival kingdoms led by hereditary rulers struggled with each other for regional dominance, much like the Mycenaean-era Greeks (see Chapter 3).

Today Maya farmers prepare their fields by cutting down small trees and brush and then burning the dead vegetation to fertilize the land. This swidden agriculture can produce high yields for a few years, but it uses up the soil's nutrients, eventually forcing people to move to more fertile land. The high population levels of the Maya classic period (250–900 C.E.) required more intensive forms of agriculture. Maya living near the major urban centers achieved high agricultural yields by draining swamps and building elevated fields. They used irrigation in areas with long dry seasons, and they terraced hillsides in the cooler highlands. Nearly every household planted a garden to provide condiments and fruits to supplement dietary staples. Maya agriculturists also managed nearby forests, favoring the growth of the trees and shrubs that were most useful to them, as well as promoting the conservation of deer and other animals hunted for food.

During the classic period, Maya city-states proliferated. The most powerful cities controlled groups of smaller dependent cities and a broad agricultural zone by building impressive religious temples and creating rituals that linked the power of kings to the gods. Classic-era cities, unlike earlier sites, had dense central precincts visually dominated by monumental architecture. These political and ceremonial centers were commonly aligned with the movements of the Sun and Venus. Open plazas were surrounded by high pyramids and by elaborately decorated palaces often built on high ground or on constructed mounds. The effect was to awe the masses drawn to these centers for religious and political rituals.

The Maya loved decoration. Nearly all of their public buildings were covered with bas-relief and painted in bright colors. Religious allegories, the genealogies of rulers, and important historical events were the most common motifs. Beautifully carved altars and stone monoliths were erected near major temples. This rich legacy of monumental architecture was constructed without the aid of wheels—no pulleys, wheelbarrows, or carts—or metal tools. Masses of men and women aided only by levers and stone tools cut and carried construction materials and lifted them into place.

The Maya cosmos was divided into three layers connected along a vertical axis that traced the course of the Sun. The earthly arena of human existence held an intermediate position between the heavens, conceptualized by the Maya as a sky-monster, and a dark underworld. A sacred tree rose through the three layers; its roots were in the underworld, and its branches reached into the heavens. The temple precincts of Maya cities physically represented essential elements of this religious cosmology. The pyramids were sacred mountains reaching to the heavens. The doorways of the pyramids were portals to the underworld.

Rulers and other members of the elite served both priestly and political functions. They decorated their bodies with paint and tattoos and wore elaborate costumes of textiles, animal skins, and feathers to project both secular power and divine sanction. Kings communicated directly with the supernatural residents of the other worlds and with deified royal ancestors through bloodletting rituals and hallucinogenic trances. Scenes of rulers drawing blood from lips, ears, and penises are common in surviving frescoes and on painted pottery.

Warfare in particular was infused with religious meaning and elaborate ritual. Battle scenes and the depiction of the torture and sacrifice of captives were frequent decorative themes. Typically, Maya military forces fought to secure captives rather than territory. Days of fasting, sacred ritual, and rites of purification preceded battle. The king, his kinsmen, and other ranking nobles actively participated in war. Elite captives were nearly always sacrificed; captured commoners were more likely to be enslaved.

The Great Plaza at Tikal   Still visible in the ruins of Tikal, in modern Guatemala, are the impressive architectural and artistic achievements of the classic-era Maya. Maya centers provided a dramatic setting for the rituals that dominated public life. Construction of Tikal began before 150 B.C.E.; the city was abandoned about 900 C.E. A ball court and residences for the elite were part of the Great Plaza.   (Martha Cooper/Peter Arnold, Inc.)

Only two women are known to have ruled Maya kingdoms. Maya women of the ruling lineages did play important political and religious roles, however. The consorts of male rulers participated in bloodletting rituals and in other important public ceremonies, and their noble blood helped legitimate the rule of their husbands. Although Maya society was patrilineal (tracing descent in the male line), there is evidence that some male rulers traced their lineages bilaterally (in both the male and the female lines). Like Lady Wac-Chanil-Ahau's son Smoking Squirrel, some rulers emphasized the female line if it held higher status. Much less is known about the lives of the women of the lower classes, but scholars believe that they played a central role in the household economy, maintaining essential garden plots and weaving, and in the management of family life.

Building on what the Olmecs had done, the Maya made important contributions to the development of the Mesoamerican calendar and to mathematics and writ-

ing. Their interest in time and in the cosmos was reflected in the complexity of their calendric system. Each day was identified by three separate dating systems. Like other peoples throughout Mesoamerica, the Maya had a calendar that tracked the ritual cycle (260 days divided into 13 months of 20 days) as well as a solar calendar (365 days divided into 18 months of 20 days, plus 5 unfavorable days at the end of the year). The concurrence of these two calendars every 52 years was believed to be especially ominous. The Maya, alone among Mesoamerican peoples, also maintained a continuous "long count" calendar, which began at a fixed date in the past that scholars have identified as 3114 B.C.E., a date that the Maya probably associated with creation.

These accurate calendric systems and the astronomical observations on which they were based depended on Maya contributions to mathematics and writing. Their system of mathematics incorporated the concept of the zero and place value but had limited notational signs.

Maya writing was a form of hieroglyphic inscription that signified whole words or concepts as well as phonetic cues or syllables. Aspects of public life, religious belief, and the biographies of rulers and their ancestors were recorded in deerskin and bark-paper books, on pottery, and on the stone columns and monumental buildings of the urban centers. In this sense every Maya city was a sacred text.

Between 800 and 900 C.E. many of the major urban centers of the Maya were abandoned or destroyed, although a small number of classic-period centers survived for centuries. This collapse was preceded in some areas by decades of urban population decline and increased warfare. Some experts have argued that the earlier destruction of Teotihuacan after 650 C.E. disrupted trade, thus undermining the legitimacy of Maya rulers who had used these goods in rituals. Other scholars suggest that growing population pressure led to environmental degradation and declining agricultural productivity. This environmental crisis, in turn, might have led to social conflict and increased levels of warfare as desperate elites sought to acquire additional agricultural land through conquest. Although little evidence has been found, some scholars have proposed that epidemic disease and pestilence were the prime causes of the catastrophe. Most probably, a combination of factors caused the end of the classic period.

THE POSTCLASSIC PERIOD IN MESOAMERICA, 900–1500

The division between classic and postclassic periods is somewhat arbitrary. Not only is there no single explanation for the collapse of Teotihuacan and many of the major Maya centers, but these events occurred over more than a century and a half. In fact, some important classic-period civilizations survived unscathed. Moreover, the essential cultural characteristics of the classic period were carried over to the postclassic. The two periods are linked by similarities in religious belief and practice, in architecture, in urban planning, and in social organization.

There were, however, some important differences between these periods. There is evidence that the population of Mesoamerica expanded during the postclassic period. Resulting pressures led to an intensification of agricultural practices and to increased warfare. The governing elites of the major postclassic states—the Toltecs and the Aztecs—responded to these harsh realities by increasing the size of their armies and by developing political institutions that facilitated their control of large and culturally diverse territories acquired through conquest.

The Mesoamerican Ball Game   From Guatemala to Arizona, archaeologists have found evidence of an ancient ball game played with a solid rubber ball on slope-sided courts shaped like a capital T. Among the Maya the game was associated with a creation myth and thus had deep religious meaning. There is evidence that some players were sacrificed. In this scene from a ceramic jar, players wearing elaborate ritual clothing—which includes heavy, protective pads around the chest and waist—play with a ball much larger than the ball actually used in such games. Some representations show balls drawn to suggest a human head.   (Dallas Art Museum/Justin Kerr)

The Toltecs

Little is known about the **Toltecs°** prior to their arrival in central Mexico. Some scholars speculate that they were originally a satellite population that Teotihuacan had placed on the northern frontier to protect against the incursions of nomads. After their migration south, the Toltecs borrowed from the cultural legacy of Teotihuacan and created an important postclassic civilization. Memories of their military achievements and the violent imagery of their political and religious rituals dominated the Mesoamerican imagination in the late postclassic period. In the fourteenth century, the Aztecs and their contemporaries erroneously believed that the Toltecs were the source of nearly all the great cultural achievements of the Mesoamerican world. As one Aztec source later recalled:

> In truth [the Toltecs] invented all the precious and marvelous things. . . . All that now exists was their discovery. . . . And these Toltecs were very wise; they were thinkers, for they originated the year count, the day count. All their discoveries formed the book for interpreting dreams. . . . And so wise were they [that] they understood the stars which were in the heavens.[3]

In fact, all these contributions to Mesoamerican culture were actually in place long before the Toltecs gained control of central Mexico. The most important Toltec innovations were instead political and military.

The Toltecs created the first conquest state based largely on military power, and they extended their political influence from the area north of modern Mexico City to Central America. Established about 968 C.E., Tula°, the Toltec capital, was constructed in a grand style (see Map 12.1). Its public architecture featured colonnaded patios and numerous temples. Although the population of Tula never reached the levels of classic-period Teotihuacan, the Toltec capital dominated central Mexico. Toltec decoration had a more warlike and violent character than the decoration of earlier Mesoamerican cultures. Nearly all Toltec public buildings and temples were decorated with representations of warriors or with scenes suggesting human sacrifice.

Two chieftains or kings apparently ruled the Toltec state together. Evidence suggests that this division of responsibility eventually weakened Toltec power and led to the destruction of Tula. Sometime after 1000 C.E., a struggle between elite groups identified with rival religious cults undermined the Toltec state. According to legends that survived among the Aztecs, Topiltzin°—one of the two rulers and a priest of the cult of Quetzalcoatl—

and his followers bitterly accepted exile in the east, "the land of the rising sun." These legendary events coincided with growing Toltec influence among the Maya of the Yucatán Peninsula. One of the ancient texts relates these events in the following manner:

> Thereupon he [Topiltzin] looked toward Tula, and then wept. . . . And when he had done these things . . . he went to reach the seacoast. Then he fashioned a raft of serpents. When he had arranged the raft, he placed himself as if it were his boat. Then he set off across the sea.[4]

After the exile of Topiltzin the Toltec state began to decline, and around 1156 C.E. northern invaders overcame Tula itself. After its destruction, a centuries-long process of cultural and political assimilation produced a new Mesoamerican political order based on the urbanized culture and statecraft of the Toltecs. Like Semitic peoples of the third millennium B.C.E. interacting with Sumerian culture (see Chapter 2), the new Mesoamerican elites were drawn in part from the invading cultures. The Aztecs of the Valley of Mexico became the most important of these late postclassic peoples.

The Aztecs

The Mexica°, more commonly known as the **Aztecs,** were among the northern peoples who pushed into central Mexico in the wake of the collapse of Tula. At the time of their arrival they had a clan-based social organization. In this new environment they began to adopt the political and social practices that they found among the urbanized agriculturalists of the valley. At first, the Aztecs served their more powerful neighbors as serfs and mercenaries. As their strength grew, they relocated to small islands near the shore of Lake Texcoco and began the construction of their twin capitals, **Tenochtitlan°** and Tlatelolco (modern Mexico City), around 1325 C.E.

Military successes allowed the Aztecs to seize control of additional agricultural land along the lakeshore. With the increased economic independence and greater political security that resulted from this expansion, the Aztecs transformed their political organization by introducing a monarchical system similar to that found in more powerful neighboring states. Clans survived to the era of Spanish conquest but increasingly lost influence to monarchs and hereditary aristocrats. Aztec rulers did not have absolute power, and royal succession was not based on primogeniture. A council of

---

Toltec (TOLL-tek)   **Tula** (TOO-la)   **Topilitzin** (tow-PEELT-zeen)

Mexica (meh-SHE-ca)   **Tenochititlan** (teh-noch-TIT-lan)

Costumes of Aztec Warriors In Mesoamerican warfare individual warriors sought to gain prestige and improve their status by taking captives. This illustration from the sixteenth-century Codex Mendoza was drawn by an Amerindian artist. It shows the Aztecs' use of distinctive costumes to acknowledge the prowess of warriors. These costumes indicate the taking of two (top left) to six captives (bottom center). The individual on the bottom right shown without a weapon was a military leader. As was common in Mesoamerican illustrations of military conflict, the captives, held by their hair, are shown kneeling before the victors.   (The Bodleian Library, Oxford, Ms. Arch. Selder. A.I. fol. 64r)

powerful aristocrats selected new rulers from among male members of the ruling lineage. Once selected, the ruler was forced to renegotiate the submission of tribute dependencies and then demonstrate his divine mandate by undertaking a new round of military conquests. War was infused with religious meaning, providing the ruler with legitimacy and increasing the prestige of successful warriors.

As the power of the ruler and aristocracy grew, the authority of kinship-based clans declined. As a result, social divisions were accentuated. These alterations in social organization and political life were made possible by Aztec military expansion. Territorial conquest allowed the warrior elite of Aztec society to seize land and peasant labor as spoils of war (see Map 12.1). In time, the royal family and highest-ranking members of the aristocracy possessed extensive estates that were cultivated by slaves and landless commoners. The Aztec lower classes received some material rewards from imperial expansion but lost most of their ability to influence or control decisions. Some commoners were able to achieve

some social mobility through success on the battlefield or by entering the priesthood, but the highest social ranks were always reserved for hereditary nobles.

The urban plan of Tenochtitlan and Tlatelolco continued to be organized around the clans, whose members maintained a common ritual life and accepted civic responsibilities such as caring for the sick and elderly. Clan members also fought together as military units. Nevertheless, the clans' historical control over common agricultural land and other scarce resources, such as fishing and hunting rights, declined. By 1500 C.E. great inequalities in wealth and privilege characterized Aztec society.

Aztec kings and aristocrats legitimated their ascendancy by creating elaborate rituals and ceremonies to distinguish themselves from commoners. One of the Spaniards who participated in the conquest of the Aztec Empire remembered his first meeting with the Aztec ruler Moctezuma° II (r. 1502–1520): "many great lords

---

Moctezuma (mock-teh-ZU-ma)

walked before the great Montezuma [Moctezuma II], sweeping the ground on which he was to tread and laying down cloaks so that his feet should not touch the earth. Not one of these chieftains dared look him in the face."[5] Commoners lived in small dwellings and ate a limited diet of staples, but members of the nobility lived in large, well-constructed two-story houses and consumed a diet rich in animal protein and flavored by condiments and expensive imports like chocolate. Rich dress and jewelry also set apart the elite. Even in marriage customs the two groups were different. Commoners were monogamous, great nobles polygamous.

The Aztec state met the challenge of feeding an urban population of approximately 150,000 by efficiently organizing the labor of the clans and additional laborers sent by defeated peoples to expand agricultural land. The construction of a dike more than 5½ miles (9 kilometers) long by 23 feet (7 meters) wide to separate the fresh and saltwater parts of Lake Texcoco was the Aztecs' most impressive land reclamation project. The dike allowed a significant extension of irrigated fields and the construction of additional chinampas. One expert has estimated that the project consumed 4 million person-days to complete. Aztec chinampas contributed maize, fruits, and vegetables to the markets of Tenochtitlan. The imposition of a **tribute system** on conquered peoples also helped relieve some of the pressure of Tenochtitlan's growing population. Unlike the tribute system of Tang China, where tribute had a more symbolic character (see Chapter 11), one quarter of the Aztec capital's food requirements was satisfied by tribute payments of maize, beans, and other foods sent by nearby political dependencies. The Aztecs also demanded cotton cloth, military equipment, luxury goods like jade and feathers, and sacrificial victims as tribute. Trade supplemented these supplies.

A specialized class of merchants controlled long-distance trade. Given the absence of draft animals and wheeled vehicles, this commerce was dominated by lightweight and valuable products like gold, jewels, feathered garments, cacao, and animal skins. Merchants also provided essential political and military intelligence for the Aztec elite. Operating outside the protection of Aztec military power, merchant expeditions were armed and often had to defend themselves. Although merchants became wealthy and powerful as the Aztecs expanded their empire, they were denied the privileges of the high nobility, which was jealous of its power. As a result, the merchants feared to publicly display their affluence.

Like commerce throughout the Mesoamerican world, Aztec commerce was carried on without money and credit. Barter was facilitated by the use of cacao,

quills filled with gold, and cotton cloth as standard units of value to compensate for differences in the value of bartered goods. Aztec expansion facilitated the integration of producers and consumers in the central Mexican economy. As a result, the markets of Tenochtitlan and Tlatelolco offered a rich array of goods from as far away as Central America and what is now the southwestern border of the United States. Hernán Cortés (1485–1547), the Spanish adventurer who eventually conquered the Aztecs, expressed his admiration for the abundance of the Aztec marketplace:

> One square in particular is twice as big as that of Salamanca and completely surrounded by arcades where there are daily more than sixty thousand folk buying and selling. Every kind of merchandise such as may be met with in every land is for sale. . . . There is nothing to be found in all the land which is not sold in these markets, for over and above what I have mentioned there are so many and such various things that on account of their very number . . . I cannot detail them.[6]

The Aztecs succeeded in developing a remarkable urban landscape. The combined population of Tenochtitlan and Tlatelolco and the cities and hamlets of the surrounding lakeshore was approximately 500,000 by 1500 C.E. The island capital was designed so that canals and streets intersected at right angles. Three causeways connected the city to the lakeshore.

Religious rituals dominated public life in Tenochtitlan. Like the other cultures of the Mesoamerican world, the Aztecs worshiped a large number of gods. Most of these gods had a dual nature—both male and female. The major contribution of the Aztecs to the religious life of Mesoamerica was the cult of Huitzilopochtli°, the southern hummingbird. As the Aztec state grew in power and wealth, the importance of this cult grew as well. Huitzilopochtli was originally associated with war, but eventually the Aztecs identified this god with the Sun, worshiped as a divinity throughout Mesoamerica. Huitzilopochtli, they believed, required a diet of human hearts to sustain him in his daily struggle to bring the Sun's warmth to the world. Tenochtitlan was architecturally dominated by a great twin temple devoted to Huitzilopochtli and Tlaloc, the rain god, symbolizing the two bases of the Aztec economy: war and agriculture.

War captives were the preferred sacrificial victims, but large numbers of criminals, slaves, and people provided as tribute by dependent regions were also sacrificed. Although human sacrifice had been practiced

---

Huitzilopochtli (wheat-zeel-oh-POSHT-lee)

since early times in Mesoamerica, the Aztecs and other societies of the late postclassic period transformed this religious ritual by dramatically increasing its scale. There are no reliable estimates for the total number of sacrifices, but the numbers clearly reached into the thousands each year. This form of violent public ritual had political consequences and was not simply the celebration of religious belief. Some scholars have emphasized the political nature of this rising tide of sacrifice, noting that sacrifices were carried out in front of large crowds that included leaders from enemy and subject states as well as the masses of Aztec society. The political subtext must have been clear: rebellion, deviancy, and opposition were extremely dangerous.

NORTHERN PEOPLES

By the end of the classic period in Mesoamerica, around 900 C.E., important cultural centers had appeared in the southwestern desert region and along the Ohio and Mississippi river valleys of what is now the United States. In both regions improved agricultural productivity and population growth led to increased urbanization and complex social and political structures. In the Ohio Valley Amerindian peoples who depended on locally domesticated seed crops as well as traditional hunting and gathering developed large villages with monumental earthworks. The introduction of maize, beans, and squash into this region from Mesoamerica after 1000 B.C.E. played an important role in the development of complex societies. Once established, these useful food crops were adopted throughout North America.

As growing populations came to depend on maize as a dietary staple, large-scale irrigation projects were undertaken in both the southwestern desert and the eastern river valleys. This development is a sign of increasingly centralized political power and growing social stratification. The two regions, however, evolved different political traditions. The Anasazi° and their neighbors in the southwest maintained a relatively egalitarian social structure and retained collective forms of political organization based on kinship and age. The mound builders of the eastern river valleys evolved more hierarchical political institutions: groups of small towns were subordinate to a political center ruled by a hereditary chief who wielded both secular and religious authority.

Southwestern Desert Cultures

Immigrants from Mexico introduced agriculture based on irrigation to present-day Arizona around 300 B.C.E. Because irrigation there allowed the planting of two crops per year, the population grew and settled village life soon appeared. Of all the southwestern cultures, the Hohokam of the Salt and Gila river valleys show the strongest Mexican influence. Hohokam sites have platform mounds and ball courts similar to those of Mesoamerica. Hohokam pottery, clay figurines, cast copper bells, and turquoise mosaics also reflect Mexican influence. By 1000 C.E. the Hohokam had constructed an elaborate irrigation system that included one canal more than 18 miles (30 kilometers) in length. Hohokam agricultural and ceramic technology spread over the centuries to neighboring peoples, but it was the Anasazi to the north who left the most vivid legacy of these desert cultures.

Archaeologists use **Anasazi,** a Navajo word meaning "ancient ones," to identify a number of dispersed though similar desert cultures located in what is now the Four Corners region of Arizona, New Mexico, Colorado, and Utah (see Map 12.2). Between 450 and 750 C.E. the Anasazi developed an economy based on maize, beans, and squash. Their successful adaptation of these crops permitted the formation of larger villages and led to an enriched cultural life centered in underground buildings called kivas. Evidence suggests that the Anasazi may have used kivas for weaving and pottery making. They produced pottery decorated with geometric patterns, learned to weave cotton cloth, and, after 900 C.E., began to construct large multistory residential and ritual centers.

One of the largest Anasazi communities was located in Chaco Canyon in what is now northwestern New Mexico. Eight large towns were built in the canyon and four more on surrounding mesas, suggesting a regional population of approximately 15,000. Many smaller villages were located nearby. Each town contained hundreds of rooms arranged in tiers around a central plaza. At Pueblo Bonito, the largest town, more than 650 rooms were arranged in a four-story block of residences and storage rooms. Pueblo Bonito had 38 kivas, including a great kiva more than 65 feet (19 meters) in diameter. Social life and craft activities were concentrated in small open plazas or

Map 12.2 Culture Areas of North America In each of the large ecological regions of North America, native peoples evolved distinctive cultures and technologies. Here the Anasazi of the arid southwest and the mound-building cultures of the Ohio and Mississippi river valleys are highlighted.

Anasazi (ah-nah-SAH-zee)

ARCTIC

SUBARCTIC

NORTHWEST

PLATEAU

PLAINS

NORTHEAST

CALIFORNIA

GREAT
BASIN

• Cahokia

Kiet Siel

Mesa
Verde

Canyon •
de Chelly

• Chaco
Canyon

SOUTHEAST

SOUTHWEST

| 0 | 300 | 600 Km. |
| 0 | 300 | 600 Mi. |

Approximate extent of Anasazi culture

Approximate extent of mound-building cultures

Mesa Verde Cliff Dwelling   Located in southern Colorado, the Anasazi cliff dwellings of Mesa Verde hosted a population of about 7,000 in 1250 C.E. The construction of housing complexes and religious buildings in the area's large caves was probably prompted by increased warfare in the region.   (David Muench Photography)

common rooms. Hunting, trade, and the need to maintain irrigation works often drew men away from the village. Women shared in agricultural tasks and were specialists in many crafts. They also were responsible for food preparation and childcare. If the practice of modern Pueblos, cultural descendants of the Anasazi, is a guide, houses and furnishings may have belonged to the women who formed extended families with their mothers and sisters.

The high-quality construction at Chaco Canyon, the size and number of kivas, and a system of roads linking the canyon to outlying towns suggest that Pueblo Bonito and its nearest neighbors exerted some kind of political or religious dominance over a large region. Some archaeologists have suggested that the Chaco Canyon culture originated as a colonial appendage of Mesoamerica, but the archaeological record provides little evidence for this

theory. Merchants from Chaco provided Toltec-period peoples of northern Mexico with turquoise in exchange for shell jewelry, copper bells, macaws, and trumpets. But these exchanges occurred late in Chaco's development, and more important signs of Mesoamerican influence such as pyramid-shaped mounds and ball courts are not found at Chaco. Nor is there evidence from the excavation of burials and residences of clear class distinctions, a common feature of Mesoamerican culture. Instead, it appears that the Chaco Canyon culture developed from earlier societies in the region.

The abandonment of the major sites in Chaco Canyon in the twelfth century most likely resulted from a long drought that undermined the culture's fragile agricultural economy. Nevertheless, the Anasazi continued in the Four Corners region for more than a century after the abandonment of Chaco Canyon. There were major centers at Mesa Verde in present-day Colorado and at Canyon de Chelly and Kiet Siel in Arizona. Anasazi settlements on the Colorado Plateau and in Arizona were constructed in large natural caves high above valley floors. This hard-to-reach location suggests increased levels of warfare, probably provoked by population pressure on limited arable land. Elements of this cultural tradition survive today among the Pueblo peoples of the Rio Grande Valley and Arizona who still live in multistory villages and worship in kivas.

Mound Builders: The Adena, Hopewell, and Mississippian Cultures

The Adena people of the Ohio River Valley constructed large villages with monumental earthworks from about 500 B.C.E. This early mound-building culture was based on traditional hunting and gathering supplemented by limited cultivation of locally domesticated seed crops. Most, but not all, of the Adena mounds contained burials. Items found in these graves indicate a hierarchical society with an elite distinguished by its access to rare and valuable goods such as mica from North Carolina and copper from the Great Lakes region.

Around 100 C.E. the Adena culture blended into a successor culture now called Hopewell, also centered in the Ohio River Valley. The largest Hopewell centers appeared in present-day Ohio; but Hopewell influence, in the form of either colonies or trade dependencies, spread west to Illinois, Michigan, and Wisconsin, east to New York and Ontario, and south to Alabama, Louisiana, Mississippi, and even Florida (see Map 12.2). For the necessities of daily life Hopewell people were dependent on hunting and gathering and a limited agriculture inherited from the Adena.

Hopewell is an early example of a North American **chiefdom**—territory that had a population of as much as 10,000 and was ruled by a chief, a hereditary leader with both religious and secular responsibilities. Chiefs organized periodic rituals of feasting and gift giving that established bonds among diverse kinship groups and guaranteed access to specialized crops and craft goods. They also managed long-distance trade, which provided luxury goods and additional food supplies.

The largest Hopewell towns in the Ohio River Valley served as ceremonial and political centers and had several thousand inhabitants. Villages had populations of a few hundred. Large mounds built to house elite burials and as platforms for temples and the residences of chiefs dominated major Hopewell centers. Chiefs and other members of the elite were buried in vaults surrounded by valuable goods such as river pearls, copper jewelry,

and, in some cases, women and retainers who seem to have been sacrificed to accompany a dead chief into the afterlife. As was true of the earlier Olmec culture of Mexico, the abandonment of major Hopewell sites around 400 C.E. has no clear environmental or political explanation.

Hopewell technology and mound building continued in smaller centers that have been linked to the development of Mississippian culture (700–1500 C.E.). As in the case of the Anasazi, some experts have suggested that contacts with Mesoamerica influenced Mississippian culture, but there is no convincing evidence to support this theory. It is true that maize, beans, and squash, all first domesticated in Mesoamerica, were closely associated with the development of the urbanized Mississippian culture. But these plants and related technologies were probably passed along through numerous intervening cultures.

The development of urbanized Mississippian chiefdoms resulted instead from the accumulated effects of small increases in agricultural productivity, the adoption of the bow and arrow, and the expansion of trade networks. An improved economy led to population growth, the building of cities, and social stratification. The largest towns shared a common urban plan based on a central plaza surrounded by large platform mounds. Major towns were trade centers where people bartered essential commodities, such as flint used for weapons and tools.

The Mississippian culture reached its highest stage of evolution at the great urban center of Cahokia, located near the modern city of East St. Louis, Illinois (see Map 12.2). At the center of this site was the largest mound constructed in North America, a terraced structure 100 feet (30 meters) high and 1,037 by 790 feet (316 by 241 meters) at the base. Areas where commoners lived ringed the center area of elite housing and temples. At its height in about 1200 C.E., Cahokia had a population of about 30,000—about the same population as the great Maya city Tikal.

Cahokia controlled surrounding agricultural lands and a number of secondary towns ruled by subchiefs. Burial evidence suggests that the rulers of Cahokia enjoyed an exalted position. In one burial more than fifty young women and retainers were apparently sacrificed to accompany a ruler on his travels after death. As at Hopewell sites, no evidence links the decline and eventual abandonment of Cahokia (which occurred after 1250 C.E.) with military defeat or civil war. Experts argue that climate changes and population pressures undermined its vitality. After the decline of Cahokia, smaller Mississippian centers continued to flourish in the southeast of the present-day United States until the arrival of Europeans.

ANDEAN CIVILIZATIONS, 200–1500

The Andean region of South America was an unlikely environment for the development of rich and powerful civilizations (see Map 12.3). Much of the region's mountainous zone is at altitudes that seem too high for agriculture and human habitation. Along the Pacific coast an arid plain posed a difficult challenge to the development of agriculture. And, to the east of the Andes Mountains, the hot and humid tropical environment of the Amazon headwaters also offered a formidable obstacle to the organization of complex societies. Yet the Amerindian peoples of the Andean area produced some of the most socially complex and politically advanced societies of the Western Hemisphere. Perhaps the harshness of the environment compelled the development of the administrative structures and social and economic relationships that became the central features of Andean civilization.

Cultural Response to Environmental Challenge

People living in the high mountain valleys and on the dry coastal plain were able to overcome the challenges posed by their environment through the effective organization of human labor. The remarkable collective achievements of Andean peoples were accomplished with a recordkeeping system more limited than the one found in Mesoamerica. A system of knotted colored cords, **khipus°**, was used to aid administration and record population counts and tribute obligations. Large-scale drainage and irrigation works and the terracing of hillsides to control erosion and provide additional farmland led to an increase in agricultural production. Andean people also undertook road building, urban construction, and even textile production collectively.

The sharing of responsibilities began at the household level. But it was the clan, or **ayllu°**, that provided the foundation for Andean achievement. Members of an ayllu held land communally. Although members claimed descent from a common ancestor, they were not necessarily related. Ayllu members thought of each other as brothers and sisters and were obligated to aid each other in tasks that required more labor than a single household could provide. These reciprocal obligations provided the

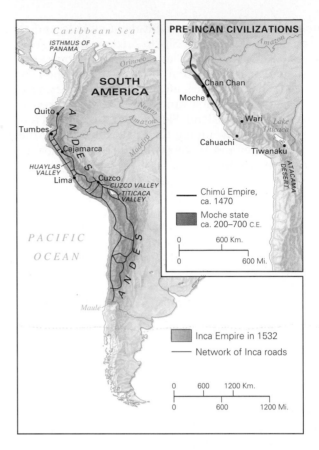

Map 12.3   Andean Civilizations, 200 B.C.E.–1532 C.E.   In response to environmental challenges posed by an arid coastal plain and high interior mountain ranges, Andean peoples made complex social and technological adaptations. Irrigation systems, the domestication of the llama, metallurgy, and shared labor obligations helped provide a firm economic foundation for powerful, centralized states. In 1532 the Inca Empire's vast territory stretched from modern Chile in the south to Colombia in the north.

model for the organization of labor and the distribution of goods at every level of Andean society. Just as individuals and families were expected to provide labor to kinsmen, members of an ayllu were expected to provide labor and goods to their hereditary chief.

With the development of territorial states ruled by hereditary aristocracies and kings after 1000 B.C.E., these obligations were organized on a larger scale. The **mit'a°** required members of ayllus to work the fields and care for the herds of llamas and alpacas owned by religious establishments, the royal court, and the aristocracy. Each allyu contributed a set number of workers for specific tasks each year. Mit'a laborers built and main-

---

khipus (KEY-pooz)   **ayllu** (aye-YOU)

mit'a (MEET-ah)

tained roads, bridges, temples, palaces, and large irrigation and drainage projects. They produced textiles and goods essential to ritual life such as beer made from maize and coca (dried leaves chewed as a stimulant and now also a source of cocaine). The mit'a system was an essential part of the Andean world for more than a thousand years.

Work was divided along gender lines, but the work of men and women was interdependent. Hunting, military service, and government were reserved largely for men. Women had numerous responsibilities in textile production, agriculture, and the home. One early Spanish commentator described the responsibilities of Andean women in terms that sound very modern:

> [T]hey did not just perform domestic tasks, but also [labored] in the fields, in the cultivation of their lands, in building houses, and carrying burdens. . . . [A]nd more than once I heard that while women were carrying these burdens, they would feel labor pains, and giving birth, they would go to a place where there was water and wash the baby and themselves. Putting the baby on top of the load they were carrying, they would then continue walking as before they gave birth. In sum, there was nothing their husbands did where their wives did not help.[7]

The ayllu was intimately tied to a uniquely Andean system of production and exchange. Because the region's mountain ranges created a multitude of small ecological areas with specialized resources, each community sought to control a variety of environments so as to guarantee access to essential goods. Coastal regions produced maize, fish, and cotton. Mountain valleys contributed quinoa (the local grain), as well as potatoes and other tubers. Higher elevations contributed the wool and meat of llamas and alpacas, and the Amazonian region provided coca and fruits. Ayllus sent out colonists to exploit the resources of these ecological niches. Colonists remained linked to their original region and kin group by marriage and ritual. Historians commonly refer to this system of controlled exchange across ecological boundaries as vertical integration, or verticality.

The historical periodization of Andean history is similar to that of Mesoamerica. Both regions developed highly integrated political and economic systems long before 1500. The pace of agricultural development, urbanization, and state formation in the Andes also approximated that in Mesoamerica. However, in the Andean region unique environmental challenges led to distinctive highland and coastal cultures with separate periodizations. Here, more than in Mesoamerica, geography influenced regional cultural integration and state formation.

Moche and Chimú

Around 200 C.E., some four centuries after the collapse of Chavín (see Chapter 4), the Moche° developed cultural and political tools that allowed them to dominate the north coastal region of Peru. Moche identity was cultural in character. They did not establish a formal empire or create unified political structures. The most powerful of the Moche urban centers, such as Cerro Blanco located near the modern Peruvian city of Trujillo (see Map 12.3), did establish hegemony over smaller towns and villages. There is also evidence that the Moche extended their political and economic control over their neighbors militarily.

Archaeological evidence indicates that the Moche cultivated maize, quinoa, beans, manioc, and sweet potatoes with the aid of massive irrigation works. At higher elevations they also produced coca, used ritually. Archaeological excavations reveal the existence of complex networks of canals and aqueducts that connected fields with water sources as far away as 75 miles (121 kilometers). These hydraulic works were maintained by mit'a labor imposed on Moche commoners and on subject peoples. The Moche maintained large herds of alpacas and llamas to transport goods across the region's difficult terrain. Their wool, along with cotton provided by farmers, provided the raw material for a thriving Moche textile production. Their meat provided an important part of the diet.

Evidence from surviving murals and decorated ceramics suggests that Moche society was highly stratified and theocratic. The need to organize large numbers of laborers to construct and maintain the irrigation system helped to promote class divisions. Wealth and power among the Moche was concentrated, along with political control, in the hands of priests and military leaders. Hierarchy was further reinforced by the military conquest of neighboring regions. The residences of the elite were constructed atop large platforms at Moche ceremonial centers. The elite literally lived above the commoners. Their power was also apparent in their rich clothing and jewelry, which confirmed their divine status and set them further apart from commoners. Moche rulers and other members of the elite wore tall headdresses. They used gold and gold alloy jewelry to mark their social position: gold plates suspended from their noses concealed the lower portion of their faces, and large gold plugs decorated their ears.

These deep social distinctions also were reflected in Moche burial practices. A recent excavation in the Lambeyeque Valley discovered the tomb of a warrior-priest who was buried with a rich treasure that included gold,

---

Moche (MO-che)

Moche Portrait Vase The Moche of ancient Peru were among the most accomplished ceramic artists of the Americas. Moche potters produced representations of gods and spirits, scenes of daily life, and portrait vases of important people. This man wears a headdress adorned by two birds and seashells. The stains next to the eyes of the birds represent tears. (Museo de Arqueologica y Antropologia, Lima/Lee Bolton Picture Library)

silver, and copper jewelry, textiles, feather ornaments, and shells. Also buried with this powerful man were two women and three men. Each retainer had one foot amputated to ensure her or his continued subservience and dependence in the afterlife.

Most commoners devoted their time to subsistence farming and to the payment of labor dues owed to their ayllu and to the elite. Both men and women were involved in agriculture, care of llama herds, and the household economy. They lived with their families in one-room buildings clustered in the outlying areas of cities and in surrounding agricultural zones.

The high quality of Moche textiles, ceramics, and metallurgy indicates the presence of numerous skilled artisans. As had been true centuries earlier in Chavín, women had a special role in the production of textiles; even elite women devoted time to weaving. Moche culture developed a brilliant representational art. Moche craftsmen produced highly individualized portrait vases that today adorn museum collections in nearly every city of the world. Ceramics were also decorated with line drawings representing myths and rituals. The most orig-

inal of Moche ceramic vessels were decorated with explicit sexual acts. The Moche also were accomplished metalsmiths, producing beautiful gold and silver objects devoted to religious and decorative functions or to elite adornment. Metallurgy served more practical ends as well: artisans produced a range of heavy copper and copper alloy tools for agricultural and military purposes.

Since we have no written sources, a detailed history of the Moche can never be written. The archaeological record makes clear that the rapid decline of the major centers coincided with a succession of natural disasters in the sixth century and with the rise of a new military power in the Andean highlands. When an earthquake altered the course of the Moche River, major flooding seriously damaged urban centers. The Moche region also was threatened by long-term climate changes. During the sixth century a thirty-year period of drought expanded the area of coastal sand dunes, and powerful winds pushed sand onto fragile agricultural lands, overwhelming the irrigation system. As the land dried, periodic heavy rains caused erosion that damaged fields and weakened the economy that had sustained ceremonial and residential centers. This succession of disasters undermined the authority of the religious and political leaders, whose privileges were based on their ability to control natural forces through rituals. Despite massive efforts to keep the irrigation canals open and the construction of new urban centers in less vulnerable valleys to the north, Moche civilization never recovered from these environmental disasters. In the eighth century, the rise of a new military power, the **Wari°,** also contributed to the disappearance of the Moche by putting pressure on trade routes that linked the coastal region with the highlands.

At the end of the Moche period the **Chimú°** developed a new and more powerful coastal civilization. Chan Chan, capital of the Chimú Empire, was constructed around 800 C.E. near the earlier Moche cultural center. After 1200 C.E. Chimú began a period of aggressive military expansion. At the apex of its power, Chimú controlled 625 miles (1,000 kilometers) of the Peruvian coast.

Within Chan Chan was a series of walled compounds, each one containing a burial pyramid. Scholars believe that each ruler built his own compound and was buried within it upon his death. Sacrifices and rich grave goods accompanied each royal burial. As with the Moche, Chimú's rulers separated themselves from the masses of society by their consumption of rare and beautiful textiles, ceramics, and precious metals as a way of suggesting the approval of the gods. Some scholars suggest that the Chimú dynasty practiced split inheritance: goods and lands of the deceased ruler went to sec-

Wari (WAH-ree) **Chimú** (chee-MOO)

ondary heirs or for religious sacrifices. The royal heir who inherited the throne was forced to construct his own residence compound and then undertake new conquests to fund his household. After the Inca conquered the northern coast in 1465, they borrowed from the rich rituals and court customs of Chimú.

Tiwanaku and Wari

After 500 C.E. two powerful civilizations developed in the Andean highlands. At nearly 13,000 feet (3,962 meters) on the high treeless plain near Lake Titicaca in modern Bolivia stand the ruins of **Tiwanaku°** (see Map 12.3). Initial occupation may have occurred as early as 400 B.C.E., but significant urbanization began only after 200 C.E. Tiwanaku's expansion depended on the adoption of technologies that increased agricultural productivity. Modern excavations provide the outline of vast drainage projects that reclaimed nearly 200,000 acres (8,000 hectares) of rich lakeside marshes for agriculture. This system of raised fields and ditches permitted intensive cultivation similar to that achieved by use of chinampas in Mesoamerica. Fish from the nearby lake and llamas added protein to a diet largely dependent on potatoes and grains. Llamas were also crucial for the maintenance of long-distance trade relationships that brought in corn, coca, tropical fruits, and medicinal plants.

The urban center of Tiwanaku was distinguished by the scale of its construction and by the high quality of its stone masonry. Large stones and quarried blocks were moved many miles to construct a large terraced pyramid, walled enclosures, and a reservoir—projects that probably required the mobilization of thousands of laborers over a period of years. Despite a limited metallurgy that produced only tools of copper alloy, Tiwanaku's artisans built large structures of finely cut stone that required little mortar to fit the blocks. They also produced gigantic human statuary. The largest example, a stern figure with a military bearing, is cut from a single block of stone 24 feet (7 meters) high.

Little is known of the social structure or daily life of this civilization. Neither surviving murals nor other decorative arts offer the suggestive guidance found in the burial goods of the Moche. Nevertheless, it is clear that Tiwanaku was a highly stratified society ruled by a hereditary elite. Most women and men devoted their time to agriculture and the care of llama herds. However, the presence of specialized artisans is evident in the high-quality construction in public buildings and in locally produced ceramics. The distribution of these ceramics to distant places suggests the presence of a specialized merchant class as well.

Many scholars portray Tiwanaku as the capital of a vast empire, a precursor to the later Inca state. It is clear that the elite controlled a large, disciplined labor force in the surrounding region. Military conquests and the establishment of colonial populations provided the highland capital with dependable supplies of products from ecologically distinct zones. And Tiwanaku cultural influence extended eastward to the jungles and southward to the coastal regions and oases of the Atacama Desert in Chile. But archaeological evidence suggests that Tiwanaku, in comparison with contemporary Teotihuacan in central Mexico, had a relatively small full-time population of around 30,000. It was not a metropolis like the largest Mesoamerican cities; it was a ceremonial and political center for a large regional population.

The contemporary site of Wari was located about 450 miles (751 kilometers) to the northwest of Tiwanaku, near the modern Peruvian city Ayacucho. The culture and technology of Wari were clearly tied to Tiwanaku, but the exact nature of this relationship remains unclear. Some scholars argue that Wari began as a dependency of Tiwanaku. Others suggest that they were joint capitals of a single empire. However, there is little evidence for either position. Clearly there were sustained cultural contacts between the two societies, but each had a unique cultural signature.

The site of Wari was larger than Tiwanaku, measuring nearly 4 square miles (10 square kilometers). The city center was surrounded by a massive wall and included a large temple. The center had numerous multifamily housing blocks. Less-concentrated housing for commoners was located in a sprawling suburban zone. Wari's development, unlike that of most other major urban centers in the Andes, appears to have occurred without central planning.

The small scale of its monumental architecture and the near absence of cut stone masonry in public and private buildings distinguish Wari from Tiwanaku. It is not clear that these characteristics resulted from the relative weakness of the elite or the absence of specialized construction crafts. Wari ceramic style also was different from that of Tiwanaku. This difference has allowed experts to trace Wari's expanding power to the coastal area earlier controlled by the Moche and to the northern highlands. Wari's military expansion occurred at a time of increasing warfare throughout the Andes. As a result, roads were built to maintain communication with remote fortified dependencies. Perhaps as a consequence of military conflict, both Tiwanaku and Wari declined to insignificance by about 1000 C.E. The Inca inherited their political legacy.

Tiwanaku (tee-wah-NA-coo)

The Inca

In little more than one hundred years, the **Inca** developed a vast imperial state, which they called "Land of Four Corners." By 1525 the empire had a population of more than 6 million inhabitants and stretched from the Maule River in Chile to northern Ecuador and from the Pacific coast across the Andes to the upper Amazon and, in the south, into Argentina (see Map 12.3). In the early fifteenth century the Inca were one of many competing military powers in the southern highlands, an area of limited political significance after the collapse of Wari. Centered in the valley of Cuzco, the Inca were initially organized as a chiefdom based on reciprocal gift giving and the redistribution of food and textiles. Strong and resourceful leaders consolidated political authority in the 1430s and undertook an ambitious campaign of military expansion.

The Inca state, like earlier highland powers, was built on traditional Andean social customs and economic practices. Tiwanaku had relied in part on the use of colonists to provide supplies of resources from distant ecologically distinct zones. The Inca built on this legacy by conquering additional distant territories and increasing the scale of forced exchanges. Crucial to this process was the development of a large, professional military. Unlike the peoples of Mesoamerica, who distributed specialized goods by developing markets and tribute relationships, Andean peoples used state power to broaden and expand the vertical exchange system that had permitted ayllus to exploit a range of ecological niches.

Like earlier highland civilizations, the Inca were pastoralists. Inca prosperity and military strength depended on vast herds of llamas and alpacas, which provided food and clothing as well as transport for goods. Both men and women were involved in the care of these herds. Women were primarily responsible for weaving; men were drivers in long-distance trade. This pastoral tradition provided the Inca with powerful metaphors that helped to shape their political and religious beliefs. They believed that the gods and their ruler shared the obligations of the shepherd to his flock—an idea akin to Old Testament references to "The Lord is my Shepherd."

Collective efforts by mit'a laborers made the Inca Empire possible. Cuzco, the imperial capital, and the provincial cities, the royal court, the imperial armies, and the state's religious cults all rested on this foundation. The mit'a system also created the material surplus that provided the bare necessities for the old, weak, and ill of Inca society. Each ayllu contributed approximately one-seventh of its adult male population to meet these collective obligations. These draft laborers served as soldiers, construction workers, craftsmen, and runners to carry messages along post roads. They also drained swamps, terraced mountainsides, filled in valley floors, built and maintained irrigation works, and built storage facilities and roads. Inca laborers constructed 13,000 miles (20,930 kilometers) of road, facilitating military troop movements, administration, and trade (see Environment and Technology: Inca Roads).

Imperial administration was similarly superimposed on existing political structures and established elite groups. The hereditary chiefs of ayllus carried out administrative and judicial functions. As the Inca expanded, they generally left local rulers in place. By leaving in place the rulers of defeated societies, the Inca risked rebellion, but they controlled these risks by means of a thinly veiled system of hostage taking and the use of military garrisons. The rulers of defeated regions were required to send their heirs to live at the Inca royal court in Cuzco. Inca leaders even required that representations of important local gods be brought to Cuzco and made part of the imperial pantheon. These measures promoted imperial integration while at the same time providing hostages to ensure the good behavior of subject peoples.

Conquests magnified the authority of the Inca ruler and led to the creation of an imperial bureaucracy drawn from among his kinsmen. The royal family claimed descent from the Sun, the primary Inca god. Members of the royal family lived in palaces maintained by armies of servants. The lives of the ruler and members of the royal family were dominated by political and religious rituals that helped to legitimize their authority (see Society and Culture: Acllas). Among the many obligations associated with kingship was the requirement to extend imperial boundaries by warfare. Thus each new ruler began his reign with conquest.

Tenochtitlan, the Aztec capital, had a population of about 150,000 in 1520. At the height of Inca power in 1530, Cuzco had a population of less than 30,000. Nevertheless, Cuzco was a remarkable place. The Inca were highly skilled stone craftsmen: their most impressive buildings were constructed of carefully cut stones fitted together without mortar. The city was laid out in the shape of a giant puma (a mountain lion). At the center were the palaces that each ruler built when he ascended to the throne, as well as the major temples. The richest was the Temple of the Sun. Its interior was lined with sheets of gold, and its patio was decorated with golden representations of llamas and corn. The ruler made every effort to awe and intimidate visitors and residents alike with a nearly continuous series of rituals, feasts, and sacrifices. Sacrifices of textiles, animals, and other goods sent as tribute dominated the city's calendar. The destruction of these valuable commodities, and a small number of human sacrifices, helped give the impression

Inca Roads

From the time of Chavín (900–250 B.C.E.), Andean peoples built roads to facilitate trade across ecological boundaries and to project political power over conquered peoples. In the fifteen and sixteenth centuries, the Inca extended and improved the networks of roads constructed in earlier eras. Roads were crucially important to Inca efforts to collect and redistribute tribute paid in food, textiles, and chicha (corn liquor).

Two roads connected Cuzco, the Inca capital in southern Peru, to Quito, Ecudaor, in the north and Chile farther south. One ran along the flat and arid coastal plain, the other through the mountainous interior. Shorter east/west roads connected important coastal and interior cities. Evidence suggests that administrative centers were sited along these routes to expedite rapid communication with the capital. Rest stops at convenient distances provided shelter and food to traveling officials and runners who carried messages between Cuzco and the empire's cities and towns. Warehouses were constructed along the roads to provide food and military supplies for passing Inca armies or to supply local laborers working in construction projects or cultivating the ruler's fields.

Because communication with regional administrative centers and the movement of troops were the central objectives of the Inca leadership, routes were selected to avoid natural obstacles and to reduce travel time. Mit'a laborers recruited from nearby towns and villages built and maintained the roads. Roads were commonly paved with stone or packed earth and often were bordered by stone or adobe walls to keep soldiers or pack trains of llamas from straying into the fields of farmers. Whenever possible, roadbeds were made level. In mountainous terrain some roads were little more than improved paths, but in flat country three or four people could walk abreast. Care was always taken to repair damage caused by rain runoff or other drainage problems.

The achievement of Inca road builders is clearest in the mountainous terrain of the interior. They built suspension bridges across high gorges and cut roadbeds into the face of cliffs. A Spanish priest living in Peru in the seventeenth century commented that the Inca roads "were magnificent constructions, which could be compared favorably with the most superb roads of the Romans."

Source: Quotation from Father Bernabe Cobo, *History of the Inca Empire. An account of the Indians' customs and origin together with a treatise on Inca legends, history, and social institutions* (Austin: University of Texas Press, 1983), 223.

Inca Road The Inca built roads to connect distant parts of the empire to Cuzco, the Inca capital. These roads are still used in Peru. (Loren McIntyre/Woodfin Camp & Associates)

Acllas

Acllas (AK-yahz) were young virgins selected by representatives of the Inca ruler to serve the cult of the Sun or be given as marriage partners and concubines to the ruler himself or to Inca nobles and favored nobles from dependencies. These young women were commonly chosen for their beauty from among the daughters of local rulers.

Our understanding of the acllas' lives comes primarily from Spanish-era sources. We know these women lived within the closely guarded walls of convent-like buildings located in the large towns of the empire and that their lives were dedicated to religious observances and the production of fine textiles.

Felipe Guaman Poma de Ayala wrote the following account in the early seventeenth century. After long neglect, his illustrated history of Inca and early Spanish colonial society has become a fundamental source for Andean history. In this text, the word Inca *refers both to the people and to their ruler. Although Guaman Poma is obviously proud of his descent from a high-ranking indigenous noble family, his description of ancient images of gods as "idols" suggests the depth of cultural change among Amerindian people after the Spanish conquest.*

During the time of the Incas certain women, who were called acllas or "the Chosen," were destined for lifelong virginity. Mostly they were confined in houses and they belonged to one of two main categories, namely sacred virgins and common virgins.

The so-called "virgins with red cheeks" entered upon their duties at the age of twenty and were dedicated to the service of the Sun, the Moon, and the Day-Star. In their whole life they were never allowed to speak to a man.

The virgins of the Inca's own shrine of Huanacauri were known for their beauty as well as their chastity. The other principal shrines had similar girls in attendance. At the less important shrines there were older virgins who occupied themselves with spinning and weaving the silk-like clothes worn by their idols. There was a still lower class of virgins, over 40 years of age and no longer very beautiful, who performed unimportant religious duties and worked in the fields or as ordinary seamstresses.

There was yet another class of aclla or "chosen," only some of whom kept their virginity and others not. These were the Inca's (the ruler of the Inca people) beautiful attendants and concubines, who were drawn from noble families and lived in his palaces. They made clothing for him out of material finer than taffeta or silk. They also prepared a maize spirit of extraordinary richness, which was matured for an entire month, and they cooked delicious dishes for the Inca. They also lay with him, but never with any other man.

Thus chastity was greatly prized in our country. It was the Inca who received our girls from the Sun and who allotted them, always as virgins, to his subjects. Until that time the man did not know the woman nor the woman the man. The man might be in Quito or Chile and might be assigned a woman from quite a different region but a contract of marriage was made with the help of the woman's brother.

What special qualities were most valued in the young women selected to be acllas? What categories of aclla does Guaman Poma describe? What were the lives of acllas like? What does this description of the Inca ruler's relationship with the acllas tell us about how he was viewed?

Source: Felipe Guaman Poma de Ayala, *Letter to a King: A Peruvian Chief's Account of Life Under the Incas and Under Spanish Rule*, ed. and trans. Christopher Dilke (New York: Dutton, 1978), 84–86.

---

of splendor and sumptuous abundance that appeared to demonstrate the ruler's claimed descent from the Sun.

Inca cultural achievement rested on the strong foundation of earlier Andean civilizations. We know that astronomical observation was a central concern of the priestly class, as in Mesoamerica; the Inca calendar, however, is lost to us. All communication other than oral was transmitted by the khipus borrowed from earlier Andean civilizations. In weaving and metallurgy, Inca technology, building on earlier regional developments, was more advanced than in Mesoamerica. Inca craftsmen produced utilitarian tools and weapons of copper and bronze as well as decorative objects of gold and silver. Inca women produced textiles of extraordinary beauty from cotton and the wool of llamas and alpacas.

Although the Inca did not introduce new technologies, they increased economic output and added to the region's prosperity. The conquest of large populations in environmentally distinct regions allowed the Inca to multiply the yields produced by the traditional ex-

Inca Tunic Andean weavers produced beautiful textiles from cotton and from the wool of llamas and alpacas. The Inca inherited this rich craft tradition and produced some of the world's most remarkable textiles. The quality and design of each garment indicated the weaver's rank and power in this society. This tunic was an outer garment for a powerful male. (From *Textile Art of Peru*. Collection created and directed by Jose Antonio de Lavalle and Jose Alejandro Gonzalez Garcia [L. L. Editores, 1989])

changes between distinct ecological niches. But the expansion of imperial economic and political power was purchased at the cost of reduced equality and diminished local autonomy. The imperial elite, living in richly decorated palaces in Cuzco and other urban centers, was increasingly cut off from the masses of Inca society. The royal court held members of the provincial nobility at arm's length, and commoners were subject to execution if they dared to look directly at the ruler's face.

After only a century of regional dominance, the Inca Empire faced a crisis in 1525. The death of the Inca ruler Huayna Capac at the conclusion of the conquest of Ecuador initiated a bloody struggle for the throne. Powerful factions coalesced around two sons whose rivalry compelled both the professional military and the hereditary Inca elite to choose sides. Civil war was the result. The Inca state controlled a vast territory spread over more than 3,000 miles (4,830 kilometers) of mountainous terrain. Regionalism and ethnic diversity had always posed a threat to the empire. Civil war weakened imperial institu-

tions and ignited the resentments of conquered peoples. On the eve of the arrival of Europeans, the destructive consequences of this violent conflict undermined the institutions and economy of Andean civilizations.

CONCLUSION

The indigenous societies of the Western Hemisphere developed unique technologies and cultural forms in mountainous regions, tropical rain forests, deserts, woodlands, and arctic regions. In Mesoamerica, North America, and the Andean region the natural environment powerfully influenced cultural development. The Maya of southern Mexico, for example, developed agricultural technologies that compensated for the tropical cycle of heavy rains followed by long dry periods. On the coast of Peru the Moche used systems of trade and mutual labor obligation to meet the challenge of an arid climate and mountainous terrain while the mound builders of North America expanded agricultural production by utilizing the rich flood plains of the Ohio and Mississippi rivers. Across the Americas, hunting and gathering peoples and urbanized agricultural societies both produced rich religious and aesthetic traditions as well as useful technologies and effective social institutions in response to local conditions. Once established, these cultural traditions proved very durable.

The Aztec and Inca Empires represented the culmination of a long developmental process that had begun before 1000 B.C.E. Each imperial state controlled extensive and diverse territories with populations that numbered in the millions. The capital cities of Tenochtitlan and Cuzco were great cultural and political centers that displayed some of the finest achievements of Amerindian technology, art, and architecture. Both states were based on conquests and were ruled by powerful hereditary elites who depended on the tribute of subject peoples. In both traditions religion met spiritual needs while also organizing collective life and legitimizing political authority.

The Aztec and Inca empires were created militarily, their survival depending as much on the power of their armies as on the productivity of their economies or the wisdom of their rulers. Both empires were ethnically and environmentally diverse, but there were important differences. Elementary markets had been developed in Mesoamerica to distribute specialized regional production, although the forced payment of goods as tribute remained important. In the Andes reciprocal labor obligations and managed exchange relationships were used to allocate goods. The Aztecs used their military to force defeated peoples to provide food, textiles and even sacrificial captives as tribute, but they left local hereditary elites in place. The Incas, in contrast, created a more centralized administrative structure managed by a trained bureaucracy.

As the Western Hemisphere's long isolation drew to a close in the late fifteenth century, both empires were challenged by powerful neighbors or by internal revolts. In earlier periods similar challenges had contributed to the decline of great civilizations in both Mesoamerica and the Andean region. In those cases, a long period of adjustment and the creation of new indigenous institutions followed the collapse of dominant powers such as the Toltecs in Mesoamerica or Tiwanaku in the Andes. With the arrival of Europeans, this cycle of crisis and adjustment would be transformed, and the future of Amerindian peoples would become linked to the cultures of the Old World.

■ Key Terms

Teotihuacan	khipu
chinampas	ayllu
Maya	mit'a
Toltecs	Moche
Aztecs	Chimú
Tenochtitlan	Tiwanaku
tribute system	Wari
Anasazi	Inca
chiefdom	acllas

■ Suggested Reading

In *Prehistory of the Americas* (1987) Stuart Fiedel provides an excellent summary of the early history of the Western Hemisphere. Alvin M. Josephy, Jr., in *The Indian Heritage of America* (1968), also provides a thorough introduction to the topic. *Canada's First Nations* (1992) by Olive Patricia Dickason is a well-written survey that traces the history of Canada's Amerindian peoples to the modern era. *Early Man in the New World,* ed. Richard Shutler, Jr. (1983), provides a helpful addition to these works. *Atlas of Ancient America* (1986) by Michael Coe, Elizabeth P. Benson, and Dean R. Snow is a useful compendium of maps and information. George Kubler, *The Art and Architecture of Ancient America* (1962), is a valuable resource, though now dated.

Eric Wolf provides an enduring synthesis of Mesoamerican history in *Sons of the Shaking Earth* (1959). A good summary of recent research on Teotihuacan is found in Esther Pasztori, *Teotihuacan* (1997). Linda Schele and David Freidel summarize the most recent research on the classic-period Maya in their excellent *A Forest of Kings* (1990). The best summary of Aztec history is Nigel Davies, *The Aztec Empire: The Toltec Resurgence*

(1987). Jacques Soustelle, *Daily Life of the Aztecs,* trans. Patrick O'Brian (1961), is a good introduction. Though controversial in some of its analysis, Inga Clendinnen's *Aztecs* (1991) is also an important contribution.

Chaco and Hohokam (1991), ed. Patricia L. Crown and W. James Judge, is a good summary of research issues. Robert Silverberg, *Mound Builders of Ancient America* (1968), supplies a good introduction to this topic.

A helpful introduction to the scholarship on early Andean societies is provided by Karen Olsen Bruhns, *Ancient South America* (1994). For the Moche see Garth Bawden, *The Moche* (1996). *The History of the Incas* (1970) by Alfred Metraux is dated but offers a useful summary. The best recent modern synthesis is María Rostworowski de Diez Canseco, *History of the Inca Realm,* trans. by Harry B. Iceland (1999). John Murra, *The Economic Organization of the Inca State* (1980), and Irene Silverblatt, *Moon, Sun, and Witches: Gender Ideologies and Class in Inca and Colonial Peru* (1987), are challenging, important works on Peru before the arrival of Columbus in the Western Hemisphere. Frederich Katz, *The Ancient Civilizations of the Americas* (1972), offers a useful comparative perspective on ancient American developments.

■ Notes

1. This summary follows closely the narrative offered by Linda Schele and David Freidel in *A Forest of Kings: The Untold Story of the Ancient Maya* (New York: Morrow, 1990), 182–186.
2. Before 1492 the inhabitants of the Western Hemisphere had no single name for themselves. They had neither a racial consciousness nor a racial identity. Identity was derived from kin groups, language, cultural practices, and political structures. There was no sense that physical similarities created a shared identity. America's original inhabitants had racial consciousness and racial identity imposed on them by conquest and the occupation of their lands by Europeans after 1492. All of the collective terms for these first American peoples are tainted by this history. *Indians, Native Americans, Amerindians, First Peoples, and Indigenous Peoples* are among the terms in common usage. In this book the names of individual cultures and states are used wherever possible. *Amerindian* and other terms that suggest transcultural identity and experience are used most commonly for the period after 1492.
3. From the Florentine Codex, quoted in Inga Clendinnen, *Aztecs* (New York: Cambridge University Press, 1991), 213.
4. Quoted in Nigel Davies, *The Toltec Heritage: From the Fall of Tula to the Rise of Tenochtitlán* (Norman: University of Oklahoma Press, 1980), 3.
5. Bernal Díaz del Castillo, *The Conquest of New Spain,* trans. J. M. Cohen (London: Penguin Books, 1963), 217.
6. Hernando Cortés, *Five Letters, 1519–1526,* trans. J. Bayard Morris (New York: Norton, 1991), 87.
7. Quoted in Irene Silverblatt, *Moon, Sun, and Witches: Gender Ideologies and Class in Inca and Colonial Peru* (Princeton, NJ: Princeton University Press, 1987), 10.

Four

INTERREGIONAL PATTERNS OF CULTURE AND CONTACT,

1200–1550

n Eurasia, overland trade along the Silk Road, which had begun before the Roman and Han Empires, reached its peak during the era of the Mongol empires. Beginning in 1206 with the rise of Genghis Khan, the Mongols linked Europe, the Middle East, Russia, Central Asia, and East Asia with threads of conquest and trade. In the century and a half of Mongol domination, some communities in Eurasia thrived on the continental connections that the Mongols' hold on the overland routes made possible, while others groaned under the tax burdens and physical devastation of Mongol rule. But whether for good or ill, Mongol power was based on the skills, strategies, and technologies of the overland trade and life on the steppes.

The impact of the Mongols was also felt by societies that remained outside Mongol rule. In Europe, Egypt, Southeast Asia, and Japan, the Mongol challenge stimulated societies that had already begun to urbanize, develop new industries, and undertake political centralization, and it accelerated many of these changes.

By 1500, Mongol dominance was past, and new powers were emerging. A new Chinese empire, the Ming, was expanding its influence in Southeast Asia. The Ottomans had captured Constantinople and overthrown the Byzantine Empire. And Christians had defeated Muslims in Spain and were laying the foundations of a new overseas empire. With the fall of the Mongol Empire, Central Asia was no longer a major crossroads of trade.

As the great overland trade of Eurasia faded, merchants, soldiers, and explorers took to the seas. The most spectacular of the early state-sponsored long-distance ocean voyages were undertaken by the Chinese admiral Zheng He. The 1300s and 1400s also saw African exploration of the Atlantic and Polynesian colonization of the central and eastern Pacific. By 1500 the navigator Christopher Columbus, sailing for Spain, had reached the Americas, and the Portuguese had sailed around the world. In earlier centuries travelers had considered a journey between Europe and East Asia as crossing the whole world. But new kinds of ships and better knowledge of the size of the globe as well as its shorelines made sub-Saharan Africa, the Indian Ocean, Asia, Europe, and finally the Americas accessible to each other with unexpected ease.

The great overland routes of Eurasia had generated massive wealth in East Asia and growing hunger for commerce in Europe. These factors animated the development of the sea trade, too. Exposure to the achievements, wealth, and resources of societies in the Americas, sub-Saharan Africa, and Asia excited the interest of the emerging European monarchies in further development and control of the seas.

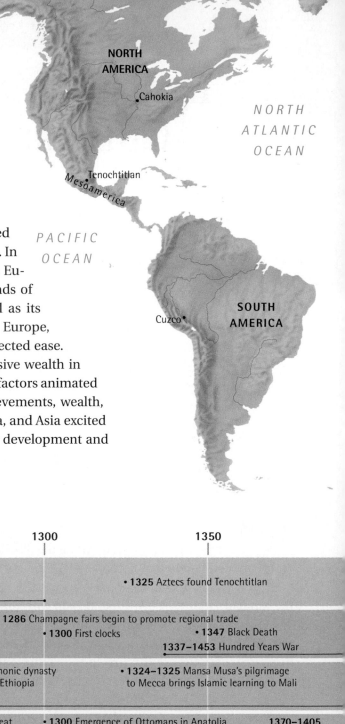

	1200	1250	1300	1350
Americas	• **1200** Population of Cahokia reaches 30,000 **1200–1300** Collapse of Anasazi centers		• **1325** Aztecs found Tenochtitlan	
Europe	• **1215** Magna Carta • **1240** Mongol conquest of Russia • **1241** Mongol invasion of Europe	• **1286** Champagne fairs begin to promote regional trade • **1300** First clocks	• **1347** Black Death **1337–1453** Hundred Years War	
Africa	Kingdom of Benin founded ca. 1250 • **1240–1500** Mali Empire	• **1270** Solomonic dynasty founded in Ethiopia	• **1324–1325** Mansa Musa's pilgrimage to Mecca brings Islamic learning to Mali	
Middle East	• **1221** Mongols attack Iran	• **1260** Mamluks defeat Mongols at Ain Jalut • **1258** Mongols take Baghdad, end Abbasid Caliphate	• **1300** Emergence of Ottomans in Anatolia **1295–1304** Rule of Muslim Il-khan Ghazan	**1370–1405** Reign of Timur
Asia and Oceania	• **1200** Polynesians settle New Zealand **1206–1227** Reign of Genghis Khan • **1206** Delhi Sultanate founded in India	• **1274, 1281** Mongol attacks on Japan Polynesians settle Hawaii **1300** • **1265–1294** Reign of Khubilai Khan	• **1336** Ashikaga Shogunate founded Yuan Empire in China **1279–1368** Ming Empire founded in China **1368** •

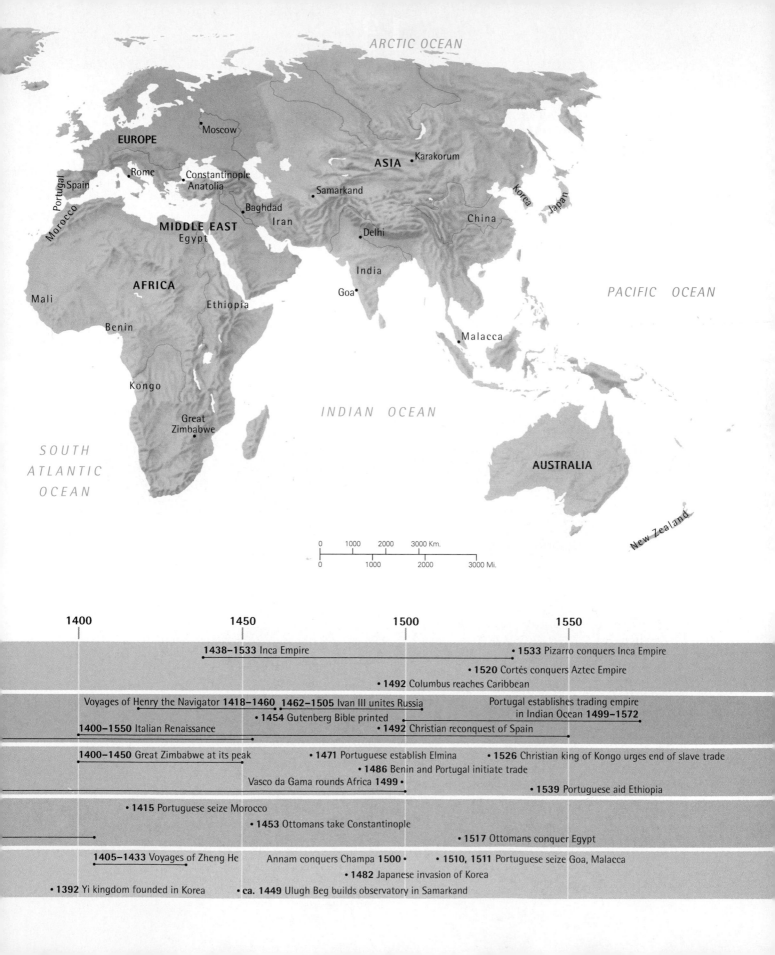

ARCTIC OCEAN

EUROPE
• Moscow

ASIA
• Karakorum

Portugal
Spain
• Rome
• Constantinople
Anatolia
• Samarkand
Korea
Japan

Morocco
MIDDLE EAST
• Baghdad
Iran
China

Egypt
• Delhi

PACIFIC OCEAN

AFRICA
India

Mali
Goa •

Ethiopia

Benin

INDIAN OCEAN

Kongo

Malacca

Great
Zimbabwe

SOUTH
ATLANTIC
OCEAN

AUSTRALIA

New Zealand

| 0 | 1000 | 2000 | 3000 Km. |
| 0 | 1000 | 2000 | 3000 Mi. |

1400   1450   1500   1550

1438–1533 Inca Empire   • 1533 Pizarro conquers Inca Empire

                                            • 1520 Cortés conquers Aztec Empire

                              • 1492 Columbus reaches Caribbean

Voyages of Henry the Navigator 1418–1460 • 1462–1505 Ivan III unites Russia   Portugal establishes trading empire
                                                                                 in Indian Ocean 1499–1572
                              • 1454 Gutenberg Bible printed

1400–1550 Italian Renaissance   • 1492 Christian reconquest of Spain

1400–1450 Great Zimbabwe at its peak   • 1471 Portuguese establish Elmina   • 1526 Christian king of Kongo urges end of slave trade

                              • 1486 Benin and Portugal initiate trade

            Vasco da Gama rounds Africa 1499 •

                                            • 1539 Portuguese aid Ethiopia

• 1415 Portuguese seize Morocco

      • 1453 Ottomans take Constantinople

                              • 1517 Ottomans conquer Egypt

1405–1433 Voyages of Zheng He   Annam conquers Champa 1500 •   • 1510, 1511 Portuguese seize Goa, Malacca

                  • 1482 Japanese invasion of Korea

• 1392 Yi kingdom founded in Korea   • ca. 1449 Ulugh Beg builds observatory in Samarkand

13

WESTERN EURASIA,
1200–1500

The Rise of the Mongols, 1200–1260 • The Fall and Rise of Islam, 1260–1500 •
Local Solidarity in Response to the Mongols
ENVIRONMENT AND TECHNOLOGY: Horses
SOCIETY AND CULTURE: Dueling Pieties

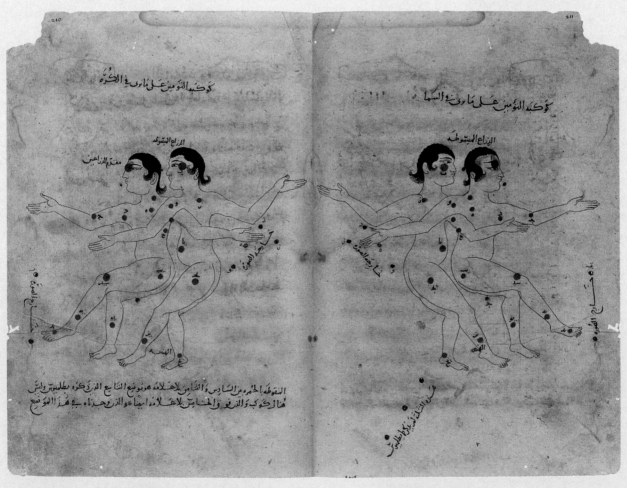

Gemini   This Persian schematic from a collection of constellations was based
on the notebooks of the Il-khan academy at Maraga.

When the Mongol leader Temüjin° was a boy, his father was murdered by a rival group. Though Temüjin's mother tried hard to shelter him (and protect him from dogs, which he feared), she could not find a safe haven for him. At the age of fifteen Temüjin sought a place for himself in the care of Toghoril°, leader of the Keraits°. Among the many warring confederations of Mongolia, the Keraits were Turkic speakers who had a strong interest in both Christianity and Buddhism. During his years with them, Temüjin learned much that would be fundamental to the power and the scope of the empire he would someday build: the charisma of personal strength, courage, and intelligence; the importance of religious tolerance; the necessity to show no mercy to determined enemies; and the versatility of the cultural and economic institutions of Central Asia.

In 1206, Temüjin was acknowledged as **Genghis Khan°**, or supreme leader, of the **Mongols** and their allies. He counted among his advisers adherents of all the major religions of the Middle East and East Asia, as well as speakers of many of the region's languages. All were able to guide him in making his rule more effective among and more appealing to the diverse civilizations of Eurasia. A contemporary historian recorded the following as Genghis's deathbed speech. It can hardly be literally true, but it captures the strategy behind Mongol success: "If you want to retain your possessions and conquer your enemies, you must make your subjects submit willingly and unite your diverse energies to a single end."[1]

Although scholars today recognize the importance of Temüjin and his successors (see Figure 13.1 on page 330) for the development of the later medieval world, the common view of the Mongols is still the one expressed in European and Asian sources of the time. The association of the Mongols with death, gore, suffering, and conflagration is nearly overwhelming. It is true that the Mongol conquests were bloody encounters, involving levels of slaughter previously unknown in many areas. It is also true that the rapid movement of Mongol soldiers, their equipment, and their captives accelerated the spread of virulent diseases, including the plague.

But Mongol rule also provided many advantages. By 1250 the Mongol Empire stretched from Poland to Siberia (see Map 13.1). By unifying much of the Eurasian landmass, the Mongol Empire promoted the movement of people and ideas from one end of Eurasia to the other. Specialized skills that had developed in various parts of the world in the preceding centuries spread rapidly throughout the Mongol domains. Trade routes improved, markets expanded, and the demand for products grew in both the Middle East and East Asia. The Silk Road was reinvigorated.

Though the period from 1200 to about 1350 is often considered the age of Mongol domination, the Mongols themselves are only one part of the story. The Mongols had limited economic and strategic interest in the areas they controlled. In most cases they permitted local cultures to survive and to continue to develop. Regions tended to become better defined in the Mongol period, partly as a result of Mongol unification of large territories, and partly because of local reactions against Mongol domination. Thus, while it is true that the Mongols stimulated economic and cultural exchange among widely separated regions, they also provoked the local reactions that allowed China, Russia, Iran, and other areas to refine their sense of difference and their search for self-rule. This was not nationalism in our modern sense of the word, but it was a stage of loyalty formation that was crucial to modern nationalism.

As you read this chapter, ask yourself the following questions:

- What accounts for the size and speed of the Mongol conquests?
- What benefits resulted from the integration of Eurasia achieved by the Mongol empire?
- What was the impact of the Il-khan Mongols' conversion to Islam?
- What was the impact of Mongol rule on Russia, Central Asia, and the Middle East?

Temüjin (TEM-uh-jin)   Toghoril (TOE-hoe-rill)
Keraits (keh-rates)   Genghis Khan (GENG-iz KAHN)

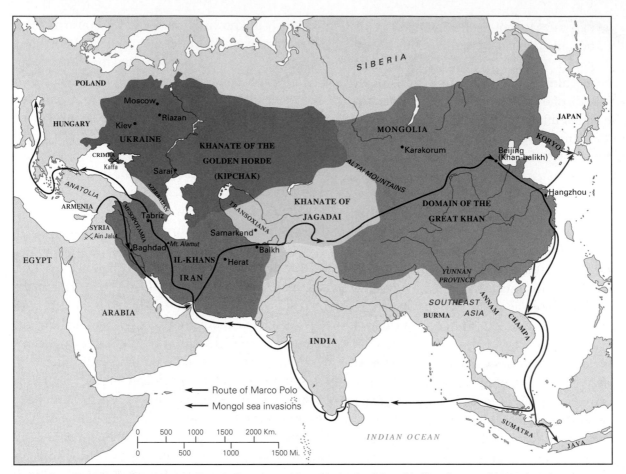

Map 13.1   The Mongol Domains in Eurasia in 1300   After the death of Genghis Khan in 1227, his empire was divided among his sons and grandsons. Son Ögödei succeeded Genghis as Great Khan. Grandson Khubilai expanded the Domain of the Great Kahn into eastern China by 1279. Grandson Hülegü was the first Il-khan in the Middle East. Grandson Batu founded the Khanate of the Golden Horde in southern Russia. Son Jagadai ruled the Jagadai Khanate in Central Asia. (From John King Fairbank, et al., *East Asia: Tradition and Transformation*, rev. ed., pp. 172, 196. Copyright © 1989 by Houghton Mifflin Company. Used by permission.)

THE RISE OF THE MONGOLS, 1200–1260

Large federations of nomads had dominated the steppes (dry, high plains) and deserts of Central Asia many times since the beginnings of recorded history. The environment, economic life, cultural institutions, and political traditions of the steppes and deserts all contributed to the expansion and contraction of empires. Similarly, the rise of the Mongols can be attributed at least as much to the long-term trends and particular pressures of Central Asia as to any special abilities of Genghis Khan and his followers.

Nomadism in Central Asia

Nomadism is a way of life forced by a scarcity of resources. Nomadic groups have by far the lowest rates of population density. To find pastures and water for their livestock, they are continually on the move. In the course of their migrations they frequently come into contact with other nomadic groups seeking the same resources, and the outcome of these encounters is commonly warfare, alliance, or both. In times of drought, conflicts increase. The result is the extermination of small groups, the growth of alliances, and frequent outmigration from groups that have grown too large. Historians believe that such a period of environmental stress afflicted northern Eurasia around 1000 C.E. and contributed to the dislocations and conflicts out of which the Mongols eventually

CHRONOLOGY

	Central Asia	Middle East	Russia
1200	**1206** Temüjin chosen Genghis Khan of the Mongols **1227** Death of Genghis Khan **1227–1241** Region of Great Khan Ögödei	**1221–1223** First Mongol attacks in Iran **1250** Mamluk regime controls Egypt and Syria **1258** Mongols sack Baghdad and kill the caliph **1260** Mamluks defeat Il-khans at Ain Jalut	**1221–1223** First Mongol attacks on Russia **1240** Mongols sack Kiev **1242** Alexander Nevskii defeats Teutonic Knights **1260** War between Il-khans and Golden Horde
1300		**1295** Il-khan Ghazan converts to Islam **1349** End of Il-khan rule **ca. 1350** Egypt infected by plague	**1346** Plague outbreak at Kaffa
	1370–1405 Reign of Timur		
1400		**1453** Ottomans capture Constantinople	**1462–1505** Ivan III unites Russia under rule of Moscow, throws off Mongol rule (1480)

emerged. Some agricultural lands became disastrously wet in this period, but lands in northern Eurasia became unusually dry, and nomadic peoples began to move south in search of new pastures.

Nomadic groups in Central Asia frequently engaged in violence, so every man was a full-time herdsman, hunter, and warrior. Like all their predecessors on the steppes, the Mongols were superb riders. They continued the ancient tradition of putting their infants on goats to accustom them to riding. And like all Central Asian warriors the Mongols were adept at shooting arrows from a galloping horse (see Environment and Technology: Horses).

Because nomads are constantly moving but also always under pressure to make their movements efficient and accurate, centralized decision making is a necessary part of their life. The relative independence of Mongol individuals and their families forced decision making to be public, and many people voiced their views. Even at the height of a military campaign nomad warriors moved with their families and their possessions and, if they disagreed with a decision, sometimes struck off on their own. The political structures of the Central Asian empires were designed to accommodate the conflicting centralizing and decentralizing forces of traditional nomadic life. Mongol groups had strong hierarchies, but the leader—the *khan*—was always required to have his decisions ratified by a council of the leaders of powerful families.

Competition for resources reinforced slavery and tribute in Central Asia. Many of the men and women captured during warfare or raids became slaves and were forced to do menial work in nomadic camps. Some individuals evidently entered into slavery willingly, to avoid starvation. Slaves were valuable for their labor and also as currency. Weak groups secured land rights and protection from strong groups by providing them with

Horses

Before the rise of the Mongols, many breeds of horses in Eurasia had been improved and specialized by cross-breeding with the large, quick, graceful horses of the Caucasus and the Middle East. The Mongols, however, preserved a form of domesticated horse that looked not very different from the prehistoric horses that Paleolithic peoples had painted on cave walls.

Mongol ponies were an excellent example of the adaptation of traditional technology (in this case horse breeding) to environment. Because they remained semiwild, they were uniquely able to survive the very cold, dry climate of Mongolia. The Mongols never fed or sheltered them, so by natural selection the breed was able to forage in snow, and to survive the plunging night temperatures.

During the Tang Empire (618–907), Central Asian ponies were crossbred with specialized strains from the Middle East to produce larger, stronger, more beautiful horses. Occasionally such horses were brought to Mongolia by the Turks and bred with the local horses. But only after the time of Genghis did the numbers of the Mongolian pony decline dramatically. The breed, or a near relative of it, now survives only in game preserves.

Charioteers, who for a time dominated warfare in ancient Middle East and East Asia, were no match for well-coordinated and well-armed light horsemen, and chariot driving disappeared as a war art wherever extensive campaigns against Central Eurasian riders occurred. The Parthians of eastern Iran, whose riding skills astonished the empires of the Middle East, were legendary for their ability to shoot arrows at the enemy while retreating from them. In China, the Xiongnu drove out the chariot and forced Chinese soldiers to fight on horseback. For similar reasons, the Huns were a revelation to Europe, which adopted the iron stirrup from them.

Central Eurasian riding skills fundamentally altered the social significance of the horse. In the ancient Middle East, the use of horse teams and chariots in warfare was extremely expensive and demanded a select group of warriors wealthy enough to maintain their equipment and powerful enough to control grazing land for their animals. Horses had to be carefully bred to be large enough to pull the chariots and carefully trained to manage their loads with rather inefficient harnessing. In Central Asia, riding was an ability that all men and women in good health possessed. It required only a rudimentary saddle and experience. The deployment of riders in warfare blurred the distinction between a riding herdsman (or hunter) and a riding soldier, and there was no specialization of function along class lines. Because Central Asians did not enclose their herds but left them to forage, no question of individual landownership arose.

In Russia, the Middle East, and East Asia, the skills necessary for the use of the horse, including breeding, tacking, and military riding, were all adapted from the nomads. The use of riders for such varied activities as postal service and military scouting changed the speed of communications and some patterns of military strategy. During the Mongol period and for centuries after, the breeding, raising, training, and maintenance of horses for warfare, in particular, dominated the government economies of all countries north of the tropics.

Mongolian Pony This resting pony wears a head collar, as specified by Ghenghis's law. (National Palace Museum, Taipei, Republic of China)

slaves, livestock, weapons, silk, or cash. Many powerful groups (such as the one to which Genghis Khan's father belonged) found that they could live almost entirely off tribute, so they spent less time and fewer resources on herding and more on the warlike activities that would secure greater tribute.

As each group grew in numbers and wealth, its political institutions became more complex. Federations arose, based on an increasing number of alliances among groups, almost always expressed in arranged marriages between the leading families. Children frequently became pawns of diplomacy: their marriages were arranged in childhood—in Temüjin's case, at the age of eight. Because of the relationship between marriage and politics, women from prestigious families were often very powerful in negotiation and management. And, when things became violent, they were just as likely as men to suffer assassination or execution.

The long-distance, seasonal movements of the Central Asia nomads created powerful channels for trade and communication. The result was great cultural diversity. Nomads aided in the spread of Manichaeism, Judaism, Christianity, Buddhism, and Islam across Central Asia. On the steppe, it was not unique to find within a single family believers in two or more of those religions, in combination with traditional shamanism (ancient practices by which special individuals visited and influenced the supernatural world). This plurality of religious practice reflected the fact that Central Eurasian nomads did not always associate ideas about rulership with ideas about religion.

Since very early times, Central Asian societies had been permeated by the idea of world rulership by a khan, who, with the aid of his shamans, would speak to and for an ultimate god, represented in Central Asia as Sky or Heaven. It was believed that this universal ruler, by virtue of his role as the speaker for Heaven, would transcend particular cultures and dominate them all. For the Mongols, the idea of universal rule was centrally important—as the words attributed to Genghis on his deathbed reflect. It permitted them to appeal to any and all religions to legitimate their conquests. And it authorized them to claim superiority over all religious leaders.

Nomads strove for economic self-sufficiency by attempting to restrict their diet to foods they could provide for themselves—primarily meat and milk—and by wearing clothes produced from pastoral animals—felt (from wool), leather, and furs. Women generally oversaw the breeding and birthing of livestock and the preparation of furs, both of which were fundamental to the nomadic economy. Nomads, however, never lived completely independent of the settled regions.

Animal Husbandry In nomadic societies, it was common for men and boys to tend to the herds in the pastures. The more technical tasks associated with animal husbandry—breeding, birthing, shearing, milking, and the processing of pelts—were usually performed by women who worked together in teams and passed their knowledge from older to younger members of the community. Various activities are depicted in this contemporary painting. (Ulan Bator Fine Arts Museum)

Iron was crucially important to Central Asian nomads. They used it in bridles and stirrups, wagons, and weapons. Nomads did not develop large mining enterprises, but they eagerly acquired iron implements in trade and reworked them to suit their own purposes. As early as the 600s, the Turks' large ironworking stations south of Mount Altai were famous. Agricultural empires in East Asia and the Middle East attempted to restrict the export of iron in any form to Central Asia, but these attempts were never successful. On the contrary, Central Asians improved many of the sedentary technologies, such as iron forging, and then exported them back to the agricultural regions. The Mongols retained the traditional Central Asian reverence for iron and the secrets of ironworking. Temüjin, Genghis Khan's personal name, means "blacksmith," and several of his prominent followers were sons of blacksmiths. The name of a later conqueror, Timur, means "iron" in Turkish.

In addition to iron, the Central Asian nomads also traded with agricultural societies to acquire wood, cotton and cotton seed, silk, vegetables, and grains. In

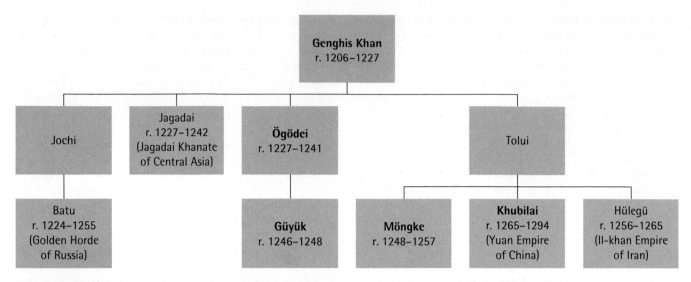

Figure 13.1   Mongol Rulers, 1206–1260   This is the family chart of the founders of the Mongol empires. All the names of those who succeeded to the position of Great Khan are shown in bold type. Those who founded the regional khanates are listed with their dates of rule.

exchange they offered wool, leather, and horses. Many nomads learned the value of permanent settlements for the farming of grains and cotton, as well as for the working of iron, and they established villages—often with the help of migrants from the agricultural regions—at strategic points. The result was extensive frontier regions, particularly east of the Caspian Sea and in northern China, where nomadic peoples and agricultural peoples interacted and created economically as well as culturally pluralistic societies.

Despite the mutual dependence of nomadic pastoralists and the settled agriculturalists, conflict between them was common. When farming societies needed land, their soldiers tried to claim additional territory. When nomads needed agricultural goods or slaves, they resorted to raiding or even large-scale invasion. Warfare tended to break out when normal trade relations between the nomads and the agriculturalists were interrupted.

The Mongol Conquests

Shortly after he was acclaimed "Great Khan" in 1206, Genghis began to carry out his plan to convince the kingdoms of Eurasia to surrender tribute to him. The next two decades saw the bursting forth of Mongol aggression. The earliest sustained action was westward, against Central Asia, the Middle East, and Russia.

Genghis Khan died in 1227, possibly of the effects of alcoholism. His son and successor, the Great Khan

Ögödei°, continued the campaigns seeking domination of China (see Figure 13.1). The Tanggut and then the Jin Empires were destroyed, and their territories were put under Mongol governors (see Chapter 14). In 1236 Genghis's grandson Batu° (d. 1255) launched a major offensive into the Russian territories and took control of all the towns along the Volga° River (see Map 13.1). Within five years he conquered Moscow and Kievan Russia, Poland, and Hungary and was ready to strike at Central Europe. Under siege by the Mongols by the 1230s, Europe would have suffered grave damage in 1241 had the Mongol forces not lifted their attack because of the death of the Great Khan Ögödei, and the necessity to head east to the Mongol capital at Karakorum for the election of a new Great Khan. After the installation of the new Great Khan, Genghis's grandson Güyük°, in 1246, Mongol pressure on the Middle East intensified. It climaxed in 1258 with the sacking of Baghdad and the murder of the last Abbasid caliph (see Chapter 9).

Historians often ask why the Mongols, who were not great in number, were able to defeat some of the most formidable armies of the time. Part of the answer lies in the combination of their extraordinary abilities on horseback and the special properties of their bows. The Mongol bow could shoot arrows one-third farther (and was significantly more difficult to pull) than Middle Eastern and European bows of the same period. The

---

Ögödei (ERG-uh-day)   **Batu** (BAH-too)   **Volga** (VOHL-gah)
Güyük (gi-yik)

composite structure of the Mongol bow and a jade thumb-ring that allowed the archer's hand to withstand the tremendous tension of the drawn bowstring also gave the archer an advantage.

Mounted Mongol archers rarely used all of the five dozen or more arrows they carried in their quivers. At the opening of battle, they shot a volley of arrows from a distance to destroy the ranks of enemy marksmen. Then they rode their swift horses nearly without challenge into sword, lance, javelin, and mace combat against the enemy's infantry. The Mongol cavalry met its match only at the Battle of Ain Jalut°, where it confronted Mamluk forces, whose war techniques also reflected the riding traditions of Central Asia. Thus it was Central Asian knowledge that stopped the Mongol advance toward the Mediterranean.

Another reason for the Mongols' success was their use of Genghis's principles of adaptability and inclusiveness. They changed their techniques for penetrating sophisticated fortifications. A typical Mongol attack began with a volley of flaming arrows, after which the Mongols hurled enormous projectiles—frequently on fire—from catapults. The first Mongol catapults were taken from the Chinese. Though easy to transport, they had short ranges and poor accuracy. From the defeated Khwarazmshahs° in Central Asia the Mongols adapted a catapult design that was half again as powerful as the Chinese catapult. They used this improved weapon against the cities of Iran and Iraq.

Residents of cities under Mongol attack faced immediate slaughter if they opened their gates to fight or slow starvation followed by slaughter if they did not. As a third alternative, the Mongols offered their prospective victims food, shelter, and protection if they surrendered without a fight. The terrible bloodletting that the Mongols inflicted on cities such as Balkh° (in present-day northern Afghanistan) in their early conquests gave staggering force to these appeals, and throughout the Middle East the Mongols found populations willing to acknowledge their overlordship in return for life. With the capture of each city the "Mongol" armies swelled in number. The conquest in the Middle East was accomplished by a small Mongol elite overseeing armies of recently recruited Turks, Iranians, and Arabs.

Through their experiences with so many different cultures the Mongols quickly learned about the rivalries among neighboring groups and found ways to take advantage of them to further the conquest. In their campaigns against the cities of Central Asia the Mongols exploited Muslims' resentment against nonbelievers. In the Middle East, where Muslims were a solid majority, the Mongols exploited Christian resentment of Muslim rule in their seizure of cities in Syria (where Christians were a large group), forcing the conversion of mosques to churches. When Hülegü° captured Baghdad in 1258, he agreed to the requests of his Christian wife that Christians be sought out and put in prominent posts.

Overland Trade and the Plague

The cosmopolitan nature of the Mongol conquests underscores the influence of the Mongols in the transmission of military technology and related scientific knowledge across Eurasia. The overland connections of the time were similarly important to the spread of civil technologies and artistic styles. A spectacular example of their importance is the leap forward in textile manufacture and trade—particularly in silk. Like their aristocratic predecessors in Central Asia, Mongol nobles had the exclusive right to wear silk, almost all bought from China. The unprecedented commercial integration of Eurasia under the Mongols brought new styles and huge quantities of silk westward. Since the material was used not only for clothing but also for wall hangings and furnishings, the presence of silk throughout the Middle East and Europe transformed the daily life of the elite and urban groups. At the same time, the trading of designs brought a mixing and merging of artistic motifs from Japan and Tibet to England and Morocco.

This trade was protected by Mongol control of the overland routes and promoted by Mongol tax policies, but it was carried out by a collection of very different peoples from all over Eurasia. Merchants hoping for wealth and prestige joined political ambassadors, learned men, and religious missionaries over long distances to the Mongol courts. These journeys produced travel literature that gives us vivid insights into the Eurasian world of the thirteenth century. Some narratives, such as that of the Venetian traveler Marco Polo° (1254–1324), freely mixed the fantastic with the factual, to the delight of the audience (Map 13.1 shows Marco Polo's route). Most important, these books left an image of the inexhaustible wealth of the Mongols, and of Asia generally, that created in Europe a persisting ambition to find easier routes to Asia for trade and conquest.

Though the accounts of these travelers mesmerized readers for centuries, their unembellished experiences were not rare for their time. In the towns they visited in Central Asia or China, they regularly encountered other

---

Ain Jalut (ine jah-LOOT)   **Khwarazmshah** (hwa-RAZZ-um-shah)
Balkh (bahlk)

Hülegü (HE-luh-gee)
Marco Polo (mar-koe POE-loe)

Passport The Mongol Empire that united Eurasia in the mid-1200s provided good roads and protection for the movement of products, merchants, and diplomats. Individuals traveling from one culture area to another encountered new languages, laws, and customs frequently. The *paisa* (from a Chinese word for "card" or "sign"), with its inscription in Mongolian, proclaimed to all that the traveler had received the ruler's permission to travel through the region. Europeans later applied the practice to travel through their small and diverse countries. The paisa was thus the ancestor of modern passports. (The Metropolitan Museum of Art, purchase bequest of Dorothy Graham Bennett, 1993 [1993.256]. Photograph 1997 The Metropolitan Museum of Art)

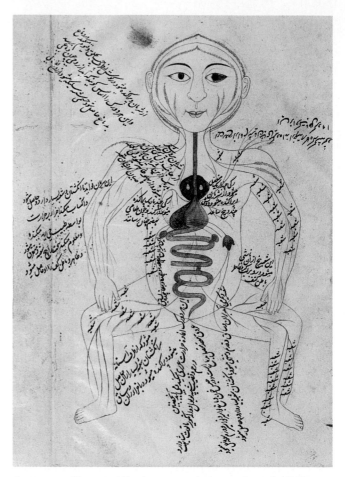

Anatomy Illustrated Persian anatomical texts from the Il-khan and Timurid periods were based on ancient Greek ideas about the functions of the body. Here, the digestive and arterial systems are depicted together because it was assumed that heat generated by digestion forced circulation of the blood. The nervous system, which was not well understood, is not included. Diagrams such as these became very important in Europe a few centuries later, as European scientists continued to build on the anatomical and physiological knowledge of the Islamic world. (Bodleian Library, Oxford, Ms. Fraser 201 fol. 104r)

Europeans, sometimes from their own home regions. Some were travelers and some were captives, but all were part of a steady flow of people across Eurasia. The economic, political, and cultural benefits of this traffic were great. Technical knowledge, whether of pharmacology, engineering, mathematics, or financial management, flowed between China and Iran.

Mongol policy and occasionally Mongol competition also widened the steady stream of knowledge between Europe and the Middle East. For instance, the wish of the Mongols in the Middle East (in the Il-khan Empire) to drive the Mongols of Russia out of the Caucasus in the 1260s helped create a half-century of complex diplomacy in which Muslims often allied themselves with the European sponsors of the Crusader states—sometimes against Christians, sometimes against the Mongols. Or to use a different case, when the Mongols in Russia granted a special trade charter to merchants from

Genoa, the Mongols in the Middle East granted a similar privilege to traders from Venice. And it was probably also by this route that the cosmological ideas and technical knowledge of scholars working under Mongol patrons were communicated to Europe and helped to profoundly change its intellectual life.

There were also great dangers to the exchange. Europe had been free of **bubonic plague** since about 700. The Middle East had seen no plague since about the year 1200. In southwestern China, however, the plague had festered in Yunnan province since the early Tang period.

In the mid-thirteenth century, Mongol troops arrived in Yunnan and established a garrison. From that point, military and supply traffic in and out of Yunnan provided the means for flea-infested rats carrying plague to be carried from Yunnan to central China, to northwestern China, and across Central Asia. Along the routes, marmots and other desert rodents were infected and passed the disease to dogs and people. The caravan traffic across Central Asia infected the oasis towns when rats and fleas disembarked from the overloaded camels, covered wagons, and the wagon-mounted felt tents of the nomads. The Mongols themselves were incapacitated by the plague during their assault on the city of Kaffa° in Crimea° in 1346. They withdrew, but the plague infiltrated Crimea. From Kaffa, both Europe and Egypt were repeatedly infected by fleas from rats on ships bound across the Mediterranean.

Bubonic plague was only one of the diseases at work weakening the resistance of urban populations in particular and unleashing new waves of latent illness. Typhus, influenza, and smallpox traveled with the plague. The combination of these and other diseases created what is often called the "great pandemic" of 1347–1352. The human and cultural damage that resulted was far greater than any of the direct consequences of the Mongol military conquests. It is tempting to associate the social disorder of conquest and the plague as twin illnesses, but it was not the Mongol invaders who brought the disease westward. Rather, disease was transmitted by the trade encouraged by Mongol protection of the Eurasian land routes. Peace and profit were the channels by which pandemic illness terrorized Eurasia in the mid-fourteenth century.

Celebrating Battle   The Mongols were in a long line of Central Asian warriors who mastered the art of shooting arrows from a galloping horse. They were renowned not only for their mobility but also for the unusual distance and accuracy their archers could attain with their distinctive compound bows. This detail from a painted bowl of the early Il-khan period illustrates a contemporary portrayal of the military skills of shooting from horseback, as well as depicting the violence of the battlefield. But it carefully avoids a fact of war in the thirteenth-century Middle East: the slaughter, starvation, and enslavement of civilians are not shown.   (Courtesy of the Freer Gallery of Art, Smithsonian Institution, Washington, DC.)

THE FALL AND RISE OF ISLAM, 1260–1500

By 1260 two distinct Mongol realms had been established in western Eurasia: the **Il-khan°** Empire and the Khanate of the **Golden Horde** (also called the Kipchak° Khanate; see Map 13.1). The Mongols under Genghis's grandson Hülegü controlled parts of Armenia and all of Azerbaijan, Mesopotamia, and Iran. The Mongols who had conquered southern Russia settled north of the Caspian Sea, establishing their capital at Sarai° on the Volga River. They became known as the Golden

Horde, and quickly established a close relationship with the Muslim Turkic nomads who had frequented the area for centuries. By the 1260s Batu's, successor as leader of the Golden Horde had declared himself a Muslim, announced his intention of avenging the murder of the caliph, and claimed the Caucasus—the region between the Black and Caspian Seas—also claimed by the Il-khans.

Mongol Rivalry

There is evidence that some members of the Mongol imperial family were believers in Islam before the Mongol assault on the Middle East, and Mongols frequently relied on Muslims as advance men and intermediaries. Muslims in the region known as Transoxiana played this critical role. In addition, certain of the Il-khans showed favoritism toward some Muslim groups. The Il-khan Hülegü, for instance, was a Buddhist but often gave privileges to the Muslim Shi'ite sect to which his most trusted adviser belonged. As a whole,

---

Kaffa (KAH-fah)   **Crimea** (cry-MEE-ah)   **Il-khan** (IL-con)
Kipchak (KIP-chahk)   **Sarai** (sah-RYE)

however, the Mongols under the command of Hülegü were slow to become exposed to the Muslim religion.

Tensions between individual Mongols and Muslims paralleled tensions between Muslim principles and Mongol culture. Many Muslims could not forgive the murder of the last Abbasid caliph. In accordance with Mongol customs for the execution of high-born persons, the caliph had been rolled in a rug and trampled to death by horses to prevent his blood from spilling on the ground. The Mongols considered the elimination of the supreme religious leader of the Muslims a necessity for their control of the region. Muslims were shocked and outraged.

The passage of time did little to reconcile Islamic doctrines with Mongol ways. Muslims were repelled by the Mongols' worship of idols, which is fundamental to shamanism but at odds with Islamic teachings on the proper use of art. Another point of contention was rituals governing animal slaughter. The shamanic method of the Mongols forbade the spilling of blood; and the Islamic code of cleanliness, *halal°*, required the draining of blood from the carcass. Litigation on this and closely related matters flooded the law courts of the Il-khans.

Islam posed other dangers to the Mongol mission in the Middle East. At the time that Hülegü was leading the Mongol armies into Iran and Iraq, Mongols were also conquering southern Russia, north of the Caspian Sea. By the 1260s the Mongol leader—Genghis's grandson Batu—in Russia had declared himself a Muslim, announced his intention to avenge the last caliph, and claimed the Caucasus, between the Black and Caspian Seas. By this route, the Mongols of the Golden Horde could gain direct access to the Il-khan territories, and particularly to the Il-khan capital at Tabriz° (see Map 13.2).

The conflict was the first between Mongol domains, and the fact that one of the parties—the Mongols of the Golden Horde—was avowedly Muslim led the leaders of Europe to believe that they could enlist the other party—the Il-khans, who were Buddhists—to drive Muslims out of contested religious sites in Syria, Lebanon, and Palestine. The result was a brief diplomatic correspondence between the Il-khan court and Pope Nicholas IV (r. 1288–1292) and an exchange of ambassadors that sent two Christian Turks—Markuz° and Rabban Sauma°—on a remarkable tour of western Europe as Il-khan ambassadors in the late 1200s.

The Buddhist Il-khans attempted to enlist the aid of European countries to eject the Golden Horde from the Caucasus. Many Christian crusaders enlisted in the Il-khan effort, and the pope later excommunicated some for doing so. For their part, the Mongols in Russia attempted to forge an alliance with the Muslim Mamluks in Egypt against the crusaders and the Il-khans. The net result was to extend the life of the Crusader kingdoms in Palestine and Syria and European influence there; the Mamluks did not succeed in completely ejecting the crusaders until the fifteenth century.

Before the Europeans could realize their plan of allying with the Mongols, the new Il-khan ruler, Ghazan° (1271–1304) declared himself a Muslim in 1295. His prime minister and confidant, **Rashid al-Din°**, a convert from Judaism to Shi'a Islam, had convinced the Il-khan to convert. In the following decades the Il-khans and the Golden Horde promoted Islam throughout their domains.

The public stance of the Il-khans as Muslims radically changed the relationship of state and religion in the Middle East. The Il-khans declared themselves the protectors and advocates of Islam, and all Mongols in the Il-khan Empire were ordered to convert to Islam. The Il-khan legal code was brought into agreement with the principles of Islam. Years passed before the Il-khans made the crucial decision to support Sunna and not Shi'a Islam.

Islam and the State

The goal of the Il-khans was to extract wealth from their domain by peaceful means whenever possible but in any case to extract the maximum. This goal was most efficiently achieved through taxation, and the Mongols became masters of extraction. The method they used is generally called **tax farming,** a practice well developed in the Middle East before the coming of the Mongols. The government sold tax-collecting contracts to small corporations, most of which were owned by merchants who might work together to finance the caravan trade, small industries, or military expeditions. The winners of the contracts were the groups that agreed to generate the most revenue for the government. They could use whatever methods they chose to collect the tax and could keep anything over the contracted amount.

The short-term results for the government were good, for with a minimum of bureaucratic overhead the state received large amounts of grain, cash, and silk. The long-term results were different. The exorbitant rates charged by the tax farmers drove many landowners into

---

halal ((haa-LAAL)   **Tabriz** (taw-BREEZE)   **Markuz** (MARK-uhz)
Rabban Sauma (rahb-bahn SAU-ma)

Ghazan (haz-zan)   **Rashid al-Din** (ra-SHEED ad-DEEN)

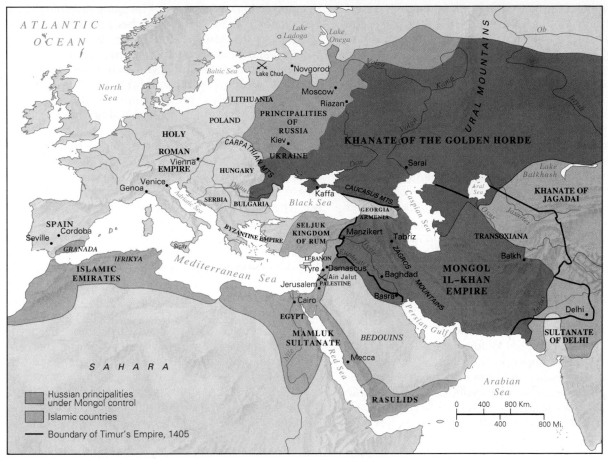

Map 13.2   Western Eurasia in the 1300s   This map of the Mongol domains in the Middle East demonstrates the delicate balance of power that was upset by Ghazan's conversion to Islam in 1295. During the conflict between the Il-khans and the Golden Horde in the 1260s, European leaders hoped to ally themselves with the Il-khans against Muslim defenders in Palestine. These hopes were abandoned after Ghazan's conversion to Islam in 1295, and the powerful alliance between the Mamluks and the Golden Horde kept the Il-khans from advancing west. Europeans hoped to exploit the conflict by enlisting the Il-khans against the Mamluks, but realized the cause was lost after Ghazan became Muslim. The Mamluks and the Golden Horde remained allies against the Il-khans, which aided Europeans in retaining their lands in Palestine and Syria.

debt and servitude and prevented the reinvestment necessary to maintain productivity. Because many taxes were collected in kind, the price of grain rose so much that the government had difficulty procuring supplies for the soldiers' granaries. As a consequence the state was forced to appropriate land to grow its own grain. This land, like religious land grants, was tax-exempt, so the tax base shrank even though the demands of the army and the Mongol nobility for revenue continued to grow.

Economic troubles were acute when Ghazan became Il-khan in 1295 and converted to Islam. To address the economic crisis, Ghazan cited the humane values of

Islam and announced his intention to lessen the government's tax demands. He also took advantage of the Mongols' international contacts to seek new methods of economic management. He believed he found one in the Chinese practice of using paper money, and he ordered the use of paper money in his domain. But the peoples of the Middle East had no previous exposure to paper money and no confidence in its value, and the economy quickly sank into a depression that lasted until after the end of the Il-khan period in 1349.

After Ghazan, the Il-khan regime experienced a slow decline that was like the decline of Mongol regimes elsewhere. The extraction of revenues for the support of the

Mongol military elite caused widespread popular unrest and resentment among local elites. Mongol nobles in the Middle East competed fiercely among themselves for the decreasing revenues, and fighting among Mongol factions destabilized the government. The fragmentation of Il-khan power aroused the expansive ambitions of the Mongols north of the Caspian. In the mid-fourteenth century, Mongols from the khanate of the Golden Horde moved through the Caucasus into the western regions of the Il-khan Empire and soon into the Il-khan's central territory, Azerbaijan. The Mongols from Russia participated in the dismemberment of the Il-khan Empire and briefly occupied its major cities.

As the power of the Il-khans in the Middle East and of the Golden Horde in Russia weakened in the fourteenth century, a new power emerged in Central Asia. The Mongol rulers there were descendants of Genghis's son Jagadai (d. 1242). Under the leader **Timur°,** the Jagadai° Khanate (see Map 13.1) drew on the political traditions of the Mongols and on Islam. The campaigns of Timur in western Eurasia were even more brutal than earlier Mongol campaigns had been. By the late fourteenth century much of the Middle East was united under his rule, and he hoped to add China. The Timurids (descendants of Timur) held the Middle East together long enough to deepen and consolidate Sunni Islamic influence, and they laid the groundwork for the later establishment in India of a Muslim Mongol regime, the Mughals, in the sixteenth century.

Timur (r. 1370–1405) was the last great Central Asian conqueror. After his time Central Asia was no longer the crossroads of Eurasia, as it had been since the earliest times.

Art and Science in Islamic Eurasia

Thanks partly to the wide-ranging cultural exchange fostered by the Mongols, the Ilkhans and Timurids presided over a brilliant period in Islamic civilization. Many of the intellectual developments of the era had a strong direct effect on Europe. Others had an indirect but equally important influence. The sharing of artistic trends and political ideas between Iran and China created the illusion in European eyes that east of the Mediterranean there existed an "Orient" that was uniform in its tastes and political cultures. In fact, the intimacy of Iran and China was a product of the centuries of Silk Road trade and only more recently of the Mongol Empire. It was not evidence of any fundamental "Oriental" character. Although Timur was not successful in his wish to reunite Iran and China, at Samarkand he made possible the advancement of some specific arts because of his practice, followed by his descendants, of forcibly concentrating scholars, artists, and craftsmen in his capital.

The historian Juvaini°, who noted Genghis Khan's deathbed speech, was a central figure in literary development. His family came from the city of Balkh, which the Mongols devastated in 1221. At that time the family switched allegiance to the Mongols, and both Juvaini and his older brother assumed high government posts. Il-khan Hülegü, seeing an opportunity to both immortalize and justify the Mongol conquest of the Middle East, enthusiastically supported Juvaini's historical projects. The result was the first comprehensive narrative describing the rise of the Mongols under Genghis Khan.

Juvaini's work and his methods—he often was critical of his subjects—inspired Rashid al-Din, the prime minister of Il-khan Ghazan, to attempt the first history of the world. It contains the earliest known general history of Europe, based on information from European monks. Editions of Rashid al-Din's world history were often richly illustrated. Pictures adapted from European paintings depicted European persons and events, and pictures adapted from Chinese paintings depicted Chinese persons and events. In this way, Chinese principles of watercolor composition and portraiture were introduced into Iran. The reproduction and distribution of Rashid al-Din's work spread throughout Eurasia knowledge of the arts and histories of the lands under Mongol rule.

The cosmopolitan influence of Rashid al-Din's world history was personified by Rashid himself. As a Jew converted to Islam, serving the Mongols and traveling very widely in their service, he was aware of many cultures and many points of view. He was in constant touch with Mongol officials in Central Asia and China. When he could not see them in person, he often wrote letters to them explaining his ideas on economic management. It was partly as a result of these lines of communication that similar financial and monetary reforms occurred at roughly the same time in Iran, Russia, and China. Rashid was above all practical. It was he who advocated conducting government in accord with the moral principles of a majority of the population, and it was he who convinced Ghazan to convert to Islam.

Under the Timurids, the magnificent achievement of the Il-khan historians was augmented. Timur himself was acquainted with the greatest historian and geographer of the age, **Ibn Khaldun°** (1332–1406), a Moroccan. Like his Mongol predecessors, Timur was an enthusiastic supporter of historical narratives in which he himself

---

Timur (tem-EER)　**Jagadai** (jahg-ah-die)

Juvaini (joo-VINE-nee)　**Ibn Khaldun** (ee-bin hal-DOON)

acted as the primary informant. In a scene reminiscent of the times when Ghazan had sat patiently answering Rashid al-Din's questions on the history of the Mongols, Timur and Ibn Khaldun sat in Damascus, exchanging historical, philosophical, and geographical viewpoints. Like Genghis, Timur saw himself as a world conqueror, so the story of his conquests was necessarily the story of the world. At their capitals of Samarkand and Herat (in modern-day Afghanistan), later Timurid rulers sponsored historical writing in both Persian and Turkish. Under them, the art of illustrating historical and fictional works, employed so strikingly in Rashid al-Din's history, reached a very high point of development.

Juvaini had accompanied Hülegü in 1256 in the campaigns against the Assassins, a radical religious sect, and he worked to preserve the historical archives that the Assassins maintained at Mount Alamut°. It was possibly the archives and libraries of the Assassins that had drawn a multitalented Shi'ite believer, **Nasir al-Din Tusi°,** to Mount Alamut, where Mongol forces took him into custody. Nasir al-Din quickly charmed Hülegü and became one of his most trusted advisers.

Nasir al-Din was interested in history, poetry, ethics, and religion, but his outstanding contributions were in mathematics and cosmology. He drew on the work of the great poet and mathematician of the Seljuk° period, Omar Khayyam° (1038?–1131), to lay the foundations for complex algebra and trigonometry. The impact of Nasir al-Din's work was considerable. A group of his followers, working at their observatory at Maraga°, an academy near the Il-khan capital of Tabriz, were able to solve a fundamental problem in classical cosmology.

Islamic scholars had preserved and elaborated on the insights of the Greeks in astronomy and mathematics. They adopted the cosmological model of Ptolemy°, which assumed a universe with the earth at its center and the sun and planets rotating around the earth in circular orbits. Astronomers knew Ptolemy's model was flawed, because the motions of the five visible planets were not in agreement with its predictions. Since Ptolemy's time, astronomers and mathematicians of the Middle East had been searching for mathematically consistent explanations that would account for the movement of the planets and reconcile them with Ptolemy's model.

Nasir al-Din proposed such a model. His approach was based on a concept of small circles rotating within a large circle, changing vectors in such a way as to account for their movement when viewed from the earth. A student of Nasir al-Din reconciled the model with the ancient Greek idea of epicycles (small circles rotating around a larger circle) to explain the movement of the moon around the earth, and here occurred the breakthrough that changed cosmological thought. The mathematical tables and geometric models of this student were later transferred in their entirety to Europe and became known to Nicholas Copernicus (1473–1543), a Polish monk and astronomer. The means of transmission is still one of the tantalizing unknowns in world history.

Astronomy and Engineering   Throughout Eurasia, observational astronomy went hand in hand not only with mathematics and calendrical science but also with engineering, as the construction of platforms, architecture for solar measurement, and armillary spheres became more sophisticated. Publication of instruction manuals helped refine the science and the technology. This manual in Persian (completed in the 1500s but illustrating activities that occurred in the Il-khan period) provides instruction on the establishment of a plumb line for an enormous outdoor armillary sphere.   (Istanbul University Library)

Alamut (ah-lah-moot)   **Nasir al-Din Tusi** (nah-zer ad-DEEN toos)
Seljuk (SEL-jook)   **Omar Khayyam** (oh-mar KIE-yam)
Maraga (mah-rah-gah)   **Ptolemy** (TOHL-uh-mee)

Copernicus adopted the lunar model as his own, virtually without revision. He then proposed that the model of lunar movement developed under the Il-khans was the proper model for planetary movement also—with the planets moving around the sun.

Europe was indebted to the Il-khans not just for cosmological insights. Perhaps because of the Central Asian nomads' traditional dependence on the stars to guide their movement, or because of the suitability of high, dry Central Asia for astronomical observation, Central Asian empires—particularly the Uigurs° and the Seljuks—had excelled in their sponsorship of observational astronomy and the making of calendars. Under the Il-khans, Maraga became a sort of world center for the prediction of lunar and solar eclipses. Astrolabes, armillary spheres, three-dimensional quadrants, and other instruments in use there were much more precise than those used earlier.

The Il-khans made a deliberate attempt to amass at their observatory astronomical data from all parts of the Islamic world, as well as from China. In this way they achieved unprecedented accuracy in the prediction of eclipses. The predictions of the Il-khan astronomers were translated into Arabic for use in the hostile Mamluk territories. Byzantine monks took them to Constantinople and translated them into Greek. They were taken to Muslim Spain and translated into Latin. They were taken to India, where the sultan of Delhi ordered them translated into Sanskrit. The Great Khan Khubilai° (see Chapter 14) was so impressed that he demanded a team of Iranians to come to Beijing to build an observatory for him. The Timurids continued to sponsor large observatories. Indeed, the Timurid ruler Ulugh Beg° (1394–1449) was an astronomer and actively participated in the construction of a great observatory at Samarkand.

Such work required a system for writing numbers that would give mathematical calculations a precision that was not possible with the numerical systems inherited—in both the Middle East and Europe—from the Greeks. By the 700s, Middle Eastern scholars had adapted the Indian numerical system, including the symbol for zero, to their own script. This advance made possible work on the level of the Nasir al-Din group. Until Leonardo of Pisa (also called Fibonacci°, the discoverer of Fibonacci's Numbers) studied Iranian texts and used them to introduce Europeans to the abacus in the 1200s, Europeans were still using the clumsy Roman numerals to do their calculations. In his text, Leonardo adapted the "Arabic" numerals of the Middle East and in this way introduced columnar calculation. With this technology, Europeans were finally able to participate again in the study of complex mathematics, astronomy and astrology, music theory, and logic—scholarship that had begun in the ancient Greek world and had been advanced in Islamic and Indian civilizations.

The Timurids continued the Seljuk and Il-khan policies of sponsoring advanced work in astronomy and mathematics that integrated the traditions of Eurasia, and they underwrote another major advance in mathematics. Ghiyas al-Din Jamshid al-Kashi°, in his studies of Chinese calendars, noted that Chinese astronomers had long used a unit for the measurement of new moons that was calculated as 1/10,000th of a day. It appears that this was the inspiration for al-Kashi's use of the decimal fraction, by which quantities less than 1 may be represented by the manipulation of a marker to show place value (a technology to which the zero was also crucial). With this means for representing decimal fractions, al-Kashi went on to propose a far more precise calculation for pi (π) than had been achieved since the value was established in classical times. This innovation was transmitted to Europe by way of Constantinople, where al-Kashi's famous work on mathematics was translated into Greek in the fifteenth century.

REGIONAL DEFINITION IN RESPONSE TO THE MONGOLS

Major features of Iran and Iraq under the Il-khans were present in many other regions that the Mongols occupied. One was a marked disparity between the fortunes of the cities and the countryside. After the conquest, the volume of safe, reliable overland trade throughout Eurasia stimulated many of the commercial cities of Iran and Iraq. But the countryside, subjected to extensive damage in the conquest, sporadically continuing violence, and crushing taxes, suffered terribly. Although from the time of Ghazan the Il-khan policy changed from maximum extraction from the rural sector to a policy that was more constructive and protective, the change came too late to stop the decline in population and further deterioration of agriculture.

There also were distinctive cultural changes under the Il-khans and Timurids. Both empires were inclined

---

Uigur (WEE-ger)   **Khubilai** (KOO-bih-lie)
Ulugh Beg (oo-look bek)   **Fibonacci** (fee-bo-NACH-chee)

Ghiyas al-Din Jamshid al-Kashi
(gee-YASS ad-DIN jam-sheed ak-KAHSH)

to promote the use of the written Persian language, often in connection with popular forms of writing such as poetry, epic writing, and songs. Similarly, both showed a strong interest in popular religious practices, especially the mystical form of Islam known as Sufism°. This interest was somewhat at odds with the official stance of the later Il-khan and the Timurid courts as adherents of Sunna orthodoxy. The elements of Persian language and steadfast devotion to Islam became indispensable to the rulers of the region.

Russia and Rule from Afar

The first conflict between Kievan Russia and the Mongols occurred in 1223, when the Mongols defeated a combined Russian and Kipchak (a Turkic people) army in southeastern Russia. The great Mongol onslaught led by Batu came in the late 1230s, when a series of defeats for the Russians culminated in the Mongol capture and pillage of the town of Riazan°. Unlike others who invaded Russia before and after, the Mongols were capable of successful winter campaigning and found that only the springtime mud of Russia hindered their cavalry. The Russian princes failed to unite to oppose the invaders, and in 1240 the central town of Kiev° fell. The princes of Hungary acknowledged the superiority of Batu shortly afterward, and the entire region came under Mongol domination.

Batu and his descendants established their own regime on the southern Russia steppe and, as discussd earlier, were known as the "Golden Horde" (see Map 13.1). This was really a collection of small khanates, many of which survived when others died out at the end of the 1300s. The White Horde, for instance, ruled much of southeastern Russia until the 1480s, and the khan of Crimea was not overthrown until 1783.

The Mongols placed their capitals at the ends of the overland caravan routes, which were the infrastructure of their empires. But in Russia only the region at the mouth of the Volga River could be connected to the steppe networks. Thus the Mongols of the Golden Horde settled well to the south and west of their Russian domains, first at (Old) Sarai just north of the Caspian Sea (see Map 13.1). As part of their rule-from-afar, the Mongols granted great privileges to the Orthodox Church, which then helped to reconcile the Russian people to their distant Mongol masters. Old Church Slavonic was revived, but chronicle-writing in Russian remained vig-

orous, and the Greek language was shunned by Russian scholars even though the khans of the Golden Horde permitted renewed contacts with Constantinople. The Russian language for the first time became the dominant written language of Russia. The Golden Horde also enlisted Russian princes to act as their agents (primarily as their tax collectors and census takers) and frequently as their ambassadors to the court of the Great Khans at Karakorum in Mongolia.

The Mongols' primary concern in Russia, as in their other domains, was the extraction of wealth. The flow of silver and gold into Mongol hands starved the local economy for currency. Like the Il-khans, the khans of the Golden Horde attempted to introduce paper money as a response to the currency shortage. So vivid was the impression left by this Mongol innovation that the word in Russian for money (*denga*°) comes from the Mongolian word for the stamp (*tamga*°) used to create paper currency.

Mongol domination strongly affected urban development and population movement in Russia, in part because of the role played by **Alexander Nevskii**° (ca. 1220–1263), the prince of Novgorod. Alexander aided in the Mongol conquest by persuading many of the Russian princes that it would be better to submit to the Mongols than to resist them. In recognition of his service, the Mongols favored both Novgorod (under Alexander's rule) and the emerging town of Moscow (under the rule of Alexander's brother Daniel). These towns eclipsed devastated Kiev as political, cultural, and economic centers during the period of Mongol domination. This, in turn, encouraged people to move northward, away from the Mongol pasture lands in the southwest, and it led to the opening of new agricultural land far north of the Caspian Sea. During the 1300s, Moscow emerged as the new center of Russia, and control of Moscow became equivalent to control of the entire country (see Map 13.2).

Russia preserved reminders of the Mongol presence for many years. Some regions of southern Russia, particularly Crimea, remained breeding grounds for the bubonic plague long after the caravans that the Mongols encouraged and protected had introduced the disease. In the late Kievan period, (1000–1230) Ukraine° had been a fertile and well-populated region. But under the Mongols, Ukraine underwent a severe loss of population. The Mongols crossed the region repeatedly in their campaigns against eastern Europe and raided it continually to punish villages that were slow to hand over their tax payments.

Sufism (SOO-fiz-uhm)   **Riazan** (ree-AH-zahn)
Kiev (kee-yef)

denga (DENG-ah))   *tamga* (TAHM-gah)   **Nevskii** (nih-EFF-skee)
Ukraine (you-CRANE)

Transformation of the Kremlin   Like many peoples of northern medieval Europe, the Russians of the Kievan period preferred to build in wood, which was easy to handle and comfortable to live in. But the fortifications of important political centers, which were vulnerable to assault, had to be made of stone. In the 1300s, the city of Moscow emerged as a leading political center, and its old palace, the Kremlin, was gradually transformed from a wooden to a stone structure. The process is depicted in this contemporary drawing.   (Novosti)

Historians debate the effect of the Mongol period of domination on the shaping of Russia. The destructiveness of the Mongol capture of Riazan, like the capture of Balkh seems to many to be typical of the Mongol conquests. In the opinion of many historians the Mongol conquest of Russia and parts of eastern Europe isolated Russia from the great currents of development in early modern Europe. These historians refer to the "Mongol yoke" and hypothesize a sluggish economy and a dormant culture under the Mongols.

Other historians offer a different interpretation. In response to the hypothesized economic damage, they point out that the Kievan economy was in decline before the coming of the Mongols and that the Kievan princes had already ceased to mint money. In addition, even though the Mongols' demands were high and their internationally oriented monetary measures sometimes inappropriate, the Russian territories regularly managed to pay their taxes in silver. These tax payments in silver suggest regular surpluses in income and an economy sufficiently well developed to make the conversion of goods to cash convenient. It also is clear that the tax burden was significantly increased not by the Mongols directly but by their tax collectors—Russian princes who often exempted their own lands from the tax and shifted the additional burden to the peasants. When the princes requested and received a lowering of the tax rate from the Mongols, the outcome was not necessarily more money in the hands of the common people.

In response to the hypothesized cultural isolation of Russia, skeptical historians point out that before the Mongol invasion, Russia was under the domination of the Byzantine Empire, which was not greatly affected by the Renaissance in western Europe. The Orthodox Church, which was strongly oriented toward Constantinople and did not encourage relations of any sort with western Europe, would have protected Russia from outside influences, with or without the influence of the Mongols.

To enhance their ability to control the country, the Mongols in Russia tended to undermine the local elites or alter the status of individuals within the elite. It does not appear that the Mongols destroyed the traditional forms of elite participation in government. There is good evidence that the structure of local government in Russia did not change significantly in this period. On the regional level, the princely families continued to battle among themselves for dominance as they had in the past. The Mongols were merely an additional factor in those struggles.

Ivan° III, the prince of Moscow (r. 1462–1505), established himself as an autocratic ruler in the late 1400s. Before Ivan, the title **tsar** (from "caesar"), by which the rulers of Russia after the Mongols were known, was used only for foreign rulers (whether the emperors of Byzantium or the Turkic khans of the steppe) dominating the disunited Russian principalities. After throwing off Mongol dominion in 1480, Russian leaders adopted the title *tsar* to show that Russia should be ruled by Russians and not from afar.

There were strong similarities between the effects of Mongol domination in Russia and in the Middle East. In Russia the Mongols ended the dominance of Kiev and

Ivan (ee-VAHN)

encouraged the rise of Moscow. In the Middle East the Mongols ended the political and cultural dominance of Baghdad and encouraged the emergence of new centers of power and commerce. Like the Mongols who first occupied Iran, the Mongols in Russia had little interest in the dominant religious system. The distance between the Mongols and the local people in Russia, prevented the Mongols from attempting to become patrons of the local religion. The result was the survival of the Russian Orthodox religious hierarchy and the strong association of the Russian Orthodox Church with Russian identity and aspirations to independence. Also, in Russia as elsewhere, the Mongols were an impetus to centralization. In the aftermath of the Mongol period, Russia's strongest leaders and its most centralized political system emerged.

Social Change and Centralization in Europe and Anatolia

Parallel to the division of the western part of the Mongol Empire between the Golden Horde and the Il-khans was the division of Europe at the same time between the political forces of the papacy and those of Frederick II of the Hohenstaufen family, who was the Holy Roman Emperor and hereditary ruler of the German territories. Raised in Sicily, Frederick (r. 1212–1250) was sympathetic to Muslim culture. When the pope threatened him with excommunication unless he participated in the Crusades in Palestine and Syria, Frederick conspired with the Mamluk rulers of Egypt and Syria to present the illusion of capturing Jerusalem.

With Europe divided between the pope and the Holy Roman Emperor, the kingdoms of eastern Europe—particularly Hungary and Poland—dealt with the onslaught of the Golden Horde on their own. Many of the eastern European princes chose to capitulate and went to (Old) Sarai to declare themselves slaves of Batu. One of the minority of the eastern groups unwilling to capitulate was the Teutonic° Knights.

Like the Knights Templar in the Middle East, the Teutonic Knights had been sent on crusade. Their goal was to Christianize the Slavic and Kipchak populations of northern Europe. Also like the Knights Templar, the Teutonic Knights were licensed to colonize their conquered territories. They imported thousands of German-speaking farmers, artisans, and clerics to populate their kingdoms. Alexander Nevskii, the prince of Novgorod, led the Mongol campaigns against the Teutonic Knights and their Finnish allies, who in 1242 lost so many of their

Teutonic (two-TOHN-ik)

Pope and Emperor   In the world history overseen by Rashid al-Din, the narratives are based on information that is often drawn from original European sources. But many of the illustrations capture the tendency of Persians to see Europeans as projections of themselves. Here, Holy Roman Emperor Frederick II—a well-known figure in the Islamic world, though not a friend to the Il-khans—and Pope Gregory IX are depicted in Persian dress and postures, their features drawn according to the artistic principles of Persian portraitists and painters of miniatures.   (Topkapi Saray Museum)

number through the ice at Lake Chud (see Map 13.2) that their power was broken and the northern Crusades virtually ceased.

Alexander Nevskii's role in the defeat of the Teutonic Knights is a reminder that the "Mongol" armies that the Europeans encountered were barely Mongol at all. Most commanders were Mongols, and historians rank one of them—Sübüdei, who was Batu's chief general in western Eurasia—as a military genius. But Mongol policies of recruitment and conscription created an international force of Mongols, Turks, Chinese, Iranians, Europeans, and at least one Englishman, who went to the Middle

East as a crusading knight and, through capture or capitulation joined the Mongol forces and turned up in the Hungarian campaigns.

Eastern Europe came under direct assault from these forces in the winter of 1241, when the Danube River froze. Sübüdei's troops rode across it and inflicted a series of dazzling defeats on the eastern European kingdoms. Mongol forces appeared at the foot of the Alps, apparently menacing northern Italy and possibly Venice. They also were on the outskirts of Vienna. Poles, Hungarians, Austrians, and Bohemians struggled frantically to safeguard themselves and mount some resistance. The rest of Europe was panicked by the sudden, terrifying onslaught.

Rumors and some written accounts described the Mongols as having bodies that were part dog. They were theorized to have come from Hell or from the caves where, it was said, Alexander the Great had banished the monsters of ancient times. They were said to be cannibals. People in Germany claimed that the Mongols were the lost tribes of Israel returned, and in the eastern German territories Jews who were thought to be in secret alliance with the invaders were lynched. In Hungary, the recently Christianized Kipchaks were accused of aiding the Mongols; some were imprisoned, and some were killed. The king of France resigned himself to the destruction of his country, accepting it as the will of God. The pope, despite his wish to keep pressure on Frederick II, authorized a crusade against the Mongols, and the liturgies for daily worship were altered to include a line begging God for deliverance from them.

It seemed that the prayers were answered. Before the Europeans could mount a united force to repel the Mongols, Sübüdei's forces withdrew in December 1241. The Great Khan Ögödei had died, and the Mongol princes wished to return to Mongolia to participate in election of Ögödei's successor as Great Khan.

After the sudden retreat of Batu's troops from Europe, several European leaders attempted to open peaceful channels of communication with the Il-khan, hoping through him to reach the Great Khan in Mongolia. Some kings of Europe, trade federations, and the pope sent embassies to Iran, and many diplomats and merchants traveled eastward toward the Mongol capital. The Mongol rulers often received merchants and craftsmen favorably, but they welcomed ambassadors from kings or from the Vatican only if they brought messages of submission from their lords (see Society and Culture: Dueling Pieties).

European embassies to the Golden Horde and to the Great Khan in Mongolia increased in number through the thirteenth century. As Europeans learned to utilize the Mongol trade routes, and to exploit Mongol divisions in the Middle East, their terror of the Mongols was replaced by their awe of, and eventual idealization of, the wealth and power of the Mongol khanates. From their contacts with the Mongols the Europeans gained their first systematic knowledge of Eurasian geography, cultural patterns, natural resources, and commerce. They learned about the use of diplomatic passports, the mining and uses of coal, movable type, high-temperature metallurgy, efficient enumeration and higher mathematics, gunpowder, and, in the fourteenth century, the casting and use of bronze cannon.

Nevertheless, Europe suffered greatly from the effects of Mongol domination of eastern Europe and Russia. The terror created by the Mongol invasions combined with other factors, such as the outbreak of bubonic plague in the late 1340s (see Chapter 16), to ignite a storm of religious questioning and anxiety, especially in regions of eastern and Central Europe that had been virtually under the hooves of the Mongol horses.

In the fourteenth century, the Mongol grip on eastern Europe was weakened, and several regions emerged from the century of Mongol pressure considerably centralized. Lithuania° was one region of Europe energized by the Mongol threat (see Map 13.2). In the mid-thirteenth century, just as Russia fell to the Mongols and eastern Europe was first invaded, Lithuania was undergoing an unprecedented degree of centralization and military strengthening. Like Alexander Nevskii, the Lithuanian leaders struck a deal with the Mongols and were able to maintain their independence. In the late 1300s, when Mongol power in Russia was waning, Lithuania capitalized on its privileged position to dominate its neighbors—particularly Poland—and ended all hopes of a revival of the power of the Teutonic Knights in eastern Europe.

In the Balkans, independent and well-organized kingdoms separated themselves from the chaos of the Byzantine Empire and thrived until the Turkic Ottomans conquered them in the 1500s and 1600s. In the history of the Mongol period we can see basic connections among eastern Europe, the Balkans, and Anatolia (then under the control of the Byzantine Empire).

Communications between the Il-khans and Constantinople gave Europe a second doorway (Spain provided the first) to the scientific and philosophical achievements of Islamic culture. Because direct Il-Khan conquests did not extend into Anatolia, the Byzantine Empire survived, and Anatolia became a haven for Turkic groups pushed eastward by the Mongols.

Lithuania (lith-oo-WAY-nee-ah)

Dueling Pieties

Much of the written communication between Europe and the Mongols survives, but only as a result of an extraordinarily complex process. Europeans wrote to the Mongols in Latin, which was normally translated into Persian when the parties reached the Il-khan territories. On the route to the Mongol capital at Karakorum, a means had to be found to translate the Persian into Mongolian. Translation could be done orally if the ambassadors received an audience with the Great Khan or his representatives. For messages going from east to west, the process was reversed.

The messages were not complicated, but each side found the other's ideas so bizarre that mistakes in translation were very often suspected. This passage in a letter from Pope Innocent IV to the Great Khan in 1245 is typical. (Innocent did not know that there was no one to receive the letter, for Ögödei had died in 1241 and Güyük had not yet been installed as the next Great Khan.)

It is not without cause that we are driven to express in strong terms our amazement that you, according to what we have heard, have invaded many countries belonging both to Christians and to others and are laying them waste in a horrible desolation, and with a fury still unabated you do not cease from breaking the bond of natural ties, sparing neither sex nor age, you rage against all indiscriminately with the sword of chastisement.

Like popes before and after him, Innocent explained that he was sending monks to convert the Great Khan to Christianity, to baptize him, and to make him not a waster of the Christian lands but their protector. Group after group of Christian missionaries tried to convert the Mongols, but all were disappointed.

When Güyük was proclaimed Great Khan in 1246, he answered Innocent's letter. He expressed befuddlement at the idea that he should be chastised for invading Christian lands and at the suggestion that he himself should be baptized. Güyük questioned Innocent's arrogance in presuming to know God's intentions:

Though you also say that I should become a trembling Christian, worship God, and be an ascetic, how do you know whom God absolves, or in truth to whom He shows mercy? How do you know that such words as you speak are with God's approval? From the rising of the sun to its setting, all the lands have been made subject to me. Who could do this contrary to the command of God?

The Great Khans shared the traditional Central Asian belief that Heaven shows its will in the unfolding of history, that victors are necessarily the messengers of Heaven's will, and that the supreme victor is the supreme messenger. As often as the popes warned the Great Khans to be baptized and submit to the guidance of the Vatican, the Great Khans responded with the simple message that they were not about to submit to the church and that all Europe had best submit to the Great Khans—or suffer the consequences.

Güyük sternly closed his letter to Innocent:

If you do not observe God's command, and if you ignore my command, I shall know you as my enemy. Likewise I shall make you understand. If you do otherwise, God knows what I know.

In 1254, the Great Khan Möngke (MERNG-keh)—the last to rule the united Mongol Empire in Eurasia—used similarly ringing rhetoric on Louis IX of France:

If, when you hear and understand the decree of the eternal God, you are still unwilling to pay attention and believe it, saying "Our country is far away, our mountains are mighty, our sea is vast," and in this confidence you bring an army against us—we know what we can do: He who made what was difficult easy and what was far away near, the eternal God, He knows.

What did the popes regard as the primary evidence that the Mongols were evil? What did the Mongols see as the basic test of their supreme righteousness?

Source: Adapted from Christopher Dawson, ed., Mission to Asia, Medieval Academy Reprints for Teaching Series (Toronto: University of Toronto Press, 1981), 75, 85–86, 204. Archaic language has been amended to make the quotations more readable.

Among such groups were the ancestors of the **Ottomans,** Turks who had come to Anatolia in the same wave of migrations as the Seljuks. The Ottomans maintained their independence because the Il-khans were preoccupied with preventing Golden Horde invasions from the north and then, in later times, Timurid incursions from the east. By 1400 the Ottomans were expanding their territory and were in conflict with the Byzantines. In 1453, the Ottomans conquered Constantinople and killed the last of the Byzantine emperors based there. The Christians of eastern Europe and Russia were stunned, and for centuries the rulers of those regions yearned to regain Constantinople from the Islamic Ottomans. But the city, renamed "Istanbul," remained the capital of the Ottoman Empire for nearly five centuries.

| **Stabilization of Mamluk Rule in Egypt** | In the Middle East, the **Mamluks°** are the outstanding example of a government that became stronger and more centralized by, and even gained |

some international support for, its resistance to the Mongol advance. (In Abbasid times, *mamluk* was a term used for military slaves; the Mamluks who established an empire in Egypt and Syria in 1250 used the name "Mamluk" for their regime and its ruling class.) The Mamluks retained control of their base in Egypt and their lands in Syria (see Map 13.2). During the campaigns against the Il-khans in the 1250s and 1260s, the crusaders allowed the Mamluks to cross Palestine to maintain lines of supply and command. The Mamluks were brilliantly successful in their campaigns against the Il-khans. This same strength was evident in the later defeat and destruction of the Crusader kingdoms. It also was demonstrated in the Mamluks' ruthless suppression of the well-organized and violent Assassins in their last remaining centers in northern Syria, which made the Mamluks one of the pillars (far more reliable than the Il-khans) of Sunni orthodoxy in the Middle East.

Mamluk society, particularly in Egypt, became very diverse. In the Abbasid and Seljuk eras, Mamluks had been Turkic immigrants from Central Asia. By the thirteenth century the military servants who gave their name to the regime were drawn from sub-Saharan Africa, from parts of Europe, and from far-flung regions of the Middle East. Under Mamluk rule, Egypt remained a military dictatorship until the forces of the Ottoman Empire conquered it in the 1500s.

The Mamluks were cosmopolitan and practical in outlook (they remained the dominant elite in Egypt until

the end of the eighteenth century). They continued their friendship with the Hohenstaufen family and sent the Syrian diarist and judge Jamal al-Din Muhammad ibn Salim° as ambassador to Frederick's son Manfred in Italy. Mamluk links with the Golden Horde, established during the conflict with the Il-khans, kept a steady stream of people and goods moving by ship between Cairo and the port of Kaffa in Crimea, the primary point of embarkation for carriers of bubonic plague to the Mediterranean.

From the late 1300s to the very end of the 1700s, the Mamluks and their successors continued to import soldiers from Crimea. At the height of the fourteenth-century pandemic, around 1350, Egypt may have lost as much as a third of its population. Lebanon, Palestine, and Syria all had many towns receiving caravan traffic from the east and ship traffic from the Mediterranean. The plague spread swiftly through the populations of those towns, but the epidemic was brief there. Egypt, however, was continually reinfected by the traffic from Crimea, where plague lingered into the modern period.

CONCLUSION

Basic features of nomadic society afforded the Mongols the military capabilities and the organizational habits to begin their conquests in Central Asia. They were ready to adopt any useful technologies and to incorporate men from anywhere into their forces. The decentralized structure of the Mongol Empire facilitated even more innovation, because the regional khans were free to forge their own relationships with local elites, cultures, and economies.

This freedom to innovate on the part of the regional Mongol leaders was complemented by communications with very distant regions. The combination of distant influences and local interactions explains much of the change in western Eurasia during this time. The Il-khans' involvement in Iranian society eventually led them to listen to Rashid ad-Din's advice and convert to Islam. In Russia, however, the Mongols were removed from Russian society, both physically and politically, and never developed an interest in or identification with the local culture. On the surface it may appear that these are two opposite results—in one case the Mongols converted to the local religion and in another they had little contact with it—but actually they are not so very different. In

---

Mamluk (MAM-look)

ibn Salim (ee-bin sah-leem)

both the Islamic Middle East and Christian Russia, the local population was free to practice its religion as in earlier times.

Yet this should not be understood as meaning that the Mongols had no important impact. During the Il-khan period, the local language, Persian, became more influential as a literary language in Iran. Similarly, Russian emerged as a literary language in Russia. In both cases, local spoken languages that had had inferior status in comparison to foreign, classical languages became more established, and the amount written in them increased. The Mongol governments contributed to these changes by weakening traditional elites.

The effects of the bubonic plague in Europe parallel effects of Mongol domination in Iran and Russia. Traditional elites were weakened, and Latin lost some ground to local vernacular languages. In all these areas, the effects on literature and literacy would survive for centuries.

In Iran, the Timurids, by their patronage of Sunni doctrine, inspired their opponents to identify with Shi'ism and often with ecstatic sects such as Sufism. Thus, both positively and negatively, the period of Il-khan and Timurid domination established the terms of regional definition. Similarly, it was both by positive and negative influences that the Mongols helped to establish the terms of regional definition in Russia. To efficiently control the Russian territories, the Mongols stabilized the rule of the Russian princes and solidified the control of powerful families over certain towns and cities. In this way, native control was unbroken during Mongol domination of Russia and parts of eastern Europe.

To understand the full impact of the Mongol conquests, it is important to compare the experiences of the Mongol domains to the Mongol peripheries. The directly controlled domains frequently gained local definition and cultural coherence under the Mongols, and many sectors of the economy benefited from their participation in the Eurasian trade system. But in general their century or so of subjugation left them drained of wealth, sometimes demographically depressed, and deprived of the technological stimulation they might have gained had the Mongols not imposed on them nearly a century of peace.

The peripheries, in contrast, frequently integrated themselves with the Mongol trade networks and enjoyed a flow of information, experience, and often wealth (as in the cases of Genoa and Venice) that aided in their growth. Under military pressure from the Mongols they often tightened and strengthened their leadership (as in the cases of Lithuania, the Ottomans, and the Mamluks), or they explored new working alliances (as between the Mamluks and the Holy Roman Emperor).

■ Key Terms

Genghis Khan	tax farming
Mongols	Timur
steppe	Ibn Khaldun
nomadism	Nasir al-Din Tusi
bubonic plague	Alexander Nevskii
Il-khan	tsar
Golden Horde	Ottomans
Rashid al-Din	Mamluks

■ Suggested Reading

An enormous amount has been written on the history of the Mongol Empire. An accessible recent introduction, now available in paperback, is David Morgan's *The Mongols* (1986). A more specialized study is Thomas T. Allsen, *Mongol Imperialism: The Policies of the Grand Qan Möngke in China, Russia, and the Islamic Lands, 1251–1259* (1987). Also in paperback is René Grousset's classic *The Empire of the Steppes: A History of Central Asia* (1970; reprint, 1988). Two accessible but scholarly texts link early and modern Mongol history and culture: Sechin Jagchid and Paul Hyer, *Mongolia's Culture and Society* (1979), and Larry Moses and Stephen A. Halkovic, Jr., *Introduction to Mongolian History and Culture* (1985). Tim Severin's *In Search of Chinggis Khan* (1992) is a fascinating revisit by a modern writer to the paths of Genghis's conquest. The demographic effects of the Mongol conquests are outlined by William H. McNeill in *Plagues and Peoples* (1976), and Joel Mokyr discusses the technological effects in *The Lever of Riches: Technological Creativity and Economic Progress* (1990). For a thesis of global development that connects commercial development in Europe to the Eurasian trade routes of the Mongol era, see Janet L. Abu-Lughod, *Before European Hegemony: The World System A.D. 1250–1350* (1989).

The history of Central Asia during the Mongol period, when it first came under the rule of the Jagadai Khanate, is important but difficult. An interesting overview is S. A. M. Adshead, *Central Asia in World History* (1993). The most recent scholarly study of Timur is Beatrice Manz, *The Rise and Rule of Tamerlane* (1989).

The only "primary" document relating to Genghis Khan, *Secret History of the Mongols*, has been reconstructed in Mongolian from Chinese script and has been variously produced in scholarly editions by Igor de Rachewilz and Francis Woodman Cleaves, among others. Paul Kahn produced a readable prose English paraphrase of the work in 1984. Also of interest is the only version of the *Secret History* by a modern Mongol author: *The History and the Life of Chinggis Khan: The Secret History of the Mongols, Translated and Annotated by Urgunge Onon* (1990). Outstanding among recent biographies of Genghis Khan are Leo de Hartog, *Genghis Khan, Conqueror of the World* (1989); Michel Hoang, *Genghis Khan*, trans. Ingrid Canfield

(1991); and Paul Ratchnevsky, *Genghis Khan: His Life and Legacy*, trans. and ed. Thomas Nivison Haining (1992), which is most detailed on Genghis's childhood and youth.

The best single volume in English on the Mongols in Russia is Charles Halperin, *Russia and the Golden Horde: The Mongol Impact on Medieval Russian History* (1987). A more detailed study is John Lister Illingworth Fennell, *The Crisis of Medieval Russia, 1200–1304* (1983), and those with a special interest might consult Devin DeWeese, *Islamization and Native Religion in the Golden Horde* (1994).

No single volume in English has yet been devoted to a history of the Il-khans. David Morgan, cited above, is a Persianist, and his chapters on the Il-khans in *The Mongols* (1986) are presently the best general introduction to the history of the Il-khans in Azerbaijan and Iran. Interestingly, the great historians of the Il-khan period have been translated into several European languages. Available in English are Juvaini's history of the Mongols, Joveyni, 'Ala al-Din 'Ata Malek, *The History of the World-Conqueror*, translated from the text of Mirza Muhammad Qazvini by John Andrew Boyle (1958); a small portion of Rashid al-Din's work translated by David Talbot Rice, *The Illustrations to the World History of Rashid al-Din*, ed. Basil Gray (1976); and *The Successors of Genghis Khan*, trans. John Andrew Boyle (1971). Equally important as illustrative reading are works re-lated to Ibn Battuta. See C. Defremery and B. R. Sanguinetti, eds., *The Travels of Ibn Battuta,* A.D. *1325–1354,* translated with revisions and notes from the Arabic text by H. A. R. Gibb (1994), and Ross E. Dunn, *The Adventures of Ibn Battuta, a Muslim Traveler of the 14th Century* (1986).

For Europe, a lively and well-known narrative is James Chambers, *The Devil's Horsemen: The Mongol Invasion of Europe* (1979). Many of the individuals who traveled from Europe to the Mongol courts—not only Marco Polo but also the Franciscan friars John of Plano Carpini and William of Rubruck—have had their accounts translated and annotated in modern editions. Christopher Dawson, ed., *Mission to Asia* (1955; reprint, 1981), is a compilation of some of the best known. But see also Frances Wood, *Did Marco Polo Really Go to China?* (1995). There is also some published material on the travels of Rabban Sauma, a Christian Turk, to Europe; the most recent and most comprehensive is Morris Rossabi, *Visitor from Xanadu* (1992).

■ Note

1. Quotation adapted from Desmond Martin, *Chingis Khan and His Conquest of North China* (Baltimore: The John Hopkins Press, 1950), 303.

14

EASTERN EURASIA,
1200–1500

Mongol Domination in Eastern Eurasia, 1200–1368 • The Early Ming Empire, 1368–1500 • Centralization and Militarism in East Asia, 1200–1500

ENVIRONMENT AND TECHNOLOGY: From Gunpowder to Guns

SOCIETY AND CULTURE: Everyday Law in Ming China

Defending Japan Japanese warriors board Mongol warships with swords to prevent the landing of the invasion force, its cavalry, and siege machines.

After the Mongols conquered northern China in the 1230s, Great Khan Ögödei° told his newly recruited Confucian adviser, Yelu Chucai°, that he planned to turn the heavily populated North China Plain into a pasture for livestock. According to the records, Yelu reacted calmly to this startling plan but argued that taxing the existing cities and villages would bring greater wealth. The Great Khan chose the gentler approach, though the tax system that he instituted was not the fixed-rate method traditional to China but the oppressive tax farming already in use in the Il-khan Empires in the Middle East.

In the early years of the Mongol occupation the Chinese suffered under this system. But there were also benefits, particularly in trade, science, and technology. The Mongols secured routes of transport and communication. They also forced the exchange of experts and advisers between eastern and western Eurasia. These practices led to the rapid spread of information, ideas, and skills.

The effects of the Mongol domination of eastern Eurasia varied from one region to another. China and in some ways Korea gained new unity and definition from the Mongol interlude but suffered great losses of agricultural wealth and population. Japan and northern Vietnam (then called Annam) shared—in very different ways—the complex effects of being at the margins of the Mongol Empire. Song° China and Korea were able to resist the Mongols for decades; Japan and northern Vietnam were attacked by the Mongols but not conquered. This resistance prolonged the warfare in eastern Asia through nearly the entire thirteenth century, a far longer period than in western Eurasia.

The Mongols rapidly appropriated technological developments, particularly in warfare, and carried them westward. As a consequence, the Mongol period of the technologies of gunpowder, metal casting, and the building of wagons and bridges were refined and spread, and large-scale trade in iron ore, sulfur, coal, and copper created new economies in eastern Eurasia. China and Korea were beneficiaries of the techno-

logical developments of the century of warfare in the 1200s, though their societies struggled for decades to recover from the social impact of the Mongol century.

As you read this chapter, ask yourself the following questions:

- What were the major effects of Mongol rule on Chinese government, economy, and culture?
- What stimulated the economic growth of the early Ming period?
- What impact did developments of the Mongol period have on state formation in Korea, Japan, and Vietnam?

MONGOL DOMINATION IN EASTERN EURASIA, 1200–1368

The Mongol conquest of southern China in 1279 marked the end of the prolonged struggle of the Southern Song Empire (1127–1279) against northern invaders—a struggle that had produced a new centralization of government and many technological advances. After destroying the Tanggut and Jin Empires in northern China, Genghis's grandson Khubilai° established a new empire based in China, the Yuan°. Integrating Korea into his empire and maintaining close relations with the Il-khans, Khubilai created a system that allowed technologies improved in the Song period to be disseminated throughout Eurasia, while technologies and sciences of the Islamic world became more accessible in China than at any time since the Tang° Empire (618–906).

The Mongol Conquests, 1206–1279

In 1206 Temüjin° became Genghis Khan, supreme leader of the Mongols. In less than ten years the Mongols subdued other powerful federations of the steppes, and in 1215 Genghis Khan led the attack on the Jin capital at Beijing°. The first Mongol invasions of Russia and the Middle East (see Chapter 13) were occurring about the same time as the extensive campaigns

---

Ögödei (ERG-uh-day) Yelu Chucai (yay-loo CHOO-tsye)
Song (soong)

Khubilai (KOO-bih-lie) Yuan (yu-wenn) Tang (tahng)
Temüjin (TEM-uh-jin) Beijing (bay-JING)

CHRONOLOGY

	Central Asia and Mongolia	China and Southeast Asia	Korea and Japan
1200	**1206** Temüjin chosen Genghis Khan of the Mongols **1227** Death of Genghis Khan **1265** Khubilai becomes last Great Khan; destruction of Karakorum	**1234** Mongols conquer northern China **1271** Founding of Yuan Empire **1279** Mongol conquest of Southern Song **1283** Yuan invades Annam **1293** Yuan attacks Java	**1258** Mongols conquer Koryo rulers in Korea **1274, 1281** Mongols attack Japan
1300			
		1368 Ming Empire founded	**1333–1338** End of Kamakura Shogunate in Japan, beginning of Ashikaga **1392** Founding of Yi kingdom in Korea
1400	**1405** Death of Timur	**1403–1424** Reign of Yongle **1405–1433** Voyages of Zheng He **1449** Mongol attack on Beijing **1471–1500** Annam conquers Champa	

against the Tanggut and Jin Empires in the early 1220s. Genghis died in 1227, but the conquest of China continued under his son Ögödei. By 1234, the Mongols controlled most of northern China and were threatening the Southern Song.

Although the earliest purpose of the Mongol campaigns was not to conquer these regions but to convince the rulers to render tribute, Ögödei was far more interested in ruling the territories. He established the Mongol imperial capital at Karakorum°, and between 1240 and 1260 it attracted merchants, ambassadors, missionaries, and adventurers from all over Eurasia. When the European missionary Giovanni di Piano Carpini (John of Plano Carpini) visited Karakorum in 1246, he found it isolated (see Map 14.1) but well populated and cosmopolitan.

The Mongol Empire was united from 1206 to about 1265, and during that period the khans of the Golden Horde, the khans of the Jagadai domains in Central Asia, and the Il-khans in the Middle East were subordinate to the Great Khan in Mongolia. The Great Khan was chosen in gatherings of Mongol aristocrats that took years to come to a conclusion. While they were deliberating and

Karakorum (kah-rah-KOR-um)

debating, the widow of the deceased Great Khan sometimes acted as head of the government. After Ögödei's death in 1241, the Mongol Empire began to disintegrate. When Khubilai declared himself Great Khan in 1265, the descendants of Jagadai and other lineages refused to accept him. Karakorum was destroyed in the fighting, and Khubilai created a new capital for himself at what is now Beijing. In 1271 he declared himself founder of the **Yuan Empire.**

The Jagadai descendants continued to dominate Central Asia, where they nursed a hatred of Khubilai and the Yuan Empire. The political prestige of the Jagadai Khanate and the ability of the Jagadai Mongols to defend themselves prevented the absorption of Central Asia by the Yuan. Moreover, the independence of the Jagadai khans contributed to the tendency of Central Asian Mongols to continue to strengthen their ties to Islam and to Turkic language and culture. Both the Islamic and the Turkic links were important to the rise of Timur (r. 1370–1405) in the later fourteenth century (Timur's empire is described in Chapter 13). The long-standing enmity between the Jagadai ruling family and the Yuan Empire may also have inspired Timur's unfulfilled wish to conquer China.

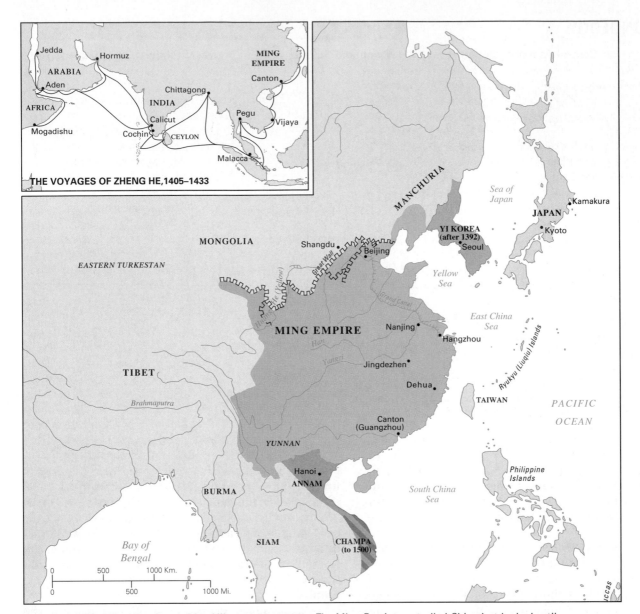

Map 14.1 The Ming Empire and Its Allies, 1368–1500 The Ming Empire controlled China but had a hostile relationship with peoples in Mongolia and Central Asia who had been under the rule of the Mongol Yuan emperors. Mongol attempts at conquest by sea, which are marked on this map, were continued by the Ming mariner Zheng He. Between 1405 and 1433 he sailed to Southeast Asia and then beyond, to India, the Persian Gulf, and East Africa.

After the Yuan Empire destroyed Southern Song in 1279, the state of Annam—in what is now northern Vietnam—was the next logical target. Mongol troops crossed south of the Red River and attacked Hanoi three times. On each occasion they occupied the city, attained an agreement for the paying of tribute, and then withdrew. In 1283 Kubilai's forces moved farther south, invading Champa in what is now southern Vietnam and making it a tribute na-

tion as well. Then Khubilai attempted to subjugate Java. In 1293 a combined Mongol, Uigur, and Chinese force, numbering perhaps forty thousand, set out from the southeast China coast. They arrived in Java but became embroiled in an internal dispute and wasted their resources without conquering the island. In Southeast Asia, as in eastern Europe, the ultimate extension of Mongol effort and the limits of Mongol war techniques were reached.

Partly because of their experiences with the formal Islamic and Christian heirarchies in the Middle East and Russia, the Mongols were quick to communicate with religious leaders in eastern Eurasia. In China, Buddhist and Daoist leaders visited the Great Khan and, like the Muslims and Christians from western Eurasia, believed that they had all but convinced him to accept their beliefs. But only the religious leaders of Tibet seem to have exercised real influence over the Mongol rulers. The Tibetan idea of a militant universal ruler, bringing the whole world under control of the Buddha and thus pushing it nearer to salvation, was in agreement with the ancient idea of universal rulership in Central Asia.

The Mongol Great Khan personally oversaw the governance of Tibet and reinforced the dominance of Lamaism, a Tibetan variant of Buddhism. A **lama°** was a teacher of special techniques for contacting the deities. Tibetan Buddhism became increasingly familiar to Mongol nobles during the 1200s and 1300s.

The Yuan Empire, 1279–1368

Khubilai Khan was the Mongol ruler who best understood the advantages of the Chinese traditions of imperial rule. He gave his oldest son a Chinese name and had Confucianists participate in the boy's education. In his public announcements and often in the ways he allowed the law to be crafted, Khubilai was careful to see that Confucian conventions were acknowledged. He made **Beijing,** in northern China, his capital in 1265.

Like the capitals of the Il-khans and of the Golden Horde, Beijing was located at a critical spot on the overland trade routes that were the infrastructure of the Mongol world. The city was the eastern terminus of the caravan routes that began near Tabriz and Sarai. The routes were reinforced by the imperial horseback courier system, which established hundreds of stations and protected trails over Central Asia.

Khubilai created the spirit, if not all the features that remain today, of Beijing, naming it his Great Capital (Dadu) or, as it was also called, City of the Khan (*khan-balikh°*, Marco Polo's "Cambaluc"). Khubilai ordered massive mud walls of rammed earth built around Beijing, and a tiny portion of them can still be seen. The main streets were made wider and broader. Khubilai's engineers developed linked lakes and artificial islands at the city's northwest edge as a closed imperial complex. As a summer retreat, Khubilai maintained the palace and parks at Shangdu°, now in Inner Mongolia. This was "Xanadu°" celebrated by the English poet Samuel Taylor Coleridge; its "stately pleasure dome" was the hunting preserve where Khubilai and his courtiers practiced the traditional skills of riding and shooting.

When the Mongols came to Chinese territory in the 1220s, there was no "China" as we think of it today. Northern China was under the control of the Tanggut Empire and of the Jin. China south of the Yellow River was ruled by the Southern Song. Part of southwestern China was controlled by the state of Nanzhao. These states had different languages, different writing systems, and different forms of government. Each had a distinctive elite culture. The Great Khans destroyed all these regional regimes and encouraged the restoration or preservation of many features of Chinese government and society, creating a reunited China that was to survive long after the end of Mongol rule.

The Mongols did not merely copy and perpetuate the style of government that had developed under the Song. They introduced many distinctive practices and large numbers of immigrant professionals. As they had in the Middle East, they put primary emphasis on counting the population and collecting taxes. In the early period, direct taxation was replaced by tax farming in the Middle Eastern style. For this purpose the Yuan government brought Persian, Arab, Uigur, and Turkic administrators to China to staff the offices of taxation and finance. The Yuan relied on Muslim scholars to lead the offices of calendar making and astronomy.

By law, the status of individuals was dictated by where they or their ancestors had come from. Mongols had the highest social ranking; below them were Central Asians and Middle Easterners, northern Chinese, and finally southern Chinese. This apparent racial ranking, it should be noted, was also a hierarchy of functions. The Mongols were the conquering caste, the warriors of the empire. Central Asians and Middle Easterners contributed the highly valued political functions of census taking, tax collection, and managing the calendar. The northern Chinese had come under Mongol control almost two generations before the southern Chinese and thus outranked them. The southern Chinese, the last to be conquered, were strongest in their attachment to the principles of Confucian thought.

Despite Khubilai's attempts to include "Confucians" (a formal and hereditary status under the Yuan Empire) in the Yuan government, most saw that their role was much weaker than it had been before the Mongols came. Many were alienated from the Yuan government because of their comparatively low status and their philosophical objections to the conquest. The Confucians, for instance, criticized the elevation in status of merchants. In the Yuan Empire, merchants were a privileged group,

---

lama (LAH-mah)   *khan-balikh* (kahn-BAL-ik)
Shangdu (shahng-DOO)   **Xanadu** (ZAH-nah-doo)

and most were of Central Asian or Middle Eastern origin or were northern Chinese. Similarly, the Confucians regarded doctors as at best technicians and at worst heretical practitioners of Daoist mysticism. The Yuan, however, encouraged the practice of medicine, and the very long process of integrating the medical and herbal knowledge of China and the rest of Eurasia began under the Yuan.

In China as in the Middle East, the Mongols redistricted the country for purposes of census taking and administration. The Mongols organized China into provinces that were much larger than earlier units had been and were under the jurisdiction of provincial governors, tax collectors, and garrison commanders. The creation of the provinces—a strong assertion of Mongol ownership—marked a radical change and increased central control over selected matters.

The impact of Mongol rule on the economy is difficult to assess because of the scarcity of contemporary records and the hostility of later Chinese accounts of the period. Many cities seem to have prospered—the cities of north China that were on the caravan routes, the cities of the interior that were on the Grand Canal, and the well-developed cities along the coast. The reunification of the country revitalized trade between north and south China, fulfilling the original purpose of the Grand Canal. Early in the Yuan period, Khubilai discovered that it was more economical to move grain from south China to Beijing by sea than by land, so the ports of eastern China also were invigorated. The reintegration of East Asia (though not Japan) with the overland Eurasian trade further stimulated the urban economies.

The privileges and prestige that merchants enjoyed under the Mongols changed urban life and the economy of China. The old Chinese elites were eligible for only a limited number of posts in the government, so the great families who in the past had spent their fortunes on educating their sons for government service needed to find other uses for their money. Many gentry families chose to enter the world of commerce, despite their sense of a loss of prestige.

Most commercial activities, from the financing of caravans to tax farming to lending money to the Mongol aristocracy, were managed through corporations—groups of individual investors who behaved as single commercial and legal units and shared the risk of doing business. The forerunners of these corporations were caravan-financing groups in Central Asia and the Middle East, and early Yuan-period corporations were operated mostly by Central Asians and Middle Easterners. Chinese quickly began to purchase an interest in them, however; and soon most corporations were mixed in membership and many were entirely Chinese-owned.

Credit was a great issue in the Yuan period, partly because Mongol conquests damaged the agricultural base from which taxes were drawn, and partly because

Mongol Couple   Mongols who settled in China adopted many of the country's practices, including the use of tombs and of portraits on tomb walls, of the sort depicted here. In accordance with Mongol custom, which for a time became influential among northern Chinese, the man and woman are portrayed side by side. (From *Wenwu*, 1986, #4, pp. 40–46)

the Mongol aristocracy absorbed much more wealth than it ever generated. The imperial government issued paper money in an attempt to solve its economic shortages. Small amounts of paper money had been used in China for centuries, but the massive amounts of unsecured notes issued by the Yuan failed to earn the trust of the population.

The improved stability of copper coins partially offset the failure of the paper currency. During the Song, exports of copper coins to Japan had caused a severe coin shortage in China. The shortage elevated the coins' value and distorted the price ratio of copper to silver. The Mongols cut off trade with Japan, which coincidentally stabilized the value of copper coins, somewhat encouraging trade and credit throughout the Yuan Empire.

The financial and commercial life of Yuan China inspired the gentry to live in cities rather than in the countryside, a change from earlier times. Cities began to cater to the tastes of merchants instead of the traditional scholars. Specialized shops selling clothing, grape wine, furniture, and properly butchered meats (reflecting customers' religious convictions) were common. Teahouses thrived—particularly those featuring sing-song girls, drum singers, operas, and other arts previously considered coarse. One result was a lasting linguistic change: the rise of literature written in the style of everyday speech and the increasing influence of the northern, Mongolian-influenced Chinese language that in the West is often called Mandarin.

In the countryside, where 90 percent of the people lived, **cottage industries** linked to the urban economies continued to advance. The cultivation of mulberry trees and cotton fields and the construction of new irrigation systems (encouraged by the Mongols, who favored the irrigation systems of the Middle East), dams, and water wheels were all common features of village technology. Some of the most famous treatises on planting, harvesting, threshing, and butchering were published in this period. Villagers continued to worship as local gods technological innovators such as Huang Dao Po°, who in the Yuan period brought her special knowledge of cotton growing, spinning, and weaving from her native Hainan Island to the fertile Yangzi Delta.

Overall, however, the Yuan period was a dark one for farmers and other residents of the rural villages. The vast majority of farmers depended on staple crops. After the initial conquests, the Mongol princes evicted many farmers. Those who remained were subjected to the exactions and the brutality of the tax farmers, their agents, and their enforcers. There is evidence that by the end of the 1200s the Mongol government in China, as in Iran, had begun to change its policy from exploitation of farmers to protection and encouragement. But the change came too late. Many farmers had been forced into servitude or homelessness, and dams and dikes had been so neglected that flooding, particularly of the Yellow River, was recurring and disastrous.

The hardships in the countryside took a toll on the size of the population. If Song records of population levels before the Mongol conquest and the Ming census taken after the overthrow of the Mongols are reliable (each may be exaggerated in one direction or another), China may have lost as much as 40 percent of its population in the eighty years of Mongol rule. Many localities in northern China may have lost as much as five-sixths of their populations during the 1200s and early 1300s.

The reasons were complex. One was the continuous warfare of the 1220s due to effective resistance by the Southern Song. Another was the massive, continuous, southward movement of people attempting to flee not only the Mongols but the flooding of the Yellow River. This migration might explain why population losses in northern China were greater than in southern China and why the population along the Yangzi River markedly increased.

Perhaps more important was the effect of bubonic plague and its attendant diseases, which were spread by the constant population movements of the period. The Mongol opening of Yunnan° to first-time rule by a government based in China exposed the lowlands to plague (see Map 14.1). Cities may have been better equipped to lessen or avoid outbreaks than the countryside. Rural portions of northern China were extensively affected by plague in the 1300s, and it is probable that the south was exposed before then. Privations in the countryside may have been extreme enough to depress the rate of population growth, particularly if the traditional practice of female infanticide was employed.

Scientific Exchange

During the Mongol period, technological, medical, mathematical, and astronomical knowledge was vigorously shared from one end of Eurasia to the other. Khubilai in China and Hülegü° in Iran were brothers, and their primary advisers were constantly in touch. The economic and financial policies of the Yuan Empire and the Il-khans were similar, and so was their devotion to the sponsorship of engineering, astronomy, and mathematics.

Huang Dao Po (hwahng DOW poh)

Yunnan (YOON-nahn)   **Hülegü** (HE-luh-gee)

Il-khan science and technology were exported to China and Korea. Muslims from the Middle East oversaw most of the weapons manufacture and engineering projects for Khubilai's armies.

From China, the Il-khans imported scholars and texts that helped them understand technological advances new to them. These included the use of sighting tubes for isolating astronomical objects, stabilized on sling-shot-shaped equatorial mounts; mechanically driven armillary spheres; and new techniques for measuring the movement of the moon. Khubilai commissioned a team of Iranians to come to Beijing to construct an observatory and an institute for astronomical studies similar to the Il-khans facility at Maraga. For the remainder of the imperial period in China, maintaining and staffing the observatory was considered an imperial responsibility.

In mathematics as well, the Yuan Empire promoted an integration of Chinese skills with new ideas from the Middle East. The Chinese had contributed the concept of fractions to Middle Eastern mathematics, and Middle Easterners coming to China brought with them the latest developments in algebra and trigonometry. Chinese mathematicians were encouraged to develop and publish their treatises.

The influence of Islamic doctors and Persian medical texts—particularly in anatomy, pharmacology, and opthalmology—was also strong in China during the Yuan. The Yuan emperors—particularly Khubilai, who suffered from alcoholism and gout—gave doctors an influential position. Chinese scholarship on herbs, drugs, and potions was well developed before the Mongol period, but the introduction of new seeds and formulas from the Middle East stimulated an explosion of experimentation and publication.

Dispersal of the Mongols

In the 1340s, power contests among the Mongol princes shredded the political fabric of the Yuan Empire. By the 1360s China was engulfed in local rebellions by farmers and local civil wars by Mongols. In the chaos a charismatic Chinese leader, Zhu Yuanzhang°, was able to mount a massive campaign that ultimately destroyed the Yuan Empire and in 1368 brought China under control of his new empire, the Ming. Though the Ming government was unfriendly to the memory of the Yuan Empire, many Mongols—as well as the Muslims, Jews, and Christians who had come with them—remained in China, some as farmers, some as shepherds, and some as high-ranking scholars and officials. In most cases their descendants took Chinese names and became part of the diverse cultural world of China.

Mongol power in Eurasia did not come to an end in 1368. New Mongol leaders prevented Ming armies from controlling Mongolia and Turkestan, and Timur held much of Central Asia and Iran. The reconcentration of Mongols on the steppes fostered Mongol unity. Islam united some Mongol groups; Tibetan Buddhism, others.

When the Yuan Empire disintegrated, some retreating Mongols joined Tungusic-speaking peoples of northeastern Asia who depended on hunting, gathering, and fishing. The Tungus—some of them were reindeer-riding nomads—were often seen in trading villages. Their languages and their dress were slightly affected by the Mongols, but in general the Tungus were too scattered and mobile to be effectively subjugated. In extreme northeastern Asia, they continued their traditional way of life and, by means of the Aleutian Islands, maintained contact with the peoples of Alaska, who were their cultural and linguistic distant relatives.

Manchuria (see Map. 14.1), with strong linguistic and cultural ties to the Tungus, was more thickly populated than extreme northeastern Asia and had a good number of farmers. Since the 600s a steady influx of Chinese and Korean settlers had worked to develop the agriculture and towns of the region. Manchuria came under Mongol control and became the Mongols' steppingstone to Korea. Using Mongolian terms and Mongol organizational institutions, the dominant indigenous people—the Jurchens, who had once ruled the area as part of the Jin Empire—made gains in economic and military power. By the late 1400s the Jurchens were a challenge to control of Manchuria by the Ming Empire in China.

Warfare among these groups became increasingly frequent after the disintegration of the Yuan Empire. The growing disorder hindered overland Eurasian trade, which remained an important economic resource for the Mongols of Central Asia.

The Mongols controlling Central Asia were less technologically innovative than their ancestors of the Genghis era, but they were superb traditional warriors and posed a persistent threat to agricultural areas. This meant trouble for Ming China, which hoped to bring all the Mongols under its domination and to convince them to participate in the tributary system. The Mongols did participate, but only to the extent that doing so made it easy for them to trade with the Chinese. Otherwise, they were hostile. Ming attempts to suppress a resurgence of Mongol power led, in the mid-1400s, to a disastrous war in which the Mongols captured the Ming emperor and in 1449 attacked Beijing.

Zhu Yuanzhang (JOO yuwen-JAHNG)

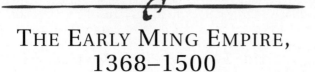

THE EARLY MING EMPIRE, 1368–1500

After the fall of the Yuan to the Ming in 1368, the intense need for technological advances in warfare waned, while population growth reduced the need for mechanization in agriculture and some manufacturing. Eastern Eurasia became a wealthy and culturally brilliant region. But the fact that Ming China had no technologically innovative, ambitious rivals on its northern frontier contributed to a slowdown in technological change.

Ming China on a Mongol Foundation

During the chaotic last decades of the Yuan Empire, Zhu Yuanzhang, who had been a monk, a soldier, and a bandit, vanquished his rivals in rebellion. In 1368 he established the **Ming Empire** and ruled as Hongwu (r. 1368–1398). Zhu said that his dedication to rebellion was inspired by the deaths of his parents and other family members from famine and disease, which he blamed on Mongol misrule. He also drew encouragement from radical Buddhist beliefs in the coming of a new age of salvation. As Emperor Hongwu, he oversaw the establishment of a distinct, highly centralized, militarily formidable empire.

In many ways the change from Yuan to Ming was more ideological than structural. The Ming were strong in their nationalist passions, and partly to symbolize their rejection of the Mongols, they established their imperial capital at Nanjing° ("southern capital") on the Yangzi River, rather than at Beijing ("northern capital") (see Map 14.1). The Ming were aggressive in their attempts to intimidate the remaining Mongols and the other peoples of Central and Southeast Asia. In these wars, they used Confucianism to depict the Ming emperor as the champion of civilization and virtue, justified in making war on uncivilized "barbarians."

The reaction against the Mongols had a vivid impact on early Ming policies regarding trade and money. Hongwu moved to choke off the close relations with Central Asia and the Middle East that had been part of the Mongol trade system. He imposed strict limits on imports and closed much of the border to foreigners. He also attempted to eradicate paper money and to force all tax and commercial payments to be made in silver.

When these extreme measures proved unhealthy for the economy, they were changed, but they are evidence of the vigorous early Ming rejection of Yuan practices.

Nevertheless, in its basic outlines the Ming government resembled that of the Yuan. Ming rulers employed Mongols who could translate communications between the Ming court and the Mongol powers remaining in Central Asia and Mongolia. They retained the provincial structure. In a continuation of Mongol social legislation, the Ming observed hereditary professional categories. The Ming also retained Muslims for making calendars and running their new observatory at Nanjing (a replica of Khubilai's observatory at Beijing), and they continued to use the calendar promulgated by the Mongols.

Ming continuities with the Yuan were even more evident after an imperial prince staged a coup d'état and then ruled as **Yongle**° from 1403 to 1424. He returned the capital to Beijing, enlarging and improving the imperial complex that Khubilai had built. It was mainly during the Yongle reign that the central part of this complex—the **Forbidden City**—took on its present character, with moats, outer vermilion walls, golden roofs, and alabaster bridges. Yongle intended this combination fortress, religious site, bureaucratic center, and imperial residential park to overshadow the imperial architecture at Nanjing, and today it is the most imposing traditional architectural complex that survives.

Economic revitalization was another consideration. Yongle restored commercial links with the Middle East. Because the hostile Mongols still controlled much of the territory through which the land routes passed, Yongle sought to establish a connection by sea. In their first half-century the Ming emperors also pursued the Mongol program of aggression against Southeast Asia, and Annam became a Ming province. Control of Annam and access to Southeast Asia also helped inspire the expeditions of the trusted imperial eunuch **Zheng He**°, from 1405 to 1433.

The Chinese and many of the peoples of Southeast Asia had been exchanging seafaring knowledge for many centuries. Tens of thousands of Chinese descendants had settled throughout Southeast Asia, in the regions ringing the Indian Ocean, almost certainly in some parts of coastal Australia, and possibly in some sites in eastern Africa. From one point of view, Zheng He was merely retracing the routes that the Chinese had been exploring for centuries. The difference was that his expeditions were sponsored by the emperor, at great cost. In any event, he was a superb sea captain who believed that his exploits were measurably increasing the glory of Emperor Yongle, whom he served unflinchingly.

Nanjing (nahn-JING)

Yongle (yoong-LAW)   **Zheng He** (JEHNG HUH)

Forbidden Spaces   The general shape of the imperial complex at Beijing and the set of artificial lakes at its northwest corner were built under the Mongol ruler Khubilai Khan in the late 1200s. It was during the Yongle period (1403–1424) of the Ming, however, that the architectural style was set. In addition to the gold-tiled roofs and the vermilion walls, the Forbidden City is noted for its marble-paved courtyards and three large central palaces, all set on a north-south axis that was part of a spatial pattern that the Forbidden City's planners believed would give it supernatural protection. (Reproduced by permission of the Commercial Press [Hong Kong] Limited, from *The Forbidden City*)

Zheng He was a Muslim. His father and grandfather had made the pilgrimage to Mecca, so Zheng He had a good knowledge of the Middle East. His religion also made him an effective ambassador to the states of the Indian subcontinent, which was the destination of his first three voyages. On subsequent journeys similar ships reached Hormuz, sailed along the southern coast of the Arabian peninsula and the northeast coast of Africa, and reached as far south, perhaps, as the Strait of Madagascar (see Map 14.1).

An important objective of Zheng He's early voyages was to visit Chinese merchant communities in Southeast Asia, affirm their allegiance to the Ming Empire, and demand taxes from them. When a community on Sumatra resisted, Zheng He's marines slaughtered the men of the community to set an example. The Ming court also hoped to advertise the reversal of Hongwu policies opposing foreign trade and to establish lucrative commercial relationships with the Middle East and possibly with Africa.

A great increase in long-distance trade with these regions did not result. The primary achievement was to introduce the Ming Empire to new countries and to sign them on as tributary states. Zheng He's expeditions added as many as fifty new tributaries. The result was sporadic embassies to Beijing from rulers in India, the Middle East, Africa, and Southeast Asia. An early ruler of Brunei° died in Beijing during such a visit and was buried at the Chinese capital with great pomp and ceremony. Many of the expeditions also brought exotic animals—

Brunei (broo-NIE)

the most beloved by the Chinese court was the giraffe—that lived for a time in the Ming imperial zoo.

Historians have long been intrigued by the extraordinary adventure in Chinese seafaring that began under the command of Zheng He in 1405 and continued sporadically until the 1430s, after both Yongle and Zheng He were dead. The feat itself was remarkable, involving ships of unprecedented size and a very well documented survey of nearly the entire Indian Ocean, long before voyages of a similar scale were undertaken by Europeans. Many historians consider Zheng He's expeditions as an early form of exploration that could have opened a period of Chinese military and colonial domination of a large part of the globe. Having accomplished long-distance navigation far in advance of the Europeans, why did the Chinese not develop seafaring for commercial and military gain?

Much of the answer requires setting aside superficial similarities to the European voyages and instead looking at the fundamental characteristics of the Zheng He expeditions. The designs of the enormous junks and of the compasses that Zheng He used were not new, and neither were his navigation techniques or geograhical concepts. Most dated from the Song period. Any empire based in China since the eleventh century that for any reason wanted to spread its reputation through the sponsorship of such voyages could have done so. But neither the Song nor the Yuan had considered it worth the trouble.

The expectation that the voyages would create new commercial opportunities or awe overseas Chinese and foreign nations into immediate submission to Yongle was not realized. In the meantime, Japanese piracy along the coast intensified, and the Mongol threat in the north and west grew. The human and financial demands of fortifying the north, remodeling and strengthening Beijing, and outfitting military expeditions against the Mongols were more than enough for a government that had outgrown its initial enthusiasm for world dominion.

Perhaps the Zheng He voyages are best seen as what people at the time understood them to be: the personal project of Emperor Yongle. This ruler, who had wrested control from a branch of the imperial family in 1403, always felt that he had to prove his worthiness. In Beijing he accomplished most of the intense building that now represents the Forbidden City. He sponsored gigantic encyclopedia projects designed to collect and organize all known knowledge and literature. And he prosecuted effective campaigns against the peoples of Mongolia and northeastern Asia. His nearest model for what he wished to achieve in the voyages west may well have been Khubilai Khan, who also hoped to use enormous fleets of large ships to demand the submission of Japan and

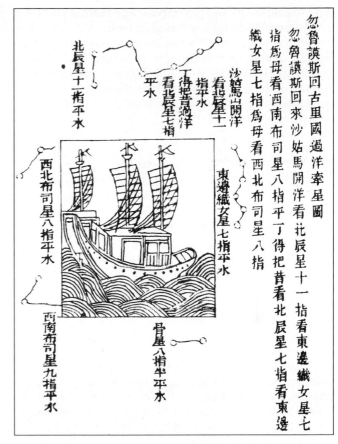

How to Navigate   The navigational techniques that Zheng He and his crew used were well established and tested, as his manual shows. Ships were precisely guided by reference to the Pole Star, and the routes to India, the Middle East, and East Africa were well known. The manual underscores that Zheng He's mission was not to explore but to carry out political and if possible economic mandates.   (From *Wubei zhi* [records of military preparations], 1621)

Southeast Asia. Indeed, Yongle's self-image was so like that of Khubilai that his political enemies spread the rumor that Yongle was a Mongol.

It is important to remember that the cessation of the voyages did not represent a Chinese turning-away from the sea. Zheng He's phenomenal fleet was only one episode in the saga of Chinese seafaring, which continued to be wide ranging and vigorous after Zheng He's voyages ceased. The question to be answered is not about Chinese involvement with the sea but about the Ming emperors' lack of interest in centralizing the organization of such voyages, funding them with government money, and turning them to military uses. The Ming empire was a large, complex, and constantly challenged land-based empire, and the Ming emperors saw little reason to attempt to impose and sustain rule over distant and far-flung sea-based colonies. It is true that before the year 1500 Europeans were engaged in sea-based exploration that brought them to East Asia. But the Zheng He voyages were not the same phenomenon, and it would be a mistake to think that the cessation of the voyages was a major miscalculation by the Ming emperors.

Technology and Population

The economy of Ming China fueled the enrichment of East Asia—and attracted ambitious Europeans. But Ming advances showed less dependence on technological innovation than had been evident in the Song. Innovation continued in all areas of the Ming economy but became less frequent and less important, particularly in agriculture. Agricultural productivity peaked by about the mid-1400s and remained level for more than a century. The slowdown in innovation is apparent in comparisons of Ming China to Song China, or Ming China to its contemporary economies in East Asia.

The slowing of technological development seems to have occurred first in mining and metallurgy, during the Yuan period. The Mongol conquest brought peace to China, and peace removed the pressure to constantly manufacture weapons. Especially striking is the apparent loss of the knowledge required to make high-quality bronze and steel. When instruments were cast for Khubilai's observatory at Beijing, the work was done by Central Asian and Middle Eastern technicians. The failure in China to preserve Song knowledge of high-temperature metallurgy has not been fully explained.

At roughly the time that Chinese metallurgy began to stagnate, Japan made dramatic advances and quickly surpassed China in the production of swords demanding steel of extremely high quality. It appears that copper, iron, and steel had become very expensive commodities in China (remember that the early Ming government preferred metal coins to paper money)—so expensive that farm implements and well-caps made of these materials became prohibitive to manufacture. Shipbuilding also declined sharply, particularly after the death of Emperor Yongle in 1424. There were fewer advances in printing, timekeeping, or agricultural technology. Innovations in the mechanization of weaving seem to have continued through the fifteenth century but were rare after 1500.

The slowing of technological development might be partly due to a significant shift in the career patterns of educated men. During the Yuan period, when few posts in the government were open to Chinese, many wealthy families had turned to commercial pursuits, investing in trading ventures and agriculture. The Ming government reactivated the old examination system, employed large numbers of educated men in government, and deprived the economy of the participation of some of its best educated, most ambitious men.

The Ming economy also may have suffered from a labor glut, which lowered the incentives for mechanization. At the end of the Yuan period in 1368, the population was perhaps as low as 60 million. By 1400 it rebounded to nearly 100 million. This growth constituted a boom to which the economy may have adjusted awkwardly. The rapid growth in population shifted economic importance away from commercial agriculture, where innovation had been rewarded in the Song period, to the production of staples—primarily wheat, millet and barley in the north and rice in the south. Staple crops, though necessary to sustain farming families and feed the rest of the population, did not offer the profit margins of specialized commercial crops and did not provide farmers with money to pay for capital improvements.

Also, the materials necessary for the building of machines had become scarce. The Ming government attempted to limit the mining of metals, partly to reinforce the value of metal coins and partly to control and tax the industry. Iron and bronze were difficult for farmers to obtain. Wood was becoming expensive because of the deforestation of southern and central China during the Ming period, when trees were cut to provide houses and coffins for the expanding population. Farmers who could not acquire plows had little need for draft animals, harnesses, or crops that required deep planting.

In warfare, the Ming faced few technological challenges. The Mongols whom the Ming confronted in the north fought on horseback with simple weapons. The Ming fought back with technology that was nearly as old: arrows, scattershot mortars, and explosive canisters. The Ming used a small number of cannon, but selectively. They were not under pressure to innovate and advance in the technologies of warfare, as the Song had been (see Environment and Technology: From Gunpowder to Guns).

The Ming state, unlike the Song, did not encourage the rapid dissemination and application of technology. Fear of **technology transfer**—whether from the state to the people or from China to foreign nations—seems evident in much of the behavior of the Ming government. Encyclopedias of practical knowledge were produced in the early Ming period, but chapters on gunpowder and guns were censored. Ming shipyards and ports were closed to avoid contact with Japanese pirates and

From Gunpowder to Guns

The word *gunpowder* suggests a substance invented for the gun, but in fact gunpowder had a variety of uses long before guns appeared. Gunpowder was used in China and Korea to do the excavation necessary for mining, canal building, and irrigation. Alchemists in China used formulas related to gunpowder to construct noxious gas pellets that they believed would not only paralyze enemies but also expel evil spirits. Certainly, the devices reduced disease-carrying insects, a critical aid to the colonization of malarial regions in China and Southeast Asia. And gunpowder was used in the Mongol Empire for fireworks displays on ceremonial occasions, delighting European visitors to Karakorum who saw them for the first time.

China is often credited with the invention of gunpowder. But anecdotal evidence in Chinese records gives credit for its introduction to a Sogdian Buddhist monk of the 500s and thus suggests that gunpowder was a Central Asian invention. The monk described the wondrous alchemical transformation of elements produced by a combination of charcoal and saltpeter. In this connection he also mentioned sulfur. Naphtha distillation, too, seems to have been a skill first developed in Central Asia, for some of the earliest devices for distilling naphtha have been found in the Gandhara region (in modern Pakistan).

By the eleventh century, the Chinese had made and used flamethrowers powered by the slow igniting of naphtha, sulfur, or gunpowder in a long tube. They used these weapons not only to intimidate and injure foot soldiers and horses but also to set fire to thatched roofs in hostile villages and, occasionally, the rigging of enemy ships.

During their war against the Mongols, the Song learned to enrich saltpeter to increase the amount of nitrate in gunpowder and thereby produce forceful explosions that could destroy bridges and buildings. Launched from catapults, canisters filled with the explosive material could rupture fortifications and inflict mass casualties. Ships could be set afire or sunk by explosives hurled from a distance.

The Song also seem to have been the first to experiment with the construction of metal gun barrels from which to fire projectiles propelled by the explosion of gunpowder. The earliest of these gun barrels were broad and squat and were carried on special wagons to their emplacements. From the mouths of the barrels projected saltpeter mixed with scattershot minerals to be ignited by the firing of the gun. The Chinese and then the Koreans also learned to use gunpowder to shoot masses of arrows—sometimes flaming arrows—at enemy fortifications. But it was the Mongols who used Song expertise to devise cannon.

In 1280, in the aftermath of the conquest of the Southern Song, the Yuan Empire produced a device featuring a projectile that completely filled the mouth of the cannon and thus concentrated the explosive force. The Yuan used cast bronze for the barrel and iron for the cannonball. The new weapon could be aimed better and shot farther than the earlier devices of the Song. Its ability to smash through brick, wood, and flesh without suffering destruction itself was unprecedented.

Knowledge of the cannon and cannonball moved westward across Eurasia. By the end of the thirteenth century, more accurate, more mobile cannon were being produced in the Middle East. By 1327, small, squat cannon called "bombards" were being produced and used in Europe.

Launching Flaming Arrows   Song soldiers used gunpowder to launch flaming arrows.   (British Library)

SOCIETY & CULTURE

Everyday Law in Ming China

When used carefully, legal documents can provide insights into daily life. Court documents, collections of legal cases, and guidebooks for judges and lawyers can all be valuable. In Ming China, law was a well-developed profession with an extensive printed literature. The following are two cases from a text illustrating when domestic complaints have gone far enough to justify legal action.

You are old and your son is dead. The candle of your life flickers, and is about to go out. By the intervention of friends a young man is engaged to care for you. How were you to know that, after he has lived with you for three years, when you have cared for him as if he were your son, he takes it into his head to betray your trust? He becomes wild and stubborn, wants to take your money and grain and run off. If you let him have his way, he will leave. But if you scold him and make him stay, he will hate you.

Sue!

You have been adopted by a childless man, and helped him build up the family property. Later, your father takes a concubine, and she has a son. The concubine wants to gain control of the property, so she has turned your father against you. One day for no reason he beat you, pulled your hair, bit your elbow to the bone, knocked out your front teeth. The woman beat you with a club, wounding you all over. Still not satisfied, the woman actually accuses you to the authorities.

Sue!

What principles of fairness seem to be behind these cases? How do you imagine these issues were addressed before it became the custom to go to court? Do you think it is important that these passages come from a training book for lawyers?

Source: Adapted from translated passages in John D. Langlois, Jr., "Ming Law," in *The Cambridge History of China,* vol. 8, *The Ming Dynasty,* 1368–1644, part 2, ed. Denis Twitchett and Frederick W. Mote (New York: Cambridge University Press, 1998), 206.

prevent Chinese from migrating to Southeast Asia. Guns and cannon, known from contacts with the Middle East and later with Europeans, were not manufactured or used on any significant scale. Advanced printing techniques were not developed. When printed editions of rare books from the Tang or Song periods were desired, they were purchased from Korea. When superior steel was needed, it was purchased from Japan. New crops, such as sweet potatoes, were available but not adopted.

The technological disparities between China and Europe that were to attract the attention of historians looking at the later Ming period were foreshadowed by the early Ming technology gap with Korea and Japan. For the first time Korea moved ahead of China in the design and production of firearms and ships and in the sciences of weather prediction and calendar making. And for the first time Japan surpassed China in mining and metallurgy and in the manufacture of novel household goods. Nevertheless, it is important to remember that the issue is not "advancement" or "development." Ming China lagged in technological innovation, but it led the world in the generation of massive wealth, and in Korea and Japan this wealth fueled innovation by energetic merchants who hoped to tap into the China markets.

The Ming Achievement

The early Ming period—the late 1300s and the 1400s—was a time of cultural brilliance. The distinctive Ming achievements in literature, the decorative arts, and painting sprang from both the wealth and the consumerism of the time. The period was creative, but also contentious. Ming legal records show the enthusiasm of landed families—and lawyers—for resolving complex personal disputes in court (see Society and Culture: Everyday Law in Ming China).

The interest in plain writing that had been encouraged during the Yuan period came to fruition in some of the world's earliest novels. One of the most famous, *Water Margin,* was based on the raucous drum-song performances of the Yuan period (and was loosely related

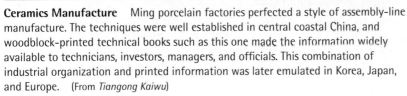

Ceramics Manufacture   Ming porcelain factories perfected a style of assembly-line manufacture. The techniques were well established in central coastal China, and woodblock-printed technical books such as this one made the information widely available to technicians, investors, managers, and officials. This combination of industrial organization and printed information was later emulated in Korea, Japan, and Europe.   (From *Tiangong Kaiwu*)

Ming Ware   Before the Ming, the most prized porcelain in China was celadon ware, normally in a single shade of green or light blue. Patterned porcelain also existed, but it was the early Ming that refined the painting of cobalt blues on white porcelain. Ming designs were celebrated throughout East Asia and highly prized in the Middle East. Despite the great variety of patterns and colors in Ming porcelain, the blue-and-white combination remains the primary image of Ming ware.   (Victoria & Albert Museum)

to Chinese opera). A group of dashing Chinese bandits struggle against Mongol rule, much as Robin Hood and his merry men resist Norman rule in the English legends of an earlier century. The fictional work distorts many of the original stories on which it is based, and it is clear that many authors were involved in its final commission to paper and print.

One of the early Ming authors of *Water Margin*, Luo Guanzhong°, is believed to be the author of *Romance of the Three Kingdoms*. Based on a much older series of story cycles, the saga in some ways resembles the Arthurian stories. It describes the attempts of an upright but doomed war leader and his talented followers to restore the Han Empire of ancient times and resist the power of the cynical but brilliant villain, Cao Cao. *Romance of the Three Kingdoms* and *Water Margin* expressed much of the militant but joyous pro-China sentiment of the early Ming and remain among the most appreciated fictional works in China.

Perhaps the best-known accomplishments of the early Ming were advances in porcelain making. The great imperial ceramic works at Jingdezhen° was a constant site not only of technological improvement but also of the organization and rationalization of labor. Ming patterns—most famous is the blue-on-white widely recognized as "Ming ware"—were stimulated in the 1400s by motifs from India, Central Asia, and the Middle East. Ming porcelain was among the most prized commercial products of Eurasia, and Ming industrial organization seems to have responded effectively to increased international demand.

Luo Guanzhong (LAW GWAHB-JOONG)

Jingdezhen (JING-deh-JUHN)

Other Ming goods for which demand was great were furniture, lacquered screens, and silk, all of which were eagerly transported by both Chinese and foreign merchants to distant markets in Southeast Asia and the Pacific, India, the Middle East, and East Africa.

CENTRALIZATION AND MILITARISM IN EAST ASIA, 1200–1500

As in western Eurasia, in eastern Eurasia areas at the margins of the Mongol advance were more likely to centralize their government and develop a sense of local solidarity. The experiences of East Asian countries apart from China were various. The Mongols conquered Korea after a difficult war of resistance, and Korean elites were drawn into close association with the leaders of the Yuan Empire. Japan managed to escape Mongol conquest.

Korea, like China, emerged from the Mongol period with significant social and economic disadvantages but with a revitalized interest in its vernacular language and its history. Korean merchants continued to develop international connections established in the Mongol period, and Korean armies proved effective in the struggle to establish a new kingdom and in the campaigns to ward off piracy. Japan and Annam, in contrast, were shaped to a certain extent by pressure from the Mongols but did not suffer the economic depletion of conquered territories. They responded to the fall of the Yuan Empire with more effective, ambitious, and expansive regimes.

Korea from the Mongols to the Yi, 1231–1500

During the 1200s, the battle against the Southern Song led the Mongols to seek greater control of the coasts of East Asia. They hoped to find new launching sites for naval expeditions against the south and for strategic points to choke off Song sea trade. Korea offered such possibilities.

When the Mongols attacked in 1231, the leader of a prominent Korean family assumed the role of military commander and protector of the king (not unlike the shoguns of Japan). Under this leader, Korean forces waged a defensive war against the Mongol invaders for over twenty years, until the countryside and the Korean armies were exhausted. Korea's losses in the war were heavy. One of the most important wooden buildings in East Asia, the nine-story pagoda at Hwangnyong-sa°, was destroyed, and the wooden printing blocks of the *Tripitaka*°—a ninth-century masterpiece of printing art—were burned. In 1258 the Korean military commander was killed by his own underlings. Soon afterward, the Koryo° king surrendered to the Mongols, and his family was joined by marriage to the family of the Great Khan.

By the middle 1300s the Koryo kings were mostly Mongol by descent and were comfortable with the Mongolian language, dress, and customs. Many lived in Beijing, and travel by the kings, princes, their families, and their entourages between China and Korea was steady. In this way, the Mongols exposed Korea to direct influence from the most current philosophical and artistic styles of Yuan China, such as neo-Confucianism, Chan Buddhism (in Korea, called *Sŏn*), and celadon ceramics.

The capacity of the Mongol Empire to facilitate the sharing of information among distant cultures strongly influenced Korea. Since the tenth century Korea had been somewhat isolated. Under the Mongols, the growing of cotton began in southern Korea and gunpowder arrived for the first time. The arts of astronomical observation and mathematics were introduced to Korea as a unified science of calendar making, eclipse prediction, and vector calculation. The direct influence of Central Asia is evident in Korean celestial clocks built for the royal observatory at Seoul. A superficial resemblance to Chinese celestial clocks is apparent, but the mechanics and astronomical orientation are Islamic in inspiration. The Mongol conquest opened new avenues of advancement to Korean scholars willing to learn Mongolian, to Korean landowners willing to open their lands to falconry and to grazing, and to Korean merchants able to capitalize on the new royal traffic to Beijing. In this and other ways, the Mongols encouraged the rise of a new landed and educated class in Korea.

Koryo attachment to the Mongol imperial family became so strong that when the Yuan Empire fell in 1368, Koryo decided to remain loyal to the Mongols and had to be forced to recognize the new Ming Empire in China. But within a generation, Koryo collapsed and was succeeded by the **Yi**° kingdom in 1392.

Korea's new royal family, the Yi, was anxious to reestablish a local identity. Like Russia and China after the Mongols, the Yi regime in Korea publicly rejected the period of Mongol domination. But much of Yi government administration adopted Mongol practices and institutions. Mongol-style land surveys, techniques in the administration of military garrisons, and taxation in kind were all continued.

Hwanghnyong-sa (hwahng-NEEYAHNG-sah)
Tripitaka (tri-PIH-tah-kah)   **Koryo** (KAW-ree-oh)   **Yi** (YEE)

Like the Ming Empire, the Yi kingdom revived the study of the Confucian classics. This scholarly activity required the Korean elites to retain their knowledge of Chinese, and it also showed the dedication of the state to the promotion of reading and study. The revival of interest in the Confucian classics may have been the primary factor leading to a key technological breakthrough in printing technology.

Koreans began using Chinese woodblock printing in the 700s. This technology was well suited to China, where a large number of literate men wanted copies of a comparatively small number of texts. But in Korea, comparatively few men could read, and those who could were interested in a wide range of texts. Movable wooden or ceramic type had been used in Korea since the early thirteenth century and may have been invented there. But texts printed from this movable type were frequently inaccurate and difficult to read. In the 1400s Yi printers, working directly with the king, developed a reliable device to anchor the pieces of type to the printing plate: they replaced the old beeswax adhesive with solid copper frames. The legibility of the printed page improved, and high-volume, accurate reproduction of many pages in rapid succession became possible. In combination with the creation in Korea of the phonetic *han'gul°* writing system, this printing technology laid the foundation for a very high rate of literacy in Korea.

Displaying their willingness to adapt and shape Eurasian knowledge imported by the Mongols, the Yi Koreans used the astronomical arts of the Koryo period to develop a meteorological science of their own. Redesigned and newly invented instruments to measure wind speed and rainfall, the first of their kind, augmented the astronomical clock and armillary spheres of the royal observatory at Seoul. A local calendar based on minute comparisons with the calendrical systems of China and the Islamic world was perfected. Interest in commercial agriculture also sparked improvements in the production and use of fertilizer, the transplanting of seedlings in rice paddies, and the engineering of reservoirs (of which there were thousands in Yi times), all disseminated through the powerful new publishing abilities of the Yi government.

Yi agriculture was so well developed that the growing of cash crops became common (this is roughly the reverse of what was happening in Ming China). **Cotton,** introduced under the Mongols, was the primary cash crop. It was so highly valued by the state that it was accepted as payment for taxes. Demand was stimulated by the need of the large and frequently mobilized Yi army for cotton uniforms. Cotton also displaced traditional

han'gul (HAHN-goor)

Movable Type   The improvement of cast bronze tiles, each showing a single character, made it no longer necessary to cast or carve whole pages. Individual tiles could be moved from page frame to page frame. In Korea, where this set was cast, movable type that was more stable in the frame and gave a more pleasing appearance was produced, and all parts of East Asia eventually adopted this form of printing for cheap, popular books. In the mid-1400s Korea also experimented with a fully phonetic form of writing, which in combination with movable type allowed Koreans unprecedented levels of literacy and access to printed works. (Courtesy, Yushin Yoo)

fabrics in the clothing worn by the Korean civil elite. Artisans built cotton gins and spinning wheels, often powered by water, to produce this profitable cloth. In mechanizing the processing of cotton, Korea advanced more rapidly than China. Soon, Korea was exporting considerable amounts of cotton to both China and Japan.

Koreans were innovators in military technology. Yi military campaigns were directed both against the northern part of the country, where Jurchens and other northeastern peoples threatened Yi control of the Yalu River, and also against the coasts, where pirates previously had operated at will and driven harassed farmers inland. Although both the Yuan and the Ming withheld the formula for destructive gunpowder from the Korean government, Korean officials acquired the information by subterfuge. By the later 1300s they had mounted cannon on their patrol ships and used gunpowder-driven arrow launchers against enemy personnel and to propel flaming arrows into the rigging of enemy ships. In combination with Koreans' skill in armoring ships, these techniques made the Yi navy, though small, a formidable defense force.

Political Transformation in Japan, 1274–1500

Once Korea was conquered in the mid-thirteenth century, Japan was the Mongols' likely next stop. It was easily accessible by sea from Korea's southern tip, and from Japan's islands the coast of southern China might be controlled. But, as the Mongols were stopped in the west by the Mamluks (see Chapter 13), so they were stopped in the east by the Japanese.

The Mongols launched their first naval expedition against Japan in 1274. The invading force was diverse and imposing. It included not only the horses and riders of the Mongols but also light catapults and incendiary and explosive projectiles manufactured by the Chinese. Some captains of the fleet, and many archers, were Koreans. Additional warriors were drawn from the Jurchens and other peoples from northeastern Asia, many of whom were excellent archers and experienced sailors. In numbers—perhaps thirty thousand combatants—and in technical outfitting, the expedition presented a clear threat to the independence of Japan. But it was not equal to the weather of Hakata° Bay on the north side of Kyushu° Island (see Map 14.2). Although the Mongol forces were able to land and inflict stunning damage on mounted Japanese warriors, a storm prevented them from establishing a base on the beach. The Mongols returned to their ships and sailed back to Korea.

The appearance of the Mongol invasion force with its superior military technology made a deep impression on the leaders of Japan and hastened social and political changes already under way. At the time Japan was organized under the Kamakura° Shogunate (established in 1185), although another powerful family actually exercised control. The military leader—the shogun—distributed land and privileges to his followers, who paid him tribute and supplied him with soldiers. Based on the balancing of power among regional warlords, this system was fairly stable, but it was also decentralized. Lords in the north and east of Japan's main island were remote from those in the south and west; little united them beyond their declared devotion to the emperor and the shogun. The Mongol threat served to pull them together because it was alien, terrifying, and prolonged.

Hakata (HAH-kah-tah)   Kyushu (KYOO-shoo)
kamakura (kah-mah-KOO-rah)

Map 14.2   Korea and Japan, 1200–1500   The proximity of Korea and of northern China to Japan gave the Mongols the opportunity for launching their enormous fleets. They were defeated by the warriors of the Kamakura Shogunate, which controlled most of the three islands (Honshu, Shikoku, and Kyushu) of central Japan.

After the initial foray in 1274, Khubilai sent envoys to Japan demanding submission. Japanese leaders executed the ambassadors and began preparations to defend against a new attack. In the past, ambitious local military commanders had frequently ignored the civil code that limited their power. Now, in response to the Mongol attack, the shogun took steps to centralize his military government and strengthen the position of mid-level military officials. The influence of warlords from the south and west of Honshu (Japan's main island) and from the island of Kyushu, which was closest to the expected point of attack, rose.

Japanese military planners attempted to imitate what they had observed of Mongol war tactics. Efforts were made to retrain Japanese warriors and outfit them for defense against the advanced weaponry of the attackers. Farm laborers were drafted from all over the country to construct defensive fortifications at Hakata and other points along the Honshu and Kyushu coasts. This effort demanded, for the first time, a national system to move resources toward western points rather than toward the imperial or shogunal centers to the east.

The Mongols attacked again in 1281. They came in a sea force greater than any ever before amassed. They brought 140,000 warriors, including Mongols, Chinese, Koreans, and Jurchens, as well as thousands of horses, in hundreds of ships. Since the first Mongol attack, however, the Japanese had built a wall cutting off Hakata Bay from the mainland. The wall deprived the Mongol forces of a reliable landing point. As Mongol ships lingered offshore, Japanese swordsmen rowed out to board them. With their supremely strong and sharp steel swords, they hacked the startled invaders to pieces. After a standoff lasting months, a typhoon struck and sent perhaps half of the Mongol ships to the bottom of the sea. The remainder of the fleet returned to the mainland, never again to harass Japan. The Japanese gave thanks to the "wind of the Gods"—*kamikaze*°—for driving away the Mongols.

The well-founded belief that the Mongols still posed a threat continued to influence Japanese development. On his deathbed in 1294 Khubilai was indeed planning a third expedition to Japan. His successors did not carry through with it, but the shoguns did not know that the Mongols had given up the idea of conquering Japan. They continued to make plans for coastal defense well into the fourteenth century. This planning helped to consolidate the social position of Japan's warrior elite. It also stimulated the development of a national infrastructure for trade and communication. But the Kamakura Shogunate was structured around the idea that finances would be regionally collected and regionally dispersed. The costs of a more centralized system of roads and defenses strained the small central treasury.

At least one member of the imperial family—which for centuries had lived in seclusion without exercising real political power—saw opportunities in the weakening of the shoguns. Between 1333 and 1338 the emperor Go-Daigo tried to reclaim power from the shoguns, igniting a civil war that destroyed the Kamakura system. In 1338 a new shogunate, the **Ashikaga**°, was established. The new government, not threatened by Mongols, was based at the imperial center of Kyoto.

Political authority was more relaxed in the Ashikaga Shogunate than in the Kamakura, and provincial warlords enjoyed renewed independence. Around their imposing castles, they sponsored the development of market towns, religious institutions, and schools. The application of technologies imported in earlier periods,

kamikazi (KUM-i-kuh-zee) **Ashikaga** (ah-shee-KAH-gah)

Painting by Sesshu Sesshu Toyo (1420–1506) is renowned as the creator of a distinctive style in ink painting that contrasted with the Chinese styles that predominated earlier in Japan. He owed much of his training to the development of Japanese commerce in the period of the Ashikaga Shogunate. As a youth he traveled to China, where he first learned his techniques. As he developed his style, a market for his art developed among the merchant communities of the Ashikaga period, and spread to other urban elites. (Collection of the Tokyo National Museum)

including water wheels, improved plows, and Champa rice, increased the productivity of the land.

The growing wealth and relative peace of the period stimulated artistic creativity, most of which reflected the Zen Buddhist beliefs of the warrior elite. In the simple elegance of the architecture and gardens, in the contemplative landscapes of artists such as Sesshu Toyo, and in the eerie, stylized performances of the No theater, the unified aesthetic code of Zen became established in the Ashikaga era.

Despite the technological advancement, artistic productivity, and rapid urbanization of this period, the progressive aggrandizement of the warlords and their followers led to regional military hostilities. By the later 1400s these conflicts were so severe that they resulted in the near destruction of the warlords. In the aftermath of the great Onin War in 1477, Kyoto was devastated and the Ashikaga Shogunate remained a central government only in name. Ambitious but low-ranking warriors began to scramble for control of the provinces. They were aided by the revival of trade with continental Asia.

After the fall of the Yuan Empire, trade among China, Korea, and the islands of Japan and Okinawa resumed. Japan benefited from the development of firearms in China and Korea by exporting copper, sulfur, and other raw materials. The folding fan, invented in Japan during the period of isolation, and swords, for which Japan quickly became famous, became desireable items in Korea and China. From China, Japan imported primarily books and porcelain. This trade, in combination with Japan's volatile political environment, produced energetic partnerships between warlords and local merchants. All of them worked to strengthen their own towns and treasuries through exploitation of the overseas trade and, sometimes, through piracy.

The Emergence of Vietnam, 1200–1500

The states of Annam (in what is now northern Vietnam) and **Champa** (in what is now southern Vietnam) had an uneasy relationship in the centuries before the Mongol invasions. Annam (once called Dai Viet) had established close relations with empires based in China and had been subject to the Tang Empire. Chinese political ideas, social philosophies, dress, religion, and language heavily influenced its official culture. Champa, in contrast, had a close relationship with the trading networks of the Indian Ocean, and its official culture was marked by a strong influence from Indian religion, language, architecture, and dress. In the Song period, when Annam was not formally subject to China and was less threatening to its southern neighbor, Champa had entered into the trade and tribute relationship with China that distributed the fast-ripening Champa rice throughout East Asia.

The Mongols exacted submission and tribute from both Annam and Champa, but after the fall of the Yuan the old conflicts between Annam and Champa resurfaced. By 1400 they were at war with each other. Taking advantage of Annam's concentration on its southern border, Ming troops occupied Hanoi and installed a puppet government. The puppet government lasted almost thirty years, then was destroyed in a war for Annamese independence. Annam returned to the tributary status it had held in the Song Empire.

But as was the case with Lithuania, the Ottomans, Egypt, and Korea, Annam's struggle against a greater empire inspired expansionist dreams of its own when the Ming were distracted by Mongol challenges in the mid-1400s. In a series of ruthless campaigns, Annamese armies defeated the forces of Champa. By 1500 the conquest was complete. Champa disappeared, and the ancestor of the modern state of Vietnam was born.

The new state, still called Annam, reinforced its centralization with Confucian bureaucratic government and an examination system. But it differed from Chinese practices in two important ways. The Vietnamese legal code preserved the tradition of group landowning and decision making within the villages. It also preserved women's property rights. Both developments probably had roots in an early rural culture based on the growing of rice in wet paddies, but by this time the Annamese considered them distinctive features of their own culture.

CONCLUSION

The effects of the Mongol period in eastern Eurasia differed from region to region. Within different societies, some groups prospered while others suffered.

In China, the Mongols destroyed the empires that had divided the region. They consolidated China as a geographical entity, and they standardized Chinese elite. China was enriched by new access to scientific, commercial, and cultural influences from Central Asia and the Middle East.

Though merchants, artists, and some officials flourished under the Yuan, the farming majority suffered. By the time the Mongol rulers realized that they were destroying the basis of the wealth they hoped to tax, the damage was done. The country was engulfed in a growing number of rebellions, infighting among Mongol princes, and floods.

But the impact of the Yuan Empire was not as fleeting as the empire itself. The Ming Empire pursued many projects inspired by the Mongols, including completion of the Forbidden City and conquests in Southeast Asia. They also showed the indirect influence of the period of Mongol domination, as they sponsored cultural and commercial measures intended to limit or purge foreign influences, and restore what they saw as the classical civilization of China.

With the Ming established in 1368, the population began a rapid recovery. For decades this increased tax revenues, fed hungry labor markets, and allowed the recovery of profitable farm land. The rapid reversal of the isolationist economic policies of the Hongwu period stimulated Ming industries, particularly procelain, which brought tremendous prosperity to China's ports, water transport systems, and industrial centers. Demand grew, labor remained cheap, credit was ample, and the currency was stable.

The concentrations of wealth created huge markets into which merchants from all parts of China tapped, as well as ambitious and technologically innovative manufacturers in Korea and Japan. A powerful economic engine was operating—it simply happened that its mechanisms did not promote technological innovation in China itself.

The close connections forged between Korea and China in the period of Mongol domination clearly aided in their commercial growth. Innovations in printing as well as in the Korean script helped accelerate the spread of knowledge. It also strengthened Yi programs to establish an extensive literature on Korean history. Koreans used sciences to which they had unusual access under the Mongols to develop very precise methods of minimizing their vulnerability to floods and droughts while maximizing their use of cash crops. The growth of the Yi state, and its many military enterprises, stimulated all industries associated with cotton, mining, and forestry.

Japan's decentralized system of military rule, the shogunate, was challenged by the prolonged threat of Mongol invasion. The threat reinforced the status of the warrior elites, and altered the regional balances of power. When the Mongol threat ended, Japan experienced a strong economic stimulus from the reestablishment of trade relations with China, stimulating advances in metallurgy and ceramics. The wealth of the Ashikaga period resulted not only from overseas trade but also from increasing productivity of the land. This wealth accelerated urbanization and produced a brilliant period in the arts.

In Vietnam, the period of Mongol attacks in the late 1200s threatened both Annam and Champa. Ming China subjugated Annam in the late 1300s, but this fueled a strong movement for ending Chinese interference. When the Ming became distracted by their problems with the remaining Mongol powers in the north, Annam quickly threw off Ming control and proceeded to obliterate Champa as an indepdent state. This laid the foundations of modern Vietnam—one of several cases of peripherally challenged states, throughout Eurasia, that experienced a period of expansoin, independence, and increased national consciousness after the period of Mongol domination had passed.

■ Key Terms

Yuan Empire	Forbidden City
lama	Zheng He
Khubilai Khan	technology transfer
Beijing	Yi
cottage industries	cotton
Manchuria	*kamikaze*
Ming Empire	Ashikaga Shogunate
Yongle	Champa

■ Suggested Reading

See Chapter 13 for works on the general history of the Mongols. For China under the Mongols see Morris Rossabi's *Khubilai Khan: His Life and Times* (1988). On the effects of the Mongol period on economy and technology in Yuan and Ming China see Mark Elvin, *The Pattern of the Chinese Past* (1973); Joel Mokyr, *The Lever of Riches: Technological Creativity and Economic Progress* (1990); and Joseph Needham, *Science in Traditional China* (1981). Also see the important interpretation of Ming economic achievement in Andre Gunder Frank, *ReORIENT: Global Economy in the Asian Age* (1998).

Scholarly studies in English on the early Ming period are not so well developed as studies on some other periods of Chinese history, but the publication of *The Cambridge History of China, vol. 8, The Ming Dynasty 1368–1644, part 2*, ed. Denis Twitchett and Frederick W. Mote (1998) improves the situation. See also Albert Chan, *The Glory and Fall of the Ming Dynasty* (1982), and Edward L. Farmer, *Early Ming Government: The Evolution of Dual Capitals* (1976).

On early Ming literature see Lo Kuan-chung, *Three Kingdoms: A Historical Novel Attributed to Luo Guanzhong*, translated and annotated by Moss Roberts (1991); Pearl Buck's translation of *Water Margin*, entitled *All Men Are Brothers*, 2 vols. (1933), and a later translation by J. H. Jackson, *Water Margin, Written by Shih Nai-an* (1937); Richard Gregg Irwin, *The Evolution of a Chinese Novel: Shui-hu-chuan* (1953); Ellen Widmer, *The Margins of Utopia: Shui-hu hou-chuan and the Literature of Ming Loyalism* (1987); and Shelley HsÜeh-lun Chang, *History and Legend: Ideas and Images in the Ming Historical Novels* (1990).

On Ming painting see James Cahill, *Parting at the Shore: Chinese Painting of the Early and Middle Ming Dynasty* (1978). See also selected essays in Paul S. Ropp, ed., *Heritage of China* (1990).

The Zheng He expeditions are extensively discussed in secondary works. A classic interpretation is Joseph R. Levenson, ed., *European Expansion and the Counter-Example of Asia, 1300–1600* (1967). More recent scholarship is available in Philip Snow, *The Star Raft* (1988), and a full and lively account is Louise Levathes, *When China Ruled the Seas* (1993).

For a general history of Korea in this period see Andrew C. Nahm, *Introduction to Korean History and Culture* (1993); Ki-Baik Lee, *A New History of Korea* (1984); and William E. Henthorn, *Korea: The Mongol Invasions* (1963). On a more specialized topic see Joseph Needham et al., *The Hall of Heavenly Records: Korean Astronomical Instruments and Clocks, 1380–1780* (1986).

For narrative histories of Japan, see also John W. Hall and Toyoda Takeshi, eds., *Japan in the Muromachi Age* (1977), and H. Paul Varley, trans., *The Onin War: History of Its Origins and Background with a Selective Translation of the Chronicle of Onin* (1967). On the Mongol invasion see Yamada Nakaba, *Ghenko, the Mongol Invasion of Japan, with an Introduction by Lord Armstrong* (1916), and the novel *Fûtô* by Inoue Yasushi, translated by James T. Araki as *Wind and Waves* (1989). On the No theater and Zen aesthetics there is a great deal of writing. Perhaps most direct and charming are Donald Keene, *No: The Classical Theatre of Japan* (1966), and Ueda Makoto, trans., *The Old Pine Tree and Other Noh Plays* (1962).

15

TROPICAL AFRICA AND ASIA,
1200–1500

Tropical Lands and Peoples • New Islamic Empires • Indian Ocean Trade •
Social and Cultural Change

ENVIRONMENT AND TECHNOLOGY: The Indian Ocean Dhow
SOCIETY AND CULTURE: Personal Styles of Rule in India and Mali

East African Pastoralists Herding large and small livestock has long
been a way of life in drier parts of the tropics.

ultan Abu Bakr° customarily offered his personal hospitality to all distinguished visitors arriving at his city of Mogadishu, an Indian Ocean port on the northeast coast of Africa. In 1331 he provided food and lodging for Muhammad ibn Abdullah ibn Battuta° (1304–1369), a young Muslim scholar from Morocco, who had set out to explore the Islamic world. Having already completed a pilgrimage to Mecca and traveled throughout the Middle East, Ibn Battuta was touring the trading cities of the Red Sea and East Africa. Subsequent travels took him to Central Asia and India, China and Southeast Asia, Muslim Spain, and sub-Saharan West Africa. Logging some 75,000 miles (120,000 kilometers) in his twenty-nine years of travel, Ibn Battuta became the most widely traveled man of his times. For this reason his journal, which describes where he went and what he saw, is a valuable historical source for these lands.

Other Muslim princes and merchants welcomed Ibn Battuta as graciously as did the ruler of Mogadishu. Hospitality was a noble virtue among Muslims, who ignored visitors' physical and cultural differences. Although the Moroccan traveler noted that Sultan Abu Bakr had skin darker than his own and spoke a different native language (Somali), that was of little consequence. They were brothers in faith when they prayed together at Friday services in the Mogadishu mosque, where the sultan greeted his foreign guest in Arabic, the common language of the Islamic world: "You are heartily welcome, and you have honored our land and given us pleasure." When Sultan Abu Bakr and his jurists heard and decided cases after the mosque service, they used the law code familiar in all the lands of Islam.

Islam was not the only thing that united Africa and southern Asia. The most basic links among the diverse peoples of these regions were products of the tropical enviornment itself. A network of land and sea trade routes joined their lands. Older than Islam, these routes were important for spreading beliefs and technologies as well as goods. Ibn Battuta made his

way down the coast of East Africa in merchants' ships and joined their camel caravans across the Sahara to West Africa. His path to India followed overland trade routes, and a merchant ship carried him on to China.

As you read this chapter, ask yourself the following questions:

- How did environmental differences shape cultural differences in tropical Africa and Asia?
- How did cultural and ecological differences promote trade in specialized goods from one place to another?
- How did trade and other contacts promote state growth and the spread of Islam?

TROPICAL LANDS AND PEOPLES

To obtain food, the people who inhabited the tropical regions of Africa and Asia used methods that generations of experimentation had proved successful, whether at the desert's edge, in grasslands, or in tropical rain forests. Much of their success lay in learning how to blend human activities with the natural order, but their ability to modify the environment to suit their needs was also evident in irrigation works and mining.

The Tropical Environment

Because of the angle of earth's axis, the sun's rays warm the **tropics** year-round. The equator marks the center of the tropical zone, and the Tropic of Cancer and Tropic of Capricorn mark its outer limits. As Map 15.1 shows, Africa lies almost entirely within the tropics, as do southern Arabia, most of India, and all of the Southeast Asian mainland and islands.

Lacking the hot and cold seasons of temperate lands, the Afro-Asian tropics have their own cycle of rainy and dry seasons caused by changes in wind patterns across the surrounding oceans. Winds from a permanent high-pressure air mass over the South Atlantic deliver heavy rainfall to the western coast of Africa during much of the year. However, in December and January

---

Abu Bakr (a-BOO BAK-uhr)   **Ibn Battuta** (IB-uhn ba-TOO-tuh)

CHRONOLOGY

	Tropical Africa	Tropical Asia
1200	**1230s** Mali Empire founded	**1206** Delhi Sultanate founded in India
1300	**1270** Solomonic dynasty in Ethiopia founded **1324–1325** Mansa Musa's pilgrimage to Mecca	**1298** Delhi Sultanate annexes Gujarat
1400	**1400s** Great Zimbabwe at its peak **1433** Tuareg retake Timbuktu, Mali declines	**1398** Timur sacks Delhi, Delhi Sultanate declines
1500		**1500** Port of Malacca at its peak

large high-pressure zones over northern Africa and Arabia produce a southward movement of dry air that limits the inland penetration of the moist ocean winds.

In the lands around the Indian Ocean the rainy and dry seasons reflect the influence of alternating winds known as **monsoons**. A gigantic high-pressure zone over the Himalaya° Mountains that is at its peak from December to March produces a strong southward air movement (the northeast monsoon) in the western Indian Ocean. This is southern Asia's dry season. Between April and August a low-pressure zone over India creates a northward movement of air from across the ocean (the southwest monsoon) that brings southern Asia its heaviest rains. This is the wet season.

Along with geographical features, these wind and rain patterns are responsible for the variations in tropical lands, from desert to rain forest. Where rainfall is exceptionally abundant, as in the broad belt along the equator in coastal West Africa and west-central Africa, the natural vegetation is dense tropical rain forest. Rain forests also characterize Southeast Asia and parts of coastal India. Somewhat lighter rains produce other tropical forests. The English word *jungle* comes from an Indian word for the tangled undergrowth in the tropical forests that once covered most of India.

Although heavy rainfall is common in some of the tropics, other parts rarely see rain at all. Stretching clear across the width of northern Africa is the world's largest desert, the Sahara. This arid zone continues eastward across northwest India. Another desert zone occupies southwestern Africa. The lands between the deserts and the rain forests that are favored with moderate amounts of moisture during the rainy seasons form the majority of tropical India and Africa. These lands and range from fairly wet woodlands to the much drier grasslands characteristic of much of East Africa.

Other variations in tropical climate result from altitude. Thin atmospheres at high altitudes can hold less of the tropical heat than can atmospheres at lower elevations. The volcanic mountains of eastern Africa rise to such heights that some are covered with snow all or part of the year. The Himalayas that form the northern frontier of India are also snowcapped and so high that they block the movement of cold air into the northern India plains, giving this region a more tropical climate than its latitude would suggest. The many plateaus of inland Africa and the Deccan° Plateau of central India also make these regions somewhat cooler than the coastal plains.

The mighty rivers that rise in these mountains and plateaus redistribute water far from where it falls. Heavy rains in the highlands of Central Africa and Ethiopia supply the Nile's annual floods that make Egypt bloom in the desert. On its long route to the Atlantic, the Niger River of West Africa arcs northward to the Sahara's edge, providing waters to the trading cities along its banks. In like fashion, the Indus River provides nourishing waters from the Himalayas to arid northwest India. The Ganges° and its tributaries provide valuable moisture to northeastern India during the dry season. Mainland Southeast Asia's great rivers, such as the Mekong, are similarly valuable.

Himalaya (him-uh-LAY-uh)

Deccan (de-KAN)   **Ganges** (GAN-jeez)

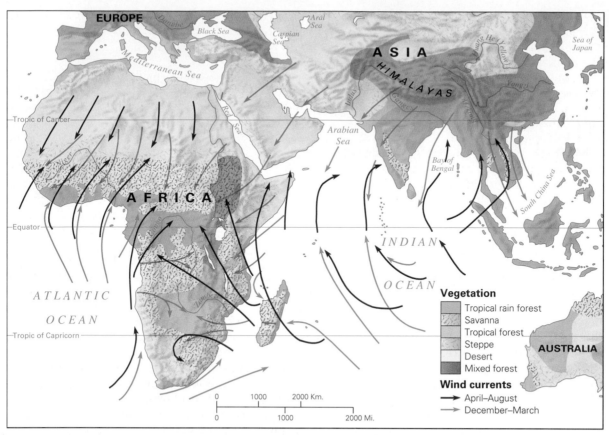

Map 15.1 Africa and the Indian Ocean Basin: Physical Characteristics Seasonal wind patterns control rainfall in the tropics and produce the different tropical vegetation zones to which human societies have adapted over thousands of years. The wind patterns also dominated sea travel in the Indian Ocean.

Human Ecosystems

Thinkers in temperate lands once imagined that, because of the absence of a harsh winter season, surviving in the tropics was as easy as picking wild fruit off a tree. In fact, mastering the tropics' many different environments was a long and difficult struggle. A careful observer touring the tropics in 1200 would have noticed how much the differences in societies could be attributed to their particular ecosystems—that is, to how human groups made use of the plants, animals, and other resources of their physical environments. Tropical peoples' success in adapting to their natural worlds was fundamental to all their other achievements.

Long before 1200, most tropical Africans and Asians had taken up raising domesticated plants and animals as the best way to feed themselves. But people in some environments found it preferable to rely primarily on wild food that they obtained by hunting, fishing, and gather-

ing. This was true of Pygmy° hunters in the dense forests of Central Africa. Their small size itself was a physical adaptation that permitted them to pursue their prey through dense undergrowth. Hunting also was a way of life in the upper altitudes of the Himalayas and in some desert environments. A Portuguese expedition led by Vasco da Gama visited the arid coast of southwestern Africa in 1497 and recorded the presence there of a healthy group of people who lived off both land and sea creatures, feeding themselves on "the flesh of seals, whales, and gazelles, and the roots of wild plants."

Fishing was a highly skilled and successful form of food gathering everywhere in the region, along all the major lakes and rivers as well as in the oceans, though it might be combined with farming. The ocean fishermen of East Africa and Southeast Asia were particularly distinguished, as were those of coastal India. The boating

Pygmy (PIG-mee)

skills of fishermen often led to their playing an important role in ocean trade.

In areas too arid for agriculture, tending herds of domesticated animals was common. Knowledge of local waterholes and observation of the scattered rains enabled pastoralists, unencumbered by bulky personal possessions and elaborate dwellings, to find adequate grazing for their animals in all but the severest droughts. They fed themselves with milk from their herds and with grain and vegetables obtained from farmers in exchange for hides and meat. The world's largest concentration of pastoralists was in the arid and semiarid lands of northeastern Africa and Arabia. Like Ibn Battuta's host at Mogadishu, some Somali were urban dwellers, but most grazed their herds of goats and camels in the desert hinterland of the Horn of Africa. The western Sahara sustained herds of sheep and camels belonging to the Tuareg°, whose intimate knowledge of the desert also made them invaluable as guides to caravans, such as the one **Ibn Battuta** joined on the two-month journey across the desert. Along the Sahara's southern edge the cattle-herding Fulani° people gradually extended their range during this period, and by 1500 they were found throughout the western and central Sudan. A few weeks after encountering the hunter-gatherers of southern Africa, Vasco da Gama's expedition bartered for meat with a pastoral people possessing fat cattle and sheep.

Although food gathering and animal husbandry continued, farming was the dominant way of life for most tropical peoples between 1200 and 1500. The density of agricultural populations was closely tied to the adequacy of rainfall and soils. South and Southeast Asia were generally much better watered than tropical Africa, and the farmers on the Asian plains practiced intensive cultivation. Their high yields supported dense populations. In 1200 there were probably over 100 million people living in South and Southeast Asia, more than four-fifths of them on the fertile Indian mainland. This was three times the number of people living in all of Africa at that time and nearly twice as many as in Europe, though still a little less than the population of China.

Because of India's lush vegetation, one Middle Eastern writer of the time identified it as "the most agreeable abode on earth . . . its delightful plains resemble the garden of Paradise."[1] Rice cultivation was particularly important in places such as the fertile Ganges plain of northeast India, mainland Southeast Asia, and southern China. In drier areas tropical farmers grew grains (such as wheat, sorghum, millet, and ensete) and legumes (such as peas and beans), whose ripening cycle

matched the pattern of the rainy and dry seasons. A variety of tubers and tree crops were characteristic of farming in rain-forest clearings.

By the year 1200 human migrations had spread many useful domesticated plants and animals around the tropics. Bantu-speaking farmers (see Chapter 8) had introduced grains and tubers from West Africa throughout the southern half of the continent. Bananas, brought to southern Africa centuries earlier by mariners from Southeast Asia, had become the staple food for people farming the rich soils around the Great Lakes of East Africa. Yams and cocoyams of Asian origin had spread across equatorial Africa. Asian cattle breeds grazed contentedly in pastures throughout Africa, and coffee of Ethiopian origin would shortly become a common drink in the Middle East.

The spread of farming did not always create permanent changes in the natural environment. In most parts of sub-Saharan Africa and many parts of Southeast Asia until quite recent times, the basic form of cultivation was extensive rather than intensive. Instead of enriching fields with manure and vegetable compost so they could be cultivated year after year, farmers abandoned fields every few years when the natural fertility of the soil was exhausted, and they cleared new fields. Ashes from the brush, grasses, and tree limbs that were cut down and burned gave the new fields a significant boost in fertility. Even though a great deal of work was needed to clear the fields initially, modern research suggests that such shifting cultivation was an efficient use of labor in areas where soils were not naturally rich in nutrients.

Water Systems and Irrigation

In parts of the tropics environmental necessity and population pressure led to the adoption of more intensive forms of agriculture. A rare area of intensive cultivation in sub-Saharan Africa was the inland delta of the Niger River, where large crops of rice were grown using the river's naturally fertilizing annual floods. The rice was probably sold to the trading cities along the Niger bend.

One of the great challenges of the tropical environment in parts of Asia was the uneven distribution of rainfall during the year. Unlike pastoralists who could move their herds to the water, farmers had to find ways of moving the water to their crops. Farmers met the challenge by conserving some of the monsoon rainfall for use during the drier parts of the year. Farming communities in Vietnam, Java, Malaya, and Burma constructed terraced hillsides with special water-control systems for growing rice. Water-storage dams and irrigation canals were also

---

Tuareg (TWAH-reg)　Fulani (foo-LAH-nee)

becoming common in both north and south India. For example, during these centuries villagers in southeast India built a series of stone and earthen dams across rivers to store water for gradual release through elaborate irrigation canals. Over many generations these canals were extended to irrigate more and more land. Although these dams and channels covered large areas, they were relatively simple structures that local people could keep working by routine maintenance.

As had been true since the days of the first river-valley civilizations (see Chapter 2), the largest irrigation systems in the tropics were government public works projects. Under the government of the **Delhi° Sultanate** (1206–1526) northern India acquired extensive new water-control systems. Ibn Battuta commented appreciatively on a large reservoir, constructed under one ruler in the first quarter of the thirteenth century, that supplied the city of Delhi with water. Enterprising farmers planted sugar cane, cucumbers, and melons along the reservoir's rim as the water level fell during the dry season. In the fourteenth century the Delhi Sultan built in the Ganges plain a network of irrigation canals that were not surpassed in size until the nineteenth century. These irrigation systems made it possible to grow crops throughout the year.

Since the tenth century the Indian Ocean island of Ceylon (modern Sri Lanka°) had been home to the greatest concentration of irrigation reservoirs and canals in the world. These facilities enabled the powerful Sinhalese° kingdom in arid northern Ceylon to support a large population. There was another impressive water-works in Southeast Asia, where a system of reservoirs and canals served Cambodia's capital city Angkor°.

Yet such complex systems were vulnerable to disruption. Between 1250 and 1400 the irrigation complex in Ceylon fell into ruin when invaders from South India disrupted the Sinhalese government. The population of Ceylon then suffered from the effects of malaria, a tropical disease spread by mosquitoes breeding in the irrigation canals. The great Cambodian system fell into ruin in the fifteenth century when the government that maintained it collapsed. Neither system was ever rebuilt.

The vulnerability of complex irrigation systems built by powerful governments suggests an instructive contrast. Although village-based irrigation systems could be damaged by invasion and natural calamity, they usually bounced back because they were the product of local initiative, not centralized direction, and they depended on simpler technologies.

Mineral Resources

Metalworking was another way in which people made use of natural resources. Skilled metalworkers furnished their customers with tools, weapons, and decorative objects. The mining and processing of metals was also important for long-distance trade.

Iron was the most abundant of the metals worked in the tropics. People in most parts of the tropical world produced sufficient quantities of iron tools and implements to satisfy their own needs. The iron hoes, axes, and knives that enabled farmers to clear and cultivate their fields seem to have been used between 1200 and 1500 to open up the rain forests of coastal West Africa and Southeast Asia for farming. Iron-tipped spears and arrows improved hunting success. Needles were used in sewing clothes, nails in building. The skill of Indian metalsmiths was renowned, especially in making strong and beautiful swords. So great was the skill of African iron smelters and blacksmiths that they were believed to possess magical powers.

Also of special importance in Africa were copper and its alloys. In the Copperbelt of southeastern Africa, copper mining was in full production in the fourteenth and fifteenth centuries. The refined metal was cast into large X-shaped ingots (metal castings). Local coppersmiths worked these ingots into wire and decorative objects. Copper mining was also important in the western Sudan, where Ibn Battuta described a mining town that produced two sizes of copper bars that were used as a currency in place of coins. Some coppersmiths in West Africa during these centuries skillfully cast copper and brass (an alloy of copper and zinc) statues and heads that are considered among the masterpieces of world art. These works were made by the "lost-wax" method, in which molten metal melts a thin layer of wax sandwiched between clay forms, replacing the "lost" wax with hard metal.

Africans also possessed an international reputation for their production of gold, which was exported in quantity across the Sahara and into the Indian Ocean and Red Sea trades. Gold was mined and collected from stream beds along the upper Niger River and farther south in modern Ghana°. In the hills south of the Zambezi° River (in modern Zimbabwe°) archaeologists have discovered thousands of mine shafts, dating from 1200, that were sunk up to a 100 feet (30 meters) into the ground to get at gold ores. Although panning for gold remained important in the streams descending from the mountains of

---

Delhi (DEL-ee)   **Sri Lanka** (sree LAHNG-kuh)
Sinhalese (sin-huh-LEEZ)   **Angkor** (ANG-kor)

Ghana (GAH-nuh)   **Zambezi** (zam-BEE-zee)
Zimbabwe (zim-BAHB-way)

the rise of powerful states and profitable commercial systems. When considering the better-documented lives of rulers and merchants described later in this chapter, ask yourself: Could the caravans have crossed the Sahara without the skilled guidance of desert pastoralists? Could the trade of the Indian Ocean have reached its full importance were it not for the seafaring skills of the coastal fishermen? Could the city-based empires of Delhi and Mali have endured without the food taxed from rural farmers? Could the long-distance trade routes have prospered without the precious metals, spices, and grains produced by such ordinary folks?

King and Queen of Ife   This copper-alloy work shows the royal couple of the Yoruba kingdom of Ife, the oldest and most sacred of the Yoruba kingdoms of southwestern Nigeria. The casting dates to the period between 1100 and 1500, except for the reconstruction of the male's face, the original of which shattered in 1957 when the road builder who found it accidentally struck it with his pick.   (Andre Held, Switzerland)

NEW ISLAMIC EMPIRES

The empires of Mali in West Africa and Delhi in northern India were the two largest and richest tropical states of the period between 1200 and 1500. Both utilized Islamic administrative and military systems introduced from the Islamic heartland, but in other ways these two Muslim sultanates were very different. **Mali** was founded by an indigenous African dynasty that had earlier adopted Islam through the peaceful influence of Muslim merchants and scholars. In contrast, the Delhi Sultanate of northern India was founded and ruled by invading Turkish and Afghan Muslims. Mali depended heavily for its wealth on its participation in the trans-Saharan trade, but long-distance trade played only a minor role in Delhi's wealth.

Mali in the Western Sudan

The consolidation of the Middle East and North Africa under Muslim rule during the seventh and eighth centuries (see Chapter 9) greatly increased the volume of trade along the routes that crossed the Sahara. In the centuries that followed, the faith of Muhammad gradually spread to the lands south of the desert, which the Arabs called the *bilad al-sudan°*, "land of the blacks."

The role of force in spreading Islam south of the Sahara was limited. Muslim Berbers invading out of the desert in 1076 caused the collapse of Ghana, the empire that preceded Mali in the western Sudan (see Chapter 8), but their conquest did little to spread Islam. To the east, the Muslim attacks that destroyed the Christian Nubian

northern India, the gold and silver mines in India seem to have been exhausted by this period. For that reason, Indians imported from Southeast Asia and Africa considerable quantities of gold for jewelry and temple decoration.

Metalworking and food-producing systems were important to tropical peoples for two reasons. First, most people made a successful livelihood through such skilled exploitation of their environment. Second, the labors and skills of such ordinary people made possible

bilad al-sudan (bih-LAD uhs–soo-DAN)

Map of the Western Sudan (1375) A Jewish geographer on the Mediterranean island of Majorca drew this lavish map in 1375, incorporating all that was known in Europe about the rest of the world. This portion of the Catalan Atlas shows a North African trader approaching the king of Mali, who holds a gold nugget in one hand and a golden scepter in the other. A caption identifies the black ruler as Mansa Musa, "the richest and noblest king in all the land." (Bibliothèque Nationale de France)

kingdoms on the upper Nile in the late thirteenth century opened that area to Muslim influences, but Christian Ethiopia successfully withstood Muslim advances. Instead, the usual pattern for the spread of Islam south of the Sahara was through gradual and peaceful conversion. The expansion of commercial contacts in the western Sudan and on the East African coast greatly promoted the process of conversion. Most Africans found meaning and benefit in the teachings of Islam and found it suited their interests. The first sub-Saharan African state to adopt the new faith was Takrur° in the far western Sudan, whose rulers accepted Islam about 1030.

Shortly after the year 1200 Takrur expanded in importance under King Sumanguru°. Then in about 1240 Sundiata°, the upstart leader of the Malinke° people, handed Sumanguru a major defeat. Even though both leaders were Muslims, the Malinke legends recall their battles as the clash of two powerful magicians, suggesting how much old and new beliefs mingled. Legends say that Sumanguru was able to appear and disappear at will, assume dozens of shapes, and catch arrows in mid-

flight. Sundiata defeated Sumanguru's much larger forces through superior military maneuvers and by successfully wounding his adversary with a special arrow that robbed him of his magical powers. This victory was followed by others that created Sundiata's Mali empire (see Map 15.2).

Mali, like Ghana before it, depended on a well-developed agricultural base and control of the lucrative regional and trans-Saharan trade routes. But Mali differed from Ghana in two ways. First, it was much larger. Mali controlled not only the core trading area of the upper Niger but the gold fields of the Niger headwaters to the southwest as well. Second, its rulers were Muslims, who fostered the spread of Islam among the political and trading elites of the empire. Control of the important gold and copper trades and contacts with North African Muslim traders gave Mali and its rulers unprecedented prosperity.

Under the Mali ruler **Mansa Kankan Musa°** (r. 1312–1337), the empire's reputation for wealth spread far and wide. Mansa Musa's pilgrimage to Mecca in 1324–1325, in fulfillment of his personal duty as a Muslim, also

---

Takrur (TAHK-roor) **Sumanguru** (soo-muhn-GOO-roo)
Sundiata (soon-JAH-tuh) **Malinke** (muh-LING-kay)

Mansa Kankan Musa (MAHN-suh KAHN-kahn MOO-suh)

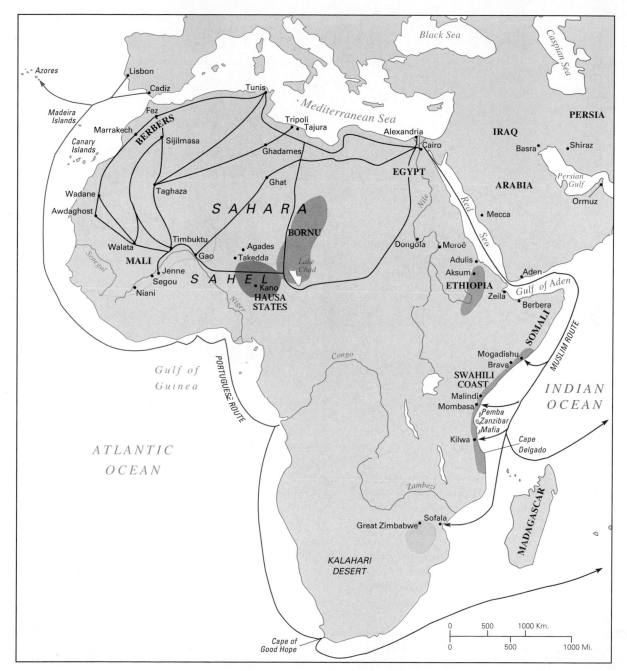

Map 15.2   Africa, 1200–1500   Many African states had beneficial links to the trade that crossed the Sahara and the Indian Ocean. Before 1500, sub-Saharan Africa's external ties were primarily with the Islamic world.

became an occasion for him to display the exceptional wealth of his empire. As befitted a powerful ruler, he traveled with a large entourage. Besides his senior wife and 500 of her ladies in waiting and their slaves, one account says there were also 60,000 porters and a vast

caravan of camels carrying supplies and provisions. Even more lavish was the gold that Mansa Musa is reported to have taken along. For purchases and gifts he took 80 packages of gold each weighing 122 ounces (3.8 kilograms). In addition, 500 slaves each carried a golden

Sankore Mosque, Timbuktu
The wall and tower at the left and center represent traditional styles of construction in clay in a region where building stone is rare. At its peak in the fourteenth through the sixteenth centuries, Timbuktu was a major emporium for trade at the southern edge of the Sahara and a center of Islamic religion and education. (Aldona Sabalis/Photo Researchers, Inc.)

staff. When the entourage passed through Cairo, Mansa Musa was so lavish with his gifts that the value of gold was depressed for years.

Mansa Musa returned from his pilgrimage eager to promote the religious and cultural influence of Islam in his empire. He built new mosques and opened Quranic schools in the cities along the Niger bend. When Ibn Battuta visited Mali from 1352 to 1354, during the reign of Mansa Musa's successor Mansa Suleiman° (r. 1341–1360), the practice of Islam in the empire met with his approval. He lauded Malians for their faithful recitation of prayers and for their zeal in teaching children the Quran.

Ibn Battuta also had high praise for Mali's government. He reported that "complete and general safety" prevailed in the vast territories ruled by Suleiman and that foreign travelers had no reason to fear being robbed by thieves or having their goods confiscated if they died. (For Ibn Battuta's account of the sultan's court and his subjects' respect see Society and Culture: Personal Styles of Rule in India and Mali.)

Two centuries after Sundiata founded the empire, Mali began to disintegrate. When Mansa Suleiman's suc-cessors proved to be less able rulers, rebellions broke out among the diverse peoples who had been subjected to Malinke rule. Avid for Mali's wealth, other groups attacked from without. The desert Tuareg retook their city of Timbuktu° in 1433. By 1500 the rulers of Mali had dominion over little more than the Malinke heartland.

The cities of the upper Niger survived Mali's collapse, but some of the western Sudan's former trade and intellectual life moved east to other African states in the central Sudan. Shortly after 1450 the rulers of several of the Hausa city-states adopted Islam as their official religion. The Hausa states were also able to increase their importance as manufacturing and trading centers, becoming famous for their cotton textiles and leatherworking. Also expanding in the late fifteenth century was the central Sudanic state of Kanem-Bornu°. It was descended from the ancient kingdom of Kanem, whose rulers had accepted Islam in about 1085. At its peak about 1250, Kanem had absorbed the state of Bornu south and west of Lake Chad and gained control of important trade routes crossing the Sahara. As Kanem-Bornu's armies conquered new territories in the late fifteenth century, they also spread the rule of Islam.

Mansa Suleiman (MAHN-suh SOO-lay-mahn)

Timbuktu (tim-buk-TOO) **Kanem-Bornu** (KAH-nuhm–BOR-noo)

Personal Styles of Rule in India and Mali

Ibn Battuta wrote vividly of the powerful men who ruled the Muslim states he visited. His account of Sultan Muhammad ibn Tughluq of Delhi reflects the familiarity he acquired during a long stay in India in the 1340s.

Muhammad is a man who, above all others, is fond of making presents and shedding blood. There may always be seen at his gate some poor person becoming rich, or some living one condemned to death. His generous and brave actions, and his cruel and violent deeds, have obtained notoriety among the people. In spite of this, he is the most humble of men, and the one who exhibits the greatest equity. The ceremonies of religion are dear to his ears, and he is very severe in respect of prayer and the punishment which follows its neglect.... When drought prevailed ... the Sultan gave orders that provisions for six months should be supplied to all the inhabitants of Delhi from the royal granaries ....

One of the most serious charges against this Sultan is that he forced all the inhabitants of Delhi to leave their homes. [After] the people of Delhi wrote letters full of insults and invectives against [him,] the Sultan ... decided to ruin Delhi, so he purchased all the houses and inns from the inhabitants, paid them the price, and then ordered them to remove to Daulatabad ....

The greater part of the inhabitants departed, but [h]is slaves found two men in the streets: one was paralyzed, the other blind. They were brought before the sovereign, who ordered the paralytic to be shot away from a *manjanik* [catapult], and the blind man to be dragged from Delhi to Daulatabad, a journey of forty days' distance. The poor wretch fell to pieces during the journey, and only one of his legs reached Daulatabad.

In contrast, Ibn Battuta's describes Mansa Suleiman of Mali, whom he visited in 1353, in remote and impersonal terms that accord with African political traditions.

On certain days the sultan holds audiences in the palace yard, where there is a platform under a tree ... carpeted with silk, [over which] is raised the umbrella, ... surmounted by a bird in gold, about the size of a falcon. The sultan comes out of a door in a corner of the palace, carrying a bow in his hand and a quiver on his back. On his head he has a golden skullcap, bound with a gold band which has narrow ends shaped like knives, more than a span in length. His usual dress is a velvety red tunic, made of the European fabrics called mutanfas. The sultan is preceded by his musicians, who carry gold and silver [two-stringed guitars], and behind him come three hundred armed slaves. He walks in a leisurely fashion, affecting a very slow movement, and even stops and looks round the assembly, then ascends [the platform] in the sedate manner of a preacher ascending a mosque-pulpit. As he takes his seat, the drums, trumpets, and bugles are sounded. Three slaves go at a run to summon the sovereign's deputy and the military commanders, who enter and sit down ....

The blacks are of all people the most submissive to their king and the most abject in their behavior before him. They swear by his name, saying *Mansa Suleiman ki* [by Mansa Suleiman's law]. If he summons any of them while he is holding an audience in his pavilion, the person summoned takes off his clothes and puts on worn garments, removes his turban and dons a dirty skullcap and enters with his garments and trousers raised knee-high. He goes forward in an attitude of humility and dejection, and knocks the ground hard with his elbows, then stands with bowed head and bent back listening to what he says. If anyone addresses the king and receives a reply from him, he uncovers his back and throws dust over his head and back, for all the world like a bather splashing himself with water. I used to wonder how it was that they did not blind themselves.

How can the kind and cruel sides of Sultan Muhammad be reconciled? What role would Islam have played in his generosity? Could cruelty have brought any benefits to the ruler of a conquest state? How did Mansa Suleiman's ritual appearances serve to enhance his majesty? What attitudes toward Suleiman do his subjects' actions suggest? How different were the ruling styles of Muhammad and Suleiman?

Source: The first excerpt is from Henry M. Elliot, *The History of India as Told by Its Own Historians* (London: Trübner and Co., 1869–1871) 3:609–614. The second excerpt is adapted from H. A. R. Gibb, ed., *Selections from the Travels of Ibn Battuta in Asia and Africa* (London: Cambridge University Press, 1929), pp. 326–327. Copyright © 1929. Reprinted with permission of the Cambridge University Press.

The Delhi Sultanate in India

The arrival of Islam in India was more violent than in West Africa. Having long ago lost the defensive unity of the Gupta Empire (see Chapter 7), the divided states of northwest India were subject to raids by Afghan warlords from the early eleventh century. Motivated by a wish to spread their Islamic faith and by a desire for plunder, the raiders looted Hindu and Buddhist temples of their gold and jewels, kidnapped women for their harems, and slew Indian defenders by the thousands.

In the last decades of the twelfth century a new Turkish dynasty, armed with powerful crossbows, mounted a furious assault that succeeded in capturing the important northern Indian cities of Lahore and Delhi. The Muslim warriors could fire crossbows from the backs of their galloping horses thanks to the use of iron stirrups. One partisan Muslim chronicler recorded, "The city [Delhi] and its vicinity was freed from idols and idol-worship, and in the sanctuaries of the images of the [Hindu] Gods, mosques were raised by the worshippers of one God."[2] The invaders' strength was bolstered by a ready supply of Turkish adventurers from Central Asia eager to follow individual leaders and by the unifying force of their common religious faith. Although Indians fought back bravely, their small states, often at war with one another, were unable to present an effective united front.

Between 1206 and 1236 the Muslim invaders extended their rule over the Hindu princes and chiefs in much of northern India. Sultan Iltutmish° (r. 1211–1236) consolidated the conquest of northern India in a series of military expeditions that made his empire the largest state in India (see Map 15.3). He also secured official recognition of the Delhi Sultanate as a Muslim state by the caliph of Baghdad. Although the looting and destruction of temples, enslavement, and massacres continued, especially on the frontiers of the empire, the incorporation of north India into the Islamic world marked the beginning of the Muslim invaders' transformation from brutal conquerors to somewhat more benign rulers. Hindus whose land came under the control of foreign Muslim military officials were accorded special measures of protection that freed them from persecution in return for the payment of a special tax. Yet Hindus never forgot the intolerance and destruction of their first contacts with the invaders.

To the astonishment of his ministers, Iltutmish passed over his weak and pleasure-seeking sons and designated as his heir his beloved and talented daughter Raziya°. When they questioned the unprecedented idea of a woman ruling a Muslim state, he said, "My sons are devoted to the pleasures of youth: no one of them is qualified to be king. . . . There is no one more competent to guide the State than my daughter." In fact, his wish was not immediately carried out after his death, but after seven months of rule by her inept brother—whose great delight was riding his elephant through the bazaar, showering the crowds with coins—the ministers relented and put Raziya on the throne.

A chronicler of the time who knew her explained why the reign of this able ruler lasted less than four years (r. 1236–1240):

> Sultan Raziya was a great monarch. She was wise, just, and generous, a benefactor to her kingdom, a dispenser of justice, the protector of her subjects, and the leader of her armies. She was endowed with all the qualities befitting a king, but that she was not born of the right sex, and so in the estimation of men all these virtues were worthless. May God have mercy upon her![3]

Doing her best to prove herself a proper king, Raziya dressed like a man and rode at the head of her troops atop an elephant. Nothing, however, could overcome the prejudices of the Turkish chiefs against a woman ruler. In the end, she was imprisoned and later killed by a robber while trying to escape.

After a half-century of stagnation and rebellion, the ruthless but efficient policies of Sultan Ala-ud-din Khalji° (r. 1296–1316) increased his control over the empire's outlying provinces. Successful frontier raids and high taxes kept his treasury full, wage and price controls in Delhi kept down the cost of maintaining a large army, and a network of spies stifled intrigue. When a Mongol threat from the northeast eased, Ala-ud-din's forces extended the sultanate's southern flank, seizing the rich trading state of **Gujarat**° in 1298. Then troops drove into south India and briefly held the southern tip of the Indian peninsula.

At the time of Ibn Battuta's visit, Delhi's ruler was Sultan Muhammad ibn Tughluq° (r. 1325–1351), who received his visitor at his palace's celebrated Hall of a Thousand Pillars. The world traveler praised the sultan's piety and generosity—traditional Muslim virtues—but also recounted his cruelties (see Society and Culture: Personal Styles of Rule in India and Mali). In keeping with these complexities, the sultan resumed against independent Indian states a policy of aggressive expansion that enlarged the sultanate to its greatest extent. He bal-

---

Iltutmish (il-TOOT-mish) **Raziya** (rah-ZEE-uh)

Ala-ud-din Khalji (uh-LAH–uh-DEEN KAL-jee)
Gujarat (goo-juh-RAHT) **Tughluq** (toog-LOOK)

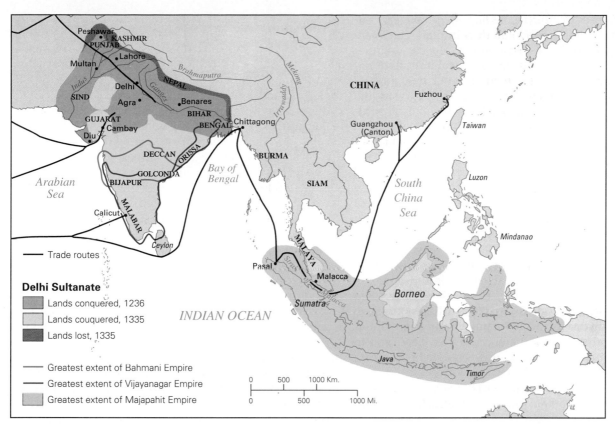

Map 15.3   South and Southeast Asia, 1200–1500   The rise of new empires and the expansion of maritime trade reshaped the lives of many tropical Asians.

anced that policy with one of religious toleration intended to win the loyalty of Hindus and other non-Muslims. He even attended Hindu religious festivals. However, his successor Firuz Shah° (r. 1351–1388) alienated powerful Hindus by taxing the Brahmins, preferring to cultivate good relations with the Muslim elite. Muslim chroniclers praised him for constructing forty mosques, thirty colleges, and a hundred hospitals.

A small minority in a giant land, the Turkish rulers relied on terror to keep their subjects submissive, on harsh military reprisals to put down rebellion, and on pillage and high taxes to sustain the ruling elite in luxury and power. Even under its most enlightened rulers, the Delhi Sultanate was probably more a burden than a benefit to most of its subjects. Although this criticism could be made of most large states of this time (including Mali), the sultanate's rulers never lost the disadvantage of their foreign origins and their practice of a religion alien to most of their subjects. Over time their hostility to any Hindu participation moderated as some Hindus

were incorporated into the administration. Some members of the ruling elite also married women from prominent Hindu families, though the brides had to become Muslims.

Personal and religious rivalries within the Muslim elite, as well as the discontent of the Hindus, threatened the Delhi Sultanate with disintegration whenever it showed weakness and finally hastened its end. In the mid-fourteenth century Muslim nobles challenged the sultan's dominion and successfully established the Bahmani° kingdom (1347–1482), which controlled the Deccan Plateau. To defend themselves against the southward push of Bahmani armies, the Hindu states of South India united to form the Vijayanagar° Empire (1336–1565), which at its height controlled the rich trading ports on both coasts of south India and held Ceylon as a tributary state.

The conflict between Vijayanagar and the Bahmani was as much a struggle among different elites as it was a conflict between Muslims and Hindus, since both states

Firuz Shah (fuh-ROOZ shah)

Bahmani (bah MAHN-ee)   **Vijayanagar** (vee-juh-yah-NAH-gar)

pursued policies that turned a blind eye to religious differences when doing so favored their interests. Bahmani rulers sought to balance devotion to Muslim domination, on the one hand, with the practical importance of incorporating the leaders of the majority Hindu population into the government, marrying Hindu wives, and appointing Brahmins to high offices, on the other. Vijayanagar rulers hired Muslim cavalry specialists and archers to strengthen their military forces, and they formed an alliance with the Muslim-ruled state of Gujarat.

By 1351, when all of South India was independent of Delhi's rule, much of north India was also in rebellion. In the northeast, Bengal successfully broke away from the sultanate in 1338, becoming a center of the mystical Sufi tradition of Islam (see Chapter 9). In the west, Gujarat regained its independence by 1390. The weakening of Delhi's central authority revived Mongol interests in the area. In 1398 the Turko-Mongol leader Timur (see Chapter 13) seized the opportunity to invade and captured the city of Delhi. When his armies withdrew the next year, dragging vast quantities of pillage and tens of thousands of captives behind them, the largest city in southern Asia lay empty and in ruins. The Delhi Sultanate never recovered.

For all its shortcomings, the Delhi Sultanate was important in the development of centralized political authority in India. It established a bureaucracy headed by the sultan, who was aided by a prime minister and provincial governors. There were efforts to improve food production, promote trade and economic growth, and establish a common currency. Despite the many conflicts that Muslim conquest and rule provoked, Islam gradually acquired a permanent place in South Asia. Yet the mixture of indigenous political traditions with these Islamic practices served to distinguish the Delhi Sultanate, like Mali, from the states in the Middle East, where Islam had first flourished.

INDIAN OCEAN TRADE

Food producers sustained tropical Africa and Asia. Sultans and kings directed its political affairs. Merchants were a third force uniting the tropics. Their maritime network stretched across the Indian Ocean from the Islamic heartlands of Iran and Arabia to Southeast Asia. Connecting routes extended to Europe, Africa, and China. The world's richest maritime trading network at this time, the Indian Ocean routes also facilitated the spread of Islam.

Monsoon Mariners

Between 1200 and 1500 the volume of trade in the Indian Ocean increased, stimulated by the prosperity of Islamic and Mongol empires in Asia, of Latin Europe, as well as of Africa and Southeast Asia. The demand for luxuries for the wealthy—precious metals and jewels, rare spices, fine textiles, and other manufactures—rose. The construction of larger ships made shipments of bulk cargoes of ordinary cotton textiles, pepper, food grains (rice, wheat, barley), timber, horses, and other goods profitable. And when the collapse of the Mongol Empire in the fourteenth century disrupted overland trade routes across Central Asia, the Indian Ocean routes assumed greater strategic importance in tying together the peoples of Eurasia and Africa.

Some goods were transported from one end of this trading network to the other, but few ships or crews made a complete circuit. Instead the Indian Ocean trade was divided into the two legs: from the Middle East across the Arabian Sea to India and from India across the Bay of Bengal to Southeast Asia (see Map 15.4).

The characteristic cargo and passenger ship of the Arabian Sea was the **dhow**° (see Environment and Technology: The Indian Ocean Dhow). Large numbers of these ships were constructed in Malabar coastal ports of southwestern India. They grew from an average capacity of 100 tons in 1200 to 400 tons in 1500. On a typical expedition a dhow might sail west from India to Arabia and Africa on the northeast monsoon winds (December to March) and return on the southwest monsoons (April to August). Small dhows kept the coast in sight. Relying on the stars to guide them, skilled pilots steered large vessels by the quicker route straight across the water. A large dhow could sail from the Red Sea to mainland Southeast Asia in from two to four months, but few did so. Eastbound cargoes and passengers from dhows reaching India were likely to be transferred to junks, which dominated the eastern half of the Indian Ocean and the South China Sea.

The largest, most technologically advanced, and most seaworthy vessels of this time, junks had been developed in China and spread with Chinese influence. They were built from heavy spruce or fir planks held together with enormous nails. The space below the deck was divided into watertight compartments to minimize flooding in case of damage to the ship's hull. According to Ibn Battuta, the largest junks had twelve sails made of bamboo and carried a crew of a thousand men, of whom

---

dhow (dow)

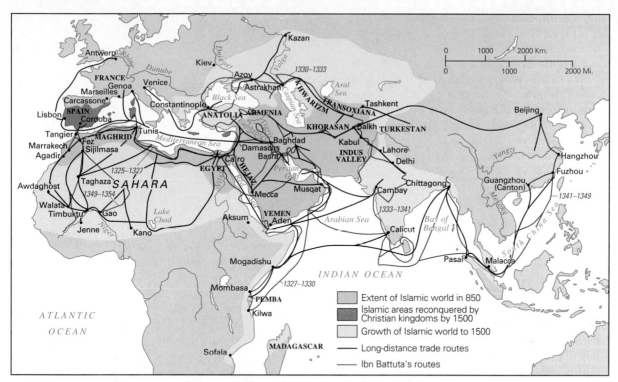

Map 15.4 Arteries of Trade and Travel in the Islamic World, to 1500 Ibn Battuta's journeys across Africa and Asia made use of land and sea routes along which Muslim traders and the Islamic faith had long traveled.

four hundred were soldiers. A large junk might have up to a hundred passenger cabins and could carry a cargo of over 1,000 tons. Chinese junks dominated China's foreign shipping to Southeast Asia and India, but not all of the junks that plied these waters were under Chinese control. During the fifteenth century, vessels of this type also were built in Bengal and Southeast Asia and were sailed by local crews.

The trade of the Indian Ocean was decentralized and cooperative. Commercial interests, not political authorities, united the several distinct regions that participated in it (see Map 15.4). The **Swahili° Coast** supplied gold from inland areas of eastern Africa. Ports around the Arabian peninsula supplied horses and goods from the northern parts of the Middle East, the Mediterranean, and eastern Europe. At the center of the Indian Ocean trade, merchants in the cities of coastal India received goods from east and west, sold some locally, passed others along, and added vast quantities of Indian goods to the trade. The Strait of Malacca°, between the

eastern end of the Indian Ocean and the South China Sea, was the meeting point of trade from Southeast Asia, China, and the Indian Ocean. In each region certain ports functioned as giant emporia for the trade, consolidating goods from smaller ports and inland areas for transport across the seas. The operation of this complex trading system can best be understood by looking at some of these regions and their emporia in greater detail.

Africa: The Swahili Coast and Zimbabwe

Trade expanded steadily along the East African coast from about 1250, giving rise to between thirty and forty separate city-states by 1500. Archaeological excavations reveal that after 1200 many mud and thatch African fishing villages were rebuilt with new masonry buildings, sometimes three or four stories high. Archaeology also reveals the growing presence of imported glass beads, Chinese porcelain, and other exotic goods. The people of the coast and island shared a common culture and and a common language, African in

---

Swahili (swah-HEE-lee) **Malacca** (meh-LAK-eh)

The Indian Ocean Dhow

The sailing vessels that crossed the Indian Ocean shared the diversity of that trading area. The name by which we know them, *dhow*, comes from the Swahili language of the East African coast. The planks of teak from which their hulls were constructed were hewn from the tropical forests of south India and Southeast Asia. Their pilots, who navigated by stars at night, used the ancient technique that Arabs had used to find their way across the desert. Some pilots used a magnetic compass, which originated in China.

Dhows came in various sizes and designs, but they all had two distinctive features in common. The first was hull construction. The hulls of dhows consisted of planks that were sewn together, not nailed. Cord made of fiber from the husk of coconuts or other materials was passed through rows of holes drilled in the planks. Because cord is weaker than nails, outsiders considered this shipbuilding technique strange. Marco Polo fancifully suggested that it indicated sailors' fear that large ocean magnets would pull any nails out of their ships. More probable explanations are that pliant sewn hulls were cheaper to build than rigid nailed hulls and were less likley to be damaged if the ships ran aground on coral reefs.

The second distinctive feature of dhows was their triangular (lateen) sails made of palm leaves or cotton. The sails were suspended from tall masts and could be turned to catch the wind.

The sewn hull and lateen sails were technologies developed centuries earlier, but there were two innovations between 1200 and 1500. First, a rudder positioned at the stern (rear end) of the ship replaced the large side oar that formerly had controlled steering. Second, shipbuilders increased the size of dhows to accommodate bulkier cargoes.

Dhow   This modern model shows the vessel's main features.
(National Maritime Museum, London)

grammar and vocabulary but enriched with many Arabic and Persian terms and written in Arabic script. In time these people became known as "Swahili," from the Arabic name *sawahil° al-sudan*, meaning "shores of the blacks."

Until shortly before Ibn Battuta's visit in 1331 the northern city of Mogadishu had been the Swahili Coast's most important commercial center, but in the fourteenth century the southern city of Kilwa surpassed it in importance. After visiting Kilwa, Ibn Battuta declared it "one of the most beautiful and well-constructed towns in the world." He noted that its dark-skinned inhabitants were devout and pious Muslims, and he took special pains to praise their ruler as a man rich in the traditional Muslim virtues of humility and generosity.

Oral traditions associate the Swahili Coast's commercial expansion with the arrival of Arab and Iranian merchants, but what had attracted them? In Kilwa's case the answer is gold. By the late fifteenth century the city was exporting a ton of gold a year. The gold was mined by inland Africans much farther south. Much of it came from or passed through a powerful state on the plateau south of the Zambezi River, whose capital city is known

---

sawahil (suh-WAH-hil)

Royal Enclosure, Great Zimbabwe   Inside these oval stone walls the rulers of the trading state of Great Zimbabwe lived. Forced to enter the enclosure through a narrow corridor between two high walls, visitors were meant to be awestruck.   (Courtesy of the Department of Information, Rhodesia)

as **Great Zimbabwe.** At its peak in about 1400, the city which occupied 193 acres (78 hectares) may have had 18,000 inhabitants.

Between about 1250 and 1450, local African craftsmen built stone structures for Great Zimbabwe's rulers, priests, and wealthy citizens. The largest structure, a walled enclosure the size and shape of a large football stadium, served as the king's court. Its drystone walls were up to 17 feet (5 meters) thick and 32 feet (10 meters) high. Inside the walls were many buildings, including a large conical stone tower. The stone ruins of Great Zimbabwe are one of the most famous historical sites in sub-Saharan Africa.

Like Mali, the Great Zimbabwe state rested on a mixed farming and cattle-herding economy, but depended on long-distance trade for its wealth. It first prospered in a regional trade based on copper ingots from the upper Zambezi Valley, salt, and local manufactures. The great expansion in the export of gold into the Indian Ocean in the fourteenth and fifteenth centuries brought Zimbabwe to the peak of its political and economic power. However, historians suspect that the city's residents depleted nearby forests for firewood while their cattle overgrazed surrounding grasslands. The result was an ecological crisis that hastened the empire's decline in the fifteenth century.

Arabia: Aden and the Red Sea

The city of **Aden°** had a double advantage in the Indian Ocean trade. Most of the rest of Arabia was desert, but monsoon winds brought Aden enough rainfall to supply drinking water to a large population and to grow grain for export. In addition, Aden's location (see Map 15.2) made it a convenient stopover for trade with India, the Persian Gulf, East Africa, and Egypt. Aden's merchants sorted out the goods from one place and sent them on to another: cotton cloth and beads from India, spices from Southeast Asia, horses from Arabia and Ethiopia, pearls from the Red Sea, luxurious manufactures from Cairo, slaves, gold, and ivory from Ethiopia, and grain, opium, and dyes from Aden's own hinterland.

Aden (AY-den)

Ibn Battuta sailed from Mecca through the Red Sea to Aden in 1331, probably wedged in among bales of trade goods. He commented at length on the great wealth of Aden's leading merchants, telling a story about the slave of one merchant who paid the fabulous sum of 400 dinars for a ram in order to keep the slave of another merchant from buying it. Instead of punishing the slave for this extravagance, the master freed him as a reward for outdoing his rival. Ninety years later a Chinese Muslim visitor, Ma Huan, found "the country . . . rich, and the people numerous," living in stone residences several stories high.

Common commercial interests generally promoted good relations among the different religions and cultures of this region. For example, in the mid-thirteenth century a wealthy Jew from Aden named Yosef settled in Christian Ethiopia, where he acted as an adviser. South Arabia had been trading with neighboring parts of Africa since before the times of King Solomon of Israel. The dynasty that ruled Ethiopia after 1270 claimed descent from Solomon and from the South Arabian princess Sheba. Solomonic Ethiopia's consolidation was associated with a great increase in trade through the Red Sea port of Zeila°, including slaves, amber, and animal pelts, which went to Aden and on to other destinations.

Nevertheless, some religious and political conflict occurred. In the fourteenth century the Sunni Muslim king of Yemen sent materials for the building of a large mosque in Zeila, but the local Somalis (who were Shi'ite Muslims) threw the stones into the sea. The result was a year-long embargo of Zeila ships in Aden. In the late fifteenth century Ethiopia's territorial expansion and efforts to increase control over the trade provoked conflicts with Muslims who ruled the coastal states of the Red Sea.

India: Gujarat and the Malabar Coast

The state of Gujarat in western India prospered as its ports shared in the expanding trade of the Arabian Sea and the rise of the Delhi Sultanate. Blessed with a rich agricultural hinterland and a long coastline, Gujarat attracted new trade after the Mongol capture of Baghdad in 1258 disrupted the northern land routes. Gujarat's forcible incorporation into the Delhi Sultanate in 1298 had mixed results. The state suffered from the violence of the initial conquest and from subsequent military crackdowns, but it also prospered from increased trade with Delhi's wealthy ruling class. Independent again after 1390, the Muslim rulers of Gujarat extended their control over neighboring Hindu states and regained their preeminent position in the Indian Ocean trade.

The state derived much of its wealth from its export of cotton textiles and indigo to the Middle East and Europe, largely in return for gold and silver. Gujaratis also dominated the trade from India to the Swahili Coast, selling cotton cloth, carnelian beads, and foodstuffs in exchange for ebony, slaves, ivory, and gold. During the fifteenth century traders expanded their trade from Gujarat eastward to the Strait of Malacca. These Gujarati merchants helped spread the Islamic faith among East Indian traders, some of whom even imported specially carved gravestones from Gujarat.

Unlike Kilwa and Aden, Gujarat was important for its manufactures as well as its commerce. According to the thirteenth-century Venetian traveler Marco Polo, Gujarat's leatherworkers dressed enough skins in a year to fill several ships to Arabia and other places and also made beautiful sleeping mats for export to the Middle East "in red and blue leather, exquisitely inlaid with figures of birds and beasts, and skilfully embroidered with gold and silver wire," as well as leather cushions embroidered in gold. Later observers considered the Gujarati city of Cambay the equal of cities in Flanders and northern Italy (see Chapter 16) in the size, skill, and diversity of its textile industries. Gujarat's cotton, linen, and silk cloth, as well as its carpets and quilts, found a large market in Europe, Africa, the Middle East, and Southeast Asia. Cambay also was famous for its polished gemstones, gold jewelry, carved ivory, stone beads, and both natural and artificial pearls. At the height of its prosperity in the fifteenth century, this substantial city's well-laid-out streets and open places boasted with fine stone houses with tiled roofs. Although most of Gujarat's overseas trade was in the hands of its Muslim residents, members of its Hindu merchant caste profited so much from related commercial activities that their wealth and luxurious lives were the envy of other Indians.

Gujarat's importance in trade and manufacturing was duplicated farther south in the cities of the Malabar Coast. Calicut° and other coastal cities prospered from their commerce in locally made cotton textiles and locally grown grains and spices, and as clearing-houses for the long-distance trade of the Indian Ocean. The Malabar Coast was united under a loose federation of its Hindu rulers, presided over by the Zamorin° (ruler) of Calicut. As in eastern Africa and Arabia, rulers were generally tolerant of other religious and ethnic groups who were important to commercial profits. Most trading activity lay in the hands of Muslims, many originally from Iran and Arabia, who intermarried with local Indian Muslims. Jewish merchants also operated from Malabar's trading cities.

Zeila (ZEYE-luh)

Calicut (KAL-ih-cut)   **Zamorin** (ZAH-much-ruhn)

Southeast Asia: The Rise of Malacca

At the eastern end of the Indian Ocean, the principal passage into the South China Sea was through the Strait of Malacca between the Malay Peninsula and the island of Sumatra (see Map 15.3). As trade increased in the fourteenth and fifteenth centuries, this commercial choke point became the object of considerable political rivalry. The mainland kingdom of Siam gained control of most of the upper Malay Peninsula, while the Java-based kingdom of Majapahit° extended its dominion over the lower Malay Peninsula and much of Sumatra. Majapahit, however, was not strong enough to suppress a nest of Chinese pirates who had gained control of the Sumatran city of Palembang° and preyed on ships sailing through the strait. In 1407 a fleet sent by the Chinese government smashed the pirates' power and took their chief back to China for trial.

Weakened by internal struggles, Majapahit was unable to take advantage of China's intervention. The chief beneficiary of the safer commerce was the newer port of **Malacca** (or Melaka), which dominated the narrowest part of the strait. Under the leadership of a prince from Palembang, Malacca had quickly grown from an obscure fishing village into an important port by means of a series of astute alliances. Nominally subject to the king of Siam, Malacca also secured an alliance with China that was sealed by the visit of the imperial fleet in 1407. The conversion of an early ruler from Hinduism to Islam helped promote trade with the Gujarati and other Muslim merchants who dominated so much of the Indian Ocean commerce. Merchants also appreciated Malacca's security and low taxes.

Besides serving as the meeting point for traders from India and China, Malacca also served as an emporium for Southeast Asian trade: rubies and musk from Burma, tin from Malaya, gold from Sumatra, as well as cloves and nutmeg from the Moluccas (or Spice Islands as Europeans later dubbed them) to the east. Shortly after 1500, when Malacca was at its height, one resident counted eighty-four languages spoken among the merchants gathered there, who came from as far away as Turkey, Ethiopia, and the Swahili Coast. Four officials administered the large foreign merchant communities: one official for the very numerous Gujaratis, one for other Indians and Burmese, one for Southeast Asians, and one for the Chinese and Japanese. Malacca's wealth and its cosmopolitan residents set the standard for luxury in Malaya for centuries to come.

Majapahit (mah-jah-PAH-hit)
Palembang (pah-lem-BONG)

SOCIAL AND CULTURAL CHANGE

State growth, commercial expansion, and the spread of Islam between 1200 and 1500 led to many changes in the social and cultural life of tropical peoples. The political and commercial elites at the top of society grew in size and power. To serve their needs, the number of slaves increased considerably. There were also changes in the lives of women in different social classes. The spread of Islamic practices and beliefs in many parts of the African and Asian tropics was a major aspect of social and cultural change, evident from the fact that the words *Sahara, Sudan, Swahili,* and *monsoon* are all Arabic in origin. Even so, traditional religious and social customs remained important.

Architecture, Learning, and Religion

As in other periods of history, social and cultural changes were more obvious in the cities than in rural areas. Some urban change was physical. As Ibn Battuta and other travelers observed, wealthy merchants and ruling elites spent lavishly on new mansions, palaces, and places of worship. In architecture, as well as in education and religious practice, the spread of Islam was a major force for change in many tropical societies.

Most of the places of worship that survive from this period exhibit fascinating blends of older traditions and new influences. African Muslims produced strikingly rendered Middle Eastern mosque designs in local building materials: sun-baked clay and wood in the western Sudan; coral stone on the Swahili Coast. Many mosques in Gujarat were influenced by the styles of Hindu temple architecture and even incorporated pieces of older structures. The congregational mosque at Cambay, built in 1325 with courtyard, cloisters, and porches typical of Islamic mosques, was assembled primarily out of pillars, porches, and arches taken from sacked Hindu and Jain° temples of earlier generations. The congregational mosque erected at the Gujarati capital of Ahmadabad° in 1423 was the culmination of a mature Hindu-Muslim architecture. It had an open courtyard typical of mosques everywhere, but the surrounding verandas incorporated many typical Gujarati details and architectural conventions.

Jain (jine)
Ahmadabad (AH-muhd-ah-bahd)

Church of Saint George, Ethiopia King Lalibela, who ruled the Christian kingdom of Ethiopia between about 1180 and 1220, had a series of churches carved out of solid volcanic rock to adorn his kingdom's new capital (also named Lalibela). The church of Saint George, excavated to a depth of 40 feet (13 meters) and hollowed out inside, has the shape of a Greek cross. (S. Sassoon/Robert Harding Picture Library)

Even more unusual than these Islamic architectural amalgams were the Christian churches of King Lalibela° of Ethiopia, constructed during the first third of the thirteenth century. As part of his new capital, Lalibela directed Ethiopian sculptors to carve eleven churches out of solid rock, each commemorating a sacred Christian site in Jerusalem. These unique structures carried on an old Ethiopian tradition of rock sculpture, though on a far grander scale.

Mosques, churches, and temples were centers of education as well as prayer. Muslims promoted literacy among their sons (and sometimes their daughters) so that they could read the religion's classic texts. Ibn Battuta reported seeing several boys in Mali who had been placed in chains until they completed memorizing passages of the Quran. In sub-Saharan Africa the spread of Islam was associated with the spread of literacy, which had previously been confined largely to Christian Ethiopia. Initially literacy was in Arabic, but in time Arabic characters were used to write local languages.

India already had a long literate heritage, so the impact of Islam on literacy there was less dramatic. Arabic spread among Indian scholars along with Persian (the language of Iran), which was considered more refined. Many new works of prose and poetry were written in **Urdu°**, a Persian-influenced literary form of Hindi written in Arabic characters. Muslims also introduced papermaking in India, a second-century Chinese invention that had spread through the Indian Ocean trade routes. Paper facilitated the distribution of written texts in India, even though they still had to be copied by hand.

Although most of the education was concerned with basic literacy and the recitation of the Quran, advanced Muslim scholars studied Islamic law, theology, and administration, as well as classical Greek works of mathematics, medicine, and science. By the sixteenth century in the West African city **Timbuktu,** there were over 150 Quranic schools, and advanced classes were held in the mosques and homes of the leading clerics. So great was the demand for books that they were the most profitable item to bring from North Africa to Timbuktu. At his death in 1536 one West African scholar, al-Hajj Ahmed of Timbuktu, possessed some seven hundred volumes, an unusually large library for that time. In Southeast Asia, Malacca became a center of Islamic learning from which scholars spread Islam throughout the region. Other im-

---

Lalibela (LAH-lee-BEL-uh)

Urdu (ER-doo)

portant centers of learning developed in Muslim India, particularly in Delhi, the capital.

These changes in architecture and education were results of the spread of Islam as a religion. Even where Islam entered as the result of conquest, as in India, conversions were rarely forced. Example and persuasion seem to have been far more effective. The communities of Muslim merchants throughout the region, along with the large number of Muslim warriors and administrators who moved into India during these centuries, attracted interest in their religion. Many Muslims were active missionaries for their faith and worked hard to persuade others of its superiority.

Muslim domination of long-distance trade and markets was particularly important in fostering the adoption of Islam. Many commercial transactions took place between people of different religions, but trust was most easily established among individuals who shared the common code of morality and law that Islam provided. For this reason many local merchants were attracted to Islam. From the major trading centers along the Swahili Coast, in the Sudan, in coastal India, and in Southeast Asia, Islam's influence spread along regional trade routes.

Another important way in which Islam spread was through marriage. Most of the foreign Muslims who settled in tropical Africa and Asia were single men. They often married local women, whom they required to be (or become) Muslims and to raise their children in the Islamic faith. Since Islam permitted a man to have up to four legal wives and many men took concubines as well, some wealthy men had dozens of children. In large elite Muslim households the many servants, both free and enslaved, were also required to be Muslims. Although such conversions were not fully voluntary, individuals could still find personal fulfillment in the Islamic faith.

In parts of southern Asia the upheavals of this period also promoted the spread of Islam. In India, Islamic invasions practically destroyed the last strongholds of long-declining Buddhism. In 1196 the great Buddhist center of study at Nalanda° in Bihar° was overrun, its manuscripts were burned, and thousands of its monks were killed or driven into exile in Nepal and Tibet. Buddhism became a minor faith in the land of its birth (see Chapter 8), while Islam, swelled by substantial immigration, emerged as India's second most important religion. Hinduism was still India's dominant faith in 1500, but in most of maritime Southeast Asia the combined impact of Mongol invasion and the peaceful expansion of Mus-

---

Nalanda (nuh-LAN-duh)   Bihar (bee-HAHR)

Qutb Minar, India   A ruler of the Delhi Sultanate built this unusually tall minaret and mosque near Delhi in the early thirteenth century to display the power of Islam. Five times a day the muezzin climbed the 240-foot (73-meter) tower of red sandstone and white marble to call Muslims to prayer.   (Jean-Louis Nou)

lim merchants led to the displacement of Hinduism by Islam.

Some peoples outside the cities were attracted to Islam in this period. The seed of Islamic belief was planted among the pastoral Fulani of West Africa and Somali of northeastern Africa, as well as among pastoralists in northwest India. Low-caste rural Bengalis also began to adopt Islam, perhaps because they saw more hope in the universalism of Islam than in the fixed inequalities of the Hindu hierarchy. Yet the spread of Islam was not a simple process by which one set of beliefs was replaced by new ones. Islam too was changed by the cultures of the regions it penetrated, developing African, Indian, and Indonesian varieties.

Social and Gender Distinctions

The political, commercial, and religious changes of these centuries significantly affected class structure and the status of at least some women. The gap between the elites and the masses widened. It is not clear that the poor became poorer—the 50 percent of the harvest that peasants in India paid in tax to the Delhi Sultanate may have been no more than what they formerly had paid to local lords—but the rich surely became richer and more numerous as a result of conquests and commerce.

A growth in slavery accompanied the rising prosperity of the elites. Many slaves were the product of wars of expansion by the powerful new states. The campaigns of conquest and pillage in India, according to Islamic sources, reduced hundreds of thousands of Hindu "infidels" to slavery. The courts of the ruling elites of Delhi overflowed with slaves. Sultan Ala ud-Din owned 50,000; Firuz Shah had 180,000, including 12,000 skilled artisans. Sultan Tughluq sent 100 male slaves and 100 female slaves as a gift to the emperor of China in return for a similar gift. His successor prohibited any more exports of slaves, perhaps because of reduced supplies in the smaller empire.

In Africa, the growth of powerful states also had led to an increase in domestic slavery, as well as to a rising export trade in slaves. As Ibn Battuta reported, Mali and Bornu sent slaves across the Sahara to North Africa, including beautiful maidens and eunuchs (castrated males). The expanding Ethiopian Empire regularly sent captives for sale to Aden traders at Zeila. According to modern estimates, about 2.5 million enslaved Africans were sent across the Sahara and the Red Sea between 1200 and 1500. Some slaves were also shipped from the Swahili Coast to India, where Africans played conspicuous roles in the navies, armies, and administrations of some Indian states, especially in the fifteenth century. A few African slaves even found their way to China, where a Chinese source dating from about 1225 says rich families preferred gatekeepers whose bodies were "black as lacquer."

The status of slaves varied enormously, depending on their skill and sex. Relatively few in this period were used as field hands because "free" labor was so abundant and cheap. Most slaves were trained for special purposes. In some places, skilled trades and military service were dominated by hereditary castes of slaves, some of whom were rich and powerful. Indeed, the earliest rulers of the Delhi Sultanate were military slaves, though their status had long ceased to be a disadvantage. A slave general in the western Sudan named Askia Muhammad seized control of the Songhai Empire (Mali's successor) in 1493. Less fortunate were slaves who did hard menial work, such as the men and women who mined copper in Mali.

In all wealthy households there was a tremendous demand for slaves to be employed as servants. Ibn Battuta observed large numbers at the sultan of Mali's palace. Some servants were males, including the eunuchs who guarded the harems of wealthy Muslims, but most household slaves were females. Female slaves were also in great demand as entertainers and concubines. Having a concubine from every part of the world was a rich man's ambition in some Muslim circles. One of Firuz Shah's nobles was said to have two thousand harem slaves, including women from Turkey and China.

Sultan Ala ud-Din's campaigns against Gujarat at the end of the thirteenth century yielded a booty of twenty thousand maidens in addition to innumerable younger children of both sexes. The supply of captives became so great that the lowest grade of horse sold for five times as much as an ordinary female slave destined for service, although beautiful young virgins destined for the harems of powerful nobles commanded far higher prices. Some decades later when Ibn Battuta was given ten girls captured from among the "infidels," he commented: "Female captives [in Delhi] are very cheap because they are dirty and do not know civilized ways. Even the educated ones are cheap." It would seem fairer to say that such slaves were cheap because the large numbers offered for sale had made them so.

How much the status of tropical women—whether slave or free—changed during this period is a subject needing more study. No one has yet offered a general opinion about Africa. Based on a reading of contemporary Hindu legal digests and commentaries, some authors speculate that the position of Hindu women may have improved somewhat compared to earlier periods, but in the absence of detailed information it is impossible to be sure. Hindu women continued to suffer from social and religious disabilities, but some restrictions on their lives may have been relaxed—or, at the very least, not expanded. For example, the ancient practice of sati°—that is, of an upper-caste widow throwing herself on her husband's funeral pyre—remained a meritorious act strongly approved by social custom. But Ibn Battuta leaves no doubt that, in his observation at least, sati was strictly optional. Since the Hindu commentaries devote considerable attention to the rights of widows without sons to inherit their husbands' estates, one may conclude that sati was exceptional.

It remained the custom for Indian girls to be given in marriage before the age of puberty, although the consummation of the marriage was not to take place until

---

sati (suh-TEE)

the young woman was ready. Wives were expected to observe far stricter rules of fidelity and chastity than were their husbands and could be abandoned for many serious breaches. But women often were punished by lighter penalties than men for offenses against law and custom.

A female's status was largely determined by the status of her male master—father, husband, or owner. Women usually were not permitted to play the kind of active roles in commerce, administration, or religion that would have given them scope for personal achievements. Even so, women possessed considerable skills within those areas of activity that social norms allotted to them.

Besides child rearing, one of the most widespread female skills was food preparation. So far historians have paid little attention to the development of culinary skills, but preparing meals that were healthful and tasty required much training and practice, especially given the limited range of foods available in most places. One kitchen skill that has received greater attention is brewing, perhaps because men were the principal consumers. In many parts of Africa women commonly made beer from grains or bananas. These mildly alcoholic beverages, taken in moderation, were a nutritious source of vitamins and minerals. Socially they were an important part of male rituals of hospitality and relaxation that promoted social harmony.

Women's activities were not confined to the hearth, however. Throughout tropical Africa and Asia women did much of the farm work. They also toted home heavy loads of food, firewood, and water for cooking balanced on their heads. Other common female activities included making clay pots for cooking and storage and making clothing. In India the spinning wheel, introduced by the Muslim invaders, greatly reduced the cost of making yarn for weaving. Spinning was a woman's activity done in the home; the weavers were generally men. Marketing was a common activity among women, especially in West Africa, where they sold their agricultural surplus and pottery and other craftwork.

It is difficult to judge how the spread of Islam affected the status of women. Women of some social classes found their status improved by becoming part of a Muslim household. The rare exception, such as Sultan Raziya, might even command supreme authority. Of course, many other women were incorporated into Muslim households as servants, concubines, and slaves.

Yet not all places that adopted Islam accepted all the social customs of the Arab world. In Mali's capital Ibn Battuta was appalled that Muslim women both free and slave did not completely cover their bodies and veil their faces when appearing in public. He considered their nakedness an offense to women's (and men's) modesty.

Indian Woman Spinning, ca. 1500 This drawing of a Muslim woman by an Indian artist shows the influence of Persian styles. The spinning of cotton fiber into thread—women's work—was made much easier by the spinning wheel, which the Muslim invaders introduced. Men then wove the threads into the cotton textiles for which India was celebrated. (British Library, Oriental and Indian Office Library, Or 3299, f. 161)

In another part of Mali he berated a Muslim merchant from Morocco for permitting his wife to sit on a couch and chat with a male friend of hers. The husband replied, "The association of women with men is agreeable to us and part of good manners, to which no suspicion attaches." Ibn Battuta's shock at this "laxity" and his refusal to ever visit the merchant again reveal the patriarchal precepts that were dear to most elite Muslims. So does the fate of Sultan Raziya of Delhi.

CONCLUSION

With nearly 40 percent of the world's population and over a quarter of its habitable land, tropical Africa and Asia was a large and diverse place. In the centuries between 1200 and 1500 commercial, political, and cultural expansion drew the region's peoples closer together. The Indian Ocean became the world's most important and richest trading area. The Delhi Sultanate brought the greatest political unity to India since the decline of the Guptas. Mali extended the political and trading role pioneered by Ghana in the western Sudan. The growth of trade and empires was closely connected with the enlargement of Islam's presence in the tropical world along with the introduction of greater diversity into Islamic practice.

But if change was an important theme of this period, so too was social and cultural stability. Most tropical Africans and Asians never ventured far outside the rural communities where their families had lived for generations. Their lives followed the familiar pattern of the seasons, the cycle of religious rituals and festivals, and the stages from childhood to elder status. Custom and necessity defined occupations. Most people engaged in food production by farming, herding, and fishing; some specialized in crafts or religious leadership. Based on the accumulated wisdom about how best to deal with their environment, such village communities were remarkably hardy. They might be ravaged by natural disaster or pillaged by advancing armies, but over time most recovered. Empires and kingdoms rose and fell in these centuries, but the villages endured.

In comparison, social, political, and environmental changes taking place in the Latin West, described in the next chapter, were in many ways more profound and disruptive. And, after 1500, changes there had great implications for tropical peoples.

■ Key Terms

tropics	dhow
Ibn Battuta	Swahili Coast
monsoon	Great Zimbabwe
Delhi Sultanate	Aden
Mali	Malacca
Mansa Kankan Musa	Urdu
Gujarat	Timbuktu

■ Suggested Reading

The trading links among the lands around the Indian Ocean have attracted the attention of recent scholars. A fine place to begin is Patricia Risso, *Merchants and Faith: Muslim Commerce and Culture in the Indian Ocean* (1995). More ambitious and perhaps more inclinded to overreach the evidence is Janet Abu-Lughod, *Before European Hegemony: The World System, A.D. 1250–1350* (1989), which may usefully be read with K. N. Chaudhuri, *Asia Before Europe: Economy and Civilization of the Indian Ocean from the Rise of Islam to 1750* (1991). Students will find clear summaries of Islam's influences in tropical Asia and Africa in Ira Lapidus, *A History of Islamic Societies* (1988), part II, and of commercial relations in Philip D. Curtin, *Cross-Cultural Trade in World History* (1984).

Greater detail about tropical lands is found in regional studies. For Southeast Asia see Nicholas Tarling, ed., *The Cambridge History of Southeast Asia*, vol. 1 (1992); John F. Cady, *Southeast Asia: Its Historical Development* (1964); and G. Coedes, *The Indianized States of Southeast Asia*, ed. Walter F. Vella (1968). India is covered comprehensively by R. C. Majumdar, ed., *The History and Culture of the Indian People*, vol. 4, *The Delhi Sultanate*, 2d ed. (1967); with brevity by Stanley Wolpert, *A New History of India*, 6th ed. (1999); and from an intriguing perspective by David Ludden, *A Peasant History of South India* (1985). For advanced topics see Tapan Raychaudhuri and Irfan Habib, eds., *The Cambridge Economic History of India*, vol. 1, *c. 1200–c. 1750* (1982).

Africa in this period is well served by the later parts of Graham Connah's *African Civilizations: Precolonial Cities and States in Tropical Africa: An Archaeological Perspective* (1987) and in greater depth by the relevant chapters in D. T. Niane, ed., *UNESCO General History of Africa*, vol. 4, *Africa from the Twelfth to the Sixteenth Century* (1984), and in Roland Oliver, ed., *The Cambridge History of Africa*, vol. 3, *c. 1050 to c. 1600* (1977).

For accounts of slavery and the slave trade see Salim Kidwai, "Sultans, Eunuchs and Domestics: New Forms of Bondage in Medieval India," in *Chains of Servitude: Bondage and Slavery in India*, ed. Utsa Patnaik and Manjari Dingwaney (1985), and the first two chapters of Paul E. Lovejoy, *Transformations in Slavery: A History of Slavery in Africa* (1983).

Three volumes of Ibn Battuta's writings have been translated by H. A. R. Gibb, *The Travels of Ibn Battuta, A.D. 1325–1354* (1958–1971). Ross E. Dunn, *The Adventures of Ibn Battuta: A Muslim of the 14th Century* (1986), provides a modern retelling of his travels with commentary. For annotated selections see Said Hamdun and Noël King, *Ibn Battuta in Black Africa* (1995).

The most accessible survey of Indian Ocean sea travel is George F. Hourani, *Arab Seafaring*, expanded ed. (1995). For a Muslim Chinese traveler's observations see Ma Huan, *Ying-yai Shenglan, "The Overall Survey of the Ocean's Shore" [1433]*, trans. and ed. J. V. G. Mills (1970). Another valuable contemporary account of trade and navigation in the Indian Ocean is G. R. Tibbetts, *Arab Navigation in the Indian Ocean Before the Coming of the Portuguese, Being a Translation of the Kitab al-Fawa'id . . . of Ahmad b. Majidal-Najdi* (1981).

■ Notes

1. Tarikh-i-Wassaf, in Henry M. Elliot, *The History of India as Told by Its Own Historians*, ed. John Dowson (London: Trübner and Co., 1869–1871), 2:28.
2. Hasan Nizami, Taju-l Ma-asir, ibid., 2:219.
3. Minhaju-s Siraj, Tabakat-i Nasiri, ibid., 2:332–333.

16

THE LATIN WEST,
1200–1500

Rural Growth and Crisis • Urban Revival • Learning, Literature, and the
Renaissance • Political and Military Transformations
ENVIRONMENT AND TECHNOLOGY: The Clock
SOCIETY AND CULTURE: Blaming the Black Death on the Jews, Strasbourg, 1349

Making Wine   In this Flemish tapestry, workers use a mechanical press
and foot stomping to crush grapes for wealthy vineyard owners.

n the summer of 1454, the man who in four years would become pope was pessimistic about the future of Latin Christendom. Aeneas Sylvius Piccolomini° was trying to stir up support for a crusade to halt the Muslim advances that were engulfing southeastern Europe. Just a year earlier, the Ottoman Turks had captured the Greek Christian city of Constantinople and showed no sign of stopping. But he doubted anyone could persuade the rulers of the Christian Europe to take up arms together, for, he lamented, "Christendom has no head whom all will obey—neither the pope nor the emperor receives his due."

Another problem was that Christian European states were more inclined to fight with each other than to join a common front against the Turks. French and English armies had been battling for over a century. The German emperor presided over dozens of states that were virtually independent of his control. The Spanish and Italians were divided into numerous kingdoms and principalities that often turned to war. With only slight exaggeration Aeneas Sylvius moaned, "Every city has its own king, and there are as many princes as there are households."

This lack of unity, he believed, was due to Europeans being so preoccupied with personal welfare and material gain that they would never sacrifice themselves to stop the Turkish armies. Both pessimism about human nature and materialism had increased during the previous century, after a devastating plague had carried off a third of western Europe's population.

Yet despite all these divisions, disasters, and wars, historians now see the period from 1200 to 1500 (Europe's later Middle Ages) as a time of unusual progress. The avarice and greed Aeneas Sylvius lamented were the dark side of the material prosperity that was most evident in the cities with their splendid architecture, institutions of higher learning, and cultural achievements. Frequent wars caused havoc and destruction, but in the long run they promoted the development of more powerful weapons and more unified monarchies.

A European fifty years later would have known that the Turks did not overrun Europe, that a truce in the Anglo-French conflict would hold, and that explorers sent by Portugal and a newly united Spain would extend Europe's reach to other continents. In 1454 Aeneas Sylvius knew only what had been, and the conflicts and calamities of the past made him shudder.

Although their contemporary Muslim and Byzantine neighbors commonly called western Europeans "Franks," western Europeans ordinarily referred to themselves as "Latins." That term underscored their allegiance to the Latin rite of Christianity (and to its patriarch, the pope) as well as the use of the Latin language by their literate members. The **Latin West** deserves special attention because its achievements during this period had profound implications for the future of the world. The region was emerging from the economic and cultural shadow of its Islamic neighbors and, despite grave disruptions caused by plague and warfare, boldly setting out to extend its dominance. Some common elements promoted the Latin West's remarkable resurgence: competition, the pursuit of success, and the effective use of borrowed technology and learning.

As you read this chapter, ask yourself the following questions:

- How well did inhabitants of the Latin West deal with their natural environment?
- How did warfare help rulers in the Latin West acquire the skills, weapons, and determination that enabled them to challenge other parts of the world?
- How did superior technology in the Latin West promote excellence in business, learning, and architecture?
- How much did the region's achievements depend on its own people and how much on things borrowed from Muslim and Byzantine neighbors?

Aeneas Sylvius Piccolomini (uh-NEE-uhs SIL-vee-uhs pee-kuh-lo-MEE-nee)

CHRONOLOGY

	Technology and Environment	Culture	Politics and Society
1200	**1200s** Use of crossbows and longbows becomes widespread; windmills in increased use	**1210s** Religious orders founded: Teutonic Knights, Franciscans, Dominicans **1225–1274** Thomas Aquinas, monk and philosopher **1265–1321** Dante Alighieri, poet **ca. 1267–1337** Giotto, painter	**1200s** Champagne fairs flourish **1204** Fourth Crusade launched **1215** Magna Carta issued
1300	**1300** First mechanical clocks in the West **1315–1317** Great Famine **1347–1351** Black Death **ca. 1350** Growing deforestation	**1300–1500** Rise of universities **1304–1374** Francesco Petrarch, humanist writer **1313–1375** Giovanni Boccaccio, humanist writer **ca. 1340–1400** Geoffrey Chaucer, poet **1389–1464** Cosimo de' Medici, banker **ca. 1390–1441** Jan van Eyck, painter	**1337** Start of Hundred Years War **1381** Wat Tyler's Rebellion
1400	**1400s** Large cannon in use in warfare; hand-held firearms become prominent **ca. 1450** First printing with movable type in the West **1454** Gutenberg Bible printed	**1449–1492** Lorenzo de' Medici, art patron **1452–1519** Leonardo da Vinci, artist **ca. 1466–1536** Erasmus of Rotterdam, humanist **1472–1564** Michelangelo, artist **1492** Expulsion of Jews from Spain	**1415** Portuguese take Ceuta **1431** Joan of Arc burned as witch **1453** End of Hundred Years War; Turks take Constantinople **1469** Marriage of Ferdinand of Aragon and Isabella of Castile **1492** Fall of Muslim state of Granada

RURAL GROWTH AND CRISIS

Between 1200 and 1500 the Latin West brought more land under cultivation, adopted new farming techniques, and made greater use of machinery and mechanical forms of energy. Yet for most rural Europeans—more than nine out of ten people were rural—this period was a time of calamity and struggle. Most rural men and women worked hard for meager returns and suffered mightily from the effects of famine, epidemics, warfare, and social exploitation. After the devastation caused from 1347 to 1351 by the plague known as the Black Death, social changes speeded up by peasant revolts released many persons from serfdom and brought some improvements to rural life.

Peasants, Population, and Plague

In 1200 most western Europeans were serfs, obliged to till the soil on large estates owned by the nobility and the church (see Chapter 10). In return for the use of a portion of their lord's land, serfs had to give their lord a share of their harvests and perform numerous labor

Rural French Peasants   Many scenes of peasant life in winter are visible in this small painting by the Flemish Limbourg brothers from the 1410s. Above the snow-covered beehives one man chops firewood, while another drives a donkey loaded with firewood to a little village. At the lower right a woman, blowing on her frozen fingers, heads past the huddled sheep and hungry birds to join other women warming themselves in the cottage (whose outer wall the artists have cut away).   (Musée Conde, Chantilly, France/Art Resource, NY)

services for him. Lords and serfs were not motivated to introduce extensive improvements in farming practices because each side knew it would get only part of the larger harvest such efforts would bring.

As a consequence of the inefficiency of farming practices and their obligations to landowners, peasants received meager returns for their hard work. Despite the existence of numerous religious holidays, peasant culti-

vators labored some 54 hours a week in their fields. More than half of that labor was in support of the local nobility. Each noble household typically rested on the labors of from fifteen to thirty peasant families. The standard of life in the lord's stone castle or manor house stood in sharp contrast to the peasant's one-room thatched cottage containing little furniture and no luxuries.

Scenes of rural life show both men and women at work in the fields, although there is no reason to believe that equality of labor meant equality of decision making at home. In the peasant's hut as elsewhere in medieval Europe, women were subordinate to men. The influential theologian Thomas Aquinas° (1225–1274) spoke for his age when he argued that, although both men and women were created in God's image, there was a sense in which "the image of God is found in man, and not in woman: for man is the beginning and end of woman; as God is the beginning and end of every creature."[1]

Rural poverty was not simply the product of inefficient farming methods and social inequality. It also resulted from the rapid growth of Europe's population. In 1200 China's population may have surpassed Europe's by two to one; by 1300 the population of each was about 80 million. China's population fell because of the Mongol conquest (see Chapter 14). Why Europe's more than doubled between 1100 and 1445 is uncertain. Some historians believe that the reviving economy may have stimulated the increase. Others argue that warmer-than-usual temperatures reduced the number of deaths from starvation and exposure while the absence of severe epidemics lessened deaths from disease.

Whatever the causes, more people required more productive ways of farming and new agricultural settlements. One new technique gaining widespread acceptance in northern Europe increased the amount of farmland available for producing crops. Instead of following the custom of leaving half of their land fallow (uncultivated) every year to regain its fertility, some farmers tried a new **three-field system.** They grew crops on two-thirds of their land each year and planted the third field in oats. The oats stored nitrogen and rejuvenated the soil, and it could be used to feed plow horses. In much of Europe, however, farmers continued to let half of their land lie fallow and to use oxen (less efficient but cheaper than horses) to pull their plows.

Population growth also led to the foundation of new agricultural settlements. In the twelfth and thirteenth centuries large numbers of Germans migrated into the fertile lands east of the Elbe River and into the eastern Baltic states. Knights belonging to Latin Christian religious orders slaughtered or drove away native inhabi-

Aquinas (uh-KWY-nuhs)

tants who had not yet adopted Christianity. For example, during the thirteenth century, the Order of Teutonic Knights conquered, resettled, and administered a vast area along the eastern Baltic that later became Prussia (see Map 16.3 on page 412). Other Latin Christians founded new settlements on lands conquered from the Muslims and Byzantines in southern Europe and on Celtic lands in the British Isles.

By draining swamps and clearing forests, people also brought new land under cultivation within the existing boundaries of the Latin West. But as population continued to rise, some people had to farm lands that had poor soils or were vulnerable to flooding, frost, or drought. The result was a decline in average crop yields after 1250 and an increase in the number of people living at the edge of starvation, vulnerable to even slight changes in the food supply resulting from bad weather or the disruptions of war. According to one historian, "By 1300, almost every child born in western Europe faced the probability of extreme hunger at least once or twice during his expected 30 to 35 years of life."[2] One unusually cold spell led to the Great Famine of 1315–1317, during which starvation was widespread in Europe.

In time the cumulative effect of such crises might have reduced the population to a size that existing agricultural methods could more readily support. However, what actually eased population pressure was not famine but the **Black Death.** This terrible plague seems to have originated in India and then struck Mongol armies attacking the city of Kaffa° on the Black Sea in 1346 (see Chapter 13). A year later Genoese° traders in Kaffa carried the disease back to Italy and southern France. During the next two years the Black Death spread across Europe, in some places carrying off two-thirds of the population. Overall the epidemic may have killed one of every three western Europeans by the time it subsided.

The plague's symptoms were ghastly to behold. Victims developed boils the size of eggs in their groins and armpits, black blotches on their skin, foul body odors, and severe pain. In most cases, death came within a few days. To prevent the plague from spreading, town officials closed their gates to people from infected areas and burned the victims' possessions. Such measures helped to spare some communities but could not halt the advance of the disease across Europe (see Map 16.1). It is now known that the Black Death was the bubonic plague, a disease that was spread not just from person to person but also by the bites of fleas that infested the fur of certain rats. But even if medieval Europeans had been aware of that route of infection, they could have done little to eliminate the rats, which thrived on urban refuse.

The plague left its mark not only physically but psychologically, bringing home to people how sudden and unexpected death could be. In response to the plague some people became more religious, giving money to the church or hitting themselves with iron-tipped whips to atone for their sins. Others chose to enjoy life while they still had it, spending their money on fancy clothes, feasts, and drinking. Whatever their mood, most people soon resumed their daily routines. Life went on.

Although population gradually rebounded from the losses caused by the Black Death, recovery was slow and uneven because of periodic returns of plague. By 1400 Europe's population had regained only the levels of 1200. Not until after 1500 did it rise above its preplague levels. Meanwhile, China was recovering from its thirteenth-century losses (see Chapter 14).

Social Rebellion

In addition to its demographic and psychological effects, the Black Death set off social changes in western Europe. Skilled and manual laborers who survived demanded higher pay for their services. At first authorities tried to freeze wages at the old levels. Seeing such repressive measures as a plot by the rich, peasants rose up against wealthy nobles and churchmen. During a widespread revolt in France in 1358, known as the Jacquerie, peasants looted castles and killed dozens of persons. Urban unrest also took place. In a large revolt led by Wat Tyler in 1381, English peasants invaded London, calling for an end to all forms of serfdom and to most kinds of manorial dues. Angry demonstrators murdered the archbishop of Canterbury and many royal officials. Authorities put down these rebellions with even greater bloodshed and cruelty, but they could not stave off the higher wages and other social changes the rebels demanded.

Serfdom practically disappeared in western Europe as peasants bought their freedom or ran away. Many free persons who got higher wages from the landowners saved their money and bought their own land in depopulated areas. Many large English landowners who could no longer afford to hire enough fieldworkers to farm their lands began pasturing sheep for their wool. Others grew less labor-intensive crops or made greater use of draft animals and labor-saving tools. Because the plague had not killed wild and domesticated animals, more meat was available for each survivor and more leather for shoes. Thus the welfare of the rural masses generally improved after the Black Death, though the gap between rich and poor remained wide.

In urban areas employers had to raise wages to attract enough workers to replace those killed by the

---

Kaffa (KAH-fah) **Genoese** (JEN-oh-eez)

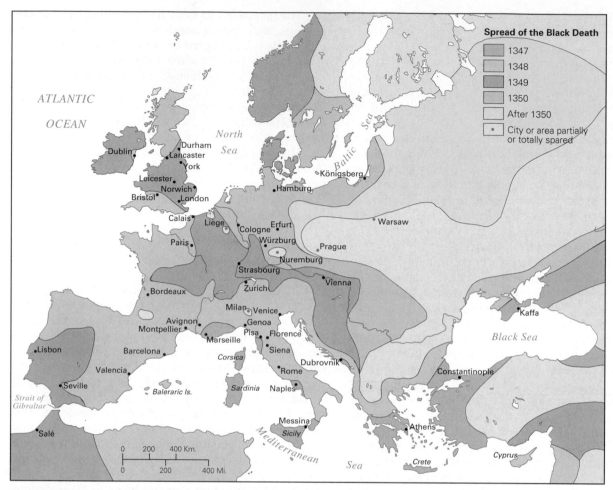

Map 16.1 The Black Death in Fourteenth–Century Europe   Spreading out of southwestern China along the routes opened by Mongol expansion, the plague reached the Black Sea port of Kaffa in 1346. This map documents its deadly progress year by year from there into the Mediterranean and north and east across the face of Europe.

plague. Guilds (see below) found it necessary to reduce the period of apprenticeship. Competition within crafts also became more common. Although the overall economy shrank with the decline in population, per capita production actually rose.

Mills and Mines

Despite calamities and conflicts, the use of mechanical energy, mining, and metallurgy grew so much in the centuries before 1500 that some historians have spoken of an "industrial revolution" in medieval Europe. That may be too strong a term, but the landscape fairly bristled with mechanical devices. Mills powered by water or wind were used to grind grain and flour,

saw logs into lumber, crush olives, tan leather, make paper, or perform other useful tasks.

England's many rivers had some 5,600 functioning watermills in 1086. After the year 1200 such mills spread rapidly across the western European mainland. By the early fourteenth century entrepreneurs had crammed 68 watermills into a one-mile section of the Seine° River in Paris. A mill's **water wheel** could be turned by the flow of a river beneath it or by the weight of water falling over the top of the wheel. For maximum efficiency, dams were built to ensure a steady flow of water throughout the year. Some watermills in France and England were designed to harness the power of ocean tides.

Seine (sen)

Watermills on the Seine River in Paris Sacks of grain were brought to these mills under the bridge called the Grand Pont to be ground into flour. The water wheels were turned by the river flowing under them. Gears translated the vertical motion of the wheels into the horizontal motion of the millstones. (Bibliothèque Nationale de France)

Windmills also were common, especially in dry lands like Spain, where the flow of rivers was too irregular for efficient watermills, and in northern Europe, where the power of the wind could be tapped even in winter when ice made water wheels useless. Neither type of mill was a new invention nor unique to Europe. Water wheels and windmills had long been common in the Islamic world, but people in the medieval Latin West used such devices to harness the power of nature on a much larger scale than did people elsewhere.

Mills were expensive to build, but nature furnished the energy to run them for free. Over time, mills returned great profits to their owners. Some mills were built by individuals or monasteries, but most were built by groups of investors. The ability of mill owners to grow rich by using wind or water power to grind grain often aroused the jealousy of their neighbors. In his *Canterbury Tales* the English poet Geoffrey Chaucer (c. 1340–1400) captured millers' unsavory reputation (not always deserved) by portraying a miller as "a master-hand at stealing grain" by pushing down on the balance scale with his thumb.[3]

Waterpower also made possible such a great expansion of iron making that some historians say Europe's real Iron Age was in the later Middle Ages, not in antiquity. Water powered the stamping mills that broke up the iron, the trip hammers that pounded it, and the bellows (first documented in the West in 1323) that raised temperatures to the point where the iron was liquid enough to be poured into molds. Blast furnaces capable of producing high-quality iron are documented from 1380. The finished products included everything from armor to nails, from horseshoes to agricultural tools.

The demand for iron stimulated iron mining in many parts of Europe. In addition, new silver, lead, and copper mines in Austria and Hungary supplied metal for coins and church bells, cannon and statues. Techniques of deep mining developed in Central Europe were introduced farther west in the latter part of the fifteenth century. A building boom led to more stone quarrying in France during the eleventh, twelfth, and thirteenth centuries than during all of the millennia of ancient Egypt.

The rapid growth of industry produced significant changes in the landscape. Towns grew outward and new ones were founded, dams and canals changed the flow of rivers, and the countryside was scarred by quarry pits and mines tunneled into hillsides. Pollution sometimes became a serious problem. Urban tanneries (factories that cured and processed leather) dumped acidic wastewater back into streams, where it mixed with human waste and the runoff from slaughterhouses. The first recorded antipollution law was passed by the English Parliament in 1388, although enforcement was difficult.

One of the most dramatic environmental changes during these centuries was deforestation. Trees were cut to provide timber for buildings and for ships. Tanneries stripped bark to make acid for tanning leather. Many forests were cleared to make room for farming. The use of wood for fuel, especially by the glass and iron industries, was also a great consumer of forests. Charcoal—used to produce the high temperatures that the glass, iron, and other industries required—was made by controlled burning of oak or other hardwood. It is estimated that a single iron furnace could consume all the trees within five-eighths of a mile (1 kilometer) in just 40 days. As a consequence of all these demands, many once-dense forests in western Europe were greatly depleted in the later Middle Ages, except for those that powerful landowners protected as hunting preserves.

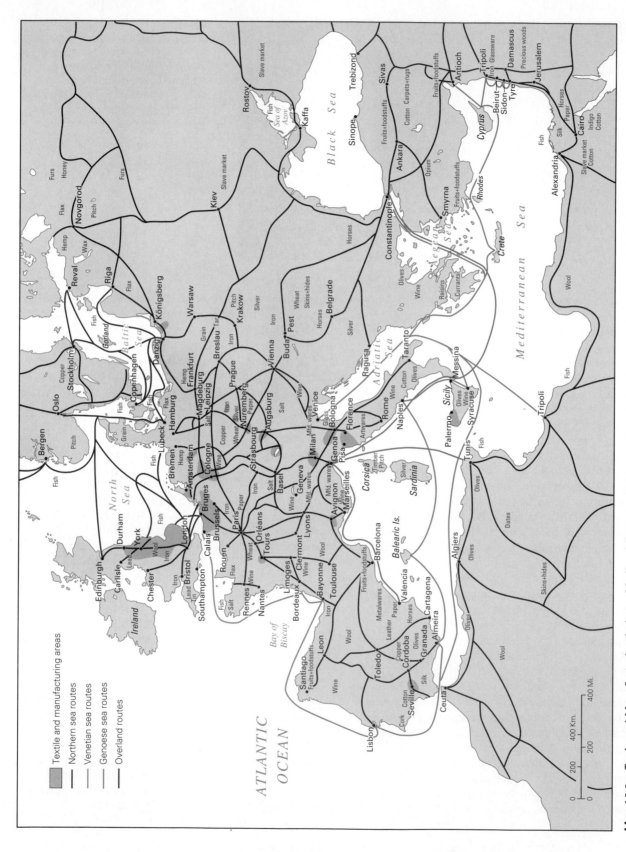

Map 16.2   Trade and Manufacturing in Later Medieval Europe   The economic revival of European cities was associated with great expansion of commerce. Notice the concentration of wool and linen textile manufacturing in northern Italy, the Netherlands, and England; the importance of trade in various kinds of foodstuffs; and the slave-exporting markets in Cairo, Kiev, and Rostov.

Urban Revival

In the tenth century not a single town in the Latin West could compare in wealth and comfort—still less in size—with the cities in the Byzantine Empire and the Islamic caliphates. Yet by the later Middle Ages wealthy commercial centers stood all along the Mediterranean, Baltic, and Atlantic, as well as on major rivers draining into these bodies of water (see Map 16.2). The greatest cities in the East were still larger, but those in the West were undergoing greater commercial, cultural, and administrative changes. Their prosperity was visible in impressive new churches, guild halls, and residences. This urban revival is a measure of the Latin West's recovery from the economic decline that had followed the collapse of the Roman Empire (see Chapter 10) as well as an illustration of how the West's rise was aided by its ties to other parts of the world.

Trading Cities

Most urban growth in the Latin West after 1200 was due to the continuing growth of trade and manufacturing. The greatest part of the trade was between cities and their hinterlands, but long-distance trade also stimulated urban revival. Cities in northern Italy in particular benefited from maritime trade with the bustling port cities of the eastern Mediterranean and, through them, with the great markets of the Indian Ocean and East Asia. In northern Europe commercial cities in the County of Flanders (roughly today's Belgium) and around the Baltic Sea profited from growing regional networks and from overland and sea routes to the Mediterranean.

Two events in the thirteenth century strengthened Italian trade with the eastern Mediterranean. One was the Venetian-inspired assault in 1204 against the city of Constantinople, which dominated the passage between the Mediterranean and Black Seas. Misleadingly named the "Fourth Crusade," this assault by Latin Christians on Greek Christians had little to do with the religious differences between them and much to do with Venice's desire to gain better access to the rich trade of the East. By crippling Byzantine power, Venetians were able to seize the strategic island of Crete in the eastern Mediterranean and expand their trading colonies around the Black Sea. The other boon to Italian trade was the westward expansion of the Mongol Empire, which opened trade routes from the Mediterranean to China (see Chapter 13).

To take advantage of that trade, the young Marco Polo set out from Venice in 1271 on the long trek across Central Asia. After reaching the Mongol court, the talented Marco spent many years serving the emperor Khubilai Khan as an ambassador and as the governor of a Chinese province. Marco later authored a fabulous account of these adventures and of the treacherous return voyage through the Indian Ocean that finally brought him back to Venice in 1295, after an absence of twenty-four years. Yet even in relatively prosperous Venice, few who had not seen for themselves could believe that Asian lands could be so wealthy.

When the disintegration of the Mongol Empire in the fourteenth century halted direct European contact with distant Asian markets, Venetian merchants purchased eastern silks and spices brought by other middlemen to Constantinople, Beirut, and Alexandria. Three times a year galleys (ships powered by some sixty oarsmen each) sailed in convoys of two or three from Venice, bringing back some 2,000 tons of goods. Other merchants began to explore new overland or sea routes.

Venice was not the only Latin city whose trade expanded in the thirteenth century. The sea trade of Genoa on the west coast of northern Italy probably equaled that of Venice. Genoese merchants built up colonies on the shores of the eastern Mediterranean and around the Black Sea as well as in the western Mediterranean. In northern Europe an association of trading cities known as the **Hanseatic° League** conducted extensive trade in the Baltic, including the newly conquered coasts of Prussia, and as far east as Novgorod in Russia and westward across the North Sea to London.

By the late thirteenth century, Genoese galleys from the Mediterranean and Hanseatic ships from the Baltic were converging on a third area, the trading and manufacturing cities in Flanders. In the Flemish towns of Bruges°, Ghent°, and Ypres° skilled artisans turned raw wool from English sheep into a fine cloth that was softer and smoother than the coarse "homespuns" from simple village looms. Dyed in vivid hues, these Flemish textiles appealed to wealthy Europeans who formerly had imported their fine textiles from Asia.

Along the overland route connecting Flanders and northern Italy important trading fairs developed in the Champagne° region of Burgundy. The Champagne fairs began as regional markets, meeting once or twice a year, where manufactured goods, livestock, and farm produce were exchanged. When Champagne came under the control of the king of France at the end of the twelfth

---

Hanseatic (han-see-AT-ik)   **Bruges** (broozh)
Ghent (gent [hard *g* as in *get*])   **Ypres** (EE-pruh)
Champagne (sham-PAIN)

Flemish Weavers, Ypres   The spread of textile weaving gave employment to many people in the Netherlands. The city of Ypres in Flanders (now northern Belgium) was an important textile center in the thirteenth century. This drawing from a fourteenth-century manuscript shows a man and a woman weaving cloth on a horizontal loom, while a child makes thread on a spinning wheel. (Stedelijke Openbare Bibliotheek, Ypres)

century, royal guarantees of safe conduct to all merchants turned the regional markets into international fairs. A century later fifteen Italian cities had permanent consulates in Champagne to represent the interests of their citizens. The fairs were also important for currency exchange and other financial transactions. During the fourteenth century the volume of trade grew so large that it became cheaper to send Flemish woolens to Italy by sea rather than overland on pack animals. As a consequence, the fairs of Champagne lost some of their international trade but remained important regional markets.

Textile manufacturing also spread beyond Flanders. In the late thirteenth century the English monarchy raised taxes on the export of raw wool, making it more profitable to turn wool into cloth in England rather than in Flanders. Flemish textile specialists crossed the English Channel and introduced the spinning wheel and other devices to England. As a consequence the number of sacks of raw wool exported annually from England fell from 35,000 at the beginning of the fourteenth century

to 8,000 in the mid-fifteenth, while exports of English wool cloth rose from 4,000 pieces just before 1350 to 54,000 a century later.

Florence was also developing as a wool-making center. Local banking families financed the production of much of the high-quality cloth that in the past Florence had bought from the Flemish cities. In 1338, Florence manufactured 80,000 pieces of cloth, while importing only 10,000. These changes in the textile industry show how competition promoted the spread of manufacturing and encouraged new specialties.

The growing textile industries made extensive use of windmills and water wheels. The power of wind and water was channeled through gears, pulleys, and belts to drive all sorts of machinery. The thriving textile industry in Flanders, for example, used mills to clean and thicken woven cloth by beating it in water, a process known as fulling. Another application of mill power was in papermaking. Although papermaking had been common in China and the Muslim world for centuries before it spread to southern Europe in the thirteenth century,

Westerners were the first to use machines to do the heavy work in its manufacturing.

In the fifteenth century Venice surpassed its European rivals in the volume of its trade in the Mediterranean as well as across the Alps into Central Europe. Its skilled craftspeople also manufactured luxury goods once obtainable only from eastern sources, notably silk and cotton textiles, glassware and mirrors, jewelry, and paper. At the same time exports of Italian and northern European woolens to the eastern Mediterranean were also on the rise. In the space of a few centuries western European cities had used the eastern trade to increase their prosperity and then reduce their dependence on eastern goods.

Civic Life

Trading cities in Europe offered people more social freedom than rural places. Most northern Italian and German cities were independent states, much like the port cities of the Indian Ocean basin (see Chapter 15). Other European cities held special royal charters that exempted them from the authority of local nobles. Because of their autonomy, they were able to adapt to changing market conditions more quickly than were cities in China and the Islamic world that were controlled by imperial authorities. Social mobility was also easier in the Latin West because anyone who lived in a chartered city for over a year might claim freedom. Thus cities became a refuge for all sorts of ambitious individuals, whose labor and talent added to their wealth.

Cities were also home to most of Europe's Jews. The largest population of Jews was in Spain, where earlier Arab rulers had made them welcome. Many commercial cities elsewhere welcomed Jews for their manufacturing and business skills. Despite the official protection they received from some Christian princes and kings, Jews were subject to violent religious persecutions or expulsions in times of crisis, such as during the Black Death (see Society and Culture: Blaming the Black Death on the Jews, Strasbourg, 1349). In 1492 the Spanish monarchs expelled all Jews in the name of religious and ethnic purity. In all of the medieval West only the papal city of Rome left its Jews undisturbed throughout the centuries before 1500.

Opportunities for individual enterprise in European cities came with many restrictions. Within most towns and cities powerful associations known as guilds dominated civic life. A **guild** was an association of craft specialists, such as silversmiths, or of merchants who worked in a particular trade. Each guild regulated the

Jewish Procession, 1517   This delegation of wealthy Jews paid their respects to the newly elected Pope Martin V and sought the papacy's continued support of their community's traditional rights and privileges. Pope Martin granted their wishes and, as was common, the pope's personal physician was a Jew.   (Bibliothèque Nationale de France)

business practices of its members and the prices they charged. Guilds also trained apprentices and promoted members' interests with the city government. By denying membership to outsiders and all Jews, guilds perpetuated the interests of the families that already were members. Guilds also perpetuated male dominance of most skilled jobs.

Nevertheless, despite serious restrictions, in a few places women were able to join guilds either on their own or as the wives, widows, or daughters of male guild members. Large numbers of poor women also toiled in nonguild jobs in urban textile industries and in the food and beverage trades, generally receiving lower wages than their male counterparts.

Blaming the Black Death on the Jews, Strasbourg, 1349

Prejudice against Jews was common in the Latin West. This selection is from the official chronicles of the upper-Rhineland towns.

In the year 1349 there occurred the greatest epidemic that ever happened. Death went from one end of the earth to the other, on that side and this side of the [Mediterranean] sea. . . . This epidemic also came to Strasbourg in the summer of [that] year, and . . . about sixteen thousand people died.

In the matter of this plague the Jews throughout the world were reviled and accused in all lands of having caused it through the poison which they are said to have put into the water and the wells—that is what they were accused of—and for this reason the Jews were burnt all the way from the Mediterranean into Germany, but not in Avignon, for the pope protected them there.

. . . The deputies of the city of Strasbourg were asked what they were going to do with their Jews. They answered and said that they knew no evil of them. [The town-council was deposed. A new council gave in to the mob and arrested the Jews.]

On Saturday—that was St. Valentine's Day—they burnt the Jews on a wooden platform in their cemetery. There were about two thousand people of them. Those who wanted to baptize themselves were spared. Many small children were taken out of the fire and baptized against the will of their fathers and mothers. And everything that was owed to the Jews was cancelled, and the Jews had to surrender all pledges and notes that they had taken for debts. The council, however, took the cash that the Jews possessed and divided it among the working-men proportionately. The money was indeed the thing that killed the Jews. If they had been poor and if the feudal lords had not been in debt to them, they would not have been burnt.

To what extent was the massacre of the Strasbourg Jews due to fear of the plague, to prejudice, and to greed? Why did some officials try to protect them?

Source: Jacob R. Marcus, ed., *The Jew in the Medieval World: A Source Book, 315–1791* (1938; reprint, Westport, CT: Greenwood, 1975), 45–47. Reprinted with permission of the Hebrew Union College Press, Cincinnati.

For many women marriage to wealthy men could be a means of social advancement. One of Chaucer's *Canterbury Tales* concerns a woman from Bath, a city in southern England, who became wealthy by marrying a succession of old men for their money (and then two other husbands for love), "aside from other company in youth." She was also a skilled weaver, Chaucer says: "In making cloth she showed so great a bent, / She bettered those of Ypres and of Ghent."

By the fifteenth century, the growth of commerce had given rise to a new class of wealthy merchant-bankers. They operated on a vast scale and specialized in money changing, loans, and investments made on behalf of other parties. Merchants great and small used their services, but the merchant-bankers also handled the financial transactions of ecclesiastical and secular officials. They arranged for the transmission to the pope of funds known as Peter's pence, a collection taken up annually in every church in the Latin West. They also ad-

vanced large sums of money to the princes and kings of Europe to support their wars and lavish courts. Some merchant-bankers even developed their own news services, gathering information on any topic that could affect their businesses.

Florence pioneered new banking services. Its financiers invented checking accounts, organized private shareholding companies (the forerunners of modern corporations), and improved bookkeeping techniques. In the fifteenth century, the Medici° family of Florence operated banks in Italy, Flanders, and London. Medicis also controlled the government of Florence and were important patrons of the arts. By 1500 the greatest banking family in western Europe was the Fuggers° of Augsburg, who had ten times the Medici bank's lending capital. Starting out as cloth merchants under Jacob "the Rich"

Medici (MED-ih-chee)   **Fuggers** (FOOG-uhrz)

(1459–1525), the family branched into many other activities, including the trade in Hungarian copper, essential for casting cannon.

Most money lenders were Jews because Latin Christians generally considered charging interest (usury) sinful. Christian bankers had to devise ways to profit from loans indirectly in order to get around the Latin Church's condemnation of usury. Some borrowers agreed to repay a loan in another currency at a rate of exchange favorable to the lender. Others added to the borrowed sum a "gift" in thanks to the lender. For example, in 1501 church officials agreed to repay a loan of 6,000 gold ducats in five months to the Fuggers along with a "gift" of 400 ducats, amounting to an effective interest rate of 16 percent a year. In fact, the return was much smaller since the church failed to repay the loan on time.

Despite the money to be made by some, for most residents of western European cities poverty and squalor was the norm. Even for the wealthy, European cities generally lacked civic amenities, such as public baths and water supply systems, that had existed in the cities of Western antiquity and still survived in cities of the Islamic Middle East.

Gothic Cathedrals

Among the skilled people in greatest demand in the thriving cities of late medieval Europe were master builders and associated craftsmen. The finest and most expensive buildings these craftsmen designed and erected were **Gothic cathedrals**. Cities competed with one another in the magnificence of their guild halls, town halls, and other structures (see Environment and Technology: The Clock). But it was these new cathedrals, which made their appearance in about 1140 in France, that were the architectural wonders of their times.

One distinctive feature of the new cathedrals was the pointed, or Gothic, arch, which replaced the older round, or Roman, arch. Another was the external (flying) buttresses that stabilized the high, thin stone columns below the arches. Using this method of construction, master builders were able to push the Gothic cathedrals to great heights and to fill the outside walls with giant windows depicting religious scenes in brilliantly colored stained glass. During the next four centuries, interior heights went ever higher, towers and spires pierced the heavens, and walls became dazzling curtains of stained glass.

Cathedrals were designed and built by men with little or no formal education and limited understanding of the mathematical principles of modern civil engi-

Strasbourg Cathedral Only one of the two spires originally planned for this Gothic cathedral was completed when work ceased in 1439. But the Strasbourg Cathedral was still the tallest masonry structure of medieval Europe. This engraving is from 1630. (Courtesy of the Trustees of the British Museum)

neering. Master masons sometimes miscalculated, and parts of some overly ambitious cathedrals collapsed. The record-high choir vault of Beauvais Cathedral, for instance—154 feet (47 meters) in height—came tumbling down in 1284. But practical experience was the greatest teacher, and as builders constantly invented novel solutions to the problems they encountered, success rose from the rubble of their mistakes. The cathedral spire in Strasbourg reached 466 feet (142 meters) into the air—as high as a 40-story building. The heights achieved by Gothic cathedrals were unsurpassed until the twentieth century.

The Clock

Clocks were a prominent feature of the Latin West in the late medieval period. The Song-era Chinese had built elaborate mechanical clocks centuries earlier (see Chapter 11), but the West was the first part of the world where clocks became a regular part of urban life. Whether mounted in a church steeple or placed on a bridge or tower, mechanical clocks proclaimed Western people's delight with mechanical objects, concern with precision, and display of civic wealth.

The word *clock* comes from a word for bell. The first mechanical clocks that appeared around 1300 in western Europe were simply bells with an automatic mechanical device to strike the correct number of hours. The most elaborate Chinese clock had been powered by falling water, but this was impractical in cold weather. The levers, pulleys, and gears of European clocks were powered by a weight hanging from a rope wound around a cylinder. An "escapement" lever regulated the slow, steady unwinding.

Enthusiasm for building expensive clocks came from various parts of the community. For some time, monks had been using devices to mark the times for prayer. Employers welcomed chiming clocks to regulate the hours of their employees. Universities used them to mark the beginning and end of classes. Prosperous merchants readily donated money to build a splendid clock that would display their city's wealth. The city of Strasbourg, for example, built a clock in the 1350s that included statues of the Virgin, the Christ Child, and the three Magi, a mechanical rooster, the signs of the zodiac, a perpetual calendar, and an astrolabe—and it could play hymns too!

By the 1370s and 1380s clocks were common enough for their measured hours to displace the older system that varied the length of the hour in proportion to the length of the day. Previously, for example, the London hour had varied from 38 minutes in winter to 82 minutes in summer. By 1500 clocks had numbered faces with hour and minute hands. Small clocks for indoor use were also in vogue. Though not very accurate by today's standards, these clocks were still a great step forward. Some historians consider the clock the most important of the many technological advances of the later Middle Ages because it fostered so many changes during the following centuries.

Early Clock   This weight-driven clock dates from 1454. (Bodleian Library Oxford, Ms. Laud Misc. 570, 25v.)

LEARNING, LITERATURE, AND THE RENAISSANCE

Throughout the Middle Ages people in the Latin West lived amid reminders of the achievements of the Roman Empire. They wrote and worshiped in a version of its language, traveled its roads, and obeyed some of its laws. Even the vestments and robes of medieval popes, kings, and emperors were modeled on the regalia of Roman officials. Yet early medieval Europeans lost touch with much of the learning of Greco-Roman antiquity. More vivid was the biblical world they heard about in the Hebrew and Christian scriptures.

Intellectuals in the Latin West struggled to recover the learning and values of of the Greco-Roman classical past. A small revival of learning associated with the court of Charlemagne in the ninth century was followed by a larger *renaissance* (rebirth) in the twelfth century. Many growing cities became centers of intellectual and artistic life. One expression of this cultural revival was found in the universities established across the Latin West after 1200. In the mid-fourteenth century the pace of intellectual and artistic life quickened in what is often called the **Renaissance,** which began in northern Italy and later spread to northern Europe. Some Italian authors saw the Italian Renaissance as a sharp break with an age of darkness. A more balanced view might reveal this era as the high noon of a day that had been dawning for several centuries.

Universities and Scholarship

Before 1100 Byzantine and Islamic scholarship generally surpassed scholarship in Latin Europe. When southern Italy was wrested from the Byzantines and Sicily and Toledo from the Muslims in the eleventh century, many manuscripts of Greek and Arabic works came into Western hands and were translated into Latin for readers eager for new ideas. The manuscripts included works of ancient philosophy by Plato and Aristotle° and Greek treatises on medicine, mathematics, and geography that were previously unknown to medieval Latin Christians. In addition, some scientific and philosophical writings by medieval Muslims came into the Latin West. The works of the Iranian philosopher Ibn Sina° (980–1037),

known in the West as Avicenna°, were particularly influential. The Jewish scholarly community contributed significantly to the translation and explication of Arabic and other manuscripts.

As in the early Middle Ages (see Chapter 10), Christian monasteries were important centers of learning, and the church was an important advocate of scholarship. Joining the older monastic schools after 1200 were new institutions of higher education: independent colleges. The thirteenth century saw the foundation of two new religious orders, the Dominicans and the Franciscans, some of whose most talented members would have distinguished careers as university professors.

The colleges established in Paris and Oxford in the late twelfth and thirteenth centuries may have been modeled after similarly endowed places of study long known in the Islamic world—madrasas, which provided subsidized housing for poor students and paid the salaries of their teachers. The Latin West, however, was the first part of the world to establish modern **universities,** degree-granting corporations specializing in multidisciplinary research and advanced teaching. Between 1300 and 1500 the twenty oldest universities in the Latin West were joined by some sixty others. Some of the first universities were started by students; others were founded as guilds to which all the professors of a city belonged. These teaching guilds, like the guilds overseeing manufacturing and commerce, set the standards for membership in their profession, trained apprentices and masters, and defended their professional interests.

Universities set the curriculum of study for each discipline and instituted comprehensive final examinations for degrees. After passing exams at the end of their apprenticeship, students received a first diploma known as a "license" to teach. More advanced students, who completed longer training and defended a masterwork of scholarship, became "masters" and "doctors." The colleges of Paris were gradually absorbed into the city's university, but the colleges of Oxford and Cambridge remained independent, self-governing organizations.

Universally recognized degrees, well-trained professors, and exciting new texts promoted the rapid spread of universities in late medieval Europe. Because all university courses were taught in Latin, students and masters could move freely across political and linguistic lines, seeking out the university that offered the courses they wanted and that had the most interesting professors. Universities offered a variety of programs of study but generally were identified with a particular specialty.

Aristotle (AR-ih-stah-tahl)   **Ibn Sina** (IB-uhn SEE-nah)

Avicenna (av-uh-SEN-uh)

Bologna° was famous for the study of law; Montpellier and Salerno specialized in medicine; Paris and Oxford were best known for theology.

The prominence of theology partly reflected the fact that many students were destined for ecclesiastical careers, but theology was also seen as "queen of the sciences"—the central discipline that encompassed all knowledge. For this reason thirteenth-century theologians sought to synthesize the newly rediscovered philosophical works of Aristotle, as well as the commentaries by Avicenna, with the revealed truth of the Bible. Their daring efforts to synthesize reason and faith were known as **scholasticism°.**

The most notable scholastic work was the *Summa Theologica°*, issued between 1267 and 1273 by Thomas Aquinas, a brilliant Dominican priest who was a professor of theology at the University of Paris. Although Aquinas's exposition of Christian belief organized on Aristotelian principles was later accepted as a masterly demonstration of the reasonableness of Christianity, scholasticism upset many traditional thinkers. Some church authorities even tried to ban Aristotle from the curriculum. There also was much rivalry between the leading Dominican and Franciscan theological scholars over the next two centuries. However, the considerable freedom of medieval universities from both secular and religious authorities enabled the new ideas of accredited scholars eventually to prevail over the fears of church administrators.

Humanists and Printers

The intellectual achievements of the later Middle Ages were not confined to the universities. Talented writers of this era made important contributions to literature and literary scholarship. A new technology in the fifteenth century helped bring works of literature and scholarship to a larger audience.

Dante Alighieri° (1265–1321) completed a long, elegant poem, the *Divine Comedy*, shortly before his death. This supreme expression of medieval preoccupations tells the allegorical story of Dante's journey through the nine circles of hell and the seven terraces of purgatory, followed by his entry into Paradise. His guide through hell and purgatory is the Roman poet Virgil. His guide through Paradise is Beatrice, a woman whom he had loved from afar since childhood and whose death inspired him to write the poem.

The *Divine Comedy* foreshadows some of the literary fashions of the later Italian Renaissance. Like Dante, later Italian writers made use of Greco-Roman classical themes and mythology and sometimes chose to write not in Latin but in the vernacular languages spoken in their regions, in order to reach a broader audience (Dante used the vernacular spoken in Tuscany°.)

The English poet Geoffrey Chaucer was another vernacular writer of this era. Many of his works show the influence of Dante, but he is most famous for the *Canterbury Tales*, the lengthy poem written in the last dozen years of his life. These often humorous and earthy tales, told by fictional pilgrims on their way to the shrine of Thomas à Becket in Canterbury, are cited several times in this chapter because they present a marvelous cross-section of medieval people and attitudes.

Dante also influenced a literary movement that began in his native Florence in the mid-fourteenth century. The writers of the fourteenth and fifteenth centuries who championed the traditions pioneered by Dante are **humanists.** The term refers to their interest in grammar, rhetoric, poetry, history, and moral philosophy (ethics)—subjects known collectively as the humanities, an ancient discipline. With the brash exaggeration characteristic of new intellectual fashions, humanist writers such as the poet Francesco Petrarch° (1304–1374) and the poet and storyteller Giovanni Boccaccio° (1313–1375) proclaimed a revival of respect for the classical Greco-Roman tradition, which, they claimed, for centuries had lain buried under the rubble of the Middle Ages.

This idea of a rebirth of learning long dead too readily dismisses the efforts of scholars at the monasteries and universities who for centuries had been recovering all sorts of Greco-Roman learning and the writers such as Dante (whom the humanists revered) who anticipated humanist interests by a generation. Yet it is hard to exaggerate the beneficial influences of the humanists on their own times and later, as educators, advisers, and reformers. The humanists' greatest influence was in reforming secondary education. They introduced a curriculum centered on the languages and literature of Greco-Roman antiquity, which they felt provided intellectual discipline, moral lessons, and refined tastes. This curriculum dominated European secondary schools well into the twentieth century. Humanist influence in

---

Bologna (buh-LOHN-yuh)   scholasticism (skoh-LAS-tih-sizm)
Summa Theologica (SOOM-uh thee-uh-LOH-jih-kuh)
Dante Alighieri (DAHN-tay ah-lee-GYEH-ree)

Tuscany (TUS-kuh-nee)
Franceso Petrarch (fran-CHES-koh PAY-trahrk)
Giovanni Boccaccio (jo-VAH-nee boh-KAH-chee-oh)

the universities was less and came mostly after 1500. Despite the humanists' influence, theology, law, medicine, and branches of philosophy other than ethics remained prominent in university education during this period.

Though some humanists followed Dante in composing literary works in vernacular languages, many tried to duplicate the elegance of classical Latin and (to a lesser extent) Greek, which they revered as the pinnacle of learning, beauty, and wisdom. Boccaccio is most famous for his vernacular writings, which resemble Dante's, and especially for the *Decameron*, an earthy work that has much in common with Chaucer's boisterous tales. Under Petrarch's influence, however, Bocaccio turned to writing in classical Latin.

As humanist scholars of the fifteenth century mastered Latin and Greek, they turned their language skills to restoring the original texts of Greco-Roman writers and of the Bible. By comparing many different manuscripts, they eliminated errors introduced by generations of copyists. To aid in this task, Pope Nicholas V (r. 1447–1455) created the Vatican Library, buying scrolls of Greco-Roman writings and paying to have accurate copies and translations made. Working independently, the respected Dutch scholar Erasmus° of Rotterdam (ca. 1466–1536) produced a critical edition of the New Testament in Greek. Erasmus was able to correct many errors and mistranslations in the Latin text that had been in general use throughout the Middle Ages. In later years, this humanist priest and theologian also wrote—in classical Latin—influential moral guides including the *Enchiridion militis christiani* (*The Manual of the Christian Knight*, 1503) and *The Education of a Christian Prince* (1515).

The influence of the humanists was enhanced after 1450 because new printing technology increased the availability of their critical editions of ancient texts, literary works, and moral guides. The Chinese were the first to use carved wood blocks for printing (see Chapter 14), and block-printed playing cards from China were circulating in Europe before 1450. Then, around 1450, three technical improvements revolutionized printing: (1) movable pieces of type consisting of individual letters, (2) new ink suitable for printing on paper, and (3) the **printing press,** a mechanical device that pressed inked type onto sheets of paper.

The man who did most to perfect printing was Johann Gutenberg° (ca. 1394–1468) of Mainz. The Gutenberg Bible of 1454, the first book in the West printed from

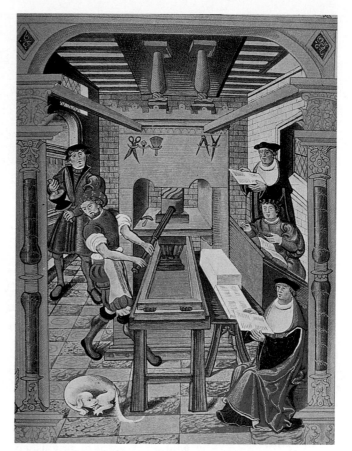

A French Printshop, 1537   A workman operates the "press," quite literally a screw device that presses the paper to the inked type. Other employees examine the printed sheets, each of which holds four pages. When folded, the sheets make a book. (Giraudon/Art Resource, NY)

movable type, was a beautiful and finely crafted work that bore witness to the printer's years of diligent experimentation. As printing spread to Italy and France, humanists worked closely with printers. Erasmus worked for years as an editor and proofreader for the great Italian scholar-printer Aldo Manuzio (1449–1515) in Venice. Manuzio's press published many critical editions of classical Latin and Greek texts.

By 1500 at least 10 million printed works had issued forth from presses in 238 towns in western Europe. Though the days of mass-produced paperbacks were still in the future, the printers and humanists had launched a revolution that was already having an effect on students, scholars, and a growing number of literate people who could gain access to ancient texts as well as to unorthodox political and religious tracts.

Erasmus (uh-RAZ-muhs)
Johann Gutenberg (yoh-HAHN GOO-ten-burg)

The Medici Family   This detail of a mural painting of 1459 by Benozzo Gozzoli depicts the arrival of the Magi at the birthplace of the Christ Child, but the principal figures in this detail are important members of the wealthy Medici family of Florence and their entourage in costumes of their day. The African bowman on the left is an interesting detail, showing how common African servants and slaves became in southern Europe during the Renaissance. (Florence, Palazzo Medici-Riccardi)

Renaissance Artists

The fourteenth and fifteenth centuries were as distinguished for their masterpieces of painting, sculpture, and architecture as they were for their scholarship. Although artists continued to depict biblical subjects, the spread of Greco-Roman learning led many artists, especially in Italy, to portray Greco-Roman deities and mythical tales. Another popular trend was depicting the scenes of daily life.

However, neither daily life nor classical images were entirely new subjects. Renaissance art, like Renaissance scholarship, owed a major debt to earlier generations. The Florentine painter Giotto° (ca. 1267–1337) had a formidable influence on the major Italian painters of the fifteenth century who credited him with singlehandedly reviving the "lost art of painting." In his religious scenes Giotto replaced the stiff, staring figures of the Byzantine style, which were intended to overawe viewers, with more natural and human portraits with whose emotions of grief and love viewers could identify. Rather than floating on backgrounds of gold leaf, his saints inhabit earthly landscapes.

Another important contribution to the early Italian Renaissance was a new painting technology from north

of the Alps. The Flemish painter Jan van Eyck° (ca. 1390–1441) mixed his pigments with linseed oil in place of the diluted egg yolk of earlier centuries. Oil paints were slower drying and more versatile, and they gave pictures a superior luster. Van Eyck's use of the technique for his own masterfully realistic paintings on religious and domestic themes was quickly copied by talented painters of the Italian Renaissance.

The great Italian Leonardo da Vinci° (1452–1519), for example, used oil paints for his famous *Mona Lisa.* Renaissance artists like Leonardo were masters of many media. His other works include the fresco (painting in wet plaster) *The Last Supper*, bronze sculptures, as well as imaginative designs for airplanes, submarines, and tanks. Leonardo's younger contemporary Michelangelo° (1472–1564) painted frescoes of biblical scenes on the ceiling of the Sistine Chapel in the Vatican, sculpted statues of David and Moses, and designed the dome for a new Saint Peter's Basilica.

The patronage of wealthy and educated merchants and prelates did much to foster an artistic blossoming in the cities of northern Italy and Flanders. The Florentine

Giotto (JAW-toh)

Jan van Eyck (yahn vahn-IKE)
Leonardo da Vinci (lay-own-AHR-doh dah-VIN-chee)
Michelangelo (my-kuhl-AN-juh-low)

banker Cosimo de' Medici (1389–1464), for example, spent immense sums on paintings, sculpture, and public buildings. His grandson Lorenzo (1449–1492), known as "the Magnificent," was even more lavish. The church was also an important source of artistic commissions. Seeking to restore Rome as the capital of the Latin Church, the papacy° launched a building program culminating in the construction of the new Saint Peter's Basilica and a residence for the pope.

These scholarly and artistic achievements exemplify the innovation and striving for excellence of the Late Middle Ages. The new literary themes and artistic styles of this period had lasting influence on Western culture. But the innovations in the organization of universities, in printing, and in oil painting had wider implications, for they were later adopted by cultures all over the world.

POLITICAL AND MILITARY TRANSFORMATIONS

Stronger and more unified states and armies developed in western Europe in parallel with the economic and cultural revivals. In no case were transformations smooth and steady, and the political changes unfolded somewhat differently in each state (see Map 16.3). During and after the prolonged struggle of the Hundred Years War, French and English monarchs forged closer ties with the nobility, the church and the merchants. The consolidation of Spain and Portugal was linked to crusades against Muslim states. In Italy and Germany, however, political power remained in the hands of small states and loose alliances.

Monarchs, Nobles, and the Church

Thirteenth-century states still shared many features of early medieval state (see Chapter 10). Hereditary monarchs occupied the peak of the political pyramid, but their powers were limited by modest treasuries and the rights possessed by others. Below them came the powerful noblemen who controlled vast estates and whose advice and consent was often required on important matters of state. The church, jealous of its traditional rights and independence, was another powerful body within each kingdom. Towns, too, had acquired many rights and privileges. Indeed, the towns in Flanders, the Hanseatic League, and Italy were nearly independent from royal interference. The power within kingdoms, however, was far from balanced and clearly defined, as some examples will illustrate.

In theory nobles were vassals of the reigning monarchs and were obliged to furnish them with armored knights in time of war. In practice vassals sought to limit the monarch's power and protect their own rights and privileges. The nobles' privileged economic and social position rested on the large estates that had been granted to their ancestors in return for supporting and training knights in armor to serve in a royal army.

In the year 1200 knights were still the backbone of western European fighting forces, but two changes in weaponry were bringing into question their central military role and thus the system of estates that supported them. The first involved the humble arrow. Improved crossbows could shoot metal-tipped arrows with such force that they could pierce helmets and light body armor. Professional crossbowmen, hired for wages, became increasingly common and much feared. Indeed, a church council in 1139 outlawed the crossbow as being too deadly for use against Christians. The ban was largely ignored. The second innovation in military technology that weakened the feudal system was the firearm. This Chinese invention, using gunpowder to shoot stone or metal projectiles (see Environment and Technology: Explosive Power in Chapter 14), further transformed the medieval army.

The church also resisted royal control. In 1302 the outraged Pope Boniface VIII (r. 1294–1303) went so far as to assert that divine law made the papacy superior to "every human creature," including monarchs. This theoretical claim of superiority was challenged by force. Issuing his own claim of superiority, King Philip "the Fair" of France (r. 1285–1314) sent an army to arrest the pope. After this treatment hastened Pope Boniface's death, Philip engineered the election of a French pope who established a new papal residence at Avignon° in southern France in 1309.

With the support of the French monarchy, a succession of popes residing in Avignon improved church discipline—but at the price of compromising the papacy's neutrality in the eyes of other rulers. Papal authority was further eroded by the **Great Western Schism** (1378–1415), a period when rival papal claimants at Avignon and Rome vied for the loyalties of Latin Christians. The conflict was eventually resolved by returning the papal residence to its traditional location, the city of Rome. The papacy regained its independence, but the long crisis broke the pope's ability to challenge the rising power of the larger monarchies.

---

papacy (PAY-puh-see)

Avignon (ah-vee-NYON)

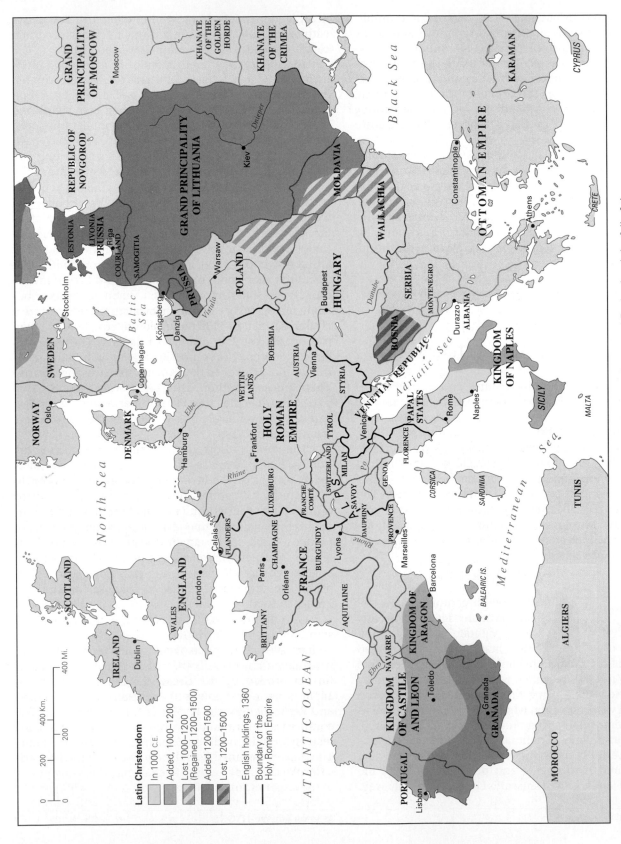

Map 16.3   Europe in 1453   This year marked the end of the Hundred Years War between France and England and the fall of the Byzantine capital city of Constantinople to the Ottoman Turks. Muslim advances into southeastern Europe were offset by the Latin Christian reconquests of Islamic holdings in southern Italy and the Iberian Peninsula and by the conversion of Lithuania.

King Philip gained an important advantage at the beginning of his dispute with Pope Boniface when he persuaded a large council of French nobles to grant him the right to collect a new tax, which sustained the monarchy for some time. Earlier, by adroitly using the support of the towns, the saintly King Louis IX of France (r. 1226–1270) had been able to issue ordinances that applied throughout his kingdom without first obtaining the nobles' consent. But later kings' efforts to extend royal authority sparked prolonged resistance by the most powerful vassals.

In 1200, in the smaller kingdom of England, royal power was already well centralized as a result of consolidation that had taken place after the Norman conquest of 1066. The Anglo-Norman kings also extended their realm by assaults on their Celtic neighbors. Between 1200 and 1400 they incorporated Wales and reasserted control over most of Ireland. Nevertheless, English royal power was far from absolute. In the span of just three years the ambitions of King John (r. 1199–1216) were severely set back. First he was compelled to acknowledge the pope as his overlord (1213). Then he lost his bid to reassert claims to Aquitaine in southern France (1214). Finally he was forced to sign Magna Carta ("Great Charter," 1215), which affirmed that monarchs were subject to established law, confirmed the independence of the church and the city of London, and guaranteed nobles' hereditary rights.

Separate from the challenges to royal authority presented by the church and the nobles were the alliances and conflicts generated by the hereditary nature of monarchial rule. Monarchs and their vassals both entered into strategic marriages with a view to increasing their lands and their wealth. Such marriages showed scant regard for the emotions of the wedded parties or for "national" interests. Besides unhappiness for the parties involved, these marriages often led to conflicts over far-flung inheritances. Although these dynastic struggles and shifting boundaries make European politics seem chaotic in comparison with the empires of Asia, some important changes were emerging from them. Aided by the changing technology of war, monarchs were strengthening their authority and creating more stable (but not entirely fixed) state boundaries within which the nations of western Europe would in time develop. Nobles lost autonomy and dominance on the battlefield but retained their social position and important political roles.

The Hundred Years War

A key example of the transformation in politics and fighting methods was the long conflict between the king of France and his vassals known as the **Hundred Years War** (1337–1453). These vassals included the kings of England (for lands that belonged to their Norman ancestors), the counts of prosperous and independent-minded Flanders in the north, the dukes of Brittany, and the dukes of Burgundy. In typical fashion, the conflict grew out of a marriage alliance.

The marriage of Princess Isabella of France to King Edward II of England (r. 1307–1327) was meant to ensure that this powerful vassal remained loyal to the French monarchy. However, none of Isabella's three brothers, who served in turn as kings of France, produced a male heir, so Isabella's son, King Edward III of England (r. 1327–1377), laid claim to the French throne in 1337. After French courts instead awarded the throne to a more distant (and more French) cousin, Edward decided to fight for his rights. Other vassals joined in a series of battles for the French throne that persisted until 1453.

The new military technology shaped the conflict. Early in the war French cavalry was reinforced by hired Italian crossbowmen, but arrows from another late medieval innovation, the English longbow, nearly annihilated the French force. Adopted from the Welsh, the 6-foot (108-meter) longbow could shoot farther and more rapidly than the crossbow. Although arrows from longbows could not pierce armor, in concentrated volleys they often found gaps in the knights' defenses or struck their less-well-protected horses. To defend against these weapons, armor became heavier and more encompassing, making it harder for a knight to move. A knight who was pulled off his steed by a foot soldier armed with a pike (hooked pole) was usually unable to get up to defend himself.

In later stages of the Hundred Years War firearms became more prominent. At first cannon were more likely to spook the horses with their smoke and noise than hit these rapidly moving targets. Then as cannon grew larger, they proved quite effective in blasting holes through the heavy walls of medieval castles and towns. The first use of such artillery against the French, in the Battle of Agincourt (1415), gave the English an important victory.

The English gains that followed were halted by a young French peasant woman, Joan of Arc. Believing she was instructed by God to save France, she donned a knight's armor and rallied the French troops that defeated the English in 1429 just as they seemed close to conquering France. Shortly after this victory, Joan had the misfortune to fall into English hands. She was tried by English churchmen for being a witch and was burned at the stake in 1431.

In the final battles of the Hundred Years War, French forces used large cannon to demolish the walls of once-secure castles held by the English and their allies. The truce that ended the struggle in 1453 left the French monarchy in firm control.

New Monarchies in France and England

To contemporaries the advantage in the Hundred Years War seemed to shift first to one side and then to the other, but in retrospect the war can be seen as a watershed that helped produce **new monarchies** in France and England. These monarchies differed from their medieval predecessors in having greater centralization of power, more fixed "national" boundaries, and stronger representative institutions.

Barred from their efforts to add France to their domains, English monarchs after 1453 directed their efforts to consolidating control over territory within the British Isles, though the Scots strongly defended their independence. With the English defeated, the French monarchs also turned to consolidating their control over powerful noble families, especially when these happened to be headed by women. First, Mary of Burgundy (1457–1482) was forced to surrender most of her family's vast holdings to the king of France. Then in 1491, Anne of Brittany was compelled to marry the king of France, a step that led to the eventual incorporation of her duchy° into France.

Nobles' resistance was undermined by changes in military technology. The smaller and more mobile cannon developed in the late fifteenth century proved very effective in battles and against castle walls. And improvements in hand-held firearms—by the late fifteenth century they could pierce even the heaviest armor—led to the final rout of the armored knight. These changes in military hardware meant that armies depended less on knights and more on bowmen, pikemen, musketeers, and specialized artillery units.

Because payment for the new armed forces came from the royal treasury, the new monarchies needed a way to finance their standing armies. Some funds came from nobles who were willing to convert their obligations to monarchs into money payments and to cough up taxes for wars they supported. For example, in 1439 and 1445 Charles VII of France (r. 1422–1461) won from his vassals the right to levy a new tax on land. The tax not only enabled him to pay the costs of the current war with England but provided the financial base of the French monarchy for the next 350 years.

Taxes on merchants were another source of new revenue. King Edward III was the first English ruler to tax the wool trade, which provided most of the funds for fighting the Hundred Years War. Some Christian princes and kings taxed Jewish merchants or extorted large contributions from wealthy towns in return for their protection. Individual merchants sometimes curried royal favor with loans, even though such debts could be difficult or dangerous to collect. For example, the wealthy fifteenth-century French merchant Jacques Coeur° gained many social and financial benefits for himself and his family by lending money to important members of the French court, but he was ruined when his jealous debtors accused him of murder and had his fortune confiscated.

A third source of revenue was the church. The clergy in a kingdom often agreed to make a voluntary contribution to support a war. English and French monarchs gained further control of church funds in the fifteenth century by winning the right to appoint important church officials in their realms. In so doing, the monarchs were not abandoning the church. Indeed, they often used state power to enforce religious orthodoxy in their realms more vigorously than the popes had ever been able to do. But, as reformers complained, the church's spiritual mission was often subordinated to political and economic concerns.

As a result of these complex dynastic and military struggles, political power in England and France had shifted by the end of the fifteenth century in favor of the monarchs and away from the nobility and the church. But the shift was only partial. Nobles retained their social position and their roles as government officials and military officers. Moreover, in both England and France in 1500 monarchs had to deal with representative institutions that had not existed in 1200. The English Parliament had become a permanent check on royal power: the House of Lords contained all the great nobles and English church officials; the House of Commons represented the towns and the leading citizens of the counties. In France a similar representative body known as the Estates General represented the church, the nobles, and the towns, though its rights were not so well entrenched as the English Parliament's.

Iberian Unification

The growth of Spain and Portugal into strong, centralized states was also shaped by struggles between kings and vassals, dynastic marriages and mergers, and warfare. But Spain and Portugal's **reconquest of Iberia** from Muslim rule was also a crusade to expand the boundaries of Latin Christianity. Such religious zeal did not rule out personal gain. The Christian Iberian knights who gradually pushed the borders of their kingdoms southward knew that to the victors would go

---

duchy (DUTCH-ee)

Coeur (cur)

the spoils. The spoils included irrigated farmland capable of producing an abundance of food, rich cities of glittering Moorish architecture, and ports offering access to the Mediterranean and the South Atlantic. Victorious Christian knights were often rewarded with a grant over the land and people in a newly conquered territory. Serving God, growing rich, and living off the labor of others became a way of life for the Iberian nobility.

The reconquest advanced in waves over several centuries; there were long pauses to consolidate the conquered territory and unify the Christian kingdoms. Toledo was taken in 1085 and made into a Christian outpost. The Atlantic port of Lisbon fell in 1147 with the aid of English crusaders on their way to capture the Holy Land. It became the new capital of Portugal and the kingdom's leading city, displacing the older capital of Oporto, whose name (meaning "the port") is the root of the word *Portugal*. The reconquest quickened in the thirteenth century. A Christian victory in 1212 broke the back of Muslim power in Iberia. During the next few decades Portuguese and Castilian forces captured the beautiful and prosperous cities of Cordova (1236) and Seville (1248) and in 1249 drove the Muslims from the southwestern corner of Iberia, known as Algarve° ("the west" in Arabic). Only the small kingdom of Granada hugging the Mediterranean coast remained in Muslim hands.

By incorporating Algarve in 1249, Portugal attained its modern territorial limits and turned to settling and revitalizing its newly acquired lands. The resettlement of peasants in these lands south of Lisbon did much to weaken serfdom in Portugal. After a long pause to colonize, Christianize, and consolidate this land, Portugal took the Christian reconquest to North Africa. In 1415, Portuguese knights seized the port city of Ceuta° in Morocco, where they learned more of the caravan trade in gold and slaves from south of the Sahara (see Chapter 15). During the next few decades Portuguese mariners sailed down the Atlantic coast of Africa in an effort to gain access to this rich trade and to make contact with African Christian allies (see Chapter 17).

Although it took the other Iberian kingdoms much longer to complete the reconquest, the struggle served to bring them together and to keep their Christian religious zealotry at a high pitch. The marriage of Princess Isabella of Castile and Prince Ferdinand of Aragon in 1469 led to the permanent union of their kingdoms into Spain a decade later when they inherited their respective thrones. Their conquest of Granada in 1492 secured the final piece of Muslim territory in Iberia for the new kingdom.

The year 1492 was also memorable because of Ferdinand and Isabella's sponsorship of the voyage from

Seville led by Christopher Columbus to the riches of the Indian Ocean (see Chapter 17). But a third event that year was as momentous an extension of the Spanish crusading mentality. Less than three months after Granada's fall, the monarchs ordered all Jews to be expelled from their kingdoms, and efforts to force the remaining Muslims to convert or leave led to a Muslim revolt at the end of 1499 that was not put down until 1501. The Spanish rulers expelled the last Muslims in 1502. Portugal also ordered the expulsion of all Jews from its kingdom in 1496, including 100,000 who had fled from Spain.

CONCLUSION

From an ecological perspective the later medieval history of the Latin West is a story of triumphs and disasters. Westerners excelled in harnessing the inanimate forces of nature with their windmills, water wheels, and sails. They mined and refined the mineral wealth of the earth, although localized pollution and deforestation were among the results. But their inability to improve food production and distribution as rapidly as their population grew created a demographic crisis that became a demographic calamity when the Black Death swept through Europe in the mid-fourteenth century.

From a regional perspective the centuries from 1200 to 1500 witnessed the coming together of the basic features of the modern West. States were of moderate size but had exceptional military capacity honed by frequent wars with one another. The ruling class, convinced that economic strength and political strength were inseparable, promoted the welfare of the urban populations that specialized in trade, manufacturing, and finance—and taxed their profits. Autonomous universities fostered intellectual excellence, and printing diffused the latest advances in knowledge. Art and architecture reached peaks of design and execution that set the standard for subsequent centuries. Perhaps most fundamentally, later medieval western Europe was a society fascinated by tools and techniques. In commerce, warfare, industry, and navigation, new inventions and improved versions of old ones underpinned the region's continuing dynamism.

From a global perspective these centuries marked the Latin West's change from a region dependent on cultural and commercial flows from the East to a region poised to export its culture and impose its power on other parts of the world. It is one of history's great ironies that many of the tools that the Latin West used to challenge Eastern supremacy had originally been borrowed from the East. Medieval Europe's mills, printing,

---

Algarve (ahl-GAHRV)   **Ceuta** (say-OO-tuh)

firearms, and navigational devices owed much to Eastern designs, just as its agriculture, alphabet, and numerals had in earlier times. Western European success depended as much on strong motives for expansion as on adequate means. Long before the first voyages overseas, population pressure, religious zeal, economic motives, and intellectual curiosity had expanded the territory and resources of the Latin West. From the late eleventh century onward such expansion of frontiers was notable in the English conquest of Celtic lands, in the establishment of crusader and commercial outposts in the eastern Mediterranean and Black Seas, in the massive German settlement east of the Elbe River, and in the reconquest of southern Iberia from the Muslims. The early voyages into the Atlantic were an extension of similar motives in a new direction.

■ Key Terms

Latin West	universities
three-field system	scholasticism
Black Death	humanists (Renaissance)
water wheel	printing press
Hanseatic League	Great Western Schism
guild	Hundred Years War
Gothic cathedrals	new monarchies
Renaissance (European)	reconquest of Iberia

■ Suggested Reading

A fine guide to the Latin West (including its ties to eastern Europe, Africa, and the Middle East) is Robert Fossier, ed., *The Cambridge Illustrated History of the Middle Ages*, vol. 3, *1250–1520* (1986). Denys Hay, *Europe in the Fourteenth and Fifteenth Centuries*, 2d ed. (1989), is comprehensive and up-to-date. For the West's economic revival and growth see Robert S. Lopez, *The Commercial Revolution of the Middle Ages, 950–1350* (1976), and Harry A. Miskimin, *The Economy of Early Renaissance Europe, 1300–1460* (1975).

For fascinating primary sources see James Bruce Ross and Mary Martin McLaughlin, eds., *The Portable Medieval Reader* (1977) and *The Portable Renaissance Reader* (1977). *The Notebooks of Leonardo da Vinci*, ed. Pamela Taylor (1960), show this versatile genius at work.

Technological change is surveyed by Arnold Pacey, *The Maze of Ingenuity: Ideas and Idealism in the Development of Technology* (1974); Jean Gimpel, *The Medieval Machine: The Industrial Revolution of the Middle Ages* (1977); and William H. McNeill, *The Pursuit of Power: Technology, Armed Force, and Society Since A.D. 1000* (1982). For a key aspect of the environment see Roland Bechmann, *Trees and Man: The Forest in the Middle Ages* (1990).

Charles Homer Haskins, *The Rise of the Universities* (1923; reprint, 1957), is a brief, lighthearted introduction; more detailed and scholarly is Olef Pedersen, *The First Universities: Studium Generale and the Origins of University Education in Europe* (1998). Johan Huizinga, *The Waning of the Middle Ages* (1924), is the classic account of the "mind" of the fifteenth century. A multitude of works deal with the Renaissance but few in any broad historical context. Lisa Jardine, *Worldly Goods: A New History of the Renaissance* (1996), is well illustrated and balanced; see also John R. Hale, *The Civilization of Europe in the Renaissance* (1995).

For social history see Georges Duby, *Rural Economy and Country Life in the Medieval West* (1990), for the earlier centuries. George Huppert, *After the Black Death: A Social History of Early Modern Europe* (1986), takes the analysis past 1500. Brief lives of individuals are found in Eileen Power, *Medieval People*, new ed. (1997), and Frances Gies and Joseph Gies, *Women in the Middle Ages* (1978). More systematic are the essays in Mary Erler and Maryanne Kowaleski, eds., *Women and Power in the Middle Ages* (1988). Vita Sackville-West, *Saint Joan of Arc* (1926; reprint, 1991), is a readable introduction to this extraordinary person.

Key events in the Anglo-French dynastic conflict are examined by Christopher Alland, *The Hundred Years War: England and France at War, ca. 1300–ca. 1450* (1988). Joseph F. O'Callaghan, *A History of Medieval Spain* (1975), provides the best one-volume coverage; for more detail see Jocelyn N. Hillgarth, *The Spanish Kingdoms*, 2 vols. (1976, 1978). Barbara W. Tuchman, *A Distant Mirror: The Calamitous 14th Century* (1978), gives a popular account of the crises of that era. P. Ziegler, *The Black Death* (1969), supplies a thorough introduction.

The Latin West's expansion is well treated by Robert Bartlett, *The Making of Europe: Conquest, Colonization, and Cultural Change* (1993); J. R. S. Phillips, *The Medieval Expansion of Europe*, new ed. (1998); and P. E. Russell, *Portugal, Spain and the African Atlantic, 1343–1492* (1998).

Francis C. Oakley, *The Western Church in the Later Middle Ages* (1985), is a reliable summary of modern scholarship. Kenneth R. Stow, *Alienated Minority: The Jews of Medieval Latin Europe* (1992), provides a fine survey up through the fourteenth century. For pioneering essays on the Latin West's external ties see Khalil I. Semaan, ed., *Islam and the Medieval West: Aspects of Intercultural Relations* (1980).

■ Notes

1. Quoted in Marina Warner, *Alone of All Her Sex: The Myth and Cult of the Virgin Mary* (New York: Random House, 1983), 179.
2. Harry Miskimin, *The Economy of the Early Renaissance, 1300–1460* (Englewood Cliffs, NJ: Prentice-Hall, 1969), 26–27.
3. Quotations here and later in the chapter are from Geoffrey Chaucer, *The Canterbury Tales*, trans. Nevill Coghill (New York: Penguin Books, 1952), 25, 29, 32.

17

THE MARITIME REVOLUTION,
to 1550

Global Maritime Expansion Before 1450 • Iberian Expansion, 1400–1550 •
Encounters with Europe, 1450–1550
ENVIRONMENT AND TECHNOLOGY: Vasco da Gama's Fleet
SOCIETY AND CULTURE: European Male Sexual Dominance Overseas

Columbus Prepares to Cross the Atlantic, 1492   This later representation shows Columbus
with the ships, soldiers, priests, and seamen that were part of Spain's enterprise.

I n 1511 the young Ferdinand Magellan sailed from Europe around the southern tip of Africa and eastward across the Indian Ocean as a member of the first Portuguese expedition to explore the East Indies (maritime Southeast Asia). Eight years later, this time in the service of Spain, he headed an expedition that sought to demonstrate the feasibility of reaching the East Indies by sailing westward from Europe. By the middle of 1521 Magellan's expedition had achieved its goal by sailing across the Atlantic, rounding the southern tip of South America, and crossing the Pacific Ocean—but at a high price.

One of the five ships that had set out from Spain in 1519 was wrecked on a reef, and the captain of another deserted and sailed back to Spain. The passage across the vast Pacific took much longer than anticipated, resulting in the deaths of dozens of sailors due to starvation and disease. In the Philippines, Magellan himself was killed on April 27, 1521, while aiding a local king who had promised to become a Christian. Magellan's successor met the same fate a few days later.

To consolidate their dwindling resources, the expedition's survivors burned the least seaworthy of their remaining three ships and transferred the men and supplies from that ship to the smaller *Victoria*, which continued westward across the Indian Ocean, around Africa, and back to Europe. Magellan's flagship, the *Trinidad*, tried unsuccessfully to recross the Pacific to Central America. The *Victoria*'s return to Spain on September 8, 1522, was a crowning example of Europeans' new ability and determination to make themselves masters of the oceans. A century of daring and dangerous voyages backed by the Portuguese crown had opened new routes through the South Atlantic to Africa, Brazil, and the rich trade of the Indian Ocean. Rival voyages sponsored by Spain since 1492 had opened new contacts with the American continents. Now the unexpectedly broad Pacific Ocean had been crossed as well. A maritime revolution was under way that would change the course of history.

That new maritime skill marked the end of an era in which the flow of historical influences tended to move from east to west. Before 1500, most overland and maritime expansion had come from Asia, as had

the most useful technologies and the most influential systems of belief. Asia also had been home to the most powerful states and the richest trading networks. The Iberians set out on their voyages of exploration to reach Eastern markets, and their success began a new era in which the West gradually became the world's center of power, wealth, and innovation.

The maritime revolution created many new contacts, alliances, and conflicts. Some ended tragically for individuals like Magellan. Some were disastrous for entire populations: Amerindians, for instance, suffered conquest, colonization, and a rapid decline in numbers. Sometimes the results were mixed: Asians and Africans found both risks and opportunities in their new relations with the visitors from Europe.

As you read this chapter, ask yourself the following questions:

- Why did Portugal and Spain undertake voyages of exploration?
- Why do the voyages of Magellan and other Iberians mark a turning point in world history?
- What were the consequences for the different peoples of the world of the new contacts resulting from these voyages?

GLOBAL MARITIME EXPANSION BEFORE 1450

S ince ancient times travel across the salt waters of the world's seas and oceans had been one of the great challenges to people's technological ingenuity. Ships had to be sturdy enough to survive heavy winds and waves, and pilots had to learn how to cross featureless expanses of water to their destination. In time ships, sails, and navigational techniques perfected in the more protected seas were tried on the vast, open oceans.

However complex the solutions and dangerous the voyages, the rewards of sea travel made it all worthwhile. For ships could move goods and people more quickly and cheaply than any form of overland travel then possible. Because of its challenges and rewards, sea travel attracted adventurers. To cross the unknown waters, find new lands, and open up new trade or settlements was an

CHRONOLOGY

	Pacific Ocean	Atlantic Ocean	Indian Ocean
Pre 1400	**400–1300** Polynesian settlement of Pacific islands	**770–1200** Viking voyages **1300s** Settlement of Madeira, Azores, Canaries **Early 1300s** Mali voyages	
1400 to 1500		**1418–1460** Voyages of Henry the Navigator **1440s** Slaves from West Africa **1482** Portuguese at Gold Coast and Kongo **1486** Portuguese at Benin **1488** Bartolomeu Dias reaches Indian Ocean **1492** Columbus reaches Caribbean **1493** Columbus returns to Caribbean (second voyage) **1498** Columbus reaches mainland of South America (third voyage) **1492–1500** Spanish conquer Hispaniola	**1405–1433** Voyages of Zheng He **1497–1498** Vasco da Gama reaches India
1500 to 1550	 **1519–1522** Magellan expedition	**1500** Cabral reaches Brazil **1513** Ponce de León explores Florida **1519–1520** Cortés conquers Aztec Empire **1531–1533** Pizarro conquers Inca Empire	**1505** Portuguese bombard Swahili Coast cities **1510** Portuguese take Goa **1511** Portuguese take Malacca **1515** Portuguese take Hormuz **1535** Portuguese take Diu **1538** Portuguese defeat Ottoman fleet **1539** Portuguese aid Ethiopia

exciting prospect. For these reasons some men on every continent had long turned their attention to the sea.

By 1450 much had been accomplished and much remained undone. Daring mariners had discovered and settled most of the islands of the Pacific, the Atlantic, and the Indian Oceans. The greatest success was the trading system that united the peoples around the Indian Ocean. But no individual had yet crossed the Pacific in either direction. Even the narrower Atlantic was a barrier that kept the peoples of the Americas, Europe, and Africa in ignorance of each other's existence. The inhabitants of Australia were likewise completely cut off from contact with the rest of humanity. All this was about to change.

The Pacific Ocean

The vast distances Polynesian peoples voyaged out of sight of land across the Pacific Ocean are one of the most impressive feats in maritime history before 1450 (see Map 17.1). Though they left no written records, it is now clear that over several thousand years intrepid mariners from the Malay° Peninsula of Southeast Asia explored and settled the island chains of the East Indies and moved onto New Guinea and the smaller islands of Melanesia°. Beginning some time before the

Malay (May-LAY)   **Melanesia** (mel-uh-NEE-zhuh)

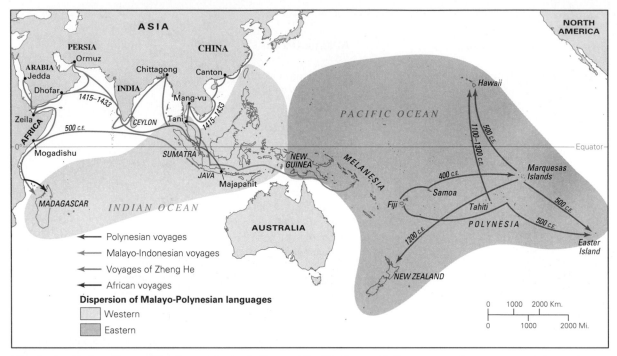

Map 17.1 Exploration and Settlement in the Indian and Pacific Oceans Before 1500 Over many centuries mariners originating in Southeast Asia gradually colonized the islands of the Pacific and Indian Oceans. The Chinese voyages led by Zheng He in the fifteenth century were lavish official expeditions.

Common Era (C.E.), a new wave of expansion from the area of Fiji brought the first humans to the islands of the central Pacific known as Polynesia. The easternmost of the Marquesas° Islands were reached about 400 C.E.; Easter Island, 2,200 miles (3,540 kilometers) off the coast of South America, was settled a century later. From the Marquesas Polynesian sailors sailed to the Hawaiian Islands as early as 500 C.E. They settled New Zealand about 1200. Then between 1100 and 1300, new voyages northward from Tahiti to Hawaii brought more Polynesian settlers across the more than 2,000 nautical miles (4,000 kilometers) to Hawaii.

Until recent decades some historians argued that Polynesians could have reached the eastern Pacific islands only by accident because they lacked navigational devices to plot their way. Others wondered how Polynesians could have overcome the difficulties, illustrated by Magellan's flagship, *Trinidad*, of sailing eastward across the Pacific. In 1947 one energetic amateur historian of the sea, Thor Heyerdahl°, argued that Easter Island and Hawaii were actually settled from the Americas. He

sought to prove his theory by sailing his balsawood raft *Kon Tiki* westward from Peru.

Although some Amerindian voyagers did use ocean currents to travel northward from Peru to Mexico between 300 and 900 C.E., there is now considerable evidence that the settlement of the islands of the eastern Pacific was the result of planned expansion by Polynesian mariners. The first piece of evidence is the fact that the languages of these islanders are all closely related to the languages of the western Pacific and ultimately to those of Malaya. The second is the finding that accidental voyages could not have brought sufficient numbers of men and women for founding a new colony along with all the plants and domesticated animals that were basic to other Polynesian islands.

In 1976 a Polynesian crew led by Ben Finney used traditional navigational methods to sail an ocean canoe from Hawaii south to Tahiti. The *Hokulea* was a 62-foot-long (19-meter-long) double canoe patterned after old oceangoing canoes that sometimes were as long as 120 feet (37 meters). Not only did the *Hokulea* prove seaworthy, but, powered by an inverted triangular sail and steered by paddles (not by a rudder), it was able to sail across the winds at a sharp enough angle to make the dif-

---

Marquesas (mar-KAY-suhs)　**Heyerdahl** (HIGH-uhr-dahl)

Polynesian Canoes   Pacific Ocean mariners sailing canoes such as these, shown in an eighteenth-century painting, made epic voyages of exploration and settlement. A large platform connects two canoes at the left, providing more room for the members of the expedition, and a sail supplements the paddlers. ("Tereoboo, King of Owyhee, bringing presents to Captain Cook," D. L. Ref. p. xx 2f. 35. Courtesy, The Dixon Library, State Library of New South Wales)

ficult voyage, just as ancient mariners must have done. Perhaps even more remarkable, the *Hokulea*'s crew was able to navigate to their destination using only their observation of the currents, stars, and evidence of land.

The Indian Ocean

While Polynesian mariners were settling Pacific islands, other Malayo-Indonesians were sailing westward across the Indian Ocean and colonizing the large island of Madagascar off the southeastern coast of Africa. These voyages continued through the fifteenth century. To this day the inhabitants of Madagascar speak Malayo-Polynesian languages. However, part of the island's population is descended from Africans who had crossed the 600 miles (1,000 kilometers) from the mainland to Madagascar, most likely in the centuries just before 1500.

Other peoples had been using the Indian Ocean for trade since ancient times. The landmasses of Southeast Asia and eastern Africa that enclose the Indian Ocean's sides, and the Indian subcontinent that juts into its middle, provided coasts that seafarers might safely follow and coves for protection. Moreover, seasonal winds known as monsoons are so predictable and steady that navigation using sailing vessels called dhows° was less difficult and dangerous in ancient times than elsewhere.

The rise of medieval Islam gave Indian Ocean trade an important boost. The great Muslim cities of the Middle East provided a demand for valuable commodities. Even more important were the networks of Muslim traders that tied the region together. Muslim traders shared a common language, ethic, and law and actively spread their religion to distant trading cities. By 1400 there were Muslim trading communities all around the Indian Ocean.

The Indian Ocean traders operated largely independently of the empires and states that they served, but in East Asia imperial China's rulers were growing more and more interested in these wealthy ports of trade. In 1368 the Ming dynasty overthrew Mongol rule and began expansionist policies to reestablish China's predominance and prestige abroad.

Having restored Chinese dominance in East Asia, the Ming next moved to establish direct contacts with

---

dhow (dow)

Chinese Junk   This modern drawing shows how much larger one of Zheng He's ships was than one of Vasco da Gama's vessels. Watertight interior bulkheads made junks the most seaworthy large ships of the fifteenth century. Sails made of pleated bamboo matting hung from the junk's masts and a stern rudder provided steering. European ships of exploration, though smaller, were faster and more maneuverable. (Dugald Stermer)

the peoples around the Indian Ocean. In choosing to send out seven imperial fleets between 1405 and 1433, the Ming may have been motivated partly by curiosity. The fact that most of the ports the fleets visited were important in the Indian Ocean trade suggests that enhancing China's commerce was also a motive. Yet because the expeditions were far larger than needed for exploration or promoting trade, their main purpose probably was to inspire awe of Ming power and achievements.

The Ming expeditions into the Indian Ocean basin were launched on a scale that reflected imperial China's resources and importance. The first consisted of sixty-two specially built "treasure ships," large Chinese junks each about 300 feet long by 150 feet wide (90 by 45 meters). There were also at least a hundred smaller vessels, most of which were larger than the flagship in which Columbus later sailed across the Atlantic. Each treasure ship had nine masts, twelve sails, many decks, and a carrying capacity of 3,000 tons (six times the capacity of Columbus's entire fleet). One expedition carried over 27,000 individuals, including infantry and cavalry troops. The ships would have been armed with small cannon, but in most Chinese sea battles arrows from highly accurate crossbows dominated the fighting.

At the command of the expeditions was Admiral **Zheng He°** (1371–1435). A Chinese Muslim with ancestral connections to the Persian Gulf, Zheng was a fitting emissary to the increasingly Muslim-dominated Indian Ocean basin. The expeditions carried other Arabic-speaking Chinese as interpreters.

One of these interpreters kept a journal recording the customs, dress, and beliefs of the people visited, along with the trade, towns, and animals of their countries. Among his observations were these: exotic animals such as the black panther of Malaya and the tapir of Sumatra; beliefs in legendary "corpse headed barbarians" whose heads left their bodies at night and caused infants to die; the division of coastal Indians into five classes, which correspond to the four Hindu varna and a separate Muslim class; the fact that traders in the rich Indian trading port of Calicut° could perform error-free calculations by counting on their fingers and toes rather than using the Chinese abacus. After his return, the interpreter went on tour in China, telling of these exotic places and "how far the majestic virtue of [China's] imperial dynasty extended."[1]

Zheng He (jung huh)   **Calicut** (KAL-ih-kut)

The Chinese "treasure ships" carried rich silks, precious metals, and other valuable goods intended as gifts for distant rulers. In return those rulers sent back gifts of equal or greater value to the Chinese emperor. Although the main purpose of these exchanges was diplomatic, they also stimulated trade between China and its southern neighbors. For that reason they were welcomed by Chinese merchants and manufacturers. Yet commercial profits could not have offset the huge cost of the fleets.

Interest in new contacts was not confined to the Chinese side. In 1415–1416 at least three trading cities on the Swahili° Coast of East Africa sent delegations to China. The delegates from one of them, Malindi, presented the emperor of China with a giraffe, creating quite a stir among the normally reserved imperial officials. Such African delegations may have encouraged more contacts, for the next three of Zheng's voyages were extended to the African coast. Unfortunately no documents record how Africans and Chinese reacted to each other during these historic meetings between 1417 and 1433. It appears that China's lavish gifts stimulated the Swahili market for silk and porcelain. An increase in Chinese imports of pepper from southern Asian lands also resulted from these expeditions.

Had the Ming court wished to promote trade for the profit of its merchants, Chinese fleets might have continued to play a dominant role in Indian Ocean trade. But some high Chinese officials opposed increased contact with peoples whom they regarded as barbarians with no real contribution to make to China. Such opposition caused a suspension in the voyages from 1424 to 1431, and after the final expedition of 1432 to 1433, no new fleets were sent out. Later Ming emperors focused their attention on internal matters in their vast empire. China's withdrawal left a power vacuum in the Indian Ocean.

The Atlantic Ocean

The greatest mariners of the Atlantic in the early Middle Ages were the Vikings. These northern European raiders and pirates used their small, open ships to attack coastal European settlements for several centuries. They also discovered and settled one island after another in the North Atlantic during these warmer than usual centuries. Like the Polynesians, the Vikings had neither maps nor navigational devices, but they managed to find their way wonderfully well using their knowledge of the heavens and the seas.

The Vikings first settled Iceland in 770. From there some moved on to Greenland in 982, and by accident one group sighted North America in 986. Fifteen years later Leif Ericsson established a short-lived Viking settlement on the island of Newfoundland, which he called Vinland. When a colder climate returned after 1200, the northern settlements in Greenland went into decline, and Vinland became only a mysterious place mentioned in Norse sagas.

Some southern Europeans also used the maritime skills they had acquired in the Mediterranean and coastal Atlantic to explore the Atlantic. In 1291 two Vivaldo brothers from Genoa set out to sail through the South Atlantic and around Africa to India. They were never heard of again. Other Genoese and Portuguese expeditions into the Atlantic in the fourteenth century discovered (and settled) the islands of Madeira°, the Azores°, and the Canaries.

There is also written evidence of African voyages of exploration in the Atlantic in this period. The celebrated Syrian geographer al-Umari (1301–1349) relates that when Mansa Kankan Musa°, the ruler of the West African empire of Mali, passed through Egypt on his lavish pilgrimage to Mecca in 1324, he told of voyages to cross the Atlantic undertaken by his predecessor, Mansa Muhammad. Muhammad had sent out four hundred vessels with men and supplies, telling them, "Do not return until you have reached the other side of the ocean or if you have exhausted your food or water." After a long time one canoe returned, reporting the others had been swept away by a "violent current in the middle of the sea." Muhammad himself then set out at the head of a second, even larger, expedition, from which no one returned.

In addition to sailing up the Pacific coast, early Amerindian voyagers from South America also colonized the West Indies. By the year 1000 Amerindians known as the **Arawak°** had moved up from the small islands of the Lesser Antilles (Barbados, Martinique, Guadaloupe) and into the Greater Antilles (Cuba, Hispaniola, Jamaica, and Puerto Rico) as well as into the Bahamas (see Map 17.2). Their route was followed in later centuries by the Carib, who by the late fifteenth century had overrun most Arawak settlements in the Lesser Antilles and were raiding parts of the Greater Antilles. From the West Indies Arawak and Carib also undertook voyages to the North American mainland.

Swahili (swah-HEE-lee)

Madeira (muh-DEER-uh)   Azores (A-zorz)
Mansa Kankan Musa (MAHN-suh KAHN-kahn MOO-suh)
Arawak (AR-uh-wahk)

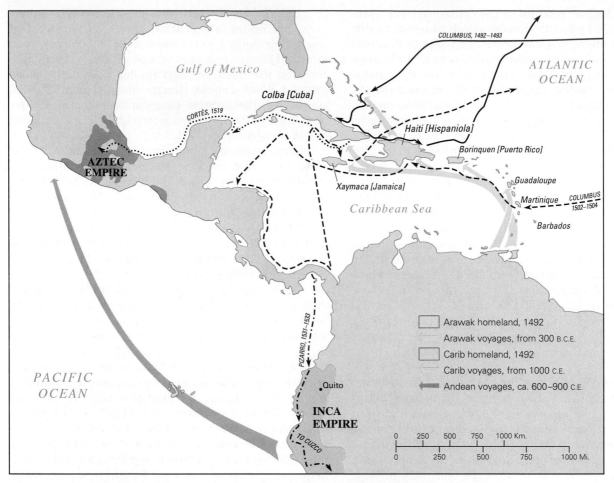

Map 17.2   Middle America to 1533   Early Amerindian voyages from South America brought new settlers to the West Indies and western Mexico. The arrival of Europeans in 1492 soon led to the conquest and depopulation of Amerindians.

EUROPEAN EXPANSION, 1400–1550

The preceding survey shows that maritime expansion occurred in many parts of the world before 1450. The epic sea voyages sponsored by the Iberian kingdoms of Portugal and Spain are of special interest because they began a maritime revolution that profoundly altered the course of world history. The Portuguese and Spanish expeditions ended the isolation of the Americas and increased global interaction. The influence in world affairs of the Iberians and other Europeans who followed them overseas rose steadily in the centuries after 1500.

Iberian overseas expansion was the product of two related phenomena. First, Iberian rulers had strong economic, religious, and political motives to expand their contacts and increase their dominance. Second, improvements in their maritime and military technologies gave them the means to master treacherous and unfamiliar ocean environments, seize control of existing maritime trade routes, and conquer new lands.

Background to European Expansion

Why did Iberian kingdoms decide to sponsor voyages of exploration in the fifteenth century? Part of the answer lies in the individual ambitions and adventurous personalities of these states' leaders. Another part of the answer can be found in long-term tendencies in Europe and the Mediterranean. In many ways these voyages continued four trends evident in the Latin West since about the year 1000: (1) the revival of urban life and trade, (2) a struggle with Islamic powers for dominance of the Mediterranean that mixed religious motives with the desire for trade with distant lands, (3) growing intellectual curiosity about the outside world, and (4) a peculiarly European alliance between merchants and rulers.

The city-states of northern Italy took the lead in all of these developments. By 1450 they had well established trade links to northern Europe, the Indian Ocean, and the Black Sea, and their merchant princes had also sponsored an intellectual and artistic Renaissance. But there were two reasons why Italian states did not take the lead in exploring the Atlantic, even after the expansion of the Ottoman Empire disrupted their trade to the East and led other Christian Europeans to launch new religious wars against the Ottomans in 1396 and 1444. The first was that the trading states of Venice and Genoa preferred to continue the system of alliances with the Muslims that had given their merchants privileged access to the lucrative trade from the East. The second was that the ships of the Mediterranean were ill suited to the more violent weather of the Atlantic. However, many individual Italians played leading roles in the Atlantic explorations.

In contrast, the special history and geography of the Iberian kingdoms led them in a different direction. Part of that special history was centuries of anti-Muslim warfare that dated back to the eighth century when Muslim forces overran most of Iberia. By about 1250 the Iberian kingdoms of Portugal, Castile, and Aragon had conquered all the Muslim lands in Iberia except the southern kingdom of Granada. United by a dynastic marriage in 1469, Castile and Aragon conquered Granada in 1492. These territories were gradually amalgamated into Spain, sixteenth-century Europe's most powerful state.

Christian militancy continued to be an important motive for both Portugal and Spain in their overseas ventures. But the Iberian rulers and their adventurous subjects were also seeking material returns. With only a modest share of the Mediterranean trade, they were much more willing than the Italians to take risks to find new routes through the Atlantic to the rich trades of Africa and Asia. Moreover, both were participants in the shipbuilding changes and the gunpowder revolution that were under way in Atlantic Europe. Though not centers of Renaissance learning, both were especially open to new geographical knowledge. Finally, both states were blessed with exceptional leaders.

Portuguese Voyages

Portugal's decision to invest significant resources in new exploration rested on well-established Atlantic fishing and a history of anti-Muslim warfare. When the Muslim government of Morocco in northwestern Africa showed weakness in the fifteenth century, the Portuguese went on the attack, beginning with the city of Ceuta° in 1415. This assault combined aspects of a religious crusade, a plundering expedition, and a military tournament in which young Portuguese knights displayed their bravery. The capture of this rich North African city, whose splendid homes, they reported, made those of Portugal look like pigsties, also made the Portuguese better informed about the caravans that brought gold and slaves to Ceuta from the African states south of the Sahara. Despite the capture of several more ports along Morocco's Atlantic coast, the Portuguese were unable to push inland and gain access to the gold trade. So they sought more direct contact with the gold producers by sailing down the African coast.

The attack on Ceuta was led by the young Prince Henry (1394–1460), third son of the king of Portugal. Because he devoted the rest of his life to promoting exploration of the South Atlantic, he is known as **Henry the Navigator.** His official biographer emphasized Henry's mixed motives for exploration—converting Africans to Christianity, making contact with existing Christian rulers in Africa, and launching joint crusades with them against the Ottomans. Prince Henry also wished to discover new places and hoped that such new contacts would be profitable. His initial explorations were concerned with Africa. Only later did reaching India become an explicit goal of Portuguese explorers.

Despite being called "the Navigator," Prince Henry himself never ventured much farther from home than North Africa. Instead, he founded a sort of research institute at Sagres° for studying navigation and collecting information about the lands beyond Muslim North Africa. His staff drew on the pioneering efforts of Italian merchants, especially the Genoese, who had learned some of the secrets of the trans-Saharan trade, and of fourteenth-century Jewish cartographers who used information from Arab and European sources to produce remarkably accurate sea charts and maps of distant places. Henry also oversaw the collection of new geographical information from sailors and travelers and sent out ships to explore the Atlantic. His ships established permanent contact with the islands of Madeira in 1418 and the Azores in 1439.

Ceuta (say-OO-tuh)   **Sagres** (SAH-gresh)

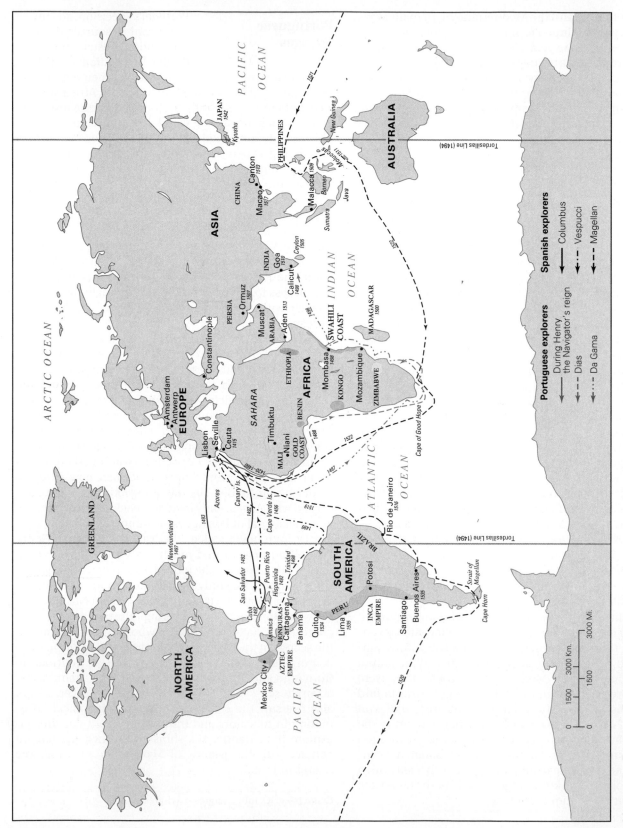

Map 17.3 European Exploration, 1420–1542 Portuguese and Spanish explorers showed the possibility and practicality of inter-continental maritime trade. Before 1540 European trade with Africa and Asia was much more important than that with the Americas, but after the Spanish conquest of the Aztec and Inca Empires transatlantic trade began to increase. Notice the Tordesillas line, which in theory separated the Spanish and Portuguese spheres of activity.

Henry also devoted his resources to solving the technical problems faced by mariners sailing in unknown waters and open seas. His staff studied and improved navigational instruments that had come into Europe from China and the Islamic world. These instruments included the magnetic compass, first developed in China, and the astrolabe, an instrument of Arab or Greek invention that enabled mariners to determine their location at sea by measuring the position of the sun or the stars in the night sky. Even with such instruments, however, voyages still depended most on the skill and experience of the navigators.

Another achievement of Portuguese mariners was the design of vessels appropriate for the voyages of exploration. The galleys in use in the Mediterranean were powered by large numbers of oarsmen and were impractical for long ocean voyages. The square sails of the three-masted European ships of the North Atlantic were propelled by friendly winds but could not sail at much of an angle against the wind. The voyages of exploration made use of a new vessel, the **caravel**°. Caravels were small, only one-fifth the size of the largest European ships of their day and of the large Chinese junks. Their size permitted them to enter shallow coastal waters and explore upriver, but they were strong enough to weather ocean storms. When equipped with lateen sails, caravels had great maneuverability and could sail deeply into the wind; when sporting square Atlantic sails, they had great speed. The addition of small cannon made them good fighting ships as well. The caravels' economy, speed, agility, and power justified a contemporary's claim that they were "the best ships that sailed the seas."[2]

To conquer the seas, pioneering captains had to overcome crew's fears that the South Atlantic waters were boiling hot and contained ocean currents that would prevent any ship entering them from ever returning home. It took Prince Henry fourteen years—from 1420 to 1434—to coax an expedition to venture beyond southern Morocco (see Map 17.3). The crew's fears proved unfounded, but the next stretch of coast, 800 miles (1,300 kilometers) of desert, offered little of interest to the explorers. Finally in 1444 the mariners reached the Senegal River and the well-watered and -populated lands below the Sahara beginning at what they named "Cape Verde" (Green Cape) because of its vegetation.

In the years that followed, Henry's explorers made an important addition to the maritime revolution by learning how to return speedily to Portugal. Instead of battling the prevailing northeast trade winds and currents back up the coast, they discovered that by sailing

Astrolabe   This ancient navigational instrument was critical to the fifteenth-century voyages of exploration because it enabled mariners to find their locations at sea from the angle of the sun above the horizon. This unusually elaborate Italian example is from about 1500. (Museum für Kunst und Gewerbe, Hamburg)

northwest into the Atlantic to the latitude of the Azores, ships could pick up prevailing westerly winds that would blow them back to Portugal. The knowledge that ocean winds tend to form large circular patterns helped explorers discover many other ocean routes.

To pay for the research, the ships, and the expeditions during the many decades before the voyages became profitable, Prince Henry drew partly on the income of the Order of Christ, a military religious order of which he was the governor. The Order of Christ had inherited the properties and crusading traditions of the Order of Knights Templar, which had disbanded in 1314. The Order of Christ received the exclusive right to promote Christianity in all the lands that were discovered, and the Portuguese emblazoned their ships' sails with the crusaders' red cross.

The first financial return from the voyages came from selling into slavery Africans captured by the Portuguese in raids on the northwest coast of Africa and the Canary Islands during the 1440s. The total number of Africans captured or purchased on voyages exceeded eighty thousand by the end of the century and rose steadily thereafter. However, the gold trade quickly became more important than the slave trade as the Portuguese made contact with the trading networks that

---

caravel (KAR-uh-vel)

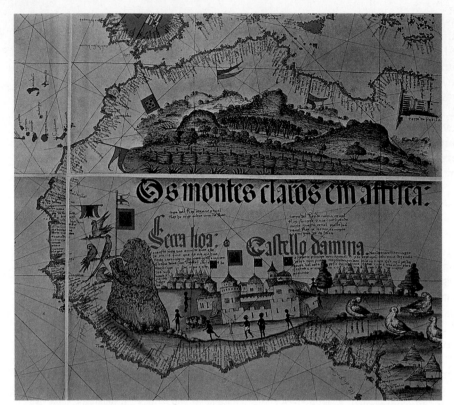

Portuguese Map of Western Africa, 1502 This map shows in great detail a section of African coastline that Portuguese explorers charted and named in the fifteenth century. The cartographer illustrated the African interior, which was almost completely unknown to Europeans, with drawings of birds and views of coastal sights: Sierra Leone (*Serra lioa*), named for a mountain shaped like a lion, and the Portuguese Castle of the Mine (*Castello damina*) on the Gold Coast. (From the American Geographical Society Collection, University of Wisconsin–Milwaukee Library)

flourished in West Africa and reached across the Sahara. By 1457 enough African gold was coming back to Portugal for the kingdom to issue a new gold coin called the *cruzado* (crusade), another reminder of how deeply the Portuguese entwined religious and secular motives.

By the time of Prince Henry's death in 1460, his explorers had established a secure base of operations in the uninhabited Cape Verde Islands, explored 600 miles (950 kilometers) of coast beyond Cape Verde, as far as what they named Sierra Leone° (Lion Mountain). From there they knew the coast of Africa curved sharply toward the east. It had taken the Portuguese four decades to cover the 1,500 miles (2,400 kilometers) from Lisbon to Sierra Leone; it took only three decades to explore the remaining 4,000 miles (6,400 kilometers) to the southern tip of the African continent.

The Portuguese crown continued to sponsor voyages of exploration, but speedier progress resulted from the growing participation of private commercial interests. In 1469 a prominent Lisbon merchant named Fernão Gomes purchased from the Crown the privilege of exploring 350 miles (550 kilometers) of new coast a year for five years in return for a monopoly on the trade he developed there. During the period of his contract, Gomes discovered the uninhabited island of São Tomé° on the equator; in the next century it became a major source of sugar produced with African slave labor. He also explored what later Europeans called the **Gold Coast,** which became the headquarters of Portugal's West African trade.

The final thrust down the African coast was spurred along by the expectation of finding a passage around Africa to the rich trade of the Indian Ocean. **Bartolomeu Dias** was the first Portuguese explorer to round the southern tip of Africa (in 1488) and enter the Indian Ocean. In 1497–1498 a Portuguese expedition led by **Vasco da Gama** sailed around Africa and reached India (see Environment and Technology: Vasco da Gama's Fleet). In 1500 ships in an expedition under Pedro Alvares Cabral°, while swinging wide to the west in the South Atlantic to catch the winds that would sweep them around southern Africa and on to India, came on the eastern coast of South America, laying the basis for Portugal's later claim to Brazil. The gamble that Prince Henry had begun eight decades earlier was about to pay off handsomely.

Sierra Leone (see- ER-uh lee-OWN

São Tomé (sow toh-MAY)   **Cabral** (kah-BRAHL)

Vasco da Gama's Fleet

The four small ships that sailed from Lisbon in June 1497 for India may seem a puny fleet compared to the sixty-two Chinese vessels that Zheng He had led into the Indian Ocean ninety-five years earlier. But given the fact that China had a hundred times as many people as Portugal, Vasco da Gama's fleet represented at least as great a commitment of resources. In any event, the Portuguese expedition had a far greater impact on the course of history. Having achieved its aim of inspiring awe at China's greatness, the Chinese throne sent out no more expeditions after 1432. Although da Gama's ships seemed more odd than awesome to Indian Ocean observers, that modest fleet began a revolution in global relations.

Portugal spared no expense in ensuring that the fleet would make it to India and back. Craftsmen built extra strength into the hulls to withstand storms at the tip of Africa as powerful as the ones Dias had encountered in 1488. Also, small enough to be able to navigate any shallow harbors and rivers they might encounter, the ships were crammed with specially strengthened casks and barrels of water, wine, oil, flour, meat, and vegetables far in excess of

what was required even on a voyage that would take the better part of a year to reach India. Arms and ammunition were also in abundance.

Three of da Gama's ships were rigged with square sails on two masts for speed and a lateen sail on the third mast. The fourth vessel was a caravel with lateen sails. Each ship carried three sets of sails and plenty of extra rigging so as to be able to repair any damages due to storms. The crusaders' red crosses on the sails signaled one of the expedition's motives.

The captains and crew—Portugal's most talented and experienced—received extra pay and other rewards for their service. Yet there was no expectation that the unprecedented sums spent on this expedition would bring any immediate return. According to a contemporary chronicle, the only immediate return the Portuguese monarch received was "the knowledge that some part of Ethiopia and the beginning of Lower India had been discovered." However, the scale and care of the preparations suggest that the Portuguese expected the expedition to open up profitable trade to the Indian Ocean. And so it did.

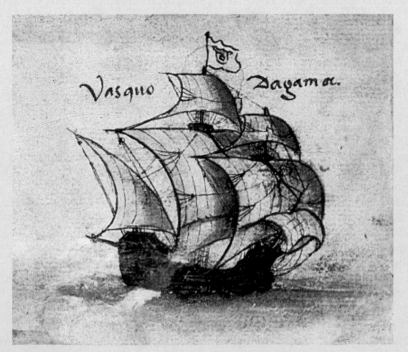

Vasco da Gama's Flagship
This vessel carried the Portuguese captain on his second expedition to India in 1505. (The Pierpont Morgan Library/Art Resource, NY)

Spanish Voyages

Portugal's century-long efforts to explore the South Atlantic are a testimony to planning and persistence. Spain's early discoveries owed more to haste and blind luck. Throughout most of the fifteenth century, the Spanish kingdoms had been preoccupied with internal affairs: completion of the reconquest of southern Iberia; amalgamation of the various dynasties; the conversion or expulsion of religious minorities. Only in the last decade of the century were Spanish monarchs ready to turn again to overseas exploration, by which time the Portuguese had already found a new route to the Indian Ocean.

The leader of their overseas mission would be **Christopher Columbus** (1451–1506), a Genoese mariner. His three voyages between 1492 and 1498 would reveal the existence of vast lands across the Atlantic, whose existence and whose inhabitants were entirely new to the "old world" peoples of Eurasia and Africa. But Columbus was frustrated rather than fulfilled by his momentous discovery, for his intention had been to find a new route to the Indian Ocean even shorter than the one the Portuguese were pioneering.

As a younger man Columbus had gained considerable experience of the South Atlantic while participating in Portuguese explorations along the African coast, but he had become convinced there was a shorter way to reach the riches of the East than the route around Africa. By his reckoning (based on a serious misreading of a ninth-century Arab authority), the Canaries were a mere 2,400 nautical miles (4,450 kilometers) from Japan. The actual distance was five times as far.

It was not easy for Columbus to find a sponsor willing to underwrite the costs of testing his theory that one could reach Asia by sailing west. Portuguese authorities twice rejected his plan, first in 1485 following a careful study and again in 1488 after Dias had established the feasibility of a route around Africa. Columbus received a more sympathetic hearing in 1486 from Castile's able ruler, Queen Isabella, but no commitment of support. After a four-year study a Castilian commission appointed by Isabella concluded that a westward sea route to the Indies rested on many questionable geographical assumptions, but Columbus's persistence finally won over the queen and her husband, King Ferdinand of Aragon. In 1492 they agreed to fund a modest expedition. Their elation at expelling the Muslims from Granada may have put them in a favorable mood.

Columbus recorded in his log that he and his mostly Spanish crew of ninety men "departed Friday the third day of August of the year 1492," toward "the regions of India." Their mission, the royal contract stated, was "to discover and acquire certain islands and mainland in the Ocean Sea." He carried letters of introduction from the Spanish sovereigns to Eastern rulers, including one to the "Grand Khan" (meaning the Chinese emperor). Also on board was a Jewish convert to Christianity whose knowledge of Arabic was expected to facilitate communication with the peoples of eastern Asia. The expedition traveled in three small ships, the *Santa María*, and two caravels, the *Santa Clara* (nicknamed the *Niña*), and a third vessel now known only by its nickname, the *Pinta*.

The expedition began well. Other attempts to explore the Atlantic west of the Azores had been impeded by unfavorable headwinds. But on earlier voyages along the African coast, Columbus had learned that he could find west-blowing winds in the latitudes of the Canaries, which is why he chose that southern route. After reaching the Canaries, he had the *Niña*'s lateen sails replaced with square sails, for he knew that from then on speed would be more important than maneuverability.

In October 1492 the expedition reached the islands of the Caribbean. Columbus insisted on calling the inhabitants "Indians" because he believed that the islands were part of the East Indies. A second voyage to the Caribbean in 1493 did nothing to change his mind. Even when, two months after Vasco da Gama reached India in 1498, Columbus first sighted the mainland of South America on a third voyage, he stubbornly insisted it was part of Asia. But by then other Europeans were convinced he had discovered islands and continents previously unknown to the Old World. Amerigo Vespucci's explorations, first on behalf of Spain and then for Portugal, led mapmakers to name the new continents "America" after him, rather than "Columbia" after Columbus.

To prevent disputes arising from their efforts to exploit their new discoveries and to spread Christianity among the people there, Spain and Portugal agreed to split the world between them. The Treaty of Tordesillas°, negotiated by the pope in 1494, drew an imaginary line down the middle of the North Atlantic Ocean. Lands east of the line in Africa and southern Asia could be claimed by Portugal; lands to the west in the Americas were reserved for Spain. Cabral's discovery of Brazil, however, gave Portugal a valid claim to the part of South America that bulged east of the line.

But if the Tordesillas line were extended around the earth, where would Spain's and Portugal's spheres of influence divide in the East? Given Europeans' ignorance of the earth's true size in 1494, it was not clear whether the Moluccas°, whose valuable spices had been a goal of the Iberian voyages, were on Portugal's or Spain's side of the line. The missing information concerned the size

---

Tordesillas (tor-duh-SEE-yuhs)   **Moluccas** (muh-LOO-kuhz)

of the Pacific Ocean. By chance, in 1513 a Spanish adventurer named Vasco Núñez de Balboa° crossed the isthmus (a narrow neck of land) of Panama from the east and sighted the Pacific Ocean on the other side. And the 1519 expedition of **Ferdinand Magellan** (ca. 1480–1521) was designed to complete Columbus's interrupted westward voyage by sailing around the Americas and across the Pacific, whose vast size no European then guessed. The Moluccas turned out to lie well within Portugal's sphere, as Spain formally acknowledged in 1529.

Magellan's voyage laid the basis for Spanish colonization of the Philippine Islands after 1564. Nor did Magellan's death prevent him from being considered the first person to encircle the globe, for a decade earlier he had sailed from Europe to the East Indies as part of an expedition sponsored by his native Portugal. His two voyages took him across the Tordesillas line, through the separate spheres claimed by Portugal and Spain—at least until other Europeans began demanding a share. Of course, in the year 1500 European claims were largely theoretical. Portugal and Spain had only modest settlements overseas.

Although Columbus failed to find a new route to the East, the consequences of his voyages for European expansion were momentous. Those who followed in his wake laid the basis for Spain's large colonial empires in the Americas and for the empires of other European nations. In turn, these empires promoted, among the four Atlantic continents, the growth of a major new trading network whose importance rivaled and eventually surpassed that of the Indian Ocean network. The more immediately important consequence was Portugal's entry into the Indian Ocean, which quickly led to a major European presence and profit. Both the eastward and the westward voyages of exploration marked a tremendous expansion of Europe's role in world history.

♪

ENCOUNTERS WITH EUROPE, 1450–1550

European actions alone did not determine the consequences of the new contacts that Iberian mariners had opened. The ways in which Africans, Asians, and Amerindians perceived their new visitors and interacted with them also influenced their future relations. Some welcomed the Europeans as potential allies; others viewed them as rivals or enemies. In general, Africans and Asians had little difficulty in recognizing the benefits and dangers that European contacts might bring. However, the long isolation of the Amerindians from the rest of the world added to the strangeness of their encounter with the Spanish and made them more vulnerable to the unfamiliar diseases that these explorers inadvertently introduced.

Western Africa

Many Africans along the West African coast were eager for trade with the Portuguese. It would give them new markets for their exports and access to imports cheaper than those that reached them through the middlemen of the overland routes to the Mediterranean. This reaction was evident along the Gold Coast of West Africa, first visited by the Portuguese in 1471. Miners in the hinterland had long sold their gold to African traders, who took it to the trading cities along the southern edge of the Sahara, where it was sold to traders who had crossed the desert from North Africa. Recognizing that they might get more favorable terms from the new sea visitors, coastal Africans were ready to negotiate with the royal representative of Portugal who arrived in 1482 seeking permission to erect a trading fort.

The Portuguese noble in charge and his officers (likely including the young Christopher Columbus, who had entered Portuguese service in 1476) were eager to make a proper impression. They dressed in their best clothes, erected and decorated a reception platform, celebrated a Catholic Mass, and signaled the start of negotiations with trumpets, tambourines, and drums. The African king, Caramansa, staged his entrance with equal ceremony, arriving with a large retinue of attendants and musicians. Through an African interpreter, the two leaders exchanged flowery speeches pledging goodwill and mutual benefit. Caramansa then gave his permission for a small trading fort to be built, assured, he said, by the appearance of these royal delegates that they were honorable persons, unlike the "few, foul, and vile" Portuguese visitors of the previous decade.

Neither side made a show of force, but the Africans' upper hand was evident in Caramansa's warning that if the Portuguese failed to be peaceful and honest traders, he and his people would simply move away, depriving their post of food and trade. Trade at the post of Saint George of the Mine (later called Elmina) enriched both sides. From there the Portuguese crown was soon purchasing gold equal to one-tenth of the world's production at the time. In return, Africans received large quantities of goods that Portuguese ships brought from Asia, Europe, and other parts of Africa.

Balboa (bal-BOH-uh)

Afro–Portuguese Ivory   A skilled ivory carver from the kingdom of Benin probably made this saltcellar. Intended for a European market, it depicts a Portuguese ship on the cover and Portuguese nobles around the base. However European the subject, the craftsmanship is typical of Benin. (Courtesy of the Trustees of the British Museum)

Early contacts generally involved a mixture of commercial, military, and religious interests. Some African rulers were quick to appreciate that the European firearms could be a useful addition to their spears and arrows in conflicts with their enemies. Because African religions did not presume to have a monopoly on religious knowledge, coastal rulers were also willing to test the value of Christian practices, which the Portuguese eagerly promoted. The rulers of Benin and Kongo, the two largest coastal kingdoms, invited Portuguese missionaries and soldiers to accompany them into battle to test the Christians' religion along with their muskets.

After a century of aggressive expansion, the kingdom of Benin in the Niger Delta was near the peak of its power when it first encountered the Portuguese. Its oba (king) presided over an elaborate bureaucracy from a spacious palace in his large capital city, also known as Benin. In response to a Portuguese visit in 1486, the oba sent an ambassador to Portugal to learn more about the homeland of these strangers. Then he established a royal monopoly on trade with the Portuguese, selling pepper and ivory tusks (to be taken back to Portugal) as well as stone beads, textiles, and prisoners of war (to be resold at Elmina). In return, the Portuguese merchants provided Benin with copper and brass, fine textiles, glass beads, and a horse for the king's royal procession. In the early sixteenth century, as the demand for slaves for the Portuguese sugar plantations on the nearby island of São Tomé grew, the oba first raised the price of slaves and then imposed restrictions that limited their sale.

Portuguese efforts to persuade the king and nobles of Benin to accept the Catholic faith ultimately failed. Early kings showed some interest, but after 1538 the rulers declined to receive further missionaries. They also closed the market in male slaves for the rest of the sixteenth century. Exactly why Benin chose to limit its contacts with the Portuguese is uncertain, but the rulers clearly had the power to control how much interaction they wanted.

Farther south, on the lower Congo River, relations between the kingdom of Kongo and the Portuguese began similarly but had a quite different outcome. Like the oba of Benin, the *manikongo*° (king of Kongo) sent delegates to Portugal, established a royal monopoly on trade with the Portuguese, and expressed interest in missionary teachings. Deeply impressed with the new religion, the royal family made Catholicism the kingdom's official faith. But Kongo, lacking ivory and pepper, had less to trade than Benin. So to acquire the goods brought by Portugal and to pay the costs of the missionaries, it had to sell more and more slaves.

Soon the manikongo began to lose his royal monopoly over the slave trade. In 1526 the Christian manikongo, Afonso I (r. 1506–ca. 1540), wrote to his royal "brother," the king of Portugal, begging for his help in stopping the trade because unauthorized Kongolese were kidnapping and selling people, even members of good families. Afonso's appeal that contacts be limited to "some priests and a few people to teach in the schools, and no other goods except wine and flour for the holy sacrament" received no reply. Other subjects took advantage of the manikongo's weakness to rebel against his authority. Indeed, after 1540 the major part of the slave trade from this part of Africa moved farther south.

---

manikongo (mah-NEE-KONG-goh)

Eastern Africa

Different still were the reactions of the Muslim rulers of the trading coastal states of eastern Africa. As Vasco da Gama's fleet sailed up the coast in 1498, most rulers gave the Portuguese a cool reception, suspicious of the intentions of these visitors who painted crusaders' crosses on their sails. But the ruler of one of the cities, Malindi, saw in the Portuguese an ally who could help him expand their trading position and provided da Gama with a pilot to guide him to India. The suspicions of most rulers were justified seven years later when a Portuguese war fleet bombarded and looted most of the coastal cities of eastern Africa in the name of Christ and commerce, though they spared Malindi.

Another eastern African state that saw potential benefit in an alliance with the Portuguese was Christian Ethiopia. In the fourteenth and early fifteenth centuries, Ethiopia faced increasing conflicts with Muslim states along the Red Sea. Emboldened by the rise of the Ottoman Turks, who had conquered Egypt in 1517 and launched a major fleet in the Indian Ocean to counter the Portuguese, the talented warlord of the Muslim state of Adal launched a furious assault on Ethiopia. Adal's decisive victory in 1529 reduced the Christian kingdom to a precarious state. At that point Ethiopia's contacts with the Portuguese became crucial.

For decades, delegations from Portugal and Ethiopia had been exploring a possible alliance between their states based on their mutual adherence to Christianity. A key figure was Queen Helena of Ethiopia, who acted as regent for her young sons after her husband's death in 1478. In 1509 Helena sent a letter to "our very dear and well-beloved brother," the king of Portugal, along with a gift of two tiny crucifixes said to be made of wood from the cross on which Christ had died in Jerusalem. In her letter she proposed an alliance of her land army and Portugal's fleet against the Turks. No such alliance was completed by the time Helena died in 1522. But as Ethiopia's situation grew increasingly desperate, renewed appeals for help were made.

Finally a small Portuguese force commanded by Vasco da Gama's son Christopher reached Ethiopia in 1539, at a time when what was left of the empire was being held together by another woman ruler. With Portuguese help the queen rallied the Ethiopians to renew their struggle. Christopher da Gama was captured and tortured to death, but the Muslim forces lost heart when their leader was mortally wounded in a later battle. Portuguese aid helped the Ethiopian kingdom save itself from extinction, but a permanent alliance faltered because Ethiopian rulers refused to transfer their Christian affiliation from the patriarch of Alexandria to the Latin patriarch of Rome (the pope) as the Portuguese wanted.

As these examples illustrate, African encounters with the Portuguese before 1550 varied considerably, as much because of the strategies and leadership of particular African states as because of Portuguese policies. Africans and Portuguese might become royal brothers, bitter opponents, or partners in a mutually profitable trade, but Europeans remained a minor presence in most of Africa in 1550. By then the Portuguese had become far more interested in the Indian Ocean trade.

Indian Ocean States

Vasco da Gama's arrival on the Malabar Coast of India in May 1498 did not make a great impression on the citizens of Calicut. After more than ten months at sea, many members of the crew were in ill health. And da Gama's four small ships were far less imposing than the Chinese fleets of gigantic junks that had called at Calicut sixty-five years earlier and no larger than many of the dhows that filled the harbor of this rich and important trading city. The *samorin* (ruler) of Calicut and his Muslim officials showed mild interest in the Portuguese as new trading partners, but the gifts da Gama had brought for the samorin evoked derisive laughter. Twelve pieces of fairly ordinary striped cloth, four scarlet hoods, six hats, and six wash basins seemed inferior goods to those accustomed to the luxuries of the Indian Ocean trade. When da Gama tried to defend his gifts as those of an explorer, not a rich merchant, the samorin cut him short, asking whether he had come to discover men or stones: "If he had come to discover men, as he said, why had he brought nothing?"

Coastal rulers soon discovered that the Portuguese had no intention of remaining poor competitors in the rich trade of the Indian Ocean. Upon da Gama's return to Portugal in 1499 the jubilant King Manuel styled himself "Lord of the Conquest, Navigation, and Commerce of Ethiopia, Arabia, Persia, and India," setting forth the ambitious scope of his plans. Previously the Indian Ocean had been an open sea, used by merchants (and pirates) of all the surrounding coasts. Now the Portuguese crown intended to make it Portugal's sea, the private property of the Portuguese alone, which others might use only on Portuguese terms.

The ability of little Portugal to assert control over the Indian Ocean stemmed from the superiority of its ships and weapons over the smaller and lightly armed merchant dhows. In 1505 the Portuguese fleet of 81 ships and some 7,000 men bombarded Swahili Coast cities. Next on the list were Indian ports. Goa, on the west coast of India, fell to a well-armed fleet in 1510, becoming the base from which the Portuguese menaced the trading

Portuguese in India   In the sixteenth century Portuguese men moved to the Indian Ocean basin to work as administrators and traders. This Indo-Portuguese drawing from about 1540 shows a Portuguese man speaking to an Indian woman, perhaps making a proposal of marriage. (Ms. 1889, c. 97, Biblioteca Casanateunse Rome. Photo: Humberto Nicoletti Serra)

cities of Gujarat° to the north and Calicut and other Malabar Coast cities to the south. The port of Hormuz, controlling the entry to the Persian Gulf, was taken in 1515. Aden, at the entrance to the Red Sea, with its intricate natural defenses was able to preserve its independence. The addition of the Gujarati port of Diu in 1535 consolidated Portuguese dominance of the western Indian Ocean.

Meanwhile, Portuguese explorers had been reconnoitering the Bay of Bengal and the waters farther east. The independent city of Malacca° on the strait between the Malay Peninsula and Sumatra became the focus of their attention. During the fifteenth century Malacca had become the main entrepôt° (a place where goods are stored or deposited and from which they are distributed) for the trade from China and Japan, from India, and from the Southeast Asian mainland and the Moluccas. Among the city's more than 100,000 residents an early Portuguese counted eighty-four different languages, including those of merchants from as far west as Cairo, Ethiopia, and the Swahili Coast of East Africa. Many non-Muslim residents supported letting the Portuguese join this cosmopolitan trading community, perhaps to offset the growing solidarity of Muslim traders. In

1511, however, the Portuguese seized this strategic trading center with a force of a thousand fighting men, including three hundred recruited in southern India.

Force was not always necessary. On the China coast local officials and merchants interested in profitable new trade with the Portuguese persuaded the imperial government to allow the Portuguese to establish a trading post at Macao° in 1557. Operating from Macao, Portuguese ships nearly monopolized the trade between China and Japan.

In the Indian Ocean the Portuguese used their control of the major port cities to enforce an even larger trading monopoly. They required all spices to be carried in Portuguese ships, as well as all goods on the major ocean routes such as between Goa and Macao. In addition, the Portuguese also tried to control and tax other Indian Ocean trade by requiring all merchant ships entering and leaving one of their ports to carry a Portuguese passport and to pay customs duties. Portuguese patrols seized vessels that attempted to avoid these monopolies, confiscated their cargoes, and either killed the captain and crew or sentenced them to forced labor.

Reactions to this power grab varied. Like the emperors of China, the Mughal° emperors of India largely ignored Portugal's maritime intrusions, seeing their interests as maintaining control over their vast land possessions. The Ottomans responded more aggressively. From 1501 to 1509 they supported Egypt's fleet of fifteen thousand men against the Christian intruders. Then, having absorbed Egypt into their empire, the Ottomans sent another large expedition against the Portuguese in 1538. Both expeditions failed because the Ottoman galleys were no match for the faster, better-armed Portuguese vessels in the open ocean. However, the Ottomans retained the advantage in the Red Sea and Persian Gulf, where they had many ports of supply.

The smaller trading states of the region were even less capable of challenging Portuguese domination head on, since their mutual rivalry impeded the formation of any common front. Some chose to cooperate with the Portuguese as the best way to maintain their prosperity and security. Others engaged in evasion and resistance. Two examples illustrate the range of responses among Indian Ocean peoples.

The merchants of Calicut put up some of the most sustained local resistance. In retaliation the Portuguese embargoed all trade with Aden, Calicut's principal trading partner, and centered their trade on the port of Cochin, which had once been a dependency of Calicut. Some Calicut merchants became adept at evading the

---

Gujarat (goo-juh-RAHT)   **Malacca** (muh-LAH-kuh)
entrepôt (ON-truh-poh)

Macao (muh-COW)   **Mughal** (MOO-gahl)

patrol, but the price of resistance was the shrinking of Calicut's importance as Cochin gradually became the major pepper-exporting port on the Malabar Coast.

The traders and rulers of the state of Gujarat farther north had less success in keeping the Portuguese at bay. At first they resisted Portuguese attempts at monopoly and in 1509 joined Egypt's failed effort to sweep the Portuguese from the Arabian Sea. But in 1535, finding his state at a military disadvantage due to Mughal attacks, the ruler of Gujarat made the fateful decision to allow the Portuguese to build a fort at Diu in return for their support. Once established, the Portuguese gradually extended their control, so that by midcentury they were licensing and taxing all Gujarati ships. Even after the Mughals (who were Muslims) took control of Gujarat in 1572, the Mughal emperor Akbar permitted the Portuguese to continue their maritime monopoly in return for allowing one pilgrim ship a year to sail to Mecca without paying the Portuguese any fee.

The Portuguese never gained complete control of the Indian Ocean trade, but their domination of key ports and the main trade routes during the sixteenth century brought them considerable profit, which they sent back to Europe in the form of spices and other luxury goods. The effects were dramatic. The Portuguese sold the large quantities of pepper that they exported for less than the price charged by Venice and Genoa for pepper obtained through Egyptian middlemen, thus breaking the Italian cities' monopoly.

In Asia the consequences were equally startling. Asian and East African traders were at the mercy of Portuguese warships, but their individual responses affected their fates. Some were devastated. Others prospered by meeting the Portuguese demands or evading their patrols. Because the Portuguese were ocean-based, they had little impact on the Asian and African mainland, in sharp contrast to what was occurring in the Americas.

The Americas

In the Americas the Spanish established a vast *territorial* empire, in contrast to the *trading* empires the Portuguese created in Africa and Asia. This outcome had little to do with differences between the two Iberian kingdoms, except for the fact that the Spanish kingdoms had somewhat greater resources to draw on. The Spanish and Portuguese monarchies had similar motives for expansion and used identical ships and weapons. Rather, the isolation of the Amerindian peoples made their responses to outside contacts different from the responses of peoples in Africa and the Indian Ocean cities. In dealing with the small communities in the Caribbean, the first European settlers resorted to conquest and plunder rather than trade. This practice was later extended to the more powerful Amerindian kingdoms on the American mainland. The spread of deadly new diseases among the Amerindians after 1518 weakened their ability to resist.

The first Amerindians to encounter Columbus were the Arawak of Hispaniola (modern Haiti and the Dominican Republic) in the Greater Antilles and the Bahamas to the north (see Map 17.2). They cultivated maize (corn), cassava (a tuber), sweet potatoes, and hot peppers, as well as cotton and tobacco, and they met their other material needs from the sea and wild plants. Although they were skilled at mining and working gold, the Arawak did not trade gold over long distances as Africans did, and they had no iron. The Arawak at first extended a cautious welcome to the Spanish but were unprepared to sell them large quantities of gold. Instead, they told Columbus exaggerated stories about gold in other places to persuade him to move on.

When Columbus made his second trip to Hispaniola, in 1493, he brought with him several hundred settlers from southern Iberia who hoped to make their fortune and missionaries who were eager to persuade the Indians to accept Christianity. The settlers stole gold

Arawak Women Making Tortillas   This sixteenth-century woodcut depicts techniques of food preparation in the West Indies. The woman at the left grinds cornmeal on a *metate*. The woman in the center pats cornmeal dough flat and fries the tortillas. The third woman serves tortillas with a bowl of stew. (Courtesy of the John Carter Brown Library at Brown University)

European Male Sexual Dominance Overseas

European expansion and colonization were overwhelmingly the work of men. Missionaries chose to remain celibate; other men did not, as these two letters make clear. The first letter, dated 1495, is from Michele de Cuneo, an officer on Columbus's second voyage across the Atlantic.

While I was in the boat I captured a very beautiful Carib woman, whom the said Lord Admiral [Columbus] gave to me, and with whom, having taken her into my cabin, she being naked according to their custom, I conceived desire to take pleasure. I wanted to put my desire into execution but she did not want it and treated me with her finger nails in such a manner that I wished I had never begun. But seeing that, (to tell you the end of it all), I took a rope and thrashed her well, for which she raised such unheard of screams that you would not have believed your ears. Finally we came to an agreement in such manner that I can tell you that she seemed to have been brought up in a school of harlots.

The second letter, dated 1550, is from an Italian Jesuit missionary in India to Ignatius Loyola, the founder of the Society of Jesus (the Jesuits), in Rome.

Your reverence must know that the sin of licentiousness is so widespread in these regions [India] that no check is placed upon it, which leads to great inconveniences, and to great disrespect of the sacraments. I say this of the Portuguese, who have adopted the vices and customs of the land without reserve, including the evil custom of buying droves of slaves, male and female, just as if they were sheep, large and small. There are countless men who buy droves of girls and sleep with all of them, and subsequently sell them. There are innumerable married settlers who have four, eight, or ten female slaves and sleep with them, as is common knowledge. This is carried to such excess that there was one man in Malacca who had twenty-four women of various races, all of whom were his slaves, and all of whom he enjoyed. I quote this city because it is a thing that everybody knows. Most men, as soon as they can afford to buy a female slave, almost invariably use her as a girl-friend (*amiga*), besides many other dishonesties, in my poor understanding.

What circumstances made it nearly impossible for the women in question to resist the European men's advances? What phrases in the letters suggest that the writers attribute some responsibility for these encounters to the sexual license of the women involved? Are such inferences credible?

Source: The first letter is reprinted from Samuel Eliot Morison, trans. and ed., *Journals and Other Documents in the Life and Voyages of Christopher Columbus* (New York: Heritage Press, 1963), 212. The second letter is from C. R. Boxer, *The Portuguese Seaborne Empire, 1415–1825* (New York: Knopf, 1969). Copyright © 1969 by C. R. Boxer. Reprinted by permission of Alfred A. Knopf, Inc.

---

ornaments, confiscated food, and raped women (see Society and Culture: European Male Sexual Dominance Overseas), provoking the Hispaniola Arawak to war in 1495. In this and later conflicts, horses and body armor gave the Spaniards a great advantage. Tens of thousands of Arawak were slaughtered. Those who survived were forced to pay a heavy tax in gold, spun cotton, and food. Any who failed to meet the quotas were condemned to forced labor. Meanwhile, the cattle, pigs, and goats introduced by the settlers devoured the Arawak's food crops, causing deaths from famine and disease. A governor appointed by the Spanish crown in 1502 forced the Arawak remaining on Hispaniola to be laborers under the control of Spanish settlers.

The actions of the Spanish in the Antilles were reflections of Spanish actions and motives during the wars against the Muslims in Spain in the previous centuries: seeking to serve God by defeating nonbelievers and placing them under Christian control—and becoming rich in the process. Individual **conquistadors**° (conquerors) extended that pattern around the Caribbean. Some attacked the Bahamas to get gold and labor as

---

conquistador (kon-KEY-stuh-dor)

Coronation of Emperor Moctezuma
This painting by an unnamed Aztec artist depicts the Aztec ruler's coronation. Moctezuma, his nose pierced by a bone, receives the crown from a prince in the palace at Tenochtitlan. (Oronz)

both became scarce on Hispaniola. Many Arawak from the Bahamas were taken to Hispaniola as slaves. Juan Ponce de León (1460–1521), who had participated in the conquest of Muslim Spain and the seizure of Hispaniola, conquered the island of Borinquen (Puerto Rico) in 1508 and then in 1513 explored southeastern Florida.

An ambitious and ruthless nobleman, **Hernán Cortés°** (1485–1547), led the most audacious expedition to the mainland. Cortés left Cuba in 1519 with six hundred fighting men and most of the island's stock of weapons to assault the Mexican mainland in search of slaves and to establish trade. But when the expedition learned of the rich Aztec Empire in central Mexico, Cortés brought to the American mainland, on a massive scale, the exploitation and conquest that had begun in the Greater Antilles.

The Aztecs themselves had conquered their vast empire only during the pervious century, and many of the Amerindians they had subjugated were far from loyal subjects. Many resented the tribute they had to pay the Aztecs, the forced labor, and the large-scale human sacrifices to the Aztec gods. Many subject people saw the Spaniards as powerful human allies against the Aztecs and gave them their support. Like the Caribbean people, the Amerindians of Mexico had no precedent by which to judge these strange visitors.

Later accounts suggest that some believed Cortés to be the legendary ruler Quetzalcoatl°, whose return to earth had been prophesied, and treated him with great deference. Another consequence of millennia of isolation was far more significant: the lack of acquired immunity to the diseases of the Old World. Smallpox was the most deadly of the early epidemics that accompanied the Spanish conquistadores. It appeared for the first time on the island of Hispaniola late in 1518. An infected member of the Cortés expedition then transmitted smallpox to Mexico in 1519, where it spread with deadly efficiency.

From his glorious capital city Tenochtitlan°, the Aztec emperor **Moctezuma° II** (r. 1502–1520) sent messengers to greet Cortés and figure out whether he was god or man, friend or foe. Cortés advanced steadily toward the capital, Tenochtitlan, overcoming Aztec opposition with cavalry charges and steel swords and gaining the support of thousands of Amerindian allies from among the unhappy subjects of the Aztecs. When the Spaniards were near, the emperor went out in a great procession, dressed in all his finery, to welcome Cortés with gifts and flower garlands.

Cortés (kor-TEZ)

Quetzalcoatl (ket-zahl-COH-ah-tal)
Tenochtitlan (teh-noch-TIT-lan)
Moctezuma (mock-teh-ZOO-ma)

Despite Cortés's initial promise that he came in friendship, Moctezuma quickly found himself a prisoner in his own palace. His treasury was looted, its gold melted down. Soon a battle was raging in and about the capital between the Spaniards (helped by their new Amerindian allies) and the Aztecs and their supporters. Briefly the Aztecs gained the upper hand. They destroyed half of the Spanish force and four thousand of the Spaniards' Amerindian allies, and they sacrificed to their gods fifty-three Spanish prisoners and four horses, displaying their severed heads in rows on pikes. Reinforced by troops from Cuba, Cortés was able to regain the advantage by means of Spanish cannon and clever battle strategies. The capture of Tenochtitlan in 1520 was also greatly facilitated by the spread of smallpox, which weakened and killed more of the city's defenders than died in the fighting. One source remembered that the disease "spread over the people as a great destruction." The bodies of the afflicted were covered with oozing sores, and large numbers soon died. It is likely that many Amerindians as well as Europeans saw the devastating spread of this disease as due to supernatural forces.

After the capital fell, the conquistadores took over other parts of Mexico. Then some Spaniards began eyeing the vast Inca Empire, stretching nearly 3,000 miles (5,000 kilometers) south from the equator and containing half of the population in South America. The Inca had conquered the inhabitants of the Andes Mountains and the Pacific coast of South America during the previous century, and their rule was not fully accepted by all of the peoples whom they had defeated.

With the vast Pacific Ocean on one side of their realm and the sparsely inhabited Amazon forests on the other, it is not surprising that Inca rulers believed they controlled most of the world worth controlling. Theirs was a great empire with highly productive agriculture, exquisite stone cities (such as the capital, Cuzco), and rich gold and silver mines. The power of the Inca emperor was sustained by beliefs that he was descended from the Sun God and by an efficient system of roads and messengers that kept him informed about major events in the empire. Yet all was not well.

At the end of the 1520s, before even a whisper of news about the Spanish reached them, smallpox claimed countless Amerindian lives, perhaps including the Inca emperor in 1530. Even more devastating was the threat awaiting the empire from **Francisco Pizarro°** (ca. 1478–1541) and his motley band of 180 men, 37 horses, and two cannon.

With limited education and some military experience, Pizarro had come to the Americas in 1502 at the age of twenty-five to seek his fortune. He had participated in the conquest of Hispaniola and in Balboa's expedition across the isthmus of Panama. By 1520 Pizarro was a wealthy landowner and official in Panama, yet he gambled his fortune on more adventures, exploring the Pacific coast to a point south of the equator, where he learned of the riches of the Inca. With a license from the king of Spain, he set out from Panama in 1531 to conquer them.

In November 1532 Pizarro arranged to meet the new Inca emperor, **Atahualpa°** (r. 1531–1533), near the Andean city of Cajamarca°. With supreme boldness and brutality, Pizarro's small band of armed men seized Atahualpa off a rich litter borne by eighty nobles as it passed through an enclosed courtyard. Though surrounded by an Inca army of at least forty thousand, the Spaniards were able to use their cannon to create confusion while their swords sliced the emperor's lightly armed retainers and servants to pieces by the thousands. The strategy to replicate the earlier Spanish conquest of Mexico was working.

Noting the glee with which the Spaniards seized gold, silver, and emeralds, the captive Atahualpa offered them what he thought would satisfy even the greediest among them in exchange for his freedom: a roomful of gold and silver. But when the ransom of 13,400 pounds (6,000 kilograms) of gold and 26,000 pounds (12,000 kilograms) of silver was paid, the Spaniards gave Atahualpa a choice: he could be burned at the stake as a heathen or baptized as a Christian and then strangled. He chose the latter. His death and the Spanish occupation broke the unity of the Inca Empire.

In 1533 the Spaniards took Cuzco and from there set out to conquer and loot the rest of the empire. The defeat of a final rebellion in 1536 spelled the end of Inca rule. Five years later Pizarro himself met a violent death at the hands of Spanish rivals, but the conquest of the mainland continued. Incited by the fabulous wealth of the Aztecs and Inca, conquistadores extended Spanish conquest and exploration in South and North America, dreaming of new treasuries to loot.

Patterns of Dominance

Within fifty years of Columbus's first landing in 1492, the Spanish had located and occupied all of the major population centers of the Americas, and the penetration of the more thinly populated areas was well under way. In no

Pizarro (pih-ZAHR-oh)

Atahualpa (ah-tuh-WAHL-puh)
Cajamarca (kah-hah-MAHR-kah)

other part of the world was European dominance so complete. Why did the peoples of the Americas suffer a fate so different from that of peoples in Africa and Asia? Why were the Spanish able to erect a vast land empire in the Americas so quickly? Three factors seem crucial.

First, long isolation from the rest of humanity made the inhabitants of the Americas vulnerable to new diseases. The unfamiliar illnesses first devastated the native inhabitants of the Caribbean islands and then spread to the mainland. Contemporaries estimated that between 25 and 50 percent of those infected with smallpox died. Repeated epidemics inhibited Amerindians' ability to regain control. Because evidence is very limited, estimates of the size of the population before Columbus's arrival vary widely, but there is no disputing the fact that the Amerindian population fell sharply during the sixteenth century. The Americas became a "widowed land," open to resettlement from across the Atlantic.

A second major factor was Spain's superior military technology. Steel swords, protective armor, and horses gave the Spaniards an advantage over their Amerindian opponents in many battles. Though few in number, muskets and cannon also gave the Spaniards a significant psychological edge. However, it should not be forgotten that the Spanish conquests depended heavily on large numbers of Amerindian allies armed with weapons the same as those of the people they defeated. But perhaps the Spaniards' most decisive military advantage came from the no-holds-barred fighting techniques they had developed during a long history of warfare at home.

The third factor in Spain's conquest of the New World was patterns previously established in the Spanish reconquest of Granada in 1492. The reconquest provided precedents for forced labor, forced conversion, and the incorporation of conquered lands into a new empire.

The same three factors help explain the quite different outcomes elsewhere. Because of centuries of contacts before 1500, Europeans, Africans, and Asians shared the same Old World diseases. Only small numbers of very isolated peoples in Africa and Asia suffered the demographic calamity that undercut Amerindians' ability to retain control of their lands. The Iberians enjoyed a military advantage at sea, as the conquest of the Indian Ocean trade routes showed, but on land they had no decisive advantage against more numerous indigenous people who were not weakened by disease. Everywhere, Iberian religious zeal to conquer non-Christians went hand in hand with a desire for riches. In Iberia and America conquest brought wealth. But in Africa and Asia, where existing trading networks were already well established, Iberian desire for wealth from trade restrained or negated the impulse to conquer.

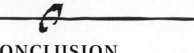

CONCLUSION

Historians agree that the century between 1450 and 1550 was a major turning point in world history. It was the beginning of an age to which they have given various names: the "Vasco da Gama epoch," the "Columbian era," the "age of Magellan," or simply the "modern period." During those years European explorers opened new long-distance trade routes across the world's three major oceans, for the first time establishing regular contact among all the continents. By 1550 those who followed them had broadened trading contacts with sub-Saharan Africa, gained mastery of the rich trade routes of the Indian Ocean, and conquered a vast land empire in the Americas.

As dramatic and momentous as these events were, they were not completely unprecedented. The riches of the Indian Ocean trade that brought a gleam to the eye of many Europeans had been developed over many centuries by the trading peoples who inhabited the surrounding lands. European conquests of the Americas were no more rapid or brutal than the earlier Mongol conquests of Eurasia. Even the crossing of the Pacific had been done before, though in stages.

What gave this maritime revolution unprecedented importance had more to do with what happened after 1550 than with what happened earlier. Europeans' overseas empires would endure longer than the Mongols' and would continue to expand for three-and-a-half centuries after 1550. Unlike the Chinese, the Europeans did not turn their backs on the world after an initial burst of exploration. Not content with dominance in the Indian Ocean trade, Europeans opened in the Atlantic a maritime network that grew to rival the Indian Ocean network in the wealth of its trade. They also pioneered regular trade across the Pacific. The maritime expansion begun in the period from 1450 to 1550 marked the beginning of a new age of growing global interaction.

■ Key Terms

Zheng He	**Christopher Columbus**
Arawak	**Ferdinand Magellan**
Henry the Navigator	**conquistadors**
caravel	**Hernán Cortés**
Gold Goast	**Moctezuma**
Bartolomeu Dias	**Francisco Pizarro**
Vasco da Gama	**Atahualpa**

■ Suggested Reading

There is no single survey of the different expansions covered by this chapter, but the selections edited by Joseph R. Levenson, *European Expansion and the Counter Example of Asia, 1300–1600* (1967), remain a good introduction to Chinese expansion and Western impressions of China. Janet Abu-Lughod, *Before European Hegemony: The World System, A.D. 1250–1350* (1989), is a stimulating speculative reassessment of the importance of the Mongols and the Indian Ocean trade in the creation of the modern world system; she summarizes her thesis in the American Historical Association (AHA) booklet *The World System in the Thirteenth Century: Dead-End or Precursor?* (1993).

The Chinese account of Zheng He's voyages is Ma Huan, *Ying-yai Sheng-lan: "The Overall Survey of the Ocean's Shores"* [1433], ed. and trans. J. V. G. Mills (1970). A reliable guide to Polynesian expansion is Jesse D. Jennings, ed., *The Prehistory of Polynesia* (1979), especially the excellent chapter "Voyaging," by Ben R. Finney, which encapsulates his *Voyage of Rediscovery: A Cultural Odyssey Through Polynesia* (1994). The medieval background to European intercontinental voyages is summarized by Felipe Fernandez-Armesto, *Before Columbus: Exploration and Colonization from the Mediterranean to the Atlantic, 1229–1492* (1987).

A simple introduction to the technologies of European expansion is Carlo M. Cipolla, *Guns, Sails, and Empires: Technological Innovation and the Early Phases of European Expansion, 1400–1700* (1965; reprint, 1985). More advanced is Roger C. Smith, *Vanguard of Empire: Ships of Exploration in the Age of Columbus* (1993).

The European exploration is well documented and the subject of intense historical investigation. Clear general accounts based on the contemporary records are Boies Penrose, *Travel and Discovery in the Age of the Renaissance, 1420–1620* (1952); J. H. Parry, *The Age of Reconnaissance: Discovery, Exploration, and Settlement, 1450–1650* (1963); and G. V. Scammell, *The World Encompassed: The First European Maritime Empires, c. 800–1650* (1981).

An excellent general introduction to Portuguese exploration is C. R. Boxer, *The Portuguese Seaborne Empire, 1415–1825* (1969). More detail can be found in Bailey W. Diffie and George D. Winius, *Foundations of the Portuguese Empire, 1415–1580* (1977); A. J. R. Russell-Wood, *The Portuguese Empire: A World on the Move* (1998); and Luc Cuyvers, *Into the Rising Sun: The Journey of Vasco da Gama and the Discovery of the Modern World* (1998). John William Blake, ed., *Europeans in West Africa, 1450–1560* (1942), is an excellent two-volume collection of contemporary Portuguese, Castilian, and English sources. Elaine Sanceau, *The Life of Prester John: A Chronicle of Portuguese Exploration* (1941), is a very readable account of Portuguese relations with Ethiopia. *The Summa Oriental of Tomé Pires: An Account of the East, from the Red Sea to Japan, Written in Malacca and India in 1512–1515,* trans. Armando Cortesão (1944), provides a detailed firsthand account of the Indian Ocean during the Portuguese's first two decades there.

The other Iberian kingdoms' expansion is well summarized by J. H. Parry, *The Spanish Seaborne Empire* (1967). Samuel Eliot Morison's *Admiral of the Ocean Sea: A Life of Christopher Columbus* (1942) is a fine scholarly celebration of the epic mariner, also available in an abridged version as *Christopher Columbus, Mariner* (1955). More focused on the shortcomings of Columbus and his Spanish peers is Tzvetan Todorov, *The Conquest of America,* trans. Richard Howard (1985). Marvin Lunenfeld, ed., *1492: Discovery, Invasion, Encounter* (1991), critically examines contemporary sources and interpretations. William D. Phillips and Carla Rhan Phillips, *The Worlds of Christopher Columbus* (1992), examines the mariner and his times in terms of modern concerns. Peggy K. Liss, *Isabel the Queen: Life and Times* (1992), is a sympathetic examination of Queen Isabella of Castile. Detailed individual biographies of each of the individuals in Pizarro's band are the subject of James Lockhart's *Men of Cajamarca: A Social and Biographical Study of the First Conquerors of Peru* (1972). A firsthand account of Magellan's expedition is Antonio Pigafetta, *Magellan's Voyage: A Narrative Account of the First Circumnavigation,* available in a two-volume edition (1969) that includes a facsimile reprint of the manuscript.

The trans-Atlantic encounters of Europe and the Americas are described by J. H. Elliott, *The Old World and the New, 1492–1650* (1970). Alfred W. Crosby, *The Columbian Voyages, the Columbian Exchange, and Their Historians* (1987), available as an AHA booklet, provides a brief overview of the first encounters in the Americas and their long-term consequences. The early chapters of Mark A. Burkholder and Lyman L. Johnson, *Colonial Latin America,* 2d ed. (1994), give a clear and balanced account of the Spanish conquest.

The perceptions of the peoples European explorers encountered are not usually so well documented. John Thornton, *Africa and Africans in the Making of the Atlantic World, 1400–1800,* 2d ed. (1998), examines Africans' encounters with Europeans, importance in the Atlantic economy, and impact in the New World. *The Broken Spears: The Aztec Account of the Conquest of Mexico,* ed. Miguel Leon-Portilla (1962), presents Amerindian chronicles in a readable package, as does Nathan Wachtel, *The Vision of the Vanquished: The Spanish Conquest of Peru Through Indian Eyes* (1977). Anthony Reid, *Southeast Asia in the Age of Commerce, 1450–1680,* 2 vols. (1988, 1993), deals with events in that region.

■ Notes

1. Ma Huan, *Ying-yai Sheng-lan: "The Overall Survey of the Ocean's Shores,"* ed. Feng Ch'eng-Chün, trans. J. V. G. Mills (Cambridge, England: Cambridge University Press, 1970), 180.
2. Alvise da Cadamosto in *The Voyages of Cadamosto and Other Documents,* ed. and trans. G. R. Crone (London: Hakluyt Society, 1937), 2.

PART FIVE

The Globe Encompassed, 1500–1750

European voyages of exploration greatly expanded global commercial, cultural, and biological exchanges between 1500 and 1750. Europeans built new commercial empires that grew stronger with each passing century. The Portuguese had begun the mastery of the seas by opening trade with sub-Saharan Africa and seizing control of maritime trading networks in the Indian Ocean. Then European colonization in the Americas stimulated the growth of a new Atlantic economy. From its colonial base in Mexico, Spain also pioneered new trade routes across the Pacific to the Philippines and China. In time, the Dutch, French, and English expanded these profitable maritime trading networks.

Commerce and colonization led to new interregional demographic and cultural exchanges. The introduction of unfamiliar diseases caused severe population losses in the Americas. To meet the resulting acute labor shortage, Europeans introduced enslaved Africans in ever-growing numbers. Europeans and Africans brought new languages, religious practices, music, and forms of personal adornment to the New World. Some Europeans who spent time overseas adopted new ways and developed new tastes that they later brought back with them when they returned to Europe.

In Asia and Africa, most important changes continued to come from internal causes rather than European expansion. The Islamic world saw the growth of regional empires in the Middle East, South Asia, and West Africa and continued its expansion into sub-Saharan Africa, southeastern Europe, and southern

Asia. Secure from external penetration, China experienced military expansion and population growth, and the expansion of educational institutions reinforced traditional values among China's upper classes. In Japan, a strong new national government promoted economic development and stemmed foreign influence, and the development of an indigenous merchant class widened the gap between popular and elite cultures.

Some of the farthest-reaching cultural changes in this period occurred in Europe. Reformers challenged established religious and political institutions, and new scientific discoveries and humanist concerns raised questions about traditional Western values and beliefs.

Important ecological changes occurred in areas of rising population and economic activity. The spread of new plants and animals around the world enhanced food supplies and altered landscapes. Forests were cut down to meet the increasing need for farmland, lumber, and fuel. But the most significant environmental changes resulted from the growing mastery of the winds and currents that propelled European ships across the world's oceans. Europeans' leadership in navigational technology went hand in hand with their emerging dominance in military technology. Lacking an expanding economic base, the great Islamic empires and China fell behind the smaller European nations in military strength. After 1750, the consequences of this widening technological and economic gap were to become momentous.

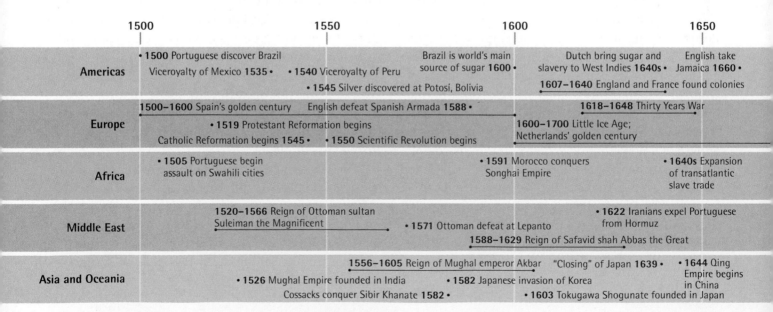

	1500	1550	1600	1650
Americas	• 1500 Portuguese discover Brazil Viceroyalty of Mexico 1535 •	• 1540 Viceroyalty of Peru • 1545 Silver discovered at Potosí, Bolivia	Brazil is world's main source of sugar 1600 •	Dutch bring sugar and slavery to West Indies 1640s • 1607–1640 England and France found colonies	English take Jamaica 1660 •
Europe	1500–1600 Spain's golden century • 1519 Protestant Reformation begins Catholic Reformation begins 1545 •	English defeat Spanish Armada 1588 • • 1550 Scientific Revolution begins	1618–1648 Thirty Years War 1600–1700 Little Ice Age; Netherlands' golden century	
Africa	• 1505 Portuguese begin assault on Swahili cities		• 1591 Morocco conquers Songhai Empire	• 1640s Expansion of transatlantic slave trade
Middle East		1520–1566 Reign of Ottoman sultan Suleiman the Magnificent	• 1571 Ottoman defeat at Lepanto 1588–1629 Reign of Safavid shah Abbas the Great	• 1622 Iranians expel Portuguese from Hormuz
Asia and Oceania		1556–1605 Reign of Mughal emperor Akbar • 1526 Mughal Empire founded in India Cossacks conquer Sibir Khanate 1582 •	"Closing" of Japan 1639 • • 1582 Japanese invasion of Korea • 1603 Tokugawa Shogunate founded in Japan	• 1644 Qing Empire begins in China

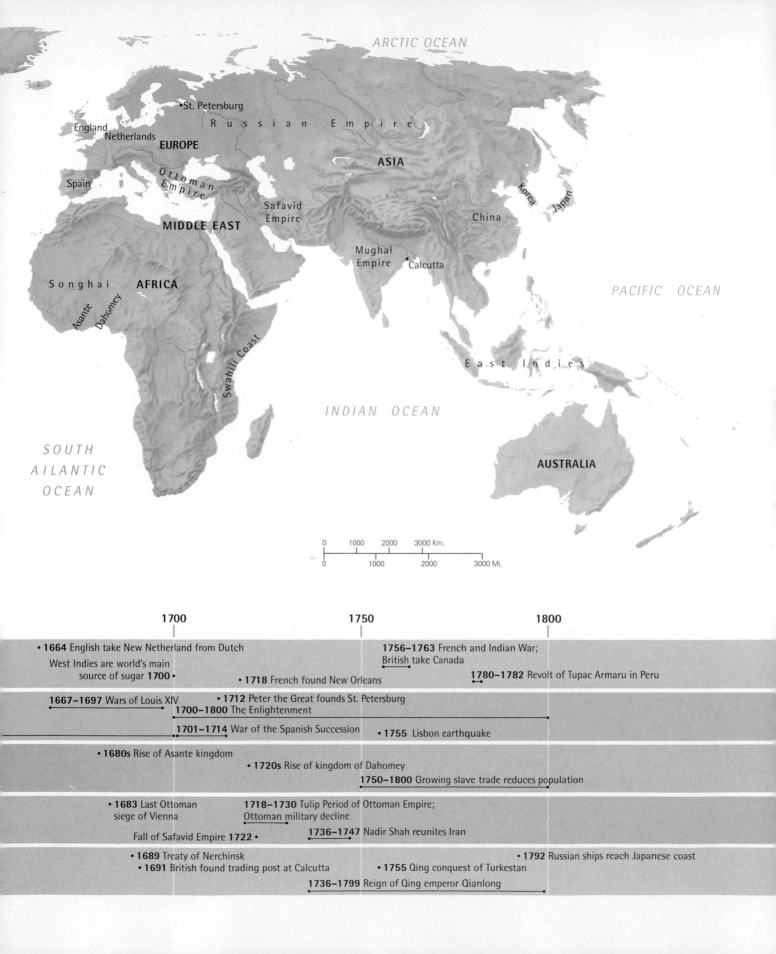

ARCTIC OCEAN

R u s s i a n   E m p i r e

St. Petersburg

England
Netherlands
EUROPE

ASIA

Spain

Ottoman Empire

Korea
Japan

MIDDLE EAST

Safavid Empire

China

Songhai
AFRICA

Mughal Empire
Calcutta

PACIFIC OCEAN

Asante
Dahomey

Swahili Coast

East Indies

INDIAN OCEAN

SOUTH
ATLANTIC
OCEAN

AUSTRALIA

| 0 | 1000 | 2000 | 3000 Km. |
| 0 | 1000 | 2000 | 3000 Mi. |

1700   **1750**   **1800**

• **1664** English take New Netherland from Dutch

1756–1763 French and Indian War;
British take Canada

West Indies are world's main
source of sugar **1700** •

• **1718** French found New Orleans

1780–1782 Revolt of Tupac Armaru in Peru

1667–1697 Wars of Louis XIV   • **1712** Peter the Great founds St. Petersburg

1700–1800 The Enlightenment

1701–1714 War of the Spanish Succession

• **1755** Lisbon earthquake

• **1680s** Rise of Asante kingdom

• **1720s** Rise of kingdom of Dahomey

1750–1800 Growing slave trade reduces population

• **1683** Last Ottoman
siege of Vienna

1718–1730 Tulip Period of Ottoman Empire;
Ottoman military decline

Fall of Safavid Empire **1722** •

1736–1747 Nadir Shah reunites Iran

• **1689** Treaty of Nerchinsk

• **1792** Russian ships reach Japanese coast

• **1691** British found trading post at Calcutta

• **1755** Qing conquest of Turkestan

1736–1799 Reign of Qing emperor Qianlong

THE TRANSFORMATION OF EUROPE,

1500–1750

Religious and Political Innovations • Building State Power • Urban Society and Commercial Technology • Rural Society and the Environment • The Realm of Ideas

ENVIRONMENT AND TECHNOLOGY: Mapping the World

SOCIETY AND CULTURE: Witchcraft

The Harvesters, 1565, by Pieter Bruegel, the Elder
A successful wheat harvest was necessary to feed bread- and pasta-eating Europe.

n the winter of 1697–1698 Tsar° Peter I, the young ruler of Russia, traveled in disguise through the Netherlands and England, eager to discover how western European societies were becoming so powerful and wealthy. A practical man, Peter paid special attention to ships and weapons, even working for a time as a ship's carpenter in the Netherlands. With great insight, he perceived that western European success owed as much to trade and toleration as to technology. Trade generated the money to spend on weapons, while toleration attracted talented persons fleeing persecution.

Upon his return to Russia, Peter resolved to "open a window onto Europe," to reform features of his vast empire that he believed were backward. He ended the servile status of women and personally trimmed his noblemen's long beards to conform to Western styles. Peter also put the skilled technical advisers he brought back with him to work on modernizing Russia's industry and military forces. His reformed armies soon gained success against Sweden for possession of a port on the Baltic Sea and against the Ottoman Turks for access to the warm waters of the Black Sea. Then Peter turned to redesigning Russia's government on a German model. He built a new palace like King Louis XIV's and copied the French king's rituals of absolute royal power.

As Peter's actions imply, by the end of the seventeenth century, western European achievements in state administration, warfare, business, and ideas were setting standards that others wished to imitate. Along with maritime expansion (examined in Chapter 17), these internal transformations promoted Western global ascendancy. Yet such achievements did not come smoothly. Warfare, poverty, persecution, and environmental degradation were also widespread in Europe between 1500 and 1750.

As you read this chapter, ask yourself the following questions:

- Was Tsar Peter right in thinking that military, economic, and political changes were moving western Europe ahead of other parts of the world?

---

tsar (zahr)

- What were the immediate and long-term consequences of those changes and others in European religious and scientific ideas?
- How did the many conflicts and rapid changes of this period affect ordinary men and women in Europe?

RELIGIOUS AND POLITICAL INNOVATIONS

Two bitter struggles in the early sixteenth century marked the end of Europe's medieval era and the beginning of the early modern period. One was the Reformation, a movement that introduced many religious reforms but shattered the ideal of Latin Christian unity. The other was an unsuccessful attempt to unite Christian Europe politically in order to block the inroads of the Muslim armies of the Ottoman Empire.

Instead of achieving unity, early modern Europe was plagued by division and persistent warfare among its national monarchies. Yet such disunity helped foster Europe's growing strength in the world. Competition and conflict promoted technological, administrative, social, and economic changes that propelled western Europe ahead of the more unified and peaceful empires of China and India and even ahead of the militarily aggressive Ottoman Empire.

Religious Reformation, 1517–1563

In 1500 the **papacy,** the central government of Latin Christianity, was simultaneously gaining stature and suffering from corruption and dissent. Economic prosperity produced larger donations and tax receipts, allowing popes to fund ambitious construction projects in Rome, their capital city. During the sixteenth century Rome gained fifty-four new churches and other buildings that showcased the artistic **Renaissance** then under way. However, the church's wealth and power also attracted some ambitious men, some of whose personal lives became the source of scandal.

The jewel of the new building projects was the magnificent new Saint Peter's Basilica in Rome. The unprecedented size and splendor of this church were intended to glorify the Christian faith, display the skill of Renaissance artists and builders, and enhance the standing of

Martin Luther   This detail of a painting by Lucas Cranach (1547) shows the Reformer preaching in his hometown church at Wittenberg.   (Church of St. Marien, Wittenberg, Germany/The Bridgeman Art Library, New York and London)

the papacy. Such a project required refined tastes and vast sums of money.

The skillful overseer of the design and financing of the new Saint Peter's was Pope Leo X (r. 1513–1521), a member of the wealthy Medici° family of Florence, famous for its patronage of the arts. Pope Leo's artistic taste was superb and his personal life free from scandal, but he was more a man of action than a spiritual leader. One technique that he used to raise funds for the basilica was to authorize an **indulgence**—a forgiveness of the punishment due for past sins, granted by church authorities as a reward for a pious act such as making a pilgrimage, saying a particular prayer, or making a donation to a religious cause.

Medici (MED-ih-chee)

In one German state where the new indulgence was being preached lived a young professor of sacred scripture named Martin Luther (1483–1546), whose personal religious quest had led him to forsake money and marriage for a life of prayer and self-denial in a monastery. Luther had found consolation in the passage in Saint Paul's Epistle to the Romans that argued that salvation came not by "doing certain things" but from religious faith. Thus Luther was very upset by the indulgence preachers, who he thought emphasized the act of giving money more than the faith behind the act. He wrote to Pope Leo, asking him to stop the abuses and challenged the preachers to a debate on the theology of indulgences.

This theological dispute quickly escalated into a contest between two strong-minded men. Largely ignoring Luther's theological objections, Pope Leo regarded his letter as a challenge to papal power and acted to silence him. During a debate in 1519 a papal representative led Luther into open disagreement with some church doctrines, for which the papacy condemned him. Blocked in his effort to reform the church from within, Luther burned the papal bull (document) of condemnation, rejecting the pope's authority and beginning the movement known as the **Protestant Reformation.**

Accusing those whom he called "Romanists" (Roman Catholics) of relying on "good works," Luther insisted that the only way to salvation was through faith in Jesus Christ. He further declared that Christian belief must be based on the word of God in the Bible and on Christian tradition, not on the authority of the pope, as Catholics held. Eventually his conclusions led him to abandon his monastic prayers and penances and to marry a former nun.

Today Roman Catholics and most Lutherans have resolved their differences on many theological issues. But in the sixteenth century, stubbornness on both sides made reconciliation impossible.

Inspired by Luther, others raised their voices to denounce the ostentation and corruption of church leaders and to call for a return to authentic Christian practices and beliefs. John Calvin (1509–1564), a well-educated Frenchman who turned from the study of law to theology after experiencing a religious conversion, became a highly influential Protestant leader. As a young man in 1535, Calvin published *The Institutes of the Christian Religion*, a masterful synthesis of Christian teachings. Much of the *Institutes* was traditional medieval theology, but in two respects Calvin's teaching differed from that of Roman Catholics and Lutherans. First, while agreeing with Luther's emphasis on faith over works, Calvin denied that even human faith could merit salvation. Salvation, said Calvin, was God's free gift to those

CHRONOLOGY

		Politics and Culture	Environment and Technology	Warfare
1500		1500s Spain's golden century 1519 Protestant Reformation begins 1540s Scientific Revolution begins 1545 Catholic Reformation begins	Mid-1500s Improved windmills and increasing land drainage in Holland	1526–1571 Ottoman wars 1546–1555 German Wars of Religion 1562–1598 French Wars of Religion 1566–1648 Netherlands Revolt
		Late 1500s Witchhunts increase	1590s Dutch develop flyboats; Little Ice Age begins	
1600		1600s Holland's golden century	1600s Depletion of forests growing 1609 Galileo's astronomical telescope	1618–1648 Thirty Years War 1642–1648 English Civil War 1652–1678 Anglo-Dutch Wars 1667–1697 Wars of Louis XIV 1683–1697 Ottoman wars
1700		1700s The Enlightenment begins	1682 Canal du Midi completed	1700–1721 Great Northern War 1701–1714 War of the Spanish Succession
			1750 English mine nearly 5 million tons of coal a year 1755 Lisbon earthquake	

God "predestined" for it. Second, Calvin went further than Luther in curtailing the power of ordained clergymen and in simplifying religious rituals. Calvinist congregations elected their own governing committees and in time created regional and national synods (councils) to regulate doctrinal issues. Calvinists also displayed simplicity in dress, life, and worship. In an age of ornate garments, they wore simple black clothes, avoided ostentatious living, and worshiped in churches devoid of statues, most musical instruments, stained-glass windows, incense, and vestments.

The Reformers appealed to religious sentiments, but political and social agendas also inspired many who joined them. Part of the appeal of Lutheranism to German-speakers was in reaction to the power of Italians in the Catholic Church. Peasants and urban laborers sometimes defied their masters by adopting a different faith. Neither tradition had a special attraction for women, since both Protestants and Roman Catholics believed in male dominance in the church and the family. Most Protestants, however, rejected the medieval tradition of celibate priests and nuns and advocated Christian marriage for all adults.

Shaken by the intensity of the Protestant Reformers' appeal, the Catholic Church undertook its own reforms. A council that met at the city of Trent, in northern Italy, in three sessions between 1545 and 1563 issued decrees reforming the education, discipline, and practices of the Roman Catholic clergy. The council also reaffirmed the supremacy of the pope and clarified Catholic beliefs (including those concerning indulgences) in light of Protestant challenges. Also important to this **Catholic Reformation** were the activities of a new religious order—the Society of Jesus, or "Jesuits," that Ignatius of Loyola (1491–1556), a Spanish nobleman, founded in 1534. Well-educated Jesuits helped stem the Protestant tide and win back some adherents by their teaching and preaching (see Map 18.1). Other Jesuits became important missionaries overseas (see Chapters 19 and 22).

Given the complexity of the issues and the intensity of the emotions that the Protestant Reformation stirred, it is not surprising that violence often flared up. Both

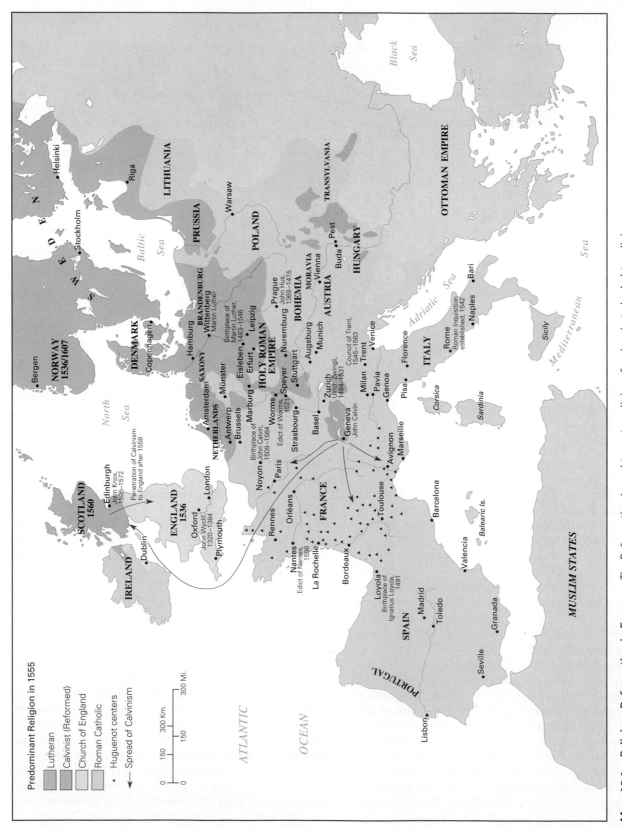

Map. 18.1 Religious Reformation in Europe The Reformation brought greater religious freedom but also led to religious conflict and persecution. In many places the Reformation accelerated the trend toward state control of religion and added religious differences to the motives for wars among Europeans.

Legend (Predominant Religion in 1555):
- Lutheran
- Calvinist (Reformed)
- Church of England
- Roman Catholic
- Huguenot centers
- Spread of Calvinism

sides persecuted and sometimes executed those of differing views. Bitter "wars of religion," fought over a mixture of religious and secular issues, continued in parts of western Europe until 1648.

The Failure of Empire, 1519–1556

Meanwhile, there was also trouble in another great medieval institution, the **Holy Roman Empire,** a loose federation of Germanic states and principalities. The threat that the Ottoman Turks posed by their advances into southeastern Europe stirred interest in a pan-European coalition to stop the Muslim advances. Hope centered on a young man named Charles (1500–1557), descended from the powerful **Habsburg°** family of Austria and the rulers of Burgundy on his father's side and from the rulers of Spain on his mother's. After the death of his maternal grandfather in 1516, Charles inherited the Spanish thrones of Castile and Aragon along with their extensive European and American possessions. At the death of his paternal grandfather in 1519, the young king inherited the Austrian Habsburg possessions and also secured election as Emperor Charles V, ruler of the Holy Roman Empire, which the Habsburgs had headed for three generations (see Map 18.2).

A Latin Christian coalition led by Charles eventually halted the Ottomans at the gates of Vienna in 1529, but did not end Ottoman attacks, which continued on and off until 1697. Charles's efforts to forge his several possessions into Europe's strongest state met strong resistance. King Francis I of France, who had lost to Charles in the election for Holy Roman Emperor, openly supported the Muslim Turks to weaken his rival. Nor were the heads of the many states within the Holy Roman Empire eager to share their powers and revenues with the emperor. Luther's Reformation played into their hands. In the imperial Diet (assembly) many German princes, swayed partly by Luther's appeals to German nationalism, also opposed Charles, a French-speaking emperor who defended the papacy. Some Lutheran princes enriched themselves by seizing the church's lands within their states in the name of reform. The new kingdom of Prussia (created in 1701) came into being in lands that a Lutheran prince had seized from a Catholic religious order in 1525.

After decades of bitter squabbles turned to open warfare in 1546 (the German Wars of Religion), Charles V finally gave up his efforts at unification, abdicated control of his various possessions to different heirs, and retired to a monastery. To his son Philip went the throne of Spain, Europe's most powerful state then in the midst of its golden age. Administration of the war-torn Holy Roman Empire went to his brother Ferdinand, who ended the lost war against Lutheranism and the German princes. By the Peace of Augsburg (1555), he recognized the princes' right to choose whether Catholicism or Lutheranism would prevail in their particular states, and he allowed them to keep church lands they had seized before 1552.

Thus two institutions that had symbolized Western unity during the Middle Ages—the papacy and the Holy Roman Empire—were seriously weakened by the mid-sixteenth century. Luther emerged from a monastery to break the papacy; Charles retired to a monastery, broken by opposition to an effective pan-European empire. Both the papacy and the Holy Roman Empire continued to exist, but national kingdoms assumed much of the religious and political leadership in western Europe. Indeed, the collapse of religious and imperial unity was partly the work of ambitious monarchs eager to enhance their own power by bringing all other institutions under their control and preventing the emergence of any imperial superpower.

Royal Centralization, 1500–1750

Talented rulers and their able ministers guided the rise of these European kingdoms. When the system of monarchical succession worked best, it brought to the throne a creative, energetic young person who gained experience and won loyalty over many decades. By good fortune the leading states produced many such talented, hard-working, and long-lived rulers. Spain had only six rulers in the two centuries from 1556 to 1759, and France had but five between 1574 and 1774 (see Table 18.1). The long reigns of the Tudor monarchs Henry VIII and his Protestant daughter Elizabeth I helped stabilize sixteenth-century England, but their Stuart successors were twice overthrown by revolution during the next century.

Successful monarchs depended heavily on their chief advisers, who also eased the transition between rulers. Cardinal Jiménez° guided the nineteen-year-old Charles V's entry to the throne of Spain. Cardinal Richelieu° oversaw the policies of the young Louis XIII in France, and Richelieu's successor Cardinal Mazarin° guided the youthful Louis XIV, who came to the throne at the age of five. By the seventeenth century, kings were beginning to draw on the talents of successful businessmen, such as Jean Baptiste Colbert° (1619–1683), Louis

---

Habsburg (HABZ-berg)

Jiménez (he-MEH-nes)   Richelieu (ree-shuh-LYOO)
Mazarin (MAZ-uh-rin, maz-uh-RAN)   Colbert (kohl-BEAR)

Map. 18.2 **The European Empire of Charles V** Charles was Europe's most powerful ruler from 1519 to 1556, but he failed to unify the Christian West. In addition to being the elected head of the Holy Roman Empire, he was the hereditary ruler of the Spanish realms of Castile and Aragon and the possessions of the Austrian Habsburgs in Central Europe. The map does not show his extensive holdings in the Americas and Asia.

Table 18.1   **Rulers in Early Modern Western Europe**

Spain	France	England/Great Britain
Habsburg Dynasty	**Valois Dynasty**	**Tudor Dynasty**
Charles I (1516–1556) (Holy Roman-Emperor Charles V) Philip II (1556–1598)	Francis I (1515–1547) Henry II (1547–1559) Francis II (1559–1560) Charles IX (1560–1574) Henry III (1574–1589)	Henry VIII (1509–1547) Edward VI (1547–1553) Mary I (1553–1558) Elizabeth I (1558–1603)
	Bourbon Dynasty	**Stuart Dynasty**
Philip III (1598–1621) Philip IV (1621–1665) Charles II (1665–1700)	Henry IV (1589–1610)[a] Louis XIII (1610–1643) Louis XIV (1643–1715)	James I (1603–1625) Charles I (1625–1649)[a, b] (Puritan Republic, 1649–1660) Charles II (1660–1685) James II (1685–1688)[b] William III (1689–1702) and Mary II (1689–1694) Anne (1702–1714)
Bourbon Dynasty		
Philip V (1700–1746)		**Hanoverian Dynasty**
	Louis XV (1715–1774)	George I (1714–1727) George II (1727–1760)
Ferdinand VI (1746–1759)		

[a]Died a violent death.   [b]Was overthrown.

XIV's able minister of finance. In Great Britain, Robert Walpole, the powerful prime minister from 1721 to 1742, dominated the early Hanoverian kings.

Able monarchs and their advisers worked to enhance royal authority by limiting the autonomy of the church. Well before the Reformation, rulers in Spain, Portugal, and France had gained control over church appointments and had used church revenues to enhance royal power. This absorption of the church into the state helps explain why religious uniformity became a hot political issue. Following the pattern used by his predecessors to suppress Jewish and Muslim practices, King Philip II of Spain used an ecclesiastical court, the Spanish Inquisition, to bring into line those who resisted his authority. It was the one institution common to his three Spanish kingdoms. Suspected Protestants, as well as critics of the king, found themselves accused of heresy, an offense punishable by death. Even those who were acquitted of the charge learned not to oppose the king again.

In France, Prince Henry of Navarre switched his faith from Calvinist to Catholic after gaining the military advantage in the French Wars of Religion (1562–1598), so that, as King Henry IV (the first of the Bourbon kings), he

would share the faith of the majority of his subjects. His son and grandson, Kings Louis XIII and Louis XIV (see Table 18.1), were as devoted to French Catholic religious uniformity as their counterparts in Spain. In 1685 Louis XIV even revoked the Edict of Nantes°, by which his grandfather had granted religious freedom to his Protestant supporters in 1598.

Elsewhere, the Protestant Reformation made it easier for monarchs to increase their control of the church. The church in England lost its remaining autonomy after the pope turned down King Henry VIII's petition for an annulment of his marriage to Katharine of Aragon. Distressed that Katharine had not furnished him with a male heir, Henry had the English archbishop of Canterbury annul the marriage in 1533. The breach with Rome was sealed the next year when Parliament made the English monarch head of the Church of England.

Henry used his authority to disband monasteries and convents. He gave some of their landholdings to his powerful allies and sold others to pay for his new navy. In other respects religion changed little under Henry and his successors, despite growing pressures from English

---

Nantes (nahnt)

Calvinists known as Puritans to "purify" the Anglican church of Catholic practices and beliefs. In 1603, the first Stuart king, James I, dismissed a Puritan petition to eliminate bishops with the statement "No bishops, no king"—a reminder of the essential role that bishops played in royal administration.

In addition to gaining control of the church, western European kings and queens enhanced their powers by promoting national institutions. In 1500 many of the separate provinces of Spain and France had their own laws and institutions, reflecting their piecemeal acquisition by inheritance and conquest. By 1750 there was more uniformity in law and administration. Seventeenth-century French kings took two steps to decrease local power. They appointed *intendants*°, new royal officials to enforce their orders in the provinces. They also used the army to tear down the fortifications behind which powerful nobles and towns had often asserted their independence.

The growth of a common language, especially among the elites, further strengthened national unity. In Spain the Castilian dialect gained currency. In France people increasingly imitated the speech of Paris. The Protestant emphasis on reading the Bible in vernacular languages (instead of in Latin) speeded up the replacement of many dialects with standardized national languages. Luther's magnificent translation of the Bible into the High German of Saxony laid the basis for modern German. The biblical translation prepared under the direction of King James I did the same for English, as did Calvin's translation for French. Important new secular literatures also helped to standardize national languages. These included the English plays of William Shakespeare (1564–1616), the French satires of François Rabelais° (1483–1553), the Spanish novel *Don Quixote* by Miguel de Cervantes° (1547–1616), and *The Lusiads*, an epic poem celebrating overseas exploration, by the Portuguese poet Luís de Camões° (1524?–1580).

Absolutism and Constitutionalism

The absence of any constitutional check on a ruler's power is called **absolutism.** Many seventeenth- and eighteenth-century European monarchs admired absolutism and tried to put it into practice. But monarchs trying to concentrate power in their own hands had to confront the representative assemblies that traditionally had to approve important royal actions such as making war and levying new taxes. As we have seen, the princes in the imperial Diet of the Holy Roman Empire effectively resisted Charles V. In contrast, French kings succeeded in circumventing the Estates General. In England, Parliament checked royal power and established **constitutionalism,** a system of government that subjects the ruler's power to limits specified by law and custom.

In France the Estates General represented the traditional rights of three groups: the clergy, the nobility, and the towns (that is, townspeople with wealth and high status). The Estates General was able to assert itself during the sixteenth-century French Wars of Religion, when the monarchy was weak. But, except in 1614 when Queen Marie de Medici was ruling in the name of her young son, the Bourbon kings refused to call it into session. Unable to impose new taxes without summoning the Estates General, Louis XIV turned to his astute finance minister, Colbert, who devised new, efficient tax collection methods that tripled the amount of money reaching the royal treasury. To increase the tax base, Colbert also promoted economic development both in France and overseas. When Louis XIV's wars (1667–1697) and high living strained the treasury to the breaking point, the king raised additional sums by selling high offices, again bypassing the Estates General.

Louis XIV's gigantic new palace at Versailles° symbolized the French monarch's triumph over the traditional rights of the nobility. Capable of housing ten thousand people and surrounded by elaborately landscaped grounds and parks, the palace can be seen as a sort of theme park of royal absolutism. Required to spend much of their time at elaborate ceremonies and banquets centered on the king, the nobles who lived at Versailles were kept away from the real politics of the kingdom. According to one of them, the duke of Saint-Simon°, "no one was so clever in devising petty distractions" as the king. So successful was Versailles in taming the nobles that not only Tsar Peter in Russia but other kings, princes, and even a powerful German archbishop built imitations of it.

As eager as his French counterparts to promote royal absolutism, King Charles I of England (see Table 18.1) ruled for eleven years without summoning Parliament, his kingdom's representative body. To raise money, he coerced "loans" from wealthy subjects and twisted tax laws to new uses. Then in 1640, a rebellion in Scotland forced him to summon the members of Parliament to approve new taxes to pay for an army. Noblemen and churchmen sat in the House of Lords. Representatives

---

intendants (in-TEN-dants)   **Rabelais** (RAB-uh-lay)
Cervantes (ser-VAHN-tees)   **Camões** (kuh-MOINSH)

Versailles (vuhr-SIGH)   **Saint-Simon** (san see-MON)

Versailles, 1722   This painting by P.-D. Martin shows the east expanse of buildings and courtyards that make up the palace complex built by King Louis XIV.   (Giraudon/Art Resource, NY)

from the towns and counties sat in the House of Commons. Before authorizing new taxes, Parliament insisted on strict guarantees that the king would never again ignore its traditional rights. These King Charles refused to grant. When he ordered the arrest of his leading critics in the House of Commons in 1642, he plunged the kingdom into civil war.

Defending Parliament's traditional rights were the rich commoners and the well-organized religious Puritans, who had not given up on their plans to cleanse the English church of Catholic traits. Supporting the king were most of the established nobility and the conservative northern parts of the kingdom. When Charles refused to compromise even after being defeated on the battlefield, a "Rump" Parliament purged of his supporters ordered him executed in 1649 and replaced the monarchy with a Puritan Republic under the Puritan general Oliver Cromwell.

Cromwell expanded England's power overseas and imposed firm control over Ireland and Scotland, but he was as unwilling as the Stuart kings to share power with Parliament. After his death the Stuart line was restored in 1660, and for a time it was unclear which side had won the English Civil War.

However, when King James II refused to respect Parliament's rights and had his heir baptized a Roman Catholic, Parliament offered the throne to his Protestant daughter Mary and her Dutch husband, Prince William of Orange. Their triumphal arrival in England forced James into exile in the bloodless Glorious Revolution of 1688. This time, there was no doubt about the outcome. The Bill of Rights of 1689 specified that Parliament had to be called "frequently" and had to consent to changes in laws and to the raising of an army in peacetime. Another law reaffirmed the official status of the Church of England but gave religious toleration to Puritans.

BUILDING STATE POWER

The growing power of early modern European rulers, whether absolutist or constitutional, would have been of modest global significance if they had not achieved notable success in two other important areas. One was developing some of the world's most powerful armed forces. The other was ensuring sufficient economic growth to support the heavy costs of royal administration and warfare.

War and Diplomacy

Warfare was almost constant in early modern Europe (see the Chronology at the beginning of the chapter). These struggles for dominance first produced a dramatic change in the size, skill, and weapons of armed forces and then an advance in diplomacy. The military revolution began in the Late Middle Ages when firearms became the preferred weapons of war: cannon replaced catapults as siege weapons, muskets displaced lances and crossbows, and gun-toting commoners on foot supplanted aristocratic knights on horseback.

The numbers of men in arms increased steadily throughout the early modern period. Spanish armies doubled in size from about 150,000 in the 1550s to 300,000 in the 1630s. French forces, about half the size of the Spanish in the 1630s, grew to 400,000 by the early eighteenth century. Even smaller European states built up impressive armies. Sweden, with under a million people, had one of the finest and best-armed military forces in seventeenth-century Europe. Prussia, with fewer than 2 million inhabitants in 1700, devoted so many resources to building a splendid army that it became one of Europe's major powers. Only England did not maintain a standing army in peacetime, but the Royal Navy protected the island nation from invasion.

Large armies required effective command structures. Long before the development of modern field communications systems, European armies, in the words of a modern historian, "evolved . . . the equivalent of a central nervous system, capable of activating technologically differentiated claws and teeth."[1] New signaling techniques improved control of battlefield maneuvers. Better discipline was achieved by frequent marching drills, which trained troops to obey orders instantly and gave them a close sense of comradeship. First developed in the Netherlands during a long struggle for independence from Spain, the drilling techniques were quickly imitated by the best armies in Europe.

Military victories by the giant armies were not assured, however. New fortifications able to withstand cannon bombardments made cities harder to capture, and battles between evenly matched armies often ended in stalemates, as in the Thirty Years War (1618–1648). Victory in war increasingly depended on naval superiority. Warships were redesigned to accommodate several tiers of cannon that had the power to blow holes in the thick sides of enemy ships. Improved four-wheel carriages made cannon easier to pull back and reload.

The rapid changes in naval warfare are evident in two fleets used by Philip II of Spain. In 1571 a combined Spanish and Italian fleet of 200 ships met an even larger Ottoman force off Lepanto on the Greek coast. Both fleets consisted principally of oar-powered galleys, which had only light armaments. To attack, one galley rammed another so that armed men could climb aboard for hand-to-hand combat. Four hours after the battle began, the remains of 200 Ottoman galleys littered the sea's surface, and the waters were red with the blood of 30,000 slain men. The Christian coalition's victory resulted from the valor of Spanish troops and the superior firepower of a handful of specially built Venetian ships.

A very different Spanish fleet, the Catholic Armada, sailed from Lisbon in 1588 hoping to repeat the Lepanto success over the Protestant enemies of the north. The complex mission of these 130 heavily armed ships was to replace the Protestant ruler of England, Queen Elizabeth, with a Roman Catholic, then put down the rebellion in the Netherlands, and finally intervene on the Catholic side in the French Wars of Religion. But history did not repeat itself. The English could fire more rapidly because of their new cannon carriages, and their smaller, quicker ships successfully evaded the ram-and-board technique, which the Spanish retained from their Mediterranean victory. Moreover, a chance storm, celebrated by the English as a providential "Protestant wind," scattered and sank many Spanish ships that had survived the sea battles, thus dooming Philip's other plans for the armada.

The armada's defeat signaled the end of Spain's military dominance in Europe. By the time of the Thirty Years War, France had recovered from its Wars of Religion to become Europe's most powerful state. With twice the population of Spain at their command, France's forceful kings of the Bourbon dynasty could field Europe's largest armies, whether to squelch domestic unrest, extend France's boundaries, or intervene in the affairs of neighboring states.

After emerging from its own civil conflicts in 1689, England became France's major rival. By then England ruled a North American empire as well as Ireland, and in 1707 England merged with Scotland to become Great

Austrian Siege of Belgrade, 1688   The Ottoman Turks, in control of the Balkan Peninsula since the early sixteenth century, again assaulted the city of Vienna in 1683. Revitalized Austrian Habsburg armies successfully defended their capital and then took the offensive against the Muslim invaders, retaking Hungary and capturing the city of Belgrade, south of the Danube River. Although the Turks soon regained Belgrade, the annexation of Hungary doubled the size of the Austrian Empire and altered the balance of power in southeastern Europe.   (Giraudon/Art Resource, NY)

Britain. England's rise as a sea power had begun in the time of King Henry VIII, who spent heavily on ships and promoted a domestic iron-smelting industry to supply cannon. Queen Elizabeth's victorious fleet of 1588 was considerably improved by the copying of innovative ship designs from the Dutch in the second half of the seventeenth century. The Royal Navy grew in numbers, surpassing the French fleet by the early eighteenth century.

In a series of eighteenth-century wars, beginning with the War of the Spanish Succession (1701–1714), the combination of Britain's naval strength and the land armies of its Austrian and Prussian allies was able to block French expansionist efforts and prevent the Bourbons from uniting the thrones of France and Spain. This defeat of the French monarchy's empire-building efforts illustrated the principle of **balance of power** in international relations: the major European states formed temporary alliances to prevent any one state from becoming too powerful.

Russia emerged as a major power in Europe after Peter the Great's modernized armies defeated Sweden in the Great Northern War (1700–1721). During the next two centuries, though adhering to four different branches of Christianity, the great powers of Europe—Catholic France, Anglican Britain, Catholic Austria, Lutheran Prussia, and Orthodox Russia (see Map 18.3)—maintained an effective balance of power in Europe by shifting their alliances for geopolitical rather than religious reasons.

Politics and the Economy

To pay the extremely heavy military costs of their wars, European rulers had to increase their revenues. The most successful of them after 1600 promoted mutually beneficial alliances with the rising commercial elites. Both parties understood that trade thrived where government taxation and regulation were not excessive, where courts enforced contracts and collected debts, and where military power stood ready to protect overseas expansion by force when necessary.

Spain, sixteenth-century Europe's mightiest state, illustrates how the financial drains of an aggressive military policy and the failure to promote economic development

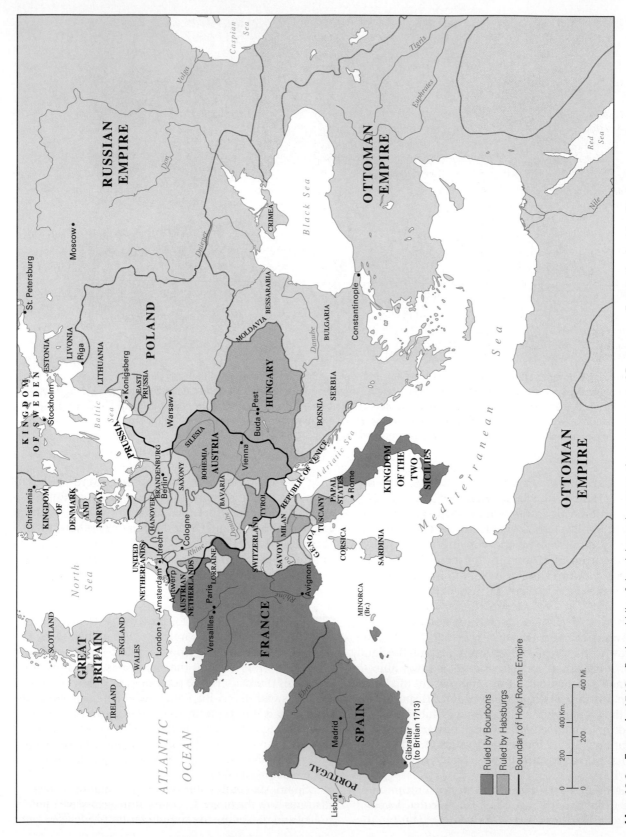

Map. 18.3   Europe in 1740   By the middle of the eighteenth century the great powers of Europe were France, the Austrian Empire, Great Britain, Prussia, and Russia. Spain, the Holy Roman Empire, and the Ottoman Empire were far weaker in 1740 than they had been two centuries earlier.

could lead to decline. Expensive wars against the Ottomans, northern European Protestants, and rebellious Dutch subjects caused the treasury of King Philip II to default on its debts four times. Moreover, the Spanish rulers' concerns for religious uniformity and traditional aristocratic privilege further undermined the country's economy. In the name of religious uniformity they expelled Jewish merchants, persecuted Protestant dissenters, and forced tens of thousands of skilled farmers and artisans into exile because of their Muslim ancestry. While exempting the landed aristocracy from taxation, Spanish rulers imposed high sales taxes that discouraged manufacturing.

For a time, vast imports of silver and gold bullion from Spain's American colonies filled the government treasury. These bullion shipments also contributed to severe inflation (rising prices), worst in Spain but bad throughout the rest of western Europe as well. A Spanish saying captured the problem: American silver was like rain on the roof—it poured down and washed away. Huge debts for foreign wars drained bullion from Spain to its creditors. More wealth flowed out to purchase manufactured goods and even food in the seventeenth century.

The rise of the Netherlands as an economic power stemmed from opposite policies. The Spanish crown had acquired these resource-poor but commercially successful provinces as part of Charles V's inheritance. But King Philip II's decision to impose Spain's ruinously heavy sales tax and enforce Catholic orthodoxy drove the Dutch to revolt in 1566 and again in 1572. Those measures would have discouraged business and driven away the Calvinists, Jews, and others who were essential to Dutch prosperity. The Dutch fought with skill and ingenuity, raising and training an army and a navy that were among the most effective in Europe. By 1609 Spain was forced to agree to a truce that recognized the autonomy of the northern part of the Netherlands. In 1648, after eight decades of warfare, the independence of these seven United Provinces of the Free Netherlands (to give their full name) became final.

Rather than being ruined by the long war, the United Netherlands emerged in the seventeenth century as the dominant commercial power in Europe and the world's greatest trading nation. During this golden century the wealth of the Netherlands multiplied instead of flowing away. This economic success owed much to a decentralized government. During the long struggle against Spain, the provinces united around the prince of Orange, their sovereign, who served as commander-in-chief of the armed forces. But in economic matters each province was free to pursue its own interests. The maritime province of Holland grew rich by favoring commercial interests.

Holland's many towns and cities were filled with skilled craftsmen. Factories and workshops turned out goods of exceptional quality at a moderate price and on a vast scale. The textile industry concentrated on the highly profitable finishing and printing of cloth, transforming into fine textiles the cloth spun and woven by low-paid workers. Other factories refined West Indian sugar, brewed beer from Baltic grain, cut Virginia tobacco, and made imitations of Chinese ceramics. Holland's printers published books in many languages, free from the censorship imposed by political and religious authorities in neighboring countries. For a small province, barely above sea level, lacking timber and other natural resources, this was a remarkable achievement.

Amsterdam, Holland's major city, was seventeenth-century Europe's financial center and major port. From there Dutch ships dominated the sea trade of Europe, carrying over 80 percent of the trade to Spain from northern Europe, even while Spain and the Netherlands were at war. The Dutch dominance of Atlantic and Indian Ocean trade was such that, by one estimate, they conducted more than half of all the oceangoing commercial shipping in the world (for details see Chapters 20 and 21).

After 1650 the Dutch faced growing competition from the English, who were developing their own close association of business and government. In a series of wars (1652–1678) England used its naval might to break Dutch dominance in overseas trade and to extend England's colonial empire. With government support, the English merchant fleet doubled between 1660 and 1700, and foreign trade rose by 50 percent. As a result, state revenue from customs duties tripled. During the eighteenth century Britain's trading position strengthened still more.

The debts run up by the Anglo-Dutch Wars helped persuade the English monarchy to greatly enlarge the government's role in managing the economy. The outcome has been called a "financial revolution." The government increased revenues by taxing the formerly exempt landed estates of the aristocrats and by collecting taxes directly. Previously private individuals known as tax farmers had advanced the government a fixed sum of money; in return they could keep whatever money they were able to collect from taxpayers. To secure cash quickly for warfare and other emergencies and to reduce the burden of debts from earlier wars, England also followed the Dutch lead in creating a central bank, from which the government was able to obtain long-term loans at low rates.

The French government was also developing its national economy, especially under Colbert. He streamlined tax collection, promoted French manufacturing

Port of Amsterdam   Ships, barges and boats of all types are visible in this busy seventeenth-century scene. The large building in the center is the Admiralty House, which housed the headquarters of the Dutch East India Company.   (Mansell Collection/Time Inc.)

and shipping by imposing taxes on foreign goods, and improved transportation within France itself. Yet the power of the wealthy aristocrats kept the French government from following England's lead in taxing wealthy landowners, collecting taxes directly, and securing low-cost loans. Nor did France succeed in managing its debt as efficiently as England. (The role of governments in promoting overseas trade is discussed in Chapter 20.)

URBAN SOCIETY AND COMMERCIAL TECHNOLOGY

Just as palaces were early modern Europe's centers of political power, cities were its economic power centers. The urban growth under way since the eleventh century was accelerating and spreading. In 1500, Paris was the only northern European city with over 100,000 inhabitants. By 1700, both Paris and London had populations over 500,000, Amsterdam had burgeoned from a fishing village to a metropolis of some 200,000, and twenty other European cities contained over 60,000 people.

The cities' growth depended primarily on the prosperous merchants who managed the great expansion of regional and overseas commerce. Improved business techniques and manufacturing technologies also added to the cities' prosperity, but wealth was unevenly distributed.

Urban Social Classes

In about 1580 the mayor of the French city of Bordeaux° asked a group of visiting Amerindian chiefs what impressed them most about European cities. The chiefs are said to have expressed astonishment at the disparity between the fat, well-fed people and the poor, half-starved men and women in rags. Why, the visitors wondered, did the poor not grab the rich by the throat or set fire to their homes? The contrasts of wealth in European cities were indeed startling, and social tension often ran high.[2]

Bordeaux (bor-DOH)

The French called the well-off who dominated the cities **bourgeoisie**° (town dwellers). Their wealth came from manufacturing, finance, and especially trade, both regional and overseas.

Grain for bread was brought by carts and barges from the surrounding countryside or, in the largest cities of western Europe, transported by special fleets from the eastern Baltic lands. Other fleets brought wine from southern to northern Europe. Parisians downed 100,000 barrels of wine a year at the end of the seventeenth century. The poor also consumed large amounts of beer. In 1750 Parisian breweries made 23 million quarts (22 million liters) for local consumption, another stimulus to the grain trade. In the seventeenth and eighteenth centuries wealthier urban classes could buy exotic luxuries imported from the far corners of the earth—Caribbean and Brazilian sugar and rum, Mexican chocolate, Virginian tobacco, North American furs, East Indian cotton textiles and spices, and Chinese tea.

As related above, the rise of the bourgeoisie was aided by mutually beneficial alliances with monarchs who saw economic growth as the best means of increasing state revenues. Unlike the old nobility, who shunned productive labor, members of the bourgeoisie devoted long hours to their businesses and poured their profits into new business ventures or other investments rather than spending them. Even so, they still had enough money to live comfortably in large houses with many servants.

Like merchants in the Islamic world, Europe's merchants relied on family and ethnic networks. In addition to families of local origin, many northern European cities contained merchant colonies from Venice, Florence, Genoa, and other Italian cities. In Amsterdam and Hamburg lived Jewish merchants who had fled religious persecution in Iberia. Other Jewish communities expanded out of eastern Europe into the German states, especially after the Thirty Years War. Armenian merchants from Iran were moving into the Mediterranean and became important in Russia in the seventeenth century.

Europe's cities were home not only to the well-off bourgeoisie, but also to craftworkers and many poor people. From 10 to 20 percent of the city dwellers were so poor they were exempt from taxation. This number included only the "deserving poor," whom officials considered permanent residents. Cities contained large numbers of "unworthy poor"—recent migrants from impoverished rural areas, peddlers traveling from place to place, and beggars (many with horrible deformities and

sores) who tried to survive on charity. There were also criminals, usually organized in gangs, ranging from youthful pickpockets to highway robbers.

Some people managed to improve their lot in life and others slipped lower, but most followed the careers of their parents.

In contrast to the arranged marriages common in much of the rest of the world, young men and women in early modern Europe generally chose their own spouses and after marriage set up their own households instead of living with their parents. The sons and daughters of craftworkers and the poor had to delay marriage until they could afford to live on their own. Young men had to serve a long apprenticeship to learn a trade. Young women had to work—helping their parents, as domestic servants, or in some other capacity—to save money for the dowry they were expected to bring into the marriage. A dowry was the money and household goods—the amount varied by social class—that enabled a young couple to begin marriage independent of their parents. The typical groom in early modern Europe could not hope to marry before his late twenties, and his bride would be a few years younger—in contrast to the rest of the world, where people usually married in their teens.

Marriage also came late in bourgeois families. One reason for the delay was to allow men to finish their education. Bourgeois parents did not formally arrange their children's marriages, but the fact that nearly all found spouses within their social class strongly suggests that parents promoted marriages that forged business alliances with other families.

Bourgeois parents were very concerned that their children have the education and training necessary for success. They promoted the establishment of municipal schools to provide a solid education, including Latin and perhaps Greek, for their sons, who were then sent abroad to learn modern languages or to a university to earn a law degree. Legal training was useful for conducting business and was a prerequisite for obtaining government judgeships and treasury positions. Daughters were less likely to be groomed for a business career, but wives often helped their husbands as bookkeepers and sometimes inherited businesses.

Besides enabling young people to be independent of their parents, the late age of marriage in early modern Europe also held down the birthrate and thus limited family size. Even so, about one-tenth of the births in a city were to unmarried women, often servants, who generally left their infants on the doorsteps of churches, convents, or rich families. Despite efforts to raise such abandoned children, many perished. Delayed marriage

---

bourgeoisie (boor-zwah-ZEE)

The Fishwife, 1572   Women were essential partners in most Dutch family businesses. This scene by the Dutch artist Adriaen van Ostade shows a woman preparing fish for retail sale. (Rijksmuseum-Stichting)

profit, the banks invested these funds in real estate, local industries, loans to governments, and overseas trade.

Another commercial innovation was the **joint-stock company,** which sold shares to individuals. Often backed by a government charter, such companies offered a way to raise large sums for overseas enterprises while spreading the risks (and profits) among many investors (the operation of chartered joint-stock companies in the overseas trade is examined in Chapter 20). After the initial offerings, investors could buy and sell shares in specialized financial markets called **stock exchanges,** an Italian innovation transferred to the cities of northwestern Europe in the sixteenth century. The greatest stock market in the seventeenth and eighteenth centuries was the Amsterdam Exchange, founded in 1530. Large insurance companies also emerged in this period, and insuring long voyages against loss became a standard practice after 1700 (see Chapter 20).

Changes in technology also facilitated economic growth. As in the case of military developments, this was more an age of technological refinement and multiplication than innovation. For example, water wheels—a traditional source of mechanical energy for mills and factories—gradually increased in size. In the Dutch province of Holland, improved systems of gears made it possible to adapt windmills for new uses, such as driving a saw. Information about new devices was spread by means of printed manuals on machinery, metallurgy, agriculture, and other technical subjects.

Improvements in water transport expanded Europe's superb natural network of seas and navigable rivers for moving bulk items such as grain, wine, and timber. The Dutch built numerous canals to drain the lowlands for agriculture and for transport. Other canals, with elaborate systems of locks to cross hills, were built in France, Germany, Italy, and England. One of the most important was the 150–mile (240–kilometer) Canal du Midi in France, built by the French government between 1661 and 1682 to link the Atlantic and the Mediterranean.

The expansion of maritime trade led to new designs for merchant ships. In this, too, the Dutch played a dominant role. Using timber imported from northern Europe, shipyards in Dutch ports built ships for their own vast fleets and for export. Especially successful was the *fluit,* or "flyboat," a large-capacity cargo ship developed in the 1590s. It was inexpensive to build and required only a small crew. Another successful type of merchant ship, the heavily armed "East Indiaman," helped the Dutch establish their supremacy in the Indian Ocean. The Dutch also excelled at mapmaking (see Environment and Technology: Mapping the World).

also had links to the existence of public brothels, where young men could satisfy their lusts in cheap and impersonal encounters with unfortunate young women, often newly arrived from impoverished rural villages. Nevertheless, rape was a common occurrence, usually perpetrated by gangs of young men who attacked young women rumored to be free with their favors. Some historians believe that such gang rapes reflect poor young men's jealousy at older men's easier access to women.

Commercial Techniques and Technology

The expansion of trade in early modern Europe prompted the development of new techniques to manage far-flung business enterprises and invest the profits they produced. As elsewhere in the world, most businesses in Europe operated with family-owned funds or money borrowed from private moneylenders. But a key change in Europe was the rise of large financial institutions to serve the interests of big business and big government. In the seventeenth century, private Dutch banks developed such a reputation for security that wealthy individuals and governments from all over western Europe entrusted them with their money. To make a

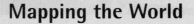

Mapping the World

In 1602 the Jesuit missionary Matteo Ricci in China printed an elaborate map of the world. Working from maps produced in Europe and incorporating the latest knowledge gathered by European maritime explorers, Ricci introduced two changes to make the map more appealing to his Chinese hosts. He labeled it in Chinese characters, and he split his map down the middle of the Atlantic so that China lay in the center. This version pleased Chinese elites, who considered China the "Middle Kingdom" surrounded by lesser states. A copy of Ricci's map in six large panels adorned the emperor's Beijing palace.

The stunningly beautiful maps and globes of sixteenth-century Europe were the most complete, detailed, and useful representations of the earth that any society had ever produced. The best mapmaker of the century was Gerhard Kremer, who is remembered as Mercator (the merchant) because his maps were so useful to European ocean traders. By incorporating the latest discoveries and scientific measurements, Mercator could depict the outlines of the major continents in painstaking detail, even if their interiors were still largely unknown to outsiders.

To represent the spherical globe on a flat map, Mercator drew the lines of longitude as parallel lines. Because such lines actually meet at the poles, Mercator's projection greatly exaggerated the size of every landmass and body of water distant from the equator. However, Mercator's rendering offered a very practical advantage: sailors could plot their course by drawing a straight line between their point of departure and their destination. Because of this useful feature the Mercator projection of the world remained in common use until quite recently. To some extent, its popularity came from the exaggerated size this projection gave to Europe. Like the Chinese, Europeans liked to think of themselves as at the center of things. Europeans also understood their true geographical position better than people in any other part of the world.

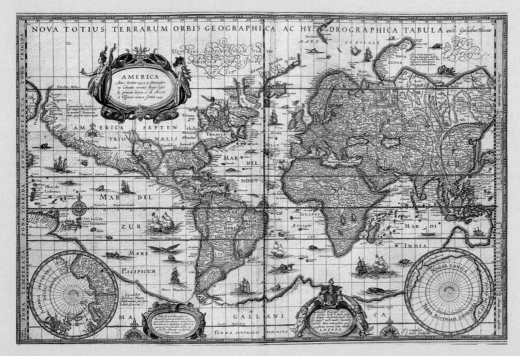

Dutch World Map, 1641
It is easy to see why the Chinese would not have liked to see their empire at the far right edge of this widely printed map. Besides the distortions caused by the Mercator projection, geographical ignorance exaggerates the size of North America and Antarctica.   (Courtesy of the Trustees British Museum)

RURAL SOCIETY AND THE ENVIRONMENT

For all its new political, military, and commercial strengths, early modern Europe rested on a fragile agrarian base. The techniques and efficiency of European agriculture had improved little since 1300. Bad years brought famine; good ones provided only small surpluses. Social tensions and conflicts multiplied as warfare, environmental deterioration, and adverse economic conditions worsened the circumstances of most rural Europeans between 1500 and 1750.

The Struggle for Food

Under the pressure of social and environmental change and inflation, the condition of the average person in western Europe seems to have worsened sharply during the century after 1530. Peasants in England were reduced to a diet of black bread and little else. Elsewhere people starved. Wars and other human-engineered calamities were partly to blame. In Spain the old nobility was responsible for the consolidation of landownership and the impoverishment of the peasantry. By 1600 only 3 percent of the population controlled 97 percent of the land. When Spanish landowners decided that they could increase their incomes by turning cropland into pastures for their sheep, food production and population declined.

Rural Europeans also felt the adverse effects of a century of relatively cool climate that began in the 1590s. During this **Little Ice Age,** average temperatures fell only a few degrees, but the effects were startling. Glaciers in the Alps grew much larger. Rivers and canals important to commerce froze solid from bank to bank. In some places during the coldest years, the growing season shrank by two months. As a result, food crops ripened more slowly during cooler summers and were often damaged by early fall frosts. In spring late frosts withered the tender shoots of newly planted crops.

People could survive a smaller-than-average harvest in one year with reserves left from the year before. But when one cold year followed another, the consequences were devastating. Records show that when average summer temperatures in northern Europe were 2.7°F (1.5°C) lower in 1674 and 1675 and again in 1694 and 1695, deaths due to malnutrition and cold increased sharply.

The cold spell of 1694–1695 caused a famine in Finland that carried off between a quarter and a third of the population.

By 1700, new crops from the Americas were helping the rural poor avoid starvation. At first eaten only in desperate times, potatoes and maize (corn) became staples for the rural poor in the eighteenth century because they yielded more abundant food from small garden plots. Potatoes sustained life in northeastern and Central Europe and in Ireland. Peasants along the Mediterranean who could not afford to eat the wheat they raised for urban markets grew maize for their own consumption.

Deforestation

Another threat to rural life came from **deforestation.** Early modern Europeans cut down their great hardwood forests to provide timbers for ships, lumber for buildings, wagons, and barrels, fuel for heating and cooking, and charcoal for smelting ores and other industrial processes. Each of the three hundred ironworks in England in the late seventeenth century consumed a thousand loads of oak a year. Wood shortages resulting from such high consumption led to increased imports of timber and charcoal from more heavily forested Scandinavian countries and Russia. Sweden used its vast forest resources to become a major iron producer in the seventeenth century. After 1716 Russia was Europe's largest producer of iron.

Because of this consumption of wood for Europe's rising population and expanding economy, forest depletion emerged as a serious issue in the seventeenth and eighteenth centuries. The shortages were particularly acute in England, where one early-seventeenth-century observer lamented: "within man's memory, it was held impossible to have any want of wood in England. But . . . at present, through the great consuming of wood . . . and the neglect of planting of woods, there is a great scarcity of wood throughout the whole kingdom."[3] Shortages in England drove the price of ordinary firewood up five times faster than other prices between the late fifteenth and the mid-seventeenth centuries.

High wood prices encouraged the use of coal as an alternative fuel. England's coal mining increased twelvefold from 210,000 tons in 1550 to 2.5 million tons in 1700. From 1709, coke—coal refined to remove impurities—gradually replaced charcoal in the smelting of iron. These new demands drove English coal production to nearly 5 million tons a year by 1750.

France was much more forested than England, but increasing consumption there caused Colbert to predict that "France will perish for lack of wood." By the late

Winter in Flanders, 1565   This January scene by the Flemish artist Pieter Bruegel, the Elder, shows many everyday activities. At left, men return from trapping hares, and the women under the sign singe the bristles off a slaughtered pig. On the frozen ponds, people skate and play hockey and curling. An old woman carries a load of faggots across the bridge. A February scene that Bruegel painted as part of this series shows the snow all melted. A few decades later, however, winters became longer and colder.   (Kunsthistorisches Museum, Vienna/The Bridgeman Art Library, New York and London)

eighteenth century, deforestation was becoming an issue even in Sweden and Russia. New laws in France and England designed to protect the forests were largely inspired by fears of shortages for naval vessels, whose keels required high-quality timbers of exceptional size and particular curvature. Although wood consumption remained high, rising prices encouraged some individuals to plant trees for future harvest.

Everywhere in Europe the rural poor felt the depletion of the forests most strongly. For centuries they had depended on woodlands for abundant supplies of wild nuts and berries, free firewood and building materials, and wild game. Many poor men and women flocked to the cities in hopes of finding better jobs, but most were disappointed. As we have seen, begging, theft, and prostitution were the result.

Peasantry and Gentry

The bright side of rural life in western Europe was the remarkable personal freedom of the peasantry in comparison with people of similar status in many other parts of the world. Serfdom, which bound men and women to land owned by a local lord, declined sharply after the great plague of the mid-fourteenth century. Most remaining serfs in western Europe gained their freedom by 1600. By that date slavery in southern Iberia, which had been sustained by large numbers of captives from Africa, had also come to an end. Coincidentally, the disappearance of serfdom in western Europe was paralleled by the introduction of serfdom in much of early modern eastern Europe.

Legal freedom in western Europe did little to make the peasants' lives safe and secure. Peasants with surplus crops to sell benefited from the higher prices brought about by inflation, but the broader trend was for peasants to fall deeper and deeper into debt until they lost their land. This transformation of rural ownership was accelerated by the desire of many successful members of the bourgeoisie to use their wealth to raise their social status. Retiring from their professions and buying country estates gained them admission to the ranks of gentry. These new owners of rural estates affected the lifestyle of the old aristocracy and sometimes received the aristocracy's exemption from taxation, but they did not have titles of nobility.

The gentry loaned money to impoverished peasants and to members of the nobility and in time increased their ownership of land. Some families sought aristocratic husbands for their daughters. The old nobility found such alliances attractive because of the large dowries that rich merchants provided. In France a family could gain the exemption from taxation by living in gentility for three generations. The same family could gain noble status more quickly by purchasing a title. French kings sold so many new patents of nobility that people came to distinguish the new *noblesse de robe°* (dress nobility) from the medieval *noblesse d'épée°* (sword nobility).

Rural misery in early modern Europe provoked many rebellions. For example, in 1525 peasant rebels in the Alps attacked both nobles and clergy as representatives of the privileged and landowning classes. They had no love for merchants either, whom they denounced for lending at interest and charging high prices. Rebellions multiplied as rural conditions worsened. In southwestern France alone some 450 uprisings occurred between 1590 and 1715, many of them set off by food shortages and tax increases. The exemption of the wealthy from taxation was a frequent souce of complaint. A rebellion in southern France in 1670 began when a mob of townswomen attacked the tax collector. It quickly spread to the country, where peasant leaders cried, "Death to the people's oppressors!" Authorities dealt severely with such revolts and executed or maimed their leaders.

In 1750 most Europeans still lived in general wretchedness. Modest improvements in food production in some places were overwhelmed by population growth. Even in the prosperous Dutch towns half of the population lived in acute poverty. Some rural poor in the eighteenth century worked at home spinning yarn and weaving cloth from materials supplied by entrepreneurs. So many single women supported themselves by spinning yarn that *spinster* became the normal English word for an unmarried woman.

---

noblesse de robe (no-BLES deh ROHB)
noblesse d'épée (no-BLES day-PAY)

THE REALM OF IDEAS

New ideas and old beliefs pulled early modern Europeans in several different directions, even after the Reformation controversies subsided. The hold of biblical and traditional folk beliefs on the thinking of most people showed itself in widespread new fears about witches and the power of the Devil. The Renaissance helped sharpen the influence of writings from Greco-Roman antiquity on educated people. A few thinkers broke new scientific ground in deciphering the motion of the planets and constructing mathematical models of the force of gravitation. In time, the new scientific ideas encouraged some to reevaluate traditional social and political systems, with important implications for the period after 1750.

Traditional Thinking and Witch-Hunts

Prevailing European ideas about the natural world blended two distinct traditions. The older was made up of stories and beliefs from local folk cultures and pre-Christian religions, which had not lost their hold on the minds of most Europeans. On to this tradition was grafted the biblical traditions of the Christian and Jewish scriptures, heard by all in church and read by growing numbers in vernacular translations. In the minds of most people ideas of magic and folk spirits mixed with Christian teachings about miracles, saints, and devils.

Like people in other parts of the world, most early modern Europeans believed that natural events could have supernatural causes. When crops failed or domestic animals died unexpectedly, many people blamed unseen spirits. People also attributed human triumphs and tragedies to supernatural causes. When an earthquake destroyed much of Lisbon, Portugal's capital city, in November 1755, for example, both educated and uneducated saw the event as a punishment sent by God. A Jesuit charged it "scandalous to pretend that the earthquake was just a natural event." An English Protestant leader agreed, comparing Lisbon's fate with that of Sodom, the city that God destroyed because of the sinfulness of its citizens, according to the Hebrew Bible.

Nowhere was the belief in unseen forces more evident than in the extraordinary series of **witch-hunts** that swept across northern Europe in the late sixteenth and seventeenth centuries. It is estimated that secular and church authorities tried over a hundred thousand people—some three-fourths of them women—for prac-

SOCIETY & CULTURE

Witchcraft

The elderly widow whose account follows was fairly typical of the kind of person accused of witchcraft in the Holy Roman Empire. Her confession, given in 1587, mentions activities commonly associated with witches: fornicating with devils, murdering children, desecrating the Blessed Sacrament, causing destructive storms, and night flying—though on a pitchfork, not a broomstick.

The herein mentioned, malefic and miserable woman, Walpurga Hausmännin, now imprisoned and in chains, has, upon kindly questioning and also torture, . . . confessed her witchcraft and admitted the following. When one-and-thirty years ago, she became a widow, she cut corn for Hans Schlumperger, of this place, together with his former servant, Bis im Pfarrhof, by name. Him she enticed with lewd speeches and gestures and they convened that they should, on an appointed night, meet in her, Walpurga's, dwelling, there to indulge in lustful intercourse. So when Walpurga in expectation of this, sat awaiting him at night in her chamber, meditating upon evil and fleshy thoughts, it was not the said bondsman who appeared unto her, but the Evil One in the latter's guise and raiment and indulged in fornication with her. . . . After the act of fornication she saw and felt the cloven foot of her whoremonger, and that his hand was not natural, but as if made of wood. She was greatly affrighted thereat and called upon the name of Jesus, whereupon the Devil left her and vanished.

On the ensuing night the Evil Spirit visited her again in the same shape and whored with her. . . . Further, the above-mentioned Walpurga confesses that she oft and much rode on a pitchfork by night with her paramour, but not far on account of her duties [as a midwife].

Since she surrendered to the Devil, she had seemingly oft received the Blessed Sacrament of the true Body and Blood of Jesus Christ, apparently by the mouth, but had not partaken of it, but (which once more is terrible to relate) had always taken it out of her mouth again and delivered it up to Feder-lin, her paramour. At their nightly gatherings she had oft with her other playfellows trodden under foot the Holy and Blessed Sacrament and the image of the Holy Cross. . . . .

He also compelled her to do away with and to kill young infants at birth, even before they had been taken to Holy Baptism. This she did whenever possible. . . . She had used the said little bones to manufacture hail; this she was wont to do once or twice a year. . . .

After all this, the Judges and Jury of the Court of this Town of Dillingen . . . at last unanimously gave the verdict that the aforesaid Walpurga Hausmännin be punished and dispatched from life to death by burning at the stake as being a maleficent and well-known witch and sorceress, convicted according to the context of Common Law and the Criminal Code of the Emperor Charles V and the Holy Roman Empire. All her goods and chattels and estate left after her to go to the Treasury of our Most High Prince and Lord. The aforesaid Walpurga to be led, seated on a cart, to which she is tied, to the place of her execution, and her body first to be torn five times with red-hot irons. . . . But since for nineteen years she was a licensed and pledged midwife of the city of Dillingen, yet has acted so vilely, her right hand with which she did such knavish tricks is to be cut off at the place of execution. Neither are her ashes after burning to remain lying on the ground, but are thereafter to be carried to the nearest flowing water and thrown thereinto.

Under what circumstances did the widow confess to these deeds? Why was she so brutally executed?

Source: *The Fugger News-Letters*, ed. Victor von Klarwill, trans. Pauline de Chary (London: John Lane, The Bodley Head Ltd., 1924); reissued as *News and Rumor in Renaissance Europe: The Fugger Newsletters*, trans. Pauline de Chary (New York: Putnam, 1959), 137–139, 142–143.

---

ticing witchcraft. Some were acquitted, some recanted, but over half were executed. The trial records make it clear that both the accusers and the accused believed that it was possible for angry and jealous individuals to use evil magic and the power of the Devil to cause people and domestic animals to sicken and die or cause crops to wither in the fields. Torture and badgering questions persuaded many accused witches to confess to casting spells and to describe in vivid detail their encounters with the Devil and their attendance at night-time assemblies of witches (see Society and Culture: Witchcraft).

Modern historians have sought other explanations for these witch-hunts. The fact that many of the accused were older women, especially widows, may reflect the widespread belief that women not directly under the control of fathers or husbands were likely to turn to evil. The fear of people rebelling against those in authority was well founded.

Modern research, however, also stresses that at least some of those accused in early modern Europe may really have tried to use witchcraft and the powers of the Devil to harm their enemies. The Reformation had focused attention on the Devil and may have helped revive older fears of witchcraft. In parts of the world where belief in witchcraft is still strong, witch-hunts often arise at times of social stress, and people who are marginalized by poverty and by the suspicions of others often relish the celebrity that public confession brings. Self-confessed "witches" may even find release from the guilt they feel for wishing evil on their neighbors.

No single reason can explain the rise in witchcraft accusations and fears in early modern Europe, but, for both the accusers and the accused, there are plausible connections between the witch-hunts and rising social tensions, rural poverty, and environmental strains. Far from being a bizarre aberration, witch-hunts reflected the larger social climate of early modern Europe.

The Scientific Revolution

Ideas about the natural world were influenced by folk and Christian traditions and by writings from Greco-Roman antiquity that had been revived during the Renaissance. Among intellectuals prevailing ideas were based on the physics of Aristotle. The Greek philosopher taught that everything on earth was reducible to four elements. The surface of the earth was composed of the two heavy elements, earth and water. The atmosphere was made up of two lighter elements, air and fire, which floated above the ground. Higher still were the sun, moon, planets, and stars, which, according to Aristotelian physics, were so light and pure that they floated in crystalline spheres. This division between the ponderous, heavy earth and the airy, celestial bodies accorded perfectly with the common-sense perception that all heavenly bodies revolved around the earth.

The prevailing conception of the universe was also influenced by the mathematical tradition derived from the ancient Greek mathematician Pythagoras, who proved the validity of the famous theorem that still bears his name: In a right triangle, the squares of the hypotenuse is equal to the sum of the squares of the other two sides ($a^2 + b^2 = c^2$). Pythagoreans attributed to mystical properties the ability of simple mathematical equations to describe physical objects. They attached special significance to the simplest (to them perfect) geometrical shapes: the circle (a point rotated around another point) and the sphere (a circle rotated on its axis). They believed that celestial objects were perfect spheres orbiting the earth in perfectly circular orbits.

In the sixteenth century, however, the careful observations and mathematical calculations of some daring and imaginative European investigators began to challenge these prevailing conceptions of the physical world. These pioneers of the **Scientific Revolution** demonstrated that the workings of the universe could be explained by natural causes.

Over the centuries, observers of the nighttime skies had plotted the movements of the heavenly bodies, and mathematicians had worked to fit these observations into the prevailing theories of circular orbits. To make all the evidence fit, they had come up with eighty different spheres and some ingenious theories to explain the many seemingly irregular movements. Pondering these complications, a Polish monk and mathematician named Nicholas Copernicus (1473–1543) came up with a mathematically simpler solution: switching the center of the different orbits from the earth to the sun would reduce the number of spheres that were needed.

Copernicus did not challenge the idea that the sun, moon, and planets were light, perfect spheres, or that they moved in circular orbits. But his placement of the sun, not the earth, at the center of things began a revolution in understanding about the structure of the heavens and about the central place of humans in the universe. To escape the anticipated controversies, Copernicus delayed the publication of his heliocentric (sun-centered) theory until after his death in 1543.

Other astronomers, including the Danish Tycho Brahe (1546–1601) and his German assistant Johannes Kepler (1571–1630), strengthened and improved on Copernicus's model, showing that planets actually move in elliptical, not circular orbits. The most brilliant of the Copernicans was the Italian Galileo Galilei° (1564–1642). In 1609 Galileo built a telescope through which he took a closer look at the heavens. Able to magnify distant objects thirty times beyond the powers of the naked eye, Galileo saw that heavenly bodies were not the perfectly smooth spheres of the Aristotelians. The moon, he re-

---

Galileo Galilei (gal-uh-LAY-oh gal-uh-LAY-ee)

ported in *The Starry Messenger* (1610), had mountains and valleys; the sun had spots; other planets had their own moons. In other words, the earth was not alone in being heavy and changeable.

At first, the Copernican universe found more critics than supporters because it so directly challenged not just popular ideas but the intellectual synthesis of classical and biblical authorities. How, demanded Aristotle's defenders, could the heavy earth move without producing vibrations that would shake the planet apart? Is the Bible wrong, asked the theologians, when the Book of Joshua says that, by God's command, "the sun [not the earth] stood still . . . for about a whole day" to give the ancient Israelites victory in their conquest of Palestine? If Aristotle's physics was wrong, worried other traditionalists, would not the theological synthesis built on other parts of his philosophy be open to question?

Intellectual and religious leaders encouraged political authorities to suppress the new ideas. Most Protestant leaders, following the lead of Martin Luther, condemned the heliocentric universe as contrary to the Bible. Catholic authorities waited longer to act. After all, both Copernicus and Galileo were Roman Catholics. Copernicus had dedicated his book to the pope, and another pope, Gregory XIII, in 1582 had used the latest astronomical findings to issue a new and more accurate calendar (still used today). Galileo ingeniously argued that the conflict between scripture and science was only apparent: the word of God revealed in the Bible was expressed in the imperfect language of ordinary people, but in nature God's truth was revealed more perfectly in a language that could be learned by careful observation and scientific reasoning.

Unfortunately, Galileo also ridiculed those who were slow to accept his findings, charging that Copernican ideas were "mocked and hooted at by an infinite multitude . . . of fools." Smarting under Galileo's stinging sarcasm, some Jesuits and other critics got his ideas condemned by the Roman Inquisition in 1616, which put *The Starry Messenger* on the Index of Forbidden Books and prohibited Galileo from publishing further on the subject. (In 1992 the Catholic Church officially retracted its condemnation of Galileo.)

Despite official opposition, printed books spread the new scientific ideas among scholars across Europe. In England, Robert Boyle (1627–1691) used experimental methods and a trial-and-error approach to examine the inner workings of chemistry. He and fellow members of the Royal Society were enthusiastic missionaries of mechanical science and fierce opponents of the Aristotelians.

Galileo in 1624   This engraving by Ottavio Leone shows the Italian scientist in full vigor at age sixty, before he was hounded by the Roman Inquisition.   (British Museum)

Meanwhile, English mathematician Isaac Newton (1642–1727) was carrying Galileo's demonstration that the heavens and earth share a common physics to its logical conclusion. Newton formulated a set of mathematical laws that all physical objects obeyed. It was the force of gravity—not angels—that governed the elliptical orbits of heavenly bodies. It was gravitation (and the resistance of air) that caused cannonballs to fall back to earth. From 1703 until his death Newton served as president of the Royal Society, using his prestige to promote the new science that came to bear his name.

As the condemnation of Galileo demonstrates, many religious and intellectual leaders viewed the new science with suspicion or outright hostility. Yet the principal pioneers of the Scientific Revolution were all convinced that scientific discoveries and revealed religion were not in conflict. At the peak of his fame Newton promoted a series of lectures devoted to proving the validity of Christianity. However, by showing that the Aristotelians and biblical writers held ideas about the natural world that were naive and unfactual, these pioneers opened the door to others who used reason to challenge a broader range of unquestioned traditions and superstitions. The world of ideas was forever changed.

The Early Enlightenment

Advances in scientific thought had few practical applications until long after 1750. But they inspired governments and private groups in many countries to reexamine the reasonableness of everything from agricultural methods to laws, religion, and social hierarchies. The belief that human reason could discover the laws that governed social behavior and were just as scientific as the laws that governed physics energized a movement known as the **Enlightenment.** Like the Scientific Revolution, this movement was the work of a few "enlightened" individuals who often faced bitter opposition from the political, intellectual, and religious establishment. Leading Enlightenment thinkers became accustomed to having their books burned or banned and spent long periods in exile to escape being imprisoned themselves.

Influences besides the Scientific Revolution affected the Enlightenment. The Reformation had aroused many to champion one creed or another, but partisan bickering and bloodshed led others to doubt the superiority of any theological position and to recommend toleration of all religions. The killing of suspected witches also shocked many thoughtful people. The leading French thinker Voltaire (the pen name of François Marie Arouet, 1694–1778) declared: "No opinion is worth burning your neighbor for."

Accounts of cultures in other parts of the world also led some European thinkers to question assumptions about the superiority of European political institutions, moral standards, and religious beliefs. Reports of Amerindian life, though romanticized, led some to conclude that those whom they had called savages were in many ways nobler than European Christians. Matteo Ricci, a Jesuit missionary to China whose journals made a strong impression in Europe, contrasted the lack of territorial ambition of the Chinese with the constant warfare in the West and attributed the difference to the fact that China was wisely ruled by educated men whom he called "Philosophers."

Another influence on the "enlightened" thinkers of the eighteenth century was the English Revolution. In the wake of the Glorious Revolution of 1688 and the English Bill of Rights, the English political philosopher John Locke (1632–1704), who had lived in the Netherlands during the period of Oliver Cromwell's Puritan Republic, published his influential *Second Treatise of Civil Government* (1690). Locke disputed the prevailing idea that government was sacred and that kings ruled by divine right. He argued that rulers derived their power from the consent of the governed, who surrendered some of their rights to the state so that they might better preserve their lives, liberty, and property. Locke challenged the continental monarchs' often-repeated claim that they held absolute authority over their subjects. He believed that absolute monarchy was incompatible with civil society, and he wrote that monarchs, like everyone else, were subject to the law that laid the basis for the compact that brought civil society into existence. If monarchs overstepped the law, Locke argued, citizens had not only the right but the duty to rebel. The consequences of this idea are considered in Chapter 23.

Although many circumstances shaped "enlightened" thinking, the new scientific methods and discoveries provided the clearest model for changing European society. Voltaire posed the issues in these terms: "it would be very peculiar that all nature, all the planets, should obey eternal laws" but a human being, "in contempt of these laws, could act as he pleased solely according to his caprice." The English poet Alexander Pope (1688–1774) made a similar point in verse: "Nature and Nature's laws lay hidden in night; / God said, 'Let Newton be' and all was light."

The Enlightenment was more a frame of mind than a coherent movement. Individuals who embraced it drew inspiration from different sources and promoted different agendas. By 1750 its proponents were clearer about what they disliked than about what new institutions should be created. Some "enlightened" thinkers thought society could be made to function with the mechanical orderliness of planets spinning in their orbits. Nearly all were optimistic that—at least in the long run—human beliefs and institutions could be improved. This belief in progress would help foster political and social revolutions after 1750, as Chapter 23 recounts.

Despite the enthusiasm the Enlightenment aroused in some circles, it was decidedly unpopular with many absolutist rulers and with most clergymen. Europe in 1750 was neither enlightened nor scientific. It was a place where political and religious divisions, growing literacy, and the printing press made possible the survival of the new ideas that profoundly changed life in future centuries.

CONCLUSION

Historians use the word *revolution* to describe many different changes taking place in Europe between 1500 and 1750. The inflation of the sixteenth century has been called a price revolution, the expansion of trade a commercial revolution, the reform of state spending a financial revolution, the changes in weapons and warfare a military revolution. We have also encountered a scientific revolution and the religious revolution of the Reformation.

These important changes in early modern European government, economy, society, and thought were parts of a dynamic process that began in the later Middle Ages and led to even bigger industrial and political revolutions before the eighteenth century was over. Yet the years from 1500 to 1750 were not simply—perhaps not even primarily—an age of progress for Europe. For many, the ferocious competition of European armies, merchants, and ideas was a wrenching experience. The growth of powerful states extracted a terrible price in death, destruction, and misery. The Reformation brought greater individual choice in religion but widespread religious persecution as well. Individual women rose or fell with their social class, but few gained equality with men. The expanding economy benefited members of the emerging merchant elite and their political allies, but most Europeans became worse off as prices rose faster than wages. New scientific and enlightened ideas ignited new controversies long before they yielded any tangible benefits.

The historical significance of this period of European history is clearest when viewed in a global context. What stands out are the powerful and efficient European armies, economies, and governments, which were envied, and sometimes imitated, by other people such as Tsar Peter the Great. Seen from a global perspective, the balance of political and economic power shifted slowly but inexorably in the Europeans' favor from 1500 to 1750. In 1500 the Ottomans threatened Europe. By 1750, as the remaining chapters of Part Five detail, Europeans had brought the world's seas and a growing part of its land and people under their control. No single group of Europeans accomplished this. The Dutch eclipsed the pioneering Portuguese and Spanish; then the English and French bested the Dutch. Competition, too, was a factor in the European success.

Other changes in Europe during this period had no great overseas significance yet. The more representative and financially stable government begun in Britain, the new ideas of the Scientific Revolution and the Enlightenment, and the innovations in agriculture and manufacturing were still of minor importance. Their full effects in furthering Europeans' global dominion were felt after 1750, as Parts Six and Seven will explore.

■ Key Terms

papacy	balance of power
Renaissance (Europe)	bourgeoisie
indulgence	joint-stock company
Protestant Reformation	stock exchange
Catholic Reformation	Little Ice Age
Holy Roman Empire	deforestation
Habsburg	witch-hunt
absolutism	Scientific Revolution
constitutionalism	Enlightenment

■ Suggested Reading

Overviews of this period include Euan Cameron, *Early Modern Europe* (1999), and H. G. Koenigsberger, *Early Modern Europe: Fifteen Hundred to Seventeen Eighty-Nine* (1987). Global perspectives can be found in Fernand Braudel, *Civilization and Capitalism, 15th–18th Century*, trans. Siân Reynolds, 3 vols. (1979), and Immanuel Wallerstein, *The Modern World-System*, vol. 2, *Mercantilism and the Consolidation of the European World-Economy, 1600–1750* (1980).

Excellent introductions to social and economic life are George Huppert, *After the Black Death: A Social History of Early Modern Europe* (1986), and Carlo M. Cipolla, *Before the Industrial Revolution: European Society and Economy, 1000–1700*, 2d ed. (1980). Peter Burke, *Popular Culture in Early Modern Europe* (1978), offers a broad treatment of nonelite perspectives, as does Robert Jütte, *Poverty and Deviance in Early Modern Europe* (1994). For more economic detail see Robert S. DuPlessis, *Transitions to Capitalism in Early Modern Europe* (1997); Myron P. Gutmann, *Toward the Modern Economy: Early Industry in Europe, 1500–1800* (1988); and Carlo M. Cipolla, ed., *The Fontana Economic History of Europe*, vol. 2, *The Sixteenth and Seventeenth Centuries* (1974). Merry E. Wiesner summarizes a body of new research in *Women and Gender in Early Modern Europe* (1994).

Technological and environmental changes are the focus of Geoffrey Parker, *Military Revolution: Military Innovation and the Rise of the West, 1500–1800*, 2d ed. (1996); William H. McNeill, *The Pursuit of Power: Technology, Armed Force, and Society Since A.D. 1000* (1982); Robert Greenhalgh Albion, *Forests and Sea Power: The Timber Problem of the Royal Navy, 1652–1862*

(1965); Emmanuel Le Roy Ladurie, *Times of Feast, Times of Famine: A History of Climate Since the Year 1000*, trans. Barbara Bray (1971); and Jean M. Grove, *The Little Ice Age* (1988). Robert C. Allen, *Enclosure and the Yeoman: The Agricultural Development of the South Midlands, 1450–1850* (1992), focuses on England.

Steven Stapin, *The Scientific Revolution* (1998), and Hugh Kearney, *Science and Change, 1500–1700* (1971) are accessible introductions. Thomas S. Kuhn, *The Structure of Scientific Revolution*, 3d ed. (1996), and A. R. Hall, *The Scientific Revolution, 1500–1800: The Formation of the Modern Scientific Attitude*, 2d ed. (1962), are classic studies. Carolyn Merchant, *The Death of Nature: Women, Ecology and the Scientific Revolution* (1980), tries to combine several broad perspectives. *The Sciences in Enlightened Europe*, ed. W. Clark, J. Golinski, and S. Schaffer (1999), examines particular topics in a sophisticated way. Dorinda Outram, *The Enlightenment* (1995), provides a recent summary of research.

An excellent place to begin examining the complex subject of witchcraft is Brian Levack, *The Witch-Hunt in Early Modern Europe*, 2d ed. (1995). Anne Llewellyn Barstow, *Witchcraft: A New History of the European Witch Hunts* (1994), offers a postmodern interpretation; other up-to-date perspectives can be found in J. Barry, M. Hester, and G. Roberts, eds., *Witchcraft in Early*

Modern Europe: Studies in Culture and Belief (1998), and Carlo Ginzburg, *The Night Battles: Witchcraft and Agrarian Cults in the Sixteenth and Seventeenth Centuries*, trans. John and Anne Tedechi (1983). Cross-cultural perspectives are presented by Lucy Mair, *Witchcraft* (1969), and Geoffrey Parrinder, *Witchcraft: European and African* (1963).

Good single-country surveys are J. A. Sharpe, *Early Modern England: A Social History*, 2d ed. (1997); Emmanuel Le Roy Ladurie, *The Royal French State, 1460–1610* (1994) and *The Ancien Régime: A History of France, 1610–1774* (1998); Jonathan Israel, *The Dutch Republic: Its Rise, Greatness and Fall, 1477–1806* (1995); and James Casey, *Early Modern Spain: A Social History* (1999).

■ Notes

1. William H. McNeill, *The Pursuit of Power: Technology, Armed Force, and Society Since a A.D. 1000* (Chicago: University of Chicago Press, 1982), 124.
2. Michel de Montaigne, *Essais*, ch. 31, "Des Cannibales."
3. Quoted by Carlo M. Cipolla, "Introduction," *The Fontana Economic History of Europe*, vol. 2, *The Sixteenth and Seventeenth Centuries* (Glasgow: Collins/Fontana Books, 1974), 11–12.

19

THE DIVERSITY OF AMERICAN COLONIAL SOCIETIES,

1530–1770

The Columbian Exchange • Spanish America and Brazil • English and
French Colonies in North America • Colonial Expansion and Conflict
ENVIRONMENT AND TECHNOLOGY: The Silver Refinery at Potosí, Bolivia, 1700
SOCIETY AND CULTURE: Colonial Wealth and the Exploitation of Indigenous Peoples

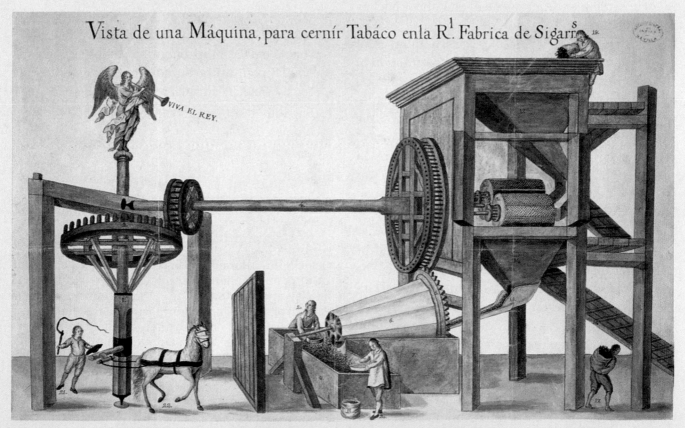

Tobacco Factory Machinery in Colonial Mexico City   The tobacco factory in eighteenth-century Mexico City
used a horse-driven mechanical shredder to produce snuff and cigarette tobacco.

*S*hulush Homa—an eighteenth-century Choctaw leader called "Red Shoes" by the English—faced a dilemma. For years he had befriended the French who had moved into the lower Mississippi Valley, protecting their outlying settlements from other indigenous groups and producing a steady flow of deerskins for trade. In return, he received guns and gifts as well as honors previously given only to chiefs. Though born a commoner, he had parlayed his skillful politicking with the French—and the shrewd distribution of the gifts he received—to enhance his position in Choctaw society. Then his fortunes turned. In the course of yet another war between England and France, the English cut off French shipping. Faced with followers unhappy over his sudden inability to supply French guns, Red Shoes decided to make a deal with the English. Unfortunately, the new tactic backfired. His former allies, the French, put a price on his head, which was soon collected. His murder in 1747 launched a Choctaw civil war, a conflict that left French settlements unprotected and the Choctaw people weakened.

The story of Red Shoes reveals a number of themes from the period of European colonization of the Americas. First, although the wars, epidemics, and territorial loss associated with European settlement threatened Amerindians, many adapted the new technologies and new political possibilities to their own purposes and thrived—at least for a time. In the end, though, the best that they could achieve was a holding action. The people of the Old World were coming to dominate the people of the New.

Second, after centuries of isolation, the Americas were being drawn into global events, influenced by the political and economic demands of Europe. The influx of Europeans and Africans resulted in a vast biological and cultural transformation, as the introduction of new plants, animals, diseases, peoples, and technologies fundamentally altered the natural environment of the Western Hemisphere. This was not a one-way transfer, however. The technologies and resources of the New World contributed to profound changes in the Old. Staple crops introduced from the Americas provided highly nutritious foods that helped fuel a population spurt in Europe, Asia, and Africa. As we saw in Chapter 18, riches and products funneled from the Americas changed economic, social, and political relations in Europe.

Third, the fluidity of the Choctaw's political situation reflects the complexity of colonial society, where Amerindians, Europeans, and Africans all contributed to the creation of new cultures. Although similar processes took place throughout the Americas, the particulars varied from place to place, creating a diverse range of cultures. The society that arose in each colony reflected the colony's mix of native peoples, its connections to the slave trade, and the characteristics of the European society establishing the colony. As the colonies matured, new concepts of identity developed, and those living in the Americas began to see themselves as unique.

As you read this chapter, ask yourself the following questions:

- How did the development of European colonies in the Americas alter the natural environment?
- What were the most important differences in the colonial political institutions and economies created by Spain, Portugal, England, and France?
- How important was forced labor to the European colonies?

THE COLUMBIAN EXCHANGE

The term **Columbian Exchange** refers to the transfer of peoples, animals, plants, and diseases between the New and Old Worlds. The European invasion and settlement of the Western Hemisphere opened a long era of biological and technological transfers that altered American environments. Within a century of first settlement, the domesticated livestock and major agricultural crops of the Old World (the known world before Columbus's voyage) had spread over much of the Americas, and the New World's useful staple crops had enriched the agricultures of Europe, Asia, and Africa. Old World diseases

CHRONOLOGY

	Spanish America	Brazil	British America	French America
1500	**1518** Smallpox arrives in Caribbean **1535** Creation of Viceroyalty of New Spain **1540s** Creation of Viceroyalty of Peru **1542** New Laws outlaw Amerindian enslavement **1545** Silver discovered at Potosí, Bolivia	**1540–1600** Era of Amerindian slavery **After 1540** Sugar begins to dominate the economy		**1524–1554** Jacques Cartier's voyages to explore Newfoundland and Gulf of St. Lawrence
1600	**1625** Population of Potosí reaches 120,000	**By 1620** African slave trade provides majority of plantation workers	**1583** Unsuccessful effort to establish colony on Newfoundland **1607** Jamestown founded **1620** Plymouth founded **1660** Slave population in Virginia begins period of rapid growth **1664** English take New York from Dutch	**1608** Quebec founded
1700	**1700** Last Habsburg ruler of Spain dies **1713** First Bourbon ruler of Spain crowned	**1750–1777** Reforms of marquis de Pombal	**1756–1763** French and Indian War	**1699** Louisiana founded **1760** English take Canada

that entered the Americas with European immigrants and African slaves devastated indigenous populations. These dramatic population changes weakened native peoples' capacity for resistance and facilitated the transfer of plants, animals, and related technologies. As a result, the colonies of Spain, Portugal, England, and France became vast arenas of cultural and social experimentation.

Demographic Changes

Because of their long isolation from other continents (see Chapter 17), the peoples of the New World lacked immunity to diseases introduced from the Old World. As a result, death rates among Amerindian peoples during the epidemics of the early colonial period were very high. The lack of reliable data has frustrated efforts to measure the deadly impact of these diseases. Scholars disagree about the size of the precontact population but generally agree that, after contact, Old World diseases overwhelmed native populations. According to one estimate, in the century that followed the triumph of Hernán Cortés in 1521, the population of central Mexico fell from a high somewhere between 13 million and 25 million to approximately 700,000. In this same period nearly 75 percent of the Maya population disappeared. In the region of the Inca Empire, population fell from about 9 million to approximately 600,000. Brazil's native population was similarly ravaged, falling from 2.5 million to under a million within a century of the arrival of the Portuguese. The most conservative estimates of population loss begin with smaller precontact populations but accept that epidemics had a catastrophic effect.

Smallpox, which arrived in the Caribbean in 1518, was the most deadly of the early epidemics. In Mexico and Central America, 50 percent or more of the Amerindian population died during the first wave of smallpox epidemics. The disease then spread to South America with equally devastating effects. Measles arrived in the New World in the 1530s and was followed by diphtheria, typhus, influenza, and, perhaps, pulmonary plague. Mortality was often greatest when two or more diseases struck at the same time. Between 1520 and 1521 influenza in combination with other ailments attacked the Cakchiquel of Guatemala. Their chronicle recalls:

> Great was the stench of the dead. After our fathers and grandfathers succumbed, half the people fled to the fields. The dogs and vultures devoured the bodies. . . . So it was that we became orphans, oh my sons! . . . We were born to die![1]

By the mid-seventeenth century, malaria and yellow fever were also present in tropical regions. The deadliest form of malaria arrived with the African slave trade. It ravaged the already reduced native populations and afflicted European immigrants as well. Most scholars believe that yellow fever was also brought from Africa, but new research suggests that the disease was present before the conquest in the tropical low country near present-day Veracruz on the Gulf of Mexico. Whatever its origins, yellow fever killed Europeans in the Caribbean Basin and in other tropical regions nearly as efficiently as smallpox had earlier extinguished Amerindians. Syphilis is the only significant disease believed to have been transferred from the Americas to Europe.

The development of English and French colonies in North America in the seventeenth century led to similar patterns of contagion and mortality. In 1616 and 1617 epidemics nearly exterminated many of New England's indigenous groups. French fur traders transmitted measles, smallpox, and other diseases as far as Hudson Bay and the Great Lakes. Although there is very little evidence that Europeans consciously used disease as a tool of empire, the deadly results of contact clearly undermined the ability of native peoples to resist settlement.

Transfer of Plants and Animals

Even as epidemics swept through the indigenous population, the New and the Old Worlds were participating in a vast exchange of plants and animals that radically altered diet and lifestyles in both regions. All the staples of southern European agriculture—such as wheat, olives,

The Columbian Exchange   After the conquest, the introduction of plants and animals from the Old World dramatically altered the American environment. Here an Amerindian woman is seen milking a cow. Livestock sometimes destroyed the fields of native peoples, but cattle, sheep, pigs, and goats also provided food, leather, and wool.   (From Martinez Compañon, *Trujillo del Perú*, V.II, E 79. Photo: Imaging services, Harvard College Library)

grapes, and garden vegetables—were being grown in the Americas in a remarkably short time after contact. African and Asian crops—such as rice, bananas, coconuts, breadfruit, and sugar cane—were soon introduced as well. Native peoples remained loyal to their traditional staples but added many Old World plants to their diet. Citrus fruits, melons, figs, and sugar as well as onions, radishes, and salad greens all found a place in Amerindian cuisines.

In return the Americas offered the Old World an abundance of useful plants. The New World staples—

maize, potatoes, and manioc—revolutionized agriculture and diet in parts of Europe, Africa, and Asia (see Environment and Technology: Amerindian Foods in Africa, in Chapter 20). Many experts assert that the rapid growth of world population after 1700 resulted in large measure from the spread of these useful crops, which provided more calories per acre than any of the Old World staples except rice. Beans, squash, tomatoes, sweet potatoes, peanuts, chilies, and chocolate also gained widespread acceptance in the Old World. The New World also provided the Old with plants that provided dyes, medicinal plants, varieties of cotton, and tobacco.

The introduction of European livestock had a dramatic impact on New World environments and cultures. Faced with few natural predators, cattle, pigs, horses, and sheep, as well as pests like rats and rabbits, multiplied rapidly in the open spaces of the Americas. On the vast plains of present-day southern Brazil, Uruguay, and Argentina, herds of wild cattle and horses exceeded 50 million by 1700. Large herds of both animals also appeared in northern Mexico and what became the southwest of the United States.

Where Old World livestock spread most rapidly, environmental changes were most dramatic. Many priests and colonial officials noted the destructive impact of marauding livestock on Amerindian agriculturists. The first viceroy of Mexico, Antonio de Mendoza, wrote to the Spanish king, "May your Lordship realize that if cattle are allowed, the Indians will be destroyed." Sheep, which grazed grasses close to the ground, were also an environmental threat. Yet the viceroy's stark choice misrepresented the complex response of indigenous peoples to these new animals.

Wild cattle on the plains of South America, northern Mexico, and Texas provided indigenous peoples with abundant supplies of meat and hides. In the present-day southwestern United States, the Navajo became sheepherders and expert weavers of woolen cloth. Even in the centers of European settlement, individual Amerindians turned European animals to their own advantage by becoming muleteers, cowboys, and sheepherders.

No animal had a more striking effect on the cultures of native peoples than the horse, which increased the efficiency of hunters and the military capacity of warriors on the plains. The horse permitted the Apache, Sioux, Blackfoot, Comanche, Assiniboine, and others to hunt more efficiently the vast herds of buffalo in North America. The horse also revolutionized the cultures of the Araucanian (or Mapuche) and Pampas peoples in South America.

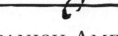

SPANISH AMERICA AND BRAZIL

The frontiers of conquest and settlement expanded rapidly. Within one hundred years of Columbus's first voyage to the Western Hemisphere, the Spanish Empire in America included most of the islands of the Caribbean, Mexico, the American southwest, Central America, the Caribbean and Pacific coasts of South America, the Andean highlands, and the vast plains of the Rio de la Plata region (a region that includes the modern nations of Argentina, Uruguay, and Paraguay). Portuguese settlement in the New World developed more slowly. But before the end of the sixteenth century, Portugal occupied most of the Brazilian coast.

Early settlers from Spain and Portugal sought to create colonial societies based on the institutions and customs of their homelands. They viewed society as a vertical arrangement of estates (classes of society), as uniformly Catholic, and as an arrangement of patriarchal extended-family networks. And they moved quickly to establish in the new colonies the religious, social, and administrative institutions that were familiar to them.

Despite the imposition of foreign institutions and the massive loss of life caused by epidemics in the sixteenth century, indigenous peoples exercised a powerful influence on the development of colonial societies. Aztec and Inca elite families sought to protect their traditional privileges and rights through marriage or less formal alliances with the Spanish settlers. They also often used colonial courts to defend their claims to land. In Spanish and Portuguese colonies, indigenous military allies and laborers proved crucial to the development of European settlements. Nearly everywhere, Amerindian religious beliefs and practices survived beneath the surface of an imposed Christianity. Amerindian languages, cuisines, medical practices, and agricultural techniques also survived the conquest and influenced the development of Latin American culture.

The African slave trade added a third cultural stream to colonial Latin American society. At first, African slaves were concentrated in plantation regions of Brazil and the Caribbean (see Chapter 20), but by the end of the colonial era, Africans and their descendants were living throughout Latin America, enriching colonial societies with their traditional agricultural practices, music, religious beliefs, cuisine, and social customs.

State and Church

The Spanish crown moved quickly to curb the independent power of the conquistadors and to establish royal authority over both the defeated native populations and the rising tide of European settlers. Created in 1524, the **Council of the Indies** in Spain supervised all government, ecclesiastical, and commercial activity in the Spanish colonies. Geography and technology, however, limited the Council's real power. Local officials could not be controlled too closely, because a ship needed more than two hundred days to make a roundtrip voyage from Spain to Veracruz, Mexico, and additional months of travel were required to reach Lima, Peru.

As a result of these difficulties of communication, the viceroy of New Spain and the viceroy of Peru, the highest-ranking Spanish officials in the colonies, enjoyed broad power. But the two viceroyalties in their jurisdiction were also vast territories with geographic obstacles to communication. Created in 1535, the Viceroyalty of New Spain, with its capital in Mexico City, included Mexico and the southwest of what is now the United States, Central America, and the islands of the Caribbean. The Viceroyalty of Peru, with its capital in Lima, was formed in the 1540s to govern Spanish South America (see Map 19.1). Each viceroyalty was divided into a number of judicial and administrative districts. Until the seventeenth century, almost all of the officials appointed to high positions in Spain's colonial bureaucracy were born in Spain. Eventually, economic mismanagement in Spain forced the Crown to sell appointments to these positions, and, as a result, local-born members of the colonial elite gained many offices.

In the sixteenth century Portugal concentrated its resources and energies on Asia and Africa. Because early settlers found neither mineral wealth nor rich native empires in Brazil, the Portuguese king hesitated to set up expensive mechanisms of colonial government in the New World. Seeking to promote settlement but limit costs, the king in effect sublet administrative responsibilities in Brazil to court favorites by granting twelve hereditary captaincies in the 1530s. After mismanagement and inadequate investment doomed this experiment, the king appointed a governor-general in 1549 and made Salvador, in the northern province of Bahia, Brazil's capital. In 1720 the first viceroy of Brazil was named.

The government institutions of the Spanish and Portuguese colonies had a more uniform character and were much more extensive and costly than those later established in North America by France and Great Britain. Taxes paid by the silver and gold mines of Spanish America and in Brazil by the sugar plantations and after 1690 by gold mines funded large and intrusive colonial bureaucracies. These institutions made the colonies more responsive to the initiatives of Spain and Portugal, but they also thwarted local economic initiative and political experimentation.

The Catholic Church became the primary agent for the introduction and transmission of Christian belief as well as European language and culture in both Spanish America and Brazil. It undertook the conversion of Amerindians, ministered to the spiritual needs of European settlers and their children, and promoted intellectual life through the introduction of the printing press and formal education.

Spain and Portugal justified their American conquests by assuming an obligation to convert native populations to Christianity. This religious objective was sometimes forgotten, and some members of the clergy were themselves exploiters of native populations. Nevertheless, the effort to convert America's native peoples expanded Christianity on a scale similar to its earlier expansion in Europe at the time of Constantine in the fourth century. In Mexico alone hundreds of thousands of conversions and baptisms were achieved within a few years of the conquest.

The Catholic clergy sought to achieve their evangelical ends by first converting members of the Amerindian elites, in the hope that they could persuade others to follow their example. Franciscan missionaries in Mexico hoped to train members of the indigenous elite for the clergy. These idealistic efforts had to be abandoned when church authorities discovered that many converts were secretly observing old beliefs and rituals. The trial and punishment of two converted Aztec nobles for heresy in the 1530s highlighted this problem. Three decades later, Spanish clergy resorted to torture, executions, and the destruction of native manuscripts to eradicate traditional beliefs and rituals among the Maya. Repelled by these events, the church hierarchy ended both the violent repression of native religious practice and efforts to recruit an Amerindian clergy.

Despite its failures, the Catholic clergy did provide native peoples with some protections against the abuse and exploitation of Spanish settlers. The priest **Bartolomé de Las Casas** (1474–1566) was the most influential defender of the Amerindians in the early colonial

Map. 19.1   Colonial Latin America in the Eighteenth Century
Spain and Portugal controlled most of the Western Hemisphere in the eighteenth century. In the sixteenth century they had created new administrative jurisdictions—viceroyalties—to defend their respective colonies against European rivals. Taxes assessed on colonial products helped pay for this extension of governmental authority.

NEW FRANCE

Mississippi

ENGLISH COLONIES
(Independence declared, 1776)

Colorado

Effective frontier
of Spanish settlement

ATLANTIC
OCEAN

Silver

Silver   **COAHUILA**

Río Grande

Gulf of Mexico

FLORIDA
(Ceded to England, 1763–1783)

VICEROYALTY OF NEW SPAIN   (1535)

Havana

Sugar cane
Beef
Tobacco

HAITI [SAINT DOMINGUE]
(Ceded to France, 1697)

Silver
Guadalajara •   **BAJÍO LEÓN**   Silver
Mexico City •   Veracruz
Silver

Sugar cane
Indigo

Sugar cane

Beef   Sugar cane

PUERTO RICO

Cacao   **BRITISH
HONDURAS**   JAMAICA
(Conquered by England, 1655)   SANTO DOMINGO   Sugar cane

Sugar
cane
Cochineal   Guatemala •   Silver

Cochineal
Cacao
Indigo   *Caribbean
Sea*

Pearls

Sugar cane

Caracas •   Cacao

Magdalena   Gold

GUIANA

Suárez

• Bogotá

**VICEROYALTY OF
NEW GRANADA**
(Separated from
Viceroyalty of Peru,
1717, 1739)

Amazon

Quito •

ANDES

Forest
products

PACIFIC
OCEAN

**VICEROYALTY
OF PERU**
(1590s)   Sugar cane

**VICEROYALTY
OF BRAZIL**
(1720)

Pernambuco •

Sugar
cane

Lima •

Sugar
cane

• Cuzco   Sugar
cane •   Bahia

Cacao

• La Paz

Chuquisaca
• (La Plata; Sucre)
Silver   • Potosí

Paraná

Diamonds
Gold

Yerba
Tobacco   São Paulo •   Rio de Janeiro
(Capital, 1763)

ANDES

**VICEROYALTY OF
LA PLATA**
(Separated from
Viceroyalty of Peru,
1776)

Wheat

Beef and
hides

Spanish colonies

Viceroyalty of New Spain

Viceroyalty of New Granada

Viceroyalty of Peru and Audiencia of Chile

Viceroyalty of La Plata

Portuguese colonies

Viceroyalty of Brazil

**AUDIENCIA
OF CHILE**
(Retained by
Viceroyalty of Peru,
1776)

Santiago •
Buenos Aires •   Montevideo

Beef and
hides

Claimed but
not settled by Spain

| 0 | 500 | 1000 Km. |
| 0 | 500 | 1000 Mi. |

Islas Malvinas
(Falkland Islands)

Cape Horn

Saint Martín de Porres (1579–1639)   Martín de Porres was the illegitimate son of a Spanish nobleman and his black servant. Eventually recognized by his father, he entered the Dominican Order in Lima, Peru. Known for his generosity, he experienced visions and gained the ability to heal the sick. As was common in colonial religious art, the artist celebrates Martín de Porres's spirituality while representing him doing the type of work assumed most suitable for a person of mixed descent.   (Mint Museum of Art, Charlotte, NC)

1542—reform legislation that outlawed the enslavement of Amerindians and limited other forms of forced labor.

European clergy arrived in the colonies with the intention of transmitting Catholic Christian belief and ritual without alteration. But the large size of Amerindian populations and their geographic dispersal over a vast landscape thwarted this objective. Linguistic and cultural differences among native peoples also inhibited missionary efforts. These problems frustrated Catholic missionaries and sometimes led to repression and cruelty. But the limited success of evangelization permitted the appearance of what must be seen as an Amerindian Christianity that blended Catholic Christian beliefs with important elements of traditional native cosmology and ritual. Most commonly, indigenous beliefs and rituals came to be embedded in the celebration of saints' days or Catholic rituals associated with the Virgin Mary. The Catholic clergy and most European settlers viewed this evolving mixture as the work of the Devil or as evidence of Amerindian inferiority. Instead it was one component of the process of cultural borrowing and innovation that contributed to a distinct and original Latin American culture.

The terrible loss of Amerindian population caused by epidemics and growing signs of resistance to conversion led the Catholic Church to redirect most of its resources from native regions in the countryside to growing colonial cities and towns with large European populations after 1600. One important outcome of this altered mission was the founding of universities and secondary schools and the stimulation of urban intellectual life. Over time, the church became the richest institution in the Spanish colonies, controlling ranches, plantations, and vineyards as well as serving as the society's banker.

Colonial Economies

The silver mines of Peru and Mexico and the sugar plantations of Brazil dominated the economic development of colonial Latin America. The mineral wealth of the New World fueled the early development of European capitalism and funded Europe's greatly expanded trade with Asia. Profits produced in these economic centers also promoted the growth of colonial cities, concentrated scarce investment capital and labor resources, and stimulated the development of livestock raising and agriculture in neighboring rural areas (see Map 19.1). Once established, this colonial dependence on mineral and agricultural exports left an enduring social and economic legacy in Latin America.

period. He arrived in Hispaniola in 1502 as a settler and initially lived off the forced labor and appropriated goods of Amerindians. Deeply moved by the deaths of so many Amerindians and by the misdeeds of the Spanish, Las Casas gave up this way of life and entered the Dominican Order, later becoming the first bishop of Chiapas, in southern Mexico. For the remainder of his long life Las Casas served as the most important advocate for native peoples, writing a number of books that detailed their mistreatment by the Spanish. His most important achievement was the enactment of the New Laws of

Gold worth millions of pesos was extracted from mines in Latin America, but silver mines in the Spanish colonies generated the most wealth and therefore exercised the greatest economic influence. The first important silver strikes occurred in Mexico in the 1530s and 1540s. In 1545 the single richest silver deposit in the Americas was discovered at **Potosí°,** in what is now Bolivia, and until 1680 the silver production of Bolivia and Peru dominated the Spanish colonial economy. After this date Mexican silver production greatly surpassed that of the Andean region.

A large labor force was needed to mine silver. The metal was extracted from deep shafts, and the refining process was complex. Silver mines supported farming, livestock raising, and even textile production, which, in turn, promoted urbanization and the elaboration of regional commercial relations. Silver mining also greatly altered the environment.

At first, silver was extracted from ore by smelting: the ore was crushed in giant stamping mills then packed with charcoal in a furnace and fired. Within a short time this wasteful use of forest resources for fuel destroyed forests near the mining centers. Faced with rising fuel costs, Mexican miners developed an efficient method of chemical extraction that relied on mixing mercury with the silver ore (see Environment and Technology: The Silver Refinery at Potosí, Bolivia, 1700). But this process, too, had severe environmental costs. Mercury was a poison, and its use contaminated the environment and sickened the Amerindian work force. Silver yields and profits increased with mercury amalgamation, but the environmental costs were high.

From the time of Columbus indigenous populations had been compelled to provide labor for European settlers in the Americas. Until the 1540s in Spanish colonies, Amerindian peoples were divided among the settlers and were forced to provide them with labor or with textiles, food, or other goods. This form of forced labor was called the **encomienda°.** As epidemics and mistreatment led to the decline in Amerindian population, reforms such as the New Laws sought to eliminate the encomienda. The discovery of silver in both Peru and Mexico, however, led to new forms of compulsory labor. In the mining region of Mexico, Amerindian populations had been greatly reduced by epidemic diseases. Therefore, from early in the colonial period, Mexican silver miners relied on free-wage laborers. Peru's Amerindian population survived in larger numbers, allowing the Spanish to impose a form of labor called the mita°.

Potosí (poh-toh-SEE)   encomienda (in-co-mee-EN-dah)
mita (MEE-tah)

Rural Blacksmiths in Colonial Peru   In colonial Latin America husbands, wives, and older children commonly worked together whether in agriculture or in urban occupations. Because few artisans earned enough to hire help, they often relied on their familes for assistance. In this illustration from Peru a rural blacksmith works alongside his wife.   (From Martinez Compañon, Trujillo del Perú, v.II, E 105. Photo: Imaging Services, Harvard College Library)

Under this system, one seventh of adult male Amerindians were compelled to work for six months each year in mines, or on farms and in textile factories. The most dangerous working conditions existed in the silver mines where workers were forced to carry heavy bags of ore up fragile ladders to the surface.

This colonial institution was a corrupted version of the Inca-era mit'a (see Chapter 12), which had been both a labor tax that supported elites and a reciprocal labor obligation that allowed kin groups to produce surpluses of essential goods that provided for the elderly and incapacitated. In the Spanish mita, few Amerindian workers

The Silver Refinery at Potosí, Bolivia, 1700

The silver refineries of Spanish America were among the largest and most heavily capitalized industrial enterprises in the Western Hemisphere during the colonial period. By the middle of the seventeenth century the mines of Potosí, Bolivia, had attracted a population of more than 120,000.

The accompanying illustration shows a typical refinery (*ingenio*). Aqueducts carried water from large reservoirs on nearby mountainsides to the refineries. The water wheel shown on the right drove two sets of vertical stamps that crushed ore. Each iron-shod stamp was about the size and weight of a telephone pole. Crushed ore was sorted, dried, and mixed with mercury and other catalysts to extract the silver. The amalgam was then separated by a combination of washing and heating. The end result was a nearly pure ingot of silver that was later assayed and taxed at the mint.

Silver production carried a high environmental cost. Forests were cut to provide fuel and the timbers needed to shore up mine shafts and construct stamping mills and other machinery. Unwanted base metals produced in the refining process poisoned the soil. In addition, the need for tens of thousands of horses, mules, and oxen to drive machinery and transport material led to overgrazing and widespread erosion.

A Bolivian Silver Refinery, 1700 The silver refineries of Spanish America were among the largest industrial establishments in the Western Hemisphere. (Courtesy, Fundacao Biblioteca Nacional, Rio de Janeiro)

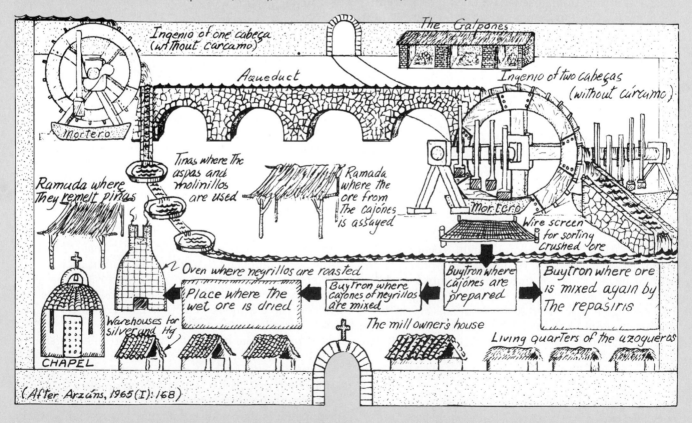

could survive on their wages. Wives and children were commonly forced to join the workforce to help meet expenses (see Society and Culture: Colonial Wealth and the Exploitation of Indigenous Peoples). Even those who remained behind in the village were forced to send food and cash to support mita workers.

As the Amerindian population fell with each new epidemic, some of Peru's villages were forced to shorten the period between mita obligations. Instead of serving every seven years, many men were forced to return to mines after only a year or two. Unwilling to accept mita service and the other tax burdens imposed on Amerindian villages, large numbers of Amerindians abandoned traditional agriculture and moved permanently to Spanish mines and farms as wage laborers. The long-term result of these individual decisions weakened Amerindian village life and promoted the assimilation of Amerindians into Spanish-speaking Catholic colonial society.

Before the settlement of Brazil the Portuguese had already developed sugar plantations that depended on slave labor on the Atlantic islands of Madeira, the Azores, the Cape Verdes, and São Tomé. Because of the success of these early experiences, they were able to quickly transfer this profitable form of agriculture to Brazil. After 1550, sugar production expanded rapidly in the northern provinces of Pernambuco and Bahia. By the seventeenth century, sugar dominated the Brazilian economy.

The sugar plantations of colonial Brazil always depended on slave labor. At first the Portuguese sugar planters enslaved Amerindians captured in war or seized from their villages. They used Amerindian men as field hands, although in this indigenous culture women had primary responsibility for agriculture. Any effort to resist or flee led to harsh punishments. Thousands of Amerindian slaves died during the epidemics that raged across Brazil in the sixteenth and seventeenth centuries. This terrible loss of Amerindian life and the rising profits of the sugar planters led to the development of an internal slave trade dominated by settlers from the southern region of São Paulo. To supply the rising labor needs of the sugar plantations of the northeast, slave raiders pushed into the interior, even attacking Amerindian populations in neighboring Spanish colonies. Many of the most prominent slavers were the sons of Portuguese fathers and Amerindian mothers.

Amerindian slaves remained an important source of labor and slave raiding a significant business in frontier regions into the eighteenth century. But sugar planters eventually came to rely more on African than Amerindian slaves. Although African slaves at first cost much more than Amerindian slaves, planters found them to be more productive and more resistant to disease. As profits from the plantations increased, imports of African slaves rose from an average of 2,000 per year in the late sixteenth century to approximately 7,000 per year a century later, outstripping the immigration of free Portuguese settlers. Between 1650 and 1750, for example, more than three African slaves arrived in Brazil for every free immigrant from Europe.

Within Spanish America, the mining centers of Mexico and Peru eventually exercised global economic influence. American silver increased the European money supply, promoting commercial expansion and, later, industrialization. Large amounts of silver also flowed across the Pacific to the Spanish colony of the Philippines, where it was exchanged for Asian spices, silks, and pottery. Spain tried to limit this trade, but the desire for Asian goods in the colonies was so strong that there was large-scale trade in contraband goods.

The rich mines of Peru, Bolivia, and Mexico stimulated urban population growth as well as commercial links with distant agricultural and textile producers. The population of the city of Potosí, high in the Andes, reached 120,000 inhabitants by 1625. This rich mining town became the center of a vast regional market that depended on Chilean wheat, Argentine livestock, and Ecuadorian textiles.

The sugar plantations of Brazil played a similar role in integrating the economy of the south Atlantic region. The ports of Bahia and Rio de Janeiro in Brazil exchanged sugar, tobacco, and reexported slaves from Brazil for yerba (Paraguayan tea), hides, livestock, and silver produced in neighboring Spanish colonies. Portugal's increasing openness to British trade also allowed Brazil to become a conduit for an illegal trade between Spanish colonies and Europe. At the end of the seventeenth century the discovery of gold in Brazil helped overcome this large region's currency shortage and promoted further economic integration.

Both Spain and Portugal attempted to control the trade of their American colonies. Spain's efforts were more ambitious, granting first Seville and then Cádiz monopoly trade rights. Similar monopoly privileges were then awarded to the merchant guilds of Lima, Peru, and Mexico City. Because ships returning to Spain with silver and gold were often attacked by foreign naval forces and pirates, Spain came to rely on convoys escorted by warships to supply the colonies and return with silver and gold. By 1650, Portugal had instituted a similar system of monopoly trade and fleets. The combination of monopoly commerce and convoy systems

Colonial Wealth and the Exploitation of Indigenous Peoples

The conditions imposed on indigenous peoples in the Spanish colonies generated contentious debates from the early sixteenth century to the end of the colonial period. Two Spanish naval officers who accompanied a French scientific expedition to South America in the mid-eighteenth century wrote the following description.

Without having to assume anything that cannot be proved absolutely or exaggerating to stretch the truth, we can agree indisputably that all the wealth produced in the Indies [Spain's American colonies], even what is consumed there, stems from the toil of the Indians. From close observation one sees that Indians work the silver and gold mines, cultivate the fields, and raise the livestock. In a word, there is no heavy labor that the Indians do not perform. They are so badly recompensed for their work that if one wanted to find out what the Spaniards paid them, he would discover it to be nothing except consistently cruel punishment, worse than that meted out in the galleys.... The gold and silver which the Spaniards acquire at the expense of the natives' sweat and toil never falls into the hands of the Indians.

[T]hose who contribute most are the ones who enjoy its fruits least and are the most poorly paid for the most arduous tasks....

There are two ways to remedy the abuse perpetrated on the free and mita Indians [the mita was a forced labor system]. The most reasonable and just method would be to eliminate the mita entirely and have free labor work the haciendas, mines, obrajes [textile mills] and everything else....

In the second place it would be fitting to prohibit completely all physical punishment of the Indians in the haciendas and obrajes under severe penalties.

How important were Amerindians to the economy of the Spanish Empire? How did these two visitors judge the treatment of Amerindian peoples? What remedies did these authors suggest?

Source: Jorge Juan and Antonio de Ulloa, *Discourse and Political Reflections on the Kingdom of Peru,* ed. John J. Tepaske and Besse A. Clement (Norman: University of Oklahoma Press, 1978), 126–148.

---

protected shipping and facilitated the collection of taxes, but these measures also slowed the flow of European goods to the colonies and kept prices high. Frustrated by these restraints, colonial populations established illegal commercial relations with the English, French, and Dutch. By the middle of the seventeenth century a majority of European imports were arriving in Latin America illegally.

Society in Colonial Latin America

With the exception of a few early viceroys, few members of Spain's great noble families came to the New World. *Hidalgos°*—lesser nobles—were well represented, as were Spanish merchants, artisans, miners, priests, and lawyers. Small numbers of criminals, beggars, and prosti-

---

hidalgos (ee-DAHL-goes)

tutes also found their way to the colonies. This flow of immigrants from Spain was never large, and Spanish settlers were always a tiny minority in a colonial society numerically dominated by Amerindians and rapidly growing populations of Africans, **creoles** (whites born in America to European parents), and people of mixed ancestry.

Conquistadors and early settlers who received from the Crown grants of labor and tribute goods (encomienda) from Amerindian communities as rewards for service to Spain dominated colonial society in early Spanish America. These *encomenderos* sought to create a hereditary social and political class comparable to the nobles of Europe. But their systematic abuse of Amerindian communities and the catastrophic loss of Amerindian life during the epidemics of the sixteenth century undermined their position. They also confronted the growing power of colonial viceroys, judges, and bishops appointed by the king.

By the end of the sixteenth century, the elite of Spanish America included both European immigrants and creoles. Europeans dominated the highest levels of the church and government as well as commerce. Creoles commonly controlled colonial agriculture and mining. Wealthy creole families with extensive holdings in land and mines often sought to increase their family prestige by arranging for their daughters to marry successful Spanish merchants and officials. Often richer in reputation than in wealth, immigrants from Spain welcomed the opportunity to forge these connections. Although tensions between Spaniards and creoles were inevitable, most elite families had members from both groups.

Before the Europeans arrived in the Americas, the native peoples were members of a large number of distinct cultural and linguistic groups. Cultural diversity and class distinctions were present even in the highly centralized Aztec and Inca empires. The loss of life provoked by the European conquest undermined this rich social and cultural complexity, and the imposition of Catholic Christianity further eroded ethnic boundaries among native peoples. Colonial administrators and settlers broadly applied the racial label "Indian," which facilitated the imposition of special taxes and labor obligations while at the same time erasing long-standing class and ethnic differences.

Indigenous Amerindian elites survived only briefly in the Spanish colonies and Brazil. Some of the conquistadors and early settlers married or established less formal relations with elite Amerindian women, but fewer of these alliances occurred after European women began to arrive. By 1600 the descendants of the most powerful Amerindian families were indistinguishable from the descendants of the village leaders who had been subordinate to them. Both groups of hereditary leaders, however, had proved indispensable to the first Spanish colonists, helping the Spaniards to organize draft labor and collect taxes. Some descendants of both groups prospered in the colonial period as ranchers, muleteers, and merchants; many others lived in the same materially deprived conditions as Amerindian commoners.

Thousands of blacks participated in the conquest and settlement of Spanish America. The majority were European-born Catholic slaves who came to the New World with their masters. Some free blacks immigrated voluntarily. More than four hundred blacks, most of them slaves, participated in the conquest of Peru and Chile. In the fluid social environment of the conquest era, many slaves gained their freedom. Some simply fled from their masters. Juan Valiente escaped his master in Mexico, participated in Francisco Pizarro's conquest of the Inca Empire, and later became one of the most prominent early settlers of Chile, where he was granted Amerindian laborers in an encomienda.

The status of the black population of colonial Latin America declined with the opening of a direct slave trade with Africa (for details, see Chapter 20). Africans were culturally different from the Afro-Iberian slaves and freedmen who accompanied the conquerors. Afro-Iberians commonly had deep roots in Spain or Portugal, their language was Spanish or Portuguese, and their religion was Catholicism. African slaves were different in language, religious belief, and cultural practice, and these differences were viewed by settlers as signs of inferiority, ultimately serving as a justification for slavery. By 1600 anyone with black ancestry was barred from positions in church and government as well as from many skilled crafts.

The rich mosaic of African identities was retained in colonial Latin America. Many cultural groups struggled in slavery to retain their languages, religious beliefs, and marriage customs. But, in regions with large slave majorities, these cultural and linguistic barriers often divided slaves and made resistance more difficult. Over time, elements from many African traditions blended and mixed with European (and in some cases Amerindian) language and beliefs to forge distinct local cultures. The rapid growth of an American-born slave population accelerated this process of cultural change.

Slave resistance took many forms, including sabotage, malingering, running away, and rebellion. Although many slave rebellions occurred, colonial authorities were always able to reestablish control. Groups of runaway slaves, however, were sometimes able to defend themselves for years. In both Spanish America and Brazil communities of runaways (called *quilombos*° in Brazil and *palenques*° in Spanish colonies) were common. The largest quilombo was Palmares, where thousands of slaves defended themselves against Brazilian authorities for sixty years until they were finally overrun in 1694.

Slaves were skilled artisans, musicians, servants, artists, cowboys, and even soldiers. However, the vast majority worked in agriculture. Conditions for slaves were worst on the sugar plantations of Brazil and the Caribbean, where harsh discipline, brutal punishments, and backbreaking labor were common. Because planters preferred to buy male slaves, there was always a gender imbalance on plantations. As a result, neither the traditional marriage and family patterns of Africa nor those of Europe developed. The disease environment of the tropics, as well as the poor housing, diet, hygiene, and medical care offered to slaves, also weakened slave families.

---

quilombos (key-LOM-bos)   *palenques* (pah-LEN-kays)

Painting of Castas This is an example of a common genre of colonial Spanish American painting. In the eighteenth century there was increased interest in ethnic mixing, and wealthy colonials as well as some Europeans commissioned sets of paintings that showed mixed families. Commonly the paintings also indicated what the artist believed was an appropriate class setting. In this painting a richly dressed Spaniard is depicted with his Amerindian wife dressed in European clothing. Notice that the painter has the mestiza daughter look to her European father for guidance. (Private Collection. Photographer: Camilo Garza/Fotocam, Monterrey, Mexico)

The colonial development of Brazil was distinguished from that of Spanish America by the absence of rich and powerful indigenous civilizations such as those of the Aztecs and Inca and by lower levels of European immigration. Nevertheless, Portuguese immigrants came to exercise the same domination in Brazil as the Spanish exercised in their colonies. The growth of cities and the creation of imperial institutions eventually duplicated in outline the social structures found in Spanish America, but with an important difference. By the early seventeenth century, Africans and their American-born descendants were the largest racial group in Brazil. As a result, Brazilian colonial society (unlike Spanish Mexico and Peru) was influenced more by African culture than by Amerindian culture.

Both Spanish and Portuguese law provided for manumission, the granting of freedom to individual slaves. The majority of those gaining their liberty had saved money and purchased their own freedom. This was easiest to do in cities, where slave artisans and market women had the opportunity to earn and save money. Only a tiny minority of owners freed slaves without demanding compensation. Household servants were the most likely beneficiaries of this form of manumission. Only about 1 percent of the slave population gained freedom each year through manumission. However, because slave women received the majority of manumissions and because children born subsequently were considered free, the free colored population grew rapidly.

Within a century of settlement, groups of mixed descent were in the majority in many regions. There were few marriages between Amerindian women and European men, but less formal relationships were common. Few European or creole fathers recognized their mixed offspring, who were called **mestizos**°. Nevertheless, this rapidly expanding group came to occupy a middle position in colonial society, dominating urban artisan trades and small-scale agriculture and ranching. In frontier regions many members of the elite were mestizos, some proudly asserting their descent from the Amerindian elite. The African slave trade also led to the appearance of new American ethnicities. Individuals of mixed European and African descent—called **mulattoes**—came to occupy intermediate position in the tropics similar to the social position of mestizos in Mesoamerica and the Andean region. In Spanish Mexico and Peru and in Brazil, mixtures of Amerindians and Africans were also common.

All these mixed-descent groups were called *castas*° in Spanish America. Castas dominated small-scale retailing and construction trades in cities. In the countryside, many small ranchers and farmers as well as wage laborers were castas. Members of these mixed groups who gained high status or significant wealth generally spoke Spanish or Portuguese, observed the requirements of Catholicism, and, whenever possible, lived the life of Europeans in their residence, dress, and diet.

---

mestizo (mess-TEE-zoh)   **castas** (CAZ-tahs)

ENGLISH AND FRENCH COLONIES IN NORTH AMERICA

The North American colonial empires of England and France and the colonies of Spain and Portugal had many characteristics in common (see Map 19.1). The governments of England and France hoped to find easily extracted forms of wealth or great indigenous empires like those of the Aztecs or Inca. Like the Spanish and Portuguese, English and French settlers responded to native peoples with a mixture of diplomacy and violence. African slaves proved crucial to the development of all four colonial economies.

Important differences, however, distinguished North American colonial development from the Latin American model. The English and French colonies were developed nearly a century after Cortés's conquest of Mexico and initial Portuguese settlement in Brazil. The intervening period witnessed significant economic and demographic growth in Europe. It also witnessed the Protestant Reformation, which helped to propel English and French settlement in the Americas. By the time England and France secured a foothold in the Americas, the regions of the world were also more interconnected commercially. Distracted by ventures elsewhere and by increasing military confrontation in Europe, neither England nor France imitated the large and expensive colonial bureaucracies established by Spain and Portugal. As a result, private companies and individual proprietors played a much larger role in the development of English and French colonies. Particularly in the English colonies, this practice led to greater regional variety in economic activity, political institutions and culture, and social structure than was evident in the colonies of Spain and Portugal.

Early English Experiments

England's first efforts to gain a foothold in the Americas produced more failures than successes. The first attempt was made by a group of West Country gentry and merchants led by Sir Humphrey Gilbert. Their effort in 1583 to establish a colony in Newfoundland, off the coast of Canada, quickly failed. After Gilbert's death in 1584, his half-brother Sir Walter Raleigh organized private financing for a new colonization scheme. A year later, 108 men attempted a settlement on Roanoke Island, off the coast of present-day North Carolina. Afflicted with poor leadership, undersupplied, and threatened by Amerindian groups, the colony was abandoned within a year. Another effort to settle Roanoke was made in 1587. Because the Spanish Armada was threatening England, no relief expedition was sent to Roanoke until 1590. When help finally arrived, there was no sign of the 117 men, women, and children who had attempted settlement. Raleigh's colonial experiment was abandoned.

In the seventeenth century, England renewed its effort to establish colonies in North America. England continued to rely on private capital to finance settlement and continued to hope that the colonies would become sources of high-value products such as silk, citrus, and wine. New efforts to establish American colonies were influenced also by English experience in colonizing Ireland after 1566. In Ireland land had been confiscated, cleared of its native population, and offered for sale to English investors. The city of London, English guilds, and wealthy private investors all purchased Irish "plantations" and then recruited "settlers." By 1650 investors had sent nearly 150,000 English and Scottish immigrants to Ireland. Indeed, Ireland attracted six times as many colonists in the early seventeenth century as did New England.

The South

London investors, organized as the privately funded Virginia Company, took up the challenge of colonizing Virginia in 1606. A year later 144 settlers disembarked at Jamestown, an island 30 miles (48 kilometers) up the James River in the Chesapeake Bay region. Additional settlers arrived in 1609. The investors and settlers hoped for immediate profits, but these unrealistic dreams were soon dashed. Although the location was easily defended, it was a swampy and unhealthy place; nearly 80 percent of all settlers in Jamestown in the first fifteen years died from disease or Amerindian attacks. There was no mineral wealth, no passage to Asia, and no docile and exploitable native population. By concentrating their energies on the illusion of easy wealth, settlers failed to grow enough food and were saved on more than one occasion by the generosity of neighboring Amerindian peoples.

In 1624 the English crown was forced to dissolve the Virginia Company because of its mismanagement of the colony. Freed from the company's commitment to Jamestown's unhealthy environment, colonists pushed deeper into the interior, developing a sustainable economy based on furs, timber, and, increasingly, tobacco. The profits from tobacco soon attracted new immigrants and new capital. Along the shoreline of Chesapeake Bay and the rivers that fed it, settlers spread out, developing plantations and farms. Colonial Virginia's population remained dispersed. In Latin America, large and powerful cities dominated by viceroys and royal courts and networks of secondary towns flourished. In contrast, in colonial Virginia no city of any significant size developed.

Colonists in Latin America had developed systems of forced labor to develop the region's resources. Encomienda, mita, and slavery were all imposed on indigenous peoples, and later the African slave trade compelled the migration of millions of additional forced laborers to the colonies of Spain and Portugal. The English settlement of the Chesapeake Bay region added a new system of compulsory labor to the American landscape: **indentured servants.** Ethnically indistinguishable from free settlers, indentured servants eventually accounted for approximately 80 percent of all English immigrants to Virginia and the neighboring colony of Maryland. Young men and women unable to pay for their transportation to the New World accepted indentures (contracts) that bound them to a term ranging from four to seven years of labor in return for passage, a small parcel of land, and some tools and clothes. During the seventeenth century, approximately fifteen hundred indentured servants, mostly male, arrived each year (see Chapter 20 for details on the indentured labor system). Planters were less likely to lose money if they purchased the cheaper limited contracts of indentured servants instead of purchasing African slaves during the period when both groups suffered high mortality rates. As life expectancy in the colony improved, planters began to purchase more slaves. They calculated that greater profits could be secured by paying the higher initial cost of slaves owned for life than by purchasing the contracts of indentured servants bound for short periods of time. As a result, Virginia's slave population grew rapidly from 950 in 1660 to 120,000 by 1756.

By the 1660s many of the elements of the mature colony were in place in Virginia. Colonial government was administered by a Crown-appointed governor and his council, as well as by representatives of towns meeting together as the **House of Burgesses.** When these representatives began to meet alone as a deliberative body, they initiated a form of democratic representation that distinguished the English colonies of North America from the colonies of other European powers. Ironically, this expansion in colonial liberties and political rights occurred along with the dramatic increase in the colony's slave population. The intertwined evolution of American freedom and American slavery gave England's southern colonies a unique and conflicted political character that endured even after independence.

At the same time, the English colonists were expanding settlements to the South. The Carolinas at first prospered from the profits of the fur trade. Fur traders pushed into the interior, eventually threatening the French trading networks based in New Orleans and Mobile. Native peoples eventually provided over a hundred thousand deerskins annually to this profitable commerce. The environmental and cultural costs of the fur trade were little appreciated at the time. As Amerindian peoples hunted more intensely, the natural balance of animals and plants was disrupted in southern forests. The profits of the fur trade altered Amerindian culture as well, leading villages to place less emphasis on subsistence hunting and fishing and traditional agriculture. Deepening dependencies on European products, including firearms, metal tools, textiles and alcohol, further altered Amerindian life.

Although increasingly brought into the commerce and culture of the Carolina colony, indigenous peoples were being weakened by epidemics, alcoholism, and a rising tide of ethnic conflicts generated by competition for hunting grounds. Conflicts among indigenous peoples—now armed with firearms—became more deadly. Many Amerindians captured in these wars were sold as slaves to local colonists, who used them as agricultural workers or exported them to the sugar plantations of the Caribbean islands. Dissatisfied with the terms of trade imposed by fur traders and angered by this slave trade, Amerindians launched attacks on English settlements in the early 1700s. Their defeat by colonial military forces led inevitably to new seizures of Amerindian land by European settlers.

The northern part of the Carolinas had been settled from Virginia and followed that colony's mixed economy of tobacco and forest products. Slavery expanded slowly in this region. Charleston and the interior of South Carolina followed a different path. Settled first by planters from the Caribbean Island of Barbados in 1670, this colony soon developed an economy based on plantations and slavery in imitation of the colonies of the Caribbean and Brazil. In 1729 North and South Carolina became separate colonies.

Despite an unhealthy climate, the prosperous rice and indigo plantations near Charleston attracted a diverse array of immigrants and an increasing flow of African slaves. African slaves were present from the founding of Charleston. They were instrumental in introducing irrigated rice agriculture along the coastal lowlands and in developing indigo (a plant that produced a blue dye) plantations at higher elevations away from the coast. Slaves were often given significant responsibilities. As one planter sending two slaves and their families to a frontier region put it: "[They] are likely young people, well acquainted with Rice & every kind of plantation business, and in short [are] capable of the management of a plantation themselves."[2]

As profits from rice and indigo rose, the importation of African slaves created a black majority in South Carolina. African languages and Gullah (a dialect with African and English roots), as well as African religious beliefs and diet, strongly influenced this unique colonial culture. African slaves were more likely than American-born slaves to rebel or run away. In South Carolina's largest slave uprising, the Stono Rebellion of 1739, Africans played a major role. After a group of about twenty slaves, many of them African Catholics who sought to flee south to Spanish Florida, seized firearms, about a hundred slaves from nearby plantations joined them. The colonial militia soon defeated the rebels and executed many of them, but the rebellion shocked slave owners throughout England's southern colonies and led to greater repression.

Colonial South Carolina was the most hierarchical society in British North America. Planters controlled the economy and political life. The richest maintained households both in the countryside and in Charleston, the largest city in the southern colonies. Small farmers, cattlemen, artisans, merchants, and fur traders held an intermediate but clearly subordinate social position. Native peoples remained influential participants in colonial society through commercial contacts and alliances, but they were increasingly marginalized. As had occurred in colonial Latin America, the growth of a large mixed population blurred racial and cultural boundaries. On the frontier, the children of white men and Indian women held an important place in the fur trade. In the plantation regions and Charleston, the offspring of white men and black women often held preferred positions within the slave work force or, if they had been freed, as carpenters, blacksmiths, or in other skilled trades.

New England

The colonization of New England by two separate groups of Protestant dissenters, Pilgrims and Puritans, put the settlement of this region on a different course. The **Pilgrims,** who came first, wished to break completely with the Church of England, which they believed was still essentially Catholic. Unwilling to confront the power of the established church and the monarch, they sought an opportunity to pursue their spiritual ends in a new land. As a result, in 1620 approximately one hundred settlers—men, women, and children—established the colony of Plymouth on the coast of present-day Massachusetts. Although nearly half of the settlers died during the first winter, the colony survived. Plymouth benefited from strong leadership and the discipline and cooperative nature of the settlers. Nevertheless, this experiment in creating a church-directed community failed. The religious enthusiasm and purpose that at first sustained the Pilgrims was dissipated by new immigrants who did not share the founders' religious beliefs, and by geographic dispersal to new towns. In 1691, Plymouth was absorbed into the larger Massachusetts Bay Colony of the Puritans.

The **Puritans** wished to "purify" the Church of England, not break with it. They wanted to abolish its hierarchy of bishops and priests, free it from governmental interference, and limit membership to people who shared their beliefs. Subjected to increased discrimination in England for their efforts to transform the church, large numbers of Puritans began emigrating from England in 1630.

The Puritan leaders of the Massachusetts Bay Company—the joint-stock company that had received a royal charter to finance the Massachusetts Bay Colony—carried with them from England to Massachusetts the company charter, which spelled out company rights and obligations as well as the direction of company government. By bringing the charter with them, they limited Crown efforts to control them; the Crown could revoke but not alter the terms of the charter. By 1643, more than 20,000 Puritans had settled in the Bay Colony.

Immigration to Massachusetts differed from immigration to the Chesapeake and to South Carolina. Most newcomers to Massachusetts arrived with their families. Whereas 84 percent of Virginia's population in 1625 was male, Massachusetts had a normal gender balance in its population almost from the beginning. It was also the healthiest of England's colonies. The result was a rapid natural increase in population. The population of Massachusetts quickly became more "American" than the population of the colonies to the south or in the Caribbean, whose survival depended on a steady flow of new English immigrants to counter the high mortality rates. Massachusetts also was more homogeneous and less hierarchical than the southern colonies.

Political institutions evolved out of the terms of the company charter. A governor was elected, along with a council of magistrates drawn from the board of directors of the Massachusetts Bay Company. Disagreements between this council and elected representatives of the towns led, by 1650, to the creation of a lower legislative house that selected its own speaker and began to develop procedures and rules similar to those of the House of Commons in England. The result was greater autonomy and greater local political involvement than in the colonies of Latin America.

Economically, Massachusetts differed dramatically from the southern colonies. Agriculture met basic needs, but poor soils and harsh climate offered no opportunity to develop cash crops like tobacco or rice. To pay for imported tools, textiles, and other essentials, the colonists needed to discover some profit-making niche in the growing Atlantic market. Fur, timber and other forest products, and fish provided the initial economic foundation, but New England's economic well-being soon depended on providing commercial and shipping services in a dynamic and far-flung commercial arena that included the southern colonies, the smaller Caribbean islands, Africa, and Europe.

In Spanish and Portuguese America, heavily capitalized monopolies (companies or individuals given exclusive economic privileges) dominated international trade. In New England, by contrast, merchants survived by discovering smaller but more sustainable profits in diversified trade across the Atlantic. The colony's commercial success rested on market intelligence, flexibility, and streamlined organization. The success of this development strategy is demonstrated by urban population growth. With 16,000 inhabitants in 1740, Boston, capital of Massachusetts Bay Colony, was the largest city in British North America. This coincided with the decline of New England's once-large indigenous population, which had been dramatically reduced by a combination of epidemics and brutal military campaigns.

Lacking a profitable agricultural export like tobacco, New England did not develop the extreme social stratification of the southern plantation colonies. Slaves and indentured servants were present, but in very small numbers. New England was ruled by the richest colonists and shared the racial attitudes of the southern colonies, but it also was the colonial society with fewest differences in wealth and status and with the most uniformly British and Protestant population in the Americas.

The Middle Atlantic Region

Much of the future success of English-speaking America was rooted in the rapid economic development and remarkable cultural diversity that appeared in the Middle Atlantic colonies—diversity that grew in part from non-European origins. In 1624 the Dutch West India Company established the colony of New Netherland and located its capital on Manhattan Island. The colony was poorly managed and underfinanced from the start, but its location commanded the potentially profitable and strategically important Hudson River. Dutch merchants established with the **Iroquois Confederacy**—an alliance among the Mohawk, Oneida, Onondaga, Cayuga, and Seneca peoples—and with other native peoples alliances and trading relationships that gave them access to the rich fur trade of Canada. When confronted by an English military expedition in 1664, the Dutch surrendered without a fight. James, duke of York and later King James II of England, became proprietor of the colony, which was renamed New York.

New York was characterized by tumultuous politics and corrupt public administration. The colony's success was guaranteed in large measure by the development of New York City as a commercial and shipping center. Located at the mouth of the Hudson River, the city played an essential role in connecting the region's grain farmers to the booming markets of the Caribbean and southern Europe. By the early eighteenth century, New York Colony had a diverse population that included (in addition to English colonists) Dutch, German, and Swedish settlers as well as a large slave community.

Pennsylvania began as a proprietary colony and as a refuge for Quakers, a persecuted religious minority. In 1682 William Penn secured an enormous grant of territory (nearly the size of England) because the English king Charles II was indebted to Penn's father. As proprietor (owner) of the land, Penn had sole right to establish a government, subject only to the requirement that he provide for an assembly of freemen.

Penn quickly lost control of the colony's political life, but the colony enjoyed remarkable success. By 1700 Pennsylvania had a population of more than 21,000, and Philadelphia, its capital, soon passed Boston to become the largest city in the British colonies. Healthy climate, excellent land, relatively peaceful relations with native peoples (prompted by Penn's emphasis on negotiation rather than warfare), and access through Philadelphia to good markets led to rapid economic and demographic growth in the colony.

Both Pennsylvania and South Carolina were grain-exporting colonies, but they were very different societies. South Carolina's rice plantations required large numbers of slaves. In Pennsylvania, free workers, including a large number of German families, produced the bulk of the colony's grain crops on family farms. As a result, Pennsylvania's economic expansion in the late seventeenth century occurred without reproducing South Carolina's hierarchical and repressive social order. By the early eighteenth century, however, the prosperous city of Philadelphia did have a large population of black slaves and freedmen. Many were servants in the homes of wealthy merchants, but the fast-growing economy offered many opportunities in skilled trades as well.

The Home of Sir William Johnson, British Superintendent for Indian Affairs, Northern District As the colonial era drew to a close, the British attempted to limit the cost of colonial defense by negotiating land settlements between native peoples and settlers. These agreements were doomed by the growing tide of western migration. William Johnson (1715–1774) maintained a fragile peace along the northern frontier by building strong personal relations with influential leaders of the Mohawk and other members of the Iroquois Confederacy. His home in present-day Johnstown, New York, shows the mixed nature of the frontier—the relative opulence of the main house offset by the two defensive blockhouses built for protection. ("Johnson Hall," by E. L. Henry. Courtesy, Albany Institute of History and Art)

French America

Patterns of French settlement more closely resembled those of Spain and Portugal than of England. The French were committed to missionary activity among Amerindian peoples and emphasized the extraction of natural resources—furs rather than minerals. The navigator and promoter Jacques Cartier first stirred France's interest in North America. In three voyages between 1524 and 1542, he explored the region of Newfoundland and the Gulf of St. Lawrence. A contemporary of Cortés and Pizarro, Cartier also hoped to find mineral wealth, but the stones he brought back to France turned out to be quartz and iron pyrite, "fool's gold."

The French waited more than fifty years before establishing settlements in North America. Coming to Canada after spending years in the West Indies, Samuel de Champlain founded the colony of **New France** at Quebec°, on the banks of the St. Lawrence River, in 1608. This location provided ready access to Amerindian trade routes, but it also compelled French settlers to take sides in the region's ongoing warfare. Champlain allied New France with the Huron and Algonkian peoples, traditional enemies of the powerful Iroquois Confederacy. Although French firearms and armor at first tipped the balance of power to France's native allies, the members of the Iroquois Confederacy proved to be resourceful and persistent enemies.

The European market for fur, especially beaver, fueled French settlement. Young Frenchmen were sent to live among native peoples to master their languages and customs. These **coureurs de bois°,** or runners of the woods, often began families with indigenous women,

---

Quebec (kwuh-BEC) **coureurs de bois** (koo-RUHR day BWA)

Canadian Fur Trader   The fur trade provided the economic foundation of early Canadian settlement. The trade depended on a mix of native and European skills and resources. The fur trader's canoe was developed from native technology to carry large loads over great distances.   (Hudson's Bay Company Archives, Provincial Archives of Manitoba)

and they and their children, who were called *métis*°, helped to direct the fur trade, guiding French expansion to the west and south. Amerindians actively participated in this trade because they quickly came to depend on the goods they received in exchange for furs—firearms, metal tools and utensils, textiles, and alcohol. This change in the material culture of the native peoples led to overhunting, which rapidly transformed the environment and led to the depletion of beaver and deer populations. It also increased competition among native peoples for hunting grounds, thus promoting warfare.

The proliferation of firearms made indigenous warfare more deadly. The Iroquois Confederacy responded to the increased military strength of France's Algonkian allies by forging commercial and military links with Dutch and later English settlements in the Hudson River Valley. Well armed by the Dutch and English, the Iroquois Confederacy nearly eradicated the Huron in 1649 and in-

métis (may-TEES)

flicted a series of humiliating defeats on the French. At the high point of their power in the early 1680s, Iroquois hunters and military forces gained control of much of the Great Lakes region and the Ohio River Valley. A large French military expedition and a relentless attack focused on Iroquois villages and agriculture finally checked Iroquois power in 1701.

Spain had effectively limited the spread of firearms in its colonies. But the fur trade, together with the growing military rivalry between Algonkian and Iroquois peoples and their respective French and English allies, led to the rapid spread of firearms in North America. Use of firearms in hunting and warfare moved west and south, reaching indigenous plains cultures that previously had adopted the horse introduced by the Spanish. This intersection of horse and gun frontiers in the early eighteenth century dramatically increased the military power and hunting efficiency of the Sioux, Comanche, Cheyenne, and other indigenous peoples, and slowed the pace of European settlement in the North American west.

In French Canada, the Jesuits led the effort to convert native peoples to Christianity. Building on earlier evangelical efforts in Brazil and Paraguay, French Catholic missionaries mastered native languages, created boarding schools for young boys and girls, and set up model agricultural communities for converted Amerindians. The Jesuits' greatest successes coincided with a destructive wave of epidemics and renewed warfare among native peoples in the 1630s. Eventually, churches were established throughout Huron and Algonkian territories. Nevertheless, local culture persisted. In 1688 a French nun who had devoted her life to instructing Amerindian girls expressed the frustration of many missionaries with the resilience of indigenous culture:

> We have observed that of a hundred that have passed through our hands we have scarcely civilized one. . . . When we are least expecting it, they clamber over our wall and go off to run with their kinsmen in the woods, finding more to please them there than in all the amenities of our French house.[3]

As epidemics undermined conversion efforts in mission settlements and evidence of indigenous resistance to conversion mounted, the church redirected some of its resources from the evangelical effort to the larger French settlements, founding schools, hospitals, and churches.

Responsibility for finding settlers and supervising the colonial economy was first granted to a monopoly company chartered in France. Even though the fur trade flourished, population growth was slow. Founded at about the same time as French Canada, Virginia had twenty times as many European residents as Canada by

1627. After the establishment of royal authority in the 1660s, Canada's French population increased but remained at only 7,000 in 1673. Although improved fiscal management and more effective colonial government did promote a limited agricultural expansion, the fur trade remained important. It is clear that Canada's small settler population and the fur trade's dependence on the voluntary participation of Amerindians allowed indigenous peoples to retain greater independence and more control over their traditional lands than was possible in the colonies of Spain, Portugal, or England. Unlike these colonial regimes, which sought to transform ancient ways of life or force the transfer of native lands, the French were compelled to treat indigenous peoples as allies and trading partners. This permitted indigenous peoples to more gradually adapt to new religious, technological, and market realities.

Despite Canada's small population, limited resources, and increasing vulnerability to attack by the English and their indigenous allies, the French aggressively expanded to the west and south. Louisiana was founded in 1699, but by 1708 there were fewer than 300 soldiers, settlers, and slaves in the territory. Like Canada, Louisiana depended on the fur trade, exporting more than 50,000 deerskins in 1726. And also as in Canada, Amerindians, driven by a desire for European goods, eagerly embraced this trade. In 1753 a French official reported a Choctaw leader as saying, "[The French] were the first . . . who made [us] subject to the different needs that [we] can no longer now do without."[4]

France's North American colonies were threatened by a series of wars fought by France and England and by the population growth and increasing prosperity of neighboring English colonies. The "French and Indian War" (also known as the Seven Years War, 1756–1763), however, proved to be the final contest for North American empire (see Map 19.2). England committed a larger military force to the struggle and, despite early defeats,

Map. 19.2   European Claims in North America, 1755–1763   The results of the French and Indian War dramatically altered the map of North America. France's losses precipitated conflicts between Amerindian peoples and the rapidly expanding population of the British colonies.

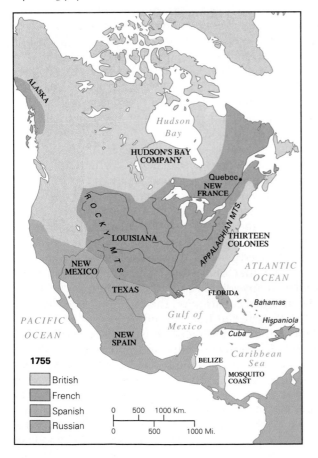

took the French capital of Quebec in 1759. Although resistance continued briefly, French forces in Canada surrendered in 1760. The peace agreement forced France to yield Canada to the English and cede Louisiana to Spain. The differences between French and English colonial realities were suggested by the petition of one Canadian indigenous leader to a British officer after the French surrender. "[W]e learn that our lands are to be given away not only to trade thereon but also to them in full title to various [English] individuals. . . . We have always been a free nation, and now we will become slaves, which would be very difficult to accept after having enjoyed our liberty so long."[5] With the loss of Canada the French concentrated their efforts on their sugar-producing colonies in the Caribbean (see Chapter 20).

COLONIAL EXPANSION AND CONFLICT

In the last decades of the seventeenth century, all of the European colonies in the Americas began to experience a long period of economic and demographic expansion. The imperial powers responded by strengthening their administrative and economic controls in the colonies. They also sought to force colonial populations to pay a larger share of the costs of administration and defense. These efforts at reform and restructuring coincided with a series of imperial wars fought along Atlantic trade routes and in the Americas. France's loss of its North American colonies was one of the most important results of these struggles. Equally significant, colonial populations throughout the Americas became more aware of separate national identities and more aggressive in asserting local interests against the will of distant monarchs.

Imperial Reform in Spanish America and Brazil

Spain's Habsburg dynasty ended when the Spanish king Charles II died without an heir in 1700 (see Table 18.1). After thirteen years of conflict involving the major European powers and factions within Spain, Philip of Bourbon, grandson of Louis XIV of France, gained the Spanish throne. Under Philip V and his Bourbon heirs, Spain's colonial administration and tax collection were reorga-

nized. Spain's reliance on convoys protected by naval vessels was abolished, more colonial ports were permitted to trade with Spain, and intercolonial trade was expanded. Spain also created new commercial monopolies to produce tobacco, some alcoholic beverages, and chocolate. Also, the Spanish navy was strengthened, and trade in contraband was more effectively policed.

For most of the Spanish Empire, the eighteenth century was a period of remarkable economic expansion associated with population growth. Amerindian populations began to recover from the early epidemics, the flow of Spanish immigrants increased, and the slave trade to the plantation colonies was expanded. Mining, the heart of the Spanish colonial economy, increased as silver production in Mexico and Peru rose steadily into the 1780s. Agricultural exports also expanded: tobacco, dyes, hides, chocolate, cotton, and sugar joined the flow of goods to Europe.

But these reforms carried unforeseen consequences that threatened the survival of the Spanish Empire. Despite expanded silver production, the economic growth of the eighteenth century was led by the previously minor agricultural and grazing economies of Cuba, the Rio de la Plata region, Venezuela, Chile, and Central America. These export economies were less able than the mining economies of Mexico and Peru to weather breaks in trade caused by imperial wars. Each such disruption forced landowning elites in Cuba and the other regions to turn to alternative, often illegal, trade with English, French, or Dutch merchants. By the 1790s, the wealthiest and most influential sectors of Spain's colonial society had come to view the Spanish Empire as an impediment to prosperity and growth.

Bourbon political and fiscal reforms also contributed to a growing sense of colonial grievance by limiting creoles' access to colonial offices and by imposing new taxes and monopolies on colonial production. Consumer and producer resentment, for example, led to rioting when the Spanish established monopolies on tobacco, cacao (chocolate), and brandy. Because these reforms produced a more intrusive and expensive colonial government that interfered with established business practices, many colonists saw these changes as an abuse of the informal constitution that had long governed the empire. Only in the Bourbon effort to expand colonial militias in the face of English threats did creoles find opportunity for improved status and greater responsibility.

In addition to tax rebellions and urban riots, colonial policies also provoked Amerindian uprisings. Most spectacular was the rebellion initiated in 1780 by the Peruvian Amerindian leader José Gabriel Condorcanqui. Once in rebellion, he took the name of his Inca ancestor

Market in Rio de Janeiro   In many of the cities of colonial Latin America female slaves and black free women dominated retail markets. In this scene from late colonial Brazil, Afro-Brazilian women sell a variety of foods and crafts.   (Sir Henry Chamberlain, *Views and Costumes of the City and Neighborhoods of Rio de Janeiro*, London, 1822)

Tupac Amaru°, who had been executed as a rebel in 1572. **Tupac Amaru II** was well connected in Spanish colonial society. He had been educated by the Jesuits and was actively involved in trade with the silver mines at Potosí. Despite these connections, he still resented the abuse of Amerindian villagers.

Historians still debate the objectives of this rebellion. Tupac Amaru's own pronouncements did not clearly state whether he sought to end local injustices or overthrow Spanish rule. It appears that a local Spanish judge who challenged Tupac Amaru's hereditary rights provided the initial provocation, but that Tupac Amaru was ultimately driven by the conviction that colonial authorities were oppressing the indigenous people. As thousands joined him, he dared to contemplate the overthrow of Spanish rule.

Amerindian communities suffering under the mita and tribute obligations provided the majority of Tupac Amaru's army. He also received some support from creoles, mestizos, and slaves. After his capture, he was brutally executed, as were his wife and fifteen other

Tupac Amaru (TOO-pack a-MAH-roo)

family members and allies. Even after his execution Amerindian rebels continued the struggle for more than two years. By the time Spanish authority was firmly reestablished, more than a hundred thousand lives had been lost and enormous amounts of property destroyed.

Brazil experienced a similar period of expansion and reform after 1700. Portugal created new administrative positions and gave monopoly companies exclusive rights to little-developed regions. Here, too, a more intrusive colonial government led to rebellions and plots, including open warfare in 1707 between "sons of the soil" and "outsiders" in São Paulo. The most aggressive period of reform occurred during the ministry of the marquis of Pombal (1750–1777). The Pombal reforms were made possible by an economic expansion fueled by the discovery of gold in the 1690s and diamonds after 1720 as well as by the development of markets for coffee and cotton. This new wealth paid for the importation of nearly 2 million African slaves. In Spanish America, a reinvigorated Crown sought to eliminate contraband trade. Portugal, however, had fallen into the economic orbit of England, and Brazil's new prosperity fueled a new wave of English imports.

Reform and Reorganization in British North America

England's efforts to reform and reorganize its North American colonies began earlier than the Bourbon initiative in Spanish America. After the period of Cromwell's Puritan Republic, the restored Stuart king, Charles II, undertook an ambitious campaign to establish greater Crown control over the colonies. Between 1651 and 1673 a series of Navigation Acts sought to severely limit colonial trading and colonial production that competed directly with English manufacturers. James II also attempted to increase royal control over colonial political life. Royal governments replaced orginal colonial charters as in Massachusetts and proprietorships as in the Carolinas. Because the New England colonies were viewed as centers of smuggling, the king temporarily suspended their elected assemblies. At the same time, he appointed colonial governors and granted them new fiscal and legislative powers.

James II's overthrow in the Glorious Revolution of 1688 ended this confrontation, but not before colonists were provoked to resist and, in some cases, rebel. They overthrew the governors of New York and Massachusetts and removed the Catholic proprietor of Maryland. William and Mary restored relative peace, but these conflicts alerted the colonists to the potential for aggression by the English government. Colonial politics would remain confrontational until the American Revolution.

During the eighteenth century the English colonies experienced renewed economic growth and attracted a new wave of European immigration, but social divisions were increasingly evident. The colonial population in 1770 was more urban, more clearly divided by class and race, and more vulnerable to economic downturns. Crises were provoked when imperial wars with France and Spain disrupted trade in the Atlantic, increased tax burdens, forced military mobilizations, and provoked frontier conflicts with the Amerindians. On the eve of the American Revolution, England defeated France and weakened Spain. The cost, however, was great. Administrative, military, and tax policies imposed to gain empirewide victory alienated much of the American colonial population.

CONCLUSION

The New World colonial empires of Spain, Portugal, France, and England had many characteristics in common. All subjugated Amerindian peoples and introduced large numbers of enslaved Africans. Within all four empires, forests were cut down, virgin soils were turned with the plow, and Old World animals and plants were introduced. Colonists in all four applied the technologies of the Old World to the resources of the New, producing wealth and exploiting the commercial possibilities of the emerging Atlantic market.

Each of the New World empires also reflected the distinctive cultural and institutional heritages of its colonizing power. Mineral wealth allowed Spain to develop the most centralized empire. Political and economic power was concentrated in the great capital cities of Mexico City and Lima. Portugal and France pursued objectives similar to Spain's in their colonies. However, neither Brazil's agricultural economy nor France's Canadian fur trade produced the financial resources that made possible the centralized control achieved by Spain. Nevertheless, all three of these Catholic powers were able to impose and enforce significant levels of religious and cultural uniformity, relative to the British.

Greater cultural and religious diversity characterized British North America. Colonists were drawn to British North America from throughout the British Isles and included participants in all of Britain's numerous religious traditions. They were joined by German, Swedish, French Huguenot, and Dutch immigrants. British colonial government varied somewhat from colony to colony and was more responsive to local interests. Thus colonists in British North America were better able than colonists in the areas controlled by Spain, Portugal, and France to respond to changing economic and political circumstances. Most important, the British colonies attracted many more European immigrants than did the other New World colonies. Between 1580 and 1760, French colonies received 60,000 immigrants, Brazil 523,000, and the Spanish colonies 678,000. Within a shorter period—between 1600 and 1760—the British settlements welcomed 746,000. Population in British North America—free and slave combined—then reached an extraordinary 2.5 million by 1775.

By the eighteenth century, colonial societies across the Americas had matured as wealth increased, populations grew, and contacts with the rest of the world became more common (see Chapter 20). Colonial elites were more confident of their ability to define and defend local interests. Colonists were in general increasingly aware of their unique and distinctive cultural identities and willing to defend American experience and practice in the face of European presumptions of superiority. Moreover, influential groups in all the colonies were drawn toward the liberating ideas of Europe's Enlightenment. In the open and less inhibited spaces of the Western Hemisphere, these ideas (as Chapter 23 examines) soon provided a potent intellectual basis for opposing the continuation of empire.

———————————————

■ Key Terms

Columbian Exchange	indentured servant
Council of the Indies	House of Burgesses
Bartolomé de Las Casas	Pilgrims
Potosí	Puritans
encomienda	Iroquois Confederacy
creoles	New France
mestizo	coureurs de bois
mulatto	Tupac Amaru II

■ Suggested Reading

Alfred W. Crosby, Jr., is justifiably the best-known student of the Columbian Exchange. See his *The Columbian Exchange: Biological and Cultural Consequences of 1492* (1972) and *Ecological Imperialism* (1986). William H. McNeill, *Plagues and People* (1976), puts the discussion of the American exchange in a world history context. Elinor G. K. Melville, *A Plague of Sheep: Environmental Consequences of the Spanish Conquest of Mexico* (1994), is the most important recent contribution to this field.

Colonial Latin America, 2d ed. (1994), by Mark A. Burkholder and Lyman L. Johnson, provides a good introduction to colonial Latin American history. *Early Latin America* (1983) by James Lockhart and Stuart B. Schwartz and *Spain and Portugal in the New World, 1492–1700* (1984) by Lyle N. McAlister are both useful introductions as well.

The specialized historical literature on the American colonial empires is extensive and deep. A sampling of useful works follows. For the early colonial period see Inga Clendinnen, *Ambivalent Conquests* (1987); James Lockhart, *The Nahuas After the Conquest* (1992); and John Hemming, *Red Gold: The Conquest of the Brazilian Indians* (1978). Nancy M. Farriss, *Maya Society Under Spanish Rule: The Collective Enterprise of Survival* (1984), is also one of the most important books on colonial Spanish America. For the Catholic Church see William Taylor, *Magistrates of the Sacred: Priests and Parishioners in Eighteenth-Century Mexico* (1996). Lyman L. Johnson and Sonya Lipsett-Rivera, *The Faces of Honor* (1999), provides a good introduction to the culture of honor. For the place of women see Asunción Lavrin, ed., *Sexuality and Marriage in Colonial Latin America* (1989). On issues of class R. Douglas Cope, *The Limits of Racial Domination* (1994), is recommended. On the slave trade, Herbert S. Klein, *The Middle Passage* (1978), and Philip D. Curtin, *The Atlantic Slave Trade: A Census* (1969), are indispensable. Frederick P. Bowser, *The African Slave in Colonial Peru, 1524–1650* (1973); Mary C. Karasch, *Slave Life and Culture in Rio de Janeiro, 1808–1850* (1986); and Stuart B. Schwartz, *Sugar Plantations in the Formation of Brazilian Society: Bahia, 1550–1835* (1985), are excellent introductions to the African experience in two very different Latin American societies.

Among the useful general studies of the British colonies are Charles M. Andrews, *The Colonial Period of American History: The Settlements,* 3 vols. (1934–1937); David Hackett Fischer, *Albion's Seed: Four British Folkways in America* (1989); and Gary B. Nash, *Red, White, and Black: The Peoples of Early America,* 2d ed. (1982). On the economy see John J. McCusker and Russell R. Menard, *The Economy of British America, 1607–1789* (1979). For slavery see David Brion Davis, *The Problem of Slavery in Western Culture* (1966); Allan Kulikoff, *Tobacco and Slaves: The Development of Southern Cultures in the Chesapeake, 1680–1800* (1986); and Peter H. Wood, *Black Majority: Negroes in Colonial South Carolina from 1670 Through the Stono Rebellion* (1974). Two very useful works on the relations between Europeans and Indians are James Merrill, *The Indians' New World: Catawbas and Their Neighbors from European Contact Through the Era of Removal* (1989); and Daniel H. Usner, Jr., *Indians, Settlers, and Slaves in a Frontier Exchange Economy: The Lower Mississippi Valley Before 1783* (1992).

For late colonial politics see Gary B. Nash, *Urban Crucible: Social Change, Political Consciousness, and the Origins of the American Revolution* (1979); Bernard Bailyn, *The Origins of American Politics* (1986); Jack P. Greene, *The Quest for Power: The Lower Houses of Assembly in the Southern Royal Colonies* (1963); and Richard Bushman, *King and People in Provincial Massachusetts* (1985). On immigration see Bernard Bailyn, *The Peopling of British North America* (1986).

On French North America, William J. Eccles, *France in America,* rev. ed. (1990), is an excellent overview; see also his *The Canadian Frontier, 1534–1760* (1969). G. F. G. Stanley, *New France, 1701–1760* (1968), is also an important resource. R. Cole Harris, *The Seigneurial System in Canada: A Geographical Study* (1966), provides an excellent analysis of the topic. Harold Innis, *The Fur Trade in Canada: An Introduction to Canadian Economic History* (1927), remains indispensable. Also of value are Cornelius Jaenen, *The Role of the Church in New France* (1976), and Alison L. Prentice, *Canadian Women: A History* (1988).

■ Notes

1. Quoted in Alfred W. Crosby, Jr., *The Columbian Exchange: Biological and Cultural Consequences of 1492* (Westport, CT: Greenwood, 1972), 58.
2. Quoted ibid.
3. Quoted in R. Douglas Francis, Richard Jones, and Donald B. Smith, *Origins: Canadian History to Confederation* (Toronto: Holt, Rinehart, and Winston of Canada, 1992), 52.
4. Quoted in Daniel H. Usner, Jr., *Indians, Settlers and Slaves in a Frontier Exchange Economy: The Lower Mississippi Valley Before 1783,* Institute of Early American History and Culture Series (Chapel Hill: University of North Carolina Press, 1992), 96.
5 Quoted in Cornelius J. Jaenen, "French and Native Peoples in New France," in J. M. Bumsted, *Interpreting Canada's Past,* vol. 1, 2d ed. (Toronto: Oxford University Press, 1993), 73.

20

THE ATLANTIC SYSTEM AND AFRICA,
1550–1800

Plantations in the West Indies • Plantation Life in the Eighteenth Century •
Creating the Atlantic Economy • Africa, the Atlantic, and Islam
ENVIRONMENT AND TECHNOLOGY: Amerindian Foods in Africa
SOCIETY AND CULTURE: A Maroon Village in French Guiana, 1748

Caribbean Sugar Mill   The wind mill crushes sugar cane whose juice
is boiled down in the smoking building next door.

As the ship bearing a cargo of slaves from West Africa neared the West Indian island of Barbados in 1757, the English crew gave a joyful shout, glad that this leg of their trading tour around the Atlantic was over. Since leaving England, some of their number had died of African tropical diseases, and one crewman had been flogged to death for insubordination. The survivors, thankful to put the risk of disease and slave insurrection behind them, looked forward to returning to England.

However, one of the slaves on board, Olaudah Equiano°, recorded in his biography that the sight of Barbados filled the shackled Africans with apprehension. Although fortunate to have survived long weeks of suffocating heat and loathsome smells packed side by side in the cargo hold, the captive African men, women, and children feared they were going to be eaten by the white people who rushed to inspect them after the ship anchored in the harbor of Bridgetown. To ease the new arrivals' panic, local sugar planters sent veteran slaves on board to assure them in several African languages that they would not be eaten. Instead, most were destined to work on the island's sugar plantations. After landing, Equiano relates, he and his companions were relieved to discover that most of the island's inhabitants were Africans. The eleven-year-old Equiano found many of his own Igbo° people there.

After examining the slaves for physical defects, the local merchants divided them into "parcels" of several slaves each and penned them in a yard, in Equiano's words, "like so many sheep in a fold without regard to sex or age." A few days later they were sold to the planters, not by auction but in a terrifying "scramble." At the beat of a drum, buyers rushed into the yard and seized the parcel of slaves they wanted. "In this manner," Equiano commented, "without scruple, are relations and friends separated, most of them never to see each other again."

By the 1750s, Barbados was past its prime as a sugar colony, so Equiano and some companions were shipped to the colony of Virginia. There for a time he was put to work weeding; he later worked on a ship. In 1766 at the age of twenty-one, Equiano was able to buy his freedom with money he earned in private trading. He worked as a seaman and then resided in England, where he married and joined the campaign against the slave trade.

The slave trade and the plantations in the West Indies, Virginia, and elsewhere in the Americas were crucial pieces of a new **Atlantic system.** This network of trading links moved not only goods and wealth but also people and cultures around the Atlantic world.

As you read this chapter, ask yourself the following questions:

- How did participation in the Atlantic system affect Europe, Africa, and the Americas?
- How and why did European businessmen, with the help of their governments, put this trading system together?
- How and why did the West Indies and other places in the Americas become centers of African population and culture?
- How did sub-Saharan Africa's expanding contacts in the Atlantic compare with its contacts with the Islamic world?

PLANTATIONS IN THE WEST INDIES

The West Indies was the first place in the Americas reached by Columbus and the first part of the Americas where native populations collapsed. It took a long time to repopulate these islands from abroad and forge new economic links between them and other parts of the Atlantic. But after 1650, sugar plantations, African slaves, and European capital made these islands a major center of the Atlantic economy.

Olaudah Equiano (oh-LAU-duh ay-kwee-AHN-oh)
Igbo (EE-boh)

Colonization Before 1650

Spanish settlers introduced sugar-cane cultivation into the West Indies shortly after 1500, but soon these colonies fell into neglect as attention shifted to colonizing the American mainland. After 1600 the West Indies revived as a focus of colonization, this time by northern Europeans interested in growing tobacco and other crops. In the 1620s and 1630s English colonization societies founded small European settlements on Montserrat°, Barbados°, Trinidad°, and other Caribbean islands, while the French colonized Martinique°, Guadeloupe°, and some other islands. Because of greater support from their government, the English colonies prospered first, largely by growing tobacco for export.

This New World leaf, long used by Amerindians for recreation and medicine, was finding a new market among seventeenth-century Europeans. Despite the opposition of individuals like King James I of England, who condemned tobacco smoke as "dangerous to the eye, hateful to the nose, harmful to the brain, and dangerous to the lungs," the habit spread. By 1614 tobacco was reportedly being sold in seven thousand shops in and around London, and some English businessmen were dreaming of a tobacco trade as valuable as Spain's silver fleets.

Turning such pipe dreams into reality was not easy. Diseases, hurricanes, and attacks by the Carib and the Spanish scourged the early French and English West Indies colonists. They also suffered from shortages of supplies from Europe and shortages of labor sufficient to clear and plant virgin land with tobacco. Two changes improved the colonies' prospects. One was the formation of **chartered companies.** To promote national claims without government expense, France and England gave groups of private investors monopolies over trade to their West Indies colonies in exchange for the payment of an annual fee. The other change was that the companies began to provide free passage to the colonies for poor Europeans. These indentured servants paid off their debt by working three or four years for the established colonists (see Chapter 19).

Under this system the French and English population on several tobacco islands grew rapidly in the 1630s and 1640s. By the middle of the century, however, the Caribbean colonies were in crisis because of stiff competition from milder Virginia-grown tobacco, also cultivated by indentured servants. The cultivation of sugar cane, introduced in the 1640s by Dutch investors expelled from Brazil, provided the Caribbean colonies a way out of this crisis. In the process their labor force changed from mostly European to mostly African.

The Portuguese had introduced sugar cultivation into Brazil from islands along the African coast after 1550 and had soon introduced enslaved African labor as well (see Chapter 19). By 1600 Brazil was the Atlantic world's greatest sugar producer. Some Dutch merchants invested in Brazilian sugar plantations so that they might profit from transporting the sugar across the Atlantic and distributing it in Europe. However, in the first half of the seventeenth century the Dutch were fighting for their independence from the Spanish crown, which then ruled Portugal and Brazil. As part of that struggle, the Dutch government chartered the **Dutch West India Company** in 1621 to carry the conflict to Spain's overseas possessions.

Not just a disguised form of the Dutch navy, the Dutch West India Company was a private trading company. Its investors expected the company's profits to cover its expenses and pay them dividends. After the capture of a Spanish treasure fleet in 1628, the company used some of the windfall to pay its stockholders a huge dividend and the rest to finance an assault on Brazil's valuable sugar-producing areas. By 1635 the Dutch company controlled 1,000 miles (1,600 kilometers) of northeastern Brazil's coast. Over the next fifteen years the new Dutch owners improved the efficiency of the Brazilian sugar industry, and the company prospered by supplying the plantations with enslaved Africans and European goods and carrying the sugar back to Europe.

Like its assault on Brazil, the Dutch West India Company's entry into the African slave trade combined economic and political motives. It seized the important West African trading station of Elmina from the Portuguese in 1638 and took their port of Luanda° on the Angolan coast in 1641. From these coasts the Dutch shipped slaves to Brazil and the West Indies. Although the Portuguese were able to drive the Dutch out of Angola after a few years, Elmina remained the Dutch West India Company's headquarters in West Africa.

Once free of Spanish rule in 1640, the Portuguese crown turned its attention to reconquering Brazil. By 1654 Portuguese armies had driven the last of the Dutch sugar planters from Brazil. Some of the expelled planters transplanted their capital and knowledge of sugar production to small colonies, which the Dutch had founded earlier as trading bases with Spanish colonies; others in-

---

Montserrat (mont-suh-RAHT)   **Barbados** (bahr-BAY-dohs)
Trinidad (TRIN-ah-dad)   **Martinique** (mahr-tee-NEEK)
Guadeloupe (gwah-duh-LOOP)

Luanda (loo-AHN-duh)

CHRONOLOGY

	West Indies	Atlantic	Africa
1500	**ca. 1500** Spanish settlers introduce sugar-cane cultivation	**1530** Amsterdam Exchange opens	**1500–1700** Gold trade predominates
			1591 Morocco conquers Songhai
1600	**1620s and 1630s** English and French colonies in Caribbean	**1621** Dutch West India Company chartered	**1638** Dutch take Elmina
	1640s Dutch bring sugar plantation system from Brazil		
	1655 English take Jamaica		
		1660s English Navigation Acts	
	1670s French occupy western half of Hispaniola	**1672** Royal African Company chartered	**1680s** Rise of Asante
		1698 French *Exclusif*	
1700	**1700** West Indies surpass Brazil in sugar production	**1700 to present** Atlantic system flourishing	**1700–1830** Slave trade predominates
			1720s Rise of Dahomey
			1730 Oyo makes Dahomey pay tribute
	1760 Tacky's rebellion in Jamaica		
	1795 Jamaican Maroon rebellion		

troduced the Brazilian system into English and French Caribbean islands. This was a momentous turning point in the history of the Atlantic economy.

Sugar and Slaves

The Dutch infusion of expertise and money revived the French colonies of Guadeloupe and Martinique, but the English colony of Barbados best illustrates the dramatic transformation that sugar brought to the seventeenth-century Caribbean. In 1640 Barbados's economy depended largely on tobacco, mostly grown by European settlers, both free and indentured. By the 1680s sugar had become the colony's principal crop, and enslaved Africans were three times as numerous as Europeans. Exporting up to 15,000 tons of sugar a year, Barbados had become the wealthiest and most populous of England's American colonies. By 1700, the West Indies had surpassed Brazil as the world's principal source of sugar.

The expansion of sugar plantations in the West Indies required a sharp increase in the volume of the slave trade from Africa (see Figure 20.1). During the first half of the seventeenth century about 10,000 slaves a year had arrived from Africa. Most were destined for Brazil and the mainland Spanish colonies. In the second half of the century the trade averaged 20,000 slaves a year. More than half were intended for the English, French, and Dutch West Indies and most of the rest for Brazil. A century later the volume of the Atlantic slave trade was three times larger.

The shift in favor of African slaves was a product of many factors. Recent scholarship has cast doubt on the once-common assertion that Africans were more suited than Europeans to field labor, since newly arrived Africans and Europeans both died in large numbers in the American tropics. Africans' slightly higher survival rate was not decisive because mortality was about the same among later generations of blacks and whites born in the West Indies and acclimated to its diseases.

The West Indian historian Eric Williams also refuted the idea that the rise of African slave labor was primarily motivated by prejudice. Citing the West Indian colonies' prior use of enslaved Amerindians and indentured Europeans, along with European convicts and prisoners of war, he argued, "Slavery was not born of racism: rather, racism was the consequence of slavery."[1] Williams suggested the shift was due to the lower cost of African labor.

Yet slaves were far from cheap. Cash-short tobacco planters in the seventeenth century preferred indentured

Figure 20.1   Transatlantic Slave Trade from Africa, 1551–1850

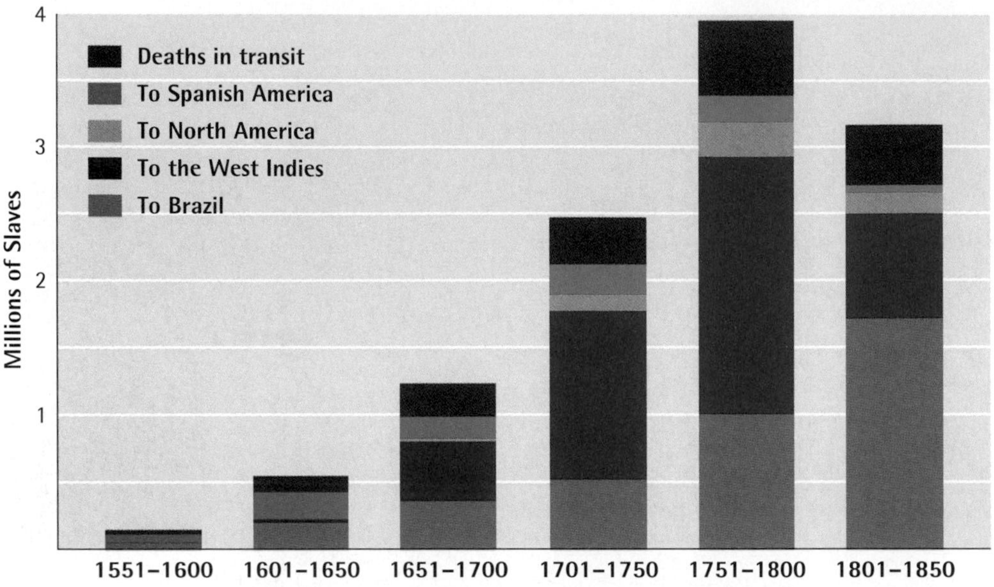

Legend:
- Deaths in transit
- To Spanish America
- To North America
- To the West Indies
- To Brazil

Y-axis: Millions of Slaves (0 to 4)

X-axis: 1551–1600, 1601–1650, 1651–1700, 1701–1750, 1751–1800, 1801–1850

Source: Philip D. Curtin, *The Atlantic Slave Trade: A Census* (Madison: University of Wisconsin Press, 1969), tables 33, 34, 65; Paul E. Lovejoy, "The Volume of the Atlantic Slave Trade: A Synthesis," *Journal of African History* 23 (1982): 473–501; David Eltis, *Economic Growth and the Ending of the Transatlantic Slave Trade* (New York: Oxford University Press, 1987), table A8.

Europeans because they cost half as much as African slaves. Poor European men and women were willing to work for little in order to get to the Americas, where they could acquire their own land cheaply at the end of their term of service. However, as the cultivation of sugar spread after 1750, rich speculators drove the price of land in the West Indies up so high that end-of-term indentured servants could not afford to buy it. As a result, poor Europeans chose to indenture themselves in the mainland North American colonies, where cheap land was still available. Rather than raise wages to attract European laborers, Caribbean sugar planters switched to slaves.

Rising sugar prices helped the West Indian sugar planters afford the higher cost of African slaves. The fact that the average slave lived seven years, while the typical indentured labor contract was for only three or four years, also made slaves a better investment. The planters could rely on the Dutch and other traders to supply them with enough new slaves to meet the demands of the expanding plantations. Rising demand for slaves (see Figure 20.1) drove their sale price up steadily during the eighteenth century. These high labor costs were one more factor favoring large plantations over smaller operations.

PLANTATION LIFE IN THE EIGHTEENTH CENTURY

To find more land for sugar plantations, France and England founded new Caribbean colonies. In 1655 the English had wrested the island of Jamaica from the Spanish (see Map 19.1). The French seized the western half of the large Spanish island of Hispaniola in the 1670s. During the eighteenth century this new French colony of Saint Domingue° (present-day Haiti) became the greatest producer of sugar in the Atlantic world, while Jamaica surpassed Barbados as England's most important sugar colony. The technological, environmental, and social transformation of these island colonies illustrates the power of the new Atlantic system.

Saint Domingue (san doh-MANGH)

Plantation Scene, Antigua, British West Indies   Even in this romanticized painting the slave's simple earthen huts contrast sharply with the planter's elegant great house on the rising ground on the left. Notice the large church in the center background and the women performing domestic tasks.   (West India Committee)

Technology and Environment

The cultivation of sugar cane was fairly straightforward. From fourteen to eighteen months after planting, the canes were ready to be cut. The roots continued to produce new shoots that could be harvested about every nine months. Only simple tools were needed: spades for planting, hoes to control the weeds, and sharp machetes to cut the canes. What made the sugar plantation a complex investment was that it had to be a factory as well as a farm. Freshly cut canes needed to be crushed within a few hours to extract the sugary sap. Thus, for maximum efficiency, each plantation needed its own expensive crushing and processing equipment.

At the heart of the sugar works was the mill where canes were crushed between sets of heavy rollers. Small mills could be turned by animal or human power, but larger, more efficient mills needed more sophisticated sources of power. Eighteenth-century Barbados went in heavily for windmills, and the French sugar islands and Jamaica used costly water-powered mills often fed by elaborate aqueducts.

From the mill, lead-lined wooden troughs carried the cane juice to a series of large copper kettles in the boiling shed, where the excess water boiled off, leaving a thick syrup. Workers poured the syrup into conical molds in the drying shed. The sugar crystals that formed in the molds were packed in wooden barrels for shipment to Europe. The dark molasses that drained off was made into rum in yet another building, or it was barreled for export.

To make their operation more efficient and profitable, investors gradually increased the size of the typical West Indian plantation from around 100 acres (40 hectares) in the seventeenth century to at least twice that size in the eighteenth century. Some plantations were even larger. In 1774 Jamaica's 680 sugar plantations averaged 441 acres (178 hectares) each; some spread over 2,000 acres (800 hectares). Jamaica specialized so heavily in sugar production that the island had to import most of its food. Saint Domingue had a comparable number of plantations of smaller average size but generally higher productivity. The French colony was also more diverse in its economy. Although sugar production was paramount, some planters raised provisions for local consumption of crops such as coffee and cacao for export.

In some ways the mature sugar plantation was environmentally responsible. The crushing mill was powered by water, wind, or animal power, not fossil fuels. The boilers were largely fueled by burning the crushed canes, and the fields were fertilized by manure of the cattle. In two respects, however, the plantation was very damaging to the environment: soil exhaustion and deforestation.

Repeated cultivation of a single crop removes from the soil more nutrients than animal fertilizer and fallow periods can restore. Instead of rotating sugar with other crops in order to restore the nutrients naturally, planters found it more profitable to clear new lands when yields declined too much in the old fields. When land close to the sea was exhausted, planters moved on to new islands. Many of the English who first settled Jamaica were from Barbados, and the pioneer planters on Saint Domingue came from older French sugar colonies. In the second half of the eighteenth century Jamaican sugar production began to fall behind that of Saint Domingue, which still had access to virgin land. Thus the plantations of this period were not a stable form of agriculture but one that gradually laid waste to the landscape.

Deforestation, the second form of environmental damage, continued a trend begun in the sixteenth century. The Spanish had cut down some forests in the Caribbean to make pastures for the cattle they introduced. Sugar cultivation rapidly accelerated land clearing. Forests near the coast were the first to disappear, and by the end of the eighteenth century only land in the interior of the islands retained dense forests.

Other changes, combined with soil exhaustion and deforestation, profoundly altered the ecology balance of the West Indies. By the eighteenth century nearly all of the domesticated animals and cultivated plants in the Caribbean were ones that Europeans had introduced. The Spanish had brought cattle, pigs, and horses, all of which multiplied so rapidly that no new imports had been necessary after 1503. They had also introduced new plants. Of these, bananas and plantain from the Canary Islands were a valuable addition to the food supply, and sugar and rice formed the basis of plantation agriculture, along with native tobacco. Other food crops arrived with the slaves from Africa, including okra, black-eyed peas, yams, grains such as millet and sorghum, and mangoes. Many of these new animals and plants were useful additions to the islands, but they crowded out indigenous species.

The most tragic and dramatic transformation in the West Indies occurred in the human population. Chapter 17 detailed how the indigenous Arawak peoples of the large islands were wiped out by disease and abuse within fifty years of Columbus's first voyage. As the plantation economy spread, the Carib surviving on the smaller islands were also pushed to the point of extinction. Far earlier and more completely than in any mainland colony, the West Indies were repeopled from across the Atlantic—first from Europe and then from Africa.

Slaves' Lives

During the eighteenth century, West Indian plantation colonies were the world's most polarized societies. On most islands 90 percent or more of the inhabitants were slaves. Power resided in the hands of a **plantocracy,** a small number of very rich men who owned most of the slaves and most of the land as well. Between the slaves and the masters might be found only a few others—a few estate managers and government officials and, in the French islands, some small farmers, both white and black. Thus it is only a slight simplification to describe eighteenth-century Caribbean society as being made up of a large, abject class of slaves and a small, powerful class of masters.

The profitability of a Caribbean plantation depended on extracting as much work as possible from the slaves. Their long workday might stretch to eighteen hours or more when the cane harvest and milling were in full swing. Sugar plantations achieved exceptional productivity through the use of force and the threat of force. As Table 20.1 shows, on a typical Jamaican plantation about 80 percent of the slaves actively engaged in productive tasks; the only exceptions were infants, the seriously ill, and the very old. Everyone on the plantation, except those disabled by age or infirmity, had an assigned task.

Table 20.1 also illustrates how slave labor was organized by age, sex, and ability. As in other Caribbean colonies, only 2 or 3 percent of the slaves served as house servants. About 70 percent of the able-bodied slaves worked in the fields, generally in one of three labor gangs. A "great gang," made up of the strongest slaves in the prime of life, did the heaviest work, such as breaking up the soil at the beginning of the planting season. A second gang of youths, elders, and less fit slaves did somewhat lighter work. A "grass gang," composed of children under the supervision of an elderly slave, was responsible for weeding and other simple work, such as collecting grass for the animals. Women formed the majority of the field laborers, even in the great gang. Nursing mothers took their babies with them to the fields. Slaves too old for field labor tended the toddlers.

Because slave ships brought twice as many males as females from Africa, men outnumbered women on Caribbean plantations. As Table 20.1 shows, a little over half of the adult males were employed in nongang work. Some tended the livestock, including the mules and oxen that did the heavy carrying work; others were skilled tradesmen, such as blacksmiths and carpenters. The most important artisan slave was the head boiler, who oversaw the delicate process of reducing the cane sap to crystallized sugar and molasses.

Table 20.1   Slave Occupations on a Jamaican Sugar Plantation, 1788

Occupations and Conditions	Men	Women	Boys and Girls	Total
Field laborers	62	78		140
Tradesmen	29			29
Field drivers	4			4
Field cooks		4		4
Mule-, cattle-, and stablemen	12			12
Watchmen	18			18
Nurse		1		1
Midwife		1		1
Domestics and gardeners		5	3	8
Grass-gang			20	20
Total employed	**125**	**89**	**23**	**237**
Infants			23	23
Invalids (18 with yaws)				32
Absent on roads				5
Superannuated [elderly]				7
Overall total				**304**

Source: Adapted from "Edward Long to William Pitt," in Michael Craton, James Walvin, and David Wright, eds., *Slavery, Abolition, and Emancipation* (London: Longman, 1976), 103. Used by permission of Pearson Education Limited.

Punishment for Slaves   In addition to whipping and other cruel punishments, slave owners devised other ways to shame and intimidate slaves into obedience. This metal face mask prevented the wearer from eating or drinking.   (By permission of the Syndics of Cambridge University Library)

Skilled slaves received rewards of food and clothing or time off for good work, but the most common reason for working hard was to escape punishment. A slave gang was headed by a privileged male slave, appropriately called the **"driver,"** whose job was to ensure that the gang completed its work. Since production quotas were high, slaves toiled in the fields from sunup to sunset, except for meal breaks. Those who fell behind due to fatigue or illness soon felt the sting of the whip. Openly rebellious slaves, who refused to work, disobeyed orders, or tried to escape, were punished with flogging, confinement in irons, or mutilation. On a Virginia plantation Equiano was shocked to see a woman slave being punished with an "iron muzzle" that "locked her mouth so fast that she could scarcely speak, and could not eat nor drink."

Even though slaves did not work in the fields on Sunday, it was no day of rest, for they had to farm their own provisioning grounds, maintain their dwellings, and do other chores, such as washing and mending their rough clothes. Sunday markets, where slaves sold small amounts of produce or animals they had raised to get a little spending money, were common in the British West Indies.

Except for occasional holidays—including the Christmas-week revels in the British West Indies—there was little time for recreation and relaxation. Slaves might sing in the fields, but singing was simply a way to distract themselves from their fatigue and the monotony of the work. There was certainly no time for schooling, and no willingness to educate slaves, beyond skills useful to the plantation.

Time for family life was also inadequate. Although the large proportion of young adults in plantation colonies ought to have led to a high rate of natural increase, the opposite occurred. Poor nutrition and overwork lowered fertility. A woman who did become pregnant found it difficult to carry a child to term while continuing heavy fieldwork or to ensure her infant's survival. As a result of these conditions, along with disease and accidents from dangerous mill equipment, deaths heavily outnumbered births on West Indian plantations (see Table 20.2). Life expectancy for slaves in nineteenth-century Brazil was only 23 years of age for males and 25.5 years for females. The figures were probably similar for the eighteenth-century Caribbean. A callous opinion, common among slave owners in the Caribbean and in parts of Brazil, held that it was cheaper to import a youthful new slave from Africa than to raise one to the same age on a plantation.

The harsh conditions of plantation life played a major role in shortening slaves' lives, but the greatest killer was disease. The very young were carried off by dysentery caused by contaminated food and water. Slaves newly arrived from Africa went through the period of adjustment to a new environment, known as **seasoning,** during which one-third on average died of unfamiliar diseases. Slaves also suffered from diseases brought with them, including malaria. On the plantation profiled in Table 20.1, for example, more than half of the slaves incapacitated by illness had yaws, a painful and debilitating skin disease common in Africa. As a consequence, only slave populations in the healthier temperate zones of North America experienced natural increase; those in tropical Brazil and the Caribbean had a negative rate of growth.

Such high mortality greatly added to the volume of the Atlantic slave trade, since plantations had to purchase new slaves every year or two just to replace those who died (see Table 20.2). The additional imports of slaves to permit the expansion of the sugar plantations meant that the majority of slaves were African-born on most West Indian plantations. As a result, African religious beliefs, patterns of speech, styles of dress and adornment, and music were prominent parts of West Indian life.

Given the harsh conditions of their lives, it is not surprising that slaves in the West Indies often sought to regain the freedom into which most had been born. Individual slaves often ran away, hoping to elude the men and dogs who would track them. Sometimes large groups of plantation slaves rose in rebellion against their bondage and abuse. For example, a large rebellion in Jamaica in 1760 was led by a slave named Tacky, who had been a chief on the Gold Coast of Africa. One night his followers broke into a fort and armed themselves. Joined by slaves from other nearby plantations, they stormed several plantations, setting them on fire and killing the planter families. Tacky died in the fighting that followed, and three other rebel leaders stoically endured cruel deaths by torture that were meant to deter others from rebellion.

Because they believed rebellions were usually led by slaves with the strongest African heritage, European planters tried to curtail African cultural traditions. They required slaves to learn the colonial language and discouraged the use of African languages by deliberately mixing slaves from different parts of Africa. In French and Portuguese colonies, slaves were encouraged to adopt Catholic religious practices, though African deities and beliefs also survived. In the British West Indies, where only Quaker slave owners encouraged Christianity among their slaves before 1800, African herbal medicine remained strong, as did African beliefs concerning nature spirits and witchcraft.

Table 20.2   Birth and Death on a Jamaican Sugar Plantation, 1779–1785

Year	Born Males	Born Females	Purchased	Died Males	Died Females	Proportion of Deaths
1779	5	2	6	7	5	1 in 26
1780	4	3	–	3	2	1 in 62
1781	2	3	–	4	2	1 in 52
1782	1	3	9	4	5	1 in 35
1783	3	3	–	8	10	1 in 17
1784	2	1	12	9	10	1 in 17
1785	2	3	–	0	3	1 in 99
Total	19	18	27	35	37	
	Born 37			Died 72		

Source: From "Edward Long to William Pitt," in Michael Craton, James Walvin, and David Wright, eds., *Slavery, Abolition, and Emancipation* (London: Longman, 1976), 105. Used by permission of Pearson Education Limited.

Free Whites and Free Blacks

The lives of the small minority of free people were very different from the lives of slaves. In the French colony of Saint Domingue, which had nearly half of the slaves in the Caribbean in the eighteenth century, free people fell into three distinct groups. First, at the top of free society were the wealthy owners of large sugar plantations (the *grand blancs*°, or "great whites"), who dominated the economy and society of the island. Second came less-well-off Europeans (*petits blancs*°, or "little whites"). Most of them raised provisions for local consumption and crops such as coffee, indigo, and cotton for export, relying on their own and slave labor. Third came the free blacks. Though nearly as numerous as the free whites and engaged in similar occupations, they ranked below whites socially. A few free blacks became wealthy enough to own their own slaves.

The dominance of the plantocracy was even greater in British colonies. Whereas sugar constituted about half of Saint Domingue's exports, in Jamaica the figure was over 80 percent. Such concentration on sugar cane left much less room for small cultivators, white or black, and confined most landholding to a few larger owners. Three-quarters of the farmland in Jamaica at midcentury belonged to individuals who owned 1,000 acres (400 hectares) or more.

One source estimated that a planter had to invest nearly £20,000 ($100,000) to acquire even a medium-size Jamaican plantation of 600 acres (240 hectares) in 1774. A third of this money went for land on which to grow sugar and food crops, pasture animals, and cut timber and firewood. A quarter of the expense was for the sugar works and other equipment. The largest expense was to purchase 200 slaves at about £40 ($200) each. In comparison, the wage of an English rural laborer at this time was about £10 ($50) a year (one-fourth the price of a slave), and the annual incomes in 1760 of the ten wealthiest noble families in Britain averaged only £20,000 each.

Reputedly the richest Englishmen of this time, West Indian planters often translated their wealth into political power and social prestige. The richest planters put their plantations under the direction of managers and lived in Britain, often on rural estates that once had been the preserve of country gentlemen. Between 1730 and 1775 seventy of these absentee planters secured election to the British Parliament, where they formed an influential voting bloc. Those who resided in the West Indies had political power as well, for the British plantocracy controlled the colonial assemblies.

The Unknown Maroon of Saint-Domingue This modern sculpture by Albert Mangonès celebrates the brave but perilous life of a run-away slave, who is shown drinking water from a seashell. (Albert Mangonès, "The Unknown Maroon of Saint-Domingue." From Richard Price, *Maroon Societies*, Johns Hopkins University Press. Reproduced with permission.)

Most Europeans in plantation colonies were single males. Many of them took advantage of slave women for sexual favors or took slave mistresses. A slave owner who fathered a child by a female slave often gave both mother and child their freedom. In some colonies such **manumission** (a legal grant of freedom to an individual slave) produced a significant free black population. By the late eighteenth century, free blacks were more numerous than slaves in most of the Spanish colonies. They were almost 30 percent of the black population of Brazil, and they existed in significant numbers in the French colonies. Free blacks were far less common in the British colonies and the United States, where manumission was rare.

As in Brazil (see Chapter 19), escaped slaves constituted another part of the free black population. In the Caribbean runaways were known as **maroons,** Maroon communities were especially numerous in the mountainous interiors of Jamaica and Hispaniola as well as in the island parts of the Guianas° (see Society and Culture:

---

grands blancs (grawn blawnk)   *petits blancs* (pay-TEE blawnk)

Guianas (guy-AHN-uhs)

A Maroon Village in French Guiana). The Jamaican Maroons, after withstanding several attacks by the colony's militia, signed a treaty in 1739 that recognized their independence in return for their cooperation in stopping new runaways and suppressing slave revolts. Similar treaties with the large maroon population in the Dutch colony of Surinam (Dutch Guiana) recognized their possession of large inland regions.

CREATING THE ATLANTIC ECONOMY

At once archaic in their cruel system of slavery and oddly modern in their specialization in a single product, the West Indian plantation colonies were the bittersweet fruits of a new Atlantic trading system. Changes in the type and number of ships crossing the Atlantic illustrate the rise of this new system. The Atlantic trade of the sixteenth century calls to mind the treasure fleet, an annual convoy of from twenty to sixty ships laden with silver and gold bullion from Spanish America. Two different vessels typify the far more numerous Atlantic voyages of the late seventeenth and eighteenth centuries. One was the sugar ship, returning to Europe from the West Indies or Brazil crammed with barrels of brown sugar destined for further refinement. At the end of the seventeenth century an average of 266 sugar ships sailed every year just from the small island of Barbados. The second type of vessel was the slave ship. At the trade's peak between 1760 and 1800, some 300 ships, crammed with an average of 250 African captives each, crossed the Atlantic to the Americas each year.

Many separate pieces went into the creation of the new Atlantic economy. Besides the plantation system itself, three other elements merit further investigation: new economic institutions, new partnerships between private investors and governments in Europe, and new working relationships between European and African merchants. The new trading system is a prime example of how European capitalist relationships were reshaping the world.

Capitalism and Mercantilism

The Spanish and Portuguese voyages of exploration in the fifteenth and sixteenth centuries were government ventures, and both countries tried to keep their overseas trade and colonies royal monopolies (see Chapters 17 and 18). Monopoly control, however, proved both expensive and inefficient. The success of the Atlantic economy in the seventeenth and eighteenth centuries owed much to private enterprise, which made trading venues more efficient and profitable. European private investors were attracted by the profits they could make from an established and growing trading and colonial system, but their successful participation in the Atlantic economy depended on new institutions and a significant measure of government protection that reduced the likelihood of catastrophic loss.

Two European innovations enabled private investors to fund the rapid growth of the Atlantic economy. One was the ability to manage large financial resources through mechanisms that modern historians have labeled **capitalism.** The essence of early modern capitalism was a system of large financial institutions—banks, stock exchanges, and chartered trading companies—that enabled wealthy investors to reduce risks and increase profits. Originally developed for business dealings within Europe, the capitalist system expanded overseas in the seventeenth century, when slow economic growth in Europe led many investors to seek greater profits abroad.

Banks were a central capitalist institution. By the early seventeenth century, Dutch banks had developed such a reputation for security that individuals and governments from all over western Europe entrusted them with large sums of money. To make a profit, the banks invested these funds in real estate, local industries, loans to governments, and overseas trade.

Individuals seeking returns higher than the low rate of interest paid by banks could purchase shares in a joint-stock company, a sixteenth-century forerunner of the modern corporation. Shares were bought and sold in specialized financial markets called stock exchanges. The Amsterdam Exchange, founded in 1530, became the greatest stock market in the seventeenth and eighteenth centuries. To reduce risks in overseas trading, merchants and trading companies bought insurance on their ships and cargoes from specialized companies that agreed to cover losses.

The capitalism of these centuries was buttressed by **mercantilism,** policies adopted by European states to promote their citizens' overseas trade and accumulate capital in the form of precious metals. Mercantilist policies strongly discouraged citizens from trading with foreign merchants and used armed force when necessary to secure exclusive relations.

Chartered companies were one of the first examples of mercantilist capitalism. A charter issued by the government of the Netherlands in 1602 gave the Dutch East India Company a legal monopoly over all Dutch trade in the Indian Ocean. This privilege encouraged private in-

SOCIETY & CULTURE

A Maroon Village in French Guiana, 1748

Runaway slaves, called maroons, *were common in planta-tion colonies. Colonial officials regularly tried to recapture them and destroy their villages. In 1748 a captured maroon youth named Louis gave the following testimony to officials in French Guiana in South America.*

He declared and admitted that he has been a maroon for about eighteen moons [lunar months] with Rémy, his father, and other Negroes belonging to [M. Gourgues]; that Rémy having displeased the said M. Gourgues and having been whipped by him, had planned this marronage having first gotten together a supply of . . . cassava and bananas for the trip . . . ; that after an unknown number of weeks, a certain André [guided them] to the maroon village . . . ; that in the said village there are twenty-seven houses and three open sheds . . . ; that the said houses belong to and are inhabited by twenty-nine strong male Negroes . . . , twenty-two female Negroes . . . , nine Negro boys, and twelve Negro girls, making in all seventy-two slaves. . . .

[Louis further declared that the captain of the village,] Bernard, nicknamed Couacou, . . . takes care of wounds [with herbal medicines,] baptizes with holy water and recites daily prayer. . . . That no member of the troop has died during the past two years.

That the captain's orders are obeyed perfectly; it is in his yard that prayers are recited in the morning and evening, as they are on well-run plantations; those who are sick recite their prayers in their houses.

That André either whips or has whipped those who deserve punishment. . . . That André and some of his trusted followers make sorties from time to time to recruit new members in the area. . . . That no whites ever entered the village, nor any Negroes other than the ones who are recruited . . . and who promise never to betray them nor to run away, under penalty of being hunted down and killed. . . .

That whenever land has to be cleared, everyone works together, and that once a large area has been burned, everyone is allotted a plot according to the needs of the family to plant and maintain. That the wild pigs that they kill frequently are divided among them, as is other large game, even fish that they dry when there are large numbers of them. . . .

That . . . they maintain and repair their arms themselves, keeping them in good condition at all times, but that when having hunted a great deal they are without powder and shot, . . . they use tiny stones, which . . . are found in abundance in the area. . . .

That the women spin cotton when the weather is bad and work in the fields in good weather. That [men] weave cotton cloth, which serves to make skirts for the women and loincloths for the men; that this cotton material is woven piece by piece and then assembled and decorated with Siamese cotton thread. . . .

That they get salt from the ashes of the Maracoupy palm. That they make a beverage out of sweet potatoes, yams, bananas, and various grains, in addition to their [cassava beer].

That they store all their belongings in [baskets, and they all] are equipped with axes and machetes and that there are spares . . . and that they have no tools other than a few files, gimlets, and hammers; that they have no saws or adzes [wood-working axes]. That they had at the said Negro village two Negro drums, which they played on certain holidays.

What is the significance of the maroons employing African forms of communal ownership, herbal medicine, brewing, cloth making, and musical instruments? How much did they rely on tools, weapons, beliefs, and practices that they acquired from the French?

Source: Richard Price, ed., *Maroon Societies: Rebel Slave Communities in the Americas,* 2d ed. (Baltimore: Johns Hopkins University Press, 1979), 313–318. Reprinted by permission of the Johns Hopkins University Press.

vestors to buy shares in the company. They were amply rewarded when Dutch East India Company captured control of the long-distance trade routes in the Indian Ocean from the Portuguese (see Chapter 21). As we have seen, a sister firm, the Dutch West India Company, was chartered in 1621 to engage in the Atlantic trade and to seize sugar-producing areas in Brazil and African slaving ports from the Portuguese.

Such successes inspired other governments to set up their own chartered companies. In 1672, a royal charter placed all English trade with West Africa in the hands of a new **Royal African Company,** which established its headquarters at Cape Coast Castle, just east of Elmina on the Gold Coast. The French government also played an active role in chartering companies and promoting overseas trade and colonization. Jean Baptiste Colbert°, King Louis XIV's minister of finance from 1661 to 1683, chartered French East India and French West India Companies to reduce French colonies' dependence on Dutch and English traders.

French and English governments also used military force in pursuit of commercial dominance, especially to break the trading advantage of the Dutch in the Americas. Restrictions on Dutch access to French and English colonies provoked a series of wars with the Netherlands between 1652 and 1678 (see Chapter 18), during which the larger English and French navies defeated the Dutch and drove the Dutch West India Company into bankruptcy.

With Dutch competition in the Atlantic reduced, the French and English governments moved to revoke the monopoly privileges of their chartered companies. England opened trade in Africa to any English subject in 1698 on the grounds that ending monopolies would be "highly beneficial and advantageous to this kingdom." It was hoped that such competition would also cut the cost of slaves to West Indian planters, though the demand for slaves soon drove the prices up again.

Such new mercantilist policies fostered competition among a nation's own citizens, while using high tariffs and restrictions to exclude foreigners. In the 1660s England had passed a series of Navigation Acts that confined trade with its colonies to English ships and cargoes. The French called their mercantilist legislation, first codified in 1698, the *Exclusif*°, highlighting its exclusionary intentions. Other mercantilist laws defended manufacturing and processing interests in Europe against competition from colonies, imposing prohibitively high taxes on any manufactured goods and refined sugar imported from the colonies.

As a result of such mercantilist measures, the Atlantic became Britain, France, and Portugal's most important overseas trading area in the eighteenth century. Britain's imports from its West Indian colonies in this period accounted for over one-fifth of the value of total British imports. The French West Indian colonies played an even larger role in France's overseas trade. Only the Dutch, closed out of much of the American trade, found Asian trade of greater importance (see Chapter 21). Profits from the Atlantic economy, in turn, promoted further economic expansion and increased the revenues of European governments.

Colbert (kohl-BEAR)
Exclusif (ek-skloo-SEEF)

The Great Circuit and the Middle Passage

At the heart of the Atlantic system was a great clockwise network of trade routes known as the **Great Circuit** (see Map 20.1). It began in Europe, ran south to Africa, turned west across the Atlantic Ocean to the Americas, and then swept back to Europe. Like Asian sailors in the Indian Ocean, Atlantic mariners depended on the prevailing winds and currents to propel their ships. What drove the ships as much as the winds and currents was the desire for the profits that each leg of the circuit was expected to produce.

The first leg, from Europe to Africa, carried European manufactures—notably metal bars, hardware, and guns—as well as great quantities of cotton textiles brought from India. Some of these goods were traded for West African gold, timber, and other products, which were taken back to Europe. More goods went to purchase slaves, who were transported across the Atlantic to the plantation colonies in the part of the Great Circuit known as the **Middle Passage.** On the third leg, plantation goods from the colonies returned to Europe. Each leg of the circuit carried goods from where they were abundant and relatively cheap to where they were scarce and therefore more valuable. Thus, in theory, each leg of the Great Circuit could earn much more than its costs, and a ship that completed all three legs could return a handsome profit to its owners. In practice, shipwrecks, deaths, piracy, and other risks could turn profit into loss.

The three-sided Great Circuit is only the simplest model of Atlantic trade. Many other trading voyages supplemented the basic circuit. Cargo ships made long voyages from Europe to the Indian Ocean, passed southward through the Atlantic with quantities of African gold and American silver, and returned with the cotton textiles necessary to the African trade. Other sea routes brought to the West Indies manufactured goods from Europe or foodstuffs and lumber from New England. In addition, some Rhode Island and Massachusetts merchants participated in a "Triangular Trade" that carried rum to West Africa, slaves to the West Indies, and molasses and rum back to New England. There was also a considerable two-way trade between Brazil and Angola, which exchanged Brazilian liquor and other goods for slaves. On another route, Brazil and Portugal exchanged sugar and gold for European imports.

Map. 20.1   The Atlantic Economy   By 1700 the volume of maritime exchanges among the Atlantic continents had begun to rival the trade of the Indian Ocean basin. Notice the trade in consumer products, slave labor, precious metals, and other goods. A silver trade to East Asia laid the basis for a Pacific Ocean economy.

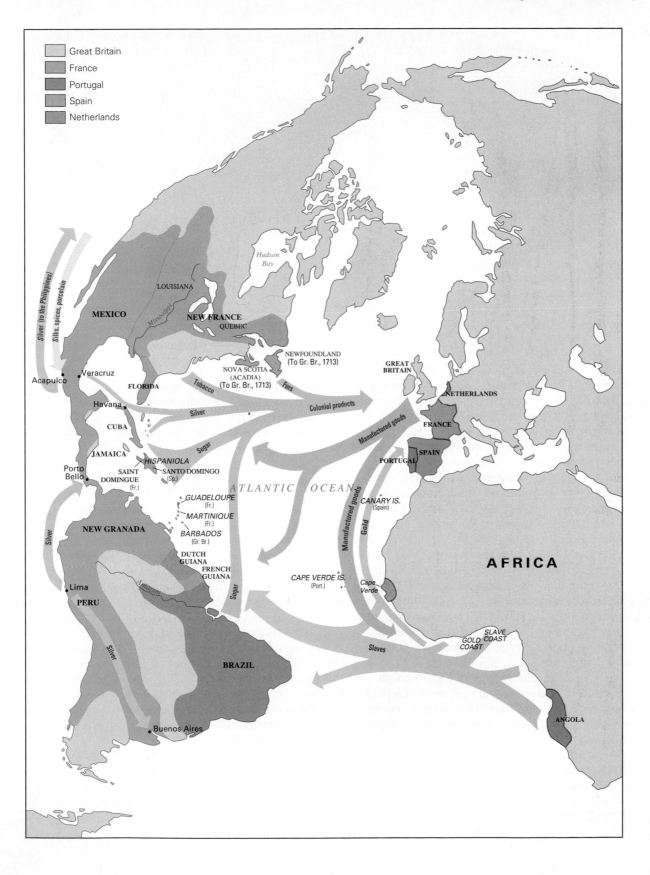

Great Britain
France
Portugal
Spain
Netherlands

Silver (to the Philippines)
Silks, spices, porcelain

Hudson
Bay

LOUISIANA

Mississippi

MEXICO

NEW FRANCE
QUEBEC

NEWFOUNDLAND
(To Gr. Br., 1713)

NOVA SCOTIA
(ACADIA)
(To Gr. Br., 1713)

GREAT
BRITAIN

Acapulco

Veracruz

FLORIDA

Tobacco

Furs

NETHERLANDS

Havana

Silver

Colonial products

Manufactured goods

FRANCE

SPAIN

CUBA

Sugar

PORTUGAL

JAMAICA

Porto
Bello

SAINT
DOMINGUE
(Fr.)

HISPANIOLA

SANTO DOMINGO
(Sp.)

A T L A N T I C   O C E A N

GUADELOUPE
(Fr.)

CANARY IS.
(Spain)

Manufactured goods

MARTINIQUE
(Fr.)

Silver

NEW GRANADA

BARBADOS
(Gr. Br.)

DUTCH
GUIANA
FRENCH
GUIANA

Gold

AFRICA

Amazon

CAPE VERDE IS.
(Port.)

Cape
Verde

Lima

Silver

PERU

Sugar

SLAVE
COAST

GOLD
COAST

Slaves

Silver

BRAZIL

Buenos Aires

ANGOLA

Slave Ship   This model of the English vessel *Brookes* shows the specially built section of the hold where enslaved Africans were packed together during the Middle Passage. Girls, boys, and women were confined separately.
(Wilberforce House Museum, Hull, Humberside, UK/The Bridgeman Art Library, London and New York)

European interests dominated the Atlantic system. The manufacturers who supplied the trade goods and the investors who provided the capital were all based in Europe, but so too were the principal consumers of the plantation products. Before the seventeenth century, sugar had been rare and fairly expensive in western Europe. By 1700 annual consumption of sugar in England had risen to about 4 pounds (nearly 2 kilograms) per person. Rising western European prosperity and declining sugar prices promoted additional consumption, starting with the upper classes and working its way down the social ladder. People spooned sugar into popular new beverages imported from overseas—tea, coffee, and chocolate—to overcome the beverages' natural bitterness. By 1750 annual sugar consumption in Britain had doubled, and it doubled again to about 18 pounds (8 kilograms) per person by the early nineteenth century (well below the American average of about 100 pounds [45 kilograms] a year in 1960).

The flow of sugar to Europe depended on another key component of the Atlantic trading system: the flow of slaves from Africa (see Map 20.2). The rising volume of the Middle Passage also measures the Atlantic system's expansion. During the first 150 years after the European discovery of the Americas, some 800,000 Africans had begun the journey across the Atlantic. During the boom in sugar production between 1650 and 1800, the slave trade amounted to nearly 7,500,000. Of the survivors, over half landed in the West Indies and nearly a third in

Brazil. Plantations in North America imported another 5 percent, and the rest went to other parts of Spanish America (see Figure 20.1).

In these peak decades, the transportation of slaves from Africa was a highly specialized trade, although it regularly attracted some amateur traders hoping to make a quick profit. Most slaves were carried in ships that had been specially built or modified for the slave trade by the construction between the ships' decks of additional platforms on which the human cargo was packed as tightly as possible.

Seventeenth-century mercantilist policies placed much of the Atlantic slave trade in the hands of chartered companies. During their existence the Dutch West India Company and the English Royal African Company each carried about 100,000 slaves across the Atlantic. In the eighteenth century, private English traders from Liverpool and Bristol controlled about 40 percent of the slave trade. The French, operating out of Nantes and Bordeaux, handled about half as much, but the Dutch hung on to only 6 percent. The Portuguese supplying Brazil and other places had nearly 30 percent of the Atlantic slave trade, in contrast to the 3 percent carried in North American ships.

To make a profit, European slave traders had to buy slaves in Africa for less than the cost of the goods they traded in return. Then they had to deliver as many healthy slaves as possible across the Atlantic for resale in the plantation colonies. The treacherous voyage to the

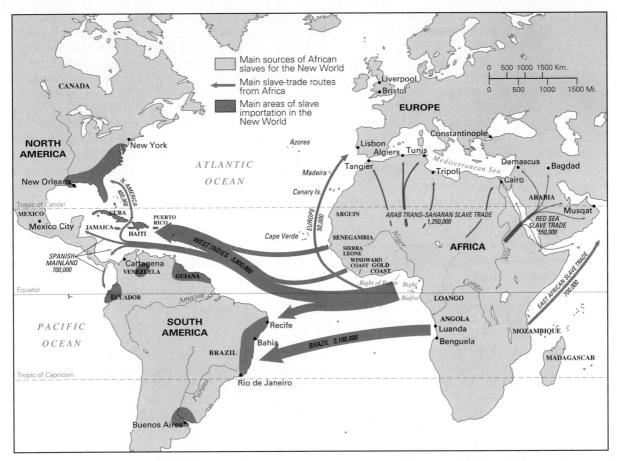

Map. 20.2   The African Slave Trade, 1500–1800   After 1500 a vast new trade in slaves from sub-Saharan Africa to the Americas joined the ongoing slave trade to the Islamic states of North Africa, the Middle East, and India. The West Indies were the major destination of the Atlantic slave trade, followed by Brazil.

Americas lasted from six to ten weeks. Some ships completed it with all of their slaves alive, but large, even catastrophic, losses of life were common. On average between 1650 and 1800, about one slave in every six perished during the Middle Passage (see Figure 20.1).

Some deaths resulted from the efforts of the captives to escape. On his voyage Equiano witnessed two of his Igbo countrymen, who were chained together, jump into the sea, "preferring death to such a life of misery." To inhibit such attempts, African men were confined below deck during most of the voyage, and special netting was installed around the outside of the ship. Some slaves fell into deep psychological depression, known to contemporaries as "fixed melancholy," from which many perished. Others, including Equiano, refused to eat, so forced feeding was used to keep slaves alive. When opportunities presented themselves (nearness to land,

illness among the crew), some cargoes of enslaved Africans tried to overpower their captors. Such "mutinies" were rarely successful and were put down with brutality that occasioned further losses of life.

Other deaths during the Middle Passage were due to the ill treatment slaves received. Although it was in the interests of the captain and crew to deliver their slave cargo in good condition, whippings, beatings, and even executions were used to maintain order and force the captives to take nourishment. Moreover, the dangers and brutalities of the slave trade were so notorious that many ordinary seamen shunned such work. As a consequence, cruel and brutal characters abounded among the officers and crews on slave ships.

Although examples of unspeakable cruelties are common in the records, most deaths in the Middle Passage were the result of disease rather than abuse, just as on the plantations. Dysentery spread by contaminated food and water caused many deaths. Others died of contagious diseases such as smallpox carried by persons whose infections were not detected during the medical examinations of slaves prior to boarding. Such maladies spread quickly in the crowded and unsanitary confines of the ships, claiming the lives of many slaves already physically weakened and mentally traumatized by their ordeals.

Crew members who were in close contact with the slaves were equally exposed to the epidemics and regularly suffered heavy losses. Moreover, sailors often fell victim to tropical diseases, such as malaria, to which Africans had acquired resistance. It is a measure of the callousness of the age, as well as the cheapness of European labor, that over the course of a Great Circuit voyage the proportion of crew deaths could be as high as the slave deaths on the Middle Passage.

AFRICA, THE ATLANTIC, AND ISLAM

The Atlantic system took a terrible toll in African lives both during the Middle Passage and under the harsh conditions of plantation slavery. Many other Africans died while being marched to African coastal ports for sale overseas. The overall effects on Africa of these losses and of other aspects of the slave trade have been the subject of considerable historical debate. It is clear that the trade's impact depended on the intensity and terms of different African regions' involvement.

Any assessment of the Atlantic system's effects in Africa must also take into consideration the fact that some Africans profited from the trade by capturing and selling slaves. They chained the slaves together or bound them to forked sticks for the march to the coast, then bartered them to the European slavers for trade goods. The effects on the enslaver were different from the effects on the enslaved. Finally, a broader understanding of the Atlantic system's effects in sub-Saharan Africa comes from comparisons with the effects of Islamic contacts.

The Gold Coast and the Slave Coast As Chapter 17 showed, early European visitors to Africa's Atlantic coast were interested more in trading than in colonizing or controlling the continent. As the Africa trade mushroomed after 1650, this pattern continued. African

kings and merchants sold slaves and other goods at many new coastal sites, but the growing slave trade did not lead to any substantial European colonization.

The transition to slave trading was not sudden. Even as slaves were becoming Atlantic Africa's most valuable export, nonslave goods such as gold, ivory, and timber remained a significant part of the total trade. For example, during its eight decades of operation from 1672 to 1752, the English Royal African Company made 40 percent of its profits from dealings in gold, ivory, and forest products. In some parts of West Africa, such nonslave exports remained predominant even at the peak of the trade.

African merchants were very discriminating about what merchandise they received in return for slaves or other goods. A European ship that arrived with goods of low quality or not suited to local tastes found it hard to purchase a cargo at a profitable price. European guidebooks to the African trade carefully noted the color and shape of beads, the pattern of textiles, the type of guns, and the sort of metals that were in demand on each section of the coast. In the early eighteenth century, the people of Sierra Leone had a strong preference for large iron kettles, brass pans were preferred on the Gold Coast, and iron and copper bars were in demand in the Niger Delta, where smiths turned them into useful objects (see Map 20.3).

Although preferences for merchandise varied, Africans' greatest demands were for textiles, hardware, and guns. Of the goods the Royal African Company traded in West Africa in the 1680s, over 60 percent were Indian and European textiles, 30 percent hardware and weaponry. Beads and other jewelry formed 3 percent. The rest consisted of cowrie shells that were used as money. In the eighteenth century, tobacco and rum from the Americas became welcome imports.

Both Europeans and Africans naturally attempted to drive the best bargain for themselves and sometimes engaged in deceitful practices. The strength of the African bargaining position, however, may be inferred from the fact that as the demand for slaves rose, so too did their price in Africa. In the course of the eighteenth century the goods needed to purchase a slave on the Gold Coast doubled and in some places tripled or quadrupled.

West Africans' trading strengths were reinforced by African governments on the Gold and Slave Coasts that made Europeans observe African trading customs and prevented them from taking control of African territory. Rivalry among European nations, each of which established its own trading "castles" along the Gold Coast, also reduced Europeans' bargaining strength. In 1700 the head of the Dutch East India Company in West Africa,

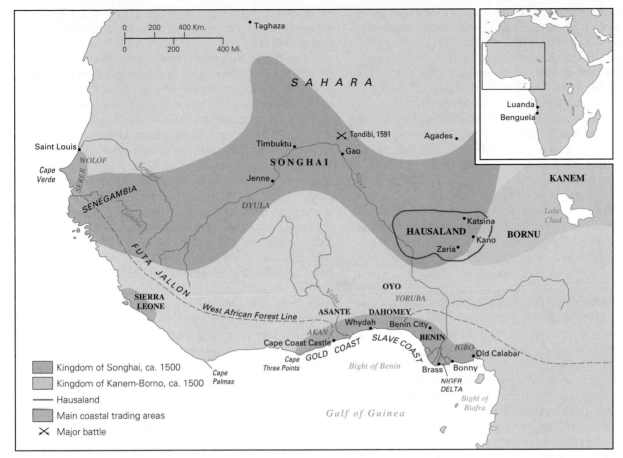

Map. 20.3   West African States and Trade, 1500–1800   The Atlantic and the trans-Saharan trade brought West Africans new goods and promoted the rise of powerful states and trading communities. The Moroccan invasion of Songhai and Portuguese colonization of the Angolan ports of Luanda and Benguela showed the political dangers of such relations.

Willem Bosman°, bemoaned the fact that, to stay competitive against the other European traders, his company had to include large quantities of muskets and gunpowder in the goods it exchanged, thereby adding to Africans' military power.

Bosman also related that before being allowed to buy slaves at Whydah on the Slave Coast his agents first had to pay the king a substantial customs duty and buy at a premium price whatever slaves the king had to sell. By African standards, Whydah was a rather small kingdom controlling only that port and its immediate hinterland. In 1727 it was annexed by the larger kingdom of Dahomey°, which maintained a strong trading position with Europeans at the coast. Dahomey's rise in the 1720s

depended heavily on the firearms that the slave trade supplied for its well-trained armies of men and women.

In the cases of two of Dahomey's neighbors, the connections between state growth and the Atlantic trade were more complex. One was the inland Oyo° kingdom to the northeast. Oyo cavalry overran Dahomey in 1730 and forced it to pay an annual tribute to keep its independence. The other was the newer kingdom of Asante°, west of Dahomey along the Gold Coast, which expanded rapidly after 1680. Both Oyo and Asante participated in the Atlantic trade, but neither kingdom was so dependent on it as Dahomey. Overseas trade formed a relatively modest part of the economies of these large and populous states and was balanced by their extensive overland trade with their northern neighbors and with

Willem Bosman (VIL-uhm boos-MAHN)
Dahomey (dah-HOH-mee)

Oyo (aw-YOH)   **Asante** (uh-SHAN-tee)

states across the Sahara. Like the great medieval empires of the western Sudan, Oyo and Asante were stimulated by external trade but not controlled by it.

How did African kings and merchants obtain slaves for sale? Bosman dismissed misconceptions prevailing in Europe in his day. "Not a few in our country," he wrote to a friend in 1700, "fondly imagine that parents here sell their children, men their wives, and one brother the other. But those who think so, do deceive themselves; for this never happens on any other account but that of necessity, or some great crime; but most of the slaves that are offered to us are prisoners of war, which are sold by the victors as their booty."[2] Other accounts agree that prisoners taken in war were the greatest source of slaves for the Atlantic trade, but it is difficult to say how often capturing slaves for export was the main cause of warfare. "Here and there," conclude two respected historians of Africa, "there are indications that captives taken in the later and more peripheral stages of these wars were exported overseas, but it would seem that the main impetus of conquest was only incidentally concerned with the slave-trade in any external direction."[3]

An early-nineteenth-century king of Asante had a similar view: "I cannot make war to catch slaves in the bush, like a thief. My ancestors never did so. But if I fight a king, and kill him when he is insolent, then certainly I must have his gold, and his slaves, and his people are mine too. Do not the white kings act like this?"[4] English rulers had indeed sentenced seventeenth-century Scottish and Irish prisoners to forced labor in the West Indies. One may imagine that the African and the European prisoners did not share their kings' view that such actions were legitimate.

The Bight of Biafra and Angola

In the eighteenth century the slave trade expanded eastward to the Bight (bay) of Biafra. In contrast to the Gold and Slave Coasts, where strong kingdoms predominated, the densely populated interior of the Bight of Biafra contained no large states. Even so, the powerful merchant princes of the coastal ports still made European traders give them rich presents. Because of the absence of sizable states, there were no large-scale wars and consequently few prisoners of war. Instead, kidnapping was the major source of slaves, as Equiano's autobiography indicates. In about 1756, while their parents were away working in the fields, the eleven-year-old Equiano and his younger sister were snatched from their yard by two men and a woman. After passing through many hands, Equiano finally reached a coastal port, where, he relates,

he was astonished at the sight of the slave ship and alarmed at his first sight of "white men with horrible looks, red faces, and loose hair." By then he had become separated from his sister, whose fate he never learned.

As Equiano discovered on his way to the coast, some inland African merchants were experienced in procuring debtors, victims of kidnapping, and convicted criminals and shepherding them through a network of markets to the coast. The largest inland traders of the Bight of Biafra were the Aro of Arochukwu, who used their control of a famous religious oracle to enhance their prestige. The Aro cemented their business links with powerful inland families and the coastal merchants through gifts and marriage alliances.

As the volume of the Atlantic trade along the Bight of Biafra expanded in the late eighteenth century, some inland markets evolved into giant fairs with different sections specializing in slaves and imported goods. An English ship's doctor reported that in the 1780s slaves were "bought by the black traders at fairs, which are held for that purpose, at a distance of upwards of two hundred miles from the sea coast." He reported seeing from twelve hundred to fifteen hundred enslaved men and women arriving at the coast from a single fair.[5]

The local context of the Atlantic trade was different south of the Congo estuary at Angola, the greatest source of slaves for the Atlantic trade (see Map 20.2). This was also the one place along the Atlantic coast where a single European nation, Portugal, controlled a significant amount of territory. Except when overrun by the Dutch for a time in the seventeenth century, Portuguese residents of the main coastal ports of Luanda and Benguela° served as middlemen between the caravans that arrived from the far interior and the ships that crossed from Brazil. From the coastal cities Afro-Portuguese traders guided large caravans of trade goods inland to exchange for slaves at special markets. Some markets met in the shadow of Portuguese frontier forts; powerful African kings controlled others.

Many of the slaves sold at these markets were prisoners of war captured by expanding African states. By the late eighteenth century, slaves sold from Angolan ports were prisoners of wars fought from as far as 600 to 800 miles (1,000 to 1,300 kilometers) inland. Many were victims of wars of expansion fought by the giant federation of Lunda kingdoms. As elsewhere in Africa, such prisoners usually seem to have been a byproduct of African wars rather than the purpose for which the wars were fought.

Benguela (ben-GWAY-luh)

Queen Nzinga of Angola, 1622   This formidable African woman went to great lengths to maintain her royal dignity when negotiating a treaty for her brother with the Portuguese governor of Luanda. To avoid having to stand in his presence, she had one of her women bend herself into a human seat. Nzinga later ruled in her own name and revolted against the Portuguese with the aid of Dutch and African allies.   (Jean-Loup Charmet)

Recent research has linked other enslavement with environmental crises in the hinterland of Angola.[6] During the eighteenth century these southern grasslands periodically suffered severe droughts, which drove famished refugees to better-watered areas. Powerful African leaders gained control of such refugees in return for supplying them with food and water. These leaders built up their followings by assimilating refugee children, along with adult women, who were valued as food producers and for reproduction. However, they often sold into the Atlantic trade the adult make refugees, who were more likely than the women and children to escape or challenge the ruler's authority. Rising Angolan leaders parceled out the Indian textiles, weapons, and alcohol they received in return for such slaves as gifts to attract new followers and to cement the loyalty of their established allies.

The most successful of these inland Angolan leaders became heads of powerful new states that stabilized areas devastated by war and drought and repopulated them with the refugees and prisoners they retained. The slave frontier then moved farther inland. This cruel system worked to the benefit of a few African rulers and merchants at the expense of the many thousands of Africans who were sent to death or perpetual bondage in the Americas.

Although the organization of the Atlantic trade in Africa varied, it was based on a partnership between European and African elites. To obtain foreign textiles, metals, and weapons, African rulers and merchants sold slaves and many other products. Most of the exported slaves were prisoners taken in wars associated with African state growth. But strong African states also helped offset the Europeans' economic advantage and hindered them from taking control of African territory. Even in the absence of strong states, powerful African merchant communities everywhere dominated the movement of goods and people. The Africans who gained from these exchanges were the rich and powerful few. Many more Africans were losers in these exchanges.

Comparing European and Islamic Contacts

The growing European influence in Atlantic Africa has a parallel in the continuing Islamic influence along the southern border of the Sahara and in eastern Africa. There are striking similarities and differences in the political, commercial, and cultural impacts of these two external influences on sub-Saharan Africa between 1500 and 1800.

Despite all their commercial expansion in the centuries before 1800, Europeans had acquired control of little African territory. Their trading posts along the Gold and Slave Coasts were largely dependent on the goodwill of local African rulers. Only on islands and in Angola did the Atlantic trade lead to significant European colonies. Ironically, the largest European colony in Africa before 1800, the Dutch East India Company's Cape Colony at the southern tip of the continent, was tied to the Indian Ocean trade, not to the Atlantic trade. The Cape Colony did not export slaves; rather the 25,750 slaves in its population were mostly derived from persons *imported* from Madagascar, South Asia, and the East Indies.

Muslim territorial dominance was more extensive. Arab conquests in the seventh century permanently brought North Africa into the Muslim world. Muslim practices and traders spread south of the Sahara, but Arab and North African Muslims had little success in extending their territorial dominance southward before 1500. During the sixteenth century, all of North Africa except Morocco was annexed to the new Ottoman Islamic empire, while Ethiopia lost extensive territory to other Muslim conquerors (see Chapter 17).

In the 1580s Morocco began a southward expansion aimed at gaining control of the Saharan trade. To that end it sent a military expedition of 4,000 men and 10,000 camels from Marrakesh to attack the indigenously ruled Muslim empire of Songhai° in the western Sudan. Half of the men perished on their way across the desert. The remainder, armed with 2,500 muskets, succeeded in besting Songhai's army of 40,000 cavalry and foot soldiers in 1591, reducing the empire to a shadow of its former self. Although Morocco was never able to annex the western Sudan, for the next two centuries the occupying troops extracted a massive tribute of slaves and goods from the local population and collected tolls from passing merchants.

Morocco's destruction of Songhai weakened the trans-Saharan trade in the western Sudan. Caravans continued to cross the desert bringing textiles, hard-ware, and weapons, but much of the trade shifted eastward to the central Sudan. Except for the absence of alcohol (which was prohibited to Muslims), these goods were similar to those in the Atlantic trade. There was also a continuation of the salt trade southward from Saharan mines. Communities of Dyula° traders in the western Sudan and Hausa traders in the central Sudan distributed these imports and local goods throughout West Africa. They also collected goods for shipment northward, including gold, caffeine-rich kola nuts from Asante and other parts of the forest (a stimulant allowed by Muslim law), African textiles and leather goods, as well as slaves.

Fewer slaves crossed the Sahara than crossed the Atlantic, but their numbers were substantial. It is estimated that between 1600 and 1800 about 850,000 slaves trudged across the desert's various routes (see Map 20.2). A nearly equal number of slaves from sub-Saharan Africa entered the Islamic Middle East and India by way of the Red Sea and the Indian Ocean.

The tasks that African slaves performed in the Islamic world were very different from their tasks in the Americas. In the late seventeenth and eighteenth centuries, Morocco's rulers employed an army of 150,000 slaves obtained from the south to keep them in power. Other slaves worked for Moroccans on sugar plantations, as servants, and as artisans. In contrast to the makeup of the Atlantic slave trade, the majority of the slaves crossing the desert were women, intended to serve wealthy households as concubines and servants. The trans-Saharan slave trade also included a much higher proportion of children than did the Atlantic trade, including eunuchs meant for eventual service as harem guards. It is estimated that only one in ten of these boys survived the surgical removal of their genitals.

The central Sudanese kingdom of Bornu illustrates some aspects of trans-Saharan contacts. This ancient Muslim state had grown and expanded in the sixteenth century as the result of guns imported from the Ottoman Empire. Bornu retained many captives from its wars, or sold them as slaves to the north in return for the firearms and horses that underpinned the kingdom's military power. Bornu's king, Mai Ali, conspicuously displayed his kingdom's new power and wealth while on four pilgrimages to Mecca between 1642 and 1667. On the last, an enormous entourage of slaves—said to number fifteen thousand—accompanied him.

Like Christians, Muslims of this period saw no moral impediment to owning and trading in slaves. Indeed, Is-

---

Songhai (song-GAH-ee)

Dyula (JOO-lah)

lam recognized the *jihad* (holy war) as a means by which their religion could be spread and considered enslaving "pagans" to be a meritorious act because it brought them into the faith. Although Islam forbade the enslavement of Muslims, some Muslim states south of the Sahara did not strictly observe that law. Ahmad Baba, a Muslim scholar of Timbuktu, in a 1614 treatise on slavery lamented that the enslavement of free Muslims was much practiced, notably by Muslim Hausa rulers.

A West African named Ayuba Suleiman Diallo° may serve as a revealing example of an enslaved Muslim. In 1730 his father, a prominent Muslim scholar, sent Ayuba to sell two slaves to an English ship on the Gambia River so as to buy paper and other necessities. On his way home a few days later, other Africans kidnapped Ayuba, shaved his head to make him appear to have been a war captive, and sold him to the same English ship. A planter from Maryland purchased Ayuba. Soon after, an English scholar, impressed by Ayuba's knowledge of Arabic and his elevated social origins, bought his freedom and arranged for him to return home.[7]

Because of sub-Saharan Africa's long and deep exposure to Islam, Muslim cultural influences were much greater than European ones before 1800. The Arabic language, long dominant in North Africa, continued to expand as a means of communication among scholars and merchants south of the Sahara. The Islamic religion also increased the number of its adherents south of the desert, reaching well beyond the urban centers that had been its medieval strength.

In contrast, African conversion to Christianity was limited to coastal Angola and the immediate vicinity of small European trading posts. The use of European languages was also largely confined to the trading coasts. Still it is notable that some African merchants sent their sons to Europe to learn European ways. One of these young men, Philip Quaque°, was educated in England and ordained as a priest in the Church of England and became the official chaplain of the Cape Coast Castle from 1766 until his death in 1816. Not only men of Quaque's stature but many African merchants learned to write a European language. A leading trader of Old Calabar on the Bight of Biafra kept a diary in pidgin English in the late eighteenth century.

The interesting details of the lives of elite and culturally sophisticated individuals such as Ayuba Suleiman and Philip Quaque must not distract us from the grim, sordid details of this era of slave trading. It is easy to re-

---

Ayuba Suleiman Diallo (ah-YOO-bah SOO-lay-mahn JAH-loh)
Quaque (KWAH-kay)

Ayuba Suleiman Diallo (1701–??)   Known as Job ben Solomon to the Maryland planter who owned him as a slave from 1731 to 1735, this Muslim from the West African state of Bondu was able to regain his freedom and return to Africa. Notice the booklet of Quranic verses around his neck.   (British Library)

joice in Ayuba's return to Africa while forgetting the unrecorded fates of the two persons whom he sold into slavery. In admiring Quaque's achievement of a position second only to the British governor on the Gold Coast, we should not overlook that his principal duties were to tend the spiritual needs of the slave traders, not the slaves. Unfortunately, surviving records tell us much less about the large number of Africans who suffered than about the small number who prospered from the European and Muslim trades.

Despite uncertainty over many details, it is still possible to assess some of the effects of the Atlantic and Islamic trades on sub-Saharan Africa. One key issue is how the European and Islamic slave trades affected Africa's population. Most scholars who have looked deeply into the question agree on two points: (1) the effect of slave exports could not have been large when measured against the population of the entire continent, but (2) losses in regions that contributed heavily to the slave trade were severe. The lands behind the Slave Coast are thought to have been acutely affected. The large slave

Amerindian Foods in Africa

The migration of European plants and animals across the Atlantic to the New World was one side of the Columbian Exchange (see Chapter 19). The Andean potato, for example, became a staple crop of the poor in Europe, and cassava (a Brazilian plant cultivated for its edible roots) and maize (corn) moved across the Atlantic to Africa.

Maize was a high-yielding grain that could produce much more food per acre than many grains indigenous to Africa. The varieties of maize that spread to Africa were not modern high-bred "sweet corn" but starchier types found in white and yellow corn meal. Cassava—not well known to modern North Americans except perhaps in the form of tapioca—became the most important New World food in Africa. Truly a marvel, cassava had the highest yield of calories per acre of any staple food and thrived even in poor soils and during droughts. Both the leaves and the root could be eaten. Ground into meal, the root could be made into a bread that would keep for up to six months, or it could be fermented into a beverage.

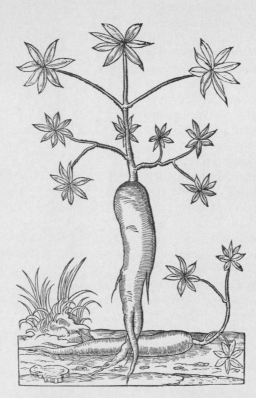

Cassava Plant   Both the leaves and the starchy root of the cassava plant could be eaten. (Engraving from André Thevet, *Les Singularitez de la Franc Antarctique.* Paris: Maurice de la Porte, 1557). Courtesy of the James Bell Library, University of Minnesota)

Cassava and maize were probably introduced accidentally into Africa by Portuguese ships from Brazil that discarded leftover supplies after reaching Angola. It did not take long for local Africans to recognize the food value of these new crops, especially in drought-prone areas. As the principal farmers in Central Africa, women must have played an important role in learning how to cultivate, harvest, and prepare these foods. By the eighteenth century, Lunda rulers hundreds of miles from the Angolan coast were actively promoting the cultivation of maize and cassava on their royal estates in order to provide a more secure food supply.

Some historians of Africa believe that in the inland areas these Amerindian food crops provided the nutritional base for a population increase that partially offset losses due to the Atlantic slave trade. By supplementing the range of food crops available and by enabling populations to increase in once lightly settled or famine-prone areas, cassava and maize, along with peanuts and other New World legumes, permanently altered Africans' environmental prospects.

---

trade may also have caused serious depopulation in Angola. To some extent, however, losses from famine in this region may have been reduced by the increasing cultivation of high-yielding food plants from the Americas (see Environment and Technology: Amerindian Foods in Africa).

Although both foreign Muslims and Europeans obtained slaves from sub-Saharan Africa, there was a significant difference in the numbers they obtained and thus in the overall effects of the two slave trades. Between 1550 and 1800 some 8 million Africans were exported into the Atlantic trade, four times as many as were taken from sub-Saharan Africa to North Africa and the Middle East. The families of all those sent abroad suffered from their individual loss, but the ability of the population to replenish its numbers through natural increase depended on the proportion of women lost to these slave trades. The much higher proportion of women in the Muslim slave trade would have multiplied its lasting effects on sub-Saharan African populations.

It is impossible to assess with precision the complex effects of the goods received in sub-Saharan Africa from these trades. Africans were very particular about what they received, so it is unlikely that they could have been consistently cheated. Some researchers have suggested that imports of textiles and metals undermined African weavers and metalworkers, but most economic historians calculate that on a per capita basis the volume of these imports was too small to have idled many African artisans. Imports supplemented rather than replaced local production. The goods received in sub-Saharan Africa were intended for consumption and thus did not serve to develop the economy. Likewise, the sugar, tea, and chocolate Europeans consumed did little to promote economic development in Europe. However, both African and European merchants profited from trading these consumer goods. Because they directed the whole Atlantic system, Europeans gained far more wealth than Africans.

Historians disagree in their assessment of how deeply European capitalism dominated Africa before 1800, but Europeans clearly had much less political and economic impact in Africa than in the West Indies or in other parts of the Americas. Still, it is significant that Western capitalism was expanding rapidly in the seventeenth century, while the Ottoman Empire, the dominant state of the Middle East, was entering a period of economic and political decline (see Chapter 27). The tide of influence in Africa was thus running in the Europeans' direction.

CONCLUSION

The new Atlantic trading system had great importance and momentous implications for world history. In the first phase of their expansion Europeans had conquered and colonized the Americas and captured major Indian Ocean trade routes. The development of the Atlantic system showed Europeans' ability to move beyond the conquest and capture of existing systems to create a major new trading system that could transform a region almost beyond recognition.

The West Indies felt the transforming power of capitalism more profoundly than did any other place outside Europe in this period. The establishment of sugar plantation societies was not just a matter of replacing native vegetation with alien plants and native peoples with Europeans and Africans. More fundamentally it made these once-isolated islands part of a dynamic trading system controlled from Europe. To be sure, the West Indies was not the only place affected. Parts of northern Brazil were touched as deeply by the sugar revolution, and other parts of the Americas were yielding to the power of European colonization and capitalism.

Africa played an essential role in the Atlantic system, importing trade goods and exporting slaves to the Americas. Africa, however, was less dominated by the Atlantic system than were Europe's American colonies. Africans remained in control of their continent and interacted culturally and politically with the Islamic world more than with the Atlantic.

Historians have seen the Atlantic system as a model of the kind of highly interactive economy that became global in later centuries. For that reason the Atlantic system was a milestone in a much larger historical process, but not a monument to be admired. Its transformations were destructive as well as creative, producing victims as well as victors. Yet one cannot ignore that the system's awesome power came from its ability to create wealth. As the next chapter describes, southern Asia and the Indian Ocean basin were also beginning to feel the effects of Europeans' rising power.

■ Key Terms

Atlantic system	maroon
chartered company	capitalism
Dutch West India Company	mercantilism
plantocracy	Royal African Company
driver	Great Circuit
seasoning	Middle Passage
manumission	

■ Suggested Reading

The global context of early modern capitalism is examined by Immanuel Wallerstein, *The Modern World-System*, 3 vols. (1974–1989); by Fernand Braudel, *Civilization and Capitalism, 15th–18th Century*, 3 vols. (1982–1984); and in two volumes of scholarly papers edited by James D. Tracy: *The Rise of Merchant Empires* (1990) and *The Political Economy of Merchant Empires* (1991). Especially relevant are the chapters in *The Rise of Merchant Empires* by Herbert S. Klein, summarizing scholarship on the Middle Passage, and by Ralph A. Austen, on the trans-Saharan caravan trade between 1500 and 1800.

The best general introductions to the Atlantic system are Philip D. Curtin, *The Rise and Fall of the Plantation Complex* (1990), and Herbert S. Klein, *The Atlantic Slave Trade* (1999) and David

Ellis, *The Rise of African Slavery in the Americas* (2000). Recent scholarly articles on subjects considered in this chapter are available in *The Atlantic Slave Trade: Effects on Economies, Societies, and Peoples in Africa, the Americas and Europe*, ed. Joseph E. Inikori and Stanley L. Engerman (1992); in *Slavery and the Rise of the Atlantic System*, ed. Barbara L. Solow (1991); and in *Africans in Bondage: Studies in Slavery and the Slave Trade*, ed. Paul Lovejoy (1986). Pieter Emmer has edited a valuable collection of articles on *The Dutch in the Atlantic Economy, 1580–1880: Trade, Slavery, and Emancipation* (1998).

Edward Reynolds, *Stand the Storm: A History of the Atlantic Slave Trade* (1993), provides a brief overview of research on that subject. A useful collection of primary and secondary sources is David Northrup, ed., *The Atlantic Slave Trade* (1994). Hugh Thomas's *The Slave Trade: The Story of the Atlantic Slave Trade, 1440–1870* (1999), and Basil Davidson's *The Atlantic Slave Trade*, rev. ed. (1980), are other useful historical narratives.

The cultural connections among African communities on both sides of the Atlantic are explored by John Thornton, *Africa and Africans in the Making of the Atlantic World, 1400–1800*, 2d ed. (1998), and Margaret E. Crahan and Franklin W. Knight, eds., *Africa and the Caribbean: The Legacies of a Link* (1979). See also the collection edited by Richard Price, *Maroon Societies: Rebel Slave Communities in the Americas*, 2d ed. (1979).

Herbert S. Klein's *African Slavery in Latin America and the Caribbean* (1986) is an exceptionally fine synthesis of recent research on New World slavery, including North American slave systems. The larger context of Caribbean history is skillfully surveyed by Eric Williams, *From Columbus to Castro: The History of the Caribbean* (1984), and more simply surveyed by William Claypole and John Robottom, *Caribbean Story*, vol. 1, *Foundations*, 2d ed. (1990). Michael Craton, James Walvin, and David Wright, eds., *Slavery, Abolition, and Emancipation* (1976), is a valuable collection of primary sources about slavery in the British West Indies.

Roland Oliver and Anthony Atmore, *The African Middle Ages, 1400–1800* (1981), summarize African history in this period. Students can pursue specific topics in more detail in Richard Gray, ed., *The Cambridge History of Africa*, vol. 4 (1975), and B. A. Ogot, ed., *UNESCO General History of Africa*, vol. 5 (1992).

For recent research on slavery and the African, Atlantic, and Muslim slave trades with Africa see Paul Lovejoy, *Transformations in Slavery: A History of Slavery in Africa* (1983); Claire C. Robertson and Martin A. Klein, eds., *Women and Slavery in Africa* (1983); and Patrick Manning, *Slavery and African Life: Occidental, Oriental, and African Slave Trades* (1990). Case studies are found in J. E. Inikori, ed., *Forced Migration: The Impact of the Export Slave Trade on African Societies* (1982). *The Interesting Narrative of the Life of Olaudah Equiano* (1789) exists in several old and modern editions, and a critical edition of the portion relevant to the slave trade is reprinted in Philip D. Curtin, ed., *Africa Remembered: Narratives by West Africans from the Era of the Slave Trade* (1968, 1997), along with other African voices.

Those interested in Islam's cultural and commercial contacts with sub-Saharan Africa will find useful information in James L. A. Webb, Jr., *Desert Frontier: Ecological and Economic Change along the Western Sahel, 1600–1850* (1995); Elizabeth Savage, ed., *The Human Commodity: Perspectives on the Trans-Saharan Slave Trade* (1992); and J. Spencer Trimingham, *The Influence of Islam upon Africa* (1968).

■ Notes

1. Eric Williams, *Capitalism and Slavery* (Charlotte: University of North Carolina Press, 1944), 7.
2. Willem Bosman, *A New and Accurate Description of Guinea, etc.* (London, 1705), quoted in David Northrup, ed., *The Atlantic Slave Trade* (Lexington, MA: D. C. Heath, 1994), 72.
3. Roland Oliver and Anthony Atmore, *The African Middle Ages, 1400–1800* (Cambridge, England: Cambridge University Press, 1981), 100.
4. King Osei Bonsu, quoted in Northrup, ed., *The Atlantic Slave Trade*, 93.
5. Alexander Falconbridge, *Account of the Slave Trade on the Coast of Africa* (London: J. Phillips, 1788), 12.
6. Joseph C. Miller, "The Significance of Drought, Disease, and Famine in the Agriculturally Marginal Zones of West-Central Africa," *Journal of African History* 23 (1982) 17–61.
7. In Philip D. Curtin, ed., *Africa Remembered: Narratives by West Africans from the Era of the Slave Trade* (Madison: University of Wisconsin Press, 1968).

21

SOUTHWEST ASIA AND THE INDIAN OCEAN,

1500–1750

The Ottoman Empire, to 1750 • The Safavid Empire, 1502–1722 • The Mughal Empire, 1526–1761 • Trade Empires in the Indian Ocean, 1600–1729

ENVIRONMENT AND TECHNOLOGY: Metal Currency and Inflation

SOCIETY AND CULTURE: Indian Merchants in Russia

Ottoman Astronomers   Instruments shown include an astrolabe, a quadrant, and an hourglass.

nthony Jenkinson, merchant-adventurer for the Muscovy Company, founded in 1555 to develop trade with Russia, was the first Englishman to set foot in Iran. Eight years after the first English ship dropped anchor at Archangel on the White Sea in Russia's frigid north, Jenkinson made his way through Russia, down the Volga River, and across the Caspian Sea. The local ruler he met when he disembarked in 1561 in northwestern Iran was an object of wonder, "richly apparelled with long garments of silk, and cloth of gold, embroidered with pearls of stone; upon his head was a *tolipane* [headdress shaped like a tulip] with a sharp end pointing upwards half a yard long, of rich cloth of gold, wrapped about with a piece of India silk of twenty yards long, wrought in gold richly enameled, and set with precious stones; his earrings had pendants of gold a handful long, with two rubies of great value, set in the ends thereof."

Moving on to Qazvin°, Iran's capital, Jenkinson met the shah, whom the English referred to as the "Great Sophie" (apparently from Safavi°, the name of the ruling family). "In lighting from my horse at the Court gate, before my feet touched the ground, a pair of the Sophie's own shoes . . . were put upon my feet, for without the same shoes I might not be suffered to tread upon his holy ground."[1] After presenting a letter from Queen Elizabeth in Latin, English, Hebrew, and Italian but finding no one capable of reading it, he managed nevertheless to propose trade between England and Iran. The shah rejected the idea, since diverting Iranian silk from the markets of the Ottoman sultans, with whom he was negotiating a truce after a half-century of intermittent war, would have been undiplomatic.

Though Central Asia's bazaars were only meagerly supplied with goods, as Jenkinson and later merchants discovered, the idea of bypassing the Ottomans in the eastern Mediterranean and trading directly with Iran through Russia remained tempting. By the same token, the Ottomans were tempted by the idea of outflanking Safavid Iran. In 1569, an Ottoman army tried unsuccessfully to dig a 40-mile (64-kilometer) canal between the Don River, which opened into the Black Sea, and the Volga, which flowed into the Caspian. Their objective was to enable Ottoman ships to reach the Caspian and attack Iran from the north.

The Ottomans' foe was Russia, then ruled by Tsar Ivan IV (r. 1533–1584), known as Ivan the Terrible or Awesome. Ivan transformed his principality from a second-rate power into the sultan's primary competitor in Central Asia. In the river-crossed steppe, where Turkic nomads had long enjoyed uncontested sway, Slavic Christian Cossacks from the region of the Don and Dnieper Rivers used armed wagon trains and river craft fitted with small cannon to push southward and establish a Russian presence.

A contest for trade with or control of Central Asia was natural after the centrality conferred on the region by three centuries of Mongol and Turkic conquest, highlighted by the campaigns of Genghis Khan and Timur. But as we shall see, changes in the organization of trade were sapping the vitality of the Silk Road. Wealth and power were shifting to European seaborne empires linking the Atlantic with the Indian Ocean. Though the Ottomans were a formidable naval power in the Mediterranean, neither they nor the Safavid shahs in Iran nor the Mughal emperors of India deployed more than a token navy in the southern seas.

As you read this chapter, ask yourself the following questions:

- What were the advantages and disadvantages of a land as opposed to a maritime empire?
- What role did religion play in political alliances and rivalries and in the formation of states?
- How did trading patterns change between 1500 and 1750?

Ↄ

THE OTTOMAN EMPIRE, TO 1750

The most long-lived of the post-Mongol Muslim empires was the **Ottoman Empire,** founded around 1300. By extending Islamic conquests into eastern Europe, starting in the late fourteenth century, and by taking Syria and Egypt from the Mamluk rulers in the early

---

Qazvin (kaz-VEEN)   **Safavi** (SAH-fah-vee)

CHRONOLOGY

	Ottoman Empire	Safavid Empire	Mughal Empire	Europeans in the Indian Ocean States
1500	**1514** Selim I defeats Safavid shah at Chaldiran; conquers Egypt and Syria (1516–1517) **1520–1566** Reign of Suleiman the Magnificent; peak of Ottoman Empire **1529** First Ottoman siege of Vienna	**1502–1524** Shah Ismail establishes Safavid rule in Iran **1514** Defeat by Ottomans at Chaldiran limits Safavid growth	**1526** Babur defeats last sultan of Delhi at Panipat **1539** Death of Nanak, founder of Sikh religion **1556–1605** Akbar rules in Agra; peak of Mughal Empire	**1511** Portuguese seize Malacca from local Malay ruler
1600	**1571** Ottoman naval defeat at Lepanto **1610** End of Anatolian revolts	**1587–1629** Reign of Shah Abbas the Great; peak of Safavid Empire **1622** Iranians oust Portuguese from Hormuz after 108 years		**1565** Spanish establish their first fort in the Philippines **1600** English East India Company founded **1602** Dutch East India Company founded **1606** Dutch reach Australia **1641** Dutch seize Malacca from Portuguese **1650** Omani Arabs capture Musqat from Portuguese
1700	**1718–1730** Tulip Period; military decline apparent to Austria and Russia	**1722** Afghan invaders topple last Safavid shah **1736–1747** Nadir Shah temporarily reunites Iran; invades India (1739)	**1658–1707** Aurangzeb imposes conservative Islamic regime **1690** British found city of Calcutta **1739** Iranians under Nadir Shah sack Delhi	**1698** Omani Arabs seize Mombasa from Portuguese **1742** Expansion of French Power in India

sixteenth, the Ottomans seemed to recreate the might of the original Islamic caliphate, the empire established by the Muslim Arab conquests in the seventh century. However, the empire was actually more similar to the new centralized monarchs of France and Spain (see Chapter 18) than to any medieval model.

Enduring more than five centuries, until 1922, the Ottoman Empire survived several periods of wrenching change, some caused by internal problems, others by the growing power of European adversaries. These periods of change reveal the problems faced by huge, land-based empires around the world.

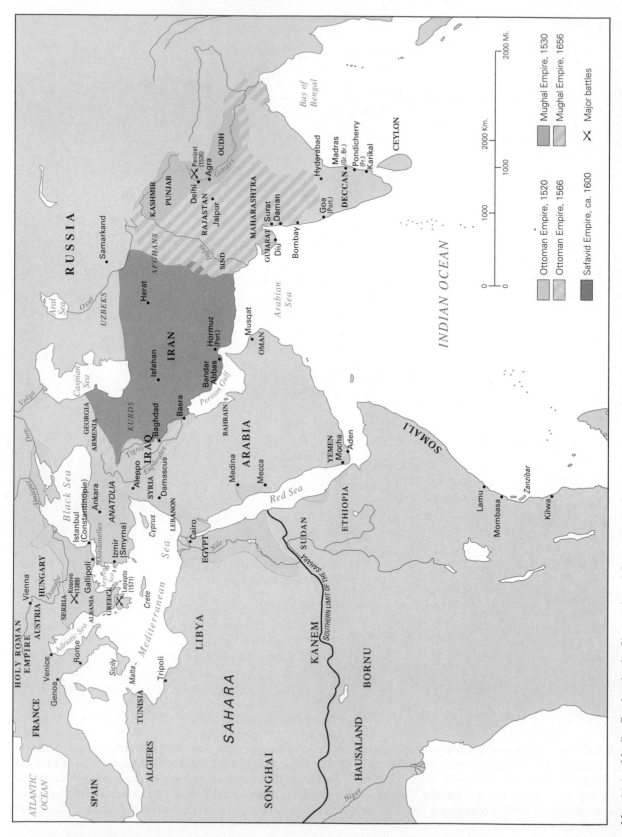

Map 21.1 Muslim Empires in the Sixteenth and Seventeenth Centuries   Iran, a Shi'ite state flanked by Sunni Ottomans on the west and Sunni Mughals on the east, had the least exposure to European influences. Ottoman expansion across the southern Mediterranean Sea intensified European fears of Islam. The areas of strongest Mughal control dictated that Islam's spread into southeast Asia would be heavily influenced by merchants and religious figures from Gujarat instead of from eastern India.

Aya Sofya Mosque in Istanbul   Orginally a Byzantine cathedral, Aya Sofya (in Greek, Hagia Sophia) was transformed into a mosque after 1453, and four minarets were added. It then became a model for subsequent Ottoman mosques. To the right behind it is the Bosporus strait dividing Europe and Asia, to the left the Golden Horn inlet separating the old city of Istanbul from the newer parts. The gate to the Ottoman sultan's palace is to the right of the mosque. The pointed tower to the left of the dome is part of the palace.   (Robert Frerck/Woodfin Camp & Associates)

Expansion and Frontiers

The Ottoman Empire grew from a tiny state in northwestern Anatolia established around 1300 on the strength of Turkish nomad warriors and a few Christian converts to Islam (see Map 21.1). The empire grew because of three factors: (1) the shrewdness of its founder Osman (from which the name "Ottoman" comes) and his descendants, (2) control of a strategic link between Europe and Asia at Gallipoli° on the Dardanelles strait, and (3) the creation of an army that took advantage of the traditional skills of the Turkish cavalryman and the new military possibilities presented by gunpowder.

At first, Ottoman armies concentrated on Christian enemies in Greece and the Balkans, in 1389 conquering a strong Serbian kingdom at the Battle of Kosovo° (in present-day Yugoslavia). Much of southeastern Europe and Anatolia was under the control of the sultans by 1402, when Bayazid° I, "the Thunderbolt," confronted Timur's challenge from Central Asia. After Timur defeated and captured Bayazid at the Battle of Ankara (1402), a generation of civil war followed, until Mehmed° I reunified the sultanate.

During a century and a half of fighting for territory both east and west of Constantinople, the sultans had repeatedly eyed the heavily fortified capital of the slowly dying Byzantine Empire. In 1453, Sultan Mehmed II, "the Conqueror," laid siege to Constantinople. His forces used enormous cannon to bash in the city's walls, dragged warships over a high hill from the Bosporus strait to the city's inner harbor to get around its sea defenses, and finally penetrated the city's land walls through a series of direct infantry assaults. The fall of Constantinople—henceforth commonly known as Istanbul—brought to an end over eleven hundred years of Byzantine rule and made the Ottomans seem invincible.

In 1514, at the Battle of Chaldiran (in Armenia), Selim° I, "the Inexorable," ended a potential threat on his eastern frontier from the new and expansive realm of the Safavid shah in Iran (see below). Although further wars were to be fought with Iran, the general border between the Ottomans and their eastern neighbors was essentially established at this time, leaving Iraq a contested and repeatedly ravaged frontier province.

When Selim conquered the Mamluk Sultanate of Egypt and Syria in 1516 and 1517, the Red Sea became the Ottomans' southern frontier. As for the Ottomans'

Gallipoli (gah-LIP-po-lee)   Kosovo (KO-so-vo)
Bayazid (BAY-yan-zeed)   Mehmed (MEH-met)

Selim (seh-LEEM)

western frontier, the rulers of the major port cities of Algeria and Tunisia, some of them Greek or Italian converts to Islam, voluntarily joined the empire in the early sixteenth century, thereby greatly strengthening its Mediterranean fleets.

The sultan who presided over the greatest Ottoman assault on Christian Europe was **Suleiman° the Magnificent** (r. 1520–1566), known to his subjects as Suleiman Kanuni, "the Lawgiver." The son of Selim I, Suleiman seemed unstoppable as he conquered Belgrade in 1521, expelled the Knights of the Hospital of St. John from the island of Rhodes the following year, and laid siege to Vienna in 1529. Vienna was saved by the lateness of the season and the need to retreat before the onset of winter more than by military action. In later centuries, Ottoman historians looked back on the reign of Suleiman as the period when the imperial system worked to perfection and spoke of it as the golden age of Ottoman greatness.

While Ottoman armies pressed deeper and deeper into eastern Europe, the sultans also sought to control the Mediterranean. Between 1453 and 1502, the Ottomans fought the opening rounds of a two-century war with Venice, the most powerful of Italy's commercial city-states. From the Fourth Crusade of 1204 onward, Venice had assembled a profitable maritime empire that included major islands such as Crete and Cyprus along with strategic coastal strongpoints in Greece. Venice thereby became more than just a trading nation. Its island sugar plantations, exploiting cheap slave labor, competed favorably with Egypt in the international trade of the fifteenth century. With their rivals the Genoese, trading through the strategic island of Chios, the Venetians stifled Ottoman maritime activities in the Aegean Sea.

The initial fighting left Venice in control of its lucrative islands for another century. But it also left Venice a reduced military power compelled to pay tribute to the Ottomans. The Ottomans, like the Chinese, were willing to let other nations carry trade to and from their ports— they preferred trade of this sort—so long as those other nations acknowledged Ottoman authority. It never occurred to them that a sea empire held together by flimsy ships could truly rival a great land empire fielding an army of a hundred thousand men.

In the south, Muslims of the Red Sea and Indian Ocean region were accustomed to trading by way of Egypt and Syria. In the early sixteenth century, merchants from southern India and Sumatra sent emissaries to Istanbul requesting naval support against the Portuguese. The Ottomans responded vigorously to Portuguese threats close to their territories, such as at Aden at the southern entrance to the Red Sea, but their efforts farther afield were insufficient to stifle growing Portuguese domination.

Eastern luxury products still flowed to Ottoman markets. Portuguese power was territorially limited to fortified coastal points, such as Hormuz at the entrance to the Persian Gulf, Goa in western India, and Malacca in Malaya (see Chapter 17). Why commit major resources to subduing an enemy whose main threat was a demand that merchant vessels, mostly belonging to non-Ottoman Muslims, buy protection from Portuguese attack? The Ottomans did send a small naval force to Indonesia, but they never formulated a consistent or aggressive policy with regard to political and economic developments in the Indian Ocean.

Central Institutions

Heirs of the military traditions of Central Asia, the Ottoman army originally consisted of lightly armored mounted warriors skilled at shooting a short bow made of compressed layers of bone, wood, and leather. The conquest of Christian territories in the Balkans in the late fourteenth century, however, gave the Ottomans access to a new military resource: Christian prisoners of war induced to serve as military slaves.

Slave soldiery had a long history in Islamic lands. The Mamluk Sultanate of Egypt and Syria was built on that practice. The Mamluks, however, acquired their new blood from slave markets in Central Asia. Enslaving Christian prisoners, an action of questionable legality in Islamic law, was an Ottoman innovation. Converted to Islam, these "new troops," called *yeni cheri* in Turkish and "**Janissary**"° in English, gave the Ottomans unusual military flexibility.

Christians by upbringing, the Janissaries had no misgivings about fighting against Turks and Muslims when the sultans wished to expand in western Asia. Since horseback riding and bowmanship were not part of their cultural backgrounds, they readily accepted the idea of fighting on foot and learning to use guns, which at that time were still too heavy and awkward for a horseman to load and fire. The Janissaries lived in barracks and trained all year round. Up to the middle of the sixteenth century, they were barred both from holding jobs and from marrying.

The process of selection for Janissary training changed early in the fifteenth century. The new system, called the ***devshirme***° (literally "selection"), imposed a regular levy of male children on Christian villages in the Balkans and occasionally elsewhere. Devshirme children

---

Suleiman (SOO-lay-man)

Janissary (JAN-nih-say-ree)   *devshirme* (dev-sheer-MEH)

were placed with Turkish families to learn their language and then were sent to the sultan's palace in Istanbul for an education that included instruction in Islam, military training, and, for the most talented, what we might call liberal arts. This regime, sophisticated for its time, produced not only the Janissary soldiers but also, from among the chosen few who received special training in the inner service of the palace, senior military commanders and heads of government departments up to the rank of grand vizier.

The Ottoman Empire became cosmopolitan in character. The sophisticated court language, Osmanli° (the Turkish form of *Ottoman*), shared basic grammar and vocabulary with the Turkish spoken by Anatolia's nomads and villagers, but Arabic and Persian elements made it as distinct from that language as the Latin of educated Europeans was from the various Latin-derived Romance languages. Everyone who served in the military or the bureaucracy and conversed in Osmanli was considered to belong to the *askeri*°, or "military," class. Members of this class were exempt from taxes and owed their well-being to the sultan. The mass of the population, whether Muslims, Christians, or Jews—Jews flooded into Ottoman territory after their expulsion from Spain in 1492 (see Chapter 17)—constituted the *raya*°, literally "flock of sheep."

By the beginning of the reign of Sultan Suleiman the Magnificent, the Ottoman Empire was the most powerful and best-organized state in either Europe or the Islamic world. Its military was balanced between mounted archers, primarily Turks supported by grants of land in return for their military service, and Janissaries, Turkified Albanians, Serbs, and Macedonians paid from the central treasury and trained in the most advanced weaponry. The galley-equipped navy was manned by Greek, Turkish, Algerian, and Tunisian sailors, usually under the command of an admiral from one of the North African ports.

The balance of the Ottoman land forces brought success to Ottoman arms in recurrent wars with the Safavids, who were much slower to adopt firearms, and in the inexorable conquest of the Balkans. Expansion by sea was less dramatic. A major expedition against Malta that would have given the Ottomans a foothold in the western Mediterranean failed in 1565. Combined Christian forces also achieved a massive naval victory at the Battle of Lepanto, off Greece, in 1571. But Ottoman resources were so extensive that in a year's time they had replaced all of the galleys sunk in that battle.

Under the land-grant system, resident cavalrymen administered most rural areas in Anatolia and the

Ottoman Glassmakers on Parade   Celebrations of the circumcisions of the sultan's sons featured parades organized by the craft guilds of Istanbul. This float features glassmaking, a common craft in Islamic realms. The most elaborate glasswork included oil lamps for mosques and colored glass for the small stained-glass windows below mosque domes.   (Topkapi Saray Museum)

Balkans. They maintained order, collected taxes, and reported for each summer's campaign with their horses, retainers, and supplies, all paid for from the taxes they collected. When not campaigning, they stayed at home. Some historians maintain that these cavalrymen, who did not own their land, had little interest in encouraging production or introducing new technologies, but since a militarily able son often succeeded his father, the grant holders did have some interest in productivity.

The Ottoman conception of the world saw the sultan providing justice for his "flock of sheep" (raya) and the military protecting them. In return, the raya paid the taxes that supported both the sultan and the military. In reality, the sultan's government, like most large territorial governments in premodern times, remained comparatively isolated from the lives of most subjects. Arab, Turkish, and Balkan townsfolk depended on local notables and religious leaders to represent them before Ottoman provincial governors and their staffs. Islam was the ruling religion and gradually became the majority religion in Balkan regions such as Albania and Bosnia that had large numbers of converts. Thus the law of Islam (the Shari'a°), as interpreted by local *ulama*° (religious

Osmanli (os-MAHN-lee)   *askeri* (AS-keh-ree)   *raya* (RAH-yah)

Shari'a (sha-REE-ah)   *ulama* (oo-leh-MAH)

Metal Currency and Inflation

Inflation occurs when the quantity of goods and services available for purchase remains stable while the quantity of money in circulation increases. With more money in their pockets, people are willing to pay more to get what they want. Prices go up, and what people think of as the value of money goes down.

Today, with paper money and electronic banking, governments try to control inflation by regulating the printing of money or by other means. Prior to the nineteenth century, money consisted of silver and gold coins, and governments did not keep track of how much money was in circulation. As long as the annual production of gold and silver mines was quite small, inflation was not a worry. In the sixteenth and seventeenth centuries, however, precious metal poured into Spain from silver and gold mines in the New World, but there was no increase in the availability of goods and services. The resulting inflation triggered a "price revolution" in Europe—a general tripling of prices between 1500 and 1650. In Paris in 1650, the price of wheat and hay was fifteen times higher than the price had been in 1500.

This wave of inflation worked its way east, contributing to social disorder in the Ottoman Empire. European traders had more money available than Ottoman merchants and could outbid them for scarce commodities. Lacking silver and gold mines,

the Ottoman government reduced the amount of precious metal in Ottoman coins. This made the problem worse. Hit hardest were people who had fixed incomes. Cavalrymen holding land grants worth a set amount each year were unable to equip themselves for military campaigns. Students living on fixed scholarships went begging.

Safavid Iran needed silver and gold to pay for imports from Mughal India, which imported few Iranian goods. Iranians sold silk to the Ottoman Empire for silver and gold, worsening the Ottoman situation, and then passed the precious metal on to India. Everyday life in Iran depended on barter or locally minted copper coinage, both more resistant to inflation. Copper for coins was sometimes imported from China.

Though no one then grasped the connection between silver production in Mexico and the trade balance between Iran and India, the world of the sixteenth and seventeenth centuries was becoming more closely linked economically than it had ever been before.

Set of Coin Dies   The lower die, called the anvil die, was set in a piece of wood. A blank disk of gold, silver, or copper was placed on top of it. The hammer die was placed on top of the blank and struck with a hammer to force the coin's image onto it.   (Courtesy, Israel Museum, Jerusalem)

---

scholars), conditioned urban institutions and social life. Local customs prevailed among non-Muslims and in many rural areas; and non-Muslims looked to their own religious leaders for guidance in family and spiritual matters.

Crisis of the Military State, 1585–1650

As military technology evolved, cannon and lighter-weight firearms played an ever-larger role on the battlefield. Accordingly, the size of the Janissary corps—and its cost to the government—grew steadily, and the role of the Turkish cavalry, which continued to

disdain firearms even as they became lighter and easier to use, diminished. To fill state coffers and pay the Janissaries, in the mid-sixteenth century the sultan started reducing the number of landholding cavalrymen. Revenues previously spent on their living expenses and military equipment went directly into the imperial treasury. Some of the displaced cavalrymen, armed and unhappy, became a restive element in rural Anatolia.

At about the same time, in the late sixteenth century, inflation caused a flood of cheap silver from the New World (see Environment and Technology: Metal Currency and Inflation) affected many of the remaining landholders restricted by law to collecting a fixed amount of taxes. Their purchasing power declined so much that they were unable to report for military service. This delinquency, however, played into the hands of the sultan's government, which wanted to reduce the cavalry and increase the Janissary corps and thus made no reforms to allow landholders to keep their land grants. As land was returned to the state, more and more cavalrymen joined the ranks of dispossessed troopers. Students and professors in *madrasas* (religious colleges) similarly found it impossible to live on fixed stipends from madrasa endowments.

Constrained by religious law from fundamentally changing the tax system, the government levied emergency surtaxes to obtain enough funds to pay the Janissaries and bureaucrats. For additional military strength, particularly in its wars with Iran, the government reinforced the Janissary ranks with partially trained, salaried soldiers hired for the duration of a campaign. Once the summer campaign season was over, however, these soldiers found themselves out of work and short on cash.

This complicated situation resulted in revolts that devastated Anatolia between 1590 and 1610. Former landholding cavalrymen, short-term soldiers released at the end of the campaign season, peasants overburdened by emergency taxes, and even impoverished students of religion formed bands of marauders. Anatolia experienced the worst of the rebellions and suffered greatly from emigration and the loss of agricultural production. But an increase in banditry, made worse by the government's inability to stem the spread of muskets among the general public, beset other parts of the empire as well.

In the meantime, the Janissaries took advantage of their growing influence to gain relief from prohibitions on their marrying and engaging in business. Janissaries who involved themselves in commerce lessened the burden on the state budget, and married Janissaries who enrolled sons or relatives in the corps made it possible in the seventeenth century for the government to save state funds by abolishing the devshirme system with its traveling selection officers. These savings, however, were more than offset by the increase in the total number of Janissaries and in their steady deterioration as a military force, which necessitated the hiring of more and more supplemental troops.

Economic Change and Growing Weakness, 1650–1750

A very different Ottoman Empire emerged from this period of crisis. The sultan once had led armies. Now he mostly resided in his palace and had little experience of the real world. This manner of living resulted from a gradually developed policy of keeping the sultan's male relatives confined to the palace to prevent them from plotting coups or meddling in politics. The sultan's mother and the chief eunuch overseeing the private quarters of the palace thus became important arbiters of royal favor, and even of succession to the sultanate, and the affairs of government were overseen more and more by the chief administrators—the grand viziers. (Ottoman historians draw special attention to the negative influence of women in the palace after the time of Suleiman, but to some degree they are reflecting traditional male, and Muslim, fears about women in politics.)

The devshirme had been discontinued, and the Janissaries had taken advantage of their increased power and privileges to make membership in their corps hereditary. Together with several other newly prominent infantry regiments, they involved themselves in crafts and trading, both in Istanbul and in provincial capitals such as Cairo, Aleppo, and Baghdad. This activity took a toll on their military skills, but they continued to be a powerful faction in urban politics that the sultans could neither ignore nor reform.

Land grants in return for military service also disappeared. Tax farming arose in their place. Tax farmers paid specific taxes, such as customs duties, in advance in return for the privilege of collecting a greater amount from the actual taxpayers. In one instance, two tax farmers advanced the government 18 million akches (small silver coins) for the customs duties of the Aegean port of Izmir°, and collected a total of 19,169,203 akches for a profit of 6.5 percent.

Rural administration, already disrupted by the rebellions, suffered from the transition to tax farms. The former landholders had been military men who readily kept order on their lands in order to maintain their incomes. Tax farmers were less likely to live on the land, and their tax collection rights could vary from year to year. The imperial government, therefore, faced greater administrative burdens and came to rely heavily on powerful provincial governors or on wealthy men who purchased lifelong tax collection rights that prompted them to behave more or less like private landowners.

Rural disorder and decline in administrative control sometimes opened the way for new economic opportunities. The port of Izmir, known to Europeans by the ancient name "Smyrna," had a population of around 2,000 in 1580. By 1650 the population had increased almost twentyfold to between 30,000 and 40,000. Along with refugees from the Anatolian uprisings and from European pirate attacks along the coast came European merchants and large colonies of Armenians, Greeks, and Jews. A French traveler in 1621 wrote: "At present, Izmir

---

Izmir (IZ-meer)

has a great traffic in wool, beeswax, cotton, and silk, which the Armenians bring there instead of going to Aleppo . . . because they do not pay as many dues.[2]

Izmir was able to transform itself between 1580 and 1650 from a small Muslim Turkish town into a multiethnic, multireligious, multilinguistic entrepôt because of the Ottoman government's inability to control trade and the slowly growing dominance of European traders in the Indian Ocean. Spices from the East, though still traded in Aleppo and other long-established Ottoman centers, were not to be found in Izmir. Aside from Iranian silk brought in by caravan, European traders at Izmir purchased local agricultural products—dried fruits, sesame seeds, nuts, and olive oil. As a consequence local farmers who previously had grown grain for subsistence shifted their plantings more and more to cotton and other cash crops, including, after its introduction in the 1590s, tobacco, which quickly became popular in the Ottoman Empire despite government prohibitions. In this way the agricultural economy of western Anatolia, the Balkans, and the Mediterranean coast—the Ottoman lands most accessible to Europe (see Map 21.1)—became enmeshed in the seventeenth century in a growing European commercial network.

At the same time, Ottoman military power slowly ebbed. The ill-trained Janissaries sometimes resorted to hiring substitutes to go on campaign, and the sultans relied on partially trained seasonal recruits and on armies raised by the governors of frontier provinces. By the middle of the eighteenth century, it was obvious to the Ottomans' Austrian and Russian opponents that the empire was in decline. On the eastern front, however, Ottoman exhaustion after many wars was matched by the demise in 1722 of their perennial adversary, the Safavid state of Iran.

The Ottoman Empire lacked both the wealth and the inclination to match European economic advances. Overland trade from the east dwindled as political disorder in Safavid Iran cut deeply into Iranian silk production (see below). Coffee, an Arabian product that rose from obscurity in the fifteenth century to become the rage first in the Ottoman Empire and then in Europe, was grown in the highlands of Yemen and exported by way of Egypt. By 1770, however, Muslim merchants trading in the Yemeni port of Mocha° (literally "the coffee place") were charged 15 percent in duties and fees. But European traders, benefiting from trade agreements with the Ottoman Empire going back to the time of Mehmed the Conqueror, paid little more than 3 percent.

Such trade agreements led to European domination of Ottoman import and export trade by sea. Nevertheless, the Europeans did not control strategic ports in the Mediterranean comparable to Malacca in the Indian Ocean and Hormuz on the Persian Gulf, so their economic power stopped short of colonial settlement and direct political administration in Ottoman territories.

A few astute Ottoman statesmen observed the growing disarray of the empire and advised the sultans to reestablish the land-grant and devshirme systems of Suleiman's reign. But to most people the downward course of imperial power was far from evident, much less the reasons behind it. Ottoman historians named the period between 1718 and 1730 the "**Tulip Period**" because of the craze for high-priced tulip bulbs that swept Ottoman ruling circles. The craze replicated a Dutch tulip mania that had begun in the mid-sixteenth century, when the flower was introduced into Holland from Istanbul, and peaked in 1636 with particularly rare bulbs going for 2,500 florins apiece—the value of twenty-two oxen. Far from seeing Europe as the enemy that eventually would dismantle the weakening Ottoman Empire, the Istanbul elite experimented with European clothing and furniture styles and purchased printed books from the empire's first (and short-lived) press.

In 1730, however, the gala soirees, at which guests watched turtles with candles on their backs wander in the dark through massive tulip beds, gave way to a conservative Janissary revolt with strong religious overtones. Sultan Ahmed III abdicated, and the leader of the revolt, Patrona Halil°, an Albanian former seaman and stoker of the public baths, swaggered around the capital for several months dictating government policies before he was seized and executed.

The Patrona Halil rebellion confirmed the perceptions of a few that the Ottoman Empire was facing severe difficulties. But decay at the center spelled benefit elsewhere. In the provinces, ambitious and competent governors, wealthy landholders, urban notables, and nomad chieftains were well placed to take advantage of the central government's weakness. By the middle of the eighteenth century, groups of Mamluks had regained a dominant position in Egypt, and Janissary commanders had become virtually independent rulers in Baghdad. In central Arabia, Muhammad ibn Abd al-Wahhab's conservative Sunni movement had begun its remarkable rise beyond the reach of Ottoman power. Although no region declared full independence, the sultan's power was slipping away to the advantage of a broad array of lower officials and upstart chieftains in all parts of the empire, and the Ottoman economy was reorienting itself toward Europe.

Mocha (MOH-kuh)

Patrona Halil (pa-TROH-nuh ha-LEEL)

Safavid Shah with Attendants and Musicians   This painting by Ali-Quli Jubbadar, a European convert to Islam working for the Safavid armory, reflects Western influences. Notice the use of light and shadow to model faces and the costume of the attendant to the shah's right. The shah's waterpipe indicates the spread of tobacco, a New World crop, to the Middle East.   (Courtesy of Oriental Institute, Academy of Sciences, Leningrad. Reproduced from *Album of Persian and Indian Miniatures* [Moscow, 1962], ill. no. 98)

THE SAFAVID EMPIRE, 1502–1722

The **Safavid Empire** of Iran (see Map 21.1) resembled its long-time Ottoman foe in many ways: it initially relied militarily on cavalry paid through land grants; its population spoke several different languages; it was oriented inward away from the sea; and urban notables, nomadic chieftains, and religious scholars served as intermediaries between the people and the government. It also had distinct qualities that to this day set Iran off from its neighbors: it derived part of its legitimacy from the pre-Islamic dynasties of ancient Iran, and it adopted the Shi'ite form of Islam.

The Rise of the Safavids

Timur had been a great conqueror. But his children and grandchildren contented themselves with modest realms in Afghanistan and Central Asia, while a number of would-be rulers vied for control elsewhere. In Iran itself, the ultimate victor in a complicated struggle for power among Turkish chieftains was Ismail°, a boy of Kurdish, Iranian, and Greek ancestry, the hereditary leader of a militant Sufi brotherhood named "Safaviya" for his ancestor Safi

al-Din. In 1502, at the age of sixteen, Ismail proclaimed himself shah of Iran. At around the same time, he declared that from that time forward his realm would be devoted to **Shi'ite Islam,** which revered the family of Muhammad's son-in-law Ali, and he called on all his subjects to abandon their Sunni beliefs.

Most of the members of the Safavi brotherhood were Turkish-speakers from nomadic groups known as *qizilbash°*, or "redheads," because of their distinctive turbans. They believed that Ismail was practically a god incarnate, and they fought ferociously on his behalf. If Ismail wished his state to be Shi'ite, his word was law to the qizilbash. The Iranian subject population, however, was not so easily persuaded. Neighboring lands received Sunni refugees from Safavid rule. Their preaching and intriguing helped stoke the fires that kept Ismail (d. 1524) and his son Tahmasp° (d. 1576) engaged in war after war. It took a century and a series of brutal persecutions to make Iran an overwhelmingly Shi'ite land. The transformation also required the importation of Arab Shi'ite scholars from Lebanon and Bahrain to institute Shi'ite religious education at a high level.

Although Ismail's reasons for compelling Iran's conversion to Shi'ism are unknown, the effect of this radical act was to create a deep chasm between Iran and its neighbors, all of which were Sunni. Iran became a truly separate country for the first time since its incorporation into the Islamic caliphate in the seventh century.

Ismail (IS-ma-eel)

qizilbash (KIH-zil-bahsh)   **Tahmasp** (tah-MAHSP)

Society and Religion

The imposition of Shi'ite belief made permanent the split between Iran and its neighbors, but differences between them had long been in the making. Persian, written in the Arabic script from the tenth century onward, had emerged as the second language of Islam. By 1500, an immense library of legal and theological writings; epic, lyric, and mystic poetry; histories; and drama and fiction had come into being. Iranian scholars and writers normally read Arabic as well as Persian and sprinkled their writings with Arabic phrases, but their Arab counterparts were much less inclined to learn Persian. Even handwriting styles differed, Iranians preferring highly cursive forms of the Arabic script.

This divergence between the two language areas had intensified after the Mongols destroyed Baghdad, the capital of the Islamic caliphate, in 1258 and diminished the importance of Arabic-speaking Iraq. Syria and Egypt had become the heartland of the Arab world while Iran developed largely on its own, having more extensive contacts with India—where Muslim rulers favored the Persian language—than with the Arabs.

In the heyday of the Islamic caliphate in the seventh through ninth centuries, cultural styles had radiated in all directions from Baghdad. In the post-Mongol period—a time of immense artistic creativity and innovation in Iran, Afghanistan, and Central Asia—styles in the East went their own separate ways. Painted and molded tiles and tile mosaics, often in vivid turquoise blue, became the standard exterior decoration of mosques in Iran but never were used in Syria and Egypt. Persian poets raised morally instructive and mystical-allegorical verse to peaks of perfection that had no reflection in Arabic poetry, generally considered to be in a state of decline.

The Turks, who steadily came to dominate the political scene from Bengal to Algeria, generally preferred Persian as a vehicle for literary or religious expression. The Mamluks in Egypt and Syria showed greatest respect for Arabic. The Turkish language, which had a vigorous tradition of folk poetry, developed only slowly, primarily in the Ottoman Empire, as a language of literature and administration. Ironically, Ismail Safavi was a noted religious poet in the Turkish language of his qizilbash followers, and his mortal adversary, the Ottoman Selim I (r. 1512–1520), was known for the elegance of his Persian poetry.

To be sure, Islam itself provided a tradition that crossed ethnic and linguistic borders. Mosque architecture differed, but Iranians, Arabs, and Turks, as well as Muslims in India, all had mosques. They also had madrasas that trained the ulama to sustain and interpret the Shari'a as the all-encompassing law of Islam. Yet local understandings of the common tradition differed substantially.

All Sufi orders had distinctive rituals and concepts of mystical union with God. These orders also were present in pre-Safavid Iran, but Iran stood out as the land where Sufism most often fused with militant political objectives. The Safavi Order was not the first to deploy armies and use the point of a sword to promote love of God. The Safavid shahs were unique, however, in eventually banning, somewhat ineffectively, all Sufi orders from their domain.

Even prior to Shah Ismail's imposition of Shi'ism, therefore, Iran had become a distinctive society. Nevertheless, the impact of Shi'ism was significant. Shi'ite doctrine says that all temporal rulers, regardless of title, are temporary stand-ins for the **"Hidden Imam":** the twelfth descendant of Ali, who was the prophet Muhammad's cousin and son-in-law. Shi'ites believe that leadership of the Muslim community rests solely with divinely appointed Imams from Ali's family, that the twelfth descendant (the Hidden Imam) disappeared as a child in the ninth century, and that the Shi'ite community will lack a proper religious authority until he returns. Some Shi'ite scholars concluded that the faithful should calmly accept the world as it was and wait quietly for the Hidden Imam's return. Others maintained that they themselves should play a stronger role in political affairs because they were best qualified to know the Hidden Imam's wishes. These two positions, which still play a role in Iranian Shi'ism, tended to enhance the self-image of the ulama as independent of imperial authority and stood in the way of religious scholars becoming subordinate government functionaries, as happened with many Ottoman ulama.

Shi'ism also affected the psychological life of the people. Commemoration of the martyrdom of Imam Husayn (d. 680), Ali's son and the third Imam, during the first two weeks of every lunar year regularized an emotional outpouring with no parallel in Sunni lands. Day after day for two weeks (as they do today) preachers recited the woeful tale to crowds of weeping believers, and elaborate street processions, often organized by craft guilds, paraded chanting and self-flagellating men past crowds of reverent onlookers. Passion plays in which Husayn and his family are mercilessly killed by the agents of the caliph became a unique form of Iranian public theater.

Of course, Shi'ites elsewhere observed some of the same rites of mourning for Imam Husayn, particularly in the Shi'ite pilgrimage cities of Karbala and Najaf° in

---

Najaf (NAH-jaf)

Ottoman Iraq. But the impact of these rites on society as a whole was especially great in Iran, where 90 percent of the population was Shi'ite. Over time, the subjects of the Safavid shahs came to feel more than ever a people apart, even though many of them had been Shi'ite for only two or three generations.

A Tale of Two Cities: Isfahan and Istanbul

Isfahan° became Iran's capital in 1598 by decree of **Shah Abbas I** (r. 1587–1629). Outwardly, Istanbul and Isfahan looked quite different. Built on seven hills on the south side of the narrow Golden Horn inlet, Istanbul boasted a skyline punctuated by the gray stone domes and thin, pointed minarets of the great imperial mosques. Their design was inspired by Hagia Sophia, the Byzantine cathedral converted to a mosque and renamed Aya Sofya after 1453 (see page 525). The mosques surrounding the royal plaza in Isfahan, in contrast, had unobtrusive minarets and brightly tiled domes that rose to gentle peaks. High walls surrounded the sultan's palace in Istanbul. Shah Abbas in Isfahan focused his capital on the giant royal plaza, which was large enough for his army to play polo, and he used an airy palace overlooking the plaza to receive dignitaries and review his troops. This public image contributed to Shah Abbas being called "the Great."

The harbor of Istanbul, the primary Ottoman seaport, teemed with sailing ships and smaller craft, many of them belonging to a colony of European merchants perched on a hilltop on the north side of the Golden Horn. Isfahan, far from the sea, was only occasionally visited by Europeans. Most of its trade was in the hands of Jews, Hindus, and especially a colony of Armenian Christians brought in by Shah Abbas and settled in a suburb of the city.

Beneath these superficial differences, the two capitals had much in common. Wheeled vehicles were scarce in hilly Istanbul and nonexistent in Isfahan, which was within the broad zone where camels supplanted wheeled transport after the rise of the Arab caravan cities in the pre-Islamic centuries. In size and layout both cities were built for walking and, aside from the royal plaza in Isfahan, lacked the open spaces common in contemporary European cities. Away from the major mosque complexes, streets were narrow and irregular. Houses crowded against each other in dead-end lanes. Open areas were interior courtyards where residents could enjoy their privacy. Artisans and merchants organized themselves into guilds that had strong social and

Masjid–i Shah (Royal Mosque) in Isfahan   This masterpiece of Safavid architecture reflects several highlights of Iranian craftsmanship. The tile mosaics include different styles of Arabic calligraphy: a cursive version with long uprights in a band around the dome; below that, a partially squared-off script between the window grills; and below that, and on the minaret, completely orthogonal words set within polygons. The flowery pattern on the dome recalls the designs of Persian carpets. Notice the difference between this minaret and the Ottoman minarets in the illustration on page 525.   (Walter H. Hodge/Peter Arnold, Inc.)

religious as well as economic bonds. The shops of each guild adjoined each other in the markets.

Women were seldom seen in public, even in Istanbul's mazelike covered market or in Isfahan's long, serpentine bazaar. At home, the women's quarters—called *anderun*°, or "interior," in Iran and *harem*, or "forbidden area," in Istanbul—were separate from the public rooms where the men of the family received visitors. In both areas, low cushions, charcoal braziers for warmth, carpets, and small tables constituted most of the furnishings. In Iran and the Arab provinces, shelves and niches for books could be cut into the thick, mud-brick walls. Residences in Istanbul were usually built of wood. Glazed tile in geometric or floral patterns covered the walls of wealthy men's reception areas.

The private side of family life has left few traces, but it is apparent that women's society—consisting of wives, children, female servants, and sometimes one or more eunuchs—was not entirely cut off from the outside world. Ottoman court records reveal that women, using male agents, were very active in the urban real estate market. Often they were selling inherited shares of their father's estate, but some both bought and sold real estate on a regular basis and even established religious

---

Isfahan (is-fah-HAHN)

anderun (an-deh-ROON)

Istanbul Family on the Way to a Bath House   Public baths, an important feature of Islamic cities, set different hours for men and women. Young boys, such as the lad in the turban shown here, went with their mothers and sisters. Notice that the children wear the same styles as the adults.   (Osterreichische Nationalbibliothek)

to adolescent boys were neither unusual nor hidden. Women who appeared in public—aside from non-Muslims, the aged, and the very poor—were likely to be slaves. Miniature paintings frequently depict female dancers, musicians, and even acrobats in attitudes and costumes that range from decorous to decidedly erotic.

Despite social similarities, the overall flavors of Isfahan and Istanbul were not the same. Isfahan had its prosperous Armenian quarter across the river from the city's center, but it was not a truly cosmopolitan capital, just as the peoples of the Safavid realm were not remarkably diverse. Like other rulers of extensive land empires, Shah Abbas located his capital toward the center of his domain within comparatively easy reach of any threatened frontier. Istanbul, in contrast, was a great seaport and crossroads located on the straits separating the sultan's European and Asian possessions. People of all sorts lived or spent time in Istanbul—Venetians, Genoese, Arabs, Turks, Greeks, Armenians, Albanians, Serbs, Jews, Bulgarians, and more. In this respect Istanbul conveyed the cosmopolitan character of major seaports from London to Canton (Guangzhou) and belied the fact that its prosperity rested on the vast reach of the sultan's territories rather than on the voyages of its merchants.

endowments for pious purposes. The fact that Islamic law, unlike some European codes, permitted a wife to retain her property after marriage gave some women a stake in the general economy and a degree of independence from their spouses. Women also appeared in other types of court cases, where they often testified for themselves, for Islamic courts did not recognize the role of attorney. Although comparable Safavid court records do not survive, historians assume that a parallel situation prevailed in Iran.

European travelers commented on the veiling of women outside the home, but miniature paintings indicate that ordinary female garb consisted of a long, ample dress with a scarf or long shawl pulled tight over the forehead to conceal the hair. Lightweight trousers, either close-fitting or baggy, were often worn under the dress. This mode of dress was not far different from that of men. Poor men wore light trousers, a long shirt, a jacket, and a hat or turban. Wealthier men wore over their trousers ankle-length caftans, often closely fitted around the chest. The norm for both sexes was complete coverage of arms, legs, and hair.

Public life was almost entirely the domain of men. Poetry and art, both somewhat more elegantly developed in Isfahan than in Istanbul, were as likely to extol the charms of beardless boys as pretty women. Despite religious disapproval of homosexuality, attachments

Economic Crisis and Political Collapse

The silk fabrics of northern Iran, monopolized by the shahs, were the mainstay of the Safavid Empire's foreign trade. However, the manufacture that eventually became most powerfully associated with Iran was the deep-pile carpet made by knotting colored yarns around stretched warp threads. Different cities produced distinctive carpet designs. Women and girls did much of the actual knotting work.

Carpets with geometrical or arabesque designs appear in Timurid miniature paintings, but no knotted "Persian rug" survives from the pre-Safavid era. One of the earliest dated carpets was produced in 1522 to adorn the tomb of Shaikh Safi al-Din, the fourteenth-century founder of the Safavi Order. This use indicates the high value accorded these products within Iran. One German visitor to Isfahan remarked: "The most striking adornment of the banqueting hall was to my mind the carpets laid out over all three rostra in a most extravagant fashion, mostly woolen rugs from Kirman with animal patterns and woven of the finest wool."[3]

Overall, Iran's manufacturing sector was neither large nor notably productive. Most of the shah's subjects, whether Iranians, Turks, Kurds, or Arabs, lived by subsistence farming or herding. Neither area of activity recorded significant technological advances during the Safavid period. Large sections of the country were granted to the qizilbash nomads in return for their furnishing mounted warriors for the army. These lands were held by the groups in common, however, and were not subdivided into individual landholdings as in the Ottoman Empire. Thus many people in rural areas lived according to the will of a nomad chieftain who had little interest in building the agricultural economy.

The Safavids, like the Ottomans, had difficulty finding the money to pay troops armed with firearms. This crisis occurred somewhat later in Iran because of its greater distance from Europe. By the end of the sixteenth century, it was evident that a more systematic adoption of cannon and firearms in the Safavid Empire would be needed to hold off the Ottomans and the Uzbeks° (Turkish rulers who had succeeded the Timurids on Iran's Central Asian frontier; see Map 21.1). Like the Ottoman cavalry a century earlier, however, the warriors furnished by the nomad leaders were not inclined to trade in their bows for firearms. Shah Abbas responded by establishing a slave corps of year-round soldiers and arming them with guns.

The Christian converts to Islam who initially provided the manpower for the new corps were mostly captives taken in raids on Georgia in the Caucasus°. Some became powerful members of the court. They formed a counterweight to the nomad chiefs just as the Janissaries had earlier challenged the landholding Turkish cavalry in the Ottoman Empire. Under the strong hand of Shah Abbas, the inevitable rivalries and intrigues between the factions were kept under control. His successors were less fortunate.

In the late sixteenth century, the inflation caused by cheap silver spread into Iran; then overland trade through Safavid territory declined because of mismanagement of the silk monopoly after Shah Abbas's death in 1629. As a result, the country faced the unsolvable problem of finding money to pay the army and bureaucracy. Trying to unseat the nomads from their lands to regain control of taxes was more difficult and more disruptive militarily than the piecemeal dismantlement of the land-grant system in the Ottoman Empire. The nomads were still a cohesive military force, and pressure from the center simply caused them to withdraw to their mountain pastures until the pressure subsided. By 1722, the government had become so weak and commanded so little support from the nomadic groups that an army of marauding Afghans was able to capture Isfahan and effectively end Safavid rule.

Despite Iran's long coastline, the Safavids never possessed a navy. The Portuguese seized the strategic Persian Gulf island of Hormuz in 1517 and were expelled only in 1622, when the English ferried Iranian soldiers to the attack. Land-oriented rulers, the shahs relied on the English and Dutch for naval support and never considered competing with them at sea. Nadir Shah, a general who emerged from the confusion of the Safavid fall to reunify Iran briefly between 1736 and 1747, purchased some naval vessels from the English and used them in the Persian Gulf. But his navy decayed after his death, and Iran did not have a navy again until the twentieth century.

THE MUGHAL EMPIRE, 1526–1761

What distinguished the Indian empire of the Mughal° sultans from the empires of the Ottomans and Safavids was the fact that India was a land of Hindus ruled by a Muslim minority. To be sure, the Ottoman provinces in the Balkans, except for Albania and Bosnia, remained mostly Christian, but the remainder of the Ottoman Empire was overwhelmingly Muslim with small Christian and Jewish minorities. The Ottoman sultans made much of their control of Mecca and Medina and resulting supervision of the annual pilgrimage caravans just as the Safavids fostered pilgrimages to a shrine in Mashhad in northeastern Iran for their overwhelmingly Shi'ite subjects.

India, in contrast, was far from the Islamic homelands (see Map 21.1). Muslim dominion in India was the result of repeated military campaigns from the early eleventh century onward, and the Mughals had to contend with the Hindus' long-standing resentment of the destruction of their culture by Muslims. The Balkan peoples had struggled to maintain their separate identities in relation to the Byzantines, the crusaders, and one another before arrival of the Turks. The peoples of the Indian subcontinent, in contrast, had used centuries of freedom from foreign intrusion to forge a distinctive Hindu civilization that could not easily accommodate the world-view of Islam. Thus the challenge facing the Mughals was not just conquering and organizing a large territorial state but also finding a formula for Hindu-Muslim coexistence.

Uzbeks (UHZ-bex) **Caucasus** (CAW-kuh-suhs)

Mughal (MOH-guhl)

**New Year Celebration at the Court of Shah Jahan
(r. 1628–1658)**   The Pre-Islamic Iranian tradition of celebrating
the New Year (in Persian *No Ruz*, "New Day") on March 21, the
vernal equinox, spread with Islamic rule. The dancing girls are a
characteristically Indian aspect of the celebration.   (The Royal
Collection © Her Majesty Queen Elizabeth II)

Political Foundations

Babur° (1483–1530), the founder
of the **Mughal Empire,** was a
Muslim descendant of Timur.
Though *Mughal* is Persian for
"Mongol," the Timurids were of Turkic rather than Mongol origin. Timur's marriage to a descendant of Genghis
Khan had earned him the Mongol designation "son-in-
law," but he and his descendants, like the Ottomans,
could never claim the mantle of Genghisid political legitimacy that came naturally to lesser rulers in Central Asia
and in the Crimea north of the Black Sea.

Invading from Central Asia, Babur defeated the last
Muslim sultan of Delhi at the Battle of Panipat in 1526.
But even though this victory marked the birth of a brilliant and powerful state in India, Babur's descendants
continued to think of Central Asia as their true home,
from time to time expressing intentions of recapturing
Samarkand and referring to its Uzbek ruler—a genuine
descendant of Genghis Khan—as a governor rather than
an independent sovereign.

India proved to be the primary theater of Mughal
accomplishment, however. Babur's grandson **Akbar**
(r. 1556–1605), a brilliant but mercurial man whose lifelong illiteracy betrayed his upbringing in the wilds of
Afghanistan, established the central administration of
the expanding state. Under him and his three successors—the last of whom died in 1707—all but the southern tip of India fell under Mughal rule, administered first
from Agra and then from Delhi°.

Akbar granted land revenues to military officers and
government officials in return for their service. Ranks,
called *mansabs°,* some high and some low, entitled their
holders to revenue assignments. As in the other Islamic
empires, revenue grants were not considered hereditary,
and the central government kept careful track of their is-
suance.

With a population of 100 million, a thriving trading
economy based on cotton cloth, and a generally efficient
administration, India under Akbar was probably the
most prosperous empire of the sixteenth century (see
Society and Culture: Indian Merchants in Russia). He
and his successors faced few external threats and experienced generally peaceful conditions in their northern
Indian heartland. Nevertheless, they were capable of
squandering immense amounts of blood and treasure to
subdue Hindu kings and rebels in the Deccan region or
Afghans on their western frontier (see Map 21.1).

Foreign trade boomed at the port of Surat in the
northwest, which also served as an embarkation point
for pilgrims on their way to Mecca. Like the Safavids, the
Mughals had no navy or merchant ships. The government saw the Europeans—now primarily Dutch and English, the Portuguese having lost most of their Indian
ports—less as enemies than as shipmasters whose naval
support could be procured as needed in return for trading privileges. It never questioned the wisdom of selling
Indian cottons for European coin—no one understood
how cheap silver had become in Europe—and shipping
them off to European customers in English and Dutch
vessels.

Babur (BAH-bur)

Delhi (DEL-ee)   *mansabs* (MAN-sabz)

Indian Merchants in Russia

Overland commerce through Central Asia continued throughout this period. Few traders from eastern lands reached western Europe, but trading missions from India visited Russia, and a small but important colony of Indian merchants developed in Astrakhan, at the mouth of the Volga River, where they dealt primarily in cotton and silk cloth.

In 1675, Indian merchants in Moscow informed Russian officials that:

In the Indian state the highest demand for Russian goods is for high-priced sables—10, 20, 30 roubles a pair, good, red broad cloth and green broad cloth, red leather, walrus teeth, coral, large middle sized and small mirrors, gold and silver velvet and Turkish velvet. . . . And the Indian rulers love Borzoi dogs. (p. 91)

One Indian merchant of Astrakhan, Marwar Bara, wrote in 1735:

Previously there were favorable conditions for trade from India to Russia and merchants comfortably went [abroad]. Each year about two hundred exported . . . goods, and then when disturbances occurred in Persia and passage became difficult because of robbers the number of merchants declined year by year. Now exceedingly few came, less than eighty. (p. 128)

Nevertheless, in 1777 the Russian governor of Astrakhan complained:

It is not a secret that they, the Indians, having trade with Russian subjects, attempt, in exchange for Russian money and for goods, to receive Russian silver money, and especially heavy silver of the best kind with the portrait of Peter the Great. . . . Silver is in short supply in Russia and is aggravated by these noncitizens, the Indians. (p. 111)

How do the circumstances of Indian traders in Russia compare with those of Europeans in India? How do the goods exchanged between India and Russia compare with goods exchanged across the Indian Ocean?

Source: Stephen Frederic Dale, *Indian Merchants and Eurasian Trade, 1600–1750* (Cambridge: Cambridge University Press, 1994).

Hindus and Muslims

India had not been dominated by a single ruler since the time of Harsha Vardhana (r. 606–647). Hindus were horrified by Muslim destruction of Hindu cultural monuments, the expansion of Muslim territory, and the practice, until Akbar's time, of enslaving prisoners of war and compelling them to convert to Islam. But Hindu efforts to oppose Muslim rule were piecemeal rather than concerted. The Mughal state, in contrast, inherited traditions of unified imperial rule both from the Islamic caliphate and from the more recent examples of Genghis Khan and Timur.

Those Mongol-based traditions did not necessarily mean religious intolerance. Seventy percent of the *mansabdars*° (officials holding land revenues) appointed under Akbar were Muslim soldiers born outside India, but 15 percent were Hindus. Most of the Hindu appointees were warriors from the north called **Rajputs**°, one of whom rose to be a powerful revenue minister. Their status as mansabdars was a manifestation of the policy of religious accommodation adopted by Akbar and his successors.

Akbar was the most illustrious ruler of his dynasty. He differed from his Ottoman and Safavid counterparts—Suleiman the Magnificent and Shah Abbas the Great—in his striving for social harmony and not just for more territory and revenue. He succeeded to the throne at the age of thirteen, and his actions at first were dominated by a regent and then by his strong-minded childhood nurse. At the age of twenty, he took command of the government. He married a Rajput princess, whose name is not recorded, and welcomed her father and brother to the court in Agra.

---

mansabdars (man-sab-DAHRZ)

Rajputs (RAHJ-putz)

Other rulers might have used such a marriage as a means of humiliating a subject group. But Akbar signaled by this marriage his desire for reconciliation and even intermarriage between Muslims and Hindus. A year later he rescinded the head tax that Muslim rulers traditionally levied on tolerated non-Muslims. This measure was more symbolic than real because the tax had not been regularly collected, but the gesture helped cement the allegiance of the Rajputs.

Akbar longed for an heir. Much to his relief, his Rajput wife gave birth to a son in 1569, ensuring that future rulers would have both Muslim and Hindu ancestry.

Akbar ruled that in legal disputes between two Hindus, decisions would be made according to village custom or Hindu law as interpreted by local Hindu scholars. Shari'a law was in force for Muslims. Akbar made himself the legal court of last resort in a 1579 declaration that he was God's infallible earthly representative. Thus appeals could be made to Akbar personally, a possibility not usually present in Islamic jurisprudence.

Akbar also made himself the center of a new "Divine Faith" incorporating Muslim, Hindu, Zoroastrian, Sikh°, and Christian beliefs. He was strongly attracted by Sufi ideas, which permeated the religious rituals he instituted at his court. To promote serious consideration of his religious principles, he oversaw, from a catwalk high above the audience, debates among scholars of all religions assembled in his octagonal private audience chamber. When courtiers uttered the Muslim exclamation "Allahu Akbar"—"God is great"—they also understood it in its second grammatical meaning: "God is Akbar." Akbar's religious views did not survive him, but the court culture he fostered, reflecting a mixture of Muslim and Hindu traditions, flourished until his zealous great-grandson Aurangzeb° (r. 1658–1707) reinstituted many restrictions on Hindus.

Mughal and Rajput miniature paintings reveled in precise portraits of political figures and depictions of scantily clad women, even though they brought frowns to the faces of pious Muslims, who deplored the representation of human beings in art. Most of the leading painters were Hindus. In poetry, in addition to the florid style of Persian verse favored at court, a new taste developed for poetry and prose in the popular language of the Delhi region. The Turkish word *ordu,* meaning "army," led to the modern descendant of this language being called *Urdu* in Pakistan (in India it is called *Hindi*).

Akbar's policy of toleration does not explain the pattern of conversion to Islam in Mughal India. Some scholars maintain that most converts came from members of the lowest Hindu social groups, or castes, who hoped to improve their lot in life, but there is little data to confirm this theory. Others argue that Sufi brotherhoods, which developed strongly in India, led the way in converting people to Islam, but this proposition has not been proved. The most heavily Muslim regions were in the valley of the Indus River and east Bengal. The Indus center dates from the establishment of Muslim rule there as early as the eighth century.

A careful study of local records and traditions from east Bengal indicates that the eastward movement of the delta of the Ganges River and the spread of rice cultivation into forest clearings played the primary role in conversions to Islam there. Mansabdars (mostly Muslims) with land grants in east Bengal contracted with local entrepreneurs to collect a labor force, cut down the forest, and establish rice paddies. Some of the entrepreneurs were Hindus, but most were non-Sufi Muslim religious figures. Like the Hindus, those Muslims used religion, represented by the construction of mosques and shrines, as a cement to maintain their farming communities. Most natives of the region were accustomed to worshiping local forest deities rather than the main Hindu gods. So the shift to Islam represented a move to a more sophisticated, literate culture appropriate to their new status as farmers producing for the commercial rice market. Gradual religious change of this kind often produced Muslim communities whose social customs differed little from those in neighboring Hindu communities. In east Bengal, common Muslim social institutions, such as madrasas, the ulama, and law courts, were little in evidence.

Another change in Indian religious life in the Mughal period was the appearance of **Sikhism** in the Punjab region of northwest India. Nanak (1469–1539), the religion's first *guru* (spiritual teacher), stressed meditation as a means of seeking enlightenment and drew from both Muslim and Hindu imagery in his teachings. His followers formed a single community without differences of caste. However, after Aurangzeb ordered the ninth guru beheaded in 1675 for refusing to convert to Islam, the tenth and final guru dedicated himself to avenging his father's death and reorganized his followers into "the army of the pure," a religious order dedicated to defending Sikh beliefs. These devotees signaled their faith by leaving their hair uncut; carrying a comb, a steel bracelet, and a sword or dagger; and wearing military-style breeches. By the eighteenth century, the Mughals were encountering fierce opposition from the Sikhs as well as from Hindu guerrilla forces in the rugged and ravine-scarred province of Maharashtra on India's west coast.

Sikh (sick) **Aurangzeb** (ow-rang-ZEB)

Central Decay and Regional Challenges 1707–1761

Mughal power did not long survive Aurangzeb's death in 1707. Some historians consider the land-grant system a central element in the rapid decline of imperial authority, but other factors were at play as well. Aurangzeb's additions to Mughal territory in southern India were not all well integrated into the imperial structure, and a number of strong regional powers arose to challenge Mughal military supremacy. The Marathas proved a formidable enemy as they carved out a swath of territory across India's middle, and Sikhs, Hindu Rajputs, and Muslim Afghans exerted intense pressure from the northwest. A climax came in 1739 when Nadir Shah, the warlord who had seized power in Iran after the fall of the Safavids, invaded the subcontinent and sacked Delhi, which Akbar's grandson had rebuilt and beautified as the Mughal capital some decades before. The "peacock throne," the priceless, jewel-encrusted symbol of Mughal gandeur, was carried off to Iran as part of the booty. Another throne was found for the later Mughals to sit on; but their empire, which survived in name to 1857, was finished.

In 1723, Nizam al-Mulk°, the powerful vizier of the Mughal sultan, gave up on the central government and established his own nearly independent state at Hyderabad in the eastern Deccan. Other officials bearing the title *nawab*°, Anglicized as "nabob," became similarly independent in Bengal and Oudh° in the northeast, as did the Marathas farther west. In the northwest, simultaneous Iranian and Mughal weakness allowed the Afghans to establish an independent kingdom.

Some of these regional powers, and the smaller princely states that arose on former Mughal territory, were prosperous and benefited from the removal of the sultan's heavy hand. Linguistic and religious communities, freed from the religious intolerance instituted during the reign of Aurangzeb, similarly enjoyed greater opportunity for political expression. However, this disintegration of central power favored the intrusion of European adventurers.

Joseph François Dupleix° took over the presidency of the French stronghold of Pondicherry° in 1741 and began a new phase of European involvement in India. He captured the English trading center of Madras and used his small contingent of European and European-trained Indian troops to become a power broker in southern India. Though offered the title *nawab,* Dupleix preferred to

operate behind the scenes, using Indian princes as puppets. His career ended in 1754 when he was called home. Deeply involved in wars in Europe, the French government was unwilling to pursue further adventures in India. Dupleix's departure opened the way for the British, whose ventures in India are described in Chapter 26.

Trade Empires in the Indian Ocean, 1600–1729

It is no coincidence that the Mughal, Safavid, and Ottoman Empires declined simultaneously in the seventeenth and eighteenth centuries. Complex changes in military technology and in the world economy, along with the increasing difficulty of basing an extensive land empire on military forces paid through land grants, affected them all adversely. The opposite was true for seafaring countries intent on turning trade networks into maritime empires. Improvements in ship design, navigation accuracy, and the use of cannon gave an ever-increasing edge to European powers competing with local seafaring peoples. Moreover, the development of joint-stock companies in which many merchants pooled their capital provided a flexible and efficient financial instrument for exploiting new possibilities. The English East India Company was founded in 1600, the Dutch East India Company in 1602.

Although the Ottomans, Safavids, and the Mughals did not seriously contest the growth of Portuguese and then Dutch, English, and French maritime power, the majority of non-European shipbuilders, captains, sailors, and traders were Muslim. Groups of Armenian, Jewish, and Hindu traders were also active, but they remained almost as aloof from the Europeans as the Muslims did. The presence in every port of Muslims following the same legal traditions and practicing their faith in similar ways cemented the Muslims' trading network. Islam, from its very outset in the life and preachings of Muhammad (570–632), was always congenial to trade and traders. Unlike Hinduism, it was a proselytizing religion, a factor that encouraged the growth of coastal Muslim communities as local non-Muslims were drawn into Muslim commercial activities, converted, and intermarried with Muslims from abroad.

Although European missionaries, particularly the Jesuits, tried to extend Christianity into Asia and Africa

Nizam al-Mulk (nee-ZAHM al-MULK)   *nawab* (NAH-wab)
Oudh (OW-ad)   Dupleix (doo-PLAY)
Pondicherry (pon-dir-CHEH-ree)

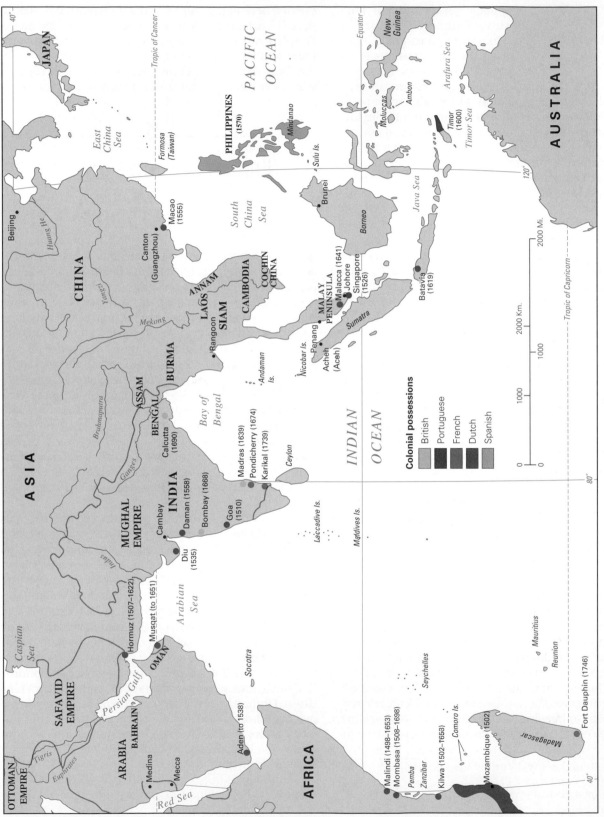

Map 21.2   European Colonization in the Indian Ocean to 1750   Since Portuguese explorers were the first Europeans to reach India by rounding Africa, Portugal gained a strong foothold in both areas. Rival Spain was barred from colonizing the region by the Treaty of Tordesillas in 1494, which limited Spanish efforts to lands west of a line drawn through the mid-Atlantic Ocean. The line carried around the globe provided justification of Spanish colonization in the Philippines. French, British, and Dutch colonies date from after 1600 when joint stock companies provided a new stimulus for overseas commerce.

(see Chapters 17 and 22), most Europeans, the Portuguese excepted, were less inclined than the Muslims were to treat local converts or the offspring of mixed marriages as full members of their communities. As a consequence, Islam spread extensively into East Africa and Southeast Asia during precisely the time of rapid European commercial expansion. Even without the support of the Muslim land empires, Islam became a source of resistance to growing European domination.

Muslims in the East Indies

Historians disagree about the chronology and manner of Islam's spread in Southeast Asia. Arab traders were well known in southern China as early as the eighth century, so Muslims probably reached the East Indies at a similarly early date. Nevertheless, the dominance of Indian cultural influences in the area for several centuries thereafter indicates that early Muslim visitors had little impact on local beliefs. Clearer indications of conversion and the formation of Muslim communities date from roughly the fourteenth century. The strongest overseas linkage is to the port of Cambay in India (see Map 21.2) rather than to the Arab world. Islam took root first in port cities and in some royal courts and spread inland slowly, possibly transmitted by itinerant Sufis.

Although appeals to the Ottoman sultan for support against the Europeans ultimately proved of little use, Islam as a political ideology strengthened resistance to Portuguese, Spanish, and Dutch intruders. When the Spaniards conquered the Philippines during the decades following the establishment of their first fort in 1565 (see Chapter 17), they encountered Muslims on the southern island of Mindanao° and the nearby Sulu archipelago. They called them "Moros," the Spanish term for their old enemies, the Muslims of North Africa. In the ensuing Moro wars, the Spaniards portrayed the Moros as greedy pirates who raided non-Muslim territories for slaves. In fact, they were political, religious, and commercial competitors whose perseverance enabled them to establish the Sulu Empire based in the southern Philippines, one of the strongest states in Southeast Asia from 1768 to 1848.

Other local kingdoms that looked on Islam as a force to counter the aggressive Christianity of the Europeans included the actively proselytizing Brunei° Sultanate in northern Borneo and the **Acheh° Sultanate** in northern Sumatra. At its peak in the early seventeenth century, Acheh succeeded Malacca as the main center of Islamic expansion in Southeast Asia. It prospered from trade in pepper and cotton cloth from Gujarat in India. Acheh declined after the Dutch seized Malacca from Portugal in 1641.

How well Islam was understood in these Muslim kingdoms is open to question. In Acheh, for example, a series of women ruled between 1641 and 1699. This practice came to an end when local Muslim scholars obtained a ruling from scholars in Mecca and Medina that Islam did not approve of female rulers. This ruling became a turning point after which scholarly understandings of Islam gained greater prominence in the East Indies.

Historians have theorized that the first propagators of Islam in Southeast Asia were merchants, Sufi preachers, or both. The scholarly vision of Islam, however, took root in the sixteenth century by way of pilgrims returning from years of study in Mecca and Medina. Islam was the primary force in the dissemination of writing in the region. Some of the returning pilgrims wrote in Arabic, others in Malay or Javanese. As Islam continued to spread, *adat,* a form of Islam rooted in pre-Muslim religious and social practices, retained its preeminence in rural areas over practices centered on the Shari'a, the religious law. But the royal courts in the port cities began to heed the views of the pilgrim teachers, as in their condemnation of female rulers. Though different in many ways, both varieties of Islam provided believers with a firm basis of identification in the face of the growing European presence. Christian missionaries gained most of their converts in regions that had not yet converted to Islam, such as the northern Philippines.

Muslims in East Africa

The East African ports that the Portuguese began to visit in the fifteenth century were governed by Muslim rulers but were not linked politically (see Map 21.2). People living in the millet and rice lands of the Swahili Coast—from the Arabic *sawahil°* meaning "coasts"—had little contact with those in the dry hinterlands. Throughout this period, the East African lakes region and the highlands of Kenya witnessed unprecedented migration and relocation of peoples because of drought conditions that persisted from the late sixteenth through most of the seventeenth century.

Cooperation among the trading ports of Kilwa, Mombasa, and Malindi was hindered by the thick bush country that separated the cultivated tracts of coastal

Mindanao (min-duh-NOW)   Brunei (BROO-nie)
Acheh (AH-cheh)

sawahil (suh-WAH-hil)

Portuguese Fort Guarding Musqat Harbor   Musqat in Oman and Aden in Yemen, the best harbors in southern Arabia, were targets for imperial navies trying to establish dominance in the Indian Ocean. Mosqat's harbor is small and circular with one narrow entrance overlooked by this fortress. The palace of the sultan of Oman is still located at the opposite end of the harbor. (Robert Harding Picture Library)

land and by the fact that the ports competed with one another in the export of ivory; ambergris° (a whale byproduct used in perfumes); and forest products such as beeswax, copal tree resin, and wood (Kilwa also exported gold). In the eighteenth century, slave trading, primarily to Arabian ports but also to India, increased in importance. Because Europeans—the only peoples who kept consistent records of slave-trading activities—played a minor role in this slave trade, few records have survived to indicate its extent. Perhaps the best estimate is that 2.1 million slaves were exported between 1500 and 1890, a little over 12.5 percent of the total traffic in African slaves during that period (see Chapter 20).

The Portuguese conquered all of the coastal ports from Mozambique northward except Malindi, with whose ruler Portugal cooperated. A Portuguese description of the ruler indicates some of the cloth and metal goods that Malindi imported, as well as some local manufactures:

> The King wore a robe of damask trimmed with green satin and a rich [cap]. He was seated on two cushioned chairs of bronze, beneath a rough sunshade of crimson satin attached to a pole. An old man, who attended him as a page, carried a short sword in a silver sheath. There were many players on [horns], and two trumpets of ivory richly carved and of the size of a man, which were blown through a hole in the side, and made sweet harmony with the [horns].[4]

Initially, the Portuguese favored the port of Malindi, which caused the decline of Kilwa and Mombasa. Repeatedly plagued by local rebellion, Portuguese power suffered severe blows when the Arabs of **Oman** in southeastern Arabia captured their south Arabian stronghold at Musqat (1650) and then went on in support of African resistance to seize Mombasa (1698), which had become the Portuguese capital in East Africa. The Portuguese briefly retook Mombasa but lost control permanently in 1729. From then on, the Portuguese had to content themselves with Mozambique in Africa and a few remaining ports in India (Goa) and farther east (Macao and Timor).

The Omanis created a maritime empire of their own, but one that worked in greater cooperation with the African populations. The Bantu language of the coast, broadened by the absorption of Arabic, Persian, and Portuguese loanwords, developed into **Swahili**°, which was spoken throughout the region. Arabs and other Muslims who settled in the region intermarried with local families, giving rise to a mixed population that played an important role in developing a distinctive Swahili culture.

Islam also spread in the southern Sudan in this period, particularly in the dry areas away from the Nile River. This growth coincided with a waning of Ethiopian power as a result of Portugal's stifling of trade in the Red Sea. Yet no significant contact developed between the emerging Muslim Swahili culture and that of the Muslims in the Sudan, to the north.

---

ambergris (AM-ber-grees)

Swahili (swah-HEE-lee)

The Coming of the Dutch

The Dutch played a major role in driving the Portuguese from their possessions in the East Indies. They were better organized than the Portuguese through the Dutch East India Company (see Chapter 20). Just as the Portuguese had tried to dominate the trade in spices, so the Dutch concentrated at first on the spice-producing islands of Southeast Asia. The Portuguese had seized Malacca, a strategic town on the narrow strait at the end of the Malay Peninsula, from a local Malay ruler in 1511 (see Chapter 17). The Dutch took it away from them in 1641, leaving Portugal little foothold in the East Indies except the islands of Ambon° and Timor (see Map 21.2).

Although the United Netherlands was one of the least autocratic countries of Europe, the governors-general appointed by the Dutch East India Company deployed almost unlimited powers in their efforts to maintain their trade monopoly. They could even order the execution of their own employees for "smuggling"—that is, trading on their own. Under strong governors-general, the Dutch fought a series of wars against Acheh and other local kingdoms on Sumatra and Java. In 1628 and 1629, their new capital at **Batavia,** now the city of Jakarta on Java, was besieged by a fleet of fifty ships belonging to the sultan of Mataram°, a Javanese kingdom. The Dutch held out with difficulty and eventually prevailed when the sultan was unable to get effective help from the English.

Suppressing local rulers, however, was not enough to control the spice trade once other European countries adopted Dutch methods, became more knowledgeable about where goods might be acquired, and started to send more ships to Southeast Asia. In the course of the eighteenth century, therefore, the Dutch gradually turned from being a middleman for Southeast Asian producers and European buyers to being a producer of crops in areas they controlled, notably in Java. Javanese teak forests yielded high-quality lumber, and coffee, transplanted from Yemen, grew well in the hilly regions of western Java. In this new phase of colonial export production, Batavia developed from being the headquarters town of a far-flung enterprise to being the administrative capital of a conquered land.

Beyond the East Indies, the Dutch utilized their discovery of a band of powerful eastward-blowing winds (called the "Roaring Forties" because they blow throughout the year between 40 and 50 degrees south latitude) to reach Australia in 1606. In 1642 and 1643 Abel Tasman became the first European to set foot on Tasmania and New Zealand and to sail around Australia, signaling European involvement in that region (see Chapter 26).

Ambon (am-BOHN)　Mataram (MAH-tah-ram)

CONCLUSION

That a major shift in world economic and political alignments was well under way by the late seventeenth century was scarcely perceivable in those parts of Asia and Africa ruled by the Ottoman and Mughal sultans and the Safavid shahs. They focused their efforts on conquering more and more land, sometimes at the expense of Christian Europe or Hindu India, but also at one another's expense since the Sunni-Shi'ite division justified Iranian attacks on its neighbors and vice versa.

To be sure, more and more trade was being carried in European vessels, particularly after the advent of joint-stock companies in 1600; and Europeans had enclaves in a handful of port cities and islands. But the age-old tradition of Asia was that imperial wealth came from control of broad expanses of agricultural land. Except in the case of state monopolies, such as Iranian silk, governments did not greatly concern themselves with what farmers planted. They relied mostly on land taxes, usually indirectly collected via holders of land-grants or tax farmers, rather than on customs duties or control of markets to fill the government coffers.

With ever-increasing military expenditures, these taxes fell short of the rulers' needs. Few people realized, however, that this was a problem basic to the entire economic system rather than a temporary revenue shortfall. Imperial courtiers pursued their luxurious ways, poetry and the arts continued to flourish, and the quality of manufacturing and craft production remained generally high. Eighteenth century European observers, luxuriating in the prosperity gained from their ever increasing control of the Indian Ocean, marvelled no less at the riches and industry of these eastern lands than at the fundamental weakness of their political and military systems.

■ Key Terms

Ottoman Empire	Mughal Empire
Suleiman the Magnificent	Akbar
Janissary	*mansabs*
devshirme	Rajputs
Tulip Period	Sikhism
Safavid Empire	Acheh Sultanate
Shi'ite Islam	Oman
Hidden Imam	Swahili
Shah Abbas I	Batavia

■ Suggested Reading

The best comprehensive and comparative account of the post-Mongol Islamic land empires, with an emphasis on social history, is Ira Lapidus, *A History of Islamic Societies* (1988). For a work of similar scope concentrating on intellectual history see Marshall G. S. Hodgson, *The Venture of Islam*, vol. 3, *The Gunpowder Empires and Modern Times* (1974).

Ottoman origins are well covered in Cemal Kafadar, *Between Two Worlds* (1995). On the Ottoman Empire, the standard political history is Stanford J. Shaw, *History of the Ottoman Empire and Modern Turkey*, vol. 1, *Empire of the Ghazis: The Rise and Decline of the Ottoman Empire, 1280–1808* (1976). Jason Goodwin, *Lords of the Horizons: A History of the Ottoman Empire* (1999), offers a more readable and journalistic account. For a collection of articles on nonpolitical matters see Halil Inalcik and Donald Quataert, eds., *An Economic and Social History of the Ottoman Empire, 1300—1914* (1994).

The world's foremost Ottoman historian, Halil Inalcik, analyzes the history and structure of the empire in *The Ottoman Empire: The Classical Age, 1300–1600* (1989). For a sociological analysis of change in the seventeenth century see Karen Barkey, *Bandits and Bureaucrats* (1994).

Among the specialized studies of cities and regions that give a good sense of some of the major changes in Ottoman society and economy after the sixteenth century are Daniel Goffman, *Izmir and the Levantine World, 1550–1650* (1990); Abraham Marcus, *The Middle East on the Eve of Modernity: Aleppo in the Eighteenth Century* (1989); and Bruce McGowan, *Economic Life in the Ottoman Empire: Taxation, Trade, and the Struggle for Land, 1600–1800* (1981).

Questions relating to religious minorities in the Ottoman Empire are best covered by the articles in Benjamin Braude and Bernard Lewis, eds., *Christians and Jews in the Ottoman Empire: The Functioning of a Plural Society* (1982). The role of women in the governance of the empire is skillfully treated by Leslie Pierce, *The Imperial Harem: Women and Sovereignty in the Ottoman Empire* (1993). Ralph S. Hattox, *Coffee and Coffeehouses: The Origins of a Social Beverage in the Medieval Near East* (1988), is an excellent contribution to Ottoman social history.

The most comprehensive treatment of the history of Safavid Iran is in the articles in Peter Jackson and Laurence Lockhart, eds., *The Cambridge History of Iran*, vol. 6, *The Timurid and Safavid Periods* (1986). The articles by Hans Roemer in this volume provide the best political narratives of the pre-Safavid and Safavid periods. Roger Savory's important article on the structure of the Safavid state is available in a more extensive form in his *Iran Under the Safavids* (1980).

For the artistic side of Safavid history, abundantly illustrated, see Anthony Welch, *Shah Abbas and the Arts of Isfahan* (1973). Said Amir Arjomand, *The Shadow of God and the Hidden Imam: Religion, Political Order, and Societal Change in Shiite Iran from the Beginning to 1890* (1984), contains the best analysis of the complicated relationship between Shi'ism and monarchy. Safavid economic history is not well developed, but useful studies have been published by Ann K. S. Lambton, *Landlord and Peasant in Persia: A Study of Land Tenure and Land Revenue Administration*, rev. ed. (1991), and Mehdi Keyvani, *Artisans and Guild Life in the Later Safavid Period: Contribution to the Social-Economic History of Persia* (1982).

A highly readable work that situates the Mughal Empire within the overall history of the subcontinent is Stanley Wolpert, *A New History of India*, 4th ed. (1993). For a broad treatment of the entire development of Islamic society in India with emphasis on the Mughal period see S. M. Ikram, *History of Muslim Civilization in India and Pakistan* (1989). Wheeler Thackston has made a lively translation of Babur's autobiography in *The Baburnama: Memoirs of Babur, Prince and Emperor* (1996). For a comprehensive history of the Mughals see John F. Richards, *The Mughal Empire* (1993). Irfan Habib has edited an extensive collection of articles on the Mughal Empire in its prime entitled *Akbar and His India* (1997). For the history of the Sikhs see W. H. McLeod *The Sikhs: History, Religion, and Society* (1989). Two specialized works on the economic and trading history of India are Ashin Das Gupta and M. N. Pearson, eds., *India and the Indian Ocean, 1500–1800* (1987), and Stephen Frederic Dale, *Indian Merchants and Eurasian Trade, 1600–1750* (1994).

The history of East Africa in this period is not well documented, but B. A. Ogot, ed., *UNESCO General History of Africa*, vol. 5, *Africa from the Sixteenth to the Eighteenth Century* (1992), provides a useful collection of articles. See also Tom Spear *The Swahili*, (1984) and James de Vere Allen, *Swahili Origins* (1993).

For a brief, general introduction to the relations between the Muslim land empires and the development of Indian Ocean trade see Patricia Risso, *Merchants and Faith: Muslim Commerce and Culture in the Indian Ocean* (1995). Esmond Bradley Martin and Chryssee Perry Martin have written a popular and well-illustrated work on the western Indian Ocean entitled *Cargoes of the East: The Ports, Trade and Culture of the Arabian Seas and Western Indian Ocean* (1978). C. R. Boxer, *The Dutch Seaborne Empire, 1600–1800* (1973), is a classic account of all aspects of Dutch maritime expansion.

■ Notes

1. Quoted in Sarah Searight, *The British in the Middle East* (New York: Atheneum 1970), 36.
2. Daniel Goffman, *Izmir and the Levantine World, 1550–1650* (Seattle: University of Washington Press, 1990), 52.
3. Quoted in Peter Jackson and Laurence Lockhart, eds., *The Cambridge History of Iran*, vol. 6, *The Timurid and Safavid Periods* (New York: Cambridge University Press, 1986), 703.
4. Esmond Bradley Martin and Chryssee Perry Martin, *Cargoes of the East: The Ports, Trade and Culture of the Arabian Seas and Western Indian Ocean* (1978), 17.

22

EASTERN EURASIA,
1500–1800

New Patterns of Contact in Eurasia • The Triumph of the Russian Empire •
The Late Ming and Early Qing Empires, 1500–1800 • Decentralization and
Innovation in Tokugawa Japan, to 1800
ENVIRONMENT AND TECHNOLOGY: Women and Tokugawa Technology
SOCIETY AND CULTURE: Style and Conversion: Christian Rivalries in Beijing

Russian Ambassadors to Holland Display Their Furs, 1500s Representatives from Muscovy impressed
the court of the German prince Maximillian II of Regensburg with their sable coats and caps.

In the 1650s, two enormous and expanding empires battled for control of Siberia, the Amur° River basin, and the Pacific coast of northern Asia. Hardy Russian scouts, mostly Cossacks, came east across the tundra, hoping to stake an early claim to the great Amur waterway. They built wooden forts on its northern bank, but they were countered by Manchu agents of the Qing° Empire based in China, which hoped to secure Qing territories north of Korea and to secure the same stretch of Pacific coast the Russians sought. The Manchus built wooden forts on the southern bank of the Amur.

Neither empire sent large forces into the Amur territories, and the contest was mostly a struggle for the goodwill of the local Evenk and Dagur peoples. The Qing emperor emphasized the importance of treading lightly in the struggle and well understood the principles of espionage:

> Upon reaching the lands of the Evenks and the Dagurs you will send to announce that you have come to hunt deer. Meanwhile, keep a careful record of the distance and go, while hunting, along the northern bank of the Amur until you come by the shortest route to the town of Russian settlement at Albazin. Thoroughly reconnoitre its location and situation. I don't think the Russians will take a chance on attacking you. If they offer you food, accept it and show your gratitude. If they do attack you, don't fight back. In that case, lead your people and withdraw into our own territories. For I have a plan of my own.[1]

That delicacy gives a false impression of the intensity of the struggle between these two great empires. The contest was partly for dominance in the new northeast Asian economy of furs, timber, and metals concentrated in Siberia, Manchuria, and Yakutsk. But even without the attraction of those specific resources, the Amur River would have been critical in the interplay of the two empires, because each had an overriding need to protect itself against the other. The kingdoms of Europe, and even Europe's emerging sea-based empires, were small in territory and weak in economic influence in comparison with these titanic Eurasian empires.

Where the Russian and Qing Empires faced each other—in Central Asia, in Mongolia, and in Northeast Asia—they had to expend great resources conquering and defending lands that in the long run yielded very little profit. But for either to have flinched would have meant disaster at the hands of the other.

In 1689, the Qing and Russian Empires formalized their stand-off with a treaty establishing a border and a set of customs regulations. Russia was denied access to the Pacific coast east of the Amur, but the Russians exploited a more northerly route to explore the North Pacific and colonize the northwestern coast of North America. The Russian and Qing Empires still sought ways around each other but apparently were evenly matched. Only the intrusion of the smaller, product-poor empires of Europe eventually upset the balance and permitted one of the Eurasian giants to outflank the other.

The Russian and Qing Empires were part of a regional power system in which size, agriculture, and infrastructure for overland communication and transport were of the greatest importance. In their struggle to maintain their power when challenged by the new empires of Europe, the Russian and Qing Empires faced common problems and experienced similar outcomes. The response of Japan was spectacularly different. That small, relatively remote nation had been a minor player in Asian affairs but was able to withstand economic and political changes more effectively than Asia's greatest empires.

As you read this chapter, ask yourself the following questions:

- What did the Russian and Qing Empires have in common? How do their similarities explain the tensions between them?

- What were the Russian and Qing attitudes toward Europe in the times of Peter the Great and Emperor Kangxi? What were the long-term consequences of these attitudes?

- What explains the comparative speed of Japanese economic and technological development in the 1700s?

Amur (AH-moor)   **Qing** (ching)

CHRONOLOGY

	Russia	China and Central Asia	Korea and Japan
1500	**1547** Ivan IV tsar		
	1582 Cossacks conquer Khanate of Sibir		**1582** Japanese invasion of Korea
1600		**1601** Matteo Ricci active in Ming China	**1600** Decisive battle begins Tokugawa Shogunate
	1613–1645 Rule of Mikhail, the first Romanov tsar	**1644** Qing conquest of Beijing	**1649** Closing of Japan
		1662–1722 Rule of Emperor Kangxi	
	1689–1725 Rule of Peter the Great	**1689** Treaty of Nerchinsk with Russia	
1700		**1691** Qing control of Inner Mongolia	**1702** Trial of the Forty-seven Ronin
	1712 St. Petersburg becomes Russia's capital	**1736–1795** Rule of Emperor Qianlong	
		1755 Qing conquest of Turkestan	
	1762–1796 Rule of Catherine the Great		**1792** Russian ships first spotted off the coast of Japan
	1799 Alaska becomes a Russian colony		

NEW PATTERNS OF CONTACT IN EURASIA

Between 1500 and 1800 several fundamental factors transformed the routes of contact and commerce in Eurasia. During the period of Mongol domination of Eurasia in the thirteenth century, overland trade connecting Iran, southern Russia, and China had thrived. But the Ming rulers, who came to power in China in 1368, did not control Central Asia as the Mongols had done. Instead, local leaders in Central Asia fought for dominance over the trading routes and commercial centers. After 1500, no single power controlled all of Central Asia, and no unified economic policy protected and promoted trade. Large and ambitious empires based in the Middle East, in Russia, and in China competed for control of parts of Central Asia, and this competition deepened their conflicts with the remaining Mongol groups and further depressed both travel and profitable trade.

Samarkand°, Bukhara°, Kashgar° and other oasis cities that had been rich and cosmopolitan in the days when overland trade was vigorous became isolated. Their governors were often hostile to outside influences. As the 1500s passed, the transporting of many goods by caravan between East Asia and the Middle East was neither cheap nor reliable.

The troubles afflicting Central Asia in this period might have been overcome in the interests of profitable trade, but a new venue of commerce had opened: Along the southern and eastern coasts of Eurasia, merchants from Europe, the Middle East, and Asia were taking advantage of the new global trade connections. Seaborne trade was now cheaper, faster, and more reliable than overland trade. Goods once transported across the interior of Eurasia could be moved more efficiently around its edges, and many new goods were available from the sea-connected economies.

Samarkand (SAM-mar-kahnd)   **Bukhara** (boo-CAR-ruh)
Kashgar (kahsh-gar)

Ancient Asian ports that had become rich from centuries of trade found new economic stimulation from the development of European commerce. China, and later Japan, were also beneficiaries of this new trade in the old ports. And after 1700, the development of a global commercial interest in the Pacific magnified the importance of the sea and control of its main trade routes. China, Japan, and other coastal economies of East Asia participated in the trade and sought means of cushioning the effects of globalization on their own economies and societies. Russia, in contrast, had to enter a period of renewed and more militant expansion or risk being left out of the Pacific trade.

The Land-Based Empires of Eurasia

The Portuguese, Spanish, and Dutch Empires relied on the sea for contact with their colonies. As relatively small empires, they had few major strategic worries and could exercise a wide range of options in their territorial roamings and commercial and military activities. For the Ottoman, Russian, Mughal, and Ming Empires, things were very different. They were land-based empires and much larger than the sea-based empires of Europe. Their self-defense was extremely expensive, they had fewer choices than their smaller European contemporaries about where to expand and how to enrich themselves after they expanded.

Even though the commercial importance of Central Asia had declined steeply by 1500, the region remained the strategic center of gravity for the land-based Eurasian empires, because this was where each was most vulnerable to attack by an ambitious rival. Much of Central Asia, however, was arid steppes or desert, crossed by formidable mountain ranges. Maintaining garrisons in these regions was extremely expensive, for food, weapons, animals, and even building materials had to be brought in from far away. The best hope of eventually making these territories self-supporting lay in the development of agriculture and mining, which required the introduction of large-scale irrigation, crops able to thrive in cold, dry climates, extensive new roads, and large numbers of settlers or prisoners to serve as laborers. All the land-based empires achieved some success in agriculture and mining, but the costs were so steep that often there was no profit.

The challenge to make large, unprofitable areas in the land-based Eurasian empires self-supporting through environmental change strengthened two tendencies that were already strong. First, it reinforced the emphasis on agriculture as the predominant source of wealth and government tax revenues. Although these empires were interested in new industries and sea communications, they had little choice but to concentrate on agriculture. Second, it reinforced the tendency toward political centralization, which was to be important in the Russian and Qing Empires in the late 1600s. If the herculean task of environmental transformation across Central Asia and parts of northern Asia was to be achieved, imperial governments had to be in full command of the massive resources necessary for development of the infrastructure. Forced labor by the domestic population persisted in the Russian and Qing Empires after it was abandoned in Europe; in Russia serfdom became more brutal and widespread in the seventeenth and eighteenth centuries than ever before. Rulers and their advisers believed that the strategic concerns were so great that there could be no interference in policy-making from the aristocracy, low-level bureaucrats, or anyone else.

In the long run, these empires were at a disadvantage in the competition with the sea-based empires of Europe. The Europeans concentrated on the colonization of profitable areas, linked the development of commerce to the enrichment of their central governments, and enlisted the aid of joint-stock companies and other semiprivate organizations to acquire and develop territories. Between 1500 and about 1800, the land-based empires of Eurasia were the largest administrative and economic systems in the world, but they posed more of a danger to each other than they faced from any of the sea-based empires of Europe.

New Global Influences: The Society of Jesus and the East India Companies

The European entry into sea trade and communications that so challenged Russia and the Qing was not at first a project of empires or even of states. In the sixteenth and seventeenth centuries, new global organizations such as the Society of Jesus and the East India Companies created ties between Asia, Europe, and the Americas. The **Jesuits** often preceded traders, explorers, and conquerors to those regions that were newly known to Europe. One of the first Jesuits, Francis Xavier, went to India in the mid-sixteenth century looking for converts and later traveled throughout Southeast and East Asia. He spent two years in Japan and died in 1552 in China. Following Xavier, other Jesuits had a significant influence in China and presented to Europeans an intriguing picture of Asian life.

China reaped some material benefits from contact with the Jesuits. Chinese converts to Catholicism were important in introducing European techniques of crop

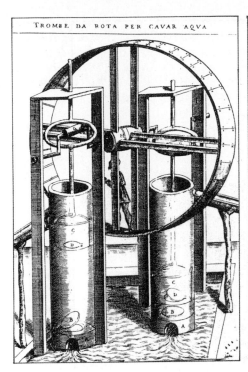

TROMBE DA ROTA PER CAVAR AQVA

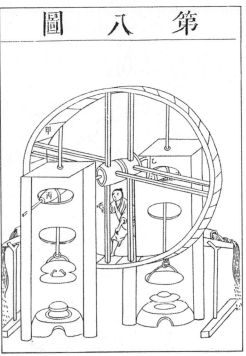

圖 八 第

production, irrigation, and engineering. The outstanding Jesuit of late Ming China, Matteo Ricci° (1552–1610), became expert in the Chinese language and an accomplished scholar of the Confucian classics. He and other Jesuits in China made a deep impression on the Ming elites at Beijing° and also in the wealthy, cosmopolitan cities of the Yangzi River delta and the southern China coast. Ricci himself was deeply affected by Chinese literature and philosophy. In his time and after, Jesuits remained important in transmitting to Europe knowledge of Chinese classical culture and translations of Chinese philosophical works. The high regard in which many European thinkers of the 1600s and early 1700s held the rulers of China was very much due to the activities of the Jesuits. The Society of Jesus was the most prominent transmitter of European science and technology to China, and of Chinese philosophy and literature to Europe.

European merchants arrived in East Asia by the time of the Jesuits arrival. First came the Portuguese, who after 1500 dominated the spice trade of the Moluccas and Java and the trade routes around India. The Spanish also were interested in the trade and established a small base on the island of Taiwan, off the coast of southeast China

(and not at the time part of the Ming Empire). Soon after 1600, the Dutch dislodged the Portuguese and Spanish from Taiwan. To secure their influence in East Asia and to discredit their rivals, representatives of the Dutch East India company (VOC) willingly complied with Chinese rituals by which foreigners were supposed to acknowledge the moral superiority of the emperor of China. They performed the ritual *kowtow* (in which the visitor knocked his head on the floor while crawling toward the throne) to the Ming emperor in China. The Dutch also got along well with the rulers of Japan and retained exclusive permission to live on the island of Deshima°, off Nagasaki°, after other Europeans were banned from the country. Outside Japan, however, the VOC faced a strong rival in the East India Company of England, chartered by Queen Elizabeth I in 1600.

The European trading companies and the Jesuits are examples of the global organizations that became conduits of trade and knowledge between Asia and Europe. The two-way communication that they made possible sparked enormous changes in how the opposite ends of Eurasia related to each other. But in the 1700s these organizations were viewed with suspicion by imperial authorities in Europe as well as in Asia.

Matteo Ricci (ma-TAY-o REE-chee) **Beijing** (bay-JING)   **Deshima** (DUH-shee-ma) **Nagasaki** (nah-gah-SAH-kee)

The Russian Empire

- Russia in 1533
- Russia in1598
- Russia in 1721
- Russia in 1796
- ■ Fort

PACIFIC
OCEAN

Novo Arkhangelsk
(Sitka)
TLINGIT

BRITISH NORTH AMERICA
(CANADA)

RUSSIAN
AMERICA
(ALASKA)

ALEUTS

INUIT

INUIT

INUIT

CHUKCHI

INUIT

KORYAKS

Bering
Sea

Bering

Strait

GREENLAND

ARCTIC
OCEAN

Petropavlovsk
ALEUTS
Kamchatka
Peninsula

Zashiversk

Okhotsk

Sea of
Okhotsk

Sakalin

Barents
Sea

Kara
Sea

Novaya Zemiya

S I B E R I A

Zhigansk   Yakutsk

EVENKI   YAKUTS   LAMUTS

EVENKI

SWEDEN

Arkhangelsk

FINLAND

St. Petersburg

Baltic
Sea

Riga

Novgorod

URAL MOUNTAINS

Obdorsk

SAMOYEDS

OSTYAKS

Surgut

TARTARS

Verkhoturye

TUNGUSY

OSTYAKS

Bratsk

Krasnoyarsk
Irkutsk

Nerchinsk

MANCHURIA

PRUSSIA

Moscow

Smolensk

POLAND

Nizhni
Novgorod

Kiev

UKRAINIANS

Saratov

Samara

COSSACKS

Biysk

Omsk

MONGOLIA

Q I N G
E M P I R E

AUSTRIA

COSSACKS

KAZAKS

OTTOMAN EMPIRE

Black Sea

GEORGIA

Aral
Sea

Caspian
Sea

AFGHANISTAN

PERSIA

TIBET

NEPAL

BHUTAN

BURMA

I N D I A

THE TRIUMPH OF THE RUSSIAN EMPIRE

The shift in intensity of exchange toward the seas and away from inland Asia presented both challenges and opportunities to the rising Russian Empire. The fragmentation of political power in Central Asia lessened the pressure on the Russian rulers to defend themselves on their southern border with Turkestan. Instead, they could turn their attention toward eastern Eurasia, including Mongolia and **Siberia,** and even to the Pacific coast. It was still necessary to maintain western and southern boundaries against the Ottoman Empire. But the rise of the European empires diminished this need somewhat, because the Europeans not only held the line against further Ottoman expansion in the Balkans but began to challenge and distract the Ottomans in the eastern Mediterranean.

The Rise of Romanov Power

After the dissolution of Mongol power in Russia, the city of Moscow became the foundation for a new state, **Muscovy°,** the territory surrounding the city of Moscow. By 1500, Muscovy was the dominant political force in the lands that had been controlled by the Kievan state. The process of unification forced by Muscovy was very difficult. By the mid-sixteenth century, Novgorod, which had been independent since the twelfth century and had maintained close connections with Sweden, was absorbed. To mark the extension of Muscovy and of his personal power, the Muscovite ruler Ivan IV ("the Terrible") assumed the title **tsar** (from "caesar") in 1547. Within a few years Ivan expanded Russia's borders far to the east through the conquest of the Khanates of Kazan and Astrakhan and the northern Caucausus region (see Map 22.1).

The westward extension of the territories ruled by Ivan IV and his successors did not progress much thereafter. Sweden and Poland, the dominant powers in northeastern Europe, prevented Russian expansion westward. Instead, Russia had to defend itself more strenuously on the European front. In the early seventeenth century Swedish and Polish forces briefly occupied Moscow on separate occasions, and Russian politics were rent by prolonged and deadly rivalries for the tsarship.

In the midst of this "Time of Troubles" the old line of Muscovite rulers was finally deposed, and the Russian aristocracy—the *boyars°*—allowed one of their own, **Mikhail Romanov°,** to become tsar (r. 1613–1645). But this dynastic change did not resolve the social and political tensions resulting from boyar resistance to further centralization of political power. Equally destabilizing were attacks from Sweden, Poland, and the Ottoman Empire.

The early Romanov rulers realized that consolidation of their own authority and successful competition with neighboring powers went together. Options for Russian expansion were limited. The Ottoman Empire controlled the Balkans, and the Safavid rulers of Iran dominated southern Central Asia. Trade with Europe was blocked as well because Sweden controlled the Baltic Sea, the Ottomans the Black Sea, and Iran the access to the surviving overland routes. As we will see, the obvious direction for expansion—east—provided the Russian Empire both its greatest possibilities for conquest and its greatest conflicts with old and new powers.

Russians and Turks

Most of the peoples who defined themselves as "Russian" during the Kievan period were speakers of a language closely related to other Slavic languages, and they tended to live as farmers, hunters, builders, scribes, or merchants. Surrounding Russia to the north, east, and parts of the south were speakers of Turkic languages who tended to live as herders, caravan workers, and soldiers. Language was not a solid defining line between peoples: Turkic-speakers had lived among Russian-speakers for centuries and in many instances were indistinguishable from Russians. Nevertheless, despite instances of cooperation, suspicion between Russian and Turkic peoples remained strong. Hostility increased when the Ottoman Empire emerged as a great power in the Caucasus and in the Balkans. The Romanovs felt those two regions were critical to Russia's security and were eager to control them.

Under the Romanov dynasty, the divisions between Russians and Turks tended to be represented as conflicts

Map 22.1   The Expansion of Russia, 1500–1800   Sweden and Poland initially blocked Russian expansion in Europe, while the Ottoman Empire blocked the southwest. In the sixteenth century, Russia began to expand east, toward Siberia and the Pacific Ocean. By the end of the rule of Catherine the Great in 1796, Russia encompassed all of northern and northeastern Eurasia.

Muscovy (MUSS-koe-vee)   *boyar* (BOY-ar)
Romanov (ROE-man-off or roe-MAN-off)

between Christians and "infidels" or between the civilized and the "barbaric". Despite this rhetoric, it is important to understand that the interplay of Turkic (Central Asian) Russian (Slavic) influences was what produced the Russian Empire. These cultural groups were defined not by blood ties but by the way in which they lived.

A revealing example is the **Cossacks.** Their name comes from a Turkic word for a warrior or mercenary and is related to the modern name Kazakh. The word *Cossack* in various forms seems to have first emerged in the Ukraine, where it referred to bands of people living on the steppes, herding or robbing for their livelihoods. But the Cossacks of the Ukraine were a diverse group. Many were escaped serfs from Muscovy or Lithuania; others were wandering Turks or Cumans, Poles, Hungarians, or Mongols. Who their ancestors were was irrelevant. What mattered was that they lived in close-knit bands, were superb riders and fighters, and were feared by both the villagers and the legal authorities. Poland enlisted Cossacks to be the front line against the Ottomans. The Cossacks also proved to be a danger to their Polish patrons.

The Muscovite and early Romanov rulers decided to take no chances with the Cossacks and moved to crush them as an independent political force in the Ukraine. But Russia also desired to exploit the Cossacks' extraordinary military spirit and skills. The empire reached an accommodation with them, enrolling them in special military regiments and allowing them to live in autonomous villages. In return the Cossacks performed distinctive service for Russia, not only defending against Swedish and Ottoman incursions in the west but leading campaigns for exploration, conquest, and settlement in the east.

The Cossacks were an example of the ways in which Russia combined elements considered "Turk" with those considered "Russian." They displayed the military skills of Asian horsemen but were Russian-speakers, Christians, and in most cases willing participants in the building of the Russian Empire. Although Russian rulers and churchmen often tried to draw a strong line between the realm of the Russian and the realm of the Turk, this artificial distinction was at odds with the historical realities of the Russian Empire.

Peter the Great, r. 1689–1725

Much of the rhetoric that drew distinctions between "Russians" and "Turks" was connected to the age of **Peter the Great,** who ruled Russia from 1689 to 1725 (see Chapter 18). Peter was determined to secure a warm-water port on the Black Sea, and his first priority was to build a small but formidable navy that could blockade Ottoman ports. Peter described his wars with the Ottoman Empire as a new crusade to liberate Constantinople (now Istanbul) from the Muslim sultans. He also claimed the right to function as the legal protector of Orthodox Christians living in the Balkan territories under Ottoman rule. Peter's forces seized the port of Azov in 1696, but the fortress was lost again in 1713 and Russian expansion southward was blocked for the rest of Peter's reign. The need for a Black Sea port and Russia's role as the protector of Orthodox Christians, however, were not forgotten.

Peter was more successful in his campaigns in the west. In the long and costly Great Northern War (1700–1721), Peter's modernized armies broke Swedish control of the Baltic Sea, establishing direct contacts between Russia and Europe. Previously the courts of western Europe had regarded Russia as backward, brutal, and alien. But Peter's striking intelligence, his imposing physical presence, his open admiration of European architecture, art, and military technology, and his disarming willingness to engage in physical labor while learning carpentry, shipbuilding, and architecture had made him a European celebrity and generally improved the European opinion of Russia.

Peter's victory in the Great Northern War forced the European powers to recognize Russia as a major power for the first time. Taking advantage of his new prestige in Europe, he built a new city, St. Petersburg, on land captured from Sweden. In 1712 the city became Russia's capital. Peter intended St. Petersburg to be a model to Russian elites seeking to absorb European culture and a demonstration to Europeans of Russian sophistication. Houses were to be built of stone and brick, in the baroque style then fashionable in western Europe. Nobles were ordered to wear western styles and shave their beards. Peter attempted to end the traditional seclusion of upper-class Russian women, by requiring officials, officers, and merchants to bring their wives to the social gatherings he organized in the capital.

There was also a political objective in building the new capital: Peter intended to break the power of the boyars by sharply reducing their traditional roles in government and the army. The old boyar council of Moscow was replaced by a group of advisers in St. Petersburg whom the tsar appointed. Members of the traditional nobility continued to serve as generals and admirals, but officers in Peter's modern, professional army and navy were promoted according to merit, not birth.

Peter was interested in European technology and in some of Europe's culture, but he had no intention of following the movement of the Netherlands and Britain toward political liberalization. The goal of westernization was to strengthen the Russian state and the institutions of personal power that the Russians called **autocracy.** A decree of 1716 proclaimed that the tsar "is not obliged to answer to anyone in the world for his doings, but possesses power and authority over his kingdom and land, to rule them at his will and pleasure as a Christian ruler." Under this expansive definition of his role, Peter brought the Russian Orthodox Church firmly under state control, built factories and iron and copper foundries to provide munitions and supplies for the military, and increased the burdens of taxes and forced labor on the serfs. **Serfs**— the great mass of Russian people, forced by law and custom to work the land of their overlords—could have been freed as part of Peter's reform. But there was no move to abolish serf status, because the Russian Empire was dependent on serfs for the production of basic foodstuffs. It was locked in the struggle of the Eurasian land empires, and political centralization remained critical to the strategic challenges it faced.

The Russian Drive Eastward

Long before Peter's time, Russian rulers realized that the eastern frontier was wide open to Russian expansion because no other great empire controlled the northern tier of Asia. Living there were small groups of native peoples who relied on hunting and fishing for their survival and who had not assembled the complex military organizations and weaponry of the empires to the west and south. Russian exploration of Siberia began in the time of Ivan IV and was led by a Cossack, Yermak Timofeyovich°. Yermak's troops attacked the only political power in the region, the Khanate of Sibir, and by force of their rifles destroyed the khanate in 1582. Yermak himself did not survive to return to Moscow, but Cossacks remained in the forefront of Russian campaigns to conquer and settle Siberia. Most historians believe that Cossacks founded all the major towns of Russian Siberia.

Siberian furs and timber were the first valued resources; after 1700, gold, coal, and iron also became important. From the early seventeenth century the tsar used Siberia as a penal colony for criminals and political prisoners. By the 1650s, Cossack explorers had claimed the Amur Valley for the Russian Empire, and many villages along the Amur River were rendering tribute to Russian officials. Through the 1650s, clashes occurred between

---

Yermak Timofeyovich (YAIR-mak tih-mo-FAY-oh-vich *or* tih-mo-fay-OH-vich)

these soldiers and soldiers of the Qing Empire stationed near the river. To deprive the Russians of the goods rendered by the Amur villagers, the Qing Empire forcibly resettled native peoples westward in Qing territory.

By the late 1600s the Russian and Qing Empires also were competing for influence in Mongolia and Central Asia. The Mongol federations were attempting to maintain their independence by playing the Russians and Qing against each other. Both the Russian and the Qing rulers saw that their interests lay in a diplomatic agreement that would delineate their borders in Mongolia, Siberia, and the Amur River Valley, as well as fix trade and tariff regulations across their borders. The Treaty of Nerchinsk in 1689 was a strategic coup for both empires, and it was reinforced in the Treaty of Kiakhta in 1727.

The immediate results were two. First, Mongol groups lost the leverage they had gained by exploiting Russian and Qing competition. Thereafter, the Mongols steadily declined as a power, and the Qing Empire quickly consolidated its control over Mongolia and Central Asia. Second, with a fixed boundary and Siberia inside it, Russia could concentrate on further eastern expansion, all the way to the Pacific and, by logical extension, into North America.

The ramifications of Russia's arrival at the Pacific were apparent by the mid-1700s, as British expeditions explored not only the Hawaiian Islands but also the Alaskan coast. They were alert to the extraordinary possibilities of pelt gathering in the American northwest. Sable and fox furs were precious goods in both Europe and China, and the British looked for ways to add seal and beaver furs to the markets. Furs from the eastern part of North America had traded in Europe for a century and become the foundation of the charter companies. But to exploit the fur market in China without a ruinous overhead, traders would have to secure and process furs on the west coast of America. The economic possibilities of the fur trade in northwestern America fired the imagination of English and American entrepreneurs. But within a few decades Russia dominated Alaska, and Russian traders were active along the entire western coast of North America.

The drive to the east brought Russia control of the rich natural resources of Siberia and the strategically important Amur River and put Russia into a position to dominate the lucrative fur and shipping industries of the North Pacific. This expansion of the empire was started by the rulers of Muscovy, had its most dramatic developments under Peter, and was sustained by Peter's successors. When Catherine the Great (r. 1762–1796) died, Russian reach extended from Poland in the west to Alaska in the east, from the Barents Sea in the north to the

Power and Youth   Emperor Kangxi (left) and Peter the Great (right) were contemporaries, great rulers, and rivals for control of Central and Northeast Asia. Both were child-emperors who outwitted their elders to achieve personal rule and then pursued all avenues of knowledge to strengthen their empires. But their youthful portraits show differences: Peter is depicted here while he was a student in Holland in 1697, learning engineering and shipbuilding. Kangxi, in a portrait from about 1690, preferred to be portrayed as a refined scholar. (left: The Palace Museum, Beijing; right: Collection, Countess Bobrinskoy/Michael Holford)

Caspian Sea in the south, and was still growing. Catherine ruled the world's largest land empire, the survivor of a form of Eurasian empire that had prized large territories, agriculture, logging, fishing, and furs. It shared these qualities with its old rival, the Qing Empire.

THE LATER MING AND EARLY QING EMPIRES, 1500–1800

By the time the Qing Empire was fighting Russia for control of Northeast Asia, it was in its own right a very large and growing empire. Only a half-century earlier, however, the ancestors of the Qing rulers were local chiefs trying to protect the economic enterprises of their followers in Manchuria from regulation by the **Ming Empire** based in China. Though the Ming Empire did not control Mongolia, Turkestan, or Tibet, it was a large empire with a rich and complex economy. It was militarily and politically influential, positioned at the center of an international tributary system, mounting effective military campaigns against Vietnam and the Mongols, and defending Korea against Japanese invasion. It would have been difficult for anybody to predict that in such a short period the Ming Empire would be destroyed and the Qing would assume control of China. Was the achievement due primarily to Ming weakness or to Qing strengths?

The End of the Ming

Historians are puzzled by the Ming decline because of the brilliance of the earlier Ming period. The unusual economic and cultural achievements of the Ming period continued until 1600. Ming manufacturers had transformed the global economy with their techniques for the assembly-line production of porcelain. By the 1500s Europe knew about the high-grade blue-on-white porcelain commonly used by the elites of China. Portuguese merchants not only began importing the products to Europe but requested special designs that imitated European pitchers and bowls that otherwise would have been made of metal or wood. Many of these commissioned items featured distinctive gold fittings and designs that Chinese artisans copied from European paintings. By 1600 the Dutch were also heavily involved in this trade, and wealthy families in Europe were becoming accustomed to the fine new porcelain, which they called "china." An international market eager for Ming porcelain, as well as for silk and lacquered furniture, stimulated the commercial development of East Asia, the Indian Ocean, and Europe.

This apparent golden age, however, was beset by serious problems that by the year 1600 left the Ming Empire economically exhausted, politically deteriorating, and technologically lagging behind both its East Asian neighbors and Europe. Some of these problems were the result of natural disasters associated with climate change and disease. There is evidence of climate change in the seventeenth century. Annual temperatures dropped, reached a low point about 1645, then remained low until the early 1700s. The last decades of the Ming were a time of agricultural distress, migration of peoples out of less productive areas, and the spread of epidemic diseases. Large uprisings that speeded the end of the Ming Empire were fueled by the dissatisfaction of tenant farmers and day workers squeezed by high rents, low wages, and poor crop yields. The devastation caused by these uprisings resulted in steep declines in local populations and grinding distress for individuals who were left. Climate change also may have contributed to external pressure on the Ming, as Manchus and Mongols sought to protect their productive lands from Ming control and to acquire land along the Ming borders.

Other kinds of global change also affected China. As Europeans colonized Mexico and Central America, they exploited the new sources of silver and flooded the global trade networks with silver coins. As China became more involved in this trade in the 1500s and early 1600s, silver flowed into China in exchange for goods sold to Europe. Silver dollars from the Spanish Empire were fully accepted in the Chinese economy, and the Chinese government began to mint its own silver coins and remint foreign silver in imitation of the Spanish design.

As the amount of silver in circulation rose, its relative value fell. Nevertheless, the Ming government maintained a strict ratio in price between silver coins and copper coins. Taxes and the prices of commodities were tied to the vlaue of silver, and most transactions required the conversion of copper coinage to silver. As silver declined in value, more and more copper was needed to make purchases and pay taxes. In a time of worsening economic and population conditions, the decline in the value of silver and consequent inflation in prices and taxes hit the rural population especially hard. The Ming government found it increasingly difficult to maintain order and eventually was overwhelmed by rebellious forces.

Environmental and economic stress do not in themselves destroy societies. Indeed both the eastern Mongols and the Manchus centralized their political systems and increased the territories under their control in the 1600s, all at the expense of the Ming Empire. The importance of global factors in the demise of the Ming must be placed in the context of the special factors operating on China.

Ming cities were culturally and commercially vibrant. Many large landowners and absentee landlords lived in the cities, as well as officials, artists, and rich merchants who had purchased ranks or prepared their sons for the examinations. The elites had created a brilliant culture in which novels, operas, poetry, porcelain, and painting were all closely interwoven. Owners of small businesses catering to the urban elites could make money through printing, tailoring, running restaurants, or selling paper, ink, ink-stones, and writing brushes. The imperial government also marketed to the urban elites by operating factories for the production of ceramics and silks. Enormous government complexes at Jingdezhen° and at Dehua° invented assembly-line techniques and produced large quantities of high-quality ceramics for sale in China and abroad. But by the end of the Ming period the factories were plagued by disorder and inefficiency. The situation became so bad during the late sixteenth and seventeeth centuries that workers held strikes with increasing frequency. During a work action at Jingdezhen in 1601, workers threw themselves into the kilns to protest working conditions.

Yet the urban and industrial sectors of later Ming society fared much better than the rural, agricultural sector. After a period of economic growth and recovery from the population decline of the thirteenth century, the rural Ming economy did not continue strong growth. After the beginning of the sixteenth century, China had knowledge, gained from European traders, of new crops from Africa and America. But they were introduced very slowly, and neither rice-growing regions in southern China nor wheat-growing regions in northern China experienced a meaningful increase in productivity during the second half of the Ming period. After 1500, economic depression in the countryside, combined with recurring epidemics in central and southern China, kept population growth in check. The Ming population—about a

---

Jingdezhen (JING-deh-JUHN)   **Dehua** (duh-HUA)

hundred million—at its height probably did not much surpass that of the Song dynasty four hundred years earlier.

The Ming also were under constant pressure from the powerful Mongol federations of Central Asia. In the late 1500s large numbers of Mongols were unified again. This time, Tibetan religion was used to centralize power in the hands of a Mongol khan. To legitimate his power, the khan designated for the first time a **dalai lama°,** or universal teacher, of Tibetan Buddhism. The unification of the Mongols in the 1500s was a significant step in the reemergence of Mongolia as a regional military power around 1600. In its last decades the Ming Empire was squeezed by Mongol forces on the west and north.

In 1582 Japanese warriors invaded Korea, which was a Ming tributary state. The invasions threw East Asia into crisis. The **Manchus,** an agriculturally based people who controlled the region north of Korea, contributed troops to an international force under Ming leadership. The Koreans employed all the technological and military skill for which the Yi period was renowned. General Yi Son-sin devised and employed the covered warships, or "turtle boats," that intercepted a portion of Japanese fleet.

The effects of the Japanese invasion were lasting. The impoverished Ming had to pay a high price to bring the Manchus into the struggle. In addition, the strain of repelling the invasions hastened the Ming decline in military strength. In Korea, the factionalism afflicting the Yi court before the Japanese arrived was worsened by the devastation resulting from the invasion and the struggle for leadership after the invaders were turned back. Korea was so weakened that the Manchus soon brought the country under their sway.

For the entire later Ming period, the boundaries of the empire were critical to its health, and conditions at the boundaries are an indication of the difficulties the later Ming Empire endured. The Mongols remained strong in the north. The Manchus grew stronger in the northeast and severed the traditional relationship between China and Korea. In the southwest, there were repeated uprisings among native peoples crowded by the immigration of Chinese farmers. The Ming could not look to the seas for relief. Pirates, often of Japanese or partial Japanese ancestry, based themselves in Okinawa and in Taiwan and roamed the southeastern coast of China, frequently looting inadequately protected trading towns. Ming military resources, concentrated against the Mongols and the Manchus in the north, could not be deployed to make the coasts hospitable to Chinese traders who were not themselves connected to the pirates. Frustrated by conditions and despairing of ever making a living at home, many southern Chinese migrated to all areas of Southeast Asia, where they began to profit from the sea trading networks of the Indian Ocean.

After decades of weakening control, the Ming ruler was deposed when rebellious forces under the leadership of Li Zicheng° captured Beijing. The imperial family left the city, but a Ming general entered into an agreement with Manchu leaders, inviting them to take Beijing from the rebels. The Qing did so in the summer of 1644 but did not restore the Ming. They claimed China for their own and began a forty-year conquest of the rest of the Ming territories.

It was some years before all hope was lost for the Ming. The Ming imperial family thought they could appeal to the Catholic Church for help in resisting the invaders. On November 4, 1650, from the remote highlands of Southeast Asia, Grand Dowager Empress Wang° sent a delegation of Jesuits to Rome to ask the pope to "take pity on us sinners in God's presence and, when we die, to bestow a special absolution." Wang noted that all members of the imperial family had been converted and said that if the papacy would help repel the Manchus "ambassadors will be dispatched to perform proper ceremonies at the altars of Saints Peter and Paul." Michel Boym°, the Jesuit priest acting as Wang's envoy, did not reach Rome until 1652 and could gain no papal audience until 1656. Then, with an encouraging letter from Pope Alexander VI, Boym returned to a China nearly conquered by the Manchus, who refused to let him travel inland from Canton. By that time Wang and her family were dead. Boym himself died attempting to contact them and was buried in the highlands between China and Vietnam in 1659.[2]

Power and Trade in the Early Qing

The **Qing Empire** was ruled by a Manchu imperial family, and Manchus were the leaders of the military forces. But Manchus were a very small portion of the population, and from its beginnings the empire was dependent on diverse peoples for its achievements. Peoples of Mongol, Korean, Cossack, and Turkic descent were all important in one way or another. Some Jesuits also were helpers, particularly after the collapse of Ming resistance. But the most important population in the Qing Empire was the Chinese, particularly the millions who deserted the Ming as Qing forces entered the country. Though the Qing style

---

dalai lama (DAH-lie LAH-mah)

Li Zicheng (lee ZUH-cheng)   **Wang** (wahng)
Michel Boym (mee-SHELL bwam)

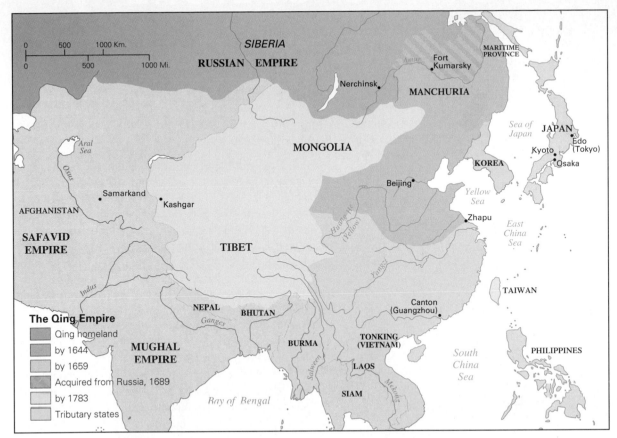

Map 22.2   The Qing Empire, 1644–1783   The Qing Empire began in Manchuria and captured north China in 1644. Between 1644 and 1783 the Qing conquered all the former Ming territories and added Taiwan, the lower Amur River basin, Inner Mongolia, eastern Turkestan, and Tibet. The resulting state was more than twice the size of the Ming Empire.

of rule was multilingual and international and the Qing were keenly focused on large strategic issues relating to competition with the Russian Empire, the overwhelming majority of officials, soldiers, merchants, and farmers were Chinese.

Before the year 1700 the Qing gained south China, and for the first time the island of Taiwan was incorporated into an empire based in China (see Map 22.2). At the time, the Qing Empire was also conquering Mongolia and Central Asia. The seventeenth and eighteenth centuries in China—particularly the reigns of the Kangxi° (r. 1662–1722) and Qianlong° (r. 1736–1796) emperors—were the period of greatest economic, military, and cultural achievement.

The early Qing emperors wished to foster economic and demographic recovery in China. They repaired the

roads and waterworks, lowered transit taxes, mandated comparatively low rents and interest rates, and established economic incentives for resettlement of the areas devastated during the peasant rebellions of the late Ming period. Foreign trade was encouraged. Korean ambassadors and students were numerous in Beijing and readily absorbed the tastes of the Qing elite. Vietnam, Burma, and Nepal sent regular embassies to the Qing tribute court and carried the latest Chinese fashions back home. Overland routes of communication from Samarkand to Korea were revived, though their economic and cultural influence was a shadow of what it had been under the Mongols in the 1200s. Nevertheless, through its Central Asian conquests the Qing Empire gained access to the superior horses of Afghanistan, gained new sources of coal, iron, gold, and silver, and eventually was able to eliminate the military danger of the Mongols.

Kangxi (KAHNG-shee)   **Qianlong** (chee-YEN-loong)

Style and Conversion: Christian Rivalries in Beijing

The Treaty of Nerchinsk (1689) presented new opportunities for Russian missionaries in Beijing to continue their work of ministering to Russians in Beijing as well as spreading Orthodox Christianity in China. They failed to gain converts, largely because they did not learn Chinese. But they believed their failure was due to the interference of the Jesuits, who had arrived before them, knew Chinese, and made themselves indispensable in diplomatic communications between the Qing and Russian courts. In 1722 leaders of the Orthodox Church wrote the following comment to the new head of the Russian mission in Beijing.

I t would be prudent if you kept your rank of bishop a secret, because your status might arouse opposition among our enemies—especially our main enemies, the Jesuits. They are constantly creating troubles between us and others, as well as strife among ourselves, in order to frustrate our good works. Of course it could not be otherwise, for remember that Jesus cried out to the Father, "Lord, have I not sown good seed? Where have these weeds come from?" And the Lord said, "The Devil has done this."

For their part, the Jesuits considered the Russian missionaries hopelessly unpersuasive, not only because of their limitations of language but also because of their poverty. Russians traveled overland, by caravan, to Beijing, which was very expensive. Once there, they lived on a very small allowance from the Qing court, and they were often short of food and fuel, not to mention new clothes. The relatively independent and wealthy Jesuits considered the Russian missionaries unprepared for international experience, as Matteo Ripa made clear in his report to the Vatican on the Russian mission in Beijing, probably in 1718.

I sent a present to the head of the mission, then visited him. His manners were courteous and dignified, and his dress remarkably neat. With me, he pretended to be a Roman Catholic (despite the fact he was obviously Orthodox), speaking just enough Latin to be understood. He told me that a priest who was ill and in bed could speak Latin, and so I went to visit him, but all I could get out of him was the word "intelligit, intelligit, [he understands, he understands]" over and over. The head of the mission told me that the congregation is limited to descendants of Russian prisoners of war. They cannot convert the Chinese because they don't speak Chinese, and besides they have so few priests that they have no time for any but their flock of Russians.

The truth is, their church services have no ceremony at all, and they allow men and women to worship together, which in China is considered abominable. And though the head of the mission looks elegant, the priests on his staff look very shabby. To make matters worse, the priests play in the streets in front of the mission. In China this is absolutely uncouth, and no respectable person would do it.

What do you think accounts for the tensions between the Jesuits and Russian Orthodox churchmen in China? What were they really competing for?

Source: Eric Widmer, The Russian Ecclesiastical Mission in Peking During the Eighteenth Century (Cambridge, MA: Harvard East Asian Research Center, 1976), 44, 63. © The President and Fellows of Harvard College 1976. Reproduced by permission of the Harvard University Asia Center.

Emperor Kangxi

The early Qing conquest of Beijing and north China was carried out under the leadership of a group of Manchu aristocrats who dominated the first Qing emperor based in China and were regents for his young son, who was declared emperor in 1662. This child-emperor, Kangxi, spent several years doing political battle with his regents, and in 1669 he gained real as well as formal control of the government by executing his chief regent. **Kangxi** was then sixteen. He was an intellectual prodigy who mastered classical Chinese, Manchu, and Mongolian at an early age and memorized the Chinese classics. He was a successful military commander who personally led troops in the great campaigns that brought Mongolia under Qing control by 1691. He battled with and then made peace with the Russian Empire and negotiated complex domestic political crises. His reign, lasting until his death in 1722, was marked not only by great expansion of the empire but by great stability as well.

Part of the effectiveness of Qing expansion in the Kangxi era was due to Qing willingness to incorporate ideas and technologies from different regions. Before the invasion of China, the Qing already were using the Mongol system of political organization. They also adapted a program of religious legitimation of the emperor's power that was Tibetan in origin but had been used by Mongol emperors. Many of the agricultural policies of the early Qing state were influenced by Korean and Chinese practices.

As the Qing conquest was consolidated in north China, south China, and Northeast Asia, maps in the European style—reflecting the century of Jesuit influence at the Ming court—were created as practical guides to the newly conquered regions and as symbols of Qing dominance. Kangxi considered introducing the European calendar, but protests were so strong that an anti-Jesuit backlash developed among the Confucian elites, and the plan was dropped. The emperor himself remained friendly with the Jesuits and frequently discussed scientific and philosophical issues with them (see Society and Culture: Style and Conversion: Christian Rivalries in Beijing). When he fell ill with malaria in the 1690s, he relied on Jesuit medical expertise (in this case, the use of quinine) for his recovery. He ordered the creation of illustrated books in Manchu detailing European anatomical and pharmaceutical knowlege. The Jesuits also lectured Kangxi on mathematics, astronomy, and European civilization generally.

To gain converts among the Chinese elite, the Jesuits made important compromises in their religious teaching. The most important was their toleration of Confucian ancestor worship. The matter caused great controversy between the Jesuits and their Catholic rivals in China, the Franciscans and Dominicans, and also between the Jesuits and the pope. In 1690 the disagreement reached a high pitch. Kangxi wrote to Rome supporting the Jesuit position, but the matter was dropped, inconclusively, in the early 1700s. By that time, the influx of Jesuits to China had slowed, and for the remainder of the 1700s a very small population of Jesuits remained at the Qing court.

The exchange of information between the Qing and the Europeans that Kangxi had fostered was never one-way. When the Jesuits informed the Qing court on matters of anatomy, for instance, the Qing were able to demonstrate to the Jesuits an early form of inoculation, called **variolation,** that had been used to stem the spread of smallpox after the Qing conquest of Beijing. The technique was the inspiration for the vaccines later developed by Europeans. Similarly, the enormous imperial factories that produced porcelain inspired the industrial management of practices of Josiah Wedgwood in England.

Transferring European Designs, Canton   By 1750, both Chinese and European merchants at Canton were dependent on the expansion of commerce between Europe and the Qing Empire for their fortunes. For centuries Chinese factories had produced special products in porcelain, silk, and lacquerware for European markets. By the end of the 1700s, even the trade itself was an object of commercialization: Here, a painting specially made for export shows a Canton artisan carefully transferring European designs to a glass painting that is itself specially made for export.   (V & A Picture Library)

Tea and Diplomacy

The brilliant successes of the Qing in conquest and trade excited admiration in Europe. Things Chinese—or things that looked to Europeans as if they could be Chinese—were demanded by the wealthy and the aspiring middle classes of Europe. Not only silk, porcelain, and tea were being avidly consumed, but also cloisonné jewelry, tableware and decorative items, lacquered and jeweled room dividers, painted fans, carved jade and ivory (which originated in Africa and was finished in China). Perhaps the most striking Chinese influence on the transformation of European interior life in this period was wallpaper—an adaptation of the Chinese practice of covering walls with enormous loose-hanging watercolors or calligraphy scrolls. By the mid-1700s, special workshops throughout China were producing wallpaper and other consumer items according to the specifications of European merchants. The items were shipped to Canton for export to Europe.

In political philosophy, too, the Europeans felt they had something to learn from the early Qing emperors. In the late 1770s, poems supposedly written by Emperor Qianlong were translated into French and disseminated through the intellectual circles of western Europe. These works depicted the Qing emperors as benevolent despots who campaigned against superstition and ignorance, curbed the excesses of the aristocracy, and patronized science and the arts. European intellectuals who were questioning the political systems of their own societies found the image of a practical, secular, compassionate ruler intriguing. Voltaire proclaimed the Qing emperors model philosopher-kings and advocated such rulership as a protection against the growth of aristocratic privilege. Though Jesuit interest in China was in decline by this time, the works of the Jesuits stimulated interest in the languages and civilizations of East Asia and an intensification of European efforts to establish communications with China.

The Qing were eager to expand China's economic influence but were determined to control the trade very strictly. The purposes of this regulation were to allow the imperial family to enjoy the benefits of taxation of the trade and to limit piracy on the seas and smuggling inland. The system that the Qing used for regulating trade permitted only one market point for each foreign sector. Overland trade from Central Asia was directed to Kashgar, trade from Japan was directed to a city on the eastern coast near Shanghai, and all trade from the South China Sea was directed to Canton on the southern coast. Since Europeans came to China by way of the Indian Ocean and Southeast Asia, they were included in the South China Sea sector and permitted to trade only at Canton.

This system worked well enough for European traders until the late 1700s. Britain had become an important presence in East Asia, using its bases in India and Singapore to move eastward to China. The directors of the East India Company (EIC) believed that China's technological achievements and gigantic potential markets made China the key to limitless profit. China had tea, rhubarb, porcelain, and silk to offer. Dutch merchants enriched themselves by transporting these goods to Europe for centuries, but by the early 1700s the EIC dominated the community of European "factories"—the combined residences and offices of the European merchants residing in Canton—and British families such as the Barings, Jardines, and Mathesons had established themselves as quasi-political powers.

Tea from China became enormously popular in England. It had earlier been a prized import to Russia, Central Asia, and the Middle East, all of which knew it by its northern Chinese name, *cha*, and all of which acquired it by the overland Eurasian routes of medieval and early modern times. Western Europe, however, acquired tea from sea routes first exploited by the Portuguese and Dutch and thus knew it by its name in the Fujian province of coastal China and Taiwan: *te*. From the time of its introduction to England in the mid-1600s, tea displaced chocolate and coffee as the preferred drink.

English traders, whether members of the EIC or independent businessmen, considered the potential of trade with China to be obstructed by the Qing trade system. Great fortunes were being made in the tea trade, but the English had not found a product to sell to China. They believed that China was a vast unexploited market, with hundreds of millions of potential consumers of lamp oil made from whale blubber, cotton grown in India or the American south, or guns manufactured in London or Connecticut. Particularly after the loss of the thirteen American colonies, Britain feared that its markets would diminish and believed that only the Qing trade system—the "Canton system," as the British called it—stood in the way of opening new paths for commerce.

The British government worried about Britain's massive trade deficit with China. Because the Qing Empire rarely bought anything from Britain, British silver poured into China to pay for the imported tea and other products. The Qing government, whose revenues were declining in the later 1700s while its expenses rose, needed the silver. But in Britain the imbalance of payments stirred anxiety and anger over the allegedly unfair restrictions that the Qing Empire placed on the import of foreign goods. To make matters worse, the East India Company had managed its worldwide holdings badly, and as it teetered on bankruptcy, its attempts to manipulate Parliament became increasingly intrusive. The British government attempted to limit the actions and privileges of the EIC but thought that only the opening of the China trade and increasing competition from British merchants would finally dissolve the outmoded EIC. In 1792 George Macartney was dispatched to China to open diplomatic relations with the Qing Empire and attempt to revise the trade system.

The **Macartney mission** to China, which extended into 1793, was a fiasco. Qing officials were not expecting Macartney and would not allow him to travel from Canton to Beijing. Moreover, they did not accept his credentials, and Macartney did not know how to make any headway through the Qing bureaucracy. There were prolonged disputes about rituals. Macartney was ordered to perform the kowtow, but he refused. He asked Qing officials to bow before a portrait of the king of England, and they refused. The basic issues were unresolvable. Britain wished the Qing Empire to abandon its trade system because it was benefiting only the troublesome EIC. Britain wished the Qing to open Chinese ports to a wide range of competing British firms, one of which might eventually find a product that would be popular in China and help to reverse the trade imbalance. The Qing, however, had no interest in changing the system. The EIC was not a Qing problem; the Qing were submitting British traders to no restrictions that did not also apply to all other foreign merchants; the system provided revenue to the imperial family and lessened serious piracy problems. Macartney left China humiliated by his inability to persuade the Qing to make changes. Many people at home suspected he had in fact performed the kowtow, humiliating not only himself but all of Britain.

Dutch, French, and Russian embassies soon attempted to achieve what Macartney had failed to do, When they failed also, European frustration with the Qing mounted. The great European admiration for China of the early 1700s faded, and China was considered despotic, self-satisfied, and unrealistic. Political solutions seemed impossible because the Qing court would not communicate with foreign envoys or observe the simplest rules of the diplomatic system familiar to Europeans.

There occurred here a subtle shift in the position of Russia. In the time of Peter the Great and of the Emperor Kangxi, the two great empires had faced each other in a special contest and had found a sophisticated means of resolving or at least suspending their differences. They had used a diplomatic system, relying on Jesuits as interpreters, to create treaties establishing formal borders and customs procedures. But in those times Russia and the Qing were struggling for control of Central Asia and Mongolia and had similar strengths and weaknesses. By the last decade of the eighteenth century, Russia was committed to sea exploration, colonization of overseas territories, and the creation of a European-style empire. It had moved beyond its Eurasian land empire context, and was leaning toward the European consensus that the Qing Empire was keeping in place an unreasonable and outdated trade system. The Qing emperors at the end of the 1700s did not understand the importance of this Russian shift or anticipate the ways in which it would work to destroy the status quo that the two gigantic empires had once enjoyed.

Population and Social Stress

When Macartney and his entourage visited China in 1792–1793, they were carefully guided through the most prosperous cities and the most productive farmland. They did not see evidence of the economic and environmental decline that had begun to affect China in the last decades of the 1700s. The population explosion had intensified demand for rice and wheat, for land to be opened for the planting of crops imported from Africa and the Americas, and for more thorough exploitation of land already in use.

The narratives of Marco Polo's adventures in the 1200s had already fixed in the European imagination the image of packed, affluent Chinese cities, and between the time of Marco Polo and the time of the Macartney mission the Chinese population tripled.

This growth was partly the result of the peace that the Qing enforced. In addition, foreign crops known in the late Ming but not widely exploited then were commonly used in the Qing period to supplement or replace traditional crops. For instance, in regions of northern China, years of planting wheat and barley had exhausted the soil near the surface. In these areas, the introduction of corn from America temporarily revived agricultural productivity because the roots of corn extend deep into the soil to seek their nutrients. In central and southern China, the use of sweet potatoes and other crops from Africa made possible the cultivation of land not suitable for rice or wheat. As Macartney observed, field crops were sown in neat rows by mechanical seeders—at a time when most farmers in Europe still used the broadcast method, which wasted much of the seed.

The early Qing population exploded and reached between 350 million and 400 million by the end of the 1700s. But because of the efficiency of Chinese agriculture, population growth that had driven the per capita area of arable land to one-third of what it had been a century before had not yet created general poverty.

Whatever woodlands remained in China at the beginning of the 1700s were rapidly diminishing by the end of the century. Houses could be built of brick, but erosion became a serious problem because of deforestation. As erosion advanced, the danger of flooding grew, but government corruption and general inefficiency limited efforts to prevent flooding or recover from its effects. Dams and dikes were not maintained, and silted-up river channels were not dredged. By the end of the eighteenth century the Grand Canal was nearly unusable, and the towns that bordered it were starved for commerce.

The result was localized misery in many parts of interior China by the year 1800. Environmental deterioration and the decline of agriculture prompted many people to move. They sought seasonal jobs in better-off agricultural areas, or they worked in low-status jobs such as barge puller, charcoal burner, or nightsoil carrier. Many drifted to the cities to make their way by begging, prostitution, or theft. In central and southwestern China, where farmers had been impoverished by serious flooding, rebellions became endemic. Often joining in revolt were various indigenous peoples, who were largely concentrated in the less fertile lands in the south and in the northern and western borderlands of the empire (see Map 22.3).

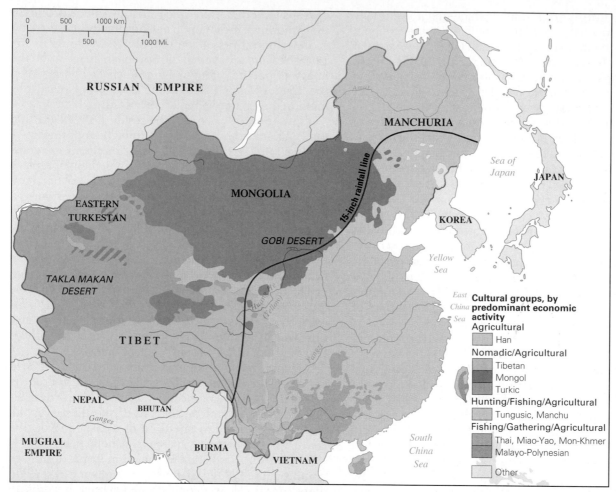

Map 22.3 Climate and Diversity in the Qing Empire The Qing Empire encompassed different environmental zones, and the climate differences corresponded to population density and cultural divisions. Wetter regions to the east of the 15-inch rainfall line also contained the most densely populated 20 percent of Qing land. The drier, less densely populated 80 percent of the Empire was home to the greatest portion of peoples who spoke languages other than Chinese. Many were nomads, fishermen, hunters, or farmers who raised crops other than rice.

The Qing Empire was outgrowing the state's control. The Qing government employed about the same number of officials as the Ming even though the Qing Empire was twice the size of the Ming geographically and nearly four times its size in terms of population. To maintain local control, the Qing depended on working alliances with local elites, including gentry and aspiring official families. But this dependence undercut the government's ability to enforce tax regulations and to control standards for admission to government service. The resulting semi-privatization of governance in the late 1700s promoted a situation in which corruption was widespread, military policies were inconsistent and ineffective, banditry was growing, and government revenues were shrinking.

The Qing fell victim to some of the basic characteristics of the land-based empires. To defend itself against Russia, it had conquered a huge stretch of territory extending from Turkestan—brought under military occupation in 1755—to Northeast Asia, and the costs of maintaining it were enormous. Population growth and the need to transport food to nonagricultural areas stressed the food and grain systems. The need to invest in agriculture and in transport infrastructure limited investment in new industries and heightened government interest in taxing foreign trade. Russia was attempting to move out of that mode by turning toward European-style imperialism and industrialization. Japan, China's neighbor, was poised for an entirely different response.

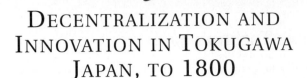

DECENTRALIZATION AND INNOVATION IN TOKUGAWA JAPAN, TO 1800

Like East Asia under the Qing rulers, Japan under the Tokugawa° shoguns had to deal with the transition from the intense militarization of the early 1600s to the comparative peace of the 1700s, while at the same time facing a decrease in state revenues and mounting European pressure for contact. In nearly every respect, the Japanese reaction to these problems strongly contrasted with the Qing response, with lasting consequences for Japan.

Shogunate and Economy

Japan's centralized political system had broken down in the twelfth century, when the first of the decentralized military governments—the shogunates—had been created. By 1500, civil war had brought a new warrior class to power, and the second of Japan's shogunates—the Ashikaga—was a loosely organized system of regional lords giving their loyalty to their leader, the shogun, who gave his loyalty to the secluded emperor. The extreme decentralization of the Ashikaga period fostered wars among ambitious local lords, and during the later 1500s infighting among the leaders engulfed the country.

In 1600 a new shogun, Tokugawa Ieyasu°, declared victory. Though Japan was brought under a single military government, the structure of the **Tokugawa Shogunate** had a very important influence over the development of the Japanese economy in the early modern period. The regional lords who fought for Tokugawa Ieyasu in the final battle in 1600 were understood to have an especially close relationship with the shogun. The shogun's original intention was to reward the lords who had supported him with well-developed rice lands in central Japan—relatively close to the shogunal capital—and to punish those who had not supported him by granting them remote, undeveloped lands at the northern and southern extremes of the Japanese islands.

The emperor of Japan had no political power; he remained at Kyoto°, the medieval capital. The Tokugawa shoguns built a new capital for themselves at Edo° (now Tokyo). A well-maintained road connected Kyoto and Edo, and trade and trading centers developed along this route.

The shogun was served by the regional lords, each of whom maintained a castle town, a small bureaucracy, a population of warriors—**samurai°**—and military support personnel, and often an academy. The result of this controlled decentralization was the establishment of well-spaced urban centers, between which there was frequent traffic. Because Tokugawa shoguns required the lords to visit Edo frequently, good roads, traffic, and commerce linked Edo to three of the four main islands of Japan. The shogun paid the lords in rice, and the lords paid their followers in rice. To meet their personal expenses, recipients of rice had to convert a large portion of it into cash. This transaction stimulated the development of rice exchanges at Edo and at Osaka°, where merchants speculated in rice prices.

Because of the domestic peace of the Tokugawa era, the warrior class had to adapt itself to the growing bureaucratic needs of the state. As the samurai became better educated, more attuned to the tastes of the civil elite, and more interested in conspicuous consumption, merchants dealing in silks, *sake°* (rice wine), fans, porcelain, lacquerware, books, and loans were well positioned to exploit the new opportunities. The state attempted—unsuccessfully—to curb the independence of the merchants when the economic well-being of the samurai was threatened, particularly when rice prices went too low or interest rates on loans were too high.

The 1600s and 1700s were centuries of high achievement in artisanship and commerce (see Environment and Technology: Women and Tokugawa Technology). Japanese skills in steel making, pottery, and lacquerware were joined by excellence in the production and decoration of porcelain, thanks in no small part to Korean experts brought back to Japan after the invasion of 1582. In the early 1600s manufacturers and merchants amassed enormous family fortunes. Several of the most important industrial and financial companies—for instance, the Mitsui° companies—had their origins in *sake* or beer breweries of the early Tokugawa period, then branched out into manufacturing, finance, and transport.

Wealthy industrial families usually cultivated close alliances with their regional lords and, if possible, with the shogun himself. In this way they could weaken the strict control of merchant activity that was an official part of Tokugawa policy. By the end of the 1700s, the industrial families of Tokugawa Japan held the key to modernization and the development of heavy industry, particularly in the prosperous provinces. Their political

---

Tokugawa (toe-koo-GAH-wah)   Ieyasu (ee-yeh-YAH-soo)
Kyoto (kee-YO-toe)   Edo (ED-doe)

samurai (SAH-moo-rie)   Osaka (OH-sah-kah)   *sake* (SAH-kay)
Mitsui (MIT-soo-ee)

Women and Tokugawa Technology

In the early modern period, the balance between available resources and demand was better in Japan than in China. In Qing China, population rapidly outstripped farmers' ability to increase agricultural output. In addition, the population of China was unevenly distributed, and when the population far exceeded the demand for labor, not everyone who needed work could find it. In such circumstances, social expectations forced many working women to relinquish skilled, specialized jobs to men and to consider themselves lucky if they were able to find low-paying, unskilled work.

In Tokugawa Japan, by contrast, women's labor remained valuable through the 1700s and became increasingly specialized. Women were regularly employed in the countryside and in the industries of the towns. In Japan as in China, they were indispensable in agricultural labor. But in Japan, because of social coherence and the comparative uniformity of the work in all regions, women's roles were well integrated with those of men, and women maintained a role in both the political and the economic life of the village. As mechanization was introduced, the value of women's work did not decline. Indeed, women's skills actually became more specialized, and mechanization became a normal part of their work.

The silk industry traditionally had been dominated by women working at home, where they oversaw the breeding and feeding of silkworms and the production of raw silk. In the Tokugawa period, these skills were mechanized—sometimes on so large a scale that the making of silk could no longer be considered a cottage industry. Nevertheless, the demand for labor remained so high that women were able to maintain their role in silk weaving.

Women also were important in mining. They were believed to have special intuition for separating desired metals from the surrounding stone, and certainly their skills at this task were very well developed. Mining was a lowly trade that was expected to attract humble workers. But as the Tokugawa economy grew, the demand for iron, copper, silver, and gold increased, and women workers remained critical to the advancement of industry, despite their low social standing. Watercolors and drawings of the period commonly depict the integration of women into the Tokugawa economic scene.

There was, however, a firm ceiling above which Tokugawa women could not rise. Although they enjoyed more economic leverage than their equally hard-working counterparts in China and Korea, they had no property rights. Moreover, despite the fact that Tokugawa women maintained their position in mechanized trades, they generally were not instructed in the most advanced techniques until after they married, because if a girl were instructed at a very young age, and then married, for the remainder of her life her skills would benefit not her own birth family but the family of her husband. Thus, when increasing complexity demanded earlier and more prolonged training in some trades, women in Japan began to lose their place in industry.

Silk Weaving by Japanese Women Before the emergence of large factories, this sort of work could be done in the home or at a shared village site. (From Hishikawa Moronobu *Wakoku hyakujo* [1695]. Reproduced courtesy of the Harvard-Yenching Library)

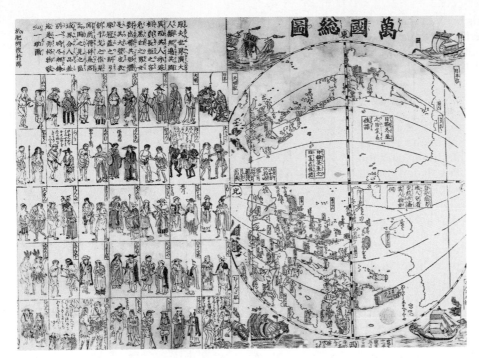

Comprehensive Map of the Myriad Nations   Thanks to the "Dutch studies" scholars and to overseas contacts, many Japanese were well informed about the cultures, technologies, and political systems of various parts of the world. This combination map and ethnographic text of 1671 enthusiastically explores the differences among the many peoples living or traveling in Asia. The map of the Pacific hemisphere has the north pole on the left and south pole on the extreme right of the drawing.   (British Museum/Fotomas Index)

influence was critical to the later transformation of Japan into an industrialized society.

The "Closing" of Japan

Like China, Japan at the end of the 1500s was a target of missionary activity by the Jesuits. But while members of the Chinese elite were open to the Jesuits so long as they accommodated Confucian values and became acquainted with Chinese culture, Japanese elite converts to Catholic Christianity were comparatively few. Missionaries could selectively gain the favor of regional lords while bypassing the shogunal court in Edo, which was consistently hostile to Christianity. This was the case with Date Masamuni°, the fierce and independent warlord of northern Honshu°, who sent his own embassy to the Vatican in 1613, by way of the Philippines (where there were significant communities of Japanese merchants and pirates) and Mexico City.

Generally, Christianity was more successful among farmers in the countryside. Jesuits had their greatest success in the southern and eastern regions of Japan. But in the late 1630s these regions were the scenes of massive uprisings by farmers impoverished by local rents and taxes. The rebellions, which were ruthlessly suppressed, were blamed on Christian influence. Hundreds of Japanese Christians were crucified as a warning to others; belief in Christianity was banned by law; and in 1649 the shogunate ordered the closing of the country, making it illegal and punishable by death for foreigners to come in or for Japanese to leave.

The purpose of the closing was to prevent the spread of foreign influence in Japan, not necessarily to exclude from Japan knowledge of foreign cultures. A few Europeans, primarily the Dutch, were permitted to reside on the small island of Deshima near Nagasaki, and a few Japanese were licensed to supply their needs. Curious about Western ways, these intermediaries concentrated first on learning Dutch, so the knowledge that they acquired and that eventually spread from Nagasaki was known as "Dutch studies." It included information about European weapons technology, shipbuilding, mathematics and astronomy, anatomy and medicine, and geography. In the 1700s some Japanese theorists advocated that Japan should abandon its decentralized, agriculturally oriented system in favor of the more centralized, mercantilistic systems used by European empires.

The closing of Japan was ignored by some of the regional lords whose fortunes depended on overseas trade with Korea, Okinawa°, Taiwan, China, and Southeast Asia. The "outer" lords at the northern and southern extremes of Japan tended to be under less control by the shoguns. Many of them not only pursued overseas trade and piracy but also claimed dominion over islands between Japan

---

Date Masamuni (dah-tay mah-sah-moo-nee)   **Honshu** (hahn-shoo)

Okinawa (oh-kee-NAH-wah)

and Korea to the east and over islands between Japan and Taiwan to the south, including present-day Okinawa. The southern Japanese lords became wealthy and powerful by controlling sea trade—so powerful that the shogunate could no longer master them.

Elite Decline and Social Crisis

Sea trade was only one factor in the reversal of the relative fortunes of the "inner" and the "outer" lords. Population growth was putting a great strain on the well-developed lands of central Japan. In the remote provinces, where the lords had sponsored programs to settle and develop new agricultural lands, the rate of economic growth far outstripped the growth rate in centrally located domains.

Also destabilizing the Tokugawa government in the 1700s was the shogunate's inability to stabilize rice prices and halt the economic decline of the samurai. To finance their living, the samurai had to convert their rice to cash in the market. The Tokugawa government realized that the rice brokers might easily enrich themselves at the expense of the samurai if the price of rice, and the rate of interest, were not strictly controlled. Laws designed to regulate both had been passed early in the Tokugawa period, and laws requiring moneylenders to forgive samurai debts were added later. But these laws were not always enforced, sometimes because neither the lords nor the samurai wished them to be. By the early 1700s members of both groups were dependent on the willingness of merchants to provide them credit.

The Tokugawa shoguns strongly resisted the forces tending to weaken the samurai and to strengthen the merchant class. Their legitimacy rested on their ability to reward and protect the interests of the lords and samurai who had supported the Tokugawa conquest. But the Tokugawa government, like the governments of the Qing Empire, Korea, and Vietnam, accepted the Confucian idea that agriculture should be the basis of state wealth and that merchants should occupy lowly positions in society because of their reputed lack of moral character.

Governments throughout East Asia used Confucian philosophy to attempt to limit the influence and power of merchants. The Tokugawa government, however, was at a special disadvantage. Its decentralized system limited its ability to regulate merchant activities and actually stimulated the growth of commercial activities. In the first two centuries of the Tokugawa Shogunate—from 1600 to 1800—the economy grew faster than the population. Household amenities and cultural resources that in China were found only in the cities were common in the Japanese countryside. Despite official disapproval, merchants and others involved in the growing

Woodblock Print of the "Forty-Seven Ronin" Story   The saga of the forty-seven ronin and the avenging of their fallen leader has fascinated the Japanese public since the event occurred in 1702. This watercolor from the Tokugawa period shows the leaders of the group pausing on the snowy banks of the Sumida River in Edo (Tokyo) before storming their enemy's residence. (Jean-Pierre Hauchecorne Collection)

economy enjoyed relative freedom and influence in eighteenth-century Japan. They produced a vivid culture of their own, fostering the development of *kabuki* theater, colorful woodblock prints and silkscreened fabrics, and restaurants.

The ideological and social crisis of Tokugawa Japan's transformation from a military to a civil society is captured in the "Forty-seven Ronin°" incident of 1702. A young regional lord was provoked by a senior minister into drawing his sword at the shogun's court. For this offense the young lord was sentenced to commit *seppuku°*, the ritual suicide of the samurai. His own followers then became *ronin*, "masterless samurai," obliged by the traditional code of the warrior to avenge their deceased master. They broke into the house of the senior minister who had provoked their own lord, and they killed him and others in his household. Then they withdrew to a temple

---

ronin (ROH-neen)   *seppuku* (SEP-poo-koo)

in Edo and petitioned the shogun to acknowledge their obligation to be loyal to their lord and avenge his death.

A legal debate began in the shogun's government. To deny the righteousness of the ronin would be to deny samurai values. But to approve their actions would create social chaos, undermine laws against murder, and deny the shogunal government itself the right to try cases of samurai violence. The shogun ruled that the ronin had to die but would be permitted to die honorably by committing *seppuku*.

This solution exposed a fatal contradiction in the structure of shogunal government. To maintain a state based on military values, the state must place the military itself outside the law. Centralization, standardization of laws, and the ability of the state to enforce law for protection of the public would be impossible. The purity of purpose of the ronin is still celebrated in Japan, but since the time of the case of 1702, Japanese writers, historians, and teachers have recognized that the self-sacrifice of the ronin for the sake of upholding civil law was necessary.

The Tokugawa Shogunate put into place a political and economic system that fostered innovation, but the government itself could not exploit it. Thus during the Tokugawa period the government remained quite traditional while other segments of society developed new methods of productivity and management.

CONCLUSION

In the early eighteenth century Eurasia was dominated by the struggle of two enormous, land-based empires to defend themselves against each other and to acquire lands that would be at least marginally profitable. Because their needs were so similar, they often competed for the same resources, from Turkestan to Northeast Asia. Russia and the Qing Empire depended on large transportation systems, intense agricultural production, and coerced labor from their domestic populations. They preserved social systems that obligated a majority of the population to work the land but withheld the right to landownership. At the center of their political structures were powerful emperors with the economic and legal resources to command armies, engineering teams, and explorers at a distance. Not surprisingly, each empire had its most brilliant period—under Peter the Great and Emperor Kangxi—when the throne was occupied by a talented, energetic, and far-sighted ruler.

There were also distinct differences between these empires. The Qing court was generally open to many kinds of foreign influences and used ideas, institutions, and technologies from a wide range of sources. But distance and circumstance limited Qing contact with Europe. The Qing could not control which Europeans came to the Qing territories and thus encountered only merchants and missionaries. The merchants did not make much of an impression. The Jesuits were influential in philosophy, mathematics, astronomy, and other issues of concern to them. But they were not an inexhaustible resource for the Kangxi emperor, who was brilliant and inquisitive. From the Jesuits he got very little insight into the emergence of European empires, their tactics, or their goals.

Peter the Great banned the Jesuits from Russia, considering them a subversive and backward influence. St. Petersburg gave Peter a "window" into Europe, and from that vantage point his choices of what to learn from the Europeans and what to reject were unlimited. Among his choices were architecture, engineering, shipbuilding, and military technologies of all kinds. He knew how to exploit the symbolism of European emperorship, and perhaps he knew how to avoid tendencies toward liberalization represented by some Enlightenment thinkers. He understood the meaning of the new European use of the sea, and he foresaw the importance of America in the developing global economy. He set Russian rulers on a path tending toward European practices of diplomacy and imperialism and away from the static values of the huge land empires.

Russia and the Qing represent variations on an imperial pattern not shared by their neighbor Japan. Instead of pursuing centralization, standardization, and strengthening of the ruler, Japan was decentralized. Each local lord developed his own economic and political center, but there was enough connection at the level of the shogun's court for nationwide roadways and trade systems to thrive. Local lords had great incentive to develop their lands, and many turned to overseas opportunities in legitimate trade or in piracy. Despite the official policy of keeping merchants down, in practice merchants worked with the regional lords to develop local enterprises, sustain local samurai, and outfit local soldiers. Many regions of Tokugawa Japan created innovative means of financing local industry and developed unique relationships with other countries, particularly the islands of the western Pacific. In 1792, when Russian ships exploring the North Pacific turned toward the Japanese coast, the local lord used his own forces to chase them away. All local lords understood that they would be on their own as foreign incursions increased. After centuries of competition with, independence from, and often disobedience to the shogunate, they were to have a very different response to foreign challenges from either of their huge imperial neighbors.

Key Terms

Jesuits	Peter the Great	Qing Empire
Siberia	autocracy	Kangxi
Muscovy	serfs	variolation
tsar	Ming Empire	Macartney Mission
Mikhail Romanov	dalai lama	Tokugawa Shogunate
Cossacks	Manchus	*samurai*

Suggested Reading

There is a great deal of literature focused on the Jesuits' history in various countries. See these general histories: Christopher Hollis, *The Jesuits: A History* (1968), and Georg Schurhammer, *Francis Xavier: His Life, His Times*, trans. M. Joseph Costelloe, (1973–1982). For East Asia in the sixteenth and seventeenth centuries see Michael Coopers, S.J., *Rodrigues the Interpreter: An Early Jesuit in Japan and China* (1974). For China see David E. Mungello, *Curious Land: Jesuit Accommodation and the Origins of Sinology* (1985), and Jonathan D. Spence, *The Memory Palace of Matteo Ricci* (1984). For Japan see C. R. Boxer, *The Christian Century in Japan, 1549–1650* (1951). See also Cornelius Wessels, *Early Jesuit Travellers in Central Asia, 1603–1721* (1924). On European images of and interactions with China connected to the Jesuits, see the relevant portions of Jonathan D. Spence, *The Chan's Great Continent: China in Western Minds* (1998), and Joanna Waley-Cohen, *The Sextants of Beijing: Global Currents in Chinese History* (1999).

On the East India companies see John E. Wills, *Pepper, Guns, and Parleys: The Dutch East India Company and China, 1662–1681* (1974); Dianne Lewis, *Jan Compagnie in the Straits of Malacca, 1641–1795* (1995); John Keay, *The Honourable Company: A History of the English East India Company* (1991); Brian Gardner, *The East India Company* (1971); and Lucy Stuart Sutherland, *The East India Company in Eighteenth-Century Politics* (1952). On the development of global commerce in tea, coffee, and cocoa see the relevant chapters in Roy Porter and Mikuláš Teich, *Drugs and Narcotics in History* (1995).

On early modern Russian history, see W. E. Brown, *A History of Eighteenth-Century Russia* (1980), and Robert O. Crummey, *Aristocrats and Servitors: The Boyar Elite in Russia, 1613–1689* (1983). On Peter the Great there is a very extensive collection of works. Among the best-known recent books are Matthew Smith Anderson, *Peter the Great* (1978); Robert K. Massie, *Peter the Great: His Life and World* (1980); and Lindsey Hughes, *Russia in the Age of Peter the Great: 1682–1725* (1998). On the effect of Peter's reforms on the serfs and on the military see Elise K. Wirtschafter, *From Serf to Russian Soldier* (1990). For Russian naval development and Russian influence in the Pacific and in America see Glynn Barratt, *Russia in Pacific Waters, 1715–1825: A Survey of the Origins of Russia's Naval Presence in the North and South Pacific* (1981), and Howard I. Kushner, *Conflict on the Northwest Coast: American-Russian Rivalry in the Pacific Northwest, 1790–1867* (1975).

For China during the transition from the Ming to Qing periods see James W. Tong, *Disorder Under Heaven: Collective Violence in the Ming Dynasty* (1991); Frederic Wakeman, *The Great Enterprise* (1985); and Lynn Struve, *Voices from the Ming-Qing Cataclysm: In Tiger's Jaws* (1993). On the history of the Manchus and of the Qing Empire see Evelyn Sakakida Rawski, *The Last Emperors* (1999), and Pamela Kyle Crossley, *The Manchus* (1997).

On Chinese society generally in this period see two classic (though slightly dated) works by Ping-ti Ho: *The Ladder of Success in Imperial China: Aspects of Social Mobility, 1368–1911* (1962), and *Studies in the Population of China 1368–1953* (1959); and see the general study by Susan Naquin and Evelyn S. Rawski, *Chinese Society in the Eighteenth Century* (1987). On the two greatest of the Qing emperors and their times see Jonathan D. Spence, *Emperor of China; Self Portrait of K'ang Hsi, 1654–1722*, (1974). For a more scholarly treatment see Lawrence D. Kessler, *K'ang-hsi and the Consolidation of Ch'ing Rule, 1661–1684* (1976); Jonathan D. Spence, *Ts'ao Yin and the K'ang-hsi Emperor: Bondservant and Master* (1966); and Harold Kahn, *Monarchy in the Emperor's Eyes: Image and Reality in the Ch'ien-lung Reign* (1971).

On the Qing trade systems see John E. Wills, *Embassies and Illusions: Dutch and Portuguese Envoys to K'ang-hsi, 1666–1687* (1984), and Craig Clunas, *Chinese Export Art and Design* (1987).

There is a great deal published on the Macartney mission, much of it originating in the diaries and memoirs of the participants. See the exhaustively detailed Alain Peyrefitte, *The Immobile Empire*, trans. Jon Rothschild (1992). For a more theoretical discussion see James L. Hevia, *Cherishing Men from Afar: Qing Guest Ritual and the Macartney Embassy of 1793* (1995).

On Japan in this period see Chie Nakane and Shinzaburo Oishi *Tokugawa Japan: The Social and Economic Antecedents of Modern Japan*, trans. Conrad Totman (1990), and Tessa Morris-Suzuki, *The Technological Transformation of Japan from the Seventeenth to the Twenty-First Century* (1994). Mary Elizabeth Berry, *Hideyoshi* (1982), is an account of the reunification of Japan at the end of the sixteenth century and the invasion of Korea. On technological advancement, capital formation, and competition in the Tokugawa period see the classic by Thomas C. Smith, *Agrarian Origins of Modern Japan* (1959); the first chapter of Albert Craig, *Choshu in the Meiji Restoration* (1961); John Whitney Hall and Marius B. Jansen, eds., *Studies in the Institutional History of Early Modern Japan* (1968); and John G. Roberts, *Mitsui: Three Centuries of Japanese Business* (1973).

Notes

1. Adapted from G. V. Melikhov, "Manzhou Penetration into the Basin of the Upper Amur in the 1680s," in S. L. Tikhvinshii, ed., *Manzhou Rule in China* (Moscow: Progress Publishers, 1983).

2. See Lynn Struve, *Voices from the Ming-Qing Cataclysm: In Tiger's Jaws* (New Haven, CT: Yale University Press, 1993), 235–237.

PART
SIX

REVOLUTIONS RESHAPE THE WORLD,

1750–1870

CHAPTER 23
REVOLUTIONARY CHANGES IN THE ATLANTIC WORLD, 1750–1850

CHAPTER 24
THE EARLY INDUSTRIAL REVOLUTION, 1760–1851

CHAPTER 25
NATION BUILDING AND ECONOMIC TRANSFORMATION IN THE AMERICAS, 1800–1890

CHAPTER 26
AFRICA, INDIA, AND THE NEW BRITISH EMPIRE, 1750–1870

CHAPTER 27
THE OTTOMAN EMPIRE AND EAST ASIA, 1800–1870

Between 1750 and 1870, dramatic political, economic, and social changes affected nearly every part of the world. The beginnings of industrialization, the American and French Revolutions, and revolutions for independence in Latin America challenged the existing order in the West. In Africa, Asia, and the Middle East, the expansion of European commercial and military power combined with powerful internal transformations to challenge long-established institutions.

In the West, the American, French, and Haitian Revolutions unleashed forces of nationalism and social reform. At this time, the Industrial Revolution introduced technologies and patterns of work that made industrial societies wealthier, more socially fluid, and militarily more powerful than nonindustrial, traditional societies. Even while Europe's colonial empires in the Western Hemisphere were being dismantled, the Industrial Revolution was fueling European economic expansion, which undermined traditional producers in distant places such as Asia and Africa. When this economic penetration was resisted, as it was in East Asia, the industrializing nations of the West used military force to open markets.

Great Britain expanded its empire by establishing colonial rule in distant Australia, New Zealand, and India. India alone had a population larger than the combined populations of all the colonies that Europe lost in the Americas. The Atlantic slave trade was ended by an international abolitionist movement and by Great Britain's use of diplomacy and naval power. European economic influence expanded in Africa. Invigorated by this exchange, some African states created new institutions and introduced new economic sectors.

The Ottoman Empire, the Qing Empire, and Japan were deeply influenced by the expansion of Europe and the United States. Each society met the Western challenge with reform programs that preserved traditional structures while adopting elements of Western technology and organization. The Ottoman court introduced reforms in education, the military, and law and created the first constitution in an Islamic state. The Qing Empire survived the period of European expansion, but a series of military defeats and civil war seriously compromised China's centralization efforts. Japan experienced the most revolutionary change, abolishing its ancient political system and initiating radical top-down transformations.

The economic, political, and social revolutions that began in the mid-eighteenth century shook the foundations of European culture and led to the expansion of Western power across the globe. Societies throughout Asia, Africa, and Latin America responded to cross-cultural contacts. Some resisted foreign intrusion by using local culture and experience as a guide. Others adopted Western commercial policies, industrial technologies, and government institutions.

	1750	1775	1800	
Americas	1754–1763 French and Indian War	U.S. Declaration of Independence 1776 •	Louisiana Purchase by United States 1803 • • 1789 U.S. Constitution ratified • 1791 Slaves revolt in Haiti	1809–1825 Wars for independence in Spanish America
Europe	• ca. 1750 Industrial Revolution begins in Britain 1756–1763 Seven Years War		1789–1799 French Revolution 1799–1815 Rule of Napoleon in France	1814–1815 Congress of Vienna
Africa		Britain takes Cape Colony 1795 •	Sokoto Caliphate founded 1809 • Shaka founds Zulu kingdom 1818 •	
Middle East		Muhammad Ali founds dynasty in Egypt 1805 •	1789–1807 Reign of Ottoman sultan Selim III • 1798 Napoleon invades Egypt	
Asia and Oceania	• 1755 Qing conquest of Turkestan East India Company rule of Bengal begins 1765 •	1769–1778 Captain Cook's exploration of Australia, New Zealand	White Lotus Rebellion in China 1796–1804 Britain takes Ceylon 1798 •	East India Company creates Bombay presidency 1818 •

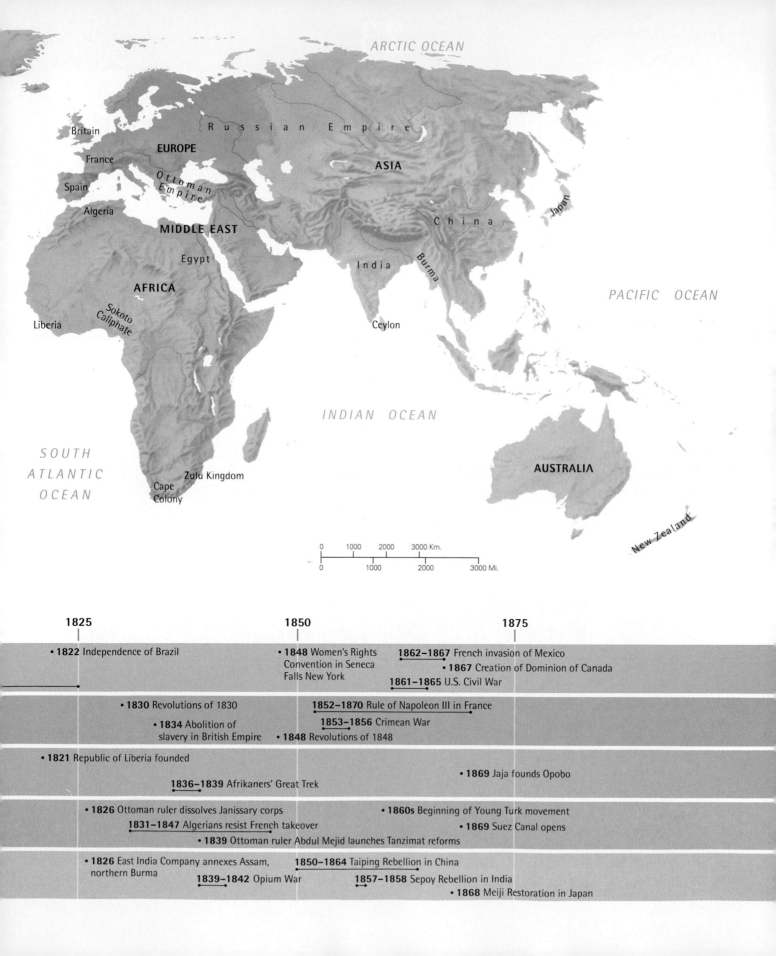

ARCTIC OCEAN

Britain

EUROPE

France

Spain

Algeria

Russian Empire

Ottoman Empire

ASIA

Japan

China

MIDDLE EAST

Egypt

India

Burma

AFRICA

Sokoto Caliphate

Liberia

Ceylon

PACIFIC OCEAN

INDIAN OCEAN

SOUTH ATLANTIC OCEAN

Zulu Kingdom

Cape Colony

AUSTRALIA

New Zealand

| 0 | 1000 | 2000 | 3000 Km. |
| 0 | 1000 | 2000 | 3000 Mi. |

1825　　　　　　**1850**　　　　　　**1875**

• **1822** Independence of Brazil

• **1848** Women's Rights Convention in Seneca Falls New York

1862–1867 French invasion of Mexico

• **1867** Creation of Dominion of Canada

1861–1865 U.S. Civil War

• **1830** Revolutions of 1830

1852–1870 Rule of Napoleon III in France

• **1834** Abolition of slavery in British Empire

1853–1856 Crimean War

• **1848** Revolutions of 1848

• **1821** Republic of Liberia founded

• **1869** Jaja founds Opobo

1836–1839 Afrikaners' Great Trek

• **1826** Ottoman ruler dissolves Janissary corps

• **1860s** Beginning of Young Turk movement

1831–1847 Algerians resist French takeover

• **1869** Suez Canal opens

• **1839** Ottoman ruler Abdul Mejid launches Tanzimat reforms

• **1826** East India Company annexes Assam, northern Burma

1850–1864 Taiping Rebellion in China

1839–1842 Opium War

1857–1858 Sepoy Rebellion in India

• **1868** Meiji Restoration in Japan

23

Revolutionary Changes in the Atlantic World,

1750–1850

Prelude to Revolution: The Eighteenth-Century Crisis •
The American Revolution, 1775–1800 • The French Revolution, 1789–1815 •
Revolution Spreads, Conservatives Respond, 1789–1850
ENVIRONMENT AND TECHNOLOGY: The Pencil
SOCIETY AND CULTURE: The Women of Revolutionary France

Execution of Louis XVI The execution of the French king in 1793 was the most shocking and dramatic signal that the "Old Order" was about to be swept away.

*O*n the evening of August 14, 1791, more than two hundred slaves and black freedmen met in secret in the plantation district of northern Saint Domingue° (present-day Haiti) to set the date for an armed uprising against local slave owners. Although the delegates agreed to delay the attack for a week, violence began almost immediately. During the following decade, slavery was abolished, military forces from Britain and France were defeated, and Haiti achieved independence.

This meeting was provoked by news and rumors about revolutionary events in France that had spread through the island's slave community. Events in France also had divided the island's white population into competing camps of royalists (supporters of France's King Louis XVI) and republicans (supporters of democracy). The free mixed-race population initially gained some political rights from the French Assembly but was then forced to rebel when the slave-owning elite reacted violently.

Among those planning the insurrection was a black freedman named François Dominique Toussaint. He proved to be one of the most remarkable representatives of the revolutionary era, later taking the name Toussaint L'Ouverture°. He organized the rebels into a potent military force, negotiated with the island's royalist and republican factions and with representatives of Great Britain and France, and wrote his nation's first constitution. Commonly portrayed as a fiend by slave owners throughout the Western Hemisphere, Toussaint became for slaves a towering symbol of resistance to oppression.

The Haitian slave rebellion was an important episode in the long and painful political and cultural transformation of the modern Western world. Economic expansion and the growth of trade were creating unprecedented wealth. The first stage of the Industrial Revolution (see Chapter 24) increased manufacturing productivity and led to greater global interdependence, new patterns of consumerism, and altered social structures. At the same time, intellectuals were questioning the traditional place of monarchy and religion in society. An increasingly powerful class of merchants, professionals, and manufacturers created by the emerging economy provided an audience for these new intellectual currents and began to press for a larger political role.

This revolutionary era turned the Western world "upside down." The *ancien régime*°, the French term for Europe's old order, rested on medieval principles: politics dominated by powerful monarchs, intellectual and cultural life dominated by religion, and economics dominated by a hereditary agricultural elite. In the West's new order, politics was opened to vastly greater participation, science and secular inquiry took the place of religion in intellectual life, and economies were increasingly opened to competition.

This radical transformation did not take place without false starts and temporary setbacks. Imperial powers resisted the loss of colonies; monarchs and nobles struggled to retain their ancient privileges; and the church fought against the claims of science. Revolutionary steps forward were often matched by reactionary steps backward. The liberal and nationalist ideals of the eighteenth-century revolutionary movements were only imperfectly realized in Europe and the Americas in the nineteenth century. Despite setbacks, belief in national self-determination and universal suffrage, and a passion for social justice continued to animate reformers into the twentieth century.

As you read this chapter, ask yourself the following questions:

- How did imperial wars among European powers provoke revolution?
- In what ways were the revolutions, expanded literacy, and new political ideas linked?
- How did revolution in one country help to incite revolution elsewhere?
- Why were the revolutions in France and Haiti more violent than the American Revolution?

Saint Domingue (san doe-MANG)
Toussaint L'Ouverture (too-SAN loo-ver-CHORE)

ancien régime (ahn-see-EN ray-ZHEEM)

PRELUDE TO REVOLUTION: THE EIGHTEENTH-CENTURY CRISIS

In large measure, the cost of wars fought among Europe's major powers over colonies and trade precipitated the revolutionary era that began in 1775 with the American Revolution. Britain, France, and Spain were the central actors in these global struggles, but other imperial powers were affected as well. Unpopular and costly wars had been fought earlier and paid for with new taxes. But changes in the Western intellectual and political environments led to a much more critical response. Any effort to extend the power of a monarch or impose new taxes now raised questions about the rights of individuals and the authority of political institutions.

Colonial Wars and Fiscal Crises

The rivalry among European powers intensified in the early 1600s when the newly independent Netherlands began an assault on the American and Asian colonies of Spain and Portugal. The Dutch attacked Spanish treasure fleets in the Caribbean and Pacific and seized parts of Portugal's colonial empire in Brazil and Angola. Europe's other emerging sea power, Great Britain, also attacked Spanish fleets and seaports in the Americas. By the end of the seventeenth century, expanding British sea power had checked Dutch commercial and colonial ambitions and ended the Dutch monopoly of the African slave trade.

As Dutch power ebbed, Britain and France began a long struggle for political preeminence in western Europe and for territory and trade outlets in the Americas and Asia. Both the geographic scale and the expense of this conflict expanded during the eighteenth century. Nearly all of Europe's great powers were engaged in the War of the Spanish Succession (1701–1714). War between Britain and Spain, begun in 1739 over smuggling in the Americas, quickly broadened into a generalized European conflict, the War of the Austrian Succession (1740–1748). Conflict between French and English settlers in North America then helped ignite a long war that altered the colonial balance of power. When Britain finally won the Seven Years War (1756–1763), known as the French and Indian War in America, it not only gained undisputed control of North America east of the Mississippi River but also forced France to surrender most of its holdings in India.

The enormous costs of these conflicts distinguished them from earlier wars. Traditional taxes collected in traditional ways no longer covered the obligations of governments. For example, at the end of the Seven Years War in 1763, Britain's war debt had reached £137 million. Although Britain's total budget before the war had averaged only £8 million, annual interest on the war debt alone came to exceed £5 million. Even as European economies expanded because of increased trade and the early stages of the Industrial Revolution, fiscal crises overtook one European government after another. In an intellectual environment transformed by the Enlightenment, the need for new revenues provoked debate and confrontation within a vastly expanded and more critical public.

The Enlightenment and the Old Order

The complex and diverse intellectual movement called the **Enlightenment** applied the methods and questions of the Scientific Revolution of the seventeenth century to the study of human society. Dazzled by Copernicus's ability to explain the structure of the solar system and Newton's representation of the law of gravity, European intellectuals began to apply the logical tools of scientific inquiry to other questions. Some labored to systematize knowledge or organize reference materials. For example, Carolus Linnaeus° (a Swedish botanist known by the Latin form of his name) sought to categorize all living organisms, and Samuel Johnson published a comprehensive English dictionary with over forty thousand definitions. In France Denis Diderot° worked with other Enlightenment thinkers to create a compendium of human knowledge, the thirty-five-volume *Encyclopédie*.

Other thinkers pursued lines of inquiry that challenged long-established religious and political institutions. Some argued that if scientists could understand the laws of nature then surely similar forms of disciplined investigation might reveal laws of human nature. Others wondered whether society and government might be better regulated and more productive if guided by science rather than by hereditary rulers and the church. These new perspectives and the intellectual optimism that fed them were to help guide the revolutionary movements of the late eighteenth century.

The English political philosopher John Locke (1632–1704) argued in 1690 that governments were created to protect life, liberty, and property and that the people had

---

Carolus Linnaeus (kar-ROLL-uhs lin-NEE-uhs)
Denis Diderot (duh-nee DEE-duh-roe)

CHRONOLOGY

	The Americas	Europe
1750	**1756–1763** French and Indian War	**1756–1763** Seven Years War
1775	**1770** Boston Massacre **1776** American Declaration of Independence **1778** United States alliance with France **1783** Treaty of Paris ends American Revolution	
	1791 Slaves revolt in Saint Domingue (Haiti)	**1789** Storming of Bastille begins French Revolution **1793–1794** Reign of Terror in France **1795–1799** The Directory rules France **1799** Napoleon overthrows the Directory
1800	**1798** Toussaint L'Ouverture defeats British in Haiti **1804** Haitians defeat French invasion and declare independence	**1804** Napoleon crowns himself emperor **1814** Napoleon abdicates; Congress of Vienna opens **1815** Napoleon defeated at Waterloo **1830** Greece gains independence; revolution in France overthrows Charles X **1848** Revolutions in France, Austria, Germany, Hungary, and Italy

a right to rebel when a monarch violated these natural rights. Locke's closely reasoned theory began with the assumption that individual rights were the foundation of civil government. In *The Social Contract,* published in 1762, the French-Swiss intellectual Jean-Jacques Rousseau° (1712–1778) asserted that the will of the people was sacred and that the legitimacy of the monarch depended on the consent of the people. Although both men beleived that government rested on the will of the people rather than divine will, Locke emphasized the importance of individual rights, and Rousseau envisioned the people acting collectively because of their shared historical experience.

All Enlightenment thinkers were not radicals like Rousseau. There was never a uniform program for political and social reform, and the era's intellectuals often disagreed about principles and objectives. The Enlightenment is commonly associated with hostility toward religion and monarchy, but few European intellectuals openly expressed republican or atheist sentiments. The church was most commonly attacked when it attempted to censor ideas or ban books. Critics of monarchial authority were as likely to point out violations of ancient custom as to suggest democratic alternatives. Even Voltaire, one of the Enlightenment's most critical intel-

lects and one of the era's great celebrities, believed that Europe's monarchs were likely agents of political and economic reform, and he wrote favorably of China's Qing° emperors.

Indeed, sympathetic members of the nobility and reforming European monarchs such as Charles III of Spain (r. 1759–1788), Catherine the Great of Russia (r. 1762–1796), Joseph II of Austria (r. 1780–1790), and Frederick the Great of Prussia (r. 1740–1786) actively sponsored and promoted the dissemination of new ideas, providing patronage for many intellectuals. They recognized that elements of the Enlightenment critique of the ancien régime buttressed their own efforts to expand royal authority at the expense of religious institutions, the nobility, and regional autonomy. Goals such as the development of national bureaucracies staffed by civil servants selected on merit, the creation of national legal systems, and the modernization of tax systems united many of Europe's monarchs and intellectuals. Monarchs also understood that the era's passion for science and technology held the potential of fattening national treasuries and improving economic performance (see Environment and Technology: The Pencil). Periodicals disseminating new technologies often gained the patronage of these reforming monarchs.

Jean-Jacques Rosseau (zhahn-zhock roo-SOE)

Qing (ching)

The Pencil

From early times, Europeans had used sharp points, lead, and other implements to sketch, make marks, and write brief notes. At the end of the seventeenth century, a source of high-quality graphite was discovered at Borrowdale in northwestern England. Borrowdale graphite gained acceptance among artists, artisans, and merchants. At first, pure graphite was simply wrapped in string. By the eighteenth century, pieces of graphite were being encased in wooden sheaths and resembled modern pencils. Widespread use of this useful tool was retarded by the limited supply of high-quality graphite from the English mines.

The English crown periodically closed the Borrowdale mines or restricted production to keep prices high and maintain adequate supplies for future needs. As a result, artisans in other European nations developed alternatives that used lower-quality graphite or, most commonly, graphite mixed with sulfur and glues.

The major breakthrough occurred in 1793 in France when war with England ruptured trade links. The government of revolutionary France responded to the shortage of graphite by assigning a thirty-nine-year-old scientist, Nicolas-Jacques Conté, to find an alternative. Conté had earlier promoted the military use of balloons and conducted experiments with hydrogen. He also had had experience using graphite alloys in the development of crucibles for melting metal.

Within a short period, Conté produced a graphite that is the basis for most lead pencils today. He succeeded by mixing finely ground graphite with potter's clay and water. The resulting paste was dried in a long mold, sealed in a ceramic box, and fired in an oven. The graphite strips were then placed in a wooden case. Although some believed the Conté pencils were inferior to the pencils made from Borrowdale

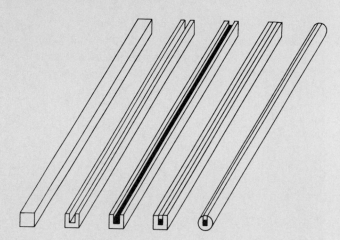

Pencils Wartime necessity led to invention of the modern pencil in France. (Drawing by Fred Avent for Henry Petroski. Reproduced by permission)

graphite, Conté produced a very serviceable pencil that could be produced in uniform quality and unlimited amounts.

Henry Petroski, summarizing the achievement of Conté in his *The Pencil*, wrote: "The laboratory is really the modern workshop. And modern engineering results when the scientific method is united with experience with the tools and products of craftsmen.... Modern engineering, in spirit if not in name, would come to play a more and more active role in turning the craft tradition into modern technology, with its base of research and development."

Source: This discussion depends on Henry Petroski, *The Pencil: A History of Design and Circumstance* (New York: Knopf, 1990); the quotation is from pp. 50–78. Drawing by Fred Avent for Henry Petroski. Reproduced by permission.

Though willing to embrace reform proposals when they served royal interests, Europe's monarchs moved quickly to suppress or ban radical ideas that promoted republicanism or directly attacked religion. However, too many channels of communication were open to permit a thoroughgoing suppression of these ideas. In fact, censorship tended to enhance intellectual reputations, and persecuted intellectuals generally found patronage in the courts of foreign rivals.

Many of the major intellectuals of the Enlightenment maintained an extensive correspondence with each other as well as with political leaders. This communication led to numerous firsthand contacts among the intellectuals of different nations and helped to create a coherent assault on what was typically called ignorance—beliefs and values associated with the ancien régime. Rousseau, for example, briefly sought refuge in Britain, where the Scottish philosopher David Hume befriended him. Similarly, Voltaire sought patronage and protection in England and later Prussia.

Women were instrumental in the dissemination of the new ideas. In England educated middle-class women purchased and discussed the books and pamphlets of the era. Some were important contributors to intellectual life as writers and commentators, raising by example and in argument the issue of the rights of women. In Paris wealthy women made their homes centers of debate, intellectual speculation, and free inquiry. Their salons brought together philosophers, social critics, artists, and members of the aristocracy and commercial elite. Unlike their contemporaries in England, the women of the Parisian salons used their social standing more to direct the conversations of men rather than to give vent to their own opinions.

The intellectual ferment of the era deeply influenced the expanding middle class in Europe and the Western Hemisphere. Members of this class were eager consumers of books and the inexpensive newspapers and journals that were widely available in the eighteenth century. This broadening of the intellectual audience overwhelmed traditional institutions of censorship. Scientific discoveries, new technologies, and controversial work on human nature and politics also were discussed in the thousands of coffeehouses and teashops opening in major cities and market towns.

Many European intellectuals were interested in the Americas. Some Europeans continued to dismiss the New World as barbaric and inferior, but others used idealized accounts of the New World to support their critiques of European society. These thinkers looked to Britain's North American colonies for confirmation of their belief that human nature unconstrained by the corrupted practices of Europe's old order would quickly produce material abundance and social justice. More than any other American, the writer and inventor **Benjamin Franklin** came to symbolize both the natural genius and the vast potential of America.

Born in 1706 in Boston, the young Franklin was apprenticed to his older brother, a printer. At seventeen he ran away to Philadelphia, where he succeeded as a printer and publisher, best known for his *Poor Richard's Almanac*. By age forty-two he was a wealthy man. He retired from active business to pursue writing, science, and public affairs. In Philadelphia, Franklin was instrumental in the creation of the organizations that later became the Philadelphia Free Library, the American Philosophical Society, and the University of Pennsylvania.

His contributions were both practical and theoretical. He was the inventor of bifocal glasses, the lightning rod, and an efficient wood-burning stove. In 1751 he published a scientific work on electricity, *Experiments and Observations on Electricity*, that established his intellectual reputation in Europe. Intellectuals heralded the book as proof that the simple and unsophisticated world of America was a particularly hospitable environment for genius.

Franklin was also an important political figure. He served Pennsylvania as a delegate to the Albany (New York) Congress in 1754, which sought to coordinate colonial defense against attacks by the French and their Amerindian allies. Later he was a Pennsylvania delegate to the Continental Congress that issued the Declaration of Independence in 1776. His service in England as colonial lobbyist and later as the Continental Congress's ambassador to Paris allowed him to cultivate his European reputation. Franklin's wide achievement, witty conversation, and careful self-promotion make him a symbol of the era. In him the Enlightenment's most radical project, the freeing of human potential from the inhibitions of inherited privilege, found its most agreeable confirmation.

As Franklin's career demonstrates, the Western Hemisphere shared in the debates of Europe. New ideas penetrated the curricula of many colonial universities and appeared in periodicals and books published in the New World. As scientific method was applied to economic and political questions, colonial writers, scholars, and artists on both sides of the Atlantic were drawn into a debate that eventually was to lead to the rejection of colonialism itself. This radicalization of the colonial intellectual community was provoked by the European monarchies' efforts to reform colonial policies. As European authorities swept away colonial institutions and long-established political practices without consultation, colonial residents had to acknowledge that their status as colonies meant perpetual subordination to European rulers. Among people compelled to recognize this structural dependence and inferiority, the idea that government authority ultimately rested on the consent of the governed was potentially explosive.

Folk Cultures and Popular Protest

While intellectuals and the reforming royal courts of Europe were embracing the rational and secular enthusiasms of the Enlightenment, most people in Western society remained loyal to competing cultural values grounded in the preindustrial past. These regionally distinct folk cultures were framed by the memory of shared local historical experience and nourished by religious practices encouraging emotional release. They emphasized the obligations that people had to each other and local, rather than national, loyalties. Though never formally articulated, these cultural traditions composed a coherent expression of the mutual rights and obligations connecting the people and their rulers. Rulers who violated the constraints of these understandings were likely to face violent opposition.

In the eighteenth century, European monarchs sought to increase their authority and to centralize power by reforming tax collection, judicial practice, and public administration. Although monarchs viewed these changes as reforms, the common people often saw them as violations of sacred customs and sometimes expressed their outrage in bread riots, tax protests, and attacks on royal officials. These violent actions were not efforts to overturn traditional authority. They were efforts to preserve custom and precedent. In Spain and the Spanish colonies, for example, protesting mobs commonly asserted the apparently contradictory slogan

"Long live the King. Death to bad government." They expressed loyalty and love of their monarch while at the same time assaulting his officials and preventing the implementation of changes to long-established customs.

Folk cultures were threatened by other kinds of reform as well. Rationalist reformers of the Enlightenment sought to bring order and discipline to the citizenry by banning or by altering in form the numerous popular cultural traditions—such as harvest festivals, religious holidays, and country fairs—that enlivened the drudgery of everyday life. These events were popular celebrations of sexuality and individuality as well as occasions where masked and costumed celebrants mocked the greed, pretension, and foolishness of government officials, the wealthy, and the clergy. Hard drinking, gambling, and blood sports like cockfighting and bearbaiting were all popular activities in this preindustrial mass culture. Because these customs were viewed as corrupt and decadent by reformers influenced by the Enlightenment,

Beer Street (1751) This engraving by William Hogarth shows an idealized London street scene where beer drinking is associated with manly strength, good humor, and prosperity. The self-satisfied corpulent figure in the left foreground has been reading a copy of the king's speech to Parliament. We can imagine him offering a running commentary to his drinking companions as he reads. (The Art Archive Limited)

governments undertook efforts to substitute civic rituals, patriotic anniversaries, and institutions of self-improvement. These challenges to custom—like the efforts at political reform—often provoked protests, rebellions, and riots.

The efforts of ordinary men and women to resist the growth of government power and the imposition of new cultural forms provide an important political undercurrent to much of the revolutionary agitation and conflict from 1750 to 1850. Spontaneous popular uprisings and protests punctuated nearly every effort at reform in the eighteenth century. But these popular actions gained revolutionary potential only when they coincided with ideological divisions and conflicts within the governing class itself. In America and France the old order was swept away when the protests and rebellions of the rural and urban poor coincided with the appearance of revolutionary leaders who followed Enlightenment ideals in the effort to create secular republican states. Likewise, a slave rebellion in Saint Domingue (Haiti) achieved revolutionary potential when it attracted the support of black freedmen and disaffected poor whites who had been radicalized by news of the French Revolution.

THE AMERICAN REVOLUTION, 1775–1800

In British North America, clumsy efforts to reform colonial tax policy to cover rising defense expenditures and to diminish the power of elected colonial legislatures outraged a populace accustomed to greater local autonomy. Once begun, the American Revolution ushered in a century-long process of political and cultural transformation in Europe and the Americas. By the end of this revolutionary century, the authority of monarchs had been swept away or limited by constitutions, and religion had lost its dominating place in Western intellectual life. Moreover, the medieval idea of a social order determined by birth had been replaced by a capitalist vision that emphasized competition and social mobility.

Frontiers and Taxes

After defeating the French in 1763, the British government faced two related problems in its North American colonies. As settlers quickly pushed into Amerindian lands west of the Appalachian Mountains and across the Ohio River, the British government saw the likelihood of armed con-

flict with Amerindian peoples. Already burdened with debts from the French and Indian War, Britain desperately wanted to avoid additional expenditures for frontier defense. Because of the possibility of frontier conflict and the need to hold down defense costs, Britain tried to get the colonists to shoulder more of the costs of imperial defense and colonial administration.

Every effort to impose new taxes or prevent the settlement of the trans-Appalachian frontier provoked angry protests in the colonies. The situation was made politically explosive by the confrontational and impolitic way in which a succession of weak British governments responded. Because George III (r. 1760–1820) relied upon cabinet ministers selected from among court favorites without regard to parliamentary support, the common response to colonial protests was incendiary bluster and weak enforcement. British government in the period after 1763 was a dangerous combination of qualities: both overbearing and weak.

When the British replaced the French in the Great Lakes region, they angered indigenous peoples by refusing to follow the French practice of paying rent for frontier forts and giving gifts to Amerindian allies. They also reduced the prices paid for furs. Amerindians had become accustomed to the goods they received in exchange for furs, especially firearms, gunpowder, textiles, and alcohol. To get these commodities, they had greatly intensified their hunting practices, endangering some species. Relations deteriorated quickly as settlers and white fur traders pushed across the Appalachians, adding new pressures to the natural environment.

Britain soon demonstrated that it was unable to negotiate the diplomatic and military challenges inherent in the relationship between Amerindians and settlers. Led by Pontiac, an Ottawa chief, a broad alliance of native peoples successfully drove the British military from frontier outposts and then raided deep into the settled areas of Virginia and Pennsylvania. Although this Amerindian alliance was defeated decisively within a year, the potential for renewed violence existed all along the frontier.

The British government's panicked reaction to Pontiac's challenge was the Proclamation of 1763. It sought to establish an effective western limit for settlement. The proposed boundary threw into question the claims of thousands of already established farmers without effectively protecting Amerindian land. No one was satisfied. A decade later the British government irritated the colonists even more when it attempted to slow settlement in contested regions east of the Mississippi and north of the Ohio. The Quebec Act of 1774 annexed disputed lands to the province of Quebec, thus denying eastern colonies the authority to distribute lands claimed as a result of original charters. Colonists saw the Quebec Act as punitive and tyrannical, and Amerindian peoples received no relief from the continuous assault on their land.

Frontier wars were costly and destructive but did not threaten British authority directly. The British government's campaign of fiscal reforms and new taxes, however, sparked a political confrontation that ultimately led to rebellion. New commercial regulations that increased the cost of foreign molasses and endangered colonial exports cut into New England's profitable trade with Spanish and French Caribbean sugar colonies. Britain also outlawed the colonial practice of issuing paper money, a custom made necessary by the colonies' chronic balance-of-payments deficits. These actions, which restricted trade and limited the money supply, provoked widespread anger. Colonial legislatures formally protested, and angry colonists organized boycotts of British goods.

The Stamp Act of 1765 imposed a tax, to be paid in scarce coin, on all legal documents, newspapers, pamphlets, and nearly all other types of printed material. Propertied colonists, including holders of high office and members of the colonial elite, took leading roles in the resulting protests. They used fiery political language, even calling Britain's rulers "parricides" and "tyrants." In 1765 representatives from the colonies met in New York City to protest, and women from many of the most prominent colonial families organized boycotts of British goods. Organizations such as the Sons of Liberty held public meetings, intimidated royal officials, and developed committees to enforce the boycotts. The combination of violent protest and trade boycott forced the repeal of the Stamp Act in 1766. But new taxes and duties were soon imposed, and parliament granted colonial governors new powers, even sending British troops to quell urban riots.

The result was a new round of boycotts, which cut colonial imports of British goods by two-thirds. Angry colonists also destroyed property and bullied or attacked royal officials. The mob practice of covering despised British functionaries with hot tar and feathers became a symbol of American lawlessness for the British public. Unable to control the streets, British authorities reacted by threatening traditional liberties, even dissolving the colonial legislature of Massachusetts.

The cycle of confrontation in Boston prompted the British government to dispatch a warship and two regiments of soldiers to reestablish control of Boston's streets. Conflicts soon occurred when off-duty British soldiers sought part-time employment, further enraging Boston's working class, which was suffering through a

The Tarring and Feathering of a British Official, 1774   This illustration from a British periodical shows the unfortunate John Malcomb, commissioner of customs at Boston. By the mid-1770s, British periodicals were focusing public opinion on mob violence and the breakdown of public order in the colonies. British critics of colonial political protests viewed the demand for liberty as little more than an excuse for mob violence.   (The Granger Collection, New York)

period of low wages and high unemployment. Support for a complete break with Britain grew after March 5, 1770, when a British force fired on an angry Boston crowd, killing five civilians. This "Boston Massacre," which seemed to expose the naked force on which colonial rule rested, radicalized public opinion throughout the colonies.

Parliament attempted to calm public opinion by repealing some of the taxes and duties, then stumbled into another crisis by granting the British East India Company a monopoly for importing tea to the colonies. This monopoly raised anew the constitutional issue of Parliament's right to tax the colonies. It also offended wealthy colonial merchants, who were excluded from this profitable commerce. The crisis came to a head in the already politically overheated port of Boston when tea worth £10,000 was dumped into the harbor by protesters disguised as Amerindians. Britain responded by appointing a military man, Thomas Gage, as governor of Massachusetts and by closing the port of Boston. Public order in Boston now depended on British troops, and public administration was in the hands of a general. This militarization of colonial government in Boston undermined Britain's constitutional authority and made a military test of strength inevitable.

The Course of Revolution, 1775–1783

As the crisis mounted, new governing bodies created by patriot leaders effectively deposed many British governors, judges, and customs officers. The new institutions of colonial government created laws, appointed justices, and even took control of colonial militias. Simultaneously, radical leaders organized crowds to intimidate loyalists—people who were pro-British—and to enforce the boycott of British goods.

By the time elected representatives met in Philadelphia as the Continental Congress in 1775, blood had already been shed when patriot militia met British troops at Lexington and Concord, Massachusetts (see Map 23.1). Events were propelling the colonies toward revolution. Congress assumed the powers of government, creating a currency and organizing an army. **George Washington** (1732–1799), a Virginia planter who had served in the French and Indian War, was named commander.

Popular support for independence was given a hard edge by the angry rhetoric of thousands of street-corner speakers and the inflammatory pamphlet *Common Sense*, written by Thomas Paine, a recent immigrant from England. Paine's pamphlet alone sold 120,000 copies. On July 4, 1776, Congress approved the Declaration of Independence, the document that proved to be the most enduring statement of the revolutionary era's ideology:

> We hold these truths to be self evident: That all men are created equal; that they are endowed by their creator with certain unalienable rights; that among these are life, liberty and the pursuit of happiness; that, to secure these rights, governments are instituted among men, deriving their just powers from the consent of the governed.

The Declaration's affirmation of popular sovereignty and individual rights influenced the language of revolution and popular protest around the world.

Hoping to shore up British authority, Great Britain sent an expeditionary force of 32,000 soldiers and an armada of more than 400 ships to pacify the colonies. By 1778, British land forces numbered 50,000 supported by 30,000 German mercenaries. But this military commitment proved futile. Despite the existence of a large loyalist community in the colonies, the British army found it difficult to control the countryside. Although British forces won most of the battles, Washington slowly built a competent Continental army and civilian support networks that provided supplies and financial resources.

The real problem for the British government was its inability to discover a compromise solution that would satisfy colonial grievances. Half-hearted efforts to resolve the bitter conflict over taxes failed, and a later offer to roll back the clock and reestablish the administrative arrangements of 1763 made little headway. Independence had been declared, and blood had been shed. Overconfidence and poor leadership prevented the British from finding a political solution before revolutionary institutions were in place and the armies engaged. By allowing confrontation to occur, the British government lost the opportunity to mobilize and give direction to the large numbers of loyalists and pacifists in the colonies.

Along the Canadian border, both sides solicited Amerindians as potential allies and feared them as potential enemies. For over a hundred years, members of the powerful Iroquois Confederacy—Mohawk, Oneida, Onondaga, Cayuga, Seneca, and (after 1722) Tuscarora—had protected their traditional lands with a combination of diplomacy and warfare, playing a role in all the colonial wars of the eighteenth century. Just as the American Revolution forced neighbors and families to join the rebels or remain loyal, it divided the Iroquois, who fought on both sides. The Mohawk proved to be the most valuable of British allies among the Iroquois.

The Mohawk loyalist leader **Joseph Brant** (Thayendanegea°) organized Britain's most potent fighting force along the Canadian border. Portrayed in the propaganda of the revolutionaries as a symbol of Amerindian savagery, Brant organized raids along the northern frontier that earned him the title "Monster" Brant. Actually, he was a man who moved easily between European and Amerindian cultures. Educated by missionaries, he was fluent in English and helped to translate Protestant religious tracts into Mohawk. He was tied to many of the wealthiest loyalist families through his sister, formerly the mistress of Sir William Johnson, Britain's superintendent of Indian affairs for North America. Brant had traveled to London and had an audience with George III. He

---

Thayendanegea (ta YEHN dah NEY geh ah)

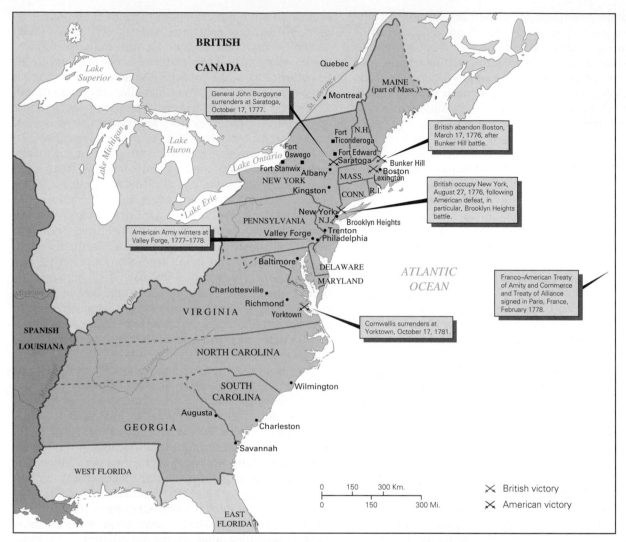

BRITISH

CANADA

Quebec

MAINE
(part of Mass.)

General John Burgoyne
surrenders at Saratoga,
October 17, 1777.

Montreal

Lake Superior

Lake Huron

Lake Michigan

Fort
Oswego

Fort
Ticonderoga

Fort Edward

N.H.

British abandon Boston,
March 17, 1776, after
Bunker Hill battle.

Lake Ontario

Fort Stanwix

Saratoga

Bunker Hill

Albany

Boston

Lexington

MASS.

NEW YORK

Kingston

CONN.   R.I.

Lake Erie

New York

British occupy New York,
August 27, 1776, following
American defeat, in
particular, Brooklyn Heights
battle.

PENNSYLVANIA

N.J.

Brooklyn Heights

Valley Forge

Trenton

Philadelphia

American Army winters at
Valley Forge, 1777–1778.

Ohio

Baltimore

DELAWARE

*ATLANTIC
OCEAN*

MARYLAND

Missouri

Charlottesville

Richmond

Franco–American Treaty
of Amity and Commerce
and Treaty of Alliance
signed in Paris, France,
February 1778.

VIRGINIA

Yorktown

SPANISH

Cornwallis surrenders at
Yorktown, October 17, 1781.

LOUISIANA

Tennessee

NORTH CAROLINA

Mississippi

SOUTH
CAROLINA

Wilmington

Augusta

GEORGIA

Charleston

Savannah

WEST FLORIDA

| 0 | 150 | 300 Km. |
| 0 | 150 | 300 Mi. |

✕ British victory

✕ American victory

EAST
FLORIDA

Map 23.1   The American Revolutionary War   The British army won most of the major battles, and British troops held most of the major cities. Even so, the American revolutionaries eventually won a comprehensive military and political victory.

had been embraced by London's aristocratic society and initiated into one of the most exclusive secret clubs.

The defeat in late 1777 of Britain's general John Burgoyne by General Horatio Gates at Saratoga, New York, put the future of the Mohawk at risk. This victory gave heart to patriot forces that had recently suffered a string of defeats, and it led to destructive attacks on Iroquois villages. Brant's supporters fought on to the end of the war, but patriot victories along the frontier curtailed Iroquois political and military power. Brant eventually joined the loyalist exodus to Canada and led an effort to integrate the Iroquois into the market economy of the settlers. For these Americans the revolution did not mean the protection of life and property.

The British defeat at Saratoga convinced France, in 1778, to enter the war as an ally of the United States. French military help proved crucial, supplying American forces and forcing the British to defend their colonies in the Caribbean. The French contribution was most clear in the final decisive battle, fought at Yorktown, Virginia (see Map 23.1). An American army, supported by French soldiers, besieged a British army led by General Charles Cornwallis. With escape cut off by a French fleet, Cornwallis surrendered to Washington as the British military band played "The World Turned Upside-Down."

This victory effectively ended the war. The Continental Congress sent representatives to the peace conference that followed with instructions to work in tandem with the French. Believing that France was more concerned with containing British power than with guaranteeing a strong United States, America's peace delegation negotiated directly with Britain and gained a generous settlement. The Treaty of Paris (1783) granted unconditional independence and established generous boundaries for the former colonies. The United States, in return, promised to repay prewar debts due to British merchants and to allow loyalists to recover property confiscated by patriot forces. In the end, loyalists were poorly treated and thousands of them, including Brant and other Mohawk, decided to leave for Canada.

The Construction of Republican Institutions, to 1800

Even before the Declaration of Independence, most of the colonies had created new governments. After independence, ignoring the British example of an unwritten constitution, leaders in each of the new states (as the former colonies were called) summoned constitutional conventions to draft formal charters and submitted the results to voters for ratification. Europeans were fascinated by the drafting of written constitutions and by the formal ratification of these constitutions by a vote of the people. Many of these documents were quickly translated and published in Europe. Here was the social contract of Locke and Rousseau made manifest. Remembering conflicts between royal governors and colonial legislatures, the authors of state constitutions placed severe limits on executive authority but granted legislatures greater powers than in colonial times. Many states also inserted in their constitutions a bill of rights to provide further protection against government tyranny.

An effective constitution for the new national government was developed more slowly and hesitantly. The Second Continental Congress sent the Articles of Confederation—the first constitution of the United States—to the states for approval in 1777, but it was not accepted by all the states until 1781. It created a one-house legislature in which each state was granted a single vote. A simple majority of the thirteen states was sufficient to pass minor legislation, but nine votes were necessary for declaring war, imposing taxes, and coining or borrowing money. Executive power was to be exercised by committees, not by a president. Given the intended weakness of this government, it is remarkable that it successfully organized the human and material resources to defeat Great Britain.

With the coming of peace, many of the most powerful political figures in the United States began an effort to fashion a new constitution. The Confederation government proved unable to enforce unpopular requirements of the peace treaty such as the recognition of loyalist property claims, the payment of prewar debts, and even the payment of military salaries and pensions. In September 1786 Virginia invited the other states to discuss the government's failure to deal with trade issues. This led to a call for a new convention to meet in Philadelphia nine months later. A rebellion led by Revolutionary War veterans in western Massachusetts gave the assembling delegates a sense of urgency.

The **Constitutional Convention,** which began meeting in May 1787, achieved a nonviolent second American Revolution. The delegates pushed aside the announced purpose of the convention—"to render the constitution of the federal government adequate to the exigencies of the union"—and in secret undertook to write a new constitution. George Washington was elected presiding officer. His reputation and popularity provided the solid foundation on which the delegates could contemplate an alternative political model. The real leader of the convention was James Madison of Virginia.

Debate focused on several issues: representation, electoral procedures, executive powers, and the relationship between the federal government and the states. Compromise solutions included distribution of political power among the executive, legislative, and judicial branches and the division of authority between the federal government and the states. The final compromise provided for a two-house legislature: the lower house (the House of Representatives) to be elected directly by voters and the upper house (the Senate) to be elected by state legislatures. The chief executive—the president—was to be elected indirectly by "electors" selected by ballot in the states (each state had a number of electors equal to the number of its representatives and senators).

Although the U.S. Constitution created the most democratic government of the era, only a minority of the adult population was given full rights. In some northern states where large numbers of free blacks had fought with patriot forces, there was hostility to the continuation of slavery, but southern leaders were able to protect it. Slaves were denied any participation in the political process. Slave states, however, were permitted to count three-fifths of the slave population in the calculations that determined number of congressional representatives, thus multiplying the political power of the slave-owning class in the national government. Southern delegates also gained a twenty-year continuation of the slave trade to 1808 and a fugitive slave clause that required all states to return runaway slaves to their masters.

Women were powerfully affected by their participation in revolutionary politics and by the changes in the economy brought on by the break with Britain. Women had led prewar boycotts and during the war had organized relief and charitable organizations. Nevertheless, they were denied political rights in the new republic. New Jersey briefly stood as an exception. Without specifically excluding women, the framers of that state's constitution had granted the right to vote to free residents who met modest property-holding requirements. As a result, women and African-Americans who met property requirements were able to vote in New Jersey until 1807, when lawmakers eliminated this right.

THE FRENCH REVOLUTION, 1789–1815

The French Revolution undermined traditional monarchy as well as the power of the Catholic Church and the hereditary aristocracy but, unlike the American Revolution, did not create an enduring form of representative democracy. The colonial revolution in North America, however, did not confront so directly the entrenched privileges of an established church, monarchy, and aristocracy, and the American Revolution produced no symbolic drama comparable to the public beheading of the French king Louis XVI in early 1793. Among its achievements, the French Revolution expanded mass participation in political life and radicalized the democratic tradition inherited from the English and American experiences. But in the end, the passions unleashed in France by revolutionary events could not be sustained, and popular demagogues and the dictatorship of Napoleon stalled democratic reform.

French Society and Fiscal Crisis

French society was divided into three groups. The clergy, called the First Estate, numbered about 130,000 in a nation of 28 million. The Catholic Church owned about 10 percent of the nation's land and extracted substantial amounts of wealth from the economy in the form of tithes and ecclesiastical fees. Despite its substantial wealth, the church was exempted from nearly all taxes. The clergy was organized hierarchically, and members of the hereditary nobility held almost all the upper positions in the church.

The 300,000 members of the nobility, the Second Estate, controlled about 30 percent of the land and retained ancient rights on much of the rest. Nobles held the vast majority of high administrative, judicial, military, and church positions. Though traditionally barred from some types of commercial activity, nobles were important participants in wholesale trade, banking, manufacturing, and mining. Like the clergy, this estate was hierarchical: important differences in wealth, power, and outlook separated the higher from the lower nobility. The nobility was also a highly permeable class: the Second Estate in the eighteenth century saw an enormous infusion of wealthy commoners who purchased administrative and judicial offices that conferred noble status.

The Third Estate included everyone else, from wealthy financier to homeless beggar. The bourgeoisie°, or middle class, grew rapidly in the eighteenth century. There were three times as many members of this class in 1774, when Louis XVI took the throne, as there had been in 1715, at the end of Louis XIV's reign. Commerce, finance, and manufacturing accounted for much of the wealth of the Third Estate. Wealthy commoners also owned nearly a third of the nation's land. This literate and socially ambitious class supported an expanding publishing industry, subsidized the fine arts, and purchased many of the extravagant new homes being built in Paris and other cities.

Peasants accounted for 80 percent of the French population. Artisans and other skilled workers, small shopkeepers and peddlers, and small landowners held a more privileged position in society. They owned some property and lived decently when crops were good and prices stable. By 1780 poor harvests had increased their cost of living and led to a decline in consumer demand for their products. They were rich enough to fear the loss of their property and status, well educated enough to be aware of the growing criticism of the king, but too poor and marginalized to influence policy.

The nation's poor were a large, growing, and troublesome sector. The poverty and vulnerability of peasant families forced younger children to seek seasonal work away from home and led many to crime and beggary. That raids by roving vagabonds threatened isolated farms was one measure of this social dislocation. In Paris and other French cities, the vile living conditions and unhealthy diet of the working poor were startling to visitors from other European nations. Urban streets swarmed with beggars and prostitutes. Paris alone had 25,000 prostitutes in 1760. The wretchedness of the French poor is perhaps best indicated by the growing

---

bourgeoisie (boor-zwah-ZEE)

problem of child abandonment. On the eve of the French Revolution at least forty thousand children a year were given up by their parents. The convenient fiction was that these children would be adopted; in reality the majority died of neglect.

Unable to afford decent housing, obtain steady employment, or protect their children, the poor periodically erupted in violent protest and rage. In the countryside violence was often the reaction when the nobility or clergy increased dues and fees. In towns and cities an increase in the price of bread often provided the spark, for bread prices largely determined the quality of life of the poor. These explosive episodes, however, were not revolutionary in character. The remedies sought were conventional and immediate rather than structural and long-term. That was to change when the Crown tried to solve its fiscal crisis.

The expenses of the War of the Austrian Succession began the crisis. Louis XV (r. 1715–1774) first tried to impose new taxes on the nobility and on other groups that in the past had enjoyed exemptions. But this effort failed in the face of widespread protest and the refusal of the Parlement of Paris, a court of appeal that heard appeals from local courts throughout France, to register the new tax. The crisis deepened when debts from the Seven Years War compelled the king to impose emergency fiscal measures. Again, the king met resistance from the Parlement of Paris. In 1768 frustrated authorities exiled the members of that Parlement and pushed through a series of unpopular fiscal measures. When the twenty-two-year-old Louis XVI assumed the throne in 1774, he attempted to gain popular support by recalling the exiled members of the Parlement of Paris, but he soon learned that provincial parlements had also come to see themselves as having a constitutional power to check any growth in monarchial authority.

In 1774 Louis's chief financial adviser warned that the government could barely afford to operate; as he put it, "the first gunshot [act of war] will drive the state to bankruptcy." Despite this warning, the French took on the heavy burden of supporting the American Revolution, delaying collapse by borrowing enormous sums and disguising the growing debt in misleading fiscal accounts. By the end of the war with Britain, more than half of France's national budget was required to service the debt alone. It soon became clear that fiscal reforms and new taxes, not new loans, were necessary.

In 1787 the desperate king called an Assembly of Notables to approve a radical and comprehensive reform of the economy and fiscal policy. Despite the fact that the members of this assembly were selected by the king's advisers from the high nobility, the judiciary, and the clergy, it proved unwilling to act as a rubber stamp for the proposed reforms or new taxes. Instead, these representatives of France's most privileged classes sought to protect their interests by questioning the competence of the king and his ministers to supervise the nation's affairs.

Protest Turns to Revolution, 1789–1792

In frustration, the king dismissed the Notables and attempted to implement some reforms on his own, but his effort was met by an increasingly hostile judiciary and by popular demonstrations. Because the king was unable to extract needed tax concessions from the French elite, he was forced to call the **Estates General,** the French national legislature, which had not met since 1614. The narrow self-interest and greed of the rich—who would not tolerate an increase in their taxes—rather than the grinding poverty of the common people, had created the conditions for political revolution.

In late 1788 and early 1789 members of the three estates came together throughout the nation to discuss grievances and elect representatives who would meet at Versailles°. The Third Estate's representatives were mostly men of property, but there was anger directed against the king's ministers and an inclination to move France toward constitutional monarchy with an elected legislature. Many nobles and members of the clergy sympathized with the reform agenda of the Third Estate, but deep internal divisions over procedural and policy issues limited the power of the First and the Second Estates.

Traditionally the three estates met separately, and a positive vote by two of the three was required for action. Tradition, however, was quickly overturned when the Third Estate refused to conduct business until the king ordered the other two estates to sit with it in a single body. During a six-week period of stalemate many parish priests from the First Estate began to meet with the commoners. When this expanded Third Estate declared itself the **National Assembly,** the king and his advisers recognized that the reformers intended to force them to accept a constitutional monarchy.

After being locked out of their meeting place, the Third Estate appropriated an indoor tennis court and pledged to write a constitution. The Oath of the Tennis Court ended Louis's vain hope that he could limit the agenda to fiscal reform. The king's effort to solve the

---

Versailles (vuhr-SIGH)

nation's fiscal crisis was being connected in unpredictable ways to the central ideas of the era: the people were sovereign, and the legitimacy of political institutions and individual rulers ultimately depended on their carrying out the people's will. Louis prepared for a confrontation with the National Assembly by moving military forces to Versailles. But before he could act, the people of Paris intervened.

A succession of bad harvests beginning in 1785 had propelled bread prices upward throughout France and provoked an economic depression as demand for nonessential goods collapsed. By the time the Estates General met, nearly a third of the Parisian work force was unemployed. Hunger and anger marched hand in hand through working-class neighborhoods.

When the people of Paris heard that the king was massing troops in Versailles to arrest the representatives, crowds of common people began to seize arms and mobilize. On July 14, 1789, a crowd searching for military supplies attacked the Bastille°, a medieval fortress used as a prison. The futile defense of the Bastille cost ninety-eight lives before its garrison surrendered. Enraged, the attackers hacked the commander to death and then paraded through the city with his head and that of Paris's chief magistrate stuck on pikes.

These events coincided with uprisings by peasants in the country. Peasants sacked manor houses and destroyed documents that recorded their traditional obligations. They refused to pay taxes and dues to landowners and seized common lands. Forced to recognize the fury raging through rural areas, the National Assembly voted to end traditional obligations and to reform the tax system. Having forced acceptance of their narrow agenda, the peasants ceased their revolt.

These popular uprisings strengthened the hand of the National Assembly in its dealings with the king. One manifestation of this altered relationship was passage of the **Declaration of the Rights of Man.** There were clear similarities between the language of this declaration and the U.S. Declaration of Independence. Indeed, Thomas Jefferson, who had written the American document, was U.S. ambassador to Paris and offered his opinion to those involved in the drafting of the French statement. The French declaration, however, was more sweeping in its language than the American one. Among the enumerated natural rights were "liberty, property, security, and resistance to oppression." The Declaration of the Rights of Man also guaranteed free expression of ideas, equality before the law, and representative government.

Parisian Stocking Mender The poor lived very difficult lives. This woman uses a discarded wine barrel as a shop where she mends socks. (Private collection)

While delegates debated political issues in Versailles, the economic crisis worsened in Paris. Women employed in the garment industry and in small-scale retail businesses were particularly hard hit. Because the working women of Paris faced high food prices every day as they struggled to feed their families, their anger had a hard edge. Public markets became political arenas where the urban poor met daily in angry assembly. Here the revolutionary link between the material deprivation of the French poor and the political aspirations of the French bourgeoisie was forged.

On October 5, market women organized a crowd of thousands to march the 12 miles (19 kilometers) to Versailles (see Society and Culture: The March to Versailles on page 588). Once there, they forced their way into the National Assembly to demand action from the frightened representatives: "the point is that we want bread."

Bastille (bass-TEEL)

Parisian Women Marching on Versailles   When the market women of Paris marched to Versailles and forced the royal family to return to Paris with them, they altered the course of the French Revolution. In this drawing the women are armed with pikes and swords and drag a cannon. Only the woman on the far left is clearly middle class, and she is pictured hesitating or turning away from the resolute actions of the poor women around her.   (Bibliothèque nationale de France)

The crowd then entered the royal apartments, killed some of the king's guards, and searched for Queen Marie Antoinette°, whom they loathed as a symbol of extravagance. Eventually, the crowd demanded that the royal family return to Paris. Preceded by the heads of two aristocrats carried on pikes and hauling away the palace's supply of flour, the triumphant crowd escorted the royal family to Paris.

With the king's ability to resist democratic change overcome by the Paris crowd, the National Assembly achieved a radically restructured French society in the next two years. It passed a new constitution that dramatically limited monarchial power and abolished the nobility as a hereditary class. Economic reforms swept away monopolies and trade barriers within France. The Legislative Assembly (the new constitution's name for the National Assembly) seized church lands to use as collateral for a new paper currency, and priests—who were to be elected—were put on the state payroll. When the government tried to force priests to take a loyalty oath, however, many Catholics joined a growing counterrevolutionary movement.

At first, many European monarchs had welcomed the weakening of the French king, but by 1791 Austria and Prussia threatened to intervene in support of the monarchy. The Legislative Assembly responded by declaring war. Although the war went badly at first for French forces, people across France responded patriotically to foreign invasions, forming huge new volunteer armies and mobilizing national resources to meet the challenge. By the end of 1792 French armies had gained the upper hand everywhere.

The Terror, 1793–1794

In this period of national crisis and foreign threat, the French Revolution entered its most radical phase. A failed effort by the king and queen to escape from Paris and find foreign allies cost the king any remaining popular support. As foreign armies crossed into France, his behavior was increasingly viewed as treasonous. On August 10, 1792, a crowd similar to the one that had marched on Versailles

---

Antoinette (ann twah-NET)

SOCIETY & CULTURE

The March to Versailles

Marie-Rose Barré, a 20-year old lace worker, participated in one of the most dramatic events of the French Revolution, the march of Parisian market women to Versailles in October 1789. The initial object of the march was to protest the high cost of bread. Once in Versailles, the crowd forced King Louis XVI and his family to return to Paris. In her testimony given shortly afterward to the Paris municipal council, Barré avoided any suggestion that she had been a leader of the march or that she had threatened the royal family.

. . . on October 5 last, at about eight o'clock in the morning, going to take back some work, she was stopped at the Pont Notre Dame by about a hundred women who told her that it was necessary to go with them to Versailles to ask for bread there. Not being able to resist this great number of women, she decided to go with them. At the hamlet at the Point-du-Jour, two young men, unknown to her, who were on foot and going their way, told them that they were running a great risk, that there were cannon mounted at the bridge at Saint-Cloud. This did not prevent them from continuing on their way. . . . At Versailles they found the King's Guards lined up in three ranks before the palace. A gentleman dressed in the uniform of the King's Guard . . . came to ask them what they wanted of the King, recommending peaceful behavior on their part. They answered that they were coming to ask him for bread. This gen-

tleman was absent for a few minutes and then returned to take four of them to introduce them to the King. The deponent was one of the four. . . .

They spoke first to M. de Saint-Priest, and then to His Majesty, whom they asked for bread. His Majesty answered them that he was suffering at least as much as they were, to see them lacking it, and that so far as he was able he had taken care to prevent them from experiencing a dearth. . . . The King promised them to have the flour escorted and said that if it depended on him, they would have bread then and there. They took leave of His Majesty and were led, by a gentleman in a blue uniform with red piping, into the apartments and courts of the palace to the ranks of the Flanders regiment, to which they called out. "Vive Le Roi!" It was then about nine o'clock. After this, they retired into a house on Rue Satory and went to bed in a stable.

Is it likely that someone pressured to join this march would have been selected to meet with the king to present the protestors' grievances? Does the king's concern for the plight of the poor ring true?

Source: Philip Dawson, ed., *The French Revolution* (Englewood Cliffs, N.J.: Prentice-Hall, Inc., 1967), pp. 66–67. Reprinted with permission of Simon & Schuster. Copyright © 1967 by Prentice-Hall, Inc., renewed 1995 by Philip Dawson.

---

invaded his palace in Paris and forced the king to seek protection in the Legislative Assembly. The Assembly suspended the king, ordered his imprisonment, and called for the formation of a new National Convention to be elected by the vote of all men.

Rumors of counterrevolutionary plots kept working-class neighborhoods in an uproar. In September mobs surged through the city's prisons, killing nearly half of the prisoners. Swept along by popular passion, the newly elected National Convention convicted Louis XVI of treason, sentencing him to death and proclaiming France a republic. The guillotine ended the king's life in January 1793. Invented in the spirit of the era as a more humane way to execute the condemned, this machine was to become the bloody symbol of the revolution.

The National Convention—the new legislature of the new First Republic of France—convened in September. Almost all of its members were from the middle class, and nearly all were **Jacobins°**—the most uncompromising democrats. Deep political differences, however, separated moderate Jacobins—called "Girondists°," after a region in southern France—and radicals known as "the Mountain." Members of the Mountain—so named because their seats were on the highest level in the assembly hall—were more sympathetic than the Girondists to the demands of the Parisian working class and more impatient with parliamentary procedure and constitutional constraints on government action. The Mountain

---

Jacobin (JAK-uh-bin) **Girondist** (juh-RON-dist)

Playing Cards from the French Revolution   Even playing cards could be used to attack the aristocracy and Catholic Church. In this pack of cards, "Equality" and "Liberty" replaced kings and queens.   (Jean-Loup Charmet)

came to be dominated by **Maximilien Robespierre°**, a young, little-known lawyer from the provinces who had been influenced by Rousseau's ideas.

With the French economy still in crisis and Paris suffering from inflation, high unemployment, and scarcity, Robespierre used the popular press and political clubs to forge an alliance with the volatile Parisian working class. His growing strength in the streets allowed him to purge the National Convention of his enemies and to restructure the government. Executive power was placed in the hands of the newly formed Committee of Public Safety, which created special courts to seek out and punish domestic enemies.

Among the groups that lost ground were the active feminists of the Parisian middle class and the working-class women who had sought the right to bear arms in defense of the Revolution. These women had provided decisive leadership at crucial times, helping propel the Revolution toward a widened suffrage and a more democratic structure. Armed women had actively participated in every confrontation with conservative forces. It is ironic that the National Convention—the revolutionary era's most radical legislative body, one elected by universal male suffrage—chose to repress the militant feminist forces that had prepared the ground for its creation.

Faced with rebellion in the provinces and foreign invasion, Robespierre and his allies unleashed a period of repression called the Reign of Terror (1793–1794). During the Terror, approximately 40,000 people were executed or died in prison, and another 300,000 were thrown into prison. New actions against the clergy were also approved, including the provocative measure of

Robespierre (ROBES-pee-air)

forcing priests to marry. Even time was subject to revolutionary change. A new republican calendar created twelve thirty-day months divided into ten-day weeks. Sunday, with its Christian meanings, disappeared from the calendar.

By the spring of 1794 the Revolution was secure from foreign and domestic enemies, but repression, now institutionalized, continued. Among the victims were some who had been Robespierre's closest political collaborators during the early stage of the Terror. The execution of these former allies prepared the way for Robespierre's own fall by undermining the sense of invulnerability that had secured the loyalty of his remaining partisans in the National Convention. After French victories eliminated the immediate foreign threat, conservatives in the Convention felt secure enough to vote for the arrest of Robespierre on July 27, 1794. Over the next two days, Robespierre and nearly a hundred of his remaining allies were executed by guillotine.

Reaction and Dictatorship, 1795–1815

Purged of Robespierre's collaborators, the Convention began to undo the radical reforms. It removed many of the emergency economic controls that had been holding down prices and protecting the working class. Gone also was toleration for violent popular demonstrations. When the Paris working class rose in protest in 1795, the Convention approved the use of overwhelming military force. Another retreat from radical objectives was signaled when the Catholic Church was permitted to regain much of its former influence. The church's confiscated wealth, however, was not returned.

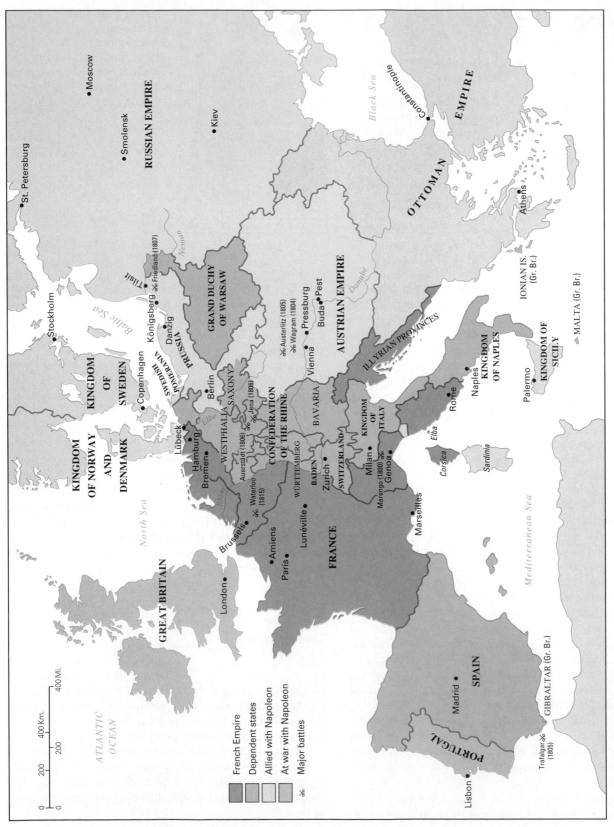

Map 23.2 Napoleon's Europe, 1810 By 1810, Great Britain was the only remaining European power at war with Napoleon. Because of the loss of the French fleet at the Battle of Trafalgar in 1805, Napoleon was unable to threaten Britain with invasion, and Britain was able to actively assist the resistance movements in Spain and Portugal, thereby helping to weaken French power.

A more conservative constitution was also ratified. It protected property, established a voting process that reduced the power of the masses, and created a new executive authority, the Directory. Once installed in power, however, the Directory proved unable to end the foreign wars or solve domestic economic problems.

After losing the election of 1797, the Directory suspended the results. The republican phase of the Revolution was clearly dead. Legitimacy was now based on coercive power rather than on elections. Two years later, **Napoleon Bonaparte** (1769–1821), a brilliant young general in the French army, seized power. Just as the American and French Revolutions had been the start of the modern democratic tradition, the military intervention that brought Napoleon to power in 1799 marked the advent of another modern form of government: popular authoritarianism.

The American and French Revolutions had resulted in part from conflicts over representation. If the people were sovereign, what institutions best expressed popular will? In the United States, the answer was to expand the electorate and institute representative government. The French Revolution had taken a different direction with the Reign of Terror. Interventions on the floor of the National Convention by market women and soldiers, the presence of common people at revolutionary tribunals and at public executions, and expanded military service were all forms of political communication that satisfied, temporarily, the French people's desire to influence their government. Napoleon tamed these forms of political expression to organize Europe's first popular dictatorship. He succeeded because his military reputation promised order to a society exhausted by a decade of crisis, turmoil, and bloodshed.

In contrast to the National Convention, Napoleon proved capable of realizing France's dream of dominating Europe and providing effective protection for persons and property at home. Negotiations with the Catholic Church led to the Concordat of 1801. This agreement gave French Catholics the right to freely practice their religion, and it recognized the French government's authority to nominate bishops and retain priests on the state payroll. In his comprehensive rewriting of French law, the Civil Code of 1804, Napoleon won the support of the peasantry and of the middle class by asserting two basic principles inherited from the moderate first stage of the French Revolution: equality in law and protection of property. Even some members of the nobility became supporters after Napoleon declared himself emperor and France an empire in 1804. However, the discrimination against women that had begun during the Terror was extended by the Napoleonic Civil Code. Women were denied basic political rights and were able to participate in the economy only with the guidance and supervision of their fathers and husbands.

While providing personal security, the Napoleonic system denied or restricted many individual rights. Free speech and free expression were limited. Criticism of the government, viewed as subversive, was proscribed, and most opposition newspapers disappeared. Spies and informers directed by the minister of police enforced these limits to political freedom. Thousands of the regime's enemies and critics were questioned or detained in the name of domestic tranquillity.

Ultimately, the Napoleonic system depended on the success of French arms and French diplomacy (see Map 23.2). From Napoleon's assumption of power until his fall, no single European state could defeat the French military. Even powerful alliances like that of Austria and Prussia were brushed aside with humiliating defeats and forced to become allies of France. Only Britain, protected by its powerful navy, remained able to thwart Napoleon's plans to dominate Europe. His effort to mobilize forces for an invasion of Britain failed in late 1805 when the British navy defeated the French and allied Spanish fleets off the coast of Spain at the Battle of Trafalgar.

Desiring to extend French power again to the Americas, Napoleon invaded Portugal in 1807 and Spain in 1808. French armies soon became tied down in a costly conflict with Spanish and Portuguese patriots who had forged an alliance with the only available European power, Great Britain. Frustrated by events on the Iberian Peninsula and faced with a faltering economy, Napoleon made the fateful decision to invade Russia. In June 1812 Napoleon began his campaign with the largest army ever assembled in Europe, approximately 600,000 men. After fighting an inconclusive battle at Borodino, Napoleon pressed on to Moscow. Five weeks after occupying Moscow, he was forced to retreat by Russian patriots who set the city on fire and by approaching armies. He ordered a retreat, but the brutal Russian winter and attacks by Russian forces destroyed his army. A broken and battered fragment of 30,000 men returned home to France.

After the debacle in Russia, Austria and Prussia deserted Napoleon and entered an alliance with England and Russia. Unable to defend Paris, Napoleon was forced to abdicate the French throne in April 1814. The allies exiled Napoleon to the island of Elba off the coast of Italy and restored the French monarchy. The next year Napoleon escaped from Elba and returned to France. But his moment had passed. He was defeated by an allied army at Waterloo, in Belgium, after only one hundred days in power. His final exile was on the distant island of St. Helena in the South Atlantic, where he died in 1821.

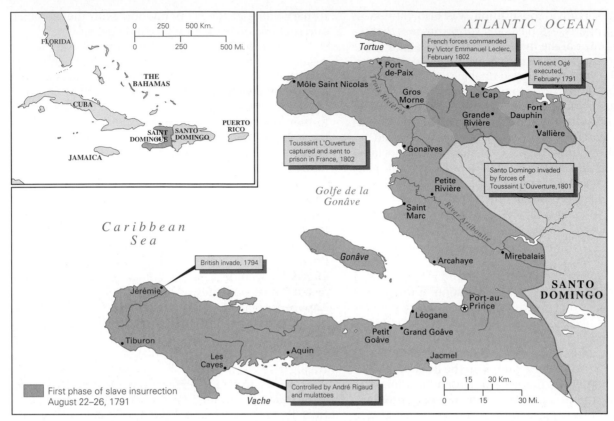

Map 23.3   The Haitian Revolution   On their way to achieving an end to slavery and gaining national independence, the Haitian revolutionaries were forced to defeat British and French military interventions as well as the local authority of the slave masters.

REVOLUTION SPREADS, CONSERVATIVES RESPOND, 1789–1850

Even as the dictatorship of Napoleon eliminated the democratic legacy of the French Revolution, revolutionary ideology was spreading and taking hold in Europe and the Americas. In Europe, the French Revolution promoted nationalism and republicanism. In the Americas, the legacies of the American and French Revolutions led to a new round of struggles for independence. News of revolutionary events in France destabilized the colonial regime in Saint Domingue (present-day Haiti), a small French colony on the western half of the island of Hispaniola, and resulted in the first successful slave rebellion. In Europe, however, the spread of revolutionary fervor was checked by reaction as monarchs formed an alliance to protect themselves from further revolutionary outbreaks.

The Haitian Revolution, 1789–1804

In 1789 the French colony of Saint Domingue was among the richest European colonies in the Americas. Its plantations produced sugar, cotton, indigo, and coffee. The colony produced two-thirds of France's tropical imports and generated nearly one-third of all French foreign trade. This impressive wealth depended on a brutal slave regime. Saint Domingue's harsh punishments and poor living conditions were notorious throughout the Caribbean. The colony's high mortality and low fertility rates created an insatiable demand for African slaves. As a result the majority of the colony's 500,000 slaves in 1790 were African-born.

In 1789, when news of the calling of France's Estates General arrived on the island, wealthy white planters sent a delegation to Paris charged with seeking more home rule and greater economic freedom for Saint Domingue. The free mixed-race population, the ***gens de couleur°,*** also sent representatives. These delegates were mostly drawn from the large class of slave-owning small planters and urban merchants. They focused on gaining the end to race discrimination and the achievement of political equality with whites. They did not seek freedom for slaves, because the most prosperous gens de couleur were slave owners themselves. As the French Revolution became more radical, the gens de couleur forged an alliance with sympathetic French radicals, who came to identify the colony's wealthy planters as royalists and aristocrats.

The political turmoil in France weakened the ability of colonial administrators to maintain order. The authority of colonial officials was no longer clear, and the very legitimacy of slavery was being challenged in France. In the vacuum that resulted, rich planters, poor whites, and the gens de couleur each pursued their narrow interests, engendering an increasingly bitter and confrontational struggle. Given the slaves' hatred of the brutal regime that oppressed them and the accumulated grievances of the free people of color, there was no way to limit the violence once the control of the slave owners slipped. When Vincent Ogé°, leader of the gens de couleur mission to France, returned to Saint Domingue to organize a military force, planter forces captured, tortured, and executed him. This cruelty was soon repaid in kind.

By 1791 whites, led by the planter elite, and the gens de couleur were engaged in open warfare. This breach between the two groups of slave owners gave the slaves an opening. A slave rebellion began on the plantations of the north and spread throughout the colony (see Map 23.3). Plantations were destroyed, masters and overseers killed, and crops burned. An emerging rebel leadership that combined elements of African political culture with revolutionary ideology from France mobilized and directed the rebelling slaves.

The rebellious slaves eventually gained the upper hand under the leadership of **François Dominique Toussaint L'Ouverture,** a former domestic slave, who created a more disciplined military force. Toussaint was politically strengthened in 1794 when the radical National Convention in Paris abolished slavery in all French possessions. He overcame his rivals in Saint Domingue, defeated a British expeditionary force in 1798, and then

Toussaint L'Ouverture Negotiating with the British   The former slave Toussaint L'Ouverture led the successful slave rebellion in Saint Domingue (Haiti). He then defended the revolution against British and French military intervention. Notice that in this print Toussaint seems to command the scene, directing the attention of the British officers to the document that he holds in his hand. (Bibliothèque nationale de France)

led an invasion of neighboring Santo Domingo, freeing the slaves there. Toussaint continued to assert his loyalty to France but gave the French government no effective role in local affairs.

As reaction overtook revolution in France, both the abolition of slavery and Toussaint's political position were threatened. When the Directory contemplated the reestablishment of slavery, Toussaint protested,

> Do they think that men who have been able to enjoy the blessing of liberty will calmly see it snatched away? They supported their chains only so long as they did not know any condition of life more happy than slavery. But today when they have left it, if they had a thousand lives they would sacrifice them all rather than be forced into slavery again.[1]

---

gens de couleur (zhahn deh koo-LUHR)   **Ogé** (oh-ZHAY)

In 1802 Napoleon sent a large military force to Saint Domingue to reestablish both French authority and slavery (see Map 24.3). At first the French forces were successful. Toussaint was captured and sent to France, where he died in prison. Eventually, however, the loss of thousands of lives to yellow fever and the resistance of the revolutionaries turned the tide. Visible in the resistance to the French were small numbers of armed women. During the early stages of the Haitian Revolution very few slave women had taken up arms, although many had aided Toussaint's forces in support roles. But after a decade of struggle and violence, more Haitian women were politically aware and willing to join the armed resistance. In 1804 Toussaint's successors declared independence, and the free republic of Haiti joined the United States as the second independent nation in the Western Hemisphere. But independence and emancipation were achieved at a terrible price. Tens of thousands had died, the economy was destroyed, and public administration was corrupted by more than a decade of violence. Political violence and economic stagnation were to trouble Haiti throughout the nineteenth century.

The Congress of Vienna and Conservative Retrenchment, 1815–1820

From 1814 to 1815 representatives of Britain, Russia, Austria, and Prussia met as the **Congress of Vienna** to reestablish political order in Europe. While they were meeting, Napoleon escaped from Elba, then was defeated at Waterloo. The French Revolution and Napoleon's imperial ambitions had threatened the very survival of the European old order. Ancient monarchies had been overturned and dynasties replaced with interlopers. Long-established political institutions had been tossed aside, and long-recognized international borders had been ignored. The very existence of the nobility and church had been put at risk. Under the leadership of the Austrian foreign minister, Prince Klemens von Metternich° (1773–1859), the allies worked together in Vienna to create a comprehensive peace settlement that they hoped would safeguard the conservative order.

The central objective of the Congress of Vienna was to roll back the clock in France. Because the participants believed that a strong and stable France was the best guarantee of future peace, the French monarchy was reestablished and France's 1792 borders were recognized. Most of the continental European powers received some territorial gains, for Metternich sought to offset French strength with a balance of power. In addition, Austria, Russia, and Prussia formed a separate alliance to confront more actively the revolutionary and nationalist energies that the French Revolution had unleashed. In 1820 this "Holy Alliance" acted decisively to defeat liberal revolutions in Spain and Italy. By repressing republican and nationalist ideas in universities and the press, the Holy Alliance also attempted to meet the potential challenge posed by subversive ideas. Metternich's program of conservative retrenchment succeeded in the short term, but powerful ideas associated with liberalism and nationalism remained a vital part of European political life throughout the nineteenth century.

Nationalism, Reform, and Revolution, 1821–1850

Despite the power of the conservative monarchs, popular support for national self-determination and democratic reform grew throughout Europe. Greece had been under Ottoman control since the fifteenth century. In 1821, Greek patriots launched an independence movement. Metternich and other conservatives opposed Greek independence, but European artists and writers enamored with the cultural legacy of ancient Greece rallied political support for intervention. After years of struggle, Russia, France, and Great Britain forced the Ottoman Empire to recognize Greek independence in 1830.

Louis XVIII, brother of the executed Louis XVI, had been placed on the throne of France by the victorious allies in 1814. He ruled as a constitutional monarch until his death in 1824 and was followed to the throne by his brother, Charles X. Charles attempted to rule in the pre-revolutionary style of his ancestors, repudiating the constitution in 1830. Unwilling to accept this reactionary challenge, the people of Paris rose up and forced Charles to abdicate. His successor was his cousin Louis Philippe° (r. 1830–1848), who accepted the reestablished constitution and extended voting privileges.

At the same time, in both the United States and Great Britain, democratic reform movements appeared. In the United States after 1790, new states with constitutions granting voting rights to most free males joined the original thirteen states. After the War of 1812, the right to vote was expanded in the older states as well. This broadening of the franchise led in 1828 to the election of the populist president Andrew Jackson (see Chapter 25).

However, revolutionary violence in France made the British aristocracy and the conservative Tory Party fearful of expanded democracy and mass movements of any kind. In 1815 the British government passed the Corn

---

Metternich (MET-uhr-nik)

Louis Philippe (loo-EE-fee-LEEP)

The Revolution of 1830 in Belgium   After the 1830 uprising that overturned the restored monarchy in France, Belgians rose up to declare their independence from Holland. In Poland and Italy, similar uprisings, combining nationalism and a desire for self-governance, failed. This painting by Baron Gustaf Wappers romantically illustrates the popular nature of the Belgian uprising by bringing to the barricades men, women, and children drawn from both the middle and the working classes.   (Musées royaux des Beaux-Arts de Belgique, Brussels)

Laws, which limited the importation of foreign grains. This law favored the profits of wealthy landowners that produced grain at the expense of the poor who were forced to pay more for their bread. When poor consumers organized to overturn these laws, the government outlawed most public meetings, using troops to crush protest in Manchester. Reacting against these policies, reformers gained the passage of laws that increased the power of the House of Commons, redistributed votes from agricultural to industrial districts, and increased the number of voters by nearly 50 percent. Although the most radical demands of these reformers, called Chartists, were defeated, new labor and economic reforms addressing the grievances of workers were passed (see Chapter 24).

Despite the achievement of Greek independence and limited political reform in France and Great Britain, conservatives continued to hold the upper hand in Europe. Finally, in 1848, the desire for democratic reform

and national self-determination and the frustrations of urban workers led to upheavals across Europe. The **Revolutions of 1848** began in Paris, where members of the middle class and workers united to overthrow the regime of Louis Philippe and create the Second French Republic. Adult men were given voting rights, slavery was abolished in French colonies, the death penalty was ended, and a ten-hour workday was legislated for Paris. But Parisian workers' demand for programs to reduce unemployment and lower prices provoked conflicts with the middle class, which wanted to protect property rights. When workers rose up against the government, French troops were called out to crush them. Desiring the reestablishment of order, the French elected Louis Napoleon, nephew of the former emperor, president in December 1848. Three years later, he overturned the constitution as a result of popular plebiscite and, after ruling briefly as dictator, became Emperor Napoleon III. He remained in power until 1871.

Reformers in Hungary, Italy, Bohemia, and elsewhere pressed for greater national self-determination in 1848. When the Austrian monarchy hesitated to meet such demands, students and workers in Vienna took to the streets to force political reforms similar to those sought in Paris. With revolution spreading throughout the Austrian Empire, Metternich, the symbol of reaction, fled Vienna in disguise. Little lasting change occurred, however, because the new Austrian emperor, Franz Joseph (r. 1848–1916) was able to use Russian military assistance and loyal Austrian troops to reestablish central authority.

Middle-class reformers and workers in Berlin joined forces in an attempt to compel the Prussian king to accept a liberal constitution and seek unification of the German states. But the Constituent Assembly called to write a constitution and arrange for national integration became entangled in diplomatic conflicts with Austria and Denmark. As a result, Frederick William IV (r. 1840–1861) was able to reassert his authority, thwarting both constitutional reform and unification.

Despite their heroism on the barricades of Paris, Vienna, Rome, and Berlin, the revolutionaries of 1848 failed to gain either their nationalist or their republican objectives. Monarchs retained the support not only of aristocrats but also of professional militaries, largely recruited from among peasants who had little sympathy for urban workers. Revolutionary coalitions, in contrast, were fragile and lacked clear objectives. Workers' demands for higher wages, lower prices, and labor reform often drove their middle-class allies into the arms of the reactionaries.

CONCLUSION

This era of revolution was, in large measure, the product of a long period of costly warfare among the imperial nations of Europe. Using taxes and institutions inherited from the past, England and France found it increasingly difficult to fund distant wars in the Americas or in Asia. Royal governments attempting to impose new taxes met with angry resistance. The spread of literacy and the greater availability of books helped create a European culture more open to reform or revolutionary change of existing institutions. The ideas of Locke and Rousseau guided critics of monarchy toward a new political culture of elections and representative institutions. Each new development served as example and provocation for new revolutionary acts. French officers who took part in the American Revolution helped ignite the French Revolution. Black freemen from Haiti traveled to France to seek their rights and returned to spread revolutionary passions. Each revolution had its own character. The revolutions in France and Haiti proved to be more violent and destructive than the American Revolution. Revolutionaries in France and Haiti, facing a more strongly entrenched and more powerful opposition and greater social inequalities, responded with greater violence.

The conservative retrenchment that followed the defeat of Napoleon succeeded in the short term. Monarchy, multinational empires, and the established church retained their hold on the loyalty of millions of Europeans and could count on the support of many of Europe's wealthiest and most powerful individuals. But liberalism and nationalism continued to stir revolutionary sentiment. The contest between adherents of the old order and partisans of change was to continue well into the nineteenth century. In the end, the nation-state, the Enlightenment legacy of rational inquiry, broadened political participation, and secular intellectual culture were to prevail. This outcome was determined in large measure by the old order's inability to satisfy the new social classes that appeared with the emerging industrial economy. The material transformation produced by industrial capitalism could not be contained in the narrow confines of a hereditary social system, nor could the rapid expansion of scientific learning be contained within the doctrines of traditional religion.

The revolutions of the late eighteenth century began the transformation of Western society, but they did not complete it. Only a minority gained full political rights. Women achieved full political rights only in the twentieth century. Democratic institutions, as in revolutionary France, often failed. Moreover, as Chapter 25 will discuss, slavery endured in the Americas past the mid-1800s, despite the revolutionary era's enthusiasm for individual liberty.

■ Key Terms

Enlightenment	Jacobins
Benjamin Franklin	Maximilien Robespierre
George Washington	Napoleon Bonaparte
Joseph Brant	*gens de couleur*
Constitutional Convention	François Dominique
Estates General	Toussaint L'Ouverture
National Assembly	Congress of Vienna
Declaration of the Rights of Man	Revolutions of 1848

■ Suggested Reading

The American Revolution has received a great amount of attention from scholars. Colin Bonwick, *The American Revolution* (1991), and Edward Countryman, *The American Revolution* (1985), provide excellent introductions. Edmund S. Morgan, *The Challenge of the American Revolution* (1976), remains a major work of interpretation. Gordon S. Wood, *The Radicalism of the American Revolution* (1992), is a brilliant examination of the ideological and cultural meanings of the Revolution. See also William Howard Adams, *The Paris Years of Thomas Jefferson* (1997). Lance Banning, *The Sacred Fire of Liberty: James Madison and the Founding of the Federal Republic* (1995), is a convincing revision of the story of Madison and his era. For the role of women in the American Revolution see Linda K. Kerber, *Women of the Republic: Intellect and Ideology in Revolutionary America* (1980), and Mary Beth Norton, *Liberty's Daughters: The Revolutionary Experience of American Women, 1750–1800* (1980). Also recommended is Norton's *Founding Mothers and Fathers: Gendered Power and the Forming of American Society* (1996). Among the many works that deal with African-Americans and Amerindians during the era, see Sylvia Frey, *Water from Rock: Black Resistance in a Revolutionary Age* (1991); Barbara Graymont, *The Iroquois in the American Revolution* (1972); and William N. Fenton, *The Great Law and the Longhouse: A Political History of the Iroquois Confederacy* (1998).

For intellectual life in the era of the French Revolution see Anne Goldgar, *Impolite Learning: Conduct and Community in the Republic of Letters, 1680–1750* (1995), and Dena Goodman, *The Republic of Letters: A Cultural History of the Enlightenment* (1994). For the "underside" of this era see *Shaping History: Ordinary People in European Politics, 1500–1700* (1998), by Wayne Te Brake, for a discussion of "folk culture." François Furet, *Interpreting the French Revolution* (1981), breaks with interpretations that emphasize class and ideological interpretations. Georges Lefebve, *The Coming of the French Revolution*, trans. R. R. Palmer (1947), presents the classic class-based analysis. George Rudé, *The Crowd in History: Popular Disturbances in France and England* (1981), remains the best introduction to the role of mass protest in the period. Lynn Hunt, *The Family Romance of the French Revolution* (1992), examines the gender content of revolutionary politics. For the role of women see Joan Landes, *Women and the Public Sphere in the Age of the French Revolution* (1988), and the recently published *The Women of Paris and Their French Revolution* (1998) by Dominique Godineau. Felix Markham, *Napoleon* (1963), and Robert B. Holtman, *The Napoleonic Revolution* (1967), provide reliable summaries of the period.

The Haitian Revolution has received less extensive coverage than the revolutions in the United States and France. C. L. R. James, *The Black Jacobins*, 2d ed. (1963), is the classic study. Anna J. Cooper, *Slavery and the French Revolutionists, 1788–1805* (1988), also provides an overview of this important topic. Carolyn E. Fick, *The Making of Haiti: The Saint Domingue Revolution from Below* (1990), is the best recent synthesis. David P. Geggus, *Slavery, War, and Revolution* (1982), examines the British role in the revolutionary period. See also David Barry Gaspar and David Patrick Geggus, eds., *A Turbulent Time: The French Revolution and the Greater Caribbean* (1997).

For the revolutions of 1830 and 1848 see Arthur J. May, *The Age of Metternich, 1814–48*, rev. ed. (1963), for a brief survey. Henry Kissinger's *A World Restored* (1957) remains among the most interesting discussions of the Congress of Vienna. Eric Hobsbawm's *The Age of Revolution* (1962) provides a clear analysis of the class issues that appeared during this era. Paul Robertson's *Revolutions of 1848: A Social History* (1960) remains a valuable introduction. See also Peter Stearns and Herrick Chapman, *European Society in Upheaval* (1991). For the development of European social reform movements see Albert Lindemann, *History of European Socialism* (1983).

For national events in Hungary see István Deák's examination of Hungary, *The Lawful Revolution: Louis Kossuth and the Hungarians, 1848–49* (1979). For Germany, see Theodore S. Hamerow, *Restoration, Revolution, and Reaction, 1815–1871* (1966), For French events see Roger Price, *A Social History of Nineteenth-Century France* (1987). Barbara Taylor, *Eve and the New Jerusalem: Socialism and Feminism in the Nineteenth Century* (1983), analyzes connections between workers' and women's rights issues in England.

■ Note

1. Quoted in C. L. R. James, *The Black Jacobins*, 2d ed., rev. (New York: Vintage Books, 1963), 196.

24

THE EARLY INDUSTRIAL REVOLUTION,

1760–1851

Causes of the Industrial Revolution • The Technological Revolution •
The Impact of the Industrial Revolution • Ideological and Political Responses
to Industrialization • Industrialization and the Nonindustrial World
ENVIRONMENT AND TECHNOLOGY: "The Annihilation of Time and Space"
SOCIETY AND CULTURE: Charles Babbage, Ada Lovelace, and the "Analytical Engine"

Opening of the Saltash Bridge over the Tamar River in England in 1859   During the celebrations,
a steam locomotive pulled a train over the bridge while a steam-powered paddle wheeler passed underneath.

In January 1840, a shipyard in Britain launched a radically new ship. The *Nemesis* had an iron hull, a flat bottom so it could navigate in shallow waters, and a steam engine to power it upriver and against the wind. The ship was heavily armed. In November it arrived off the coast of China. Though ships from Europe had been sailing to China for three hundred years, the *Nemesis* was the first steam-powered iron gunboat seen in Asian waters. A Chinese observer noted: "Iron is employed to make it strong. The hull is painted black, weaver's shuttle fashion. On each side is a wheel, which by the use of coal fire is made to revolve as fast as a running horse. . . . At the vessel's head is a Marine God, and at the head, stern, and sides are cannon, which give it a terrific appearance. Steam vessels are a wonderful invention of foreigners, and are calculated to offer delight to many."[1]

Instead of offering delight, the *Nemesis* and other steam-powered warships that soon joined it steamed up the Chinese rivers, bombarded forts and cities, and brought in troops and supplies. With this new weapon, Britain, a small island nation half a world away, was able to defeat the largest and most populated country in the world in its own heartland.

The *Nemesis* was no isolated invention. Its outstanding features—steam power and cheap iron—were part of a larger phenomenon, the **Industrial Revolution,** that involved dramatic innovations in manufacturing, mining, transportation, and communications and equally rapid changes in society and commerce. New technologies and new social and economic arrangements allowed the industrializing countries—first Britain, followed by western Europe and the United States—to unleash massive increases in production and productivity, exploit the world's natural resources as never before, and transform the environment and human life in unprecedented ways.

The distribution of this power and wealth was very uneven. The people who owned and controlled these innovations amassed wealth and power over nature and over other people. Workers and their children were harmed, for industrialization widened the gap between rich and poor.

The effect of the Industrial Revolution around the world was also very uneven. The first countries to industrialize grew in wealth and power. But in Russia and eastern Europe, we cannot speak of an industrial revolution until the end of the nineteenth century. In Egypt, India, and a few other non-Western countries, the economic and military power of the European countries soon stifled the tentative beginnings of industrialization. China and other regions without industry were easily taken advantage of. The disparity between the industrial and the nonindustrial countries that exists today dates from the early nineteenth century.

As you read this chapter, ask yourself the following questions:

- What caused the Industrial Revolution?
- What were the key innovations that increased productivity and drove industrialization?
- What was the impact of these changes on the society and environment of the industrializing countries?
- How did the Industrial Revolution affect the relations between the industrialized and the nonindustrialized parts of the world?

CAUSES OF THE INDUSTRIAL REVOLUTION

What caused the Industrial Revolution, and why did it begin in England in the late eighteenth century? These are two of the great questions of history. The basic precondition of this momentous event seems to have been economic development propelled by population growth, an agricultural revolution, the expansion of trade, and an openness to innovation.

Population

The population of Europe rose in the eighteenth century—slowly at first, faster after 1780, then even faster in the early nineteenth century. The fastest growth took place in England and Wales. Population there rose from 5.5 million in 1688 to 9 million in 1801 and to 18 million by 1851—increases never before experienced in history.

The growth of population resulted from more reliable food supplies and more widespread resistance to disease. We know that industrialization was not the cause, for the populations of China and eastern and southern Europe were also growing. We also know that the population boom did not cause industrialization. But when economic growth and population growth occurred together, they reinforced each other.

More dependable food supplies and job opportunities led people to marry at an earlier age and have more children. A high birthrate meant a large percentage of children in the general population. In the early nineteenth century some 40 percent of the population of Britain was under fifteen years of age. This high proportion of youths explains both the vitality of the British people in that period and the widespread use of child labor. People also migrated at an unprecedented rate—from the countryside to the cities, from Ireland to England, and, more generally, from Europe to the Americas. Thanks to immigration, the population of the United States rose from 4 million in 1791 to 9.6 million in 1820 to 31.5 million in 1860—faster growth than in any other part of the world at the time.

The Agricultural Revolution

Innovations in manufacturing, energy, transportation, and communications could only have taken place alongside a simultaneous revolution in farming that provided food for city dwellers and forced poorer peasants off the land. This **agricultural revolution** began long before the eighteenth century. One important aspect was the acceptance of the potato, introduced from South America centuries earlier. In the cool and humid regions of Europe, from Ireland to Russia, potatoes yielded two or three times more food per acre than grain. Maize (American corn) was grown across Europe from southwestern France to the Balkans. Turnips, legumes, and clover did not deplete the soil and could be fed to cattle, sources of milk and meat. Additional manure from cattle in turn fertilized the soil for other crops.

Only prosperous landowners with secure titles to their land could afford the risks of new methods and new crops. Rich landowners therefore "enclosed" the land—that is, consolidated their holdings—and took over the commons that in the past had been open to all. Once in control of the land, they could make their tenants drain and improve the soil, breed better livestock, and introduce crop rotation. The security of small-scale tenant farmers and sharecroppers depended on traditional methods and rural customs such as gleaning in others' fields after the harvest, pasturing their animals on common village lands, and gathering firewood in common woods. This "enclosure movement" turned tenants and sharecroppers into landless farm laborers. Many moved to the cities to seek work; others became homeless migrants and vagrants; others emigrated.

In eastern Europe, as in Britain, large estates predominated and aristocratic landowners used such improvements to increase their wealth and political influence. In western Europe, enclosure was hampered by the fact that the law gave secure property rights to numerous small farmers.

Trade and Inventiveness

In most of Europe, the increasing demand that accompanied economic growth was met by increasing production in traditional ways. Roads were improved, so stagecoaches could travel faster. Royal manufacturers trained additional craftsmen to produce fine china, silks, and carpets by hand. In rural areas much production was carried out through the putting-out system. Merchants delivered fibers, leather, and other raw materials to craftspeople (often farmers in the off-season), and picked up the finished products.

The growth of the population and food supply was accompanied by the growth of trade. Most of it was local trade in traditional goods and services. But a growing share consisted of simple goods that even middle-class people could afford: sugar, tea, cotton textiles, iron hardware, pottery. Products from other parts of the world like tea and sugar, required extensive networks of shipping and finance.

In the late eighteenth century, technology and innovation fascinated educated people throughout Europe and eastern North America. The French *Encyclopédie* contained thousands of articles and illustrations of handicrafts. The American Benjamin Franklin, like many others, experimented with electricity. The Montgolfier brothers invented a hot-air balloon. Claude Chappe created the first semaphore telegraph. French artillery officers and the American Eli Whitney proposed making guns with interchangeable parts.

Britain and Continental Europe

Economic growth was evident everywhere in the North Atlantic area, yet industrialization did not take place everywhere at once. To understand why, we must look at the peculiar role of Great Britain.

Britain enjoyed a rising standard of living during the eighteenth century, thanks to good harvests, a growing

CHRONOLOGY

	Technology	Economy, Society, and Politics
1750		
	1759 Josiah Wedgwood opens pottery factory	
	1764 Spinning jenny	
	1769 Richard Arkwright's water frame; James Watt patents steam engine	**1776** Adam Smith's *Wealth of Nations*
	1779 First iron bridge	**1776–1783** American Revolution
	1785 Boulton and Watt sell steam engines; Samuel Crompton's mule	**1789–1799** French Revolution
	1793 Eli Whitney's cotton gin	
1800	**1800** Alessandro Volta's battery	**1804–1815** Napoleonic Wars
	1807 Robert Fulton's *Clermont*	**1820s** U.S. cotton industry begins
	1820s Construction of Erie Canal	
	1829 *Rocket,* first steam-powered locomotive	**1833** Factory Act in Britain
		1834 German Zollverein; Robert Owen's Grand National Consolidated Trade Union
	1837 Wheatstone & Cooke's telegraph	
	1838 First ships steam across the Atlantic	
	1840 *Nemesis* sails to China	
	1843 Samuel Morse's Baltimore–to–Washington telegraph	**1846** Repeal of British Corn Laws
		1847–1848 Irish famine
1850	**1851** Crystal Palace opens in London	**1848** Collapse of Chartist movement; Revolutions in Europe
		1854 First cotton mill in India

population, and a booming overseas trade. Until the mid-eighteenth century, the British were better known for their cheap imitations than for their innovations or quality products. But they put inventions into practice more quickly than other people, as the engineer John Farey told a parliamentary committee in 1829: "The prevailing talent of English and Scotch people is to apply new ideas to use and to bring such applications to perfection, but they do not imagine as much as foreigners."

Britain was the world's leading exporter of tools, guns, hardware, and other craft goods (see Map 24.1). Its mining and metal industries employed engineers willing to experiment with new ideas. It had the largest merchant marine and produced more ships, naval supplies, and navigation instruments than other countries.

Before 1790, Britain had a more fluid society than the rest of Europe. The English royal court was less ostentatious than the courts of France, Spain, or Austria. Its aristocracy was less powerful, and the lines separating the social classes were less sharply drawn. Political power was not as centralized as on the European continent, and the government employed fewer bureaucrats and officials. Members of the gentry, and even some aris-

tocrats, married into merchant families. Intermarriage among the families of petty merchants, yeoman farmers, and town craftsmen was common. Guilds, which resisted innovation, were relatively weak. Ancestry remained important, but wealth also commanded respect. A businessman with enough money could buy a landed estate, a seat in Parliament, and the social status that accompanied them.

At a time when transportation by land was very costly, Great Britain had good water transportation, thanks to its indented coastline, navigable rivers, and growing network of canals. It had a unified internal market, with none of the duties and tolls that goods had to pay every few miles in France. This encouraged specialization and trade.

Britain was highly commercial. More people there were involved in production for export and in trade and finance than in any other major country. It was especially active in overseas trade with the Americas, West Africa, the Middle East, and India. It had financial and insurance institutions able to support growing business enterprises and a patent system that offered inventors the hope of rich rewards. The example of men who be-

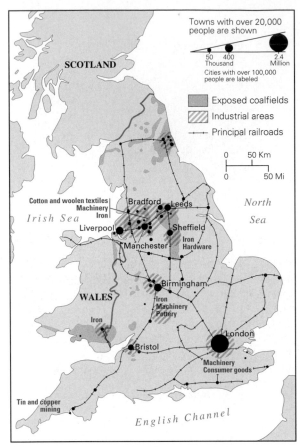

Map 24.1   The Industrial Revolution in Britain, ca. 1850
The first industries arose in northern and western England.
These regions had abundant coal and iron-ore deposits for
the iron industry and a moist climate and fast-flowing rivers,
factors important for the cotton-textile industry.

came wealthy and respected for their inventions—such as Richard Arkwright, the cotton magnate, and James Watt, the steam engine designer—stimulated others.

In the eighteenth century, the economies of continental Europe underwent a dynamic expansion, thanks to the efforts of individual entrepreneurs and investors. Yet growth was still hampered by high transportation costs, misguided government regulations, and rigid social structures. The Low Countries were laced with canals, but the terrain elsewhere in Europe made canal building costly and difficult. The ruling monarchies made some attempts to import British techniques and organize factory production, but they all floundered for lack of markets or management skills. From 1789 to 1815, Europe was the scene of revolutions and wars. War created opportunities for suppliers of weapons, uniforms, metal goods, food, and horses. The insecurity of the times and the interruption of trade with Britain weakened the incentive to invest in new technologies.

The political revolutions swept away the restrictions of the old regimes. After 1815, when peace returned, the economies of western Europe were ready to begin industrializing. Industrialization first took hold in Belgium and northern France, as their businessmen visited Britain to observe the changes and to spy out industrial secrets. In spite of British laws forbidding the emigration of skilled workers and the export of textile machinery, many slipped through. By the 1820s, several thousand Britons were at work on the continent of Europe setting up machines, training workers in the new methods, and even starting their own businesses.

Acutely aware of Britain's head start and of the need to stimulate their own industrialization, European governments took action. They created technical schools. They eliminated internal tariff barriers, tolls, and other hindrances to trade. They encouraged the formation of joint-stock companies and banks to channel private savings into industrial investments. On the European continent, as in Britain, cotton was the first industry. The mills of France, Belgium, and Germany served local markets but could not compete abroad with the more advanced British industry. By 1830, the political climate in western Europe was as favorable to business as Britain's had been a half-century earlier.

THE TECHNOLOGICAL REVOLUTION

Five revolutionary innovations spurred industrialization: (1) mass production through the division of labor, (2) new machines and mechanization, (3) a great increase in the supply of iron, (4) the steam engine and the changes it made possible in industry and transportation, and (5) the electric telegraph.

Mass Production: Pottery

The pottery industry offers a good example of **mass production,** the making of many identical items by breaking the process into simple repetitive tasks. East Asian potters had long known how to make fine glazed porcelain, or "china." In Europe before the mid-eighteenth century only the wealthy could afford fine porcelain imported from Asia. Middle-class people used pewter tableware, and the poor ate from wooden or earthenware bowls. Several royal manufactures—Meissen in Saxony, Delft in Holland, and Sèvres in France—were founded to produce exquisite handmade products for the courts and aristocracy, but their products were much too expensive for mass consumption. Meanwhile, more and more Europeans acquired a taste for tea, cocoa, and coffee, and wanted porcelain that would not spoil the flavor of hot beverages. This demand created opportunities for inventive entrepreneurs.

Britain, like other countries, had many small pottery workshops where craftsmen made a few plates and cups at a time. Much of this activity took place in a part of the Midlands that possessed good clay, coal for firing, and lead for glazing. There **Josiah Wedgwood** opened a pottery business in 1759. Today, the name Wedgwood is associated with expensive, highly decorated china. But Wedgwood's most important contribution lay in producing ordinary porcelain cheaply, by means of the **division of labor.**

To do so, he subdivided the work into highly specialized and repetitive tasks, such as unloading the clay, mixing it, pressing flat pieces, dipping the pieces in glaze, putting handles on cups, packing kilns, and carrying things from one part of his plant to another. He substituted the use of molds for the potter's wheel wherever possible, a change that not only saved labor but created identical plates and bowls that could be stacked. Wedgwood was also interested in new technologies. He invested in toll roads and canals so that clay could be shipped economically from southwestern England to his factories in the Midlands. In 1782, to mix clay and grind flint, he purchased one of the first steam engines to be used in industry.

These were radical departures from the age-old methods of craftsmanship. But the division of labor, strict discipline, and new machinery allowed Wedgwood to lower the cost of his products while improving their quality, and to offer his wares for sale at lower prices. His factory grew far larger than his competitors' factories and employed several hundred workers. His own salesmen traveled throughout England touting his goods.

Wedgwood's interest in applying technology to manufacturing was connected with his membership in the Birmingham Lunar Society, a group of manufacturers, scientists, and inventors who met when the moon was full so they could see their way home after dark. This critical mass of creative thinkers willing to exchange ideas and discoveries encouraged the atmosphere of experimentation and innovation that characterized late-eighteenth-century England. Similar societies through-

Wedgwood's Potteries   In Staffordshire, England, Josiah Wedgwood established a factory to mass-produce beautiful and inexpensive china. The bottle-shape buildings are kilns in which thousands of pieces of china could be fired at one time. Kilns, factories, and housing were all mixed together in pottery towns, and smoke from burning coal filled the air.   (Mary Evans Picture Library)

out Britain were creating a vogue for science and giving the word *progress* a new meaning: "change for the better."

Mechanization: The Cotton Industry

The cotton industry, the largest industry in this period, illustrates the role of **mechanization,** the use of machines to do work previously done by hand. Cotton cloth had long been the most common fabric in China, India, and the Middle East, where it was spun and woven by hand. The cotton plant did not grow in Europe, but the cloth was so much cooler, softer, and cleaner than wool that wealthy Europeans developed a liking for this costly import. When the powerful English woolen industry persuaded Parliament to forbid the import of cotton cloth into England, it stimulated attempts to import cotton fiber and make the cloth locally. Here was an opportunity for enterprising inventors to reduce costs with labor-saving machinery.

To turn inventions into successful businesses, inventors had to link up with entrepreneurs or become businessmen themselves. Making a working prototype often took years, even decades, and many inventions led to dead ends. History remembers the successful, but even they struggled against great odds (see Society and Culture: Charles Babbage, Ada Lovelace, and the "Analytical Engine").

Beginning in the 1760s, a series of inventions revolutionized the spinning of cotton thread. The first was the spinning jenny, invented in 1764, which drew out the cotton fibers and twisted them into thread. The jenny was simple, cheap to build, and easy for one person to operate. Early models spun six or seven threads at once, later ones up to eighty. The thread, however, was soft and irregular and could be used only in combination with linen.

In 1769 **Richard Arkwright** invented another spinning machine, the water frame, which produced thread strong enough to be used without linen. Arkwright was both a gifted inventor and a successful businessman. His machine was larger and more complex than the jenny and required a source of power such as a water wheel, hence the name "water frame." To obtain the necessary energy, he installed many machines in one building, next to a fast-flowing river. The resemblance to a flour mill gave such enterprises the name cotton mill.

In 1785 Samuel Crompton patented a machine that combined the best features of the jenny and the water frame. This device, called a mule, produced a thread that was both strong and fine enough to be used in the finer qualities of cotton called muslin. The mule could make a finer, more even thread than any human, and at a lower cost. Now British industry could undersell high-quality handmade cotton cloth from India. As a result, British cotton output increased tenfold between 1770 and 1790.

The boom in thread production and the soaring demand for cloth created bottlenecks in weaving. Inventors in England rose to the challenge. The first power loom was introduced in 1784 but was not perfected until after 1815. Other inventions of that period included carding machines, chlorine bleach, and cylindrical printing presses. By the 1830s large English textile mills powered by steam engines were turning raw cotton into printed cloth. This was a far cry from the cottage industries of the previous century.

Mechanization offered two advantages: (1) productivity for the manufacturer and (2) price for the consumer. Whereas in India it took 500 hours to spin a pound of cotton, the mule of 1790 could do so in 3 person-hours, and the self-acting mule—an improved version introduced in 1830—required only 80 minutes. Cotton mills needed very few skilled workers, and managers often hired children to tend the spinning machines. The same was true of power looms, which gradually replaced handloom weaving: the number of power looms rose from 2,400 in 1813 to 500,000 by 1850. Meanwhile, the price of cloth fell by 90 percent from 1782 to 1812 and kept on dropping.

The industrialization of Britain made cotton into America's most valuable crop. In the 1790s, most of Britain's cotton came from India, as the United States produced a mere 750 tons, mostly long-staple cotton from South Carolina. In 1793, the American Eli Whitney patented his cotton gin, a simple device that separated the bolls from the fiber and made the growing of short-staple cotton economical. This invention permitted the spread of cotton farming into Georgia, then into Alabama, Mississippi, and Louisiana, and finally as far west as Texas. By the late 1850s the southern states were producing a million tons of cotton a year, five-sixths of the world's total.

With the help of British craftsmen who introduced jennies, mules, and power looms, Americans developed a cotton industry in the 1820s. By 1840, the United States had 1,200 cotton mills, two-thirds of them in New England, powered by water rather than steam.

The Iron Industry

Iron making also was transformed during the Industrial Revolution. Throughout Eurasia and Africa, iron had been in use for thousands of years for tools, swords and other weapons, and household items such as knives, pots, hinges, and locks. In the eleventh century, during the Song period, Chinese forges had produced cast iron in large quantities. Production declined after the Song, but iron continued to be common and inexpensive in China. Wherever iron was produced, however, deforestation eventually drove up the cost of charcoal (used for smelting) and restricted output. Furthermore, iron had to be repeatedly heated and hammered to drive out impurities, a difficult and costly process. Because of limited wood supplies and the high cost of skilled labor, iron was a rare and valuable metal outside China before the eighteenth century.

A major breakthrough occurred in 1709 when Abraham Darby discovered that coke (coal from which the impurities have been cooked out) could be used in place of charcoal. The resulting metal was of lower quality than charcoal-iron but much cheaper to produce, for coal was

SOCIETY & CULTURE

Charles Babbage, Ada Lovelace, and the "Analytical Engine"

In the early nineteenth century, many professions relied on tables of numbers such as logarithms, astronomical positions, and actuarial data. Calculated by hand, these tables were full of arithmetic and typographical errors. In 1820, while correcting such a table, the English mathematician Charles Babbage exclaimed: "I wish to God these calculations had been executed by steam." Babbage went on to devise a machine—he called it the "Difference Engine"—to perform calculations and print out the results as flawlessly as a power loom produced cloth. While a prototype was being built, he designed the "Analytical Engine," which could interpret instructions inserted on punched cards and could alter its calculations in response to the results of previous calculations.

One of Babbage's assistants, Ada, the countess of Lovelace, translated an article by the Italian military engineer, L. F. Menabrea, about the Analytical Engine for the magazine Taylor's Scientific Memoirs. *In his autobiography, published in 1864, Babbage recalled: "The late Countess of Lovelace informed me that she had translated the memoir of Menabrea. I asked why she had not herself written an original paper on a subject with which she was so intimately acquainted? To this Lady Lovelace replied that the thought had not occurred to her. I then suggested that she should add some notes to Menabrea's memoir; an idea which was immediately adopted. ... The notes of the Countess of Lovelace extend to about three times the length of the original memoir. Their author has entered fully into almost all the very difficult and abstract questions concerned with the subject.*

In the notes that she added to Menabrea's article, Ada Lovelace wrote the following:

The distinctive characteristic of the Analytical Engine, and that which has rendered it possible to endow mechanism with such extensive faculties as bid fair to make this engine the executive right-hand of abstract algebra, is the introduction into it of the principle which Jacquard devised for regulating, by means of punched cards, the most complicated patterns in the fabrication of brocaded stuffs [fabrics]. ...

The bounds of *arithmetic* were outstepped the moment the idea of applying the cards had occurred; and the Analytical Engine does not occupy common ground with mere "calculating machines." It holds a position wholly its own; and the considerations it suggests are most interesting in their nature. ... A new, a vast, and a powerful language is developed for the future use of analysis, in which to wield its truths so that these may become of more speedy and accurate practical application for the purposes of mankind than the means hitherto in our possession have rendered possible. Thus not only the mental and the material, but the theoretical and the practical in the mathematical world, are brought into more intimate and effective connexion with each other. We are not aware of its being on record that anything partaking in the nature of what is so well designated the *Analytical Engine* has been hitherto proposed, or even thought of, as a practical possibility, any more than the idea of a thinking or of a reasoning machine.

In short, Babbage invented the computer.

The first working computers were not built until a hundred years later, but Babbage is honored as the first person to imagine such a machine. And the widely used programming language Ada is named after his friend, the countess of Lovelace.

Is "a thinking or ... a reasoning machine" a good description of a computer? Because Babbage's Analytical Engine did not use electricity, can it really be called a computer?

Source: From Philip Morison and Emily Morison, eds., *Charles Babbage and His Calculating Engines: Selected Writings by Charles Babbage and Others* (New York: Dover, 1961), 68, 251–252. © Copyright 1961. Reprinted by permission of Dover Publications.

Crystal Palace Interior   The Crystal Palace, built for the Universal Exposition of 1851, was the largest structure in England. It was made entirely prefabricated of iron and glass and was a forerunner of the great railroad stations of the late nineteenth century and the skyscrapers of the twentieth. (Guildhall Library, Corporation of London, The Bridgeman Art Library, London and New York)

plentiful. In 1784 Henry Cort found a way to remove some of the impurities in coke-iron by puddling—stirring the molten iron with long rods. By 1790 four-fifths of Britain's iron was made with coke; other countries still used charcoal. Coke-iron was cheaper and less destructive of forests, and it allowed a great expansion in the size of individual blast furnaces, substantially reducing the cost of iron. There seemed almost no limit to the quantity of iron that could be produced with coke. Britain's iron production began rising fast, from 17,000 tons in 1740 to 3 million tons in 1844, as much as in the rest of the world put together.

In turn, there seemed no limit to the amount of iron that an industrializing society would purchase or to the novel applications for this cheap and useful material. In 1779 the iron manufacturer Abraham Darby III (grand-

son of the first Abraham Darby) built a bridge of iron across the Severn River. In 1851 Londoners marveled at the **Crystal Palace,** a huge greenhouse made entirely of iron and glass and large enough to enclose the tallest trees.

The idea of interchangeable parts originated in the eighteenth century, when French army officers attempted, without success, to persuade gun makers to produce precisely identical parts. The craftsmen continued to use traditional methods to make gun parts that had to be fitted together by hand. By the mid-nineteenth century, however, interchangeable-parts manufacturing had been adopted in the manufacture of firearms, farm equipment, and sewing machines. At the Crystal Palace exhibition of 1851, Europeans called it the "American system of manufactures." In the next hundred years, the use of machinery to mass-produce consumer items was to become the hallmark of American industry.

The Steam Engine

Although the mechanization of manufacturing was very important, the most revolutionary invention of the Industrial Revolution was surely the **steam engine,** a mechanical substitute for human and animal power as well as wind and water power. By the late seventeenth century many activities were experiencing serious bottlenecks for lack of energy. In particular, deep mines filled with water faster than horses could pump it out.

Scientists understood the concept of atmospheric pressure and had created experimental devices to turn heat into motion, but they had not found a way to put those devices to practical use. Then, between 1702 and 1712, Thomas Newcomen developed the first practical steam engine, a crude and inefficient device. Its voracious appetite for fuel mattered little in coal mines, where fuel was cheap, but it was too costly for other uses.

James Watt, an instrument maker at Glasgow University in Scotland, was asked to repair the university's model Newcomen engine. Watt realized that the engine wasted fuel because the cylinder had to be alternately heated and cooled. He developed a separate condenser—a vessel into which the steam was allowed to escape after it had done its work, leaving the cylinder always hot and the condenser always cold. Watt patented his idea in 1769. He enlisted the help of the iron manufacturer Matthew Boulton to turn his invention into a commercial product. In 1785, Boulton and Watt began selling steam engines to manufacturers of iron, pottery, and cotton.

Watt's steam engine was the most celebrated invention of the eighteenth century. Because there seemed almost no limit to the amount of coal in the ground, steam-generated energy seemed an inexhaustible source of power, and steam engines could be used where animal, wind, and water power were lacking. Without the steam engine, industrialization would have been a limited phenomenon.

Inspired by the success of Watt's engine, inventors in France in 1783, in the United States in 1787, and in England in 1788 put steam engines on boats. The need to overcome great distances in the United States explains why the first commercially successful steamboat was Robert Fulton's *Clermont*, which steamed between New York City and Albany in 1807.

Soon steamboats were launched on other American rivers, especially the Ohio and the Mississippi, gateways to the midwest. In the 1820s, the Erie Canal linked the Atlantic seaboard with the Great Lakes and opened Ohio, Indiana, and Illinois to European settlement. Steamboats proliferated west of the Appalachian Mountains; by 1830 some three hundred plied the Mississippi and its tributaries. To counter the competition from New York State, Pennsylvania built a thousand miles of canals by 1840. The United States was fast becoming a nation that moved by water.

Oceangoing steam-powered ships were much more difficult to build than riverboats, for the first steam engines used so much coal that no ship could carry more than a few days' worth. The *Savannah*, which crossed the Atlantic in 1819, was a sailing ship with an auxiliary steam engine that was used for only 90 hours of its 29-day trip. But engineers soon developed more efficient engines, and in 1838 two steamers, the *Great Western* and the *Sirius*, crossed the Atlantic on steam power alone. Elsewhere, sailing ships held their own until late in the century, for world trade was growing so fast that there was enough business for ships of every kind.

On land as on water, the problem was not imagining uses for steam-powered vehicles but building ones that worked, for steam engines were too heavy and weak to pull any weight. After Watt's patent expired in 1800, inventors experimented with lighter, more powerful high-pressure engines—an idea Watt had rejected as too dangerous. In 1804, the engineer Richard Trevithick built an engine that consumed twelve times less than Newcomen's and three times less than Watt's. With it, he built several steam-powered vehicles able to travel on roads or rails.

Horses could pull heavier wagons on wooden or iron rails than on cobblestone roads. By the 1820s England had many horse-powered railways. On one of them, the Stockton and Darlington Railway, the chief engineer, George Stephenson, began using steam locomotives in 1825. Four years later, the owners of the Liverpool and Manchester Railway organized a contest between steam-powered locomotives and horse-drawn wagons. Stephenson and his son Robert easily won the contest with their locomotive *Rocket*, which pulled a 20-ton train at up to 30 miles (48 kilometers) per hour. After that triumph, a railroad-building mania that lasted for twenty years swept Britain. The first lines linked towns and mines with the nearest harbor or waterway. In the late 1830s, passenger traffic soared, and entrepreneurs built lines between the major cities and then to small towns as well. Railroads were far cheaper, faster, and more comfortable than stagecoaches, and millions of people got in the habit of traveling.

The De Witt Clinton Locomotive, 1835–1840   The De Witt Clinton was the first steam locomotive built in the United States. The high smokestack let the hot cinders cool so they would not set fire to nearby trees, an important consideration at a time when eastern North America was still covered with forests. The three passenger cars are clearly horse-carriages fitted with railroad wheels.   (Corbis)

In the United States, entrepreneurs built railroads as fast and cheaply as possible with an eye to quick profits, not long-term durability. By the 1840s, 6,000 miles (10,000 kilometers) of track radiated westward from Boston, New York, Philadelphia, and Baltimore and connected these cities to one another. The boom of the 1840s was dwarfed by the mania of the 1850s, when 21,000 miles (34,000 kilometers) of new track were laid, much of it westward across the Appalachians to Memphis, St. Louis, and Chicago. After 1856, the trip from New York to Chicago, which once took three weeks by boat and on horseback, could be made in forty-eight hours. More than anything else, it was the railroads that opened up the midwest, turning the vast prairie into wheat fields and pasture for cattle to feed the industrial cities of the eastern United States.

Railways triggered the industrialization of Europe (see Map 24.2). Belgium, independent since 1830, quickly copied the British. In France and Prussia, the state planned and supervised railroad construction from the start. This delayed construction until the mid-1840s. When it began, however, it had a greater impact than in Britain, for it not only satisfied the long-standing need for transportation, but also stimulated the iron, machinery, and construction industries.

Abundant coal and iron-ore deposits determined the concentration of industries in a swath of territories running from northern France through Belgium and the Ruhr district of western Germany to Silesia in Prussia (now part of Poland). In the 1850s and 1860s, the states of Germany experienced an industrial boom, as did France and Belgium.

Borsig Ironworks in Germany in the 1840s This foundry was built to supply rails, locomotives, and other iron products to the German railroads, then under construction. (Deutsches Technikmuseum Berlin. Photo: Hans-Joachim Bartsch. Bildarchiv Preussischer Kulturbesitz)

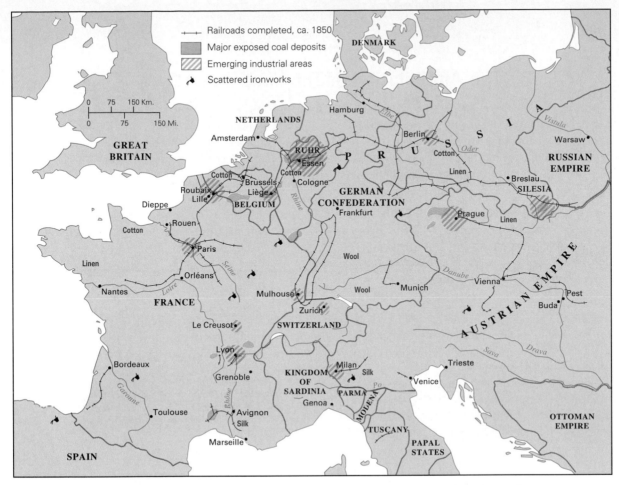

Map 24.2   Industrialization in Europe, ca. 1850   In 1850 industrialization was in its early stages on the European continent. The first industrial regions were comparatively close to England and possessed rich coal deposits: Belgium and the Ruhr district of Germany. Politics determined the location of railroads. Notice the star-shaped French network of rail lines emanating from Paris and the lines linking the different parts of the German Confederation.

Communication over Wires

The advent of railroads coincided with the development of the **electric telegraph.** After the Italian scientist Alessandro Volta invented the battery in 1800, making it possible to produce an electric current, many inventors tried to apply electricity to communication. The first practical telegraphy systems were developed almost simultaneously in England and America. In England, Wheatstone and Cooke introduced a five-needle telegraph in 1837; it remained in use until the early twentieth century. That same year, the American Samuel Morse introduced a code of dots and dashes that could be transmitted with a single wire; in 1843, he erected a line between Washington and Baltimore.

By the late 1840s, telegraph wires were being strung throughout the eastern United States and western Europe. In 1851, the first submarine telegraph cable was laid across the English Channel from England to France; it was the beginning of a network that eventually enclosed the entire globe. The world was rapidly shrinking, to the applause of Europeans and Americans for whom speed was a clear measure of progress (see Environmental and Technology: "The Annihilation of Time and Space"). No longer were communications limited to the speed of which a ship could sail or a horse could gallop.

"The Annihilation of Time and Space"

In the 1780s it took from five to eight months to sail from England to India, and a European writing a letter to someone in India usually had to wait two years for an answer. Fifty years later, when the first steamships and telegraph lines appeared, telegraph pioneer William O'Shaughnessy, serving with the British army in India, wrote:

> The progress of science is hourly adding to the catalogue of triumphs effected by the sagacity of man over the seeming impossibilities of nature. . . . A conquest still greater than all which I have quoted would be the annihilation of time and space in the accomplishment of correspondence.

By 1870, the voyage to India had been shortened to three weeks, and correspondents could expect answers to their letters in less than two months. What O'Shaughnessy called "the annihilation of time and space" had begun.

The telegraph had an even more astonishing impact on global communications. Beginning in the 1860s, cables laid on the ocean floor allowed telegrams to be sent across oceans as readily as on land. When the first cable to India was completed in June 1870, the chairman of the Eastern Telegraph Company, John Pender, sent a telegram to Bombay and received an answer 4 minutes and 22 seconds later. The *Daily Telegraph* of London reported this astonishing news:

> Aladdin . . . must have dropped his wonderful lamp in sheer amazement and neglect, and sold his magic ring for old gold. Time itself is telegraphed out of existence. Today communicates on one hand with Yesterday, on the other, with tomorrow.

The easy, almost instantaneously communication with any country in the world that we take for granted today began in the mid-nineteenth century. Since that time, communications technologies have made the world a much smaller and more intimate place—for those who can afford them.

Source: Sir William Brooke O'Shaughnessy, "Memoranda Relative to Experiments on the Communication of Telegraphic Signals by Induced Electricity," *Journal of the Asiatic Society of Bengal* (September 1839): 720–721. Quoted in G. R. M. Garatt, *One Hundred Years of Submarine Cables* (London: HMSO, 1950), 29.

Transatlantic Steamship Race   In 1838, two ships equipped with steam engines, the *Sirius* and the *Great Western*, steamed from England to New York. Although the *Sirius* left a few days earlier, the *Great Western*—shown here arriving in New York harbor—almost caught up with it, arriving just four hours after the *Sirius*. This race inaugurated regular transatlantic steamship service.   (Courtesy of the Mariner's Museum, Newport News, VA)

Overcrowded London   The French artist Gustave Doré depicted the tenements of industrial London where workers and their families lived. This drawing shows crowded and unsanitary row houses, each one room wide, with tiny back yards, and a train steaming across a viaduct overhead.   (Prints Division, New York Public Library, Astor, Lenox, and Tilden Foundations)

THE IMPACT OF THE INDUSTRIAL REVOLUTION

Although inventions were the most visible aspect of the Industrial Revolution, many other changes in society, politics, and the economy took place, interacting with one another. At first, the changes were quite local: smoky cities, slum neighborhoods, polluted water, child labor in mines and textile mills. By the mid-nineteenth century, the worst local effects were being alleviated. Replacing them on a national or even international scale were more complex problems: business cycles, labor conflicts, and the transformation of entire regions into industrial landscapes.

The New Industrial Cities

The most dramatic environmental changes brought about by industrialization occurred in the towns. Never before had towns grown so fast. London, one of the largest cities in Europe in 1700 with 500,000 inhabitants, grew to 959,000 by 1800, and to 2,363,000 by 1850; it was then the largest city the world had ever known. Smaller towns grew even faster. Manchester, a small town of 20,000 in 1758, reached 400,000 a century later, an eightfold increase. Liverpool grew sixfold in sixty years, from 82,000 in 1801 to 472,000 in 1861. New York City, already 100,000 strong in 1815, reached 600,000 (including Brooklyn) in 1850. These were not isolated instances. In some areas, towns merged and formed megalopolises, such as Greater London, the English Midlands, central Belgium, and the Ruhr district of Germany.

Industrialization made some people very prosperous. A great deal of this new wealth went into the building of fine homes, churches, museums, and theaters in wealthy neighborhoods in London, Berlin, and New York. Much of the beauty of London dates from the time of the Industrial Revolution. Yet, by all accounts, the industrial cities grew much too fast, and much of the growth occurred in the poorest neighborhoods.

As poor migrants streamed in from the countryside, developers built cheap, shoddy row houses for them to rent. These tenements were dangerously overcrowded. Often, several families had to live in one small room.

Sudden population growth, overcrowding, and inadequate municipal services conspired to make urban problems more serious than in earlier times. Town dwellers recently arrived from the country brought country ways with them. People threw their sewage and trash out the windows to be washed down the gutters in the streets. The poor kept pigs and chickens, the rich kept horses, and pedestrians stepped into the street at their own risk. Factories and workers' housing were mixed together. Air pollution from burning coal, a problem since the sixteenth century, got steadily worse. Londoners in particular breathed dense and noxious coal smoke. Although humans tolerated the burning of coal, it was too polluting for smelting iron or baking bread. People drank water drawn from wells and rivers contaminated by sewage and industrial runoff. The River Irwell, which ran through Manchester, was, in the words of one visitor, "considerably less a river than a flood of liquid manure."

"Every day that I live," wrote an American visitor to Manchester, "I thank Heaven that I am not a poor man with a family in England." In his poem "Milton," William Blake (1757–1827) expressed the revulsion of sensitive people at the spoliation of England's "mountains green" and "pleasant pastures":

> And did the Countenance Divine
> Shine forth upon our clouded hills?
> And was Jerusalem builded here
> Among these dark Satanic Mills?

Railroads invaded the towns. Railroad companies built their stations as close to the heart of cities as they could. On the outskirts of cities, railroad yards, sidings, and repair shops covered acres of land, surrounded by miles of warehouses and workers' housing. Farther out, far from the dangerous and polluted cities where their factories were located, newly rich industrialists created an environment halfway between country homes and townhouses: the first suburbs.

Under these conditions, diseases proliferated. To the long list of preindustrial urban diseases such as small-pox, dysentery, and tuberculosis, industrialization added new ailments. Rickets, a bone disease caused by lack of sunshine, became endemic in dark and smoky industrial cities. Steamships brought cholera from India, causing great epidemics that struck the poor neighborhoods especially hard. In the 1850s, when the average life expectancy in England was forty years, it was only twenty-four years in Manchester, and around seventeen years in Manchester's poorest neighborhoods, because of the high infant mortality. Observers of nineteenth-century industrial cities documented the horrors of slum life in vivid detail. Their shocking reports led to municipal reforms, such as garbage removal, water and sewage systems, and parks and schools. These measures began to alleviate the ills of urban life after the mid-nineteenth century.

Rural Environments

Long before the Industrial Revolution began, practically no wilderness areas were left in Britain and very few in western Europe. Almost every piece of land was covered with fields, forests, or pastures shaped by human activity, or by towns; yet humans continued to alter the environment. The most serious problem was deforestation. People cut timber to build ships and houses, to heat homes, and to manufacture bricks, iron, glass, beer, bread, and many other items.

Americans transformed their environment even faster than Europeans. Land in North America seemed practically free for the taking, and, east of the Appalachian Mountains, settlers viewed forests not as a valuable resource but as a hindrance to development. In their haste to "open up the West," pioneers felled trees and burned them, built houses and abandoned them, and then moved on. The cultivation of cotton was especially harmful. Planters cut down forests, grew cotton for a few years until it depleted the soil, then moved west, abandoning the land to scrub pines. This was slash-and-burn agriculture on an industrial scale.

At that time, America seemed immune to human depredations. Americans thought of nature as an obstacle to be overcome and dominated. This mindset persisted long after the entire continent was occupied and the environment truly endangered.

Paradoxically, in some ways industrialization actually relieved pressures on the environment in Britain. Raw materials once grown on British soil (for example, wood, hay, and wool) were replaced by materials found underground (iron ore and coal) or obtained overseas (cotton). While Russia, Sweden, the United States, and other forested countries continued to smelt iron with charcoal, the British substituted coke made from coal. As the British population increased, and land grew scarcer, the cost of growing feed for horses rose, creating incentives to find new, less land-hungry means of transportation. Likewise, as iron became cheaper and wood more expensive, ships and many other things formerly made of wood began to be made of iron.

To contemporaries, the most obvious changes in rural life were brought about by the new transportation systems. In the eighteenth century, France had a national network of quality roads, which Napoleon extended into Italy and Germany. In Britain, local governments' neglect of the roads that served long-distance traffic led to the formation of private enterprises—"Turnpike Trusts"— that built numerous toll roads. For heavy goods, horse-drawn wagons were too costly even on good roads. The growing volume of heavy freight triggered canal-building booms in Britain, France, and the Low Countries in the late eighteenth century. Some canals, like the duke of Bridgewater's canal in England, connected coal mines to towns or navigable rivers. Others linked navigable rivers and created national transportation networks.

Canals were marvels of construction, with deep cuts, tunnels, and even aqueducts that carried barges over rivers. They also were a sort of school where engineers learned skills they were able to apply to the next great transportation system: the railroads. They laid track across rolling country by cutting deeply into hillsides and erecting daringly long bridges of stone and iron across valleys. Lesser lines snaked their way to small towns hidden in remote valleys. Soon, clanking trains pulled by puffing, smoke-belching locomotives were invading long-isolated districts.

Thus, in the century after industrialization began, the landscape of industrializing countries was transformed more rapidly than ever before. But the ecological changes, like the technological and economic changes that caused them, were only beginning.

Working Conditions

Industrialization offered new opportunities to the enterprising. Carpenters, metalworkers, and machinists were in great demand. Since industrial machines were fairly simple, some workers became engineers or went into business for themselves. The boldest in England moved to the European Continent, the Americas, or India, taking their skills with them to establish new industries.

The successful, however, were a minority. Most industrial jobs were unskilled, repetitive, and boring. Factory work did not vary with the seasons or the time of day but began and ended by the clock. Workdays were long, there were few breaks, and foremen watched constantly. Workers who performed one simple task over and over had little sense of achievement or connection to the final product. Industrial accidents were common and could ruin a family. Unlike even the poorest preindustrial farmer or artisan, factory workers had no control over their tools, jobs, or working hours.

Industrial work, by definition, was physically removed from the home. This had a major impact on women and on family life. Women workers were concentrated in textile mills, partly because of ancient traditions, partly because textile work required less strength than metalworking, construction, or hauling. On average, women earned one-third to one-half as much as men. Young unmarried women worked to support themselves or to save for marriage. Married women took factory jobs when their husbands were unable to support the family. Mothers of infants faced a hard choice: whether to leave their babies with wet-nurses at great expense and danger or to bring them to the factory and keep them quiet with opiates. Rather than working together as family units, husbands and wives increasingly worked in different places.

Even where factory work was available, it was never the main occupation of working women in the early years of industrialization. Most young women who sought paid employment became domestic servants in spite of the low pay, drudgery, and risk of sexual abuse by male employers. Women with small children tried hard to find work they could do at home, such as laundry, sewing, embroidery, millinery, or taking in lodgers.

Even with both parents working, poor families found it hard to make ends meet. As in preindustrial societies, parents thought children should contribute to their upkeep as soon as they were able to. The first generation of workers brought their children with them to the factories and mines as early as age five or six; they had little choice, since there were no public schools or day-care centers. Employers encouraged the practice and even hired orphans. They preferred children because they were cheaper and more docile than adults and were better able to tie broken threads or crawl under machines to sweep the dust.

In Arkwright's cotton mills, two-thirds of the workers were children. In another mill, 17 percent were under ten years of age and 53 percent were between ten and seventeen; they worked 14 to 16 hours a day and were beaten if they made a mistake or fell asleep. Mine operators used children to pull coal carts along the low passageways from the coal face to the mine shaft. In the mid-nineteenth century, when the British government began restricting child labor, mill owners increasingly recruited Irish immigrants.

Cotton Mill in Early-Nineteenth-Century New England These machines, called self-acting mules, could spin hundreds of threads at once. Most of the workers tending the mules were women and children. (The Granger Collection, New York)

American industry began on a somewhat different note than the British. In the early nineteenth century, Americans still remembered their revolutionary ideals. When Francis Cabot Lowell built a cotton mill in Massachusetts, he deliberately hired the unmarried daughters of New England farmers, promising them decent wages and housing in dormitories under careful moral supervision. Other manufacturers eager to combine profits with morality followed his example. But soon the profit motive won out and manufacturers imposed longer hours, harsher working conditions, and lower wages. The young women protested: "As our fathers resisted with blood the lordly avarice of the British ministry, so we, their daughters, never will wear the yoke which has been prepared for us." When they went on strike, the factory owners replaced them with Irish immigrant women willing to accept lower pay and worse conditions.

While the cotton boom enriched planters, merchants, and manufacturers, African-Americans paid for it with their freedom. In the 1790s, 700,000 slaves of African descent lived in the United States, but their numbers were diminishing and the founders of the American republic did not consider slavery a serious problem. The rising demand for cotton and the abolition of the African slave trade in 1808 caused an increase in the price of slaves. As the "Cotton Kingdom" expanded, the number of slaves rose through natural increase and the reluctance of slaveowners to free their slaves. By 1850 the United States had 3,200,000 slaves, 60 percent of whom grew cotton. Similarly, Europe's and North America's surging demand for tea and coffee prolonged slavery in the sugar plantations of the West Indies and caused it to spread to the coffee-growing regions of southern Brazil.

Slavery was not, as white American southerners maintained, a "peculiar institution"—a consequence of biological differences, biblical injunctions, or African traditions. Slavery was part and parcel of the Industrial Revolution, just as much as child labor in Britain, the clothes that people wore, and the beverages they drank.

Changes in Society

Industrialization accentuated the polarization of society and disparities of income. In his novel *Sybil; or, The Two Nations*, the British politician Benjamin Disraeli° (1804–1881) spoke of "Two nations between whom there is no intercourse and no sympathy, who are as ignorant of each other's habits, thoughts, and feelings as if they were dwellers in different zones, or inhabitants of different planets . . . the rich and the poor."

Disraeli (diz-RAY-lee)

In Britain, the worst-off were those who clung to an obsolete skill or craft. The cotton-spinning boom of the 1790s briefly brought prosperity to weavers. Their high wages and low productivity, however, induced inventors to develop power looms. As a result, by 1811 the wages of handloom weavers had fallen by a third; by 1832, by two-thirds. Even by working more hours, they could not escape destitution.

The wages and standard of living of factory workers did not decline steadily like those of handloom weavers; they fluctuated wildly. During the war years 1792 to 1815, the price of food, on which the poor spent most of their income, rose faster than wages. The result was widespread hardship. Then, in the 1820s, real wages and public health began to improve. Industrial production grew at over 3 percent a year, pulling the rest of the economy along. Prices fell and wages rose. Even the poor could afford comfortable, washable cotton clothes and underwear.

Improvement, however, was not steady. One reason was the effect of **business cycles**—recurrent swings from economic hard times to recovery and growth, then back to hard times and a repetition of the sequence. When demand fell, businesses contracted or closed, and workers found themselves unemployed without any savings or insurance. Hard times returned in the "hungry forties." In 1847–1848 the potato crop failed in Ireland. One-quarter of the Irish population died in the resulting famine, and another quarter emigrated to England and America. On the European continent, the negative effects of economic downturns were tempered by the existence of small family farms to which urban workers could return when they were laid off.

Overall, the benefits of industrialization—cheaper food, clothing, and utensils—did not improve workers' standard of living until the 1850s. The real beneficiaries of the Industrial Revolution were the middle class. In Britain, landowning gentry and merchants had long shared wealth and influence. In the late eighteenth century, a new group arose: entrepreneurs whose money came from manufacturing. Most, like Arkwright and Wedgwood, were the sons of middling shopkeepers, craftsmen, or farmers. Their enterprises were usually self-financed, for little capital was needed to start a cotton-spinning or machine-building business. Many tried and some succeeded, largely by plowing their profits back into the business. A generation later, in the nineteenth century, some newly rich industrialists bought their way into high society.

Before the Industrial Revolution, wives of merchants had often participated in the family business; occasionally, widows managed sizable businesses on their own.

With industrialization came a "cult of domesticity" to justify removing middle-class women from contact with the business world. Instead, they became responsible for the home, the servants, the education of children, and the family's social life.

Middle-class people who attributed their success, often correctly, to their own efforts and virtues believed in individual responsibility: if some people could succeed through hard work, thrift, and temperance, then those who did not succeed had no one but themselves to blame for their failure. Many workers, however, newly arrived from rural districts, earned too little to save for the long stretches of unemployment they periodically experienced, and the squalor and misery of life in factory towns led to a noticeable increase in drunkenness on paydays. While the life of the poor remained brutal, the well-to-do—with no hypocrisy—espoused sobriety, thrift, industriousness, and responsibility. This moral position was a middle-class expression of sincere concern coupled with feelings of helplessness in the face of terrible social problems.

IDEOLOGICAL AND POLITICAL RESPONSES TO INDUSTRIALIZATION

Changes as profound as the Industrial Revolution could not occur without political ferment and ideological conflict. So many other momentous events took place during those years—the American Revolution (1776–1783), the French Revolution (1789–1799), the Napoleonic Wars (1804–1815), the reactions and revolts that periodically swept over Europe after 1815—that we cannot neatly separate out the consequences of industrialization from the rest. But it is clear that the Industrial Revolution strengthened the ideas of laissez faire° and socialism and sparked workers' protests.

Laissez Faire and Its Critics

The most celebrated exponent of **laissez faire** ("let them do") was Adam Smith (1723–1790), a Scottish economist. In *The Wealth of Nations* (1776) Smith argued that if individuals

laissez faire (lay-say fair)

were allowed to seek their personal gain, the effect, as though guided by an "invisible hand," would be to increase the general welfare. Except to protect private property, the government should refrain from interfering in business; it should even allow duty-free trade with foreign countries.

Although it was true that governments at the time were incompetent at regulating their national economies, it was becoming obvious that industrialization was not improving the general welfare but was for some causing great misery. Two other thinkers, Thomas Malthus (1766–1834) and David Ricardo (1772–1832), attempted to explain the poverty they saw without changing the basic premises of laissez faire. The cause of the workers' plight, Malthus and Ricardo said, was the population boom, which outstripped the food supply and led to falling wages. The workers' poverty, they claimed, was as much a result of "natural law" as the wealth of successful businessmen, and the only way the working class could avoid mass famine was to delay marriage and practice self-restraint and sexual abstinence.

Laissez-faire provided an ideological justification for a special kind of capitalism: banks, stock markets, and chartered companies allowed investors to obtain profits with reasonable risks but with much less government control and interference than in the past. In particular, removing guild and other restrictions allowed businesses to employ women and children and keep wages low.

Business people in Britain eagerly adopted laissez-faire ideas that justified their activities and kept the government at bay. But not everyone accepted the grim conclusions of the "dismal science," as economics was then known. Jeremy Bentham (1748–1832) believed that it was possible to maximize "the greatest happiness of the greatest number," if only a Parliament of enlightened reformers would study the social problems of the day and pass appropriate legislation; his philosophy became known as utilitarianism.

The German economist Friedrich List (1789–1846) rejected laissez faire and free trade as a British trick "to make the rest of the world, like the Hindus, its serfs in all industrial and commercial relations." To protect their "infant" industries from British competition, he argued, countries like Germany had to erect high tariff barriers. On the European continent, List's ideas were as influential as those of Smith and Ricardo and led to the formation of the Zollverein°, a customs union of most of the German states in 1834.

Positivists and Utopian Socialists

Bentham optimistically advocated gradual improvements. In contrast, some French social thinkers, moved by sincere concern for the poor, offered a radically new vision of a just civilization. Espousing a philosophy called **positivism,** the count of Saint-Simon (1760–1825) argued that the scientific method could solve social as well as technical problems. He recommended that the poor, guided by scientists and artists, form workers' communities under the protection of benevolent business leaders. These ideas found no following among workers, but they attracted the enthusiastic support of bankers and entrepreneurs, inspired by visions of railroads, canals, and other symbols of progress.

Meanwhile, the **utopian° socialism** of Charles Fourier (1768–1837), who loathed capitalists, imagined an ideal society in which groups of sixteen hundred workers would live in dormitories and work together on the land and in workshops where music, wine, and pastries would soften the hardships of labor. For this idea, critics called him "utopian"—a dreamer, after the Greek word *utopia* meaning "nowhere."

The person who came closest to creating a utopian community was the Englishman Robert Owen (1771–1858), a successful cotton manufacturer who believed that industry could provide prosperity for all. Conscience-stricken by the appalling plight of the workers, Owen took over the management of New Lanark, a mill town south of Glasgow. He improved the housing and added schools, a church, and other amenities. He also testified before Parliament against child labor and for government inspection of working conditions, thereby angering his fellow industrialists.

Protests and Reforms

Workers benefited little from the ideas of these middle-class philosophers. Instead, they resisted the harsh working conditions in their own ways. They changed jobs frequently. They often were absent, especially on Mondays. And when they were not closely watched, the quality of their work was likely to be poor.

Periodically, workers rioted or went on strike. Protests coincided with periods of high food prices and with downturns in the business cycle that left many unemployed. In some places, craftsmen broke into factories and destroyed the machines that threatened their livelihoods. Such acts of resistance did nothing, however, to change the nature of industrial work. Not until

---

Zollverein (TSOLL-feh-rine)

utopian (you-TOE-pee-uhn)

workers learned to act together could they hope to have much influence.

Gradually they formed benevolent societies and organizations to demand universal male suffrage and shorter workdays. In 1834 Robert Owen organized the Grand National Consolidated Trade Union to lobby for an eight-hour workday; it gained half a million members but failed a few months later in the face of government prosecution of trade-union activities. The Chartist movement had more success, gathering petitions by the thousands to present to Parliament. Although Chartism collapsed in 1848, it left a legacy of labor organizing.

Eventually, mass movements persuaded political leaders to look into the abuses of industrial life, despite the prevailing laissez-faire philosophy. In the 1820s and 1830s, the British Parliament began investigating conditions in the factories and mines. The Factory Act of 1833 prohibited the employment of children under age nine in textile mills. It also limited the working hours of children between the ages of nine and thirteen to eight hours a day and the daily working hours of fourteen- to eighteen-year-olds to twelve. The Mines Act of 1842 prohibited the employment of all women and of boys under age ten underground. Several decades passed before the government appointed enough inspectors to enforce the new laws.

Most important was the struggle over the Corn Laws—tariffs on imported grain. Their repeal in 1846, in the name of "free trade," was designed to lower the cost of food for workers and thereby allow employers to pay lower wages. A victory for laissez-faire, the repeal also represented a victory for the rising class of manufacturers, merchants, and investors over the conservative landowners who had long dominated politics.

The British learned to seek reform through accommodation. On the European continent, in contrast, the revolutions of 1848 revealed widespread discontent with repressive governments but failed to soften the hardships of industrialization.

INDUSTRIALIZATION AND THE NONINDUSTRIAL WORLD

The spread of the Industrial Revolution to western Europe and North America in the early nineteenth century delayed industrialization elsewhere. In most places, trade with the industrial countries meant exporting raw materials, not locally made handicraft products. In the few countries whose governments were tempted to imitate the West, cheap Western imports, backed by the power of Great Britain, thwarted the spread of industry for a century or more.

We will consider three places where industrialization did *not* occur in this period: Russia, whose society and institutions delayed industrialization by a century, and Egypt and India, where industrialization was stifled at the outset. In these three cases, we can discern the outlines of the Western domination that has characterized the history of the world since the late nineteenth century.

Russia

Russia had been in close contact with western Europe since the seventeenth century. Its aristocrats spoke French, its army was modeled on the armies of western Europe, and it participated in European wars and diplomacy. Yet Russia differed from western Europe in one important aspect: it had almost no middle class. Thus industrialization there arose not from the initiative of local entrepreneurs but by government decree and through the work of foreign engineers.

Tsar Nicholas I (r. 1825–1855) built the first railroad in Russia from St. Petersburg, the capital, to his summer palace in 1837. A few years later, he insisted that the trunk line from St. Petersburg to Moscow run in a perfectly straight line. American engineers built locomotive workshops in Russia, and British engineers set up textile mills. These projects, though well publicized, were oddities in a society where most people were serfs tied to the estates of powerful noble landowners and towns were few and far apart.

Until the late nineteenth century, the Russian government's interest in industry was limited and hesitant. An industrial revolution, to be successful, required large numbers of educated and independent-minded artisans and entrepreneurs. Suspicious of Western ideas, especially anything smacking of liberalism, socialism, or revolution, the Russian government feared the spread of literacy and of modern education beyond the minimum needed to train the officer corps and the bureaucracy. Rather than run the risk of allowing a middle class and a working class to arise that might challenge its control, the regime of Nicholas I kept the peasants in serfdom and preferred to import most industrial goods and pay for them with exports of grain and timber.

Russia aspired to Western-style economic development. But fear of political change caused the country to fall further behind western Europe, economically and technologically, than it had been a half-century before. When France and Britain went to war against Russia in 1854, they faced a Russian army equipped with obsolete weapons and bogged down for lack of transportation.

Steam Tractor in India   Power machinery was introduced slowly into India because of the abundance of skilled low-cost labor. In this scene, a steam tractor fords a shallow stream, to the delight of onlookers. The towerlike construction on the right is probably a pier for a railroad bridge.   (Billie Love Historical Collection)

Egypt

Like Russia, Egypt began to industrialize in the early nineteenth century. The driving force was its ruler, Muhammad Ali (1769–1849), a man who was to play a major role not only in the history of Egypt but in the Middle East and East Africa as well (see Chapter 26). He wanted to build up the Egyptian economy and military in order to become less dependent on the Ottoman sultan, his nominal overlord. To do so, he imported advisers and technicians from Europe and built cotton mills, foundries, shipyards, weapons factories, and other industrial enterprises. To pay for all this, he made the peasants grow wheat and cotton, which the government bought at a low price and exported at a profit. He also imposed high tariffs on imported goods in order to force the pace of industrialization.

Muhammad Ali's efforts, however, fell afoul of the British, who did not want a powerful country threatening to interrupt the flow of travelers and mail cross Egypt, the shortest route between Europe and India. When Egypt went to war against the Ottoman Empire in 1839, Britain intervened and forced Muhammad Ali to eliminate all import duties in the name of free trade. Unprotected, Egypt's fledgling industries could not compete with the flood of cheap British products. Thereafter,

Egypt exported raw cotton and imported manufactured goods and became, in effect, an economic dependency of Britain.

India

Until the late eighteenth century, India had been the world's largest producer and exporter of cotton textiles, handmade by skilled spinners and weavers. The British East India Company took over large parts of India just as the Industrial Revolution was beginning in Britain. Thus cheap British factory-made textiles began flooding into India duty-free, putting first spinners and then handloom weavers out of work. Unlike Britain, India had no factories to which displaced handicraft workers could turn for work. Most of them became landless peasants, eking out a precarious living.

Like other tropical regions, India became an exporter of raw materials and an importer of British industrial goods. To hasten the process, British entrepreneurs and colonial officials introduced railroads into the subcontinent. The construction of India's railroad network began in the mid-1850s, along with coal mining to fuel the locomotives and the installation of telegraph lines to connect the major cities.

Some Indian entrepreneurs saw opportunities in the atmosphere of change that the British created. In 1854 the Bombay merchant Cowasjee Nanabhoy Davar imported an engineer, four skilled workers, and several textile machines from Britain and started India's first textile mill. This was the beginning of India's cotton industry. But, despite many gifted entrepreneurs, India's industrialization proceeded at a snail's pace, for the government was in British hands and the British did nothing to encourage Indian industry.

CONCLUSION

In the period from 1760 to 1851, the new technologies of the Industrial Revolution greatly increased humans' power over nature. Goods could be manufactured in vast quantities at low cost. People and messages could travel at unprecedented speeds. In addition to utilizing the energy produced by muscle power, wind, and water, humans gained access to the energy stored in coal. Faster than ever before, humans turned woodland into farmland, dug canals and laid tracks, bridged rivers and cut through mountains, and covered the countryside with towns and cities.

This newfound power over nature, far from benefiting everyone, increased the disparities between individuals and societies. Industrialization brought forth entrepreneurs—whether in the mills of England or on plantations in the American south—with enormous power over their employees or slaves, a power that they found easy and profitable to abuse. Some people acquired great wealth while others lived in poverty and squalor. Middle-class women were restricted to the care of their homes and children. Many working-class women had to leave home to earn wages in factories or as domestic servants. These changes in work and family life provoked intense debates among intellectuals. Some defended the disparities in the name of laissez faire; others criticized the injustices that industrialization brought. Society was slow to bring these abuses under control.

By the 1850s, the Industrial Revolution had spread from Britain to western Europe and the United States, and its impact was being felt around the world. To make a product that was sold on every continent, the British cotton industry used African slaves, American land, British machines, and Irish workers. Iron ships and steam engines shifted the historic balance between Europe and China. After the 1850s—as we shall see in Chapter 29—no part of the world remained untouched by the power of industry.

Key Terms

Industrial Revolution	Crystal Palace
agricultural revolution	steam engine
(eighteenth century)	James Watt
mass production	electric telegraph
Josiah Wedgwood	business cycle
division of labor	laissez faire
mechanization	positivism
Richard Arkwright	utopian socialism

Suggested Readings

General works on the history of technology give pride of place to industrialization. For an optimistic overview see Joel Mokyr, *The Lever of Riches: Technological Creativity and Economic Progress* (1990). Other important recent works include James McClellan III and Harold Dorn, *Science and Technology in World History* (1999); David Landes, *The Wealth and Poverty of Nations* (1998); and Ian Inkster, *Technology and Industrialization: Historical Case Studies and International Perspectives* (1998).

There is a rich literature on the British industrial revolution, beginning with T. S. Ashton's classic *The Industrial Revolution, 1760–1830*, published in 1948 and often reprinted.

The impact of industrialization on workers is the theme of E. P. Thompson's classic work *The Making of the English Working Class* (1963), but see also E. R. Pike, *"Hard Times": Human Documents of the Industrial Revolution* (1966). The role of women is most ably revealed in Lynn Y. Weiner, *From Working Girl to Working Mother: The Female Labor Force in the United States, 1820–1980* (1985), and in Louise Tilly and Joan Scott, *Women, Work, and Family* (1978).

European industrialization is the subject of J. Goodman and K. Honeyman, *Gainful Pursuits: The Making of Industrial Europe: 1600–1914* (1988); John Harris, *Industrial Espionage and Technology Transfer: Britain and France in the Eighteenth Century* (1998); and David Landes, *The Unbound Prometheus: Technological Change and Industrial Development in Western Europe from 1750 to the Present* (1972). On the beginnings of American industrialization see David Jeremy, *Artisans, Entrepreneurs and Machines: Essays on the Early Anglo-American Textile Industry, 1770–1840* (1998).

On the environmental impact of industrialization see Richard Wilkinson, *Poverty and Progress: An Ecological Perspective on Economic Development* (1973), and Richard Tucker and John Richards, *Global Deforestation in the Nineteenth-Century World Economy* (1983).

The first book to treat industrialization as a global phenomenon is Peter Stearns, *The Industrial Revolution in World History* (1993); see also Louise Tilly's important article "Connections" in *American Historical Review* (February 1994).

Note

1. *Nautical Magazine* 12 (1843): 346.

25

NATION BUILDING AND ECONOMIC TRANSFORMATION IN THE AMERICAS, 1800–1890

Independence in Latin America, 1800–1830 • The Problem of Order, 1825–1890 • The Challenge of Economic and Social Change

ENVIRONMENT AND TECHNOLOGY: The McCormick Reaper

SOCIETY AND CULTURE: Villages in New England and Mexico

The Train Station in Orizaba, Mexico, 1877   In the last decades of the nineteenth century, Mexico's political leaders actively promoted economic development. The railroad became the symbol of this ideal.

n 1862, seeing Mexico divided by violent factional conflicts and the United States convulsed by the Civil War, Napoleon III seized the opportunity to project French power into the Americas by sending a large military force to Mexico. Mexican conservatives who resented their government's efforts to introduce democratic reforms and limit the power of the Catholic Church supported the invasion. After driving the liberal president, Benito Juárez°, from Mexico City, Napoleon III and a group of Mexican conservatives in 1864 convinced Archduke Maximilian of Habsburg, brother of Emperor Franz Joseph of Austria, to accept the throne of Mexico.

Although Maximilian embraced Mexican patriotic symbols and accepted some of Juárez's reforms, he failed to win popular support. Armed resistance by Mexican liberals and diplomatic pressure by the United States after the conclusion of the Civil War led to a French pullout. Then, on the morning of June 19, 1867, a Mexican firing squad executed Maximilian. His young wife Charlotte, daughter of King Leopold of Belgium, was in Europe trying to convince the emperor of France or the pope to intervene to save her husband when news of his death swept her into madness. For Mexicans, the defeat and execution of Maximilian signaled an end to intervention and the triumph of republicanism.

The independence of Britain's thirteen North American colonies set in motion a radical transformation of the New World. Spurred by the revolutionary examples of the United States and France (see Chapter 23) and buttressed by Enlightenment ideology, which exalted political freedom, most of the Spanish and Portuguese colonies in the New World gained independence in the early decades of the nineteenth century. As the French intervention in Mexico illustrates, however, European powers were ready to challenge the sovereignty of many of the new American nations.

Through the nineteenth century, the new nations in the Western Hemisphere wrestled with the difficult questions that independence raised. If colonies could reject submission to imperial powers, could not regions with distinct cultures, social structures, and economies refuse to accept the political authority of the newly formed nation-states? How could nations born in revolution accept the political strictures of written constitutions—even those they wrote themselves? How could the ideals of liberty and freedom expressed in those constitutions be reconciled with the denial of rights to Amerindians, slaves, recent immigrants, and women?

While trying to resolve these political questions, the new nations also attempted to promote economic growth. But just as the legacy of class and racial division thwarted the realization of political ideals, colonial economic development, with its emphasis on agricultural and mining exports, inhibited efforts to promote diversification and industrialization.

As you read this chapter, ask yourself the following questions:

- What were the causes of the revolutions for independence in Latin America?
- What major political challenges did Western Hemisphere nations face in the nineteenth century?
- How did abolitionism, the movement for women's rights, and immigration change the nations of the Western Hemisphere?
- How did industrialization and new agricultural technologies affect the environment?

INDEPENDENCE IN LATIN AMERICA, 1800–1830

As the eighteenth century drew to a close, Spain and Portugal held vast colonial possessions in the Western Hemisphere, although their power had declined relative to that of their British and French rivals. Both Iberian empires had reformed colonial administration and strengthened their military forces in the eighteenth century. Despite these efforts, the same economic and political forces that had undermined British rule in the

---

Benito Juárez (beh-NEE-toh WAH-rez)

colonies that became the United States were present in Spanish America and Brazil.

Roots of Revolution, to 1810

Wealthy colonial residents of Latin America were frustrated by the political and economic power of colonial officials and angered by high taxes and imperial monopolies. By 1800, the examples of the American and French Revolutions had stirred enthusiasm for self-government (see Chapter 23). The great works of the Enlightenment as well as revolutionary documents like the Declaration of Independence and the Declaration of the Rights of Man circulated widely in Latin America. But it was Napoleon's decision to invade Portugal (1807) and Spain (1808), not revolutionary ideas, that ignited Latin America's struggle for independence.

In 1808 the royal family of Portugal fled to Brazil. King John VI maintained his court there for over a decade. In Spain, in contrast, Napoleon forced King Ferdinand VII to abdicate and placed his own brother, Joseph Bonaparte, on the throne. Spanish patriots fighting against the French created a new political body, the Junta° Central, to administer the areas they controlled. Most Spaniards viewed the Junta as a temporary patriotic institution created to govern Spain while the king remained a French prisoner. The Junta, however, claimed the right to exercise the king's powers over Spain's colonies, and this claim provoked a crisis.

Large numbers of colonists in Spanish America, perhaps a majority, favored obedience to the Junta Central. A vocal minority, which included many wealthy and powerful individuals, objected. The dissenters argued that they were subjects of the king, not dependents of the Spanish nation. They wanted to create local juntas and govern their own affairs until Ferdinand regained the throne. Spanish loyalists in the colonies resisted this tentative assertion of local autonomy and thus provoked armed uprisings. In late 1808 and 1809, popular movements overthrew Spanish colonial officials in Venezuela, Mexico, and Bolivia and created local juntas. In each case, Spanish officials quickly reasserted control and punished the leaders. Their harsh repression, however, further polarized public opinion in the colonies and gave rise to a greater sense of a separate American nationality. By 1810 Spanish colonial authorities were facing a new round of revolutions more clearly focused on the achievement of independence.

Junta (HUN-tah)

Simón Bolívar   Simón Bolívar was the greatest of Latin America's independence-era leaders. There are many portraits of Bolívar, each suggesting distinct elements of his political legacy. This portrait shows him in uniform and cape mounted on a white horse. His gaze is focused on the horizon, suggesting his unique ability to foresee the future's challenges.   (Organization of American States)

Spanish South America, 1810–1825

In Caracas (the capital city of modern Venezuela), a revolutionary Junta led by creoles (colonial-born whites) declared independence in 1811. Although this group espoused popular sovereignty and representative democracy, its leaders were large landowners who defended slavery and opposed full citizenship for the black and mixed-race majority. Their aim was to expand their own privileges by eliminating Spaniards from the upper levels of Venezuela's government and from the church. The junta's narrow agenda spurred loyalists in the colonial administration and church hierarchy to rally thousands of free blacks and

CHRONOLOGY

	United States and Canada	Mexico and Central America	South America
1800	**1789** U.S. Constitution ratified **1803** Louisiana Purchase		
	1812–1815 War of 1812	**1810–21** Mexican movement for independence	**1808** Portuguese royal family arrives in Brazil **1808–1809** Revolutions for independence begin in Spanish South America
1825	**1837** Texas gains independence from Mexico **1845** Texas admitted as a state		**1822** Brazil gains independence
		1846–1848 War between Mexico and the United States **1847–1870** Caste War	
1850	**1848** Women's Rights Convention in Seneca Falls, New York **1861–1865** Civil War **1867** Creation of Dominion of Canada	**1862–1867** French invade Mexico	**1865–1870** Argentina, Uruguay, and Brazil wage war against Paraguay **1870s** Governments of Argentina and Chile begin final campaigns against indigenous peoples
1875	**1876** Sioux and allies defeat United States Army in Battle of Little Bighorn		**1879–1881** Chile wages war against Peru and Bolivia **1888** Abolition of slavery in Brazil

slaves to defend the Spanish Empire. Faced with this determined resistance, the revolutionary movement placed overwhelming political authority in the hands of its military leader **Simón Bolívar°** (1783–1830), who later became the preeminent leader of the independence movement in Spanish South America.

The son of wealthy Venezuelan planters, Bolívar had studied both the classics and the works of the Enlightenment. He used the force of his personality to mobilize political support and to hold the loyalty of his troops. Defeated on many occasions, Bolívar successfully adapted his objectives and policies to attract new allies and build coalitions. Although initially opposed to the abolition of slavery, for example, he agreed to support emancipation in order to draw slaves and freemen to his cause and to gain supplies from Haiti. Bolívar was also capable of

using harsh methods to ensure victory. Attempting to force resident Spaniards to join the rebellion in 1813, he proclaimed: "Any Spaniard who does not ... work against tyranny in behalf of this just cause will be considered an enemy and punished; as a traitor to the nation, he will inevitably be shot by a firing squad."[1]

Between 1813 and 1817 military advantage shifted back and forth between the patriots and loyalists. Bolívar's ultimate success was aided by his decision to enlist demobilized English veterans of the Napoleonic Wars and by a military revolt in Spain in 1820. The English veterans, hardened by combat, helped improve the battlefield performance of Bolívar's army. The revolt in Spain forced Ferdinand VII—he was restored to the throne in 1814 after the defeat of Napoleon—to accept a constitution that limited the powers of both the monarch and the church. Colonial loyalists who for a decade had fought to maintain the authority of monarch and church viewed those reforms as unacceptably liberal.

Simón Bolívar (see-MOAN bow-LEE-varh)

OREGON COUNTRY
(Joint U.S.-British occupation)

BRITISH NORTH AMERICA
(Gr. Br.)

Mississippi

UNITED STATES

Colorado

Rio Grande

MEXICO
1821

San Antonio

Gulf of Mexico

Mexico City

Veracruz

ATLANTIC OCEAN

BAHAMA IS.
(Gr. Br.)

Havana

CUBA
(Spain)

HAITI 1804

PUERTO RICO (Spain)

JAMAICA (Gr. Br.)

BRITISH HONDURAS (Gr. Br.)

GUATEMALA
Guatemala

UNITED PROVINCES OF CENTRAL AMERICA
1823–1839

Caribbean Sea

Panama

Caracas

TRINIDAD (Gr. Br.)

VENEZUELA

BR. GUIANA (Gr. Br.)

DUTCH GUIANA (Neth.)

FRENCH GUIANA (France)

Socorro
Bogotá

Magdalena

GRAN COLOMBIA
1819–1830

Galápagos Islands

Quito

ECUADOR

Amazon

EMPIRE OF BRAZIL
1822

PERU
1824

Lima

Bahia

PACIFIC OCEAN

BOLIVIA
1825

La Paz

Sucre

Paraná

PARAGUAY
1811

São Paulo

Rio de Janeiro

CHILE
1817

UNITED PROVINCES OF THE RÍO DE LA PLATA
1816

Valparaíso
Santiago

URUGUAY
1828

ARGENTINA

Buenos Aires
Bahía Blanca

Montevideo

1811 Year independence gained

Colony

0   500   1000 Km.

0   500   1000 Mi.

PATAGONIA
(Disputed between Argentina and Chile)

Islas Malvinas
(Falkland Islands)

With the king's supporters divided, momentum swung irreversibly to the patriots. After liberating present-day Venezuela, Colombia, and Ecuador, Bolívar's army occupied the area that is now Peru and Bolivia (named for Bolívar). Finally defeating the last Spanish armies in 1824, Bolívar and his closest supporters attempted to draw the former Spanish colonies into a formal confederation. The first step was to forge Venezuela, Colombia, and Ecuador into a single nation: Gran Colombia (see Map 25.1). With Bolívar's encouragement, Peru and Bolivia also experimented with unification. Despite his prestige, however, all of these initiatives had failed by 1830.

Buenos Aires (the capital city of modern Argentina) was the second important center of revolutionary activity in Spanish South America. In Buenos Aires, news of Ferdinand VII's abdication led to the creation of a junta, organized by militia commanders, merchants, and ranchers, which overthrew the viceroy in 1810. To deflect the opposition of loyalists and Spanish colonial officials, the junta claimed loyalty to the imprisoned king. After Ferdinand regained the Spanish throne, however, junta leaders dropped this pretense. In 1816 they declared independence as the United Provinces of the Río de la Plata.

Patriot leaders in Buenos Aires at first sought to retain control over the territory of the Viceroyalty of Río de la Plata, which had been created in 1776 and included modern Argentina, Uruguay, Paraguay, and Bolivia. But Spanish loyalists in Uruguay and Bolivia and a separatist movement in Paraguay defeated these ambitions. Even within the territory of Argentina, the government in Buenos Aires was unable to control regional rivalries and political differences. As a result, the region rapidly descended into political chaos.

A weak succession of juntas, collective presidencies, and dictators soon lost control over much of the interior of Argentina. However, in 1817 the government in Buenos Aires did manage to support a mixed force of Chileans and Argentines led by José de San Martín° (1778–1850), who crossed the Andes Mountains to attack Spanish military forces in Chile and Peru. During this campaign, San Martín's most effective troops were former slaves, who had gained their freedom by enlisting in the army, and gauchos, the cowboys of the Argentine pampas (prairies). After gaining victory in Chile, San Martín pushed on to Peru in 1820 but failed to gain a clear victory there. The violent and destructive uprising of Tupac Amaru II in 1780 had traumatized the Andean region and colonists fearful that support for independence might unleash another Amerindian uprising. Unable to make progress, San Martín surrendered command of patriot forces in Peru to Simón Bolívar, who overcame final Spanish resistance in 1824.

Mexico, 1810–1823

In 1810, Mexico was Spain's richest and most populous colony. Its silver mines were the richest in the world, and the colony's capital, Mexico City, was larger than any city in Spain. Mexico also had the largest population of Spanish immigrants among the colonies. Spaniards dominated the government, church, and economy of Mexico. When news of Napoleon's invasion of Spain reached the colony, conservative Spaniards in Mexico City overthrew the local viceroy because he was too sympathetic to the Creoles. This action by Spanish loyalists underlined the new reality: with the king of Spain in a French prison, colonial authority now rested on brute force.

The first stage of the revolution against Spain occurred in central Mexico. In this region wealthy ranchers and farmers had aggressively forced many Amerindian communities from their traditional agricultural lands. A series of crop failures and epidemics further afflicted the region's rural poor. At the same time, miners and the urban poor faced higher food prices and rising unemployment. With the power of colonial authorities weakened by events in Spain, anger and fear spread through towns and villages in central Mexico.

On September 16, 1810, **Miguel Hidalgo y Costilla°**, parish priest of the small town of Dolores, rang the church bells, attracting thousands. In a fiery speech he urged the crowd to rise up against the oppression of Spanish officials. Tens of thousands of the rural and urban poor joined his movement. They lacked military discipline and adequate weapons but knew who their oppressors were, spontaneously attacking the ranches and mines that had been exploiting them. Many Spaniards and colonial-born whites were murdered or assaulted. At first, wealthy Mexicans were sympathetic to Hidalgo's objectives, but they eventually supported Spanish authorities when they recognized the threat that the angry masses following Hidalgo posed to them. The military

Map 25.1 Latin America by 1830   By 1830, patriot forces had overturned the Spanish and Portuguese Empires of the Western Hemisphere. Regional conflicts, local wars, and foreign interventions challenged the survival of many of these new nations following independence.

José de San Martín (hoe-SAY deh san mar-TEEN)
Miguel Hidalgo y Costilla (mee-GEHL ee-DAHL-go ee cos-TEA-ah)

tide quickly turned against Hidalgo, and he was captured, tried, and executed in 1811.

The revolution continued under the leadership of another priest, **José María Morelos°,** a former student of Hidalgo. A more adept military and political leader than his mentor, Morelos created a formidable fighting force and, in 1813, convened a congress that declared independence and drafted a constitution. Despite these achievements, loyalist forces also proved too strong for Morelos. He was defeated and executed in 1815.

Although small numbers of insurgents continued to wage war against Spanish forces, colonial rule seemed secure in 1820. However, news of the military revolt in Spain unsettled the conservative groups and church officials who had defended Spanish rule against Hidalgo and Morelos. In 1821 Colonel Agustín de Iturbide° and other loyalist commanders forged an alliance with remaining insurgents and declared Mexico's independence. The conservative origins of Mexico's transition to independence were highlighted by the decision to create a monarchial form of government and crown Iturbide as emperor. In early 1823, however, the army overthrew Iturbide and Mexico became a republic.

Brazil, to 1831

The arrival of the Portuguese royal family in Brazil in 1808 helped to maintain the loyalty of the colonial elite and to stimulate the local economy. After the defeat of Napoleon in Europe, the Portuguese government called for King John VI to return to Portugal. He at first resisted this pressure. Then in 1820 the military uprising in Spain provoked a sympathetic liberal revolt in Portugal, and the Portuguese military garrison in Rio de Janeiro forced the king to permit the creation of juntas. John recognized that he needed to take dramatic action to protect his throne. In 1821, he returned to Portugal. Hoping to protect his claims to Brazil, he left his son Pedro in Brazil as regent.

By 1820, the Spanish colonies along Brazil's borders had experienced ten years of revolution and civil war, and some, like Argentina and Paraguay, had gained independence. Unable to ignore these struggles, some Brazilians began to reevaluate Brazil's relationship with Portugal. Many Brazilians resented their homeland's economic subordination to Portugal. The arrogance of Portuguese soldiers and bureaucrats led others to talk openly of independence. Rumors circulated that Portuguese troops were being sent to discipline Brazil and force the regent Pedro to join his father in Lisbon.

José María Morelos (hoe-SAY mah-REE-ah moh-RAY-los)
Agustín de Iturbide (ah-goos-TEEN deh ee-tur-BEE-deh)

Unwilling to return to Portugal and committed to maintaining his family's hold on Brazil, Pedro aligned himself with the rising tide of independence sentiment. In 1822, he declared Brazilian independence. Pedro's decision launched Brazil into a unique political trajectory. Unlike its neighbors, which became constitutional republics, Brazil gained independence as a constitutional monarchy with Pedro I, heir to the throne of Portugal, as emperor.

Pedro I was committed both to monarchy and to many liberal principles. He directed the writing of the constitution of 1824, which provided for an elected assembly and granted numerous protections for political opposition. But he made powerful enemies by attempting to protect the Portuguese who remained in Brazil from arbitrary arrest and seizure of their property. More dangerously still, he opposed slavery in a nation dominated by the slave-owning class. In 1823 Pedro I anonymously published an article that characterized slavery as a "cancer eating away at Brazil." Despite opposition, he then concluded a treaty with Great Britain to end Brazilian participation in the slave trade in 1830. The political elite of Brazil's slave-owning regions opposed the treaty and for nearly two decades worked tirelessly to prevent enforcement. Pedro also continued his father's costly commitment of military forces to control neighboring Uruguay. As military losses and costs rose, the Brazilian public grew impatient. A small but vocal minority that opposed the monarchy and sought the creation of a democracy used these issues to rally public opinion against the emperor.

Confronted by street demonstrations and violence between Brazilians and Portuguese, Pedro I abdicated the throne in 1831 in favor of his five-year-old son Pedro II. After a nine-year regency, Pedro II assumed full powers as emperor of Brazil. He reigned until he was overthrown by republicans in 1889.

THE PROBLEM OF ORDER, 1825–1890

All the newly independent nations of the Western Hemisphere had difficulties establishing stable political institutions. The idea of popular sovereignty found broad support across the hemisphere. As a result, written constitutions and elected assemblies were put in place, often before the actual achievement of independence. Even in the hemisphere's two monarchies, Mexico and Brazil, the emperors sought to legitimize their rule by accepting constitutional limits on their authority and by the creation of representative assemblies. Nevertheless, widespread support for constitutional order and for representative government failed to prevent bitter factional conflict, regionalism, and the appearance of charismatic political leaders and military uprisings.

Constitutional Experiments

In reaction to the arbitrary and tyrannical authority of colonial rulers, revolutionary leaders in both the United States and Latin America espoused constitutionalism. They believed that the careful description of political powers in written constitutions offered the best protection for individual rights and liberties. In practice, however, many new constitutions proved unworkable. In the United States, George Washington, James Madison, and other leaders became dissatisfied with the nation's first constitution, the Articles of Confederation. They led the effort to write a new constitution, which was put into effect in 1789. In Latin America, few constitutions survived the rough-and-tumble of national politics. Between 1811 and 1833 Venezuela and Chile alone ratified and then rejected a combined total of nine constitutions.

Important differences in colonial political experience influenced later political developments in the Americas. The ratification of a new constitution in the United States was the culmination of a long historical process that had begun with the development of English constitutional law and continued under colonial charters. Many more residents of the British North American colonies had had the experience of voting and holding political office than was true in the colonial societies of Portuguese or Spanish America. The British colonies provided opportunities for holding elective offices in town governments and colonial legislatures, and, by the time of independence, citizens had grown accustomed to elections, political parties, and factions. In contrast, constitutional government and elections were only briefly experienced in Spanish America between 1812 and 1814—while Ferdinand VII was a prisoner of Napoleon—and this short period was disrupted by the early stages of the revolutions for independence. Brazil had almost no experience with popular politics before independence. Despite these differences in experience and constitutional forms, every new republic in the Americas initially limited the right to vote to free men of property.

Democratic passions and the desire for effective self-rule led to significant political reform in the Americas, even in some of the region's remaining colonies. British Canada was divided into separate colonies and territories each with a separate and distinct government. Political life in each colony was dominated by a provincial governor and appointed advisory councils drawn from the local elite. Elected assemblies existed within each province, but they exercised limited power. Agitation to end oligarchic rule and make government responsive to the will of the assemblies led to armed rebellion in 1837. In the 1840s Britain responded by establishing responsible government in each of the Canadian provinces, allowing limited self-rule. By the 1860s regional political leaders interested in promoting economic development realized that railroads and other internal improvements required a government with a "national" character. Moreover, civil war in the U.S. and raids from U.S. territory into Canada by Irish nationalists focused attention on the need to protect the border. Negotiations led to the **Confederation of 1867,** which included the provinces of Ontario, Quebec, New Brunswick, and Nova Scotia. The Confederation that created the new Dominion of Canada with a central government in Ottawa (see Map 25.2) was hailed by one observer as the "birthday of a new nationality." [2]

The path to effective constitutional government was rockier to the south. Because neither Spain nor Portugal had permitted anything like the elected legislatures and municipal governments of colonial North America, the drafters of Latin American constitutions were less constrained by practical political experience. As a result, many of the new Latin American nations experimented with untested political institutions. For example, Simón Bolívar, who wrote the first constitutions of five South American republics, included in Bolivia's constitution a fourth branch of government that had "jurisdiction over the youth, the hearts of men, public spirit, good customs, and republican ethics."

Most Latin American nations found it difficult to define the political role of the Catholic Church after independence. In the colonial period the Catholic Church was a religious monopoly that controlled all levels of education, and dominated intellectual life. Many early constitutions aimed to reduce this power by making education secular and by permitting the practice of other religions. The church reacted by organizing its allies and financing conservative political movements. In Mexico, Colombia, Chile, and Argentina conflicts between liberals who sought the separation of church and state and supporters of the church's traditional powers dominated political life until late in the nineteenth century.

Limiting the power of the military proved to be another significant stumbling block to the creation of constitutional governments in Latin America. The wars for independence elevated the prestige of military leaders. When the wars were over, Bolívar and other military commanders seldom proved willing to subordinate themselves to civilian authorities. At the same time, frustrated

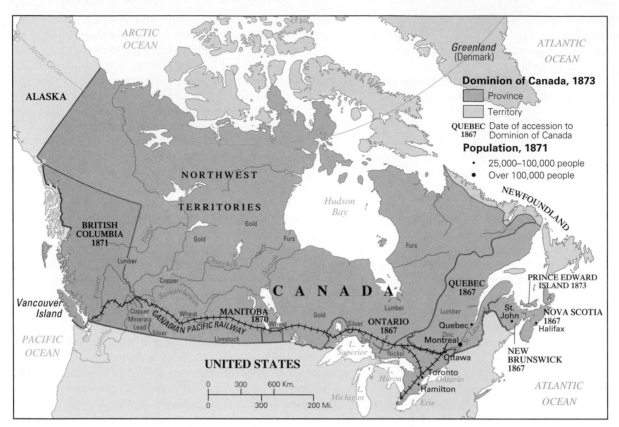

Map 25.2   Dominion of Canada, 1873   Although independence was not yet achieved and settlement remained concentrated along the U.S. border, Canada had established effective political and economic control over its western territories by 1873.

by the often-chaotic workings of constitutional democracy, few citizens were willing to support civilian politicians in any contest with the military. As a result, many Latin American militaries successfully resisted civilian control. Brazil, ruled by Emperor Pedro I, was the principal exception to this pattern.

Personalist Leaders

Successful patriot leaders in both the United States and Latin America gained mass followings during the wars for independence. They recruited and mobilized popular support by using patriotic symbols and by carefully associating their actions with national objectives. After independence, many patriot military leaders were able to use their personal followings to gain national political leadership. George Washington's ability to dominate the political scene in the early republican United States anticipated the later political ascendancy of revolutionary heroes such as Iturbide in Mexico and Bolívar in Gran Colombia. In each case, military reputation provided the foundation for personal political power. These **personalist leaders** relied on their ability to mobilize and direct the masses of these new nations rather than on the authority of constitutions and laws. Their model was Napoleon, who rose from the French army to become emperor, not John Madison, the primary author of the U.S. Constitution. In Latin America, a personalist leader who gained and held political power without constitutional sanction was called a *caudillo°*.

Latin America's slow development of stable political institutions made personalist politics more influential than was the case in the United States (see Society and Culture: Villages in New England and Mexico). Nevertheless, charismatic politicians in the United States such as Andrew Jackson did sometimes challenge constitutional limits to their authority, as did the caudillos of Latin

---

caudillo (kouh-DEE-yoh)

Villages in New England and Mexico

Born in Scotland, Fanny Calderón de la Barca lived briefly in Boston. She married a Spanish diplomat who later became ambassador to Mexico. She was a very critical observer of Mexican customs and culture. In this brief selection from Life in Mexico, *published in 1843, she compares village life in Mexico and New England. We can see clearly Calderón de la Barca's obvious affection for her native land and prejudice against Mexico. Historians often deal with biased or prejudiced sources and develop strategies to overcome these weaknesses to order to illuminate the past. This source challenges us to overcome the author's prejudice in order to undertake a comparative analysis of why Mexico and the United States developed so differently in response to the opportunities and challenges of the nineteenth century.*

If anyone wishes to try the effect of strong contrast, let him come direct from the United States to this country; but it is in the villages especially that the contrast is most striking. Travelling in New England, for example, we arrive at a small village. We see four new churches, proclaiming four different sects; religion suited to all customers. These wooden churches or meeting houses are all new, all painted white. . . . Houses, churches, stores, and taverns, all are of a piece. They are suited to the present emergency, whatever that may be, though they will never make fine ruins. Everything proclaims prosperity, equality, consistency; the past forgotten, the present all and all, and the future taking care of itself. . . . No beggars.

Transport yourself in imagination [to] Mexico. The Indian huts, with their half-naked inhabitants, and little gardens full of flowers; the huts themselves built either of clay or the [stones of a ruined building]. . . . [T]he church, gray and ancient, but strong as if designed for eternity; with its saints and virgins, and martyrs and relics, its gold and silver and precious stones, whose value could buy up all the spare lots in the New England village; the [beggar] with scarce a rag to cover him, kneeling on the marble pavement. . . . Here, everything reminds us of the past; of the conquering Spaniards, who seemed to build for eternity; impressing each work with their own solid, grave, and religious character; of the triumphs of Catholicism. . . . It is the present that seems like a dream, a pale reflection of the past. All is decaying and growing fainter, and men seem trusting to some unknown future which they may never see. One government has been abandoned, and there is none in its place. One revolution follows another, yet the remedy is not found. Let them beware lest half a century later, they be awakened from their delusion.

How does Fanny Calderón de la Barca attempt to connect the visual differences between New England and Mexican villages to differences in culture? What does she say about how these two societies regarded their pasts and futures? What threat does the author seem to see in Mexico's future? Find one example of bias in her comparison.

Source: Fanny Calderón de la Barca, *Life in Mexico* (1843), reprinted in an abridged form in Lewis Hanke, ed., *Latin America: A Historical Reader* (Boston: Little, Brown, 1974), 440–441.

America. Unlike Latin America, however, the United States never experienced an armed rebellion that overturned the results of an election.

Throughout the Western Hemisphere, charismatic military men played key roles in attracting mass support for independence movements that were commonly dominated by colonial elites. Although this popular support was often decisive in the struggle for independence, the first constitutions of nearly all the American republics excluded large numbers of poor citizens from full political participation. But nearly everywhere in the Americas marginalized groups found populist leaders to articulate their concerns and challenge these limits on their political participation. Using informal means, these leaders sought to influence the selection of officeholders and to place their concerns in the public arena. Despite their success in overturning the deference-based politics of the colonial past, this populist political style at times threatened constitutional order and led to dictatorship.

Andrew Jackson of the United States and **José Antonio Páez°** of Venezuela were political leaders whose powerful personal followings allowed them to challenge constitutional limits to their authority. During the independence

---

José Antonio Páez (hoe-SAY an-TOE-nee-oh PAH-eez)

wars in Venezuela and Colombia, Páez (1790–1873) organized and led Bolívar's most successful cavalry force. Like most of his followers, Páez was uneducated and poor, but his physical strength, courage, and guile made him a natural guerrilla leader and helped him build a powerful political base in Venezuela. Páez described his authority in the following manner: "[the soldiers] resolved to confer on me the supreme command and blindly to obey my will, confidant . . . that I was the only one who could save them."[3] Able to count on the personal loyalty of his followers, Páez was seldom willing to accept the constitutional authority of a distant president.

After defeating the Spanish armies, Bolívar pursued his dream of forging a permanent union of former Spanish colonies modeled on the federal system of the United States. But he underestimated the strength of nationalist sentiment unleashed during the independence wars. Páez and other Venezuelan leaders resisted the surrender of their hard-won power to Bolívar's Gran Colombia government in distant Bogotá (the capital city of modern Colombia). When Bolívar's authority was challenged by political opponents in 1829, Páez declared Venezuela's independence. Merciless to his enemies and indulgent with his followers, Páez ruled the country as president or dictator for the next eighteen years. Despite implementing an economic program favorable to the elite, Páez remained popular with the masses by skillfully manipulating popular political symbols. Even as his personal wealth grew through land acquisitions and commerce, Páez took care to present himself as a common man.

Andrew Jackson (1767–1845) was the first president of the United States born in humble circumstances. A self-made man who eventually acquired substantial property and owned over a hundred slaves, Jackson was extremely popular among frontier residents, urban workers, and small farmers. Although he was notorious for his untidy personal life as well as for dueling, his courage, individualism, and willingness to challenge authority helped him lead a successful political career as judge, general, congressman, senator, and president.

During his military career, Jackson proved to be impatient with civilian authorities. Widely known because of his victories over the Creek and Seminole peoples, he was elevated to the pinnacle of American politics by his celebrated defeat of the British at the Battle of New Orleans in 1815 and by his seizure of Florida from the Spanish in 1818. In 1824 he received a plurality of the popular votes cast for the presidency, but he failed to win a majority of the electoral votes and was denied the presidency when the House of Representatives chose John Quincy Adams.

Jackson's followers viewed his landslide election victory in 1828 and reelection in 1832 as the triumph of democracy over the entrenched aristocracy. In office Jackson challenged constitutional limits on his authority, substantially increasing presidential power at the expense of Congress and the Supreme Court. Like Páez, Jackson was able to dominate national politics by blending a populist political style that celebrated the virtues and cultural enthusiasms of common people with support for policies that promoted the economic interests of some of the nation's most powerful propertied groups.

Personalist leaders were common in both Latin America and the United States, but Latin America's weaker constitutional tradition, more limited protection of property rights, lower literacy levels, and less-developed communications systems provided fewer checks on the ambitions of popular politicians. The Constitution of the United States was never suspended, and no national election result in the United States was ever successfully overturned by violence. Latin America's personalist leaders, however, often ignored constitutional restraints on their authority, and election results seldom determined access to presidential power. As a result, by 1900, every Latin American nation had experienced periods of dictatorship.

The Threat of Regionalism

After independence, new national governments were generally weaker than the colonial governments they replaced. In debates over tariffs, tax and monetary policies, and, in many nations, slavery and the slave trade, regional elites often were willing to lead secessionist movements or to provoke civil war rather than accept laws that threatened their interests. Some of the hemisphere's newly independent nations did not survive these struggles; others lost territories to aggressive neighbors.

In Spanish America, all of the postindependence efforts to forge large multistate federations failed. Central America and Mexico maintained their colonial-era administrative association following independence in 1821. After the overthrow of Iturbide's imperial rule in Mexico in 1823, however, regional politicians split with Mexico and created the independent Republic of Central America. Regional rivalries and civil wars during the 1820s and 1830s forced the breakup of that entity as well and led to the creation of five separate nations. Bolívar attempted to maintain the colonial unity of Venezuela, Colombia, and Ecuador by creating the nation of Gran Colombia with its capital in Bogotá. But even before his death in 1830, not only Venezuela but also Ecuador had become independent states.

During colonial times, Argentina, Uruguay, Paraguay, and Bolivia had been united in a single viceroyalty with its capital in Buenos Aires. With the defeat of Spain, political leaders in Paraguay, Uruguay, and Bolivia declared their independence from Buenos Aires. Argentina, the area that remained after this breakup, was itself nearly overwhelmed by these powerful centrifugal forces. After independence, Argentina's liberals took power in Buenos Aires. They sought a strong central government to promote secular education, free trade, and immigration from Europe. Conservatives dominated the interior provinces. They supported the Catholic Church's traditional control of education as well as the protection of local textile and winemaking industries from European imports. When, in 1819, political leaders in Buenos Aires imposed a national constitution that ignored these concerns, the conservatives of the interior rose in rebellion.

After a decade of civil war and rebellions, a powerful local caudillo, Juan Manuel de Rosas°, came to power. For more than two decades he dominated Argentina, running the nation as if it were his private domain. The economy expanded under Rosas, but his use of intimidation, mob violence, and assassination created many enemies. In 1852 an alliance of foreign and domestic enemies overthrew him, but a new cycle of provincial rivalry and civil war prevented the creation of a strong central government until 1861.

Regionalism threatened the United States as well. The defense of state and regional interests played an important role in the framing of the U.S. Constitution. Many important constitutional provisions represented compromises forged among competing state and regional leaders. The creation of a Senate with equal representation from each state, for example, was an attempt to calm small states, which feared they might be dominated by larger states. The formula for representation in the House of Representatives was also an effort to compromise the divisions between slave and free states. Yet, despite these constitutional compromises, the nation was still threatened by regional rivalries.

Slavery increasingly divided the nation into two separate and competitive societies. A rising tide of immigration to the northern states in the 1830s and 1840s began to move the center of political power in the House of Representatives away from the south. Many southern leaders sought to protect slavery by expanding it to new territories. They supported the Louisiana Purchase in 1803 (see Map 25.3). This agreement with France transferred to the United States a vast territory extending from the Gulf of Mexico to Canada. Southern leaders also supported statehood for Texas and war with Mexico (discussed later in the chapter).

The territorial acquisitions proved a mixed blessing to the defenders of slavery because they forced a national debate about slavery itself. Should slavery be allowed to expand into new territories? Could slavery be protected if new territories eligible for statehood were overwhelmingly free?

In 1860 Abraham Lincoln (1809–1865), who was committed to checking the spread of slavery, was elected president of the United States. In response, the planter elite in the southern states chose the dangerous course of secession from the federal Union. The seceding states formed a new government, the Confederate States of America, known as the Confederacy. Lincoln was able to preserve the Union, but his victory was purchased at an enormous cost. The U.S. Civil War (1861–1865), waged by southern Confederate forces and northern Union (U.S.) forces, was the most destructive conflict in the history of the Western Hemisphere. More than 600,000 lives were lost before the Confederacy surrendered in 1865. The Union victory led to the abolition of slavery. It also transferred national political power to a northern elite committed to industrial expansion and federal support for the construction of railroads and other internal improvements.

The Confederate States of America was better prepared politically and economically for independence than were the successful secessionist movements that broke up Gran Colombia and other Spanish American federations. Nevertheless, the Confederacy failed, in part because of poor timing. The new nations of the Western Hemisphere were most vulnerable during the early years of their existence; indeed, all the successful secessions occurred within the first decades following independence. In the case of the United States, southern secession was defeated by an experienced national government legitimated and strengthened by more than seventy-five years of stability and reinforced by economic and population growth.

Foreign Interventions and Regional Wars

With the exception of the U.S. Civil War, in the nineteenth century the scale of military conflict was far smaller in the Western Hemisphere than in Europe. Nevertheless, wars often determined national borders, access to natural resources, and control of markets in the hemisphere. Even after independence, some Western Hemisphere nations had to defend themselves against Europe's great powers. Contested national borders and regional rivalries also led to wars between Western Hemisphere nations. By the end of the nineteenth century, the United States, Brazil, Argentina, and Chile

---

Juan Manuel de Rosas (huan man-WELL deh ROH-sas)

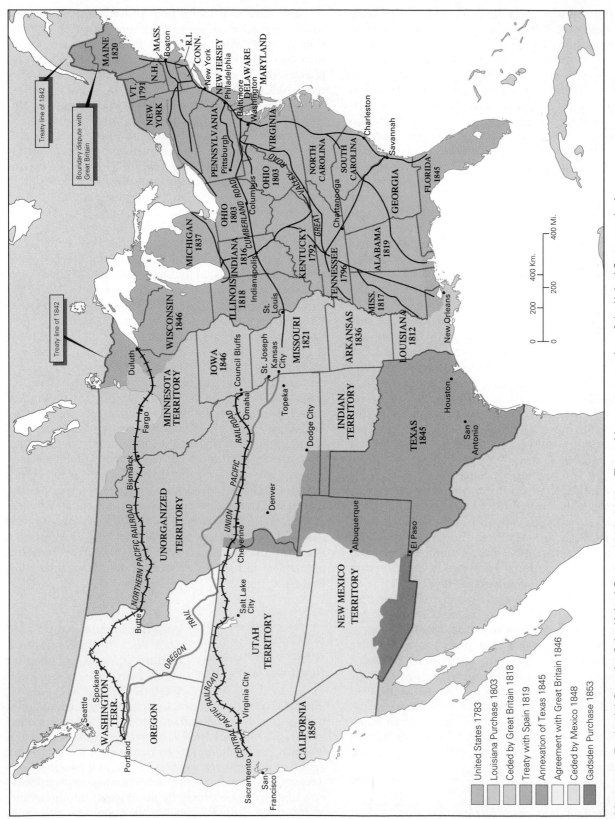

Map 25.3 Territorial Growth of the United States, 1783–1853 The rapid western expansion of the United States resulted from aggressive diplomacy and warfare against Mexico and Amerindian peoples. Railroad development helped integrate the trans-Mississippi west and promote economic expansion.

Benito Juárez's Triumph over the French   Benito Juárez overcame humble origins to lead the overthrow of Emperor Maximilian and the defeat of French imperialism. He remains a powerful symbol of secularism and republican virtue in Mexico. In this 1948 mural by José Clemente Orozco, Juárez's face dominates a scene of struggle that pits Mexican patriots against the allied forces of the Catholic Church, Mexican conservatives, and foreign invaders.   (Museo Nacional de Historia/CENIDIAP-INBA)

had successfully waged wars against their neighbors and established themselves as regional powers.

Within thirty years of independence, the United States fought a second war with England—the War of 1812 (1812–1815). The weakness of the new republic was symbolized by the burning of the White House and Capitol by British troops in 1814. This humiliation was soon overcome, however, and by the end of the nineteenth century the United States was the hemisphere's greatest military power. Its war against Spain in 1898–1899 created an American empire that reached from the Philippines in the Pacific Ocean to Puerto Rico in the Caribbean Sea.

Europe also challenged the sovereignty of Latin American nations. During the first decades after independence, Argentina faced British and French naval blockades, and British naval forces systematically violated Brazil's territorial waters to stop the importation of slaves. Mexico faced graver threats to its sovereignty, defeating a weak Spanish invasion in 1829 and then a French assault on the city of Veracruz in 1838.

The French used Mexico's inability to repay a loan as an excuse for an invasion in 1862. Mexico had been weakened by a destructive war between conservatives and liberals (1858–1862), and the conservatives allied themselves with the French invaders. The French army quickly forced the president of Mexico, **Benito Juárez,** to flee Mexico City. The French then installed the Austrian Habsburg Maximilian as emperor of Mexico. Juárez, the orphaned child of Amerindian parents, organized an effective military resistance and after years of warfare drove the French army out of Mexico in 1867. After capturing Maximilian, Juárez ordered his execution.

Wars between Western Hemisphere nations commonly produced more enduring results. The United States greatly expanded its land area through military conflicts. In the 1820s Mexico had encouraged Americans to immigrate to Texas, which at that time was part of Mexico. By the early 1830s Americans outnumbered Mexican nationals in Texas by four to one and were aggressively challenging Mexican laws such as the prohibition of slavery. In 1835 political turmoil in Mexico led to a rebellion in Texas by an alliance of Mexican liberals and American settlers. Mexico was defeated in a brief war, and in 1837 Texas became an independent nation. In

1845 the United States made Texas a state, provoking war with Mexico a year later. Mexican forces fought well, but U.S. forces captured Mexico City, and the United States imposed a punitive peace treaty in 1848. Compounding the loss of Texas in 1837, the treaty of 1848 forced Mexico to cede vast territories to the United States, including present-day Texas, New Mexico, Arizona, and California. In return Mexico received $15 million. When gold was discovered in California in 1848, the magnitude of Mexico's loss became clear.

In two wars with neighbors, Chile established itself as the leading military and economic power on the west coast of South America. Between 1836 and 1839, Chile defeated the Confederation of Peru and Bolivia. In 1879 Chilean and British investors in nitrate mines located in the Atacama Desert, a disputed border region, provoked a new war with Peru and Bolivia. The Chilean army and navy won a crushing victory in 1881, forcing Bolivia to cede its only outlet to the sea and Peru to yield the mining districts.

Argentina and Brazil fought over control of Uruguay in the 1820s, but a military stalemate eventually forced them to recognize Uruguayan independence. In 1865 Argentina and Uruguay joined Brazil to wage war against Paraguay. After five years of warfare, the Paraguayan dictator Francisco Solano López° and more than 20 percent of the population of Paraguay were dead. Paraguay suffered military occupation, lost territory to the victors, and was forced to open its markets to foreign trade.

Native Peoples and the Nation-State

Both diplomacy and military action shaped relations between the Western Hemisphere's new nation-states and the indigenous peoples living within them. During late colonial times, to avoid armed conflict and to limit the costs of frontier defense, Spanish, Portuguese, and British imperial governments attempted to limit the expansion of settlements into territories already occupied by Amerindians. With independence, the colonial powers' role as mediator for and protector of native peoples ended.

Still-independent Amerindian peoples posed a significant military challenge to many Western Hemisphere republics. Weakened by civil wars and constitutional crises, many of the new nations were less able to maintain frontier peace than the colonial governments had been. After independence, Amerindian peoples in Argentina, the United States, Chile, and Mexico succeeded in pushing back some frontier settlements. But despite these early victories, native military resistance was finally overcome by the end of the 1880s in both North and South America.

After the American Revolution, the rapid expansion of agricultural settlements threatened native peoples in North America. Between 1790 and 1810 tens of thousands of settlers entered territories guaranteed to Amerindians in treaties with the United States. In Ohio alone more than 200,000 white settlers were present by 1810. Indigenous leaders responded by seeking the support of British officials in Canada and by forging broad indigenous alliances. American forces decisively defeated one such Amerindian alliance in 1794 at the Battle of Fallen Timbers in Ohio. After 1800 two Shawnee leaders, the brothers **Tecumseh°** and Prophet (Tenskwatawa), created a larger and better-organized alliance among southern and western Amerindian peoples and gained some support from Great Britain. In 1811 American military forces attacked and destroyed the ritual center of the alliance, Prophet Town. The final blow came during the War of 1812 when Tecumseh, fighting alongside his British allies, was killed in battle.

In the 1820s white settlers forced native peoples living in Ohio, southern Indiana and Illinois, southwestern Michigan, most of Missouri, central Alabama, and southern Mississippi to cede their land. The 1828 presidential election of Andrew Jackson, a veteran of wars against native peoples, brought matters to a head. In 1830 Congress passed the Indian Removal Act, forcing the resettlement of the Cherokee, Creek, Choctaw, and other eastern peoples to land west of the Mississippi River. The removal was carried out in the 1830s, and nearly half of the forced migrants died on this journey, known as the Trail of Tears.

Amerindians living on the Great Plains offered formidable resistance to the expansion of while settlement. By the time substantial numbers of white buffalo hunters, cattlemen, and settlers reached the American west indigenous peoples were skilled users of horses and firearms. These technologies had transformed the cultures of the Sioux, Comanche, Pawnee, Kiowa, and other Plains peoples. The improved efficiency of the buffalo hunt reduced their dependence on agriculture. As a result, women, whose primary responsibility had been raising crops, lost prestige and social power to male hunters. Living arrangements also changed as the single-family tepees of migratory buffalo hunters replaced the multigenerational lodges of the traditional farming economy.

During the U.S. Civil War, native peoples experienced a disruption of their trade with Eastern merchants and the suspension of treaty indemnities. After the war,

Francisco Solano López (fran-CEES-co so-LAN-oh LOH-pez)

Tecumseh (teh-CUM-sah)

Navajo Leaders Gathered in Washington to Negotiate As settlers, ranchers, and miners pushed west in the nineteenth century, leaders of Amerindian peoples were forced to negotiate territorial concessions with representatives of the U.S. government. In order to impress Amerindian peoples with the wealth and power of the United States, many of their leaders were invited to Washington, D.C. This photo shows Navajo leaders and their Anglo translators in Washington, D.C., in 1874. (#5851 Frank McNill Collection, State Records Center & Archives, Sante Fe, NM)

ever more settlers pushed onto the plains. Buffalo herds were hunted to near extinction for their hides, and land was lost to farmers and ranchers. During nearly four decades of armed conflict with the United States Army, Amerindian peoples were forced to give up their land and their traditional ways. The Comanche, who had dominated the southern plains during the period of Spanish and Mexican rule, were forced by the U.S. government to cede most of their land in Texas in 1865. The Sioux and their allies resisted. In 1876 they overwhelmed General George Armstrong Custer and the Seventh Cavalry in the Battle of Little Bighorn (in the southern part of the present-day state of Montana). But finally the Sioux also were forced to accept reservation life. Military campaigns in the 1870s and 1880s then broke the resistance of the Apache.

The indigenous peoples of Argentina and Chile experienced a similar trajectory of adaptation, resistance, and defeat. Herds of wild cattle provided indigenous peoples with a limitless food supply, and horses and metal weapons increased their military capacities. Thus, for a while, the native peoples of Argentina and Chile effectively checked the southern expansion of agriculture and ranching. Amerindian raiders operated within 100 miles (160 kilometers) of Buenos Aires into the 1860s. Unable to defeat these resourceful enemies, the governments of Argentina and Chile relied on an elaborate system of gift giving and prisoner exchanges to maintain peace on the frontier. By the 1860s, however, population increase, political stability, and military modernization allowed Argentina and Chile to take the offensive.

In the 1870s the government of Argentina used overwhelming military force to crush native resistance. Thousands of Amerindians were killed, and survivors were driven onto marginal land. In Chile the story was the same. When civil war and an economic depression weakened the Chilean government at the end of the 1850s, the Mapuches° (called "Araucanians" by the Spanish) attempted to push back frontier settlements. Despite early successes, the Mapuches were defeated in the 1870s by modern weaponry. In Chile, as in Argentina and the United States, military campaigns against native peoples were justified by demonizing the Amerindians. Newspaper editorials and the speeches of politicians portrayed Amerindians as brutal and cruel, and as obstacles to progress. In April 1859, a Chilean newspaper commented:

> The necessity, not only to punish the Araucanian race, but also to make it impotent to harm us, is well recognized . . . as the only way to rid the country of a million evils. It is well understood that they are odious and prejudicial guests in Chile . . . conciliatory measures have accomplished nothing with this stupid race—the infamy and disgrace of the Chilean nation.[4]

Political divisions and civil wars within the new nations sometimes provided an opportunity for long-pacified native peoples to rebel. In the Yucatán region of Mexico, the owners of henequen (the agave plant that produces fiber used for twine) and sugar plantations had forced

Mapuches (mah-POO-chez)

many Maya° communities off their traditional agricultural lands, reducing thousands of them to peonage. This same regional elite declared itself independent of the government in Mexico City that was convulsed by civil war in the late 1830s. The Mexican government was unable to reestablish control because it faced the greater threat of invasion by the United States. Seeing their oppressors divided, the Maya rebelled in 1847. This well-organized and popular uprising, known as the **Caste War,** nearly returned the Yucatán to Maya rule. Grievances accumulated over more than three hundred years led to great violence and property destruction. The Maya were not defeated until the war with the United States ended. Even then Maya rebels retreated to unoccupied territories and created an independent state, which they called the "Empire of the Cross." Organized around a mix of traditional beliefs and Christian symbols, this indigenous state resisted Mexican forces to 1870. A few defiant Maya strongholds survived until 1901.

THE CHALLENGE OF ECONOMIC AND SOCIAL CHANGE

During the nineteenth century, the newly independent nations of the Western Hemisphere struggled to realize the Enlightenment ideals of freedom and individual liberty that had helped to ignite the revolutions for independence. The achievement of these objectives was slowed by the persistence of slavery and other oppressive colonial-era institutions. Cultural and racial diversity also presented obstacles to reform. Nevertheless, by century's end reform movements in many of the hemisphere's nations had succeeded in ending the slave trade, abolishing slavery, expanding voting rights, and assimilating immigrants from Asia and Europe.

The consequences of increased industrialization and greater involvement in the evolving world economy challenged the region's political stability and social arrangements. A small number of nations embraced industrialization, but most Western Hemisphere economies became increasingly dependent on the export of agricultural goods and minerals during the nineteenth century. While the industrializing nations of the hemisphere became richer than the nations that remained

Maya (MY-ah)

exporters of raw materials, all the region's economies became more vulnerable and volatile as a result of greater participation in international markets. Like contemporary movements for social reform, efforts to assert national economic control produced powerful new political forces.

The Abolition of Slavery

In both the United States and Latin America, strong anti-slavery sentiments were expressed during the struggles for independence. In nearly all the new nations of the Western Hemisphere, revolutionary leaders asserted universal ideals of freedom and citizenship that contrasted sharply with the reality of slavery. Men and women who wanted to outlaw slavery were called **abolitionists.** Despite the efforts of abolitionists, slavery survived in much of the hemisphere until the 1850s. In regions where the export of plantation products was most important—such as the United States, Brazil, and Cuba—the abolition of slavery was achieved with great difficulty.

In the United States, slavery was weakened by abolition in some northern states and by the termination of the African slave trade in 1808. But this progress was stalled by the profitable expansion of cotton agriculture after the War of 1812. In Spanish America, tens of thousands of slaves gained freedom by joining revolutionary armies during the wars for independence. After independence, most Spanish American republics prohibited the slave trade. Counteracting that trend was the growing international demand for sugar and coffee, products traditionally produced on plantations by slaves. As prices rose for plantation products in the first half of the nineteenth century, Brazil and Cuba (the island remained a Spanish colony until 1899) increased their imports of slaves.

During the long struggle to end slavery in the United States, American abolitionists argued that slavery offended both morality and the universal rights asserted in the Declaration of Independence. Abolitionist Theodore Weld articulated the religious objection to slavery in 1834:

> No condition of birth, no shade of color, no mere misfortune of circumstance, can annul the birth-right charter, which God has bequeathed to every being upon whom he has stamped his own image, by making him a free *moral agent* [emphasis in original], and that he who robs his fellow man of this tramples upon right, subverts justice, outrages humanity . . . and sacrilegiously assumes the prerogative of God.[5]

Two groups denied full rights of citizenship under the Constitution, women and free African-Americans, played important roles in the abolition of slavery. Women served on the executive committee of the American Anti-Slavery Society and produced some of the most effective propaganda against slavery. Eventually, thousands of women joined the abolitionist cause, where they provided leadership and were effective speakers and propagandists. When social conservatives attacked this highly visible public role, many women abolitionists responded by becoming public advocates of female suffrage as well.

Frederick Douglass, a former slave, became one of the most effective abolitionist speakers and writers. Other more radical black leaders pushed the abolitionist movement to accept the inevitability of violence. They saw civil war or slave insurrection as necessary for the ending of slavery. One argued passionately that slaves should "RISE AT ONCE, en masse, and THROW OFF THEIR FETTERS" (capitalization in original).

In the 1850s the growing electoral strength of the newly formed Republican Party forced a confrontation between slave and free states. After the election of Abraham Lincoln in 1860, the first of the thirteen southern states that formed the Condeferacy seceded from the Union. During the Civil War, pressure for emancipation rose as tens of thousands of black freemen and escaped slaves joined the Union army. Hundreds of thousands of other slaves fled their masters' plantations and farms for the protection of advancing northern armies. In 1863, in the midst of the Civil War and two years after the abolition of serfdom in Russia (see Chapter 27), President Lincoln began the abolition of slavery by issuing the Emancipation Proclamation, which ended slavery in rebel states not occupied by the Union army. Final abolition was accomplished after the war, in 1865, by the Thirteenth Amendment to the Constitution.

In Brazil slavery survived more than two decades after it was abolished in the United States. Progress toward abolition was not only slower in Brazil but also depended on foreign pressure. In 1830 Brazil signed a treaty with the British ending the slave trade. Despite this agreement, Brazil illegally imported over a half-million more African slaves before the British navy finally forced compliance in the 1850s. In the 1850s and 1860s the Brazilian emperor, Pedro II, and many liberals worked to abolish slavery, but their desire to find a form of gradual emancipation acceptable to slave owners slowed progress.

During the war with Paraguay (1865–1870), large numbers of slaves joined the Brazilian army in exchange for freedom. Their loyalty and heroism undermined the military's support for slavery. Educated Brazilians in-

A Former Brazilian Slave Returns from Military Service   The heroic participation of black freemen and slaves in the Paraguayan War (1885–1870) led many Brazilians to advocate the abolition of slavery. The original caption for this drawing reads: "On his return from the war in Paraguay: Full of glory, covered with laurels, after having spilled his blood in defense of the fatherland and to free a people from slavery, the volunteer sees his own mother bound and whipped! Awful reality!"   (Courtesy, Fundacao Biblioteca Nacional, Brazil)

creasingly viewed slavery as an obstacle to economic development and an impediment to democratic reform. In the 1870s, as abolitionist sentiment grew, reformers forced the passage of laws providing for the gradual emancipation of slaves. When political support for slavery weakened in the 1880s, growing numbers of slaves forced the issue by fleeing from bondage. By the 1880s, however, army leaders were resisting demands that they capture and return runaway slaves. Legislation abolishing slavery finally was passed by the Brazilian parliament and accepted by the emperor in 1888.

The plantations of the Caribbean region received almost 40 percent of all African slaves shipped to the New World. As a result, throughout the region tiny white minorities lived surrounded by slave and free colored majorities. At the end of the eighteenth century, the slave rebellion in Saint Domingue (see Chapter 23) spread terror across the Caribbean. Because of fear that any effort to overthrow colonial rule might unleash new slave rebellions, there was little enthusiasm among free settlers in Caribbean colonies for independence. Nor did local support for abolition appear among white settlers or free colored populations. Thus abolition in most Caribbean colonies commonly resulted from political decisions made in Europe by colonial powers.

Nevertheless, like slaves in Brazil, the United States, and Spanish America, slaves in the Caribbean helped propel the movement toward abolition by rebelling, running away, and resisting in more subtle ways. Although initially unsuccessful, the rebellions that threatened other French Caribbean colonies after the Haitian Revolution (1789–1804)) weakened France's support for slavery. Jamaica and other British colonies also experienced rebellions and saw the spread of communities of runaways. In Spanish Cuba as well, slave resistance forced increases in expenditures for police forces in the nineteenth century.

After 1800, the profitability of sugar plantations in the British West Indian colonies declined, and a coalition of labor groups, Protestant dissenters, and free traders in Britain pushed for the abolition of slavery. Britain, the major participant in the eighteenth-century expansion of slavery in the Americas, ended its participation in the slave trade in 1807. It then negotiated a series of treaties with Spain, Brazil, and other importers of slaves to eliminate the slave trade to the Americas. Once these treaties were in place, British naval forces acted to force compliance.

Slavery in British colonies was abolished in 1834. However, the law compelled "freed" slaves to remain with former masters as "apprentices." Abuses by planters and resistance to apprenticeship by former slaves led to complete abolition in 1838. A decade later slavery in the French Caribbean was abolished after upheavals in France led to the overthrow of the government of Louis Philippe (see Chapter 23).

Slavery lasted longest in Cuba and Puerto Rico, Spain's remaining colonies. Britain's use of diplomatic pressure and naval force to limit the arrival of African slaves weakened slavery after 1820. More important, however, was the growth of support for abolition in these colonies. Both Cuba and Puerto Rico had larger white and free colored populations than did the Caribbean colonies of Britain and France. As a result, there was less fear in Cuba and Puerto Rico that abolition would lead to the political ascendancy of former slaves (as had occurred in Haiti). In Puerto Rico, where slaves numbered approximately thirty thousand, local reformers sought and gained the abolition of slavery in 1873. In the midst of a decade-long war to defeat forces seeking the independence of Cuba, the Spanish government moved

gradually toward abolition. Initially, slave children born after September 18, 1868, were freed but obligated to work for their former masters for eighteen years. In 1880 all other slaves were freed on the condition that they serve their masters for eight additional years. Finally, in 1886, these conditions were eliminated, slavery was abolished, and Cuban patriots forged the multiracial alliance that was to initiate a war for Cuban independence in 1895 (See Chapter 29).

Immigration

During the colonial period, free Europeans were a minority among immigrants to the Western Hemisphere. Between 1500 and 1760, African slaves entering the Western Hemisphere outnumbered European immigrants by nearly two to one. Another 4 million or so African slaves were imported before the effective end of the slave trade at the end of the 1850s. As the African slave trade came to an end, the arrival of millions of immigrants from Europe and Asia in the nineteenth century contributed to the further transformation of the Western Hemisphere. This new wave of immigration fostered rapid economic growth and the occupation of frontier regions in the United States, Canada, Argentina, Chile, and Brazil. It also promoted urbanization. By century's end, nearly all of the hemisphere's fastest-growing cities (Buenos Aires, Chicago, New York, and São Paulo, for example) had large immigrant populations.

During the nineteenth century, Europe provided the majority of immigrants to the Western Hemisphere. For much of the century, these people came primarily from western Europe, but after 1870 most came from southern and eastern Europe. The scale of immigration increased dramatically in the second half of the century. The United States received approximately 600,000 European immigrants in the 1830s, 1.5 million in the 1840s, and then 2.5 million per decade until 1880. In the 1890s an astonishing total of 5.2 million immigrants arrived. European immigration to Latin America also increased dramatically after 1880. Combined immigration to Argentina and Brazil rose from just under 130,000 in the 1860s to 1.7 million in the 1890s. By 1910, 30 percent of the Argentine population was foreign-born, more than twice the proportion in the U.S. population. Argentina was an extremely attractive destination for European immigrants, receiving more than twice as many immigrants as Canada between 1870 and 1930. Even so, immigration to Canada increased tenfold during this period.

Asian immigration to the Western Hemisphere increased after 1850. Between 1849 and 1875, approximately 100,000 Chinese immigrants arrived in Peru and another 120,000 entered Cuba. Canada attracted about 50,000 Chinese in the second half of the century. The United States, however, was the primary North American destination for Chinese immigrants, receiving 300,000 between 1854 and 1882. India also contributed to the social transformation of the Western Hemisphere, sending more than a half-million immigrants to the Caribbean region. British Guiana alone received 238,000 immigrants from the Asian subcontinent.

Despite the obvious economic benefits that accompanied this inflow of people, hostility to immigration mounted in many nations. Nativist political movements argued that large numbers of foreigners could not be successfully integrated into national political cultures. By the end of the century, fear and prejudice led many governments in the Western Hemisphere to limit immigration or to distinguish between "desirable" and "undesirable" immigrants, commonly favoring Europeans over Asians.

Asians faced more obstacles to immigration than did Europeans and were more often victims of violence and extreme forms of discrimination in the New World. In the 1870s and 1880s anti-Chinese riots erupted in many western cities in the United States. Congress responded to this wave of racism by passing the Chinese Exclusion Act in 1882, which eliminated most Chinese immigration. In 1886 fears that Canada was being threatened by "inferior races" led to the imposition of a head tax that made immigration to Canada more difficult for Chinese families. During this same period, strong anti-Chinese prejudice surfaced in Peru, Mexico, and Cuba. Japanese immigrants in Brazil and East Indians in the English-speaking Caribbean faced similar prejudice.

Immigrants from Europe also faced prejudice and discrimination. In the United States, Italians were commonly portrayed as criminals or anarchists. In Argentina, social scientists attempted to prove that Italian immigrants were more violent and less honest than the native-born population. Immigrants from Spain were widely stereotyped in Argentina as miserly and dishonest. Eastern European Jews seeking to escape pogroms and discrimination at home found themselves barred from many educational institutions and professional careers in both the United States and Latin America. Negative stereotypes were invented for German, Swedish, Polish, and Middle Eastern immigrants as well. The perceived grievances used to justify these common prejudices were remarkably similar from Canada to Argentina. Immigrants, it was argued, threatened the well-being of native-born workers by accepting low wages, and they threatened national culture by resisting assimilation.

Many intellectuals and political leaders wondered if the evolving mix of culturally diverse populations could sustain a common citizenship. As a result, efforts were directed toward compelling immigrants to assimilate.

Arrest of Labor Activist in Buenos Aires
The labor movement in Buenos Aires grew in numbers and became more radical with the arrival of tens of thousands of Italian and Spanish immigrants. Fearful of socialist and anarchist unions, the government of Argentina used an expanded police force to break strikes by arresting labor leaders.   (Archivo General de la Nacion, Buenos Aires)

Schools became cultural battlegrounds where language, cultural values, and patriotic feelings were transmitted to the children of immigrants. Across the hemisphere, school curricula were revised to promote national culture. Ignoring Canada's large French-speaking population, an English-speaking Canadian reformer commented on recent immigration: "If Canada is to become in a real sense a nation, if our people are to become one people, we must have one language."[6] Fear and prejudice led to the singing of patriotic songs, the veneration of national flags and other symbols, and the writing of national histories that emphasized patriotism and civic virtue. Nearly everywhere in the Americas schools worked to create homogeneous national cultures.

American Cultures

Despite discrimination, immigrants continued to stream into the Western Hemisphere, introducing new languages, living arrangements, technologies, and work customs. Immigrants altered the politics of many of the hemisphere's nations as they sought to influence government policies. Where immigrants arrived in the greatest numbers, they put enormous pressure on housing, schools, and social welfare services. To compensate for their isolation from home, language, and culture, immigrants often created ethnically based mutual aid societies, sports and leisure clubs, and neighborhoods. Ethnic organizations and districts provided valuable social and economic support for recent arrivals while sometimes worsening the fears of the native-born that immigration posed a threat to national culture.

Immigrants were changed by their experiences in their adopted nations and by programs that forced them to accept new cultural values through education or, in some cases, service in the military. The modification of the language, customs, values, and behaviors of a group as a result of contact with people from another culture is called **acculturation.** Immigrants and their children, in turn, made their mark on the cultures of their adopted nations. They learned the language spoken in their adopted countries as fast as possible in order to improve their earning capacity. At the same time, words and phrases from their languages entered the language of the host nations. Languages as diverse as Yiddish and Italian strongly influenced American English, Argentine Spanish, and Brazilian Portuguese. Dietary practices introduced from Europe and Asia altered the cuisine of nearly every American nation. In turn, immigrants commonly added native foods to their diets, especially the hemisphere's abundant and relatively cheap meats.

American popular music changed as well. For example, the Argentine tango, based on African-Argentine rhythms, was transformed by new instrumentation and orchestral arrangements brought by Italian immigrants. Mexican ballads blended with English folk music in the U.S. southwest, and Italian operas played to packed houses in Buenos Aires. Sports, games of chance, and fashion also experienced this process of borrowing and exchange.

Union movements and electoral politics in the hemisphere also felt the influence of new arrivals who aggressively sought to influence government and improve working conditions. The labor movements of Mexico, Argentina, and the United States, in particular, were influenced by the anarchist and socialist beliefs of European immigrants. Mutual benevolent societies and less formal ethnic associations pooled resources to help immigrants open businesses, aid the immigration of their relatives, or bury their family members. They also established links with political movements, sometimes exchanging votes for favors.

Women's Rights and the Struggle for Social Justice

The abolition of slavery in the Western Hemisphere did not end racial discrimination or provide full political rights for every citizen. Not only blacks but also women, new immigrants, and native peoples in nearly every Western Hemisphere nation suffered the effects of political and economic discrimination. During the second half of the nineteenth century, reformers struggled to remove these limits on citizenship while also addressing the welfare needs of workers and the poor.

In 1848 a group of women angered by their exclusion from an international antislavery meeting issued a call for a meeting to discuss women's rights. The **Women's Rights Convention** at Seneca Falls, New York, issued a statement that said in part, "We hold these truths to be self-evident: that all men and women are equal." While moderates focused on the issues of greater economic independence and full legal rights, increasing numbers of women demanded the right to vote. Others lobbied to provide better conditions for women working outside the home, especially in textile factories. Sarah Grimké responded to criticism of women's activism:

This has been the language of man since he laid aside the whip as a means to keep woman in subjection. He spares her body, but the war he has waged against her mind, her heart, and her soul, has been no less destructive to her as a moral being. How monstrous is the doctrine that woman is to be dependent on man![7]

Progress toward equality between men and women was equally slow in Canada and Latin America. Canada's first women doctors received their training in the United States because no woman was able to receive a medical degree in Canada until 1895. Full enfranchisement occurred in Canada in the twentieth century, but Canadian women did gain the right to vote in some provincial and municipal elections before 1900. Like women in the United States, Canadian women provided leadership in temperance, child welfare, and labor reform movements. Argentina and Uruguay were among the first Latin American nations to provide public education for women. Both nations introduced coeducation in the 1870s. Chilean women gained access to some careers in medicine and law in the 1870s. In Argentina, the first woman doctor graduated from medical school in 1899. In Brazil, where many women were active in the abolitionist movement, four women graduated in medicine by 1882. Throughout the hemisphere, more rapid progress was achieved in lower status careers that threatened male economic power less directly, and by the end of the century, women dominated elementary school teaching throughout the Western Hemisphere.

From Canada to Argentina and Chile, the majority of working-class women had no direct involvement in these reform movements, but in their daily lives they succeeded in transforming gender relations. By the end of the nineteenth century, large numbers of poor women worked outside the home on farms, in markets, and, increasingly, in factories. Many bore full responsibility for providing for their children. Whether men thought women should remain in the home or not, by the end of the century women were unambiguously present in the economy (see also Chapter 28).

Throughout the hemisphere there was little progress toward eliminating racial discrimination. Blacks were denied the vote throughout the southern United States. They also were subjected to the indignity of segregation—consigned to separate schools, hotels, restaurants, seats in public transportation, and even water fountains. Racial discrimination against men and women of African descent was also common in Latin America, though seldom spelled out in legal codes. Unlike the southern states of the United States, Latin American nations did not insist on formal racial segregation or permit lynching. Nor did they enforce a strict color line. Many men and women of mixed background were able to enter the skilled working class or middle class. Latin Americans tended to view racial identity across a continuum of physical characteristics rather than in the narrow terms of black and white that defined race relations in the United States.

The Children's Aid Society of Toronto   Throughout the Western Hemisphere, women led the effort to develop social welfare institutions. Their leadership was most clearly evident in providing protection for poor and abandoned children. This photo shows a social worker and children sitting on the front step of the Children's Aid Society of Toronto in 1895.   (City of Toronto Archives, #SC1-3)

The successful movements to abolish slavery in Latin America did not lead to an end to racial discrimination. But some of the participants in the abolition struggles later organized to promote racial integration in their societies. They demanded access to education, the right to vote, and greater economic opportunity, pointing out the economic and political costs paid by poor countries that denied full rights to all citizens. Their success depended on political organization and the forging of alliances with sympathetic white politicians. Black intellectuals also struggled to overturn racist stereotypes. In Brazil, Argentina, and Cuba, as in the United States, political and literary magazines celebrating black cultural achievement became powerful weapons in the struggle against racial discrimination. Despite these efforts, men and women of African descent continued to suffer discrimination everywhere in the Americas at century's end.

Development and Underdevelopment

Although the Atlantic economy experienced three periods of economic contraction during the nineteenth century, nearly all the nations of the Western Hemisphere were richer in 1900 than in 1800. The Industrial Revolution, worldwide population growth, and an increasingly integrated world market stimulated economic expansion (see Environment and Technology: The McCormick Reaper). Wheat, corn, wool, meats, and nonprecious minerals joined the region's earlier exports of silver, sugar, dyes, coffee, and cotton. During the nineteenth century, the United States was the only Western Hemisphere nation to industrialize, but nearly every government promoted new economic activities. Throughout the hemisphere investments were made in roads, railroads, canals, and telegraphs to better serve distant markets. In addition, tariff and monetary policies helped to foster economic diversification and growth. Yet only three Western Hemisphere nations—the United States, Canada, and Argentina—achieved individual income levels similar to those in western Europe by 1900.

New demands for copper, zinc, lead, coal, and tin unleashed by the Industrial Revolution led to mining booms in the western United States and in Mexico and Chile. Unlike the small-scale and often short-term gold- and silver-mining operations of the colonial era, the mining companies of the late nineteenth century were heavily capitalized international corporations that could bully governments and buy political favors. During this period, European or North American corporations owned most new mining enterprises in Latin America. Petroleum development, which occurred at the end of the century, followed this pattern as well.

New technology accelerated economic integration, but the high cost of this technology often increased dependence on foreign capital. Many of the hemisphere's governments promoted railroads by granting tax benefits, free land, and monopoly rights to both domestic and foreign investors. By 1890 vast areas of the Great Plains in the United States and Canada, the Argentine pampas, and the northern part of Mexico were producing grain and livestock for foreign markets opened by the development of railroads. Steamships also lowered the cost of transportation to distant markets, and the telegraph stimulated expansion by speeding the spread of information about the demand for and availability of products.

The acquisition of bundles of new technologies at the same time often multiplied the cumulative effects of individual technologies. In Argentina, for example, the railroad, telegraph, barbed wire, and refrigeration all appeared within a single generation in the 1870s and 1880s. Although Argentina had had abundant livestock herds since the colonial period, the great distance separating Argentina from Europe's markets prevented Argentine cattle raisers from efficiently exporting either fresh meat or live animals. Technology changed this situation. The combination of railroads and the telegraph lowered freight costs and improved information about markets. Steamships shortened trans-Atlantic crossings. Refrigerated ships made it possible to sell meat from Argentina's pampas in the markets of Europe. As land values rose and livestock breeding improved, new investments were protected by barbed wire, the first inexpensive fencing available on the nearly treeless plains.

Despite these shared experiences, growing interdependence and increased competition produced deep structural differences among Western Hemisphere economies by 1900. Two distinct economic tracks became clearly visible. One led to industrialization and prosperity, what is now called **development.** The other continued colonial dependence on the export of raw materials and low-wage industries, now commonly called **underdevelopment.** By the end of the nineteenth century, material prosperity was greater and economic development was more diversified in English-speaking North America than in the nations of Latin America. With a temperate climate, vast fertile prairies, and an influx of European immigrants, Argentina was the only Latin American nation to imitate the prosperity of the United States and Canada in the nineteenth century.

These important differences in regional economic development were due in part to cyclical swings in international markets. When the United States gained independence in 1783, the world capitalist economy was in the first years of a four-decade period of rapid growth. With a large merchant fleet, a diversified economy that included some manufacturing, and adequate banking and insurance services, the United States benefited from the expansion of the world economy. Rapid population growth due in large measure to immigration, high levels of individual wealth, widespread landownership, and relatively high literacy rates also fostered rapid economic development in the United States.

Canada's struggle for greater political autonomy, which culminated in the Confederation of 1867, coincided with a second period of global economic expansion. Canada also benefited from its special trading relationship with Britain, the world's preeminent industrial nation, and from a rising tide of immigrants after 1850.

The McCormick Reaper

The McCormick reaper was one of the great industrial success stories of the nineteenth century. McCormick reapers and other agricultural implements dominated agriculture and gained export markets throughout the Western Hemisphere and Europe. By leading the mechanization of agriculture, the McCormick Havesting Machine Company reduced labor costs and promoted the development of large-scale commercial farming in the midwestern United States and Canada. Aided by mechanization, wheat production grew by 70 percent in the 1850s alone.

Cyrus McCormick and his family began building reapers in their blacksmith shop in Rockbridge County, Virginia, in 1840. In the early years, slaves owned by the family helped hand-craft the reapers from raw materials found locally. Although McCormick faced competition from other manufacturers, the business grew quickly, in part because McCormick was a great promoter who effectively used advertising to develop his business. As demand rose, he increased production by adding new skilled workers and by licensing other manufacturers to produce the company's reapers.

These licensing agreements caused problems of quality control that led McCormick to move all the company's production to a custom-built factory in Chicago in 1848. Production in the new factory quickly reached 1,500 units per year, far outstripping the 200 units per year produced in the Virginia operation. Nearly all this increase came from adding skilled workers and from the closer supervision of subcontractors who supplied blades and other parts. By 1876, 14,000 reapers were produced.

At the end of the 1870s, Cyrus broke with his brother, Leander, and brought in a factory manager who had worked at Colt firearms and the Wilson Sewing Machine Company. Under this new leadership, the company introduced a new industrial process that emphasized standardization and the use of special-purpose machine tools for fabrication. Production reached 48,000 units in 1885 and then soared to 100,000 in 1889. These changes in technology and production methods, however, changed the work force from skilled to unskilled labor and contributed to increased numbers of strikes and work stoppages.

Source: This discussion follows the analysis in David A. Hounshell, *From the American System to Mass Production, 1800–1932: The Development of Manufacturing Technology in the United States* (Baltimore: Johns Hopkins University Press, 1984), 153–189.

The McCormick Reaper
In the nineteenth century, the machine age arrived in the countryside. The McCormick reaper increased productivity and also promoted the concentration of land in grain producing regions of the United States. (Navistar International Harvester Archives)

The Introduction of New Technologies Changes the Mining Industry Powerful hydraulic technologies were introduced in western mining sites in the United States. This early photo shows how high power water jets could transform the natural environment. (Colorado Historical Society)

Nevertheless, some regions within each of these prosperous North American nations—Canada's Maritime Provinces and the southern part of the United States, for example—demonstrated the same patterns of underdevelopment found in Latin America.

Latin American nations gained independence in the 1820s, when the global economy was contracting due to the end of the Napoleonic Wars and market saturation provoked by the early stages of European industrialization. During the colonial period the region's economic resources had been concentrated on the production of agricultural and mining exports. After independence those raw-material exports faced increased competition. Although these sectors experienced periods of great prosperity in the nineteenth century, their markets experienced sharp moves not only up but down. The history of these specialized Latin American economies, subject to periodic problems of oversupply and low prices, was one of boom and bust. The efforts of Latin American

governments to gain competitive market advantages by defeating union activity, holding down wages, and opening markets to foreign manufactures further complicated the movement toward industrialization.

Weak governments, political instability, and, in some cases, civil war also slowed Latin American economic development. A comparative examination of Western Hemisphere economic history makes clear that stable and reliable public administration is a necessary part of the development process. Because Latin America was dependent on capital and technology obtained from abroad, Great Britain and, by the end of the century, the United States often were able to impose unfavorable trade conditions or even intervene militarily to protect investments. The combined impact of these domestic and international impediments to development became clear when Mexico, Chile, and Argentina failed to achieve high levels of domestic investment in manufacturing late in the nineteenth century, despite a rapid accumulation of wealth induced by a rising tide of income derived from traditional exports.

Altered Environments

Population growth, economic expansion, new technologies, and the introduction of plants and animals to new regions dramatically altered the Western Hemisphere's environment. Many of Cuba's forests were cut in the early nineteenth century to expand sugar production. The expansion of livestock raising put heavy pressure on fragile environments in Argentina, Uruguay, southern Brazil, and the southwestern United States. Other forms of commercial agriculture also threatened the environment. Farmers in South Carolina and Georgia gained a short-term increase in cotton production by abandoning crop rotation after 1870, but this practice quickly led to soil exhaustion and erosion. The use of plows on the North American prairies and the Argentine pampa eliminated many native grasses and increased the threat of soil erosion. Coffee planters in Brazil exhausted soil fertility with a destructive cycle of overplanting followed by expansion onto forest reserves cleared by cutting and burning.

Rapid urbanization also put heavy pressure on the environment. New York, Chicago, Rio de Janeiro, Buenos Aires, and Mexico City were among the world's fastest-growing cities in the nineteenth century. Governments strained to keep up with the need for sewers, clean water, and garbage disposal. A rising demand for building materials led to the rapid spread of the timber industry in many countries. Under the Timber and Stone Act of

1878, more than 3.5 million acres (1.4 million hectares) of public land in the United States had been claimed at low cost by 1900. Similar transfers of land from public to private ownership occurred in Argentina and Brazil.

As the mining frontier advanced into Nevada, Montana, and California after 1860, erosion and pollution resulted. Similar results occurred in other mining areas. The expansion of nitrate mining and, later, open-pit copper mining in Chile scarred and polluted the environment. The state of Minas Gerais in Brazil experienced a series of mining booms that began with gold in the late seventeenth century and continued with iron ore in the nineteenth. By the end of the century, its red soil was ripped open, its forests were depleted, and the resulting erosion was uncontrolled. Similar devastation afflicted parts of Bolivia and Mexico.

Efforts to meet increasing domestic demand for food and housing and to satisfy foreign demands for exports led to environmental degradation but also contributed significantly to the growth of the world economy and to regional prosperity. By the end of the nineteenth century, small-scale conservation efforts were under way in many nations, and the first national parks and nature reserves had been created. But when confronted by a choice between economic growth and environmental protection, all of the hemisphere's nations embraced growth.

CONCLUSION

The nineteenth century witnessed enormous changes in the Western Hemisphere. With the exception of Canada and many Caribbean islands, colonial controls were removed by century's end. The powerful new political ideas of the Enlightenment and an increased sense of national identity contributed to the desire for independence and self-rule. The success of the American and Haitian revolutions began the assault on the colonial order, transforming the hemisphere's politics. Napoleon's invasion of Portugal and Spain then helped initiate the movement toward independence in Latin America.

Once colonial rule was overturned, the creation of stable and effective governments proved difficult. Powerful personalist leaders resisted the constraints imposed by constitutions. National governments often confronted divisive regional political movements. From Argentina in the south to the United States in the north regional political rivalries provoked civil wars that challenged the very survival of the new nations. Foreign military interventions and wars with native peoples also consumed resources and determined national boundaries. The effort to fulfill the promise of universal citizenship led to struggles to end slavery, extend civil and political rights to women and minorities, and to absorb new immigrants. These objectives were only partially achieved.

Industrialization had a transforming effect on the hemisphere as well. Wealth, political power, and population were increasingly concentrated in urban areas. Bankers and manufacturers, not farmers and plantation owners, directed national destinies. The United States, the most industrialized nation in the Americas, played an aggressive economic role in the region's affairs and used its growing military power as well. Industrialization altered the natural environment in dramatic ways. Modern factories consumed huge amounts of raw materials and energy. Copper mines in Chile and Mexico, Cuban sugar plantations, Brazilian coffee plantations, and Canadian lumber companies all left their mark on the natural environment, and all had ties to markets in the United States. The concentration of people in cities in the United States and Latin America put pressure on water supplies, sewage treatment, and food supplies.

By 1900, however, the hemisphere's national governments were much stronger than they had been at independence. Latin America lagged behind the United States and Canada in institutionalizing democratic political reforms, but Latin American nations in 1900 were stronger and more open than they had been in 1850. By 1900, all of the hemisphere's nations also were better able to meet the threats of foreign intervention and regionalism. Among the benefits resulting from the increased strength of national governments were the abolition of slavery and the extension of political rights to formerly excluded citizens.

Serious challenges remained. Amerindian peoples were forced to resettle on reservations, were excluded from national political life, and, in some countries, remained burdened with special tribute and tax obligations. Women began to enter occupations previously reserved to men but still lacked full citizenship rights. The baneful legacy of slavery and colonial racial stratification remained a barrier to many men and women. The benefits of economic growth were not equitably distributed among the nations of the Western Hemisphere or within individual nations. In 1900 nearly every American nation was wealthier, better educated, more democratic, and more populous than at independence. But they also were generally more vulnerable to distant economic forces, more profoundly split between haves and have-nots, and more clearly divided into a rich North and a poorer South.

■ Key Terms

Simón Bolívar	Tecumseh
Miguel Hidalgo y Costilla	Caste War
José María Morelos	abolitionists
Confederation of 1867	acculturation
personalist leaders	Women's Rights Convention
Andrew Jackson	development
José Antonio Páez	underdevelopment
Benito Juárez	

■ Suggested Reading

For the independence era in Latin America see John Lynch, *The Spanish American Revolutions, 1808–1826*, 2d ed. (1986); Jay Kinsbruner, *Independence in Spanish America* (1994); and A. J. R. Russell-Wood, ed., *From Colony to Nation: Essays on the Independence of Brazil* (1976).

The postindependence political and economic struggles in Latin America can be traced in David Bushnell and Neil Macaulay, *The Emergence of Latin America in the Nineteenth Century* (1988). Tulio Halperin-Donghi, *The Contemporary History of Latin America* (1993), and E. Bradford Burns, *The Poverty of Progress: Latin America in the Nineteenth Century* (1980), argue in different ways that Latin America's economic and social problems originated in unfavorable trade relationships with more-developed nations. See also an excellent collection of essays, Leslie Bethell, ed., *The Cambridge History of Latin America*, vol. 3, *From Independence to c. 1870* (1985).

There is an enormous literature on politics and nation building in the United States and Canada. Among the many worthy studies of the United States are William J. Cooper, *The South and the Politics of Slavery, 1828–1856* (1978); Kenneth M. Stampp, *America in 1857* (1991); and Lawrence Frederick Kohl, *The Politics of Individualism: Parties and the American Character in the Jacksonian Era* (1989). For Canada see J. M. S. Careless, *The Union of the Canadas: The Growth of Canadian Institutions, 1841–1857* (1967); Ged Martin, ed., *The Causes of Canadian Confederation* (1990); and Arthur I. Silver, *The French-Canadian Idea of Confederation, 1864–1900* (1982).

The social and cultural issues raised in this chapter are also the subject of a vast literature. For an excellent history of the immigration era see Walter Nugent, *Crossing: The Great Transatlantic Migrations, 1870–1914* (1992). See also Gunther Barth, *Bitter Strength: A History of Chinese in the United States, 1850–1870* (1964), and Nicolás Sánchez-Albornoz, *The Population of Latin America: A History* (1974).

On the issue of slavery see David Brion Davis, *Slavery and Human Progress* (1984); George M. Frederickson, *The Black Image in the White Mind: The Debate on Afro-American Character and Destiny, 1817–1914* (1971); and Benjamin Quarles, *Black Abolitionists* (1969). For the women's rights movement see Ellen C. Du Bois, *Feminism and Suffrage: The Emergence of an Indepen-*

dent Woman's Movement in the Nineteenth Century (1984), and Lori D. Ginzberg, *Women and the Work of Benevolence: Morality, Politics, and Class in the Nineteenth-Century United States* (1990). Among numerous excellent studies of Indian policies see Robert M. Utley, *The Indian Frontier of the American West, 1846–1890* (1984). On those topics for Canada see J. R. Miller, *Skyscrapers Hide the Heavens: A History of Indian White Relations in Canada* (1989); Olive Patricia Dickason, *Canada's First Nations* (1993); and Alison Prentice, *Canadian Women: A History* (1988).

For abolition in Latin America and the Caribbean see Rebecca Scott, *Slave Emancipation in Cuba: The Transition to Free Labor, 1860–1899* (1985); Robert Conrad, *The Destruction of Brazilian Slavery, 1850–1888* (1973); and William A. Green, *British Slave Emancipation: The Sugar Colonies and the Great Experiment, 1830–1865*. An introduction to the place of women in Latin American society is found in Francesca Miller, *Latin American Women and the Search for Social Justice* (1991), and Jane Jaquette, ed., *The Women's Movement in Latin America* (1989). See also David Barry Gaspar and Darlene Clark Hine, eds., *More Than Chattel: Black Women and Slavery in the Americas* (1996).

An introduction to environmental consequence of North American development is provided by William Cronon, *Nature's Metropolis: Chicago and the Great West* (1991); Joseph M. Petulla, *American Environmental History* (1973); and Donald Worster, *Rivers of Empire: Water, Aridity, and the Growth of the American West* (1985). For Brazil see Warren Dean, *With Broadax and Firebrand: The Destruction of the Brazilian Atlantic Forest* (1995); and for Argentina, Uruguay, and Chile, Alfred Crosby, *Ecological Imperialism: The Biological Expansion of Europe, 900–1900* (1986).

■ Notes

1. Quoted in Lyman L. Johnson, "Spanish American Independence and Its Consequences," in *Problems in Modern Latin American History: A Reader,* ed. John Charles Chasteen and Joseph S. Tulchin (Wilmington, DE: Scholarly Resources, 1994), 21.
2. Quoted in Margaret Conrad, Alvin Finkel, and Cornelius Jaenen, *History of the Canadian Peoples*, vol. 1 (Toronto: Copp Clark Pittman Ltd., 1993), 606–607.
3. José Antonio Páez, *Autobiografía del General José Antonio Páez,* vol. 1 (Nueva York: Hallety Breen, 1869), 83.
4. Quoted in Brian Loveman, *Chile: The Legacy of Hispanic Capitalism* (New York: Oxford University Press, 1979), 170.
5. Quoted in Bernard Bailyn, David Brion Davis, David Herbert Donald, John L. Thomas, Robert H. Wiebe, and Gordon S. Wood, *The Great Republic: A History of the American People* (Lexington, MA: D. C. Heath, 1981), 398.
6. J. S. Woodsworth in 1909, quoted in R. Douglas Francis, Richard Jones, and Donald B. Smith, *Destinies: Canadian History Since Confederation*, 2d ed. (Toronto: Holt, Rinehart and Winston, 1992), 141.
7. Sarah Grimké, "Reply to the Massachusetts Clergy," in Nancy Woloch, ed., *Early American Women: A Documentary History, 1600–1900* (Belmont, CA: Wadsworth, 1992), 343.

26

AFRICA, INDIA, AND THE NEW BRITISH EMPIRE,

1750–1870

Changes and Exchanges in Africa • India Under Company Rule • Britain's Eastern Empire

ENVIRONMENT AND TECHNOLOGY: Whaling

SOCIETY AND CULTURE: Ceremonials of Imperial Domination

Indian Railroad Station, 1866   British India built the largest network of railroads in Asia. People of every social class traveled by train.

n 1782 Tipu Sultan inherited the throne of the state of Mysore°, which his father had made the most powerful state in South India. The ambitious and talented new ruler also inherited a healthy distrust of the British East India Company's territorial ambitions. Before the company could invade Mysore, Tipu Sultan launched his own attack in 1785. He then sent an embassy to France in 1788 seeking an alliance against Britain. Neither of these ventures was immediately successful.

Not until a decade later did the French agree to a loose alliance with Tipu Sultan as part of their plan to challenge Britain's colonial and commercial supremacy in the Indian Ocean. General Napoleon Bonaparte invaded Egypt in 1798 to threaten British trade routes to India and hoped to use the alliance with Tipu Sultan to drive the British out of India. The French invasion of Egypt went well enough at first, but a British naval blockade and the ravages of disease crippled the French force. When the French withdrew, another military adventurer, Muhammad Ali, commander of the Ottoman army in Egypt, took advantage of the situation to revitalize Egypt and expand its rule.

Meanwhile, Tipu's struggle with the East India Company was going badly. A military defeat in 1792 forced him to surrender most of his coastal lands. Despite the loose alliance with France, he was unable to stop further British advances. Tipu lost his life in 1799 while defending his capital against a British assault. Mysore was divided between the British and their Indian allies.

As these events illustrate, talented local leaders and European powers were both vying to expand their influence in South Asia and Africa between 1750 and 1870. Midway through that period, it was by no means clear who would gain the upper hand. Britain and France were as likely to fight each other as they were to fight any Asian or African state. In 1800, the two nations were engaged in their third major war for overseas supremacy since 1750. By 1870, however, Britain had gained a decisive advantage over France.

The new British empire in the East included the subcontinent of India, settler colonies in Australia and New Zealand, and a growing network of trading outposts. By 1870 Britain had completed the campaign to replace the overseas slave trade from Africa with "legitimate" trade and had spearheaded new Asian and South Pacific labor migrations into a rejuvenated string of tropical colonies.

As you read this chapter, ask yourself the following questions:

- Why were the British able to gain decisive advantages in distant lands?
- Why were Asians and Africans so divided, some choosing to cooperate with the Europeans while others resisted their advances?
- How important an advantage were Britain's weapons, ships, and economic motives?
- How much of the outcome was the result of advance planning, and how much was due to particular individuals or to chance?
- By 1870, how much had the British and the different peoples of Africa and Asia gained or lost?

CHANGES AND EXCHANGES IN AFRICA

During the century before 1870, Africa underwent dynamic political changes and a great expansion of foreign trade. Indigenous African leaders as well as Middle Eastern and European imperialists built powerful new states or expanded old ones. As the continent's external slave trades to the Americas and to Islamic lands died slowly under British pressure, trade in goods such as palm oil, ivory, timber, and gold grew sharply. In return Africans imported large quantities of machine-made textiles and firearms. These complex changes are best understood by looking at African regions separately.

Mysore (my-SORE)

CHRONOLOGY

	Empire	Africa	India
1750			**1756** Black Hole of Calcutta **1765** East India Company (EIC) rule of Bengal begins
	1763 End of Seven Years War **1769–1778** Captain James Cook explores New Zealand and eastern Australia **1795** End of Dutch East India Company	**1795** Britain takes Cape Colony **1798** Napoleon invades Egypt	**1798** Britain annexes Ceylon **1799** EIC defeats Mysore
1800		**1805** Muhammad Ali seizes Egypt	
	1808 Britain outlaws slave trade	**1808** Britain takes over Sierra Leone **1809** Sokoto Caliphate founded **1818** Shaka founds Zulu kingdom **1821** Foundation of Republic of Liberia; Egypt takes control of Sudan	**1818** EIC creates Bombay Presidency **1826** EIC annexes Assam and northern Burma **1828** Brahmo Samaj founded
	1834 Britain abolishes slavery	**1831–1847** Algerians resist French takeover **1836–1839** Afrikaners' Great Trek **1840** Omani sultan moves capital to Zanzibar	**1834** Indentured labor migrations begin
1850	**1867** End of Atlantic slave trade **1877** Queen Victoria becomes Empress of India	**1869** Jaja founds Opobo **1889** Menelik unites modern Ethiopia	**1857–1858** Sepoy Rebellion leads to end of EIC rule and Mughal rule **1885** First Indian National Congress

New States in Southern and Inland West Africa

Internal forces produced clusters of new states in two parts of sub-Saharan Africa between 1750 and 1870. In southern Africa changes in warfare gave rise to a powerful Zulu kingdom and other new states. In inland West Africa Islamic reformers created the gigantic Sokoto° Caliphate and companion states (see Map 26.1).

In the fertile coastlands of southeastern Africa (in modern South Africa), the Nguni° peoples for many centuries had pursued a life based on cattle and agriculture. Small independent chiefdoms suited their political needs until a serious drought hit the region at the beginning of the nineteenth century. Out of the conflict for grazing and farming lands an upstart military genius named Shaka (r. 1818–1828) in 1818 created the **Zulu** kingdom. Strict military drill and close-combat warfare featuring oxhide shields and lethal stabbing spears made the Zulu the most powerful and most feared fighters in southern Africa.

Shaka expanded his kingdom by raiding his African neighbors, seizing their cattle, and capturing their women and children. Breakaway military bands spread this system of warfare and state building inland to the high plateau country, across the Limpopo River (in modern Zimbabwe°), and as far north as Lake Victoria. As the power and population of these new kingdoms increased, so too did the number of displaced and demoralized refugees around them.

To protect themselves from the Zulu, some neighboring Africans created their own states. The Swazi kingdom consolidated north of the Zulu, and the kingdom of Lesotho° grew by attracting refugees to strongholds in

---

Sokoto (SOH-kuh-toh)   Nguni (ng-GOO-nee)

Zimbabwe (zim-BAH-bway)   Lesotho (luh-SOO-too)

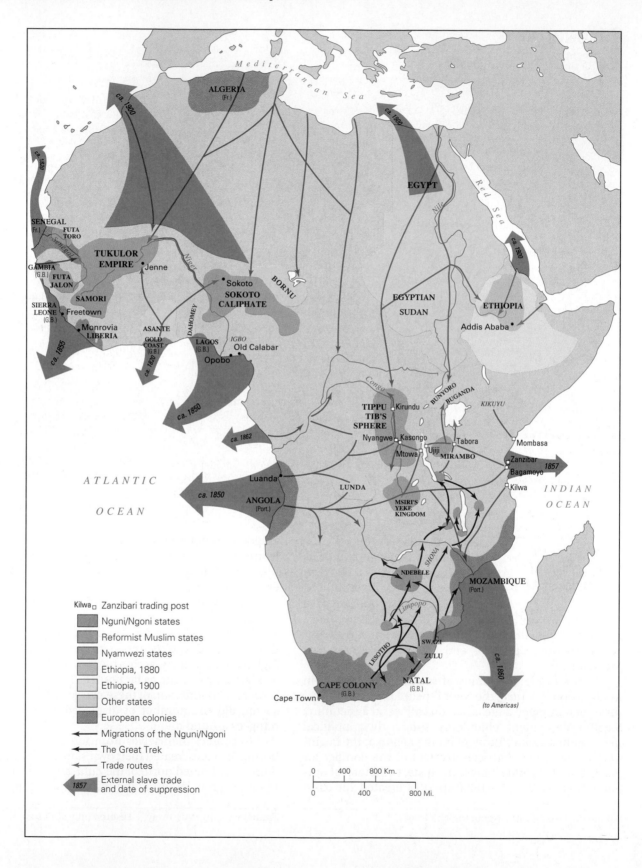

Kilwa □ Zanzibari trading post
■ Nguni/Ngoni states
■ Reformist Muslim states
■ Nyamwezi states
■ Ethiopia, 1880
■ Ethiopia, 1900
■ Other states
■ European colonies
← Migrations of the Nguni/Ngoni
← The Great Trek
← Trade routes
← *1857* External slave trade and date of suppression

Map 26.1   Africa in the Nineteenth Century   Expanding internal and overseas trade drew much of Africa into global networks, but foreign colonies in 1870 were largely confined to Algeria and southern Africa. Growing trade, Islamic reform movements, and other internal forces created important new states throughout the continent.

southern Africa's highest mountains. Both Lesotho and Swaziland survive as independent states to this day.

Although Shaka ruled for little more than a decade, he succeeded in creating a new national identity as well as a new kingdom. He grouped all the young people in his domains by age into regiments. Regiment members lived together and immersed themselves in learning Zulu lore and customs, including fighting methods for the males. A British trader named Henry Francis Fynn expressed his "astonishment at the order and discipline" he found everywhere in the Zulu kingdom. He witnessed public festivals of loyalty to Shaka at which regiments of young men and women numbering in the tens of thousands danced around the king for hours. Parades showed off the king's enormous herds of cattle, a Zulu measure of wealth.

Meanwhile, Islamic reform movements were creating another cluster of powerful states in the savannas of West Africa. Islam had been a force in the politics and cities of this region for centuries, but it had made only slow progress among most rural people. As a consequence, most Muslim rulers had found it prudent to tolerate the older religious practices of their rural subjects. In the 1770s, local Muslim scholars began preaching the need for a vigorous reform of Islamic practices. They condemned the accommodations Muslim rulers had made with older traditions and called for a forcible conquest of rural "pagans." The reformers followed a classic Muslim pattern: a *jihad* (holy war) added new lands, where governments enforced Islamic laws and promoted the religion's spread among conquered people.

The largest of the new Muslim reform movements occurred in the Hausa° states (in what is now northern Nigeria) under the leadership of Usuman dan Fodio° (1745–1817), a Muslim cleric of the Fulani° people. He charged that the Hausa kings, despite their official profession of Islam, were "undoubtedly unbelievers . . . because they practice polytheistic rituals and turn people away from the path of God." Distressed by the lapses of a former pupil, the king of Gobir, Usuman issued a call in

Hausa (HOW-suh)
Usuman dan Fodio (OO-soo-mahn dahn FOH-dee-oh)
Fulani (foo-LAH-nee)

Zulu in Battle Dress, 1838   Elaborate costumes helped impress opponents with the Zulu's strength. Shown here are long-handled spears and thick leather shields. The stabbing spear is not shown. (Killie Campbell Africana Library. Photo: Jane Taylor/Sonia Halliday)

1804 for a jihad to overthrow him. Muslims unhappy with their social or religious position spread the movement to other Hausa states. The successful armies united the conquered Hausa states and neighboring areas under a caliph (sultan) who ruled from the city of Sokoto. The **Sokoto Caliphate** (1809–1906) was the largest state in West Africa since the fall of Songhai in the sixteenth century.

As in earlier centuries, these new Muslim states became centers of Islamic learning and reform. Schools for training boys in Quranic subjects spread rapidly, and the great library at Sokoto attracted many scholars. Although officials permitted non-Muslims within the empire to follow their religions in exchange for paying a special tax, they suppressed public performances of dances and ceremonies associated with traditional religions. During the jihads, many who resisted the expansion of Muslim rule were killed, enslaved, or forced to convert.

Sokoto's leaders sold some captives into the Atlantic slave trade and many more into the trans-Saharan slave trade, which carried ten thousand slaves a year, mostly women and children, across the desert to North Africa and the Middle East. Slavery also increased greatly within the Sokoto Caliphate and other new Muslim states. It is estimated that by 1865 there were more slaves in the Sokoto Caliphate than in any remaining slaveholding state in the Americas.[1] Most of the enslaved persons raised food, making possible the seclusion of free women in their homes in accordance with reformed Muslim practice.

Modernization and Expansion in Egypt and Ethiopia

While new states were arising elsewhere, the ancient African states of Egypt and Ethiopia in northeastern Africa were undergoing a period of growth and **modernization.** Napoleon's invading army had withdrawn from Egypt by 1801, but the shock of this display of European strength and Egyptian weakness was long lasting. The successor to Napoleon's rule was **Muhammad Ali** (1769–1849), who eliminated his rivals and ruled Egypt from 1805 to 1848. He began the political, social, and economic reforms that created modern Egypt.

Muhammad Ali's central aim was to give Egypt sufficient military strength to prevent another European conquest, but he was pragmatic enough to make use of European experts and techniques to achieve that goal. His reforms transformed Egyptian landholding, increased agricultural production, and created a modern administration and army. To train candidates for the army and administration, Muhammad Ali set up a European-style state school system and opened a military college at Aswan°. To pay for these ventures and for the European experts and equipment that he imported, he required Egyptian peasants to cultivate cotton and other crops for export.

In the 1830s Muhammad Ali headed the strongest state in the Islamic world and the first to employ Western methods and technology for modernization. The process was far from a blind imitation of the West. Rather, the technical expertise of the West was combined with Islamic religious and cultural traditions. For example, the Egyptian printing industry, begun to provide Arabic translations of technical manuals, turned out critical editions of Islamic classics and promoted a revival of Arabic writing and literature later in the century.

By the end of Muhammad Ali's reign in 1848, the modernization of Egypt was well under way. The population had nearly doubled, trade with Europe had expanded by almost 600 percent, and a new class of educated Egyptians had begun to replace the old ruling aristocracy. Egyptians were replacing many of the foreign experts, and the fledgling program of industrialization was providing the country with its own textiles, paper, weapons, and military uniforms. The demands on peasant families for labor and military service, however, were acutely disruptive.

Ali's grandson Ismail° (r. 1863–1879) placed even more emphasis on westernizing Egypt. "My country is no longer in Africa," Ismail declared, "it is in Europe."[2] His efforts increased the number of European advisers in Egypt—and Egypt's debts to French and British banks. In the first decade of his reign, revenues increased thirty-fold and exports doubled (largely because of a huge increase in cotton exports during the American Civil War). By 1870 there was a network of new irrigation canals, 800 miles (1,300 kilometers) of railroads, a modern postal service, and the dazzling new capital city of Cairo. When the market for Egyptian cotton collapsed after the American Civil War, however, Egypt's debts to British and French investors led to the country's partial occupation.

From the middle of the century, state building and reform also were under way in the ancient kingdom of Ethiopia, whose rulers had been Christian for fifteen hundred years. Weakened by internal divisions and the pressures of its Muslim neighbors, Ethiopia was a shadow of what it had been in the sixteenth century, but under Emperor Téwodros° II (r. 1833–1868) and his successor Yohannes° IV (r. 1872–1889) most highland regions were brought back under imperial rule. The only large part of ancient Ethiopia that remained outside Emperor Yohannes's rule was the Shoa kingdom, ruled by King Menelik° from 1865. When Menelik succeeded Yohannes as emperor in 1889, the merger of their separate realms created the modern boundaries of Ethiopia.

Beginning in the 1840s, Ethiopian rulers purchased modern weapons from European sources and created strong armies loyal to the ruler. Emperor Téwodros also encouraged the manufacture of weapons locally. With the aid of Protestant missionaries his craftsmen even constructed a giant cannon capable of firing a half-ton shell. However, his efforts to coerce more technical aid by holding some British officials captive backfired when the British invaded instead. As the British forces advanced, Téwodros committed suicide to avoid being taken prisoner. Satisfied that their honor was avenged, the British withdrew. Later Ethiopian emperors kept up the program of reform and modernization.

Aswan (AS-wahn)

Ismail (is-MAH-eel)   Téwodros (tay-WOH-druhs)
Yohannes (yoh-HAHN-nehs)   Menelik (MEN-uh-lik)

Téwodros's Mighty Cannon   Like other modernizers in the nineteenth century, Emperor Téwodros of Ethiopia sought to reform his military forces. In 1861 he forced resident European missionaries and craftsmen to build guns and cannon, including this 7-ton behemoth nicknamed "Sebastapol" after the Black Sea port that had been the center of the Crimean War. It took five hundred men to haul the cannon across Ethiopia's hilly terrain.   (From Hormuzd Rassam, *Narrative of the British Mission to Theodore, King of Abyssinia, II,* London 1869, John Murray)

European Invaders and Explorers

More lasting than Britain's punitive invasion of Ethiopia was France's conquest of Algeria, a move that anticipated the general European "Scramble for Africa" after 1870. Equally pregnant with future meaning was the Europeans' exploration of the inland parts of Africa in the middle decades of the century.

Long an exporter of grain and olive oil to France, the North African state of Algeria had even supplied Napoleon with grain for his 1798 invasion of Egypt. The failure of French governments to repay this debt led to many disputes between Algeria and France and eventually to a serving of diplomatic relations in 1827, after the ruler of Algeria, annoyed with the French ambassador, allegedly struck him with a fly whisk. Three years later an unpopular French government, hoping to stir French nationalism with an easy overseas victory, attacked Algeria on the pretext of avenging this insult.

The invasion of 1830 proved a costly mistake. The French government was soon overthrown, but the war in Algeria dragged on for eighteen years. The attack by an alien Christian power united the Algerians behind 'Abd al-Qadir°, a gifted and resourceful Muslim holy man. To achieve victory, the French built up an army of over 100,000 that broke Algerian resistance by destroying farm animals and crops and massacring villagers by the tens of thousands. After 'Abd al-Qadir was captured and exiled in 1847, the resistance movement fragmented, but the French occupiers faced resistance in the mountains for another thirty years. Poor European settlers, who rushed in to take possession of Algeria's rich coastlands, numbered 130,000 by 1871.

Meanwhile, a more peaceful European intrusion was penetrating Africa's geographical secrets. Small expeditions of adventurous explorers, using their own funds or financed by private geographical societies, were seeking to uncover the mysteries of inner Africa that had eluded Europeans for four centuries. Besides discovering more about the course of Africa's mighty rivers, these explorers wished to assess the continent's mineral wealth or convert the African millions to Christianity.

'Abd al-Qadir (AHB-dahl-KAH-deer)

Many of the explorers were concerned with tracing the course of Africa's great rivers. Explorers learned in 1795 that the Niger River in West Africa flowed from west to east (not the other way as had often been supposed) and in 1830 that the great morass of small streams entering the Gulf of Guinea was in fact the Niger Delta.

The north-flowing Nile, whose annual floods made Egypt bloom, similarly attracted explorers bent on finding the headwaters of the world's longest river. In 1770 Lake Tana in Ethiopia was established as a major source, and in 1861–1862 Lake Victoria (named for the British sovereign) was found to be the other main source.

In contrast to the heavily financed expeditions with hundreds of African porters that searched the Nile, the Scottish missionary David Livingstone (1813–1873) organized modest treks through southern and Central Africa. The missionary doctor's primary goal was to scout out locations for Christian missions, but he was also highly influential in tracing the course of the Zambezi River, between 1853 and 1856. He named its greatest waterfall for the British monarch Queen Victoria. Livingstone also traced the course of the upper Congo River, where in 1871 he was met by the Welsh-American journalist Henry Morton Stanley (1841–1904) on a publicity-motivated search for the "lost" missionary doctor. On an expedition from 1874 to 1877, Stanley descended the Congo River to its mouth.

One of the most remarkable features of the explorers' experiences in Africa was their ability to move unmolested from place to place. The strangers were seldom harmed without provocation. Stanley preferred large expeditions that fought their way across the continent, but Livingstone's modest expeditions, which posed no threat to anyone, regularly received warm hospitality.

Abolition and Legitimate Trade in Coastal West Africa

No sooner was the mouth of the Niger River discovered than eager entrepreneurs began to send expeditions up the river to scout out its potential for trade. Along much of coastal West Africa, commercial relations with Europeans remained dominant between 1750 and 1870. The value of trade between Africa and the other Atlantic continents more than doubled between the 1730s and the 1780s, then doubled again by 1870.[3] Before about 1825 the slave trade accounted for most of that increase, but thereafter African exports of vegetable oils, gold, ivory, and other goods drove overseas trade to new heights.

Europeans played a critical role in these changes in Africa's overseas trade. The Atlantic trade had arisen to serve the needs of the first European empires, and its transformation was linked to the ideas and industrial needs of Britain's new economy and empire.

One step in the Atlantic slave trade's extinction was the successful slave revolt in Saint Domingue in the 1790s (see Chapter 23). It ended slavery in the largest plantation colony in the West Indies, and elsewhere in the Americas it inspired slave revolts that were brutally repressed. As news of the slave revolts and their repression spread, humanitarians and religious reformers called for an end to the slave trade. Since it was widely believed that African-born slaves were more likely to rebel than were persons born into slavery, support for abolition of the slave trade was found even among Americans wanting to preserve slavery. In 1808 both Great Britain and the United States made carrying and importing slaves from Africa illegal for their citizens. Most other Western countries followed suit by 1850, but few enforced abolition with the vigor of the British.

Once the world's greatest slave traders, the British became the most aggressive abolitionists. Britain sent a naval patrol to enforce the ban along the African coast and negotiated treaties allowing the patrol to search other nations' vessels suspected of carrying slaves. During the half-century after 1815, Britain spent some $60 million (£12 million) in its efforts to end the slave trade, a sum equal to the profits British slave traders had made in the fifty years before 1808.

Although British patrols captured 1,635 slave ships and liberated over 160,000 enslaved Africans, the trade proved difficult to stop, for Cuba and Brazil continued to import huge numbers of slaves. Such demand drove prices up and persuaded some African rulers and merchants to continue to sell slaves and to help foreign slavers evade the British patrols. After British patrols quashed the slave trade along the Gold Coast, the powerful king of Asante° even tried to persuade a British official in 1820 that reopening the trade would be to their mutual profit. Because the slave trade moved to other parts of Africa, the trans-Atlantic slave trade did not end until 1867.

The demand for slaves in the Americas claimed the lives and endangered the safety of untold numbers of Africans, but the trade also satisfied other Africans' desires for the cloth, metals, and other goods that European traders brought in return. To continue their access to those imports, Africans expanded their **"legitimate" trade** (exports other than slaves). They revived old trades or developed new exports as the Atlantic slave trade was shut down. On the Gold Coast, for example, annual exports of gold climbed to nearly 25,000 ounces (750 kilograms) in the 1840s and 1850s, compared to 10,000 ounces (300 kilograms) in the 1790s.

Asante (uh-SHAHN-tee)

The most successful of the new exports from West Africa was palm oil, a vegetable oil used by British manufacturers for soap, candles, and lubricants. Though still a major source of slaves until the mid-1830s, the trading states of the Niger Delta simultaneously emerged as the permier exporters of palm oil. In inland forests men climbed tall oil palms and cut down large palm-nut clusters, which women pounded to extract the thick oil. Coastal African traders bought the palm oil at inland markets and delivered it to European ships at the coast.

The dramatic increase in palm-oil exports—from a few hundred tons at the beginning of the century to tens of thousands of tons by midcentury—did not require any new technology, but it did alter the social structure of the coastal trading communities. Coastal traders grew rich and used their wealth to buy large numbers of male slaves to paddle the giant dugout canoes that transported palm oil from inland markets along the narrow delta creeks to the trading ports. Niger Delta slavery could be as harsh and brutal as slavery on New World plantations, but it offered some male and female slaves a chance to gain wealth and power. Some female slaves who married big traders exercised great authority over junior members of trading households. Male slaves who supervised canoe fleets were well compensated, and a few even became wealthy enough to take over the leadership of the coastal "canoe houses" (companies). The most famous, known as "Jaja" (ca. 1821–1891), rose from being a canoe slave to the head of a major canoe house. To escape discrimination by free-born Africans, in 1869 he founded the new port of Opobo, which he ruled as king. In the 1870s Jaja of Opobo was the greatest palm-oil trader in the Niger Delta.

Another effect of the suppression of the slave trade was the spread of Western cultural influences in West Africa. To serve as a base for their anti-slave-trade naval squadron, in 1808 the British had taken over the small colony of Sierra Leone°. Over the next several years, 130,000 men, women, and children taken from "captured" vessels were liberated in Sierra Leone. Christian missionaries helped settle these impoverished and dispirited **recaptives** in and around Freetown, the capital. In time the mission churches and schools made many willing converts among such men and women.

Sierra Leone's schools also produced a number of distinguished graduates. For example, Samuel Adjai Crowther (1808–1891), freed as a youth from a slave ship in 1821 by the British squadron, became the first Anglican bishop in West Africa in 1864, administering a pioneering diocese along the lower Niger River. James

Sierra Leone (see-ER-uh lee-OWN)

King Jaja of Opobo   This talented man rose from slavery in the Niger Delta port of Bonny to head one of the town's major palm-oil trading firms, the Anna Pepple House, in 1863. Six years later, Jaja founded and ruled his own trading port of Opobo. (Reproduced from *West Africa: An Introduction to Its History*, by Michael Crowder, by courtesy of the publishers, Addison Wesley Longman)

Africanus Horton (1835–1882), the son of a slave liberated in Sierra Leone, became a doctor and the author of many studies of West Africa.

Other Western cultural influences came from people of African birth or descent returning to their ancestral homeland in this era. In 1821, to the south of Sierra Leone, free black Americans began a settlement that grew into the Republic of Liberia, a place of liberty at a time when slavery was illegal and flourishing in the

United States. After their emancipation in 1865 other African-Americans moved to Liberia. Emma White, a literate black woman from Kentucky, moved from Liberia to Opobo in 1875, where King Jaja employed her to write his commercial correspondence and run a school for his children. Edward Wilmot Blyden (1832–1912), born in the Danish West Indies and proud of his West African parentage, emigrated to Liberia in 1851 and became a professor of Greek and Latin (and later Arabic) at the fledgling Liberia College. Free blacks from Brazil and Cuba chartered ships to return to their West African homelands, bringing with them Roman Catholicism, architectural motifs, and clothing fashions from the New World. Although the number of Africans exposed to Western culture in 1870 was still small, this influence grew rapidly.

Slaves and Secondary Empires in Eastern Africa

When British patrols hampered the slave trade in West Africa, slavers moved southward and then around the tip of southern Africa to eastern Africa. There the Atlantic slave trade joined an existing trade in slaves to the Islamic world that also was expanding. Two-thirds of the 1.2 million slaves exported from eastern Africa in the nineteenth century went to markets in North Africa and the Middle East; the other third went to plantations in the Americas and to European-controlled Indian Ocean islands.

Slavery also became more prominent within eastern Africa itself. Between 1800 and 1873, Arab and Swahili owners of clove plantations along the coast purchased some 700,000 slaves from inland eastern Africa to do the labor-intensive work of harvesting this spice. The plantations were on Zanzibar Island and in neighboring territories belonging to the Sultanate of Oman, an Arabian kingdom on the Persian Gulf that had been expanding its control over the East African coast since 1698. The sultan had even moved his court to Zanzibar in 1840 to take better advantage of the burgeoning trade in cloves. Zanzibar also was an important center of slaves and ivory. Most of the ivory was shipped to India, where much of it was carved into decorative objects for European markets.

Ivory caravans came to the coast from hundreds of miles inland under the direction of African and Arab merchants. Some of these merchants brought large personal empires under their control by using capital they had borrowed from Indian bankers and modern firearms they had bought from Europeans and Americans. Some trading empires were created by inland Nyamwezi° traders, who worked closely with the indigenous Swahili° and Arabs in Zanzibar to develop the long-distance caravan routes.

The largest of these personal empires, along the upper Congo River, was created by Tippu Tip (ca. 1830–1905), a trader from Zanzibar, who was Swahili and Nyamwezi on his father's side and Omani Arab on his mother's. Livingstone, Stanley, and other explorers who received Tippu Tip's gracious hospitality in the remote center of the continent praised their host's intelligence and refinement. On an 1876 visit, for example, Stanley recorded in his journal that Tippu Tip was "a remarkable man," a "picture of energy and strength" with "a fine intelligent face: almost courtier-like in his manner."

Tippu Tip also composed a detailed memoir of his adventures in the heart of Africa, written in the Swahili language of the coast. In it he mocked innocent African villagers for believing that his gunshots were thunder. As the memoir and other sources make clear, these modern rifles not only felled countless elephants for their ivory tusks but also inflicted widespread devastation and misery on the people of this isolated area.

One can blame Tippu Tip and other Zanzibari traders for the pillage and havoc in the once-peaceful center of Africa, along with their master, the sultan of Oman. However, the circle of responsibility was still broader. Europeans supplied the weapons used by the invaders and were major consumers of ivory and cloves. For this reason histories have referred to the states carved out of eastern Africa by the sultans of Oman, Tippu Tip, and others as "secondary empires," in contrast to the empire that Britain was establishing directly. At the same time, Britain was working to bring the Indian Ocean slave trade to an end in eastern Africa. British officials pressured the sultan of Oman into halting the Indian Ocean slave trade from Zanzibar in 1857 and ending the import of slaves into Zanzibar in 1873.

Egypt's expansion southward during the nineteenth century can also be considered a secondary empire. Muhammad Ali had pioneered the conquest of the upper Nile, in 1821 establishing at Khartoum° a major base that became the capital of the Egyptian Sudan. A major reason for his invasion of Sudan was to secure slaves for his army so that more Egyptian peasants could be left free to grow cotton for export. From the 1840s unscrupulous traders of many origins, leading forces armed with European weapons, pushed south to the modern frontiers of Uganda and Zaire in search of cattle, ivory, and slaves. They set one African community against another and reaped profit from the devastation they sowed.

Nyamwezi (nn-nyahm-WAY-zee)   Swahili (swah-HEE-lee)
Khartoum (khar-TOOM)

British Mem–Sahib, ca. 1782   This charming painting by a Bengali artist shows Lady Impey, wife of the British East India Company's chief justice of Bengal, surrounded by her Indian servants in a room that mixes Indian and European decor. The Hindi word *sahib* was an honorific title; *mem-sahib* was the Anglo-Indian feminine form reserved for European women.   (The Art Archive Ltd.)

INDIA UNDER BRITISH RULE

The people of South Asia felt the impact of European commercial, cultural, and colonial expansion more immediately and profoundly than did the people of Africa. While Europeans were laying claim to only small parts of Africa between 1750 and 1870, nearly all of India (with three times the population of all of Africa) came under Britain's direct or indirect rule. During the 250 years after the founding of East India Company in 1600, British interests commandeered the colonies and trade of the Dutch, fought off French and Indian challenges, and picked up the pieces of the decaying Mughal° Empire. By 1763 the French were stymied, in 1795 the Dutch East India Company was dissolved, and in 1858 the last Mughal emperor was dethroned, leaving the vast subcontinent in British hands.

Mughal (MOO-guhl

Company Men

As Mughal power weakened in the eighteenth century, Europeans were not the first outsiders to make a move. In 1739, Iranian armies defeated the Mughal forces, sacked Delhi, and returned home with vast amounts of booty. Indian states also took advantage of Mughal weakness to assert their independence. By midcentury, the Maratha° Confederation, a coalition of states in central India, controlled more land than the Mughals did (see Map 26.2). Also ruling their own powerful states were the **nawabs**° (a term used for Muslim princes who were deputies of the Mughal emperor, though in name only): the nawab of Bengal in the northeast; the nawab of Arcot in the southeast, Haidar Ali (1722–1782)—the father of Tipu Sultan and ruler of the southwestern state of Mysore; and many others.

British, Dutch, and French companies were also eager to expand their profitable trade into India in the eighteenth century. Such far-flung European trading

Maratha (muh-RAH-tuh)   **nawab** (NAH-wab)

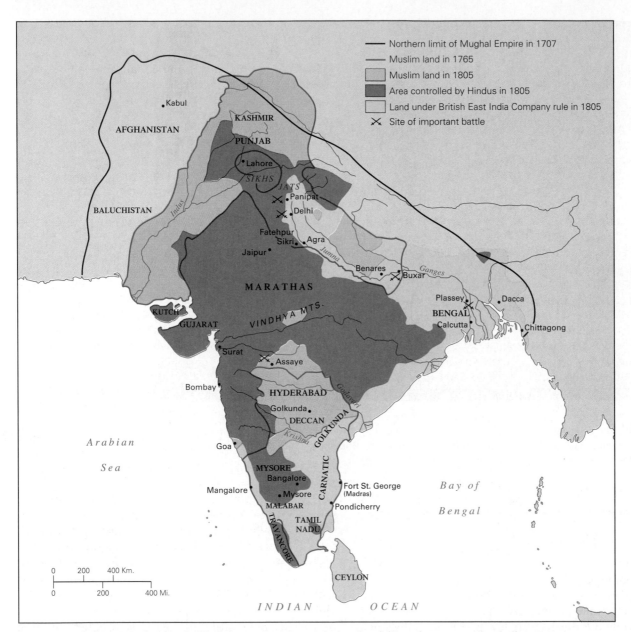

Map 26.2   India, 1707–1805   As Mughal power weakened during the eighteenth century, other Indian states and the British East India Company expanded their territories.

companies were speculative and risky ventures in 1750. Their success depended on hard-drinking and ambitious young "Company Men," who used hard bargaining, and hard fighting when necessary, to persuade Indian rulers to allow them to establish trading posts at strategic points along the coast. To protect their fortified warehouses from attack by other Europeans or by native states, the companies hired and trained Indian troops known as **sepoys°**. In divided India these private armies came to hold the balance of power.

In 1691 the East India Company (EIC) had convinced the nawab of the large state of Bengal in northeast India to let the company establish a fortified outpost at the fishing port of Calcutta. A new nawab, pressing claims

sepoy (SEE-poy)

for additional tribute from the prospering port, overran the fort in 1756 and imprisoned a group of EIC men in a cell so small that many died of suffocation. To avenge their deaths in this "Black Hole of Calcutta," a large EIC force from Madras, led by the young Robert Clive, overthrew the nawab. The weak Mughal emperor was persuaded to acknowledge the East India Company's right to rule Bengal in 1765. Fed by the tax revenues of Bengal as well as by profits from trade, the EIC was on its way. Calcutta grew into a city of 250,000 by 1788.

In southern India, Clive had used EIC forces from Madras to secure victory for the British Indian candidate for nawab of Arcot during the Seven Years War (1756–1763), thereby gaining an advantage over French traders who had supported the loser. The defeat of Tipu Sultan of Mysore at the end of the century (described at the start of the chapter) secured south India for the company and prevented a French resurgence.

Along with Calcutta and Madras, the third major center of British power in India was Bombay, on the western coast. There, after a long series of contests with the Maratha Confederation rulers, the East India Company gained a decisive advantage in 1818, annexing large territories to form the core of what was called the "Bombay Presidency." Some states were taken over completely, as Bengal had been, but very many others remained in the hands of local princes who accepted the political control of the company.

The Raj and the Rebellion, 1818–1857

In 1818 the East India Company controlled an Empire with more people than in all of western Europe and fifty times the population of the colonies the British had lost in North America. One thrust of **British raj** (reign) was to remake India on a British model through administrative and social reform, economic development, and the introduction of new technology. But at the same time the company men—like the Mughals before them—had to temper their interference with Indian social and religious customs lest they provoke rebellion or lose the support of their Indian princely allies. For this reason and because of the complexity of the task of ruling such a vast empire, there were many inconsistencies in Britain's policies toward India.

The main policy was to create a powerful and efficient system of government. British rule before 1850 relied heavily on military power—170 sepoy regiments and 16 European regiments. Another policy very much in the interests of India's new rulers was to disarm approximately 2 million warriors who had served India's many states and turn them to civilian tasks, mostly cultivation. A third policy was to give freer rein to Christian missionaries eager to convert and uplift India's masses. Few converts were made, but the missionaries kept up steady pressure for social reforms.

Another key British policy was to substitute ownership of private property for India's complex and overlapping patterns of landholding. In Bengal this reform worked to the advantage of large landowners, but in Mysore the peasantry gained. Private ownership made it easier for the state to collect the taxes that were needed to pay for the costs of administration, the army, and economic reform.

Such policies of "westernization, Anglicization, and modernization," as they have been called, were only one side of British rule. The other side was the bolstering of "traditions"—both real and newly invented. In the name of tradition the Indian princes who ruled nearly half of British India were frequently endowed by their British overlords with greater power and splendor and longer tenure than their predecessors had ever had. Hindu and Muslim holy men were able to expand their "traditional" power over property and people far beyond what had ever been the case in earlier times. Princes, holy men, and other Indians frequently used claims of tradition to resist British rule as well as to turn it to their advantage. The British rulers themselves invented many "traditions"—including elaborate parades and displays—half borrowed from European royal pomp, half freely improvised from Mughal ceremonies (see Society and Culture: Ceremonials of Imperial Domination).

The British and Indian elites danced sometimes in close partnership, sometimes in apparent opposition. But the ordinary people of India suffered. Women of every status, members of subordinate Hindu castes, the "untouchables" and "tribals" outside the caste system, and the poor generally found less benefit in the British reforms and much new oppression in the taxes and "traditions" that exalted their superiors' status.

The transformation of British India's economy was also doubled-edged. On the one hand, British raj created many new jobs as a result of the growth of internal and external trade and the expansion of agricultural production, such as in opium in Bengal—largely for export to China (see Chapter 27)—coffee in Ceylon (an island off the tip of India), and tea in Assam (a state in northeastern India). On the other hand, competition from cheap cotton goods produced in Britain's industrial mills drove many Indians out of the handicraft textile industry. In the eighteenth century India had been the world's greatest exporter of cotton textiles; in the nineteenth century India increasingly shipped raw cotton fiber to Britain.

Ceremonials of Imperial Domination

These excerpts from a letter written to Queen Victoria by the viceroy of India, Lord Lytton, describe the elaborate ceremonies the colony staged in 1876 in anticipation of her being named "Empress of India" and the effects they had on the Indian princes who governed many parts of India. Although British India's power still rested on the threat of military force, its leaders grew increasingly skilled at using symbolic displays of authority and material rewards to win the support of Indian allies.

The day before yesterday (December 23), I arrived, with Lady Lytton and all my staff at Delhi. . . . I was received at the [railroad] station by all the native chiefs and princes, and, . . . after shaking hands . . . , I immediately mounted my elephant, accompanied by Lady Lytton, our two little girls following us on another elephant. The procession through Delhi to the camp . . . lasted upwards of three hours. . . . The streets were lined for many miles with troops; those of the native princes being brigaded with those of your Majesty. The crowd along the way, behind the troops, was dense, and apparently enthusiastic; the windows, walls, and housetops being thronged with natives, who salaamed, and Europeans, who cheered as we passed along. . . .

My reception by the native princes at the station was most cordial. The Maharaja of Jeypore (who has lighted the Viceroy's camp with gas of his own manufacture) informed Sir John Strachey that India had never seen such a gathering as this, in which not only all the great native princes (many of whom have never met before), but also chiefs and envoys from Khelat, Burmah, Siam, and the remotest parts of the East, are assembled to do homage to your Majesty. . . .

On Tuesday (December 26) from 10 A.M. till past 7 P.M., I was, without a moment's intermission, occupied in receiving visits from native chiefs, and bestowing on those entitled to them the banners, medals, and other honours given by your Majesty. The durbar, which lasted all day and long after dark, was most successful. . . . Your Majesty's portrait, which was placed over the Viceregal throne in the great durbar tent, was thought by all to be an excellent likeness of your Majesty. The native chiefs examined it with special interest.

On Wednesday, the 27th, I received visits from native chiefs, as before, from 10 A.M. til 1 P.M., and from 1:30 P.M. to 7:30 P.M., was passed in returning visits. I forgot to mention

that on Tuesday and Wednesday evenings I gave great State dinners to the Governors of Bombay and Madras. Every subsequent evening of my stay at Delhi was similarly occupied by state banquets and receptions [for officials, foreign dignitaries, and] many distinguished natives. After dinner on Thursday, I held a levee [reception], which lasted till one o'clock at night, and is said to have been attended by 2,500 persons—the largest, I believe, ever held by any Viceroy or Governor-General in India.

. . . your Majesty will, perhaps, allow me to mention, in connection with [the ruler of Kashmir], one little circumstance which appears to me very illustrative of the effect which the assemblage has had on him and others. In the first interviews which took place months ago between myself and Kashmir, . . . I noticed that, though perfectly courteous, he was extremely mistrustful of the British Government and myself. . . . On the day following the Imperial assemblage, I had another private interview with Kashmir for the settlement of some further details. His whole manner and language on this last occasion were strikingly different. [He said:] "I am now convinced that you mean nothing that is not for the good of me and mine. Our interests are identical with those of the empire. Give me your orders and they shall be obeyed."

What is significant about the fact that Lord Lytton and his family arrived in Delhi by train and then chose to move through the city on elephants? What impression did the viceroy intend to create in the minds of the Indian dignitaries by assembling so many of them together and bestowing banners, medals, and honors on them? What might account for the Indian ruler of Kashmir's remarkable change of attitude toward the viceroy and the empire? How differently might a member of the Indian middle class or an unemployed weaver have reacted?

Source: Lady Betty Balfour, *The History of Lord Lytton's Indian Administration, 1876 to 1880* (London: Longmans, Green, and Co., 1899), 116–121, 132.

Even the beneficial economic changes introduced under Britain rule were disruptive, and there were no safety nets for the needy. Thus local rebellions by displaced ruling elites, disgruntled religious traditionalists, and the economically dispossessed were almost constant during the first half of the nineteenth century. Officials' greatest concern was over the continuing loyalty of Indian sepoys in the East India Company's army. Their numbers had increased to 200,000 in 1857, along with 38,000 British officers. Armed with the latest rifles and disciplined in fighting methods, the sepoys had a potential for successful rebellion that other groups lacked.

In fact, discontent was growing among Indian soldiers. In the early decades of EIC rule, most sepoys came from Bengal, one of the first states the company had annexed. The Bengali sepoys resented the active recruitment of other ethnic groups into the army after 1848, such as Sikhs° from Punjab and Gurkhas from Nepal. Many high-caste Hindus objected to a new law in 1856 requiring new recruits to be available for service overseas in the growing Indian Ocean empire, for their religion prohibited ocean travel. The replacement of the standard military musket by the far more accurate Enfield rifle in 1857 also caused problems. Soldiers were ordered to use their teeth to tear open the ammunition cartridges, which were greased with animal fat. Hindus were offended by this order if the fat came from cattle, which they considered sacred. Muslims were offended if the fat came from pigs, which they considered unclean.

Although the cartridge-opening procedure was quickly changed, the initial discontent grew into rebellion by Hindu sepoys in May 1857. British troubles mushroomed when Muslim sepoys, peasants, and discontented elites joined in. The rebels asserted old traditions to challenge British authority: sepoy officers in Delhi proclaimed their loyalty to the Mughal emperor; others rallied behind the Maratha leader Nana Sahib. The rebellion was put down by March 1858, but it shook this piecemeal empire to its core.

Historians have attached different names and meanings to the events of 1857 and 1858. Concentrating on the technical fact that the uprising was an unlawful action by soldiers, nineteenth-century British historians labeled it the **"Sepoy Rebellion"** or the "Mutiny," and these names are still commonly used. Seeing in these events the beginnings of the later movement for independence, some modern Indian historians have termed it the "Revolution of 1857." In reality, it was much more than a simple mutiny, because it involved more than soldiers, but it was not yet a nationalist revolution, for the rebels' sense of a common Indian national identity was weak.

Sikh (seek)

Political Reform and Industrial Impact, 1858–1900

Whatever it is called, the rebellion of 1857–1858 was a turning point in the history of modern India. Some say it marks the beginning of modern India. In its wake Indians gained a new centralized government, entered a period of rapid economic growth, and began to develop a new national consciousness.

The changes in government were immediate. In 1858 Britain eliminated the last traces of Mughal and Company rule. In their place, a new secretary of state for India in London oversaw Indian policy, and a new government-general in Delhi acted as the British monarch's viceroy on the spot. A proclamation by Queen Victoria in November 1858 guaranteed all Indians equal protection of the law and the freedom to practice their religions and social customs; it also assured Indian princes that so long as they were loyal to the queen British India would respect their control of territories and "their rights, dignity and honour."[4]

British rule continued to emphasize both tradition and reform after 1857. At the top, the British viceroys lived in enormous palaces amid hundreds of servants and gaudy displays of luxury meant to convince Indians that the British viceroys were legitimate successors to the Mughal emperors. They treated the quasi-independent Indian princes with elaborate ceremonial courtesy and maintained them in splendor. When Queen Victoria was proclaimed "Empress of India" in 1877 and periodically thereafter, the viceroys put on great pageants known as **durbars.** The most elaborate of all was the durbar at Delhi in 1902 to celebrate the coronation of King Edward VII, at which Viceroy Lord Curzon honored himself with a 101-gun salute and a parade of 34,000 troops in front of 50 princes and 173,000 lesser visitors.

Behind the pomp and glitter, a powerful and efficient bureaucracy controlled the Indian masses. Members of the elite **Indian Civil Service** (ICS), mostly graduates of Oxford and Cambridge Universities, held the senior administrative and judicial posts. Numbering only a thousand at the end of the nineteenth century, these men visited the villages in their districts, heard lawsuits and complaints, and passed judgments. Beneath them were a far greater number of Indian officials and employees. Recruitment into the ICS was by open examinations. In theory any British subject could take these exams. But they were given in England, so in practice the system worked to exclude Indians. In 1870 only one Indian was a member of the ICS. Subsequent reforms by Viceroy Lord Lytton led to fifty-seven Indian appointments by 1887, but there the process stalled.

The key reason blocking qualified Indians' entry into the upper administration of their country was the racist contempt most British officials felt for the people they ruled. When he became commander-in-chief of the Indian army in 1892, Lord Kitchener declared:

> It is this consciousness of the inherent superiority of the European which had won for us India. However well educated and clever a native may be, and however brave he may have proved himself, I believe that no rank we can bestow on him would cause him to be considered an equal of the British officer.

A second transformation of India after 1857 resulted from involvement with industrial Britain. The government invested millions of pounds sterling in harbors, cities, irrigation canals, and other public works. British interests felled forests to make way for tea plantations, persuaded Indian farmers to grow cotton and jute for export, and created great irrigation systems to alleviate the famines that periodically decimated whole provinces. As a result, India's trade expanded rapidly.

Most of the exports were agricultural commodities for processing elsewhere: cotton fiber, opium, tea, silk, and sugar. In return India imported manufactured goods from Britain, including the flood of machine-made cotton textiles that severely undercut Indian hand-loom weavers. The effects on individual Indians varied enormously. Some women found new jobs, though at very low pay, on plantations or in the growing cities, where prostitution flourished. Others struggled to hold families together or ran away from abusive husbands. Everywhere in India poverty remained the norm.

The Indian government also promoted the introduction of new technologies into India not long after their appearance in Britain. Earlier in the century there were steamboats on the rivers and a massive program of canal building for irrigation. Beginning in the 1840s, a railroad boom (paid for out of government revenues) gave India its first national transportation network, followed shortly by telegraph lines. Indeed, in 1870 India had the greatest rail network in Asia and the fifth largest in the world. Originally designed to serve British commerce, the railroads were owned by British companies, constructed with British rails and equipment, and paid dividends to British investors. Ninety-nine percent of the railroad employees were Indians, but Europeans occupied all the top positions—"like a thin film of oil on top of a glass of water, resting upon but hardly mixing with [those] below," as one official report put it.

Although some Indians opposed the railroads at first because the trains mixed people of different castes, faiths, and sexes, the Indian people took to rail travel with great enthusiasm. Indians rode trains on business,

on pilgrimage, and in search of work. In 1870 over 18 million passengers traveled along the network's 4,775 miles (7,685 kilometers) of track, and more than a half-million messages were sent up and down the 14,000 miles (22,500 kilometers) of telegraph wire. By 1900 India's trains were carrying 188 million passengers a year.

But the freer movement of Indian pilgrims and the flood of poor Indians into the cities also promoted the spread of cholera°, a disease transmitted through water contaminated by human feces. Cholera deaths rose rapidly during the nineteenth century, and eventually the disease spread to Europe. In many Indian minds *kala mari* ("the black death") was a divine punishment for failing to prevent the British takeover. This chastisement also fell heavily on British residents, who died in large numbers. In 1867 officials demonstrated the close connection between cholera and pilgrims who bathed in and drank from sacred pools and rivers. The installation of a new sewerage system (1865) and a filtered water supply (1869) in Calcutta dramatically reduced cholera deaths there. Similar measures in Bombay and Madras also led to great reductions, but most Indians lived in small villages where famine and lack of sanitation kept cholera deaths high. In 1900 an extraordinary four out of every thousand residents of British India died of cholera. Sanitary improvements lowered the rate later in the twentieth century.

Rising Indian Nationalism, 1828–1900

Ironically, both the successes and the failures of British India stimulated the development of Indian nationalism. Stung by the inability of the rebellion of 1857 to overthrow British rule, some thoughtful Indians began to argue that the only way for Indians to regain control of their destiny was to reduce their country's social and ethnic divisions and promote Pan-Indian nationalism.

Individuals such as Rammohun Roy (1772–1833) had promoted development along these lines a generation earlier. A Western-educated Bengali from a Brahmin family, Roy was a successful administrator for the British East India Company and a thoughtful student of comparative religion. His Brahmo Samaj° (Divine Society), founded in 1828, attracted Indians who sought to reconcile the values they found in the West with the ancient religious traditions of India. They supported efforts to reform some Hindu customs, including the restrictions on widows and the practice of child marriage. They

cholera (KAHL-uhr-uh)   Bramo Samaj (BRAH-moh suh-MAHJ)

advocated reforming the caste system, encouraged a monotheistic form of Hinduism, and urged a return to the founding principles found in the Upanishads, ancient sacred writings of Hinduism.

Roy and his supporters had backed earlier British efforts to reform or ban some practices they found repugnant. Widow burning (*sati*°) was outlawed in 1829 and slavery in 1843. Reformers sought to correct other abuses of women: prohibitions against widows remarrying were revoked in 1856, and female infanticide was made a crime in 1870.

Although Brahmo Samaj remained an influential movement after the rebellion of 1857, many Indian intellectuals turned to Western secular values and nationalism as the way to reclaim India for its people. In this process the spread of Western education played an important role. Roy had studied both Indian and Western subjects, mastering ten languages in the process, and helped found the Hindu College in Calcutta in 1816. Other Western-curriculum schools quickly followed, including Bethune College in Calcutta, the first secular school for Indian women, in 1849. European and American missionaries played a prominent role in the spread of Western education. In 1870 there were 790,000 Indians in over 24,000 elementary and secondary schools, and India's three universities (established in 1857) awarded 345 degrees. Graduates of these schools articulated a new Pan-Indian nationalism that transcended regional and religious differences.

Many of the new nationalists came from the Indian middle class, which had prospered from the increase of trade and manufacturing. Such educated and ambitious people were angered by the obstacles that British rules and prejudices put in the way of their advancement. Hoping to increase their influence and improve their employment opportunities in the Indian government, they convened the first **Indian National Congress** in 1885. The members sought a larger role for Indians in the Civil Service. They also called for reductions in military expenditures, which consumed 40 percent of the government's budget, so that more could be spent on alleviating the poverty of the Indian masses. The Indian National Congress promoted unity among the country's many religions and social groups, but most early members were upper-caste Western-educated Hindus and Parsis (members of a Zoroastrian religious sect descended from Persians). The Congress effectively voiced the opinions of elite Indians, but until it attracted the support of the masses, it could not hope to challenge British rule.

BRITAIN'S EASTERN EMPIRE

In 1750 Britain's empire was centered on slave-based plantation and settler colonies in the Americas. A century later its main focus was on commercial networks and colonies in the East. In 1750 the French and Dutch were also serious contenders for global dominion. A century later they had been eclipsed by the British colossus straddling the world. Several distinct changes facilitated this expansion and transformation of Britain's overseas empire: a string of military victories pushed aside other rivals for overseas trade and colonies; new policies favored free trade over mercantilism; and changes in shipbuilding techniques increased the speed and volume of maritime commerce. Linked to these changes were new European settlements in southern Africa, Australia, and New Zealand and the growth of a new long-distance trade in indentured labor.

Colonial Rivalries and Trading Networks

As the story of Tipu Sultan told at the beginning of this chapter illustrates, France was still a serious rival to Britain for dominion in the Indian Ocean at the end of the eighteenth century. However, France's defeats in the wars of French Revolution (see Chapter 23) ended Napoleon's dream of restoring French dominance overseas. The wars also dismantled much of the Netherlands' Indian Ocean empire. When French armies occupied the Netherlands, the Dutch ruler, who had fled to Britain in January 1795, authorized the British to take over Dutch possessions overseas, to keep them out of French hands. During 1795 and 1796 British forces quickly occupied the Cape Colony at the tip of southern Africa, the strategic Dutch port of Malacca on the strait between the Indian Ocean and the South China Sea, and the island of Ceylon (see Map 26.3).

Then the British occupied Dutch Guiana° and Trinidad in the southern Caribbean. In 1811 they even seized the island of Java, the center of the Netherlands' East Indian empire. British forces had also attacked French possessions, gaining control of the islands of Mauritius° and Réunion in the southwestern Indian Ocean. At the end of the Napoleonic Wars in 1814, Britain returned Java to the Dutch and Réunion to the French but kept the Cape Colony, British Guiana (once

---

sati (suh-TEE)

Guiana (ghee-AH-nuh)   **Mauritius** (moh-RIH-uhs)

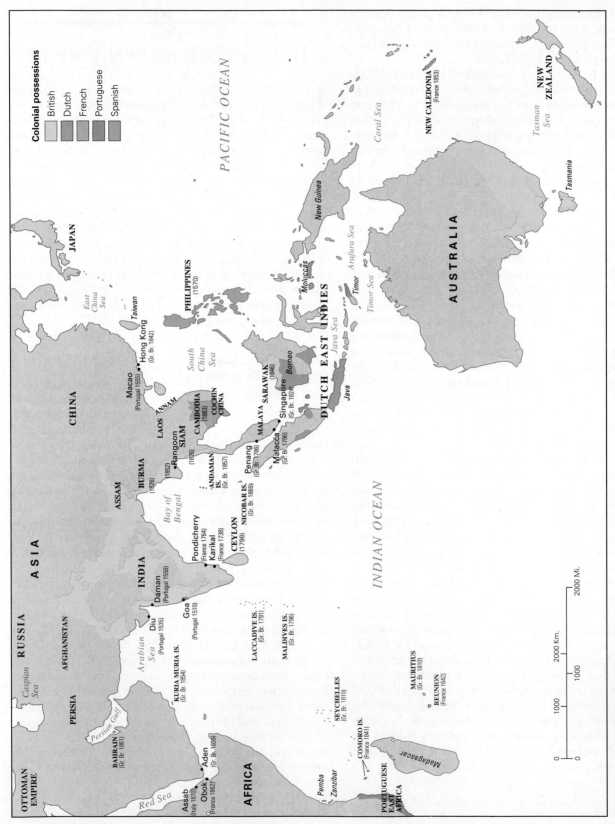

Map 26.3 European Possessions in the Indian Ocean and South Pacific, 1870 After 1750, French and British competition for new territories generally expanded the European presence established earlier by the Portuguese, Spanish, and Dutch. By 1870 the British controlled much of India, were settling Australia and New Zealand, and possessed important trading enclaves throughout the region.

part of Dutch Guiana), Trinidad, Ceylon, Malacca, and Mauritius.

The Cape Colony was valuable because of Cape Town's strategic importance as a supply station for ships making the long voyages between Britain and India. With the port city came some twenty thousand descendants of earlier Dutch and French settlers who occupied far-flung farms and ranches in its hinterland. Despite their European origins, these people thought of themselves as permanent residents of Africa and were beginning to refer to themselves as "Afrikaners°" ("Africans" in their dialect of Dutch). British governors prohibited any expansion of the white settler frontier because such expansion invariably led to wars with indigenous Africans. This decision, along with the imposition of laws protecting African rights within Cape Colony (including the emancipation of slaves in 1834), alienated many Afrikaners.

Between 1836 and 1839, parties of Afrikaners embarked on a "Great Trek," leaving British-ruled Cape Colony for the fertile high *veld* (plateau) to the north that two decades of Zulu wars had depopulated. The Great Trek led to the foundation of three new settler colonies in southern Africa by 1850: the Afrikaners' Orange Free State and Transvaal on the high veld and the British colony of Natal on the Indian Ocean coast. Although firearms enabled the settlers to win some important battles against the Zulu and other Africans, they were still a tiny minority surrounded by the populous and powerful independent African kingdoms that had grown up at the beginning of the century. A few thousand British settlers came to Natal and the Cape Colony by midcentury, but these colonies' strategic importance to Britain was only as stopovers for shipping between Britain and British India.

Meanwhile, another strategic British outpost was being established in Southeast Asia. One prong of the advance was led by Thomas Stamford Raffles, who had governed Java during the period of British occupation from 1811 to 1814. After Java's return to the Dutch, Raffles helped the British East India Company establish a new free port at Singapore in 1824, on the site of a small Malay fishing village with a superb harbor. By attracting British merchants and Chinese businessmen and laborers, Singapore soon became the center of trade and shipping between the Indian Ocean and China. Along with Malacca and other possessions on the strait, Singapore formed the "Straits Settlements," which British India administered until 1867.

Further British expansion in Malaya (now Malaysia) did not occur until after 1874, but in neighboring Burma

Afrikaner (af-rih-KAHN-uhr)

Great Trek Aided by African Servants   The ox-drawn wagons of the Afrikaners struggled over the Drakensberg Mountains to the high plains in an effort to escape British control.   (Hulton Getty/Liaison)

it came more quickly. Burma had emerged as a powerful kingdom by 1750, with plans for expansion. In 1785 Burma tried to annex neighboring territories of Siam (now Thailand) to the east, but a coalition of Thai leaders thwarted Burmese advances by 1802. Burma next attacked Assam to the west, but this action led to war with British India, which was concerned for the security of its own frontier with Assam. After a two-year war, India annexed Assam in 1826 and occupied two coastal provinces of northern Burma. As rice and timber trade from these provinces grew important, the occupation became permanent, and in 1852 British India annexed the port of Rangoon and the rest of coastal Burma.

Imperial Policies and Shipping

Through such piecemeal acquisitions, by 1870 Britain had added several dozen colonies to the twenty-six colonies it had in 1792, after the loss of the thirteen in North America (see Chapter 23). Nevertheless, historians usually portray Britain in this period as a reluctant empire builder, its leaders unwilling to acquire new outposts that could prove difficult and expensive to administer. This apparent contradiction is resolved when one recognizes that the underlying goal of most British imperial expansion during these decades was trade rather than territory. Most of the new colonies were meant to serve as ports in the growing network of shipping that encircled the globe or as centers of production and distribution for those networks.

This new commercial expansion was closely tied to the needs of Britain's growing industrial economy and reflected a new philosophy of overseas trade. Rather than rebuilding the closed, mercantilist network of trade with its colonies, Britain sought to trade freely with all parts of the world. Free trade was also a wise policy in light of the independence of so many former colonies in the Americas (see Chapter 25).

Whether colonized or not, more and more African, Asian, and Pacific lands were being drawn into the commercial networks created by British expansion and industrialization. As was pointed out earlier, uncolonized parts of West Asia became major exporters to Britain of vegetable oils for industrial and domestic use and forest products for dyes and construction, while areas of eastern Africa free of European control exported ivory that ended up as piano keys and decorations for the elegant homes of the industrial middle class. From the far corners of the world came coffee, cocoa, and tea for the tables of the new industrial classes in Britain and other parts of Europe (along with sugar to sweeten these beverages), and indigo dyes and cotton fibers for their expanding textile factories.

In return, the factories of the industrialized nations supplied manufactured goods at very attractive prices. By the mid-nineteenth century a major part of their textile production was destined for overseas markets. Sales of cotton cloth to Africa increased 950 percent from the 1820s to the 1860s. British trade to India grew 350 percent between 1841 and 1870 while India's exports increased 400 percent. Trade with other regions also expanded rapidly. In most cases such trade benefited both sides, but there is no question that the industrial nations were the dominant partners.

A second impetus to global commercial expansion was the technological revolution in the construction of oceangoing ships under way in the nineteenth century. The middle decades of the century were the golden age of the sailing ship. Using iron to fasten timbers together permitted shipbuilders to construct much larger vessels. Merchant ships in the eighteenth century rarely exceeded 300 tons, but after 1850 swift American-built **clipper ships** of 2,000 tons were commonplace in the British merchant fleet. Huge canvas sails hung from tall masts made the streamlined clippers faster than earlier vessels. Ships from the East Indies or India had taken six months to reach Europe in the seventeenth century; after 1850 the new ships could complete the voyage in half that time.

This increase in size and speed lowered shipping costs and further stimulated maritime trade. The growth in size and numbers of ships increased by the tonnage of British merchant shipping by 400 percent between 1778 and 1860. To extend the life of such ships in tropical lands, clippers intended for Eastern service generally were built of teak and other tropical hardwoods from new British colonies in South and Southeast Asia. Although tropical forests began to be cleared for rice and sugar plantations as well as for timbers, the effects on the environment and people of Southeast Asia came primarily after 1870.

Colonization of Australia and New Zealand

The development of new ships and shipping contributed to a third form of British rule in the once-remote South Pacific. In contrast to the rule over an indigenous population in India or the commercial empire overseen from Singapore and Cape Town, in the new British colonies of Australia and New Zealand British settlers displaced indigenous populations, just as they had done in North America.

Portuguese mariners had sighted the continent of Australia in the early seventeenth century, but its remoteness made the land of little interest to Europeans. However, after the English adventurer Captain James Cook made the first systematic European exploration of New Zealand and the fertile eastern coast of Australia between 1769 and 1778, expanding shipping networks brought in growing numbers of visitors and settlers.

At the time of Cook's visits Australia was the home of about 650,000 hunting and gathering people, whose Melanesian° ancestors had settled there some 40,000 years earlier. The two islands of New Zealand, lying 1,000 miles (1,600 kilometers) southeast of Australia, were inhabited by about 250,000 Maori°, who practiced hunting, fishing, and simple forms of agriculture, which their Polynesian ancestors had introduced around 1200 C.E. Because of their long isolation from the rest of humanity, the populations of Australia and New Zealand were as vulnerable as the Amerindians had been to unfamiliar

---

Melanesian (mel-uh-NEE-zhuhn)
Maori (MOW-ree [*ow* as in *cow*])

diseases introduced by new overseas contacts. By the late nineteenth century only 93,000 aboriginal Australians and 42,000 Maori survived. By then they were outnumbered and dominated by British settler populations.

The first permanent British settlers in Australia were 736 convicts, of whom 188 were women, sent into exile from British prisons in 1788. For the next few decades Australian penal colonies grew slowly and had only slight contact with the indigenous population, whom the British called "Aborigines." However, the discovery of gold in 1851 brought a flood of free European settlers (and some Chinese) and hastened the end of the penal colonies. After 1850 tens of thousands of British settlers received government-subsidized passages "down under" on the improved sailing ships of that era, although the voyage still took more than three months. By 1860 the settler population had reached 1 million, and it doubled over the next fifteen years.

British settlers were drawn more slowly to New Zealand. Some of the first were temporary residents along the coast who slaughtered seals and exported seal pelts to Western countries to be made into men's felt hats. A single ship in 1806 took away sixty thousand sealskins. By the early 1820s overhunting had nearly exterminated the seal population. Sperm whales were also hunted extensively near New Zealand for their oil, used for lubrication, soap, and lamps; ambergris°, an ingredient in perfume; and bone, used in women's corsets (see Environment and Technology: Whaling). Military action that overcame Maori resistance, a brief gold rush, and the availability of faster ships and subsidized passages attracted more British immigrants after 1860. The colony especially courted women immigrants to offset the preponderance of single men. By the early 1880s, fertile agricultural lands of this farthest frontier of the British Empire had a settler population of 500,000.

The model that in 1867 had formed the giant Dominion of Canada out of the very diverse and thinly settled colonies of British North America was applied to the newer colonies in Australia and New Zealand. In 1901 Australia emerged from the federation of six separate colonies. New Zealand became a separate colony in 1840 and a self-governing dominion in 1907.

Britain's policies toward its settler colonies in Canada and the South Pacific were shaped by a desire to avoid the conflicts that had led to the American Revolution in the eighteenth century. By gradually turning over governing power to the colonies' inhabitants, Britain accomplished three things. It satisfied the settlers' desire

ambergris (AM-ber-grees)

British Proclamation to the Australian Aborigines, ca. 1830 Affixed to trees in rural areas, this poster was intended to convey to the indigenous population the message that the European settlers wanted to be their friends and the settler government would punish murders of either race with equal severity. The poster failed to produce mutual trust.   (Tasmanian Museum & Art Gallery)

for greater control over their own territories, it muted demands for independence, and it made the colonial governments responsible for most of their own expenses. Indigenous peoples were outvoted by the settlers or even excluded from voting. An 1897 Australian law segregated the remaining Aborigines onto reservations, where they lacked the rights of Australian citizenship. The requirement that voters had to be able to read and write English kept Maori from voting in early New Zealand elections, but four seats in the lower house of the legislature were reserved for Maori from 1867.

ENVIRONMENT + TECHNOLOGY

Whaling

The rapid expansion of whaling aptly illustrates the growing power of technology over nature in this period. Many contemporaries, like many people today, were sickened by the killing of the planet's largest living mammals. American novelist Herman Melville captured the conflicting sentiments in his epic whaling story, *Moby Dick* (1851). One of his characters enthusiastically explains why the grisly and dangerous business existed:

> But, though the world scorns us as whale hunters, yet does it unwittingly pay us the profoundest homage; yea, an all abounding adoration! for almost all the tapers, lamps, and candles that burn around the globe, burn, as before so many shrines, to our glory!

Melville's character overstates the degree to which whale oil dominated illumination and does not mention its many other industrial uses. Neither does he describe the commercial importance of whalebone (baleen). For a time its use in corsets allowed fashionable women to achieve the hourglass shape that fashion dictated. Whalebone's use for umbrella stays, carriage springs, fishing rods, suitcase frames, combs, brushes, and many other items made it the plastic of its day.

New manufacturing technologies went hand in hand with new hunting technologies. The revolution in ship design enabled whalers from Europe and North America to extend the hunt into the southern oceans off New Zealand. By the nineteenth century whaling ships were armed with guns that shot a steel harpoon armed with vicious barbs deep into the whale. In the 1840s explosive charges on harpoon heads ensured the whale's immediate death. Yet, as this engraving of an expedition off New Zealand shows, flinging small harpoons from rowboats in the open sea continued to be part of the dangerous work.

Another century of extensive hunting devastated many whale species before international agreements finally limited the killing of these giant sea creatures.

South Pacific Whaling   One boat was swamped, but the hunters killed the huge whale.   (The Granger Collection, New York)

Asian Laborers in British Guiana The manager of the sugar estate reposes on the near end of the gallery of his house with the proprietor's attorney. At the other end of the gallery European overseers review the plantation's record books. In the yard, cups of lifeblood are being drained from bound Chinese and Indian laborers. This allegorical drawing by a Chinese laborer represents the exploitation of Asian laborers by Europeans. (Boston Athenaeum)

In other ways the new settler colonies were more progressive. Australia developed very powerful trade unions, which improved the welfare of skilled and semi-skilled urban white male workers, promoted democratic values, and exercised considerable political clout. In New Zealand, where sheep raising was the main occupation, populist and progressive sentiments promoted the availability of land for the common person. Australia and New Zealand were also among the first states in the world to grant women the right to vote, beginning in 1894.

New Labor Migrations

Europeans were not the only people to transplant themselves overseas in the mid-nineteenth century. Between 1834 and 1870 large numbers of Indians, Chinese, and Africans responded to labor recruiters, especially to work overseas on sugar plantations. In the half-century after 1870 tens of thousands of Asians and Pacific Islanders made similar voyages. The scale of such population movements and fact that many of these migrants traveled halfway around the world show the capacities of the new sailing ships. The power and interdependence of the British Empire are revealed in the fact that British India was the greatest source of such laborers and other British colonies were their principal destinations.

After Britain's emancipation of slaves in 1834, the freed Africans were no longer willing to work the long hours they had been forced to work as slaves. When given full freedom of movement in 1839, many men and women left the plantations. British colonies had to find other laborers if they were to compete successfully with sugar plantations in Cuba, Brazil, and the French Caribbean that were still using slave labor.

India's impoverished people seemed one obvious alternative. After planters on Mauritius successfully introduced Indian laborers, the Indian labor trade was extended to the British Caribbean in 1838. Free Africans were another possibility. In 1841, the British government allowed Caribbean planters to recruit Africans whom British patrols had rescued from slave ships and brought to liberation depots in Sierra Leone and elsewhere. By 1870, over a half-million Indians had left their homes for Mauritius or the British Caribbean along with nearly 40,000 Africans and over 18,000 Chinese for the British Caribbean colonies. After the French abolished slavery in 1848, their colonies also recruited 19,000 laborers from Africa and nearly 80,000 from India. Also ending slavery in 1848, Dutch Guiana recruited 57,000 new Asian workers for its plantations.

Although African slave labor was not abolished in Cuba until 1886, the rising cost of slaves led the burgeoning sugar plantations to recruit 138,000 new laborers from China between 1847 and 1873. Such labor recruitment also became the mainstay of new sugar plantations in places that had never known slave labor: after 1850 American planters in Hawaii recruited labor from China and Japan; British planters in Natal recruited from India; and those in Queensland (in northeastern Australia) relied on laborers from neighboring South Pacific islands.

Larger, faster ships made transporting laborers halfway around the world affordable, though voyages from Asia to the Caribbean still took an average of three months. Despite close regulation and supervision of shipboard conditions, the crowded accommodations on the long voyages encouraged the spread of cholera and other contagious diseases that took many migrants' lives.

All of these laborers served under **contracts of indenture,** which bound them to work for a specified period (usually from five to seven years) in return for free passage to their overseas destination. They were also paid a small salary and were provided with housing, clothing, and medical care. Indian indentured laborers also received the right to a free passage home if they worked a second five-year contract. British Caribbean colonies required that forty women be recruited for every hundred men as a way to promote family life. So many Indians chose to stay on in Mauritius, Trinidad, British Guiana, and Fiji that they constituted a third or more of the total population of these colonies by the early twentieth century.

Although many early recruits from China and the Pacific Islands were kidnapped or otherwise coerced into leaving their homes, in most cases the new indentured migrants had much in common with contemporary emigrants from Europe (described in Chapter 24). Both groups chose to leave their homelands in hopes of improving their economic and social conditions. Both earned modest salaries. Many saved to bring money back with them when they returned home, or they used their earnings to buy land or to start a business in their new countries, where large numbers chose to remain. One major difference was that people recruited as indentured laborers were generally so much poorer than emigrants from Europe that they had to accept lower-paying jobs in less desirable areas because they could not pay their own way. However, it is also true that many European immigrants into distant places like Australia and New Zealand had their passages subsidized but did

not have to sign a contract of indenture. This shows that racial and cultural preferences, not just economics, shaped the flow of labor into European colonies.

A person's decision to accept an indentured labor contract could also be shaped by political circumstances. In India, disruption brought by British colonial policies and the suppression of the 1857 rebellion contributed significantly to people's desire to emigrate. Poverty, famine, and warfare had not been strangers in precolonial India. Nor were these causes of emigration absent in China and Japan (see Chapter 27).

Not simply the creation of Western imperialism, the indentured labor trade both allured and repelled the Asians and Africans. The commercial and industrial expansion of the West created an unequal relationship but not an entirely one-sided one. Most men and women who signed indentured contracts were trying to improve their lives by emigrating, and many succeeded in manipulating the system to their own advantage. Whether for good or ill, more and more of the world's peoples saw their lives being influenced by the existence of Western colonies, Western ships, and Western markets.

CONCLUSION

What is the global significance of these complex political and economic changes in southern Asia, Africa, and the South Pacific? One perspective stresses the continuing exploitation of the weak by the strong, of African, Asian, and Pacific peoples by aggressive Europeans. In this view, the emergence of Britain as a dominant power in the Indian Ocean basin and South Pacific continues the European expansion that the Portuguese and the Spanish pioneered and the Dutch continued. Likewise, Britain's control over the densely populated lands of South and Southeast Asia and over the less populated lands of Australia and New Zealand can be seen as a continuation of the conquest and colonization of the Americas.

From another perspective what was most important about this period was not the political and military strength of the Europeans but their growing dominance of the world's commerce, especially through long-distance ocean shipping. In this view, like other Europeans, the British were drawn to Africa and southern Asia by a desire to obtain new materials.

Britain's commercial expansion in the nineteenth century, however, was increasingly the product of

Easterners' demand for industrial manufactures. The growing exchanges could be mutually beneficial. African and Asian consumers found industrially produced goods far cheaper and sometimes better than the handicrafts they replaced or supplemented. Industrialization created new markets for African and Asian goods, as in the case of the vegetable-oil trade in West Africa or cotton in Egypt and India. There also was a negative impact, in the case of the weavers of India and the damage to species of seals and whales.

The emphasis on Europeans' military and commercial strength did not mean that African, Asian, and Pacific peoples were reduced to appendages of Europe. The balance of power was shifting in the Europeans' favor between 1750 and 1870, but local cultures were still vibrant and local initiatives often dominant. Islamic reform movements and the rise of the Zulu nation had greater significance for their respective regions of Africa than did Western forces. Despite some ominous concessions to European power, Southeast Asians were still largely in control of their own destinies. Even in India, most people's lives and beliefs showed more continuity with the past than the change due to British rule.

Finally, it must not be imagined that Asians and Africans were powerless in dealing with European expansion. The Indian princes who extracted concessions from the British in return for their cooperation and the Indians who rebelled against the raj both forced the system to accommodate their needs. Moreover, some Asians and Africans were beginning to use European education, technology, and methods to transform their own societies. Leaders in Egypt, India, and other lands, like those in Russia, the Ottoman Empire, China, and Japan—the subject of Chapter 27—were learning to challenge the power of the West on its own terms. In 1870 no one could say how long and how difficult that learning process would be, but Africans and Asians would continue to shape their own futures.

■ Key Terms

Zulu	British raj
Sokoto Caliphate	Sepoy Rebellion
modernization	durbar
Muhammad Ali	Indian Civil Service
"legitimate" trade	Indian National Congress
recaptives	clipper ship
nawab	contract of indenture
sepoy	

■ Suggested Reading

Volumes 2 and 3 of *The Oxford History of the British Empire,* ed. William Roger Louis, (1998, 1999), are the most up-to-date global surveys of this period. Less Anglocentric in their interpretations are Immanuel Wallerstein's *The Modern World-System III: The Second Era of Great Expansion of the Capitalist World-Economy, 1730–1840s* (1989) and William Wodruff's *Impact of Western Man: A Study of Europe's Role in the World Economy, 1750–1960* (1982). Atlantic relations are well handled by David Eltis, *Economic Growth and the Ending of the Transatlantic Slave Trade* (1987). For the Indian Ocean basin see Sugata Bose, ed., *South Asia and World Capitalism* (1990).

Roland Oliver and Anthony Atmore provide a brief introduction to Africa in *Africa Since 1800,* 4th ed. (1994). More advanced works are J. F. Ade Ajayi, ed., *UNESCO General History of Africa,* vol. 6, *Africa in the Nineteenth Century until the 1880s* (1989), and John E. Flint, ed., *The Cambridge History of Africa,* vol. 5, *From c. 1790 to c. 1870* (1976). Although specialized literature has refined some of their interpretations, the following are excellent introductions to their subjects: J. D. Omer-Cooper, *The Zulu Aftermath* (1966); Murray Last, *The Sokoto Caliphate* (1967); A. G. Hopkins, *An Economic History of West Africa* (1973); Robert W. July, *The Origins of Modern African Thought* (1967); and Robert I. Rotberg, ed., *Africa and Its Explorers: Motives, Methods, and Impact* (1970). For eastern and northeastern Africa see Norman R. Bennett, *Arab Versus European: War and Diplomacy in Nineteenth Century East Central Africa* (1985); P. J. Vatikiotis, *The History of Modern Egypt: From Muhammad Ali to Mubarak,* 4th ed. (1991); and, for the negative social impact of Egyptian modernization, Judith Tucker, "Decline of the Family Economy in Mid-Nineteenth-Century Egypt," *Arab Studies Quarterly 1* (1979): 245–271.

Very readable introductions to India in this period are Sugata Bose and Ayeshia Jalal, *Modern South India* (1998); Burton Stein, *A History of India* (1998); and Stanley Wolpert, *A New History of India,* 6th ed. (1999). More advanced treatments in the "New Cambridge History of India" series are P. J. Marshall, *Bengal: The British Bridgehead: Eastern India, 1740–1828* (1988); C. A. Bayly, *Indian Society and the Making of the British Empire* (1988); Sugata Bose, *Peasant Labour and Colonial Capital: Rural Bengal Since 1700* (1993); and Kenneth W. Jones, *Socio-Religious Reform Movements in British India* (1989). Environmental and technological perspectives on India are offered in the appropriate parts of Daniel Headrick, *The Tentacles of Progress: Technology Transfer in the Age of Imperialism, 1850–1940* (1988); Mashav Gadgil and Ramachandra Guha, *This Fissured Land: An Ecological History of India* (1992); and David Arnold, *Colonizing the Body: State Medicine and Epidemic Disease in Nineteenth-Century India* (1993).

A good introduction to the complexities of Southeast Asian history is D. R. SarDesai, *Southeast Asia: Past and Present,* 2d ed. (1989). More detail can be found in the appropriate chapters of Nicholas Tarling, ed., *The Cambridge History of South East Asia,* 2 vols. (1992). The second and third volumes of *The Oxford History of Australia,* ed. Geoffrey Bolton (1992, 1988), deal with the period covered by this chapter. A very readable multicultural and gendered perspective is provided by *Images of Australia,* ed. Gillian Whitlock and David Carter (1992). *The Oxford Illustrated History of New Zealand,* ed. Keith Sinclair (1990), provides a wide-ranging introduction to that nation.

For summaries of recent scholarship on the indentured labor trade see David Northrup, *Indentured Labor in the Age of Imperialism, 1834–1922* (1995), and Robin Cohen, ed., *The Cambridge Survey of World Migration,* part 3, "Asian Indentured and Colonial Migration" (1995).

An outstanding analysis of British whaling is Gordon Jackson's *The British Whaling Trade* (1978). Edouard A. Stackpole's *Whales & Destiny: The Rivalry Between America, France, and Britain for Control of the Southern Whale Fishery, 1785–1825* (1972) is more anecdotal.

■ Notes

1. Paul E. Lovejoy and Jan S. Hogendorn, *Slow Death for Slavery: The Course of Abolition in Northern Nigeria, 1897–1936* (New York: Cambridge University Press, 1993).
2. Quoted in P. J. Vatikiotis, *The History of Modern Egypt: From Muhammad Ali to Mubarak,* 4th ed. (Baltimore: Johns Hopkins University Press, 1991), 74.
3. David Eltis, "Precolonial Western Africa and the Atlantic Economy," in *Slavery and the Rise of the Atlantic Economy,* ed. Barbara Solow (New York: Cambridge University Press, 1991), table 1.
4. Quoted by Bernard S. Cohn, "Representing Authority in Victorian India," in *The Invention of Tradition,* ed. Eric Hobsbawm and Terence Ranger (Cambridge, England: Cambridge University Press, 1983), 165.

27

THE OTTOMAN EMPIRE AND EAST ASIA,

1800–1870

The Ottoman Empire and the European Model • **The Qing Empire and Foreign Coercion** • **Japan from Shogunate to Empire**

ENVIRONMENT AND TECHNOLOGY: **The Web of War**

SOCIETY AND CULTURE: **Fighting the Opium Trade**

Netting Whales   During the Tokugawa, the Japanese began using nets to catch large numbers of whales, and many provinces became dependent on the new industry.

When the emperor of the Qing° (the last empire to rule China) died in 1799, the imperial court received a shock. For decades officials had known that the emperor was indulging his handsome young favorite, Heshen°, allowing him extraordinary privileges and power. Senior bureaucrats hated Heshen, suspecting him of overseeing a widespread network of corruption. They believed he had been scheming to prolong the inconclusive wars against the native Miao° peoples of southwest China in the late 1700s. Glowing reports of successes against the rebels had poured into the capital, and enormous sums of government money had flowed to the battlefields. But there was no adequate accounting for the funds, and the war persisted.

After the emperor's death, Heshen's enemies ordered his arrest. When they searched his mansion, they discovered a magnificent hoard of silk, furs, porcelain, furniture, and gold and silver. His personal cash alone exceeded what remained in the imperial treasury. The new emperor ordered Heshen to commit suicide with a rope of gold silk. The government seized Heshen's fortune, but the financial damage could not be undone. The expenses of the government were so great that it was permanently bankrupt. The declining agricultural base could not replenish the state coffers, and pressures for internal police and military action rose after 1800. Repeated investigations of the bureaucracy revealed growing corruption. Thus, in the 1800s, the Qing Empire faced increasing challenges from Europe and the United States with an empty treasury, a stagnant economy, and a troubled society.

The Qing Empire's problems were not unique. They were common to all of the land-based empires of Eurasia. During the early 1800s, rapid population growth and slow agricultural growth affected much of Eurasia. Earlier military expansion had overstretched the resources of the imperial treasuries. As these traditional regimes were experiencing economic and social crises in the 1800s, the militarily advanced sea-based powers of western Europe were pressing them for economic concessions. The result was general indebtedness—either through direct loans or failure to pay indemnities after losing military conflicts—to France, Britain, and other Western powers.

This chapter concentrates on the experiences of the Ottoman and Qing Empires. To understand the significance of the similarities between them, it is necessary to examine a dramatic contrasting case: Japan. Like the Ottoman and Qing Empires, Japan in the 1800s was in the late decades of a long-lived political system—the Tokugawa Shogunate. Also like the imperial Ottomans and Qing, the Tokugawa government saw revenues steeply declining, the agricultural base stagnating, and the central government engulfed in corruption. And finally, Japan like other East Asian countries experienced the shock of military and economic confrontation with a foreign power in the mid-1800s. But the decentralized system of rule under the Tokugawa made it impossible for Japan to attempt the top-down reforms tried by the Ottomans and Qing. Instead, Japan's first direct contact with a foreign sea power led to the destruction, not reform, of the traditional state. It was replaced by a centralized and relatively efficient order whose leaders were determined to avoid becoming victims of European expansion and to participate in the evolving colonial order in Asia.

As you read this chapter, ask yourself the following questions:

- Why did the Ottoman and Qing Empires find themselves at a disadvantage during their encounters with Europeans in the 1800s?

- What were the best options for the land-based empires facing military challenges from Europe?

- Why was Japan's experience so different from that of China?

Qing (ching)   **Heshen** (huh-shun)   **Miao** (mee-ow)

CHRONOLOGY

	Ottoman Empire	Qing Empire	Japan
			Since 1600 Decentralized rule of Tokugawa Shogunate
1800	**1789–1807** Rule of Selim III	**1794–1804** White Lotus Rebellion	
	1826 Janissary corps dissolved **1829** Greek independence **1839** Abdul Mejid begins Tanzimat reforms	**1839–1842** Opium War	
1850	**1853–1856** Crimean War	**1850–1864** Taiping Rebellion	**1853** First visit by Commodore Matthew Perry **1854** Perry returns **1858** Treaty of Kanagawa
		1856–1860 Arrow War **1860** Sack of Beijing **1862–1875** Reign of Tongzhi	**1867** Civil war **1868** Meiji Restoration
	1876 First constitution by an Islamic government		

THE OTTOMAN EMPIRE AND THE EUROPEAN MODEL

Though the Ottoman Empire experienced the problems and challenges sketched above, its position close to Europe gave it relatively early exposure to European ambitions and capabilities. The Ottoman rulers were earlier than the rulers of other Eurasian empires to experiment with financial and military modernization. Not until the mid-1800s, however, did the Ottoman government overcome entrenched opposition to change and put into place a series of reforms designed to remove the influence of religious elites from many areas of the state and economy. The reforms could not move rapidly enough to preserve the empire's independence from western Europe, but they created momentum for centralization, helped promote nationalism in the late nineteenth century, and created a practical base for the creation of a Turkish republic in the twentieth century.

Early Struggles for Reform, 1793–1807

At the end of the eighteenth century Sultan Selim° III (r. 1789–1807) introduced reforms to strengthen the military, bring provincial governors under the control of the central government, and standardize taxation and land tenure. The rise in government expenditures to implement the reforms was supposed to be offset by taxes on selected items, primarily tobacco and coffee.

These reforms failed for political reasons, more than economic. The most violent and persistent opposition came from the **Janissaries°,** the traditional corps of Ottoman military slaves. The Janissaries were originally Christian boys required to convert to Islam and serve for life in the Ottoman army. Over the years, the Janissaries became a significant political force, and their conservative attitudes dissuaded many Ottoman rulers and officials from pursuing reform.

At times the disapproval of the Janissaries produced military uprisings. An early example occurred in the

Selim (seh-LEEM)   **Janissaries** (JAN-nih-say-rees)

Change with Tradition   Change in the Ottoman armies was gradual, beginning with the introduction of European guns and artillery. To use the new weapons efficiently and safely, the Janissaries were required to modify their dress and their beards. Beards were trimmed, and elaborate headgear was reserved for ritual occasions. Traditional military units attempted to retain distinctive dress whenever possible, and one compromise was the brimless cap, the fez (shown here), adapted from the high hats that some Janissaries had traditionally worn.   (Courtesy, Turkish Ministry of Culture and Tourism. Photo: Necmettin Kulahci)

The Janissaries were not the only opponents of reform. In some parts of the empire, including Anatolia, revolts by the Janissaries were encouraged by noblemen who had been supporters of earlier imperial reforms but now feared that further reform would result in new taxes. Also opposed to reform were the congregations of Muslim councilors, the *ulama*, who distrusted the secularization of law and taxation that Selim proposed. In the face of widespread rejection of his reforms, Selim suspended his program in 1806. Nevertheless, a massive military uprising occurred at Istanbul, and the sultan was deposed and imprisoned. Reform forces rallied and recaptured the capital, but not before Selim had been executed.

Army and Society in the Early Tanzimat, 1826–1853

In 1826 Selim's cousin Sultan Mahmud° II (r.1808–1839) revived the reform movement. The fate of Selim III had taught the Ottoman court that reform needed to be more systematic and imposed more forcefully. Mahmud II was able to use the loss of Greece, formerly an Ottoman colony, as a sign of the weakness of the empire and the pressing need for reform.

Greek independence in 1829 was a complex event that had dramatic international significance. Earlier Ottoman rulers had pointed to the shattering of Byzantine rule over Greece and Anatolia as a triumph of Islamic civilization and proof of God's favor. Europeans and Russians, however, saw the capture of the former Byzantine capital, Constantinople—now the Ottoman capital, Istanbul—as justification for a new holy war to be waged

Balkans, in the Ottoman territory of **Serbia,** where Janissaries acted as provincial governors. Their control in Serbia was intensely resented by the local residents, particularly Orthodox Christians who claimed that the Janissaries abused them. In response to the charges, Selim threatened to reassign the Janissaries to the Ottoman capital at Istanbul. Suspecting that the sultan's threat signaled the beginning of the end of their political power, the Janissaries in 1805 revolted against Selim, and massacred Christians in Serbia. Selim was unable to reestablish central Ottoman rule over Serbia. Instead, the Ottoman court had to rely on the ruler of Bosnia, another Balkan province, who joined his troops with the peasants of Serbia to suppress the Janissary uprising. The threat of Russian intervention prevented the Ottomans from disarming the victorious Serbians, so Serbia became effectively independent.

Mahmud (MACH-mood)

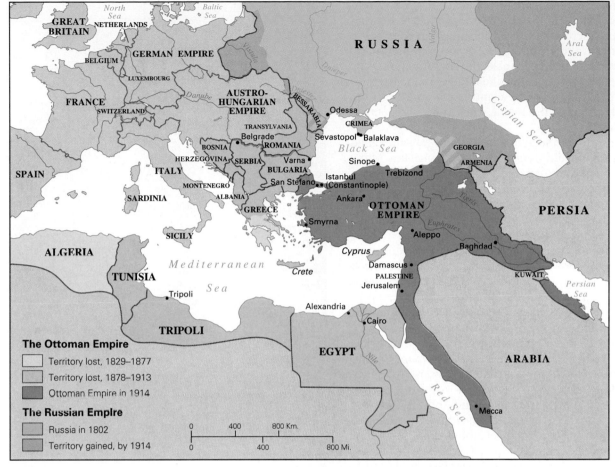

Map 27.1   Disintegration of the Ottoman Empire, 1829–1914   At its height the Ottoman Empire controlled most of the perimeter of the Mediterranean Sea. But in the 1800s Ottoman territory shrank as many countries gained their independence—frequently with the aid of France or Russia. The Black Sea, which left the Turkish coast vulnerable to assault by the Russian navy, was a weak spot that intensely contested in the Crimean dispute.

by Christian countries against the Ottoman Empire. By the early nineteenth century, interest in the classical age of Greece and Rome had intensified Europeans' desire to encourage and if possible aid the Greeks' struggle for independence from Ottoman rule. Europeans considered the war for Greek independence a campaign to recapture the classical roots of their civilization from Muslim despots, and many—including the "mad, bad and dangerous to know" English poet Lord Byron, who lost his life in the war—went to Greece to fight as volunteers. The Ottomans depended on Ibrahim Pasha° of Egypt (son of Muhammad Ali°) to preserve their rule in Greece, but the combined squadrons of the British, French, and Russian

Ibrahim Pasha (EEB-RAH-heem PAH-shah)
Muhammad Ali (moo-HAM-mad AH-lee)

fleets handily defeated him. Not only did Ottoman control of Greece end, but the Ottoman's tenuous rule in Egypt was further damaged (see Map 27.1).

Europeans trumpeted the victory of the Greeks as a triumph of European civilization over the Ottoman Empire, and Mahmud II agreed that the loss of Greece indicated a profound weakness—he considered it backwardness—in Ottoman military and financial organization. Like his predecessors, Mahmud believed that the Janissaries should be destroyed, and with popular outrage over the loss of Greece strong, he made his move in 1826. First he announced the creation of a new army corps, which would be open to the Janissaries. Then, when the Janissaries rose in revolt, he ordered loyal troops to attack the Janissary barracks and obliterate the force.

Mahmud also reduced the political power of the religious elite. To accomplish this reform, he had to restructure the bureaucracy, because education and law were to be under the authority of the civil government. Property laws too were amended, to make the charitable trusts by which religious communities and families managed their wealth subject to civil review and regulation. Even the public judgments of the ulama were to be bureaucratically regulated.

In attempting to secularize the state, Mahmud relied heavily on establishing a uniform code of civil law. Many of his ideas received their widest expression in the **Tanzimat**° ("restructuring"), a series of reforms announced by his sixteen-year-old son and successor, Abdul Mejid°, in 1839. One proclamation guaranteeing basic political rights has been compared to England's Magna Carta (1215). It called for public trials and equal protection under the law for all, whether Muslim, Christian, or Jew. It also guaranteed some rights of privacy, equalized the eligibility of men for conscription into the army, and provided for a new, formalized method of tax collecting that legally ended tax farming in the Ottoman Empire. No Islamic country had ever produced anything so nearly approaching a constitution, and the Ottoman Empire enjoyed a renewed reputation as a progressive influence in the Middle East.

The successors to Mahmud II and Abdul Mejid were less zealous in their legal ideologies and later created a mixed court system that permitted *qadi*° (religious judges) to decide certain matters. Nevertheless, the distinction between religious and secular law continued to be observed. In the mid-1800s, the commercial code was remodeled along the lines of the French system, and the rulers affirmed that trade and finance were outside the jurisdiction of religious law.

Military cadets were sent to France and the German states for training, and military uniforms were modeled on those of France. In the 1830s an Ottoman imperial school of military sciences was established at Istanbul. Instructors imported from western Europe taught chemistry, engineering, mathematics, and physics in addition to military history. Reforms in military education became the model for more general educational reforms. In 1838 the first medical school was established, for army doctors and surgeons. Later, a national system of preparatory schools was created. The subjects that were taught and many of the teachers were foreign, so the issue of whether Turkish would be a language of instruction in the new schools was a serious one. Because it was easier to import and use foreign textbooks than to write

European Exposure   Increasing exposure to French and British influence stimulated the programs of the Ottoman rulers to modernize their armies. By the time of the Crimean War, the Janissaries had been replaced by a professional military, trained in special schools, adept in the use of modern artillery, and dressed in the fashion of the European infantry and cavalry.   (Hulton Getty Liaison)

new ones in Turkish, French became the preferred language in all advanced professional and scientific training. The translation of fundamental works into Turkish was still not completed by the end of the 1800s.

The importance of educational institutions in the early reforms accelerated the growth in wealth and influence of the urban elites. At Istanbul, the capital, a cosmopolitan milieu embracing European language and culture, as well as military professionalism and an interest in progressive political reform, thrived. Newspapers—most of them in French—were founded at Istanbul, and travel to Europe—particularly to England and France—by wealthy Turks became more common. Interest in importing European military, industrial, and communications technology remained strong through the 1800s.

The Ottoman rulers quickly learned that limited improvements in military technology had unforeseen cultural and social effects. The introduction of modern weapons and drill required a change in traditional mili-

---

Tanzimat (TAHNZ-ee-MAT)   **Abdul Mejid** (ab-dul MAY-jeed)
qadi (KAW-dee)

tary dress. Beards were deemed unhygienic and, in artillery units, a fire hazard. They were restricted, along with the wearing of loose trousers and turbans. Military headgear also became controversial. European military caps, which had leather bills on the front to protect against the glare of the sun, were not acceptable because they interfered with Muslim soldiers' touching their foreheads to the ground during daily prayers. The compromise was the brimless cap now called the *fez*, which was adopted by the military and then by Ottoman civil officials in the early years of Mahmud II's reign.

Military castes had been important in traditional Ottoman society, and the changes in military dress—so soon after the suppression of the Janissaries—were recognized as an indication of the change in the social meaning of military service. A conscript army was created, and with it came educational reforms that attempted to promote secular, international, urban cultural attitudes. Among self-consciously progressive men, European dress became the fashion in the Ottoman cities of the later 1800s. Traditional dress became a symbol of the religious, the rural, and the parochial.

Secularization of the legal code had profound implications for the non-Muslim subjects of the Ottomans. Non-Muslims frequently had been required to pay extra taxes and had been excluded from certain professions, including the military, unless they converted to Islam. In addition, the role of Islamic judges in the legal process had limited non-Muslim's access to the law courts. Secularization of the law, however, gave all male subjects access to the courts. It also resulted in equalization of taxation.

The public rights and political participation granted during the Tanzimat were explicitly restricted to men. Private life, including everything connected to marriage and divorce, was left within the sphere of religious law, and at no time was there a question of political participation or reformed education for women. Indeed, the reforms actually decreased the influence of women. The political changes ran parallel to economic changes that also narrowed women's opportunities.

The influx of silver from the Americas that began in the 1600s increased the monetarization of some sectors of the Ottoman economy, particularly in the cities. Workers were increasingly paid in cash rather than goods, and businesses associated with banking, finance, and law developed. Competition drove women from the work force. Early industrial labor and the professions were not open to women, and traditional "woman's work" such as weaving was increasingly mechanized and done by men.

Nevertheless, well into the 1800s some women retained considerable power in the management and disposal of their own property. After marriage a woman was often pressured to convert her landholdings to cash in order to transfer her personal wealth to her husband's family, with whom she and her husband would reside. Until the 1820s, many women retained their say in the distribution of property through the creation of charitable trusts for their sons. Because these trusts were set up in the religious courts, they could be designed to conform to the wishes of family members, and they gave women of wealthy families an opportunity to exercise significant indirect control over property. Then, in the 1820s and 1830s, the secularizing reforms of Mahmud II transferred jurisdiction over the charitable trusts from religious courts to the state and ended women's control over their own and their families' property. In addition, reforms in the military, higher education, the professions, and commerce all bypassed women. By the late 1800s, the seclusion of women had become a highly valued symbol of Turkish nativism and Muslim traditionalism.

The Crimean War, 1853–1856

Since the reign of Peter the Great (r. 1689–1725) the Russian Empire had been attempting to expand southward at the Ottomans' expense. By 1815 Russia had pried the Georgian region of the Caucasus away from the Ottomans, and the threat of Russian intervention in Serbia had prevented the Ottomans from crushing Serbian independence. Russia seemed poised to exploit Ottoman weakness and seize key territories in the Balkans, Central Asia, and possibly the Middle East.

Between 1853 and 1856 the **Crimean° War** raged on the Black Sea and its northern shore. This extremely destructive conflict was nominally a war between the Russian and Ottoman Empires about whether Russia could claim to protect Christians in the Ottoman domains. But also involved in the dispute were Austria, Britain, France, and the Italian kingdom of Sardinia-Piedmont, all of whom sided—actively or passively—with the Ottoman Empire. These European nations feared Russia's power and influence, which they suspected would increase because of the Ottomans' weakness. The war was fought at sea as well as on land. During the prolonged sea conflict, Britain and France trapped the Russian fleet in the Black Sea. The lack of railways hampered Russian attempts to supply both its land and its sea forces. Tsar Alexander II (r. 1855–1881) abandoned the key fortress of Sevastopol in 1855 and sued for peace.

A formal alliance among Britain, France, and the Ottoman Empire blocked Russian expansion into eastern Europe and the Middle East. The terms of peace also

---

Crimean (cry-ME-uhn)

The Web of War

The lethal military technologies of the mid-nineteenth century used on battlefields in the United States, Russia, India, and China were rapidly transmitted from one conflict to the next. This dissemination was due not only to the rapid development of communications but also to the existence of a new international network of soldiers who moved from one trouble spot to another, bringing with them expertise in the use of new techniques.

General Charles Gordon (1833–1885), for instance, was commissioned in the British army in 1852, then served in the Crimean War after Britain entered on the side of the Ottomans. In 1860 he was dispatched to China. He served British forces during the Arrow War and took part in the sack of Beijing. Afterward, he stayed in China and was seconded to the Qing imperial government until the suppression of the Taipings in 1864, earning himself the nickname "Chinese" Gordon. Gordon later served the Ottoman rulers of Egypt as governor of territory along the Nile. He was killed in Egypt in 1885 while attempting to lead his Egyptian troops in defense of the city of Khartoum against an uprising by the local religious leader, the Mahdi.

Journalism played an important part in the developing web of telegraph communications that speeded orders to and from the battlefields. Readers in London could learn details of the drama occurring in the Crimea or in China within a week—or in some cases days—after they occurred. Print and, later, photographic journalism created new "stars" from these war experiences. Charles Gordon was one. Florence Nightingale was another.

In the great wars of the 1800s, the vast majority of deaths resulted from infec-tion or excessive bleeding, not from the wounds themselves. Florence Nightingale (1820–1910), while still a young woman, became interested in hospital management and nursing. She went to Prussia and France to study advanced techniques and before the outbreak of the Crimean War was credited with bringing about marked improvement in British health care. When the public reacted to news reports of the suffering in the Crimea, the British government sent Nightingale to the region. Within a year of her arrival the death rate in the military hospitals there dropped from 45 percent to under 5 percent. Her techniques for preventing septicemia and dysentery and for promoting healing therapies were quickly adopted by those working for and with her. On her return to London, Nightingale established institutes for nursing that soon were recognized around the world as leaders. She herself was lionized by the British public and received the Order of Merit in 1907, three years before her death.

The importance of Nightingale's innovations in public hygiene is underscored by the life of her contemporary, Mary Seacole (1805–1881). A Jamaican woman who volunteered to nurse British troops in the Crimean War, Seacole was excluded repeatedly from nursing service by British authorities. She eventually went to Crimea and used her own funds to run a hospital there, bankrupting herself in the process. The drama of the Crimean War moved the British public to support Seacole after her sacrifices were publicized. She was awarded medals by the British, French, and Turkish governments and today is recognized with her contemporary Florence Nightingale as an innovative field nurse and a champion of public hygiene in peacetime.

With Florence Nightingale in Crimea   Readers could see as well as read about war dramas with vivid illustrations and telegraphed copy. (The Granger Collection, New York)

We Have Got the Maxim Gun   These two representatives of the Qing Empire visited northern England after the Taiping Rebellion to examine and, if possible, purchase new weapons. They posed for a photograph after watching the famous Maxim gun shoot a tree in half.   (Peter Newark's Military Pictures)

gave Britain and France a means of checking each other's colonial ambitions in the Middle East: neither, according to the agreement that ended the war, was entitled to take Ottoman territory for its exclusive use.

The Crimean War brought significant changes to all the combatants. The tsar and his government, already beset by demands for the reform of serfdom, education, and the military, were further discredited. They plunged into reforms that slightly improved Russia's economy but profoundly destabilized its political system. In Britain and France the conflict was accompanied by massive propaganda campaigns. For the first time newspapers were an important force mobilizing public support for a war. Press accounts of British participation in the war were often so glamorized that ever since the false impression has lingered that Ottoman and Egyptian troops played a negligible role in the conflict. At the time, however, British and French military commanders noted the massive losses among Turkish troops in particular. The French press, dominant in Istanbul, promoted a sense of unity between Turkish and French society that continued to influence many aspects of Turkish urban culture.

The larger significance of the Crimean War was that it marked the transition from traditional to modern warfare (see Environment and Technology: The Web of War). The high casualty count of the war resulted in part from the clash of mechanized and unmechanized means of killing. All the combatant nations in the Crimean War once prided themselves on their effective use of highly trained cavalry to smash through the front lines of infantry. Cavalry coexisted with firearms until the early 1800s, primarily because early rifles were awkward to load, vulnerable to explosion, and not very accurate. Swift and expert cavalry could storm infantry lines during the intervals between volleys and even penetrate artillery barrages. Then in the 1830s and 1840s, **percussion caps** were widely adopted in Europe. In Crimean War battles, many cavalry units were destroyed by the rapid and relatively accurate fire of **breech-loading rifles.** That was the fate of the British "Light Brigade," which was sent to relieve an Ottoman unit surrounded by Russian troops. Cavalry were not the only victims of the new speed of the guns. Many traditional infantry units came to grief attempting to use ranks of marching, brightly coated soldiers to overwhelm lines of rapidly firing riflemen.

In the great conflicts that followed the Crimean War—the Indian Uprising, the Taiping° Rebellion in China, and the American Civil War—percussion-cap technology in combination with new designs of repeating guns led to

---

Taiping (tie-PING)

the creation of machine guns. Originally called Agar guns, then Gatling guns, machine guns resulted in a new scale of battlefield fatalities, mounting into many hundreds of thousands over only a few years. New manufacturing techniques allowed unprecedented precision in the fitting of caps and bullets within the firing chambers, creating propulsive force never before encountered so widely. Railways permitted the rapid transfer of heavy weaponry toward the front, as well as the transport of the wounded to hospitals, and also aided in the conveyance of iron and coal to manufacturing centers.

The transformation of decisive weaponry meant a change in the general ways of war. Cavalry did not immediately disappear, but the emphasis on speed and the use of light, accurate firearms by riders created more and more deadly conditions for mounted soldiers. Heavily armed infantry units pinned each other down in trenches for weeks, waiting for the enemy to be wiped out by disease or despair. Long-range artillery took on greater strategic significance and was combined with mines, early hand grenades, and mustard gas. Soldiers were reorganized, taught to scatter and shoot from trenches or from behind natural barriers, and dressed in inconspicuous colors. In such circumstances, the military began to lose its traditional connection with the aristocracy, with horses, and with ceremonial uniforms. Conscript armies took on new importance, and warfare became a political issue. Though the transformation of traditional warfare was not completed in the cycle of regional conflicts that began with the Crimean War, the process began that led toward the patterns of warfare that were to become familiar in the twentieth century.

European Patronage and Economic Decline, to 1878

After the Crimean War, declining state revenues and increasing integration with European commercial networks created hazardous economic conditions in the Ottoman Empire. Mahmud II's successors continued to secularize Ottoman financial and commercial institutions, modeling them closely on European counterparts. The Ottoman imperial bank was founded in 1840, and a few years later currency reform pegged the value of Ottoman gold coins to the British pound. Sweeping changes in the 1850s expedited the creation of banks, insurance companies, and legal firms throughout the empire. These and other reforms facilitating trade contributed to a strong demographic shift in the Ottoman Empire between about 1850 and 1880, as many people from the countryside headed for the cities Within this period many of the major cities of the empire—Istanbul, Ankara, Damascus, Cairo—doubled in size. A strong urban professional class emerged, as well as a considerable class of wage laborers. This shift was magnified by an influx into the northern Ottoman territories of refugees from Poland and Hungary, where rivalry between the European powers and the Russian Empire caused political tension and sporadic warfare.

The Ottoman reforms stimulated commerce and urbanization, but no reform could repair the chronic insolvency of the imperial government. Ottoman finances were damaged by declining revenues from agricultural yields and by widespread corruption. Some of the corruption received spectacular exposure in the early 1840s. From the conclusion of the Crimean War in 1856 on, the Ottoman government became heavily dependent on foreign loans. In return for loans, Ottoman tariffs were lowered to favor European imports, and European banks opened for business in Ottoman cities. The Ottoman currency was changed to allow more systematic conversion to European currencies. Europeans were allowed to live in Istanbul and other commercial centers in their own enclaves, subject to their own laws and exempt from Ottoman jurisdiction. This status was known as **extraterritoriality.**

As the cities prospered, they became attractive to laborers, and still more people moved from the countryside. But opportunities for wage workers reached a plateau in the bloated cities. Foreign trade brought in large numbers of imports, but—apart from the Turkish opium that American traders took to China to compete against the Indian opium of the British—few exports were sent abroad. Together with the growing national debt, these factors in the mid-1800s aggravated inflationary trends that left urban populations in a precarious position.

In the 1860s and 1870s, reform groups demanded a constitution, the possibility of a law permitting all men to vote was discussed, the prospect of the Muslims' loss of all political privilege arose. The Muslim majority was disturbed by the apparent signal that the Ottoman Empire was no longer a Muslim society. Muslims also were suspicious of the motives of Christians, many of whom were not of Turkish descent. Many Ottoman Muslims remembered attempts by Russia and France to interfere in Ottoman affairs in order to benefit Christians. Hostilities against Christians in Ottoman territories in Europe, Armenia, and the Middle East could be rationalized on the grounds of Turkish patriotism.

The decline of Ottoman power and prosperity had a strong impact on a group of urban and well-educated young men who aspired to wealth and influence. They believed that the Ottoman rulers would be forced to—or would be willing to—allow the continued domination of the empire's political, economic, and cultural life by Europeans. Inspired by the European nationalist movements of 1848 (see Chapter 23), they began to band together in the 1860s as the "Young Turks." The granting of a constitution in 1876 was regarded abroad as a great achievement because it was the first constitution to be adopted by an Islamic government. The apparent triumph of liberal reform was short lived. A *coup d'état* resulted in the enthroning of a new ruler who was hostile to democratization. A threat of war over the Balkans arose, and the imperial government used the crisis to disable the new Parliament and suspend the Constitution in 1877. But it did not quash the movement by Turks for greater independence from foreign interference. To the Young Turks, freedom from European domination required the destruction of the Ottoman Empire from within. They proposed to replace it with a Turkish national state, their "Fatherland." Though nationalism continued to be fostered by the leaders of the Young Turks—who exploited the new institutions of newspapers and private schools to spread their message—the Ottoman Empire continued its weakened existence under the sponsorship of Western powers until 1922.

THE QING EMPIRE AND FOREIGN COERCION

In 1800 the Qing Empire faced many of the crises the Ottomans had encountered, but no early reform movement of the kind initiated by Selim III emerged in China. The reasons are not difficult to understand. The Qing Empire, created by the Manchus, had distinguished itself in the 1600s for its adept maneuverings against Russia, both strategic and diplomatic. The Qing rulers had earned the admiration of the Jesuits, who transmitted to Europe a very appealing image of the emperors in China as enlightened philosopher-kings. But the failure in 1793 of the British attempt to establish diplomatic and trade relations with the Qing—the Macartney mission—turned European opinion against China, and in the very early 1800s few Europeans apart from traders based in Canton had much contact with or interest in China. For their part, the Qing rulers and bureaucrats were embroiled in some serious crises and had neither the time nor the inclination to explore new contacts with far-off Europeans. Complaints from European merchants at Canton, who chafed against the restrictions of the "Canton system" by which the Qing limited and controlled foreign trade, were brushed off.

The empire's troubles were primarily domestic and seemed depressingly familiar to Chinese historians and officials: rebellions by displaced indigenous peoples and the poor, and protests against the injustice of the local magistrates. These troubles, it was thought, could be dealt with in the usual way, by suppressing rebels and dismissing incompetent or untrustworthy officials. Unlike the Ottoman rulers of the same period, the Qing rulers of 1800 had no compelling reason to think that cataclysmic challenges were headed their way.

Economic and Social Disorder

Early Qing successes gave rise to much of the domestic and political chaos of the later period. The Qing conquest in the 1600s brought stability to central China, previously subjected to decades of rebellion and agricultural shortages. The Qing emperors encouraged the recovery of farmland, the opening of previously uncultivated areas, and the restoration and expansion of the road and canal systems. The result was a great expansion of the agricultural base together with a doubling of the population between about 1650 and about 1800. Enormous numbers of farmers, merchants, and day laborers migrated across the Qing Empire in search of less crowded conditions, and a permanent floating population of the unemployed and homeless emerged. By 1800, population strain on the land had caused serious environmental damage in some parts of central and western China. Deforestation, erosion, and soil exhaustion left swollen populations stranded on rapidly deteriorating land.

Many groups had serious grievances against the government. Minority peoples in central and southwestern China resented having been driven off their lands during the boom of the 1700s. Mongols resisted the appropriation of their grazing lands and the displacement of their traditional elites. Village vigilante organizations had grown used to policing and practically governing regions that the Qing government had become too weak to manage. And growing numbers of people mistrusted the government, suspecting that all officials were corrupt. Discontent was aggravated by the growing presence of foreign merchants and missionaries in Canton and in the Portuguese colony of Macao.

In some parts of China the Qing were hated because they themselves were a foreign conquest regime and were suspected of having sympathies with the Europeans. Indeed as the nineteenth century opened, the

White Lotus Rebellion (1794–1804)—partly inspired by a mystical ideology that predicted the restoration of the Chinese Ming dynasty and the coming of the Buddha— was raging across central China and could not be suppressed until 1804.

The White Lotus was the first large rebellion in a series of internal conflicts that continued through the 1800s. Ignited by deepening social instabilities, these movements were sometimes intensified by local ethnic conflicts and by unapproved religions. The magnitude of the conflicts was increased by the improving ability of some village militias to defend themselves (and attack others). Some of these techniques were effectively utilized by southern coastal populations attempting to fend off British invasion.

The Opium War, 1839–1842

Unlike the Ottomans, the Qing believed that the Europeans were remote and only casually interested in trade. They knew little of the enormous fortunes being made in the early 1800s by European and American merchants smuggling opium into China. They did not know that silver gained in this illegal trade was helping to finance the industrial transformation of England and the United States. But Qing officials slowly learned that Britain was not really so far away. It had colonies in India, where opium was grown. And it had a major naval base at Singapore, through which it could transport opium to East Asia.

For more than a century, British officials had been frustrated by the enormous trade deficit caused by the British demand for tea and the Qing refusal to facilitate the importation to China of any British product. In the early 1700s, a few European merchants and their Chinese partners were importing small quantities of opium, and in 1729 the first Qing law making it illegal to import opium was promulgated. By 1800, however, smuggling had increased the quantity of annual imports of opium to as many as four thousand chests. British merchants had discovered an extremely profitable trade, and a large Chinese commerce had arisen around the distribution of the drugs that foreigners brought to shore. British importers were competing with Americans, and in the early 1820s a price war raised demand so sharply that by the 1830s as many as thirty thousand chests were being imported. Addiction spread to people at all levels of Qing society, including a large number of very high-ranking officials. For a time the Qing emperor and his officials debated whether to legalize and tax opium or to more strictly enforce the existing ban on the drug. They decided to root out the use and the importation of opium,

and in 1839 they sent Lin Zexu° to Canton to deal with the matter (see Society and Culture: Fighting the Opium Trade).

Britain considered the Qing ban on the importation of opium an intolerable restraint of trade, a direct threat to Britain's economic health, and indirectly a cause for war. British naval and marine forces arrived at the south China coast in late 1839. The significance of naval power, which the Ottomans had understood but not learned to master in the Mediterranean and Black Seas, dawned on the Qing slowly. Indeed, the difference between a naval invasion and piracy was not clear to Qing strategists until the Opium War was nearly ended.

The **Opium War** (1839–1842) broke out when negotiations between the Qing and British representatives became stalemated. The war exposed the fact that the traditional, hereditary soldiers of the Qing Empire—the **Bannermen**—were, like the Janissaries of the Ottoman Empire, hopelessly obsolete. As in the Crimean War, the British attempted to keep most confrontations on the sea, where they had a distinct technological advantage. British ships landed marines who pillaged coastal cities and then returned to their ships and sailed to new destinations (see Map 27.2). The Qing had no imperial navy, and until they were able to engage the British in prolonged fighting on land, they were unable to defend themselves against British attacks. Even in the land engagements, Qing resources proved woefully inadequate. The British could quickly transport their forces by sea along the coast. Qing troops, in contrast, moved primarily on foot. Moving Qing reinforcements from central to eastern China took more than three months, and when the defense forces arrived, they were exhausted and basically without weapons.

Against the British invaders, the Bannermen used the few muskets the Qing had imported during the 1700s. The weapons were matchlocks, which required the soldiers to ignite the load of gunpowder in them by hand. Firing the weapons was dangerous, and the canisters of gunpowder that each musketeer carried on his belt was likely to explode if a fire broke out nearby—a frequent occurrence in encounters with the British artillery. A majority of the Bannermen, however, had no guns and fought with swords, knives, spears, and clubs. Soldiers under British command—many of them were Indians—carried percussion-cap rifles, which were far quicker, safer, and more accurate than the matchlocks. In addition, the long-range artillery of the British could be moved from place to place and proved deadly in the cities and villages of eastern China.

Lin Zexu (lin zuh-SHOO)

Fighting the Opium Trade

In early 1839, Lin Zexu resigned his post as a provincial governor in order to act as a special imperial commissioner at Canton. The Qing court suspected that local officials were partial to the interests of the Canton merchants, and that enforcement of an anti-opium policy would be impossible without an agent as determined and honest as Lin Zexu. Shortly after his imperial appointment, Lin wrote to Queen Victoria, hoping to persuade her to prevent British merchants from continuing the opium trade.

We find that your country is [very far] from China. Yet there are barbarian ships that strive to come here for trade for the purpose of making a great profit. . . . That is to say, the great profit made by barbarians is all taken from the rightful share of China. By what right do they in return use the poisonous drug to injure the Chinese people? Even though the barbarians may not necessarily intend to do us harm, yet in coveting profit to an extreme, they have no regard for injuring others. Let us ask, where is your conscience? I have heard that the smoking of opium is very strictly forbidden by your country; that is because the harm caused by opium is clearly understood. Since it is not permitted to do harm to your own country, then even less should you let it be passed on to the harm of other countries—how much less to China! Of all that China exports to foreign countries, there is not a single thing which is not beneficial to people: they are of benefit when eaten, or of benefit when used, or of benefit when resold: all are beneficial. Is there a single article from China that has done harm to other countries?

When open warfare broke out between the Qing and British Empires, the governments of both countries blamed Lin for the conflict. The Qing court banished him to remote Xinjiang

province. *In a letter to a friend he reflected on the consequences of Qing technology gap with Britain.*

When I was in office in [Canton] I had made plans regarding the problems of ships and cannon and a water force. Afraid that there was not enough time to build ships, I at first rented them. Afraid that there was not enough time to cast cannon and that it would not be done according to the regulations, I at first bought foreign ones. The most painful thing was that when the [harbor] was broken into, a large number of good cannon fell into the hands of the rebellious barbarians. I recall that after I had been punished two years ago, I still took the risk of calling the Emperor's attention to two things: ships and guns.

Though Lin's analysis of the predicament that the empire found itself in because of its neglect of technology was penetrating, it came too late. By the time Lin arrived at this conclusion, the Qing Empire was under such pressure from European powers and the United States that systematic, centralized reforms were very difficult to accomplish.

How do the attitudes expressed in these two passages from Lin's writings contrast with each other? How do they compare with the attitudes of Ottoman elites in the 1830s and 1840s?

Source: Adapted from Ssu-Yu Teng, Ssu-Tu-Teng, and John King Fairbank, *China's Response to the West: A Documentary Survey, 1839–1923* (Cambridge, MA: Harvard University Press, 1979), 24–29. Reprinted by permission of the publisher. Copyright © 1979 by the President and Fellows of Harvard College.

Qing commanders thought that British gunboats would ride so low in the water that they would not be able to sail up Chinese rivers, and that evacuating the coasts would protect the country from the British threat. But the British deployed new gunboats able to proceed in shallow water and moved without difficulty up the Yangzi River.

When the invaders approached Nanjing, the revered former Ming capital, the Qing decided to negotiate an end to the war. In 1842 the terms of the **Treaty of Nanking** (the British name for Nanjing) were concluded. The old Canton system was broken. The number of **treaty ports**—cities opened to foreign residents—was increased from one (Canton) to five (Canton, Xiamen,

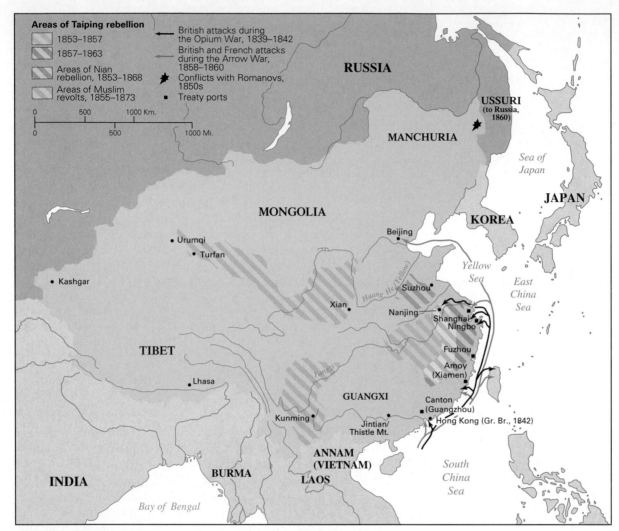

Map 27.2 Conflicts in the Qing Empire, 1839–1870 In both the Opium War of 1839–1842 and the Arrow War of 1856–1860, the sea coasts saw most of the action. Since the Qing had no imperial navy, the well-armed British ships encountered little resistance as they shelled the southern coasts. In inland conflicts, such as the Taiping Rebellion, the opposing armies were massive and slow moving. Battles on land were often prolonged attempts by one side to starve out the other side before making a major assault.

Fuzhou, Ningbo, and Shanghai°), and the island of Hong Kong became a permanent British colony. British residents in China were granted the rights of extraterritoriality. The Qing government had to agree to a low tariff of 5 percent on imports and to pay an indemnity of 21 million ounces of silver to Britain as a penalty for having started the war. A supplementary treaty the following year guaranteed **most-favored nation status** to Britain: any privileges that China granted to another country would be automatically extended to Britain as well. This

provision effectively prevented the colonization of China, because giving land to one country would have necessitated giving it to all.

With each round of treaties came a new round of privileges for foreigners. In 1860 a new treaty legalized the right of foreigners to import opium. Later, French treaties established the rights of foreign missionaries to travel extensively in the Chinese countryside and preach their religion. The number of treaty ports grew, too; by 1900 they numbered more than ninety.

The treaty system in China resulted in the colonization of small pockets of Qing territory, where foreign

---

Shanghai (shahng-hie)

merchants enjoyed the rights of extraterritoriality (the same system existed in the Ottoman Empire and elsewhere in Asia). As in the case of the Ottoman Empire, the greatest territorial losses for the Qing resulted from the actual or nominal independence of outlying regions it had dominated. In the early 1800s, Britain and Russia were both active in attempts to erase the last traces of Qing sovereignty in Central Asia. In the late 1800s France forced the court of Vietnam to end its vassalage to the Qing, while Britain encouraged Tibetan independence.

In Canton, Shanghai, and other coastal cities, Europeans and Americans maintained offices and factories in which all but a few of the local Chinese were assigned to menial labor. The foreigners built comfortable housing in zones where Chinese were not permitted to live, and they entertained themselves in exclusive restaurants and bars. Around the foreign establishments, gambling and prostitution offered employment to some of the local urban population.

Often, the work of Christian missionaries both in the cities and in the countryside was regarded as benevolent, as when the congregations sponsored hospitals, shelters, and soup kitchens or gave stipends to Chinese who attended church. But just as often the missionaries themselves were regarded as another evil. They seemed to subvert Confucian beliefs, whether by condemning ancestor worship, pressuring poor families to put their children into orphanages, or fulminating against footbinding. The growing numbers of foreigners, and their growing privileges, quickly became a target of resentment for a deeply dissatisfied, daily more impoverished, and increasingly militarized society.

The Taiping Rebellion, 1850–1864

The most startling demonstration of the inflammatory mixture of social unhappiness and foreign intrusion was the great civil war usually called the **Taiping Rebellion.** In Guangxi, where the Taiping movement originated, entrenched social problems had been generating disorders for half a century. Agriculture in the region was unstable, and many people made their living from arduous and despised trades such as disposing of human waste, making charcoal, and mining. Ethnic divisions complicated economic distress. A minority group, the Hakkas, were frequently to be found in the lowliest trades, and tensions between them and the majority were rising. It is possible that the local economy had been affected by the sharp rises and falls in the trade of opium, which after 1842 flooded the coastal and riverine portions of China, then collapsed as domestically grown opium began to dominate the market. Also, the area was

close enough to Canton to feel the cultural and economic impact of the growing number of Europeans and Americans.

All these factors were significant in the experience of Hong Xiuquan°, the founder of the Taiping movement. Hong came from a humble Hakka background. After years of study, he competed in the provincial Confucian examinations, hoping for a post in government. He failed the examinations repeatedly, and it appears that in his late thirties he suffered a nervous breakdown. Afterward he spent some time in Canton, where he met both Chinese and American Protestant missionaries, who inspired him with their teachings. Hong had his own interpretation of the Christian message. He saw himself as the younger brother of Jesus, commissioned by God to found a new kingdom on earth and drive the Manchu conquerors, the Qing, out of China. The result would be universal peace. Hong called his new religious movement the "Heavenly Kingdom of Great Peace."

Hong quickly attracted a community of believers, primarily Hakkas like himself. They believed in the prophecy of dreams and claimed they could walk on air. Hong and his rivals for leadership in the movement went in and out of ecstatic trances. They denounced the Manchus as creatures of Satan. News of the heresy reached the government, and Qing troops were sent to arrest the Taiping leaders. But the Taipings soundly repelled the imperial troops. Local loyalty to the Taipings spread quickly, their numbers multiplied, and they began to enlarge their domain.

It appears that at first the Taipings relied on Hakka sympathy and the charismatic appeal of their religious doctrine to attract followers. But as their numbers and power grew, they altered their methods of preaching and governing. They stopped enlisting Hakkas with anti-Chinese appeals and began to enlist Chinese with anti-Manchu rhetoric. They forced the populations of captured villages to join their movement, and once people were absorbed, the Taipings strictly monitored their activities. They segregated men and women and organized them into work and military teams. Women were forbidden to bind their feet (the Hakkas had never practiced footbinding), and they participated fully in farming and laboring. Brigades of women soldiers took to the field against Qing forces.

As the movement grew, it began to move toward eastern and northern China (see Map 27.2). Panic preceded the Taipings. Villagers feared being forced into Taiping units, and Confucian elites recoiled in horror from the bizarre ideology of foreign gods, totalitarian rule, and walking, working, warring women. But the

Hong Xiuquan (hoong shee-OH-chew-an)

Nanjing Encircled   For a decade the Taipings held the city of Nanjing as their capital. For years Qing and international troops attempted to break the Taiping hold. By the summer of 1864, Qing forces had built tunnels leading to the foundations of Nanjing's city walls and had planted explosives. The detonation of the explosives signaled the final Qing assault on the rebel capital. As shown here, the common people of the city, along with their starving livestock, were caught in the cross-fire. Many of the Taiping leaders escaped the debacle at Nanjing, but nearly all were hunted down and executed.   (Roger-Viollet)

huge numbers the Taipings were able to muster overwhelmed attempts at local defense. The tremendous growth in the number of Taiping followers required the movement to establish a permanent base. When the rebel army conquered Nanjing in 1853, the Taiping leaders decided to settle there and make it the capital of the new "Heavenly Kingdom of Great Peace."

At the time the Taipings were brought to a halt by the growth of their population and their organization, Qing forces attempting to defend north China against them were becoming more successful. Increasing Qing military success was due mainly to the flexibility of the imperial military commanders in the face of an unprecedented challenge. In addition, the military commanders received strong backing from a group of civilian provincial governors who had studied the techniques developed by local militia forces for self-defense. In essence, certain of the provincial governors, especially Zeng Guofan°, combined their knowledge of civilian self-defense and local terrain with more efficient organization and the use of modern weaponry. The result was the formation of new military units, in which many of the Bannermen voluntarily served under civilian governors. The Qing court agreed to special taxes to fund the new armies and acknowledged the new combined leadership of the civilian and professional force.

Zeng Guofan (zung gwoh-FAN)

When the Taipings settled into Nanjing, the new Qing armies surrounded the city, hoping to starve out the rebels. The Taipings, however, had provisioned and fortified themselves well. They also had the services of several brilliant young military commanders, who mobilized enormous campaigns in nearby parts of eastern China, scavenging supplies and attempting to break the encirclement of Nanjing. For more than a decade the Taiping leadership remained ensconced at Nanjing, and the "Heavenly Kingdom" endured.

In 1856, Britain and France, freed from their preoccupation with the Crimean War, turned their attention to China. European and American missionaries had visited Nanjing, curious to see what their fellow Christians were up to. The reports they sent home were discouraging. Hong Xiuquan and the other leaders appeared to lead lives of indulgence and abandon, and more than one missionary accused them of homosexual practices. Now having no fear of being accused of quashing an appealing Christian movement, the British and French considered the situation. Though the Taipings were not going to topple the Qing, the outbreak of a rebellion by the Nian in northern China in the 1850s was ominous. A series of simultaneous large insurrections might indeed destroy the empire. Perhaps more important, Britain and France were now considering making war on the Qing again themselves. The Qing had not observed the provisions of the treaties signed after the Opium War, and European patience was exhausted.

In 1856 the British and French launched a series of swift, brutal coastal attacks—a second opium war, called the Arrow War (1856–1860)—which culminated in a British and French invasion of Beijing and the sacking of the Summer Palace in 1860. A new round of treaties punished the Qing for not enacting all the provisions of the Treaty of Nanking. Having secured their principal objective, the British and French forces now joined the Qing in the campaign against the Taipings. Attempts to coordinate the international forces were sometimes riotous and sometimes tragic, but the injection of European weaponry and money aided in the quelling of both the Taiping and the Nian Rebellions during the 1860s.

The Taiping Rebellion ranks as the world's bloodiest civil war and the greatest armed conflict before the twentieth century. Estimates of deaths range from 20 million to 30 million. The loss of life was due primarily to starvation and disease, for most engagements consisted of surrounding the enemy holed up in fortified cities and waiting until they died, surrendered, or were so weakened that they could be easily defeated. Many sieges continued for months, and people within some cities found that after starving for a year under the occupation of the rebels they had to starve for another year under the occupation of the imperial forces. Reports of people eating grass, leather, hemp, and human flesh were widespread. The dead were rarely buried properly, and epidemic disease was common.

The area of early Taiping fighting was close to the regions of southwest China where bubonic plague had been lingering for centuries. When the rebellion was suppressed, many Taiping followers sought safety in the highlands of Laos and Vietnam, which soon showed infestation by plague. Within a few years the disease reached Hong Kong. From there it spread to Singapore, San Francisco, Calcutta, and London. In the late 1800s there was intense apprehension over the possibility of a worldwide outbreak, and Chinese immigrants were regarded as likely carriers. This fear became a contributing factor in the passage of discriminatory immigration bans on Chinese in the United States in 1882.

The Taiping Rebellion devastated the agricultural centers of China. Many of the most intensely cultivated regions of central and eastern China were depopulated and laid barren. Decades later, some were still uninhabited, and provincial population figures show that major portions of the country did not recover until the twentieth century. Cities, too, were hard hit. Shanghai, a treaty port of modest size before the rebellion, saw its population multiplied many times by the arrival of refugees from the war-blasted neighboring provinces. The city then endured months of siege by the Taipings. Major cultural centers in eastern China lost masterpieces of art and architecture, imperial libraries were burned or their collections exposed to the weather, and the printing blocks used to make books were destroyed. While the empire faced the mountainous challenge of dealing with the material and cultural destruction from the war, it also was burdened by a major ecological disaster in the north: the Yellow River changed course in 1855, destroying the south part of impoverished Shandong province with flood and leaving the former riverbed in northern Shandong to decades of drought.

Decentralization at the End of the Qing Empire

The Qing government emerged from the 1850s with no hope of achieving solvency. The treasury had been bankrupted by the corruption of the 1700s, the attempts in the very early 1800s to restore waterworks and roads, and declining yields from land taxes. By 1850, before the Taiping Rebellion had begun, the Qing government already was spending ten times more than it took in. The burden of indemnities demanded by Europeans after the Opium and Arrow Wars foreclosed any hope that the Qing would get out of debt. Vast stretches of formerly productive rice land were devastated, the population was dispersed, immediate relief for refugees was demanded, and the imperial, volunteer, foreign, and mercenary troops that had suppressed the Taipings were demanding their unpaid wages.

With the Qing government so deeply in their debt, Britain and France became active participants in the period of recovery in China that followed the rebellion. This period is sometimes called the "Tongzhi Restoration," since it occurred during the reign of Tongzhi (r. 1862–1875). To ensure that the Qing government began repaying its debt to Britain, Robert Hart was installed as inspector-general of a newly created Imperial Maritime Customs Service. The revenues he collected were split between Britain and the Qing. Britons and Americans put themselves in the employ of the Qing government as advisers and ambassadors, attempting to smooth communications between the Qing, Europe, and the United States while the imperial government started up the diplomatic machinery demanded by Europe in its latest treaties.

The real work of the recovery, however, was managed by the provincial governors who had come to the forefront in the struggle against the Taipings. To prosecute the war, they had won the right to levy their own taxes, raise their own troops, and run their own bureaucracies. These special powers were not entirely canceled when the war ended. Chief among these governors was Zeng Guofan, who oversaw programs to restore agriculture, communications, education, and publishing, as well as efforts to reform the military and industrialize armaments manufacture.

Like many provincial governors, Zeng preferred to look to the United States rather than to Britain for models and aid. He hired American advisers to run his weapons factories, shipyards, and military academies. He sponsored a daring program in which promising Chinese boys were sent to Hartford, Connecticut, to learn English, science, mathematics, engineering, and history. They returned to China to assume some of the positions previously held by foreign advisers. Though Zeng was never an advocate of participation in public life by women, he was a firm adherent of the Confucian elite view that educated mothers were a necessity, perhaps now more than ever. He not only encouraged but partly oversaw the advanced classical education of his own daughters. Zeng's death in 1872 deprived the empire of a major force for reform.

The period of recovery marked a fundamental structural change in the Qing Empire. Although the emperors after 1850 were ineffective rulers, a coalition of aristocrats supported the reform and recovery programs. If they had been unwilling to legitimate the new powers of provincial governors such as Zeng Guofan, the empire

Cixi's Allies   In the 1860s and 1870s, Cixi was a supporter of reform. In later years she was widely regarded as corrupt and self-centered and as an obstacle to reform. Her greatest allies were the court eunuchs. Introduced to palace life in early China as managers of the imperial harems, enuchs became powerful political parties at court. The first Qing emperors refused to allow the eunuchs any political influence, but by Cixi's time the eunuchs once again were a political factor.   (Freer Gallery, Smithsonian Institution)

might have evaporated within a generation. A crucial member of this alliance was Cixi°, after the 1880s known as the "Empress Dowager." Later observers, both Chinese and foreign, reviled her as a monster of corruption and arrogance. But in the 1860s and 1870s Cixi was a supporter of the provincial governors, some of whom became so powerful that they were managing Qing foreign policy as well as domestic affairs.

No longer a conquest regime dominated by a Manchu military caste and its Chinese civilian appointees, the empire came under the control of a group of reformist aristocrats and military men, independently powerful civilian governors, and a small number of foreign advisers. The Qing lacked strong, central, unified leadership, and could not recover their powers of taxation, legislation, and military command once they had been granted to the provincial governors. From the 1860s forward, the Qing Empire disintegrated into a set of large power zones in which provincial governors handed over leadership to their protégés in a pattern that the Qing court eventually could only ritually legitimate.

JAPAN FROM SHOGUNATE TO EMPIRE

The Qing Empire in the 1600s and 1700s had worked systematically to establish centralized control over China and its neighboring regions. In Japan, a completely different political organization was in place. For a thousand years Japan had had a ruler who in English is called an "emperor," but this ruler had no political power. Instead, since the twelfth century Japan had been governed by shogunates—decentralized secular government under a military leader (*shogun*) who was loyal to the emperor. This was an effective solution to the civil wars that on occasion afflicted Japan. Local lords were permitted to control their lands and populations with very little interference from the shogunate, and enough of the lords remained loyal to the shogun to prevent very frequent changes of regime.

In times of threat from outside, this system showed many weaknesses. It did not permit the coordination of resources and communications on a national scale that would be necessary to resist a major invasion from abroad. Shoguns and their advisers understood the basic weakness of the system and attempted to minimize exposure to and possible threat from foreign powers. In the early 1600s they prohibited foreigners from entering Japan and Japanese from going abroad.

The penalties for breaking these laws was death, but many Japanese ignored them anyway. The most flagrant violations were by powerful local lords in southern Japan, who ran large and very successful pirate operations or black-market trade in stolen or faked passes granting entry into the carefully regulated Qing trading ports. In their entrepreneurial activities these local lords benefited from the decentralization of the shogunal political system. But when a genuine foreign threat was suggested—as when, in 1792, Russian and British ships were spotted off the Japanese coast in separate incidents—the local lords realized that their relative independence would be no help if there was a foreign invasion.

For a time, the Tokugawa Shogunate responded to the threat of foreign invasion by attempting to strengthen its finances and its military forces, much as the more centralized Ottoman and Qing Empires had done. But unlike those empires, the Tokugawa government was limited in the measures it could decree to improve national preparedness, and it was not able to carry out a single policy to resist European and American encroachment. Instead, some of the regional lords of Japan, who did not believe the Tokugawa Shogunate had the ability or the will to protect the islands, developed their own reformed armies, arsenals, and shipyards. In 1853 the arrival of a small U.S. fleet with demands for an opening of Japan to trade with the United States started a process that ended with the destruction of the Tokugawa Shogunate by leaders of the more powerful provinces.

Collapse of the Shogunate

By the 1800s, several of the regional provinces had emerged as much wealthier and more ambitious than others. This was particularly true of Satsuma° and Choshu°, two large domains in southern Japan (see Map 27.3). Because the ancestors of their ruling houses had not been supporters of the Tokugawa lineage, they were punished by being given sparsely settled lands far from the shogunal court. Over time, this location proved to offer a distinct advantage. These regions could rapidly expand their agricultural base when more central regions had reached their limits, and Satsuma and Choshu enjoyed high rates of growth in revenue and population during the early 1800s. The remoteness and the economic vigor of these provinces also fostered a strong sense of local self-reliance.

Cixi (tsuh-shee)

Satsuma (SAT-soo-mah)   **Choshu** (CHOE-shoo)

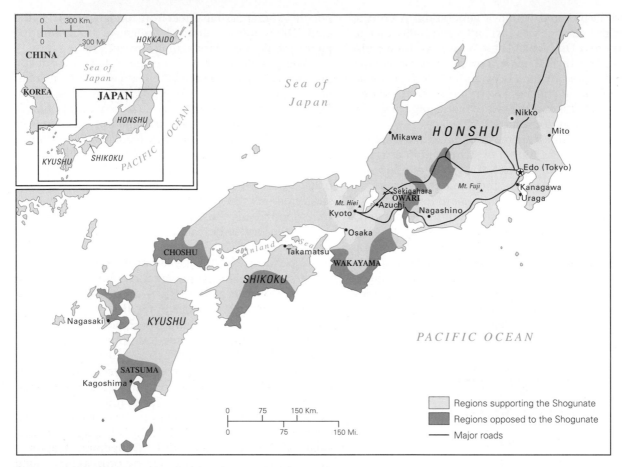

Map 27.3   Tokugawa Japan, to 1867   The Tokugawa Shogunate was the last of the decentralized governments of Japan that put primary power into the hands of a military leader and protector of the emperor. Under the Tokugawa regime, provincial leaders at the western extreme of Honshu Island—regarded as an undesirable site in the early Tokugawa period—experienced higher rates of economic growth and managerial innovation than did provincial leaders in the central provinces.

The economic and political weakness of the shogunate prompted some leaders in the Tokugawa government to attempt a restrengthening, primarily by placing new burdens on the hereditary provincial governors. Some provincial academies for aspiring soldiers, scholars, and bureaucrats became centers for the development and dissemination of a new ideology of loyalty to the shoguns, who depended on the politically weak emperors of Japan for their legitimacy. But the arrival of the American Commodore Matthew C. Perry and his fleet of what the Japanese called "black ships" in 1853 shattered the shogunate's attempts to restore its influence across the provinces. While the Japanese, like other East Asians, had been focused on intruders from their west such as the Dutch, British, French, and Russians, the Americans'

search for a route to bring pelts from northwest America across the Pacific had led them to surprise Japan with an approach from the east. Perry demanded that Japan open its ports to U.S. ships for refueling and for trade when he returned in 1854.

Perry's terms sparked a crisis in the shogunate. Consultation among the provincial governors and the shogunal officials was extensive. In the end, the shogunal advisers advocated capitulation to Perry. They pointed to China's humiliating defeats in the Opium and Arrow Wars and expressed doubt that the treaty powers in China would be discouraged from seeking other ports in East Asia. Leaders of the provincial governors opposed this view. They pointed out that the United States was not a formidable power like Britain and predicted that a

Arrivals from the East   In 1853 Commodore Matthew Perry's ships surprised the Tokugawa Shogunate by appearing not in Kyushu or southern Honshu, where European ships previously had been spotted, but at Uraga on the coast of eastern Honshu. The Japanese soon learned that Perry had come not from the south but across the Pacific from the east. The novelty of the threat unsettled the provincial leaders, who were largely responsible for their own defense. In this print done after the Meiji Restoration, the traditionally dressed local samurai go out to confront the mysterious "black ships."   (Courtesy of the Trustees of the British Museum)

refusal by Japan would result only in the Americans seeking an easier refueling location elsewhere.

In 1854, Perry's fleet returned, and representatives of the Tokugawa shogun indicated their willingness to sign the Treaty of Kanagawa°—modeled on the unequal treaties between China and the Western powers. Before provincial leaders considered the discussion closed, shogunal representatives signed the treaty in 1858. Angry and disappointed, some provincial governors began to encourage an underground movement calling for the destruction of the Tokugawa regime and the banning of foreigners from Japan.

Kanagawa (KAH-nah-GAH-wah)

Tensions between the shogunate and some provincial leaders, particularly in Choshu and Satsuma, increased in the early 1860s. British and French shelling of the southwestern coasts in 1864 further enraged provincial samurai who rejected the Treaty of Kanagawa and resented the Shogunate's inability to protect the country. Young, ambitious, educated men who faced mediocre prospects under the rigid Tokugawa class system emerged as provincial leaders. Among them, the Choshu leaders Yamagata Aritomo and Ito Hitobumi were outstanding. They realized in 1867 that they should stop warring with their rival province, Satsuma, and instead join forces to lead a rebellion against the shogunate. The civil war was intense but brief. In 1868, a new government was founded, and the young emperor Mutsuhito (r. 1868–1912) was declared "restored."

The Meiji Restoration

To destroy the old state was one thing; to create a new state with the resources and will to deal with economic and military problems was quite another. Though Japan is smaller than the landmass of either the Qing or the Ottoman Empire, its many islands are far-flung and its natural resources extremely limited. Thus the size of Japan was not necessarily a major explanation for the apparent ease with which it was reformed. Perhaps more important was the fact that, unlike the Qing and Ottoman Empires, Japan was of no great strategic importance to Europe or the United States.

American merchants expected that Japan, like China, would be a rich market for their goods, and American naval planners wanted a reprovisioning station in Japan to facilitate the movement of U.S. ships along the China coast. But neither of these considerations would have propelled the United States to initiate war with Japan in the 1850s. Also, the European powers showed only a casual interest in Japan. Thus there was no foreign effort to economically or strategically sustain the Tokugawa Shogunate, and when it was destroyed, the small group who controlled the new government—often called the Meiji° oligarchs—were unimpeded in their plans for a centralized, industrialized national state.

The ideology of the new state, known by Mutsuhito's reign name, *Meiji*, ("enlightened rule"), was one source of its power. By "restoring" the emperor, the new leaders claimed to have ended centuries of imperial seclusion and disempowerment by the shoguns. The mysticism of the emperors, nationalism, and anxiety over the foreign threat were all combined to create a decade of focused effort on the transformation of Japan from a decentralized, traditional military government to a centralized, civil, industrializing state. The nationalistic ideology of the Meiji Restoration coexisted with intense interest in European practices in government, education, industry, dress, and even popular culture.

The achievements of the **Meiji Restoration** were remarkable. The oligarchs were extraordinarily talented and far-sighted men. They overcame regional resistance to political and social reform, and gradually but systematically they effected the dissolution of the traditional provincial governorships and of the samurai class. Though the Tokugawa government had been poor, there was

Meiji (MAY-gee)

wealth in some of the provinces. The literacy rate may have been as high as 35 percent—certainly the highest in Asia at the time—and the oligarchs shrewdly exploited it in their introduction of new educational systems, a conscript army, and new communications. The government was able to establish heavy industry through the use of judicious deficit financing without extensive foreign debt, thanks to decades of experimentation with industrial development and financing in the provinces in the earlier 1800s. With a conscript army and a revamped educational system the oligarchs attempted to create a new citizenry that was literate and competent but also loyal and obedient.

CONCLUSION

The response of Japan to the challenge of the industrializing nations was a striking contrast to the responses of the Ottoman and Qing Empires. An important point of comparison is the relationship between financial resources and reform from the elite levels downward. In the Ottoman and Qing (as well as the Russian) Empires, the imperial courts attempted to mandate reforms in the military. To meet the cost, these revenue-starved empires debased their currencies, thereby stimulating inflation. To continue the reforms, they became dependent on foreign loans, which ultimately led to control of their finances, commercial strategies, and in some cases revenue-producing organs by European powers. Japan, in contrast, experienced comparatively few top-down major reforms under the Tokugawa shoguns. Instead, the decentralized provinces provided their own means of experimenting with local military improvement, new educational programs, and deficit financing before the Meiji Restoration of 1868. Afterward, they could compare their experiences and apply what they had learned.

Japan's exposure to the military and economic pressure of the sea powers was much more limited than that of the Ottoman and Qing Empires. One reason for this difference was that Japan was not an empire in the same sense. It did not control extensive trade networks and urban centers to which Britain and France wished to gain privileged access. Nor was its position, on the far eastern of the Eurasian continent, regarded as strategically significant in the West. The treaty that the United States forced on Japan was practically Japan's only experience with unequal treaties. In contrast, the Treaty of Nanking of 1842 ushered in the period of unequal treaties that resulted in the installation of a vast system of foreign privilege in China. European and American pressure on the Qing Empire became so intense that the Chinese could neither learn to finance the industries necessary for a strong military nor find a period of peace in which to develop the educational institutions that would have produced a new generation of leaders.

The Meiji oligarchs hoped that Japan's relatively remote location and relatively insignificant political status would permit it breathing space to make the revolutionary changes they envisaged. The Qing and the Ottoman rulers could only hope that mutual distrust by the European powers would limit the ambitions of any individual European state. This strategy—in China known as "using the barbarians against the barbarians"—continually embroiled the Qing Empire in short, localized wars or threatened wars with aspiring signatories in the unequal treaty system.

In the Qing territories and in the Ottoman Empire, Europeans and Americans did not need to establish colonies in order to enjoy privileged status. Neither Ottoman nor Qing lands were in need of "development" by colonial forces. Pockets of wealth—primarily in the cities—could be exploited, and this maneuvering was best done through strategic alliances or diplomacy, not by the expensive and risky methods of colonization. It is not a coincidence that both of the empires whose territorial integrity the European powers—and, in the case of China, the United States—swore to defend were ultimately derided as the "sick men" of Eurasia, unable to defend themselves against their defenders, and kept in a state of low-grade survival to provide markets, raw materials, and strategic advantages to smaller, more dynamic nations.

The Crimean War and Taiping Rebellion were watershed events in the loss of centralization and autonomy for, respectively, the Ottoman and Qing Empires. In each conflict the Eurasian empire in question emerged as nominally victorious. But both land-based empires were overextended. They suffered from declining revenues and social dislocation. Ironically, within these empires were enclaves of merchants and artisans who were enriched by the trade with Europe and America, but the imperial governments never found a way to tax these new incomes.

Much domestic wealth flowed from the Ottoman and Qing Empires to foreign countries in payment for legal as well as illegal commodities, and state resources for arms and education could not be found. Increasing pressure from Britain and France deepened the financial woes and political tensions of both empires and heightened the elite's awareness of the necessity for military reform. During the Crimean War and the Taiping Rebellion, the financial obligations of each empire and the strategic advantages of its existence led to the formation of alliances with Britain and France. And in the aftermath of the conflicts, each empire experienced serious problems with decentralization, loss of control over its borders, permanent indebtedness and inflation, a progressive loss of international and domestic credibility, and new dependence on foreign protection.

The differences between the Ottoman and Qing also are illuminating. The Ottomans made an attempt to modernize their military and make their government more efficient before the end of the 1700s. Their proximity to Europe gave them direct experience with the Napoleonic era and the rising nationalism of the 1800s. The intense struggle between France and Russia, in particular, gave the Ottomans a strategic position that made it distinctly to the advantage of France to side with the Ottomans in their territorial struggles. For their part, the Ottomans were comparatively swift in their adaptation of aspects of French culture, military practices, and commercial institutions. This adaptability sustained Ottoman political credibility in Europe through the critical period of the war for Greek independence, and later it allowed design and implementation of the reform program under Mahmud II. On the strength of that recentralization, the secular programs that defined a civil sphere and a Turkish identity gave strength to the very nationalist movement that eventually helped destroy the empire.

Unlike the Ottomans, the Qing were not able to achieve even a modest degree of recentralization. Suppression of the Taiping Rebellion required the dissolution of the traditional military structures, the regionalization of command and support, and finally the use of foreign troops. The alliance formed by Britain and France at this time was to become more active in the very late 1800s, as the European powers and the United States attempted repeatedly to prevent the colonization of Qing territory by Japan.

■ Key Terms

Janissaries	Opium War
Serbia	Bannermen
Tanzimat	Treaty of Nanking
Crimean War	treaty ports
percussion cap	most-favored-nation status
breech-loading rifle	Taiping Rebellion
extraterritoriality	Meiji Restoration

■ Suggested Reading

For the Ottoman Empire there is a large and interesting literature, much of it based on original documents, some in translation, relating to Ottoman administration throughout Europe and the Middle East. For widely available general histories see Stanford Shaw, *History of the Ottoman Empire and Modern Turkey* (1976–1977), and J.P.D.B. Kinross, *The Ottoman Centuries: The Rise and Fall of the Turkish Empire* (1977).

On the economy and society of the nineteenth-century Ottoman Empire see Huri Islamoglu-Inan, ed., *The Ottoman Empire and the World-Economy* (1987); Resat Kasaba, *The Ottoman Empire and the World Economy: The Nineteenth Century* (1988); Sevket Pamuk, *The Ottoman Empire and European Capitalism, 1820–1913: Trade, Investment, and Production* (1987); Kemal H. Karpat, *Ottoman Population, 1830–1914: Demographic and Social Characteristics* (1985); and Carter V. Findley, *Bureaucratic Reform in the Ottoman Empire: The Sublime Porte, 1789–1922* (1980). On the reform program and the emergence of national concepts see also Selim Deringil, *The Well-Protected Domains: Ideology and the Legitimation of Power in the Ottoman Empire, 1876–1909* (1998).

On the Qing Empire of the nineteenth century see Pamela Kyle Crossley, *Orphan Warriors: Three Manchu Generations and the End of the Qing World* (1990), and for a more detailed political history see Mary C. Wright, *The Last Stand of Chinese Conservatism: The T'ung-chih Restoration, 1862–1874* (1971). There is a very large literature on both the Opium War and the Taiping Rebellion, including reprinted editions of contemporary observers. For general histories of the Opium War see Peter Ward Fay, *The Opium War, 1840–1842: Barbarians in the Celestial Empire in the Early Part of the Nineteenth Century and the War by Which They Forced Her Gates Ajar* (1975); Christopher Hibbert, *The Dragon Wakes: China and the West, 1793–1911* (1970); and the classic study by Chang Hsin-pao, *Commissioner Lin and the Opium War* (1964). For a recent, more monographic study on Qing political thought in the period of the Opium War see James M. Polachek, *The Inner Opium War* (1992). On the Taiping Rebellion, enduring sources are S. Y. Têng, *The Taiping Rebellion and the Western Powers: A Comprehensive Survey* (1971), and C. A. Curwen, *Taiping Rebel: the Deposition of Li Hsiu-ch'eng* (1976); see also Caleb Carr, *The Devil Soldier: the Story of Frederick Townsend Ward* (1992). The most recent study is Jonathan D. Spence, *God's Chinese Son: The Taiping Heavenly Kingdom of Hong Xiuquan* (1996).

The classic work on the period leading to the Meiji Restoration in Japan is Albert M. Craig, *Choshu in the Meiji Restoration* (1961). See also Conrad Totman, *The Collapse of the Tokugawa Bakufu, 1862–1868* (1980), Bob Tadashi Wakabayashi, *Anti-Foreignism and Western Learning in Early-Modern Japan: The New Theses of 1825* (1986); Peter Booth Wiley with Korogi Ichiro, *Yankees in the Land of the Gods: Commodore Perry and the Opening of Japan* (1990); and George M. Wilson, *Patriots and Redeemers in Japan : Motives in the Meiji Restoration* (1992).

PART SEVEN

GLOBAL DOMINANCE AND DIVERSITY,

1850–1945

CHAPTER 28
THE NEW POWER BALANCE, 1850–1900

CHAPTER 29
THE NEW IMPERIALISM, 1869–1914

CHAPTER 30
THE CRISIS OF THE IMPERIAL ORDER, 1900–1929

CHAPTER 31
THE COLLAPSE OF THE OLD ORDER, 1929–1949

CHAPTER 32
STRIVING FOR INDEPENDENCE: AFRICA, INDIA, AND LATIN AMERICA, 1900–1949

etween 1850 and 1950, Europe, the United States, and Japan industrialized and became powerful. One cause of the power of Europe, the United States, and Japan was nationalism, a bond uniting people on the basis of a common culture or shared historical experiences. In some nations, public participation resulted in basic freedoms and strong parliamentary institutions. In others, authoritarian leaders used nationalist feelings to mobilize mass support.

Another cause of Western and Japanese power in this period was industrialization itself. New technologies and economic arrangements transformed the lives of people of all classes and professions. Work in-

creasingly took place in factories and offices, separating employment from home life, husbands from wives, children from parents. A growing proportion of married women became housewives, and compulsory education systems took over the care of children. Intensifying industrial activities transformed the natural environment. Pollution from manufacturing, long a local problem, began to affect entire regions.

Industrialization led to the creation of increasingly destructive weapons that enabled the Western powers to extend their commercial and political influence over Africa, most of Asia, and Latin America. By 1914, Britain, France, and the United States dominated over half of the area and peoples of the world.

By the time Germany and Japan entered the competition for overseas colonial empires, few unconquered territories remained.

Germany's desire to become a global power was a major cause of the First World War. The defeat of Germany did not restore the prewar equilibrium, as the victorious Allied nations had hoped. The Russian Revolution of 1917 led to the establishment of the world's first communist state. The collapse of the Ottoman Empire sparked changes in Middle Eastern societies, most dramatically in Turkey itself.

When the world economy collapsed in the 1930s, social disruption in Germany and Japan brought to power extremist politicians who sought to solve their countries' economic woes by seizing neighboring territories. Nationalism assumed its most hideous form in World War II. The war led to the massacre of millions of innocent people and the destruction of countless cities.

Domination by the great powers inspired a new generation of leaders to embrace the politics of national liberation. After decades of struggle India achieved independence in 1947. Two years later Communists led by Mao Zedong overthrew a Chinese government they denounced as too subservient to the West. In Latin America leaders turned to nationalist economic and social politics.

The year 1945 marked the end of western European dominance. Only the United States and the Soviet Union remained to compete for global influence. Meanwhile, nationalism was rapidly spreading to the rest of the world, bringing with it the urge to acquire the benefits and power of industrial technology.

	1850	1870	1890
Americas	Creation of Dominion of Canada 1867 •	U.S. Civil War **1861–1865**	British build railroads in Brazil and Argentina 1880s •	• **1890** U.S. is leading steel producer Spanish-American War **1898** • **1880–1914** Immigration from southern and eastern Europe surges
Europe	• **1851** Majority of British population living in cities • **1856** Transformation of steel and chemical industries begins	**1870–1914** Era of the New Imperialism • **1871** Unification of Germany, Italy	**1894–1906** Dreyfus affair in France
Africa	**1853–1877** Livingstone, Stanley expeditions in central Africa End of transatlantic slave trade **1867** • Gold discovered in southern Africa **1884–1886**	**1884–1885** Berlin Africa Conference	• **1880s** West Africa conquered by France and Britain • **1896** Ethiopians defeat Italian army at Adowa Nigeria becomes British protectorate **1899** •
Middle East	**1863–1879** Ismail westernizes Egypt Suez Canal opens **1869** •	• **1878** Ottoman Empire loses most of its European territories	• **1882** British occupy Egypt • **1904** Young Turk reforms in Ottoman Empire
Asia and Oceania	Direct British rule in India **1858** • • **1862** French conquer Indochina Meiji Restoration in Japan **1868** •	First Indian National Congress **1885** • Russia conquers Central Asia **1884–1887**	Boxer Rebellion in China **1900** • Sino-Japanese War **1894** • **1904–1905** Russo-Japanese War

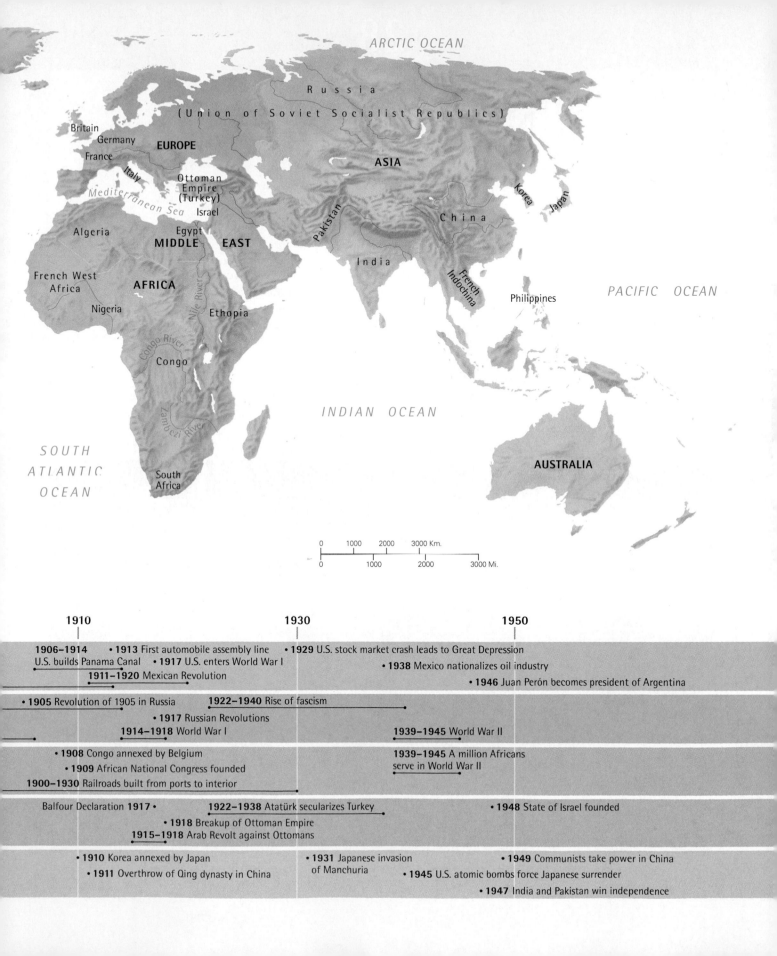

ARCTIC OCEAN

R u s s i a

(U n i o n   o f   S o v i e t   S o c i a l i s t   R e p u b l i c s)

Britain
Germany
France
EUROPE
Italy
Ottoman
Empire
(Turkey)
Israel
Mediterranean Sea

ASIA

Korea
Japan

C h i n a

Pakistan

Algeria
Egypt
MIDDLE   EAST

I n d i a

French West
Africa
AFRICA

French
Indochina

Nigeria

Philippines

PACIFIC   OCEAN

Nile River

Ethopia

Congo River

Congo

INDIAN   OCEAN

Zambezi River

SOUTH
ATLANTIC
OCEAN

AUSTRALIA

South
Africa

```
0      1000    2000    3000 Km.
|---|---|---|---|---|---|---|
0      1000    2000    3000 Mi.
```

1910   **1930**   **1950**

1906–1914 • **1913** First automobile assembly line • **1929** U.S. stock market crash leads to Great Depression
U.S. builds Panama Canal   • **1917** U.S. enters World War I   • **1938** Mexico nationalizes oil industry
   1911–1920 Mexican Revolution   • **1946** Juan Perón becomes president of Argentina

• **1905** Revolution of 1905 in Russia   **1922–1940** Rise of fascism
          • **1917** Russian Revolutions
     1914–1918 World War I   **1939–1945** World War II

• **1908** Congo annexed by Belgium   **1939–1945** A million Africans
   • **1909** African National Congress founded   serve in World War II
1900–1930 Railroads built from ports to interior

Balfour Declaration **1917** •   **1922–1938** Atatürk secularizes Turkey   • **1948** State of Israel founded
          • **1918** Breakup of Ottoman Empire
     1915–1918 Arab Revolt against Ottomans

   • **1910** Korea annexed by Japan   • **1931** Japanese invasion   • **1949** Communists take power in China
     • **1911** Overthrow of Qing dynasty in China   of Manchuria   • **1945** U.S. atomic bombs force Japanese surrender
                                          • **1947** India and Pakistan win independence

THE NEW POWER BALANCE,
1850–1900

New Technologies and the World Economy • Social Transformations •
Nationalism and the Unification of Germany • The Great Powers of Europe,
1871–1900 • New Great Powers: The United States and Japan
ENVIRONMENT AND TECHNOLOGY: Railroads and Immigration
SOCIETY AND CULTURE: Demonstrating for Women's Rights

Silk Factory in Japan   Silk manufacture, Japan's best-known industry, began to be mechanized
in the 1870s. In this factory, as in most textile mills, the workers were women.

*O*n January 18, 1871, in the Hall of Mirrors of the palace of Versailles, King Wilhelm I of Prussia was proclaimed emperor of Germany before a crowd of officers and other German rulers. This ceremony marked the unification of many small German states into one nation. Off to one side stood Prussian chancellor Otto von Bismarck°, the man most responsible for the creation of a united Germany. A few years earlier, he had declared: "The great issues of the day will be decided not by speeches and votes of the majority—that was the great mistake of 1848 and 1849—but by iron and blood." Indeed it was "blood"—that is, victories on the battlefield—rather than popular participation that had led to the unification of Germany; among the dignitaries in the Hall of Mirrors that day, only two or three were civilians. As for "iron," it meant not only weapons but, more important, the industries required to produce weapons. Thus, after 1871, nationalism, once a dream of revolutionaries and romantics, became ever more closely associated with military force and with industry.

This chapter deals with a small group of countries—Germany, France, Britain, Russia, the United States, and Japan—that we call "great powers." In the next chapter, which deals with the era of the "New Imperialism" (1870–1914), we will see how these nations used their power to conquer colonial empires in Asia and Africa and to control Latin America. Together, Chapters 28 and 29 describe an era in which a handful of wealthy industrialized nations—all but one of them of European culture—imposed on the other peoples of the world a domination more powerful than any experienced before or since.

As you read this chapter, ask yourself the following questions:

- What new technologies and industries appeared between 1850 and 1900, and how did they affect the world economy?
- How did the societies of the industrial countries change during this period?
- Why do we call certain countries "great powers" but not others?

Otto von Bismark (UTT-oh fun BIS-mark)

NEW TECHNOLOGIES AND THE WORLD ECONOMY

After 1850, industrialization took off in new directions. It spread to new countries, especially Germany and the United States, which surpassed Great Britain as the world's leading industrial powers by 1890. Small companies, like those that had flourished in Britain in the late nineteenth century, were overshadowed by large corporations, some owned by wealthy capitalists, others (especially in Russia and Japan) by governments.

New technologies based on advances in physics and chemistry revolutionized everyday life and transformed the world economy. Some of the inventions of this period—the automobile, airplane, and radio in particular—aroused tremendous excitement but did not make an impact on people's lives until after World War I (see Chapter 30). Other advances, such as the steel and chemical industries, electricity, and the spreading networks of steamships, telegraphs, and railroads, were already important by 1900.

The Steel and Chemical Industries

Steel is a special form of iron, both hard and elastic. Until the eighteenth century, it could be made only by skilled blacksmiths in very small quantities at a very high cost and thus was reserved for swords, knives, axes, and watch springs. The invention of the crucible (a container in which molten iron was stirred until it turned to steel) in the 1740s made steel cheap enough for tools, weapons, and machines. By 1850 Britain was producing some 60,000 tons a year.

Then came a series of inventions that made steel the cheapest and most versatile metal ever known. In the 1850s, William Kelly, a Kentucky iron master, discovered that air forced through molten pig iron turned it into steel without additional fuel. In 1856 the Englishman Henry Bessemer improved Kelly's method. The Bessemer converter produced steel at one-tenth the cost of the crucible method. Other new processes permitted steel to be made from scrap iron, an increasingly important raw material, and from the phosphoric iron ores common in western Europe. As a result, world steel production rose from a half-million tons in 1870 to 28 million in 1900, of which the United States produced 10 million, Germany 8, and Britain 4.9. Steel became cheap and abundant enough to make rails, bridges, ships, and even "tin" cans meant to be used once and thrown away.

Paris Lit Up by Electricity, 1900   The electric light bulb was invented in the United States and Britain, but Paris made such extensive use of the new technology that it was nicknamed "City of Lights." To mark the Paris Exposition of 1900, the Eiffel Tower and all the surrounding buildings were illuminated with strings of light bulbs while powerful spotlights swept the sky.   (Courtesy, Civiche Raccolte d'Art Applicata ed Incisioni (Raccolte Bertarelli) Photo: Foto Saporetti)

The new steel mills were hungry consumers of coal, iron ore, limestone, and other raw materials. They took up as much space as whole towns, belched smoke and particulate night and day, and left behind huge hills of slag and other waste products. Environmental degradation, long familiar in certain communities, affected entire regions such as the English Midlands, the German Ruhr, and parts of Pennsylvania.

The chemical industry followed a similar pattern. Until the late eighteenth century, chemicals were produced by trial and error in small workshops. By the early nineteenth century, soda, sulfuric acid, and chlorine bleach (used in the cotton industry) were manufactured on a large scale, especially in Britain. In 1856 the Englishman William Perkin created the first synthetic dye, aniline purple, from coal tar; the next few years were known in Europe as the "mauve decade" from the fashionable color for most women's clothes. Industry began mass-producing other organic chemicals—compounds containing carbon atoms. Toward the end of the century, German chemists synthesized red, violet, blue, brown, and black dyes as well. These bright, long-lasting colors delighted consumers but damaged the natural-dye exports of many tropical countries, especially hurting plantations in India that produced indigo, a blue vegetable dye.

Chemistry also made important advances in the manufacture of explosives. The first of these were nitrocellulose and nitroglycerin, a liquid so dangerous that it explodes when shaken. In 1866 the Swedish scientist Alfred Nobel found a way to turn nitroglycerin into a stable solid—dynamite. This and other new explosives were very useful in mining and the construction of railroads and canals. They also enabled the armies and navies of the great powers to arm themselves with increasingly accurate and powerful rifles and cannon.

The growing complexity of industrial chemistry made it one of the first fields where science and technology interacted on a daily basis. This development gave a great advantage to Germany, which had the most advanced engineering schools and scientific institutes of its time. While the British government paid little attention to science and engineering, the German government funded research and encouraged cooperation between universities and industries. By the end of the nineteenth century, Germany was the world's leading producer of dyes, drugs, synthetic fertilizers, ammonia, and nitrates used in making explosives.

Electricity

The third innovation that transformed the world of the late nineteenth century was **electricity.** At first, producing electric current was so costly that it was used only for electroplating and telegraphy. In 1831 the Englishman Michael Faraday showed that the motion of a copper wire through a magnetic field induced an electric current in the wire. Based on his

CHRONOLOGY

	Europe	United States	East Asia
1850	**1851** Majority of British population living in cities **1856** Bessemer converter; first synthetic dye **1859** Charles Darwin, *On the Origin of Species* **1861** Emancipation of serfs (Russia) **1866** Alfred Nobel develops dynamite **1867** Karl Marx, *Das Kapital*	**1865** Civil War ends; economic expansion begins **1865–1914** Surge of immigration from southern and eastern Europe	**1862–1908** Rule of Dowager Empress Cixi (China)
1870	**1871** Unification of Germany; unification of Italy **1875** Social Democratic Party founded in Germany **1882** Married Women's Property Act (Britain)	**1879** Thomas Edison develops incandescent lamp	**1868** Meiji Restoration begins modernization drive in Japan
1890	**1894–1906** Dreyfus affair (France) **1905** Revolution of 1905 (Russia)	**1890** United States is the world's leading producer of steel **1890s** "Jim Crow" laws enforce segregation in southern states **1899** United States acquires Puerto Rico and the Philippines	**1894** Sino-Japanese War **1900** Boxer Uprising (China) **1904–1905** Russo-Japanese War **1910** Japan annexes Korea

discovery, in the 1870s inventors devised efficient generators that turned mechanical energy into electric current and opened the way to a host of new applications.

Arc lamps lit up public squares, theaters, and stores. For a while, homes continued to rely on gas lamps, which produced a softer light. Then in 1879 **Thomas Edison** in the United States developed an incandescent lamp well suited to lighting small rooms. In 1882 Edison created the world's first electrical distribution network, in New York. By the turn of the century, electric lighting was rapidly replacing dim and smelly gas lamps in the cities of Europe and North America.

Other uses of electricity quickly appeared. Electric streetcars and, later, subways helped reduce the traffic jams that clogged the large cities of Europe and North America. Electric motors replaced steam engines and power belts, increasing productivity and improving workers' safety. As demand for electricity grew, engineers learned to use waterpower to produce electricity, and hydroelectric plants were built. The plant at Niagara Falls, on the border between Ontario, Canada, and New York State, opened in 1895 and produced an incredible 11,000 horsepower.

Electricity helped alleviate some environmental problems. Electric motors and lamps did not pollute the air. Power plants were built at a distance from cities. As electric trains and streetcars replaced horse-drawn trolleys and coal-burning locomotives, cities became noticeably cleaner and healthier. At the same time, electricity created a huge demand for copper, bringing Chile, Montana, and southern Africa into the world economy as never before.

Shipping and Telegraph Cables

The late nineteenth century saw a tremendous expansion of railroads and shipping, linked to growth in world trade and to technological innovations. Steam-powered ships dated back to the 1830s but were too costly at first for anything but first-class passenger traffic. Then, midcentury, a series of developments radically transformed ocean shipping. First iron, then steel, replaced the wood that had been used for hulls since shipbuilding began. Propellers replaced paddle wheels. Engineers built more powerful and fuel-efficient engines. By the turn of the century a marine engine could convert the heat produced by burning a single sheet of paper into the power to move one ton over half a mile. The average size of freighters increased from 200 tons in 1850 to 7,500 tons in 1900. Coaling stations and ports able to handle large ships were built around the world. Most of all, the Suez Canal, constructed in 1869, shortened the distance between Europe and Asia and triggered a massive switch from sail power to steam (see Chapter 29).

The steamers of the turn of the century were so costly they had to be used as efficiently as possible. As the world's fleet of merchant ships grew from 9 million to 35 million tons between 1850 and 1910, new organizations developed to make the best use of ships. One such organization was the shipping line, a company that offered fast, punctual, and reliable service on a fixed schedule. Passengers, mail, and perishable freight traveled on scheduled liners. Most ships, however, were tramp freighters that voyaged from one port to another under orders from their company headquarters in Europe or North America.

To control their ships around the globe, shipping companies used a new medium of communications: **submarine telegraph cables** laid on the ocean floor linking the continents. Cables were laid across the Atlantic in 1866, to India in 1870, to China, Japan, and Australia in 1871 and 1872, to Latin America in 1872 and 1873, to East and South Africa in 1879, and to West Africa in 1886. By the turn of the century, cables connected every country and almost every inhabited island. As the public and the press extolled the "annihilation of time and space" (see the Environment and Technology feature in Chapter 24), cables became the indispensable tools of modern shipping and business.

Railroads

By 1850 the first **railroads** had proved so successful that every industrializing country, and many that aspired to become industrial, began to build lines. The next fifty years saw a tremendous expansion of the world's rail networks. After a rapid spurt of building new lines, British railroad mileage leveled off at around 20,000 miles (over 32,000 kilometers) in the 1870s. France and Germany built networks longer than Britain's, as did Canada and Russia. When Japan began building its railway network in the 1870s, it imported several hundred engineers from the United States and

Britain. In the 1880s, it replaced them with newly trained Japanese engineers. By the early twentieth century, rail lines reached every city and province in Japan (see Map 28.1).

The largest rail network by far was the rail network of the United States. At the end of its Civil War in 1865, the United States already had 35,000 miles (over 56,000 kilometers) of track, three times as much as Britain. By 1915, the American network reached 390,000 miles (around 628,000 kilometers), more than the next seven longest networks combined.

Railroads were not confined to the industrialized nations; they could be constructed almost anywhere they would be of value to business or government. That included regions with abundant raw materials or agricultural products, like South Africa, Mexico, or Argentina, and densely populated countries like Egypt. The British built the fourth largest rail network in the world in India in order to reinforce their presence and develop trade with their largest colony (see Chapter 26).

Railroads consumed huge amounts of land. Many old cities doubled in size to accommodate railroad stations, sidings, tracks, warehouses, and repair shops. In the countryside, railroads required bridges, tunnels, and embankments. Railroads also consumed vast quantities of timber for ties to hold the rails and for bridges, often using up whole forests for miles on either side of the tracks. Throughout the world, they opened new land to agriculture, mining, and other human exploitation of natural resources, whether for the benefit of the local inhabitants, as in Europe and North America, or for a distant power, as in the colonial empires.

World Trade and Finance

Between 1850 and 1913 world trade expanded tenfold. Because steamships were much more efficient than sailing ships, the cost of freight dropped between 50 and 95 percent, making it worthwhile to ship even cheap and heavy products halfway around the world. Europe imported wheat from the United States and India, wool from Australia, and beef from Argentina, and exported coal, railroad equipment, textiles, and machinery.

The growth of world trade transformed the economies of different parts of the world in different ways. The economics of western Europe and North America, the first to industrialize, grew more prosperous and diversified. Their capitalist economies, however, were prey to sudden swings in the business cycle—booms followed by deep depressions in which workers lost their jobs and investors their fortunes. For example, because of the close

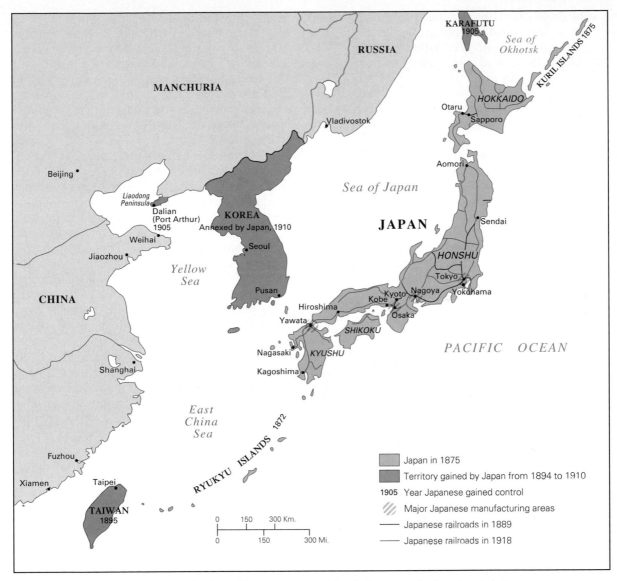

Map 28.1 Expansion and Modernization of Japan, 1868–1918 As Japan acquired modern industry, it followed the example of the European powers in seeking overseas colonies. Its colonial empire grew at the expense of its neighbors: Taiwan was taken from China in 1895. Karafuto (now Sakhalin) from Russia in 1905, and all of Korea became a colony in 1910.

connections among the industrial economies, the collapse of a bank in Austria in 1873 triggered a depression that spread to the United States, causing mass unemployment. Worldwide recessions occurred in the mid-1880s and mid-1890s as well.

In the late 1870s and early 1880s, Germany, the United States, and other late-industrializing Western nations raised tariffs to protect their industries from British

competition. Yet trade barriers could not insulate them from the business cycle, for money continued to flow almost unhindered around the world. One of the main causes of the growing interdependence of the global economy was the financial power of Great Britain. Long after German and American industries surpassed the British, Britain continued to dominate the flow of trade, finance, and information. In 1900 two-thirds of the world's submarine cables were British or passed through Britain. Over half of the world's shipping was British owned. Britain invested one-fourth of its national wealth overseas, much of it in the United States and Argentina. British money financed many of the railroads, harbors, mines, and other big projects outside Europe. While other currencies fluctuated, the pound sterling was as good as gold, and nine-tenths of international transactions used sterling.

Nonindustrial areas also were tied to the world economy as never before. They were more vulnerable to changes in price and demand than were the industrialized nations, for many of them produced raw materials that could be replaced by synthetic substitutes or alternative sources of supply. Even products in constant demand, like Cuban sugar or Bolivian tin, were subject to wild swings in price on the world market. Nevertheless, until World War I, the value of exports from the tropical countries generally remained high, and the size of their populations remained moderate.

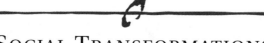

SOCIAL TRANSFORMATIONS

The technological and economic changes of the late nineteenth century sparked profound social changes in the industrial nations. A fast-growing population swelled cities to unprecedented size, and millions of Europeans emigrated to the Americas. Strained relations between industrial employers and workers spawned labor movements and new forms of radical policies. And women found their lives dramatically altered.

Population and Migrations

The population of Europe grew faster from 1850 to 1914 than ever before or since, almost doubling from 265 million to 468 million. In non-European countries with predominantly white populations—the United States, Canada, Australia, New Zealand, and Argentina—the increase was even greater because of the inflow of Europeans. There were many reasons for the mass migrations of this period: the Irish famine of 1847–1848; the persecution of Jews in Russia; poverty and population growth in Italy, Spain, Poland, and Scandinavia; and the cultural ties between Great Britain and English-speaking countries overseas. Equally important was the availability of cheap and rapid steamships and railroads serving travelers at

both ends (see Environment and Technology: Railroads and Immigration). Between 1850 and 1900, on average, 400,000 Europeans migrated overseas every year; between 1900 and 1914 the flood rose to over 1 million a year. From 1850 to 1910 the population of the United States and Canada rose from 25 million to 98 million, nearly a fourfold increase. The proportion of people of European ancestry in the world's population rose from one-fifth to one-third.

Why did the number of Europeans and their descendants overseas jump so dramatically? Much of the increase came from a drop in the death rate, as epidemics and starvation became less common. The Irish famine was the last peacetime famine in European history. As farmers plowed up the plains of North America and planted wheat, much of which was shipped to Europe, food supplies increased faster than the population. Fertilizers boosted crop yields, and canning and refrigeration made food abundant year-round. The diet of Europeans and North Americans improved as meat, fruit, vegetables, and oils became part of the daily fare of city dwellers, in winter as well as summer.

Asians also migrated in large numbers during this period, often as indentured laborers recruited to work on plantations, in mines, and on railroads. Indians went mainly to Africa, Southeast Asia, and other tropical colonies of Great Britain. Chinese emigrated to Southeast Asia and the East Indies. Many Chinese, as well as Japanese and Filipinos, went to Hawaii and California, where they encountered growing hostility from Europeans.

Urbanization and Social Structures

In 1851 Britain became the first nation to have a majority of its population living in towns and cities. By 1914, 80 percent of its population was urban, as were 60 percent of the German and 45 percent of the French populations. Cities grew to unprecedented size. London grew from 2.7 million in 1850 and to 6.6 million in 1900. New York, a small town of 64,000 people in 1800, reached 3.4 million by 1900, a fiftyfold increase. Population growth and the building of railroads and industries allowed cities to invade the countryside, swallowing nearby towns and villages. In 1800 New York had covered only the southernmost quarter of Manhattan Island, some 3 miles (nearly 8 square kilometers); by 1900 it covered 150 square miles (390 square kilometers). London in 1800 measured about 4 square miles (about 10 square kilometers); by 1900 it covered twenty times more area. In the English Midlands, in the German Ruhr, and around Tokyo Bay, towns

Urban Growth: Vienna in 1873   During the nineteenth century, European cities grew with unprecedented speed. This bird's-eye view of the Austro-Hungarian capital shows the transformation. The densely populated inner city surrounded the cathedral. In 1857 high walls that once had protected the old city from attack were torn down to make room for the Ringstrasse, a broad, tree-shaded boulevard lined with public buildings, museums, churches, and a university. Beyond the Ring, the newly wealthy bourgeoisie built new neighborhoods of large houses and apartment buildings.   (Museen der Stadt, Vienna)

fused into one another, filling in the fields and woods that once had separated them.

As cities grew, they changed in character. Newly built railroads not only brought goods into the cities on a predictable schedule but also allowed people to live farther apart. At first, only the well-to-do could afford to commute by train; by the end of the century, electric streetcars and subways allowed working-class people to live miles from their workplaces.

In preindustrial and early industrial cities, the poor crowded together in tenements, sanitation was bad, water often was contaminated with sewage, and darkness made life dangerous. New urban technologies transformed city life for all but the poorest residents. The most important change was the installation of pipes to bring in clean water and to carry away sewage. First gas lighting and then electric lighting made cities safer and more pleasant at night. By the turn of the century, municipal governments provided police and fire depart-

ments, sanitation and garbage removal, building and health inspection, schools, parks, and other amenities unheard of a century earlier.

As sanitation improved, epidemics became rare. For the first time, urban death rates fell below birthrates. The decline in infant mortality was especially significant. Confident that their children would survive infancy, couples began to limit the number of children they had, and ancient scourges like infanticide and child abandonment became less frequent. By the beginning of the twentieth century, middle- and even working-class couples began using contraceptives.

To accommodate the growing population, builders created new neighborhoods, from crowded tenements for the poor to opulent mansions for the newly rich. In the United States, planners laid out new cities, such as Chicago, on a rectangular grid, and middle-class families moved to new developments on the edges of cities. In Paris, older neighborhoods with narrow crooked streets

Railroads and Immigration

Why did so many Europeans emigrate to North America in the late nineteenth and early twentieth centuries? The quick answer is, They wanted to. Millions of people longed to escape the poverty or tyranny of their home countries and start a new life in a land of freedom and opportunity. Personal desire alone, however, does not account for the migrations. After all, poverty and tyranny existed long before the late nineteenth century. Two other factors helped determine when and where people migrated: whether they were allowed to migrate and whether they were able to.

In the nineteenth century, Asians were recruited to build railroads and work on farms. But from the 1890s on, the United States and Canada closed their doors to non-Europeans, so regardless of what they wanted, they could not move to North America. In contrast, emigrants from Europe were admitted until after the First World War.

The ability to travel was a result of improvements in transportation. Until the 1890s, most immigrants came from Ireland, England, or Germany—countries with good rail transportation to their own harbors and low steamship fares to North America. As rail lines were extended into eastern and southern Europe, more and more immigrants came from Italy, Austria-Hungary, and Russia.

Similarily, until the 1870s most European immigrants to North America settled on the east coast. Then, as the railroads pushed west, more of them settled on farms in the central and western parts of the continent. The power of railroads moved people as much as their desires did.

Emigrant Waiting Room The opening of the western region of the United States attracted settlers from the east coast and from Europe. These migrants are waiting for a train to take them to the Black Hills of Dakota during one of the gold rushes of the late nineteenth century. (Library of Congress)

and rickety tenements were replaced with broad boulevards and modern apartment buildings. Brilliantly lit by gas and electricity, Paris became the "city of lights," a model for city planners from New Delhi to Buenos Aires. The rich continued to live in inner cities that contained the monuments, churches, and palaces of preindustrial times, while workers moved to the outskirts.

Lower population densities and better transportation divided cities into industrial, commercial, and residential zones occupied by different social classes. Improvements such as water and sewerage, electricity, and streetcars always benefited the wealthy first, then the middle class, and finally the working class. In the complex of urban life, businesses of all kinds arose, and the professions—engineering, accounting, research, journalism, the law, among others—took on increased importance. The new middle class exhibited its wealth in fine houses, servants, and elegant entertainment.

In fast-growing cities such as London, New York, or Chicago, newcomers arrived so quickly that housing construction and municipal services could not keep up. Immigrants who saved their money to reunite their families could not afford costly municipal services. As a result, the poorest neighborhoods remained as overcrowded, unhealthy, and dangerous as they had been since the early decades of industrialization.

While urban environments improved in many ways, air quality worsened. Coal, burned to power steam engines and heat buildings, polluted the air, creating unpleasant and sometimes dangerous "pea-soup" fog and coating everything with a film of grimy dust. And the thousands of horses that pulled the carts and carriages covered the streets with their wastes, causing a terrible stench.

Labor Movements and Socialist Politics

Industrialization combined with the revolutionary ideas of the late eighteenth century to produce two kinds of movements—socialism and labor movements—calling for further changes. **Socialism** was an ideology developed by radical thinkers who questioned the sanctity of private property and argued in support of industrial workers against their employers. **Labor unions** were organizations formed by industrial workers to defend their interests in negotiations with employers. The socialist and labor movements were never identical. Most of the time they were allies; occasionally they were rivals.

Since the beginning of the nineteenth century, workers had united to create "friendly societies" for mutual assistance in times of illness, unemployment, or disability. Anticombination laws, however, forbade workers to strike. These laws were abolished in Britain in the 1850s and in the rest of Europe in subsequent decades. Labor unions sought not only better wages but also improved working conditions and insurance against illness, accidents, disability, and old age. They grew slowly because they required a permanent staff and a great deal of money to sustain their members during strikes. By the end of the century, British labor unions counted 2 million members, and German and American unions had a million members each.

Socialism began as an intellectual movement. By far the best-known socialist was **Karl Marx** (1818–1883), a German journalist and writer who lived most of his life in England. He combined German philosophy, French revolutionary ideas, and knowledge of British industrial conditions. He expressed his ideas succinctly in the *Communist Manifesto* (1848) and in great detail in *Das Kapital*° (1867). He argued that the capitalist system allowed the bourgeoisie (the owners of businesses and factories) to extract the "surplus value" of workers' labor—that is, the difference between workers' wages and the value of the goods they manufactured. He saw business enterprises becoming larger and more monopolistic and workers growing more numerous and impoverished with every downturn in the business cycle.

Marx provided an intellectual framework for the growing dissatisfaction with raw industrial capitalism. In the late nineteenth century, business tycoons spent money lavishly on mansions, yachts, private railroad cars, and other displays of wealth that contrasted sharply with the poverty of the workers. Even though industrial workers were not becoming poorer as Marx believed, the class struggle between workers and employers was brutally real. What Marx did was to offer a persuasive explanation of the causes of this contrast and the antagonisms it bred.

Marx was not just a philosopher; he also made a direct impact on politics. In 1864 he helped found the International Working Man's Association (later known as the First International), a movement he hoped would bring about the overthrow of the bourgeoisie. However, it attracted more intellectuals than workers. Workers found other means of redressing their grievances, such as the vote and labor unions.

Just as labor unions strove to enable workers to share in the benefits of a capitalist economy, so did electoral politics persuade workers to become part of the existing political system instead of seeking to overthrow it. The nineteenth century saw a gradual extension of the

Das Kapital (DUSS cop-ee-TALL)

right to vote throughout Europe and North America. Universal male suffrage became law in the United States in 1870, in France and Germany in 1871, in Britain in 1885, and in the rest of Europe soon thereafter. With universal male suffrage, socialist politicians could expect to capture many seats in their nations' parliaments, because the newly enfranchised working class was so numerous. The goal of the socialists was to use their voting power to gain concessions from government and eventually even to win elections.

The classic case of socialist electoral politics is the Social Democratic Party of Germany. Founded in 1875 with a revolutionary socialist program, within two years it won a half-million votes and several seats in the Reichstag° (the lower house of the German parliament). Through superb organizing efforts and important concessions wrung from the government, the party grew fast, by 1912 garnering 4.2 million votes and winning more seats in the Reichstag than any other party. In pursuit of electoral success, the Social Democrats became more reformist and less radical. By joining the electoral process, they abandoned the idea of violent revolution.

Working-class women, burdened with both job and family responsibilities, found little time for politics and were not welcome in the male-dominated trade unions or radical political parties. A few radical women, such as the anarchist Emma Goldman in the United States and the German socialist Rosa Luxemburg, became famous but never had a large following. It was never easy to reconcile the demands of workers and those of women. In 1889 the German socialist Clara Zetkin wrote: "Just as the male worker is subjected by the capitalist, so is the woman by the man, and she will always remain in subjugation until she is economically independent. Work is the indispensable condition for economic independence." Six years later, she added: "The proletarian woman cannot attain her highest ideal through a movement for the equality of the female sex, she attains salvation only through the fight for the emancipation of labor".[1]

Working-Class Women and Men

The lives of middle-class women in the Victorian Age were a mixture of luxury and discrimination, but working-class women led lives of toil and pain, considerably harder than the lives of their menfolk. Although the worst abuses of child labor had been banned in most European countries by 1850, parents expected girls as young as ten to contribute to the household. Many be-

Reichstag (RIKES-tog)

came domestic servants, commonly working sixteen or more hours a day, six and a half days a week, for little more than room and board. Their living quarters, usually in the attic or basement, contrasted with the luxurious quarters of their masters. Without appliances, much of their work was physically hard: hauling coal and water up stairs, washing laundry by hand.

Female servants were vulnerable to sexual abuse by their masters or their masters' sons. A well-known case is that of Helene Demuth, who worked for Karl and Jenny Marx all her life. At age thirty-one she bore a son by Karl Marx and put him with foster parents rather than leave the family. She was more fortunate than most, for most families fired a servant who got pregnant, rather than embarrass the master of the house.

Young women often preferred work in a factory to domestic service. Here, too, Victorian society practiced a strict division of labor by gender. Men worked in construction, iron and steel, heavy machinery, or on railroads; women worked in textiles and the clothing trades, two extensions of traditional women's household work. Appalled by the abuses of women and children in the early years of industrialization, most industrial countries passed protective legislation limiting the hours or forbidding the employment of women in the hardest and most dangerous occupations, such as mining and foundry work. Such legislation limited abuses but also reinforced gender divisions in industry, keeping women in low-paid, subordinate positions. Denied access to the better-paid jobs of foremen or machine repairmen, female factory workers earned, on average, between one-third and two-thirds of men's wages.

Married women with children were expected to stay home, even if their husbands did not make enough to support the family. Most married women of the working class had double responsibilities within the home: not only the work of child rearing and housework but also that of contributing to the family's income. Families who had room to spare, even a bed or a corner in the kitchen, took in boarders. Many women did piecework such as sewing dresses, making lace, hats, or gloves, or weaving baskets. The hardest and worst-paid work was washing other people's clothes. Often women worked at home ten to twelve hours a day and enlisted the help of their small children, perpetuating practices long outlawed in factories. Since electric lighting and indoor plumbing cost more than most working-class families could afford, even ordinary household duties like cooking and washing remained heavy burdens.

The poorest of the poor were orphans and single women with children. Unable to find jobs or support themselves at home, many turned to prostitution. The wealth of middle-class men made it easy for them to take advantage of the poverty of working-class women.

The Victorian Age and Women's "Separate Sphere"

In English-speaking countries, the period from about 1850 to 1914 is known as the **"Victorian Age."** The expression refers not only to the reign of Queen Victoria of England (r. 1837–1901) but to rules of behavior and to an ideology surrounding the family and the relations between men and women. The Victorians emphasized the differences between people more than their common humanity: white skin versus dark skin, rich versus poor, male versus female. They stressed the romantic aspects of love and marriage and both partners' duty to family and religious values. They contrasted the masculine ideals of strength and courage with the feminine virtues of beauty and kindness, and they idealized the home as a peaceful and loving refuge from the dog-eat-dog world of competitive capitalism. Although Victorian ideas contained elements of racism, sexism, and class discrimination, they were widely and sincerely felt at the time and have had an enormous impact on Western gender relations ever since.

Victorian morality claimed to be universal, yet it best fit the European upper- and middle-class family. Men and women were thought to belong in **"separate spheres."** Successful businessmen spent their time at work or relaxing in men's clubs. They put their wives in charge of rearing the children, running the household, and spending the family money to enhance the family's social status.

The word *lady,* once the feminine equivalent of *lord,* came to mean the wife of a *gentleman,* a member of the genteel bourgeoisie. As the Englishwoman Margaretta Greg explained in 1853: "A lady, to be such, must be a mere lady. She must not work for profit, or engage in any occupation that money can command, lest she invade the rights of the working classes, who live by their labour."

Before electric appliances, however, a middle-class home demanded enormous amounts of work. Not only were families larger, but middle-class couples entertained often and lavishly. To carry out all these tasks required servants. A family's status and the activities and lifestyle of the "mistress of the house" depended on the availability of servants to help her with the household tasks. Only families that employed at least one full-time servant were considered middle class.

Toward the turn of the century, modern technology began to transform middle-class homes. Plumbing eliminated the pump and the outhouse. Central heating replaced fireplaces, stoves, trips to the basement for coal, and endless dusting. Gas and electricity lit houses and cooked food without soot, smoke, and ashes. By the early twentieth century, a few wealthy families acquired the first vacuum cleaners and washing machines. Did these technological advances mean less housework for women? Not right away. As families acquired new household technologies, they raised their standards of cleanliness, thus demanding just as much labor as before.

The most important duty of middle-class women was rearing children. Unlike the rich of previous eras, who handed their children over to wet nurses and tutors, Victorian mothers nursed their own babies and showered their children with love and attention. Even those who could afford nannies and governesses remained personally involved in their children's education. However, girls received an education very different from that of boys. While boys were being prepared for the business world or the professions, girls were taught such skills as embroidery, drawing, and music, which offered no monetary reward or professional preparation but enhanced their social graces and marriage prospects.

Governments enforced legal discrimination against women. Until the end of the century, most European countries considered women minors for life—that is, subject to their fathers before marriage and to their husbands after. Even Britain, among the most progressive countries, did not give women the right to control their own property until 1882, with passage of the Married Women's Property Act.

Victorian morality frowned on careers for middle-class women. Young women could work until they got married, but only in genteel occupations such as retail and office work, never in factories. When the typewriter and telephone were introduced into the business world in the 1880s, only men could use these "high-technology" devices. Soon, however, businessmen found they could get better work at lower wages from educated young women, and operating these machines was typecast as women's work.

Jobs that required higher education, especially jobs in the professions, were closed to women. Until late in the century, few universities granted degrees to women. In the United States women's higher education was restricted to elite colleges like Smith, Wellesley, and Radcliffe in the east and to teachers' colleges in the midwest. European women had fewer opportunities. Before 1914 very few women became doctors, lawyers, or professional musicians.

The first profession open to women was teaching, as more and more countries passed laws calling for

Demonstrating for Women's Rights

Before the First World War, no country allowed all women to vote. In Britain, women who demonstrated for voting rights were known as "suffragettes." When petitions to Parliament and peaceful demonstrations had no effect, Emmeline Pankhurst, the leader of the movement, concluded that more forceful measures were required. In the following passage, she describes the tactics she devised to call attention to the cause of women's suffrage.

Whatever preparations the police department were making to prevent the demonstration, they failed because, while as usual, we were able to calculate exactly what the police department were going to do, they were utterly unable to calculate what we were able to do. We had planned a demonstration for March 4th, and this one we announced. We planned another demonstration for March 1st, but this one we did not announce. Late on the afternoon of Friday, March 1st, I drove in a taxicab, accompanied by the Hon. Secretary of the Union, Mrs. Tuke and another of our members, to No. 10 Downing Street, the official residence of the Prime Minister. It was exactly half past five when we alighted from the cab and threw our stones, four of them, through the window panes. As we expected we were promptly arrested and taken to Cannon Row police station. The hour that followed will long be remembered in London. At intervals of fifteen minutes relays of women who had volunteered for the demonstration did their work. The first smashing of glass occurred in the Haymarket and Picadilly, and greatly startled and alarmed both pedestrians and police. A large number of women were arrested, and everybody thought that this ended the affair. But before the excited populace and the frustrated shop owners' first exclamation had died down, before the police had reached the station with their prisoners, the ominous crashing and splintering of plate glass began again, this time along both sides of Regent Street and the Strand. A furious rush of police and people toward the second scene of action ensued. While their attention was taken up with occurrences in this quarter, the third relay of women began breaking the windows in Oxford Circus and Bond Street. The demonstration ended for the day at half past six with the breaking of many windows in the Strand. . . .

The demonstration had taken place in the morning, when a hundred or more women had walked quietly into Knightsbridge and walking singly along the streets demolished nearly every pane of glass they passed. Taken by surprise the police arrested as many as they would reach, but most of the women escaped.

For that two days' work something like two hundred suffragettes were taken to the various police stations, and for days the long procession of women streamed through the courts.

If the goal was to obtain the right to vote, why did the demonstrators break store windows? And why did they do so at fifteen-minute intervals?

Source: Emmeline Pankhurst, *My Own Story* (London, 1914), 211–219.

---

universal compulsory education. By 1911, for instance, 73 percent of all teachers in England were women. They were considered well suited to teaching young children and girls—an extension of the duties of Victorian mothers. Teaching, however, was judged suitable only for single women. Married women were expected to get pregnant right away and stay home taking care of their own children rather than the children of other people. In 1901, Mary Murphy, a teacher with ten years' experience, was charged with misconduct and fired from her teaching job in a Brooklyn school when she got married. After a three-year legal battle, a judge ruled that marriage was not misconduct, and she was reinstated with back pay.

A home life, no matter how busy, did not satisfy all middle-class women. Some became volunteer nurses or social workers, receiving little or no pay. Others organized to fight prostitution, alcohol, and child labor. By the turn of the century, a few were challenging male domination of politics and the law. Women suffragists, led in Britain by Emmeline Pankhurst and in the United States by Elizabeth Cady Stanton and Susan B. Anthony, demanded the right to vote. The more radical used violent tactics such as breaking windows, setting fire to

Emmeline Pankhurst Under Arrest   The leader of the British woman suffrage movement frequently called attention to her cause by breaking the law to protest discrimination against women. Here she is being arrested and carried off to jail by the police.   (Mary Evans Picture Library)

houses, or throwing themselves under horses' hoofs. (See Society and Culture: Demonstrating for Women's Rights). By 1914, women had won the right to vote in twelve states of the United States. British women did not vote until 1918.

NATIONALISM AND THE UNIFICATION OF GERMANY

The most influential idea of the nineteenth century was **nationalism**. The French revolutionaries had defined people, previously considered the subjects of a sovereign, as the citizens of a *nation*—a concept identified with a territory, the state that ruled it, and the culture of its people. Because the most widely spoken language in nineteenth-century Europe was German, the unification of most German-speaking people into a single state in 1871 had momentous consequences for the world.

Language and National Identity Before 1871

Language was usually the crucial element in creating a feeling of national unity. It was important both as a way to unite the people of a nation and as the means of persuasion by which political leaders could inspire their followers. Language was the tool of the new generation of political activists, most of them lawyers, teachers, students, and journalists. Yet language and citizenship seldom coincided.

The fit between France and the French language was exceptional. The Italian- and German-speaking peoples were divided among many small states. Living in the Austrian Empire were peoples who spoke German, Czech, Slovak, Hungarian, Polish, and other languages. Even where people spoke a common language, they could be divided by religion or institutions. The Irish, though English-speaking, were mostly Catholic, whereas the English were primarily Protestant; and in the United States, the issue of slavery divided the south from the north, creating a southern identity.

The idea of redrawing the boundaries of states to accommodate linguistic, religious, or cultural differences was revolutionary. In Italy and Germany, in 1871, it led to the forging of large new states out of many small ones. In central and eastern Europe, nationalism threatened to break up large states into smaller ones.

Until the 1860s, nationalism was associated with **liberalism,** the revolutionary middle-class ideology that emerged from the French Revolution (see Chapter 23) and asserted the sovereignty of the people and demanded constitutional government, a national parliament, and freedom of expression. The most famous nationalist of the early nineteenth century was the Italian liberal Giuseppe Mazzini° (1805–1872), the leader of the failed revolution of 1848 in Italy. Mazzini not only sought to unify the Italian peninsula into one nation but associated with like-minded revolutionaries elsewhere to bring nationhood and liberty to all peoples oppressed by tyrants and foreigners. Although the governments of Russia, Prussia, and Austria censored the new ideas, they could not be quashed. To staff bureaucracies and police forces to maintain law and order, even conservative regimes required educated personnel, and education

Giuseppe Mazzini (jew-SEP-pay mots-EE-nee)

meant universities, the seedbed of new ideas transmitted by a national language.

Although the revolutions of 1848 failed except in France (see Chapter 23), the strength of the revolutionary movements convinced conservatives that governments could not forever keep their citizens out of politics, and that mass politics, if properly managed, could strengthen rather than weaken the state. A new generation of conservative political leaders learned how to preserve the social status quo through public education, universal military service, and colonial conquests, all of which built a sense of national unity.

The Unification of Germany

Until the 1860s, the region of Central Europe where people spoke German (the former Holy Roman Empire) consisted of Prussia, the western half of the Austrian Empire, and numerous smaller states. Some German nationalists wanted to unite all Germans under the Austrian throne.

Others wanted to exclude Austria with its many non-Germanic peoples and unite all other German-speaking areas under Prussia. The divisions were also religious: Austria and southwestern Germany were Catholic; Prussia and the northeast were Lutheran. The Prussian state had two advantages: (1) the newly developed industries of the Rhineland and (2) the first European army to make use of railroads, telegraphs, breechloading rifles, steel artillery, and other products of modern industry.

The king of Prussia, Wilhelm I (r. 1861–1888), had entrusted the running of his government to his chancellor, the brilliant and authoritarian aristocrat **Otto von Bismarck** (1815–1898). Bismarck was determined to use Prussian industry and German nationalism to advance the interests of the Prussian state. In 1864, after a quick victory against Denmark, he set his sights higher.

In 1866 Prussia defeated Austria. To everyone's surprise, Prussia took no Austrian territory. Instead, Prussia and some smaller states formed the North German Confederation, the nucleus of a future Germany. Then in 1870, confident that Austria would not hinder him,

Wilhelm I Proclaimed Emperor of Germany On January 18, 1871, Prussia and the smaller states of Germany united to form the German Reich (empire). King Wilhelm I of Prussia was proclaimed kaiser (emperor) as his chancellor, Otto von Bismarck (in a white jacket), and dozens of generals and lesser princes cheered. The ceremony took place in the Great Hall of Mirrors in the palace of Versailles, near Paris, to mark Prussia's stunning victory over France. (Bismarck Museum, Friedrichsruh)

Bismarck provoked with France the war known as the "Franco-Prussian War." Prussian armies, joined by troops from southern as well as northern Germany, used their superior firepower and tactics to achieve a quick victory.

The spoils of victory included a large indemnity and two provinces of France bordering on Germany: Alsace and Lorraine. The French paid the indemnity easily enough but resented the loss of their provinces. To the Germans, this region was German because a majority of its inhabitants spoke German. To the French, it was French because it had been so when the nation of France was forged in the Revolution and because most of its inhabitants considered themselves French. These two conflicting definitions of nationalism kept enmity between France and Germany smoldering for decades. In this case, nationalism turned out to be a divisive rather than a unifying force.

Nationalism After 1871

The Franco-Prussian War of 1870–1871 changed the political climate of Europe. France became wholeheartedly liberal. The Italian peninsula became unified as the kingdom of Italy. Germany, Austria-Hungary (as the Austrian Empire had renamed itself in 1867), and Russia remained conservative and used nationalism to maintain the status quo.

All politicians tried to manipulate public opinion to bolster their governments. They were greatly aided by the press, especially cheap daily newspapers that sought to increase their circulation by publishing sensational articles about overseas conquests and foreign threats. As governments increasingly came to recognize the advantages of an educated population in the competition between states, they opened public schools in every town, opening public service jobs to women for the first time. The spread of literacy allowed politicians and journalists to appeal to the emotions of the poor, diverting their anger from their employers to foreigners and their votes from socialist to nationalist parties.

In many countries, the dominant group used nationalism to justify the imposing of its language, religion, or customs on minority populations. The Russian Empire attempted to "Russify" its diverse ethnic populations. The Spanish government made the Spanish language compulsory in the schools, newspapers, and courts of its Basque- and Catalan-speaking provinces. Immigrants to the United States were expected to learn English, to safeguard national unity.

Nationalism soon spread to other continents (see Chapters 26, 27, and 32). By the 1880s signs of national consciousness appeared in Egypt, Japan, India, and other non-Western countries, inspiring anti-Western and anti-colonial movements.

Western culture in the late nineteenth century exalted the powerful over the weak, men over women, rich over poor, Europeans over other races, and humans over nature. Some people looked to science for support of political dominance. One of the most influential scientists of the century, and the one whose ideas were most widely cited and misinterpreted, was the English biologist **Charles Darwin** (1809–1882).

As a young man, Darwin spent several years traveling through South America and the South Pacific studying plant and animal life. On his return to England, he published his explanation for the great variety of natural life forms he had seen. In *On the Origin of Species by Means of Natural Selection* (1859), he showed that the earth was extremely old and that over hundreds of thousands of years living beings had either evolved in the struggle for survival or become extinct.

The philosopher Herbert Spencer (1820–1903) and others took up Darwin's ideas of "natural selection" and "survival of the fittest" and applied them to human society. Extreme Social Darwinists developed elaborate pseudo-scientific theories of racial differences, claiming that they were the result not of history but of biology. If Europeans had conquered empires in Asia and Africa, if men had more political power than women, if workers earned less than the well-to-do, they argued, these differences must have "natural" causes. Although not based on any research, these ideas became very popular at the turn of the century, for they gave a scientific-sounding justification for the power of the privileged.

THE GREAT POWERS OF EUROPE, 1871–1900

After 1871, politicians and journalists discovered how easily they could whip up popular frenzy against neighboring countries. Military officers, impressed by the awesome power of the weapons that industry provided, began to think these weapons were invincible. Rivalries over colonial territories, ideological differences between liberal and conservative governments, and even minor border incidents or trade disagreements contributed to a growing atmosphere of international tension.

Germany at the Center of Europe

International relations revolved around a united Germany, because Germany was located in the center of Europe and had the most powerful army on the European continent. After creating a unified Germany in 1871, Bismarck declared that his country had no further territorial ambitions and put his effort into maintaining the peace in Europe. It isolate France, the only country with a grudge against Germany, he forged a loose coalition with Austria-Hungary and Russia, the other two conservative powers. Despite the competing ambitions of Austria and Russia in the Balkans, he was able to keep his coalition together for twenty years.

Bismarck proved equally adept at manipulating mass politics at home. To weaken the influence of middle-class liberals, he extended the vote to all adult men. By imposing high tariffs on manufactured goods and wheat, he gained the support of both the wealthy industrialists of the Rhineland and the great landowners of eastern Germany, traditional rivals for power. He stole the thunder of the socialists by introducing social legislation—medical, unemployment, and disability insurance and old-age pensions—long before other industrial countries. Under his leadership, the German people developed a strong sense of national unity and pride in their industrial and military power.

In 1888 Wilhelm I was succeeded by his grandson Wilhelm II (r. 1888–1918), a vulgar, insecure, and arrogant man who tried to gain respect by using bullying tactics. Within two years he had dismissed Chancellor Bismarck and surrounded himself with yes men and flatterers. Whereas Bismarck had shown little interest in acquiring colonies overseas, Wilhelm II talked about his "global policy" and demanded a colonial empire. Ruler of the nation with the mightiest army and the largest industrial economy in Europe, he felt that Germany deserved "a place in the sun."

The Liberal Powers: France and Great Britain

France, once the dominant nation in Europe, had difficulty reconciling itself to being in second place. Though a prosperous country with flourishing agriculture and a large colonial empire, the French republic had some serious weaknesses. Its population was scarcely growing; in 1911 France had only 39 million people compared to Germany's 64 million. In an age when the power of nations was roughly proportional to the size of their army, France could field an army only two-thirds the size of Germany's. Another weakness was the slow growth of French industry compared to Ger-

many's, due to the loss of the iron and coal mines of Lorraine.

The French people were deeply divided over the very nature of the state: some were monarchists and Catholic; a growing number held republican and anticlerical views. These divisions came to a head at the turn of the century over the case of Captain Alfred Dreyfus, a Jewish officer falsely convicted of spying for the Germans in 1894. French society, even families, split between those who felt that reopening the case would only dishonor the army and those who believed that letting injustice go unchallenged dishonored the nation. The case reawakened the dormant anti-Semitism in French society. Not until 1906, after twelve painful years, was Dreyfus exonerated. Yet if French political life seemed fragile and frequently in crisis, a long tradition of popular participation in politics and a strong sense of nationhood, reinforced by a fine system of universal public education, gave the French people a deeper cohesion than appeared on the surface.

Great Britain was the only other country in Europe with a democratic tradition. The British government alternated smoothly between the Liberal and Conservative Parties, and the income gap between rich and poor gradually narrowed. Nevertheless, Britain had problems that grew more apparent as time went on.

One problem was Irish resentment of English rule. Nationalism had strengthened the allegiance of the English, Scots, and Welsh to the British crown and state. But the Irish, excluded because they were Catholic and predominantly poor, felt the British were a foreign occupying force.

Another problem was the British economy. Once the workshop of the world, Great Britain had fallen behind the United States and Germany in such important industries as iron and steel, chemicals, electricity, and textiles. Even in shipbuilding and shipping, Britain's traditional specialties, Germany was catching up.

Also, Britain was preoccupied with its enormous and fast-growing empire. A source of wealth for investors and the envy of other imperialist nations, the empire was also a constant drain on Britain's finances. The revolt of 1857 against British rule in India (see Chapter 26) was crushed with difficulty and kept British politicians worried thereafter. The empire required Britain to maintain several costly fleets of warships stationed throughout the world.

For most of the nineteenth century, Britain turned its back on Europe and pursued a policy of "splendid isolation." Only once, in 1854, did it intervene militarily in Europe, joining France in the Crimean War of 1854–1856 against Russia (see Chapter 27). Britain's preoccupation with India and the shipping routes through the

The Doss House   Late-nineteenth-century cities showed more physical than social improvements. This painting by Makovsky of a street in St. Petersburg contrasts the broad avenue and impressive new buildings with the poverty of the crowd.   (The State Russian Museum/Smithsonian Institution Traveling Exhibit)

Mediterranean led British statesmen to exaggerate the Russian threat to the Ottoman Empire and to the Central Asian approaches to India. Periodic "Russian scares" and Britain's age-old rivalry with France for overseas colonies diverted the attention of British politicians away from the rise of a large, powerful, united Germany.

The Conservative Powers: Russia and Austria-Hungary

The forces of nationalism weakened rather than strengthened Russia and Austria-Hungary. The reason for this effect was that their populations were far more divided, socially and ethnically, than were the German, French, or British peoples.

Nationalism was most divisive in south-central Europe, where many different language groups lived in close proximity. In 1867 the Austrian Empire's decision to rename itself the Austro-Hungarian Empire appeased its Hungarian critics but alienated its Slavic-speaking mi-

norities. The Austro-Hungarian Empire still thought of itself as a great power, but instead of seeking conquests in Asia or Africa, it attempted to dominate the Balkans. This strategy irritated Russia, which thought of itself as the protector of Slavic peoples everywhere. The Austrian annexation of the former Turkish province of Bosnia-Herzegovina in 1908 worsened relations between the Austro-Hungarian and Russian Empires. Festering quarrels over the Balkans—the "tinderbox of Europe"—eventually pushed Europe into war (see Chapter 30).

Ethnic diversity also contributed to the instability of imperial Russia. The Polish people, never reconciled to being annexed by Russia in the eighteenth century, rebelled in 1830 and 1863–1864. The tsarist empire also included Finland, Estonia, Lavia, Lithuania, and Ukraine, the very mixed peoples of the Caucasus, and the Muslim population of Central Asia conquered between 1865 and 1881. Furthermore, Russia had the largest Jewish population in Europe, despite the harshness of its anti-Semitic laws and periodic *pogroms* (massacres), which prompted many Jews to flee to America. All in all, only 45 percent of the peoples of the tsarist empire spoke Russian. This meant that Russian nationalism and the state's attempts to impose the Russian language on its subjects were divisive instead of unifying forces in the empire.

Russia was the most misunderstood country in Europe. Its enormous size and population led many Europeans to exaggerate its military potential, but France and Britain had easily defeated Russia in the Crimean War.

In 1861, the moderate conservative Tsar Alexander II (r. 1855–1881) emancipated the peasants from serfdom. He did so partly out of a genuine desire to strengthen the bonds between the monarchy and the Russian people, and partly to promote industrialization by enlarging the labor pool. That half-hearted measure, however, did not create a modern society on the western European model. It only turned serfs into communal farmers with few skills and little capital. Though technically "emancipated," the great majority of Russians had little education, few legal rights, and no say in their government. After Alexander's assassination in 1881, his successors Alexander III (r. 1881–1894) and Nicholas II (r. 1894–1917) opposed all forms of social change. Although the Russian government employed many bureaucrats and policemen, its commercial middle class was small and had little influence. Industrialization consisted largely of state-sponsored projects, such as railroads, iron foundries, and armament factories, and led to social unrest among urban workers. Wealthy landowning aristocrats continued to dominate the Russian court and administration and succeeded in blocking most reforms.

The weaknesses in Russia's society and government became glaringly obvious during a war with Japan in 1904 and 1905. The fighting in the Russo-Japanese War took place in Manchuria, a province in northern China far from European Russia. The Russian army, which received all its supplies by means of the inefficient Trans-Siberian Railway, was soon defeated by the better trained and equipped Japanese. The Russian navy, after a long journey around Europe, Africa, and Asia, was met and sunk by the Japanese fleet at the Battle of Tsushima Strait in 1905.

The shock of defeat caused a popular uprising, the Revolution of 1905, that forced Tsar Nicholas II to grant a constitution and an elected Duma (parliament). But as soon as he was able to rebuild the army and the police, he reverted to the traditional despotism of his forefathers. Small groups of radical intellectuals, angered by the contrast between the wealth of the elite and the poverty of the common people, began plotting the violent overthrow of the tsarist autocracy.

NEW GREAT POWERS: THE UNITED STATES AND JAPAN

Since the sixteenth century, Europeans had come to regard their continent as the center of the universe and their states as the only great powers in the world. The rest of the world was either ignored or used as bargaining chips in the game of power politics. The late nineteenth century marked the high point of European power and arrogance, as the nations of Europe, in a frenzy known as the "New Imperialism," rushed to gobble up the last remaining unclaimed pieces of the world (see Chapter 29).

Yet at that very moment two nations outside Europe were becoming great powers. One of them, the United States, was inhabited mainly by people of European origin, and its rise to great-power status had been predicted early in the nineteenth century by astute observers like the French statesman Alexis de Tocqueville. The other one, Japan, seemed so distant and exotic in 1850 that no European had guessed it would join the ranks of the great powers.

The United States, 1865–1900

After the Civil War ended in 1865, the United States entered a period of vigorous growth (see Chapter 25). Hundreds of thousands of immigrants arrived every year, mainly from Russia, Italy, and Central Europe, raising the population from 39 million in 1871 to 63 million in 1891, an increase of 62 percent. Although many settled on the newly opened lands west of the Mississippi (see Map 28.2), most of the migrants moved to the towns, which mushroomed into cities in a few years. Chicago, for example, grew fourfold, from 444,000 in 1870 to 1,700,000 in 1900. In the process, the nation became an industrial giant. The rail network, already the world's longest in 1865, multiplied eleven-fold by 1915, creating the largest single integrated market in the world. To make the rails, locomotives, bridges, and other material, industry produced 20 million tons of steel annually in 1900. By then the United States had overtaken Britain and Germany as the world's leading industrial power.

This explosive growth was accomplished with few government restrictions. In fact, in the last years of the nineteenth century, the federal state, and local governments seemed to be influenced by (if not in the pay of)

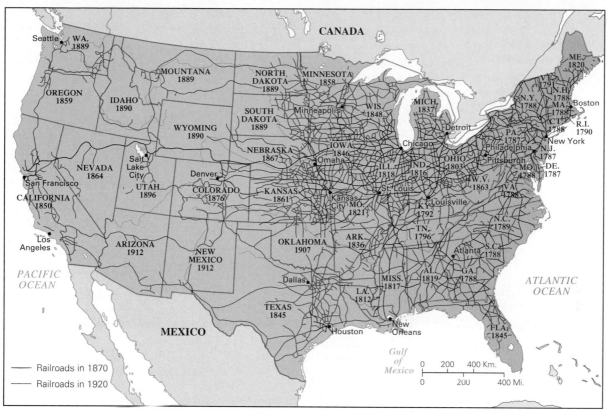

Map 28.2   The United States, 1850–1920   This map shows the expansion of the United States from the coasts into the interior of the continent. In the western half of the continent, only California and Texas were states in 1850; territories located further from the coasts became states later. The economic development, shown by the railroad lines, followed much the same pattern, radiating west and south from the northeastern states and—to a lesser extent—eastward from California.

the business sector, on which they lavished free land, tariffs, and other benefits. Giant monopolies, like John D. Rockefeller's Standard Oil Company, and steel and railroad trusts dominated American life. In this atmosphere of unfettered free enterprise, the nation got rich fast, as did its upper and middle classes.

Expansion created many victims. First among them were the American Indians. When the railroads penetrated the west after the Civil War, they brought white colonists eager to start farming, ranching, or mining. The indigenous Indians whose lands they invaded fought back with great courage but were outnumbered and outgunned. In Canada, the government tried to protect the Indians from the whites. The United States Army, however, always sided with the settlers. The U.S. government had signed numerous treaties with the Indians but tore them up when settlers demanded land. After decades of warfare, massacres, and starvation, the gov-

ernment confined the remaining Indians to reservations on the poorest lands.

The U.S. government also abandoned African-Americans in 1877, after the end of Reconstruction, especially in the defeated southern states. Though freed from slavery in 1865, most of them became sharecroppers who were at the mercy of their landowners. In the 1890s, the southern states instituted "Jim Crow" laws segregating blacks in public transportation, jobs, and schools. Not only did southern judges apply harsh laws in a biased manner, but black Americans were also subject to the lawless violence of mobs, which lynched an average of fifty blacks a year until well into the twentieth century.

Racism also affected Asian immigrants, many of whom had come to the United States to build railroads in the western states. In 1882 the U.S. government barred the Chinese from immigrating by enacting the first of many racial exclusion laws.

Deforestation   As European settlers moved into the forest regions of North America, they cut the trees for timber and to clear the land for farming. Much of Michigan, Wisconsin, and Ontario were deforested in this way. This picture shows a farmer contemplating his newly cleared land.   (State Historical Society of Wisconsin)

Working-class whites benefited little from the booming economy. Economic depressions in 1873 and 1893 caused more distress in the United States than in Europe, because the United States had few labor laws and no unemployment compensation to soften the hardships. Police or the army repressed strikes and unions. The courts consistently supported employers against their employees, capital against labor, and business against government.

Working-class women bore the brunt of repressive labor practices because they earned less than men, had more responsibilities, and seldom were members of labor unions. As in Britain, activist middle-class women organized to demand female suffrage and to fight against alcohol, prostitution, and other social evils.

The booming economy and the waves of immigrants radically transformed the environment. Timber companies clear-cut large areas of Michigan, Wisconsin, and the Appalachian Mountains to provide lumber for railroad ties and frame houses, pulp for paper, and fuel for locomotives and iron foundries. Farmers cleared the forests and plowed the prairies. Buffalo, the dominant animals of the western territories, were massacred by the hundreds of thousands to starve out the Indians and clear the land for cattle. In the west, the government be-

gan massive irrigation projects. In the industrial northeast, iron foundries, steel mills, and steam engines caused severe local air pollution.

In spite of all the assaults, the North American continent was so huge that large parts of it remained unspoiled. A few especially beautiful areas were declared national parks, beginning with Yellowstone in Wyoming in 1872, thereby marking a new state in Americans' attitude toward nature. Thanks to the efforts of naturalist John Muir and President Theodore Roosevelt (1901–1909), large parts of the western states were set aside as national forests.

Most citizens showed little interest in foreign affairs. Patriots tended to celebrate American freedom and democracy, the conquest of a huge continent, and the country's remarkable technological achievements. In this period, the inventor Thomas Edison was probably the most admired man in America.

The expansionism of the United States and its businesses did not stop at the borders but exerted a strong influence on Mexico and the Caribbean. Naval officers, bankers, and politicians urged active intervention in the Western Hemisphere. In 1899 the United States defeated Spain, annexed Puerto Rico and the Philippines, and turned Cuba into an American protectorate (see Chapter

29). Long recognized as the leading power in the Americas, the United States found itself involved in Asian affairs as well. Nevertheless, although their country was fast becoming a global power, most Americans still preferred George Washington's policy of "no European entanglements."

The Rise of Japan, 1868–1900

In the late nineteenth century, China and Japan—the two largest countries in East Asia—both felt the influence of the Western powers as never before, but their responses were completely opposite. China resisted Western influence and became weaker. Japan transformed itself into a major industrial and military power. One reason for this difference was the Western powers' heavy involvement in China and lack of strategic interest in Japan, the nation most remote from Europe by ship. But the contrast can mainly be attributed to the difference between the Chinese and Japanese elites and attitudes toward foreign cultures.

In the 1860s, China had not yet recovered from the Taiping° Rebellion (see Chapter 27), and the French and British took advantage of China's troubles to demand treaty ports where they could trade at will. The British took over China's customs and allowed the free import of opium until 1917. Foreign influence penetrated inland as well. By 1894, some two thousand Christian missionaries (many of them Americans) were founding churches, hospitals, and schools throughout the country, taking over the traditional role of the Chinese gentry. Though Christians had little success in gaining converts, the gentry resented their special privileges.

A Chinese "self-strengthening movement" tried in vain to bring about significant reforms by reducing government expenditures and eliminating corruption. The **Empress Dowager Cixi°** (r. 1862–1908) had once encouraged the construction of shipyards, arsenals, and telegraph lines. But now she opposed railways and other foreign technologies that could carry foreign influences to the interior. Government officials, who did not dare resist the Westerners outright, secretly encouraged crowds to attack and destroy the intrusive devices. They were able to slow the foreign intrusion, but in doing so, they denied themselves the best means of defense against foreign pressure.

In 1868, as we saw in Chapter 27, provincial rebels overthrew the Tokugawa Shogunate and proclaimed the "Meiji° Restoration," after the reign name (*Meiji* means

"enlightened rule") of the young Emperor Mutsuhito° (r. 1868–1912). From then until the early twentieth century, Japan was led by a remarkable group of men known as the Meiji oligarchs. Determined to protect their country from Western imperialism, they encouraged its transformation into a world-class industrial and military power. Although they claimed to be restoring the emperor to his rightful place at the head of the government, they used him as a figurehead, the embodiment of the nation in the national Shinto religion. Though imposed by an elite, the Meiji Restoration marked as profound a change as the French Revolution.

The new Japanese rulers, unlike the Chinese, were under no illusion that they could fend off the Westerners without changing their institutions or their society. In the Charter Oath issued in 1868, the young emperor included the prophetic phrase: "Knowledge shall be sought throughout the world and thus shall be strengthened the foundation of the imperial polity." It was to be the motto of a new Japan, which embraced all foreign ideas, institutions, and techniques that could strengthen the nation.

Japan had a long history of adopting ideas and patterns of culture from China and Korea; in the same spirit, the Japanese eagerly sought to learn the secrets of Western strength. To do so, the Japanese people had to acquire foreign knowledge. In the 1870s and 1880s, the government sent hundreds of students to Britain, Germany, and the United States and hired foreign experts to teach Japanese how to build railroads, organize a modern army and navy, and operate a bureaucracy.

The Meiji leaders created a government structure similar to that of imperial Germany. They introduced Western-style posts and telegraphs, railroads and harbors, banking, clocks, and calendars. They modeled the new Japanese navy on the British and the army on the Prussian. They even encouraged foreign clothing styles and pastimes.

The government was especially interested in Western technology. It opened vocational, technical, and agricultural schools and founded four imperial universities. It brought in foreign experts to advise on medicine, science, and engineering. At the newly created Imperial College of Engineering, an Englishman, William Ayrton, became the first professor of electrical engineering anywhere in the world. His students later went on to found major corporations and government research institutes.

The Japanese government also encouraged industrialization. It taxed farmers heavily to pay for the purchase of ships, machines, and other capital goods. It set up

Taiping (tie-PING)   Cixi (TSEE-she)   Meiji (MAY-gee)

Mutsuhito (moo-tsoo-HE-toe)

Yamagata Aritomo As a young man, Yamagata had joined with other provincial leaders to overthrow the Tokugawa Shogunate in 1867–1868 and form a new government. He modernized Japan's army and remained a formidable force in Japanese policymaking until his death in 1922. (Asahi Shimbun Photo)

state-owned enterprises to manufacture cloth and inexpensive consumer goods for sale abroad. The first Japanese industries, some of which had been founded in the early nineteenth century, exploited their workers ruthlessly, just as the first industries in Europe and America had done. Peasant families, squeezed by rising taxes and rents, often had to send their daughters to work in textile mills in a form of indentured servitude. In 1881, to pay off its debts, the government sold these enterprises to private investors, mainly large *zaibatsu*°, or conglomerates. But there was room for individual technological innovation as well. Thus the carpenter Toyoda Sakichi founded the Toyoda Loom Works (now Toyota Motor

zaibatsu (zye-BOT-soo)

Company) in 1906; ten years later, he patented the world's most advanced automatic loom.

In 1889 Japan promulgated a new and authoritarian constitution modeled on that of Germany, with a bicameral legislature and a cabinet led by a prime minister. But the army and navy remained free of civilian control, only wealthy men were allowed to vote, and important decisions were made without popular input or even knowledge.

By 1900 Japan was sufficiently westernized that the Western powers rescinded the unequal treaties they had imposed forty years earlier. The motive for the transformation of Japan was defensive—to protect the nation from the Western powers—but the methods that strengthened Japan against the imperial ambitions of others could also be used to carry out its own conquests. In 1876, having purchased some modern warships from Britain, Japan sent them to Korea to extort the same privileges the Westerners had obtained in Japan. This action provoked the intervention of China, which had long claimed suzerainty over Korea.

Japan's path to imperialism and independence was pointed out more vigorously by **Yamagata Aritomo.** As a young man he had been a leader of the anti-Tokugawa warriors who had effected the Meiji Restoration. In 1910 Yamagata was still leading the government. He believed that to be independent Japan had to define a "sphere of influence," to include Korea, Manchuria, and part of China. If Japan controlled this sphere, it would be secure. If other countries controlled it, Japan would be at risk. Yamagata insisted that in order to protect this sphere of influence Japan must sustain a vigorous program of military industrialization, culminating in the building of battleships. Yamagata was opposed to placing policy in the hands of a voting public, for he believed military budgets had to be protected from unpredictable political trends. He also feared popular nationalism, which could push the government into premature confrontation with dangerous imperialist powers.

Meanwhile, China was growing weaker as Japan grew stronger. In 1894, the two nations went to war. The Japanese defeated China in less than six months, forcing it to evacuate Korea, cede Taiwan and the Liaodong Peninsula, and pay a heavy indemnity. France, Germany, Britain, Russia, and the United States, upset at seeing a newcomer join the ranks of the imperialists, made Japan give up Liaodong in the name of the "territorial integrity" of China. In exchange for their "protection," the Western powers then made China grant them territorial and trade concessions, including ninety treaty ports.

In China, the humiliations suffered at the hands of Japan and the European powers led reformers around

Emperor Guangxu to press for changes inspired by the Meiji Restoration. The changes they introduced during the "Hundred Days of Reform" threatened the power and position of the Empress Dowager Cixi and the officials around her, however. In September 1898, Cixi had the emperor put under house arrest and the reforms rescinded.

In 1900, the officials who had seized power encouraged a series of antiforeign riots known as the Boxer Uprising. Military forces from the European powers, Japan, and the United States put down the riots and occupied Beijing. Emboldened by China's obvious weakness, Japan and Russia competed for possession of the mineral-rich Chinese province of Manchuria.

Japan's participation in the suppression of the Boxer Uprising demonstrated its military power in East Asia. In 1905 Japan surprised the world by defeating Russia in the Russo-Japanese War. In spite of Western attempts to restrict it to the role of junior partner, Japan continued to increase its influence. It gained control of southern Manchuria, with its industries and railroads, and established a protectorate over Korea. In 1910 it finally annexed Korea, joining the ranks of the world's colonial powers.

century, liberal political reforms had taken hold in western Europe and the United States and seemed about to triumph in Russia as well. Morality and legislation aimed at providing security for women and families, though equality between the sexes was still beyond reach.

The framework for all these changes was the nation-state. The world economy, international politics, even cultural and social issues revolved around a handful of countries—the great powers—that believed themselves in control of the destiny of the world. These included the most powerful European nations of the previous century, as well as two newcomers—the United States and Japan—that were to play important roles in the future. Seldom in history had there been such a concentration of wealth, power, and self-confidence.

The success of the great powers rested on their ability to extract resources from nature and from other societies, especially in Asia, Africa, and Latin America. In a global context, the counterpart of the rise of the great powers is the story of imperialism and colonialism. To complete our understanding of the period before 1914, let us turn now to the relations between the great powers and the rest of the world.

CONCLUSION

After World War I broke out in 1914, many people, especially in Europe, looked back on the period from 1850 to 1914 as a golden age. For some, and in certain ways, it was. Industrialization was a powerful torrent changing Europe, North America, and East Asia. While other technologies like shipping and railroads increased their global reach, new ones—electricity, the steel and chemical industries, and the global telegraph network— contributed to the enrichment and empowerment of the industrial nations. Memories of the great scourges— famines, wars, and epidemics—faded. Clean water, electric lights, and railways began to improve the lives of city dwellers, even the poor. Goods from distant lands, even travel to other continents, came within the reach of millions.

European and American society seemed to be heading toward better organization and greater security. Municipal services made city life less dangerous and chaotic. Through labor unions, workers achieved some measure of recognition and security. By the turn of the

■ Key Terms

steel	Victorian Age
electricity	"separate spheres"
Thomas Edison	nationalism
submarine telegraph cables	liberalism
railroads	Otto von Bismarck
socialism	Charles Darwin
labor unions	Empress Dowager Cixi
Karl Marx	Yamagata Aritomo

■ Suggested Reading

More has been written on the great powers in the late nineteenth century than on any previous period in their histories. The following are some interesting recent works and a few classics.

Industrialization is the subject of Peter Stearns, *The Industrial Revolution in World History* (1993), and David Landes, *The Unbound Prometheus: Technological Change and Industrial Development in Western Europe from 1750 to the Present* (1969). Two interesting works on nationalism are E. J. Hobsbawm, *Nation and Nationalism Since 1780* (1990), and Benedict Anderson, *Imagined Communities: Reflections on the Origin and Spread of Nationalism* (1991).

Barrington Moore, *The Social Origins of Dictatorship and Democracy* (1966), is a classic essay on European society. On European women see Renate Bridenthal, Claudia Koonz, and Susan Stuard, eds., *Becoming Visible: Women in European History* (1987); Patricia Branca, *Silent Sisterhood: Middle-Class Women in the Victorian Home* (1975); Louise Tilly and Joan Scott, *Women, Work, and Family* (1987); and Theresa McBride, *The Domestic Revolution: The Modernization of Household Service in England and France, 1820–1920* (1976). The history of family life is told in Beatrice Gottlieb, *The Family in the Western World from the Black Death to the Industrial Age* (1993). Albert Lindemann, *A History of European Socialism* (1983), covers the labor movements as well.

There are many excellent histories of individual countries. Germany in the late nineteenth century is well treated in Erich Eyck, *Bismarck and the German Empire* (1964). On Britain see Donald Read, *The Age of Urban Democracy: England, 1868–1914* (1994), and David Thomson, *England in the Nineteenth Century, 1815–1914* (1978). On France, Eugen Weber, *Peasants into Frenchmen* (1976), and Roger Price, *A Social History of Nineteenth-Century France* (1987), are especially recommended. A good introduction to Russian history is Hans Rogger, *Russia in the Age of Modernization and Revolution, 1881–1917* (1983).

Three very different aspects of American life are described in Carl Degler, *Out of Our Past: The Forces That Shaped Modern America* (1970); Thomas Hughes, *American Genesis: A Century of Invention and Technological Enthusiasm* (1989); and John Opie, *Nature's Nation: An Environmental History of the United States* (1998).

There are several interesting books on Japan, in particular Peter Duus, *The Rise of Modern Japan*, 2d ed. (1998), and Tessa Morris-Suzuki, *The Technological Transformation of Japan* (1994). Two fine books cover the history of modern China: John King Fairbank, *The Great Chinese Revolution, 1800–1985* (1987), and Jonathan D. Spence, *The Search for Modern China* (1990).

■ Note

1. Quoted in Bonnie S. Anderson and Judith P. Zinsser, *A History of Their Own: Women in Europe from Prehistory to the Present*, vol. 2 (New York: Harper & Row, 1988), 372, 387.

THE NEW IMPERIALISM,
1869–1914

Opening of the Suez Canal   When the canal opened in 1869, thousands of dignitaries and ordinary people gathered to watch the ships go by.

n November 1869, Empress Eugénie of France, Emperor Francis Joseph of Austria-Hungary, and sixteen hundred other dignitaries from the Middle East and Europe assembled at Port Said° in Egypt to celebrate the inauguration of the greatest construction project of the century: the **Suez Canal**. Ismail°, the khedive° (ruler) of Egypt, had invited all the Christian princes of Europe and all the Muslim princes of Asia and Africa, except the Ottoman sultan, his nominal overlord. He wanted to show that Egypt was not only independent but an equal of the great powers.

Ismail used this occasion to emphasize the harmony and cooperation between the peoples of Africa, Asia, and Europe. A French journalist wrote:

> This multitude, coming from all parts of the world, presented the most varied and singular spectacle. All races were represented. . . . We saw, coming to attend this festival of civilization, men of the Orient wearing clothes of dazzling colors, chiefs of African tribes wrapped in their great coats, Circassians in war costumes, officers of the British army of India with their shakos [hats] wrapped in muslin, Hungarian magnates wearing their national costumes.[1]

To bless the inauguration, Ismail also had invited clergy of the Muslim, Orthodox, and Catholic faiths. A reporter noted: "The Khedive . . . wished to symbolize thereby the unity of men and their brotherhood before God, without distinction of religion; it was the first time that the Orient had seen such a meeting of faiths to celebrate and bless together a great event and a great work."[2]

The canal was a great success, but not in the way Ismail intended it to be. Ships using it could travel between Europe and India in less than two weeks—much less time than the month or longer consumed by sailing around Africa and into the Indian Ocean. By lowering freight costs, the canal stimulated shipping and the construction of steamships, giving an advantage to nations that had heavy industry and a large maritime trade over land-based empires and coun-

tries that had few merchant ships. Great Britain, which long opposed construction of the canal for fear that it might fall into enemy hands, benefited more than any other nation. France, which provided half of the capital and most of the engineers, came in a distant second, for it had less trade with Asia than Britain did. Egypt, which contributed the other half of the money and most of the labor, was the loser in this affair. Instead of making Egypt powerful and independent, the Suez Canal provided the excuse for a British invasion and occupation of Egypt. Far from inaugurating an era of harmony among the peoples of three continents and three faiths, the canal triggered a wave of European domination over Africa and Asia.

Between 1869 and 1914 Germany, France, Britain, Russia, and the United States used industrial technology to impose their will on the nonindustrial parts of the world. Historians use the expression **New Imperialism** to describe this exercise of power.

As you read this chapter, ask yourself the following questions:

- What motivated the industrial nations to conquer new territories, and what means did they use?
- Which parts of the world were annexed to the new empires, and which ones became their economic dependencies?
- How did the environment change in the lands subjected to the New Imperialism?

THE NEW IMPERIALISM: MOTIVES AND METHODS

Europe had a long tradition of imperialism reaching back to the twelfth-century Crusades against the Arabs, and the United States greatly expanded its territory after achieving independence in 1783 (see Map 25.3). During the first two-thirds of the nineteenth century, the European powers continued to increase their influence overseas (see Chapter 26). The New Imperialism was characterized by an explosion of territorial conquests even more rapid than the Spanish conquests of

---

Port Said (port sah-EED)　Ismail (is-mah-EEL)
khedive (kuh-DEEV)

CHRONOLOGY

	The Scramble for Africa	Asia and Western Dominance	Imperialism in Latin America
		1862–1895 French conquer Indochina	
		1865–1876 Russian forces advance into Central Asia	
1870	**1869** Opening of the Suez Canal		**1870–1910** Railroad building boom: British companies in Argentina and Brazil; U.S. companies in Mexico.
	1874 Warfare between the British and the Asante (Gold Coast)		
	1877–1879 Warfare between the British and the Xhosa and between the British and the Zulu (South Africa)	**1878** United States obtains Pago Pago Harbor (Samoa)	
	1882 British forces occupy Egypt		
	1884–1885 Berlin Conference; Leopold II obtains Congo Free State	**1885** Britain completes conquest of Burma	
1890		**1887** United States obtains Pearl Harbor (Hawaii)	
		1894–1895 China defeated in Sino-Japanese War	
	1896 Ethiopians defeat Italian army at Adowa; warfare between the British and the Asante	**1895** France completes conquest of Indochina	**1895–1898** Cubans revolt against Spanish rule
	1898 Battle of Omdurman	**1898** United States annexes Hawaii and purchases Philippines from Spain	**1898** Spanish-American War; United States annexes Puerto Rico and Guam
	1899–1902 South African War between Afrikaners and the British	**1899–1902** U.S. forces conquer and occupy Philippines	**1901** United States imposes Platt Amendment on Cuba
	1902 First Aswan Dam completed (Egypt)	**1903** Russia completes Trans-Siberian Railway	**1903** United States backs secession of Panama from Colombia
		1904–1905 Russia defeated in Russo-Japanese War	**1904–1907, 1916** U.S. troops occupy Dominican Republic
			1904–1914 United States builds Panama Canal
1910	**1908** Belgium annexes Congo		**1912** U.S. troops occupy Nicaragua and Honduras

the sixteenth century. Between 1869 and 1914, in a land grab of unprecedented speed, Europeans seized territories in Africa and Central Asia, and both Europeans and Americans took territories in Southeast Asia and the Pacific. Approximately 10 million square miles (26 million square kilometers) and 150 million people fell under the rule of Europe and the United States in this period.

The New Imperialism, however, was more than a land grab. The imperial powers used economic and technological means to reorganize dependent regions and bring them into the world economy as suppliers of food-

stuffs and raw materials and as consumers of industrial products. In Africa and other parts of the world, this was done by conquest and colonial administration. In the Latin American republics, the same result was achieved indirectly. Those republics became economic dependencies of the United States and Europe even though they remained politically independent.

What inspired Europeans and Americans to venture overseas and impose their will on other societies? There is no simple answer to this question. Economic, cultural, and political motives were involved in each case.

Religion and Imperialism European penetration into Africa was accompanied by enthusiastic efforts to convert the Africans to Christianity. European missionaries built schools and clinics as well as churches. Here African schoolchildren are shown a picture of the Virgin Mary holding the baby Jesus, an image designed to replace traditional African religious objects. Mary and Jesus are represented as Europeans. (USGP)

peace with them. In response to border skirmishes with neighboring states, colonial agents were likely to send in troops, take over their neighbors' territories, and then inform their home governments. Governments felt obligated to back up their men-on-the-spot in order not to lose face. The great powers of Europe acquired much of West Africa, Southeast Asia, and the Pacific islands in this manner.

Cultural Motives

The late nineteenth century saw a Christian revival in Europe and North America, as both Catholics and Protestants founded new missionary societies. Their purpose was not only religious—to convert nonbelievers, whom they regarded as "heathen"—but also cultural in a broader sense. They sought to export their own norms of "civilized" behavior: they were determined to abolish slavery in Africa and bring Western education, medicine, hygiene, and monogamous marriage to all the world's peoples.

Among those attracted by religious work overseas were many women who joined missionary societies to become teachers and nurses, positions of greater authority than they could hope to find at home. Although they did not challenge colonialism directly, their influence often helped soften the harshness of colonial rule—for example, by calling attention to issues of maternity and women's health. Mary Slessor, a British missionary who lived for forty years among the people of southeastern Nigeria, campaigned against slavery, human sacrifice, and the killing of twins and, generally, for women's rights. In India, missionaries denounced the customs of child marriages and *sati* (the burning of widows on their husbands' funeral pyres). Such views often clashed with the customs of the people among whom they settled.

The sense of moral duty and cultural superiority was not limited to missionaries. Many Europeans and Americans equated technological innovations with "progress" and "change for the better." They believed that Western technology proved the superiority of Western ideas, customs, and culture. This attitude at least included the idea that non-Western peoples could achieve, through education, the same cultural level as Europeans and Americans. More harmful were racist ideas that relegated non-Europeans to a status of permanent inferiority. Social Darwinists (see Chapter 28) assigned different stages of biological development to peoples of different races and cultures. They divided humankind into several races based on physical appearance and ranked these races in a hierarchy that ranged from "civilized" at the highest level down through "semibarbarous," "barbarian," and

Political Motives

The great powers of the late nineteenth century, as well as less powerful countries like Italy, Portugal, and Belgium, were competitive and hypersensitive about their status. French leaders, humiliated by their defeat by Prussia in 1871 (see Chapter 28), sought to reestablish their nation's prestige through territorial acquisitions overseas. Great Britain, already in possession of the world's largest and richest empire, felt the need to protect India, its "jewel in the crown," by acquiring colonies in East Africa and Southeast Asia. Chancellor Otto von Bismarck had little interest in acquiring colonies, but many Germans believed that a country as important as theirs required an impressive empire overseas.

Political motives were not limited to statesmen in the capital cities. Colonial governors, even officers posted to the farthest colonial outposts, practiced their own diplomacy. They often decided on their own to claim a piece of land before some rival got it. Armies fighting frontier wars found it easier to defeat their neighbors than to make finally, at the bottom, "savage." Caucasians—whites—were always at the top of this ranking. Such ideas were often presented as an excuse for permanent rule over Africans and Asians.

Imperialism first interested small groups of explorers, clergy, and businessmen but soon attracted people from other walks of life. Young men, finding few opportunities for adventure and glory at home in an era of peace, sought them overseas as the Spanish *conquistadores* had done over three centuries earlier. At first, the European public and parliaments were indifferent or hostile to overseas adventures, but a few easy victories in the 1880s helped to overcome their reluctance. The United States was fully preoccupied with its westward expansion until the 1880s, but in the 1890s popular attention shifted to lands outside U.S. borders. Newspapers, which achieved a wide readership in the second half of the nineteenth century, discovered they could boost circulation with reports of wars and conquests. By the 1890s, imperialism was a popular cause; it was the overseas extension of the nationalism propelling the power politics of the time.

Economic Motives

The industrialization of Europe and North America stimulated the demand for minerals—copper for electrical wiring, tin for canning, chrome and manganese for the steel industry, coal for steam engines, and, most of all, gold and diamonds. The demand for such industrial crops as cotton and rubber and for stimulants such as sugar, coffee, tea, and tobacco also grew. These products were found in the tropics, but never in sufficient quantities. An economic depression lasting from the mid-1870s to the mid-1890s caused European merchants, manufacturers, and shippers to seek protection against foreign competition (see below). They argued that their respective countries needed secure sources of tropical raw materials and protected markets for their industries. Declining business opportunities at home prompted entrepreneurs and investors to look for profits from mines, plantations, and railroads in Asia, Africa, and Latin America. Since investment in countries so different from their own was extremely risky, businessmen sought the backing of their governments, preferably with soldiers.

These reasons explain why Europeans and Americans wished to expand their influence over other societies in the late nineteenth and early twentieth centuries. Yet motives alone are not enough to explain the events of that time. What made it possible to conquer a piece of Africa, to convert the "heathen," or to start a plantation was the sudden increase in the power that industrial

peoples could wield over nonindustrial peoples and over the forces of nature. Technological advances explain both the motives and the outcome of the New Imperialism.

The Tools of the Imperialists

To succeed, empire builders needed the means to achieve their objectives at a reasonable cost. These means were provided by the Industrial Revolution (see Chapter 24). In the early part of the nineteenth century, technological innovations began to tip the balance of power in favor of Europe. Europeans had dominated the oceans since about 1500, and their naval power increased still more with the introduction of steamships. The first steamer reached India in 1825 and was soon followed by regular mail service in the 1830s. The long voyage around Africa was at first too costly for cargo steamers, for coal had to be shipped from England. The building of the Suez Canal and the development of increasingly efficient engines solved this problem and led to a boom in shipping to the Indian Ocean and East Asia. Whenever fighting broke out, passenger liners were requisitioned as troopships, giving European forces greater mobility than Asians and Africans. Their advantage was enhanced even more by the development of a global network of submarine telegraph cables connecting Europe with North America in the 1860s, with Latin America and Asia in the 1870s, with Africa in the 1880s, and finally across the Pacific in 1904 (see Environment and Technology: "The Annihilation of Time and Space," in Chapter 24).

Until the middle of the nineteenth century, western Europeans were much weaker on land than at sea. Thereafter, Europeans used gunboats with considerable success in China, Burma, Indochina, and the Congo Basin. Although gunboats opened the major river basins to European penetration, the invaders often found themselves hampered by other natural obstacles. *Falciparum* malaria, found only in Africa, was so deadly to Europeans that few explorers survived before the 1850s. In 1854 a British doctor discovered that the drug quinine, taken regularly during one's stay in Africa, could prevent the disease. This and a few sanitary precautions reduced the annual death rate among whites in West Africa from between 250 and 750 per thousand in the early nineteenth century to between 50 and 100 per thousand after 1850. This reduction was sufficient to open the continent to merchants, officials, and missionaries.

Muzzleloading smoothbore muskets had been used in Europe, Asia, and the Americas since the late seventeenth century, and by the early nineteenth century they were also common in much of Africa. The development

The Battle of Omdurman In the late nineteenth century, most battles between European (or European-led) troops and African forces were one-sided encounters because of the disparity in the opponents' firearms and tactics. The Battle of Omdurman in Sudan in 1898 is a dramatic example. The forces of the Mahdi, some on horseback, were armed with spears and single-shot muskets. The British troops and their Egyptian allies, lined up in the foreground, used repeating rifles and machine guns able to shoot much farther than the Sudanese weapons. As a result, there were many Sudanese casualties but very few British or Egyptian.   (The Art Archive Limited)

of new and much deadlier firearms in the 1860s and 1870s shifted the balance of power on land between Westerners and other peoples. One of these was the breechloader, which could be fired accurately ten times as fast as, and five or six times farther than, a musket. By the 1870s armies in Europe and the United States had all switched to these new rifles. Two more innovations appeared in the 1880s: smokeless powder, which did not foul the gun or reveal the soldier's position, and repeating rifles, which could shoot fifteen rounds in fifteen seconds. In the 1890s, European and American armies began using machine guns, which could fire eleven bullets per second.

In the course of the century, Asians and Africans also acquired better firearms, mostly old weapons that Euro-

pean armies had discarded. As European firearms improved, the firepower gap widened, making colonial conquests easier than ever before. By the 1880s and 1890s, European-led forces of a few hundred could defeat non-European armies of thousands. Against the latest weapons, African and Asian soldiers armed with muskets or, in some cases, with spears did not stand a chance, no matter how numerous and courageous they were.

A classic example is the **Battle of Omdurman** in the Sudan. On September 2, 1898, 40,000 Sudanese attacked an Anglo-Egyptian expedition that had come up the Nile on six steamers and four other boats. General Horatio Kitchener's troops had twenty machine guns and four artillery pieces; the Sudanese were equipped with muskets and spears. Within a few hours, 11,000 Sudanese and 48 British lay dead. Winston Churchill, the future British prime minister, witnessed the battle and called it

> The most signal triumph ever gained by the arms of science over barbarians. Within the space of five hours the strongest and best-armed savage army yet arrayed against a modern European Power had been destroyed and dispersed, with hardly any difficulty, comparatively small risk, and insignificant loss to the victors.[3]

Colonial Agents and Administration

Once colonial agents took over a territory, their home government expected them to cover their own costs and, if possible, return some profit to the home country. The system of administering and exploiting colonies for the benefit of the home country is known as **colonialism.** In some cases, such as along the West African coast or in Indochina, there was already a considerable trade that could be taxed. In other places, profits could come only from investments and a thorough reorganization of the indigenous societies. In applying modern scientific and industrial methods to their colonies, colonialists started the transformation of Asian and African societies and landscapes that has continued to our day.

Legal experts and academics placed a great emphasis on the differences between various systems of colonial government and debated whether colonies eventually should be assimilated into the ruling nation, associated in a federation, or allowed to rule themselves. Colonies that were protectorates retained their traditional governments, even their monarchs, but had a European "resident" or "consul-general" to "advise" them. Other colonies were directly administered by a European governor. In fact, the impact of colonial rule depended much more on economic and social conditions than on narrow legal distinctions.

One important factor was the presence or absence of European settlers. In Canada, Australia, and New Zealand, whites were already in the majority by 1869, and their colonial "mother-country," Britain, encouraged them to elect parliaments and rule themselves. Where European settlers were numerous but still a minority of the population, as in Algeria and South Africa, settlers and the home country struggled for control over the indigenous population. In colonies with few white settlers, the European governors ruled autocratically.

In the early years of the New Imperialism, colonial administrations consisted of a governor and his staff, a few troops to keep order, and a small number of tax collectors and magistrates. Nowhere could colonialism operate without the cooperation of indigenous elites, because no colony was wealthy enough to pay the salaries of more than a handful of European officials. In most cases, the colonial governors exercised power through traditional rulers willing to cooperate, as in the Princely States of India (see Chapter 26). In addition, colonial governments educated a few local youths for "modern" jobs as clerks, nurses, policemen, customs inspectors, and the like. Thus colonialism relied on two rival indigenous elites.

European and American women seldom took part in the early stages of colonial expansion. As conquest gave way to peaceful colonialism and as steamships and railroads made travel less difficult, colonial officials and settlers began bringing their wives to the colonies. By the 1880s, the British Women's Emigration Association was recruiting single women to go out to the colonies to marry British settlers. As one of its founders, Ellen Joyce, explained, "The possibility of the settler marrying his own countrywoman is of imperial as well as family importance."

The arrival of white women in Asia and Africa led to increasing racial segregation. As Sylvia Leith-Ross, wife of a colonial officer in Nigeria, explained, "When you are alone, among thousands of unknown, unpredictable people, dazed by unaccustomed sights and sounds, bemused by strange ways of life and thought, you need to remember who you are, where you come from, what your standards are." Many colonial wives found themselves in command of numerous servants and expected to follow the complex etiquette of colonial entertainment in support of their husbands' official positions. Occasionally they found opportunities to exercise personal initiatives, usually charitable work involving indigenous women and children. However well meaning, their efforts were always subordinate to the work of men.

THE SCRAMBLE FOR AFRICA

Until the 1870s, African history was largely shaped by internal forces and local initiatives (see Chapter 26). Outside Algeria and southern Africa, only a handful of Europeans had ever visited the interior of Africa, and European countries possessed only small enclaves on the coasts. As late as 1879, Africans ruled more than 90 percent of the continent. Then within a decade Africa was invaded and divided among the European powers in a movement often referred to as the **"scramble" for Africa**

(See Map 29.1). This invasion affected all regions of the continent. Let us look at the most significant cases, beginning with Egypt, the wealthiest and most populated part of the continent.

Egypt

Ironically, European involvement in Egypt resulted from Egypt's attempt to free itself from Ottoman Turkish rule. Throughout the mid-nineteenth century, the khedives of Egypt had tried to modernize their armed forces; build canals, harbors, railroads, and other public works; and reorient agriculture toward export crops, especially cotton (see Chapters 24 and 26). Their interest in the Suez Canal was also part of this policy. Khedive Ismail even tried to make Egypt the center of an empire reaching south into the Sudan and Ethiopia.

These ambitions cost vast sums of money, which the khedives borrowed from European creditors at high interest rates. By 1876, Egypt's foreign debt had risen to £100 million sterling, and the interest payments alone consumed one-third of its foreign export earnings. To avoid bankruptcy, the Egyptian government sold its shares in the Suez Canal to Great Britain and accepted four foreign "commissioners of the debt" to oversee its finances. French and British bankers, still not satisfied, lobbied their governments to secure the loans by stronger measures. In 1878 the two governments obliged Ismail to appoint a Frenchman as minister of public works and a Briton as minister of finance. When high taxes caused hardship and popular discontent, the French and British persuaded the Ottoman sultan to depose Ismail. This foreign intervention provoked a military uprising under Egyptian army colonel Arabi Pasha, which threatened the Suez Canal.

Fearing for their investments, the British sent an army into Egypt in 1882. They intended to occupy Egypt for only a year or two. But theirs was a seaborne empire that depended on secure communications between Britain and India. So important was the Suez Canal to their maritime supremacy that they stayed for seventy years. During those years the British ruled Egypt "indirectly"—that is, they maintained the Egyptian government and the fiction of Egyptian sovereignty but retained real power in their own hands.

Eager to develop Egyptian agriculture, especially cotton production, the British brought in engineers and contractors to build the first dam across the Nile, at Aswan in upper Egypt. When it was completed in 1902, it was one of the largest dams in the world. It captured the annual Nile flood and released its waters throughout the year, allowing farmers to grow two, sometimes three, crops a year. This doubled the effective acreage compared with the basin system of irrigation practiced since the time of the pharaohs, in which the annual floodwaters of the Nile were retained by low dikes around the fields.

The economic development of Egypt by the British enriched a small elite of landowners and merchants, many of them foreigners. Egyptian peasants got little relief from the heavy taxes collected to pay for their country's crushing foreign debt and the expenses of the British army of occupation. Western ways that conflicted with the teachings of Islam—such as the drinking of alcohol and the relative freedom of women—offended Muslim religious leaders. Most Egyptians found British rule more onerous than that of the Ottomans. By the 1890s, Egyptian politicians and intellectuals were demanding that the British leave, but to no avail.

Western and Equatorial Africa

While the British were taking over Egypt, the French were planning to extend their empire into the interior of West Africa. Starting from the coast of Senegal, which had been in French hands for centuries, they hoped to build a railroad from the upper Senegal River to the upper Niger, to open the interior to French merchants. This in turn led the French military to undertake the conquest of the western Sudan.

Meanwhile, it was the actions of three individuals, rather than a government, that brought about the occupation of the Congo Basin, an enormous forested region in the heart of equatorial Africa (see Map 29.1). In 1879 the American journalist **Henry Morton Stanley,** who had explored the area, persuaded **King Leopold II** of Belgium to invest his personal fortune in "opening up" equatorial Africa. With Leopold's money, Stanley returned to Africa from 1879 to 1884 to establish trading posts along the southern bank of the Congo River. At the same time, an Italian explorer obtained from an African ruler living on the opposite bank, a treaty that placed the area under the "protection" of France. These events sparked a flurry of diplomatic activity.

German chancellor Bismarck called the **Berlin Conference** on Africa of 1884 and 1885. There the major powers agreed that henceforth "effective occupation"

Map 29.1   Africa in 1878 and 1914   In 1878 the European colonial presence was limited to a few coastal enclaves, plus portions of Algeria and South Africa. By 1914, Europeans had taken over all of Africa except Ethiopia and Liberia.

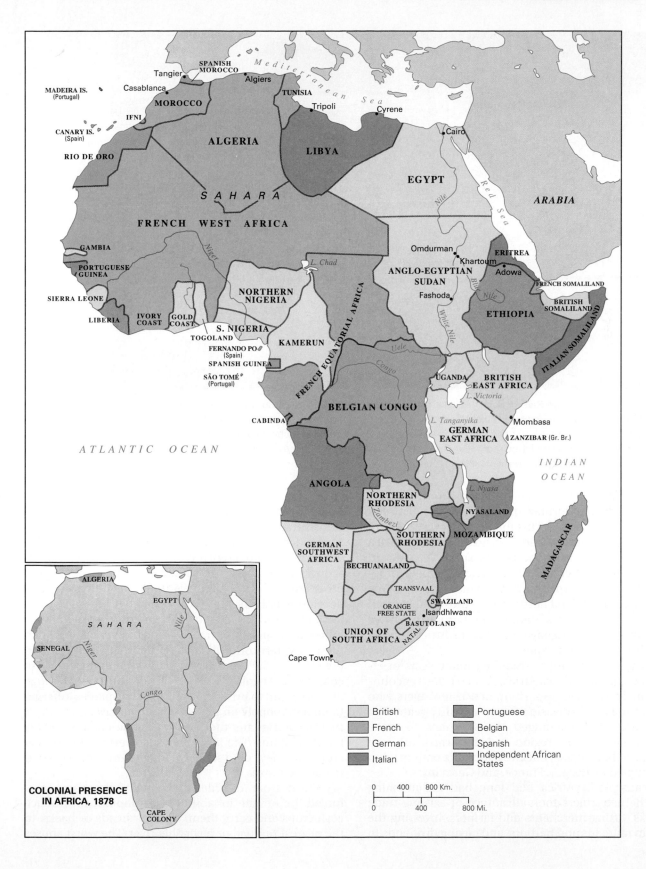

MADEIRA IS.
(Portugal)

SPANISH
MOROCCO
Tangier
Casablanca
Algiers
TUNISIA
Tripoli
Cyrene

Mediterranean Sea

CANARY IS.
(Spain)

IFNI

MOROCCO

ALGERIA

LIBYA

EGYPT

Nile

Red Sea

ARABIA

RIO DE ORO

S A H A R A

FRENCH   WEST   AFRICA

Niger

L. Chad

Omdurman
Khartoum
ERITREA

ANGLO-EGYPTIAN
SUDAN

Adowa

FRENCH SOMALILAND

GAMBIA

PORTUGUESE
GUINEA

NORTHERN
NIGERIA

Fashoda

Blue Nile

ETHIOPIA

BRITISH
SOMALILAND

SIERRA LEONE

LIBERIA

IVORY
COAST

GOLD
COAST

TOGOLAND

S. NIGERIA

White Nile

ITALIAN SOMALILAND

FERNANDO PO
(Spain)

SPANISH GUINEA

KAMERUN

FRENCH EQUATORIAL AFRICA

Uele

Congo

UGANDA

BRITISH
EAST
AFRICA

SÃO TOMÉ
(Portugal)

L. Victoria

ATLANTIC   OCEAN

BELGIAN CONGO

CABINDA

L. Tanganyika

GERMAN
EAST AFRICA

Mombasa

ZANZIBAR (Gr. Br.)

*INDIAN
OCEAN*

ANGOLA

NORTHERN
RHODESIA

L. Nyasa

NYASALAND

Zambezi

GERMAN
SOUTHWEST
AFRICA

SOUTHERN
RHODESIA

MOZAMBIQUE

MADAGASCAR

BECHUANALAND

TRANSVAAL

SWAZILAND

ORANGE
FREE STATE

Isandhlwana

BASUTOLAND

UNION OF
SOUTH AFRICA

NATAL

Cape Town

COLONIAL PRESENCE
IN AFRICA, 1878

ALGERIA

EGYPT

SAHARA

Nile

SENEGAL

Niger

Congo

CAPE
COLONY

British

French

German

Italian

Portuguese

Belgian

Spanish

Independent African
States

0   400   800 Km.

0   400   800 Mi.

A Steamboat for the Congo River   Soon after the Congo Basin was occupied by Europeans, the new colonial rulers realized they needed to improve transportation. Since access from the sea was blocked by rapids on the lower Congo River, steamboats had to be brought in sections, hauled from the coast by thousands of Congolese over very difficult terrain. This picture shows the pieces arriving at Stanley Pool, ready to be reassembled. (From H. M. Stanley, *The Congo,* vol. 2, London, 1885)

would replace the former trading relations between Africans and Europeans. This meant that every country with colonial ambitions had to send troops into Africa and participate in the division of the spoils. As a reward for triggering the "scramble" for Africa, Leopold II acquired a personal domain under the name "Congo Free State," while France and Portugal took most of the rest of equatorial Africa. In this manner, the European powers and King Leopold managed to divide Africa among themselves, at least on paper.

"Effective occupation," required many years of effort. In the interior of West Africa, French troops encountered the determined opposition of Muslim rulers who resisted the French invasion for up to thirty years. The French advance encouraged the Germans to stake claims to parts of the region and the British to move north from their coastal enclaves, until the entire region was occupied by Britain, France, and Germany.

Because West Africa had long had a flourishing trade, the new rulers took advantage of existing trade networks, taxing merchants and farmers, investing the profits in railroads and harbors, and paying dividends to

European stockholders. In the Gold Coast (now Ghana), British trading companies bought the cocoa grown by African farmers at low prices and resold it for large profits. The interior of French West Africa lagged behind. Although the region could produce cotton, peanuts, and other crops, the difficulties of transportation limited its development before 1914.

Compared to West Africa, equatorial Africa had few inhabitants and little trade. Rather than try to govern these vast territories directly, authorities in the Congo Free State, the French Congo, and the Portuguese colonies of Angola and Mozambique farmed out huge pieces of land to private concession companies, offering them a monopoly on the natural resources and trade of their territories and the right to employ soldiers and tax the inhabitants. The inhabitants, however, had no cash crops that they could sell to raise the money they needed to pay their taxes.

Freed from outside supervision, the companies forced the African inhabitants at gunpoint to produce cash crops and carry them, on their heads or backs, to the nearest railroad or navigable river. The worst abuses

Founding of South Africa   In May 1910, the *Cape Times* celebrated the founding of the Union of South Africa with a picture of Britannia releasing the dove of peace while the ship *Union* is towed out to sea.   (South African Library, Capetown)

took place in the Congo Free State, where a rubber boom lasting from 1895 to 1905 made it profitable for private companies to coerce Africans to collect latex from vines that grew in the forests. One Congolese refugee told the British consul Roger Casement who investigated the atrocities:

> We begged the white men to leave us alone, saying we could get no more rubber, but the white men and their soldiers said: 'Go. You are only beasts yourselves, you are only *nyama* (meat).' We tried, always going further into the forest, and when we failed and our rubber was short, the soldiers came to our towns and killed us. Many were shot, some had their ears cut off; others were tied up with ropes around their necks and bodies and taken away.[4]

After 1906 the British press began publicizing the horrors. The public outcry that followed, coinciding with the end of the rubber boom, convinced the Belgian government to take over Leopold's private empire in 1908.

Southern Africa

The history of southern Africa between 1869 and 1914 differs from that of the rest of the continent in several important respects. One was that the land had long attracted settlers. African pastoralists and farmers had inhabited the region for centuries. **Afrikaners,** descendants of Dutch settlers on the Cape of Good Hope, moved inland throughout the nineteenth century; British prospectors and settlers arrived later in the century; and, finally, Indians were brought over by the British and stayed.

Southern Africa attracted European settlers because of its good pastures and farmland and its phenomenal deposits of diamonds, gold, and copper, as well as coal and iron ore. This was the new El Dorado that imperialists had dreamed of since the heyday of the Spanish Empire in Peru and Mexico in the sixteenth century.

The discovery of diamonds at Kimberley in 1868 lured thousands of European prospectors as well as Africans looking for work. It also attracted the interest of Great Britain, colonial ruler of the Cape Colony, which annexed the diamond area in 1871, thereby angering the Afrikaners. Once in the interior, the British defeated the Xhosa° people in 1877 and 1878. Then in 1879 they confronted the Zulu, militarily the most powerful of the African peoples in the region.

The Zulu, led by their king Cetshwayo°, resented their encirclement by Afrikaners and British. A growing sense of nationalism and their proud military tradition led them into a war with the British in 1879. At first they

Xhosa (KOH-sah)   **Cetshwayo** (set-SHWAH-yo)

held their own, defeating the British at Isandhlwana°, but a few months later they were in turn defeated. Cetshwayo was captured and sent into exile, and the Zulu lands were given to white ranchers. Yet throughout those bitter times, the Zulu's sense of nationhood remained strong.

Relations between the British and the Afrikaners, already tense as a result of British encroachment, took a turn for the worse when gold was discovered in the Afrikaner republic of Transvaal° in 1886. In the gold rush that ensued, the British soon outnumbered the Afrikaners.

Britain's invasion of southern Africa was driven in part by the ambition of **Cecil Rhodes** (1853–1902), who once declared that he would "annex the stars" if he could. Rhodes made his fortune in the Kimberley diamond fields, founding De Beers Consolidated, a company that has dominated the world's diamond trade ever since. He then turned to politics. He led a concession company, the British South Africa Company, to push north into Central Africa, where he named two new colonies after himself: Southern Rhodesia (now Zimbabwe) and Northern Rhodesia (now Zambia). The Ndebele° and Shona peoples, who inhabited the region, resisted this invasion, but the machine guns of the British finally defeated them.

British attempts to annex the two Afrikaner republics, Transvaal and Orange Free State, and the inflow of English-speaking whites into the gold- and diamond-mining areas led to the South African War, which lasted from 1899 to 1902. At first the Afrikaners had the upper hand, for they were highly motivated, possessed modern rifles, and knew the land. In 1901, however, Great Britain brought in 450,000 troops and crushed the Afrikaner armies. Ironically, the Afrikaners' defeat in 1902 led to their ultimate victory. Wary of costly commitments overseas, the British government expected European settlers in Africa to manage their own affairs, as they were doing in Canada, Australia, and New Zealand. Thus in 1910 the European settlers created the Union of South Africa, in which the Afrikaners eventually emerged as the ruling element.

Unlike Canada, Austria, and New Zealand, South Africa had a majority of indigenous inhabitants and substantial numbers of Indians and "Cape Coloureds" (people of mixed ancestry). Yet the Europeans were both numerous enough to demand self-rule and powerful enough to deny the vote and other civil rights to the majority. In 1913 the South African parliament passed the Natives Land Act, assigning Africans to reservations and forbidding them to own land elsewhere. This and other racial policies turned South Africa into land of segregation, oppression, and bitter divisions.

Political and Social Consequences

Africa at the time of the European invasion contained a wide variety of societies. Some parts of the continent had long-established kingdoms with aristocracies or commercial towns dominated by a merchant class. In other places, agricultural peoples lived in villages without any outside government. Still elsewhere, pastoral nomads were organized along military lines. In some remote areas, people lived from hunting and gathering. It is not surprising that these societies responded in very different ways to the European invasion.

Some peoples welcomed the invaders as allies against local enemies. Under colonial rule, they sought a Western education and work in government service or in European firms. In exchange, they were often the first to receive benefits such as schools and roads.

Others, especially peoples with a pastoral or a warrior tradition, fought tenaciously. Examples abound, from the Zulu and Ndebele of southern Africa to the followers of charismatic leaders such as the Mahdi° in the eastern Sudan or Samori in the western Sudan (now Mali). In Southwest Africa (now Namibia), the pastoral Herero° people rose up against German invaders in 1904; in repressing the uprising, the Germans exterminated two-thirds of them.

Some commercial states with a long history of contact with Europeans also fought back. The kingdom of **Asante°** in Gold Coast rose up three times (in 1874, 1896, and 1900) before it was finally overwhelmed. In the Niger Delta, the ancient city of Benin, rich with artistic treasures, resisted colonial control until 1897, when a British "punitive expedition" set it on fire and carted its works of art off to Europe.

One resistance movement succeeded, to the astonishment of Europeans and Africans alike. When **Menelik** became emperor of Ethiopia in 1889 (see Chapter 26), his country was threatened by Sudanese Muslims to the west and by France and Italy, which controlled the Red Sea coast to the east. For many years, Ethiopia had been purchasing weapons. By the Treaty of Wichelle (1889), Italy agreed to sell more weapons to Ethiopia. Six years later, when Italians attempted to establish a protectorate over Ethiopia, they found the Ethiopians armed with thousands of rifles and even a few machine guns and ar-

---

Isandhlwana (ee-sawn-dull-WAH-nah)   **Transvaal** (trans-VAHL)
Ndebele (en-duh-BELL-ay)

Mahdi (MAH-dee)   **Herero** (hair-AIR-oh)   **Asante** (uh-SAWN-tay)

Victorious Ethiopians   Among the states of Africa, Ethiopia alone was able to defend itself against European imperialism. In the 1880s, hemmed in by Italian advances to its east and north and by British advances to its south and west, Ethiopia purchased modern weapons and trained its army to use them. Thus prepared, the Ethiopians defeated an Italian invasion at Adowa in 1896. These Ethiopian army officers wore their most elaborate finery to pose for a photograph after their victory.   (National Archives)

tillery pieces. Although Italy sent twenty thousand troops to attack Ethiopia, they were defeated at Adowa° in 1896 by a larger and better-trained Ethiopian army.

Most Africans neither joined nor fought the European invaders but tried to continue living as before. They found this increasingly difficult because colonial rule disrupted every traditional society. The presence of colonial officials meant that rights to land, commercial transactions, and legal disputes were handled very differently, and that traditional rulers lost all authority, except where Europeans used them as local administrators.

Changes in landholding were especially disruptive, for most Africans were farmers or herders for whom access to land was a necessity of life. In areas with a high population density, such as Egypt and West Africa, colonial rulers left peasants in place but encouraged them to grow cash crops and collected taxes on the product of their labor. Elsewhere, the new rulers declared any land that was not farmed to be "waste" or "vacant" and gave it to private concession companies or to European planters and ranchers. Africans found themselves squatters, sharecroppers, or ranch hands on land they had farmed for generations. In the worst cases, as in South Africa,

---

Adowa (AH-doe-ah)

many were forced off their lands and onto "reserves," like the Indians of North America (see Chapter 25).

Although the colonial rulers harbored designs on the land, they were even more interested in African labor. They did not want to pay wages high enough to attract workers voluntarily. Instead, they imposed various taxes, such as the hut tax or the head tax, which Africans had to pay regardless of their income. To find the money, Africans had little choice but to accept whatever work the Europeans offered. In this way, Africans were recruited to work on plantations, railroads, and other modern enterprises. In the South African mines, Africans were paid, on average, one-tenth as much as Europeans.

Some Africans came to the cities and mining camps seeking a better life than they had on the land. Many migrated great distances and stayed away for years at a time. Most migrants workers were men who left their wives and children behind in villages and on reserves. In some cases, the authorities did not allow them to bring their families and settle permanently in the towns. This caused great hardship for African women, who had to grow food for their families during the men's absences and care for sick and aged workers. Long separations between spouses also led to an increase in prostitution and to the spread of sexually transmitted diseases.

A Nigerian Woman
Remembers Her Childhood

First-person accounts of the period from 1869 to 1914 by African women are extremely rare, for few African women knew how to write and almost none wrote their memoirs. One exception is Baba of Karo, a woman from Zarewa in the Sokoto Caliphate (now northern Nigeria), who told her life story to a visiting American anthropologist. This is her recollection of the arrival of the British who conquered Sokoto between 1901 and 1903, when she was a young girl.

When I was a maiden the Europeans first arrived. Ever since we were quite small the *malams* [Quranic scholars] had been saying that the Europeans would come with a thing called a train, they would come with a thing called a motor-car, in them you would go and come back in a trice. They would stop wars, they would repair the world, they would stop oppression and lawlessness, we should live at peace with them. We used to go and sit quietly and listen to the prophecies. They would come, fine handsome people, they would not kill anyone, they would not oppress anyone, they would bring all their strange things. We were young girls when a European came with his attendants—"See, there's a white man, what has brought him?" He was asking the way to some town, we ran away and shut the door and he passed by and went on his way. . . .

I remember when a European came to Karo on a horse, and some of his foot soldiers went into the town. Everyone came out to look at them, but in Zarewa they didn't see the European. Everyone at Karo ran away—"There's a European! There's a European!" He came from Zaria with a few black men, two on horses and four on foot. We were inside the town. Later on we heard that they were there in Zaria in crowds, clearing spaces and building houses. One of my younger "sisters" was at Karo, she was pregnant, and when she saw the European she ran away and shut the door.

At that time Yusufu was the king of Karo. He did not like the Europeans, he did not wish them, he would sign their treaty. When he saw that perforce he would have to agree, so he did. We Habe [Hausa] wanted them to come, it was the Fulani [ruling class of Sokoto] who did not like it. When the Europeans came the Habe saw that if you worked for them they paid you for it, they didn't say, like the Fulani, "Commoner, give me this! Commoner, bring me that!" Yes, the Habe wanted them; they saw no harm in them. From Zaria they came to Rogo, they were building their big road to Karo City. They called out the people and said they were to come and make the road, if there were trees in the way they cut them down. The Europeans paid them with goods, they collected the villagers together and each man brought his large hoe. Money was not much use to them, so the Europeans paid them with food and other things.

The Europeans said that there were to be no more slaves; if someone said "Slave!" you could complain to the *alkali* [judge] who would punish the master who said it, the judge said "That is what the Europeans have decreed." The first order said that any slave, if he was younger than you, was your younger brother, if he was older than you he was your elder brother—they were all brothers of their master's family. No one used the world "slave" any more. When slavery was stopped, nothing much happened at our *rinji* [slave quarters] except that some slaves whom we had bought in the market ran away. Our own father went to his farm and worked, he and his son took up their large hoes; they loaned out their spare farms. Tsoho our father and Kadiri my brother with whom I live now and Balambo worked, they farmed guinea-corn and millet and groundnuts and everything; before this they had supervised the slaves' work—now they did their own. . . .

In the old days if the chief liked the look of your daughter he would take her and put her in his house; you could do nothing about it. Now they don't do that.

How did people in this part of Africa anticipate the arrival of the Europeans? Who favored their coming, and who did not? Why? What impact did the Europeans have on slavery and on labor in this area? Overall, did Baba of Karo approve or disapprove of their coming? Why?

Source: From M. F. Smith, ed., *Baba of Karo: A Woman of the Muslim Hausa* (New York: Philosophical Library, 1955), 66–68. Copyright © 1955. Reprinted by permission of Regeen Najor.

Some African women welcomed colonial rule, for it brought an end to fighting and slave raiding (see Society and Culture: A Nigerian Woman Remembers Her Childhood). A few succeeded in becoming wealthy traders or owners of livestock. On the whole, however, African women benefited less than men from the economic changes that colonialism introduced. In areas where the colonial rulers replaced communal property (traditional in most of Africa) with private property, property rights were assigned to the head of the household—that is, to the man. Almost all the jobs open to Africans, even those considered "women's work" in Europe such as nursing or domestic service, were reserved for men.

Cultural Responses

More Africans came into contact with missionaries than with any other Europeans. Missionaries, both men and women, opened schools to teach reading, writing, and arithmetic to village children. Boys were taught crafts such as carpentry and blacksmithing, while girls learned domestic skills such as cooking, laundry, and child care.

Along with basic skills, the first generation of Africans educated in mission schools acquired Western ideas of justice and progress. Samuel Ajayi Crowther, a Yoruba rescued from slavery as a boy and educated in mission schools in Sierra Leone, went on to become an Anglican minister and, in 1864, the first African bishop. Crowther thought that Africa needed European assistance in achieving both spiritual and economic development:

> Africa has neither knowledge nor skill . . . to bring out her vast resources for her own improvement. . . . Therefore to claim Africa for the Africans alone, is to claim for her the right of a continued ignorance. . . . For it is certain, unless help [comes] from without, a nation can never rise above its present state.[5]

After the first generation, many of the teachers in mission schools were African, themselves the products of a mission education. They discovered that Christian ideals clashed with the reality of colonial exploitation. As one convert wrote in 1911:

> There is too much failure among all Europeans in Nyasaland. The three combined bodies—Missionaries, Government and Companies or gainers of money—do form the same rule to look upon the native with mockery eyes. . . . If we had enough power to communicate ourselves to Europe, we would advise them not to call themselves Christendom, but Europeandom. Therefore the life of the three combined bodies is altogether

too cheaty, too thefty, too mockery. Instead of "Give," they say "Take away from." There is too much breakage of God's pure law.[6]

Christian missionaries from Europe and America were not the only ones to bring religious change to Africa. In southern and Central Africa, indigenous preachers adapted Christianity to African values and customs and founded new denominations known as "Ethiopian" churches.

Christianity proved successful in converting followers of traditional religions but made no inroads among Muslims. Instead, Islam, long predominant in northern and eastern Africa, spread southward as Muslim teachers established Quranic schools in the villages and founded Muslim brotherhoods. European colonialism unwittingly helped the diffusion of Islam. By building cities and increasing trade, colonial rule permitted Muslims to settle in new areas. As Islam—a universal religion without the taint of colonialism—became increasingly relevant to Africans, the number of Muslims in sub-Saharan Africa probably doubled between 1869 and 1914.

ASIA AND WESTERN DOMINANCE

During the period from 1869 to 1914, the pressure of the industrial powers was felt throughout Asia, the East Indies, and the Pacific islands. As trade with these regions grew in the late nineteenth century, so did their attractiveness to imperialists eager for economic benefits and national prestige.

Europeans had traded along the coasts of Asia and the East Indies since the early sixteenth century. By 1869, Britain already controlled most of India and Burma, Spain occupied the Philippines, and the Netherlands held large parts of the East Indies (now Indonesia). Between 1862 and 1895, France conquered Indochina (now Vietnam, Kampuchea, and Laos). It was the existence of these Asian colonial possessions that had inspired the building of the Suez Canal.

We have already seen the special cases of British imperialism in India (Chapter 26) and of Japanese imperialism in China and Korea (Chapter 28). Here let us look at the impact of the New Imperialism on Central and Southeast Asia, Indonesia, the Philippines, and Hawaii (see Map 29.2)

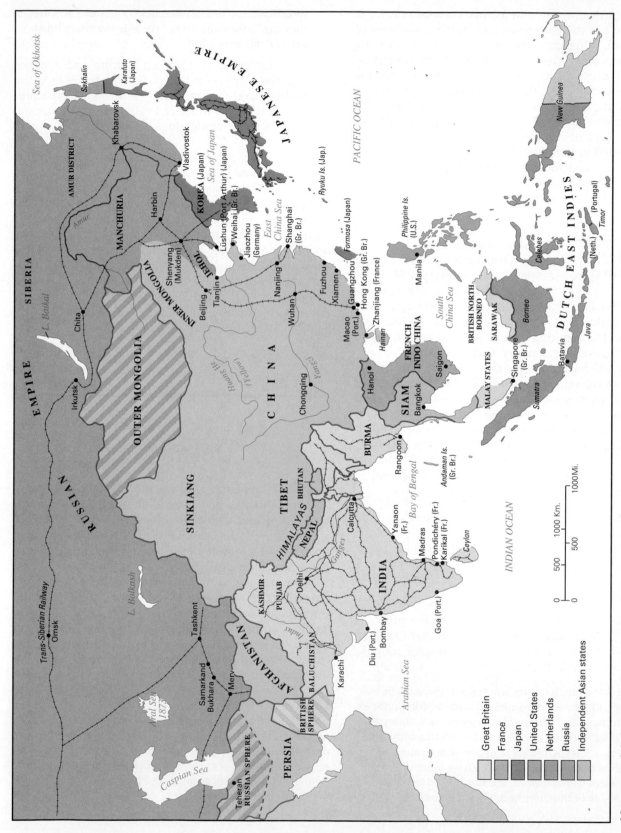

Map 29.2 Asia in 1914 By 1914, much of Asia was claimed by the colonial powers. The southern rim, from the Persian Gulf to the Pacific, was occupied by Great Britain, France, the Netherlands, and the United States. Central Asia had been incorporated into the Russian Empire. Japan, now industrialized, had joined the Western imperialist powers in expanding its territory and influence at the expense of China.

Central Asia

For over seven centuries, Russians had been at the mercy of the nomads of the Eurasian steppe extending from the Black Sea to Manchuria. When the nomadic tribesmen were united, as they were under the Mongol ruler Genghis Khan (r. 1206–1227), they could defeat the Russians; when they were not, the Russians moved into the steppe. This age-old ebb and flow ended when Russia acquired modern rifles and artillery.

Between 1865 and 1876, Russian forces advanced into Central Asia. Nomads like the Kazakhs, who lived east of the Caspian Sea, fought bravely but in vain. The fertile agricultural land of Kazakhstan attracted 200,000 Russian settlers. Although the governments of Tsar Alexander II (r. 1855–1881) and Tsar Alexander III (r. 1881–1894) claimed not to interfere in indigenous customs, they declared communally owned grazing lands "waste" or "vacant" and turned them over to farmers from Russia. By the end of the nineteenth century, the nomads were fenced out and reduced to starvation. Echoing the beliefs of other European imperialists, an eminent Russian jurist declared: "International rights cannot be taken into account when dealing with semibarbarous peoples."

South of the Kazakh steppe land were deserts dotted with oases where the fabled cities of Tashkent, Bukhara, and Samarkand served the caravan trade between China and the Middle East. For centuries the peoples of the region had lived under the protection of the Mongols and later the Qing Empire. But by the 1860s and 1870s, the Qing Empire was losing control over Central Asia (see Chapter 27), so it was fairly easy for Russian expeditions to conquer the indigenous peoples. Russia thereby acquired land suitable for cotton, along with a large and growing Muslim population.

Russian rule brought few benefits to the peoples of the Central Asian oases and few real changes. The Russians abolished slavery, built railroads to link the region with Europe, and planted hundreds of thousands of acres of cotton. Unlike the British in India, however, they did not attempt to change the customs, languages, or religious beliefs of their subjects.

Southeast Asia and Indonesia

The peoples of the Southeast Asian peninsula and the Indonesian archipelago had been in contact with outsiders—Chinese, Indians, Arabs, Europeans—for centuries. Java and the smaller islands—the fabled Spice Islands (the Moluccas)—had long been subject to Portuguese and later to Dutch domination. Until the mid-nineteenth century, however, most of the region was made up of independent kingdoms.

As in Africa, there is considerable variation in the history of different parts of the region, yet they all came under intense imperialist pressure during the nineteenth century. Burma (now Myanmar), nearest India, was gradually taken over by the British in the course of the century, until the last piece was annexed in 1885. Indochina fell piece by piece under French control until it was finally subdued in 1895. Similarly, Malaya (now Malaysia) came under British rule in stages during the 1870s and 1880s. By the early 1900s the Dutch had subdued northern Sumatra, the last part of the Dutch East Indies to be conquered. Only Siam (now Thailand) remained independent, although it lost several border provinces.

Despite their varied political histories, all these regions had features in common. They all had fertile soil, constant warmth, and heavy rains. Furthermore, the peoples of the region had a long tradition of intensive gardening, irrigation, and terracing. In those parts of the region where the population was not very dense, Europeans found it easy to import landless laborers from China and India seeking better opportunities overseas. Another reason for the region's wealth was the transfer of commercially valuable plants from other parts of the world. Tobacco, cinchona° (an antimalarial drug), manioc (an edible root crop), maize (corn), and natural rubber were brought from the Americas; sugar from India; tea from China; and coffee and oil palms from Africa. By 1914, much of the world's supply of these valuable products—in the case of rubber, almost all—came from Southeast Asia and Indonesia (see Environment and Technology: Imperialism and Tropical Ecology).

Most of the wealth of Southeast Asia and Indonesia was exported to Europe and North America. In exchange, the inhabitants of the region received two benefits from colonial rule: peace and a reliable food supply. As a result, their numbers increased at an unprecedented rate. For instance, the population of Java (an island the size of Pennsylvania) doubled from 16 million in 1870 to over 30 million in 1914.

Colonialism and the growth of population brought many social changes. The more numerous agricultural and commercial peoples gradually moved into mountainous and forest areas, displacing the earlier inhabitants who practiced hunting and gathering or shifting agriculture. The migrations of the Javanese to Borneo and Sumatra are but one example. Immigrants from China and India (see Chapter 26) changed the ethnic composition and culture of every country in the region. Thus the population of the Malay Peninsula became one-third Malay, one-third Chinese, and one-third Indian.

---

cinchona (sin-CHO-nah)

Imperialism and Tropical Ecology

Like all conquerors before them, the European imperialists of the nineteenth century exacted taxes and rents from the peoples they conquered. But they also sent botanists and agricultural experts to their tropical colonies to increase the production of commercial crops. In doing so, they radically changed the landscapes of their tropical dependencies.

The most dramatic effects were brought about by the deliberate introduction of new crops—an acceleration of the Columbian Exchange that had begun in the fifteenth century. In the early nineteenth century, tea was transferred from China to India and Ceylon. In the 1850s, British and Dutch botanists smuggled seeds of the cinchona tree from the Andes in South America to India and Java. They had to operate in secret, because the South American republics, knowing the value of this crop, prohibited the export of seeds. With the seeds, the British and Dutch established cinchona plantations in Ceylon and Java, respectively, to produce quinine, which was essential as an antimalarial drug and a flavoring for tonic water. Similarly, in the 1870s, British agents stole seeds of the rubber tree from the Amazon rain forest and transferred them to Malaya and Sumatra.

Before these transfers, vast forests covered the highlands of India, Southeast Asia, and Indonesia, precisely the lands where the new plants grew best. So European planters had the forests cut down and replaced with thousands of acres of commercially profitable trees and bushes, all lined up in perfect rows and tended by thousands of indigenous laborers to satisfy the demands of customers in faraway lands. The crops that poured forth from the transformed environments brought great wealth to the European planters and the imperial powers. In 1909 the British botanist John Willis justified the transformation in these terms:

> Whether planting in the tropics will always continue to be under European management is another question, but the northern powers will not permit that the rich and as yet comparatively undeveloped countries of the tropics should be entirely wasted by being devoted merely to the supply of the food and clothing wants of their own people, when they can also supply the wants of the colder zones in so many indispensable products.

This quotation raises important questions about trade versus self-sufficiency. If a region's economy supplies the food and clothing wants of its own people, is its output "entirely wasted"? What is the advantage of trading the prod-

Branch of a Cinchona Tree   The bark of the cinchona tree was the source of quinine, the only antimalarial drug known before 1940. Quinine made it much safer for Europeans to live in the tropics.   (From Bentley & Trimen's *Medicinal Plants.* Hunt Institute for Botanical Documentation, Carnegie Mellon University)

ucts of one region (such as the tropics) for those of another (such as the colder zones)? Is this trade an obligation? Should one part of the world (such as the "northern powers") let another refuse to develop and sell its "indispensable products"? Can you think of a case where a powerful country forced a weaker one to trade?

Source: The quotation is from John Christopher Willis, *Agriculture in the Tropics: An Elementary Treatise* (Cambridge: Cambridge University Press, 1909), 38–39.

As in Africa, European missionaries attempted to spread Christianity under the colonial umbrella. Islam, however, was much more successful in gaining new converts, for it had been established in the region for centuries and people did not consider it a religion imposed on them by foreigners.

Education and European ideas had an impact on the political perceptions of the peoples of Southeast Asia and Indonesia. Just as important was their awareness of events in neighboring Asian countries: India, where a nationalist movement arose in the 1880s (see Chapter 26); China, where modernizers were undermining the authority of the Qing (Chapter 27); and especially Japan, whose rapid industrialization culminated in its brilliant victory over Russia in the Russo-Japanese War (1904–1905) (Chapter 28). The spirit of a rising generation was expressed by a young Vietnamese writing soon after the Russo-Japanese War.

> I, . . . an obscure student, having had occasion to study new books and new doctrines, have discovered in a recent history of Japan how they have been able to conquer the impotent Europeans. This is the reason why we have formed an organization. . . . We have selected from young Annamites [Vietnamese] the most energetic, with great capacities for courage, and are sending them to Japan for study. . . . Several years have passed without the French being aware of the movement. . . . Our only aim is to prepare the population for the future.[7]

Hawaii and the Philippines, 1878–1902

By the 1890s, the United States had a fast-growing population and industries that produced more manufactured goods than they could sell at home. Merchants and bankers began to look for export markets. The political mood was also expansionist, and many echoed the feelings of the naval strategist Alfred T. Mahan°: "Whether they will or no, Americans must now begin to look outward. The growing production of the country requires it."

Some Americans had been looking outward for quite some time, especially across the Pacific to China and Japan. In 1878 the United States obtained the harbor of Pago Pago in Samoa as a coaling and naval station, and in 1887 it secured the use of Pearl Harbor in Hawaii for the same purpose. Six years later, American settlers in Hawaii deposed Queen Liliuokalani (1838–1917) and of-

fered the Hawaiian Islands to the United States. At the time President Grover Cleveland (1893–1897) was opposed to annexation, and the settlers had to content themselves with an informal protectorate. By 1898, however, the United States under President William McKinley (1897–1901) had become openly imperialistic. It annexed Hawaii for strategic reasons as a steppingstone to Asia. As the United States became ever more involved in Asian affairs, Hawaii's strategic location brought an inflow of U.S. military personnel, and its fertile land caused planters to import farm laborers from Japan, China, and the Philippines. These immigrants soon outnumbered the native Hawaiians.

While large parts of Asia were falling under colonial domination, the people of the Philippines were chafing under their Spanish rulers. The movement for independence began among young Filipinos studying in Europe. José Rizal, a young doctor working in Spain, was arrested and executed in 1896 for writing patriotic and anticlerical novels. Thereafter, the center of resistance shifted to the Philippines, where **Emilio Aguinaldo,** leader of a secret society, rose in revolt and proclaimed a republic in 1898. The revolutionaries had a good chance of winning independence, for Spain had its hands full with a revolution in Cuba (see below).

Unfortunately for Aguinaldo and his followers, the United States went to war against Spain in April 1898 and quickly overcame Spanish forces in the Philippines and in Cuba. President McKinley had not originally intended to acquire the Philippines. But after the Spanish defeat, he realized that a weakened Spain might lose the islands to another imperialist power. Japan, having recently defeated China in the Sino-Japanese War (1894–1895) and annexed Taiwan (see Chapter 28), was eager to expand its empire. So was Germany, which had taken over parts of New Guinea and Samoa and several Pacific archipelagoes during the 1880s. To forestall them, McKinley purchased the Philippines from Spain for $20 million.

The Filipinos were not eager to trade one master for another. For a while, Aguinaldo cooperated with the Americans in the hope of achieving full independence. When his plan was rejected, in 1899 he rose up again and proclaimed the independence of his country. In spite of protests by anti-imperialists in the United States, the U.S. government decided that its global interests outweighed the interests of the Filipino people. In rebel areas, a U.S. army of occupation tortured prisoners, burned villages and crops, and forced the inhabitants into "reconcentration camps." Many American soldiers tended to look on Filipinos with the same racial contempt with which Europeans viewed their colonial subjects. By the end of the insurrection in 1902, the war had cost the lives of 5,000 Americans and 200,000 Filipinos.

Mahan (mah-HAHN)

Emilio Aguinaldo In 1896, a revolt led by Emilio Aguinaldo attempted to expel Spaniards from the Philippines. When the United States purchased the Philippines from Spain two years later, the Filipino people were not consulted. Aguinaldo continued his campaign, this time against the American occupation forces, until his capture in 1901. In this picture, he appears on horseback, surrounded by some of his troops. (Corbis)

After the end of the insurrection, the United States attempted to soften its rule with public works and economic development projects. New buildings went up in the city of Manila; roads, harbors, and railroads were built; and the Philippine economy was tied ever more closely to that of the United States. In 1907 Filipinos were allowed to elect representatives to a legislative assembly; however, ultimate authority remained in the hands of a governor appointed by the president of the United States. In 1916 the Philippines were the first U.S. colony to be promised independence, a promise fulfilled thirty years later.

IMPERIALISM IN LATIN AMERICA

Nations in the Americas followed two divergent paths (see Chapter 25). In Canada and the United States there arose manufacturing industries, powerful corporations, and wealthy financial institutions. Latin America and the Caribbean exported raw materials and foodstuffs and imported manufactured goods. The poverty of their people, the preferences of their elites, and the pressures of the world economy made them increasingly dependent on the industrialized countries. Their political systems saved them from outright annexation by the colonial empires. But their natural resources made them attractive targets for manipulation by the industrial powers, including the United States, in a form of economic dependence called **free-trade imperialism.**

In the Western Hemisphere, therefore, the New Imperialism manifested itself not by a "scramble" for territories but in two other ways. In the larger republics of South America, the pressure was mostly financial and economic. In Central America and the Caribbean, it also included military intervention by the United States.

Railroads and the Imperialism of Free Trade

Latin America's economic potential was huge, for the region could produce many agricultural and mineral products in demand in the industrial countries. What was needed was a means of opening the interior to development. Railroads seemed the perfect answer.

Foreign merchants and bankers as well as Latin American landowners and politicians embraced the new technology. Starting in the 1870s, almost every country

Railroads Penetrate South America   The late nineteenth century saw the construction of several railroad networks in South America, often through rugged and dangerous terrain. This photograph shows the opening of a bridge on the Transandine Railroad in Peru. Flags were raised in honor of American construction and British ownership of the railroad.   (Tony Morrison/South American Pictures)

in Latin America acquired railroads, usually connecting mines or agricultural regions with the nearest port rather than linking up the different parts of the interior. Since Latin America did not have any steel or mechanical industries, all the equipment and building material came from Britain or the United States. So did the money to build the networks, the engineers who designed and maintained them, and the managers who ran them.

Argentina, a land of rich soil that produced wheat, beef, and hides, gained the longest and best-developed rail network south of the United States. By 1914, 86 percent of the railroads in Argentina were owned by British firms, 40 percent of the employees were British, and the official language of the railroads was not Spanish but English. The same was true of mining and industrial enterprises and public utilities throughout Latin America.

In many ways, the situation resembled that of India or Ireland, which also obtained a rail network in exchange for raw materials and agricultural products. The Argentine nationalist Juan Justo saw the parallel:

> English capital has done what English armies could not do. Today our country is tributary to England . . . the gold that the English capitalists take out of Argentina or carry off in the form of products does us no more good than the Irish get from the revenues that the English lords take out of Ireland.[8]

The difference was that the Indians and Irish had little say in the matter because they were under British rule. But in Latin America the political elites encouraged foreign companies with generous concessions as the most rapid way to modernize their countries and enrich the property owners. In countries where the majority of the poor were Indians (as in Mexico and Peru) or of African origin (as in Brazil), they were neither consulted nor allowed to benefit from the railroad boom.

American Expansionism and the Spanish-American War, 1898

After 1865, the European powers used their financial power to penetrate Latin America. But they avoided territorial acquisitions, for four reasons: (1) they were overextended in Africa and Asia; (2) there was no need, because the Latin American governments provided the political backing for the economic arrangements; (3) the Latin Americans had shown themselves capable of resisting invasions, most recently when Mexico fought off the French in the 1860s (see Chapter 25); and (4) the United States, itself a former colony, claimed to defend the entire Western Hemisphere against all outside intervention. This claim, made in the Monroe Doctrine (1823), did not prevent the United States itself from intervening in Latin American affairs.

The United States had long had interests in Cuba, the closest and richest of the Caribbean islands and a Spanish colony. American businesses had invested great sums of money in Cuba's sugar and tobacco industries, and tens of thousands of Cubans had migrated to the United States. In 1895 the Cuban nationalist José Martí started a revolution against Spanish rule. American newspapers thrilled readers with lurid stories of Spanish atrocities, businessmen worried about their investments, and politicians demanded that the U.S. government help liberate Cuba.

On February 15, 1898, the U.S. battleship *Maine* accidentally blew up in Havana harbor, killing 266 American sailors. The U.S. government immediately blamed Spain and issued an ultimatum that the Spanish evacuate Cuba. Spain agreed to the ultimatum, but the American press and Congress were eager for war, and President McKinley did not restrain them.

The Spanish-American War was over quickly. On May 1, 1898 U.S. warships destroyed the Spanish fleet at Manila in the Philippines. Two months later, the United States Navy sank the Spanish Atlantic fleet off Santiago, Cuba. By mid-August, Spain was suing for peace. U.S. Secretary of State John Hay called it "a splendid little war." The United States purchased the Philippines from Spain but took over Puerto Rico and Guam as war booty. The two islands remain American possessions to this day. Cuba became an independent republic, subject, however, to intense interference by the United States.

American Intervention in the Caribbean and Central America, 1901–1914

The nations of the Caribbean and Central America were small and poor, and their governments were corrupt, unstable, and often bankrupt. They seemed to offer an open invitation to foreign interference. A government would borrow money to pay for railroads, harbors, electric power, and other symbols of modernity. When it could not repay the loan, the lending banks in Europe or the United States would ask for assistance from their home governments, which sometimes threatened to intervene. To ward off European intervention, the United States sent in the marines on more than one occasion.

Presidents Theodore Roosevelt (1901–1909), William Taft (1909–1913), and Woodrow Wilson (1913–1921) differed sharply on the proper policy the United States should follow toward the small nations to the south. But all three felt impelled to intervene in the region. Having "liberated" Cuba from Spain, the United States forced the Cuban government to accept the Platt Amendment in 1901. The amendment gave the United States the "right to intervene" to maintain order on the island. The United States used this excuse to occupy Cuba militarily from 1906 to 1909, in 1912, and again from 1917 to 1922. In all but name, Cuba became an American protectorate. U.S. troops also occupied the Dominican Republic from 1904 to 1907 and again in 1916, Nicaragua and Honduras in 1912, and Haiti in 1915. They brought sanitation and material progress but no political improvements.

The United States was especially forceful in Panama, which was a province of Colombia. Here the issue was not corruption or debts but a more vital interest: the construction of a canal across the isthmus of Panama to speed shipping between the east and west coasts of the United States. In 1878 the Frenchman Ferdinand de Lesseps, builder of the Suez Canal, had obtained a concession from Colombia to construct a canal across the isthmus, which lay in Colombian territory. Financial scandals and yellow fever, however, doomed his project.

When the United States acquired Hawaii and the Philippines, it recognized the strategic value of a canal that would allow warships to move quickly between the Atlantic and Pacific Oceans. The main obstacle was Colombia, whose senate refused to give the United States a piece of its territory. In 1903 the U.S. government supported a Panamanian rebellion against Colombia and quickly recognized the independence of Panama. In exchange, it obtained the right to build a canal and to occupy a zone 5 miles (8 kilometers) wide on either side of it. Work began in 1904, and the **Panama Canal** opened on August 15, 1914.

The World Economy and the Global Environment

The New Imperialists were not traditional conquerors or empire builders like the Spanish conquistadors. Although their conquests were much larger (see Map 29.3), their aim was not only to extend their power over new territories and peoples but to control both the natural world and indigenous societies and put them to work more efficiently than had ever been done before. Both their goals and their methods were industrial. A railroad, for example, was an act of faith as well as a means of transportation. They expressed their belief in progress and their good intentions in the clichés of the time: "the conquest of nature," "the annihilation of time and space," "the taming of the wilderness," and "our civilizing mission."

Expansion of the World Economy

For centuries, spices, sugar, silk and other exotic or tropical products had found a ready market in Europe. The Industrial Revolution vastly expanded this demand. Imports of foods and stimulants such as tea, coffee, and cocoa increased substantially during the nineteenth century. The trade in industrial raw materials grew even faster. Some were the products of agriculture, such as cotton, jute for bags, and palm oil for soap and lubricants. Others were minerals such as diamonds, gold, and copper. There also were wild forest products that only later came to be cultivated: timber for buildings and railroad ties, cinchona bark, rubber for rainwear and tires, and gutta-percha° to insulate electric cables.

The growing needs of the industrial world could not be met by the traditional methods of production and transportation of the nonindustrial world. When the U.S. Civil War interrupted the export of cotton to England in the 1860s, the British turned to India. But they found that Indian cotton was ruined by exposure to rain and dust during the long trip on open carts from the interior of the country to the harbors. To prevent the expansion of their industry from being stifled by the technological backwardness of their newly conquered territories, the imperialists made every effort to bring those territories into the mainstream of the world market.

One great change was in transportation. The Suez and Panama Canals cut travel time and lowered freight costs dramatically. Steamships became more numerous, and as their size increased, new, deeper harbors were needed. The Europeans also built railroads throughout the world; India alone had 37,000 miles (nearly 60,000 kilometers) of track by 1915, almost as much as Germany or Russia. Railroads reached into the interior of Latin America, Canada, China, and Australia. In 1903 the Russians completed the Trans-Siberian Railway from Moscow to Vladivostok on the Pacific. Visionaries even made plans for railroads from Europe to India and from Egypt to South Africa.

Transformation of the Global Environment

The economic changes brought by Europeans and Americans also altered environments around the world. The British, whose craving for tea could not be satisfied with the limited exports available from China, introduced tea into the warm, rainy hill country of Ceylon and northeastern India. In those areas and in Java, thousands of square miles of tropical rain forests were felled to make way for tea plantations.

Economic botany and agricultural science were applied to every promising plant species. European botanists had long collected and classified exotic plants from around the world. In the nineteenth century, they founded botanical gardens in Java, India, Mauritius°, Ceylon, Jamaica, and other tropical colonies. These gardens not only collected local plants but also exchanged plants with other gardens. They were especially active in systematically transferring commercially valuable plant species from one tropical region to another. Cinchona, tobacco, sugar, and other crops were introduced, improved, and vastly expanded in the colonies of Southeast Asia and Indonesia (see Environment and Technology: Imperialism and Tropical Ecology). Cocoa and coffee growing spread over large areas of Brazil and Africa; oil-palm plantations were established in Nigeria and the Congo Basin. Rubber, used to make waterproof garments and bicycle tires, originally came from the latex of *Hevea* trees growing wild in the Brazilian rain forest. Then in the 1870s, British agents smuggled seedlings from Brazil to the Royal Botanic Gardens at Kew near London, and from there to the Botanic Garden of Singapore. These plants formed the nucleus of the enormous rubber economy of Southeast Asia.

Throughout the tropics, land once covered with forests or devoted to shifting slash-and-burn agriculture were transformed into permanent farms and plantations. Even in areas not developed to export crops, growing

---

gutta-percha (gut-tah–PER-cha)

Mauritius (maw-REE-shuss)

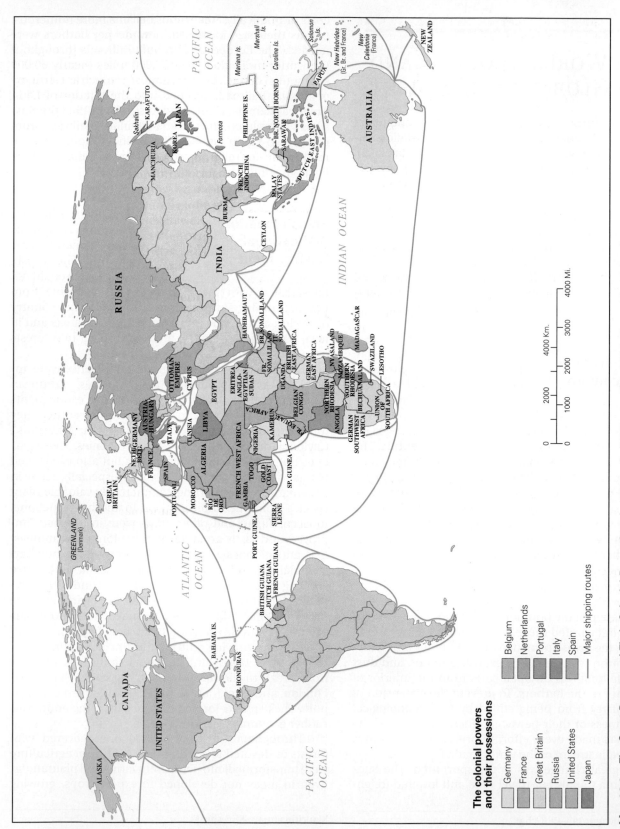

Map 29.3   The Great Powers and Their Colonial Possessions in 1913   By 1913, a small handful of countries claimed sovereignty over more than half the land area of the earth. Global power was closely connected with industries and a merchant marine, rather than with a large territory. This explains why Great Britain, the smallest of the great powers, possessed the largest empire.

The colonial powers and their possessions

- Germany
- France
- Great Britain
- Russia
- United States
- Japan

- Belgium
- Netherlands
- Portugal
- Italy
- Spain
- Major shipping routes

populations put pressure on the land. In Java and India, farmers felled trees to obtain arable land and firewood. They terraced hillsides, drained swamps, and dug wells.

Irrigation and water control transformed the dry parts of the tropics as well. In the 1830s, British engineers in India had restored ancient canals that had fallen into disrepair. Their success led them to build new irrigation canals, turning thousands of previously barren acres into well-watered, densely populated farmland. The migration of European experts spread the newest techniques of irrigation engineering around the world. By the turn of the century, irrigation projects were under way wherever rivers flowed through dry lands. In Egypt and Central Asia, irrigation brought more acres under cultivation in one forty-year span than in all previous history.

Railroads had voracious appetites for land and resources. They cut into mountains, spanned rivers and canyons with trestles, and covered as much land with their freight yards as whole cities had needed in previous centuries. They also consumed vast quantities of iron, timber for ties, and coal or wood for fuel. Most important of all, railroads brought people and their cities, farms, and industries to areas previously occupied by small, scattered populations.

Prospectors looking for valuable minerals opened the earth to reveal its riches: gold in South Africa, Australia, and Canada; tin in Nigeria, Malaya, and Bolivia; copper in Chile and Central Africa; iron ore in northern India; and much else. Where mines were dug deep inside the earth, the dirt and rocks brought up with the ores formed huge mounds near mine entrances. Open mines dug to obtain ores lying close to the surface created a landscape of lunar craters, and runoff from the minerals poisoned the water for miles around. Refineries that processed the ores fouled the environment with slag heaps and more toxic runoff.

The transformation of the land by human beings, a constant throughout history, accelerated sharply. Only the changes occurring since 1914 can compare with the transformation of the global environment that took place between 1869 and 1914.

CONCLUSION

The industrialization of the late nineteenth century increased the power of Europeans and North Americans over nature and over the peoples of other continents. They used their new-found power to conquer empires.

The opening of the Suez Canal in 1869 was the symbolic beginning of the New Imperialism. It demonstrated the power of modern industry to subdue nature by carving the land. It stimulated shipping and trade between the industrial countries and the tropics. It deepened the involvement of Europeans in the affairs of the Middle East, Africa, and Asia. From that year until 1914, not only the great powers but smaller countries too—even, in some cases, individual Europeans or Americans—had the power to decide the fate of whole countries. The motivation to conquer or control other lands surely helps explain the New Imperialism. But the means at the disposal of the imperialists—that is, the gap that opened between their technologies and forms of organization and those available to Asians, Africans, and Latin Americans—is equally important.

The new technological means and the enhanced motivations of the imperialists resulted in the most rapid conquest of territories in the history of the world. In less than half a century, almost all of Africa and large parts of Asia and Oceania were added to the colonial empires, while Latin America, nominally independent, was turned into an economic colony of the industrial powers. In the process of developing the economic potential of their empires, the colonial powers transformed natural environments around the world.

The opening of the Panama Canal in August 1914 confirmed the new powers of the industrializing nations—but with a twist, for it was the United States, a latecomer to the game of imperialism, that created the canal. In that same month, the other imperialist nations turned their weapons against one another and began a life-or-death struggle for supremacy in Europe. That conflict is the subject of the next chapter.

■ Key Terms

Suez Canal
New Imperialism
Battle of Omdurman
colonialism
"scramble" for Africa
Henry Morton Stanley
King Leopold II (Belgium)
Berlin Conference
Afrikaners
Cecil Rhodes Asante
Asante
Emperor Menelik
Emilio Aguinaldo
free-trade imperialism
Panama Canal

■ Suggested Readings

Two good introductions to imperialism are D. K. Fieldhouse, *Colonialism, 1870–1945* (1981), and Scott B. Cook, *Colonial Encounters in the Age of High Imperialism* (1996). The debate on the theories of imperialism is presented in Roger Owen and Robert Sutcliffe, *Studies in the Theory of Imperialism* (1972), and in Winfried Baumgart, *Imperialism* (1982). The British Empire is the subject of Bernard Porter, *The Lion's Share: A Short History of British Imperialism, 1850–1970* (1976).

On Africa in this period see Roland Oliver and Anthony Atmore, *Africa Since 1800*, new ed. (1994); Roland Oliver and G. N. Sanderson, eds., *From 1870 to 1905* (1985), and A. D. Roberts, ed., *From 1905 to 1940* (1986), in *The Cambridge History of Africa*; and A. Adu Boahen, ed., *Africa Under Colonial Domination, 1880–1935* (1985), in *UNESCO General History of Africa*. The European conquest of Africa is recounted in Thomas Pakenham, *The Scramble for Africa* (1991); Bruce Vandervort, *Wars of Imperial Conquest in Africa, 1830–1914* (1998); and Ronald Robinson and John Gallagher, *Africa and the Victorians: The Climax of Imperialism* (1961). Adam Hochschild's *King Leopold's Ghost: A Story of Greed, Terror, and Heroism in Colonial Africa* (1998) is a very readable account of imperialism in the Belgian Congo. The classic novel about the impact of colonial rule on African society is Chinua Achebe's *Things Fall Apart* (1958).

Imperial rivalries in Asia are the subject of Akira Iriye, *Across the Pacific: An Inner History of American-East Asian Relations*, rev. ed. (1992); David Gillard, *The Struggle for Asia, 1828–1914: A Study in British and Russian Imperialism* (1977); and Peter Hopkirk, *The Great Game: The Struggle for Empire in Central Asia* (1994). On other aspects of imperialism in Asia see Clifford Geertz, *Agricultural Involution: The Process of Ecological Change in Indonesia* (1963), especially chapters 4 and 5, and Stanley Karnow, *In Our Image: America's Empire in the Philippines* (1989).

On Latin America in this period see David Bushnell and Neill Macauley, *The Emergence of Latin America in the Nineteenth Century* (1994). Free-trade imperialism is the subject of D. C. M. Platt, *Latin America and British Trade, 1806–1914* (1973). On American expansionism see David Healy, *Drive to Hegemony: The United States in the Caribbean, 1898–1917* (1989), and Walter LaFeber, *The Panama Canal*, rev. ed. (1990).

On race relations in the colonial world see Noel Mostert, *Frontiers: The Epic of South Africa's Creation and the Tragedy of the Xhosa People* (1992), and Robert Huttenback, *Racism and Empire: White Settlers and Colored Immigrants in the British Self-Governing Colonies, 1830–1910* (1976). Gender relations are the subject of Caroline Oliver, *Western Women in Colonial Africa* (1982), and Cheryl Walker, ed., *Women and Gender in Southern Africa to 1945* (1990). David Northrup's *Indentured Labor in the Age of Imperialism, 1834–1922* (1995), discusses migrations and

labor. Franz Fanon, *The Wretched of the Earth* (1966), and Albert Memmi, *The Colonizer and the Colonized* (1967), examine colonialism from the point of view of the colonized.

The impact of technology on the New Imperialism is the subject of Daniel R. Headrick, *The Tools of Empire: Technology and European Imperialism in the Nineteenth Century* (1981) and *The Tentacles of Progress: Technology Transfer in the Age of Imperialism, 1850–1940* (1988), and Clarence B. Davis and Kenneth E. Wilburn, Jr., eds., *Railway Imperialism* (1991).

On the economic and demographic transformation of Africa and Asia see Eric Wolf, *Europe and the People Without History* (1982), especially chapters 11 and 12. The impact on the environment is the subject of R. P. Tucker and J. F. Richards, *Deforestation and the Nineteenth-Century World Economy* (1983); Donal McCracken, *Gardens of Empire: Botanical Institutions of the Victorian British Empire* (1997); Lucile H. Brockway, *Science and Colonial Expansion: The Role of the British Royal Botanic Gardens* (1979); and David Arnold and Ramchandra Guha, eds., *Nature, Culture, Imperialism: Essays on the Environmental History of South Asia* (1995).

■ Notes

1. *Journal officiel* (November 29, 1869), quoted in Georges Douin, *Histoire du règne du khédive Ismaïl* (Rome: Reale Societá di geografia d'Egitto, 1933), 453.
2. E. Desplaces in *Journal de l'Union des Deux Mers* (December 15, 1869), quoted ibid., 453.
3. Winston Churchill, *The River War: An Account of the Reconquest of the Soudan* (New York: Charles Scribner's Sons, 1933), 300.
4. "Correspondence and Report from His Majesty's Consul at Boma respecting the Administration of the Independent State of the Congo," *British Parliamentary Papers, Accounts and Papers*, 1904 (Cd. 1933), lxii, 357.
5. Robert W. July, *A History of the Africa People*, 3d ed. (New York: Charles Scribner's Sons, 1980), 323.
6. George Shepperson and Thomas Price, *Independent African* (Edinburgh: University Press, 1958), 163–164, quoted in Roland Oliver and Anthony Atmore, *Africa Since 1800*, 4th ed. (Cambridge: Cambridge University Press, 1994), 150.
7. Thomas Edson Ennis, *French Policy and Development in Indochina* (Chicago: University of Chicago Press, 1936), 178, quoted in K. M. Panikkar, *Asia and Western Dominance* (New York: Collier, 1969), 167.
8. Quoted in Stanley J. Stein and Barbara H. Stein, *The Colonial Heritage of Latin America* (New York: Oxford University Press, 1970), 151.

THE CRISIS OF THE IMPERIAL ORDER,

1900–1929

Origins of the Crisis in Europe and the Middle East • The "Great War" and the
Russian Revolutions, 1914–1918 • Peace and Dislocation in Europe, 1919–1929 •
China and Japan: Contrasting Destinies • The New Middle East •
Society, Culture, and Technology in the Industrialized World

ENVIRONMENT AND TECHNOLOGY: Cities Old and New

SOCIETY AND CULTURE: The Experience of Battle

The Western Front in World War I   In a landscape ravaged by artillery fire,
two soldiers dash for cover amid shell holes and the charred remains of a forest.

O n June 28, 1914, Archduke Franz Ferdinand, heir to the throne of Austria-Hungary, was riding in an open carriage through Sarajevo, capital of the province of Bosnia-Herzegovina, which Austria had annexed six years before. When the carriage stopped momentarily, Gavrilo Princip, member of a pro-Serbian conspiracy, fired his pistol twice, killing the archduke and his wife.

Those shots ignited a war that spread throughout Europe, then turned into a global war as the Ottoman Empire fought against Britain in the Middle East and Japan attacked German positions in China. France and Britain involved their empires in the war and brought Africans, Indians, Australians, and Canadians to Europe to fight and labor on the front lines. Finally, in 1917, the United States entered the fray.

The next three chapters tell a story of violence and hope. In this chapter, we will look at the causes of war between the great powers, the consequences of that conflict in Europe, the Middle East, and Russia, and the upheavals in China and Japan. At the same time, we will review the accelerating rate of technological change, which made the first half of the twentieth century so violent and so hopeful. Industrialization continued apace. Entirely new technologies, and the organizations that produced and applied them, made war more dangerous yet also allowed far more people to live healthier, more comfortable, and more interesting lives than ever before.

As you read this chapter, ask yourself the following questions:

- How did the First World War lead to revolution in Russia and the disintegration of several once-powerful empires?

- What role did the war play in eroding European dominance in the world?

- Why did China and Japan follow such divergent paths in this period?

- How did European and North American society and technology change in the aftermath of the war?

ORIGINS OF THE CRISIS IN EUROPE AND THE MIDDLE EAST

W hen the twentieth century opened, the world seemed firmly under the control of the great powers that you read about in Chapter 28. The first decade of the twentieth century was a period of relative peace and economic growth in most of the world. Trade boomed. Several new technologies—airplanes, automobiles, radio, and cinema—aroused much excitement. The great powers consolidated their colonial conquests of the previous decades. Their alliances were so evenly matched that they seemed, to observers at the time, likely to maintain peace. The only international war of the period, the Russo-Japanese War (1904–1905), ended quickly with a decisive Japanese victory.

However, two major changes were undermining the apparent stability of the world. In Europe, tensions mounted as Germany, with its growing industrial and military might, challenged Britain at sea and France in Morocco. The Ottoman Empire grew weaker, leaving a dangerous power vacuum. The resulting chaos in the Balkans, the unstable borderlands between a predominantly Christian Europe and a predominantly Muslim Middle East, gradually draw the European powers into a web of hostilities.

The Ottoman Empire and the Balkans

From the fifteenth to the nineteenth century, the Ottoman Empire was one of the world's richest and most powerful states. By the late nineteenth century, however, it had fallen behind economically, technologically, and militarily, and Europeans referred to it as the "sick man of Europe."

As the Ottoman Empire weakened, it began losing those outlying provinces situated closest to Europe. Macedonia rebelled in 1902–1903. In 1908 Austria-Hungary annexed Bosnia. Crete, occupied by European "peacekeepers" since 1898, merged with Greece in 1909. A year later, Albania became independent. In 1912 Italy conquered Libya, the Ottomans' last foothold in Africa. In 1912–1913 in rapid succession came two Balkan Wars in which Serbia, Bulgaria, Romania, and Greece chased the Turks out of Europe, except for a small enclave around Constantinople.

CHRONOLOGY

	Europe and North America	Middle East	East Asia
1900			1900 Boxer Rebellion in China
	1904 British-French Entente		1904–1905 Russo-Japanese
	1907 British-Russian Entente		War
1910		1909 Young Turks overthrow	
		Sultan Abdul Hamid	1911 Chinese revolutionaries led
	1912–1913 Balkan Wars	1912 Italy conquers Libya, last	by Sun Yat-sen overthrow Qing
	1914 Assassination of Archduke	Ottoman territory in Africa	dynasty
	Franz Ferdinand sparks World	1915 British defeat at Gallipoli	1915 Japan presents Twenty-
	War I		One Demands to China
	1916 Battles of Verdun and the	1916 Arab Revolt in Arabia	
	Somme		
	1917 Russian Revolutions;	1917 Balfour Declaration	
	United States enters the war		
	1918 Armistice ends World War I		
	1918–1921 Civil war in Russia		
	1919 Treaty of Versailles	1919–1922 War between Turkey	1919 May Fourth Movement in
1920	1920 First commercial radio	and Greece	China
	broadcast (United States)		
	1921 New Economic Policy in		
	Russia	1922 Egypt nominally independent	
		1923 Mustafa Kemal proclaims	
	1927 Charles Lindbergh flies	Turkey a republic	1927 Guomindang forces
	alone across the Atlantic		occupy Shanghai and expel
			Communists

The European powers meddled in the internal affairs of the Ottoman Empire, sometimes cooperatively but often as rivals. Russia saw itself as the protector of the Slavic peoples of the Balkans. France and Britain, posing as protectors of Christian minorities, controlled Ottoman finances, taxes, railroads, mines, and public utilities. Austria-Hungary coveted Ottoman lands inhabited by Slavs, thereby angering the Russians.

In reaction, the Turks began to assert themselves against rebellious minorities and meddling foreigners. Many officers in the army, the most Europeanized segment of Turkish society, blamed Sultan Abdul Hamid II (r. 1876–1909) for the decline of the empire. The group known as "Young Turks" began conspiring to force a constitution on the Sultan. They alienated other anti-Ottoman groups by advocating centralized rule and the Turkification of ethnic minorities.

In 1909 the parliament, dominated by Young Turks, overthrew Abdul Hamid and replaced him with his brother. The new regime began to reform the police, the bureaucracy, and the education system. At the same time, it cracked down on Greek and Armenian minorities. Galvanized by their defeat in the Balkan Wars, the Turks turned to Germany, the European country that had meddled least in Ottoman affairs, and hired a German general to modernize Turkey's armed forces.

Nationalism, Alliances, and Military Strategy

The assassination of the Archduke Franz Ferdinand triggered a chain of events over which military and political leaders lost control. The escalation from assassination to global war had causes that went back many years. One was nationalism, which bound citizens to their ethnic group and led them, when called upon, to kill people they viewed as enemies. Another was the system of alliances and military plans that the great powers had devised to protect themselves from their rivals. A third was Germany's yearning to dominate Europe.

Nationalism was deeply rooted in European culture. As we saw in Chapter 28, it united the citizens of France, Britain, and Germany behind their respective

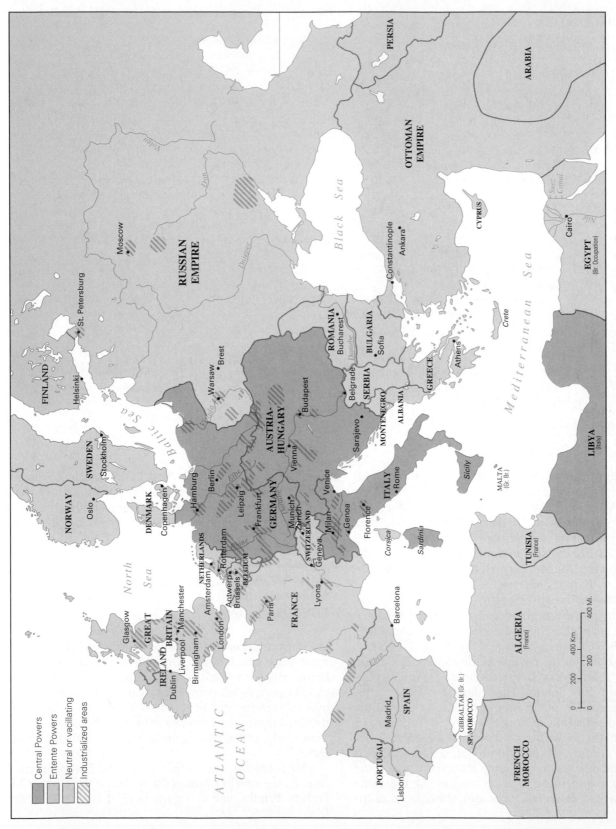

Map 30.1   Europe in 1913   On the eve of World War I, Europe was divided between two great alliance systems—the Central Powers (Germany, Austria-Hungary, and Italy) and the Entente (France, Great Britain, and Russia)—and their respective colonial empires. These alliances were not stable. When war broke out, the Central Powers lost Italy but gained the Ottoman Empire.

governments and gave them tremendous cohesion and strength of purpose. Only the most powerful feelings could inspire millions of men to march obediently into battle and sustain civilian populations through years of hardship.

Nationalism could also be a dividing rather than a unifying force. The large but fragile multinational Russian, Austro-Hungarian, and Ottoman Empires contained numerous ethnic and religious minorities. Having repressed them for centuries, the governments could never count on their full support. The very existence of an independent Serbia threatened Austria-Hungary by stirring up the hopes and resentments of its Slavic populations.

Because of the spread of nationalism, most people viewed war as a crusade for liberty or as long-overdue revenge for past injustices. In the course of the nineteenth century, as memories of the misery and carnage caused by the Napoleonic Wars faded, revulsion against war gradually weakened. The few wars fought in Europe after 1815, such as the Crimean War of 1853–1856 and the Franco-Prussian War of 1871, had been short and caused few casualties or long-term consequences. And in the wars of the New Imperialism (see Chapter 29), Europeans almost always had been victorious at a small cost in money and manpower. The well-to-do began to believe that only war could heal the class divisions in their societies and make workers unite behind their "natural" leaders.

What turned an incident in a small town in the Balkans into a conflict involving all the great powers was the system of alliances that had grown up over the previous decades. At the center of Europe stood Germany, the most heavily industrialized country in Europe. Its army was the best trained and equipped. Germany was challenging Great Britain's naval supremacy by building a series of "dreadnoughts"—heavily armed battleships. It joined Austria-Hungary and Italy in the Triple Alliance in 1882, while France allied itself with Russia. In 1904 Britain joined France in an Entente° ("understanding"), and in 1907 Britain and Russia buried their differences and formed an Entente. Europe was thus divided into two blocs of roughly equal power (see Map 30.1).

The alliance system was cursed by inflexible military planning. In 1914 western and central Europe had highly developed railroad networks but very few motor vehicles. European armies had grown to include millions of soldiers and more millions of reservists. To mobilize these forces and transport them to battle would be an enormous project requiring thousands of trains running

on precise schedules. As a result, once under way, a country's mobilization could not be canceled or postponed without creating chaos.

In the years before World War I, military planners in France and Germany had worked out elaborate railroad timetables to mobilize their respective armies in a few days. Other countries were less well prepared. Russia, a large country with an underdeveloped rail system, needed several weeks to mobilize its forces. Britain, with only a tiny volunteer army, had no mobilization plans, and German planners believed that the British would stay out of a war on the European continent. So that Germany could avoid having to fight France and Russia at the same time, German war plans called for German generals to defeat France in a matter of days, then transport their entire army by train across Germany to the Russian border before Russia could fully mobilize.

On July 28, emboldened by the backing of Germany, Austria-Hungary declared war on Serbia. Diplomats, statesmen, and monarchs sent one another frantic telegrams, but they had lost control of events, for the declaration of war triggered the general mobilization plans of Russia, France, and Germany. On July 29, the Russian government ordered general mobilization to force Austria to back down. On August 1, France honored its treaty obligation to Russia and ordered general mobilization. Minutes later Germany did likewise. Because of the rigid railroad timetables, war was now automatic.

The German plan was to wheel around through neutral Belgium and into northwestern France. The German General Staff expected France to capitulate before the British could get involved. But on August 3, when German troops entered Belgium, Britain demanded their withdrawal. When Germany refused, Britain declared war on Germany.

THE "GREAT WAR" AND THE RUSSIAN REVOLUTIONS, 1914–1918

Throughout Europe, people greeted the outbreak of war with parades and flags and hopes for a quick victory. German troops marched off to the front shouting "To Paris!" Spectators in France encouraged marching French troops with shouts of "Send me the Kaiser's moustache!" The British poet Rupert Brooke began a poem with the line: "Now God be thanked Who has matched us with His hour." The German sociologist Max

---

Entente (on-TONT)

Weber wrote: "This war, with all its ghastliness, is nevertheless grand and wonderful. It is worth experiencing." When the war began, very few imagined that their side might not win, and no one foresaw that everyone would lose.

In Russia the effect of the war was especially devastating, for it destroyed the old society, opened the door to revolution and civil war, and introduced a radical new political system. By clearing away the old, the upheaval of war prepared Russia to industrialize under the leadership of professional revolutionaries.

Stalemate, 1914–1917

The war that erupted in 1914 was known as the "Great War" until the 1940s, when a far greater one overshadowed it. Its form came as a surprise to all belligerents, from the generals on down. In the classic battles—from the time of Alexander the Great to Napoleon—that every officer studied, the advantage always went to the fastest-moving army led by the boldest general. In 1914 the generals' carefully drawn-up plans went awry from the start. Believing that a spirited attack would always prevail, French generals hurled their troops, dressed in bright blue-and-red uniforms, against the well-defended German border and suffered a crushing defeat. In battle after battle the much larger German armies defeated the French and the British. By early September they held Belgium and northern France and were fast approaching Paris.

German victory seemed assured. But German troops, who had marched and fought for a month, were exhausted, and their generals wavered. When Russia attacked eastern Germany, troops needed for the final push into France were shifted to the Russian front. A gap opened between two German armies along the Marne River, into which General Joseph Joffre moved France's last reserves. At the Battle of the Marne (September 5–12, 1914), the Germans were thrown back several miles.

During the next month, both sides spread out until they formed an unbroken line extending over 300 miles

Trench Warfare in World War I   German and Allied soldiers on the Western Front faced each other from elaborate networks of trenches. Attacking meant jumping out of the trenches and racing across a no-man's land of mud and barbed wire. Here we see Princess Patricia's Canadian Light Infantry repelling a German attack near Ypres, in northern France, in March 1915, using machine guns, rifles, and hand grenades.   (Courtesy, The Princess Patricia's Canadian Light Infantry, Regimental Museum and Archives)

The Experience of Battle

What is it like to be a soldier in the midst of a battle? Here is how the German writer Erich Maria Remarque, a veteran of World War I, described a battle from a soldier's point of view in his classic war novel All Quiet on the Western Front *(1928).*

Night again. We are deadened by the strain—a deadly tension that scrapes along one's spine like a gapped knife. Our legs refuse to move, our hands tremble, our bodies are a thin skin stretched painfully over repressed madness, over an almost irresistible, bursting roar. We have neither flesh nor muscles any longer, we dare not look at one another for fear of some incalculable thing. So we shut our teeth—it will end—it will end—perhaps we will come through.

Suddenly the nearer explosions cease. The shelling continues but it has lifted and falls behind us, our trench is free. We seize the hand-grenades, pitch them out in front of the dug-out and jump after them. The bombardment has stopped and a heavy barrage now falls behind us. The attack has come.

No one would believe that in this howling waste there could still be men; but steel helmets now appear on all sides of the trench, and fifty yards from us a machine-gun is already in position and barking.

The wire entanglements are torn to pieces. Yet they offer some obstacle. We see the storm-troops coming. Our artillery opens fire. Machine-guns rattle, rifles crack. The charge works its way across. Haie and Kropp begin with the hand-grenades. They throw as fast as they can, others pass them the handles with the strings already pulled. . . .

We recognize the smooth distorted faces, the helmets: they are French. They have already suffered heavily when they reach the remnants of the barbed wire entanglements. A whole line has gone down before our machine-guns; then we have a lot of stoppages and they come nearer.

I see one of them, his face upturned, fall into a wire cradle. His body collapses, his hands remain suspended as though he were praying. Then his body drops clean away and only his hands with the stumps of his arms, shot off, now hang in the wire.

How successful is Remarque in conveying a soldier's experiences to readers who have never been to war? How do you explain what makes men willing to fight such battles?

Source: Erich Maria Remarque, *All Quiet on the Western Front,* trans. A. W. Wheen (Boston: Little, Brown, 1958), 98–99. *Im Westen Nichts Neues,* copyright 1928 by Ullstein A. G. Copyright renewed © 1956, 1957, 1958 by Erich Maria Remarque. *All Quiet on the Western Front,* copyright © 1929, 1930 by Little, Brown and Company. All rights reserved.

(some 500 kilometers) from the North Sea to the border of Switzerland. All along this line, the **Western Front,** the opposing troops prepared their defenses. Their most potent weapons were machine guns, which provided an almost impenetrable defense against advancing infantry but were useless for the offensive because they were too heavy for one man to carry and took too much time to set up. To escape the deadly streams of bullets, soldiers dug holes for themselves in the ground, connected the holes to form shallow trenches, then dug communications trenches to the rear. Within weeks, the battlefields were scarred up with lines of trenches several feet deep, their tops protected by sandbags and their floors covered with planks. Despite all the work they put into them, the soldiers spent much of the year soaked and covered with mud (see Society and Culture: The Experience of Battle). Trenches were nothing new. What was extraordinary about this war was that the trenches along the entire Western Front were connected, leaving no gaps through which armies could advance (see Map 30.2). How, then, could either side ever hope to win?

For four years, generals on each side again and again ordered their troops to attack. They knew the casualties would be enormous, but they expected the enemy to run out of young men before their side did. In battle after battle, thousands of young men on one side climbed out of their trenches, raced across the open fields, and were mowed down by enemy machine-gun fire. Hoping to destroy the machine guns, the attacking force would saturate the entrenched enemy lines with artillery barrages. But this tactic would alert the defenders to an impending attack and allow them to rush in reinforcements and set up new machine guns. Attacking troops released poison gas to kill or blind the defenders, only to find that gas also immobilized the onrushing attackers themselves, adding to the horror of battle.

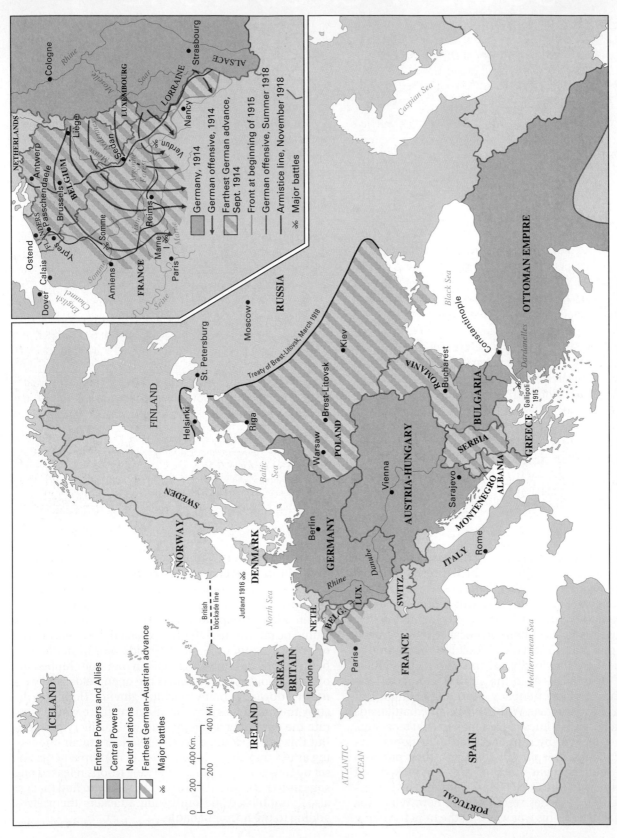

Map 30.2 The First World War in Europe Most of the fighting in World War I took place on two fronts. After an initial surge through Belgium into northern France, the German offensive bogged down for four years along the Western Front. To the east, the German armies conquered a large part of Russia during 1917 and early 1918. Despite spectacular victories in the east, Germany lost the war because its armies collapsed along the strategically important Western Front.

The year 1916 saw the bloodiest and most futile battles of the war. The Germans attacked French forts at Verdun, losing 281,000 men and causing 315,000 French casualties. In retaliation, the British attacked the Germans at the Somme River and suffered 420,000 casualties—60,000 on the first day alone—while the Germans lost 450,000 and the French 200,000.

This was not warfare as it had ever been waged before; it was mass slaughter in a moonscape of mud, steel, and flesh. Both sides attacked and defended, but neither side could win, for the armies were stalemated by trenches and machine guns. During four years of the bloodiest fighting the world had ever seen, the Western Front moved no more than a few miles one way or another.

At sea, the war was just as inconclusive. As soon as the war broke out, the British cut the German overseas telegraph cables, blockaded the coasts of Germany and Austria-Hungary, and set out to capture or sink all enemy ships still at sea. The German High Seas Fleet, built at enormous cost, seldom left port. Only once, in May 1916, did it confront the British Grand Fleet. At the Battle of Jutland, off the coast of Denmark, the two fleets lost roughly equal numbers of ships, and the Germans escaped back to their harbors.

Britain ruled the waves but not the ocean below the surface. In early 1915, in retaliation for the British naval blockade, Germany announced a blockade of Britain by submarines. Unlike surface ships, submarines could not rescue the passengers of a sinking ship or distinguish between neutral and enemy ships. German submarines attacked every vessel they could. One of their victims was British ocean liner *Lusitania*. The death toll from that attack was 1,198 people, 139 of them Americans. When the United States protested, Germany ceased its submarine campaign, hoping to keep America neutral.

Women in World War I   Women played a more important role in World War I than in previous wars. As the armies drafted millions of men, employers hired women for essential war work. This poster extolling the importance of women workers in supplying munitions was probably designed to recruit women for factory jobs.   (The Art Archive Limited)

The Home Front and the War Economy

Trench-bound armies demanded ever more weapons, ammunition, and food, so civilians had to work harder, eat less, and pay higher taxes. Textiles, coal, meat, fats, and imported products such as tea and sugar were strictly rationed. Governments gradually imposed stringent controls over all aspects of their economies. Socialists and labor unions participated actively in the war effort, for they found government regulation more to their liking than unfettered free enterprise.

The war economy transformed civilian life. In France and Britain, food rations were allocated according to need, improving nutrition among the poor. Unemployment vanished. Thousands of Africans, Indians, and Chinese were recruited for heavy labor in Europe. Employers hired women to fill jobs in steel mills, mines, and munitions plants vacated by men off to war. Some women became streetcar drivers, mail carriers, and police. Others found work in the burgeoning government bureaucracies. Many joined auxiliary military services as doctors, nurses, mechanics, and ambulance drivers; after 1917, as the war took its toll of young men, the British government established women's auxiliary units for the army, navy, and air force. Though clearly intended "for the duration only," these positions gave thousands of women a sense of participation in the war effort and a taste of personal and financial independence.

German civilians paid an especially high price for the war, for the British naval blockade severed their overseas trade. The German chemical industry developed synthetic explosives and fuel, but synthetic food was not an option. Wheat flour disappeared, replaced first by rye, then by potatoes and turnips, then by acorns and chestnuts, and finally by sawdust. After the failure of the potato crop in 1916 came the "turnip winter," when people had to survive on 1,000 calories per day, half of the normal amount that an active adult needed. Women, children, and the elderly were especially hard hit. Soldiers at the front went hungry and raided enemy lines to scavenge food.

When the war began, the British and French overran German Togo on the West African coast. The much larger German colonies of Southwest Africa and German Cameroon were conquered in 1915. In Tanganyika, the Germans remained undefeated until the end of the war.

The war also brought hardships to Europe's African colonies. The Europeans requisitioned foodstuffs, imposed heavy taxes, and forced Africans to grow export crops and sell them at low prices. Many Europeans stationed in Africa left to join the war, leaving large areas with little or no European presence. In Nigeria, Libya, Nyasaland (now Malawi), and other colonies, the combination of increased demands on Africans and fewer European officials led to uprisings that lasted for several years.

Over a million Africans served in the various armies, and perhaps three times that number were drafted as porters to carry army equipment. Faced with a shortage of young Frenchmen, France drafted Africans into its army, where many fought side by side with Europeans. The Senegalese Blaise Diagne°, the first African elected to France's Chamber of Deputies in 1914, campaigned for African support of the war effort. Put in charge of recruiting African soldiers, he insisted on equal rights for African and European soldiers and an extension of the franchise to educated Africans. These demands were only partially met.

One country grew rich during the war: the United States. For two and a half years, the United States stayed technically neutral—that is, it did not fight but did a roaring business supplying France and Britain. When the United States entered the war in 1917, businesses engaging in war production made spectacular profits. Civilians were exhorted to help the war effort by investing their savings in war bonds and growing food in backyard "victory gardens." Facing labor shortages, employers hired women and African-Americans. Employment opportunities created by the war played a major role in the migration of black Americans from the rural south to the cities of the north.

The Ottoman Empire at War

On August 2, 1914, the Turks signed a secret alliance with Germany. In November they joined the fighting, hoping to gain land at Russia's expense. But the campaign in the Caucasus proved disastrous for both armies and for the civilian populations as well. The Turks deported the Armenians, whom they suspected of being pro-Russian, from their homelands in eastern Anatolia to Syria and other parts of the Ottoman Empire. During the forced march across the mountains in the winter, hundreds of thousands of Armenians died of hunger and exposure; this massacre was a precedent for even ghastlier tragedies still to come.

The Turks also closed the Dardanelles, the strait between the Mediterranean and Black Seas (see Map 30.2). British officials, seeing little hope of victory on the Western Front, tried to force open the Dardanelles by landing troops on the nearby Gallipoli Peninsula in 1915. Turkish troops pushed the invaders back into the sea.

Having failed at the Dardanelles, the British tried to subvert the Ottoman Empire from within by promising the emir (prince) of Mecca, Hussein ibn Ali, a kingdom of his own if he would lead an Arab revolt against the Turks. In 1916 Hussein rose up and was proclaimed king of Hejaz° (western Arabia). His son **Faisal**° led an Arab army in support of the British advance from Egypt into Palestine and Syria. The Arab Revolt of 1916 did not affect the struggle in Europe, but it did contribute to the defeat of the Ottoman Empire.

The British made promises to Jews as well as Arabs. For centuries, Jewish minorities had lived in eastern and Central Europe, where they developed a thriving culture despite frequent persecutions. By the early twentieth century a nationalist movement called Zionism, led by **Theodore Herzl,** arose among those who wanted to return to their ancestral homeland in Palestine. The concept of a Jewish homeland appealed to many Europeans, Jews and gentiles alike, as a humanitarian solution to the problem of anti-Semitism.

By 1917, Chaim Weizmann°, leader of the British Zionists, had persuaded several British politicians that a

---

Blaise Diagne (blez dee-AHN-yuh)

Hejaz (HEE-jaz)   Faisal (fie-SAHL)
Chaim Weizmann (hi-um VITES-mun)

Jewish homeland in Palestine should be carved out of the Ottoman Empire and placed under British protection, thereby strengthening the Allied cause (as the Entente was now called). In November, as British armies were advancing on Jerusalem, Foreign Secretary Sir Arthur Balfour wrote that "His Majesty's Government view with favor the establishment in Palestine of a national home for the Jewish people and will use their best endeavours to facilitate the achievement of that object, it being clearly understood that nothing shall be done which may prejudice the civil and religious rights of existing non-Jewish communities in Palestine." The British did not foresee that this statement, known as the **Balfour Declaration,** would lead to conflicts between Palestinians and Jewish settlers.

Britain also sent troops to southern Mesopotamia to secure the oil pipeline from Iran. Then they moved north, taking Baghdad in early 1917. The officers for the Mesopotamian campaign were British, but most of the troops and equipment came from India. Most Indians, like other colonial subjects of Britain, supported the war effort despite the hardships it caused. Their involvement in the war bolstered the movement for Indian independence (see Chapter 32).

Double Revolution in Russia, 1917

At the beginning of the war, Russia had the largest army in the world, but its generals were incompetent, supplies were lacking, and soldiers were poorly trained and equipped. In August 1914, two Russian armies invaded eastern Germany but were thrown back. Several times the Russians defeated the Austro-Hungarian army, only to be defeated in turn by the Germans.

In 1916, after a string of defeats, the Russian army ran out of ammunition and other essential supplies. Soldiers were ordered into battle unarmed and told to pick up the rifles of fallen comrades. With so many men in the army, railroads broke down for lack of fuel and parts, and crops rotted in the fields. Civilians faced shortages and widespread hunger. In the cities food and fuel became scarce. During the bitterly cold winter of 1916–1917, factory workers and housewives had to line up in front of grocery stores before dawn in order to get something to eat. The court of Tsar° Nicholas II, however, remained as extravagant and corrupt as ever.

In early March 1917 (February by the old Russian calendar), food ran out in Petrograd (formerly called St. Petersburg), the capital. Housewives and women factory workers staged mass demonstrations. Soldiers mutinied and joined striking workers to form soviets (councils) to take over factories and barracks. A few days later, the tsar abdicated, and leaders of the parliamentary parties, led by Alexander Kerensky, formed a Provisional Government. Thus began what Russians called the "February Revolution."

Revolutionary groups formerly hunted by the tsar's police came out of hiding. Most numerous were the Social Revolutionaries, who advocated the redistribution of land to the peasants. The Social Democrats, a Marxist party, were divided into two factions: Mensheviks and Bolsheviks. The Mensheviks advocated electoral politics and reform in the tradition of European Socialists and had a large following among intellectuals and factory workers. The **Bolsheviks,** their rivals, were a small but tightly disciplined group of radicals obedient to the will of their leader, **Vladimir Lenin** (1870–1924).

Lenin, the son of a government official, became a revolutionary in his teens when his older brother was executed for plotting to kill the tsar. He spent years in exile, first in Siberia and later in Switzerland, where he devoted his full attention to organizing his followers. He professed Marx's ideas concerning class conflict (see Chapter 28), but he never visited a factory or a farm. His goal was to create a party that would lead the revolution rather than wait for it. He explained: "Classes are led by parties and parties are led by individuals. . . . The will of a class is sometimes fulfilled by a dictator."

In early April 1917, the German government, hoping to destabilize Russia, allowed Lenin to travel from Switzerland to Russia in a sealed railway car. As soon as he arrived in Petrograd, he announced his program: immediate peace, all power to the soviets, and transfers of land to the peasants and factories to the workers. This plan proved immensely popular among soldiers and workers exhausted by the war.

The next few months witnessed a tug-of-war between the Provisional Government and the various revolutionary factions in Petrograd. When Kerensky ordered another offensive against the Germans, Russian soldiers began to desert by the hundreds of thousands, throwing away their rifles and walking back to their villages. As the Germans advanced, Russian resistance melted and the government lost what little support it had.

The Bolsheviks meanwhile were gaining support among the workers of Petrograd and the soldiers and sailors stationed there. On November 6, 1917 (October 24 in the Russian calendar), they rose up and took over the city, calling their action the "October Revolution." Their sudden move surprised rival revolutionary groups that believed that a "socialist" revolution could happen

---

tsar (zahr)

only after many years of "bourgeois" rule. Lenin, however, was more interested in power than in the fine points of Marxist doctrine. He overthrew the Provisional Government and arrested Mensheviks, Social Revolutionaries, and other rivals.

Seizing Petrograd was only the first step, for the rest of Russia was in chaos. The Bolsheviks nationalized all private land and ordered the peasants to hand over their crops without compensation. The peasants, having seized their landlords' estates, resisted. In the cities, the Bolsheviks took over the factories and drafted the workers into compulsory labor brigades. To enforce his rule, Lenin created the Cheka, a secret police force with powers to arrest and execute opponents.

The Bolsheviks also sued for peace with Germany and Austria-Hungary. By the Treaty of Brest-Litovsk, signed on March 3, 1918, Russia lost territories containing a third of its population and wealth. Poland, Finland, and the Baltic states (Estonia, Latvia, and Lithuania) became independent republics. Russian colonies in Central Asia and the Caucasus broke away temporarily.

The End of the War in Western Europe, 1917–1918

Like many other Americans, President **Woodrow Wilson** wanted to stay out of the European conflict. For nearly three years he kept the United States neutral and tried to persuade the belligerents to compromise. But in late 1916, German leaders decided to starve the British into submission by using submarines to sink merchant ships carrying food supplies to Great Britain. The Germans knew that unrestricted submarine warfare was likely to bring the United States into the war, but they were willing to gamble that Britain and France would collapse before the United States could send enough troops to help them.

The submarine campaign resumed on February 1, 1917, but the German gamble failed. The British organized their merchant ships into convoys protected by destroyers, and on April 6, President Wilson asked the United States Congress to declare war on Germany.

On the Western Front, the two sides were so evenly matched in 1917 that the war seemed unlikely to end until one side or the other ran out of young men. Losing hope of winning, soldiers began to mutiny. In May 1917, before the arrival of U.S. forces, fifty-four of one hundred French divisions along the Western Front refused to attack. During the summer, Italian troops also mutinied, panicked, or deserted.

Between March and August 1918, General Erich von Ludendorff launched a series of surprise attacks that broke through the front at several places and pushed to within 40 miles (64 kilometers) of Paris. But victory eluded him. Meanwhile, every month was bringing another 250,000 American troops to the front. In August, the Allies counterattacked, and the Germans began a retreat that could not be halted, for German soldiers, many of them sick with the flu, had lost the will to fight.

In late October, Ludendorff resigned and sailors in the German fleet mutinied. Two weeks later Kaiser Wilhelm fled to Holland as a new German government signed an armistice. On November 11 at 11 A.M., the guns on the Western Front went silent.

PEACE AND DISLOCATION IN EUROPE, 1919–1929

The Great War lasted four years. It took almost twice as long for Europe to recover. Millions of people had died or been disabled, political tensions and resentments lingered, and national economies remained depressed until the mid-1920s. In the late 1920s, peace and prosperity finally seemed assured, but this hope proved to be illusory.

The Impact of the War

The war left more dead and wounded and more physical destruction than any previous conflict. It is estimated that between 8 million and 10 million people died, almost all of them young men. Perhaps twice that many returned home wounded, gassed, or shell-shocked, many of them injured for life. Among the dead were about 2 million Germans, 1.7 million Russians, and 1.7 million Frenchmen. Austria-Hungary lost 1.5 million, the British Empire a million, Italy 460,000, and the United States 115,000.

Besides ending over 8 million lives, the war dislocated whole populations, creating millions of refugees. War and revolution forced almost 2 million Russians, 750,000 Germans, and 400,000 Hungarians to flee their homes. War led to the expulsion of hundreds of thousands of Greeks from Anatolia and Turks from Greece.

Many refugees found shelter in France, which welcomed 1.5 million people to bolster its declining population. The preferred destination, however, was the United States, the most prosperous country in the world. About 800,000 immigrants succeeded in reaching it before U.S. immigration laws passed in 1921 and 1924 closed the door to eastern and southern Europeans. Canada, Australia, and New Zealand adopted similar restrictions on immigration. The Latin American republics welcomed European refugees, but their economies were hard hit by the drop in the prices of their main exports and their poverty discouraged potential immigrants.

One unexpected byproduct of the war was the great influenza epidemic of 1918–1919, which started among soldiers heading for the Western Front. This was no ordinary flu but a virulent strain that infected almost everyone on earth and killed one person in every forty. It caused the largest number of deaths in so short a time in the history of the world. Half a million Americans perished in the epidemic—five times as many as died in the war. Worldwide, some 30 million people died, 20 million in India alone.

The war also caused serious damage to the environment. No place on earth was ever so completely devastated as the scar across France and Belgium known as the Western Front. The fighting ravaged forests and demolished towns. The earth was gouged by trenches, pitted with craters, and littered with ammunition, broken weapons, chunks of concrete, and the bones of countless soldiers. After the war, it took a decade to clear away the debris, rebuild the towns, and create dozens of military cemeteries with neat rows of crosses stretching for miles. To this day, farmers plow up fragments of old weapons and ammunition, and every so often, a long-buried shell explodes. The war also hastened the buildup of industry, with mines, factories, and railroad tracks.

The Peace Treaties

In early 1919, delegates of the victorious powers met in Paris. The defeated powers were kept out until the treaties were ready for signing. Russia, in the throes of civil war, was not invited.

From the start, three men dominated the Paris Peace Conference: United States president Wilson, British prime minister David Lloyd George, and French premier Georges Clemenceau°. They ignored the Italians, who had joined the Allies in 1915. They paid even less attention to the delegates of smaller European nations and none at all to non-European nationalities. They rejected the Japanese proposal that all races be treated equally. They ignored

the Pan-African Congress organized by the African-American W. E. B. Du Bois to call attention to the concerns of African peoples around the world. They also ignored the ten thousand other delegates of various nationalities that did not represent sovereign states—the Arab leader Faisal, the Zionist Chaim Weizmann, and several Armenian delegations—who came to Paris to lobby for their causes. They were, in the words of Britain's Foreign Secretary Balfour, "three all-powerful, all-ignorant men, sitting there and carving up continents" (see Map 30.3).

Each one had his own agenda. Wilson, a high-minded idealist, wanted to apply the principle of self-determination to European affairs, by which he meant creating nations that reflected ethnic or linguistic divisions. He proposed a **League of Nations,** a world organization to safeguard the peace and foster international cooperation. His idealism clashed with the more hard-headed and self-serving nationalism of the Europeans. To satisfy his constituents, Lloyd George insisted that Germany pay a heavy indemnity. Clemenceau wanted Germany to give Alsace and Lorraine (a part of France before 1871) and the industrial Saar region to France and demanded that the Rhineland be detached from Germany to form a buffer state.

The result was a series of compromises that satisfied no one. The European powers formed a League of Nations, but the United States Congress, reflecting the isolationist feelings of the American people, refused to let the United States join. France recovered Alsace and Lorraine but was unable to detach the Rhineland and had to content itself with vague promises of British and American protection if Germany ever rebuilt its army. Britain acquired new territories in Africa and the Middle East but was greatly weakened by human losses and the disruption of its trade.

On June 28, 1919, the German delegates reluctantly signed the **Treaty of Versailles°.** Germany was forbidden to have an air force and was permitted only a token army and navy. It gave up large parts of its eastern territory to a newly reconstituted Poland. The Allies made Germany promise to pay reparations, but they did not set a figure or a period of time for payment. A "guilt clause," which was to rankle for years to come, obliged the Germans to accept "responsibility for causing all the loss and damage" of the war. The Treaty of Versailles left Germany humiliated but largely intact and potentially the most powerful nation in Europe. Establishing a peace neither of punishment nor of reconciliation, the treaty was one of the great failures in history.

Georges Clemenceau (zhorzh cluh-mon-SO)

Versailles (vuhr-SIGH)

Map 30.3   Territorial Changes in Europe After World War I   Although the heaviest fighting took place in western Europe, the territorial changes there were relatively minor; two provinces taken by Germany in 1871, Alsace and Lorraine, were returned to France. In eastern Europe, in contrast, the changes were enormous. The disintegration of the Austro-Hungarian Empire and the defeat of Russia allowed a belt of new countries to arise, stretching from Finland in the north to Yugoslavia in the south.

Meanwhile, the Austro-Hungarian Empire had fallen apart. In the Treaty of Saint-Germain° (1920) Austria and Hungary each lost three-quarters of their territory. New countries appeared in the lands lost by Russia, Germany, and Austria-Hungary: Poland, resurrected

after over a century; Czechoslovakia, created from the northern third of Austria-Hungary; and Yugoslavia, combining Serbia and the former south Slav provinces of Austria-Hungary. The new boundaries coincided with the major linguistic groups of eastern Europe, but they all contained disaffected minorities. These small nations were safe only as long as Germany and Russia lay defeated and prostrate.

Saint-Germain (san–chur-MEN)

Lenin the Orator   The leader of the Bolshevik revolutionaries was a spellbinding orator. Here Lenin is addressing Red Army soldiers in Sverdlov Square, Moscow, in 1920. At the time, the Bolsheviks were mopping up the last of the anti-Bolshevik forces and were fully engaged in a war with Poland. The fate of the Revolution depended on the fighting spirit of the Red Army soldiers and on their loyalty to Lenin. (David King Collection)

Russian Civil War and the New Economic Policy

The end of the Great War did not bring peace to all of Europe. Fighting continued in Russia for another three years. The Bolshevik Revolution had provoked Allied intervention. French troops occupied Odessa in the south, the British and Americans landed in Archangel and Murmansk in the north, and the Japanese occupied Vladivostok in the far east. Liberated Czech prisoners of war briefly seized the Trans-Siberian Railway.

Also, in December 1918, civil war broke out in Russia. The Communists—as the Bolsheviks called themselves after March 1918—held central Russia, but all the surrounding provinces rose up against them. Counterrevolutionary armies led by former tsarist officers obtained weapons and supplies from the Allies. For three years the two sides fought each other. They burned farms and confiscated crops, causing a famine that claimed 3 million victims, more than had died in Russia in seven years of fighting. By 1921, the Communists had defeated most of their enemies, for the anti-Bolshevik forces were never united and the peasants feared that a tsarist victory would mean the return of their landlords. The Communists' victory was also due to the superior discipline of their Red Army, and the military genius of their army commander, Leon Trotsky.

Finland, the Baltic states, and Poland remained independent, but the Red Army reconquered other parts of the tsar's empire one by one. In December 1920 Ukrainian Communists declared the independence of a Soviet republic of Ukraine, then in 1922 it merged with Russia to create the Union of Soviet Socialist Republics (USSR), or Soviet Union. The provinces of the Russian Empire in the Caucasus and Central Asia had also declared their independence in 1918. Although the Bolsheviks staunchly supported anticolonialist movements in Africa and Asia, they opposed what they called "feudalism" in the former Russian colonies. Also, they were eager to control the oil fields in both regions. In 1920–1921 the Red Army reconquered the Caucasus and replaced the indigenous leaders with Russians. In 1922 the new Soviet republics of Georgia, Armenia, and Azerbaijan joined the USSR. In this way the Bolsheviks rid Russia of the taint of tsarist colonialism but retained control over lands and peoples that had been part of the tsar's empire.

Years of warfare, revolution, and mismanagement ruined the Russian economy. By 1921 it had declined to one-sixth of its prewar level. Factories and railroads had shut down for lack of fuel, raw materials, and parts. Farmland had been devastated and livestock killed, causing hunger in the cities. Finding himself master of a country in ruin, Lenin decided to release the economy from party and government control. In March 1921 he announced The **New Economic Policy** (N.E.P.) It allowed peasants to own land and sell their crops, private merchants to trade, and private workshops to produce goods and sell them on the free market. Only the biggest businesses, such as banks, railroads, and factories, remained under government ownership.

The relaxation of controls had an immediate effect. Production began to climb, and food and other goods became available. In the cities, food remained scarce because farmers used their crops to feed their livestock rather than sell them. But the N.E.P. reflected no change in the ultimate goals of the Communist Party. It merely provided breathing space, what Lenin called "two steps back to advance one step forward." The Communists had every intention of creating a modern industrial economy without private property, under party guidance. This meant investing in heavy industry and electrification and moving farmers to the cities to work in the new industries. It also meant providing food for the urban workers without spending scarce resources to purchase it from the peasants. In other words, it meant making the peasants, the great majority of the Soviet people, pay for the industrialization of Russia. This turned them into bitter enemies of the Communists.

When Lenin died in January 1924, his associates jockeyed for power. The leading contenders were Leon Trotsky, commander of the Red Army, and Joseph Stalin, general secretary of the Communist Party. Trotsky had the support of many "Old Bolsheviks" who had joined the party before the Revolution. Having spent years in exile, he saw the revolution as a spark that would ignite a world revolution of the working class. Stalin, the only leading Communist who had never lived abroad, insisted that socialism could survive "in one country."

Stalin filled the party bureaucracy with individuals loyal to himself. In 1926–1927 he had Trotsky expelled for "deviation from the party line." In January 1929 he forced Trotsky to flee the country. Then, as absolute master of the party, he prepared to industrialize the Soviet Union at breakneck speed.

An Ephemeral Peace

The 1920s were a decade of apparent progress hiding irreconcilable tensions. Conservatives in Britain and France longed for a return to the stability of the prewar era—the hierarchy of social classes, prosperous world trade, and European dominance over the rest of the world. Elsewhere, all over the world, people's hopes had been raised by the rhetoric of the war, then dashed by its outcome. In Europe, Germans felt cheated out of a victory that had seemed within their grasp, and Italians were disappointed that their sacrifices had not been rewarded at Versailles with large territorial gains. In the Middle East and Asia, Arabs and Indians longed for independence; the Chinese looked for social justice and a lessening of foreign intrusion; and the Japanese hoped to expand their influence in China. In Russia, the Communists were eager to consolidate their power and export their revolution to the rest of the world.

The decade after the end of the war can be divided into two distinct periods: five years of painful recovery and readjustment (1919–1923), followed by six years of growing peace and prosperity (1924–1929). In 1923, Germany suspended reparations payments. In retaliation for the French occupation of the Ruhr, the German government began printing money recklessly, causing the most severe inflation the world had ever seen. Soon German money was worth so little that it took a wheelbarrowful to buy a loaf of bread. As Germany teetered on the brink of civil war, radical nationalists called for revenge and tried to overthrow the government. Finally, the German government issued a new currency and promised to resume reparations payments, and the French agreed to withdraw their troops from the Ruhr.

Beginning in 1924, the world enjoyed a few years of calm and prosperity. After the end of the German crisis of 1923, the western European nations became less confrontational, and Germany joined the League of Nations. The vexed issue of reparations also seemed to vanish, as Germany borrowed money from New York banks to make its payments to France and Britain, which used the money to repay their wartime loans from the United States. This triangular flow of money, based on credit, stimulated the rapid recovery of the European economies. France began rebuilding its war-torn northern zone, Germany recovered from its hyperinflation, and in the United States a boom began that was to last over five years.

While their economies flourished, governments grew more cautious and businesslike. Even the Communists, after Lenin's death, seemed to give up their attempts to spread revolution abroad. Yet neither Germany nor the Soviet Union accepted their borders with the small nations that had arisen between them. In 1922 they signed a secret pact allowing the German army to conduct maneuvers in Russia (in violation of the Versailles treaty) in exchange for German help in building up Russian industry and military potential.

The League of Nations proved adept at resolving numerous technical issues pertaining to health, labor relations, and postal and telegraph communications. But the League could carry out its main function, preserving

Rice Paddies in China   After irrigating all the level land, Chinese farmers turned to the hillsides. To grow rice even on the steepest slopes, they terraced the land and controlled the flow of water so that each field received the optimum amount that the rice shoots required.   (Julia Waterlow/Eye Ubiquitous)

the peace, only when the great powers (Britain, France, and Italy) were in agreement. Without U.S. participation, sanctions against states that violated League rules carried little weight.

CHINA AND JAPAN: CONTRASTING DESTINIES

China and Japan share a common civilization, and both have been subject to Western pressures, but their modern histories have been completely opposite. China clung much longer than Japan to a traditional social structure and economy, then collapsed into chaos and revolution (see below). Japan experienced reform from above (see Chapter 28), acquiring industry and a powerful military, which it used to take advantage of China's weakness. Their different reactions to the pressures of the West put these two great nations on a collision course.

Social and Economic Change

China's population—about 400 million in 1900—was the largest of any country in the world and growing fast. But China had little new land to put into cultivation. In 1900, peasant plots averaged between 1 and 4 acres (less than 2 hectares) apiece, half as large as they had been two generations earlier. Farming methods had not changed in centuries. Landlords and tax collectors took more than half of the harvest. Most Chinese worked incessantly, survived on a diet of grain and vegetables, and spent their lives in fear of floods, bandits, and tax collectors.

Constant labor was needed to prevent the Yellow River from bursting its dikes and flooding the low-lying fields and villages on either side. In times of war and civil disorder, when flood-control precautions were neglected, disasters ensued. Between 1913 and 1938 the river burst its dikes seventeen times, each time killing thousands of people and making millions homeless.

Japan had few natural resources and very little arable land on which to grow food for its rising population. It did not suffer from devastating floods like China, but it was subject to other natural calamities. Typhoons regularly hit its southern regions. Earthquakes periodically shook the country, which lies on the great ring of tectonic fault lines that surround the Pacific Ocean. The Kanto earthquake of 1923 destroyed all of Yokohama and half of Tokyo and killed as many as 200,000 people.

Above the peasantry, Chinese society was divided into many groups and strata. Landowners lived off the rents of their tenants. Officials, chosen through an elaborate examination system, enriched themselves from taxes and the government's monopolies on salt, iron, and other products. Wealthy merchants handled China's growing import-export trade in collaboration with foreign companies. Shanghai, China's financial and commercial center, was famous for its wealthy foreigners and its opium addicts, prostitutes, and gangsters.

Although foreign trade represented only a small part of China's economy, contact with the outside world had a tremendous impact on Chinese politics. Young men living in the treaty ports saw no chance for advancement in the old system of examinations and official positions. Some learned foreign ideas in Christian mission schools or abroad. The contrast between the squalor in which most urban residents lived and the luxury of the foreigners' enclaves in the treaty ports sharpened the resentment of educated Chinese.

Japan's population reached 60 million in 1925 and was increasing by a million a year. The crash program of industrialization begun in 1868 by the Meiji oligarchs (see Chapter 28) accelerated during the First World War, when Japan exported textiles, consumer goods, and munitions. In the war years, its economy grew four times as fast as western Europe's, eight times faster than China's.

In the 1880s, electrification was still in its infancy, so Japan became competitive very early on. Blessed with a rainy climate and many fast-flowing rivers, Japan quickly expanded its hydroelectric capacity. By the mid-1930s, 89 percent of Japanese households had electric lights, compared with 68 percent of U.S. households and 44 percent of British.

Economic growth aggravated social tensions. The *narikin* ("new rich") affected Western ways and lifestyles that clashed with the austerity of earlier times. In the big cities, *mobos* (modern boys) and *mogas* (modern girls) shocked traditionalists with their foreign ways: dancing together, wearing short skirts and tight pants, behaving like Americans. Students who flirted with dangerous thoughts were called "Marx boys."

The main beneficiaries of prosperity were the *zaibatsu*°, four giant corporations—Mitsubishi, Sumitomo, Yasuda, and Mitsui—that controlled most of Japan's industry and commerce. Farmers, who constituted half of the population, remained poor; some, in desperation, sold their daughters to textile mills or into domestic service, where young women formed the bulk of the labor force. Labor unions were weak and repressed by the police.

Japanese prosperity depended on foreign trade and imperialism in Asia. The country exported silk and light manufactures and imported almost all its fuel, raw materials, and machine tools, and even some of its food. Though less at the mercy of the weather than China, Japan was much more vulnerable to swings in the world economy.

Revolution and War, 1900–1918

In 1900, China's Empress Dowager Cixi°, who had seized power in a palace coup two years earlier, encouraged a secret society, the Righteous Fists, or Boxers, to rise up and expel all the foreigners from China. When the Boxers threatened the foreign legation in Beijing, an international force from the Western powers and Japan captured the city and forced China to pay a huge indemnity. Shocked by these events, many Chinese students became convinced that China needed a revolution to get rid of the Qing dynasty and modernize their country. In Shanghai, dissidents published works that would have been forbidden elsewhere in China.

When Cixi died in 1908, the Revolutionary Alliance led by **Sun Yat-sen**° (Sun Zhongshan, 1867–1925) prepared to take over. Sun had spent much of his life in Japan, England, and the United States, plotting the overthrow of the Qing dynasty. His ideas were a mixture of nationalism, socialism, and Confucian philosophy. His patriotism, his powerful ambition, and his tenacious spirit attracted a large following.

The military thwarted Sun's plans. After China's defeat in the war with Japan in 1895, the government had agreed to equip the army with modern rifles and machine guns. The combination of traditional regional autonomy with modern tactics and equipment led to the creation of local armies beholden to local generals known as warlords, rather than to the central government. When a regional army mutinied in October 1911, **Yuan Shikai**°, the most powerful of the regional generals, refused to defend the Qing. A revolutionary assembly at Nanjing elected Sun president of China in December 1911, and the last Qing ruler, the boy-emperor Puyi,

---

zaibatsu (zie-BOT-soo)

Cixi (tsuh-shee)   Sun Yat-sen (soon yot-SEN)
Yuan Shikai (you-AHN she-KIE)

abdicated the throne. But Sun had no military forces at his command. To avoid a clash with the army, he resigned after a few weeks, and a new national assembly elected Yuan president of the new Chinese republic.

Yuan was an able military leader, but he had no political program. When Sun reorganized his followers into a political party called **Guomindang°** (National People's Party), Yuan quashed every attempt at creating a Western-style government and harassed Sun's followers. Victory in the first round of the struggle to create a new China went to the military.

The Japanese were quick to join the Allied side in World War I. They saw the war as a golden opportunity to advance their interests while the Europeans were occupied elsewhere. The war created an economic boom, as the Japanese suddenly found their products in greater demand than before. But it also created hardships for workers, who rioted when the cost of rice rose faster than their wages.

The Japanese soon conquered the German colonies in the northern Pacific and on the coast of China, then turned their attention to the rest of China. In 1915 Japan presented China with Twenty-One Demands, which would have turned it into a virtual protectorate. Britain and the United States persuaded Japan to soften the demands but could not prevent it from keeping the German coastal enclaves and extracting railroad and mining concessions at China's expense. In protest, anti-Japanese riots and boycotts broke out throughout China. Thus began a bitter struggle between the two countries that was to last for thirty years.

Chinese Warlords and the Guomindang, 1919–1929

At the Paris Peace Conference, the great powers went along with Japan's seizure of the German enclaves in China. To many educated Chinese, this decision was a cruel insult. On May 4, 1919, students demonstrated in front of the Forbidden City of Beijing. Despite a government ban, the May Fourth Movement spread to other parts of China. A new generation was growing up to challenge the old officials, the regional generals, and the foreigners.

China's regional generals—the warlords—still supported their armies through plunder and arbitrary taxation. They frightened off trade and investment in railroads, industry, and agricultural improvement. While neglecting the dikes and canals on which the livelihood of Chinese farmers depended, they fought one another and protected the gangsters who ran the opium trade. During the warlord era, China grew poorer and only the treaty ports prospered.

Sun Yat-sen tried to make a comeback in Canton (Guangzhou) in the early 1920s. Though not a Communist, he was impressed with the efficiency of Lenin's revolutionary tactics and let a Soviet adviser reorganize the Guomindang along Leninist lines. He also welcomed members of the newly created Chinese Communist Party into the Guomindang.

When Sun died in 1925, the leadership of his party passed to Jiang Jieshi, known in the West as Chiang Kai-shek° (1887–1975). An officer and director of the military academy, Chiang trained several hundred young officers who remained loyal to him thereafter. In 1927 he determined to crush the regional warlords. As his army moved north from its base in Canton, he briefly formed an alliance with the Communists. Once his troops had occupied Shanghai, however, he allied himself with local gangsters to crush the labor unions and decimate the Communists, whom he considered a threat. He then defeated or co-opted most of the other warlords and established a dictatorship.

Chiang's government issued ambitious plans to build railroads, develop agriculture and industry, and modernize China from the top down. However, his followers were neither competent administrators like the Japanese officials of the Meiji Restoration nor ruthless modernizers like the Russian Bolsheviks. Instead, the government attracted thousands of opportunists whose goal was to "become an official and get rich" by taxing and plundering businesses. In the countryside, tax collectors and landowners squeezed the peasants ever harder, even at times of natural disasters. What little money reached the government's coffers went to the military. For twenty years after the fall of the Qing, China remained mired in poverty, subject to corrupt officials and the whims of nature.

THE NEW MIDDLE EAST

Having contributed to the Allied victory, the Arab peoples expected to have a say in the outcome of the Great War. But the victorious French and British planned to treat the Middle East like a territory open to colonial rule. The result was a legacy of instability that has persisted to this day.

Guomindang (gwo-min-dong)

Chiang Kai-shek (chang kie-shek)

Mustafa Kemal Atatürk   After World War I, Mustafa Kemal was determined to modernize Turkey on the western model. Here he is shown wearing a European-style suit and teaching the Latin alphabet.   (Stock Montage)

The Mandate System

At the Paris Peace Conference, France, Britain, Italy, and Japan proposed to divide the former German colonies and the territories of the Ottoman Empire among themselves, but their ambitions clashed with President Wilson's ideal of national self-determination. Eventually, the victors arrived at a compromise solution called the **mandate system:** colonial rulers would administer the territories but would be accountable to the League of Nations for "the material and moral well-being and the social progress of the inhabitants."

Class C Mandates—those with the smallest populations—were treated as colonies by their conquerors. South Africa replaced Germany in Southwest Africa (now Namibia). Britain, Australia, New Zealand, and Japan took over the German islands in the Pacific. Class B Mandates, larger than Class C but still underdeveloped, were to be ruled for the benefit of their inhabitants under League of Nations supervision. They were to receive autonomy at some unspecified time in the future. Most of Germany's African colonies fell into this category.

The Arab-speaking territories of the old Ottoman Empire were Class A Mandates. The League of Nations declared that they had "reached a state of development where their existence as independent nations can be provisionally recognized subject to the rendering of administrative advice and assistance by a Mandatory, until such time as they are able to stand alone." Arabs interpreted this ambiguous wording as a promise of independence. Britain and France sent troops into the region "for the benefit of its inhabitants." Palestine (now Israel), Transjordan (now Jordan), and Iraq (formerly Mesopotamia) became British mandates; France claimed Syria and Lebanon (see Map 30.4).

The Rise of Modern Turkey

At the end of the war, as the Ottoman Empire teetered on the brink of collapse, France, Britain, and Italy saw an opportunity to expand their empires, and Greece eyed those parts of Anatolia inhabited by Greeks. In 1919 French, British, Italian, and Greek forces occupied Constantinople and parts of Anatolia. By the Treaty of Sèvres (1920), the Allies made the sultan give up most of his lands.

In 1919, Mustafa Kemal, a hero of the Gallipoli campaign, had formed a nationalist government in central Anatolia with the backing of fellow army officers. After a short but fierce war against invading Greeks, his armies reconquered Anatolia and the area around Constantinople in 1922. The victorious Turks forced hundreds of thousands of Greeks from their ancestral homes in Anatolia. In response the Greek government expelled all Muslims from Greece. The ethnic diversity that had prevailed in the region for centuries ended.

As a war hero and proclaimed savior of his country, Kemal was able to impose wrenching changes on his people faster than any other reformer would have dared. An outspoken modernizer, he was eager to bring Turkey closer to Europe as quickly as possible. He abolished the

Map 30.4   Territorial Changes in the Middle East After World War I   The defeat and dismemberment of the Ottoman Empire at the end of World War I resulted in an entirely new political map of the region. The Turkish Republic inherited Anatolia and a small piece of the Balkans, while the Ottoman Empire's Arab provinces were divided between France and Great Britain as "Class A Mandates." The French acquired Syria and Lebanon and the British got Palestine (now Israel), Transjordan (now Jordan), and Iraq. Only Iran and Egypt remained as they had been.

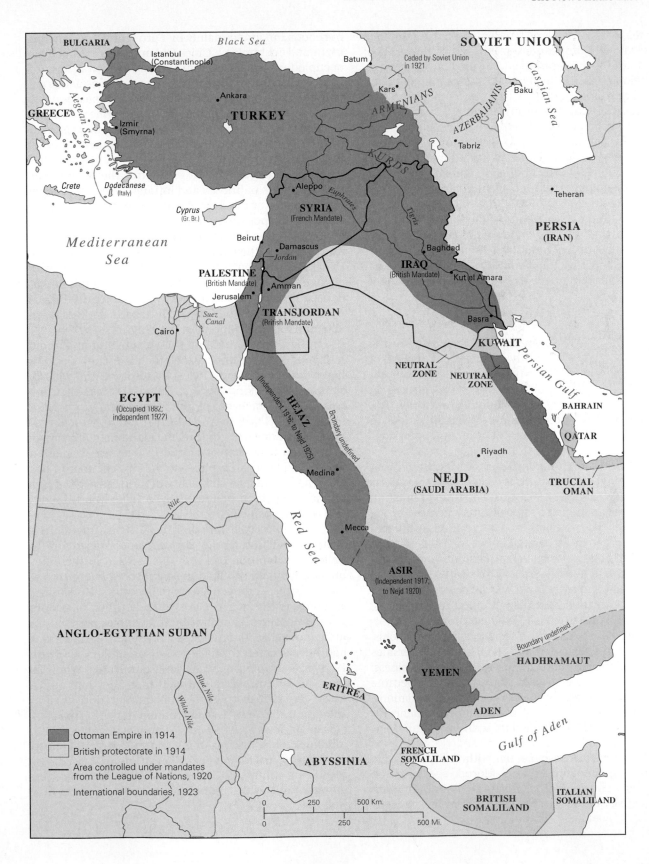

BULGARIA

Black Sea

SOVIET UNION

Istanbul
(Constantinople)

Batum

Ceded by Soviet Union
in 1921

Caspian Sea

Kars

Baku

ARMENIANS

Ankara

AZERBAIJANIS

GREECE

Aegean Sea

TURKEY

Izmir
(Smyrna)

KURDS

Tabriz

Teheran

Crete

Dodecanese
(Italy)

Aleppo

Euphrates

PERSIA
(IRAN)

Cyprus
(Gr. Br.)

SYRIA
(French Mandate)

Tigris

*Mediterranean
Sea*

Beirut

Damascus

Baghdad

Jordan

IRAQ
(British Mandate)

Kut el Amara

PALESTINE
(British Mandate)

Amman

Jerusalem

*Suez
Canal*

TRANSJORDAN
(British Mandate)

Basra

KUWAIT

Persian Gulf

Cairo

NEUTRAL
ZONE

NEUTRAL
ZONE

BAHRAIN

EGYPT
(Occupied 1882;
independent 1922)

HEJAZ
(Independent 1916 to Nejd 1925)

Boundary undefined

QATAR

Riyadh

TRUCIAL
OMAN

Medina

NEJD
(SAUDI ARABIA)

Nile

Red Sea

Mecca

ANGLO-EGYPTIAN SUDAN

ASIR
(Independent 1917;
to Nejd 1920)

Boundary undefined

HADHRAMAUT

Blue Nile

White Nile

YEMEN

ERITREA

ADEN

FRENCH
SOMALILAND

Gulf of Aden

ABYSSINIA

Ottoman Empire in 1914

British protectorate in 1914

Area controlled under mandates
from the League of Nations, 1920

International boundaries, 1923

BRITISH
SOMALILAND

ITALIAN
SOMALILAND

0   250   500 Km.

0   250   500 Mi.

sultanate, in 1923 declared Turkey a secular republic, and introduced European laws. In a radical break with Islamic tradition, he suppressed Muslim courts, schools, and religious orders and replaced the Arabic alphabet with the Latin alphabet.

Kemal attempted to westernize the traditional Turkish family. Women received civil equality, including the right to vote and be elected to the national assembly. Kemal forbade polygamy and instituted civil marriage and divorce. He even changed people's clothing, strongly discouraging women from veiling their faces and replacing the fez, until then the traditional Turkish men's hat, with the European brimmed hat. He ordered everyone to take a family name, choosing the name Atatürk ("father of the Turks") for himself. His reforms spread quickly in the cities; but in rural areas, where Islamic traditions remained strong, people resisted them for a long time.

Arab Lands and the Question of Palestine

Among the Arab people, the thinly disguised colonialism of the mandate system set off protests and rebellions, not only in the mandated territories, but even as far away as Morocco. Arabs viewed the European presence not as "liberation" from Ottoman "oppression" but as foreign occupation.

After World War I, Middle Eastern society underwent dramatic changes. Nomads disappeared from the deserts as trucks replaced camel caravans. The rural population grew fast, and many landless peasants migrated to the swelling cities. The population of the region is estimated to have increased by 50 percent between 1914 and 1939, while that of large cities such as Constantinople, Baghdad, and Cairo doubled.

The urban and mercantile middle class, encouraged by the transformation of Turkey, adopted Western ideas, customs, and styles of housing and clothing. Some families sent their sons to European secular or mission schools, then to Western colleges in Cairo and Beirut or universities abroad, to prepare for jobs in government and business. Among the educated elite were a few women who became schoolteachers or nurses. There were great variations, ranging from Lebanon, with its strong French influence, to Arabia and Iran, which retained their diverse cultural traditions.

The region in closest contact with Europe was the Maghrib—Algeria, Tunisia and Morocco—which the French army considered its private domain. Alongside the old native quarters, the French built modern neighborhoods inhabited mainly by Europeans (see Environment and Technology: Cities Old and New). France had occupied Algeria since 1830 and had encouraged European immigration. The settlers owned the best lands and monopolized government jobs and businesses while Arabs and Berbers remained poor and suffered intense discrimination. Nationalism was only beginning to appear before World War II, and the settlers quickly blocked any attempt at reform.

The British attempted to control the Middle East with a mixture of bribery and intimidation. They helped Faisal, leader of the Arab Revolt, become king of Syria. When the French ousted him, the British made him king of Iraq. They used bombers to quell rural insurrections in Iraq. In 1931 they reached an agreement with King Faisal's government: official independence for Iraq in exchange for the right to keep two air bases, a military alliance, and an assured flow of petroleum. France, meanwhile, sent thousands of troops to Syria and Lebanon to crush nationalist uprisings.

In Egypt as in Iraq, the British substituted a phony independence for official colonialism. They declared Egypt independent in 1922 but reserved the right to station troops along the Suez Canal to secure their link with India in the event of war. Most galling to the Wafd (Nationalist) Party was the British attempt to remove Egyptian troops from the Sudan, a land many Egyptians considered a colony of Egypt. Britain was successful in keeping Egypt in limbo—neither independent nor a colony—thanks to an alliance with King Farouk and conservative Egyptian politicians who feared both secular and religious radicalism.

As soon as Palestine became a British mandate in 1920, Jewish immigrants arrived, encouraged by the Balfour Declaration of 1917. Most settled in the cities, but some purchased land to establish *kibbutzim,* communal farms. Their goals were to become self-sufficient and reestablish their ties to the land of their ancestors. The purchases of land by Jewish agencies angered the indigenous Palestinians, especially tenant farmers who had been evicted to make room for settlers. In 1920–1921 riots erupted between Jews and Arabs. When far more Jewish immigrants arrived than they had anticipated, the British tried to limit immigration, thereby alienating the Jews without mollifying the Arabs. Increasingly, Jews arrived without papers, smuggled in by militant Zionist organizations. In the 1930s the country was torn by strikes and guerrilla warfare that the British could not control. In the process, Britain earned the hatred of both sides and of much of the Arab world as well.

Cities Old and New

Cities do not just grow larger; they change, sometimes radically, in response to culture and technology. The impact of cultural dominance and technological innovations on urban design is evident in these photographs of Cairo.

The European colonial presence was felt more strongly in cities than in the countryside. Cairo, the largest city in the Arab world before the British conquest, grew much larger after 1882. However, the construction of modern quarters for Europeans and wealthy Egyptians had little impact on the older quarters where most Cairenes lived. In the picture of the old quarter of Cairo in 1900 with its narrow streets and open stalls, men wear the burnoose and women cover their faces with a veil. The later picture, taken in 1904, shows Shepheard's hotel, one of the most luxurious hotels in the world, built on a broad avenue in the city's modern quarter.

The picture at left reflects the traditional architecture of hot desert countries: narrow streets, thick whitewashed walls, small windows, and heavy doors, all designed to keep out the heat of the day and protect privacy. The picture below shows the ideas Europeans brought with them about how a city should look. The wide streets and high airy buildings with windows and balconies mimic the urban design of late-nineteenth-century Paris, London, or Rome.

Cairo—Modern and Traditional The luxurious Shepheard's Hotel (below) was built in the European style on a broad avenue in the new quarter of Cairo. In stark contrast is the street (above) in the old quarter of the city: the street is narrow, the walls of the buildings are thick, and the windows small in order to protect the interiors from the heat of the sun. (Billie Love Historical Collection)

SOCIETY, CULTURE, AND TECHNOLOGY IN THE INDUSTRIALIZED WORLD

With the signing of the peace treaties, the countries that had fought for four years turned their efforts toward building a new future. The war had left a deep imprint on European society and culture. Advances in science offered astonishing new insights into the mysteries of nature and the universe. New technologies, many of them pioneered in the United States, promised to change the daily lives of millions of people.

Class and Gender

After the war, class distinctions began to fade. Many European aristocrats had died on the battlefields, and with them went their class's long domination of the army, the diplomatic corps, and other elite sectors of society. The United States and Canada had never had as rigidly defined a class structure as European societies or as elaborate a set of traditions and manners. During the war, displays of wealth and privilege seemed unpatriotic, and remained so afterward. On both sides of the Atlantic, engineers, businessmen, lawyers, and other professionals rose to prominence, increasing the relative importance of the middle class.

The activities of governments had expanded during the war and continued to grow. Governments provided housing, highways, schools, public health facilities, broadcasting, and other services. This growth of government influence created a need for thousands more bureaucrats. Department stores, banks, insurance companies, and other businesses also increased the white-collar work force.

In contrast with the middle class, the working class did not expand. The introduction of new machines and new ways of organizing work, such as the automobile assembly line that Henry Ford devised, increased workers' productivity so that greater outputs could be achieved without expanding the labor force.

Women's lives changed more rapidly in the 1920s than in any previous decade. Although the end of the war marked a retreat from wartime job opportunities, some women remained in the work force as wage earners and as salaried professionals. The young and wealthy enjoyed more personal freedoms than their mothers had before the war. They drove cars, played sports, traveled alone, and smoked in public. Emancipated from the corsets and long dresses of prewar fashion, they wore their skirts and their hair short and danced to jazz instead of waltzes, to the consternation of their elders. Others found that the upheavals of war brought more suffering than liberation. Millions of women had lost their fathers, brothers, sons, husbands, and fiancés in the war or in the great influenza epidemic. After the war, the shortage of young men caused many single women to lead lives of loneliness and destitution.

In Europe and North America advocates of women's rights—labeled "suffragettes" by their critics—had been demanding the vote for women since the 1890s. Only in New Zealand (in 1893) did women receive the vote before the twentieth century. Women in Norway were the first to obtain it in Europe, in 1915. Russian women followed in 1917, Canadian and German women in 1918. Britain gave women over age thirty the vote in 1918 and later extended it to younger women. The Nineteenth Amendment to the U.S. Constitution granted suffrage to American women in 1920. Women in Turkey began voting in 1934. Most other countries did not allow women to vote until after 1945.

In dictatorships, voting rights for women made no difference, and in democratic countries, women tended to vote like their male relatives. In the British elections of 1918—the first to include women—they overwhelmingly voted for the Conservative Party. Everywhere, their influence on politics was less radical than feminists had hoped and conservatives had feared. Even when it did not alter the political situation, however, the right to vote was a potent symbol.

Revolution in the Sciences

For two hundred years, scientists, following in Isaac Newton's footsteps, had applied the same laws and equations to astronomical observations and to laboratory experiments. At the end of the nineteenth century, however, a revolution in physics undermined all the old certainties about nature. Physicists discovered that atoms, the building blocks of matter, are not indivisible but consist of far smaller subatomic particles. In 1900 the German physicist **Max Planck** (1858–1947) found that light and energy do not flow in a continuous stream but travel in small units, which he called *quanta*. These findings seemed strange enough, but what really undermined Newtonian physics was the general theory of relativity developed by **Albert Einstein** (1879–1955), another German physicist. In 1916 Einstein announced that not only is matter made of insubstantial particles, but time, space, and mass are not fixed but are relative to one another. Other physicists said that light is made up of either waves or particles, depending on the observer, and that an experiment could determine either the speed or the position of a particle of light, but never both.

To nonscientists it seemed as though theories expressed in arcane mathematical formulas were replacing truth and common sense. Far from being mere speculation, however, the new physics promised to unlock the secrets of matter and provide humans with plentiful—and potentially dangerous—new sources of energy.

The new social sciences were even more unsettling than the new physics, for they challenged Victorian morality, middle-class values, and notions of Western superiority. Sigmund Freud (1856–1939), a Viennese physician, developed a technique—psychoanalysis—to probe the minds of his patients. He found not only rationality but also hidden layers of emotion and desire repressed by social restraints. "The primitive, savage and evil impulses have not vanished from any individual, but continue their existence, although in a repressed state," he warned. Meanwhile, sociologists and anthropologists had begun the empirical study of societies, both Western and non-Western. Before the war, the French sociologist Emile Durkheim (1858–1917) had come to the then-shocking conclusion that "there are no religions that are false. All are true in their own fashion."

If the words *primitive* and *savage* applied to Europeans as well as to other peoples, and if religions were all equally "true," then what remained of the superiority of Western civilization? Cultural relativism, as the new approach to human societies was called, was as unnerving as relativity in physics.

Although these ideas had been expressed before 1914, wartime experiences called into question the West's faith in reason and progress. Some people accepted the new ideas with enthusiasm. Others condemned and rejected them, clinging to the sense of order and faith in progress that had energized European and American culture before the war.

The New Technologies of Modernity

Some Europeans and Americans viewed the sciences with mixed feelings, but the new technologies aroused almost universal excitement. In North America, even working-class people could afford some of the new products of scientific research, inventors' ingenuity, and industrial production. Mass consumption lagged in Europe, but science and technology were just as advanced, and public fascination with the latest inventions—the cult of the modern—was just as strong.

Of all the innovations of the time, none attracted public interest as much as airplanes. In 1903 two young American mechanics, Wilbur and Orville Wright, built the first aircraft that was heavier than air and could be maneuvered in flight. From that moment on, wherever they appeared, airplanes fascinated people. During the war, the exploits of air aces relieved the tedium of news from the front. In the 1920s aviation became a sport and a form of entertainment, and flying daredevils achieved extraordinary fame by pushing their planes to the very limit—and often beyond. Among the most celebrated pilots were three Americans. Amelia Earhart was the first woman to fly across the Atlantic Ocean, and her example encouraged other women to fly. Richard Byrd flew over the North Pole in 1926. The most admired of all was Charles Lindbergh, the first person to fly alone across the Atlantic, in 1927. The heroic age of flight lasted until the late 1930s, when aviation became a means of transportation, a business, and a male preserve.

Electricity, produced in industrial quantities since the 1890s (see Chapter 28), began to transform home life. The first home use of electricity was for lighting, thanks to the economical and long-lasting tungsten bulb. Then, having persuaded people to wire their homes, electrical utilities joined manufacturers in advertising electric irons, fans, washing machines, hot plates, and other electric appliances.

Radio—or wireless telegraphy, as it was called—had served ships and the military during the war as a means of point-to-point telecommunication. After the war, amateurs used surplus radio equipment to talk to one another. The first commercial station began broadcasting in Pittsburgh in 1920. By the end of 1923, six hundred stations were broadcasting news, sports, soap operas, and advertising to homes throughout North America. By 1930, 12 million families owned radio receivers. In Europe, radio spread more slowly because governments reserved the airwaves for cultural and official programs and taxed radio owners to pay for the service.

Another medium that spread explosively in the 1920s was film. Motion pictures had begun in France in 1895 and flourished there and elsewhere in Europe, where the dominant concern was to reproduce stage plays. In the United States, filmmaking started at almost the same time, but American filmmakers considered it their business to entertain audiences rather than preserve outstanding theatrical performances. In competing for audiences, they looked to cinematic innovation, broad humor, and exciting spectacles, in the process developing styles of filmmaking that became immensely popular.

Diversity was a hallmark of the early film industry. After World War I filmmaking took root and flourished in Japan, India, Turkey, Egypt, and a suburb of Los Angeles, California, called Hollywood. American and European movie studios were both successful in exporting films, since silent movies presented no language problems. In 1929, out of an estimated 2100 films produced worldwide, 510 were made in the United States and 750 in Japan. But by then the United States had introduced the first "talking" motion picture, *The Jazz Singer* (1927), which changed all the rules. The number of Americans who went to see their favorite stars in thrilling adventures and heart-breaking romances rose from 40 million in 1922 to 100 million in 1930, at a time when the population of the country was about 120 million. Europeans had the technology and the art but neither the wealth nor the huge market of the United States. Hollywood studios began the diffusion of American culture that has continued to this day.

Health and hygiene were also part of the cult of modernity. Advances in medicine—some learned in the war—saved many lives. Wounds were regularly disinfected, and x-ray machines helped diagnose fractures. Since the late nineteenth century, scientists had known that disease-causing bacteria could be transmitted through contaminated water, spoiled food, or fecal matter. After the war, cities built costly water supply and sewage treatment systems. By the 1920s, indoor plumbing and flush toilets were becoming common even in working-class neighborhoods.

Interest in cleanliness altered private life. Doctors and home economists bombarded women with warnings and advice on how to banish germs. Soap and appliance manufacturers filled women's magazines with advertisements for products to help housewives keep their family's homes and clothing spotless and their meals fresh and wholesome. The decline in infant mortality and improvements in general health and life expectancy in this period owe as much to the cult of cleanliness as to advances in medicine.

Technology and the Environment

Two new technologies—the skyscraper and the automobile—transformed the urban environment even more radically than the railroad had done in the nineteenth century. At the end of the nineteenth century, architects had begun to design ever-higher buildings using load-bearing steel frames and passenger elevators. Major corporations in Chicago and New York competed to build the most daring buildings in the world, such as New York's 55-story Woolworth Building (1912) and Chicago's 34-story Tribune Tower (1923). A building boom in the late 1920s produced dozens of skyscrapers, culminating with the 86-story, 1,239-foot (377-meter) Empire State Building in New York, completed in 1932.

European cities restricted the height of buildings to protect their architectural heritage; Paris forbade buildings over 56 feet (17 meters) high. In innovative designs, however, European architects led the way. In the 1920s the Swiss architect Charles Edouard Jeanneret (1887–1965), known as Le Corbusier°, outlined a new approach to architecture that featured simplicity of form, absence of surface ornamentation, easy manufacture, and inexpensive materials. Among his influential designs were the main buildings of Chandigarh, the new capital of the Indian state of Punjab. Other architects—including the Finn Ero Saarinen, the Germans Ludwig Mies van der Rhoe° and Walter Gropius, and the American Frank Lloyd Wright—advanced his lines of thought and added their own to create what became known as the International Style.

While central business districts were reaching for the sky, outlying areas were spreading far out into the countryside, thanks to the automobile. The assembly line pioneered by Henry Ford mass-produced vehicles in ever-greater volume and at falling prices. By 1929, the United States had one car for every five people, five-sixths of the world's automobiles. Far from being blamed for their exhaust emissions, automobiles were praised as the solution to urban pollution. As cars replaced carts and carriages, horses disappeared from city streets, as did tons of manure.

The most important environmental effect of automobiles was suburban sprawl. Middle-class families could now live in single-family homes too spread apart to be served by public transportation. By the late 1920s, paved roads rivaled rail networks both in length and in the surface they occupied. As middle- and working-class families bought cars, cities acquired rings of automobile suburbs. Los Angeles, the first true automobile city, consisted of suburbs spread over hundreds of square miles and linked together by broad avenues. In those sections of the city where streetcar lines went out of business, the automobile, at first a plaything for the wealthy, became a necessity for commuters. Many Americans saw Los Angeles as the portent of a glorious future when everyone would have a car; only a few foresaw the congestion and pollution that would ensue.

Technological advances also transformed rural environments. Automobile owners quickly developed an interest in "motoring"—driving their vehicles out into the

Le Corbusier (luh cor-booz-YEH)
Ludwig Mies van der Rohe (LOOD-vig MEES fon der ROW-uh)

The Archetypal Automobile City   As Los Angeles grew from a modest town into a sprawling metropolis, broad avenues, parking lots, and garages were built to accommodate automobiles. By 1929, most families owned a car and streetcar lines had closed for lack of passengers. This photograph shows a street in the downtown business district.   (Ralph Morris Archives/Los Angeles Public Library)

country on weekends or on holiday trips. Farmers began buying cars and light trucks, using them to transport produce as well as passengers. Governments obliged by building new roads and paving old ones to make automobile travel smoother and safer.

Until the 1920s, horses remained the predominant source of energy for pulling plows and reapers and powering threshing machines on American farms. Only the wealthiest farmers could afford the slow and costly steam tractors. In 1915, Ford introduced a gasoline-powered tractor, and by the mid-1920s, these versatile machines began replacing horses. Larger farms profited most from this innovation, while small farmers sold their land and moved to the cities. Tractors hastened the transformation of agriculture from family enterprises to the large agribusinesses of today.

In India, Australia, and the western United States, where there was little virgin rain-watered land left to cultivate, engineers built dams and canals to irrigate dry lands. Dams offered the added advantage of producing electricity, for which there was a booming demand. The immediate benefits of irrigation—land, food, and electricity—far outweighed such distant consequences as salt deposits on irrigated lands and harm to wildlife.

CONCLUSION

In the late 1920s, it seemed as though the victors in the Great War might reestablish the prewar prosperity and European dominance of the globe. But the spirit of the 1920s was an illusion—not real peace but the eye of a hurricane.

The Great War caused a major realignment among the nations of the world. France and Britain, the two leading colonial powers, emerged economically weakened despite their victory. The war brought defeat and humiliation to Germany but did not reduce its military or industrial potential. It destroyed the old regime and the aristocracy of Russia, leading to civil war and revolution from which the victorious powers sought to isolate themselves. Two other old empires—the Austro-Hungarian and the Ottoman—were divided into many smaller and weaker nations. For a while, the Middle East seemed ripe for a new wave of imperialism. But there and throughout Asia, the war unleashed revolutionary nationalist movements that challenged European influence.

Only two countries benefited from the war. Japan took advantage of the European conflict to develop its industries and press its demands on a China weakened by domestic turmoil and social unrest. The United States emerged as the most prosperous and potentially most powerful nation, restrained only by the isolationist sentiments expressed by many Americans.

Modern technology and industrial organization had long been praised in the name of "progress" for their ability to reduce toil and disease and improve living standards. The war showed that they possessed an equally awesome destructive potential. As we shall see in the next chapter, most survivors wanted no repeat of such a nightmare. But a small minority worshiped violence and saw in the new weaponry a means to dominate those who feared conflict and death.

■ Key Terms

Western Front	Treaty of Versailles
Faisal	New Economic Policy
Theodore Herzl	Sun Yat-sen
Balfour Declaration	Yuan Shikai
Bolsheviks	Guomindang
Vladimir Lenin	mandate system
Woodrow Wilson	Max Planck
League of Nations	Albert Einstein

■ Suggested Reading

Bernadotte Schmitt and Harold C. Bedeler, *The World in the Crucible, 1914–1918* (1984), and John Keegan, *The First World War* (1999), are two engaging overviews of World War I. Imanuel Geiss, *July 1914: The Outbreak of the First World War* (1967), argues that Germany caused the conflict. Barbara Tuchman's *The Guns of August* (1962) and Alexander Solzhenitsyn's *August 1914* (1972) recount the first month of the war in detail. Keegan's *The Face of Battle* (1976) vividly describes the Battle of the Somme from the soldiers' perspective. On the technology of warfare see William H. McNeill, *The Pursuit of Power: Technology, Armed Force, and Society* (1982), and John Ellis, *The Social History of the Machine Gun* (1975). The role of women and the home front is the subject of essays in Margaret Higonnet et al., eds., *Behind the Lines: Gender and the Two World Wars* (1987), and sections of Lynn Weiner, *From Working Girl to Working Mother* (1985). The definitive work on the flu epidemic is Alfred W. Crosby, *America's Forgotten Pandemic: The Influenza of 1918* (1989). Two famous novels about the war are Erich Maria Re-

marque's *All Quiet on the Western Front* (1928) and Robert Graves's *Goodbye to All That* (1929). The war in English literature is the subject of Paul Fussell, *The Great War and Modern Memory* (1975).

For the background to the Russian Revolution read Theodore von Laue's *Why Lenin? Why Stalin?* 2d ed. (1971); but see also Richard Pipes, *The Russian Revolution* (1990), and Orlando Figes, *A People's Tragedy: The Russian Revolution, 1891–1924* (1996). The classic eyewitness account of the Revolution is John Reed's *Ten Days That Shook the World* (1919). On gender issues see Wendy Goldman, *Women, the State, and Revolution: Soviet Family Policy and Social Life, 1917–1936* (1993). The best-known novel about the Revolution and civil war is Boris Pasternak's *Doctor Zhivago* (1958).

John Maynard Keynes's *The Economic Consequences of the Peace* (1920) is a classic critique of the Paris Peace Conference. Arno Mayer's *Political Origins of the New Diplomacy, 1917–1918* (1959) analyzes the tensions and failures of great-power politics. The 1920s are discussed in Raymond Sontag's *A Broken World, 1919–1939* (1971).

The best recent book on Japan in the twentieth century is Daikichi Irokawa's *The Age of Hirohito: In Search of Modern Japan* (1995). See also Richard Storry, *A History of Modern Japan* (1982), and Tessa Morris-Suzuki, *The Technological Transformation of Japan* (1994). In the large and fast-growing literature on twentieth-century China, two general introductions are especially useful: John K. Fairbank, *The Great Chinese Revolution, 1800–1985* (1986), and Jonathan Spence, *The Search for Modern China* (1990). On the warlord and Guomindang periods see Lucien Bianco, *Origins of the Chinese Revolution, 1915–1949* (1971).

On the war and its aftermath in the Middle East see David Fromkin, *A Peace to End All Peace* (1989), and M. E. Yapp, *The Near East Since the First World War* (1991). Bernard Lewis, *The Emergence of Modern Turkey* (1968), is a good introduction. On Africa in this period see A. Adu Boahen, ed., *Africa Under Colonial Domination, 1880-1935*, volume 7 of the *UNESCO General History of Africa* (1985), and A. D. Roberts, ed., *Cambridge History of Africa*, vol. 7, *1905–1940* (1986).

The cultural transformation of Europe is captured in H. Stuart Hughes, *Consciousness and Society: The Reorientation of European Social Thought, 1890–1930* (1958). The towering intellectuals of that era are the subject of Peter Gay, *Freud: A Life for Our Time* (1988), and Abraham Pais, *Subtle Is the Lord: The Science and Life of Albert Einstein* (1982). Three books capture the enthusiastic popular response to technological innovations: David E. Nye, *Electrifying America: Social Meanings of a New Technology* (1990); Peter Fritzsche, *A Nation of Fliers: German Aviation and the Popular Imagination* (1992); and the sweeping overview by Thomas Hughes, *American Genesis: A Century of Invention and Technological Enthusiasm, 1870–1970* (1989).

THE COLLAPSE OF THE OLD ORDER,
1929–1949

The Stalin Revolution • The Depression • The Rise of Fascism •
East Asia, 1931–1945 • The Second World War • The Character of Warfare
ENVIRONMENT AND TECHNOLOGY: Biomedical Technologies
SOCIETY AND CULTURE: Preparing for Combat

German Dive-Bomber over Eastern Europe   A German ME-100 fighter plane
attacks a Soviet troop convoy on the Eastern Front

efore the First World War, the Italian futurist poets exalted violence as a noble and manly idea. Filippo Marinetti defined their creed in these words: "We want to glorify war, the world's only hygiene—militarism, deed, destroyer of anarchisms, the beautiful ideas that are death-bringing, and the subordination of women." His friend Gabriele d'Annunzio said: "If it is a crime to incite citizens to violence, I shall boast of this crime."

The war taught most survivors to abhor violence. During the 1920s, the world seemed to return to what United States president Warren Harding called "normalcy": prosperity in Europe and America, European colonialism in Asia and Africa, paternalistic U.S. domination of Latin America, and peace almost everywhere. But that euphoria did not last, for its economic underpinnings were fragile, political contentment was superficial, and the yearning to solve social problems by violent means lay close to the surface. For a few, war and domination became a creed and a goal.

In 1929 the artificial normalcy of the 1920s began to come apart. The Great Depression caused governments to turn against one another in a desperate attempt to protect their people's livelihood. As the economic crisis spread around the world, businesses went bankrupt, prices fell, factories closed, and workers were laid off. Even wholly agricultural nations and colonies suffered as markets for their exports shriveled.

While some countries accepted poverty and unemployment, others chose to solve their problems by violent means. As some nations shut their doors to Japan's products, the Japanese military tried to save their country by conquering China, which erupted in revolution. In Germany, the Depression reawakened resentments against the victors of the Great War; people who feared communism or blamed Jews for their troubles turned to Hitler and the Nazis, who promised to save their society by dominating others. In the Soviet Union, Stalin used energetic and murderous means to force his country into a communist version of the Industrial Revolution.

The result was war. The Second World War engulfed more lands and peoples and caused far more deaths and destruction than any previous conflict. At the end of it, much of Europe and East Asia lay in ruins, and millions of destitute refugees sought safety in other lands. The European colonial powers were either defeated or so weakened that they could no longer hold onto their empires when Asian and African peoples asserted their desire for independence.

As you read this chapter, ask yourself the following questions:

- How did the Soviet Union change under Stalin, and at what cost?
- What were the main causes of the Second World War?
- How was the war fought, and why did Japan and Germany lose?

THE STALIN REVOLUTION

During the 1920s, other countries ostracized the Soviet Union as it recovered from the Revolutions of 1917 and the civil war that followed (see Chapter 30). After Stalin achieved total mastery over this huge nation in early 1929, he led it through another revolution—an economic and social transformation that turned it into a great industrial and military power and intensified both admiration for and fear of communism throughout the world.

Five-Year Plans

Joseph Stalin (1879–1953) was born Joseph Vissarionovich Dzhugashvili into the family of a poor shoemaker. Before becoming a revolutionary, he studied for the priesthood. Under the name "Stalin" (Russian for "man of steel"), he played a small part in the Revolutions of 1917. He was a hard-working and skillful administrator who rose within the party bureaucracy and filled its upper ranks with men loyal to himself. By 1925, he had ousted Leon Trotsky, the best-known revolutionary after Lenin, from the party. He then proceeded to squeeze all other rivals out of positions of power, make himself absolute dictator, and transform Soviet society.

Stalin's ambition was to turn the USSR into an industrial nation. Industrialization was to serve a different

CHRONOLOGY

	Europe and North Africa	Asia and the Pacific
1930	**1931** Great Depression reaches Europe	**1931** Japanese forces occupy Manchuria
	1933 Hitler comes to power in Germany	**1934–1935** Mao leads Communists on Long March
1935	**1936** Hitler invades the Rhineland	**1937** Japanese troops invade China, conquer coastal provinces; Chiang Kai-shek flees to Sichuan
		1937–1938 Japanese troops take Nanjing
1940	**1939 (Sept. 1)** German forces invade Poland	
	1940 (March–April) German forces conquer Denmark, Norway, the Netherlands, and Belgium	
	1940 (May–June) German forces conquer France	
	1940 (June–Sept.) Battle of Britain	
	1941 (June 21) German forces invade USSR	**1941 (Dec. 7)** Japanese aircraft bomb Pearl Harbor
	1942–1943 Allies and Germany battle for control of North Africa; Soviet victory in Battle of Stalingrad (1943)	**1942 (Jan–March)** Japanese conquer Thailand, Philippines, Malaya
	1943–1944 Red Army slowly pushes Wehrmacht back to Germany	**1942 (June)** United States Navy defeats Japan at Battle of Midway
	1944 (June 6) D-day: U.S., British, and Canadian troops land in Normandy	
1945	**1945 (May 7)** Germany surrenders	**1945 (Aug. 6)** United States drops atomic bomb on Hiroshima
		1945 (Aug. 14) Japan surrenders
		1945–1949 Civil war in China
		1949 Communists defeat Guomindang; Mao proclaims People's Republic (Oct. 1)

purpose in the USSR than in other countries, however. It was not expected to produce consumer goods for a mass market, as in Britain and the United States, or to enrich individuals. Instead, its aim was to increase the power of the Communist Party domestically and the power of the Soviet Union in relation to other countries.

By building up Russia's industry, Stalin was determined to prevent a repetition of the humiliating defeat Russia had suffered at the hands of Germany in 1917. His goal was to quintuple the output of electricity and double that of heavy industry—iron, steel, coal, and machinery—in five years. To do so, he devised the first of a series of **Five-Year Plans,** a system of centralized control copied from the German experience of World War I.

Beginning in October 1928, the Communist Party and government created whole industries and cities from scratch, then recruited millions of peasants and trained them to work in the new factories and mines and offices. In every way except actual fighting, Stalin's Russia resembled a nation at war.

Rapid industrialization hastened environmental changes. Hydroelectric dams turned rivers into strings of reservoirs. Roads, canals, and railroad tracks cut the landscape. Forests and grassland were turned into farmland. From an environmental perspective, the outcome of the Five-Year Plans resembled the transformation that had occurred in the United States and Canada a few decades earlier (see Chapter 25).

Collectivization of Agriculture

Since the Soviet Union was still a predominantly agrarian country, the only way to pay for these massive investments, provide the labor, and feed the millions of new industrial workers was to squeeze the peasantry. Stalin therefore proceeded with the most radical social experiment conceived up to that time: the collectivization of agriculture.

Collectivization meant consolidating small private farms into vast collectives and making the farmers work

The Collectivization of Soviet Agriculture   One of the goals of collectivization was to introduce modern farm machinery. This poster shows delighted farmers operating new tractors and threshers.   (David King Collection)

together in commonly owned fields. Each collective was expected to supply the government with a fixed amount of food and distribute what was left among its members. Machine Tractor Stations leased agricultural machinery to several farms in exchange for the government's share of the crop. Collectives were to become outdoor factories where food was manufactured through the techniques of mass production and the application of machinery. Collectivization was an attempt to replace what Lenin called the peasants' "petty bourgeois" attitudes with an industrial way of life, the only one Communists respected. Collectivization was expected to bring the peasants once and for all under government control so they never again could withhold food supplies as they had done during the period of Lenin's New Economic Policy (see Chapter 30).

When collectivization was announced, the government mounted a massive propaganda campaign and sent party members into the countryside to enlist the farmers' support. At first all seemed to go well, but soon *kulaks*° ("fists"), the better-off peasants, began to resist giving up all their property. When soldiers came to force them into collectives at gunpoint, the kulaks burned their own crops, smashed their own equipment, and slaughtered their own livestock. Within a few months, they slaughtered half of the Soviet Union's horses and cattle and two-thirds of its sheep and goats. In retaliation, Stalin ruthlessly ordered the "liquidation of kulaks as a class" and incited the poor peasants to attack their wealthier neighbors. Over 8 million kulaks were arrested. Many were executed. The rest were sent to slave labor camps, where most starved to death.

The peasants who were left had been the least successful before collectivization and proved to be the least competent after. Many were sent to work in factories. The rest were forbidden to leave their farms. With half of their draft animals gone, they could not plant or harvest enough to meet the swelling demands of the cities. Yet government agents took whatever they could find, leaving little or nothing for the farmers themselves. After bad harvests in 1933 and 1934, a famine swept through the countryside, killing some 5 million people, about one in every twenty farmers.

Stalin's second Five-Year Plan, designed to run from 1933 to 1937, was originally intended to increase the output of consumer goods. But when the Nazis took over Germany in 1933 (see below), Stalin changed the plan to emphasize heavy industries that could produce armaments. Between 1927 and 1937 the Soviet output of metals and machines increased fourteen-fold while consumer goods became scarce and food was rationed. After a decade of Stalinism, the Soviet people were more poorly clothed, fed, and housed than they had been during the years of the New Economic Policy.

Terror and Opportunities

The 1930s brought both terror and new opportunities to the Soviet people. The forced pace of industrialization, the collectivization of agriculture, and the uprooting of millions of people could be accomplished only under duress. To prevent any possible resistance or rebellion, the NKVD, Stalin's secret police force, created a climate of suspicion and fear. The terror that pervaded the country was a

kulaks (COO-lox)

reflection of Stalin's own paranoia, for he distrusted everyone and feared for his life.

As early as 1930, Stalin had hundreds of engineers and technicians arrested on trumped-up charges of counterrevolutionary ideas and sabotage. Three years later, he expelled a million members of the Communist Party—one-third of the membership—on similar charges. He then turned on his most trusted associates.

In December 1934 Sergei Kirov, the party boss of Leningrad (formerly called Petrograd), was assassinated, perhaps on Stalin's orders. Stalin made a public display of mourning Kirov while blaming others for the crime. He then ordered a series of spectacular purge trials in which he accused most of Lenin's associates of "antiparty activities," the worst form of treason. In 1937 he had his eight top generals and many lesser officers charged with treason and executed, leaving the Red Army dangerously weakened. He even executed the head of the dreaded NKVD, which was enforcing the terror. Under torture or psychological pressure, almost all the accused confessed to the "crimes" they were charged with.

While "Old Bolsheviks" and high officials were being put on trial, terror spread steadily downward. The government regularly made demands on people that they could not meet, so everyone was guilty of breaking some regulation or other. People from all walks of life were arrested, sometimes on a mere suspicion or because of a false accusation by a jealous coworker or neighbor, sometimes for expressing a doubt or working too hard or not hard enough, sometimes for being related to someone previously arrested, sometimes for no reason at all. Millions of people were sentenced without a trial. At the height of the terror, some 8 million were sent to *gulags*° (labor camps), where perhaps a million died each year of exposure or malnutrition. To its victims, the terror seemed capricious and random. Yet it turned a sullen and resentful people into docile hard-working subjects of the party.

In spite of the fear and hardships, Stalin's regime received the support of many Soviet citizens. Suddenly, with so many people gone and new industries and cities being built everywhere, there were opportunities for those who remained, especially the poor and the young. Women entered careers and jobs previously closed to them, such as steelworkers, physicians, and office managers; but they retained their household and child-rearing duties, receiving little help from men. People who moved to the cities, worked enthusiastically, and asked no questions could hope to rise into the upper

ranks of the Communist Party, the military, the government, or the professions—where the privileges and rewards were many.

Stalin's brutal methods helped the Soviet Union industrialize faster than any country had ever done. By the late 1930s, the USSR was the world's third largest industrial power, after the United States and Germany. To foreign observers it seemed to be booming with construction projects, production increases, and labor shortages. Even anti-Communist observers admitted that only a planned economy subject to strict government control could avoid the Depression. To millions of Soviet citizens who took pride in the new strength of their country, and to many foreigners who contrasted conditions in the Soviet Union with the unemployment and despair in the West, Stalin's achievement seemed worth any price.

♫

THE DEPRESSION

On October 24, 1929—"Black Thursday"—the New York stock market went into a dive. Within days, stocks lost half of their value, and their value continued to fall for three years. Millions of investors lost money, as did the banks and brokers who had lent them money. People with savings accounts rushed to make withdrawals, causing thousands of banks to collapse.

Economic Crisis What began as a stock-market crash soon turned into the deepest and most widespread depression in history. As consumers reduced their purchases, businesses cut production. General Motors, for example, saw its sales drop by half between 1929 and 1931. Companies laid off thousands of workers, throwing them onto public charity. Business and government agencies replaced their women workers with men, arguing that men had to support their families whereas women worked only for "pin money." Jobless men deserted their families. As farm prices fell, small farmers went bankrupt and lost their land. By mid-1932, the American economy had fallen by half, and unemployment had risen to an unprecedented 25 percent of the work force. Government spending on welfare and public works was unable to restore prosperity. Many observers thought the free-enterprise system would be replaced by bread lines, soup kitchens, men selling apples on street corners, and hoboes riding freight trains.

---

gulag (GOO-log)

Two Views of the American Way   In this classic photograph, *Life* magazine photographer Margaret Bourke-White captured the contrast between advertisers' view of the ideal American family and the reality of mass poverty in a land of plenty.   (Margaret Bourke-White/LIFE Magazine © Time Inc.)

Frightened by the stock-market collapse, the New York banks called in their loans to Germany and Austria. Without American money, Germany and Austria stopped paying reparations to France and Britain, which then could not repay their war loans to America. Governments canceled both reparations payments and war loans, but it was too late to save the world economy.

In 1930 the U.S. government, hoping to protect domestic industries from foreign competition, imposed the Smoot-Hawley tariff, the highest import duty in American history. In retaliation, other countries raised their tariffs in a wave of "beggar thy neighbor" protectionism. The result was to cripple export industries and shrink world trade. By 1931 the Depression had spread to Europe. While global industrial production declined by 36 percent between 1929 and 1932, world trade dropped by a breathtaking 62 percent.

Depression in Industrial Nations

France and Britain escaped the worst of the Depression by making their colonial empires purchase their products rather than the products of other countries. Nations that relied on exports to pay for imported food and fuel, in particular Japan and Germany, suffered much more. In Germany, unemployment reached 6 million by 1932, twice as high as in Britain. Half of the German population lived in poverty. Thousands of teachers and engineers were laid off, and those who kept their jobs saw their salaries cut and their living standards fall. In Japan, the burden of the Depression fell on the farmers and fishermen, who saw their incomes drop sharply. Some, in desperation, revived the ancient practice of selling their daughters.

This massive economic upheaval had profound political repercussions. Many people in capitalist countries began calling for government intervention in the economy. In the United States, Franklin D. Roosevelt was elected president in 1932 on a "New Deal" platform of government programs to stimulate and revitalize the economy. Although the American, British, and French governments intervened in their economies, they remained democratic.

Even government control of a national economy could be jeopardized by the swings of the world market; hence nationalists everywhere yearned for autarchy, or independence from the world economy. Only two industrial nations—the United States and the Soviet Union—even came close to self-sufficiency; two others, Britain and France, survived by trading with their colonial empires. In Germany and Japan, as economic grievances worsened long-festering political resentments, radical politicians took over the economy and turned their nations into machines to make war, hoping to acquire, by war if necessary, empires large enough to support a self-sufficient economy.

Depression in Nonindustrial Regions

The Depression spread to Asia, Africa, and Latin America, but very unevenly. By 1930 India had erected a wall of import duties to protect its infant industries from foreign competition; its living standards stagnated but did not drop. Except for its coastal regions, China was little affected by trade with other countries; as we shall see, its problems were more political than economic.

Countries that depended on exports—sugar from the Caribbean, coffee from Brazil and Colombia, wheat and beef from Argentina, tea from Ceylon and Java, tin from Bolivia, and many other products—were hard hit by the Depression. Malaya, Indochina, and the Dutch East Indies produced most of the world's natural rubber. When automobile production dropped by half in the United States and Europe, so did imports of rubber, devastating the economies of Southeast Asia. During the 1920s, Cuba had been a playground for American tourists who basked in the sun and quaffed liquor forbidden at home by Prohibition. When the Depression hit, the tourists vanished and with them went Cuba's prosperity.

Throughout Latin America, unemployment and homelessness increased markedly. The industrialization of Argentina and Brazil was set back a decade or more. In response to the Depression, military officers seized power in several Latin American countries. Consciously imitating dictatorships emerging in Europe, they imposed authoritarian control over their economies, hoping to stimulate local industries and curb imports.

Outside of the USSR, only southern Africa boomed during the 1930s. As other prices dropped, gold became relatively more valuable. Copper deposits, found in Northern Rhodesia (now Zambia) and the Belgian Congo, proved to be cheaper to mine than Chilean copper. But this mining boom benefited only a small number of European and white South African mine owners. For Africans it was at best a mixed blessing, for mining offered jobs and cash wages to men while women stayed behind in the villages, farming, herding, and raising children without their husbands' help.

THE RISE OF FASCISM

The Russian Revolution and its Stalinist aftermath frightened property owners in Europe and North America. In the democracies of western Europe and North America, where there was little fear of Communist uprisings or electoral victories, middle- and upper-income voters took refuge in conservative politics. Political institutions in southern and Central Europe, in contrast, were frail and lacked popular legitimacy. The war had turned people's hopes of victory to bitter disappointment. Many were bewildered by modernity—with its cities, factories, and department stores—which they blamed on ethnic minorities, especially Jews. In their yearning for a mythical past of family farms and small shops, increasing numbers rejected representative government and sought more dramatic solutions.

Radical politicians quickly learned to use wartime propaganda techniques to appeal to a confused citizenry, especially young and unemployed men. They promised to use any means necessary to bring back full employment, stop the spread of communism, and achieve the territorial conquests that World War I had denied them. They borrowed their tactics from the Bolsheviks and their goals from the war.

Mussolini's Italy

The first country to seek radical answers was Italy. World War I, which had never been popular, left thousands of veterans who found neither pride in their victory nor jobs in the postwar economy. Unemployed veterans and violent youths banded together into *fasci di combattimento* (fighting units) to demand action and intimidate politicians. When workers threatened to strike, factory and property owners hired gangs of these *fascisti* to defend them.

Benito Mussolini (1883–1945) had once been a member of the Socialist Party, but he was expelled for supporting Italy's entry into the war. A spellbinding orator, he quickly became the leader of the **Fascist Party,** which glorified warfare and the Italian nation. By 1921 the party had 300,000 members, many of whom used violent methods to repress strikes, intimidate voters, and seize municipal governments. A year later, Mussolini threatened to march on Rome if he was not appointed prime minister. The government, composed of timid parliamentarians, gave in.

Mussolini proceeded to install Fascist Party members in all government jobs, crush all opposition parties, and jail anyone who criticized him. The party took over the press, public education, and youth activities and gave employers control over their workers. The Fascists lowered living standards but reduced unemployment and provided social security and public services. On the whole, they proved to be neither ruthless radicals nor competent administrators.

What Mussolini and the Fascist movement really excelled at was publicity: bombastic speeches, spectacular parades, news bulletins full of praise for *Il Duce°* ("the leader"), and signs everywhere proclaiming "Il Duce is always right!" Mussolini's genius was to apply the techniques of modern mass communications and advertisement to political life. Billboards, movie footage, and radio news bulletins galvanized the masses in ways never before seen in peacetime. Although his rhetoric was filled with words like *war, violence,* and *struggle,* his foreign policy was cautious. But his techniques of whipping up public enthusiasm were not lost on other radicals. By the 1930s, fascist movements had appeared in most European countries, as well as in Latin America, China, and Japan. Of all of Mussolini's imitators, none was as sinister as Adolf Hitler.

Hitler's Germany

Germany had lost the First World War after coming very close to winning. The hyperinflation of 1923 wiped out the savings of middle-class families. Less than ten years later, the Depression caused more unemployment and misery than in any other country. Millions of Germans blamed Socialists, Jews, and foreigners for their troubles. Few foresaw that they were about to get a dictatorship dedicated to war and mass murder.

Adolf Hitler (1889–1945) was born in Austria, the son of a minor government official. At the start of World War I, he joined the German army and was wounded at the front. He later looked back fondly on the clear lines of authority and the camaraderie he had experienced in battle. After the war, he used his gifts as an orator to lead a political splinter group called the National Socialist German Workers' Party—**Nazis** for short. In 1924 he led a small and unsuccessful uprising in Munich. While serving a brief jail sentence, he wrote *Mein Kampf°* (*My Struggle*), a book in which he outlined his goals and beliefs.

When it was published in 1925, *Mein Kampf* attracted little notice. Its ideas seemed so insane that almost no one took it, or its author, seriously. Hitler's ideas went far beyond ordinary nationalism. He believed that Germany should incorporate all German-speaking people, even those who lived in neighboring countries. He distinguished among a "master race" of Aryans (he meant Germans, Scandinavians, and Britons), a degenerate "Alpine" race of French and Italians, and an inferior race of Russian and eastern European Slavs, who he believed were fit only to be slaves of the master race. He reserved his most intense hatred for Jews, on whom he blamed every disaster that had befallen Germany, especially the defeat of 1918. He glorified violence, interpreting the Darwinian idea of "survival of the fittest" (see Chapter 28) to mean that in a future war the "master race" would defeat and subjugate all others.

His first goal was to repeal the humiliation and military restrictions of the Treaty of Versailles. Then he planned to annex all German-speaking territories to a greater Germany and then conquer *Lebensraum°* (room to live) at the expense of Poland and the USSR. Finally, he planned to eliminate all Jews from Europe.

From 1924 to 1930, Hitler's followers remained a tiny minority, for most Germans found his ideas too extreme. But when the Depression hit, the Nazis gained supporters among the unemployed who believed Nazi promises of jobs for all and among property owners frightened by the growing popularity of Communists. In March 1933, as leader of the largest party in Germany, Hitler became chancellor.

Once in office, he quickly assumed dictatorial power. From the Reichstag° (parliament) he obtained the power to govern by decree, legally ending democracy in Germany. He put Nazis in charge of all government agencies, educational institutions, and professional organizations. He banned all other political parties and threw their leaders into concentration camps. The Nazis deprived Jews of their citizenship and civil rights, prohibited them from marrying "Aryans," ousted them from the professions, and confiscated their property. In August 1934

Il Duce (eel DOO-chay)

Mein Kampf (mine compf)   *Lebensraum* (LAY-bens-rowm)
Reichstag (RIKES-tog)

Hitler the Orator   A masterful public speaker, Adolf Hitler often captivated mass audiences at Nazi Party rallies.   (Roger Viollet)

Hitler proclaimed himself *Führer°* ("leader") and called Germany the "Third Reich" (empire)—the third after the Holy Roman Empire of medieval times and the German Empire of 1871 to 1918.

The Nazis' economic and social policies were spectacularly effective. The government undertook massive public works projects. Businesses got contracts to manufacture weapons for the armed forces. Women, who had entered the work force during and after World War I, were urged to return to "Kinder, Kirche, Küche" (children,

---

Führer (FEW-rer)

church, kitchen), releasing jobs for men. By 1936 business was booming, unemployment was at its lowest level since the 1920s, and living standards were rising. Hitler's popularity soared because most Germans believed their economic well-being outweighed the loss of liberty.

The Road to War, 1933–1939

Hitler's goal was not prosperity or popularity but conquest. As soon as he came to office, he began to build up the armed forces. Meanwhile, he tested the reactions of the other powers through a series of surprise moves followed by protestations of peace.

In 1933 Hitler withdrew Germany from the League of Nations. France and Britain hesitated to retaliate by blockading or invading Germany. Two years later he announced that Germany was going to introduce conscription, build up its army, and create an air force—in violation of the Versailles treaty. Instead of protesting, Britain signed a naval agreement with Germany. The message was clear: neither Britain nor France was willing to risk war by standing up to Germany. The United States, absorbed in its domestic economic problems, reverted to isolationism.

In 1935, emboldened by the weakness of the democracies, Italy invaded Ethiopia, the last independent state in Africa and a member of the League of Nations. The League and the democracies protested but refused to close the Suez Canal to Italian ships or impose an oil embargo. The following year, when Hitler sent troops into the Rhineland on the borders of France and Belgium, the other powers merely protested.

By 1938 Hitler decided his rearmament plans were far enough advanced that he could afford to escalate his demands. In March, Germany invaded Austria. Most of its citizens were German-speakers and accepted the annexation of their country without protest. Then came the turn of Czechoslovakia, where a German-speaking minority lived along the German border. Hitler first demanded their autonomy from Czech rule, then their annexation to Germany. Throughout the summer he threatened to go to war. At the Munich Conference of September 1938, he met with the leaders of France, Britain, and Italy, who gave him everything he wanted without consulting Czechoslovakia. Once again, Hitler learned that aggression paid off and that the democracies would always give in.

The weakness of the democracies—now called "appeasement"—ran counter to the traditional European balance of power. It had three causes. The first was the deep-seated fear of war among all people who had lived through World War I. Unlike the dictators, politicians in the democracies could not ignore their constituents' yearnings for peace. Politicians and most other people believed that the threat of war might go away if they wished for peace fervently enough.

The second cause of appeasement was fear of communism among the conservative politicians who ruled France and Britain. Until very late in the day, they were more afraid of Stalin than of Hitler, for Hitler claimed to respect Christianity and private property. Distrust of the Soviet Union prevented them from recreating the only viable counterweight to Germany: the pre–World War I alliance of Britain, France, and Russia.

The third cause was the very novelty of fascist tactics. Britain's Prime Minister Neville Chamberlain assumed that political leaders (other than the Bolsheviks) were honorable men and that an agreement was as valid as a business contract. Thus, when Hitler promised to incorporate only German-speaking people into Germany and said he had "no further territorial demands," Chamberlain believed him.

After Munich it was too late to stop Hitler, short of war. Germany and Italy were now united in an alliance called the Axis. In March 1939 Germany invaded what was left of Czechoslovakia. Belatedly realizing that Hitler could not be trusted, France and Britain sought Soviet help. Stalin, however, distrusted the "capitalists" as much as they distrusted him. Hitler, meanwhile, offered to divide Poland between Germany and the Soviet Union. On August 23, Stalin accepted. The Nazi-Soviet Pact freed Hitler from the fear of a two-front war and gave Stalin two more years of peace to build up his armies. One week later, on September 1, 1939, German forces swept into Poland. The war was on.

EAST ASIA, 1931–1945

When the Depression hit, China and the United States erected barriers against Japanese imports. The collapse of demand for silk and rice ruined thousands of Japanese farmers; to survive, many sold their daughters into prostitution while their sons flocked to the military. Ultra-nationalists, including young army officers, resented their country's dependence on foreign trade. If only Japan had a colonial empire, they thought, it would not be beholden to the rest of the world. But Europeans and Americans had already taken most potential colonies in Asia. Japan had only Korea, Taiwan, and a railroad in Manchuria. China, however, had not yet been conquered. Japanese nationalists saw the conquest of China, with its vast population and resources, as the solution to their country's problems.

The Manchurian Incident of 1931

Meanwhile, in China the Guomindang° was becoming stronger and preparing to challenge the Japanese presence in Manchuria, a province rich in coal and iron ore. Junior officers in the Japanese army guarding the South Manchurian Railway, frustrated by the caution of their superiors, determined to take action. In September 1931, an explosion on a railroad track, probably staged, gave them an excuse to conquer the entire province. In Tokyo, weak civilian ministers were intimidated by the military. Informed after the fact, they acquiesced to the attack to avoid losing face but privately one said: "From beginning to end the government has been utterly fooled by the army."

When Chinese students, workers, and housewives boycotted Japanese goods, Japanese troops briefly took over Shanghai, China's major industrial city, and the area around Beijing. Japan thereupon recognized the "independence" of Manchuria under the name "Manchukuo°."

The U.S. government condemned the Japanese conquest. The League of Nations refused to recognize Manchukuo and urged the Japanese to remove their troops from China. Persuaded that the Western powers would not fight, Japan simply resigned from the League.

During the next few years, the Japanese built railways and heavy industries in Manchuria and northeastern China and sped up their rearmament. At home, production was diverted to the military, especially to building warships. The government grew more authoritarian, jailing thousands of dissidents. On several occasions, super-patriotic junior officers mutinied or assassinated leading political figures. The mutineers received mild punishments, and generals and admirals sympathetic to their views replaced more moderate civilian politicians.

The Chinese Communists and the Long March

Until the Japanese seized Manchuria, the Chinese government seemed to be consolidating its power and creating the conditions for a national recovery. The main challenge to the government of **Chiang Kai-shek°** came from the Communists. The Chinese Communist Party was founded in 1921 by a handful of intellectuals. For several years it lived in the shadow of the Guomindang, kept there by orders of Joseph Stalin, who expected it to subvert the government from within. All its efforts to manipulate the Guomindang and to recruit members among industrial workers came to nought in

---

Guomindang (gwo-min-dong)   Manchukuo (man-CHEW-coo-oh)
Chiang Kai-shek (chang kie-shek)

1927, when Chiang Kai-shek arrested and executed Communists and labor leaders alike. The few Communists who escaped the mass arrests fled to the remote mountains of Jiangxi°, in southeastern China.

Among them was **Mao Zedong°** (1893–1976), a farmer's son who had left home to study philosophy. He was not a contemplative thinker but a man of action whose first impulse was to call for violent effort: "To be able to leap on horseback and to shoot at the same time; to go from battle to battle; to shake the mountains by one's cries, and the colors of the sky by one's roars of anger." In the early 1920s Mao discovered the works of Karl Marx, joined the Communist Party, and soon became one of its leaders.

In Jiangxi, Mao began studying conditions among the peasants, in whom Communists had previously shown no interest. He planned to redistribute land from the wealthier to the poorer peasants, thereby gaining adherents for the coming struggle with the Guomindang army. In this, he was following the example of innumerable leaders of peasant rebellions over the centuries. His goal, however, was not just a nationalist revolution against the traditional government and foreign intervention, but a complete social revolution from the bottom up. Mao's reliance on the peasantry was a radical departure from Marxist-Leninist ideology, which stressed the backwardness of the peasants and pinned its hopes on the industrial workers. Mao therefore had to be careful to cloak his pragmatic tactics in Communist rhetoric in order to allay the suspicions of Stalin and his agents.

Mao was also an advocate of women's equality. Radical ideas such as those of Margaret Sanger, the American leader of the birth-control movement, and the feminist play *A Doll's House* by the Norwegian playwright Henrik Ibsen inspired veterans of the May Fourth Movement and young women attending universities and medical or nursing schools. Before 1927 the Communists had organized the women who worked in Shanghai's textile mills, the most exploited of all Chinese workers. Later, in their mountain stronghold in Jiangxi, they organized women farmers, allowed divorce, and banned arranged marriages and footbinding. But they did not admit women to leadership positions, for the party was still run by men whose primary task was warfare.

The Guomindang army pursued the Communists into the mountains, building small forts throughout the countryside. Rather than risk direct confrontations, Mao responded with guerrilla warfare. He harassed the army at its weak points with hit-and-run tactics, relying on the terrain and the support of the peasantry. Government

Mao on the Long March   In 1934–1935, Mao Zedong led his rag-tag army of guerrillas across the rugged mountains of southern and western China. In this romanticized painting, young Mao is speaking to a group of soldiers in spotless uniforms who look up at him with worshipful expressions.   (Library of Congress)

troops often mistreated civilians, but Mao insisted that his soldiers help the peasants, pay a fair price for food and supplies, and treat women with respect.

In spite of their good relations with the peasants of Jiangxi, the Communists gradually found themselves encircled by government forces. In 1934 Mao and his followers decided to break out of the southern mountains and trek to Shaanxi°, an even more remote province in northwestern China. The so-called **Long March** took them 6,000 miles (nearly 9,700 kilometers) in one year, 17 miles (27 kilometers) a day over desolate mountains and through swamps and deserts, pursued

Jiangxi (jang -she)   **Mao Zedong** (ma-oh zay-dong)

Shaanxi (SHAWN-she)

by the army and bombed by Chiang's aircraft. Of the 100,000 Communists who left Jiangxi in October 1934, only 4,000 reached Shaanxi a year later (see Map 31.1). Chiang's government thought it was finally rid of the Communists.

The Sino-Japanese War, 1937–1945

In Japan, politicians, senior officers, and business leaders disagreed on how to solve their country's economic problems. Some proposed a quick conquest of China; others advocated war with the Soviet Union. While their superiors hesitated, junior officers decided to take matters into their own hands.

On July 7, 1937, Japanese troops attacked Chinese forces near Beijing. As in 1931, the junior officers who ordered the attack quickly obtained the support of their commanders and then, reluctantly, of the government. Within weeks, Japanese troops seized Beijing, Tianjin, Shanghai, and other coastal cities, and the Japanese navy blockaded the entire coast of China.

Once again, the United States and the League of Nations denounced the Japanese atrocities. Yet the Western powers were too preoccupied with events in Europe and with their own economic problems to risk a military confrontation in Asia. When the Japanese sank a U.S. gunboat and shelled a British ship on the Yangzi River, the U.S. and British governments responded only with righteous indignation and pious resolutions.

The Chinese armies were large and fought bravely, but they were poorly led and armed and lost every battle. Japanese planes bombed Nanjing, Hankou, and Canton, while on the ground, soldiers broke dikes and burned villages, killing thousands of civilians. Within a year, Japan controlled the coastal provinces of China and the lower Yangzi and Yellow River Valleys, China's richest and most populated regions (see Map 31.1).

In spite of Japanese organizational and fighting skills, the attack on China did not bring the victory Japan had hoped for. The Chinese people continued to resist, either in the army or, increasingly, with the Communist guerrilla forces. Japan's periodic attempts to turn the tide by conquering one more piece of China only pushed Japan deeper into the quagmire. For the Japanese people, life became harsher and more repressive as taxes rose, food and fuel became scarce, and more and more young men were drafted. Japanese leaders belatedly realized that the war with China was a drain on the Japanese economy and manpower and that their war machine was becoming increasingly dependent on the United States for steel and machine tools and for nine-tenths of its oil.

Warfare between Chinese and Japanese was incredibly violent. In the winter of 1937–1938, Japanese troops took Nanjing, raped 20,000 women, killed 200,000 prisoners and civilians, and looted and burned the city. To slow them down, Chiang ordered the Yellow River dikes blasted open, causing a flood that destroyed 4,000 villages, killed 890,000 people, and made 12.5 million homeless. Two years later, when the Communists ordered a massive offensive, the Japanese retaliated with a "kill all, burn all, loot all" campaign, destroying hundreds of villages down to the last person, building, and farm animal.

The Chinese government, led by Chiang Kai-shek, escaped to the mountains of Sichuan in the center of the country. There he built up a huge army, not to fight Japan but to prepare for a future confrontation with the Communists. The army drafted over 3 million men, even though it had only a million rifles and could not provide food or clothing for all its soldiers. The Guomindang raised farmers' taxes, even when famine forced farmers to eat the bark of trees. Such taxes were not enough to support both a large army and the thousands of government officials and hangers-on who had fled to Sichuan. To avoid taxing its wealthy supporters, the government printed money, causing inflation, hoarding, and corruption.

From his capital of Yan'an in Shaanxi province, Mao also built up his army and formed a government. Until early 1941, he received a little aid from the Soviet Union; then, after Stalin signed a Soviet-Japanese Neutrality Pact, none at all. Unlike the Guomindang, the Communists listened to the grievances of the peasants, especially the poor, to whom they distributed land confiscated from wealthy landowners. They imposed rigid discipline on their officials and soldiers and tolerated no dissent or criticism from intellectuals. Though they had few weapons, the Communists obtained support and intelligence from farmers in Japanese-occupied territory. They turned military reversals into propaganda victories, presenting themselves as the only group in China that was serious about fighting the Japanese.

Map 31.1 Chinese Communist Movements and the Sino-Japanese War, to 1938 During the 1930s, China was the scene of a three-way war. The Nationalist government attacked and pursued the Communists, who escaped into the mountains of Shaanxi. Meanwhile, Japanese forces, having seized Manchuria in 1931, attacked China in 1937 and quickly conquered its eastern provinces.

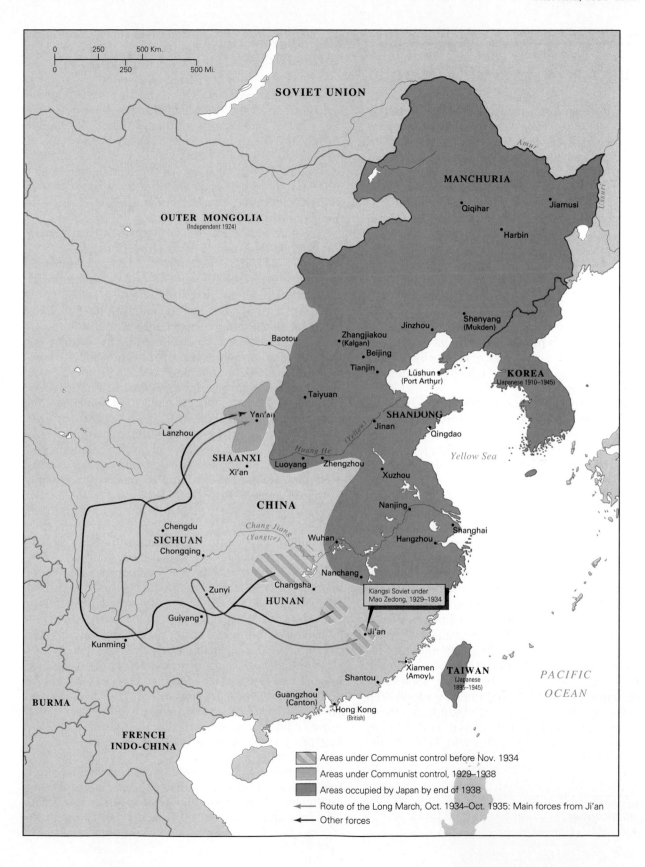

SOVIET UNION

MANCHURIA

Qiqihar
Jiamusi

Amur

Ussuri

OUTER MONGOLIA
(Independent 1924)

Harbin

Shenyang
(Mukden)

Jinzhou

Baotou

Zhangjiakou
(Kalgan)

Beijing

Tianjin

KOREA
(Japanese 1910–1945)

Lüshun
(Port Arthur)

Taiyuan

SHANDONG

Yan'an

Jinan

Lanzhou

Qingdao

Huang He   (Yellow)

SHAANXI

Yellow Sea

Xi'an

Luoyang   Zhengzhou

Xuzhou

CHINA

Nanjing

Chengdu

Chang Jiang
(Yangtze)

Shanghai

SICHUAN

Wuhan

Hangzhou

Chongqing

Nanchang

Kiangsi Soviet under
Mao Zedong, 1929–1934

Zunyi

Changsha

Guiyang   HUNAN

Ji'an

Kunming

Xiamen
(Amoy)

TAIWAN
(Japanese
1895–1945)

Shantou

PACIFIC
OCEAN

BURMA

Guangzhou
(Canton)

Hong Kong
(British)

FRENCH
INDO-CHINA

Areas under Communist control before Nov. 1934

Areas under Communist control, 1929–1938

Areas occupied by Japan by end of 1938

Route of the Long March, Oct. 1934–Oct. 1935: Main forces from Ji'an

Other forces

THE SECOND WORLD WAR

Many people feared the Second World War would be a repetition of the First. Instead, it was much bigger in every way. It was fought around the world, from Norway to New Guinea, from Hawaii to Egypt, and on every ocean. It killed far more people than World War I. It was a total war involving all productive forces and all civilians, and it showed how effectively industry, science, and nationalism could be channeled into mass destruction.

The War of Movement

Defensive maneuvers had dominated in World War I. In World War II, motorized weapons gave back the advantage to the offensive. Opposing forces moved fast, their victories hinging as much on the aggressive spirit of their commanders and the military intelligence they obtained as on numbers of troops or firepower.

The Wehrmacht°, or German armed forces, was the first to learn this lesson. It not only had tanks, trucks, and fighter planes but perfected their combined use in a tactic called *blitzkrieg*° (lightning war): fighter planes scattered enemy troops and disrupted communications, and tanks punctured the enemy's defenses and then, with the help of the infantry, encircled and captured enemy troops. At sea, the navies of both Japan and the United States had developed aircraft carriers that could launch planes against targets hundreds of miles away.

Yet the very size and mobility of the opposing forces made the fighting far different from any the world had ever seen. Instead of engaging in localized battles, armies ranged over vast theaters of operation. Countries were conquered in a matter of days or weeks. The belligerents mobilized the economies of entire continents, squeezing them for every possible resource. They tried not only to defeat their enemies' armed forces but—by means of blockades, submarine attacks on shipping, and bombing raids on industrial areas—to damage the economies that supported those armed forces. They thought of civilians not as innocent bystanders but as legitimate targets and, later, as vermin to be exterminated.

Wehrmacht (VAIR-mokt)
blitzkrieg (BLITS-creeg)

War in Europe and North Africa

It took less than a month for the Wehrmacht to conquer Poland. Britain and France declared war on Germany but took no military action. Meanwhile, the Soviet Union invaded eastern Poland and the Baltic republics of Lithuania, Latvia, and Estonia. Although the Poles fought bravely, the Polish infantry and cavalry were no match for German or Russian tanks. During the winter of 1939–1940, Germany and the Western democracies faced each other in what soldiers called a "phony war" and watched as the Soviet Union attacked Finland, which resisted for many months.

In March 1940, Hitler went on the offensive again, conquering Denmark, Norway, the Netherlands, and Belgium in less than two months. In May, he attacked France. Although the French army had as many soldiers, tanks, and aircraft as the Wehrmacht, its morale was low and it quickly collapsed. By the end of June, Hitler was master of all of Europe between Russia and Spain.

Germany still had to face one enemy: Britain. The British had no army to speak of, but they had other assets: the English Channel, the Royal Navy and Air Force, and a tough new prime minister, Winston Churchill. The Germans knew they could invade Britain only by gaining control of the airspace over the Channel, so they launched a massive air attack—the Battle of Britain—lasting from June through September. They failed, however, because the Royal Air Force had better fighters and used radar and code-breaking to detect approaching German planes.

Frustrated in the west, Hitler turned his attention eastward. So far he had gotten the utmost cooperation from Stalin, who supplied Germany with grain, oil, and strategic raw materials. Yet he had always wanted to conquer lebensraum in the east and enslave the Slavic peoples who lived there, and he feared that if he waited, Stalin would build up a dangerously strong army. In June 1941 he launched the largest attack in history, with 3 million soldiers and thousands of planes and tanks. Within five months the Wehrmacht conquered the Baltic states, Ukraine, and half of European Russia, captured a million prisoners of war, and stood at the very gates of Moscow and Leningrad (now St. Petersburg). The USSR seemed on the verge of collapse when suddenly the weather turned cold, machines froze, and the fighting came to a halt. Like Napoleon, Hitler had ignored the environment of Russia to his peril.

The next spring the Wehrmacht renewed its offensive. It surrounded Leningrad in a siege that was to cost a million lives. Leaving Moscow aside, it turned toward the Caucasus and its oil wells. In August, the Germans at-

The Enigma Machine   During World War II, German armed forces used Enigma machines like the one seen here in the vehicle of a German tank commander. With Enigmas, they could encrypt and decode radio messages, keeping them secret (they believed) from enemy code-breakers.   (Brian Johnson)

tacked **Stalingrad** (now Volgagrad), the key to the Volga River and the supply of oil. For months, German and Soviet soldiers fought over every street and every house. When winter came, the Red Army counterattacked and encircled the city. In February 1943 the remnants of the German army in Stalingrad surrendered. Hitler had lost his greatest gamble (see Map 31.2).

From Europe, the war spread to Africa. When France fell in 1940, Mussolini began imagining himself a latter-day Roman emperor and decided the time had come to realize his imperial ambitions. Italian forces quickly overran British Somaliland, then invaded Egypt. Their victories were ephemeral, however, for when the British counterattacked, Italian resistance crumbled. During 1941, British forces conquered Italian East Africa and invaded Libya as well. The Italian rout in North Africa

brought the Germans to their rescue. During 1942 the German army and the forces of the British Empire (now known as the Commonwealth) seesawed back and forth across the deserts of Libya and Egypt. At **El Alamein** in northern Egypt the British prevailed because they had more weapons and supplies. Thanks to their success at breaking German codes, they also were better informed about their enemies' plans. The Germans were finally expelled from Africa in May 1943.

War in Asia and the Pacific

The fall of France and the involvement of Britain and the USSR against Germany presented Japan with the opportunity it had been looking for. Suddenly the European colonies in Southeast Asia, with their abundant oil, rubber, and other strategic materials, seemed ripe for the taking. In July 1941, the French government allowed Japanese forces to occupy Indochina. Instead of merely complaining, the United States and Britain stopped shipments of steel, scrap iron, oil, and other products that Japan desperately needed. This left Japan with three alternatives: accept the shame and humiliation of giving up its conquests, as the Americans insisted; face economic ruin; or widen the war. Japan chose war (see Society and Culture: Preparing for Combat).

Admiral Isoroku Yamamoto, commander of the Japanese fleet, told Prime Minister Fumimaro Konoye: "If I am told to fight regardless of the consequences, I shall run wild for the first six months or a year, but I have utterly no confidence for the second or third year. . . . I hope that you will endeavor to avoid a Japanese-American war." Finally they agreed on a plan for a surprise attack on the United States Navy, followed by an invasion of Southeast Asia. They knew they could not hope to defeat the United States, but they calculated that the shock of the attack would be so great that isolationist Americans would accept the Japanese conquest of Southeast Asia as readily as they had acquiesced to Hitler's conquests in Europe.

On December 7, 1941, Japanese planes bombed the U.S. naval base at **Pearl Harbor,** Hawaii, sinking or damaging scores of warships but missing the aircraft carriers, which were at sea. Then, between January and March 1942, the Japanese bombed Hong Kong and Singapore and invaded Thailand, the Philippines, and Malaya. Within a few months they occupied all of Southeast Asia and the Dutch East Indies. The Japanese claimed to be liberating the inhabitants of these lands from European colonialism. But they soon began to confiscate food and raw materials and demand heavy labor from the

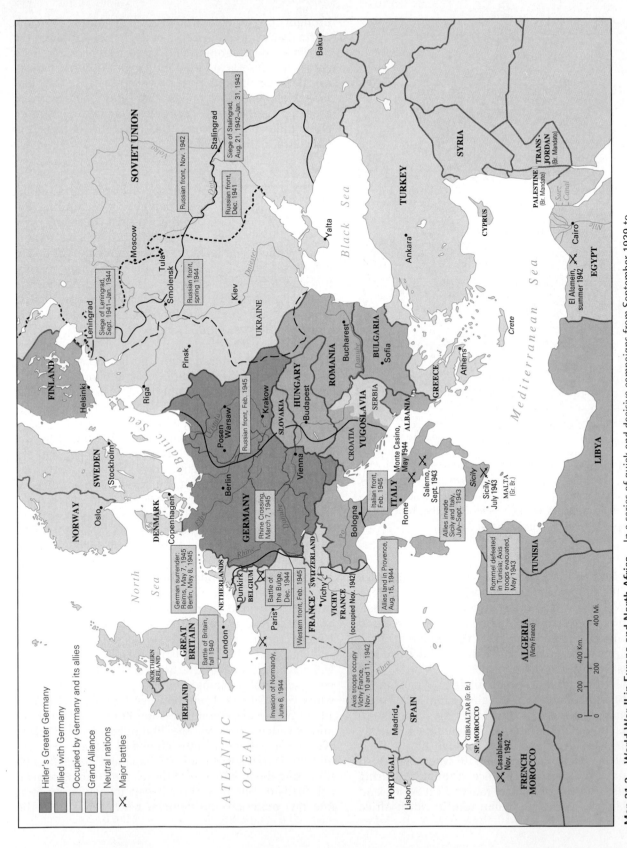

Map 31.2   World War II in Europe and North Africa   In a series of quick and decisive campaigns from September 1939 to December 1941, German forces overran much of Europe and North Africa. There followed three years of bitter fighting as the Allies slowly pushed the Germans back. This map shows the maximum extent of Germany's conquests and alliances, as well as the key battles and the front lines at various times.

Legend:
- Hitler's Greater Germany
- Allied with Germany
- Occupied by Germany and its allies
- Grand Alliance
- Neutral nations
- ✗ Major battles

Map labels:
SOVIET UNION · Baku · Stalingrad · Siege of Stalingrad, Aug. 21, 1942–Jan. 31, 1943 · Russian front, Nov. 1942 · Russian front, Dec. 1941 · Moscow · Tula · Smolensk · Russian front, spring 1944 · Kiev · Leningrad · Siege of Leningrad, Sept. 1941–Jan. 1944 · Pinsk · UKRAINE · Riga · FINLAND · Helsinki · SWEDEN · Stockholm · NORWAY · Oslo · DENMARK · Copenhagen · Warsaw · Posen · Krakow · Russian front, Feb. 1945 · SLOVAKIA · HUNGARY · Budapest · Vienna · Berlin · GERMANY · Rhine Crossing, March 7, 1945 · German surrender: Reims, May 7, 1945; Berlin, May 8, 1945 · NETHERLANDS · Dunkirk · BELGIUM · Battle of the Bulge, Dec. 1944 · Paris · Western front, Feb. 1945 · FRANCE · SWITZERLAND · VICHY FRANCE (occupied Nov. 1942) · Vichy · Allies land in Provence, Aug. 15, 1944 · Invasion of Normandy, June 6, 1944 · GREAT BRITAIN · London · Battle of Britain, fall 1940 · IRELAND · NORTHERN IRELAND · ATLANTIC OCEAN · North Sea · Baltic Sea · ROMANIA · Bucharest · BULGARIA · Sofia · CROATIA · SERBIA · YUGOSLAVIA · ALBANIA · GREECE · Athens · Crete · TURKEY · Ankara · CYPRUS · SYRIA · PALESTINE (Br. Mandate) · TRANS-JORDAN (Br. Mandate) · Suez Canal · EGYPT · Cairo · Nile · El Alamein, summer 1942 · Black Sea · Mediterranean Sea · Yalta · ITALY · Rome · Monte Casino, May 1944 · Salerno, Sept. 1943 · Italian front, Feb. 1945 · Bologna · Sicily, July 1943 · Allies invade Sicily and Italy, July–Sept. 1943 · MALTA (Gr. Br.) · LIBYA · TUNISIA · Rommel defeated in Tunisia; Axis troops evacuated, May 1943 · ALGERIA (Vichy France) · Casablanca, Nov. 1942 · FRENCH MOROCCO · SP. MOROCCO · GIBRALTAR (Gr. Br.) · SPAIN · Madrid · PORTUGAL · Lisbon · Ebro · Axis troops occupy Vichy France, Nov. 10 and 11, 1942

Scale: 0   200   400 Mi. · 0   200   400 Km.

Preparing for Combat

All armies train their recruits to face the violence of battle. Tominaga Shozo, a young officer in the Japanese army, describes his training in brutality. As you read this passage, compare it to the experience of battle in the First World War, as described by Erich Maria Remarque in the Society and Culture feature in Chapter 30.

It was July 30, 1941, when I reported in. They took me to the infantry company where I had been assigned as a second lieutenant. I was fresh from officer school. "These men are the members of the second platoon" was my only introduction to those who would be under my command. I'll never forget meeting them. . . . When I looked at the men of my platoon I was stunned—they had evil eyes. They weren't human eyes but the eyes of leopards or tigers. . . .

The next-to-last day of the exercise, Second Lieutenant Tanaka took us to the detention center. Pointing at the people in a room, all Chinese, he announced, "These are the raw materials for your trial of courage." We were astonished at how thin and emaciated they looked. Tanaka told us, "They haven't been fed for several days, so they'll be ready for their part in tomorrow's plan." He said that it was to be a test to see if we were qualified to be platoon leaders. He said we wouldn't be qualified if we couldn't chop off a head.

On the final day, we were taken out to the site of our trial. Twenty-four prisoners were squatting there with their hands tied behind their backs. They were blindfolded. A big hole had been dug—ten meters long, and more than three meters deep. The regimental commander, the battalion commanders, and the company commanders all took the seats arranged for them. Second Lieutenant Tanaka bowed to the regimental commander and reported, "We shall now begin." He ordered a soldier on fatigue duty to haul one of the prisoners to the edge of the pit; the prisoner was kicked when he resisted. The soldier finally dragged him over and forced him to his knees. Tanaka turned toward us and looked into each of our faces in turn. "Heads should be cut off like this," he said, unsheathing his army sword. He scooped water from a bucket with a dipper. Then poured it over both sides of the blade. Swishing off the water, he raised his sword in a long arc. Standing behind the prisoners, Tanaka steadied himself, legs spread apart, and cut off the man's head with a shout, "Yo!" The head flew more than a meter away. Blood spurted up in two fountains from the body and sprayed the hole.

After witnessing this demonstration, Lieutenant Tominaga Shozo is required to do the same to another prisoner. He writes:

At that moment I felt something change inside me. I don't know how to put it, but I gained strength somewhere in my gut. . . . We returned to our companies. Until that day I had been overwhelmed by the sharp eyes of my men when I called the roll each night. That night I realized I was not self-conscious at all in front of them. I didn't even find their eyes evil anymore.

Why did Tominaga Shozo first think the soldiers had "evil eyes," then change his mind? What was the purpose of training officers to kill prisoners?

Source: Tominaga Shozo, "Qualifying as a Leader," in Haruko Taya Cook and Theodore F. Cook, *Japan at War: An Oral History* (New York: New Press, 1992), 40–41. Copyright © 1992. Reprinted by permission of The New Press.

---

inhabitants, whom they treated with contempt. Those who protested were brutally punished.

Japan's dream of an East Asian empire seemed within reach, for its victories surpassed even Hitler's in Europe. Yamamoto's fears were justified, however, because the United States, far from being cowed into submission, joined Britain and the Soviet Union in an alliance called the United Nations (or the Allies) and began preparing for war. In April 1942, American planes bombed Tokyo. In May the United States Navy defeated a Japanese fleet in the Coral Sea, ending Japanese plans to conquer Australia. A month later, at the **Battle of Midway,** Japan lost four of its six largest aircraft carriers. Japan did not have enough industry to replace them, for its war production was only one-tenth that of the United States. In the vastness of the Pacific Ocean, aircraft carriers held the key to victory, and without them, Japan faced a long and hopeless war (see Map 31.3).

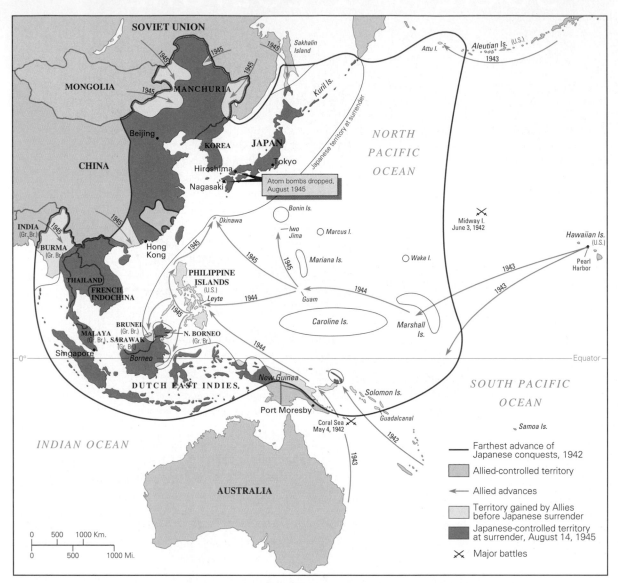

Map 31.3   World War II in Asia and the Pacific   After having conquered much of China between 1937 and 1941, Japanese forces launched a sudden attack on Southeast Asia, Indonesia, and the Pacific in late 1941 and early 1942. American forces slowly reconquered the Pacific islands and the Philippines until August 1945, when the atomic bombing of Hiroshima and Nagasaki forced Japan's surrender.

The End of the War   After the Battle of Stalingrad, the advantage on the Eastern Front shifted to the Soviet Union. By 1943 the Red Army was receiving a growing stream of supplies from factories in Russia and the United States. Slowly at first and then with increasing vigor, it pushed the Wehrmacht back toward Germany.

The Western powers, meanwhile, staged two invasions of Europe. Beginning in July 1943, they captured Sicily and invaded Italy. Mussolini resigned and Italy signed an armistice, but German troops held off the Allied advance for two years. Then on June 6, 1944—forever after known as D-day—156,000 British, American, and Canadian troops landed on the coast of Normandy in western France—the largest shipborne assault ever staged. Within a week, the Allies had more troops in France than Germany did, and by September Germany faced an Allied army of over 2 million men with half a million vehicles of all sorts. Although the Red Army was on the eastern border of Germany, ready for the final

Hiroshima After the Atomic Bomb   On August 6, 1945, an atomic bomb destroyed the city, killing over fifty thousand people. This photo shows the devastation of the city center, where only a few concrete buildings remained standing.   (Wide World Photos)

push, Hitler transferred part of the Wehrmacht westward. Despite overwhelming odds, Germany held out for almost a year, a result of the fighting qualities of its soldiers and the terror inspired by the Nazi regime, which commanded obedience to the end. On May 7, 1945, a week after Hitler committed suicide, German military leaders surrendered.

Japan fought on a while longer, in large part because the United States had aimed most of its war effort at Germany. In the Pacific, U.S. forces "leap-frogged" some heavily fortified Japanese island bases in order to capture others closer to Japan itself. By June 1944, U.S. bombers were able to attack Japan. Meanwhile, U.S. submarines sank ever larger numbers of Japanese merchant ships, gradually cutting Japan off from its sources of oil and other raw materials. In 1944 a terrible earthquake devastated the city of Nagoya, compounding the misery of war and bombing raids. After May 1945, with the Japanese air force grounded for lack of fuel, U.S. planes began destroying Japanese shipping, industries, and cities at will.

Even as their homeland was being pounded, the Japanese still held strong positions in Asia. At first, Asian nationalists such as the Indonesian Achmed Sukarno

were glad to get rid of the white colonialists and welcomed the Japanese. Yet despite its name, "Greater East Asian Co-Prosperity Sphere," the Japanese occupation was harsh and brutal. By 1945 Asians were eager to see the Japanese leave but not to welcome back the Europeans; instead, they looked forward to independence (see Chapters 32 and 33).

On August 6, 1945, the United States dropped an atomic bomb on **Hiroshima,** killing some 80,000 people in a flash and leaving about 120,000 more to die an agonizing death from burns and radiation. Three days later, another atomic bomb destroyed Nagasaki. Were these atomic weapons necessary? At the time, Americans believed that the conquest of the Japanese homeland would take more than a year and cost the lives of hundreds of thousands of American soldiers. Although some Japanese were determined to fight to the bitter end, others were willing to surrender if they could retain their emperor. Had the Allies agreed sooner to keep the monarchy, Japan might have surrendered without the nuclear devastation. On August 14, Japan offered to surrender and Emperor Hirohito himself gave the order to lay down arms. Two weeks later, Japanese leaders signed the terms of surrender. The war was officially over.

Chinese Civil War and Communist Victory

The formal Japanese surrender in September 1945 came as a surprise to the Guomindang. American transport planes flew Guomindang officials and troops to all the cities of China. The United States gave millions of dollars of aid and weapons to the Guomindang, all the while urging "national unity" and a "coalition government" with the Communists. But Chiang used American aid and all other means available to prepare for a civil war. By late 1945 he had an army of 2.7 million, more than twice the size of the Communist forces.

From 1945 to 1949 the contest between the Guomindang and the Communists intensified. Guomindang forces started with many advantages: more troops and weapons, U.S. support, and control of China's cities. But their behavior eroded whatever popular support they had. As they moved into formerly Japanese-held territory, they acted like an occupation force. They taxed the people they "liberated" more heavily than the Japanese had, looted businesses, confiscated supplies, and enriched themselves at the expense of the population. To pay its bills, Chiang's government printed money so fast that it soon lost all its value, ruining merchants and causing hoarding and shortages. In the countryside, the Guomindang's brutality alienated the peasants.

Meanwhile, the Communists obtained Japanese equipment seized by the Soviets in the last weeks of the war and American weapons brought over by deserting Guomindang soldiers. In Manchuria, where they were strongest, they pushed through a radical land reform program, distributing the properties of wealthy landowners among the poorest peasants. In battles against government forces, the higher morale and popular support they enjoyed outweighed the heavy equipment of the Guomindang, whose soldiers began deserting by the thousands.

In April 1947, as Chinese Communist forces surrounded Nanjing, the British frigate *Amethyst* sailed up the Yangzi River to evacuate British civilians. Dozens of times since the Opium War of 1839–1842, foreign powers had dispatched warships up the rivers of China to rescue their citizens, enforce their treaty rights, or intimidate the Chinese. Foreign warships deep in the heart of China were the very symbols of its weakness. This time, however, Chinese Communist artillery damaged the *Amethyst* and beat back other British warships sent to its rescue.

By 1949 the Guomindang armies were collapsing everywhere, defeated more by their own greed and ineptness than by the Communists. As the Communists advanced, high-ranking members of the Guomindang fled to Taiwan, protected from the mainland by the United States Navy. On October 1, 1949, Mao Zedong announced the founding of the People's Republic of China.

THE CHARACTER OF WARFARE

The war left an enormous death toll. Recent estimates place the figure at close to 60 million deaths, six to eight times more than in World War I. Over half of the dead were civilian victims of massacres, famines, or bombs. The Soviet Union lost between 20 million and 25 million people, more than any other country. China suffered 15 million deaths; Poland lost some 6 million, of whom half were Jewish; the Jewish people lost another 3 million outside Poland. Over 4 million Germans and over 2 million Japanese died. In much of the world, almost every family mourned one or more of its members. In contrast, Great Britain lost 400,000 people, the United States only 300,000.

Many parts of the world were flooded with refugees. Some 90 million Chinese fled the Japanese advance. In Europe, millions fled from the Nazis or the Red Army or were herded back and forth on government orders. Many refugees never returned to their homes, creating new ethnic mixtures more reminiscent of the New World than of the Old.

One reason for the terrible toll in human lives and suffering was a change in moral values, as belligerents identified not just soldiers but entire peoples as enemies. Some belligerents even labeled their own ethnic minorities as "enemies." Another reason for the devastation was the appearance of new technologies that carried destruction deep into enemy territory far beyond the traditional battlefields. Let us consider the new technologies of warfare, the changes in morality, and their lethal combination.

The War of Science

As fighting spread around the world, the features that had characterized the early years of the war—the mobilization of manpower and economies and the mobility of the armed forces—grew increasingly powerful. Meanwhile, new aspects of war took on a growing importance. One of these was the impact of science on the technology of warfare. Chemists found ways to make synthetic rubber from coal or oil. Physicists perfected radar, which warned of approaching enemy aircraft and submarines. Cryptanalysts broke enemy codes and were able to penetrate secret military communications. Pharmacologists developed antibiotics that saved the lives of countless wounded soldiers, who in any earlier war would have died of infections (see Environment and Technology: Biomedical Technologies).

Biomedical Technologies

Life expectancy at birth has nearly doubled in the past 150 years. Even in the poorest countries, life expectancy has risen from forty to sixty or seventy years. The cause of this remarkable change is threefold: clean water, immunizations, and antibiotics.

The realization that drinking water can spread disease came first to Dr. Charles Snow, who noticed the correlation between deaths from cholera and the water from a particular pump in London during an epidemic in 1854. Since then, public health officials have been very conscious of the quality of drinking water, although only wealthy cities can afford to purify and chlorinate water for all their inhabitants.

The practice of immunization goes back to the eighteenth century, when physicians in Turkey and in Europe applied infected pus from a person with smallpox (variolation) or an animal with cowpox (vaccination) to healthy persons to build up their resistance to smallpox. By the end of the nineteenth century, it became clear that immunity to many diseases could be conferred by injections of weakened bacteria. Immunizations offer the single most effective way to prevent childhood diseases and thereby increase life expectancy.

Antibiotics are more recent. In 1928 Dr. Alexander Fleming discovered that a certain mold, *Penicillin notatum,* could kill bacteria. Antibiotics were first used in large quantities in the Second World War. Along with two other innovations—synthetic antimalarial drugs and blood transfusions—antibiotics helped cut the fatality of battlefield wounds from 11 percent in World War I to 3 percent in World War II.

The remarkable success of these technologies has led people to consider good health their natural birthright. Unfortunately, the victory over disease is temporary at best. The abuse of antibiotics and of antibacterial products encourages the growth of new strains of old diseases, such as tuberculosis, which can resist all known antibiotics. And although bacterial diseases are no longer as prevalent as they once were, humans are still susceptible to viral afflictions such as influenza and AIDS.

Biotechnology in Action Campaigns to immunize children against diseases reached even remote villages, as here in Thailand. (Peter Charlesworth/Saba)

Aircraft development was especially striking. As war approached, German, British, and Japanese aircraft manufacturers developed fast, maneuverable fighter planes. U.S. industry produced aircraft of every sort but was especially noted for its heavy bombers designed to fly in huge formations and drop tons of bombs on enemy cities. The Japanese developed the Mitsubishi "Zero" fighter plane—light, fast, and agile but dangerous to fly. Unable to produce heavy planes in large numbers, Germany responded with radically new designs, including the first jet fighters, low-flying buzz bombs, and, finally, V-2 missiles, against which there was no warning or defense.

Military planners no longer dismissed the creations of civilian inventors, as they had done before World War I. Now they expected scientists to furnish secret weapons that could doom the enemy. In October 1939, President Roosevelt received a letter from physicist Albert Einstein, a Jewish refugee from Nazism, warning of the dangers of nuclear power: "There is no doubt that sub-atomic energy is available all around us, and that one day man will release and control its almost infinite power. We cannot prevent him from doing so and can only hope that he will not use it exclusively in blowing up his next door neighbor." Fearing that Germany might develop a nuclear bomb first, Roosevelt placed the vast resources of the U.S. government at the disposal of physicists and engineers, both Americans and refugees from Europe. By 1945 they had built two atomic bombs, each one powerful enough to annihilate an entire city.

Bombing Raids

German bombers damaged Warsaw in 1939 and Rotterdam and London in 1940. Yet Germany lacked a strategic bomber force capable of destroying whole cities. In this area, the British and Americans excelled. Since it was very hard to pinpoint individual buildings, especially at night, the British Air Staff under British Air Chief Marshal Arthur "Bomber" Harris decided that "operations should now be focused on the morale of the enemy civilian population and in particular the industrial workers."

In May 1942, 1,000 British planes dropped incendiary bombs on Cologne, setting fire to most of the old city. Between July 24 and August 2, 1943, 3,330 British and Americans bombers set fire to Hamburg, killing 50,000 people, mostly women and children. Later raids destroyed Berlin, Dresden, and other German cities. All in all, the bombing raids against Germany killed 600,000 people—more than half of them women and children— and injured 800,000. If the air strategists had hoped thereby to break the morale of the German people, they failed. German armament production continued to increase until late 1944, and the population remained obedient and hard working. The only effective bombing raids were those directed against oil depots and synthetic fuel plants; by early 1945, they had almost brought the German war effort to a standstill.

Japanese cities were also the targets of American bombing raids. As early as April 1942, sixteen planes launched from an aircraft carrier bombed Tokyo. Later, as American forces captured islands close to Japan, the raids intensified. Their effect was even more devastating than the fire-bombing of German cities, for Japanese cities were made of wood. In March 1945, bombs set Tokyo ablaze, killing 80,000 people and leaving a million homeless. It was a portent of worse destruction to come.

The Holocaust

In World War II, for the first time, more civilians than soldiers were deliberately put to death. The champions in the art of killing defenseless civilians were the Nazis. Their murders were not the accidental byproducts of some military goal but a calculated policy of exterminating whole races of people.

Their first targets were Jews. Soon after Hitler came to power, he deprived German Jews of their citizenship and legal rights. When eastern Europe fell under Nazi rule, the Nazis herded its large Jewish population into ghettos in the major cities, where many died of starvation and disease. Then, in early 1942, the Nazis decided to carry out Hitler's "final solution to the Jewish problem" by applying modern industrial methods to the slaughter of human beings. German companies built huge extermination camps in eastern Europe. Every day, trainloads of cattle cars arrived at the camps and disgorged thousands of captives and the corpses of those who had died of starvation or asphyxiation along the way. The strongest survivors were put to work and fed almost nothing until they died. Women, children, the elderly, and the sick were shoved into gas chambers and asphyxiated with poison gas. **Auschwitz,** the biggest camp, was a giant industrial complex designed to kill up to twelve thousand people a day. Most horrifying of all were the tortures inflicted on prisoners selected by Nazi doctors for "medical experiments." This mass extermination, now called the **Holocaust** ("burning") claimed some 6 million Jewish lives.

Besides the Jews, the Nazis also killed 3 million Polish Catholics—especially professionals, army officers, and the educated—in an effort to reduce the Polish people to slavery. They also exterminated homosexuals, Jehovah's Witnesses, Gypsies, the disabled, and the mentally ill—all in the interests of "racial purity." Whenever a German was killed in an occupied country, the Nazis retaliated by burning a village with all its inhabitants. After the invasion of Russia, the Wehrmacht was given orders to execute all captured communists, government employees, and officers. They also worked millions of prisoners of war to death or let them die of starvation.

The Holocaust   When Allied forces entered Germany, they found not only camp guards and their prisoners but also enormous numbers of corpses. This picture shows female guards at Bergen-Belsen dumping the bodies of Holocaust victims into a mass grave.   (Wide World Photos)

The Home Front in Europe and Asia

In the First World War, there had been a clear distinction between the "front" and the "home front." Not so in World War II, where rapid military movements and air power carried the war into people's homes. For the civilian populations of China, Japan, Southeast Asia, and Europe, the war was far more terrifying than their worst nightmares. Armies swept through the land, confiscating food, fuel, and anything else of value. Bombers and heavy artillery pounded cities into rubble, leaving only the skeletons of buildings, while survivors cowered in cellars and scurried like rats. Even when a city was not targeted, air-raid sirens awakened people throughout the night. In countries occupied by the Germans, the police arrested civilians, deporting many to die in concentration camps or to work as slave laborers in armaments factories. Millions fled their homes in terror, losing their families and friends. Even in Britain, which was never invaded, children and the elderly were taken from their families for their own safety and sent to live in the countryside.

The war demanded an enormous and sustained effort from all civilians, but more so in some countries than in others. In 1941, even as the Wehrmacht was routing the Red Army, the Soviets dismantled over fifteen hundred factories and rebuilt them in the Ural Mountains and Siberia, where they soon turned out more tanks and artillery than the Axis.

Half of the ships afloat in 1939 were sunk during the war, but the Allied losses were more than made up for by American shipyards, while Axis shipping was reduced to nothing by 1945. The production of aircraft, trucks, tanks, and other materiel showed a similar imbalance. Although the Axis Powers made strenuous efforts to increase their production, they could not compete with the vast outpouring of Soviet tanks and American materiel.

The Red Army eventually mobilized 22 million men; Soviet women took over half of all industrial and three-quarters of all agricultural jobs. In the other belligerent countries, women also played a major role in the war effort, replacing men in fields, factories, and offices. The Nazis, in contrast, believed that German women should stay home and bear children, and they imported 7 million "guest workers"—a euphemism for war prisoners and captured foreigners.

The Home Front in the United States

Unlike the other belligerents, the United States flourished during the war. Safe behind their oceans, Americans felt no bombs, saw no enemy soldiers, and suffered few military casualties and almost no civilian ones. The economy, still depressed in 1939, went into a prolonged boom after 1940. By 1944 the United States alone was producing twice as much as all the Axis Powers combined. Thanks to huge military orders, jobs were plentiful and opportunities beckoned. Bread lines disappeared, and nutrition and health improved. Consumer goods ranging from automobiles to nylon stockings were in short supply, and most Americans saved part of their paychecks, laying the basis for a phenomenal postwar consumer boom. Many Americans later looked back on that conflict as the "good war."

War always exalts such supposedly masculine qualities as physical courage, violence, and domination. These were the official virtues of the Axis Powers, but they were highly valued in America as well. Yet World War II also did much to weaken the hold of traditional ideas. On a much larger scale than in World War I, employers recruited women and members of racial minorities to work in jobs once reserved for white men. For example, 6 million women entered the labor force during the war, 2.5 million of them in manufacturing jobs previously considered "men's work." In a book entitled *Shipyard Diary of a Woman Welder* (1944), Augusta Clawson recalled her experiences in a shipyard in Oregon:

> The job confirmed my strong conviction—I have stated it before—what exhausts the woman welder is not the work, not the heat, nor the demands upon physical strength. It is the apprehension that arises from inadequate skill and consequent lack of confidence; and this *can* be overcome by the right kind of training. . . . I know I can do it if my machine is correctly set, and I have learned enough of the vagaries of machines to be able to set them. And so, in spite of the discomforts of climbing, heavy equipment, and heat, I enjoyed the work today because *I could do it.*

The expansion of job opportunities did not take place without friction. At the beginning, many men resisted the idea that women, especially mothers of young children, should take jobs that would take them away from their families. As the labor shortage got worse, however, employers and politicians grudgingly admitted that the government ought to help provide day care for the children of working mothers. The entry of women into the labor force proved to be one of the most significant consequences of the war. As one woman put it: "War jobs have uncovered unsuspected abilities in American women. Why lose all these abilities because of a belief that 'a women's place is in the home?' For some it is, for others not."

The war loosened racial bonds as well, bringing hardships for some and benefits for others. Seeking work in war industries, 1.2 million African-Americans migrated to the north and west. In the southwest, Mexican immigrants took jobs in agriculture and war industries. But no new housing was built to accommodate the influx of migrants to the industrial cities, and as a result many suffered from overcrowding and discrimination. Much worse was the fate of 112,000 Japanese-Americans living on the west coast of the United States; they were rounded up and herded into internment camps in the desert until the war was over, ostensibly for fear of spying and sabotage but actually because of their race.

War and the Environment

During the Depression, construction and industry had slowed to a crawl, reducing environmental stress. The war reversed this trend, sharply accelerating pressures on the environment.

One reason for the change was the fighting itself. Battles scarred the landscape, leaving behind spent ammunition and damaged equipment. Retreating armies flooded large areas of China and the Netherlands. The bombing of cities left ruins that remained visible for a generation or more. Much of the damage eventually was repaired, although the rusted hulls of ships still darken the lagoons of once-pristine coral islands in the Pacific.

The main cause of environmental stress, however, was not the fighting but the economic development that sustained it. The war's half-million aircraft required thousands of air bases, many of them in the Pacific, China, Africa, and other parts of the world that had seldom seen an airplane before. Barracks, shipyards, docks, warehouses, and other military construction sprouted on every continent.

As war industries boomed—the United States increased its industrial production fourfold during the war—so did the demand for raw materials. Mining companies opened new mines and towns in Central Africa to supply strategic minerals. Brazil, Argentina, and other Latin American countries deprived of manufactured imports began building their own steel mills, factories, and shipyards. In India, China, and Europe, timber felling accelerated far beyond the reproduction rate of trees, replacing forests with denuded land. In a few instances, the war was good for the environment. For example, submarine warfare made fishing and whaling so dangerous that fish and whale populations had a few years in which to increase.

We must keep the environmental effects of the war in perspective. Except for the destruction of cities, much of the war's impact was simply the result of industrial development only temporarily slowed by the Depression. During the war, the damage that military demand caused was tempered by restraints on civilian consumption. From the vantage point of the present, the environmental impact of the war seems quite modest in comparison with the damage inflicted on the earth by the long consumer boom that began in the post–World War II years.

CONCLUSION

Between 1929 and 1949 the old global order—conservative, colonialist, and dominated by Great Britain and France—was shattered by the Depression, the politics of violence, and the most devastating war in history. Stalin transformed the Soviet Union into an industrial giant at enormous human cost. Reacting to the Depression, which weakened the Western democracies, Hitler in Germany and military leaders in Japan prepared for a war of conquest. Though Germany and Japan achieved stunning victories at first, their forces soon faltered in the face of the greater industrial production of the United States and the Soviet Union.

The war was so destructive and spread to so much of the globe because rapidly advancing technology was readily converted from civilian to military production. Machines that had made cars could also manufacture bombers or tanks. Engineers could design factories to kill people with maximum efficiency. The accelerating technology of missiles and nuclear bombs made the entire planet vulnerable to human destruction for the first time in history.

Into the power vacuum left by the collapse of Germany and Japan stepped the two superpowers: the United States and the USSR. When the war ended, U.S. soldiers were stationed in Australia, Japan, and western Europe, and the Red Army occupied all of eastern Europe and parts of northern China. Within months of their victory, these one-time allies became ideological enemies hovering on the brink of war.

World War I had rearranged the colonial empires. In contrast, the global impact of World War II was drastic and almost immediate, because the war weakened the European colonial powers and because so much of the fighting took place in North Africa, Southeast Asia, and other colonial areas. Within fifteen years of the end of the war, almost every European colonial empire had disappeared. As the long era of European domination receded, Asians and Africans began reclaiming their independence.

■ Key Terms

Joseph Stalin	Long March
Five-Year Plans	Stalingrad
Benito Mussolini	El Alamein
Fascist Party	Pearl Harbor
Adolf Hitler	Battle of Midway
Nazis	Hiroshima
Chiang Kai-shek	Auschwitz
Mao Zedong	Holocaust

■ Suggested Reading

The literature on the period from 1929–1945 is enormous and growing fast. The following list is but a very summary introduction.

Charles Kindelberger's *The World in Depression, 1929–39* (1973) and Robert McElvaine's *The Great Depression: America, 1929–1941* (1984) provide a sophisticated economic analysis of the Depression. A. J. H. Latham's *The Depression and the Developing World, 1914–1939* (1981) gives a global perspective.

The best recent book on Japan in the twentieth century is Daikichi Irokawa's *The Age of Hirohito: In Search of Modern Japan* (1995). On Japanese expansion see W. G. Beasley, *Japanese Imperialism, 1894–1945* (1987). The race to war is covered in Akira Iriye, *The Origins of the Second World War in Asia and the Pacific* (1987); Michael Barnhart, *Japan Prepares for Total War* (1987), is short and well written.

In the large and fast-growing literature on twentieth-century China, two general introductions are especially useful: John K. Fairbank, *The Great Chinese Revolution, 1800–1985* (1986), and Jonathan Spence, *The Search for Modern China* (1990). On the warlord and Guomindang periods see Lucien Bianco, *Origins of the Chinese Revolution, 1915–1949* (1971). The Japanese invasion of China is the subject of Iris Chang, *The Rape of Nanking: The Forgotten Holocaust of World War II* (1997), and of James Hsiung and Steven Levine, eds., *China's Bitter Victory: The War with Japan, 1937–1945* (1992). Jung Chang, *Wild Swans: Three Daughters of China* (1991), is a fascinating account of women's experiences during the Revolution and the Mao era by the daughter of two Communist officials.

Among recent biographies of Stalin, see Dmitrii Volkogonov's *Stalin: Triumph and Tragedy* (1991) and Robert Tucker's *Stalin as Revolutionary, 1879–1929* (1973) and *Stalin in Power: The Revolution from Above, 1928–1941* (1990). On the transformation of the USSR, see Roy Medvedev's *Let History Judge: The Origins and Consequences of Stalinism* (1989) and Stephen Kotkin's *Magnetic Mountain: Stalinism as Civilization* (1995). Stalin's collectivization of agriculture is vividly portrayed in Robert Conquest's *Harvest of Sorrow* (1986); see also Sheila Fitzpatrick's *Stalin's Peasants: Resistance and Survival in the Russian Village After Collectivization* (1994). Conquest's *The Great Terror: A Reassessment* (1990) describes the purges of the 1930s. Alexander Solzhenitsyn, a veteran of Stalin's prisons, explores them in a detailed history, *The Gulag Archipelago, 1918–1956* (3 vols. 1974–1978), and in a short but brilliant novel *One Day in the Life of Ivan Denisovich* (1978).

Alexander De Grand provides an excellent interpretation of fascism in *Italian Fascism: Its Origins and Development*, 2d ed. (1989). William Shirer's *The Rise and Fall of the Third Reich* (1960) is a long but very dramatic eyewitness description of Nazi Germany by a journalist. The dictators are the subject of two fine biographies: Denis Mack Smith's *Mussolini* (1982) and Alan Bullock's *Hitler: A Study in Tyranny* (1965). See also A. J. P. Taylor's controversial classic *The Origins of the Second World War* (1966).

Two very detailed books on World War II are John Keegan, *The Second World War* (1990), and Gerhard Weinberg, *A World at Arms: A Global History of World War II* (1994). Particular aspects of the war in Europe are covered in Alexander Werth, *Russia at War, 1941–1945* (1965), and Conrad Crane, *Bombs, Cities, and Civilians* (1993). One of the most readable accounts of the war in Asia and the Pacific is Ronald Spector's *Eagle Against the Sun* (1988). Also see Akira Iriye, *Power and Culture: The Japanese-American War, 1941–1945* (1981), and James Hsiung and Steven Levine, eds., *China's Bitter Victory: The War with Japan, 1937–1945* (1992).

The terror of life under Nazi rule is the subject of two powerful memoirs: Anne Frank's *The Diary of a Young Girl* and Eli Wiesel's *Night* (1960). On the Holocaust see Lucy Dawidowicz, *The War Against the Jews, 1933–1945*, 2d ed. (1986); Leni Yahil, *The Holocaust: The Fate of European Jewry* (1990); and a controversial book by Daniel Goldhagen, *Hitler's Willing Executioners: Ordinary Germans and the Holocaust* (1996).

Among the many books that capture the scientific side of warfare, two are especially recommended: Richard Rhodes's long but fascinating *The Making of the Atomic Bomb* (1986), and F. H. Hinsley and Alan Stripp, eds., *Code Breakers* (1993).

Among the many books on the home front in the United States, the most vivid is Studs Terkel, *"The Good War": An Oral History of World War Two* (1984). Margaret Higonnet et al., eds., *Behind the Lines: Gender and the Two World Wars* (1987), discusses the role of women in the war.

32

STRIVING FOR INDEPENDENCE: AFRICA, INDIA, AND LATIN AMERICA, 1900–1949

Sub-Saharan Africa, 1900–1945 • The Indian Independence
Movement, 1905–1947 • The Mexican Revolution, 1910–1940 •
Argentina and Brazil, 1900–1949

ENVIRONMENT AND TECHNOLOGY: Gandhi and Technology

SOCIETY AND CULTURE: Self-Government in Africa

African Farmers in the Gold Coast African farmers in the Gold Coast (now Ghana) sold their cocoa beans to government agents. The government kept the price artifically low in order to profit on the transactions.

miliano Zapata°, leader of a peasant rebellion in the Mexican Revolution, liked to be photographed on horseback, carrying a sword and a rifle and draped with bandoliers of bullets. Mahatma Gandhi°, who led the independence movement in India, preferred to be seen sitting at a spinning wheel, dressed in a *dhoti*°, the simple loincloth worn by Indian farmers. The images they liked to project and the methods they used could not have been more opposed. Yet their goals were similar: each wanted social justice and a better life for the poor in a country free of foreign domination.

The previous two chapters focused on a world convulsed by war and revolution. The world wars involved Europe, East Asia, the Middle East, and the United States, and they sparked violent revolutions in Russia and China. They accelerated the development of aviation, electronics, nuclear power, and other technologies. Although these momentous events dominate the history of the first half of the twentieth century, parts of the world that were little touched by war also underwent profound changes in this period, partly for internal reasons and partly because of the influence of warfare and revolution in other parts of the world.

In this chapter we examine the changes that took place in three regions: in sub-Saharan Africa, in India, and in three major countries of Latin America—Mexico, Brazil, and Argentina. These three regions represent three very distinct cultures, yet they had much in common. Africa and India were colonies of Europe, both politically and economically. Though politically independent, the Latin American republics were dependent on Europe and the United States for the sale of raw materials and commodities and for imports of manufactured goods, technology, and capital. In all three regions, independence movements tried to wrest control from distant foreigners and improve the livelihood of their peoples. Their success was partial at best.

As you read this chapter, ask yourself the following questions:

- How did wars and revolutions in Europe and East Asia affect the countries of the Southern Hemisphere?
- Why did educated Indians and Africans want independence?
- What could Latin Americans do to achieve social justice and economic development? Were these two goals compatible?

SUB-SAHARAN AFRICA, 1900–1945

Of all the continents, Africa was the last to come under European rule (see Chapter 29). The first half of the twentieth century, when nationalist movements threatened European rule in Asia, was Africa's period of classic colonialism. After World War I, Britain, France, Belgium, and South Africa divided Germany's African colonies among themselves. In the 1930s, Italy invaded Ethiopia. The colonial empires reached their peak shortly before World War II.

Colonial Africa: Economic and Social Changes

Outside of Algeria, Kenya, and South Africa, few Europeans lived in Africa. In 1930, Nigeria, with a population of 20 million, was ruled by 386 British officials and by 8,000 policemen and military, of whom 150 were European. Yet even such a small presence stimulated deep social and economic changes.

Since the turn of the century, the colonial powers had built railroads from coastal cities to mines and plantations in the interior, in order to provide raw materials to the industrial world. The economic boom of the interwar years benefited few Africans. Colonial governments took lands that Africans owned communally and sold or leased them to European companies or, in eastern and southern Africa, to white settlers. Large European companies dominated wholesale commerce, while immigrants from various countries—Indians in East Africa, Greeks and Syrians in West Africa—handled much of the retail trade. Airplanes and automobiles were even more alien to the experience of Africans than railroads had been to an earlier generation.

Zapata (zeh-PAH-teh)   Gandhi (GAHN-dee)   *dhoti* (DOE-tee)

CHRONOLOGY

	Africa	India	Latin America
1900	**1900s** Railroads connect ports to the interior **1909** African National Congress founded	**1905** Viceroy Curzon splits Bengal; mass demonstrations **1906** Muslims found All-India Muslim League **1911** British transfer capital from Calcutta to Delhi	**1876–1910** Porfirio Díaz, dictator of Mexico **1911–1919** Mexican Revolution; Emiliano Zapata and Pancho Villa against the Constitutionalists
1920	**1920s** J. E. Casely Hayford organizes political movement in British West Africa	**1919** Amritsar Massacre **1929** Gandhi leads March to the Sea **1930s** Gandhi calls for independence; he is repeatedly arrested	**1917** New constitution proclaimed in Mexico **1928** Plutarco Elías Calles founds Mexico's National Revolutionary Party **1930–1945** Getulio Vargas, dictator of Brazil **1934–1940** Lázaro Cárdenas, president of Mexico
1940	**1939–1945** A million Africans serve in World War II	**1939** British bring India into World War II **1940** Muhammad Ali Jinnah demands a separate nation for Muslims **1947** Partition and independence of India and Pakistan	**1938** Cárdenas nationalizes Mexican oil industry; Vargas proclaims Estado Novo in Brazil **1943** Juan Perón leads military coup in Argentina **1946** Perón elected president of Argentina

Where land was divided into small farms, some Africans benefited from the boom. Farmers in the Gold Coast (now Ghana°) profited from the high prices of cocoa, as did palm-oil producers in Nigeria and coffee growers in East Africa. In most of Africa, women played a major role in the retail trades, selling pots and pans and other hardware, toys, cloth, and food in the markets. Many maintained their economic independence and kept their household finances separate from those of their husbands, following a custom that predated the colonial period.

For many Africans, economic development meant working in European-owned mines and plantations, often under compulsion. Colonial governments were eager to develop the resources of the territories under their control but could not afford to pay high enough wages to attract workers. Instead, they used their police powers to force Africans to work under harsh conditions for little or no pay. In the 1920s, when the government of French Equatorial Africa decided to build a railroad from Brazzaville to the Atlantic coast, a distance of 312 miles (502 kilometers), it drafted 127,000 men to carve a roadbed across mountains and through rain forests. For lack of food, clothing, and medical care, 20,000 of them died, an average of 64 deaths per mile of track.

Europeans prided themselves on bringing modern health care to Africa; yet before the 1930s, there was too little of it to help the majority of Africans, and other aspects of colonialism actually worsened public health. Migrants to cities, mines, and plantations and soldiers moving from post to post spread syphilis, gonorrhea, tuberculosis, and malaria. Sleeping sickness and smallpox epidemics raged throughout Central Africa. In recruiting men to work, colonial governments depleted rural areas of farmers needed to plant and harvest crops. Forced requisitions of food taken to feed the workers left the remaining populations undernourished and vulnerable to

---

Ghana (GAH-nuh)

Diamond Mining in Southern Africa The discovery of diamonds in the Transvaal in 1867 attracted prospectors to the area around Kimberley. The first wave of prospectors consisted of individual "diggers," including a few Africans. By the late 1870s, surface deposits had been exhausted and further mining required complex and costly machinery. After 1889, one company, De Beers Consolidated, owned all the diamond mines. This photograph shows the entrance to a mine shaft and mine workers surrounded by heavy equipment. (Royal Commonwealth Society. By permission of the Syndics of Cambridge University Library.)

diseases. Not until the 1930s did colonial governments realize the negative consequences of their labor policies and begin to invest in agricultural development and in health care for Africans.

In 1900 Ibadan° in Nigeria was the only city in sub-Saharan Africa with more than 100,000 inhabitants; fifty years later, dozens of cities had reached that size, including Nairobi° in Kenya, Johannesburg in South Africa, Lagos in Nigeria, Accra in Gold Coast, and Dakar in Senegal. Africans migrated to cities because they offered hope of jobs and excitement and, for a few, the chance to become wealthy.

However, migrations damaged the family life of those involved, for almost all the migrants were men

---

Ibadan (ee-BAH-dahn)　Nairobi (nie-ROE-bee)

leaving women in the countryside to farm and raise children. Cities built during the colonial period reflected the colonialists' attitudes with their racially segregated housing, clubs, restaurants, hospitals, and other institutions. Patterns of racial discrimination were most rigid in the white-settler colonies of eastern and southern Africa.

Religious and Political Changes

Traditional religious belief could not explain the dislocations that foreign rule, migrations, and sudden economic changes brought to the lives of Africans. Many therefore turned to one of the two universal religions, Christianity and Islam, for guidance. A major attraction of the Christian denominations was their mission schools, which taught

Self-Government in Africa

Colonialism rested on the presumption of European superiority. Nowhere was that presumption more evident than in Africa, where colonialists argued that Africans had not evolved politically and therefore would not be ready for self-rule for a long time. Here is an expression of such thinking from the pamphlet African Opportunity, *by Lord Milverton, a former governor of Nigeria.*

The African has had self-government. Until about fifty years ago he had had it for countless centuries, and all it brought him was blood-stained chaos, a brief, insecure life, haunted by fear, in which evil tradition and custom held him enslaved to superstition, hunger, disease, squalor and ruthless cruelty, even to his family and friends. For countless centuries, while all the pageant of history swept by, the African remained unmoved—in primitive savagery.

The Gold Coast nationalist J. E. Casely Hayford responded to that sort of attack by giving examples of progressive and beneficial government in precolonial Africa.

A people who could, indigenously, and without a literature, evolve the orderly representative government which obtained in Ashanti and the Gold Coast before the advent of the foreign interloper, are a people to be respected and shown consideration when they proceed to discuss questions of self-government.

How do these quotations illustrate the importance of history in an argument about the future?

Source: Quotations from Thomas Hodgkin, *Nationalism in Colonial Africa* (New York: New York University Press, 1957), 172–173.

---

both craft skills and basic literacy, providing access to employment as minor functionaries, teachers, clergy, or shopkeepers. These schools educated a new elite, many of whom learned not only skills and literacy but Western political ideas as well.

Christianity was introduced into Africa by Western missionaries, except in Ethiopia, where it was indigenous. Islam, in contrast, spread through the influence and example of African traders. Islam also emphasized literacy—in Arabic rather than in a European language—and was less disruptive of traditional African customs such as polygamy. Christianity was most successful in the coastal regions of West and South Africa, where the European influence was strongest. Islam tended to spread inland from the East African coast and southward from the Sahel° toward the West African coast.

The contrast between the liberal ideas imparted by Western education and the realities of racial discrimination under colonial rule contributed to the rise of nationalism among educated Africans. In Senegal, **Blaise Diagne°** agitated for African participation in politics and fair treatment in the French army. In the 1920s, J. E. Casely Hayford began organizing a movement for greater autonomy in British West Africa (see Society and

Culture: Self-Government in Africa). In South Africa, Western-educated lawyers and journalists founded the **African National Congress** in 1909 to defend the interests of Africans. These nationalist movements were inspired by the ideas of Pan-Africanists from America such as W. E. B. Du Bois and Marcus Garvey, who advocated the unity of African peoples around the world, as well as by European ideas of liberty and nationhood. Until World War II, however, they were small and had little influence.

The Second World War (1939–1945) had a profound effect on the peoples of Africa, even those far removed from the theaters of war. The war brought hardships, such as increased forced labor, inflation, and requisitions of raw materials. Yet it also brought hope. During the campaign to oust the Italians from Ethiopia, Emperor **Haile Selassie°** (r. 1930–1974) led his own troops into his capital Addis Ababa and reclaimed his title. A million Africans served as soldiers and carriers in Burma, North Africa, and Europe, where many became aware of Africa's role in helping the Allied war effort. They listened to Allied propaganda in favor of European liberation movements and against Nazi racism, and they returned to their countries with new and radical ideas.

Sahel (SAH-hel)   **Diagne** (dee-AHN-yuh)

Haile Selassie (HI-lee seh-LASS-ee)

The early twentieth century was a relatively peaceful period for sub-Saharan Africa. But this peace—enforced by the European occupiers—masked profound changes that were to transform African life after the Second World War. The building of cities, railroads, and other enterprises brought Africa into the global economy, often at great human cost. Colonialism also brought changes to African culture and religion, hastening the spread of Christianity and Islam. And the foreign occupation awakened political ideas that inspired the next generation of Africans to demand independence (see Chapter 33).

THE INDIAN INDEPENDENCE MOVEMENT, 1905–1947

India was a colony of Great Britain from the late eighteenth to the mid-twentieth century. Under British rule, the subcontinent acquired many of the trappings of Western-style economic development, such as railroads, harbors, modern cities, and cotton and steel mills, as well as an active and worldly middle class. The economic transformation of the region awakened in this educated middle class a sense of national dignity that demanded political fulfillment. In response, the British gradually granted India a limited amount of political autonomy while maintaining overall control. Religious and communal tensions among the Indian peoples were carefully papered over under British rule. Violent conflicts tore India apart after the withdrawal of the British in 1947 (see Map 32.1).

The Land and the People

Much of India is fertile land, but it is vulnerable to the vagaries of nature, especially droughts caused by the periodic failure of the monsoons. When the rains failed from 1896 to 1900, 2 million people died of starvation.

Despite periodic famines, the Indian population grew from 250 million in 1900 to 319 million in 1921 and 389 million in 1941. This growth created pressures in many areas. Landless young men converged on the cities, exceeding the number of jobs available in the slowly expanding industries. To produce timber for construction and railroad ties and to clear land for tea and rubber plantations, government foresters cut down most of the tropical hardwood forests that had covered the subcontinent in the nineteenth century. In spite of deforestation and extensive irrigation, the amount of land available to peasant families shrank with each successive generation. Economic development—what the British called the "moral and material progress of India"—hardly benefited the average Indian.

Indians were divided into many classes. Peasants, always the great majority, paid rents to the landowner, interest to the village moneylender, and taxes to the government and had little left to improve their land or raise their standard of living. The government protected property owners, from village moneylenders all the way up to the princes and maharajahs° who owned huge tracts of land. The cities were crowded with craftsmen, traders, and workers of all sorts, mostly very poor. Although the British had banned *sati*° (the burning of widows on their husbands' funeral pyres), in other respects women's lives changed little under British rule.

The peoples of India spoke many different languages: Hindi in the north, Tamil in the south, Bengali in the east, Gujerati around Bombay, Urdu in the northwest, and dozens of others. As a result of British rule and increasing trade and travel, English became, like Latin in medieval Europe, the common medium of communication of the Western-educated middle class. This new class of English-speaking government bureaucrats, professionals, and merchants were to play a leading role in the independence movement.

The majority of Indians practiced Hinduism and were subdivided into hundreds of castes, each affiliated with a particular occupation. Hinduism discouraged intermarriage and other social interactions among the castes and with people who were not Hindus. Muslims constituted one-quarter of the people of India but formed a majority in the northwest and in eastern Bengal. Muslim rulers had dominated northern and central India until they were displaced by the British in the eighteenth century. More reluctant than Hindus to learn English, Muslims felt discriminated against by both British and Hindus.

British Rule and Indian Nationalism

Colonial India was ruled by a viceroy appointed by the British government; the country was administered by a few thousand members of the Indian Civil Service. These men, imbued with a sense of duty toward their subjects, formed one of the most honest (if not the most efficient)

---

maharajah (mah-huh-RAH-juh)   *sati* (suh-TEE)

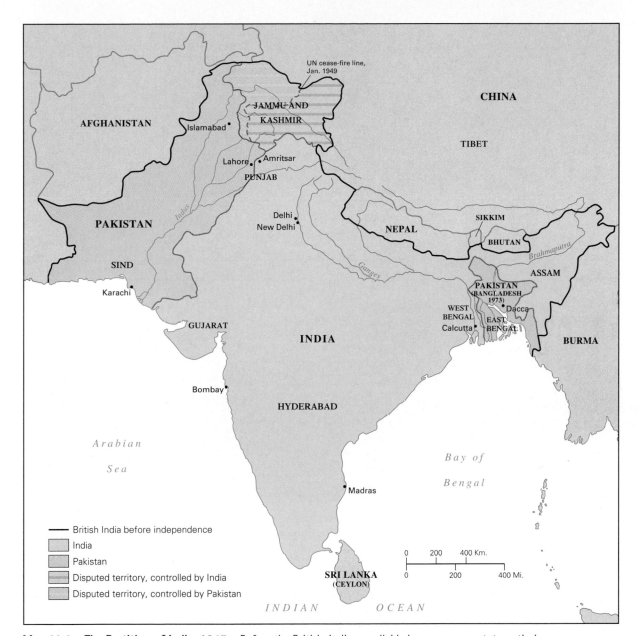

Map 32.1   The Partition of India, 1947   Before the British, India was divided among many states, ethnic groups, and religions. When the British left in 1947, the subcontinent split along religious lines. The predominantly Muslim regions of Sind and Punjab in the northwest and East Bengal in the east formed the new nation of Pakistan. The predominantly Hindu center became the Republic of India. Jammu and Kashmir remained disputed territories and poisoned relations between the two new countries.

bureaucracies of all time. Drawn mostly from the English gentry, they liked to think of India as a land of lords and peasants. They considered it their duty to protect the Indian people from the dangers of industrialization and radical politics.

As Europeans, they admired modern technology but tried to control its introduction into India so as to maximize the benefits to Britain and to themselves. For example, they encouraged railroads, harbors, telegraphs, and other communications technologies, as

Construction Site in Colonial India   British civil engineers were active throughout India building roads, railroads, and canals. Here, a British official supervises Indian workers building a bridge.   (The Billie Love Collection)

well as irrigation and plantations, because they increased India's foreign trade and strengthened British control. At the same time, they discouraged the cotton and steel industries and limited the training of Indian engineers in order to spare India the social and political upheavals that had accompanied the Industrial Revolution in Europe.

At the turn of the century, the majority of Indians—especially the peasants, landowners, and princes—accepted British rule. But the Europeans' racist attitude toward dark-skinned people increasingly offended those Indians who had learned English and absorbed English ideas of freedom and representative government and then discovered that thinly disguised racial quotas excluded them from the Indian Civil Service, the officer corps, and prestigious country clubs.

In 1885 a small group of English-speaking Hindu professionals founded a political organization called the **Indian National Congress.** For twenty years, its members respectfully petitioned the government for access to the higher administrative positions and for a voice in official decisions, but they had little influence outside intellectual circles. Then, in 1905, Viceroy Lord Curzon divided the province of **Bengal** in two to improve the efficiency of its administration. This decision, made without consulting anyone, angered not only educated Indians, who saw it as a step taken to lessen their influence, but also millions of uneducated Hindu Bengalis, who suddenly found themselves outnumbered by Muslims in East Bengal. Soon Bengal was the scene of demonstrations, boycotts of British goods, and even incidents of violence against the British.

In 1906, while the Hindus of Bengal were protesting the partition of their province, Muslims, fearful of Hindu dominance elsewhere in India, founded the **All-India Muslim League.** Caught in an awkward situation, the government responded by granting Indians a limited franchise based on wealth. Muslims, however, were on average poorer than Hindus, for many poor and low-caste Hindus had converted to Islam to escape caste discrimination. Taking advantage of these religious divisions, the British instituted separate representation and different voting qualifications for Hindus and Muslims. Then, in 1911, the British transferred the capital of India from Calcutta to Delhi°, the former capital of the Mughal° emperors. These changes disturbed Indians of all classes and religions and raised their political consciousness. Politics, once primarily the concern of westernized intellectuals, turned into two mass movements: one by Hindus and one by Muslims.

To maintain their commercial position and prevent social upheavals, the British resisted the idea that India could, or should, industrialize. Their geologists looked for minerals, such as coal or manganese, that British industry required. However, when the only Indian member of the Indian Geological Service, Pramatha Nath Bose, wanted to prospect for iron ore, he had to resign because the government wanted no part of an Indian steel industry that could compete with that of Britain. Bose joined forces with Jamsetji Tata, a Bombay textile magnate who decided to produce steel in spite of British opposition. With the help of German and American engineers and equipment, Tata's son Dorabji opened the first steel mill in India in 1911, in a town called Jamshedpur in honor of his father. Although it produced only a fraction of the steel that India required, Jamshedpur became a powerful symbol of Indian national pride. It prompted Indian nationalists to ask, why did a country that could produce its own steel need foreigners to run its government?

During World War I, Indians supported Britain enthusiastically; 1.2 million men volunteered for the army, and millions more Indians voluntarily contributed money to the government. Many expected that the British would reward such loyalty with political concessions. Others organized to demand such concessions and began demanding a voice in the government. In 1917, in response to the agitation, the British government announced "the gradual development of self-governing institutions with a view to the progressive realization of responsible government in India as an integral part of the British Empire." This sounded like a promise of self-government, but the timetable was left so vague that nationalists denounced it as a devious maneuver to postpone India's independence.

In late 1918 and early 1919, a violent influenza epidemic broke out among soldiers in the war zone of northern France. Within a few months, it spread to every country on earth and killed over 20 million people. India was especially hard hit; of the millions who died, one out of four was Indian. This dreadful toll increased the mounting political tensions. Leaders of the Indian National Congress declared that the British reform proposals were too little too late. On April 13, 1919, in the city of Amritsar in Punjab, General Reginald Dyer ordered his troops to fire into a peaceful crowd of some 10,000 demonstrators, killing at least 379 and wounding 1,200. As waves of angry demonstrations swept over India, the period of gradual accommodation between the British and the Indians came to a close.

Mahatma Gandhi and Militant Nonviolence

For the next twenty years, India teetered on the edge of violent uprisings and harsh repression, possibly even war. That it did not succumb was due to **Mohandas K. Gandhi** (1869–1948), a man known to his followers as "Mahatma," the "great soul."

Gandhi began life with every advantage. His family was wealthy enough to send him to England for his education. After his studies, he lived in South Africa, where he practiced law for the small Indian community living there. During World War I he returned to India and was one of many Western-educated Hindu intellectuals who joined the Indian National Congress.

Gandhi had some unusual political ideas. Unlike many radical political thinkers of his time, he denounced the popular ideals of power and struggle and combat. Instead, inspired by both Hindu and Christian concepts, he preached the saintly virtues of *ahimsa*° (nonviolence) and *satyagraha*° (the search for truth). He refused to countenance violence among his followers, and several times he called off demonstrations when they turned violent.

Gandhi had an affinity for the poor that was unusual even among socialist politicians. In 1921 he gave up the Western-style suits worn by lawyers and the fine raiment of wealthy Indians and henceforth wore simple peasant garb: a length of homespun cloth below his waist and a shawl to cover his torso (see Environment and Technology: Gandhi and Technology). He spoke for the farmers

---

Delhi (DEL-ee)   **Mughal** (MOO-guhl)

ahimsa (uh-HIM-sah)   *satyagraha* (suh-TYAH-gruh-huh)

Gandhi and Technology

Gandhi at the Spinning Wheel Mahatma Gandhi chose the spinning wheel as his symbol because it represented the traditional activity of millions of rural Indians whose livelihoods were threatened by industrialization. (Margaret Bourke-White, *LIFE Magazine* © Time Warner Inc.)

In the twentieth century, all political leaders but one have embraced modern industrial technology. That one exception is Gandhi.

After deciding to wear only handmade cloth, Gandhi made a bonfire of imported factory-made cloth and began spending half an hour every day spinning yarn on a simple spinning wheel, a task he called a "sacrament." The spinning wheel became the symbol of his movement. Any Indian who wished to come before him had to dress in handwoven cloth.

Gandhi had several reasons for reviving this ancient craft. One was revulsion against the materialism of the West, which he contrasted with the poverty of his own people:

The incessant search for material comforts and their multiplication is such an evil, and I make bold to say that the Europeans themselves will have to remodel their outlook if they are not to perish under the weight of the comforts to which they are becoming slaves.

Gandhi believed that foreign cotton mills had impoverished his people:

A hundred and fifty years ago, we manufactured all our cloth. Our women spun fine yarns in their own cottages, and supplemented the earnings of their husbands. . . . India grows all the cotton she needs. She exports several million bales of cotton to Japan and Lancashire and receives much of it back in manufactured calico, though she is capable of producing all the cloth and all the yarn necessary for supplying her wants by hand-weaving and hand-spinning. . . . The spinning wheel was presented to the nation for giving occupation to the millions who had, at least four months of the year, nothing to do.

But most of all, to Gandhi, the spinning wheel was a political symbol of "national consciousness and a contribution by every individual to a definite constructive national work":

If three hundred million people did the same thing every day . . . because they were inspired by the same ideal, we would have enough unity of purpose to achieve independence.

Nevertheless, Gandhi was a shrewd politician who understood the usefulness of modern devices for mobilizing the masses and organizing his followers. He wore a watch and used the telephone and the printing press to keep in touch with his followers. When he traveled by train, he rode third class—but in a third-class railroad car of his own. His goal was the independence of his country, and he pursued it with every nonviolent means he could find.

Gandhi's ideas challenge us to rethink the purpose of technology. Was he opposed on principle to all modern devices? Was he an opportunist who used those devices that served his political ends and rejected those that did not? Or did he have a higher principle that accounts for his willingness to use the telephone and the railroad but not factory-made cloth?

Source: Quotations from Louis Fischer, *Gandhi: His Life and Message for the World* (New York: New American Library, 1954), 82–83. Copyright 1954, renewed © 1982 by Louis Fischer. Used by permission of Viking Penguin, a division of Penguin Putman Inc.

and the outcasts, whom he called *harijan*°, "children of God." He attracted ever-larger numbers of followers among the poor and the illiterate, who soon began to revere him; and he transformed the cause of Indian independence from an elite movement of the educated into a mass movement with a quasi-religious aura.

Gandhi was a brilliant political tactician and a master of public relations gestures. In 1929, for instance, he led a few followers on an 80-mile (129-kilometer) walk, camped on a beach, and gathered salt from the sea in a blatant and well-publicized act of civil disregard for the government's monopoly of salt. But he discovered that unleashing the power of popular participation was one thing and controlling its direction was quite another. Within days of his "Walk to the Sea," demonstrations of support broke out all over India, in which the police killed 100 demonstrators and arrested over 60,000.

Many times, during the 1930s, Gandhi threatened to fast "unto death," and several times he did come close to death, to protest the violence of both the police and his followers and to demand independence. He was repeatedly arrested and spent a total of six years in jail. But every arrest made him more popular. He became a cult figure not only in his own country but also in the Western media. He never won a battle or an election; instead, in the words of historian Percival Spear, he made the British "uncomfortable in their cherished field of moral rectitude," and he gave Indians the feeling that theirs was the ethically superior cause.

India Moves Toward Independence

In the 1920s, slowly and reluctantly, the British began to give in to the pressure of the Indian National Congress and the Muslim League. They handed over to Indians control of "national" areas such as education, the economy, and public works. They also gradually admitted more Indians into the Civil Service and the officer corps.

India took its first tentative steps toward industrialization in the years before the First and then the Second World Wars. Indian politicians obtained the right to erect high tariff barriers against imports in order to protect India's infant industries from foreign, even British, competition. Behind these barriers, Indian entrepreneurs built plants to manufacture iron and steel, cement, paper, cotton and jute textiles, sugar, and other products. This early industrialization provided jobs, though not enough to improve the lives of the Indian peasants or urban poor. These manufactures, however, helped create a class of wealthy Indian businessmen. Far from being satisfied by the government's policies, they supported the Indian National Congress and its demands for independence. Though paying homage to Gandhi, they preferred his designated successor as leader of the Indian National Congress, **Jawaharlal Nehru**° (1889–1964). A highly educated nationalist and subtle thinker, Nehru, in contrast to Gandhi, looked forward to creating a modern industrial India.

Congress politicians won regional elections but continued to be excluded from the viceroy's cabinet, the true center of power. When World War II began in September 1939, Viceroy Lord Linlithgow declared war without consulting a single Indian. The Congress-dominated provincial governments resigned in protest and found that boycotting government office increased their popular support. When the British offered to give India its independence once the war ended, Gandhi called the offer a "postdated cheque on a failing bank" and demanded full independence immediately. His "Quit India" campaign aroused popular demonstrations against the British and provoked a wave of arrests, including his own.

As in World War I, Indians contributed heavily to the Allied war effort, supplying 2 million soldiers and enormous amounts of resources, especially timber needed for emergency construction. The Second World War divided the Indian people. Most Indian soldiers felt they were fighting to defend their country rather than to support the British Empire. The Indian National Congress, however, opposed India's participation in the war; as Nehru explained: "I would fight Japan sword in hand, but I can only do so as a free man." A small number of Indians, meanwhile, were so anti-British that they joined the Japanese side.

India's subordination to British interests was vividly demonstrated in the famine of 1943 in Bengal. Unlike previous famines, this one was caused not by drought but by the Japanese conquest of Burma, which cut off supplies of Burmese rice that normally went to Bengal. Although food was available elsewhere in India, the British army had requisitioned the railroads to transport troops and equipment in preparation for a Japanese invasion. As a result, supplies ran short in Bengal and surrounding areas, speculators hoarded what little there was, and some 2 million people starved before the army was ordered to supply food.

---

harijan (HAH-ree-jahn)

Nehru (NAY-roo)

The Partition of India   When India became independent, Muslims fled from Hindu regions, and Hindus fled from Muslims. Margaret Bourke-White photographed a long line of refugees, with their cows, carts, and belongings, trudging down a country road toward safety.   (Margaret Bourke-White, *LIFE Magazine* © Time Inc.)

Partition and Independence

When the war ended, Britain's new Labour Party government prepared for Indian independence, but deep suspicions between Hindus and Muslims complicated the process. The break between the two communities had started in 1937, when the Indian National Congress won the provincial elections and refused to share power with the Muslim League. In 1940, the leader of the League, **Muhammad Ali Jinnah**° (1876–1948) demanded what many Muslims had been dreaming of for years: a country of their own, to be called Pakistan (from "Punjab-Afghans-Kashmir-Sind" plus the Persian suffix *-stan* meaning "kingdom").

As independence approached, talks between Jinnah and Nehru broke down and battle lines were drawn. Violent rioting between Hindus and Muslims broke out in Bengal and Bihar. Gandhi's appeals for tolerance and cooperation fell on deaf ears; in despair, he retreated to his home near Ahmedabad. The British made frantic proposals to keep India united, but their authority was waning fast.

By early 1947 the Indian National Congress had accepted the idea of a partition of India into two states, one secular but dominated by Hindus, the other Muslim. In June, Lord Mountbatten, the last viceroy, decided that independence must come immediately. On August 15, British India gave way to a new India and Pakistan. The Indian National Congress, led by Nehru, formed the first government of India; Jinnah and the Muslim League established a government for the provinces that made up Pakistan.

The rejoicing over independence was marred by violent outbreaks between Muslims and Hindus. In protest against the mounting chaos, Gandhi refused to attend the independence day celebration. Throughout the land, Muslim and Hindu neighbors turned on one another, and armed members of one faith hunted down people of the other faith. For centuries Hindus and Muslims had intermingled throughout most of India. Now, leaving all their possessions behind, Hindus fled from predominantly Muslim areas, and Muslims fled from Hindu areas. Trainloads of desperate refugees of one faith were

Jinnah (jee-NAH)

attacked and massacred by members of the other or were left stranded in the middle of deserts. Within a few months, some 12 million people had abandoned their ancestral homes and a half-million lay dead. In January 1948, Gandhi died too, gunned down by an angry Hindu refugee.

THE MEXICAN REVOLUTION, 1910–1940

In the nineteenth century, Latin America achieved independence from Spain and Portugal but did not industrialize. Throughout much of the century most Latin American republics suffered from ideological divisions, unstable governments, and violent upheavals. By trading their raw materials and agricultural products for foreign manufactured goods and capital investments, they became economically dependent on the wealthier countries to the north, especially on the United States and Great Britain. Their societies, far from fulfilling the promises of their independence, remained deeply split between wealthy landowners and desperately poor peasants.

In this chapter we focus on three Latin American republics: Mexico, Brazil, and Argentina. They contained well over half of Latin America's land, population, and wealth, and their relations with other countries and their economies were quite similar. Mexico, however, underwent a traumatic social revolution, while Argentina and Brazil evolved more peaceably.

Mexico in 1910

Few countries in Latin America suffered as many foreign invasions and interventions as Mexico. A Mexican saying observed wryly: "Poor Mexico: so far from God, so close to the United States." In Mexico, the chasm between rich and poor was so deep that only a revolution could move the country toward prosperity and democracy.

Mexico was the Latin American country most influenced by the Spanish during three centuries of colonial rule. Mexico gained its independence in 1821. At the beginning of the twentieth century, Mexican society was divided into rich and poor and among persons of Spanish, Indian, and mixed ancestry. A few very wealthy families of Spanish origin, less than 1 percent of the population, owned 85 percent of Mexico's land, mostly in huge *haciendas* (estates). Closely tied to this elite were the handful of American and British companies that controlled most of Mexico's railroads, silver mines, plantations, and other productive enterprises. At the other end of the social scale were Indians and *mestizos°*, people of mixed Indian and European ancestry. Most of them were peasants who worked on the haciendas or farmed small communal plots near their ancestral villages.

The urban middle class was small and had little political influence. Few professional and government positions were open to them, and foreigners owned most businesses. Industrial workers also were few in number; the only significant groups were textile workers in the port of Veracruz on the Gulf of Mexico and railroad workers spread throughout the country.

During the colonial period, the Spanish government had made halfhearted efforts to defend Indians and mestizos from the land-grabbing tactics of the haciendas. After independence in 1821, wealthy Mexican families and American companies used bribery and force to acquire millions of acres of good agricultural land from villages in southern Mexico. Peasants lost not only their fields but also their access to firewood and pasture for their animals. Sugar, cotton, and other commercial crops replaced the cultivation of corn and beans, and peasants had little choice but to work on haciendas. To survive, they had to buy food and other necessities on credit from the landowner's store; eventually, they fell permanently into debt. Sometimes whole communities were forced to relocate.

In the 1880s, American investors purchased from the Mexican government dubious claims to more than 2.5 million acres (1 million hectares) traditionally held by the Yaqui people of Sonora, in northern Mexico. When the Yaqui resisted the expropriation of their lands, they were brutally repressed by the Mexican army.

Northern Mexicans had no peasant tradition of communal ownership, for the northern half of the country was too dry for farming, unlike the tropical and densely populated south. The north was a region of silver mines and cattle ranches, some of them enormous. It was thinly populated by cowboys and miners. The harshness of their lives and vast inequities in the distribution of income made northern Mexicans as resentful as people in the south.

Despite many upheavals in Mexico in the nineteenth century, the government in 1910 seemed in control; no

---

mestizo (mess-TEE-zoh)

one expected a revolution. For thirty-four years, General Porfirio Díaz° (1830–1915) had ruled Mexico under the motto "Liberty, Order, Progress." To Díaz, "liberty" meant freedom for rich hacienda owners and foreign investors to acquire more land. The government imposed "order" through rigged elections and a policy of *pan o palo* (bread or the stick)—that is, bribes for Díaz's supporters and summary justice for those who opposed him. And "progress" meant mainly the importing of foreign capital, machinery, and technicians to take advantage of Mexico's labor, soil, and natural resources.

During the Díaz years (1876–1910), Mexico City—with paved streets, streetcar lines, electric street lighting, and public parks—became a showplace, and new telegraph and railroad lines connected cities and towns throughout Mexico. But this material progress benefited only a handful of well-connected businessmen. The boom in railroads, agriculture, and mining at the turn of the century actually caused a decline in the average Mexican's standard of living.

Though a mestizo himself, Díaz discriminated against the nonwhite majority of Mexicans. He and his supporters tried to eradicate what they saw as Mexico's embarrassingly rustic traditions. On many middle- and upper-class tables, French cuisine replaced traditional Mexican dishes. The wealthy replaced sombreros and ponchos with European garments, and they preferred horse racing and soccer to the traditional bullfighting and cockfighting. To the educated middle class—the only group with a strong sense of Mexican nationhood—this devaluation of Mexican culture became a symbol of the Díaz regime's failure to defend national interests against foreign influences.

Revolution and Civil War, 1911–1920

Unlike the independence movement in India, the Mexican Revolution was not the work of one party with a well-defined ideology. Instead, it developed haphazardly, led by a series of ambitious but limited leaders, each representing a different segment of Mexican society.

The first was Francisco I. Madero (1873–1913), the son of a wealthy landowning and mining family, educated in the United States. When minor uprisings broke out in 1911, the government collapsed and Díaz fled into exile. In 1913, after two years as president, Madero was overthrown and murdered by one of his former supporters, General Victoriano Huerta. Woodrow Wilson (1856–

Díaz (DEE-as)

Emiliano Zapata   Zapata, the leader of a peasant rebellion in southern Mexico during the Mexican Revolution, stands in full revolutionary regalia: sword, rifles, bandoleers, boots, and sombrero.   (Brown Brothers)

1924), president of the United States, showed his displeasure by sending the United States Marines to occupy Veracruz.

The inequities of Mexican society and foreign intervention in Mexico's affairs angered Mexico's middle class and industrial workers. They found leaders in Venustiano Carranza, a landowner, and in Alvaro Obregón°, a schoolteacher. Calling themselves Constitutionalists, Carranza and Obregón organized private armies and in

Obregón (oh-bray-GAWN)

Map 32.2   The Mexican Revolution   The Mexican Revolution began in two distinct regions of the country. One was the mountainous and densely populated area south of Mexico City, particularly Morelos, homeland of Emiliano Zapata. The other was the dry and thinly populated ranch country of the north, such as Chihuahua, home of Pancho Villa. The fighting that ensued crisscrossed the country along the main railroad lines, shown on the map.

1914 succeeded in overthrowing Huerta. By then, the revolution had spread to the countryside.

As early as 1911, **Emiliano Zapata** (1879–1919), an Indian farmer, had led a revolt against the haciendas in the mountains of Morelos, south of Mexico City (see Map 32.2). His soldiers were peasants, some of them women, mounted on horseback and armed with pistols and rifles. For several years, they periodically came down from the mountains, burned hacienda buildings, and returned land to the Indian villages to which it had once belonged.

Another leader appeared in Chihuahua, a northern state where seventeen individuals owned two-fifths of the land and 95 percent of the people had no land at all. Starting in 1913, **Francisco "Pancho" Villa** (1877–1923), a former ranch hand, mule driver, and bandit, organized an army of three thousand men, most of them cowboys. They too seized land from the large haciendas, not to

rebuild traditional communities as in southern Mexico but to create family ranches.

Zapata and Villa were part agrarian rebels, part social revolutionaries. They enjoyed tremendous popular support but could never rise above their regional and peasant origins and lead a national revolution. The Constitutionalists had fewer soldiers than Zapata and Villa; but they held the major cities, controlled the country's exports of oil, and used the proceeds of oil sales to buy modern weapons. Fighting continued for years, and gradually the Constitutionalists took over most of Mexico. In 1919 they defeated and killed Zapata; Villa was assassinated four years later. An estimated 2 million people lost their lives in the civil war, and much of Mexico lay in ruins.

During their struggle to win support against Zapata and Villa, the Constitutionalists adopted many of their rivals' agrarian reforms, such as restoring communal

The Agitator, **a Mural by Diego Rivera** Diego Rivera (1886–1957) was politically committed to the Mexican Revolution and widely admired as an artist. This mural, painted at the National Agricultural School at Chapingo near Mexico City, shows a political agitator addressing peasants and workers. With one hand, the speaker points to miners laboring in a silver mine; with the other, to a hammer and sickle. (Universidad Autonoma de Chapingo/CENIDIAP-INBA)

lands to the Indians of Morelos. The Constitutionalists also proposed social programs designed to appeal to workers and the middle class. The Constitution of 1917 promised universal suffrage and a one-term presidency; state-run education to free the poor from the hold of the Catholic Church; the end of debt peonage; restrictions on foreign ownership of property; and laws specifying minimum wages and maximum hours to protect laborers. Although these reforms were too costly to implement right away, they had important symbolic significance, for they enshrined the dignity of Mexicans and the equality of Indians, mestizos, and whites, as well as of peasants and city people.

The Revolution Institutionalized, 1920–1940

In the early 1920s, after a decade of violence that exhausted all classes, the Mexican Revolution lost momentum. Only in Morelos did peasants receive land, and President Obregón and his closest associates made all important decisions. Nevertheless, the Revolution changed the social makeup of the governing class in important ways. For the first time in Mexico's history, representatives of rural communities, unionized workers, and public employees were admitted to the inner circle.

In the arts, the Mexican Revolution sparked a surge of creativity. The political murals of José Clemente Orozco and Diego Rivera and the paintings of Frida Kahlo focused on social themes, showing peasants, workers, and soldiers in scenes from the Revolution.

In 1928 Obregón was assassinated. His successor, Plutarco Elías Calles°, founded the National Revolutionary Party, or PNR (the abbreviation of its name in Spanish). The PNR was a forum where all the pressure groups and vested interests—labor, peasants, businessmen, landowners, the military, and others—worked out compromises. The establishment of the PNR gave the Mexican Revolution a second wind.

Lázaro Cárdenas°, chosen by Calles to be president in 1934, brought peasants' and workers' organizations into the party, renamed it the Mexican Revolutionary Party (PRM), and removed the generals from government positions. Then he set to work implementing the reforms promised in the Constitution of 1917. Cárdenas redistributed 44 million acres (17.6 million hectares) to peasant communes. He closed church-run schools, replacing them with government schools. He nationalized

Calles (KAH-yace)
Lázaro Cárdenas (LAH-sah-roe KAHR-dih-nahs)

the railroads and numerous other businesses. Cárdenas's most dramatic move was the expropriation of foreign-owned oil companies.

In the early 1920s, Mexico was the world's leading producer of oil, but a handful of American and British companies exported almost all of it. In 1938 Cárdenas seized the foreign-owned oil industry, more as a matter of national pride than of economics. The oil companies expected the governments of the United States and Great Britain to come to their rescue, perhaps with military force. But Mexico and the United States chose to resolve the issue through negotiation, and Mexico retained control of its oil industry.

When Cárdenas's term ended in 1940, Mexico, like India, was still a land of poor farmers with a small industrial base. The Revolution had brought great changes, however. The political system was free of both chaos and dictatorships. A small group of wealthy people no longer monopolized land and other resources. The military was tamed, the Catholic Church no longer controlled education, and the nationalization of oil had demonstrated Mexico's independence from foreign corporations and military intervention.

What did the Mexican Revolution accomplish? It did not fulfill the democratic promise of Madero's campaign, but it did allow far more sectors of the population to participate in politics. The Revolution also promised far-reaching social reforms, such as free education, higher wages and more security for workers, and the redistribution of land to the peasants. These long-delayed reforms began to be implemented during the Cárdenas administration. They fell short of the ideals expressed by the revolutionaries, but they laid the foundation for the later industrialization of Mexico.

Argentina and Brazil, 1900–1949

On the surface, Argentina and Brazil seem very different. Argentina is Spanish-speaking, temperate in climate, and populated almost exclusively by Europeans. Brazil is tropical, Portuguese-speaking, and inhabited by people of mixed European and African origin, plus a substantial Indian minority. But in the twentieth century, their economic, political, and technological experiences were remarkably similar.

The Transformation of Argentina

Most of Argentina consists of *pampas*°, flat, fertile land that is easy to till, much like the prairies of the midwestern United States and Canada. Throughout the nineteenth century, Argentina's economy was based on two exports: the hides of longhorn creole cattle and the wool of merino sheep, which roamed the pampas in huge herds. Centuries earlier, Europeans had haphazardly introduced the animals and the grasses they ate. Natural selection had made the animals tough and hardy.

At the end of the nineteenth century, railroads and refrigerator ships, which allowed the safe transportation of meat, changed not only the composition of Argentina's exports but also the way they were produced—in other words, the land itself. European consumers preferred the soft flesh of Lincoln sheep and Hereford cattle to the tough sinewy meat of creole cattle and merino sheep. The valuable Lincolns and Herefords could not be allowed to roam and graze on the pampas. They were carefully bred and received a diet of alfalfa and oats. To safeguard them, the pampas had to be divided, plowed, cultivated, and fenced with barbed wire to keep out predators and other unwelcome animals. Once fenced, the land could be used to produce wheat as well as beef and mutton. Within a few years, grasslands that had stretched to the horizon were transformed into farmland. Like the North American midwest, the pampas became one of the world's great producers of wheat and meat.

Argentina's government represented the interests of the *oligarquía*°, a very small group of wealthy landowners. Members of this elite controlled enormous haciendas where they raised cattle and sheep and grew wheat for export. They also owned fine homes in Buenos Aires°, a city that was built to look like Paris. They traveled frequently to Europe and spent so lavishly that the French coined the superlative "rich as an Argentine." They showed little interest in any business other than farming, however, and were content to let foreign companies, mainly British, build Argentina's railroads, processing plants, the public utilities. In exchange for its agricultural exports, Argentina imported almost all its manufactured goods from Europe and the United States. So important were British interests in the Argentinean economy that the language used on the railroads was not Spanish but English, and the biggest department store in Buenos Aires was a branch of Harrod's of London.

---

pampas (POM-pus)   *oligarquía* (oh-lee gar-KEE-ah)
Buenos Aires (BWAY-nihs AIR-eze)

Brazil and Argentina, to 1929

Before the First World War, Brazil produced most of the world's coffee and cacao, grown on vast estates, and natural rubber, gathered by Indians from rubber trees growing wild in the Amazon rain forest. Brazil's elite was made up of coffee and cacao planters and rubber exporters. Like their Argentinean counterparts, they spent their money lavishly on palaces in Rio de Janeiro° and on the world's most beautiful opera house in Manaus°, deep in the Amazon. They had little interest in other forms of development, let British companies build railroads, harbors, and other infrastructure, and imported all manufactured goods. At the time, this situation seemed to offer a rational division of labor that allowed each country to do what it did best. If the British did not grow coffee, why should Brazil build locomotives?

Both Argentina and Brazil had small but outspoken middle classes that demanded a share in government and looked to Europe as a model. Beneath each middle class were the poor. In Argentina these were mainly Spanish and Italian immigrants who had ended up as landless farm laborers or workers in urban packing plants. In Brazil there was a large class of sharecroppers and plantation workers, many of them descendants of slaves.

Rubber exports collapsed after 1912, replaced by cheaper plantation rubber from Southeast Asia. The outbreak of war in 1914 put an end to imports from Europe as Britain and France focused all their industries on war production and Germany was cut off entirely. To a certain extent, the United States replaced the European countries as suppliers of machinery and as consumers of coffee. European immigrants built factories to manufacture textiles and household goods. Desperate for money to pay for the war, Great Britain sold off many of its railroad, streetcar, and other companies to the governments of Argentina and Brazil.

The disruption of the old trade patterns weakened the landowning class. In Argentina, the urban middle class obtained the secret ballot and universal male suffrage in 1916 and elected a liberal politician, Hipólito Irigoyen°, as president. In Brazil, junior officers rebelled periodically against the government but accomplished little. In neither country did the urban middle class take power away from the wealthy landowners. Instead, the two classes shared power at the expense of both the landless peasants and the urban workers.

The 1920s were a period of peace and prosperity in South America, in contrast to Mexico. Trade with Europe

---

Rio de Janeiro (REE-oh day zhuh-NAIR-oh)
Manaus (meh-NOWSE)
Hipólito Irigoyen (ee-POH-lee-toe ee-ree-GO-yen)

resumed, prices received for agricultural exports remained high, and both Argentina and Brazil used profits accumulated during the war to industrialize and improve their transportation systems and public utilities. Yet as they were moving forward, new technologies again left them dependent on the advanced industrial countries.

Brazilians are justly proud that the first person to fly an airplane outside the United States was Alberto Santos-Dumont, a Brazilian. He did so in 1906 in France, where he lived most of his life and had access to engine manufacturers and technical assistance. Aviation reached Latin America after World War I, when European and American companies such as Aéropostale and Pan American Airways introduced airmail service between the cities and linked Latin America with the United States and Europe.

Before and during World War I, radio, then called "wireless telegraphy," was used not for broadcasting but for point-to-point communications. Transmitters powerful enough to send messages across oceans or continents were extraordinarily complex and expensive: their antennas covered many acres, they used as much electricity as a small town, and they cost tens of thousands of pounds sterling (millions of year-2000 dollars).

Right after the war, the major powers scrambled to build powerful transmitters on every continent to compete with the telegraph cable companies and to take advantage of the boom in international business and news reporting. At the time, no Latin American country possessed the knowledge or funds to build its own transmitters. In 1919, therefore, President Irigoyen of Argentina granted a radio concession to a German firm. France and Britain protested this decision, and eventually four powerful radio companies—one British, one French, one German, and one American—formed a cartel to control all radio communications in Latin America. This cartel set up a national radio company in each Latin American republic, installing a prominent local politician as its president, but the cartel held all the stock and therefore received all the profits. Thus, even as Brazil and Argentina were taking over their railroads and older industries, the major industrial countries controlled the diffusion of the newer aviation and radio technologies.

The Depression and the Vargas Regime in Brazil

The Depression hit Latin America as hard as it hit Europe and the United States; in many ways, it marks a more important turning point for the region than either of the world wars. As long-term customers cut back their orders, the value of agricultural and mineral exports fell by two-thirds between 1929 and 1932. Argentina and Brazil could no longer afford to import manufactured goods. An imploding economy also undermined their shaky political systems. Like European countries, Argentina and Brazil veered toward authoritarian regimes that promised to solve their economic problems.

In 1930, **Getulio Vargas°,** (1883–1953), governor of the state of Rio Grande do Sul°, staged a coup and proclaimed himself president of Brazil. He proved to be a masterful politician. He wrote a new constitution that broadened the franchise and limited the president to one term. He raised import duties and promoted national firms and state-owned enterprises, culminating in the construction of the Volta Redonda steel mill in the 1930s. By 1936, industrial production had doubled, especially in textiles and small manufactures. Brazil was on its way to becoming an industrial country. Vargas's policy, called **import-substitution industrialization,** became a model for other Latin American countries as they attempted to break away from neocolonial dependency.

The industrialization of Brazil brought all the familiar environmental consequences. Powerful new machines allowed the reopening of old mines and the digging of new ones. Cities grew as poor peasants looking for work arrived from the countryside. Around the older neighborhoods of Rio de Janeiro and São Paulo°, the poor turned steep hillsides and vacant lands into immense *favelas°* (slums) of makeshift shacks.

The countryside also was transformed. Scrubland was turned into pasture, and new acreage was planted in wheat, corn, and sugar cane. Even the Amazon rain forest—half of the land area of Brazil—was affected. In 1930, American industrialist Henry Ford invested $8 million to clear land along the Tapajós River and prepare it to become the site of the world's largest rubber plantation. Ford encountered opposition from Brazilian workers and politicians, the rubber trees proved vulnerable to diseases, and he had to abandon the project—but not before leaving 3 million acres (1.2 million hectares) denuded of trees. The ecological changes of the Vargas era, however, were but a tiny forerunner of the degradation of the Brazilian environment that was to take place later in the century.

Vargas instituted many reforms favorable to urban workers, such as labor unions, pension plans, and disability insurance, but he refused to take any measures that might help the millions of landless peasants or harm the interests of the great landowners. Although the Brazilian economy recovered from the Depression, the benefits of recovery were so unequally distributed that communist and fascist movements demanded even more radical changes.

In 1938, prohibited by his own constitution from being reelected, Vargas staged another coup, abolished the constitution, and instituted the Estado Novo°, or "New State," with himself as supreme leader. He abolished political parties, jailed opposition leaders, and turned Brazil into a fascist state. When the Second World War broke out, however, Vargas aligned Brazil with the United States and contributed troops and ships to the Allied war effort.

Despite his economic achievements, Vargas harmed Brazil. By running roughshod over laws, constitutions, and rights, he infected not only Brazil but all of South America with the temptations of political violence. It is ironic, but not surprising, that Vargas was overthrown in 1945 by a military coup.

Argentina After 1930

Economically, the Depression hurt Argentina almost as badly as it hurt Brazil. Politically, however, the consequences were delayed for many years. In 1930, General José Uriburu° overthrew the popularly elected President Irigoyen. The Uriburu government represented the large landowners and big business interests. For thirteen years the generals and the oligarquía ruled, doing nothing to lessen the poverty of the workers or the frustrations of the middle class. When World War II broke out, Argentina sympathized with the Axis but remained officially neutral.

In 1943 another military revolt flared, this one among junior officers angry at conservative politicians. It was led by Colonel **Juan Perón°** (1895–1974). The intentions of the rebels were clear:

> Civilians will never understand the greatness of our ideal; we shall therefore have to eliminate them from the government and give them the only mission which corresponds to them: work and obedience.[1]

Once in power, the officers took over the highest positions in government and business and began to lavish money on military equipment and their own salaries. Their goal, inspired by Nazi victories, was nothing less than the conquest of South America.

As the war turned against the Nazis, the officers saw their popularity collapse. Perón, however, had other

---

Getulio Vargas (jay-TOO-lee-oh VAR-gus)
Rio Grande do Sul (REE-oh GRAN-dee do SOOL)
São Paulo (sow PAL-oh)   *favela* (feh-VEL-luh)

Estado Novo (esh-TAH-doe NO-vo)
José Uriburu (hoe-SAY oo-ree-BOO-roo)
Juan Perón (hoo-AHN pair-OWN)

Eva and Juan Perón   Eva Perón was a formidable political campaigner and the real power behind her husband's rise to power. Here Eva and Juan are addressing a political rally.   (Archivo General de la Nacion, Buenos Aires)

plans. Inspired by his charismatic wife **Eva Duarte Perón°** (1919–1952), he appealed to the urban workers. Eva Perón became the champion of the *descamisados°*, or "shirtless ones," and campaigned tirelessly for social benefits and for the cause of women and children. With his wife's help, Perón won the presidency in 1946 and created a populist dictatorship in imitation of the Vargas regime in Brazil.

Like Brazil, Argentina industrialized rapidly under state sponsorship. Perón spent lavishly on social welfare projects as well as on the military, depleting the capital that Argentina had earned during the war. Though a skillful demagogue who played off the army against the navy and both against the labor unions, Perón could not create a stable government out of the chaos of coups and conspiracies. He had to back down from a plan to make Eva his vice president. When she died in 1952, he lost his political skills (or perhaps they were hers), and soon thereafter he was overthrown in yet another military coup.

Eva Duarte Perón (AY-vuh doo-AR-tay pair-OWN)
descamisados (des-cah-mee-SAH-dohs)

Mexico, Argentina, and Brazil: A Comparison

Until 1910, Mexico, Argentina, and Brazil shared a common history and similar cultures. In the first half of the twentieth century, their economies followed parallel trajectories, based on their unequal relations with the industrialized countries of Europe and North America. All three countries—indeed, all of Latin America—struggled with the failure of neocolonial economics to improve the lives of the middle class, let alone the peasants. And when the Depression hit, all three turned to state intervention and import-substitution industrialization. Like all industrializing countries, they did so by mining, farming, ranching, cutting down forests, and irrigating land, all at the expense of the natural environment.

Yet their political histories diverged radically. Mexico underwent a traumatic and profound social revolution. Argentina and Brazil, meanwhile, languished under conservative regimes devoted to the interests of wealthy landowners, sporadically interrupted by military coups and populist demagogues. Mexicans, thanks to their experience of revolution, developed an acute sense of their national identity and civic pride in their history—pride largely missing in South America. Despite shortcomings, Mexico took seriously its commitment to education, land reform, social justice, and political stability as a national goal, not merely as the campaign platform of a populist dictator.

CONCLUSION

Sub-Saharan Africa, India, and Latin America lay outside the theaters of war that engulfed most of the Northern Hemisphere, but they were deeply affected by global events and by the demands of the industrial powers. Sub-Saharan Africa and India were still under colonial rule, and their political life revolved around the yearnings of their elites for political independence and their masses for social justice. Mexico, Argentina, and Brazil were politically independent, but their economies, like those of Africa and India, were closely tied to the economies of the industrial nations with which they traded. Their deeply polarized societies and the stresses caused by their dependence on the industrial countries clashed with the expectations of ever larger numbers of their peoples.

In Mexico, these stresses brought about a long and violent revolution, out of which Mexicans forged a lasting sense of national identity. Argentina and Brazil moved toward greater economic independence, but at the price of militarism and dictatorship. In India, the conflict between growing expectations and the reality of colonial rule produced both a movement for independence and an ethnic split that tore the nation apart. In sub-Saharan Africa, demands for national self-determination and economic development were only beginning to be voiced by 1949 and were not to come to fruition until the second half of the century.

Nationalism and the yearning for social justice were the two most powerful forces for change in the early twentieth century. These ideas originated in the industrialized countries but resonated in the independent countries of Latin America as well as in colonial regions such as the Indian subcontinent and sub-Saharan Africa. However, they did not always unite people against their colonial rulers or foreign oppressors; instead, they often divided them along social, ethnic, or religious lines. Western-educated elites looked to industrialization as a means of modernizing their country and ensuring their

position in it, while peasants and urban workers supported nationalist and revolutionary movements in the hope of improving their lives. Often these goals were not compatible.

■ Key Terms

Blaise Diagne	Emiliano Zapata
African National Congress	Francisco "Pancho" Villa
Haile Selassie	Lázaro Cárdenas
Indian National Congress	Getulio Vargas
Bengal	import-substitution
All-India Muslim League	industrialization
Mohandas K. (Mahatma) Gandhi	Juan Perón
Jawaharlal Nehru	Eva Duarte Perón
Muhammad Ali Jinnah	

■ Suggested Reading

On Africa under colonial rule the classic overview is Melville Herskovits, *The Human Factor in Changing Africa* (1958). Two excellent general introductions are Roland Oliver and Anthony Atmore, *Africa Since 1800*, 4th ed. (1994), and A. E. Afigbo et al., *The Making of Modern Africa*, vol. 2, *The Twentieth Century* (1986). More detailed and challenging are *UNESCO General History of Africa*, vols. 7 and 8; *The Cambridge History of Africa*, vols. 7 and 8; and Adu Boahen, *African Perspectives on Colonialism* (1987). Outstanding novels about Africa in the colonial era include Chinua Achebe, *Arrow of God* (1964); Buchi Emecheta, *The Joys of Motherhood* (1980); and Peter Abraham, *Mine Boy* (1946).

For a general introduction to Indian history see Sumit Sarkar, *Modern India, 1885–1947* (1983), and Percival Spear, *India: A Modern History*, rev. ed. (1972). On the influenza epidemic of 1918–1919 see Alfred W. Crosby, *America's Forgotten Pandemic: The Influenza of 1918* (1989). The Indian independence movement has received a great deal of attention. Judith M. Brown's most recent book on Gandhi is *Gandhi: Prisoner of Hope* (1989). *Gandhi's Truth: On the Origin of Militant Nonviolence* (1969) by noted psychoanalyst Erik Erikson is also recommended. Two collections of memoirs of the last decades of British rule are worth looking at: Charles Allen, ed., *Plain Tales of the Raj: Image of British India in the Twentieth Century* (1975), and Zareer Masani, ed., *Indian Tales of the Raj* (1988). The transition from colonialism to partition and independence is the subject of the very readable *Freedom at Midnight* (1975) by Larry Collins and Dominique Lapierre. The environment is discussed in M. Gadgil and R. Guha, *This Fissured Land: An Ecological History of India* (1993).

Thomas Skidmore and Peter Smith, *Modern Latin America*, 3d ed. (1992), offers the best brief introduction. Two fine general overviews of modern Mexican history are Enrique Krauze, *Mexico: Biography of a Power* (1997), and Colin MacLachlan and William Beezley, *El Gran Pueblo: A History of Greater Mexico* (1994). On the Mexican Revolution, two recent books are essential: Alan Knight, *The Mexican Revolution*, 2 vols. (1986), and John M. Hart, *Revolutionary Mexico: The Coming and Process of the Mexican Revolution* (1987). But see also two classics by sympathetic Americans: Frank Tannenbaum, *Peace by Revolution: Mexico After 1910* (1933), and Robert E. Quirk, *The Mexican Revolution, 1914–1915* (1960). Mexico's most celebrated revolutionary is the subject of Manuel Machado, *Centaur of the North: Francisco Villa, the Mexican Revolution, and Northern Mexico* (1988). Mariano Azuela, *The Underdogs* (1988), is an interesting fictional account of this period. The standard work on Brazil is E. Bradford Burns, *A History of Brazil*, 3d ed. (1993). The history of modern Argentina is ably treated in David Rock, *Argentina, 1517–1987: From Spanish Colonization to Alfonsín* (1987). Mark Jefferson, *Peopling the Argentine Pampas* (1971), and Jeremy Adelman, *Frontier Development: Land, Labour and Capital on the Wheatlands of Argentina and Canada, 1890–1914* (1994), describe the transformation of the Argentinean environment.

■ Note

1. George Blanksten, *Perón's Argentina* (Chicago: University of Chicago Press, 1953), 37.

PART EIGHT

THE PERILS AND PROMISES OF A GLOBAL COMMUNITY,

1945 – 2000

he notion of a postwar era in which all the world's peoples could rejoice in the defeat of totalitarianism became increasingly hollow as the Cold War set in between the United States and the Soviet Union and more and more peoples engaged in struggles for national independence. From 1945 to 1991, conflicts between communist and noncommunist forces in emerging nations repeatedly involved the superpowers, sometimes as arms suppliers or allies, sometimes as combatants. The Korean War and the Vietnam War engaged American troops; the Soviet Union became bogged down in a war in Afghanistan. Leaders of the Third World, a group of states proclaiming nonalignment in the Cold War, tried to advance their state-building programs by playing off the United States against the Soviet Union and gaining favors from both sides.

A turning point of sorts arrived around 1975. Escalating oil prices, provoked by conflicts in the Middle East, shook the world's economic foundations. The major nuclear powers began to recognize the futility of the arms race. The countries of East Asia rapidly industrialized. And the attitudes of young people around the world increasingly clashed with those of the parental, World War II, generation.

In the relatively nonindustrialized parts of the world, population grew rapidly. Governments in Latin America, Africa, South Asia, China, and the Middle East faced serious problems in providing the necessities of life. The extension of agriculture and other pressures on resources sped the deterioration of the environment.

The dissemination of new technologies, ranging from "green revolution" agricultural practices to consumer electronics, transformed daily life. Regional cultures, many of them religiously based, felt threatened by the spread of Western consumer society and entertainment. The vision of a global culture excited some people while repelling others.

Formal relations among groups of states—the United Nations, Cold War alliances, and free trade agreements—brought the world's peoples closer together than ever before. With the emergence of a truly global community, peacekeeping, human rights, and gender equality became international issues.

As the Cold War faded rapidly from memory after 1991, the world was seen by many to lack an overarching political or economic structure. Globalization became the watchword of those most deeply committed to economic growth and high technology. Rivalry between the poor South and the rich North struck others as a better reading of world affairs. Still others looked on environmental degradation as the greatest world problem. The postwar era had certainly come to an end, but no one was certain about what was next to come.

	1950	1960	1970
Americas	• **1945** United Nations charter signed in San Francisco • **1946** International Monetary Fund and World Bank founded • **1952** U.S. tests first hydrogen bomb	• **1962** Cuban missile crisis • **1959** Cuban Revolution • **1964** Military takes power in Brazil Neil Armstrong walks on moon **1969** •
Europe	**1948–1952** Marshall Plan helps rebuild western Europe • **1949** NATO founded • **1955** Warsaw Pact formed Soviet troops crush revolt in Hungary **1956** • • **1957** Common Market founded	• **1961** Berlin Wall built Student uprising in France **1968** •
Africa	• **1948** Apartheid becomes official in South Africa Ghana first British colony in Africa to win independence **1957** • • **1958** Guinea wins independence from France	• **1960** Nigeria, Congo, Somalia, Togo win independence • **1963** Kenya independent
Middle East	• **1948** State of Israel founded; first Arab-Israeli War • **1956** Suez crisis **1954–1962** Algerian war for Independence Organization of Petroleum Exporting Countries founded **1960** •	• **1967** Six Day Arab-Israeli War
Asia and Oceania	Communist Revolution in China **1949** • **1951–1953** Korean War **1954–1975** Vietnam War • **1949** Indonesia wins independence from Netherlands	Cultural Revolution in China **1966–1969** Japan becomes world economic power **1970s** •

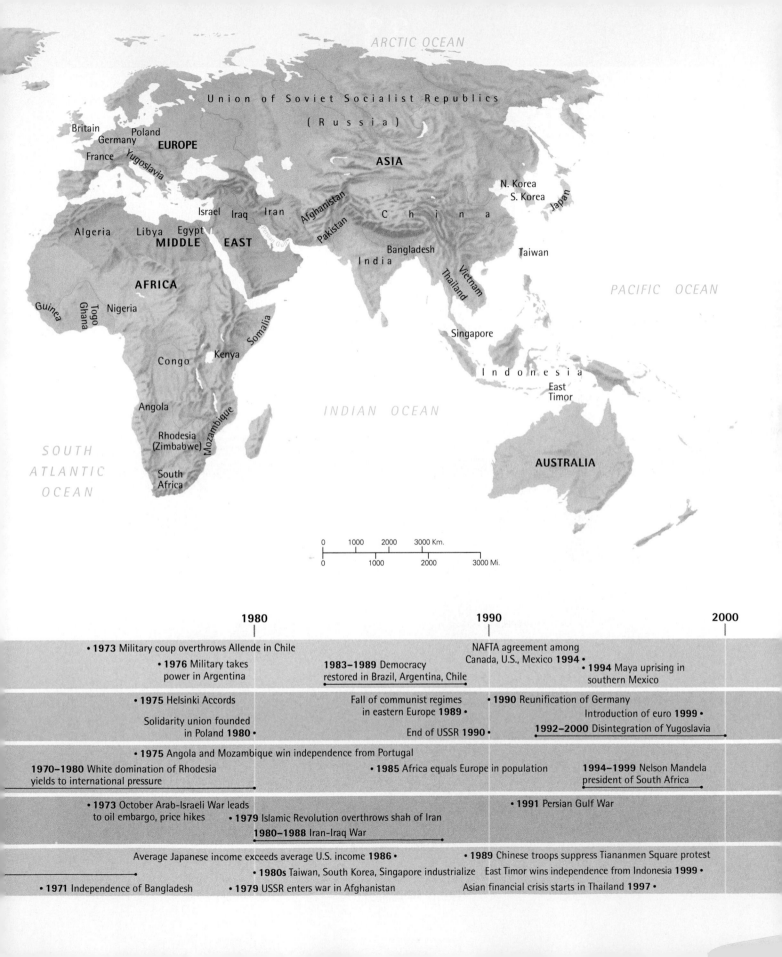

ARCTIC OCEAN

Union of Soviet Socialist Republics

(Russia)

Britain
Germany Poland
France EUROPE
Yugoslavia

ASIA

N. Korea
S. Korea
Japan

Israel Iraq Iran Afghanistan
Algeria Libya Egypt Pakistan China
MIDDLE EAST
Bangladesh
India Taiwan

AFRICA

PACIFIC OCEAN

Guinea Nigeria
Togo
Ghana
Vietnam
Thailand
Congo Kenya
Somalia
Singapore

INDONESIA
East
Timor

Angola

INDIAN OCEAN

Mozambique
Rhodesia
(Zimbabwe)

AUSTRALIA

SOUTH
ATLANTIC
OCEAN

South
Africa

| 0 | 1000 | 2000 | 3000 Km. |
| 0 | 1000 | 2000 | 3000 Mi. |

1980   **1990**   **2000**

• **1973** Military coup overthrows Allende in Chile

NAFTA agreement among
Canada, U.S., Mexico **1994** •

• **1976** Military takes
power in Argentina

1983–1989 Democracy
restored in Brazil, Argentina, Chile

• **1994** Maya uprising in
southern Mexico

• **1975** Helsinki Accords

Fall of communist regimes
in eastern Europe **1989** •

• **1990** Reunification of Germany

Introduction of euro **1999** •

Solidarity union founded
in Poland **1980** •

End of USSR **1990** •

1992–2000 Disintegration of Yugoslavia

• **1975** Angola and Mozambique win independence from Portugal

1970–1980 White domination of Rhodesia
yields to international pressure

• **1985** Africa equals Europe in population

1994–1999 Nelson Mandela
president of South Africa

• **1973** October Arab-Israeli War leads
to oil embargo, price hikes

• **1991** Persian Gulf War

• **1979** Islamic Revolution overthrows shah of Iran

1980–1988 Iran-Iraq War

Average Japanese income exceeds average U.S. income **1986** •

• **1989** Chinese troops suppress Tiananmen Square protest

• **1980s** Taiwan, South Korea, Singapore industrialize

East Timor wins independence from Indonesia **1999** •

• **1971** Independence of Bangladesh

• **1979** USSR enters war in Afghanistan

Asian financial crisis starts in Thailand **1997** •

33

THE COLD WAR AND DECOLONIZATION,

1945–1975

The Cold War • **Decolonization and Nation Building** •
Beyond a Bipolar World
ENVIRONMENT AND TECHNOLOGY: The Green Revolution
SOCIETY AND CULTURE: Silent Spring

Soviet Postal Tribute to First Woman Cosmonaut Valentina Tereshkova became
the first woman in space when she went aloft on the *Vostok-6* mission.

*I*n 1946, in a speech at Fulton, Missouri, Great Britain's wartime leader Winston Churchill said: "From Stettin in the Baltic to Trieste in the Adriatic, an iron curtain has descended across the Continent. . . . I am convinced there is nothing they [the communists] so much admire as strength, and there is nothing for which they have less respect than weakness, especially military weakness." The phrase **"iron curtain"** became a watchword of the **Cold War,** the state of political tension and military rivalry that was then beginning between the United States and its allies ("running dogs of imperialism" in Soviet parlance) and the Soviet Union and its allies ("satellites" in American parlance).

In the Atlantic Charter that Churchill and President Franklin Roosevelt issued four months before the United States entered the war in 1941, and then in the 1942 declaration signed by twenty-six "United Nations" (Roosevelt's term for the alliance against the Axis), they had looked forward to a postwar world of economic cooperation and restoration of sovereignty to peoples suffering Axis occupation and, above all, to a world where war and territorial conquest would not be tolerated. By the time Churchill delivered his "iron curtain" speech, however, Britain's electorate had voted him out of power, Harry S Truman had succeeded to the presidency after Roosevelt's death, and the Soviet Union was dominating eastern Europe and supporting communist movements in China, Iran, Turkey, Greece, and Korea. Although Soviet diplomats sat with their former allies in the newly founded United Nations Organization, confrontation rather than cooperation was the hallmark of relations between East and West.

The intensity of the Cold War, with its accompanying threat of nuclear destruction, sometimes obscured a postwar phenomenon of even greater importance. Western domination of Asia, Africa, and Latin America was largely ended, and the colonial empires of the New Imperialism were gradually dismantled. The new generation of national leaders to head the states in these regions sometimes skillfully played Cold War antagonism to their own advantage. Their real business, however, was nation building, an enterprise charged with almost insurmountable problems and conflicts.

Each land subject to imperialism had its own specific history and conditions and followed its own route to independence. Thus the new nations had a difficult time finding a collective voice in a world increasingly oriented toward two superpowers, the United States and the Soviet Union. Some sided openly with one or the other. Others banded together in a posture of neutrality and spoke with one voice about their need for economic and technical assistance and the obligation of the wealthy nations to satisfy those needs.

The Cold War military rivalry stimulated extraordinary advances in weaponry and associated technologies, but many new nations faced basic problems of educating their citizens, nurturing industry, and escaping the economic constraints imposed by their former imperialist masters. The environment suffered severe pressures, whether from oil exploration and transport to feed the growing economies of the wealthy nations or from deforestation in poor regions challenged by the need for cropland. Neither rich nor poor realized the costs associated with environmental change.

As you read this chapter, ask yourself the following questions:

- What impact did economic philosophy have on both the Cold War and the decolonization movement?
- How was a third world war averted?
- Was world domination by the superpowers good or bad for the rest of the world?

THE COLD WAR

The wartime alliance between the United States, Great Britain, and the Soviet Union had been an uneasy one. Fear of working-class revolution, which the Nazis had played upon in their rise to power, was not confined to Germany. Political and economic leaders committed to free markets and untrammeled capital investment

The Green Revolution

Concern about world food supplies grew directly out of the serious shortages that many nations faced because of the devastation and trade disruptions of World War II. The Food and Agriculture Organization of the United Nations, the Rockefeller Foundation, and the Ford Foundation took leading roles in fostering crop research and educating farmers about agricultural techniques. In 1966 the International Rice Research Institute (established in 1960–1962) began distributing seeds for an improved rice variety known as IR-8. Crop yields from this and other new varieties, along with improved farming techniques, were so impressive that the term *Green Revolution* was coined to describe a new era in agricultural history.

On the heels of the successful new rice strains came new varieties of corn and wheat. Building on twenty years of Rockefeller-funded research in Mexico, the Centro Interna-cional de Mejoramiento de Maiz y Trigo (International Center for the Improvement of Maize and Wheat) was established in 1966 under Norman Borlaug, who was awarded the Nobel Peace Prize four years later. This organization distributed around the world short, stiff-strawed varieties of wheat that were resistant to disease and responsive to fertilizer.

By 1970 other centers for research on tropical agriculture had been established in Ibadan, Nigeria, and Cali, Colombia. But the success of the Green Revolution and the growing need for its products called for a more comprehensive effort. The Consultative Group on International Agricultural Research brought together World Bank expertise, private foundations, international organizations, and national foreign aid agencies to undertake worldwide support of efforts to increase food productivity and improve natural resource management.

Miracle Rice   New strains of so-called "miracle rice" made many nations in south and southeast Asia self-sufficient in food production after decades of worry about the growth of population outstripping agricultural productivity. (Victor Englebert)

had loathed socialism in its several forms for more than a century. After World War II, the iron curtain in Europe and communist insurgencies in China and elsewhere seemed to confirm the threat of worldwide revolution.

Western leaders quickly came to perceive the Soviet Union as the nerve center of world revolution and as a military power capable of launching a war as destructive and terrible as the one recently ended. But Soviet leaders, par-ticularly after the United States and the countries of western Europe established the **North Atlantic Treaty Organization (NATO)** military alliance in 1949, felt themselves surrounded by hostile forces just when they were trying to recover from the terrible losses sustained in the war against the Axis. The distrust and suspicion between the two sides played out on a worldwide stage. The United Nations provided the venue for face-to-face debate.

CHRONOLOGY

	Cold War	Decolonization
1945		
1950	**1948–1949** Berlin airlift **1949** NATO formed **1950–1953** Korean War **1952** United States detonates first hydrogen bomb	**1947** Partition of India **1949** Dutch withdraw from Indonesia
	1955 Warsaw Pact concluded **1956** Soviet Union suppresses Hungarian revolt **1957** Soviet Union launches first artificial satellite into earth orbit	**1954** CIA intervention in Guatemala; defeat at Dienbienphu ends French hold on Vietnam **1955** Bandung Conference **1957** Ghana becomes first British colony in Africa to gain independence **1959** Fidel Castro leads revolution in Cuba
1960	**1961** East Germany builds Berlin Wall **1962** Cuban missile crisis	**1960** Shootings in Sharpeville intensify South African struggle against apartheid; Nigeria becomes independent **1962** Algeria wins independence
1970	**1975** Helsinki Accords; end of Vietnam War	**1971** Bangladesh secedes from Pakistan

The United Nations

In 1944 representatives from the United States, Great Britain, the Soviet Union, and China met and drafted specific charter proposals that finally bore fruit in the treaty called the United Nations Charter, ratified on October 24, 1945. Like the League of Nations, the **United Nations** had two main bodies: the General Assembly, with representatives from all member states; and the Security Council, with five permanent members—China, France, Great Britain, the United States, and the Soviet Union—and seven rotating members. A full-time bureaucracy headed by a Secretary General carried out the day-to-day business of both bodies. Various United Nations agencies focused on specialized international problems—for example, UNICEF (United Nations Children's Emergency Fund), FAO (Food and Agriculture Organization) and UNESCO (United Nations Educational, Scientific and Cultural Organization) (see Environment and Technology: The Green Revolution). Unlike the League of Nations, which required unanimous agreement in both of its deliberative bodies, the United Nations operated by majority vote, except that the five permanent members of the Security Council had veto power in that chamber.

All signatories to the United Nations Charter renounced war and territorial conquest. Nevertheless, peacekeeping, the sole preserve of the Security Council, became a vexing problem. The permanent members exercised their veto when necessary to protect their friends and interests. Throughout the Cold War, the United Nations was seldom able to forestall or quell international conflicts, though from time to time it sent observers or peacekeeping forces to monitor truces or agreements otherwise arrived at.

The decolonization of Africa and Asia greatly swelled the size of the General Assembly but not the Security Council. Many of the new nations looked to the United Nations for material assistance and access to a wider political world. While the vetoes of the Security Council's permanent members often stymied actions touching even indirectly on Cold War concerns, the General Assembly became an arena for expressing opinions on many issues involving decolonization, a movement that the Soviet Union strongly encouraged but the Western colonial powers resisted.

In the early years of the United Nations, General Assembly resolutions carried great weight. An example is a 1947 resolution that sought to divide Palestine into sovereign Jewish and Arab states. Gradually, though, the flood of new members produced a voting majority concerned more with poverty, racial discrimination, and the struggle against imperialism than with the Cold War. As a result, the Western powers increasingly disregarded the General Assembly, allowing the new nations of the world to have their say but not to act collectively.

Capitalism and Communism

In July 1944, with Allied victory a foregone conclusion, economic specialists representing over forty countries met at Bretton Woods, a New Hampshire resort, to devise a new international monetary system. The signatories eventually agreed to fix exchange rates while creating an International Monetary Fund (IMF) and a World Bank (formally the International Bank for Reconstruction and Development). The IMF was to use currency reserves from member nations to finance temporary trade deficits, and the **World Bank** was to provide funds for reconstructing Europe and helping needy countries after the war.

The Soviet Union attended the Bretton Woods Conference and signed the agreements, but by 1946, when they went into effect, suspicion between the Soviet Union and the United States and Britain had deepened. While the rest of the world moved to a monetary system that relied for stability on most countries holding reserves of dollars and the United States holding reserves of gold, the Soviet Union established a closed monetary system for itself and the new communist regimes in eastern Europe. In the Western countries, supply and demand determined prices; in the Soviet command economy, government priorities and agencies allocated goods and set prices, irrespective of market forces.

Many leaders from the newly independent states, having won the struggle against imperialism, preferred the Soviet Union's socialist example to the capitalism of their former colonizers. Thus the relative success of economies patterned on Eastern or Western models became an element in the Cold War rivalry. Each side trumpeted economic successes measured by such things as industrial output, changes in per capita income, and productivity gains as evidence of its superiority.

During World War II, the U.S. economy finally escaped the lingering effects of the Great Depression (see Chapter 31). Increased military spending and the draft brought full employment and high wages. The wartime conversion of factories from the production of consumer goods created pent-up demand for those goods.

With peace, the United States enjoyed prosperity and an international competitive advantage because of the massive destruction in Europe.

The economy of western Europe was heavily damaged during World War II, and in many European countries the early postwar years were bleak. With prosperity, the United States was able to support the reconstruction of western Europe. The **Marshall Plan** provided $12.5 billion to friendly European countries between 1948 and 1952. By 1961 more than $20 billion in economic aid had been disbursed. European determination backed up with American dollars spurred recovery. By 1963, a resurgent European economy had doubled 1940 output.

Western European governments generally increased their role in economic management during this period. In Great Britain, the Labour Party government of the 1950s nationalized coal, steel, railroads, and health care. The French government nationalized public utilities, the auto, banking, and insurance industries, and parts of the mining industry. These steps provided large infusions of capital for rebuilding and for acquiring new technologies.

In 1948 European governments also launched a process of economic cooperation and integration with the creation of the Organization of European Economic Cooperation (OEEC). After cooperative policies on coal and steel proved successful, some OEEC countries were ready to begin lowering tariffs to encourage the movement of goods and capital. In 1957 France, West Germany, Italy, the Netherlands, Belgium, and Luxembourg signed a treaty creating the European Economic Community, also known as the Common Market. By the 1970s the Common Market nations had nearly overtaken the United States in industrial production. The economic alliance expanded after 1970, as Great Britain, Denmark, Greece, Ireland, Spain, Portugal, Finland, Sweden, and Austria joined. The enlarged alliance called itself the **European Community (EC).**

Prosperity brought dramatic changes to European society. Average wages increased, unemployment fell, and social welfare benefits were expanded. Governments increased spending on health care, unemployment benefits, old age pensions, public housing, and grants to poor families with children. The combination of economic growth and income redistribution raised living standards and fueled demand for consumer goods. Automobile ownership, for example, grew approximately ninefold between 1950 and 1970.

The Soviet experience provided a dramatic contrast. The rapid development of a powerful Soviet state after 1917 had challenged traditional Western assumptions about economic development and social policy. From the 1920s, the Soviet state relied on bureaucratic agencies and political processes to determine the production, distribution, and price of goods. Housing, medical services, retail shops, factories, the land—even musical compositions and literary works—were viewed as collective property and were therefore regulated and administered by the state.

The economies of the Soviet Union and its eastern European allies were just as devastated at the end of the Second World War as those of western Europe. However, the Soviet command economy had enormous natural resources, a large population, and abundant energy at its disposal. Moreover, Soviet planners had made large investments in technical and scientific education, and the Soviet state had developed heavy industry in the 1930s and during the war years. As a result, recovery was rapid at first. Then, as the postwar period progressed, bureaucratic control of the economy grew less efficient, and industrial might became increasingly measured by the production of consumer goods such as television sets and automobiles rather than tons of coal and steel. In the 1970s the gap with the West widened. The Soviet

economy failed to meet domestic demand for clothing, housing, food, automobiles, and consumer electronics. Agricultural inefficiency forced the Soviet Union to rely on food imports.

The socialist nations of eastern Europe were compelled to follow the Soviet economic model, although some national differences appeared. Poland and Hungary, for example, implemented agricultural collectivization more slowly than did Czechoslovakia. Despite the differences, however, economic planners throughout the region coordinated industrialization and production plans with the Soviet Union. Significant growth occurred among the socialist economies, but the inefficiencies and failures that plagued the Soviet economy troubled them as well.

The United States and the Soviet Union competed in providing loans and grants and in supplying arms (at bargain prices) to countries willing to align with them politically. Thus the relative success or failure of capitalism and communism in Europe and the United States was not necessarily the strongest consideration in other parts of the world when the time came to construct new national economies.

Cold War Confrontation in 1959   U.S. vice president Richard M. Nixon and Soviet premier Nikita Khrushchev had a heated exchange of views during Nixon's visit to a Moscow trade fair. Two years earlier, the Soviet Union had launched the world's first space satellite.   (Seymour Raskin/Magnum Photos, Inc.)

West Versus East in Europe and Korea

For Germany, Austria, and Japan, peace brought foreign military occupation and new governments installed and controlled by the occupiers. For the Soviet Union, war's end meant opportunities for workers' movements struggling for power. Military occupation facilitated the communist victories in eastern Europe. The rapid emergence of communist regimes in Poland, Czechoslovakia, Hungary, Bulgaria, Romania, Yugoslavia, and Albania appalled Western leaders.

For the United States, the shift from viewing the Soviet Union as an ally against Germany to seeing it as a worldwide enemy took two years. In the waning days of World War II, the United States had seemed amenable to the Soviet desire for free access to the Bosphorus and Dardanelles straits that, under Turkish control, restricted naval deployments from the Black Sea to the Mediterranean. But in July 1947 the **Truman Doctrine** offered military aid to help both Turkey and Greece resist Soviet military pressure and subversion. (This initiative quickly grew into the Marshall Plan.) In 1951 Greece and Turkey were admitted to NATO. NATO's Soviet counterpart, the **Warsaw Pact,** emerged in 1955 in response to the Western powers' decision to allow West Germany to rearm within limits set by NATO (see Map 33.1).

The much-feared and long-prepared-for third great war in Europe did not occur. The Soviet Union tested Western resolve in 1948–1949 by blockading the areas of Berlin occupied by British, French, and American forces, which were surrounded by Soviet-controlled East Germany. Airlifts of food and fuel defeated the blockade. In 1961 the East German government accentuated Germany's political division by building the Berlin Wall, as much to prevent its citizens from fleeing to the noncommunist western part of the city as to keep westerners from entering East German territory. The West tested the East, in turn, by encouraging a rift between the Soviet Union and Yugoslavia. Western aid and encouragement resulted in Yugoslavia signing a defensive treaty with Greece and Turkey (but not with NATO) and deciding against joining the Warsaw Pact.

Soviet power set clear limits on how far any eastern European country might stray from Soviet domination. In 1956 Soviet troops crushed an anti-Soviet revolt in Hungary. Czechoslovakia suffered Hungary's fate in 1968. The West, a passive onlooker, had no recourse but to acknowledge that the Soviet Union had the right to intervene in the domestic affairs of any Soviet-bloc nation whenever it wished.

A more explosive crisis erupted in Korea, where the Second World War had left Soviet troops in control north of the thirty-eighth parallel and American troops in control to the south. When no agreement could be reached on holding countrywide elections, communist North Korea and noncommunist South Korea became independent states in 1948. Two years later, North Korea invaded South Korea. The United Nations Security Council, in the absence of the Soviet delegation, voted to condemn the invasion and called on members of the United Nations to come to the defense of South Korea. The ensuing **Korean War** lasted until 1953. The United States was the primary ally of South Korea. The People's Republic of China supported North Korea.

The conflict in Korea remained limited to the Korean peninsula because the United States feared that launching attacks into China might prompt China's ally, the Soviet Union, to retaliate and bring about the dreaded third world war. Americans and South Koreans advanced from a toehold in the south to the North Korean–Chinese border. Then, after China sent troops across the border, the North Koreans and the Chinese pushed the Americans and South Koreans back, and the fighting settled into a static war in the mountains along the thirty-eighth parallel. The two sides eventually agreed to a truce along that line; but the ceasefire lines remained fortified, no peace treaty was concluded, and the possibility of renewed warfare between the two Koreas continued well past the end of the Cold War.

Japan benefited from the Korean War in an unexpected way. Massive purchases of supplies by the United States and spending by American servicemen on leave provided a financial stimulus to the Japanese economy similar to the stimulus that Europe received from the Marshall Plan.

U.S. Defeat in Vietnam

A shooting war also developed in Vietnam. In 1954 United States president Dwight D. Eisenhower (1953–1961) and his foreign policy advisers debated long and hard about whether to aid France in its failing effort to sustain colonial rule in Vietnam. They decided against doing so, perceiving that the days of the European colonial empires were numbered. After winning independence, however, communist North Vietnam supported a communist guerrilla movement—the Viet Cong—against the noncommunist government of South Vietnam. At issue was the ideological and economic orientation of an independent Vietnam.

When John F. Kennedy became president (1961–1963), he and his advisers decided to support the South Vietnamese government of President Ngo Dinh Diem°.

Diem (dee-YEM)

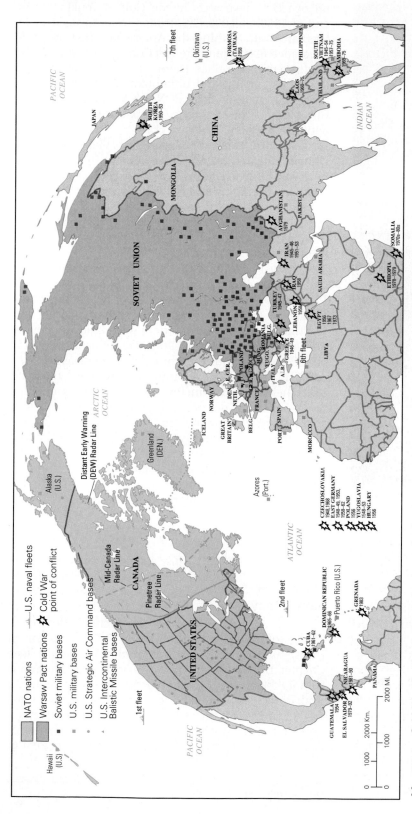

Map 33.1   Cold War Confrontation   A polar projection is shown on this map because Soviet and U.S. strategists planned to attack one another by missile in the polar region, hence the Canadian-American radar lines. Military installations along the southern border of the Soviet Union were directed primarily at China.

Legend:

- NATO nations
- Warsaw Pact nations
- Soviet military bases
- U.S. military bases
- U.S. Strategic Air Command bases
- U.S. Intercontinental Balistic Missile bases
- U.S. naval fleets
- Cold War point of conflict

Map labels include:

PACIFIC OCEAN · 7th fleet · Okinawa (U.S.) · FORMOSA (TAIWAN) 1958 · PHILIPPINES · SOUTH VIETNAM 1945–54 1957–75 · CAMBODIA 1969–75 · LAOS 1960–75 · THAILAND · JAPAN · SOUTH KOREA 1950–53 · CHINA · MONGOLIA · SOVIET UNION · INDIAN OCEAN · AFGHANISTAN 1979 · PAKISTAN · IRAN 1945–46 1951–53 · IRAQ 1958 · SAUDI ARABIA · TURKEY 1945–47 · LEBANON 1958 · EGYPT 1956 1967 1973 · GREECE 1946–49 · SOMALIA 1970s–80s · ETHIOPIA 1978–1979 · LIBYA · 6th fleet · ROMANIA · BULG. · HUNGARY · YUGO. · ITALY · ALB. · POLAND · CZECH. · E. GER. · GER. · FRANCE · BELG. · NETH. · DEN. · NORWAY · ICELAND · GREAT BRITAIN · PORT. · SPAIN · MOROCCO · ARCTIC OCEAN · Distant Early Warning (DEW) Radar Line · Greenland (DEN.) · Azores (Port.) · CZECHOSLOVAKIA 1948 1968 · EAST GERMANY 1948–49, 1953, 1958–62 · POLAND 1956 · YUGOSLAVIA 1948–53 · HUNGARY 1956 · Alaska (U.S.) · Mid-Canada Radar Line · Pinetree Radar Line · CANADA · ATLANTIC OCEAN · 2nd fleet · DOMINICAN REPUBLIC 1965–66 · Puerto Rico (U.S.) · GRENADA 1983 · CUBA 1961–62 · UNITED STATES · 1st fleet · NICARAGUA 1981–90 · PANAMA · GUATEMALA 1954 · EL SALVADOR 1979–92 · PACIFIC OCEAN · Hawaii (U.S.) · 2000 Mi. · 2000 Km. · 1000 · 0

The Vietnamese People at War   American and South Vietnamese troops burned many villages to deprive the enemy of civilian refuges. This policy undermined support for the South Vietnamese government in the countryside.   (Dana Stone/ Black Star)

on two U.S. destroyers in the Gulf of Tonkin. By the end of 1966, 365,000 U.S. troops were engaged in the **Vietnam War.** Nothing the Americans tried, however, succeeded in stopping the Viet Cong guerrillas and their North Vietnamese allies. Diem's successors turned out to be just as corrupt and unpopular as he was, and the heroic nationalist image of North Vietnam's leader Ho Chi Minh° evoked strong sympathies among many South Vietnamese.

In 1973 a treaty between North Vietnam and the United States ended U.S. involvement in the war and promised future elections. Two years later, in violation of the treaty, Viet Cong and North Vietnamese troops overran the South Vietnamese army and captured the southern capital of Saigon, renaming it Ho Chi Minh City. The two parts of Vietnam were reunited in a single state ruled from the north.

The war was bloody and traumatic. The Vietnamese had over a million casualties. The deaths of fifty-eight thousand Americans ensured that the United States would not easily be drawn into another shooting war. The war effort gave rise to serious economic problems in the United States because President Johnson refused to curtail his ambitious program of welfare measures. The conflict also stirred an antiwar movement that was instrumental in convincing the U.S. government that many Americans did not support the war. Nevertheless, at the same time, many members of the military and their civilian supporters were angry about limitations on the conduct of operations. The restrictions were designed to prevent China from entering the war and possibly touching off a nuclear confrontation, but many people saw them as depriving the armed forces of a chance for victory.

They realized that the Diem government was corrupt and unpopular, but they feared that a communist victory would encourage communist movements throughout Southeast Asia and alter the Cold War balance of power. Kennedy steadily increased the number of American military advisers from 685 to almost 16,000 while secretly encouraging the overthrow and execution of Diem in hopes of seeing a more popular and honest government come to power.

Lyndon Johnson, who became president (1963–1969) after Kennedy was assassinated, gained support from Congress for unlimited expansion of U.S. military deployment after an apparent North Vietnamese attack

The Race for Nuclear Supremacy

Just as fear of nuclear warfare affected strategic decisions in the Korean and Vietnam Wars, the existence of weapons of mass destruction affected all aspects of Cold War confrontation. The devastation of Hiroshima and Nagasaki with atomic weapons (see Chapter 31) had ushered in a new era. Nuclear weapons fed into a logic of total war that was already reaching a peak in Nazi genocide and terror bombing and in massive Allied air raids on large cities. After the Soviet Union exploded its first nuclear device in 1949, fears of a worldwide holocaust grew and then became even greater

Ho Chi Minh (hoe chee min)

when the United States exploded a far more powerful weapon, the hydrogen bomb, in 1952 and the Soviet Union followed suit less than a year later. Fear of the theft of nuclear secrets by Soviet spies fostered a sense of paranoia in the United States. The conviction that the nuclear superpowers were willing to use their terrible weapons if their vital interests were threatened spread despair around the world.

In 1954 President Eisenhower warned Soviet leaders against attacking western Europe. In response to such an attack, he said, the United States would reduce the Soviet Union to "a smoking, radiating ruin at the end of two hours." A few years later, the Soviet leader Nikita Khrushchev° offered an equally stark promise: "We will bury you." His reference was to economic competition, but the image produced in Americans was of literal burial. Rhetoric aside, both men—and their successors—had the capacity to deliver on nuclear threats, and everyone in the world knew that all-out war with nuclear weapons would produce the greatest global devastation in human history.

Everyone's worst fears seemed about to be realized in 1962 when the Soviet Union deployed nuclear-tipped missiles in Cuba in response to the U.S. installation of similar missiles in Turkey. The world held its breath. Confronted by unyielding diplomatic pressure and military threats from President Kennedy, Khrushchev backed down and pulled the missiles from Cuba. Subsequently the United States removed its missiles from Turkey. As frightening as the **Cuban missile crisis** was, the fact that the superpower leaders accepted tactical defeat rather than launch an attack gave reason for hope that nuclear weapons might be contained.

The number, means of delivery, and destructive force of nuclear weapons increased enormously. The bomb dropped on Hiroshima, equal in strength to 12,500 tons of TNT, had destroyed an entire city. By the 1960s, explosive yields were measured in megatons (millions of tons of TNT), and it became possible to load a single missile with several weapons of this scale, each of which could be targeted to a different site. When these missiles were placed on submarines, a major component of U.S. nuclear forces, defending against them seemed impossible.

Arms limitation also saw progress. In 1963, Great Britain, the United States, and the Soviet Union agreed to ban the testing of nuclear weapons in the atmosphere, in space, and under water, thus reducing the environmental danger of radioactive fallout. In 1968, the

United States and the Soviet Union together proposed a world treaty against further proliferation of nuclear weapons. It was signed by 137 countries. Not until 1972, however, did the two superpowers truly recognize the futility of squandering their wealth on ever-larger missile forces. They began the arduous and extremely slow process of negotiating weapons limits, a process made even slower by the vested interests of military officers and arms industries in each country, what President Eisenhower had called the "military-industrial complex."

In Europe, the Soviet-American arms race outran the economic ability of atomic powers France and Britain to keep pace. Instead, the European states sought to relax tensions. Between 1972 and 1975, the Conference on Security and Cooperation in Europe (CSCE) brought delegates from thirty-seven European states, the United States, and Canada to Helsinki. The goal of the Soviet Union was to gain European acceptance of the political boundaries of the Warsaw Pact nations. The Helsinki Final Act—commonly known as the **Helsinki Accords**—affirmed that no boundaries should be changed by military force. It also contained formal (but nonbinding) declarations calling for economic, social, and governmental contacts across the iron curtain, and for cooperation in humanitarian fields, a provision that paved the way for dialogue about human rights.

Space exploration was another offshoot of the nuclear arms race. The contest to build larger and more accurate missiles for delivery of warheads prompted the superpowers to prove their skills in rocketry by launching space satellites. The Soviet Union placed a small Sputnik satellite into orbit around the earth in October 1957. The United States responded with its own satellite three months later. The space race was on, a contest in which accomplishments in space were understood to signify equivalent achievements in the military sphere. Sputnik administered a deep shock to American pride and confidence, but in 1969 two Americans, Neil A. Armstrong and Edwin E. "Buzz" Aldrin, became the first humans to walk on the moon.

Despite rhetorical Cold War saber-rattling by Soviet and American leaders, the threat of nuclear war forced a measure of restraint on the superpower adversaries. Because fighting each other directly would have risked escalation to the level of nuclear exchange, they carefully avoided crises that might provoke such confrontations. Even when arming third parties to do their fighting by proxy, they set limits on how far such fighting could go. Some of these proxy combatants, however, understood the limitations of the superpowers well enough to manipulate them for their own purposes.

Khrushchev (KROOSH-chef)

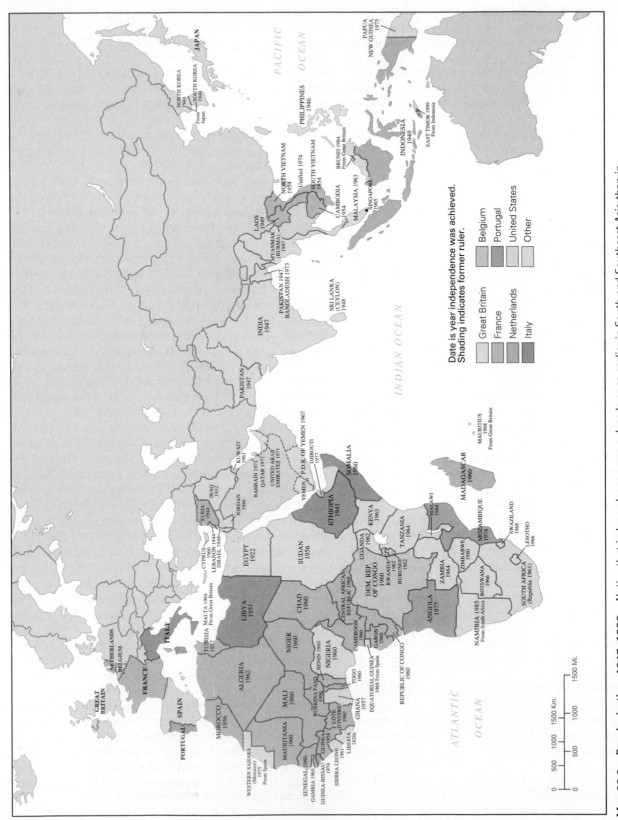

Map 33.2 Decolonization, 1947–1990 Notice that independence came a decade or so earlier in South and Southeast Asia than in Africa. Numerous countries that gained independence after World War II in the Caribbean, in South and Central America, and in the Pacific are not shown.

DECOLONIZATION AND NATION BUILDING

Whereas the losing countries in World War I—Germany, Austria-Hungary, and the Ottoman Empire—were stripped of colonies and torn apart to be reborn as new nations in the Balkans and the Middle East, it was primarily countries on the winning side in World War II—Great Britain, France, the Netherlands, Belgium—that ended up losing their colonies (see Map 33.2). However, this time decolonization did not come about through a series of war-ending treaties or through the mechanism of a League of Nations. Instead, each colony raised its demand for freedom and recognition, sometimes making that demand at the point of a bayonet. Although each country followed its own road to independence, all of the countries gaining independence shared feelings of excitement and rebirth.

Circumstances differed profoundly from place to place. In some Asian countries, where colonial rule was of long standing, newly independent states found themselves in possession of viable industries, communications networks, and education systems. In other countries, notably in Africa, decolonization gave birth to nations facing dire economic problems and internal disunity based on language or ethnicity. In Latin America, where political independence already had been achieved, the quest was for freedom from foreign economic domination, particularly by the United States.

Despite their differences, a sense of kinship arose among the new and old nations of Latin America, Africa, and Asia. As the North Americans, Europeans, and Chinese settled into the exhausting deadlock of the Cold War, visions of independence and national growth captivated the rest of the world.

New Nations in South and Southeast Asia

After partition in 1947, the independent states of India and Pakistan were strikingly dissimilar. Muslim Pakistan defined itself according to religion and quickly fell under the control of military leaders. India, a secular republic led by Prime Minister Jawaharlal Nehru, was much larger and inherited most of the considerable industrial and educational resources the British had developed, along with the larger share of trained civil servants and military officers. Ninety percent of its population was Hindu, most of the rest Muslim.

Adding to the tensions of independence (see Chapter 32) was the decision of the Hindu ruler of the northwestern state known as Jammu and Kashmir to join India without consulting his overwhelmingly Muslim subjects. War between India and Pakistan over Kashmir broke out in 1947 and ended with an uneasy truce, only to resume briefly in 1965. Though Kashmir remained a flashpoint of patriotic feeling, the two countries managed to avoid further warfare.

Despite recurrent predictions that multilingual India might break up into a number of linguistically homogeneous states, most Indians recognized that unity benefited everyone; and the country pursued a generally democratic and socialist line of development. Pakistan, in contrast, did break up. In 1971 its Bengali-speaking eastern section seceded to become the independent country of Bangladesh. Their shared political heritage notwithstanding, these South Asian countries grew steadily apart after independence, following markedly different economic, political, religious, and social paths.

As the Japanese had supported anti-British Indian nationalists, so they encouraged the dreams of some anticolonialists in the countries they had occupied in Southeast Asia. Other nationalists, particularly those belonging to communist groups, saw the Japanese as an imperialist enemy; and the harsh character of Japanese occupation eventually alienated the mass of the population in the occupied countries. Nevertheless, the defeats the Japanese inflicted on British, French, and Dutch colonial armies set an example of an Asian people standing up to European colonizers.

In the Dutch East Indies, a man named simply Sukarno (1901–1970) cooperated with the Japanese in hopes that the Dutch, who had dominated the region economically since the seventeenth century, would never return. After a military confrontation, Dutch withdrawal was finally negotiated in 1949, and Sukarno went on to become the dictator of his resource-rich but underdeveloped island nation. He ruled until 1965, when a military coup ousted him and brutally eliminated Indonesia's powerful communist party.

Elsewhere in the region, nationalist movements won independence as well. Britain granted independence to Burma (now Myanmar°) in 1948 and established the Malay Federation that same year. (Singapore, once a member of the federation, became an independent city-state itself in 1965.) In 1946 the United States kept its promise of postwar independence for the Philippine Islands but retained close economic ties and leases on military bases.

Myanmar (myahn-MAH)

In all these cases, communist insurgents plagued the departing colonial powers and the newly formed governments. The most important postwar communist movement arose in the part of Southeast Asia known as French Indochina. There Ho Chi Minh (1890–1969), who had spent several years in France during World War I, played the pivotal role. In France, Ho had joined the communist party. After training in Moscow, he returned to Vietnam to found the Indochina Communist Party in 1930. He and his supporters took refuge in China during World War II.

At war's end, the new French government was determined to keep its prewar colonial possessions. Ho Chi Minh's nationalist coalition, then called the Viet Minh, fought the French with help from the People's Republic of China. After a brutal struggle, the French stronghold of Dienbienphu° fell in 1954, marking the doom of France's colonial enterprise. Ho's Viet Minh government took over in the north, and a noncommunist nationalist government ruled in the south. Fighting between North and South Vietnam eventually became a major Cold War conflict, as we have seen.

The Struggle for Independence in Africa

The postwar French government was as determined to hold on to Algeria as it was to keep Vietnam. Since invading the country in 1830, France had followed policies very different from those of the British in India. French settlement had been strongly encouraged, and Algeria had been declared an actual part of France rather than a colony. By the mid-1950s, 10 percent of the Algerian population was French, and Algeria's economy was strongly oriented toward France. Though Islam, the religion of 90 percent, prohibited the drinking of alcohol, Algerian vineyards produced immense quantities of wine for French tables. Algerian oil and gas fields were the mainstay of the French petroleum industry.

The revolt in 1954 was pursued with great brutality by both sides. The Algerian revolutionary organization, the Front de Libération National (FLN), was supported by Egypt and other Arab countries acting on the principle that all Arab peoples should be able to choose their own governments. French colonists, however, considered the country rightfully theirs and swore to fight to the bitter end. When Algeria finally won independence in 1962, a flood of angry colonists returned to France. Their departure undermined the Algerian economy because very few Arabs had received technical training or acquired management experience. Despite bitter feel-

French Soldiers on Patrol in Algeria   The Algerian war was one of the most savage struggles for independence in the era of decolonization. The French held out a more secular, Western-style view of life but did not hesitate to intrude into homes and residential areas in search of their enemies. At independence in 1961, most Algerian leaders spoke French more readily than Arabic.   (Marc Riboud/Magnum Photos, Inc.)

ings left by the war, Algeria retained close and seemingly indissoluble economic ties to France, and Algerians increasingly fled unemployment at home by emigrating to France and taking low-level jobs.

None of the several wars for independence in sub-Saharan Africa matched the Algerian struggle in scale. But even without war, most of the new states suffered from many problems. Boundaries that the imperial powers had established in the nineteenth century did not coincide with natural geographic or ethnic divisions. Neglect of education under colonial rule left too few educated Africans to run government ministries and to staff newly established schools without European assistance. In some places, overdependence on export crops such as cacao or peanuts held economies hostage to swings in

---

Dienbienphu (dee-yen-bee-yen-FOO)

international prices. States lacked national road and railroad networks. And population growth, resulting in part from colonial improvements in medical care and public health, foreshadowed worsening poverty and unemployment as well as population pressures that would jeopardize wildlife by expanding the amount of land used for agriculture. In the 1950s and 1960s, however, enthusiasm for liberation overcame worries about these material problems.

Some of the politicians who led the nationalist movements had devoted their lives to ridding their homelands of foreign occupation. An example is Kwame Nkrumah° (1909–1972), who in 1957 became prime minister of Ghana (formerly the Gold Coast), the first British colony in Africa to achieve independence. Only a few hundred Ghanaian children of Nkrumah's generation had graduated each year from the seven-year elementary schools, and he was one of only a handful who made it through teacher training college. After graduation he spent a decade reading philosophy and theology in the United States and absorbing ideas about black pride and independence then being propounded by W. E. B. Du Bois and Marcus Garvey.

After a brief stay in Britain—where he joined Kenyan nationalist Jomo Kenyatta to found an organization devoted to African freedom—Nkrumah returned in 1947 to the Gold Coast to work for independence. The time was right. Great Britain was exhausted by war and unwilling to squander money and blood to hold restive colonies that were not sources of valuable resources. Independent Ghana thus came into being without war or protracted bloodshed. Nkrumah became president in 1960. He turned out to be more effective internationally as a spokesman for colonized peoples than he was at home as an administrator. In 1966 a group of army officers ousted him.

Jomo Kenyatta (ca. 1894–1978) traveled a more difficult road in Kenya, where a substantial number of European coffee planters strenghtened Britain's desire to retain control. A movement known as the Mau Mau, formed mostly by the Kikuyu° people, became active in 1952. As violence between settlers and Mau Mau fighters escalated, British troops hunted down the Mau Mau leaders and resettled the Kikuyu. The British charged Kenyatta with being a Mau Mau leader and held him in prison and then in internal exile for eight years during a declared state of emergency. They released him in 1961, and negotiations with the British to write a constitution for an independent Kenya followed. In 1964 Kenyatta was elected the first president of the Republic of Kenya.

He proved to be an effective, though autocratic, ruler. Kenya benefited from greater stability and prosperity than Ghana.

In contrast with the African nationalists in the British colonies and their counterparts in Algeria, African leaders in the sub-Saharan French colonies were reluctant to call for independence. They visualized change in terms of promises made in 1944 by the Free French movement of General Charles de Gaulle at a conference in Brazzaville, in French Equatorial Africa. Acknowledging the value of his African territorial base, his many African troops, and the food supplied by African farmers, de Gaulle had promised the colonial leaders who attended the conference—none of them African—more democratic government and broader suffrage, though not representation in the French National Assembly. He also had promised to abolish forced labor and imprisonment of Africans without charge; to expand education, in French only, down to the village level; to improve health services; and to open more administrative positions, though not the top ones, to Africans. The word *independence* was never mentioned at Brazzaville, but the politics of postwar colonial self-government led in that direction.

Most of the new group of African politicians seeking election in the colonies of French West Africa were trained as civil servants. Because of the French policy of job rotation, they had typically served in a number of different colonies and thus had a broad outlook. They realized that some colonies—such as Ivory Coast with its coffee and cacao exports, fishing, and hardwood forests—had good economic prospects and others, such as landlocked, desert Niger, did not. Furthermore, they recognized the importance of French public investment in the region—a billion dollars between 1947 and 1956—and their own dependence on civil service salaries, which in places totaled 60 percent of government expenditures.

As the Malagasy politician Philibert Tsirinana° said at a press conference in 1958: "When I let my heart talk, I am a partisan of total and immediate independence [for Madagascar]; when I make my reason speak, I realize that it is impossible." Charles de Gaulle, returning to power in France in 1958, at the height of the Algerian war, spoke to the issue of rationality when he said: "One cannot conceive of both an independent territory and a France which continues to aid it."

Ultimately, however, the heart prevailed everywhere. Guinea, under the dynamic leadership of Sékou Touré°, led the way in 1958. By the time Nigeria, the most

---

Kwame Nkrumah (KWAH-mee nn-KROO-muh)
Kikuyu (kih-KOO-you)

Tsirinana (tsee-REE-nah-nah)
Sékou Touré (SAY-koo too-RAY)

populous West African state, achieved independence from Great Britain in 1960, the leaders of the former French colonies of Ivory Coast (now Côte d'Ivoire), Niger, Dahomey (now Benin), Senegal, and Upper Volta (now Burkina Faso) could attend the celebrations as independent heads of state.

Decolonization in Africa presented innumerable scenes of people of European descent struggling with indigenous Africans to retain personal privileges, control of resources, and political power. Race conflict became particularly severe in the temperate southern part of the continent. African guerrillas struggled against Portuguese rule in Angola and Mozambique, prompting the Portuguese army to revolt against the home government in 1974. The new Portuguese government granted independence to its African colonies the following year. In 1980, after a ten-year fight, European settlers in the British colony of Southern Rhodesia acceded to majority African rule. The new government changed the country's name, which had honored the memory of the British imperialist Cecil Rhodes, to Zimbabwe, the name of a great stone city built by indigenous Africans long before the arrival of European settlers. This left only South Africa and neighboring Southwest Africa in the hands of ruling European minorities. The change had been swift; Africa had entered the postwar period almost entirely under European control.

After World War II, a succession of South African governments had constructed a state and society based on a policy of racial separation, or *apartheid*°. South Asians and people of mixed parentage, approximately 12 percent of the population, were classified as "nonwhite" along with the 74 percent of the population who were indigenous Africans. These groups were subjected to strict limitations on place of residence, right to travel, and access to jobs and public facilities. "Homelands" somewhat similar to Amerindian reservations in the United States were created in comparatively undesirable parts of the country. The largest and most productive tracts of land were held by the 14 percent of the population descended from Dutch and English settlers.

Rising in opposition was the African National Congress (ANC), formed in 1912. After police fired on demonstrators in the African town of Sharpeville in 1960, a lawyer named Nelson Mandela (b. 1918) organized guerrilla resistance by the ANC. Mandela was sentenced to life in prison in 1964 (see Chapter 35 Society and Culture: Nelson Mandela). The ANC continued to lead a bloody and prolonged struggle against apartheid.

---

apartheid (uh-PAHRT-ate)

The Quest for Economic Freedom in Latin America

In Latin America, independence from European rule was achieved earlier, but American and European economic domination increased (see Chapters 29 and 32). Chile's copper, Cuba's sugar, Colombia's coffee, and Guatemala's bananas were all controlled from abroad. The largest resort hotel in Havana was owned by American mobster Meyer Lansky. The communications networks of several countries were in the hands of ITT (International Telephone and Telegraph Company), a U.S. corporation.

In Mexico the Institutional Revolutionary Party, or PRI (the abbreviation of its name in Spanish), controlled the government in the postwar years. Despite PRI rhetoric about revolutionary independence and economic development, the yawning gulf between rich and poor, urban and rural, persisted. According to one estimate from the mid-1960s, not more than 300 foreign and 800 Mexican companies dominated the country, and some 2,000 families made up the industrial-financial elite. At the other end of the economic scale were peasants and the 14 percent of the population classified as Indian.

While Mexico's problems derived only partly from foreign influence and investment, Guatemala's situation was more common. Jacobo Arbenz Guzmán, elected in 1951, was typical of Latin American leaders who tried to confront the power of foreign interests. His expropriation of large estates angered large landowners, the United Fruit Company in particular. This U.S. corporation not only dominated banana exports but held vast tracts of land in reserve for possible future use. Reacting to reports that Arbenz was becoming friendly toward communism, the United States Central Intelligence Agency (CIA), in one of its first major overseas operations, prompted a takeover by the Guatemalan military in 1954. CIA intervention removed Arbenz from the scene; it also condemned Guatemala to decades of governmental instability and growing violence between leftist and rightist elements in society.

In Cuba, economic domination by the United States prior to 1960 was overwhelming. U.S. companies owned 40 percent of raw sugar production, 23 percent of nonsugar industry, 90 percent of telephone and electrical services, and 50 percent of public service railways. Many of Cuba's American-owned industries depended on factories in the United States for essential supplies. The needs of the U.S. economy largely determined Cuban foreign trade. A 1934 treaty granted Cuban sugar preferential treatment in the American market in return for American manufacturers gaining access to the Cuban market. As a consequence, by 1956 sugar accounted for

80 percent of Cuba's exports and 25 percent of Cuba's national income. But demand in the United States dictated that only 39 percent of the land owned by the sugar companies be in production. Similarly, immense deposits of nickel in Cuba went untapped because the U.S. government, which owned them, considered them only as a reserve.

Profits went north to the United States or to a small class of wealthy Cubans, many of them, like the owners of the Bacardi rum company, of foreign origin. Between 1951 and 1958 Cuba's economic growth rate was 1.4 percent per year, less than the rate of population increase; and most of the year a quarter of the working population was unemployed. Cuba's ruler during that period, Fulgencio Batista, became a symbol of corruption, repression, and foreign economic domination.

In 1959, a popular rebellion forced Batista to flee the country. Fidel Castro, the lawyer leader of the rebels, his brother Raoul Castro, and Ernesto "Che" Guevara°, who was the main theorist of communist revolution in Latin America, created a new regime. Fidel Castro (b. 1927) gave a number of speeches in the United States in the wake of his victory. Large crowds cheered him as a heroic champion against dictatorship and American economic imperialism. Within a year, his government redistributed land, lowered urban rents, and raised wages, effectively transferring 15 percent of the national income from rich to poor. Within twenty-two months the Castro government seized almost all U.S. property in Cuba and most Cuban corporations. This action resulted in a blockade by the United States, the flight of middle-class and technically trained Cubans, a drop in foreign investment, and the beginning of chronic food shortages.

Little evidence supports the view that Castro undertook his revolution to install a communist government. But at that time the East-West rivalry of the Cold War was increasingly influencing international politics, and Castro soon turned to the Soviet Union for economic aid. In doing so, he unwittingly committed his nation to economic stagnation and to dependence on a foreign power as damaging as the previous relationship with the United States had been.

In April 1961 some fifteen hundred Cuban exiles, whom the CIA had trained for a year in Guatemala, landed at the Bay of Pigs in an effort to overthrow Castro. The Cuban army defeated the attempted invasion in a matter of days, partly because the new U.S. president, John F. Kennedy, decided not to provide all the air support that the plan, which had originated in the Eisen-

---

°**Che Guevara** (chay guh-VAHR-uh)

Cuban Poster of Charismatic Leader Ernesto 'Che' Guevara A leading theorist of communist revolution in Latin America, Argentine-born Guevara was in Guatemala at the time of the CIA-sponsored coup against Jacobo Arbenz in 1954. He later met and had a strong influence on Fidel Castro. He was killed in 1967 while leading an insurgency in Bolivia. (Christopher Morris/Black Star)

hower administration, called for. The failure of the Bay of Pigs invasion tarnished the reputation of the United States and the CIA and provoked Castro into declaring that he and his revolution were and always had been Marxist-Leninist.

Challenges of Nation Building

Decolonization occurred on a vast scale. Fifty-one nations signed the United Nations Charter in the closing months of 1945. During the United Nations' first decade, twenty-five new members joined, a third of them upon gaining independence. During the next decade, forty-six more new members were admitted, nearly all of them former colonial territories.

Each of these nations had to organize and institute some form of government. Comparatively few were able to do so without experiencing coups, rewritten constitutions, or regional rebellions. Leaders did not always agree on the form independence should take. In the absence of established constitutional traditions, individual leaders frequently tried to impose their own visions by force. Most of the new nations, while trying to establish political stability, also faced severe economic challenges, including foreign ownership and operation of key resources and the need to build infrastructure. Overdependence on world demand for raw materials and on imported manufactured goods persisted in many places long after independence.

Because the achievement of political and economic goals called for educated and skilled personnel, education was another common concern in the newly emerging nations. Addressing that concern required more than building and staffing schools. In some countries, leaders had to decide which language to teach and how to inculcate a sense of national unity in students from different— and sometimes historically antagonistic—ethnic, religious, and linguistic groups. Another problem was how to provide satisfying jobs for new graduates, many of whom had high expectations because of their education.

Only rarely were the new nations able to surmount these hurdles. Even the most successful economically and educationally, such as South Korea, suffered from tendencies toward authoritarian rule. Similarly, Costa Rica, a country with a remarkably stable parliamentary regime from 1949 onward and a literacy rate of 90 percent, remained heavily dependent on world prices for agricultural commodities and on importation of manufactured goods.

BEYOND A BIPOLAR WORLD

Although no one doubted the dominating role of the East-West superpower rivalry in world affairs, the newly independent states had concerns that were primarily domestic and regional. The challenge they faced was to find a way to pursue their ends within the bipolar structure of the Cold War—and possibly to take advantage of the East-West rivalry. Where nationalist forces sought to assert political or economic independence, Cold War antagonists provided arms and political support even when the nationalist goals were quite different from those of the superpowers. For other nations, the ruinously expensive superpower arms race opened opportunities to expand their industries and export capabilities. In short, the superpowers dominated the world but did not control it. And as time progressed, they dominated it less and less.

The Third World

As one of the most successful leaders of the decolonization movement, Indonesia's President Sukarno was an appropriate figure to host a meeting in 1955 of twenty-nine African and Asian countries at Bandung, Indonesia. The conferees proclaimed solidarity among all peoples fighting against colonial rule. The Bandung Conference marked the beginning of an effort by the many new, poor, mostly non-European nations emerging from colonialism to gain more weight in world affairs by banding together. The terms **nonaligned nations** and **Third World,** which became commonplace in the following years, signaled these countries' collective stance toward the rival sides in the Cold War. If the West, led by the United States, and the East, led by the Soviet Union, represented two worlds locked in mortal struggle, the Third World consisted of everyone else.

Leaders of the so-called Third World countries preferred the label *nonaligned,* which signified freedom from membership on either side. However, many leaders in the West noted that the Soviet Union supported national liberation movements and that the nonaligned movement included communist countries such as China and Yugoslavia. As a result, they decided not to take the term *nonaligned* seriously. In a polarized world, they saw Sukarno, Nehru, Nkrumah, and Egypt's Gamal Abd al-Nasir° as stalking horses for a communist takeover of the world. This may also have been the view of some Soviet leaders, since the Soviet Union was quick to offer some of these countries military and financial aid.

For the movement's leaders, however, nonalignment was primarily a means to extract money and support from one or both superpowers. By flirting with the Soviet Union or its ally the People's Republic of China, a country could get cheap or free weapons and training and barter agreements that offered an alternative to selling agricultural or mineral products on Western-dominated world markets. The same flirtation might also prompt the United States and its allies to proffer grants and loans, cheap or free surplus grain, and investment in industry and infrastructure.

A skillfully played balancing game allowed nonaligned countries to play the two sides against each other and gain from both sides in the process. Egypt under Nasir, who had led a military coup against the Egyptian monarchy in 1952, and, after 1970, under Nasir's successor Anwar al-Sadat°, played the game well. The United States offered to build a dam at Aswan°, on the Nile River, to increase Egypt's electrical generating and irrigation capacity. When Egypt turned to the Soviet

---

Gamal Abd al-Nasir (gah-MAHL AHB-d al–NAH-suhr)
al-Sadat (al–seh-DAT)   **Aswan** (AS-wahn)

Bandung Conference, 1955   India's Jawaharlal Nehru (reading a document) was a central figure at this conference held in Indonesia to promote solidarity among nonaligned developing nations. The nonalignment movement failed to achieve the influence that Nehru, Egypt's Nasir, and Indonesia's Sukarno sought.   (Wide World Photos)

Union for arms, the United States reneged on the dam project in 1956. The Soviet Union then picked it up and in the 1960s brought it to conclusion. In 1956, Israel, Great Britain, and France conspired to invade Egypt. Their objective was to overthrow Nasir, regain the Suez Canal (he had recently nationalized it), and secure Israel from any Egyptian threat. The invasion succeeded militarily, but the United States and the Soviet Union both pressured the invaders to withdraw, thus saving Nasir's government. In 1972, Sadat evicted his Soviet military advisers but a year later used his Soviet weapons to attack Israel. After he lost that war, he announced his faith in the power of the United States to solve Egypt's political and economic problems.

Numerous other countries adopted similar balancing strategies. In each case, local leaders were trying to develop their nation's economy and assert or preserve their nation's interests. Manipulating the superpowers was simply a means toward those ends and implied very little about true ideological orientation.

Japan and China

No countries took better advantage of the opportunities presented by the superpowers' preoccupation than did Japan and China. Japan signed a peace treaty with most of its former enemies in 1951 and regained independence from American occupation the following year. Renouncing militarism and its imperialist past (see Chapter 28), Japan remained on the sidelines throughout the Korean War. Its new constitution, written under American supervision in 1946, allowed only a limited self-defense force, banned the deployment of Japanese troops abroad, and gave the vote to women.

The Japanese turned their talents and energies to rebuilding their industries and engaging in world commerce. Peace treaties with countries in Southeast Asia specified reparations payable in the form of goods and services, thus reintroducing Japan to that region as a force for economic development rather than as a military occupier. Nevertheless, bitterness over the oppression of the wartime occupying forces remained strong, and Japan had to move slowly in developing new regional markets for its manufactured goods. The Cold War isolated Japan and excluded it from most world political issues. It thus provided an exceptionally favorable environment for Japan to develop its economic strength.

Three industries that took advantage of government aid and the newest technologies paved the way for Japan's emergence as an economic superpower after 1975. Electricity was in short supply in 1950; Tokyo itself suffered evening power outages. Projects producing 60 million kilowatts of electricity were completed between 1951 and 1970, almost a third through dams on Japan's many rivers. Between 1960 and 1970 steel production more than quadrupled, reaching 15.7 percent of the total capacity of countries outside the Soviet bloc. The ship-building industry produced six times as much tonnage in 1970 as in 1960, almost half of the new tonnage produced outside the Soviet bloc.

While Japan benefited from being outside the Cold War, China was deeply involved in Cold War politics. When Mao Zedong° and the communists defeated the nationalists in 1949 and established the People's Republic of China (PRC), their main ally and source of arms was the Soviet Union. By 1956, however, the PRC and the Soviet Union were beginning to diverge politically, partly in reaction to the Soviet rejection of Stalinism and partly because of China's reluctance to be cast forever in the role of student. Mao had his own notions of communism, focusing strongly on the peasantry, whom the Soviets ignored in favor of the industrial working class.

Mao's Great Leap Forward in 1958 was supposed to vault China into the ranks of world industrial powers by maximizing the use of labor in small-scale, village-level industries. The policy failed but demonstrated Mao's willingness to carry out massive economic and social projects of his own devising.

In 1966 Mao instituted another radical nationwide program, the **Cultural Revolution.** He ordered the mass mobilization of Chinese youth into Red Guard units. His goal was to kindle revolutionary fervor in a new generation. He also wished to ward off the stagnation and bureaucratization he saw in the Soviet Union. Red Guard units criticized and purged teachers, party officials, and intellectuals for "bourgeois values," but they themselves suffered from factionalism. Internal party conflict continued until 1971, when Mao admitted that attacks on individuals had gotten out of hand. Meanwhile, small-scale industrialization resulted in record levels of agricultural and industrial production. The last years of the Cultural Revolution were dominated by radicals led by Mao's wife Jiang Qing°, who focused on restrictions on artistic and intellectual activity.

In the meantime, the rift between the PRC and the Soviet Union had opened so wide that United States President Richard Nixon (1969–1974), by reputation a staunch anticommunist, put out secret diplomatic feelers to revive relations with China. In 1971 the United States dropped objections to the PRC joining the United Nations and occupying China's permanent seat on the Security Council. This decision necessitated the expulsion from the United Nations of the Chinese nationalist government based on the island of Taiwan, which had persistently claimed to be the only legal Chinese auth-

ority. The following year, Nixon visited Beijing, making dramatically clear the new cooperation between the People's Republic of China and the United States.

The Middle East

The superpowers could not control all dangerous international disputes. Independence had come gradually to the Arab countries of the Middle East. Britain granted Syria and Lebanon independence after World War II. Other Arab countries—Iraq, Egypt, Jordan—enjoyed nominal independence during the interwar period but remained under indirect British control until the 1950s, when military coups overthrew King Faruq° of Egypt in 1952 and King Faysal° II of Iraq in 1958. King Husayn° of Jordan dismissed his British military commander in 1956 in response to the Suez crisis, but his poor desert country remained dependent on British, and later American, financial aid.

Overshadowing all Arab politics, however, was the struggle with Israel. British policy on Palestine between the wars oscillated between sentiment favoring Zionist Jews—who emigrated to Palestine, encouraged by the Balfour Declaration—and sentiment for the indigenous Palestinian Arabs, who felt themselves being pushed aside and suspected that the Zionists were aiming at an independent state. As more and more Jews sought a safe haven from persecution by the Nazis, Arabs felt more and more threatened by mass immigration. The Arabs unleashed a guerrilla uprising against the British in 1936, and Jewish groups turned to militant tactics a few years later. Occasionally, Arabs and Jews confronted each other in riots or killings, making it clear that peaceful coexistence in Palestine would be difficult or impossible to achieve.

After the war, under intense pressure to resettle European Jewish refugees, Britain conceded that it saw no way of resolving the dilemma and turned the Palestine problem over to the United Nations. In November 1947, the General Assembly voted in favor of partitioning Palestine into two states, one Jewish and one Arab. The Jewish community made plans to declare independence while the Palestinians, who felt the proposed land division was unfair, reacted in horror and took up arms. When Israel declared its independence in May 1948, neighboring Arab countries sent armies to help the Palestinians crush the newborn state.

Israel, however, prevailed on all fronts. Some 700,000 Palestinians became refugees. They found shelter in United Nations refugee camps in Jordan, Syria,

---

Mao Zedong (maow dzuh-dong) **Jiang Qing** (jyahn ching)

Faruq (fuh-ROOK) **Faysal** (FIE-suhl) **Husayn** (hoo-SANE)

Oil Crisis at the Gas Station   Dislocations in the oil industry caused by OPEC price rises that began in 1974 produced long lines at the gas pump and local shortages. The crisis brought Middle East politics home to consumers and created a negative stereotype of "oil sheikhs."   (Keza/Liaison)

Lebanon, and the Gaza Strip (a bit of coastal land on the Egyptian-Israeli border). The right of these refugees to return home remains a focal point of Arab politics. In 1967 Israel responded to threatening military moves by Egypt's Nasir by preemptively attacking Egyptian and Syrian air bases. In six days, Israel won a smashing victory. When Jordan entered the war, Israel won control of Jerusalem, which it had previously split with Jordan, and the West Bank. Acquiring all of Jerusalem satisfied Jews' deep longing to return to their holiest city, but Palestinians continued to regard Jerusalem as their destined capital, and Muslims in many countries protested Israeli control of the Dome of the Rock, a revered Islamic shrine located in the city. Israel also occupied the Gaza Strip, the strategic Golan Heights in southern Syria, and the entire Sinai Peninsula (see Map 33.3). These acquisitions resulted in a new wave of Palestinian refugees.

The rival claims to Palestine continued to plague Middle Eastern politics. The Palestine Liberation Organization (PLO), headed by Yasir Arafat°, waged guerrilla war against Israel, frequently engaging in acts of terrorism. The militarized Israelis were able to blunt or absorb these attacks and launch counterstrikes that likewise involved assassinations and bombings. Though the United States proved a firm friend of Israel, and the Soviet Union armed the Arab states, neither superpower saw the

Arafat (AR-uh-fat)

struggle between Zionism and Palestinian nationalism as a vital concern—until oil became a political issue.

The phenomenal concentration of oil wealth in the Persian Gulf states—Iran, Iraq, Kuwait, Saudi Arabia, Qatar, Bahrain, and the United Arab Emirates—was not fully realized until after World War II when demand for oil rose sharply as civilian economies recovered. As a world oversupply diminished in the face of rising demand, oil-producing states in 1960 formed the **Organization of Oil Exporting Countries (OPEC)** to promote their collective interest in higher revenues.

Oil politics and the Arab-Israeli conflict intersected in October 1973. A surprise Egyptian attack across the Suez Canal threw the Israelis into temporary disarray. Within days the war turned in Israel's favor, and an Egyptian army was trapped at the canal's southern end. The United States then arranged a ceasefire and the disengagement of forces. But before that could happen, the Arab oil-producing countries voted to embargo oil shipments to the United States and the Netherlands as punishment for their support of Israel.

The implications of oil as an economic weapon profoundly disturbed the worldwide oil industry. Prices rose—along with feelings of insecurity. In 1974 OPEC responded to the turmoil in the oil market by quadrupling prices, setting the stage for massive transfers of wealth to the producing countries and provoking a feeling of crisis throughout the consuming countries.

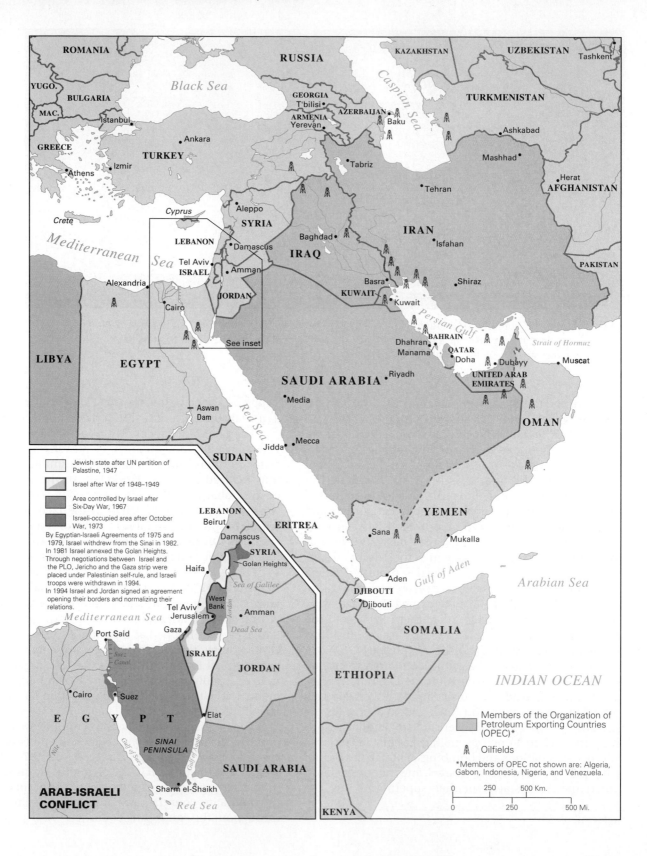

ROMANIA

YUGO.

BULGARIA

MAC.

GREECE

Athens

Istanbul

Izmir

Ankara

TURKEY

Crete

Cyprus

Mediterranean

Sea

Black Sea

RUSSIA

GEORGIA

T'bilisi

ARMENIA
Yerevan

AZERBAIJAN

Baku

Caspian Sea

Aleppo

SYRIA

Damascus

LEBANON

Tel Aviv
ISRAEL

Amman

JORDAN

Alexandria

Cairo

See inset

KAZAKHSTAN

UZBEKISTAN

Tashkent

TURKMENISTAN

Ashkabad

Mashhad

Herat

AFGHANISTAN

Tabriz

Tehran

IRAN

Isfahan

Baghdad

IRAQ

Basra

Shiraz

KUWAIT

Kuwait

Persian Gulf

BAHRAIN

Dhahran

Manama

QATAR

Doha

Strait of Hormuz

Dubayy

Muscat

UNITED ARAB
EMIRATES

PAKISTAN

LIBYA

EGYPT

Aswan
Dam

Red Sea

SAUDI ARABIA

Riyadh

Media

Mecca

Jidda

OMAN

SUDAN

ERITREA

Sana

YEMEN

Mukalla

Aden

Gulf of Aden

Arabian Sea

DJIBOUTI

Djibouti

SOMALIA

ETHIOPIA

INDIAN OCEAN

KENYA

Jewish state after UN partition of
Palestine, 1947

Israel after War of 1948–1949

Area controlled by Israel after
Six-Day War, 1967

Israeli-occupied area after October
War, 1973

By Egyptian-Israeli Agreements of 1975 and
1979, Israel withdrew from the Sinai in 1982.
In 1981 Israel annexed the Golan Heights.
Through negotiations between Israel and
the PLO, Jericho and the Gaza strip were
placed under Palestinian self-rule, and Israeli
troops were withdrawn in 1994.
In 1994 Israel and Jordan signed an agreement
opening their borders and normalizing their
relations.

LEBANON

Beirut

Damascus

SYRIA

Golan Heights

Haifa

Sea of Galilee

Mediterranean Sea

West
Bank

Tel Aviv

Jerusalem

Amman

Gaza

Dead Sea

Port Said

Suez
Canal

ISRAEL

JORDAN

Cairo

Suez

Elat

E G Y P T

Nile

Gulf of Suez

SINAI
PENINSULA

Gulf of Aqaba

SAUDI ARABIA

ARAB-ISRAELI
CONFLICT

Sharm el-Shaikh

Red Sea

Members of the Organization of
Petroleum Exporting Countries
(OPEC)*

Oilfields

*Members of OPEC not shown are: Algeria,
Gabon, Indonesia, Nigeria, and Venezuela.

0   250   500 Km.

0   250   500 Mi.

Silent Spring

The research laboratories that spawned an arsenal of new weapons during World War II also developed highly effective insecticides and herbicides. The potency of DDT was discovered in 1939, and thousands of soldiers were dusted with DDT powder to control lice. Related compounds like dieldrin and aldrin proved many times stronger. The herbicide Agent Orange was later used by the United States to defoliate jungles in Vietnam and reveal enemy infiltration routes.

In 1962, Rachel Carson, a marine biologist, published Silent Spring, a book in which she warned about lethal accumulations of insecticides and herbicides in water and soil that were causing die-offs of wildlife. She also warned of a "silent spring" resulting from the extermination of song birds. Carson's work was one of the first to describe the dangers of uncontrolled technological change and focus public attention on environmental issues.

The new chemicals come from our laboratories in an endless stream; almost five hundred annually find their way into actual use in the United States alone. The figure is staggering and its implications are not easily grasped—500 new chemicals to which the bodies of men and animals are required somehow to adapt each year, chemicals totally outside the limits of biologic experience. . . .

Along with the possibility of the extinction of mankind by nuclear war, the central problem of our age has therefore become the contamination of man's total environment with such substances of incredible potential for harm—substances that accumulate in the tissues of plants and animals and even penetrate the germ cells to shatter or alter the very material of heredity upon which the shape of the future depends.

How did Rachel Carson's warning affect subsequent government policies? What are some other examples of wartime technology affecting later civilian life?

Source: Rachel Carson, *Silent Spring* (Boston: Houghton Mifflin, 1962), 7–8.

The Emergence of Environmental Concerns

The Cold War and the massive investments made in postwar economic recovery had focused public and governmental attention on technological innovations and enormous projects such as hydroelectric dams and nuclear power stations. Only a few people, such as the marine biologist Rachel Carson (see Society and Culture: Silent Spring), warned that untested technologies and all-out drives for industrial productivity were rapidly degrading the environment. The superpowers were particularly negligent of the environmental impact of pesticide and herbicide use, automobile exhaust, industrial waste disposal, and radiation hazards.

In 1968 a wave of student unrest swept many parts of the world. At Columbia University in New York City students protested racism and the war in Vietnam. In Paris and Tokyo they rioted to reform higher education. In Mexico they were outraged at the amount of money the government was spending to host the Olympic Games. The current of youth activism grew rapidly and focused awareness on environmental problems. Earth Day was first celebrated in 1970, the year in which the United States established its Environmental Protection Agency.

The problem of finite natural resources became more broadly recognized when oil prices skyrocketed. Making gasoline engines and home heating systems more efficient and lowering highway speed limits to conserve fuel became matters of national debate in the United States while poorer countries struggled to find the money to import oil. A widely read 1972 study called

Map 33.3 Middle East Oil and the Arab-Israeli Conflict, 1947–1973 Oil resources were long controlled by private European and American companies. In the 1960s most countries, guided by OPEC, negotiated agreements for sharing control, leading eventually to national ownership. This set the stage for the use of oil as a weapon in the Arab-Israeli war of 1973 and for the succeeding oil price increases.

The Limits of Growth forecast a need to cut back on consumption of natural resources in the twenty-first century. Thus as the most dangerous moments of the Cold War seemed to be passing, ecological and environmental problems of worldwide impact vied with the superpower rivalry and Third World nation building for public attention.

CONCLUSION

The impact of the Second World War on the popular mind was so immense that for several decades people commonly referred to the time they were living in as the "postwar era," not needing to specify which war they were referring to. The Cold War and the decolonization movement seemed to arise as logical extensions of World War II. The question of who would control the parts of Europe and Asia liberated from Axis occupation led to Churchill's notion of an iron curtain dividing East and West. The war exhaustion of the European imperialist powers encouraged Asian and African peoples to seek independence and embark on building their own nations.

Intellectuals often framed their understanding of the period in terms of a philosophical struggle between capitalism and socialism dating back to the nineteenth century. But for leaders facing the challenge of governing new nations and creating viable economies, economic philosophy became inextricably intertwined with questions of how to take advantage of the Cold War rivalry between the United States and the Soviet Union.

Historians do not all agree on the year 1975 as the end of the postwar era. The end of the Vietnam War, the beginning of the world oil crisis, and the signing of the Helsinki Accords that brought a measure of agreement among Europeans on both sides of the iron curtain were pivotal events for some countries. But the number of independent countries in the world had grown enormously, and each was in the process of working out its own particular problems. What marks the mid-1970s as the end of an era, therefore, is not a single event so much as the emergence of new concerns. Young people in particular—the new generation that had no memories of World War II—seemed less concerned with the Cold War and the specter of nuclear annihilation than with newly recognized threats to the world environment and personal opportunities for making their way in the world. In the wealthier nations, this meant taking advantage of

economic growth and increasing technological sophistication. In the developing world, it meant seeking the education and employment needed for playing active roles in the drama of nation building.

■ Key Terms

Third World	Warsaw Pact
Cold War	Cultural Revolution (China)
iron curtain	European Community
nonaligned nations	Helsinki Accords
United Nations	Marshall Plan
World Bank	Organization of Petroleum
Korean War	Exporting Countries (OPEC)
Vietnam War	Truman Doctrine
Cuban missile crisis	
North Atlantic Treaty Organization (NATO)	

■ Suggested Reading

The period since 1945 has been particularly rich in memoirs by government leaders. Some that are particularly relevant to the Cold War and decolonization are Dean Acheson (United States secretary of state under Truman), *Present at the Creation* (1969); Nikita Khrushchev, *Khrushchev Remembers* (1970); and Anthony Eden (British prime minister), *Full Circle* (1960).

Geoffrey Barraclough, *An Introduction to Contemporary History* (1964), is a remarkable early effort at understanding the broad sweep of history during this period.

Scholarship on the origins of the Cold War is extensive and includes Akira Iriye, *The Cold War in Asia: A Historical Introduction* (1974); Bruce Kuniholm, *The Origins of the Cold War in the Middle East* (1980); Madelaine Kalb, *The Congo Cables: The Cold War in Africa—From Eisenhower to Kennedy* (1982); and Michael J. Hogan, *A Cross of Iron: Harry S Truman and the Origins of the National Security State* (1998). For a recent reconsideration of earlier historical viewpoints see Melvyn P. Leffler and David S. Painter (eds.), *Origins of the Cold War: An International History* (1994).

Good general histories of the Cold War include Martin Walker, *The Cold War: A History* (1993), and Walter Lafeber, *America, Russia, and the Cold War, 1945–1992* (1993). The latter puts emphasis on how the Cold War eroded American democratic values. For a look at the Cold War from the Soviet perspective see William Taubman, *Stalin's America Policy* (1981); for the American perspective see John Lewis Gaddis, *Strategies of Containment: A Critical Appraisal of Postwar American National Security Policy* (1982). The Cuban missile crisis is well covered in Graham Allison, *Essence of Decision: Explaining the Cuban*

Missile Crisis (1971), and Michael Beschloss, *The Crisis Years: Kennedy and Khrushchev, 1960–1963* (1991).

The nuclear arms race and the associated Soviet–U.S. competition in space are well covered by McGeorge Bundy, *Danger and Survival: Choices About the Bomb in the First Fifty Years* (1988), and Walter MacDougall, *The Heavens and the Earth: A Political History of the Space Age* (1985). Among the many novels illustrating the alarming impact of the arms race on the general public are Philip Wylie, *Tomorrow!* (1954), and Nevil Shute, *On the Beach* (1970). At a technical and philosophical level, Herman Kahn's *On Thermonuclear War* (1961) had a similar effect.

The end of the European empires is broadly treated by D. K. Fieldhouse, *The Colonial Empires* (1982); the British Empire in particular, by Brian Lapping, *End of Empire* (1985). For a critical view of American policies toward the decolonized world see Gabriel Kolko, *Confronting the Third World: United States Foreign Policy, 1945–1980* (1988).

For books on some of the specific episodes of decolonization treated in this chapter see, on Algeria, Alistaire Horne, *A Savage War of Peace: Algeria, 1954–1962* (1987); on Cuba, Hugh Thomas, *Cuba: The Pursuit of Freedom* (1971); on the Suez crisis of 1956, Keith Kyle, *Suez 1956* (1991); on Britain's role in the Middle East over the period of the birth of Israel, William Roger Louis, *The British Empire in the Middle East, 1945–1951* (1984); on Vietnam, George Herring, *America's Longest War: The United States and Vietnam, 1950–1975* (1986), and Stanley Karnow, *Vietnam: A History* (1991); and on Latin America, Eric Wolf, *The Human Condition in Latin America* (1972).

The special cases of Japan and China in this period are covered by Takafusa Nakamura, *A History of Showa Japan, 1926–1989* (1998); Marius B. Jansen, *Japan and China: From War to Peace, 1894–1972* (1975); and Maurice Meisner, *Mao's China and After: A History of the People's Republic* (1986). John Merrill, *Korea: The Peninsular Origins of the War* (1989), presents the Korean War as a civil and revolutionary conflict as well as an episode of the Cold War. Among the hundreds of books on the Arab-Israeli conflict, Charles D. Smith, *Palestine and the Arab-Israel Conflict* (1992), and Trevor N. Dupuy, *Elusive Victory: The Arab-Israeli Wars, 1947–1974* (1978), stand out.

34

CRISIS, REALIGNMENT, AND THE DAWN OF THE POST–COLD WAR WORLD,
1975–1991

Postcolonial Crises and Asian Economic Expansion, 1975–1990 • The End of
the Bipolar World, 1989–1991 • The Challenge of Population Growth •
Unequal Development and the Movement of Peoples •
Technological and Environmental Change

ENVIRONMENT AND TECHNOLOGY: The Personal Computer

SOCIETY AND CULTURE: China's Family-Planning Needs

Dry Docks Owned by Korea's Hyundai Corporation
Korea's rapid industrialization symbolizes Pacific Rim economic growth.

On Thursday, July 22, 1993, police officers in Rio de Janeiro's banking district attempted to arrest a young boy caught sniffing glue. In the resulting scuffle, one police officer was injured by stones thrown by a group of homeless children who lived in nearby streets and parks. Late the following night, hooded vigilantes in two cars fired hundreds of shots at a group of these children sleeping on the steps of a church. The attackers killed five children there and two more in a park. The murderers were later identified as off-duty police officers.

At that time more than 350,000 abandoned children lived in Rio's streets and parks and resorted to begging, selling drugs, stealing, and prostitution to survive. In 1993 alone death squads and drug dealers killed more than four hundred of them. Few people sympathized with the victims. One person living near the scene of the July shootings said, "Those street kids are bandits, and bandits have to die. They are a rotten branch that has to be pruned."

At the end of the twentieth century the brutality of those children's lives was an increasingly common feature of life in the developing world, where rapid population growth was outstripping economic resources.[1] Similar problems of violence, poverty, and social breakdown could be found in most developing nations.

In wealthy industrialized nations as well, politicians and social reformers worried about the effects of unemployment, family breakdown, substance abuse, and homelessness. As had been true during the eighteenth-century Industrial Revolution (see Chapter 24), dramatic economic growth, increased global economic integration, and rapid technological progress in the post–World War II period coincided with growing social dislocation and inequality. Among the most important events of the period were the emergence of new industrial powers in Asia and the precipitous demise of the Soviet Union and its socialist allies.

New challenges also appeared in the form of world population growth and large-scale migrations. Population grew most rapidly in the world's poorest nations, worsening social and economic problems and undermining fragile political institutions. In the industrialized nations the arrival of large numbers of culturally and linguistically distinct immigrants fueled economic growth but also led to the appearance of anti-immigrant political movements and, in some cases, violent ethnic conflict.

As you read this chapter, ask yourself the following questions:

- How did the Cold War affect politics in Latin America and the Middle East in the 1970s and 1980s?
- What forces led to the collapse of the Soviet Union?
- What is the relationship between the rate of population growth and the wealth of nations?
- How did technological change affect the global environment in the recent past?

POSTCOLONIAL CRISES AND ASIAN ECONOMIC EXPANSION, 1975–1989

Between 1975 and 1991, wars and revolutions provoked by a potent mix of ideology, nationalism, ethnic hatred, and religious fervor spread death and destruction through many of the world's least developed regions. These conflicts often had ties to earlier experiences of colonialism and foreign intervention, but the character and objectives of each conflict reflected a specific set of historical experiences. Throughout these decades of conflict the two superpowers sought to avoid direct military confrontation while working to gain strategic advantages. To accomplish these ends, the United States and the Soviet Union each supplied arms and financial assistance to nations or insurgent forces hostile to the other. Once they became linked to the geopolitical rivalry of the superpowers, conflicts provoked by local and regional causes tended to become more deadly and long lasting. Conflicts in which the rival super powers financed and armed competing factions or parties were called **proxy wars.**

In Latin America the rivalry of the superpowers helped to transform conflicts over political rights, social justice, and economic policies into a violent cycle of revolution, military dictatorship, and foreign meddling. In Iran and Afghanistan resentment against foreign intrusion and religiously based hostility to modernization led to revolutionary transformations. Here again superpower ambitions and regional political instability helped provoke war and economic decline. These experiences were not universal. During this same period, a small number of Asian nations experienced rapid transformation. Japan gained a position among the world's leading industrial powers while a small number of other Asian economies quickly entered the ranks of industrial and commercial powers.

The collapse of the Soviet system in eastern Europe at the end of the 1980s ended the Cold War and undermined socialist economies elsewhere. As developing and former socialist nations opened their markets to foreign investment and competition, economic transformation was often accompaniued by wrenching social change. Growing economic interconnectedness across the world coincided with increased inequality. By the early 1990s, it was clear that the world's wealthiest industrial nations were reaping most of the benefits of economic integration.

This period also witnessed a great increase in world population and in international immigration. Population growth and increased levels of industrialization had a dramatic impact on the global environment. Every continent felt the destructive effects of forest depletion, soil erosion, and pollution. Wealthy nations with slow rates of population growth found it easier to respond to these environmental challenges than did poor nations experiencing rapid population growth. These were some of the challenges facing the late twentieth century: growing inequalities among nations and within nations, rapid population expansion, and degradation of the environment.

Revolutions, Repression, and Democratic Reform in Latin America

After the Cuban Revolution Fidel Castro sought to end the domination of the United States and uplift the Cuban masses by changing the economy in fundamental ways. Both objectives led to confrontation with the United States. The Cuban Revolution was the first revolution in the Western Hemisphere to nationalize foreign investment, redistribute the wealth of the elite, and forge an alliance with the Soviet Union. The fact that a communist government could come to power and thwart efforts by the United States to overthrow it energized the revolutionary left throughout Latin America (see Chapter 33). Unable to overthrow Castro and fearful that revolution would spread across Latin America, the

United States organized its political and military allies in Latin America, determined to defeat communism at all costs.

Brazil was the first to experience the full effects of the conservative reaction to the Cuban Revolution. Claiming that Brazil's civilian political leaders could not protect the nation from communist subversion, the army overthrew the democratically elected government of President João Goulart° in 1964. The military suspended the constitution, outlawed all existing political parties, and exiled former presidents and opposition leaders. Death squads— illegal paramiliary organizations sanctioned by the government—detained, tortured, and executed thousands of citizens. The dictatorship also undertook an ambitious economic program that promoted industrialization through import substitution, using tax and tariff policies to compel foreign-owned companies to increase investment in manufacturing.

This combination of dictatorship, violent repression, and government promotion of industrialization came to be called the "Brazilian Solution." Elements of this "solution" were imposed across much of Latin America in the 1970s and early 1980s, beginning in Chile. In 1970 Chile's new president, **Salvador Allende°,** undertook an ambitious program of socialist reforms to redistribute wealth from the elite and middle classes to the poor. He also nationalized most of Chile's heavy industry and mines, including the American-owned copper companies that dominated the Chilean economy. From the beginning of Allende's presidency the administration of United States president Richard Nixon (1969–1973) worked in Chile to organize opposition to Allende's reforms and to overturn his election. Afflicted by inflation, mass consumer protests, and declining foreign trade, Allende was overthrown in 1973 by a military uprising led by General Augusto Pinochet° and supported by the United States. President Allende and thousands of Chileans died in this uprising, and thousands of others were illegally seized, tortured, and imprisoned without trial. Once in power Pinochet rolled back Allende's reforms, reduced state participation in the economy, and encouraged foreign investment.

In 1976 Argentina followed Brazil and Chile into dictatorship. Isabel Martínez de Perón° became president after the death of her husband Juan Perón in 1974 (see Chapter 32). Argentina was racked by high inflation, terrorism, and labor protests. Impatient with the policies of

---

João Goulart (juwow go-LARHT)
Salvador Allende (sal-vah-DOR ah-YEHN-day)
Augusto Pinochet (ah-GOOS-toh pin-oh-CHET)
Isabel Martínez de Perón (EES-ah-bell mar-TEEN-ehz deh pair-OWN)

CHRONOLOGY

	The Americas	Middle East	Asia	Eastern Europe
1970	**1964** Military takeover in Brazil **1970** Salvador Allende elected president of Chile **1973** Allende overthrown **1976** Military takeover in Argentina **1979** Sandinistas overthrow Anastasio Somoza in Nicaragua	**1979** Islamic Revolution overthrows shah of Iran **1980–1988** Iran-Iraq War	**1975** Vietnam war ends **1978** China opens its economy	**1978** USSR sends troops to Afghanistan
1980	**1983–1990** Democracy returns in Argentina, Brazil, and Chile **1989** United States invades Panama		**1986** Average Japanese income overtakes income in United States **1989** Tiananmen Square confrontation	**1985** Mikhail Gorbachev becomes Soviet head of state **1989** USSR withdraws troops from Afghanistan; Berlin Wall falls **1989–1991** End of communism in eastern Europe
1990	**1990** Sandinistas defeated in elections in Nicaragua	**1990** Iraq invades Kuwait **1991** Persian Gulf War		**1990** Reunification of Germany

the president, the military seized power and suspended the constitution. During the next seven years the military fought what it called the **Dirty War** against terrorism. More than nine thousand Argentines lost their lives, and thousands of others endured arrest, terrible tortures, and the loss of property.

Despite reverses in Brazil, Chile, and Argentina, however, revolutionary movements persisted elsewhere. The high-water mark of the revolutionary movement came in 1979 in Nicaragua with the overthrow of the corrupt dictatorship of Anastasio Somoza. The broad alliance of revolutionaries and reformers that gained this victory called themselves **Sandinistas°**. They took their name from Augusto César Sandino, who had led Nicaraguan opposition to U.S. military intervention between 1927 and 1932. The Sandinistas received significant political

Sandinistas (sahn-din-EES-tahs)

and financial support from Cuba and, once in power, sought to imitate the command economies of Cuba and the Soviet Union. The Nicaraguan Revolution nationalized properties owned by members of the Nicaraguan elite and U.S. citizens.

During his four-year term, United States president Jimmy Carter (1977–1980) championed human rights in the hemisphere and stopped the flow of U.S. arms to regimes with the worst records. Carter sought to placate Latin American resentment for past U.S. interventions by renegotiating the Panama Canal treaty, agreeing to the reestablishment of Panamanian sovereignty in the Canal Zone at the end of 1999. He also tried and failed to find some common ground with the Sandinistas. In 1981, Ronald Reagan became president and abandoned this policy of conciliation.

Reagan was committed to reversing the results of the Nicaraguan Revolution and defeating a revolution-

The Nicaraguan Revolution Overturns Somoza A revolutionary coalition that included Marxists drove the dictator Anastasio Somoza from power in 1979. The Somoza family had ruled Nicaragua since the 1930s and maintained a close relationship with the United States.   (Susan Meiselas/ Magnum Photos, Inc.)

ary movement in neighboring El Salvador. His options, however, were limited by the U.S. Congress, which feared that Central America might become another Vietnam. Congress resisted any suggestion that U.S. combat forces be used in Nicaragua or El Salvador and put strict limits on military aid. The Reagan administration sought to roll back the Nicaraguan Revolution by the use of punitive economic measures and by the recruitment and arming of anti-Sandinista Nicaraguans. Called Contras (counterrevolutionaries), this military force was financed by both legal and illegal funds provided by the Reagan administration.

The Contras were unable to defeat the Sandinistas, but they did gain a bloody stalemate by the end of the 1980s. Confident that they were supported by the majority of Nicaraguans and assured that the U.S. Congress was close to cutting off aid to the Contras, the Sandinistas called for free elections in 1990. But they had miscalculated and lost the election. Exhausted by more than a decade of violence, a majority of Nicaraguan voters rejected the Sandinistas and elected a middle-of-the-road coalition led by Violeta Chamorro°.

The revolutionaries of El Salvador hoped to imitate the initial success of the Sandinistas of Nicaragua. Taking their name from a martyred leftist leader of the 1930s,

the FMLN (Farabundo Martí° National Liberation Front) organized an effective guerrilla force. The United States responded by providing hundreds of millions of dollars in military assistance annually and by training units of the El Salvadoran army. Despite these investments in military modernization, the Salvadoran military was guilty of widespread human rights abuses, including the assassination of Archbishop Oscar Romero and other members of the Catholic clergy. Responding to these human rights abuses, the U.S. Congress placed strict limits on the number of U.S. military advisers that could be sent to El Salvador and tried to force political reforms. External events finally brought peace to El Salvador. With the electoral defeat of the Sandinistas in Nicaragua and the collapse of the Soviet Union (see below), popular support for the rebels' vision of a socialist El Salvador waned, and the FMLN rebels negotiated an end to the war, transforming themselves into a civilian political party.

The military dictatorships established in Brazil, Chile, and Argentina all came to an end between 1983 and 1990. In each case reports of kidnappings, tortures, and corruption by military governments undermined public support. In Argentina, the military junta's foolish decision to seize the Falkland Islands—the Argentines

---

Violeta Chamorro (vee-oh-LET-ah cha-MOR-roe)

Farabundo Martí (fah-rah-BOON-doh mar-TEE)

called them the "Malvinas"—in 1982 from Great Britain ended in an embarrassing military defeat and precipitated the return to civilian rule. The Argentine junta had helped President Reagan support the Contras in Nicaragua and believed he would keep Britain's Prime Minister Margaret Thatcher from taking military action. When the Argentine garrison in the Falklands surrendered, military rule in Argentina itself collapsed.

In Chile and Brazil the military dictatorships ended without the drama of foreign war. Despite significant economic growth under Pinochet, Chileans resented the violence and corruption of the military. In 1988 Pinochet called a plebiscite to extend his authority, but the majority vote went against him. A year later Chile elected its first civilian president in eighteen years. Brazil's military initiated a gradual transition to civilian rule in 1985 and four years later had its first popular presidential election. By 1991 nearly 95 percent of Latin America's population lived under civilian rule.

By the end of the 1980s, both oil-importing and oil-exporting nations in Latin America were in economic trouble. Brazil and other oil importers had borrowed heavily to cover budget deficits caused by high oil prices engineered by OPEC. Oil exporters such as Mexico and Venezuela at first enjoyed a windfall as prices rose. Expecting prices to remain high, they borrowed to increase production and develop refining capacity. When oil prices fell in the 1980s, they were hard-pressed to repay debts. In 1982 Mexico was forced to declare that it could not make debt payments, triggering a world financial crisis. By 1988, Latin American nations owed more than $400 billion to external lenders, and Brazil alone owed $113 billion. Debt remained an impediment to economic development in Latin America into the 1990s.

In 1991 Latin America was more dominated by the United States than it had been in 1975. In the 1980s the United States used military force to achieve its objectives on a number of occasions. In 1983, for example, President Reagan authorized a military invasion of the tiny Caribbean nation of Grenada, justifying his action by the need to protect a small number of American students from the actions of a pro-Cuban government. Six years later United States President George Bush sent a large military force into Panama to overthrow and arrest the dictator General Manuel Noriega°, who was associated with both drug smuggling and attacks on U.S. military personnel. These actions were powerful reminders to Latin Americans of prior experience with foreign intervention and occupation (see Chapter 25).

Manuel Noriega (MAN-wel no-ree-EGG-ah)

Islamic Revolutions in Iran and Afghanistan

Although the Arab-Israel conflict and the oil crisis (see Chapter 33) concerned both superpowers, the prospect of their direct military involvement remained remote. When unexpected crises developed in Iran and Afghanistan, however, significant strategic issues came to the foreground because both countries adjoined Soviet territory, thus making Soviet military intervention more likely. Exercising post–Vietnam War caution, the United States reacted to the crises with restraint. The Soviet Union chose a bolder and ultimately disastrous course.

The Iranian Revolution of 1979 proved enormously frustrating to the United States. In 1941 Muhammad Reza Pahlavi° succeeded his father as shah of Iran. In 1953, covert intervention by the United States Central Intelligence Agency (CIA) helped the shah retain his throne in the face of a movement to usurp royal power. Even when he finally nationalized the foreign-owned oil industry, the shah continued to enjoy special American support. As oil revenues increased following the price increases of the 1970s, the United States encouraged the shah to spend his nation's growing wealth on equipping the Iranian army with advanced American weaponry.

Resentment in Iran against the Pahlavi family's autocracy dated from the 1925 seizure of power by the shah's father. The shah's dependence on the United States stimulated further opposition. By the 1970s, popular resentment against the ballooning wealth of the elite families that supported the shah and the inefficiency, malfeasance, and corruption of his government led to mass opposition.

Ayatollah Ruhollah Khomeini°, a Shi'ite° philosopher-cleric who had spent most of his eighty-plus years in religious and academic pursuits, became the voice and symbolic leader of the opposition. Massive street demonstrations and crippling strikes forced the shah to flee Iran and ended the monarchy in 1979. In the Islamic Republic of Iran, which replaced the monarchy, Ayatollah Khomeini was supreme arbiter of disputes and guarantor of religious legitimacy. He oversaw a parliamentary regime that was based on European models, but he imposed religious control of legislation and public behavior. Elections were held, but the electoral process was not open to all: monarchists, communists, and other groups opposed to the idea of an Islamic Republic were barred from running for office. Shi'ite clerics

---

Reza Pahlavi (REH-zah PAH-lah-vee)
Ayatollah Ruhollah Khomeini (A-yat-ol-LAH ROOH-ol-LAH ko-MAY-nee)   **Shi'ite** (SHE-ite)

Muslim Women Mourning the Death of Ayatollah Khomeini in 1989 An Islamic revolution overthrew the shah of Iran in 1979. Ayatollah Khomeini sought to lead Iran away from the influences of Western culture and challenged the power of the United States in the Persian Gulf. (Alexandra Avakian/Woodfin Camp & Associates)

with little training for government service emerged in many of the highest posts, and stringent measures were taken to combat Western styles and culture. Universities were temporarily closed, and their faculties were purged of secularists and monarchists. Women were compelled to wear modest Islamic garments outside the house, and semi-official vigilante committees policed public morals and cast a pall over entertainment and social life.

The United States under President Carter had criticized the shah's repressive regime, but the overthrow of a long-standing ally and the creation of the Islamic Republic were blows to American prestige. The new Iranian regime was religiously doctrinaire. It also was anti-Israeli and anti-American. Khomeini saw the United States as a "Great Satan" opposed to Islam, and he helped to foster Islamic revolutionary movements elsewhere, which

threatened the interests of both the United States and Israel. In November 1979 Iranian radicals seized the U.S. embassy in Tehran and then held fifty-two diplomats hostage for 444 days. Americans felt humiliated by their inability to do anything, particularly after the failure of a military rescue attempt.

In the fall of 1980, shortly after negotiations for the release of the hostages began, **Saddam Husain°,** the ruler of neighboring Iraq, invaded Iran to topple the Islamic Republic. His own dictatorial rule rested on a secular, Arab nationalist philosophy and long-standing friendship with the Soviet Union, which had provided him with advanced weaponry. He feared that the fervor of Iran's revolutionary Shi'ite leaders would infect his own country's Shi'ite majority and threaten his power. The war pitted American weapons in the hands of the Iranians against Soviet weapons in the hands of the Iraqis, but the superpowers avoided overt involvement during eight years of bloodshed. Covertly, however, the United States sent arms to Iran, hoping to gain the release of other American hostages held by radical Islamic groups in Lebanon and to help finance the Contra war against the Sandinista government of Nicaragua. When this deal came to light in 1986, the resulting political scandal intensified American hostility toward Iran. Openly tilting toward Iraq, President Reagan sent the United States Navy to the Persian Gulf, ostensibly to protect nonbelligerent shipping. The move helped force Iran to accept a cease-fire in 1988.

While the United States faced anguish and frustration in Iran, the Soviet Union found itself facing even more serious problems in neighboring Afghanistan. Since World War II, the Soviet Union had succeeded in staying out of shooting wars by using proxies to challenge the United States. But in 1978, the Soviet Union sent its army to Afghanistan to support a fledgling communist regime against a hodgepodge of local, religiously inspired guerrilla bands that had taken control of much of the countryside.

With the United States, Saudi Arabia, and Pakistan paying, equipping, and training the Afghan rebels, the Soviet Union found itself in the same kind of unwinnable war the United States had stumbled into in Vietnam. Unable to justify the continuing drain on manpower, morale, and economic resources and facing widespread domestic discontent over the war, Soviet leaders finally withdrew their troops in 1989. The Afghan communists held on for another three years. But once rebel groups took control of the entire country they began to fight among themselves over who should rule.

Saddam Husain (sah-DAHM who-SANE)

Asian Transformation

Japan has few mineral resources and is dependent on oil imports, but the Japanese economy weathered the oil price shocks of the 1970s better than did the economies of Europe and the United States. In fact, Japan experienced a faster rate of economic growth in the 1970s and 1980s than did any other major developed economy, growing at about 10 percent a year. Average income also increased rapidly, overtaking that of the United States in 1986 and surpassing it in the 1990s.

There are some major differences between the Japanese industrial model and that of the United States. During the American occupation, Japanese industrial conglomerates, zaibatsu, (see Chapter 30) were broken up. Although ownership of major industries became less concentrated as a result, new industrial alliances appeared. There are now six major *keiretsu*° that each include firms in industry, commerce, construction, and a major bank tied together in an interlocking ownership structure. There are also minor keiretsu dominated by a major corporation, like Toyota, and including its major suppliers. These combinations of companies have close relationships with government. Government assistance in the form of tariffs and import regulations inhibiting foreign competition was crucial in the early stages of development of Japan's automobile and semiconductor industries, among others.

Through the 1970s and 1980s Japanese success at exporting manufactured goods produced huge trade surpluses with other nations, prompting the United States and the European Community to try to force an opening of the Japanese market through tough negotiating. These efforts had only limited success. In 1990 Japan enjoyed a trade surplus with the rest of the world that was twice as large as in 1985. Many experts assumed that the competitive advantages that Japan enjoyed in the 1980s would propel Japan past the United States as the world's preeminent industrial economy. But problems appeared at the end of the decade. Japanese housing and stock markets had become highly overvalued, in part because the large trade imbalances increased the monetary supply. Also, the close relationship of government, banks, and industries had led to speculation and corruption that undermined the nation's confidence.

The Japanese model of close cooperation between government and industry was imitated by a small number of Asian states. The most important of them was South Korea, which had a number of assets that helped to promote economic development. The combination of inexpensive labor, strong technical education, and substantial domestic capital reserves allowed South Korea to overcome the devastation of the Korean War in little more than a decade. Despite large defense expenditures, South Korea developed heavy industries such as steel and shipbuilding as well as consumer industries such as automobiles and consumer electronics. Japanese investment and technology transfers accelerated this process. Led by four giant corporations, which accounted for nearly half of South Korea's gross domestic product (GDP) and produced a broad mix of goods, the Korean economy began to match Japanese economic growth rates by the 1980s. Hyundai, one of the four giant corporations, manufactured products ranging from supertankers and cars to electronics and housing.

Taiwan, Hong Kong, and Singapore also developed modern industrial and commercial economies. As a result of their rapid economic growth, these three nations and South Korea were often referred to as the **Asian Tigers.** Taiwan suffered a number of political reverses, including the loss of its United Nations seat to the People's Republic of China in 1971 and the withdrawal of diplomatic recognition by the United States. Nevertheless, it achieved remarkable economic progress. In contrast with South Korea, smaller, more specialized companies led development in Taiwan. Also, Taiwan was able to gain a foothold in the economy of the People's Republic of China while maintaining its traditional markets in the United States and South Asia. Between 1955 and 1990, Taiwan's per capita GDP (gross domestic product) increased from 10 percent of the U.S. levels to 50 percent.

Hong Kong and Singapore—both small societies with extremely limited resources—also enjoyed rapid economic development. Singapore's initial economic takeoff was based on its busy port and on banking and commercial services. As capital accumulated in these profitable sectors, this society of around 3 million people diversified by building textile and electronics industries. Singapore's rate of growth in GDP was double that of Japan from 1970 to 1980. Hong Kong's economic prosperity too was tied to its port and to the development of banking and commercial services, which were increasingly tied to the growing economy of China. Hong Kong also developed a highly competitive industrial sector dominated by textile and consumer electronics production. Worried about Hong Kong's reintegration into the People's Republic of China in 1997, local capitalists moved significant amounts of capital to the United States, Canada, and elsewhere, slowing economic growth in Hong Kong.

All of these **newly industrialized economies (NIEs)** shared many characteristics that helped explain their

---

keiretsu (kay-REHT-soo)

rapid industrialization. All had disciplined and hard-working labor forces, and all invested heavily in education. For example, as early as 1980, Korea had as many engineering graduates as Germany, Britain, and Sweden combined. All had high rates of personal saving that allowed them to generously fund investment in new technology. In 1987, the saving rates in Taiwan and South Korea were three times higher than in the United States. All emphasized outward-looking export strategies. And, like Japan, all these dynamic Pacific Rim economies benefited from government sponsorship and protection. All were beneficiaries of the extraordinary expansion in world trade and international communication that permitted technology to be disseminated more rapidly than at any time in the past. As a result, newly industrializing nations began with current technologies.

In China after Mao Zedong's death in 1976, the communist leadership introduced a comprehensive economic reform that allowed more individual initiative and permitted individuals to accumulate wealth. Beginning in 1978, the Communist Party in Sichuan province freed more than six thousand firms to compete for business outside the state planning process. The results were remarkable. Under China's leader **Deng Xiaoping**° these reforms were expanded across the nation. China also began to permit foreign investment for the first time since the communists came to power in 1949. Between 1978 and the end of the 1990s foreign investors committed more than $180 billion to the Chinese economy, and Mc-Donald's, Coca-Cola, Airbus, and other foreign companies opened for business. But more than 100 million workers were still employed in state-owned enterprises, and most foreign-owned companies were segregated in special economic zones. The result was a dual industrial sector—one modern and efficient and connected to international markets, the other dominated by government and directed by political decisions.

When Mao came to power in 1949, the meaning of the Chinese Revolution was made clear in the countryside, where collective ownership and organization were imposed. Deng Xiaoping did not privatize land, but he did permit the contracting of land to individuals and families, who were free to consume or sell whatever they produced. By 1984, 93 percent of China's agricultural land was in effect in private hands and producing for the market, tripling agricultural output.

Perhaps the best measure of the success of Deng's reforms is that between 1980 and 1993 China's per capita output more than doubled, averaging more than 8 percent growth per year in comparison with the world average of slightly more than 1 percent and Japan's average of 3.3 percent. This growth was overwhelmingly the result of exports to the developed nations of the West, especially the United States. Nevertheless, per capita measures of wealth indicated that China remained a poor nation. China's per capita GDP was roughly the same as Mexico's, about $3,600 per year. By comparison, Taiwan had a per capita GDP of $14,700.

Much of China's command economy remained in place, and the leadership of the Chinese Communist Party resisted serious political reform. Deng Xiaoping's strategy of balancing change and continuity, however, helped China avoid some of the social costs and political consequences experienced by Russia and other European socialist countries that abruptly plunged into capitalism and democracy. As Chinese officials put it, "[China was] changing a big earthquake into a thousand tremors." The nation's leadership faced a major challenge in 1989. Responding to mass movements in favor of democracy across the globe and to inflation, Chinese students and intellectuals, many of whom had studied outside China, led a series of protests demanding more democracy and an end to inflation and corruption. This movement culminated in **Tiananmen Square**°, in the heart of Beijing. Hundreds of thousands of protesters gathered, refusing to leave. The government decided on the use of force. After weeks of standoff, tanks pushed into the square, killing hundreds, perhaps thousands. Many more were arrested. Although the Communist party survived this challenge, it was not clear whether rapid economic growth, increasing inequality, high levels of unemployment, and massive migration from the countryside to the cities could occur without triggering a political transformation.

THE END OF THE BIPOLAR WORLD, 1989–1991

After the end of World War II, competition between the United States and the Soviet Union and their respective allies created a bipolar world. Every conflict, no matter how local its origins, held the potential of engaging the attention of one or both of the superpowers. The Korean War, decolonization in Africa, the Vietnam War, the Cuban Revolution, hostilities between Israel and its neighbors, and numerous other events increased tension

---

Deng Xiaoping (dung shee-yao-ping)

Tiananmen (tee-yehn-ahn-men)

between the superpowers, each armed with nuclear weapons. Given this succession of provocations, budgets within both blocs were dominated by defense expenditures, and political culture everywhere was dominated by arguments over the relative merits of the two competing economic and political systems.

Few in 1980 predicted the startling collapse of the Soviet Union and the socialist nations of the Warsaw Pact. Western observers tended to see communist nations as both more uniform in character and more subservient to the Soviet Union than was true. Long before the 1980s deep divisions had appeared among communist states. Yugoslavia broke with the Soviet Union in the 1940s; China actually fought a brief border war with the Soviet Union in the 1960s; and the government of newly unified communist Vietnam invaded communist Cambodia in the 1970s. But in general, the once-independent nations and ethnic groups that had been brought within the Soviet Union and the eastern European nations seemed securely transformed by the experiences and institutions of communism. By 1990, however, nationalism was resurgent and communism was nearly finished.

Crisis in the Soviet Union

Under United States President Ronald Reagan and the Soviet Union's General Secretary Leonid Brezhnev°, the rhetoric of the Cold War remained intense. Massive new U.S. investments in armaments, including a space-based missile protection system that never became operational, placed heavy burdens on the Soviet economy, which was unable to absorb the cost of developing similar weapons. Soviet economic problems were systemic; shortages of food, consumer goods, and housing were an ongoing part of Soviet life. Obsolete industrial plants and centralized planning that stifled initiative and responsiveness to market demand led to a declining standard of living relative to the West. Government bureaucrats and Communist Party favorites received special privileges, including permission to shop in stores that stocked Western goods, but the average citizen faced long lines and waiting lists for goods. Soviet citizens contrasted their lot with the free and prosperous life of the West—depicted in the increasingly accessible Western media. The arbitrariness of the bureaucracy, the cynical manipulation of information, and deprivations created a generalized crisis in morale.

Despite the unpopularity of the war in Afghanistan and growing discontent, Brezhnev refused to modify his rigid and unsuccessful policies. But he was unable to contain an underground current of protest. In a series of powerful books, the writer Alexander Solzhenitzyn° castigated the Soviet system and particularly the Stalinist prison camps. He won a Nobel Prize in literature but was charged with treason and expelled from the country in 1974. Self-published underground writings (*samizdat°*) by critics of the regime circulated widely despite government efforts to suppress them. The physicist Andrei Sakharov and his wife Yelena Bonner protested the nuclear arms race and human rights violations and were condemned to banishment within the country. Some Jewish dissidents spoke out against anti-Semitism, but many more left for Israel or the United States.

By the time **Mikhail Gorbachev°** took up the reins of the Soviet government in 1985, war weariness, economic decay, and vocal protest had reached critical levels. Casting aside Brezhnev's hard line, Gorbachev authorized major reforms in an attempt to stave off total collapse. His policy of political openness (*glasnost*) permitted criticism of the government and Communist Party. His policy of ***perestroika°*** "restructuring" was an attempt to address long-suppressed economic problems by moving away from central state planning and toward a more open economic system. In 1989 he ended the war in Afghanistan, which had cost many lives and much money.

The Collapse of the Socialist Bloc

Events in eastern Europe were very important in forcing change on the Soviet Union. In 1980 protests by Polish shipyard workers in the city of Gdansk led to the formation of **Solidarity,** a labor union that soon enrolled 9 million members. The Roman Catholic Church in Poland, strengthened by the elevation of a Pole, Karol Wojtyla°, to the papacy as John Paul II in 1978, gave strong moral support to the protest movement.

The Polish government imposed martial law in 1980 in response to the growing power of Solidarity and its allies, giving the army effective political control. Seeing Solidarity under tight controls and many of its leaders in prison, the Soviet Union decided not to intervene. But Solidarity remained a potent force with a strong institutional structure and nationally recognized leaders. As Gorbachev loosened political controls in the Soviet Union after 1985, communist leaders elsewhere lost confidence in Soviet resolve and critics and reformers in Poland and

---

Leonid Brezhnev (leh-oh-NEED BREZ-nef)

Solzhenitzen (sol-zhuh-NEET-sin)   *samizdat* (sah-meez-DAHT)
Gorbachev (GORE-beh-CHOF)   *perestroika* (per-ih-STROY-kuh)
Karol Wojtyla (KAH-rol voy-TIL-ah)

Map 34.1   The End of Soviet Domination in Eastern Europe   The creation of new countries out of Yugoslavia and Czechoslovakia and the reunification of Germany marked the most complicated changes of national borders since World War I. The Czech Republic and Slovakia separated peacefully, but Slovenia, Croatia, Macedonia, and Bosnia and Herzegovina achieved independence only after bitter fighting.

throughout eastern Europe were emboldened (see Map 34.1).

Beleaguered Warsaw Pact governments vacillated between relaxation of control and the suppression of dissent. As the Catholic clergy in Poland had supported Solidarity, Protestant and Orthodox religious leaders aided the rise of opposition groups elsewhere. This combination of nationalism and religion provided a powerful base for opponents of the communist regimes. Threatened by these forces, communist governments sought to quiet the opposition by seeking solutions to their severe economic problems. They turned to the West for trade and financial assistance. They also opened their nations to travelers, ideas, styles, and money from Western countries, all of which accelerated the demand for change.

By the end of 1989, communist governments across eastern Europe had fallen. The dismantling of the Berlin Wall, the symbol of a divided Europe and the bipolar world, vividly represented this transformation. In Poland, Hungary, Czechoslovakia, and Bulgaria communist leaders decided that change was inevitable and initiated political reforms. In Romania the dictator Nicolae Ceausescu° refused to surrender power, thus provoking a rebellion that ended with his arrest and execution. The comprehensiveness of these changes became clear in 1990, when Solidarity leader Lech Walesa° was elected president of Poland and dissident playwright Vaclav Havel° was elected president of Czechoslovakia.

Nicolae Ceausescu (neh-koh-LIE chow-SHES-koo)
Lech Walesa (leck wah-LESS-ah)   **Vaclav Havel** (vah-SLAV hah-VEL)

Worker Unrest in Eastern Europe   After the collapse of the Soviet Union, workers such as these angry women surrounding plant managers in Minsk, capital of Belarus, demanded improvements in their working conditions. (Yuri Ivanoff/*LIFE Magazine* © Time Inc.)

Following the fall of the Berlin Wall, a tidal wave of patriotic enthusiasm swept aside the once-formidable communist government of East Germany. In the chaotic months that followed, East Germans crossed to West Germany in large numbers, and governmental services in the eastern sector nearly disappeared. Some Europeans recalled German militarism earlier in the century and worried about reunification. But there was little concrete opposition, and in 1990 Germany was reunified. Numerous problems followed reunification, including high levels of unemployment and budget deficits, but nearly fifty years of confrontation and tension across the heart of Europe seemed to end over night.

Soviet leaders looked on with dismay at the collapse of communism in the Warsaw Pact countries. They knew that similarly powerful nationalist sentiments existed within the Soviet Union as well. The year 1990 brought declarations of independence by Lithuania, Estonia, and Latvia, three small states on the Baltic Sea that the Soviet Union had annexed in 1939. And soon, violent ethnic strife erupted in the Caucasus region. Gorbachev tried to accommodate the rising pressures for change, but the tide was running too fast.

The end of the Soviet Union came suddenly in 1991 (see Map 34.2). After Communist hardliners botched a poorly conceived coup against Gorbachev, disgust with communism boiled over. Boris Yeltsin, the president of the Russian Republic and long-time member of the Communist Party, led popular resistance to the coup in Moscow and emerged as the most powerful leader in the country. Russia, the largest republic in the Soviet Union, was effectively taking the place of the disintegrating USSR. With the central government of the Soviet Union scarcely functioning, nationalism, long repressed by Soviet authorities, reappeared throughout the Soviet Union. In September 1991 the Congress of People's Deputies—the central legislature of the USSR, long subservient to the Communist Party—voted to dissolve the union. Mikhail Gorbachev went into retirement.

The ethnic and religious passions that fueled the breakup of the Soviet Union soon challenged the survival of Yugoslavia and Czechoslovakia. The dismemberment of Yugoslavia began with declarations of independence in Slovenia and Croatia in 1991. A year later, Czechoslovakia peacefully divided into the Czech Republic and Slovakia. Across eastern Europe ethnic and religious conflict was soon to turn violent.

Map 34.2 The End of the Soviet Union When Communist hardliners failed to overthrow Gorbachev in 1991, popular anti-Communist sentiment swept the Soviet Union. Following Boris Yeltsin's lead in Russia, the republics that constituted the Soviet Union declared their independence.

The Persian Gulf War, 1990–1991

The first significant conflict to occur after the breakup of the Soviet Union and the end of the Cold War was the Persian Gulf War. The immediate causes were local and bilateral. Iraq's ruler, Saddam Husain, had borrowed a great deal of money from neighboring Kuwait and sought unsuccessfully to get Kuwait's royal family to reduce the size of this debt. He was also eager to gain control of Kuwait's oil fields. Husain believed that the smaller and militarily weaker nation could be quickly defeated and suspected, as a result of a conversation with an American diplomat, that the United States would not react. The invasion came in August 1990.

Saudi Arabia, a key regional ally of the United States and a major oil producer, felt threatened by Iraq's action and helped draw the United States into the conflict. Soon the United States and its allies had concentrated an imposing military force of 500,000 in the region. With his intention to use force endorsed by the United Nations and with many Islamic nations supporting military action, President George Bush ordered an attack in early 1991. Iraq proved incapable of countering the sophisticated weaponry of the coalition. The missiles and bombs of the United States destroyed not only military targets but also "relegated [Iraq] to a pre-industrial age," reported the United Nations after the war. Although Iraq's military defeat was comprehensive, Husain remained in power and the country was not occupied. Husain, in fact, crushed an uprising in the months following this defeat. In the wake of this event the United States and its key allies imposed "no fly" zones that denied Iraq's military aircraft access to the northern and southern regions of the country. As a result, military tensions and periodic armed confrontations continued.

In the United States the results of the war were interpreted to mean that the U.S. military defeat in the Vietnam War could be forgotten and that U.S. military capability was unrivaled. Unable to deter military action by the U.S.-led coalition or to meaningfully influence the diplomacy that surrounded the war, Russia had been of little use to its former ally Iraq and its impotence was clear.

THE CHALLENGE OF POPULATION GROWTH

For most of human history population growth was viewed as beneficial, and human beings were seen as a source of wealth. Since the late eighteenth century, however, population growth has been viewed with increasing alarm. At first it was feared that food supplies could not keep up with population growth. Then social critics expressed concern that growing population would lead to class and ethnic struggle as numbers overwhelmed resources. By the second half of the twentieth century, population growth was increasingly seen as a threat to the environment. Are urban sprawl, pollution, and soil erosion inevitable results of population growth? These questions and debates remain today, but clearly population is both a cause and a result of increased global interdependency.

Demographic Transition

The population of Europe almost doubled between 1850 and 1914, putting enormous pressure on rural land and urban housing and overwhelming fragile public assistance institutions that provided some crisis assistance (see Chapter 28). This dramatic growth forced a large wave of immigration across the Atlantic, helping to develop North and South America and invigorating the Atlantic economy. Population growth also contributed to Europe's industrial revolution by lowering labor costs and increasing consumer demand.

Educated Europeans of the nineteenth century were ambivalent about the rapid increase in human population. Some saw it as a blessing that would promote economic well-being. Others warned that the seemingly relentless increase would bring disaster. Best known of these pessimists was the English cleric **Thomas Malthus,** who in 1798 argued convincingly that unchecked population growth would outstrip food production. When Malthus looked at Europe's future, he used a prejudiced image of China to terrify his European readers. A visitor to China, he claimed, "will not be surprised that mothers destroy or expose many of their children; that parents sell their daughters for a trifle; . . . and that there should be such a number of robbers. The surprise is that nothing still more dreadful should happen."[2]

The generation that came of age in the years immediately following World War II inherited a world in which the views of Malthus were casually dismissed. Industrial and agricultural productivity had multiplied supplies of food and other necessities. Cultural changes associated with expanded female employment, older age at marriage, and more effective family planning had combined to slow the rate of population increase. And by the late 1960s, Europe and other industrial societies had made what was called the **demographic transition** to lower fertility rates (average number of births per woman) and reduced mortality. The number of births in the developed nations was just adequate for the maintenance of current population levels. Thus many experts argued that the population growth then occurring in developing nations was a short-term phenomenon that would be ended by the combination of economic and social changes that had altered European patterns.

By the late 1970s, however, the demographic transition had not occurred in the Third World, and the issue of population growth had become politicized. The leaders of some developing nations actively promoted large families, arguing that larger populations would increase national power. These arguments remained a persistent part of the debate between developed and developing nations. Industrialized, mostly white, nations raised concerns about rapid population growth in Asia, Africa, and Latin America. Populist political leaders in those regions asked whether these concerns were not fundamentally racist.

The question exposed the influence of racism in the population debate and temporarily disarmed Western advocates of birth control. However, once the economic shocks of the 1970s and 1980s revealed the vulnerability of developing economies, governments in the developing world jettisoned pronatalist policy. In the 1970s Mexico's government had encouraged high fertility, and population growth in Mexico rose to 3 percent per year. By the 1980s Mexico started to promote birth control, and the annual population growth rate fell to 2.3 percent.

World population exploded in the twentieth century (see Table 34.1). At current rates of growth, world population increases by a number equal to the total population of the United States every three years. Unlike population growth in the eighteenth and nineteenth centuries, when much of the increase occurred in the

Table 34.1 Population for World and Major Areas, 1750–2050

Population Size (Millions)

Major Area	1750	1800	1850	1900	1950	1998	2050
World	791	978	1,262	1,650	2,521	5,901	8,909
Africa	106	107	111	133	221	749	1,766
Asia	502	635	809	947	1,402	3,585	5,268
Europe	163	203	276	408	547	729	628
Latin America and the Caribbean	16	24	38	74	167	504	809
North America	2	7	26	82	172	305	392
Oceania	2	2	2	6	13	30	46

Percentage Distribution

Major Area	1750	1800	1850	1900	1950	1998	2050
World	100	100	100	100	100	100	100
Africa	13.4	10.9	8.8	8.1	8.8	12.7	19.8
Asia	63.5	64.9	64.1	57.4	55.6	60.8	59.1
Europe	20.6	20.8	21.9	24.7	21.7	12.4	7.0
Latin America and the Caribbean	2.0	2.5	3.0	4.5	6.6	8.5	9.1
North America	0.3	0.7	2.1	5.0	6.8	5.2	4.4
Oceania	0.3	0.2	0.2	0.4	0.5	0.5	0.5

Source: J. D. Durand, "Historical Estimates of World Population: An Evaluation" (Philadelphia: University of Pennsylvania, Population Studies Center, 1974, mimeographed); United Nations, *The Determinants and Consequences of Population Trends,* vol. 1 (New York: United Nations, 1973); United Nations, *World Population Prospects as Assessed in 1963* (New York: United Nations, 1966); United Nations, *World Population Prospects: The 1998 Revision* (New York: United Nations, forthcoming); United Nations Population Division, Department of Economic and Social Affairs, http://www.popin.org/pop1998/4.htm.

wealthiest nations, population growth at the end of the twentieth century was overwhelmingly in the poorest nations. Fertility rates had dropped in most developing nations but remained much higher than rates in the industrialized nations. At the same time, improvements in hygiene and medical treatment caused mortality rates to fall. The result has been rapid population growth.

The Industrialized Nations

In the developed industrial nations of western Europe and in Japan at the beginning of the twenty-first century, fertility levels are so low that population will fall unless immigration increases. In Japan women have an average of 1.39 children; in Italy the number is 1.2. Sweden provides cash payments, tax incentives, and job leaves to families with children, but the average number of births there fell to 1.4 in recent years. The low fertility found in mature industrial nations is tied to higher levels of female education and employment, the material values of consumer culture, and access to contraception and abortion. Educated women now defer marriage and child

rearing until they are established in careers. An Italian woman in Bologna, the city with the lowest fertility in the world, put it this way: "I'm an only child and if I could, I'd have more than one child. But most couples I know wait until their 30's to have children. People want to have their own life, they want to have a successful career. When you see life in these terms, children are an impediment." [3]

In industrialized nations life expectancy has improved as fertility has declined. The combination of abundant food, improved hygiene, more effective medicines, and medical care has lengthened human lives. About 12.5 percent of the population was age sixty-five or over in wealthy nations in 1990. In western Europe this percentage ranged from 13 in France to 18 in Sweden. Italy soon will have more than 20 adults fifty years old or over for each five-year-old child.

The combination of falling fertility and rising life expectancy in the industrialized nations presents a challenge very different from the one foreseen by Malthus. These nations generally offer a broad array of social services, including retirement income, medical services, and housing supplements for the elderly. As the number of retirees increases relative to the number of people who are employed, the costs of these services may become unsustainable. Clearly Japan, the United States, and the nations of western Europe will have to reexamine programs that encourage early retirement.

In Russia and other former socialist nations, current birthrates are now actually lower than death rates—levels inadequate to sustain the current population size. Birthrates were already low before the collapse of the socialist system and have contracted further with recent economic problems. Since 1975 fertility rates have fallen between 20 and 40 percent across the former Soviet bloc. By the early 1980s, abortions were as common as births in much of eastern Europe.

At the same time life expectancy has also fallen. Life expectancy for Russian men is now only fifty-seven years, down almost ten years since 1980. In the Czech Republic, Hungary, and Poland, life expectancy is improving in response to improved economic conditions, but in most of the rest of eastern Europe the Russian pattern of declining life expectancy is found. High unemployment, low incomes, food shortages, and the dismantling of the social welfare system of the communist era have all contributed to this decline.

The Developing Nations

Even if the industrialized nations decided to promote an increase in family size in the twenty-first century, they would continue to fall behind the developing nations as a percentage of world population. At current rates, 95 percent of all future population growth will be in developing nations (see Map 34.3 and Table 34.1). A comparison between Europe and Africa illustrates these changes. In 1950, Europe had twice the population of Africa. By 1985, Africa had drawn even. According to projections, by 2025 Africa's population will be three times larger than Europe's. Given the performance of African economies, future generations of Africans will likely face increased levels of famine, epidemics, and social breakdown.

As the 1990s ended, other developing regions had rapid population growth as well. While all developing nations had an average birthrate of 33.6 per thousand inhabitants, Muslim countries had a rate of 42.1. This rate is more than 300 percent higher than the rate for the developed nations of the West (13.1 births per thousand). The populations of Latin America and Asia also were expanding dramatically, but at rates slower than those in sub-Saharan Africa or the Muslim nations.

Chinese Family–Planning Campaign   Hoping to slow population growth, the Chinese government has sought to limit parents to a single child. Billboards and other forms of mass advertising have been an essential part of the campaign to gain compliance with national family-planning directives.   (Picard/Sipa Press)

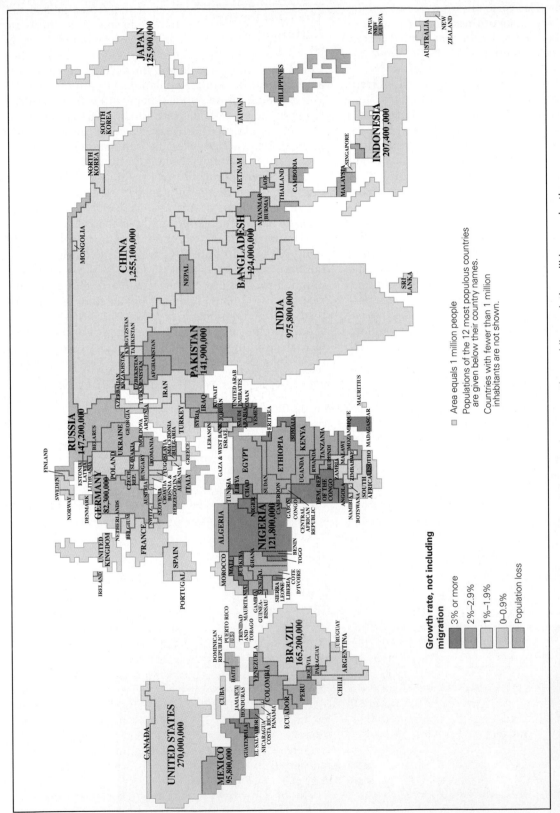

Map 34.3 World Population Growth At current rates of growth, every three years, the world's population will increase by the equivalent of a nation the size of the United States. Most of this population increase will be in some of the world's poorest nations. By 2050, for example, Pakistan, a nation of only 40 million in 1950, will surpass the United States and become the country with the world's third largest population. (National Geographic Maps 1998/10 Map Supplement Population Growth. Used by permission of National Geographic Society.)

China's Family-Planning Needs

China has the world's largest population—over a billion people. Although China enjoyed rapid economic growth in the closing years of the twentieth century, population pressures continued to present severe problems. In 1993 the Chinese economy became the world's tenth largest. Nevertheless, China's per capita GDP (gross domestic product) of $370 remained at Third World levels. Heavy pressure on families to have only one child resulted in the killing of female infants and the abandonment of children with disabilities. Peng Yu, vice minister of the State Family Planning Commission, explained the need for efforts at population control.

China is a developing country with a huge population but limited cultivated land, inadequate per capita resources and a weak economic foundation. . . . Despite continuous efforts in family planning, the huge base has created an annual net increase of around 14 million in recent years, equal to the total population of a medium-sized country. At present, per capita cultivated land in China has declined to less than 0.1 hectare, equivalent to only one-fourth the world average as are [its] per capita freshwater resources. . . . Although national income has been climbing by 25 percent annually, the increase has been eaten up by new population growth, resulting in reduced fund accumulation and also holding up the speed of economic construction. A fast-growing population has also created great difficulties in employment, education, housing, transportation, and health care. Confronted by such grim realities, to guarantee basic living conditions and constantly improve standards of living, China cannot follow the Western mode under which natural falling birth rates coincide with gradual economic growth.

The Chinese government's family-planning practices have been harshly criticized. Why has the Chinese government sought to control population growth? What effect has population growth had on the environment and economic development? What ethical questions are raised by the effort of any government to limit population growth?

Latin America's population increased from 165 million in 1950 to 405 million in 1985 and is projected to reach 778 million in 2025, despite declining birthrates.

In Asia, the populations of India and China continued to grow despite government efforts to reduce family size (see Society and Culture: China's Family-Planning Needs). In China, efforts to enforce a limit of one child per family led to large-scale female infanticide as rural families sought to produce male heirs. India's policies of forced sterilization created widespread outrage and led to the electoral defeat of the ruling Congress Party. Yet both countries achieved some successes. Between 1960 and 1982, India's birthrate fell from 48 to 34 per thousand, while China's rate declined even more sharply—from 39 to 19. Still, by 2025 both China, which today has 1.13 billion people, and India, today with 853 million, will both reach 1.5 billion.

It is unclear whether the nations of Asia, Africa, and Latin America will undergo the lowered fertility and mortality rates experienced in the West during the Industrial Revolution. Yet real progress has occurred, and fertility rates have fallen in the developing world where women have had access to education and employment outside the home.

Old and Young Populations

Population pyramids generated by demographers clearly illustrate the profound transformation in human reproductive patterns and life expectancy in the years since World War II. Figure 34.1 shows the 1985 age distributions in Pakistan, South Korea, and Sweden—nations at three different stages of economic development. Sweden is a mature industrial nation. South Korea is a rapidly industrializing nation that has surpassed many European nations in both industrial output and per capita wealth. Pakistan is a poor, traditional Muslim nation with rudimentary industrialization, low educational levels, and little effective family planning.

In 1985 nearly 50 percent of Pakistan's population was under age sixteen. The resulting pressures on the

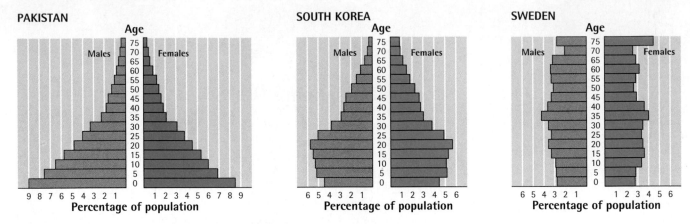

Figure 34.1   Age Structure Comparison: Islamic Nation (Pakistan), Non–Islamic Developing Nation (South Korea), and Developed Nation (Sweden), 1985   *Source:* Data from the World Bank.

economy were extraordinary. Every year 150,000 men reached age sixty-five—and another 1.2 million turned sixteen. Pakistan, therefore, had to create more than a million new jobs a year or face steadily growing unemployment and steadily declining wages. Sweden confronted a different problem. Sweden's aging population, growing demand for social welfare benefits, and declining labor pool meant that Sweden's industries faced the possibility of becoming less competitive and its citizens confronted the likelihood of declining living standards. In South Korea, a decline in fertility dramatically altered the ratio of children to adults, so that South Korea faced neither Pakistan's pressure to create jobs nor Sweden's growing demands for welfare benefits for the aged.

The demographic challenges faced by Sweden and other developed nations are less daunting than those confronting the developing nations. Poor nations must overcome problems such as shortages of investment capital, poor transportation and communication networks, and low educational levels, while they struggle to create jobs. Wealthy, well-educated, and politically stable nations can invest in robots and other new technologies to reduce labor needs and increase industrial and agricultural efficiency as their populations age.

The demographic problem and potential technological adjustments are most clearly visible in Japan. Unless current demographic patterns are reversed, Japan will have the oldest population among industrial nations by 2025. In Canada, Germany, the United States, and most other industrialized nations, young immigrants from poorer nations are entering the work force in large numbers. Japan has resisted immigration, instead investing heavily in technological solutions to the problems cre-

ated by its aging labor force. As of 1994, Japan had 75 percent of the world's industrial robots. Although Japanese industries are able to produce more goods with fewer workers, Japan will still face long-term increases in social welfare payments.

UNEQUAL DEVELOPMENT AND THE MOVEMENT OF PEOPLES

Two characteristics of the postwar world should now be clear. First, despite decades of experimentation with state-directed economic development, most nations that were poor in 1960 were as poor or poorer at the end of the 1990s. The only exceptions were a few rapidly developing Asian industrial nations and an equally small number of oil-exporting nations. Second, world population increased to startlingly high levels, and most of the increase was in the poorest nations.

The combination of intractable poverty and growing population generated a surge in international immigration. Few issues stirred more controversy. Even moderate voices sometimes framed the discussion of immigration as a competition among peoples. One commentator summarized his analysis this way: "As the better-off families of the northern hemisphere individually decide that having only one or at the most two children is sufficient, they may not recognize that they are in a small way vacating future

Table 34.2   Urban Residents as a Percentage of the Total Population in Selected Developing Nations

Nation	1960	1995
Nigeria	18	39
Tanzania	4	25
Morocco	29	48
Tunisia	40	57
India	18	28
Brazil	46	78
Mexico	51	75

Source: World Tables 1976 (Baltimore: Johns Hopkins University Press, 1976); *The Economist Book of Vital World Statistics* (Times Book: London, 1990); and *World Tables 1995* (Baltimore: Johns Hopkins University Press, 1995).

space (that is, jobs, parts of inner cities, shares of population, shares of market preferences) to faster-growing ethnic groups both inside and outside their boundaries. But that, in fact, is what they are doing."[4]

Large numbers of legal and illegal immigrants from poor nations with growing populations are entering the developed industrial nations, with the exception of Japan. Large-scale migrations within developing countries are a related phenomenon. The movement of impoverished rural residents to the cities of Asia, Africa, and Latin America (see Map 34.3 and Table 34.2) has increased steadily since the 1970s. This internal migration often serves as the first step toward migration abroad.

The Problem of Growing Inequality

Since 1945 global economic productivity has expanded more rapidly than at any other time in the past. Faster, cheaper communications and transportation have combined with improvements in industrial and agricultural technologies to create levels of material abundance that would have amazed those who experienced the first Industrial Revolution (see Chapter 24). Despite this remarkable economic expansion and growing market integration, the majority of the world's population remains in poverty. The industrialized nations of the Northern Hemisphere now enjoy a larger share of the world's wealth than they did a century ago. The thousands of homeless street children who live among the gleaming glass and steel towers of Rio's banking district can be seen as a metaphor for the social consequences of postwar economic development.

The gap between rich and poor nations has grown much wider since 1945. In 1993, Switzerland and Japan had the highest per capita GNPs (gross national products)—$35,760 and $31,490, respectively; the U.S. figure was $24,740; and Greece, the poorest nation in the European Union, had a per capita GNP of $7,220. The nations of the former Soviet Union and eastern Europe have per capita GNPs similar to those in the better-off nations of the Third World. Russia's per capita GNP in 1993 was $2,340, similar to Brazil's $2,930. Among developing economies in 1993, Algeria and Thailand had per capita GNPs of approximately $2,000, and in Nigeria, India, and China the figure was below $1,000. One billion of the world's people, approximately 20 percent, lived on less than $500 a year in 1993. This poverty was concentrated in Africa, Latin America, and Asia.

Wealth inequality within nations also grew. Regions tied to new technologies that provided competitive advantages became wealthier while other regions lost ground. In the United States, for example, the south and southwest grew richer in the last three decades relative to the older industrial regions of the midwest. Regional inequalities also appeared in developing nations. Generally, capital cities such as Buenos Aires, in Argentina, and Lagos, in Nigeria, attracted large numbers of migrants from rural areas because they offered more opportunities, even if those opportunities could not compare to the ones available in developed nations.

Even in the industrialized world, people were divided into haves and have-nots. During the presidency of Ronald Reagan (1981–1989), wealth inequality in the United States reached its highest level since the 1929 stock market crash. Some scholars estimated that the wealthiest 1 percent of households in the United States controlled more than 30 percent of the nation's total wealth. In 1992, households receiving Aid to Families with Dependent Children (AFDC) in the United States

Garbage Dump in Manila, Philippines Garbage pickers are a common feature of Third World urban development. Thousands of poor families in nearly every Third World city sort and sell bottles, aluminum cans, plastic, and newspapers to provide household income. (Geoff Tompkinson/Aspect Picture Library Ltd.)

had an average income of $4,680. In the same year the average income of the 1,059 partners in New York City's largest law firms was $957,000.[5] Even in Europe, where tax and inheritance laws redistributed wealth, unemployment, homelessness, and substandard housing were increasingly common.

Internal Migration: The Growth of Cities

Migration from rural areas to urban centers in developing nations increased threefold from 1925 to 1950. After that, the pace accelerated. Shantytowns sprawling around major cities in developing nations are commonly seen as signs of social breakdown and economic failure. Nevertheless, city life was generally better than life in the countryside. A World Bank study estimated that three out of four migrants to cities made economic gains. Residents of cities in sub-Saharan Africa, for example, were six times more likely than rural residents to have safe water. An unskilled migrant from the depressed northeast of Brazil could triple his or her income by moving to Rio de Janeiro.

As the scale of rural-to-urban migration grew, these benefits proved more elusive, however. In many West African cities, basic services were crumbling under the pressure of rapid population growth. In 1990 in Mexico City, one of the world's largest cities, more than thirty thousand people lived in garbage dumps, where they scavenged for food and clothing. Worsening conditions and the threat of crime and political instability led many governments to try to slow migration to cities and, in some cases, to return people to the countryside. Indonesia, for example, has relocated more than half a million urban residents since 1969. Despite some successes with slowing the rate of internal migration, nearly every poor nation still faces the challenge of rapidly growing cities.

Global Migration

Each year hundreds of thousands of men and women leave the developing world to emigrate to industrialized nations. After 1960 this movement increased in scale, and ethnic and racial tensions in the host nations worsened. Political refugees and immigrants faced murderous violence in Germany; growing anti-immigrant sentiment led to a new right-wing political movement in France; and an expanded Border Patrol attempted to more effectively seal the U.S. border with Mexico. By the 1990s, levels of immigration posed daunting social and cultural challenges for both host nations and immigrants.

Immigrants from the developing nations brought to host nations many of the same benefits that the great migration of Europeans to the Americas provided a century ago (see Chapter 25). Many European nations actively promoted guest worker programs and other inducements to immigration in the 1960s when an expanding European economy first confronted labor shortages. However, attitudes toward immigrants changed as the size of the immigrant population grew and as European economies slowed in the 1980s. Facing higher levels of unemployment, native-born workers saw immigrants as competitors willing to work for lower wages and less likely to support unions. However, because cultural and ethnic characteristics have traditionally formed the basis of national identity in many European countries (see Chapter 28), worsening relations between immigrants and the native-born may have been inevitable. Put simply, many Germans are unable to think of the German-born son or daughter of Turkish immigrants as a German.

Because immigrants generally are young adults and commonly retain the positive attitudes toward early marriage and large families dominant in their native cultures, immigrant communities in Europe and the United States tended to have fertility rates higher than the rates of the host populations. In Germany in 1975, for example, immigrants made up about 7 percent of the population but accounted for nearly 15 percent of all births. Although immigrant fertility rates decline with prolonged residence in industrialized societies, the family size of second-generation immigrants is still larger than that of the host population. Therefore, even without additional immigration, immigrant groups grow faster than the longer-established population. Although the fertility of the Hispanic population in the United States is lower than the rates in Mexico and other Latin American nations, Hispanic groups will contribute well over 20 percent of all population growth in the United States during the next twenty-five years.

As the Muslim population in Europe and the Asian and Latin American populations in the United States expand in the twenty-first century, cultural conflicts will test definitions of citizenship and nationality. The United States will have some advantages in meeting these challenges because of long experience with immi-

gration and relatively open access to citizenship. Yet in the 1990s the United States was moving slowly in the direction of European efforts to restrict immigration and defend a culturally conservative definition of nationality.

TECHNOLOGICAL AND ENVIRONMENTAL CHANGE

Technological innovation powered the economic expansion that began after World War II. New technologies increased productivity and disseminated human creativity. They also altered the way people lived, worked, and played. Because most of the economic benefits were concentrated in the advanced industrialized nations, technology increased the power of those nations relative to the developing world. Even within developed nations, postwar technological innovations did not benefit all classes, industries, and regions equally. There were losers as well as winners.

Population growth and increased levels of migration and urbanization led to the global expansion of agricultural and industrial production. This multiplication of farms and factories intensified environmental threats. At the end of the twentieth century, loss of rain forest, soil erosion, global warming, pollution of air and water, and extinction of species threatened the quality of life and the survival of human societies. Here again, differences between nations were apparent. Environmental protection, like the acquisition of new technology, had progressed furthest in societies with the most economic resources.

New Technologies and the World Economy

Nuclear energy, jet engines, radar, and tape recording were among the many World War II developments that later had an impact on consumers' lives. When applied to industry, new technology increased productivity, reduced labor requirements, and improved the flow of information. Pent-up demand for consumer goods also spurred new research and the development of new technologies. As the Western economies recovered from the war and incomes rose, consumers wanted new products that reduced their workloads or provided entertainment. The consumer electronics industry rapidly developed new products.

The Personal Computer

From Mainframe to Laptop
During the last forty years the computer revolution has changed the way we work. (left: Courtesy, IBM Corporation; bottom: Dagmar Fabricius/Liaison)

The period since World War II witnessed wave after wave of technological innovations. Few of them have had a greater impact on the way people work, learn, and live than the personal computer. In the 1970s computing was done on large mainframe computers owned by institutions and businesses, and IBM (International Business Machines) dominated the computer industry. By the mid-1990s desktop and laptop computers had marginalized the mainframe and dispersed the economic and political power associated with the computer. The computer industry experienced a rapid succession of revolutions made possible by the microchip and miniaturization.

Improvements in existing technologies accounted for much of the developed world's productivity increases during the 1950s and 1960s. Larger and faster trucks, trains, and airplanes cut transportation costs. Both capitalist and socialist governments made these changes possible by building highway systems, improving railroad track, and constructing airports. Governments also bore much of the cost for developing and constructing nuclear power plants.

No technology had greater significance in this period than the computer. The first computers were expensive, large, and slow. Only large corporations, governments, and universities could afford them. But by the mid-1980s desktop computers had replaced typewriters in most of the developed world's offices, and technological advances continued. Each new generation of computers was smaller, faster, and more powerful than the one before (see Environmental and Technology: The Personal Computer).

Computers also altered manufacturing. Small dedicated computers were used to control and monitor machinery in some industries. In the developed world, companies forced by competition to improve efficiency and product quality brought robots into the factory. Europe followed Japan's initiative in this field, especially in automobile production and mining. The United States introduced robots more slowly because it enjoys lower labor costs.

The transnational corporation became the primary agent of these technological changes. From the eighteenth century, powerful commercial companies have conducted business across national borders. By the twentieth century, the growing economic power of corporations in the industrialized nations allowed them to invest directly in the mines, plantations, and public utilities of less developed regions. In the post–World War II years, many of these companies became truly transnational, having multinational ownership and management. International trade agreements and open markets furthered the process. Ford Motor Company not only produced and sold cars internationally, but its shareholders, workers, and managers also had an international character. The Japanese automaker Honda imported into Japan cars it manufactured in Ohio. Similarly, German Volkswagen made cars in Mexico for sale in the United States.

As transnational manufacturers, agricultural conglomerates, and financial giants became wealthier and more powerful, they increasingly escaped the controls imposed by national governments. If labor costs were too high in Japan, antipollution measures too intrusive in the United States, or taxes too high in Great Britain,

transnational companies relocated—or threatened to do so. Governments in the developing world were often hard-pressed to control the actions of these powerful enterprises. As a result, the worst abuses of labor or of the environment usually occurred in poor nations.

Conserving and Sharing Resources

In the 1960s, environmental activists and political leaders began warning about the devastating environmental consequences of population growth, industrialization, and the expansion of agriculture onto marginal lands. Assaults on rain forests and redwoods, the disappearance of species, and the poisoning of streams and rivers raised public consciousness. Environmental damage occurred in the advanced industrial economies and in the poorest of the developing nations. Perhaps the worst environmental record was achieved in the former Soviet Union, where industrial and nuclear wastes were often dumped with little concern for environmental consequences. The accumulated effect of scientific studies and public debate led to national and international efforts to slow, if not undo, damage to the environment.

The expanding global population required increasing quantities of food, housing, energy, and other resources as the twentieth century ended. In the developed world, industrial activity increased much more rapidly than population grew, and the consumption of energy (coal, electricity, and petroleum) rose proportionally. Indeed, the consumer-driven economic expansion of the post–World War II years became an obstacle to addressing environmental problems. Modern economies depend for their well-being on the profligate consumption of goods and resources. Stock markets closely follow measures of consumer confidence—the willingness of people to buy. When consumption slows, industrial nations enter a recession. How could the United States, Germany, or Japan change consumption patterns to protect the environment without endangering corporate profits, wages, and employment levels?

Population growth since 1945 has been most dramatic in the developing countries where environmental pressures were also extreme. In Brazil, India, and China, for example, the need to expand food production led to rapid deforestation and the extension of farming and grazing onto marginal lands. The results were predictable: erosion and water pollution. Population growth in Indonesia forced the government to permit the cutting of nearly 20 percent of the total forest area. These and many other poor nations also attempted to force industrialization because they feared that their rapidly growing populations could not be provided for unless the transition from agriculture to manufacturing was completed. The argument for this policy was compelling. Why should Indians or Brazilians remain poor while Americans, Europeans, and Japanese remained rich?

Responding to Environmental Threats

Despite the gravity of environmental threats, there were many successful efforts to preserve and protect the environment. The Clean Air Act, the Clean Water Act, and the Endangered Species Act were passed in the United States in the 1970s as part of an environmental effort that included the nations of the European Community and Japan. Environmental awareness spread by means of the media and grassroots political movements, and most nations in the developed world enforced strict antipollution laws and sponsored massive recycling efforts. Many also encouraged resource conservation by rewarding energy-efficient factories and the manufacturers of fuel-efficient cars and by promoting the use of alternative energy sources such as solar and wind power.

These efforts produced significant results. In western Europe and the United States, air quality improved dramatically. In the United States, smog levels were down nearly a third from 1970 to 2000 even though the number of automobiles increased more than 80 percent. Emissions of lead and sulfur dioxide were down as well. The Great Lakes, Long Island Sound, and Chesapeake Bay were all much cleaner at the end of the century than they had been in 1970. The rivers of North America and Europe also improved. Still, more than thirty thousand deaths each year in the United States are attributed to exposure to pesticides and other chemicals.

New technologies made much of this improvement possible. Pollution controls on automobiles, planes, and factory smokestacks reduced harmful emissions. Similar progress was made in the chemical industry. Scientists identified the chemicals that threaten the ozone layer, and the phase-out of their use in new appliances and cars began.

Clearly the desire to preserve the natural environment was growing around the world. In the developed nations, continued political organization and enhanced awareness of environmental issues seemed likely to lead to step-by-step improvements in environmental policy. In the developing world and most of the former Soviet bloc, however, population pressures and weak governments were major obstacles to effective environmental policies. In China, for example, respiratory disease caused by pollution was the leading cause of death. Thus it was likely that the industrialized nations would have to fund global improvements, and the cost was likely to be high. Achieving this global redistribution of wealth and political power will be the most difficult task facing the environmental movement in the coming years.

CONCLUSION

The world was profoundly altered between 1975 and 1991. The Cold War dominated international relations to the end of the 1980s. Every conflict threatened to provoke a confrontation between the nuclear-armed superpowers, for both the United States and the Soviet Union feared that every conflict and every regime change represented a potential threat to their strategic interests. As a result, the superpowers were drawn into a succession of civil wars and revolutions. The costs in lives and property were terrible, the gains small. As defense costs escalated, the Soviet system crumbled. By 1991 the Soviet Union and the socialist Warsaw Pact had disappeared, transforming the international stage.

Latin America was pulled into the violence of the late Cold War period and paid a terrible price. The 1970s and 1980s witnessed a frontal assault on democratic institutions, a denial of human rights, and economic decline. This was the period of death squads and Dirty War. With the end of the Cold War, peace returned there and democracy began to replace dictatorship.

In the Persian Gulf, the end of the Cold War did not lead to peace. Iran and Iraq have experienced deep cycles of political turmoil, war, and foreign threats since the late 1970s.

The world also was altered by economic growth and integration, by population growth and movement, and by technological and environmental change. Led by the postwar recovery of the industrial powers and the remarkable economic expansion of Japan and the Asian Tigers, the world economy grew dramatically. The development and application of new technology contributed significantly to this process. International markets were more open and integrated than at any other time. The new wealth and exciting technologies of the postwar era were not shared equally, however. The capitalist West and a few Pacific Rim nations grew richer and more powerful while most of the world's nations remained poor.

Population growth in the developing world was one reason for this divided experience. Unable to find adequate employment or, in many cases, bare subsistence, people in developing nations migrated across borders hoping to improve their lives. These movements often provided valuable labor in the factories and farms of the developed world, but they also provoked cultural, racial, and ethnic tension. Problems of inequality, population growth, and international migration would continue to challenge the global community in the coming decades.

Technology seemed to offer some hope for meeting these challenges. Engineering, financial services, education, and other professions developed an international character thanks to the communications revolution. Ambitious and talented people in the developing world could now fully participate in global intellectual and economic life. However, most people working in the developing world remained disconnected from this liberating technology by poverty. Technology also bolstered efforts to protect the environment, providing the means to clean auto and factory emissions—even while it helped produce much of the world's pollution. Technology has been intertwined with human culture since the beginning of human history. Our ability to control and direct its use will determine the future.

■ Key Terms

proxy wars
Salvador Allende
Dirty War
Sandinistas
Ayatollah Ruhollah
  Khomeini
Saddam Husain
keiretsu
Asian Tigers
newly industrialized
  economies (NIEs)
Deng Xiaoping
Tiananmen Square
Mikhail Gorbachev
perestroika
Solidarity
Thomas Malthus
demographic transition

■ Suggested Reading

Among the works devoted to postwar economic performance are W. L. M. Adriaasen and J. G. Waardensburg, eds., *A Dual World Economy: Forty Years of Development Experience* (1989); P. Krugman, *The Age of Diminished Expectations: U.S. Economic Policy in the 1990s* (1990); B. J. McCormick, *The World Economy: Patterns of Growth and Change* (1988); and H. van der Wee, *Prosperity and Upheaval: The World Economy, 1945–1980* (1986).

For Latin America, Thomas E. Skidmore and Peter H. Smith, *Modern Latin America*, 4th ed. (1996), provides an excellent general introduction to the period 1975 to 1991. The literature on the era of repression is large. *Nunca Mas* (1986), the official report of the Argentine government, provides a moving introduction. Also see news stories in 1999 and 2000 about the arrest of Augusto Pinochet in London and the resulting legal proceedings. The movie *Official Story* (available with subtitles or dubbed) offers an effective look at the legacy of the Dirty War in Argentina. For Central America see Walter La Feber, *Inevitable Revolutions: The United States in Central America* (1983).

For the Pacific Rim see Jonathan Spence, *The Search for Modern China* (1990); Edwin O. Reischauer, *The Japanese* (1988); H. Patrick and H. Rosovsky, *Asia's New Giant: How the Japanese Economy Works* (1976); and Staffan B. Linder, *Pacific Century: Economic and Political Consequences of Asian-Pacific Dynamism* (1986).

There are many fine studies of Europe and the Soviet system. See, for example, C. Kindleberger, *Europe's Postwar Growth* (1976). More focused examinations of the Soviet bloc are provided in K. Dawisha, *Eastern Europe, Gorbachev and Reform: The Great Challenge* (1988); Barbara Engel and Christine Worobec, eds., *Russia's Women: Accommodation, Resistance, Transformation* (1990); David Remnick, *Lenin's Tomb: The Last Days of the Soviet Empire* (1993); and Charles Maier, *Dissolution: The Crisis of Communism and the End of East Germany* (1997).

The story of the Iranian Revolution and the early days of the Islamic Republic of Iran is well told by Shaul Bakhash, *The Reign of the Ayatollahs: Iran and the Iranian Revolution* (1990). Barnet Rubin, *The Fragmentation of Afghanistan* (1995), provides excellent coverage of the struggle between Soviet forces and the Muslim resistance in that country.

A number of studies examine the special problems faced by women in the postwar period. See, for example, Elisabeth Croll, *Feminism and Socialism in China* (1978); J. Ginat, *Women in Muslim Rural Society: Status and Role in Family and Community* (1982); June Hahner, *Women in Latin America* (1976); P. Hudson, *Third World Women Speak Out* (1979); A. de Souza, *Women in Contemporary India and South Asia* (1980); and M. Wolf, *Revolution Postponed: Women in Contemporary China* (1985).

For general discussions of economic, demographic, and environmental problems facing the world see R. N. Gwynne, *New Horizons? Third World Industrialization in an International Framework* (1990); W. Alonso, ed., *Population in an Interacting World* (1987); P. R. Ehrlich and A. E. Ehrlich, *The Population Explosion* (1990); James Fallows, *More like Us: Making America Great Again* (1989); Paul M. Kennedy, *Preparing for the Twenty-first Century* (1993); and J. L. Simon, *Population Matters: People, Resources, Environment and Immigration* (1990).

For issues associated with technological and environmental change see M. Feshbach and A. Friendly, *Ecocide in the U.S.S.R.* (1992); John Bellamy Foster, *Economic History of the Environment* (1994); S. Hecht and A. Cockburn, *The Fate of the Forest: Developers, Destroyers, and Defenders of the Amazon* (1989); K. Marton, *Multinationals, Technology, and Industrialization: Implications and Impact in Third World Countries* (1986); S. P. Huntington, *The Third Wave: Demoralization in the Late Twentieth Century* (1993); L. Solomon, *Multinational Corporations and the Emerging World Order* (1978); and B. L. Turner II et al., eds., *The Earth as Transformed by Human Action: Global and Regional Changes in the Biosphere over the Past 300 Years* (1990).

■ Notes

1. *New York Times,* July 24, 1993, 1.
2. Quoted in Antony Flew, "Introduction," in Thomas Robert Malthus, *An Essay on the Principle of Population and a Summary View of the Principle of Population* (New York: Penguin Books, 1970), 30.
3. "Population Implosion Worries a Graying Europe," *New York Times,* July 10, 1998.
4. Paul Kennedy, *Preparing for the Twenty-first Century* (New York: Random House, 1993), 45.
5. Andrew Hacker, "Unjust Desserts?" *New York Review of Books,* March 3, 1994, 20.

35

The End of a Global Century,

1991–2000

A Fragmented World • The Struggle for Rights •
Elements of a Global Culture
ENVIRONMENT AND TECHNOLOGY: Global Warming
SOCIETY AND CULTURE: Nelson Mandela

Orly Airport in Paris   The growing pace of transportation and communications
was a distinctive feature of late twentieth-century life.

As the year 1999 ended, *Time* magazine, in keeping with its long-standing tradition of choosing a "Person of the Year," decided to name the "Person of the Century." Instead of simply consulting among themselves or hiring a polling company to conduct a statistically sound survey, the editors conducted a poll over the Internet. Individuals with access to the Internet—well under half of the U.S. population—could vote for whomever they liked as many times as they wished. After deleting the names they considered frivolous, the editors came up with several lists of winners, ranging from revolutionaries to sports heroes. At the very top of the list was Albert Einstein; Franklin D. Roosevelt and Mahatma Gandhi were the first and second runners-up.

Time's contribution to the end-of-the-century passion for recapitulations encapsulated how many people viewed the world around them. Albert Einstein opened the door to the scientific wonders of the Atomic Age and inadvertently made possible the Cold War's "balance of terror." Franklin D. Roosevelt led the military alliance that crushed fascism in World War II, leaving the United States the world's most powerful nation. Mahatma Gandhi pioneered nonviolence in the face of injustice as a technique for winning rights and in the process helped set in motion the wave of decolonization of the post–World War II decades. And the Internet, *Time*'s technological collaborator, symbolized a revolution in communication that promised to bring the peoples of the world into ever closer contact.

Despite these emblems of the twentieth century's achievements, however, the twenty-first century dawned on a world deeply concerned about ethnic conflicts, human rights violations, environmental problems, and economic uncertainties. While powerful economic and cultural forces pushed for greater globalization, peoples in many lands sought ways to preserve or achieve autonomy and identity and safeguard human rights. While affluent individuals in the most developed countries enjoyed unprecedented prosperity, growing disparities between rich and poor, both within and among countries, cast a shadow on the future.

As you read this chapter, ask yourself the following questions:

- How did technology contribute to the process of globalization in the late twentieth century?
- What are the main sources of conflict in the post–Cold War world?
- What role does the struggle for human rights play in the contemporary world?

A FRAGMENTED WORLD

Religion, ethnicity, and race had played supporting roles during the era of empire and ideological struggle, but they took stage center with the fading of the Cold War. From the onset of the New Imperialism in the mid-nineteenth century (see Chapter 29) down to the peace settlements at the close of World War I (see Chapter 30), the European powers had readily—often arbitrarily—drawn and redrawn lines on maps. In the era of decolonization, these arbitrary boundaries became accepted borders for new nations. During the Cold War, the West tended to see local efforts to change political boundaries as communist plots; and most governments in the newly independent states were too preoccupied with the problems of governance and economic development to put much effort into attempts to redraw boundaries. To dispel fears of territorial aggression, regional groups such as the Organization of African Unity affirmed the colonial borders as national boundaries despite their lack of relationship to ethnic and linguistic realities. This generally conservative attitude toward change was reinforced by a number of violent episodes that aroused fears that the world order somehow might dissolve.

Challenges to the Nation-State

The modern state system that conceives of the world as a community of sovereign nation-states wielding absolute authority within recognized borders began with the Peace of Westphalia in 1648. Exhausted by the Thirty Years War, the Catholic and Protestant rulers of Europe signed treaties designed to bring Europe's Wars of Religion to an end. But although international commitment

CHRONOLOGY

	Politics	Economics and Society
1991		**1991** CNN covers Persian Gulf War live from Baghdad
	1992 Yugoslavia disintegrates—Croatia and Slovenia become independent states	
	1992–1995 Bosnia crisis	
	1994 Maya uprising in southern Mexico	**1993** Nobel Peace Prize to Nelson Mandela
1995	**1995** Nerve gas released in Tokyo subway	**1995** World Trade Organization founded
		1997 Asian financial crisis
	1998 Terrorist bombings of U.S. embassies in Kenya and Tanzania; India and Pakistan test atomic bombs	
	1999 Kosovo crisis; East Timor secedes from Indonesia	**1999** Nobel Peace Prize to Doctors Without Borders

to the concept of the sovereign nation-state reduced violence between states, it did not erase the passions of groups within states who felt alienated from their rulers or their rulers' religion.

Europeans subsequently worked hard to make religious toleration a reality at home. But in the parts of the world they colonized, they tended to see the local populations as divided into two opposed groups analogous to Protestants and Catholics. Divisions between Sunni and Shi'ite Muslims in the Middle East, between Hindus and Muslims in India, and between Arabs and Berbers in Algeria were all viewed through the distorting lens of European religious conflict. Instead of analyzing the specific nature of each ethnic or religious system they encountered, the United States and Europe tried in vain to establish Western-style democracy and secularism as a general formula for ensuring peace and tolerance.

The conflicts were many, extending even to countries with only small religious minorities (see Map 35.1). The Tamil-speaking Hindu population in Sri Lanka fought a prolonged and merciless guerrilla struggle throughout the 1980s and 1990s against the dominant Singhalese-speaking Buddhists. Dissidents in mostly Catholic East Timor fought for separation from Muslim Indonesia from the moment Portuguese rule ended in 1975 down to 1999, when their goal was finally achieved by popular referendum. In East Africa, Eritrea fought for and won independence from religiously and linguistically different Ethiopia in 1993. The ethnic hatreds between the Hutu people and the Tutsi people that repeatedly wracked Rwanda and Burundi spilled over into Congo (then Zaire) in 1998, overturning the long-standing dictatorship of President Joseph Mobutu. Even constitutionally secular

India saw instances of violence against Muslims and Christians in the name of Hindu nationalism.

In some instances, large-scale violence was avoided. Czechs and Slovaks agreed to divide postcommunist Czechoslovakia into the Czech Republic and the Republic of Slovakia in 1993. A brief uprising among the Maya population of southern Mexico in 1994 drew needed government attention and aid to that part of the country. And Malay-Chinese animosities in Malaysia and Indonesia were largely submerged in prosperity until economic calamity struck those countries in 1997.

In Yugoslavia, a population that had seemed harmonious until 1991 dissolved into a morass of separatist and warring groups. This conflict drew particular attention because of the complexity of the situation and its location on the border of an eastern Europe and a western Europe trying to restore connections after four decades of Iron Curtain separation. Industrial and urban Slovenia and agricultural Croatia, the most northerly parts of Yugoslavia, were predominantly Roman Catholic and had strong historic links to Austria and Hungary, respectively. Both were recognized as independent states in 1992 after brief struggles with federal Yugoslav forces.

The Yugoslavian province of Bosnia and Herzegovina faced greater difficulties. The people living there spoke Serbo-Croatian, but 40 percent were Muslims, 30 percent Eastern Orthodox Serbs, and 18 percent Croatian Catholics. The religious division dated back to Ottoman times, when this part of Yugoslavia was a border zone between Islam and Christian Europe. The murderous three-sided fighting that broke out with the declaration of Bosnian national independence in 1992 gave rise to the term **ethnic cleansing.** Originally journalists used

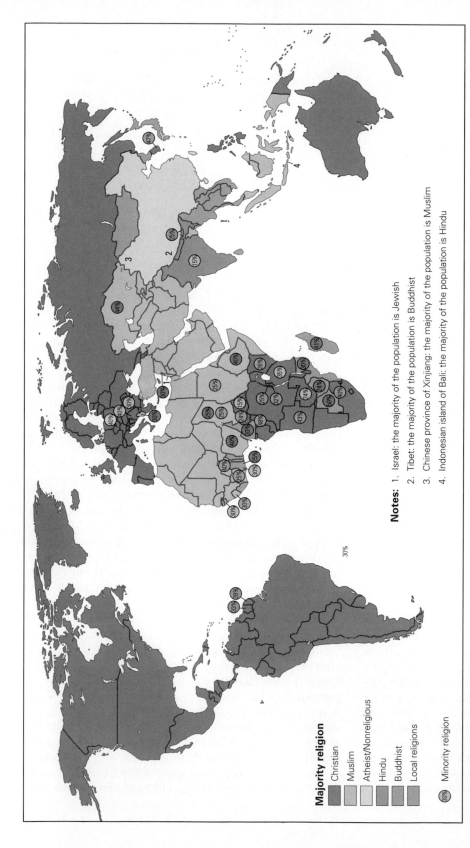

Map 35.1 World Religions Believers in Islam, Christianity, and Buddhism make up large percentages of the population in many countries. Differing forms of these religions seldom coincide with national boundaries. As religion revives as a source of social identity or a rationale for political assertion or mass mobilization, the possibility of religious activism spreading across broad geographic regions becomes greater, as does the likelihood of domestic discord in multireligious states.

Majority religion

- Christian
- Muslim
- Atheist/Nonreligious
- Hindu
- Buddhist
- Local religions

30% Minority religion

Notes: 1. Israel: the majority of the population is Jewish

2. Tibet: the majority of the population is Buddhist

3. Chinese province of Xinjiang: the majority of the population is Muslim

4. Indonesian island of Bali: the majority of the population is Hindu

Albanian Refugees from Kosovo   Lines of familiar-looking refugees from the complex Yugoslavia crisis reminded Europeans of the grim days following World War II. Parallel refugee situations in Afghanistan, Iraq, Rwanda, or Somalia had less immediacy and generated less pressure for international intervention.   (Peter Turnley/Black Star)

the term to refer to the efforts of Bosnian Serbs to evict Bosnian Muslims from their homes and destroy all vestiges of Muslim presence, from manuscripts in the national library to mosques and historic Ottoman buildings. Today the term means any effort by one racial, ethnic, or religious group to eliminate the people and culture of a different group.

The Bosnia crisis challenged the international community to consider whether one country could rightly intervene in another nation's civil war when the intervening power had no national interests at stake. Since the territories that retained the name Yugoslavia—the southern regions centered on the heavily populated province of Serbia—were helping the Bosnian Serbs, and independent Croatia was helping the Croatians of Bosnia, the question was whether anyone was going to come to the aid of the Muslims, Bosnia's largest ethnic group. No Muslim state had the capability to intervene in a major way. Iran and other Muslim states sent some

aid and charged that religious prejudice was the reason for European unwillingness to help the Muslims. Finally, after much indecision—and extensive television coverage of atrocities and wanton destruction—the United States made a cautious intervention and eventually brokered a tentative settlement in 1995.

The shooting had hardly stopped in Bosnia when tension began to heighten in Kosovo, a southern province of Yugoslavia, populated mostly by Albanian-speaking Muslims. In 1389 the Ottoman Empire defeated the kingdom of Serbia in the Battle of Kosovo, and Kosovo became an enduring and powerful symbol of Serbian national aspirations. By the 1990s, however, Serbs constituted only a minority of Kosovo's population. The NATO alliance repeatedly urged Serbia to stop mistreating the Kosovars (that is, the Albanian-speaking Muslims of Kosovo) and to permit them to participate in Yugoslavia's federal government as they had done before 1989, when Kosovo was an autonomous province within Yugoslavia. When

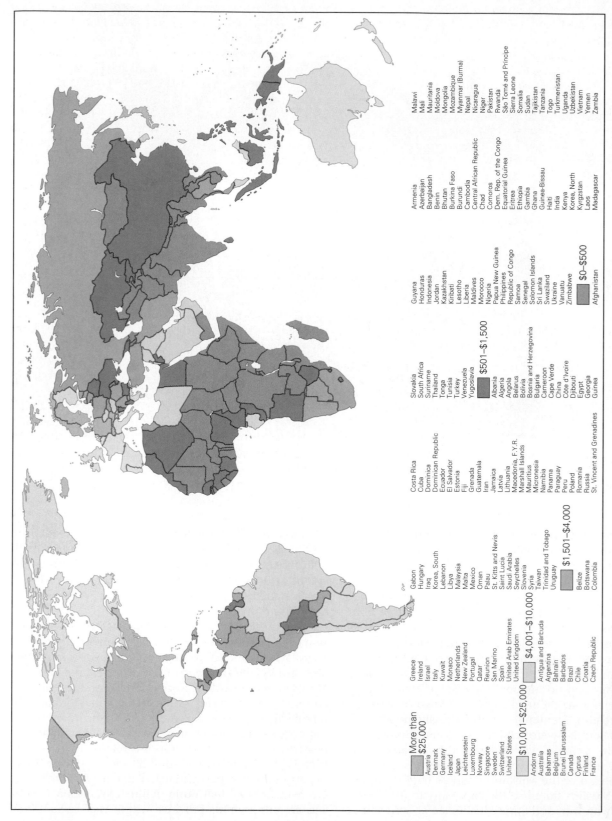

Map 35.2   Estimated GNP per Capita, 1990s   Since World War II, wealth has increasingly been concentrated in a small number of industrialized nations in the Northern Hemisphere. The cost of developing and acquiring new technologies has widened the gap between rich and poor nations.

NATO's warnings went unheeded, the United States, Britain, and France—acting under the NATO umbrella—launched an aerial war against Serbia in 1999. Suffering few casualties themselves, the NATO allies—but mainly the United States—damaged military and infrastructural targets in Serbia and forced the withdrawal of Serbian forces from Kosovo.

In the aftermath of the air attacks, no one was certain whether new principles of international action had been established. Having nearly single-handedly won the Kosovo war without losing any American lives to enemy fire, the United States had again proven its might. But it was unclear whether such things as violations of human rights, ethnic cleansing, and atrocities, on the one hand, or the military weakness of the force perpetrating the abuses, on the other, would determine when and where future U.S. or NATO interventions might occur. Chronic internal conflicts in Turkey against Kurdish-speaking peoples, and in Sudan against Christian and animist groups were cited as instances in which human rights concerns might call for international intervention. However, these trouble spots were also places where a long-standing alliance (Turkey) or geographical remoteness (Sudan) weighed heavily against intervention. Also in the aftermath of the events of Yugoslavia, the European Union took steps to organize a collective military force outside of NATO so as to have a basis for independent action in any future crisis.

Problems of the Global Economy

Issues of foreign intervention and national sovereignty also surfaced in the economic realm. In the nineteenth century the imperialist nations exported raw materials from their overseas colonies and shipped in manufactured goods, destroying local handicraft industries and making the colonies dependent on international commodity prices. If a slump occurred in the market for cotton cloth, colonial economies that depended heavily on the export of raw cotton suffered more than the economies of the imperialist nations that wove the cloth. When industrial profits were high, the imperialists invested surplus capital in industrializing nations with populations of European ancestry, such as the United States, or in building railroads, ports, and other facilities to increase commodity exports from the colonies to the industrial nations.

World economic development after World War II at first followed this pattern—that is, favoring industry in Europe and commodity production elsewhere. Marshall Plan aid by the United States to rebuild industrial western Europe was paralleled by investments by the USSR to favor industry in Russia and eastern Europe. The Caspian and Central Asian republics of the Soviet Union were left dependent on exchanging cotton, wheat, petroleum, and other basic commodities for industrial products.

The pattern gradually changed, however, partly because of Cold War conflicts. American purchases of supplies during the Korean War stimulated economic growth in Japan in the 1950s. In the 1960s and 1970s, American involvement in Vietnam entailed similar expenditures, which helped Singapore, Hong Kong, and Taiwan develop vigorous industrial economies. At the same time, Japan concluded a series of treaties formally ending World War II. Its 1965 peace treaty with South Korea, for example, a country it had exploited harshly during the decades of annexation from 1910 to 1940, was accompanied by economic agreements that fueled a strong Korean economic resurgence. These unprecedented new avenues for the international flow of money helped these East Asian countries reach levels of industrial prosperity previously enjoyed only in Europe and North America.

Other factors similarly altered the world pattern of wealth distribution (see Map 35.2). During the decade of high oil prices starting in 1974, the oil-producing states became rich, but foreign debt became a major problem for some of the world's biggest countries, including Mexico and Brazil (see Chapter 34). After the collapse of the Soviet Union in 1991, the newly independent republics in eastern Europe required enormous investment to adapt their inefficient command economies to the global marketplace. By century's end it was still unclear whether Russia's faltering economy would make a successful transition to capitalism.

At the same time, Southeast Asia boomed. Benefiting from investment and technical expertise from Japan and other industrial nations, Thailand, Malaysia, and Indonesia experienced rapid economic growth. As the world's tallest skyscraper rose in Kuala Lumpur, industry mushroomed. Deforestation proceeded with equal rapidity as hardwood trees in Indonesia and other tropical countries, including Brazil, were cut down and sold on the world market. Groups concerned with protecting animal habitats and saving species from extinction protested these assaults, but quick profits and a national interest in economic development proved of greater weight (see Environmental and Technology: Global Warming).

The fevered pace of economic growth in Asia exploded in 1997 in a financial crisis that sent currency and stock values plummeting first in Thailand and then in neighboring countries, eventually triggering serious recession in Japan and having effects as far away as Brazil. Though the damage to the industrial economies of Europe and North America was limited, slackened demand for oil in Asia caused petroleum prices to fall to historic

Global Warming

Until the 1980s, environmental alarms focused mainly on localized episodes of air and water pollution, exposure to toxic substances, waste management, and the disappearance of wilderness. The development of increasingly powerful computers and complex models of ecological interactions in the 1990s, however, made people aware of the global scope of certain environmental problems.

Many scientists and policymakers came to perceive global warming, the slow increase of the temperature of earth's lower atmosphere, as an environmental threat requiring preventive action on an international scale. The warming was caused by a layer of atmospheric gases—called *greenhouse gases* (carbon dioxide, methane, nitrous oxide, and ozone)— that allowed solar radiation to reach the earth and warm it but kept infrared energy (heat) from radiating from the earth's surface into space. Called the *greenhouse effect*, this process normally keeps the earth's temperature at a level suitable for life. However, twentieth century increases in greenhouse-gas emissions from industry, agriculture, and transportation added to this insulating atmospheric layer. Though scientists disagree about which computer model of climatic change is most reliable, many have warned that global temperature increases might melt glaciers and icecaps and raise sea levels by many feet. They also have cautioned that warming might be more intense in the polar regions and that changes in oceanic currents and wind patterns could trigger disastrous weather changes.

Though 1998 was the warmest year of modern times and 1995 the second warmest, scientists continued to disagree over the exact extent and cause of global warming. International agreements to limit greenhouse-gas production signed in 1992 and 1997 were controversial because of the effect they could have on curtailing industry in North America, Europe, and Japan—regions that contribute disproportionately high levels of greenhouse gases to the atmosphere. Leaders of developing countries fear that limits on gas emissions could cripple their plans for industrial and economic expansion. Nevertheless, if the most alarming predictions— that sea-level rises could inundate coastal regions and some of the world's largest cities—come to pass, further agreements will be needed. It is unclear whether nations are prepared to cooperate on world environmental programs that might seem to limit their sovereignty or run against their national economic interests.

Flooding in Bangladesh
Typhoon-driven floods submerge the low-lying farmlands of Bangladesh with tragic regularity. Any significant rise in the sea level will make parts of the country nearly uninhabitable.   (D. Aubert/Sygma)

Postwar Food Distribution in Iraq   Economic sanctions placed on Iraq by the United Nations after the 1991 Gulf War required international monitoring of food distribution made possible by the sale of limited amounts of Iraqi oil. Though sanctions were intended to weaken Saddam Husain, shown in the photo to the left of food distributors, hardship experienced by the general population strengthened his control and focused resentment on the United Nations.   (Samara Boustani/Sygma)

lows in 1999. This decline threatened the economies of the oil-producing states sufficiently to prod them into agreeing to production limits to bring prices back up.

The financial crises in Asia and Russia exemplified the tight interconnections within the global economy and raised the question of whether prosperous nations were obliged to rescue failing economies. A financial bailout for Mexico became a heated political issue in the United States in 1995, the year after the North American Free Trade Agreement (NAFTA), eliminating tariffs among the United States, Canada, and Mexico, went into effect. Arguing that Mexican prosperity was in the U.S. national interest, President Bill Clinton (1993–2001) pushed through a rescue plan that turned out to be successful. Other countries went to the International Monetary Fund and World Bank for assistance. These bodies made their assistance conditional on internal economic reforms that were often politically difficult, such as terminating government subsidies for basic foodstuffs and liberalizing investment.

Economic sanctions—embargoes, boycotts, freezing of assets, and restrictions on investment, all intended to harm another country's economy—became popular as a weapon, though one that only rich nations could wield. The United States, sometimes with the collaboration of its European allies, imposed severe sanctions on Iraq, Libya, Iran, Yugoslavia, and a number of other countries it had disputes with. Though the ultimate goal of such sanctions was normally to change a target government's policies, oil boycotts (Libya, Iraq) and bans on American investment (Iran) generally fell short of this objective, though they were often successful in inflicting economic damage.

In 1995, in an effort to foster and bring order to international trade, the world's major trading powers established the **World Trade Organization (WTO)** as the climax of a final round of negotiations under the rubric General Agreement on Tariffs and Trade (GATT). Charged with enforcing GATT agreements hammered out during periodic negotiating sessions over forty-seven years, the WTO seeks to reduce barriers to world trade. Despite a membership of 110 nations, however, the WTO is not without enemies, as became evident in Seattle in 1999, when street demonstrations, partly organized by American labor unions fearful of foreign competition, forced the organization to suspend a meeting.

Old Threat, New Dangers

As new military technologies gave the United States and a few other states the ability to wage war with minimal casualties to themselves, other ways of deploying violence for political ends became popular. One technique was to launch violent terrorist attacks. **Terrorism** rested on the belief that horrendous acts of violence could provoke harsh reprisals or, if repeated frequently, demonstrate such government incompetence that existing regimes would lose legitimacy and the people would look to the terrorists as a strong, organized, determined replacement. By no means a new force in world affairs, terrorism thrived in the late twentieth century because it was hard to combat and well adapted to television news coverage. Global broadcasting gave terrorist acts publicity, thus generating fear among the public and increasing the likelihood of governments losing control.

Palestinian groups dedicated to destroying Israel set the tone for later media-centered terrorism with airplane hijackings in 1968 and the capture and eventual murder of eleven Israeli athletes during the Munich Olympic Games of 1972. Both of these outrages became media events that galvanized sympathy for Israel, but they also led fearful television viewers to believe that Palestinian groups were much stronger than they actually were. Fear of Palestinian violence unquestionably contributed to the on-again, off-again peace process that Israel agreed to during secret discussions in Oslo, Norway, in 1991.

Political groups around the world staged innumerable terrorist acts, from bombings in the British Isles by the Irish Republican Army, to the assassinations in India of prime ministers Indira Gandhi (1984) and Rajiv Gandhi (1991), to the release of nerve gas in the Tokyo subway system by an apocalyptic Buddhist sect in 1995. The simultaneous bombing of U.S. embassies in Kenya and Tanzania in 1998 demonstrated the frustration and vulnerability of even the most powerful governments. Usamah bin Ladin°, a Saudi veteran of the Afghan war

---

Usamah bin Ladin (oo-SAH-mah bin LAH-din)

against the USSR, was named by the United States as the mastermind of the bombings. Yet despite a token retaliatory air attack on his base in Afghanistan, a country with which the United States had no diplomatic relations, he remained untouchable and seemingly continued his terrorist plotting against the United States.

Nuclear proliferation offered a far more plausible threat to world peace, and fear that nuclear devices would fall into the wrong hands was especially strong in government circles. During the Cold War, the world had lived with a sense of impending nuclear doom. This feeling quickly evaporated after communism collapsed in Europe in 1991. Yet thousands of nuclear weapons remained. Despite safeguards to keep them from being sold or stolen, the possibility of nuclear weapons falling into the hands of terrorists or states interested in blackmailing their neighbors could not be discounted. Nor was there adequate assurance that radioactive materials could be disposed of safely without environmental contamination.

In addition, a number of countries undertook to construct their own nuclear devices, usually in secret. Oddly, the balance of nuclear forces between the United States and the Soviet Union throughout the Cold War had increasingly come to be seen as an element of stability. Because neither side could have started a nuclear war without facing total annihilation, both sides were bound never to use their ghastly arsenals. Without the threat of mutual destruction, however, it seemed possible that one or two nuclear weapons could be used in a restricted regional context. Thus a new form of nuclear anxiety arose. The problem for the world community was **nuclear nonproliferation:** how to prevent a country like North Korea or Iraq from deploying nuclear weapons. The United States sought commitments from North Korea to refrain from developing nuclear weapons, and the United Nations used intrusive inspections of suspected nuclear facilities to disarm Iraq. But there was no assurance that either form of deterrence would prove effective in the long run. Anxiety over nuclear proliferation increased when India and Pakistan openly tested nuclear bombs and missile delivery systems in 1998.

Chemical and biological weapons, which could kill massively and indiscriminately and be delivered in missile warheads, posed a similar threat. But preventing their manufacture was more difficult. Nuclear weapons required advanced technology and large investments in factories and equipment, but lethal chemicals and biological agents could be produced by seemingly ordinary chemical and pharmaceutical plants using standard equipment. United Nations inspections of Iraqi war-

Nelson Mandela

The drama of decolonization in Africa climaxed in 1994 when Nelson Rolihlahla Mandela was elected president of South Africa in the first election open to citizens of all races. Born in 1918, Mandela became an active protester for civil rights as a college student in 1940. While working for a law degree, he helped found the Youth League of the African National Congress (ANC) in 1944.

After violent racial clashes in 1960 prompted the banning of the ANC, Mandela became its underground leader, challenging the apartheid regime (see Chapter 33) and calling for a new constitution based on democratic principles. Facing the full military mobilization of the apartheid state, he organized armed resistance and was arrested in 1962. While serving a life sentence, he refused several offers of freedom that would have required recognition of government racial policies.

In 1990, when it became evident that apartheid could not be maintained, Mandela was released and the next year elected President of the ANC. In 1993 he was awarded the Nobel Peace Prize, and in the following year he was elected president of South Africa. The following excerpt comes from his inauguration address.

O̲ur daily deeds as ordinary South Africans must produce an actual South Africa that will reinforce humanity's belief in justice, strengthen its confidence in the nobility of the human soul and sustain all our hopes for a glorious life for all. . . .

To my compatriots, I have no hesitation in saying that each one of us is as intimately attached to the soil of this beautiful country as are the jacaranda trees of Pretoria and the mimosa trees of the bushveld. . . .

That spiritual and physical oneness we all share with this common homeland explains the depth of the pain we all carried in our hearts as we saw our country tear itself apart in a terrible conflict, and as we saw it spurned, outlawed and isolated by the peoples of the world, precisely because it had become the universal base of the pernicious ideology and practice of racism and racial oppression.

We, the people of South Africa, feel fulfilled that humanity has taken us back into its bosom, that we, who were outlaws not so long ago, have today been given the rare privilege to be host to the nations of the world on our own soil. . . .

The time for the healing of wounds has come.

The moment to bridge the chasms that divide us has come.

Why was Mandela's election considered a great victory for human rights? What is the significance of Mandela's use of the word compatriot?

Source: Inauguration Address of Nelson Mandela as State President of South Africa, May 10, 1994.

---

making potential (carried out as part of the settlement of the 1991 Persian Gulf War) uncovered and destroyed extensive stocks of chemical munitions and plants for producing nerve gas and lethal germs. However, no means of preventing Iraq or any other country from developing these weapons was devised. In 1998 Iraqi resistance to inspections provoked a military confrontation with the United States and effectively terminated the inspection program. Thus the most concerted international effort to limit a country's military capability suffered a severe setback, and the issue returned to the United Nations Security Council for reconsideration.

THE STRUGGLE FOR RIGHTS

S̲ome critics chastised U.S. president Jimmy Carter in 1979 for pressing the shah of Iran to improve Iran's human rights record. His pressure, they felt, hastened the shah's downfall (see Chapter 34). However, the question of rights played an increasingly important role in international affairs in the 1990s (see Society and Culture: Nelson Mandela). While environmental and animal liberation groups pressed for extensions of the concept of rights, some religious communities deemed rights agitation an attack on their traditions. When governments were criticized on rights issues, they commonly protested that the matters were purely internal and that any interference from abroad was an attack on state sovereignty.

Human Rights

In addition to maintaining peaceful relations between states, the United Nations also aimed to protect the rights of individuals. A General Assembly resolution passed on December 10, 1948—called the **Universal Declaration of Human Rights**—contained thirty articles that it proclaimed to be "a common standard of achievement for all peoples and nations."[1] It condemned slavery, torture, cruel and inhuman punishment, and arbitrary arrest, detention, or exile. It called for freedom of movement, assembly, and thought. It asserted rights to life, liberty, and security of person; to impartial public trials; and to education, employment, and leisure. The declaration ringingly asserted the principle of equality, most fully set forth in Article 2:

> Everyone is entitled to all the rights and freedoms set forth in this Declaration, without distinction of any kind, such as race, color, sex, language, religion, or political or other opinion, national or social origin, property, birth or other status.[2]

The roots of the declaration lay mostly in European and American history. Religious tolerance emerged from Europe's bloody religious wars of the sixteenth and seventeenth centuries. The idea of inalienable rights came from the U.S. Constitution (1788) and Bill of Rights (1791) and the French Declaration of the Rights of Man (1789). The struggle against slavery and the woman suffrage movement in the nineteenth and twentieth centuries extended the concept of tolerance to all races and both sexes (see Chapters 25 and 28). The concept of social justice steadily advanced in Europe and America with the legalization of labor unions, the spread of universal education, and the establishment of government programs to care for the needy and ensure adequate standards of living for all citizens.

Not all the countries that voted for the declaration in 1948 shared this European heritage, but its principles dovetailed with humanitarian concerns in a variety of non-European cultures and nations. Most countries later joining the United Nations willingly signed the declaration because it implicitly condemned the persistence of discriminatory European colonial regimes. Despite this apparent agreement, however, some people had philosophical reservations about the declaration's formulation of human rights. They asked whether such a set of principles could be called universal when so many of the world's religious and cultural traditions had not been consulted in its drafting.

Did the declaration's assertion of total equality, for example, mean that the traditional social distinctions represented by the Hindu castes were unacceptable? Was the declaration breached by nations that used religion, language, skin color, or membership in a particular ethnic group to distinguish more privileged from less privileged citizens—a group of nations that included Israel, the United States, South Africa, and Saudi Arabia, among many others? Did the section declaring that "everyone has a right to a nationality" implicitly condemn suppressing ethnic minorities—as Turkey, Iraq, and Iran did with their Kurdish populations; China did with Tibetans; and France did with immigrant Muslims from North Africa?

Lacking mechanisms for addressing issues on this scale, human rights activists, often working through international philanthropic bodies known as **nongovernmental organizations (NGOs),** focused their efforts on easily agreed-upon violations of human decency: torture, imprisonment without trial, summary execution by government death squads, and famine relief, and refugee assistance. NGOs devoted to relieving hunger and oppression and bringing human rights abuses to world attention proliferated in the 1970s. Amnesty International, founded in 1961 and numbering a million members in 162 countries by the 1990s, concentrated on gaining freedom for people illegally imprisoned. Médecins Sans Frontières (Doctors Without Borders), founded in 1971, was awarded the Nobel Peace Prize in 1999 for the medical assistance it offered in scores of crisis situations. Even entertainers became involved in relieving suffering through Live Aid, a 1985 rock concert in London and Philadelphia that raised millions of dollars for famine assistance.

Such efforts raised the prominence of human rights as a global concern and put pressure on governments to consider human rights when making foreign policy decisions. Skeptics observed, however, that a Western country could prod a non-Western country to improve its human rights performance—for example, by barring the government from cutting off a thief's hand as stipulated by Islamic law—but reverse criticism of a Western country—for example, condemnation of persistent racial discrimination in the United States—often fell on deaf ears. Thus the human rights movement was sometimes seen not as an effort to make the world as a whole more humane but as another form of Western cultural imperialism, a club with which to beat former colonial societies into submission.

Women's Rights

No issue exemplified this dichotomy of views so clearly as women's rights. The feminist movement that peaked in the early twentieth century had concentrated on acquiring voting rights (see Chapters 28 and 30). Inspired by parallel efforts to combat racial discrimination and end the war in Vietnam, feminist activism revived in the United States in the 1960s and spread around the world. The movement focused on equal access to education and jobs and on quality-of-life matters such as ending sexual exploitation, gaining control of reproduction, and abandoning confining clothing styles. Ironically, the decades in which the feminist movement (followed by movements for gay and lesbian rights in North America and Europe) became a major force also saw sexuality become a more explicit and prominent aspect of commercial, artistic, and social life.

Feminists in the West decried the oppression of women in other parts of the world. At the same time, some non-Western women complained about the deterioration of morality and family life in the West and what they considered to be the feminists' misplaced concern with matters such as clothing. As with human rights, non-Western peoples disputed the West's definition of priorities. Western women and many secularized Muslim women protested Islam's requirement that a woman cover her head and wear loose-fitting garments to conceal the shape of her body, practices enforced by law in countries such as Iran and Saudi Arabia. Nevertheless, many outspoken Muslim women voluntarily donned concealing garments as expressions of personal belief, statements of resistance to secular dictatorship, or defenses against coarse male behavior. Some African women saw their real problems as deteriorating economic conditions, AIDS, and the customary practice of circumcising girls, a form of genital mutilation that could cause chronic infections or permanently impair sexual enjoyment.

Efforts to coordinate the struggle for women's rights internationally gained momentum in the 1970s with a series of highly publicized international conferences. But the search for a universally accepted women's rights agenda proved elusive, because of local concerns and strong disagreement on abortion and other issues. Nevertheless, a rising global tide of women's education, access to employment, political participation, and control of fertility augured well for the eventual achievement of gender equality.

Beijing Women's Conference in 1995   This gathering of women, under United Nations auspices, from every part of the world illustrated the challenges posed by women's search for equality. The Chinese government, consistent with its policies of suppressing dissent and closely regulating social life, tried to limit press access to the conference. As in many other instances, these efforts to silence or control women's voices on issues like abortion and family planning proved ineffective.   (Alesandra Boulat/Sipa Press)

Still, culturally shaped disagreement on women's rights and other philosophical and social issues persisted at the end of the twentieth century. The greatest likelihood was that the diverse peoples of the world would seldom be able to do more than agree to disagree. World developmental patterns pointed to worsening social and economic problems in Africa and growing economic power in Asia. Thus the continuing appeal of standards too closely identified with European and American values seemed to be in doubt.

ELEMENTS OF A GLOBAL CULTURE

With the disintegration of the Soviet Union into fifteen separate republics in 1990–1991, overt political imperialism seemed an increasingly distant memory (see Chapter 34). Yet concerns grew in many quarters about **cultural imperialism.** Critics complained that entertainment conglomerates were flooding the world's movie theaters and television screens with Western tastes and styles and that Western manufacturers were flooding world markets with Western goods—both relying on sophisticated advertising techniques that vigorously promoted worldwide consumption and cultural conformity. In this view, global marketing was an especially insidious effort not only to overwhelm the world with a single Western outlook shaped by capitalist ideology, but also to suppress or devalue traditional cultures and alternative ideologies; the United States was the primary culprit.

But in truth, technology, not ideology, played the central role in spreading Western culture. The idea that the West engaged in cultural imperialism rested in part on the fact that Americans invented and developed so much of the technology that formed and spread popular culture in the twentieth century. A close analysis of cultural trends reveals a diversity of voices that the case for cultural imperialism overlooks.

The Medium and the Message

After World War II, much of Europe's and Japan's industry lay in ruins, and the United States became the world's main exporter of movies. Hollywood exported an image of the United States as a land of gangsters and cowboys, pratfalls and musical romance. By the 1960s, depictions of American life broadened. Still, emphasis on crime, luxurious living, and—from the 1970s on—explicit sexuality presented a skewed but influential and fairly consistent image of America.

European and Japanese cinema recovered slowly from the war. European and Japanese filmmakers earned high marks for artistic accomplishment, but their work generally appealed to relatively small international markets. Hollywood's main international competition in the field of popular cinema came from Bombay, whose joyous musicals had wide appeal; Egypt, famed for musicals and comedies; and Hong Kong, which specialized in martial arts films. Films of high artistic merit made in the USSR, Brazil, China, India, and, after the 1979 revolution, Iran, won international prizes but did not attract mass international audiences.

Television, made possible by the invention of an electron scanning gun by the American Vladimir Zworykin° in 1928, became widely available to consumers only after World War II and did not spread to most non-Western countries until the 1960s. Hollywood's dominance in the world movie industry was not replicated in television. By the time videotape technology (invented in 1956) and satellite broadcasting (begun in 1962) became generally available, the newly independent governments resulting from decolonization were already using radio and television broadcasting for nation building and were disinclined to rely on foreign programs.

Moviemaking tended to be privately organized even in countries that imposed government censorship. In contrast, television outside the United States usually became a government monopoly, following the pattern of telegraph and postal service and radio broadcasting. Government control of news reports and approval of other programming was intended to disseminate a unified national viewpoint. Many state broadcasters eventually turned to American sources to meet the demand for shows because broadcasting American soap operas, adventure series, and situation comedies was cheaper than producing them locally. The United States, however, was not the only external source of programming. Many nations purchased shows from Brazil, Mexico, and Great Britain.

When American producers realized that satellite transmission provided an opening to an international market, MTV (Music Television) and CNN (Cable News Network) came into being. Specializing in rock music videos aimed at a youth audience, MTV became an international enterprise offering special editions in different parts of the world. Music videos shown in Uzbekistan°, for example, often featured Russian bands, and Chinese groups appeared in MTV programs shown in Singapore. CNN developed its international potential after becoming the most-viewed and informative news source during the 1991 Persian Gulf War, when it broadcast live from Baghdad. Providing news around the clock, CNN began to supplant other commercial and government news programming as the best source of information about rapidly developing events. However, CNN's fundamentally American view of the news, even

---

Vladimir Zworykin (VLAD-ih-meer ZWOR-ih-kin)
Uzbekistan (uzz-BEK-ih-stan)

Rock Concert for African Famine Relief
The Live-Aid concerts like this one in London's Wembley Stadium were organized in the late 1980s by Bob Geldof. Popular music had been used for centuries to mobilize public concern and engage the feelings of young people. Modern electronics and satellite technology amplified its impact and carried it throughout the world.   (Redferns Music Picture Library)

in its international editions, prompted some governments to limit its reception.

Zworykin's electron scanning gun also made possible the computer screen. At first, the computer industry, which mushroomed for defense and business purposes in the post–World War II decades, had little connection with television or movies. The three technologies were quite different. Movies recorded light and shadow on film. Television used electromagnetic waves. Computers were based on a digital system in which every bit of information was expressed as a combination of zeros and ones and millions of bits were required for even a simple screen display. But with adequate electronic storage capacity and enough speed in recovering stored information, every point on a photographic image or electron wave could be expressed digitally and transmitted to the computer screen as a moving picture. In the 1990s Japan introduced the first digital television broadcasting at about the time that disks containing digitized movies and computer programs with movielike action became increasingly available.

More widespread was communication over the Internet, a linkage of academic, government, and business computer networks. Developed originally for U.S. defense research in the 1960s, the Internet became a major cultural phenomenon with the proliferation of personal computers in the 1980s. With the establishment of the World Wide Web as an easy-to-use graphic interface in the 1990s, the number of Internet users skyrocketed (see Map 35.3). Myriad new companies formed to explore "e-commerce," the commercial dimension of the Internet. By century's end, many American college students were spending less time studying conventional books and scholarly resources than they were spending to explore the Web for entertainment and to accomplish class assignments.

As had happened so often throughout history, technological developments had unanticipated consequences. The new telecommunications and entertainment technologies derived disproportionately from American invention, industry, and cultural creativity (Japan became a powerful secondary factor on the industrial side in the

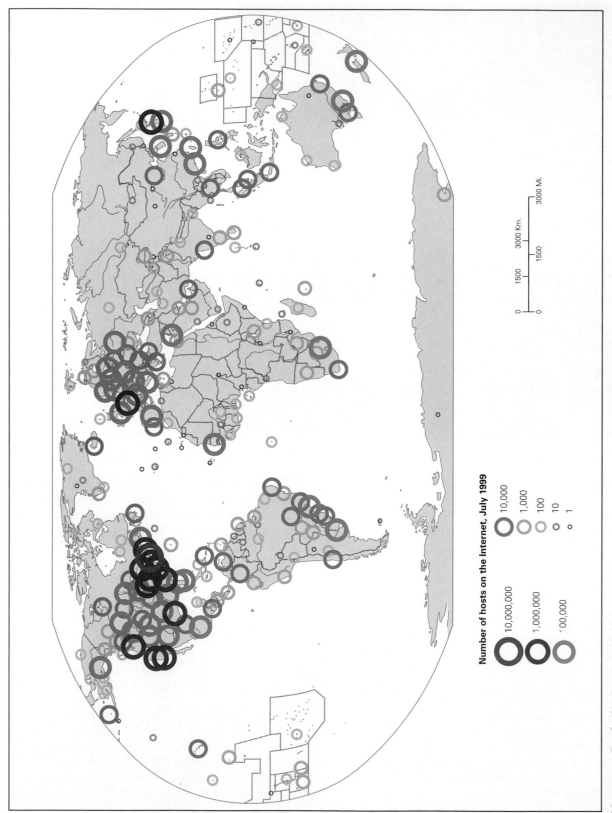

Number of hosts on the Internet, July 1999

◯ 10,000
◯ 1,000
◯ 100
∘ 10
∘ 1

◯ 10,000,000
◯ 1,000,000
◯ 00,000

Map 35.3   Per Capita Access to the Internet   Internet servers, computers through which users can connect their personal computers with the Internet, are most numerous in industrialized countries. As the Internet expands into more countries, questions of language difference will become more pronounced.   *Source:* Data from July 1999. Used with permission of Matrix Information and Directory Services, Inc. Visit our website at www.mids.org.

1970s). Thus they could be seen as portents of Western, especially American, cultural domination. But the American input was rather uneven, and the more widespread the new technologies became, the greater the opportunities they afforded to people around the world to adapt them to their own purposes.

The Spread of Popular Culture

The new technologies changed perceptions of culture. At the end of the nineteenth century, sophisticated Europeans and Americans, like earlier elite groups from imperial Rome to Ming China, valued most what they considered **high culture**—paintings, literature, and other works created to satisfy their tastes. They sneered at **popular culture** as localized entertainment for villagers and common folk—vigorous, picturesque, and quaint, but essentially vulgar. Influenced by the preferences of the European imperialist powers, modernizing elite groups around the world turned their backs on their own artistic traditions. Fascinated with everything Western, they built opera houses, established symphony orchestras, and experimented with European literary forms. Thus European notions of high culture—masterworks created exclusively by composers, artists, and thinkers of European descent—took root in many parts of the world, and non-Western cultural forms lost prestige in their own locales.

By the beginning of the twentieth century, popular culture began to become more and more visible. Illustrious European composers and choreographers had been turning to folk tunes and dances for inspiration since the eighteenth century. And the search for fresh sounds and images intensified with the advent of modernism in Europe in the mid-nineteenth century. Modernist writers, composers, and artists valued novelty and individuality of expression over classical structures and traditional formal narratives. These artists explored the workings of the subconscious rather than attempting to portray an objective reality. Since experimental or unconventional modernist works often outraged and offended patrons of the arts, the capacity to create a sensation and provoke outrage became a hallmark of modernism. Artists and composers strove to explore ever broader frontiers of feeling and experience. Some were captivated by the sounds and images of Europe's new industrial society; others drew inspiration from popular culture. Spanish artist Pablo Picasso (1881–1973), for example, borrowed the imagery of African masks in some of his paintings, circuses and carnivals in others, and newspaper typography in still others.

This mining of popular cultures by elite artists did little to inspire a wide interest in those cultures, however.

The invention of the phonograph by Thomas Edison in 1878 was the key that opened popular culture to global audiences. After three decades of further technological development, inexpensive recordings on disks became a reality. Phonograph records spread American popular music around the world. Jazz and blues had originated in the black culture of the American south at the end of the nineteenth century and moved north with black musicians in the twentieth century. The newborn recording industry made the works of pianist Jelly Roll Morton, guitar player Robert Johnson, singer Bessie Smith, and other musicians widely available.

Though blues remained primarily a black American taste, jazz recordings and jazz musicians became popular in Europe in the 1920s. The driving force behind jazz was the creative skill of black musicians such as Duke Ellington, Louis Armstrong, Ella Fitzgerald, and Billie Holiday. Orchestral composers such as the Russian Igor Stravinsky and the Frenchman Maurice Ravel utilized jazz rhythms and themes just as Picasso borrowed ideas from African masks. However, jazz remained the music of nightclubs and dance parties instead of concert halls. By World War II, black jazz musicians had become so much a part of the international image of the United States that Nazi propaganda frequently incorporated vile racial caricatures of them. Ironically, while jazz was widely perceived abroad as quintessential American popular culture, it remained largely the preserve of the African-American minority at home. Millions of white Americans preferred the more sedate tunes published by New York's commercial music houses, which employed some of the musical language of jazz but seldom displayed the black intensity of feeling and capacity for innovation.

The international popularity of jazz derived from the appeal of its rhythms and naturalness—that is, from the music itself—not from its approval by a colonial ruling class, as with the nineteenth-century vogue for grand opera. The same was true of rock 'n' roll, a dynamic, sensual, and audacious popular music that arose in the 1950s and became even more widespread than jazz. Rock grew out of black rhythm-and-blues and derived initially from innovative black American performers like Chuck Berry. The rise to international stardom in the early 1960s of Britain's Beatles helped make rock 'n' roll a worldwide phenomenon. The core of rock remained American and British, but popular musicians from all over the world recorded in rock-influenced styles. Some achieved broad acclaim, as did Jamaica's Bob Marley with his Caribbean reggae style. Others gained strong local followings by blending rock with traditional forms, as happened with Malagasy music in Madagascar and Rai music in Algeria.

Japanese Adult Male Comic Book   Comic magazines emerged after World War II as a major form of publication in Japan and a distinctive product of Japanese culture. Different series are directed to different age and gender groups. Issued weekly and running to some 300 pages in black and white, the most popular magazines sell as many copies as major news magazines do in the United States.   (Private Collection)

The rhythms and feelings of former black slaves in the American south could never have evolved into a core element of global culture without the recording industry. However, the preponderant role of the United States in the post–World War II world was also important. The equally African-inspired rhythms of the Brazilian samba and Cuban rumba, for example, never gained a significant international following comparable to that of jazz and rock 'n' roll.

In the post–World War II decades, mass production and advertising (both developed largely in the United States) opened another door to the worldwide spread of popular culture. American consumer products began to find international markets, and European, Japanese, and transnational companies soon became as aggressive as American companies in international marketing. Home-grown industries in small or poorer countries found it harder and harder to hold their own without government protection. In marketplaces around the world, imports displaced domestically produced consumer goods, from children's toys to copper cooking pots.

In the 1970s and 1980s, critics around the world identified the United States as the chief propagator of a worldwide consumer culture. This judgment seemed to be confirmed by the international cachet of American brand names like Levi's, Coca-Cola, Marlboro, Gillette, McDonald's, and Kentucky Fried Chicken. But names blazoned in neon atop the skyscrapers of Tokyo—Hitachi, Sony, Sanyo, and Mitsubishi—also commanded instant recognition, as did such European names as Nestlé, Mercedes, Pirelli, and Benetton. The concept of a globe-girdling American consumer culture had been overtaken by internationalization.

A sidewalk stand in Amman, Jordan, in 1986 featured inexpensive yellow sweatshirts bearing the legend "Oklahoma" with a large number beneath it. The shirts were made in Hong Kong; the buyers were Arabs; and the reference was to American football, then rarely played outside North America. At the same time, sidewalk stands in New York's Greenwich Village were stocked with checked Arab kaffiyas (headscarves). The internationalization of styles, as of music, had become two-way. Yet, on balance, the overall direction of change in popular culture and consumer taste during the decades following World War II was indeed toward the United States. Two years after the breakup of the Soviet Union, a shopper in Bishkek, the capital of Kyrgyzstan° in the heart of Central Asia, could buy women's underpants stenciled with a picture of a Marlboro cigarette pack, and a diner in Moscow could go to Pizza Hut for an exotic, if fairly expensive, treat.

When Marxism was challenging capitalism for world domination, Marxist theories argued that the tendency of capitalist economies to produce too many goods compelled industrialized nations to seek ever-larger markets and thereby exploit the entire world for the benefit of corporate shareholders. They interpreted the spread of American products as simply another form of imperialism, inevitably destroying local crafts, styles, and cultural traditions. But most young Turks, Nigerians, Taiwanese and others who liked to wear Levis's jeans,

---

Kyrgyzstan (KIR-gih-stan)

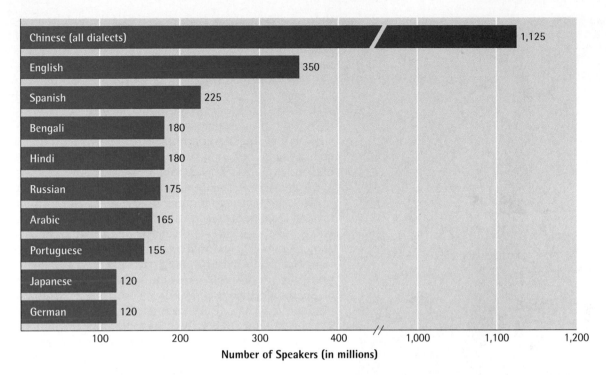

Figure 35.1   The Top Ten Languages   Numbers include all dialects of the language. For example, Chinese includes Mandarin, Wu, and less common dialects. *Source:* Andrew Dalby, *Dictionary of Languages* (New York: Columbia University Press, 1998). Published with permission of Columbia University Press, from Andrew Dalby, *Dictionary of Languages.* ©1998 as conveyed through the Copyright Clearance Center, Inc.

drink Coke, smoke Camels, and listen to rock 'n' roll had little sense of being under the thumb of the imperialists. Although their nations' economies may have been in thrall to transnational business concerns, they themselves generally felt free to condemn American foreign policy and considered their personal style preferences simply a result of living within an increasingly global culture. Thus the reality of cultural imperialism remained far more ambiguous than European imperialism had been in the days of colonial viceroys and gunboat diplomacy.

Global Connections and Elite Culture

While the globalization of popular culture became a subject of dispute, cultural links across national and ethnic boundaries at a more elite level generated less controversy. The end of the Cold War reopened intellectual and cultural contacts between former adversaries, making possible such things as Russian-American collaboration on space missions and extensive business contacts among former rivals. European and American scientific laboratories benefited as well from the intellectual gifts of an increasing number of graduate students and researchers from China, India, Pakistan, Turkey, and elsewhere. Given the scarcity of high-level research laboratories outside Europe, America, and Japan, many of these students chose to remain in their countries of training after graduation, contributing to a "brain drain" that primarily benefited the West.

In this way, technical training helped contribute to the rising importance of English as a global second language. British imperialism had planted English on every continent by the beginning of the twentieth century. Spurred by American economic and political eminence in the second half of the century, as well as by American movies and television, the language spread even as the British Empire faded away. French, by contrast, faded with the French Empire (see Figure 35.1). English became the most commonly taught second language in the world, and a number of technology-intensive industries, including air transportation and computers, used it extensively. In newly independent countries, universities

Postmodern Japanese Architecture Kiyoshi Sey Takeyama, born in 1954, designed the D-Hotel in Osaka in 1985. "Relations can often be clarified by interrupting things. . . . I built massive, incomplete walls, simultaneously expressing desire for and renunciation of communication with others. This ambivalence sums up our life in the contemporary city." Takeyama and other young Japanese architects pursue an architecture that responds more to modern Japanese culture than to the earlier modernism of the international style. (Courtesy, AMORPHE Takeyama and Associates)

that took pride in teaching in the national language often had science faculties that operated in English. The emergence of this potential global language made travel for business and pleasure increasingly easy and greatly facilitated the operations of multinational corporations.

Architectural design and engineering afford another example of globalization at the higher cultural level. The International Style pioneered by European architects in the 1920s (see Chapter 30) was the guiding aesthetic for the austere, ornament-free skyscrapers sheathed in glass that began to rise in world capitals in the 1960s. At the same time, people were traveling to

those capitals along highways that followed limited-access designs pioneered by the German autobahns and American thruways. The causeway linking the island-nation of Bahrain with mainland Saudi Arabia, for example, was indistinguishable in design from an American superhighway. The designs of new underground rail systems in Cairo, Mexico City, and Calcutta similarly reflected the internationalization of engineering and design. It became commonplace for a project in one country to be designed by an architectural firm in a second and built by a construction firm from a third.

The International Style was criticized, however, for neglecting local architectural traditions. Critics either blasted the designs for heedlessly indulging the creative fancies of the architects or complained that architects turned out boringly similar designs that imparted an unattractive uniformity to previously distinctive cities. In the United States, this criticism formed the foundation of **postmodernism,** a movement that called for abandoning the rigid rules of architectural modernism and showing greater sensitivity to history and local context, and for allowing diverse voices, such as those of minorities, to be heard. Some architects, including a growing number from non-Western countries, responded to the postmodern critique. Conventional glass and steel skyscrapers continued to be built, but liberation from the International Style permitted architects in different countries to follow their own inclinations and experiment with a broad array of forms, surface decoration, and references to earlier architectural traditions.

Postmodernism was not confined to architecture. Dance, music, literature, and cultural theory were all affected by postmodernist impulses, though the forms they took differed from one area to another. Common to much postmodernist thought was a sense that the modernist styles that composed the artistic avant-garde between 1850 and 1950 reflected the limited perspective of an elite, white, male Euro-American intelligentsia preoccupied with individualism and innovation. Against this background, postmodernism championed an aesthetic based on multicutluralism, social inclusion, historical continuity, and styles and forms from everyday life.

By fostering local diversity within the context of global change, architectural postmodernism had a substantial international impact. But it was not the only indicator of cultural change on a global scale. Among the ten winners of the Nobel Prize for Literature between 1982 and 1991 were writers from Colombia, Nigeria, Egypt, Mexico, and the West Indies. By contrast, the previous decade's winners had included only one non-European. The prize committee thus helped the world recognize the growing strength of its cultural diversity.

The West, for good or ill, dominated the early postimperialist era because the web of international contact made possible by advanced technologies had yet to reach its full extent or become accessible to most people. According to one estimate, at the end of the century, half of the world's people had never spoken on a telephone. The cultural changes spurred by technology were only in midcourse, and technology seemed likely to offer a means of releasing profound creative energies in unexpected locales.

The Endurance of Cultural Diversity

Diverse cultural traditions persisted at the twentieth century's end despite the globalization of industrial society and the integration of economic markets. Japan demonstrated that a country with a non-Western culture could perform at a high economic level. The Western concern for the individual was less valued in Japan than the ability of each individual to fit into a group, whether as a corporation employee, a member of an athletic team, or a student in a class. Moreover, the Japanese considered it unmannerly to directly contradict, correct, or refuse the request of another person.

From a Western point of view, these Japanese customs seemed to discourage individual initiative and personality development and to preserve traditional hierarchies. Japanese women, for example, even though they often worked outside the home, responded only slowly to the American and European feminist advocacy of equality in economic and social relations. However, the Japanese approach to social relations was well suited to an industrial economy. The efficiency, pride in workmanship, and group solidarity of Japanese workers, supported by closely coordinated government and corporate policies, played a major role in transforming Japan from a defeated nation with a demolished industrial base in 1945 to an economic power by the 1980s.

Japan's success in the modern industrial world called into question an assumption common in the immediate postwar era. Since industrialization was pioneered by Europeans and Americans, many Westerners thought that the spread of industrialization to different parts of the world would require the adoption of Western culture in every area of life. As awareness of the economic impact of Japanese culture and society began to spread, however, it became apparent that Taiwan and South Korea, along with Singapore and Hong Kong (a British colony before being reunited with China in 1997), were developing dynamic industrial economies of their own. Until the Asian financial crisis of 1997, Muslim Malaysia and Buddhist Thailand had appeared to be embarking on the same road to development. Had Japan been unique, or would cultural variety prove fully compatible with industrial growth and prosperity worldwide?

Clearly, the long-standing Western assumption of European and American exceptionalism—the belief that all of world history culminated in the exceptional convergence of political freedom, secularism, and industrialization in the West—needed to be abandoned. So, too, did the corollary that the twenty-first century would be as thoroughly dominated by Western culture and economic and political power as the previous two centuries had been.

Also coming into question was whether industrialization offered the only viable route to prosperity. As computer technology continued to change almost all aspects of life, perhaps in the twenty-first century countries could achieve prosperity primarily through their control of information and telecommunications.

The lesson to be drawn from the success of Japan and the other rising economic powers of Asia was not that Western technology pointed the way to universal well-being, but rather that human ingenuity and adaptability are endlessly fertile and creative. Human cultural achievement has historically followed unpredictable paths, reaching one sort of climax in one time and place and a different sort in another. In the same spirit, the future locus of spiritual and cultural achievement remained essentially unpredictable at the start of a new millennium.

CONCLUSION

The final decade of the twentieth century witnessed a burgeoning of computer and telecommunications technology that fostered the worldwide spread of popular culture while at the same time enabling businesses and financial markets to operate on a truly global scale. It also witnessed an intensification of world concerns for human rights as fears of international conflicts between great powers faded into the past. But in some respects it was more strongly marked by things that came to an end than by things that had their start.

For nearly eight decades, from the outbreak of World War I to the dissolution of the Soviet Union, a world whose economic and political destiny had seemed firmly in the grip of European imperialism witnessed an

Millennium Celebration in Sydney, Australia Uncertainties about what lay ahead for the world in the twenty-first century took a backseat to exuberant festivities as the millennium ended. The sleek modern silhouette of Sidney's opera house and the neon signs of major corporations epitomized the hopes of many. (Sydney Morning Herald/Sipa Press)

increasingly lethal struggle between competing European ideologies. The outcome of the struggle, in which all the peoples of the world eventually became principals or pawns, was often in doubt. Each camp accused the other of leading humanity down the road to slavery—slavery to fascist or communist dictators according to one side, slavery to the insatiable greed of capitalist profiteers according to the other. Each camp similarly had a vision of how it would organize the world in the event of victory. Adolf Hitler visualized a "thousand year Reich [empire]" serving the desires of an Aryan superrace. Communists spoke of a "workers' paradise" of equality and brotherhood. Responding to these oppressive visions, Western

leaders extolled the virtues of "freedom," a world order that would permit all peoples to elect their own governments and allow every individual to pursue his or her individual destiny in an open and competitive market environment.

Victory, when it came, proved far more complicated and puzzling than Western ideologues had anticipated. Though "democratization" and "economic liberalization" became watchwords of Western, and particularly American, foreign policy, many of the world's peoples proved less concerned with liberal ideology than with ethnic, linguistic, and religious quarrels, or with simply maintaining life and hope in circumstances of increasing poverty and overpopulation. Developing countries and postcommunist countries alike looked to the United States, Europe, and Japan for financial salvation, introducing democratic institutions and open markets only to the degree necessary to gain Western support.

The United States and the other major industrial countries recognized that they could not meet all of the world's demands, but they were reluctant to put too much trust in international bodies such as the United Nations, which had no financial resources beyond the dues paid by its member states. Thus the end of the global contest among European ideologies did not produce a workable model of a world community. To the contrary, local conflicts and atrocities proliferated in the 1990s, and more and more countries debated whether to seek nuclear weapons or other weapons of mass destruction in anticipation of future confrontations.

Yet while world order seemed as unattainable as ever, economic, technological, and cultural forces drew the world's peoples ever closer together. Since the victors in the world struggle had been the capitalists rather than the fascists or communists, private business and consumer economics expanded aggressively into every region of the globe, checked only by market conditions and rearguard efforts by authoritarian governments, such as that of China, to control the pace and direction of change.

For most of the world's population, the 1990s brought greater desire for and access to consumer goods, and a globalized culture became more and more a reality. But the logic of global economic growth, with its immense demands on clean water, clear air, and nonrenewable resources, made it clear that some of the world's greatest problems, including how to preserve the shared global environment for future generations of humanity, had no obvious solutions and had only begun to be addressed.

■ Key Terms

ethnic cleansing

economic sanctions

World Trade Organization (WTO)

terrorism

nuclear nonproliferation

Universal Declaration
 of Human Rights

nongovernmental
 organizations (NGOs)

cultural imperialism

high culture

popular culture

postmodernism

■ Suggested Reading

Many of the subjects in this chapter are covered by thematic essays in Richard W. Bulliet, ed., *The Columbia History of the Twentieth Century* (1998).

The Bosnian crisis is well covered in Susan L. Woodward, *Balkan Tragedy: Chaos and Dissolution After the Cold War* (1995). Other world crises involving international intervention are treated in William J. Durch, ed., *UN Peacekeeping, American Policy, and the Uncivil Wars of the* 1990s (1996). Terrorism is well covered by Bruce Hoffman, *Inside Terrorism* (1998). Gilles Kepel, *The Revenge of God: The Resurgence of Islam, Christianity, and Judaism in the Modern World* (1994), deals with recent religio-political movements. Human rights are well surveyed by Jack Donnelly, *International Human Rights,* 2d ed. (1998).

A seminal book in the awakening of the feminist movement in the 1970s is Betty Friedan, *The Feminine Mystique* (1974). For the revival of feminism in Europe see Gisela Kaplan, *Contemporary Western European Feminism* (1992). For non-Western perspectives see Phyllis Andors, *The Unfinished Liberation of Chinese Women, 1949–1980* (1983), and Chandra Talpade Mohanty, Ann Russo, and Lourdes Torres, eds., *Third World Women and the Politics of Feminism* (1991).

The interrelationships between high culture and popular culture during the twentieth century are treated from very different perspectives by Greil Marcus, *Lipstick Traces: A Secret History of the Twentieth Century* (1989), and Kurt Varnedoe, *High and Low: Modern Art and Popular Culture* (1991). The former concentrates on the avant-garde from Dada to Punk Rock, the latter on images from popular culture used in art. Two very readable books by James B. Twitchell, *Carnival Culture: The Trashing of Taste in America* (1992) and *Adcult USA: The Triumph of Advertising in American Culture* (1996), detail the rise of popular culture in the United States and present various reactions to this phenomenon.

Many interpretations of and approaches to postmodernism are sampled in Thomas Docherty, ed., *Postmodernism: A Reader* (1993). These may be compared with a classic early statement of modernism, Amédée Ozenfant, *Foundations of Modern Art* (1931).

Thomas P. Hughes, *American Genesis: A Century of Invention and Technological Enthusiasm, 1870–1970* (1989), offers a far-ranging account of the American role in twentieth-century technological change by an outstanding historian of technology. Books on films and the film industry around the world are legion. A good place to start is Gerald Mast, *A Short History of the Movies* (1986). A similar survey of jazz music is available from Marshall W. Stearns, *The Story of Jazz* (1970). For the rock video phenomenon see E. Ann Kaplan, *Rocking Around the Clock: Music Television, Postmodernism, and Consumer Culture* (1987).

Some noteworthy novels that have attempted to visualize the near future on the basis of current perceptions of technological change, environmental deterioration, and growth of transnational corporations are David Brin, *Earth* (1990), and Bruce Sterling, *Islands in the Net* (1988). See too William Gibson's "Sprawl" trilogy *Neuromancer* (1984), *Count Zero* (1987), and *Mona Lisa Overdrive* (1988).

■ Notes

1. "Universal Declaration of Human Rights," in *Twenty-five Human Rights Documents* (New York: Center for the Study of Human Rights, Columbia University, 1994), 6.
2. Ibid.

GLOSSARY

The glossary for *The Earth and Its Peoples,* 2/e is for the complete text, Chapters 1 through 35.

Abbas the Great (1571–1629) Shah of Iran (r. 1587–1629). The most illustrious ruler of the **Safavid Empire,** he moved the imperial capital to Isfahan in 1598, where he erected many palaces, mosques, and public buildings. (*p. 533*)

Abbasid Caliphate Descendants of the Prophet Muhammad's uncle, al-Abbas, the Abbasids overthrew the **Umayyad Caliphate** and ruled an Islamic empire from their capital in Baghdad (founded 762) from 750 to 1258. (*p. 234*)

abolitionists Men and women who agitated for a complete end to slavery. British abolitionists pressed for the abolition of the transatlantic slave trade in 1808 and slavery in 1834. In the United States the activities of abolitionists were one factor leading to the Civil War (1861–1865). (*p. 636*)

absolutism The theory popular in France and other early modern European monarchies that royal power should be free of constitutional checks. (*p. 452*)

Acheh Sultanate Muslim kingdom in northern Sumatra. Main center of Islamic expansion in Southeast Asia in the early seventeenth century, it declined after the Dutch seized **Malacca** from Portugal in 1641. (*p. 541*)

acculturation The adoption of the language, customs, values, and behaviors of host nations by immigrants. (*p. 640*)

acllas Women selected by Inca authorities to serve in religious centers as weavers and ritual participants. (*p. 318*)

Aden Port city in the modern south Arabian country of Yemen. It has been a major trading center in the Indian Ocean since ancient times. (*p. 385*)

African National Congress An organization dedicated to obtaining equal voting and civil rights for black inhabitants of South Africa. Founded in 1912 as the South African Native National Congress, it changed its name in 1923. Though it was banned and its leaders were jailed for many years, it eventually helped bring majority rule to South Africa. (*p. 809*)

Afrikaners South Africans descended from Dutch and French settlers of the seventeenth century. Their Great Trek founded new settler colonies in the nineteenth century. Though a minority among South Africans, they held political power after 1910, imposing a system of racial segregation called apartheid after 1949. (*pp. 665, 735*)

Agricultural Revolution(s) (ancient) The change from food gathering to food production that occurred between ca. 8000 and 2000 B.C.E. Also known as the Neolithic Revolution. (*p. 17*)

Agricultural Revolution (eighteenth century) The transformation of farming that resulted in the eighteenth century from the spread of new crops, improvements in cultivation techniques and livestock breeding, and the consolidation of small holdings into large farms from which tenants and sharecroppers were forcibly expelled. (*p. 600*)

Aguinaldo, Emilio (1869–1964) Leader of the Filipino independence movement against Spain (1895–1898). He proclaimed the independence of the Philippines in 1899, but his movement was crushed and he was captured by the United States Army in 1901. (*p. 743*)

Akbar I (1542–1605) Most illustrious sultan of the Mughal Empire in India (r. 1556–1605). He expanded the empire and pursued a policy of conciliation with Hindus. (*p. 536*)

Akhenaten Egyptian pharaoh (r. 1353–1335 B.C.E.). He built a new capital at Amarna, fostered a new style of naturalistic art, and created a religious revolution by imposing worship of the sun-disk. The Amarna letters, largely from his reign, preserve official correspondence with subjects and neighbors. (*p. 66*)

Alexander (356–323 B.C.E.) King of Macedonia in northern Greece. Between 334 and 323 B.C.E. he conquered the Persian Empire, reached the Indus Valley, founded many Greek-style cities, and spread Greek culture across the Middle East. Later known as Alexander the Great. (*p. 136*)

Alexandria City on the Mediterranean coast of Egypt founded by Alexander. It became the capital of the Hellenistic kingdom of the **Ptolemies.** It contained the famous Library and the Museum—a center for leading scientific and literary figures. Its merchants engaged in trade with areas bordering the Mediterranean and the Indian Ocean. (*p. 138*)

Allende, Salvador (1908–1973) Socialist politician elected president of Chile in 1970 and overthrown by the military in 1973. He died during the military attack. (*p. 856*)

All-India Muslim League Political organization founded in India in 1906 to defend the interests of India's Muslim minority. Led by Muhammad Ali Jinnah, it attempted to negotiate with the **Indian National Congress.** In 1940, the League began demanding a separate state for Muslims, to be called Pakistan. (See also **Jinnah, Muhammad Ali.**) (*p. 813*)

amulet Small charm meant to protect the bearer from evil. Found frequently in archaeological excavations in Mesopotamia and Egypt, amulets reflect the religious practices of the common people. (*p. 37*)

Anasazi Important culture of what is now the southwest of the United States (1000–1300 C.E.). Centered on Chaco Canyon in New Mexico and Mesa Verde in Colorado, the Anasazi culture built multistory residences and worshipped in subterranean buildings called kivas. (*p. 308*)

aqueduct A conduit, either elevated or under ground, using gravity to carry water from a source to a location—usually a city—that needed it. The Romans built many aqueducts in a period of substantial urbanization. (*p. 156*)

Arawak Amerindian peoples who inhabited the Greater Antilles of the Caribbean at the time of Columbus. (*p. 423*)

Arkwright, Richard (1732–1792) English inventor and entrepreneur who became the wealthiest and most successful textile manufacturer of the early **Industrial Revolution.** He invented the water frame, a machine that, with minimal human supervision, could spin many strong cotton threads at once. (*p. 604*)

Armenia One of the earliest Christian kingdoms, situated in eastern Anatolia and the western Caucasus and occupied by speakers of the Armenian language. (*p. 221*)

Asante African kingdom on the **Gold Coast** that expanded rapidly after 1680. Asante participated in the Atlantic economy, trading gold, slaves, and ivory. It resisted British imperial ambitions for a quarter century before being absorbed into Britain's Gold Coast colony in 1902. (*p. 736*)

Ashikaga Shogunate (1336–1573) The second of Japan's military governments headed by a shogun (a military ruler). Sometimes called the Muromachi Shogunate. (*p. 365*)

Ashoka Third ruler of the **Mauryan Empire** in India (r. 270–232 B.C.E.). He converted to Buddhism and broadcast his precepts on inscribed stones and pillars, the earliest surviving Indian writing. (*p. 184*)

Ashur Chief deity of the Assyrians, he stood behind the king and brought victory in war. Also the name of an important Assyrian religious and political center. (*p. 94*)

Asian Tigers Collective name for South Korea, Taiwan, Hong Kong, and Singapore—nations that became economic powers in the 1970s and 1980s. (*p. 861*)

Atahualpa (1502?–1533) Last ruling Inca emperor of Peru. He was executed by the Spanish. (*p. 438*)

Atlantic system The network of trading links after 1500 that moved goods, wealth, people, and cultures around the Atlantic Ocean basin. (*p. 497*)

Augustus (63 B.C.E.–14 C.E.) Honorific name of Octavian, founder of the **Roman Principate,** the military dictatorship that replaced the failing rule of the **Roman Senate.** After defeating all rivals, between 31 B.C.E. and 14 C.E. he laid the groundwork for several centuries of stability and prosperity in the Roman Empire. (*p. 151*)

Auschwitz Nazi extermination camp in Poland, the largest center of mass murder during the **Holocaust.** Close to a million Jews, Gypsies, Communists, and others were killed there. (*p. 800*)

australopithecines The several extinct species of humanlike primates that existed during the Pleistocene era (genus *Australopithecus*). (*p. 9*)

autocracy The theory justifying strong, centralized rule, such as by the **tsar** in Russia or **Haile Selassie** in Ethiopia. The autocrat did not rely on the aristocracy or the clergy for his or her legitimacy. (*p. 553*)

ayllu Andean lineage group or kin-based community. (*p. 312*)

Aztecs Also known as Mexica, the Aztecs created a powerful empire in central Mexico (1325–1521 C.E.). They forced defeated peoples to provide goods and labor as a tax. (*p. 305*)

Babylon The largest and most important city in Mesopotamia. It achieved particular eminence as the capital of the Amorite king **Hammurabi** in the eighteenth century B.C.E. and the Neo-Babylonian king Nebuchadnezzar in the sixth century B.C.E. (*p. 29*)

balance of power The policy in international relations by which, beginning in the eighteenth century, the major European states acted together to prevent any one of them from becoming too powerful. (*p. 455*)

Balfour Declaration Statement issued by Britain's Foreign Secretary Arthur Balfour in 1917 favoring the establishment of a Jewish national homeland in Palestine. (*p. 761*)

Bannermen Hereditary military servants of the **Qing Empire,** in large part descendants of peoples of various origins who had fought for the founders of the empire. (*p. 684*)

Bantu Collective name of a large group of sub-Saharan African languages and of the peoples speaking these languages. (*p. 219*)

Batavia Fort established ca.1619 as headquarters of Dutch East India Company operations in Indonesia; today the city of Jakarta. (*p. 543*)

Battle of Midway U.S. naval victory over the Japanese fleet in June 1942, in which the Japanese lost four of their best aircraft carriers. It marked a turning point in World War II. (*p. 795*)

Battle of Omdurman British victory over the Mahdi in the Sudan in 1898. General Kitchener led a mixed force of British and Egyptian troops armed with rapid-firing rifles and machine guns. (*p. 730*)

Beijing China's northern capital, first used as an imperial capital in 906 and now the capital of the People's Republic of China. (*p. 351*)

Bengal Region of northeastern India. It was the first part of India to be conquered by the British in the eighteenth century and remained the political and economic center of British India throughout the nineteenth century. The 1905 split of the province into predominantly Hindu West Bengal and predominantly Muslim East Bengal (now Bangladesh) sparked anti-British riots. (*p. 812*)

Berlin Conference (1884–1885) Conference that German chancellor Otto von Bismarck called to set rules for the partition of Africa. It led to the creation of the Congo Free State under King **Leopold II** of Belgium. (See also **Bismarck, Otto von.**) (*p. 732*)

Bhagavad-Gita The most important work of Indian sacred literature, a dialogue between the great warrior Arjuna and the god Krishna on duty and the fate of the spirit. (*p. 185*)

bipedalism The ability to walk upright on two legs, characteristic of hominids. (*p. 9*)

Bismarck, Otto von (1815–1898) Chancellor (prime minister) of Prussia from 1862 until 1871, when he became chancellor of Germany. A conservative nationalist, he led Prussia to victory against Austria (1866) and France (1870) and was responsible for the creation of the German Empire in 1871. (*p. 714*)

Black Death An outbreak of **bubonic plague** that spread across Asia, North Africa, and Europe in the mid-fourteenth century, carrying off vast numbers of persons. (*p. 397*)

Bolívar, Simón (1783–1830) The most important military leader in the struggle for independence in South America. Born in Venezuela, he led military forces there and in Colombia, Ecuador, Peru, and Bolivia. (*p. 623*)

Bolsheviks Radical Marxist political party founded by Vladimir Lenin in 1903. Under Lenin's leadership, the Bolsheviks seized power in November 1917 during the Russian Revolution. (See also **Lenin, Vladimir.**) (*p. 761*)

Bonaparte, Napoleon. See **Napoleon I.**

Borobodur A massive stone monument on the Indonesian island of Java, erected by the Sailendra kings around 800 C.E. The winding ascent through ten levels, decorated with rich relief carving, is a Buddhist allegory for the progressive stages of enlightenment. (*p. 193*)

bourgeoisie In early modern Europe, the class of well-off town dwellers whose wealth came from manufacturing, finance, commerce, and allied professions. (*p. 459*)

Brant, Joseph (1742–1807) Mohawk leader who supported the British during the American Revolution. (*p. 581*)

breech-loading rifle Gun into which the projectiles had to be individually inserted. Later guns had magazines, a compartment holding multiple projectiles that could be fed rapidly into the firing chamber. (*p. 681*)

British raj The rule over much of South Asia between 1765 and 1947 by the East India Company and then by a British government. (*p. 659*)

bubonic plague A bacterial disease of fleas that can be transmitted by flea bites to rodents and humans; humans in late stages of the illness can spread the bacteria by coughing. Because of its very high mortality rate and the difficulty of preventing its spread, major outbreaks have created crises in many parts of the world in many countries. (See also **Black Death.**) (*pp. 280, 332*)

Buddha (563–483 B.C.E.) An Indian prince named Siddhartha Gautama, who renounced his wealth and social position. After becoming "enlightened" (the meaning of *Buddha*) he enunciated the principles of Buddhism. This doctrine evolved and spread throughout India and to Southeast, East, and Central Asia. (See also **Mahayana Buddhism; Theravada Buddhism.**) (*p. 180*)

business cycles Recurrent swings from economic hard times to recovery and growth, then back to hard times and a repetition of the sequence. (*p. 615*)

Byzantine Empire Historians' name for the eastern portion of the Roman Empire from the fourth century onward, taken from "Byzantion," an early name for Constantinople, the Byzantine capital city. The empire fell to the Ottomans in 1453. (See also **Ottoman Empire.**) (*p. 250*)

caliphate Office established in succession to the Prophet Muhammad, to rule the Islamic empire; also the name of that empire. (See also **Abbasid Caliphate; Sokoto Caliphate; Umayyad Caliphate.**) (*p. 232*)

capitalism The economic system of large financial institutions—banks, stock exchanges, investment companies—that first developed in early modern Europe. *Commercial capitalism*, the trading system of the early modern economy, is often distinguished from *industrial capitalism*, the system based on machine production. (*p. 506*)

caravel A small, highly maneuverable three-masted ship used by the Portuguese and Spanish in the exploration of the Atlantic. (*p. 427*)

Cárdenas, Lázaro (1895–1970) President of Mexico (1934–1940). He brought major changes to Mexican life by distributing millions of acres of land to the peasants, bringing representatives of workers and farmers into the inner circles of politics, and nationalizing the oil industry. (*p. 820*)

Carthage City located in present-day Tunisia, founded by **Phoenicians** ca. 800 B.C.E. It became a major commercial center and naval power in the western Mediterranean until defeated by Rome in the third century B.C.E. (*p. 107*)

Caste War A rebellion of the Maya people against the government of Mexico in 1847. It nearly returned the Yucatán to Maya rule. Some Maya rebels retreated to unoccupied territories where they held out until 1901. (*p. 636*)

Catholic Reformation Religious reform movement within the Latin Christian Church, begun in response to the **Protestant Reformation.** It clarified Catholic theology and reformed clerical training and discipline. (*p. 447*)

Celts Peoples sharing a common language and culture that originated in Central Europe in the first half of the first millennium B.C.E.. After 500 B.C.E. they spread as far as Anatolia in the east, Spain and the British Isles in the west, and later were overtaken by Roman conquest and Germanic invasions. Their descendants survive on the western fringe of Europe (Brittany, Wales, Scotland, Ireland). (*p. 90*)

Champa A state formerly located in what is now southern Vietnam. It was hostile to Annam and was annexed by Annam and destroyed as an independent entity in 1500. (*p. 366*)

Champa rice Quick-maturing rice that can allow two harvests in one growing season. Originally introduced into Champa from India, it was later sent to China as a tribute gift by the Champa state. (See also **tributary system.**) (*p. 295*)

Chang'an City in the Wei Valley in eastern China. It became the capital of the Zhou kingdom and the Qin and early Han Empires. Its main features were imitated in the cities and towns that sprang up throughout the Han Empire. (*p. 164*)

Charlemagne (742–814) King of the Franks (r. 768–814); emperor (r. 800–814). Through a series of military conquests he established the Carolingian Empire, which encompassed all of Gaul and parts of Germany and Italy. Though illiterate himself, he sponsored a brief intellectual revival. (*p. 250*)

chartered companies Groups of private investors who paid an annual fee to France and England in exchange for a monopoly over trade to the West Indies colonies. (*p. 498*)

Chavín The first major urban civilization in South America (900–250 B.C.E.). Its capital, Chavín de Huántar, was located high in the Andes Mountains of Peru. Chavín became politically and economically dominant in a densely populated region that included two distinct ecological zones, the Peruvian coastal plain and the Andean foothills. (*p. 89*)

Chiang Kai-shek (Jiang Jieshi; 1887–1975) General and leader of Nationalist China after 1925. Although he succeeded **Sun Yat-sen** as head of the **Guomindang,** he became a military dictator whose major goal was to crush the communist movement led by **Mao Zedong.** (*p. 788*)

chiefdom Form of political organization with rule by a hereditary leader who held power over a collection of villages and towns. Less powerful than kingdoms and empires, chiefdoms were based on gift giving and commercial links. (*p. 311*)

Chimú Powerful Peruvian civilization based on conquest. Located in the region earlier dominated by **Moche.** Conquered by **Inca** in 1465. (*p. 314*)

chinampas Raised fields constructed along lake shores in Mesoamerica to increase agricultural yields. (*p. 301*)

city-state A small independent state consisting of an urban center and the surrounding agricultural territory. A characteristic political form in early Mesopotamia, Archaic and Classical Greece, Phoenicia, and early Italy. (See also **polis.**) (*p. 32*)

civilization An ambiguous term often used to denote more complex societies but sometimes used by anthropologists to describe any group of people sharing a set of cultural traits. (*p. 28*)

Cixi, Empress Dowager (1835–1908) Empress of China and mother of Emperor Guangxi. She put her son under house arrest, supported antiforeign movements, and resisted reforms of the Chinese government and armed forces. (*p. 721*)

clipper ship Large, fast, streamlined sailing vessel, often American built, of the mid-to-late nineteenth century rigged with vast canvas sails hung from tall masts. (*p. 666*)

Cold War (1945–1991) The ideological struggle between communism (Soviet Union) and capitalism (United States) for world influence. The Soviet Union and the United States came to the brink of actual war during the **Cuban missile crisis** but never attacked one another. The Cold War came to an end when the Soviet Union dissolved in 1991. (See also **North Atlantic Treaty Organization; Warsaw Pact.**) (*p. 831*)

colonialism Policy by which a nation administers a foreign territory and develops its resources for the benefit of the colonial power. (*p. 731*)

Columbian Exchange The exchange of plants, animals, diseases, and technologies between the Americas and the rest of the world following Columbus's voyages. (*p. 472*)

Columbus, Christopher (1451–1506) Genoese mariner who in the service of Spain led expeditions across the Atlantic, reestablishing contact between the peoples of the Americas and the Old World and opening the way to Spanish conquest and colonization. (*p. 430*)

Confederation of 1867 Negotiated union of the formerly separate colonial governments of Ontario, Quebec, New Brunswick, and Nova Scotia. This new Dominion of Canada with a central government in Ottawa is seen as the beginning of the Canadian nation. (*p. 627*)

Confucius Western name for the Chinese philosopher Kongzi (551–479 B.C.E.). His doctrine of duty and public service had a great influence on subsequent Chinese thought and served as a code of conduct for government officials. (*p. 62*)

Congress of Vienna (1814–1815) Meeting of representatives of European monarchs called to reestablish the old order after the defeat of **Napoleon I.** (*p. 594*)

conquistadors Early-sixteenth-century Spanish adventurers who conquered Mexico, Central America, and Peru. (See **Cortés, Hernán; Pizarro, Francisco.**) (*p. 436*)

Constantine (285–337 C.E.) Roman emperor (r. 312–337). After reuniting the Roman Empire, he moved the capital to Constantinople and made Christianity a favored religion. (*p.159*)

Constitutional Convention Meeting in 1787 of the elected representatives of the thirteen original states to write the Constitution of the United States. (*p. 583*)

constitutionalism The theory developed in early modern England and spread elsewhere that royal power should be subject to legal and legislative checks. (*p. 452*)

contract of indenture A voluntary agreement binding a person to work for a specified period of years in return for free passage to an overseas destination. Before 1800 most **indentured servants** were Europeans; after 1800 most indentured laborers were Asians. (*p. 670*)

Cortés, Hernán (1485–1547) Spanish explorer and conquistador who led the conquest of Aztec Mexico in 1519–1521 for Spain. (*p. 437*)

Cossacks Peoples of the Russian Empire who lived outside the farming villages, often as herders, mercenaries, or outlaws. Cossacks led the conquest of Siberia in the sixteenth and seventeenth centuries. (*p. 552*)

cottage industries Weaving, sewing, carving, and other small-scale industries that can be done in the home. The laborers, frequently women, are usually independent. (*p. 353*)

cotton The plant that produces fibers from which cotton textiles are woven. Native to India, cotton spread throughout Asia and then to the New World. It has been a major cash crop in various places, including early Islamic Iran, Yi Korea, and nineteenth-century Egypt and the United States. A related species was exploited for fiber in pre-Columbia America. (*p. 363*)

Council of the Indies The institution responsible for supervising Spain's colonies in the Americas from 1524 to the early eighteenth century, when it lost all but judicial responsibilities. (*p. 476*)

***coureurs des bois* (runners of the woods)** French fur traders, many of mixed Amerindian heritage, who lived among and often married with Amerindian peoples of North America. (*p. 489*)

creoles In colonial Spanish America, term used to describe someone of European descent born in the New World. Elsewhere in the Americas, the term is used to describe all nonnative peoples. (*p. 482*)

Crimean War (1853–1856) Conflict between the Russian and Ottoman Empires fought primarily in the Crimean Peninsula. To prevent Russian expansion, Britain and France sent troops to support the Ottomans. (*p. 679*)

Crusades (1096–1291) Armed pilgrimages to the Holy Land by Christians determined to recover Jerusalem from Muslim rule. The Crusades brought an end to western Europe's centuries of intellectual and cultural isolation. (*p. 270*)

Crystal Palace Building erected in Hyde Park, London, for the Great Exhibition of 1851. Made of iron and glass, like a gigantic greenhouse, it was a symbol of the industrial age. (*p. 606*)

Cuban missile crisis (1962) Brink-of-war confrontation between the United States and the Soviet Union over the latter's placement of nuclear-armed missiles in Cuba. (*p. 839*)

cultural imperialism Domination of one culture over another by a deliberate policy or by economic or technological superiority. (*p. 894*)

Cultural Revolution (China) (1966–1969) Campaign in China ordered by **Mao Zedong** to purge the Communist Party of his opponents and instill revolutionary values in the younger generation. (*p. 848*)

culture Socially transmitted patterns of action and expression. *Material culture* refers to physical objects, such as dwellings, clothing, tools, and crafts. Culture also includes arts, beliefs, knowledge, and technology. (*p. 11*)

cuneiform A system of writing in which wedge-shaped symbols represented words or syllables. It originated in Mesopotamia and was used initially for Sumerian and Akkadian but later was adapted to represent other languages of western Asia. Because so many symbols had to be learned, literacy was confined to a relatively small group of administrators and **scribes**. (*p. 39*)

Cyrus (600–530 B.C.E.) Founder of the Achaemenid Persian Empire. Between 550 and 530 B.C.E. he conquered Media, Lydia, and Babylon. Revered in the traditions of both Iran and the subject peoples, he employed Persians and Medes in his administration and respected the institutions and beliefs of subject peoples. (*p. 117*)

czar See **tsar.**

Dalai Lama Originally, a title meaning "universal priest" that the Mongol khans invented and bestowed on a Tibetan lama (priest) in the late 1500s to legitimate their power in Tibet. Subsequently, the title of the religious and political leader of Tibet. (*p. 556*)

Daoism Chinese school of thought, originating in the Warring States Period with Laozi (604–531 B.C.E.). Daoism offered an alternative to the Confucian emphasis on hierarchy and duty. Daoists believe that the world is always changing and is devoid of absolute morality or meaning. They accept the world as they find it, avoid futile struggles, and deviate as little as possible from the *Dao,* or "path" of nature. (See also **Confucius.**) (*p. 63*)

Darius I (ca. 558–486 B.C.E.) Third ruler of the Persian Empire (r. 521–486 B.C.E.). He crushed the widespread initial resistance to his rule and gave all major government posts to Persians rather than to Medes. He established a system of provinces and tribute, began construction of Persepolis, and expanded Persian control in the east (Pakistan) and west (northern Greece). (*p. 118*)

Darwin, Charles (1809–1882) English naturalist. He studied the plants and animals of South America and the Pacific islands, and in his book *On the Origin of Species by Means of Natural Selection* (1859) set forth his theory of **evolution.** (*p. 715*)

Declaration of the Rights of Man (1789) Statement of fundamental political rights adopted by the French **National Assembly** at the beginning of the French Revolution. (*p. 586*)

deforestation The removal of trees faster than forests can replace themselves. (*p. 462*)

Delhi Sultanate (1206–1526) Centralized Indian empire of varying extent, created by Muslim invaders. (*p. 374*)

democracy A system of government in which all "citizens" (however defined) have equal political and legal rights, privileges, and protections, as in the Greek city-state of Athens in the fifth and fourth centuries B.C.E. (*p. 127*)

demographic transition A change in the rates of population growth. Before the transition, both birth and death rates are high, resulting in a slowly growing population; then the death rate drops but the birth rate remains high, causing a population explosion; finally the birth rate drops and the population growth slows down. This transition took place in Europe in the late nineteenth and early twentieth centuries, in North America and East Asia in the mid-twentieth, and, most recently, in Latin America and South Asia. (*p. 867*)

Deng Xiaoping (1904–1997) Communist Party leader who forced Chinese economic reforms after the death of **Mao Zedong.** (*p. 862*)

development In the nineteenth and twentieth centuries, the economic process that led to industrialization, urbanization, the rise of a large and prosperous middle class, and heavy investment in education. (*p. 642*)

devshirme "Selection" in Turkish. The system by which boys from Christian communities were taken by the Ottoman state to serve as **Janissaries.** (*p. 526*)

dhow Ship of small to moderate size used in the western Indian Ocean, traditionally with a triangular sail and a sewn timber hull. (*p. 382*)

Diagne, Blaise (1872–1934) Senegalese political leader. He was the first African elected to the French National Assembly. During World War I, in exchange for promises to give French citizenship to Senegalese, he helped recruit Africans to serve in the French army. After the war, he led a movement to abolish forced labor in Africa. (*p. 809*)

Dias, Bartolomeu (1450?–1500) Portuguese explorer who in 1488 led the first expedition to sail around the southern tip of Africa from the Atlantic and sight the Indian Ocean. (*p. 428*)

diaspora A Greek word meaning "dispersal," used to describe the communities of a given ethnic group living outside their homeland. Jews, for example, spread from Israel to western Asia and Mediterranean lands in antiquity and today can be found throughout the world. (*p. 103*)

Dirty War War waged by the Argentine military (1976–1982) against leftist groups. Characterized by the use of illegal imprisonment, torture, and executions by the military. (*p. 857*)

divination Techniques for ascertaining the future or the will of the gods by interpreting natural phenomena such as, in early China, the cracks on oracle bones or, in ancient Greece, the flight of birds through sectors of the sky. (*p. 59*)

division of labor A manufacturing technique that breaks down a craft into many simple and repetitive tasks that can be performed by unskilled workers. Pioneered in the pottery works of Josiah Wedgwood and in other eighteenth-century factories, it greatly increased the productivity of labor and lowered the cost of manufactured goods. (See also **Wedgwood, Josiah.**) (*p. 603*)

driver A privileged male slave whose job was to ensure that a slave gang did its work on a plantation. (*p. 503*)

Druids The class of religious experts who conducted rituals and preserved sacred lore among some ancient Celtic peoples. They provided education, mediated disputes between kinship groups, and were suppressed by the Romans as a potential focus of opposition to Roman rule. (See also **Celts.**) (*p. 92*)

durbar An elaborate display of political power and wealth in British India in the nineteenth century, ostensibly in imitation of the pageantry of the **Mughal Empire.** (*p. 661*)

Dutch West India Company (1621–1794) Trading company chartered by the Dutch government to conduct its merchants' trade in the Americas and Africa. (*p. 498*)

economic sanctions Boycotts, embargoes, and other economic measures that one country uses to pressure another country into changing its policies. (*p. 889*)

Edison, Thomas (1847–1931) American inventor best known for inventing the electric light bulb, acoustic recording on wax cylinders, and motion pictures. (*p. 703*)

Einstein, Albert (1879–1955) German physicist who developed the theory of relativity, which states that time, space, and mass are relative to each other and not fixed. (*p. 774*)

El Alamein Town in Egypt, site of the victory by Britain's Field Marshal Bernard Montgomery over German forces led by General Erwin Rommel (the "Desert Fox") in 1942–1943. (*p. 793*)

electricity A form of energy used in telegraphy from the 1840s on and for lighting, industrial motors, and railroads beginning in the 1880s. (*p. 702*)

electric telegraph A device for rapid, long-distance transmission of information over an electric wire. It was introduced in England and North America in the 1830s and 1840s and replaced telegraph systems that utilized visual signals such as semaphores. (See also **submarine telegraph cables.**) (*p. 609*)

encomienda A grant of authority over a population of Amerindians in the Spanish colonies. It provided the grant holder with a supply of cheap labor and periodic payments of goods by the Amerindians. It obliged the grant holder to Christianize the Amerindians. (*p. 479*)

Enlightenment A philosophical movement in eighteenth-century Europe that fostered the belief that one could reform society by discovering rational laws that governed social behavior and were just as scientific as the laws of physics. (*pp. 468, 574*)

equites In ancient Italy, prosperous landowners second in wealth and status to the senatorial aristocracy. The Roman emperors allied with this group to counterbalance the influence of the old aristocracy and used the *equites* to staff the imperial civil service. (*p. 152*)

Estates General France's traditional national assembly with representatives of the three estates, or classes, in French society: the clergy, nobility, and commoners. The calling of the Estates General in 1789 led to the French Revolution. (*p. 585*)

Ethiopia East African highland nation lying east of the Nile River. (See also **Menelik II; Selassie, Haile.**) (*p. 221*)

ethnic cleansing Effort to eradicate a people and its culture by means of mass killing and the destruction of historical buildings and cultural materials. Ethnic cleansing was used by both sides in the conflicts that accompanied the disintegration of Yugoslavia in the 1990s. (*p. 883*)

European Community (EC) An organization promoting economic unity in Europe formed in 1967 by consolidation of earlier, more limited, agreements. Replaced by the European Union (EU) in 1993. (*p. 834*)

evolution The biological theory that, over time, changes occurring in plants and animals, mainly as a result of **natural selection** and genetic mutation, result in new species. (*p. 6*)

extraterritoriality The right of foreign residents in a country to live under the laws of their native country and disregard the laws of the host country. In the nineteenth and early twentieth centuries, European and American nationals living in certain areas of Chinese and Ottoman cities were granted this right. (*p. 682*)

Faisal I (1885–1933) Arab prince, leader of the Arab Revolt in World War I. The British made him king of Iraq in 1921, and he reigned under British protection until 1933. (*p. 760*)

Fascist Party Italian political party created by Benito Mussolini during World War I. It emphasized aggressive nationalism and was Mussolini's instrument for the creation of a dictatorship in Italy from 1922 to 1943. (See also **Mussolini, Benito.**) (*p. 786*)

fief In medieval Europe, land granted in return for a sworn oath to provide specified military service. (*p. 256*)

First Temple A monumental sanctuary built in Jerusalem by King Solomon in the tenth century B.C.E. to be the religious center for the Israelite god Yahweh. The Temple priesthood conducted sacrifices, received a tithe or percentage of agricultural revenues, and became economically and politically powerful. The First Temple was destroyed by the Babylonians in 587 B.C.E., rebuilt on a modest scale in the late sixth century B.C.E., and replaced by King Herod's Second Temple in the late first century B.C.E. (destroyed by the Romans in 70 C.E.) (*p. 102*)

Five-Year Plans Plans that Joseph Stalin introduced to industrialize the Soviet Union rapidly, beginning in 1928. They set goals for the output of steel, electricity, machinery, and most other products and were enforced by the police powers of the state. They succeeded in making the Soviet Union a major industrial power before World War II. (See also **Stalin, Joseph.**) (*p. 781*)

foragers People who support themselves by hunting wild animals and gathering wild edible plants and insects. (*p. 13*)

Forbidden City The walled section of Beijing where emperors lived between 1121 and 1924. A portion is now a residence for leaders of the People's Republic of China. (*p. 355*)

Franklin, Benjamin (1706–1790) American intellectual, inventor, and politician He helped to negotiate French support for the American Revolution. (*p. 577*)

free-trade imperialism Economic dominance of a weaker country by a more powerful one, while maintaining the legal independence of the weaker state. In the late nineteenth century, free-trade imperialism characterized the relations between the Latin American republics, on the one hand, and Great Britain and the United States, on the other. (*p. 744*)

fresco A technique of painting on walls covered with moist plaster. It was used to decorate Minoan and Mycenaean palaces and Roman villas, and became an important medium during the Italian Renaissance. (*p. 73*)

Funan An early complex society in Southeast Asia between the first and sixth centuries C.E. It was centered in the rich rice-growing region of southern Vietnam, and it controlled the passage of trade across the Malaysian isthmus. (*p. 191*)

Gama, Vasco da (1460?–1524) Portuguese explorer. In 1497–1498 he led the first naval expedition from Europe to sail to India, opening an important commercial sea route. (*p. 428*)

Gandhi, Mohandas K. (Mahatma) (1869–1948) Leader of the Indian independence movement and advocate of nonviolent resistance. After being educated as a lawyer in England, he returned to India and became leader of the **Indian National Congress** in 1920. He appealed to the poor, led nonviolent demonstrations against British colonial rule, and was jailed many times. Soon after independence he was assassinated for attempting to stop Hindu-Muslim rioting. (*p. 813*)

Genghis Khan (ca. 1167–1227) The title of Temüjin when he ruled the Mongols (1206–1227). It means the "oceanic" or "universal" leader. Genghis Khan was the founder of the Mongol Empire. (*p. 325*)

gens de couleur Free men and women of color in Haiti. They sought greater political rights and later supported the Haitian Revolution. (See also **L'Ouverture, François Dominique Toussaint.**) (*p. 593*)

gentry In China, the class of prosperous families, next in wealth below the rural aristocrats, from which the emperors drew their administrative personnel. Respected for their education and expertise, these officials became a privileged group and made the government more efficient and responsive than in the past. The term *gentry* also denotes the class of landholding families in England below the aristocracy. (*p. 166*)

Ghana First known kingdom in sub-Saharan West Africa between the sixth and thirteenth centuries C.E. Also the modern West African country once known as the Gold Coast. (*p. 215*)

Gold Coast (Africa) Region of the Atlantic coast of West Africa occupied by modern Ghana; named for its gold exports to Europe from the 1470s onward. (*p. 428*)

Golden Horde Mongol khanate founded by Genghis Khan's grandson Batu. It was based in southern Russia and quickly adopted both the Turkic language and Islam. Also known as the Kipchak Horde. (*p. 333*)

Gorbachev, Mikhail (b. 1931) Head of the Soviet Union from 1985 to 1991. His liberalization effort improved relations with the West, but he lost power after his reforms led to the collapse of Communist governments in eastern Europe. (*p. 863*)

Gothic cathedrals Large churches originating in twelfth-century France; built in an architectural style featuring pointed arches, tall vaults and spires, flying buttresses, and large stained-glass windows. (*p. 405*)

Grand Canal The 1,100-mile (1,700-kilometer) waterway linking the Yellow and the Yangzi Rivers. It was begun in the **Han** period and completed during the Sui Empire. (*p. 277*)

Great Circuit The network of Atlantic Ocean trade routes between Europe, Africa, and the Americas that underlay the **Atlantic system.** (*p. 508*)

Great Ice Age Geological era that occurred between ca. 2 million and 11,000 years ago. As a result of climate shifts, large numbers of new species evolved during this period, also called the Pleistocene epoch. (See also **Holocene.**) (*p. 9*)

"great tradition" Historians' term for a literate, well-institutionalized complex of religious and social beliefs and practices adhered to by diverse societies over a broad geographical area. (See also **"small tradition."**) (*p. 217*)

Great Western Schism A division in the Latin (Western) Christian Church between 1378 and 1417, when rival claimants to the papacy existed in Rome and Avignon. (*p. 411*)

Great Zimbabwe City, now in ruins (in the modern African country of Zimbabwe), whose many stone structures were built between about 1250 and 1450, when it was a trading center and the capital of a large state. (*p. 385*)

guild In medieval Europe, an association of men (rarely women), such as merchants, artisans, or professors, who worked in a particular trade and banded together to promote their economic and political interests. Guilds were also important in other societies, such as the Ottoman and Safavid empires. (*p. 403*)

Gujarat Region of western India famous for trade and manufacturing; the inhabitants are called Gujarati. (*p. 380*)

gunpowder A mixture of saltpeter, sulfur, and charcoal, in various proportions. The formula, brought to China in the 400s or 500s, was first used to make fumigators to keep away insect pests and evil spirits. In later centuries it was used to make explosives and grenades and to propel cannonballs, shot, and bullets. (*p. 289*)

Guomindang Nationalist political party founded on democratic principles by **Sun Yat-sen** in 1912. After 1925, the party was headed by **Chiang Kai-shek,** who turned it into an increasingly authoritarian movement. (*p. 769*)

Gupta Empire (320–550 C.E.) A powerful Indian state based, like its Mauryan predecessor, on a capital at Pataliputra in the Ganges Valley. It controlled most of the Indian subcontinent through a combination of military force and its prestige as a center of sophisticated culture. (See also **theater-state.**) (*p. 186*)

Habsburg A powerful European family that provided many Holy Roman Emperors, founded the Austrian (later Austro-Hungarian) Empire, and ruled sixteenth- and seventeenth-century Spain. (*p. 449*)

hadith A tradition relating the words or deeds of the Prophet Muhammad; next to the **Quran,** the most important basis for Islamic law. (*p. 241*)

Hammurabi Amorite ruler of **Babylon** (r. 1792–1750 B.C.E.). He conquered many city-states in southern and northern Mesopotamia and is best known for a code of laws, inscribed on a black stone pillar, illustrating the principles to be used in legal cases. (*p. 34*)

Han A term used to designate (1) the ethnic Chinese people who originated in the Yellow River Valley and spread throughout regions of China suitable for agriculture and (2) the dynasty of emperors who ruled from 206 B.C.E. to 220 C.E. (*p. 164*)

Hanseatic League An economic and defensive alliance of the free towns in northern Germany, founded about 1241 and most powerful in the fourteenth century. (*p. 401*)

Harappa Site of one of the great cities of the Indus Valley civilization of the third millennium B.C.E. It was located on the northwest frontier of the zone of cultivation (in modern Pakistan), and may have been a center for the acquisition of raw materials, such as metals and precious stones, from Afghanistan and Iran. (*p. 48*)

Hatshepsut Queen of Egypt (r. 1473–1458 B.C.E.). She dispatched a naval expedition down the Red Sea to Punt (possibly Somalia), the faraway source of myrrh. There is evidence of opposition to a woman as ruler, and after her death her name and image were frequently defaced. (*p. 66*)

Hebrew Bible A collection of sacred books containing diverse materials concerning the origins, experiences, beliefs, and practices of the Israelites. Most of the extant text was compiled by members of the priestly class in the fifth century B.C.E. and reflects the concerns and views of this group. (*p. 99*)

Hellenistic Age Historians' term for the era, usually dated 323–30 B.C.E., in which Greek culture spread across western Asia and northeastern Africa after the conquests of **Alexander** the Great. The period ended with the fall of the last major Hellenistic kingdom to Rome, but Greek cultural influence persisted until the spread of Islam in the seventh century C.E. (*p. 137*)

Helsinki Accords (1975) Political and human rights agreement signed in Helsinki, Finland, by the Soviet Union and western European countries. (*p. 839*)

Henry the Navigator (1394–1460) Portuguese prince who promoted the study of navigation and directed voyages of exploration down the western coast of Africa. (*p. 425*)

Herodotus (ca. 485–425 B.C.E.) Heir to the technique of *historia*—"investigation"—developed by Greeks in the late Archaic period. He came from a Greek community in Anatolia and traveled extensively, collecting information in western Asia and the Mediterranean lands. He traced the antecedents of and chronicled the **Persian Wars** between the Greek city-states and the Persian Empire, thus originating the Western tradition of historical writing. (*p. 128*)

Herzl, Theodore (1860–1904) Austrian journalist and founder of the Zionist movement urging the creation of a Jewish national homeland in Palestine. (*p. 760*)

Hidalgo y Costilla, Miguel (1753–1811) Mexican priest who led the first stage of the Mexican independence war in 1810. He was captured and executed in 1811. (*p. 625*)

Hidden Imam Last in a series of twelve descendants of Muhammad's son-in-law Ali, whom **Shi'ites** consider divinely appointed leaders of the Muslim community. In occlusion since ca. 873, he is expected to return as a messiah at the end of time. (*p. 532*)

hieroglyphics A system of writing in which pictorial symbols represented sounds, syllables, or concepts. It was used for official and monumental inscriptions in ancient Egypt. Because of the long period of study required to master this system, literacy in hieroglyphics was confined to a relatively small group of **scribes** and administrators. Cursive symbol-forms were developed for rapid composition on other media, such as **papyrus**. (*p. 44*)

high culture Canons of artistic and literary masterworks recognized by dominant economic classes. (*p. 897*)

Hinduism A general term for a wide variety of beliefs and ritual practices that have developed in the Indian subcontinent since antiquity. Hinduism has roots in ancient Vedic, Buddhist, and south Indian religious concepts and practices. It spread along the trade routes to Southeast Asia. (*p. 181*)

Hiroshima City in Japan, the first to be destroyed by an atomic bomb, on August 6, 1945. The bombing hastened the end of World War II. (*p. 797*)

history The study of past events and changes in the development, transmission, and transformation of cultural practices. (*p. 11*)

Hitler, Adolf (1889–1945) Born in Austria, Hitler became a radical German nationalist during World War I. He led the National Socialist German Workers' Party—the **Nazi Party**—in the 1920s and became dictator of Germany in 1933. He led Europe into World War II. (*p. 786*)

Hittites A people from central Anatolia who established an empire in Anatolia and Syria in the Late Bronze Age. With wealth from the trade in metals and military power based on chariot forces, the Hittites vied with New Kingdom Egypt for control of Syria-Palestine before falling to unidentified attackers ca. 1200 B.C.E. (See also **Ramesses II.**) (*p. 64*)

Holocaust Nazis' program during World War II to kill people they considered undesirable. Some 6 million Jews perished during the Holocaust, along with millions of Poles, Gypsies, Communists, Socialists, and others. (*p. 800*)

Holocene The geological era since the end of the **Great Ice Age** about 11,000 years ago. (*p. 21*)

Holy Roman Empire Loose federation of mostly German states and principalities, headed by an emperor elected by the princes. It lasted from 962 to 1806. (*pp. 260, 449*)

hominid The biological family that includes humans and humanlike primates. (*p. 9*)

Homo erectus An extinct human species. It evolved in Africa about 2 million years ago. (*p. 10*)

Homo habilis The first human species (now extinct). It evolved in Africa about 2.5 million years ago. (*p. 9*)

Homo sapiens The current human species. It evolved in Africa about 200,000 years ago. It includes archaic forms such as Neanderthals (now extinct) and all modern humans. (*p. 10*)

hoplite A heavily armored Greek infantryman of the Archaic and Classical periods who fought in the close-packed phalanx formation. Hoplite armies—militias composed of middle- and upper-class citizens supplying their own equipment—were for centuries superior to all other military forces. (*p. 126*)

horse collar Harnessing method that increased the efficiency of horses by shifting the point of traction from the animal's neck to the shoulders; its adoption favors the spread of horse-drawn plows and vehicles. (*p. 269*)

House of Burgesses Elected assembly in colonial Virginia, created in 1618. (*p. 486*)

humanists (Renaissance) European scholars, writers, and teachers associated with the study of the humanities (grammar, rhetoric, poetry, history, languages, and moral philosophy), influential in the fifteenth century and later. (*p. 408*)

Hundred Years War (1337–1453) Series of campaigns over control of the throne of France, involving English and French royal families and French noble families. (*p. 413*)

Husain, Saddam (b. 1937) President of Iraq since 1979. Waged war on Iran in 1980–1988. In 1990 he ordered an invasion of Kuwait but was defeated by United States and its allies in the Gulf War (1991). (*p. 860*)

Ibn Battuta (1304–1369) Moroccan Muslim scholar, the most widely traveled individual of his time. He wrote a detailed account of his visits to Islamic lands from China to Spain and the western Sudan. (*p. 373*)

Ibn Khaldun (1332–1406) Arab historian. He developed an influential theory on the rise and fall of states. Born in Tunis, he spent his later years in Cairo as a teacher and judge. In 1400 he was sent to Damascus to negotiate the surrender of the city, where he met and exchanged views with **Timur.** (*p. 336*)

Il-khan A "secondary" or "peripheral" khan based in Persia. The Il-khans' khanate was founded by Hülegü, a grandson of **Genghis Khan,** was based at Tabriz in modern Azerbaijan. It controlled much of Iran and Iraq. (*p. 333*)

import-substitution industrialization An economic system aimed at building a country's industry by restricting foreign trade. It was especially popular in Latin American countries such as Mexico, Argentina, and Brazil in the mid-twentieth century. It proved successful for a time but could not keep up with technological advances in Europe and North America. (*p. 823*)

Inca Largest and most powerful Andean empire. Controlled the Pacific coast of South America from Ecuador to Chile from its capital of Cuzco. (*p. 316*)

indentured servant A migrant to British colonies in the Americas who paid for passage by agreeing to work for a set term ranging from four to seven years. (*p. 486*)

Indian Civil Service The elite professional class of officials who administered the government of British India. Originally composed exclusively of well-educated British men, it gradually added qualified Indians. (*p. 661*)

Indian National Congress A movement and political party founded in 1885 to demand greater Indian participation in government. Its membership was middle class, and its demands were modest until World War I. Led after 1920 by Mohandas K. Gandhi, it appealed increasingly to the poor, and it organized mass protests demanding self-government and independence. (See also **Gandhi, Mohandas K.**) (*pp. 663, 812*)

Indian Ocean maritime system In premodern times, a network of seaports, trade routes, and maritime culture linking countries on the rim of the Indian Ocean from Africa to Indonesia. (*p. 207*)

indulgence The forgiveness of the punishment due for past sins, granted by the Catholic Church authorities as a reward for a pious act. Martin Luther's protest against the sale of indulgences is often seen as touching off the **Protestant Reformation.** (*p. 446*)

Industrial Revolution The transformation of the economy, the environment, and living conditions, occurring first in England in the eighteenth century, that resulted from the use of steam engines, the mechanization of manufacturing in factories, and innovations in transportation and communication. (*p. 599*)

investiture controversy Dispute between the popes and the Holy Roman Emperors over who held ultimate authority over bishops in imperial lands. (*p. 261*)

Iron Age Historians' term for the period during which iron was the primary metal for tools and weapons. The advent of iron technology began at different times in different parts of the world. (*p. 85*)

iron curtain Winston Churchill's term for the Cold War division between the Soviet-dominated East and the U.S.-dominated West. (*p. 831*)

Iroquois Confederacy An alliance of five northeastern Amerindian peoples (after 1722 six) that made decisions on military and diplomatic issues through a council of representatives. Allied first with the Dutch and later with the English, the Confederacy dominated the area from western New England to the Great Lakes. (*p. 488*)

Islam Religion expounded by the Prophet Muhammad (570–632 C.E.) on the basis of his reception of divine revelations, which were collected after his death into the **Quran.** In the tradition of Judaism and Christianity, and sharing much of their lore, Islam calls on all people to recognize one creator god—Allah—who rewards or punishes believers after death according to how they led their lives. (See also **hadith.**) (*p. 231*)

Israel In antiquity, the land between the eastern shore of the Mediterranean and the Jordan River, occupied by the Israelites from the early second millennium B.C.E. The modern state of Israel was founded in 1948. (*p. 98*)

Jackson, Andrew (1767–1845) First president of the United States born in humble circumstances. He was popular among frontier residents, urban workers, and small farmers. He had a successful political career as judge, general, congressman, senator, and president. After being denied the presidency in 1824 in a controversial election, he won in 1828 and was reelected in 1832. (*p. 629*)

Jacobins Radical republicans during the French Revolution. They were led by Maximilien Robespierre from 1793 to 1794. (See also **Robespierre, Maximilien.**) (*p. 588*)

Janissaries Infantry, originally of slave origin, armed with firearms and constituting the elite of the Ottoman army from the fifteenth century until the corps was abolished in 1826. See also **devshirme.** (*p. 526, 675*)

Jesuits Members of the Society of Jesus, a Roman Catholic order founded by Ignatius Loyola in 1534. They played an important part in the **Catholic Reformation** and helped create conduits of trade and knowledge between Asia and Europe. (*p. 548*)

Jesus (ca. 5 B.C.E.–34 C.E.) A Jew from Galilee in northern Israel who sought to reform Jewish beliefs and practices. He was executed as a revolutionary by the Romans. Hailed as the Messiah and son of God by his followers, he became the central figure in Christianity, a belief system that developed in the centuries after his death. (*p. 155*)

Jinnah, Muhammad Ali (1876–1948) Indian Muslim politician who founded the state of Pakistan. A lawyer by training, he joined the **All-India Muslim League** in 1913. As leader of the League from the 1920s on, he negotiated with the British and the **Indian National Congress** for Muslim participation in Indian politics. From 1940 on, he led the movement for the independence of India's Muslims in a separate state of Pakistan, founded in 1947. (*p. 816*)

joint-stock company A business, often backed by a government charter, that sold shares to individuals to raise money for its trading enterprises and to spread the risks (and profits) among many investors. (*p. 460*)

Juárez, Benito (1806–1872) President of Mexico (1858–1872). Born in poverty in Mexico, he was educated as a lawyer and rose to become chief justice of the Mexican supreme court and then president. He led Mexico's resistance to a French invasion in 1863 and the installation of Maximilian as emperor. (*p. 633*)

junk A very large flatbottom sailing ship produced in the **Tang** and **Song Empires,** specially designed for long-distance commercial travel. (*p. 288*)

Kamakura Shogunate The first of Japan's decentralized military governments. (1185–1333). (*p. 294*)

kamikaze The "divine wind," which the Japanese credited with blowing Mongol invaders away from their shores in 1281. (*p. 365*)

Kangxi (1654–1722) Qing emperor (r. 1662–1722). He oversaw the greatest expansion of the **Qing Empire.**

karma In Indian tradition, the residue of deeds performed in past and present lives that adheres to a "spirit" and determines what form it will assume in its next life cycle. The doctrines of karma and reincarnation were used by the elite in ancient India to encourage people to accept their social position and do their duty. (*p. 177*)

keiretsu Alliances of corporations and banks that dominate the Japanese economy. (*p. 861*)

khipu System of knotted colored cords used by preliterate Andean peoples to transmit information. (*p. 312*)

Khomeini, Ayatollah Ruhollah (1900?–1989) Shi'ite philosopher and cleric who led the overthrow of the shah of Iran in 1979 and created an Islamic republic. (*p. 859*)

Khubilai Khan (1215–1294) Last of the Mongol Great Khans (r. 1260–1294) and founder of the **Yuan Empire.** (*p. 351*)

Kievan Russia State established at Kiev in Ukraine ca. 879 by Scandinavian adventurers asserting authority over a mostly Slavic farming population. (*p. 267*)

Korean War (1950–1953) Conflict that began with North Korea's invasion of South Korea and came to involve the United Nations (primarily the United States) allying with South Korea and the People's Republic of China allying with North Korea. (*p. 836*)

Koryo Korean kingdom founded in 918 and destroyed by a Mongol invasion in 1259. (*p. 292*)

Kush An Egyptian name for Nubia, the region alongside the Nile River south of Egypt, where an indigenous kingdom with its own distinctive institutions and cultural traditions arose beginning in the early second millennium B.C.E. It was deeply influenced by Egyptian culture and at times under the control of Egypt, which coveted its rich deposits of gold and luxury products from sub-Saharan Africa carried up the Nile corridor. (*p. 70*)

labor union An organization of workers in a particular industry or trade, created to defend the interests of members through strikes or negotiations with employers. (*p. 709*)

laissez faire The idea that government should refrain from interfering in economic affairs. The classic exposition of laissez-faire principles is Adam Smith's *Wealth of Nations* (1776). (*p. 615*)

lama In Tibetan Buddhism, a teacher. (*p. 351*)

Las Casas, Bartolomé de (1474–1566) First bishop of Chiapas, in southern Mexico. He devoted most of his life to protecting Amerindian peoples from exploitation. His major achievement was the New Laws of 1542, which limited the ability of Spanish settlers to compel Amerindians to labor for them. (See also **encomienda.**) (*p. 476*)

Latin West Historians' name for the territories of Europe that adhered to the Latin rite of Christianity and used the Latin language for intellectual exchange in the period ca. 1000–1500. (*p. 394*)

League of Nations International organization founded in 1919 to promote world peace and cooperation but greatly weakened by the refusal of the United States to join. It proved ineffectual in stopping aggression by Italy, Japan, and Germany in the 1930s, and it was superseded by the **United Nations** in 1945. (*p. 763*)

Legalism In China, a political philosophy that emphasized the unruliness of human nature and justified state coercion and control. The **Qin** ruling class invoked it to validate the authoritarian nature of their regime and its profligate expenditure of subjects' lives and labor. It was superseded in the **Han** era by a more benevolent Confucian doctrine of governmental moderation. (*p. 62*)

"legitimate" trade Exports from Africa in the nineteenth century that did not include the newly outlawed slave trade. (*p. 654*)

Lenin, Vladimir (1870–1924) Leader of the Bolshevik (later Communist) Party. He lived in exile in Switzerland until 1917, then returned to Russia to lead the Bolsheviks to victory during the Russian Revolution and the civil war that followed. (*p. 761*)

Leopold II (1835–1909) King of Belgium (r. 1865–1909). He was active in encouraging the exploration of Central Africa and became the ruler of the Congo Free State (to 1908). (*p. 732*)

Li Shimin (599–649) One of the founders of the **Tang Empire** and its second emperor (r. 626–649). He led the expansion of the empire into Central Asia. (*p. 277*)

liberalism A political ideology that emphasizes the civil rights of citizens, representative government, and the protection of private property. This ideology, derived from the **Enlightenment,** was especially popular among the property-owning middle classes of Europe and North America. (*p. 713*)

Library of Ashurbanipal A large collection of writings drawn from the ancient literary, religious, and scientific traditions of Mesopotamia. It was assembled by the sixth century B.C.E. Assyrian ruler Ashurbanipal. The many tablets unearthed by archaeologists constitute one of the most important sources of present-day knowledge of the long literary tradition of Mesopotamia. (*p. 98*)

Linear B A set of syllabic symbols, derived from the writing system of **Minoan** Crete, used in the Mycenaean palaces of the Late Bronze Age to write an early form of Greek. It was used primarily for palace records, and the surviving Linear B tablets provide substantial information about the economic organization of Mycenaean society and tantalizing clues about political, social, and religious institutions. (*p. 75*)

Little Ice Age A century-long period of cool climate that began in the 1590s. Its ill effects on agriculture in northern Europe were notable. (*p. 462*)

llama A hoofed animal indigenous to the Andes Mountains in South America. It was the only domesticated beast of burden in the Americas before the arrival of Europeans. It provided meat and wool. The use of llamas to transport goods made possible specialized production and trade among people living in different ecological zones and fostered the integration of these zones by **Chavín** and later Andean states. (*p. 90*)

loess A fine, light silt deposited by wind and water. It constitutes the fertile soil of the Yellow River Valley in northern China. Because loess soil is not compacted, it can be worked with a simple digging stick, but it leaves the region vulnerable to devastating earthquakes. (*p. 58*)

Long March (1934–1935) The 6,000-mile (9,600-kilometer) flight of Chinese Communists from southeastern to northwestern China. The Communists, led by **Mao Zedong,** were pursued by the Chinese army under orders from **Chiang Kai-shek.** The four thousand survivors of the march formed the nucleus of a revived Communist movement that defeated the **Guomindang** after World War II. (*p. 789*)

L'Ouverture, François Dominique Toussaint (1743–1803) Leader of the Haitian Revolution. He freed the slaves and gained effective independence for Haiti despite military interventions by the British and French. (*p. 593*)

ma'at Egyptian term for the concept of divinely created and maintained order in the universe. Reflecting the ancient Egyptians' belief in an essentially beneficent world, the divine ruler was the earthly guarantor of this order. (See also **pyramid.**) (*p. 12*)

Macartney mission (1792–1793) The unsuccessful attempt by the British Empire to establish diplomatic relations with the **Qing Empire.** (*p. 560*)

Magellan, Ferdinand (1480?–1521) Portuguese navigator who led the Spanish expedition of 1519–1522 that was the first to sail around the world. (*p. 431*)

Mahabharata A vast epic chronicling the events leading up to a cataclysmic battle between related kinship groups in early India. It includes the Bhagavad-Gita, the most important work of Indian sacred literature. (*p. 185*)

Mahayana Buddhism "Great Vehicle" branch of Buddhism followed in China, Japan, and Central Asia. The focus is on reverence for **Buddha** and for bodhisattvas, enlightened persons who have postponed nirvana to help others attain enlightenment. (*p. 181*)

Malacca Port city in the modern Southeast Asian country of Malaysia, founded about 1400 as a trading center on the Strait of Malacca. Also spelled Melaka. (*p. 387*)

Malay peoples A designation for peoples originating in south China and Southeast Asia who settled the Malay Peninsula, Indonesia, and the Philippines, then spread eastward across the islands of the Pacific Ocean and west to Madagascar. (*p. 190*)

Mali Empire created by indigenous Muslims in western Sudan of West Africa from the thirteenth to fifteenth century. It was famous for its role in the trans-Saharan gold trade. (See also **Timbuktu.**) (*p. 375*)

Malthus, Thomas (1766–1834) Eighteenth-century English intellectual who warned that population growth threatened future generations because, in his view, population growth would always outstrip increases in agricultural production. (*p. 867*)

Mamluks Under the Islamic system of military slavery, Turkic military slaves who formed an important part of the armed forces of the **Abbasid Caliphate** of the ninth and tenth centuries. Mamluks eventually founded their own state, ruling Egypt and Syria (1250–1517). (*pp. 236, 344*)

Manchuria Region of Northeast Asia bounded by the Yalu River on the south and the Amur River on the east and north. (*p. 354*)

Manchus Federation of Northeast Asian peoples who founded the **Qing Empire.** (*p. 556*)

Mandate of Heaven Chinese religious and political ideology developed by the **Zhou,** according to which it was the prerogative of Heaven, the chief deity, to grant power to the ruler of China and to take away that power if the ruler failed to conduct himself justly and in the best interests of his subjects. (*p. 61*)

mandate system Allocation of former German colonies and Ottoman possessions to the victorious powers after World War I, to be administered under League of Nations supervision. (*p. 770*)

manor In medieval Europe, a large, self-sufficient landholding consisting of the lord's residence (manor house), outbuildings, peasant village, and surrounding land. (*p. 254*)

mansabs In India, grants of land given in return for service by rulers of the **Mughal Empire.** (*p. 536*)

Mansa Kankan Musa Ruler of Mali (r. 1312–1337). His pilgrimage through Egypt to **Mecca** in 1324–1325 established the empire's reputation for wealth in the Mediterranean world. (*p. 376*)

manumission A grant of legal freedom to an individual slave. (*p. 505*)

Mao Zedong (1893–1976) Leader of the Chinese Communist Party (1927–1976). He led the Communists on the **Long March** (1934–1935) and rebuilt the Communist Party and Red Army during the Japanese occupation of China (1937–1945). After World War II, he led the Communists to victory over the **Guomindang.** He ordered the **Cultural Revolution** in 1966. (*p. 789*)

maroon A slave who ran away from his or her master. Often a member of a community of runaway slaves in the West Indies and South America. (*p. 505*)

Marshall Plan U. S. program to support the reconstruction of western Europe after World War II. By 1961 more than $20 billion in economic aid had been dispersed. (*p. 834*)

Marx, Karl (1818–1883) German journalist and philosopher, founder of the Marxist branch of **socialism.** He is known for two books: *The Communist Manifesto* (1848) and *Das Kapital* (Vols. I–III, 1867–1894). (*p. 709*)

mass deportation The forcible removal and relocation of large numbers of people or entire populations. The mass deportations practiced by the Assyrian and Persian Empires were meant as a terrifying warning of the consequences of rebellion. They also brought skilled and unskilled labor to the imperial center. (*p. 95*)

mass production The manufacture of many identical products by the division of labor into many small repetitive tasks. This method was introduced into the manufacture of pottery by Josiah Wedgwood and into the spinning of cotton thread by Richard Arkwright. (See also **Arkwright, Richard; Industrial Revolution; Wedgwood, Josiah.**) (*p. 602*)

Mauryan Empire The first state to unify most of the Indian subcontinent. It was founded by Chandragupta Maurya in 324 B.C.E. and survived until 184 B.C.E. From its capital at Pataliputra in the Ganges Valley it grew wealthy from taxes on agriculture, iron mining, and control of trade routes. (See also **Ashoka.**) (*p. 184*)

Maya Mesoamerican civilization concentrated in Mexico's Yucatán Peninsula and in Guatemala and Honduras but never unified into a single empire. Major contributions were in mathematics, astronomy, and development of the calendar. (*p. 302*)

Mecca City in western Arabia; birthplace of the Prophet **Muhammad,** and ritual center of the Islamic religion. (*p. 230*)

mechanization The application of machinery to manufacturing and other activities. Among the first processes to be mechanized were the spinning of cotton thread and the weaving of cloth in late-eighteenth- and early-nineteenth-century England. (*p. 603*)

medieval Literally "middle age," a term that historians of Europe use for the period ca. 500 to ca. 1500, signifying its intermediate point between Greco-Roman antiquity and the Renaissance. (*p. 250*)

Medina City in western Arabia to which the Prophet Muhammad and his followers emigrated in 622 to escape persecution in Mecca. (*p. 231*)

megaliths Structures and complexes of very large stones constructed for ceremonial and religious purposes in **Neolithic** times. (*p. 23*)

Meiji Restoration The political program that followed the destruction of the **Tokugawa Shogunate** in 1868, in which a collection of young leaders set Japan on the path of centralization, industrialization, and imperialism. (See also **Yamagata Aritomo.**) (*p. 694*)

Memphis The capital of Old Kingdom Egypt, near the head of the Nile Delta. Early rulers were interred in the nearby **pyramids.** (*p. 43*)

Menelik II (1844–1911). Emperor of Ethiopia (r. 1889–1911). He enlarged Ethiopia to its present dimensions and defeated an Italian invasion at Adowa (1896). (*p. 737*)

mercantilism European government policies of the sixteenth, seventeenth, and eighteenth centuries designed to promote overseas trade between a country and its colonies and accumulate precious metals by requiring colonies to trade only with their motherland country. The British system was defined by the Navigation Acts, the French system by laws known as the *Exclusif.* (*p. 506*)

Meroë Capital of a flourishing kingdom in southern Nubia from the fourth century B.C.E. to the fourth century C.E. In this period Nubian culture shows more independence from Egypt and the influence of sub-Saharan Africa. (*p. 71*)

mestizo The term used by Spanish authorities to describe someone of mixed Amerindian and European descent. (*p. 484*)

Middle Passage The part of the **Great Circuit** involving the transportation of enslaved Africans across the Atlantic to the Americas. (*p. 508*)

Ming Empire (1368–1644) Empire based in China that Zhu Yuanzhang established after the overthrow of the **Yuan Empire.** The Ming emperor **Yongle** sponsored the building of the **Forbidden City** and the voyages of **Zheng He.** The later years of the Ming saw a slowdown in technological development and economic decline. (*pp. 355, 554*)

Minoan Prosperous civilization on the Aegean island of Crete in the second millennium B.C.E. The Minoans engaged in far-flung commerce around the Mediterranean and exerted powerful cultural influences on the early Greeks. (*p. 73*)

mit'a Andean labor system based on shared obligations to help kinsmen and work on behalf of the ruler and religious organizations. (*p. 312*)

Moche Civilization of north coast of Peru (200–700 C.E.). An important Andean civilization that built extensive irrigation networks as well as impressive urban centers dominated by brick temples. (*p. 313*)

Moctezuma II (1466?–1520) Last Aztec emperor, overthrown by the Spanish conquistador Hernán Cortés. (*p. 437*)

modernization The process of reforming political, military, economic, social, and cultural traditions in imitation of the early success of Western societies, often with regard for accommodating local traditions in non-Western societies. (*p. 652*)

Mohenjo-Daro Largest of the cities of the Indus Valley civilization. It was centrally located in the extensive floodplain of the Indus River in contemporary Pakistan. Little is known about the political institutions of Indus Valley communities, but the large-scale of construction at Mohenjo-Daro, the orderly grid of streets, and the standardization of building materials are evidence of central planning. (*p. 48*)

moksha The Hindu concept of the spirit's "liberation" from the endless cycle of rebirths. There are various avenues—such as physical discipline, meditation, and acts of devotion to the gods—by which the spirit can distance itself from desire for the things of this world and be merged with the divine force that animates the universe. (*p. 179*)

monasticism Living in a religious community apart from secular society and adhering to a rule stipulating chastity, obedience, and poverty. It was a prominent element of medieval Christianity and Buddhism. Monasteries were the primary centers of learning and literacy in medieval Europe. (*p. 261*)

Mongols A people of this name is mentioned as early as the records of the **Tang Empire,** living as nomads in northern

Eurasia. After 1206 they established an enormous empire under **Genghis Khan,** linking western and eastern Eurasia. (*p. 325*)

monotheism Belief in the existence of a single divine entity. Some scholars cite the devotion of the Egyptian pharaoh **Akhenaten** to the Aten (sun-disk) and his suppression of traditional goals as the earliest instance. The Israelite worship of Yahweh developed into an exclusive belief in one god, and this concept passed into Christianity and Islam. (*p. 102*)

monsoon Seasonal winds in the Indian Ocean caused by the differences in temperature between the rapidly heating and cooling landmasses of Africa and Asia and the slowly changing ocean waters. These strong and predictable winds have long been ridden across the open sea by sailors, and the large amounts of rainfall that they deposit on parts of India, Southeast Asia, and China allow for the cultivation of several crops a year. (*pp. 174, 371*)

Morelos, José María (1765–1814) Mexican priest and former student of Miguel Hidalgo y Costilla, he led the forces fighting for Mexican independence until he was captured and executed in 1814. (See also **Hidalgo y Costilla, Miguel.**) (*p. 626*)

most-favored-nation status A clause in a commercial treaty that awards to any later signatories all the privileges previously granted to the original signatories. (*p. 686*)

movable type Type in which each individual character is cast on a separate piece of metal. It replaced woodblock printing, allowing for the arrangement of individual letters and other characters on a page, rather than requiring the carving of entire pages at a time. It may have been invented in Korea in the thirteenth century. (See also **printing press.**) (*p. 293*)

Mughal Empire Muslim state (1526–1857) exercising dominion over most of India in the sixteenth and seventeenth centuries. (*p. 536*)

Muhammad (570–632 C.E.) Arab prophet; founder of religion of Islam. (*p. 230*)

Muhammad Ali (1769–1849) Leader of Egyptian modernization in the early nineteenth century. He ruled Egypt as an Ottoman governor, but had imperial ambitions. His descendants ruled Egypt until overthrown in 1952. (*p. 652*)

mulatto The term used in Spanish and Portuguese colonies to describe someone of mixed African and European descent. (*p. 484*)

mummy A body preserved by chemical processes or special natural circumstances, often in the belief that the deceased will need it again in the afterlife. In ancient Egypt the bodies of people who could afford mummification underwent a complex process of removing organs, filling body cavities, dehydrating the corpse with natron, and then wrapping the body with linen bandages and enclosing it in a wooden sarcophagus. (*p. 46*)

Muscovy Russian principality that emerged gradually during the era of Mongol domination. The Muscovite dynasty ruled without interruption from 1276 to 1598. (*p. 551*)

Muslim An adherent of the Islamic religion; a person who "submits" (in Arabic, *Islam* means "submission") to the will of God. (*p. 231*)

Mussolini, Benito (1883–1945) Fascist dictator of Italy (1922–1943). He led Italy to conquer Ethiopia (1935), joined Germany in the Axis pact (1936), and allied Italy with Germany in World War II. He was overthrown in 1943 when the Allies invaded Italy. (*p. 786*)

Mycenae Site of a fortified palace complex in southern Greece that controlled a Late Bronze Age kingdom. In Homer's epic poems Mycenae was the base of King Agamemnon, who commanded the Greeks besieging Troy. Contemporary archaeologists call the complex Greek society of the second millennium B.C.E. "Mycenaean." (*p. 74*)

Napoleon I (1769–1832). Overthrew French Directory in 1799 and became emperor of the French in 1804. Failed to defeat Great Britain and abdicated in 1814. Returned to power briefly in 1815 but was defeated and died in exile. (*p. 591*)

Nasir al-Din Tusi (1201–1274) Persian mathematician and cosmologist whose academy near Tabriz provided the model for the movement of the planets that helped to inspire the Copernican model of the solar system. (*p. 337*)

National Assembly French Revolutionary assembly (1789–1791). Called first as the Estates General, the three estates came together and demanded radical change. It passed the **Declaration of the Rights of Man** in 1789. (*p. 585*)

nationalism A political ideology that stresses people's membership in a nation—a community defined by a common culture and history as well as by territory. In the late eighteenth and early nineteenth centuries, nationalism was a force for unity in western Europe. In the late nineteenth century it hastened the disintegration of the Austro-Hungarian and Ottoman Empires. In the twentieth century it provided the ideological foundation for scores of independent countries emerging from **colonialism.** (*p. 713*)

natural selection The biological process by which variations that enhance a population's ability to survive in a particular environment become dominant in a species over very long periods and lead to the **evolution** of a new species. (*p. 6*)

nawab A Muslim prince allied to British India; technically, a semi-autonomous deputy of the Mughal emperor. (*p. 657*)

Nazi Party German political party joined by Adolf Hitler, emphasizing nationalism, racism, and war. When Hitler became chancellor of Germany in 1933, the Nazi Party became the only legal party and an instrument of Hitler's absolute rule. Its formal name was National Socialist German Workers' Party. (See also **Hitler, Adolf.**) (*p. 786*)

Nehru, Jawaharlal (1889–1964) Indian statesman. He succeeded Mohandas K. Gandhi as leader of the **Indian National Congress.** He negotiated the end of British colonial rule in India and became India's first prime minister (1947–1964). (*p. 815*)

Neo-Assyrian Empire An empire extending from western Iran to Syria-Palestine, conquered by the Assyrians of northern Mesopotamia between the tenth and seventh centuries B.C.E. They used force and terror and exploited the wealth and labor of their subjects. They also preserved and continued the cultural and scientific developments of Mesopotamian civilization. (*p. 93*)

Neo-Babylonian kingdom Under the Chaldaeans (nomadic kinship groups that settled in southern Mesopotamia in the early first millennium B.C.E.), **Babylon** again became a major political and cultural center in the seventh and sixth centuries B.C.E. After participating in the destruction of Assyrian power, the monarchs Nabopolassar and Nebuchadnezzar took over the southern portion of the Assyrian domains. By destroying the **First Temple** in Jerusalem and deporting part of the population, they initiated the **diaspora** of the Jews. (*p. 110*)

Neolithic The period of the Stone Age associated with the ancient **Agricultural Revolution(s).** It follows the **Paleolithic** period. (*p. 11*)

Nevskii, Alexander (1220–1263) Prince of Novgorod (r. 1236–1263). He submitted to the invading Mongols in 1240 and received recognition as the leader of the Russian princes under the Golden Horde. (*p. 339*)

New Economic Policy Policy proclaimed by Vladimir Lenin in 1924 to encourage the revival of the Soviet economy by allowing small private enterprises. Joseph Stalin ended the N.E.P. in 1928 and replaced it with a series of **Five-Year Plans.** (See also **Lenin, Vladimir.**) (*p. 766*)

New France French colony in North America, with a capital in Quebec, founded 1608. New France fell to the British in 1763. (*p. 489*)

New Imperialism Historians' term for the late-nineteenth- and early-twentieth-century wave of conquests by European powers, the United States, and Japan, which were followed by the development and exploitation of the newly conquered territories for the benefit of the colonial powers. (*p. 726*)

Newly Industrialized Economies (NIEs) Rapidly growing, new industrial nations of the late twentieth century, including the **Asian Tigers.** (*p. 861*)

new monarchies Historians' term for the monarchies in France, England, and Spain from 1450 to 1600. The centralization of royal power was increasing within more or less fixed territorial limits. (*p. 414*)

nomadism A way of life, forced by a scarcity of resources, in which groups of people continually migrate to find pastures and water. (*p. 326*)

nonaligned nations Developing countries that announced their neutrality in the **Cold War.** (*p. 846*)

nongovernmental organizations (NGOs) Nonprofit international organizations devoted to investigating human rights abuses and providing humanitarian relief. Two NGOs won the Nobel Peace Prize in the 1990s: International Campaign to Ban Landmines (1997) and Doctors Without Borders (1999). (*p. 892*)

North Atlantic Treaty Organization (NATO) Organization formed in 1949 as a military alliance of western European and North American states against the Soviet Union and its east European allies. (See also **Warsaw Pact.**) (*p. 832*)

nuclear nonproliferation Goal of international efforts to prevent countries other than the five declared nuclear powers (United States, Russia, Britain, France, and China) from obtaining nuclear weapons. The first Nuclear Non-Proliferation Treaty was signed in 1968. (*p. 890*)

Olmec The first Mesoamerican civilization. Between ca. 1200 and 400 B.C.E., the Olmec people of central Mexico created a vibrant civilization that included intensive agriculture, wide-ranging trade, ceremonial centers, and monumental construction. The Olmec had great cultural influence on later Mesoamerican societies, passing on artistic styles, religious imagery, sophisticated astronomical observation for the construction of calendars, and a ritual ball game. (*p. 86*)

Oman Arab state based in Musqat, the main port in the southwest region of the Arabian peninsula. Oman succeeded Portugal as a power in the western Indian Ocean in the eighteenth century. (*p. 542*)

Opium War (1839–1842) War between Britain and the **Qing Empire** that was, in the British view, occasioned by the Qing government's refusal to permit the importation of opium into its territories. The victorious British imposed the one-sided **Treaty of Nanking** on China. (*p. 684*)

Organization of Petroleum Exporting Countries (OPEC) Organization formed in 1960 by oil-producing states to promote their collective interest in generating revenue from oil. (*p. 849*)

Ottoman Empire Islamic state founded by Osman in north-western Anatolia ca. 1300. After the fall of the **Byzantine Empire,** the Ottoman Empire was based at Istanbul (formerly Constantinople) from 1453 to 1922. It encompassed lands in the Middle East, North Africa, the Caucasus, and eastern Europe. (*p. 522*)

Páez, José Antonio (1790–1873) Venezulean soldier who led Simón Bolívar's cavalry force. He became a successful general in the war and built a powerful political base. He was unwilling to accept the constitutional authority of Bolívar's government in distant Bogotá and declared Venezuela's independence from Gran Colombia in 1829. (*p. 629*)

Paleolithic The period of the Stone Age associated with the **evolution** of humans. It predates the **Neolithic** period. (*p. 11*)

Panama Canal Ship canal cut across the isthmus of Panama by United States Army engineers; it opened in 1915. It greatly shortened the sea voyage between the east and west coasts of North America. The United States turned the canal over to Panama on January 1, 2000. (*p. 746*)

papacy The central administration of the Roman Catholic Church, of which the pope is the head. (*pp. 258, 445*)

papyrus A reed that grows along the banks of the Nile River in Egypt. From it was produced a coarse, paperlike writing medium used by the Egyptians and many other peoples in the ancient Mediterranean and Middle East. (*p. 44*)

Parthians Iranian ruling dynasty between ca. 250 B.C.E. and 226 C.E. (*p. 204*)

patron/client relationship In ancient Rome, a fundamental social relationship in which the patron—a wealthy and powerful individual—provided legal and economic protection and assistance to clients, men of lesser status and means, and in return the clients supported the political careers and economic interests of their patron. (*p. 149*)

Paul (ca. 5–65 C.E.) A Jew from the Greek city of Tarsus in Anatolia, he initially persecuted the followers of Jesus but, after receiving a revelation on the road to Syrian Damascus, became a Christian. Taking advantage of his Hellenized background and Roman citizenship, he traveled throughout Syria-Palestine, Anatolia, and Greece, preaching the new religion and establishing churches. Finding his greatest success among pagans ("gentiles"), he began the process by which Christianity separated from Judaism. (*p. 156*)

pax romana Literally, "Roman peace," it connoted the stability and prosperity that Roman rule brought to the lands of the Roman Empire in the first two centuries C.E. The movement of people and trade goods along Roman roads and safe seas allowed for the spread of cultural practices, technologies, and religious ideas. (*p. 154*)

Pearl Harbor Naval base in Hawaii attacked by Japanese aircraft on December 7, 1941. The sinking of much of the U.S. Pacific Fleet brought the United States into World War II. (*p. 793*)

Peloponnesian War A protracted (431–404 B.C.E.) and costly conflict between the Athenian and Spartan alliance systems that convulsed most of the Greek world. The war was largely a consequence of Athenian imperialism. Possession of a naval empire allowed Athens to fight a war of attrition. Ultimately, Sparta prevailed because of Athenian errors and Persian financial support. (*p. 135*)

percussion caps Gunpowder-filled capsules that, when struck by the hammer of a gun, ignite the explosive charge in a gun. Their use meant that guns no longer needed to be ignited by hand. (*p. 681*)

perestroika Policy of "openness" that was the centerpiece of Mikhail Gorbachev's efforts to liberalize communism in the Soviet Union. (See also **Gorbachev, Mikhail**.) (*p. 863*)

Pericles (ca. 495–429 B.C.E.) Aristocratic leader who guided the Athenian state through the transformation to full participatory democracy for all male citizens, supervised construction of the Acropolis, and pursued a policy of imperial expansion that led to the **Peloponnesian War**. He formulated a strategy of attrition but died from the plague early in the war. (*p. 130*)

Perón, Eva Duarte (1919–1952) Wife of **Juan Perón** and champion of the poor in Argentina. She was a gifted speaker and popular political leader who campaigned to improve the life of the urban poor by founding schools and hospitals and providing other social benefits. (*p. 824*)

Perón, Juan (1895–1974) President of Argentina (1946–1955, 1973–1974). As a military officer, he championed the rights of labor. Aided by his wife **Eva Duarte Perón**, he was elected president in 1946. He built up Argentinean industry, became very popular among the urban poor, but harmed the economy. (*p. 823*)

Persepolis A complex of palaces, reception halls, and treasury buildings erected by the Persian kings **Darius I** and Xerxes in the Persian homeland. It is believed that the New Year's festival was celebrated here, as well as the coronations, weddings, and funerals of the Persian kings, who were buried in cliff-tombs nearby. (*p. 119*)

Persian Wars Conflicts between Greek city-states and the Persian Empire, ranging from the Ionian Revolt (499–494 B.C.E.) through Darius's punitive expedition that failed at Marathon (490 B.C.E.) and the defeat of Xerxes' massive invasion of Greece by the Spartan-led Hellenic League (480–479 B.C.E.). This first major setback for Persian arms launched the Greeks into their period of greatest cultural productivity. **Herodotus** chronicled these events in the first "history" in the Western tradition. (*p. 131*)

personalist leaders Political leaders who rely on charisma and their ability to mobilize and direct the masses of citizens outside the authority of constitutions and laws. Nineteenth-century examples include José Antonio Páez of Venezuela and Andrew Jackson of the United States. Twentieth-century examples include Getulio Vargas of Brazil and Juan Perón of Argentina. (See also **Jackson, Andrew; Paez, José Antonio; Perón, Juan; Vargas, Getulio**.) (*p. 628*)

Peter the Great (1672–1725) Russian tsar (r. 1689–1725). He enthusiastically introduced Western languages and technologies to the Russian elite, moving the capital from Moscow to the new city of St. Petersburg. (*p. 552*)

pharaoh The central figure in the ancient Egyptian state. Believed to be an earthly manifestation of the gods, he used his absolute power to maintain the safety and prosperity of Egypt. (*p. 42*)

Phoenicians Semitic-speaking Canaanites living on the coast of modern Lebanon and Syria in the first millennium B.C.E. From major cities such as Tyre and Sidon, Phoenician merchants and sailors explored the Mediterranean, engaged in widespread commerce, and founded **Carthage** and other colonies in the western Mediterranean. (*p. 103*)

pilgrimage Journey to a sacred shrine by Christians seeking to show their piety, fulfill vows, or gain absolution for sins. Other religions also have pilgrimage traditions, such as the Muslim pilgrimage to **Mecca** and the pilgrimages made by early Chinese Buddhists to India in search of sacred Buddhist writings. (*p. 270*)

Pilgrims Group of English Protestant dissenters who established Plymouth Colony in Massachusetts in 1620 to seek religious freedom after having lived briefly in the Netherlands. (*p. 487*)

Pizarro, Francisco (1475?–1541) Spanish explorer who led the conquest of the **Inca** Empire of Peru in 1531–1533. (*p. 438*)

Planck, Max (1858–1947) German physicist who developed quantum theory and was awarded the Nobel Prize for physics in 1918. (*p. 774*)

plantocracy In the West Indian colonies, the rich men who owned most of the slaves and most of the land, especially in the eighteenth century. (*p. 502*)

polis The Greek term for a **city-state**, an urban center and the agricultural territory under its control. It was the characteristic form of political organization in southern and central Greece in the Archaic and Classical periods. Of the hundreds of city-states in the Mediterranean and Black Sea regions settled by Greeks, some were oligarchic, others democratic, depending on the powers delegated to the Council and the Assembly. (*p. 125*)

popular culture Entertainment spread by mass communications and enjoying wide appeal. (*p. 897*)

positivism A philosophy developed by the French count of Saint-Simon. Positivists believed that social and economic problems could be solved by the application of the scientific method, leading to continuous progress. Their ideas became popular in France and Latin America in the nineteenth century. (*p. 616*)

postmodernism Post-World War II intellectual movement and cultural attitude focusing on cultural pluralism and release from the confines and ideology of Western high culture. (*p. 900*)

Potosí Located in Bolivia, one of the richest silver mining centers and most populous cities in colonial Spanish America. (*p. 479*)

printing press A mechanical device for transferring text or graphics from a woodblock or type to paper using ink. Presses using movable type first appeared in Europe in about 1450. See also **movable type.** (*p. 409*)

Protestant Reformation Religious reform movement within the Latin Christian Church beginning in 1519. It resulted in the "protesters" forming several new Christian denominations, including the Lutheran and Reformed Churches and the Church of England. (*p. 446*)

proxy wars During the **Cold War,** local or regional wars in which the superpowers armed, trained, and financed the combatants. (*p. 855*)

Ptolemies The Macedonian dynasty, descended from one of Alexander the Great's officers, that ruled Egypt for three centuries (323–30 B.C.E.). From their magnificent capital at Alexandria on the Mediterranean coast, the Ptolemies largely took over the system created by Egyptian pharaohs to extract the wealth of the land, rewarding Greeks and Hellenized non-Greeks serving in the military and administration. (*p. 138*)

Puritans English Protestant dissenters who believed that God predestined souls to heaven or hell before birth. They founded Massachusetts Bay Colony in 1629. (*p. 487*)

pyramid A large, triangular stone monument, used in Egypt and Nubia as a burial place for the king. The largest pyramids, erected during the Old Kingdom near Memphis with stone tools and compulsory labor, reflect the Egyptian belief that the proper and spectacular burial of the divine ruler would guarantee the continued prosperity of the land. (See also **ma'at.**) (*p. 42*)

Qin A people and state in the Wei Valley of eastern China that conquered rival states and created the first Chinese empire (221–206 B.C.E.). The Qin ruler, **Shi Huangdi,** standardized many features of Chinese society and ruthlessly marshalled subjects for military and construction projects, engendering hostility that led to the fall of his dynasty shortly after his death. The Qin framework was largely taken over by the succeeding **Han** Empire. (*p. 163*)

Qing Empire Empire established in China by Manchus who overthrew the **Ming Empire** in 1644. At various times the Qing also controlled Manchuria, Mongolia, Turkestan, and Tibet. The last Qing emperor was overthrown in 1911. (*p. 556*)

Quran Book composed of divine revelations made to the Prophet Muhammad between ca. 610 and his death in 632; the sacred text of the religion of **Islam.** (*p. 232*)

railroads Networks of iron (later steel) rails on which steam (later electric or diesel) locomotives pulled long trains at high speeds. The first railroads were built in England in the 1830s. Their success caused a railroad-building boom throughout the world that lasted well into the twentieth century. (*p. 704*)

Rajputs Members of a mainly Hindu warrior caste from northwest India. The Mughal emperors drew most of their Hindu officials from this caste, and **Akbar I** married a Rajput princess. (*p. 537*)

Ramesses II A long-lived ruler of New Kingdom Egypt (r. 1290–1224 B.C.E.). He reached an accommodation with the **Hittites** of Anatolia after a standoff in battle at Kadesh in Syria. He built on a grand scale throughout Egypt. (*p. 68*)

Rashid al-Din (d.1318) Adviser to the **Il-khan** ruler Ghazan, who converted to Islam on Rashid's advice. (*p. 334*)

recaptives Africans rescued by Britain's Royal Navy from the illegal slave trade of the nineteenth century and restored to free status. (*p. 655*)

reconquest of Iberia Beginning in the eleventh century, military campaigns by various Iberian Christian states to recapture territory taken by Muslims. In 1492 the last Muslim ruler was defeated, and Spain and Portugal emerged as united kingdoms. (*p. 414*)

Renaissance (European) A period of intense artistic and intellectual activity, said to be a "rebirth" of Greco-Roman culture. Usually divided into an Italian Renaissance, from roughly the mid-fourteenth to mid-fifteenth century, and a Northern (trans-Alpine) Renaissance, from roughly the early fifteenth to early seventeenth century. (*pp. 407, 445*)

Revolutions of 1848 Democratic and nationalist revolutions that swept across Europe. The monarchy in France was overthrown. In Germany, Austria, Italy, and Hungary the revolutions failed. (*p. 595*)

Rhodes, Cecil (1853–1902) British entrepreneur and politician involved in the expansion of the British Empire from South Africa into Central Africa. The colonies of Southern Rhodesia (now Zimbabwe) and Northern Rhodesia (now Zambia) were named after him. (*p. 736*)

Robespierre, Maximilien (1758–1794) Young provincial lawyer who led the most radical phases of the French Revolution. His execution ended the Reign of Terror. See **Jacobins.** (*p. 589*)

Roman Principate A term used to characterize Roman government in the first three centuries C.E., based on the ambiguous title *princeps* ("first citizen") adopted by Augustus to conceal his military dictatorship. (*p. 151*)

Roman Republic The period from 507 to 31 B.C.E., during which Rome was largely governed by the aristocratic **Roman Senate.** (*p. 148*)

Roman Senate A council whose members were the heads of wealthy, landowning families. Originally an advisory body to the early kings, in the era of the **Roman Republic** the Senate effectively governed the Roman state and the growing empire. Under Senate leadership, Rome conquered an empire of unprecedented extent in the lands surrounding the Mediterranean Sea. In the first century B.C.E. quarrels among powerful and ambitious senators and failure to address social and economic problems led to civil wars and the emergence of the rule of the emperors. (*p. 148*)

Romanization The process by which the Latin language and Roman culture became dominant in the western provinces of the Roman Empire. The Roman government did not actively seek to Romanize the subject peoples, but indigenous peoples in the provinces often chose to Romanize because of the political and economic advantages that it brought, as well as the allure of Roman success. (*p. 155*)

Romanov, Mikhail (1596–1645) Russian tsar (r. 1613–1645) A member of the Russian aristocracy, he became tsar after the old line of Muscovite rulers was deposed. (*p. 551*)

Royal African Company A trading company chartered by the English government in 1672 to conduct its merchants' trade on the Atlantic coast of Africa. (*p. 507*)

sacrifice A gift given to a deity, often with the aim of creating a relationship, gaining favor, and obligating the god to provide some benefit to the sacrificer, sometimes in order to sustain the deity and thereby guarantee the continuing vitality of the natural world. The object devoted to the deity could be as simple as a cup of wine poured on the ground, a live animal slain on the altar, or, in the most extreme case, the ritual killing of a human being. (*p. 127*)

Safavid Empire Iranian kingdom (1502–1722) established by Ismail Safavi, who declared Iran a Shi'ite state. (*p. 531*)

Sahel Savanna Belt south of the Sahara; literally "coastland" in Arabic. (*p. 215*)

samurai Literally "those who serve," the hereditary military elite of the **Tokugawa Shogunate.** (*p. 563*)

Sandinistas Members of a leftist coalition that overthrew the Nicaraguan dictatorship of Anastasia Somoza in 1979 and attempted to install a socialist economy. The United States financed armed opposition by the Contras. The Sandinistas lost national elections in 1990. (*p. 857*)

Sasanid Empire Iranian empire, established ca. 226, with a capital in Ctesiphon, Mesopotamia. The Sasanid emperors established **Zoroastrianism** as the state religion. Islamic Arab armies overthrew the empire ca. 640. (*p. 225*)

satrap The governor of a province in the Achaemenid Persian Empire, often a relative of the king. He was responsible for protection of the province and for forwarding tribute to the central administration. Satraps in outlying provinces enjoyed considerable autonomy. (*p. 118*)

savanna Tropical or subtropical grassland, either treeless or with occasional clumps of trees. Most extensive in **sub-Saharan Africa** but also present in South America. (*p. 217*)

schism A formal split within a religious community. See **Great Western Schism.** (*p. 260*)

scholasticism A philosophical and theological system, associated with Thomas Aquinas, devised to reconcile Aristotelian philosophy and Roman Catholic theology in the thirteenth century. (*p. 408*)

Scientific Revolution The intellectual movement in Europe, initially associated with planetary motion and other aspects of physics, that by the seventeenth century had laid the groundwork for modern science. (*p. 466*)

"scramble" for Africa Sudden wave of conquests in Africa by European powers in the 1880s and 1890s. Britain obtained most of eastern Africa, France most of northwestern Africa. Other countries (Germany, Belgium, Portugal, Italy, and Spain) acquired lesser amounts. (*p. 731*)

scribe In the governments of many ancient societies, a professional position reserved for men who had undergone the lengthy training required to be able to read and write using **cuneiforms, hieroglyphics,** or other early, cumbersome writing systems. (*p. 35*)

seasoning An often difficult period of adjustment to new climates, disease environments, and work routines, such as that experienced by slaves newly arrived in the Americas. (*p. 504*)

Selassie, Haile (1892–1975) Emperor of Ethiopia (r. 1930–1974) and symbol of African independence. He fought the Italian invasion of his country in 1935 and regained his throne during World War II, when British forces expelled the Italians. He ruled **Ethiopia** as a traditional **autocracy** until he was overthrown in 1974. (*p. 809*)

Semitic Family of related languages long spoken across parts of western Asia and northern Africa. In antiquity these languages included Hebrew, Aramaic, and Phoenician. The most widespread modern member of the Semitic family is Arabic. (*p. 32*)

"separate spheres" Nineteenth-century idea in Western societies that men and women, especially of the middle class, should have clearly differentiated roles in society: women as wives, mothers, and homemakers; men as breadwinners and participants in business and politics. (*p. 711*)

sepoy A soldier in South Asia, especially in the service of the British. (*p. 658*)

Sepoy Rebellion The revolt of Indian soldiers in 1857 against certain practices that violated religious customs; also known as the Sepoy Mutiny. (*p. 661*)

Serbia The Ottoman province in the Balkans that rose up against **Janissary** control in the early 1800s. After World War II the central province of Yugoslavia. Serb leaders struggled to maintain dominance as the Yugoslav federation dissolved in the 1990s. (*p. 676*)

serf In medieval Europe, an agricultural laborer legally bound to a lord's property and obligated to perform set services for the lord. In Russia some serfs worked as artisans and in factories; serfdom was not abolished there until 1861. (*pp. 254, 553*)

shaft graves A term used for the burial sites of elite members of Mycenaean Greek society in the mid-second millennium B.C.E. At the bottom of deep shafts lined with stone slabs, the bodies were laid out along with gold and bronze jewelry, implements, weapons, and masks. (*p. 75*)

shamanism The practice of identifying special individuals (shamans) who will interact with spirits for the benefit of the community. Characteristic of the Korean kingdoms of the early medieval period and of early societies of Central Asia. (*p. 292*)

Shang The dominant people in the earliest Chinese dynasty for which we have written records (ca. 1750–1027 B.C.E.). Ancestor worship, divination by means of oracle bones, and the use of bronze vessels for ritual purposes were major elements of Shang culture. (*p. 59*)

Shi Huangdi Founder of the short-lived **Qin** dynasty and creator of the Chinese Empire (r. 221–210 B.C.E.). He is remembered for his ruthless conquests of rival states, standardization of practices, and forcible organization of labor for military and engineering tasks. His tomb, with its army of life-size terracotta soldiers, has been partially excavated. (*p. 163*)

Shi'ites Muslims belonging to the branch of Islam believing that God vests leadership of the community in a descendant of Muhammad's son-in-law Ali. Shi'ism is the state religion of Iran. (See also **Sunnis**.) (*pp. 225, 531*)

Siberia The extreme northeastern sector of Asia, including the Kamchatka Peninsula and the present Russian coast of the Arctic Ocean, the Bering Strait, and the Sea of Okhotsk. (*p. 551*)

Sikhism Indian religion founded by the guru Nanak (1469–1539) in the Punjab region of northwest India. After the Mughal emperor ordered the beheading of the ninth guru in 1675, Sikh warriors mounted armed resistance to Mughal rule. (*p. 538*)

Silk Road Caravan routes connecting China and the Middle East across Central Asia and Iran. (*p. 203*)

"small tradition" Historians' term for a localized, usually nonliterate, set of customs and beliefs adhered to by a single society, often in conjunction with a **"great tradition."** (*p. 217*)

socialism A political ideology that originated in Europe in the 1830s. Socialists advocated government protection of workers from exploitation by property owners and government ownership of industries. This ideology led to the founding of socialist or labor parties throughout Europe in the second half of the nineteenth century. (See also **Marx, Karl**.) (*p. 709*)

Socrates Athenian philosopher (ca. 470–399 B.C.E.) who shifted the emphasis of philosophical investigation from questions of natural science to ethics and human behavior. He attracted young disciples from elite families but made enemies by revealing the ignorance and pretensions of others, culminating in his trial and execution by the Athenian state. (*p. 133*)

Sokoto Caliphate A large Muslim state founded in 1809 in what is now northern Nigeria. (*p. 651*)

Solidarity Polish trade union created in 1980 to protest working conditions and political repression. It began the nationalist opposition to communist rule that led in 1989 to the fall of communism in eastern Europe. (*p. 863*)

Song Empire Empire in central and southern China (960–1126) while the Liao people controlled the north. Empire in southern China (1127–1279; the "Southern Song") while the Jin people controlled the north. Distinguished for its advances in technology, medicine, astronomy, and mathematics. (*p. 285*)

Srivijaya A state based on the Indonesian island of Sumatra, between the seventh and eleventh centuries C.E. It amassed wealth and power by a combination of selective adaptation of Indian technologies and concepts, control of the lucrative trade routes between India and China, and skillful showmanship and diplomacy in holding together a disparate realm of inland and coastal territories. (See also **theaterstate**.) (*p. 192*)

Stalin, Joseph (1879–1953) Bolshevik revolutionary, head of the Soviet Communist Party after 1924, and dictator of the Soviet Union from 1928 to 1953. He led the Soviet Union with an iron fist, using **Five-Year Plans** to increase industrial production and terror to crush all opposition. (*p. 780*)

Stalingrad City in Russia, site of a Red Army victory over the Germany army in 1942–1943. The Battle of Stalingrad was the turning point in the war between Germany and the Soviet Union. Today Volgograd. (*p. 793*)

Stanley, Henry Morton (1841–1904) British-American explorer of Africa, famous for his expeditions in search of Dr. David Livingstone. Stanley helped King **Leopold II** establish the Congo Free State. (*p. 732*)

steam engine A machine that turns the energy released by burning fuel into motion. Thomas Newcomen built the first crude but workable steam engine in 1712. **James Watt** vastly improved his device in the 1760s and 1770s. Steam power was later applied to moving machinery in factories and to powering ships and locomotives. (*p. 607*)

steel A form of iron that is both durable and flexible. It was first mass-produced in the 1860s and quickly became the most widely used metal in construction, machinery, and railroad equipment. (*p. 701*)

steppes Treeless plains, especially the high, flat expanses of northern Eurasia, which usually have little rain and are covered with coarse grass. They are good lands for nomads and their herds. Living on the steppes promoted the breeding of horses and the development of military skills that were essential to the rise of the Mongol Empire. (*pp. 217, 326*)

stirrup Device for securing a horseman's feet, enabling him to wield weapons more effectively. First evidence of the use of stirrups was among the Kushan people of northern Afghanistan in approximately the first century C.E. (*p. 206*)

stock exchange A place where shares in a company or business enterprise are bought and sold. (*p. 460*)

Stone Age The historical period characterized by the production of tools from stone and other nonmetallic substances. It was followed in some places by the Bronze Age and more generally by the Iron Age. (*p. 11*)

submarine telegraph cables Insulated copper cables laid along the bottom of a sea or ocean for telegraphic communication. The first short cable was laid across the English Channel in 1851; the first successful transatlantic cable was laid in 1866. (See also **electric telegraph**.) (*p. 704*)

sub-Saharan Africa Portion of the African continent lying south of the Sahara. (*p. 216*)

Suez Canal Ship canal dug across the isthmus of Suez in Egypt, designed by Ferdinand de Lesseps. It opened to shipping in 1869 and shortened the sea voyage between Europe and Asia. Its strategic importance led to the British conquest of Egypt in 1882. (*p. 726*)

Suleiman the Magnificent (1494–1566) The most illustrious sultan of the **Ottoman Empire** (r. 1520–1566); also known as Suleiman Kanuni, "The Lawgiver." He significantly expanded the empire in the Balkans and eastern Mediterranean. (*p. 526*)

Sumerians The people who dominated southern Mesopotamia through the end of the third millennium B.C.E. They were responsible for the creation of many fundamental elements of Mesopotamian culture—such as irrigation technology, **cuneiform,** and religious conceptions—taken over by their **Semitic** successors. (*p. 32*)

Sunnis Muslims belonging to branch of Islam believing that the community should select its own leadership. The majority religion in most Islamic countries. (See also **Shi'ites.**) (*p. 225*)

Sun Yat-sen (1867–1925) Chinese nationalist revolutionary, founder and leader of the **Guomindang** until his death. He attempted to create a liberal democratic political movement in China but was thwarted by military leaders. (*p. 768*)

Swahili Bantu language with Arabic loanwords spoken in coastal regions of East Africa. (*p. 542*)

Swahili Coast East African shores of the Indian Ocean between the Horn of Africa and the Zambezi River; from the Arabic *sawahil*, meaning "shores." (*p. 383*)

Taiping Rebellion (1853–1864) The most destructive civil war before the twentieth century. A Christian-inspired rural rebellion threatened to topple the **Qing Empire.** (*p. 687*)

Tamil kingdoms The kingdoms of southern India, inhabited primarily by speakers of Dravidian languages, which developed in partial isolation, and somewhat differently, from the Aryan north. They produced epics, poetry, and performance arts. Elements of Tamil religious beliefs were merged into the Hindu synthesis. (*p. 185*)

Tang Empire Empire unifying China and part of Central Asia, founded 618 and ended 907. The Tang emperors presided over a magnificent court at their capital, Chang'an. (*p. 277*)

Tanzimat "Restructuring" reforms by the nineteenth-century Ottoman rulers, intended to move civil law away from the control of religious elites and make the military and the bureaucracy more efficient. (*p. 678*)

tax farming A government's use of private collectors to collect taxes. Individuals or corporations contract with the government to collect a fixed amount for the government and are permitted to keep as profit everything they collect over that amount. (*p. 334*)

technology transfer The communication of specific plans, designs, or educational programs necessary for the use of new technologies from one society or class to another. (*p. 358*)

Tecumseh (1768–1813) Shawnee leader who attempted to organize an Amerindian confederacy to prevent the loss of additional territory to American settlers. He became an ally of the British in War of 1812 and died in battle. (*p. 634*)

Tenochtitlan Capital of the Aztec Empire, located on an island in Lake Texcoco. Its population was about 150,000 on the eve of Spanish conquest. Mexico City was constructed on its ruins. (*p. 305*)

Teotihuacan A powerful **city-state** in central Mexico (100–75 C.E.). Its population was about 150,000 at its peak in 600. (*p. 300*)

Terrorism Political belief that extreme and seemingly random violence will destabilize a government and permit the terrorists to gain political advantage. Though an old technique, terrorism gained prominence in the late twentieth century with the growth of worldwide mass media that, through their news coverage, amplified public fears of terrorist acts. (*p. 890*)

theater-state Historians' term for a state that acquires prestige and power by developing attractive cultural forms and staging elaborate public ceremonies (as well as redistributing valuable resources) to attract and bind subjects to the center. Examples include the **Gupta Empire** in India and **Srivijaya** in Southeast Asia. (*p. 186*)

Thebes Capital city of Egypt and home of the ruling dynasties during the Middle and New Kingdoms. Amon, patron deity of Thebes, became one of the chief gods of Egypt. Monarchs were buried across the river in the Valley of the Kings. (*p. 43*)

Theravada Buddhism "Way of the Elders" branch of Buddhism followed in Sri Lanka and much of Southeast Asia. Therevada remains close to the original principles set forth by the **Buddha;** it downplays the importance of gods and emphasizes austerity and the individual's search for enlightenment. (*p. 181*)

third-century crisis Historians' term for the political, military, and economic turmoil that beset the Roman Empire during much of the third century C.E.: frequent changes of ruler, civil wars, barbarian invasions, decline of urban centers, and near-destruction of long-distance commerce and the monetary economy. After 284 C.E. Diocletian restored order by making fundamental changes. (*p. 157*)

Third World Term applied to a group of developing countries who professed nonalignment during the **Cold War.** (*p. 846*)

three-field system A rotational system for agriculture in which one field grows grain, one grows legumes, and one lies fallow. It gradually replaced two-field system in medieval Europe. (*p. 396*)

Tiananmen Square Site in Beijing where Chinese students and workers gathered to demand greater political openness in 1989. The demonstration was crushed by Chinese military with great loss of life. (*p. 862*)

Timbuktu City on the Niger River in the modern country of Mali. It was founded by the Tuareg as a seasonal camp sometime after 1000. As part of the **Mali** empire, Timbuktu became a major major terminus of the trans-Saharan trade and a center of Islamic learning. (*p. 388*)

Timur (1336–1405) Member of a prominent family of the Mongols' Jagadai Khanate, Timur through conquest gained control over much of Central Asia and Iran. He consolidated the status of Sunni Islam as orthodox, and his descendants, the Timurids, maintained his empire for nearly a century and founded the **Mughal Empire** in India. (*p. 336*)

Tiwanaku Name of capital city and empire centered on the region near Lake Titicaca in modern Bolivia (375–1000 C.E.). (*p. 315*)

Tokugawa Shogunate (1600–1868) The last of the three shogunates of Japan. (*p. 563*)

Toltecs Powerful postclassic empire in central Mexico (900–1168 C.E.). It influenced much of Mesoamerica. Aztecs claimed ties to this earlier civilization. (*p. 305*)

tophet A cemetery containing burials of young children, possibly sacrificed to the gods in times of crisis, found at **Carthage** and other **Phoenician** settlements in the western Mediterranean. (*p. 108*)

trans-Saharan caravan routes Trading network linking North Africa with **sub-Saharan Africa** across the Sahara. (*p. 210*)

Treaty of Nanking (1842) The treaty that concluded the **Opium War.** It awarded Britain a large indemnity from the **Qing Empire,** denied the Qing government tariff control over some of its own borders, opened additional ports of residence to Britons, and ceded the island of Hong Kong to Britain. (*p. 685*)

Treaty of Versailles (1919) The treaty imposed on Germany by France, Great Britain, the United States, and other Allied Powers after World War I. It demanded that Germany dismantle its military and give up some lands to Poland. It was resented by many Germans. (*p. 763*)

treaty ports Cities opened to foreign residents as a result of the forced treaties between the **Qing Empire** and foreign signatories. In the treaty ports, foreigners enjoyed **extraterritoriality.** (*p. 685*)

tributary system A system in which, from the time of the **Han** Empire, countries in East and Southeast Asia not under the direct control of empires based in China nevertheless enrolled as tributary states, acknowledging the superiority of the emperors in China in exchange for trading rights or strategic alliances. (*p. 279*)

tribute system A system in which defeated peoples were forced to pay a tax in the form of goods and labor. This forced transfer of food, cloth, and other goods subsidized the development of large cities. An important component of the Aztec and Inca economies. (*p. 307*)

trireme Greek and Phoenician warship of the fifth and fourth centuries B.C.E. It was sleek and light, powered by 170 oars arranged in three vertical tiers. Manned by skilled sailors, it was capable of short bursts of speed and complex maneuvers. (*p. 132*)

tropical rain forest High-precipitation forest zones of the Americas, Africa, and Asia lying between the Tropic of Cancer and the Tropic of Capricorn. (*p. 217*)

tropics Equatorial region between the Tropic of Cancer and the Tropic of Capricorn. It is characterized by generally warm or hot temperatures year-round, though much variation exists due to altitude and other factors. Temperate zones north and south of the tropics generally have a winter season. (*p. 370*)

Troy Site in northwest Anatolia, overlooking the Hellespont strait, where archaeologists have excavated a series of Bronze Age cities. One of these may have been destroyed by Greeks ca. 1200 B.C.E., as reported in Homer's epic poems. (*p. 76*)

Truman Doctrine Foreign policy initiated by U.S. president Harry Truman in 1947. It offered military aid to help Turkey and Greece resist Soviet military pressure and subversion. (*p. 836*)

tsar (czar) From Latin *caesar,* this Russian title for a monarch was first used in reference to a Russian ruler by Ivan III (r. 1462–1505). (*pp. 340, 551*)

Tulip Period (1718–1730) Last years of the reign of Ottoman sultan Ahmed III, during which European styles and attitudes became briefly popular in Istanbul. (*p. 530*)

Tupac Amaru II Member of Inca aristocracy who led a rebellion against Spanish authorities in Peru in 1780–1781. He was captured and executed with his wife and other members of his family. (*p. 493*)

tyrant The term the Greeks used to describe someone who seized and held power in violation of the normal procedures and traditions of the community. Tyrants appeared in many Greek **city-states** in the seventh and sixth centuries B.C.E., often taking advantage of the disaffection of the emerging middle class and, by weakening the old elite, unwittingly contributing to the evolution of **democracy.** (*p. 127*)

Uigurs A group of Turkic-speakers who controlled their own centralized empire from 744 to 840 in Mongolia and Central Asia. (*p. 284*)

ulama Muslim religious scholars. From the ninth century onward, the primary interpreters of Islamic law and the social core of Muslim urban societies. (*p. 238*)

Umayyad Caliphate First hereditary dynasty of Muslim caliphs (661 to 750). From their capital at Damascus, the Umayyads ruled an empire that extended from Spain to India. Overthrown by the **Abbasid Caliphate.** (*p. 232*)

umma The community of all Muslims. A major innovation against the background of seventh-century Arabia, where traditionally kinship rather than faith had determined membership in a community. (*p. 231*)

underdevelopment The condition experienced by economies that depend on colonial forms of production such as the export of raw materials and plantation crops with low wages and low investment in education. (*p. 642*)

United Nations International organization founded in 1945 to promote world peace and cooperation. It replaced the **League of Nations.** (*p. 833*)

Universal Declaration of Human Rights A 1946 United Nations covenant binding signatory nations to the observance of specified rights. (*p. 892*)

universities Degree-granting institutions of higher learning. Those that appeared in Latin West from about 1200 onward became the model of all modern universities. (*p. 407*)

Urdu A Persian-influenced literary form of Hindi written in Arabic characters and used as a literary language since the 1300s. (*p. 388*)

utopian socialism A philosophy introduced by the Frenchman Charles Fourier in the early nineteenth century. Utopian socialists hoped to create humane alternatives to industrial capitalism by building self-sustaining communities whose inhabitants would work cooperatively. (See also **socialism.**) (*p. 616*)

Vargas, Getulio (1883–1954) Dictator of Brazil from 1930 to 1945 and from 1951 to 1954. Defeated in the presidential election of 1930, he overthrew the government and created Estado Novo ("New State"), a dictatorship that emphasized industrialization and helped the urban poor but did little to alleviate the problems of the peasants. (*p. 823*)

variolation The technique of enhancing immunity by exposing patients to dried mucous taken from those already infected. (*p. 559*)

varna/jati Two categories of social identity of great importance in Indian history. *Varna* are the four major social divisions: the *Brahmin* priest class, the *Kshatriya* warrior/administrator class, the *Vaishya* merchant/farmer class, and the *Shudra* laborer class. Within the system of *varna* are many *jati,* regional groups of people who have a common occupational sphere, and who marry, eat, and generally interact with other members of their group. (*p. 177*)

vassal In medieval Europe, a sworn supporter of a king or lord committed to rendering specified military service to that king or lord. (*p. 256*)

Vedas Early Indian sacred "knowledge"—the literal meaning of the term—long preserved and communicated orally by

Brahmin priests and eventually written down. These religious texts, including the thousand poetic hymns to various deities contained in the Rig Veda, are our main source of information about the Vedic period (ca. 1500–500 B.C.E.). (*p. 175*)

Victorian Age The reign of Queen Victoria of Great Britain (r. 1837–1901). The term is also used to describe late-nineteenth-century society, with its rigid moral standards and sharply differentiated roles for men and women and for middle-class and working-class people. (See also **"separate spheres."**) (*p. 711*)

Vietnam War (1954–1975) Conflict pitting North Vietnam and South Vietnamese communist guerrillas against the South Vietnamese government, aided after 1961 by the United States. (*p. 838*)

Villa, Francisco "Pancho" (1878–1923) A popular leader during the Mexican Revolution. An outlaw in his youth, when the revolution started, he formed a cavalry army in the north of Mexico and fought for the rights of the landless in collaboration with **Emiliano Zapata.** He was assassinated in 1923. (See also **Zapata, Emiliano.**) (*p. 819*)

Wari Andean civilization culturally linked to **Tiwanaku,** perhaps beginning as colony of Tiwanaku. (*p. 314*)

Warsaw Pact The 1955 treaty binding the Soviet Union and countries of eastern Europe in an alliance against the **North Atlantic Treaty Organization.** (*p. 836*)

Washington, George (1732–1799) Military commander of the American Revolution. He was the first elected president of the United States (1789–1799). (*p. 581*)

water wheel A mechanism that harnesses the energy in flowing water to grind grain or to power machinery. It was used in many parts of the world but was especially common in Europe from 1200 to 1900. (*p. 398*)

Watt, James (1736–1819) Scot who invented the condenser and other improvements that made the **steam engine** a practical source of power for industry and transportation. The watt, an electrical measurement, is named after him. (*p. 607*)

Wedgwood, Josiah (1730–1795) English industrialist whose pottery works were the first to produce fine-quality pottery by industrial methods. (*p. 603*)

Western Front A line of trenches and fortifications in World War I that stretched without a break from Switzerland to the North Sea. Scene of most of the fighting between Germany, on the one hand, and France and Britain, on the other. (*p. 757*)

Wilson, Woodrow (1856–1924) President of the United States (1913–1921) and the leading figure at the Paris Peace Conference of 1919. He was unable to persuade the U.S. Congress to ratify the **Treaty of Versailles** or join the **League of Nations.** (*p. 762*)

witch-hunt The pursuit of people suspected of witchcraft, especially in northern Europe in the late sixteenth and seventeenth centuries. (*p. 464*)

Women's Rights Convention An 1848 gathering of women angered by their exclusion from an international antislavery meeting. They met at Seneca Falls, New York to discuss women's rights. (*p. 640*)

World Bank A specialized agency of the United Nations that makes loans to countries for economic development, trade promotion, and debt consolidation. Its formal name is the International Bank for Reconstruction and Development. (*p. 834*)

World Trade Organization (WTO) An international body established in 1995 to foster and bring order to international trade. (*p. 889*)

Xiongnu A confederation of nomadic peoples living beyond the northwest frontier of ancient China. Chinese rulers tried a variety of defenses and stratagems to ward off these "barbarians," as they called them, and finally succeeded in dispersing the Xiongnu in the first century C.E. (*p. 168*)

Yamagata Aritomo (1838–1922) One of the leaders of the **Meiji Restoration.** (*p. 722*)

Yi kingdom (1392–1910) The Yi dynasty ruled Korea from the fall of the **Koryo** kingdom to the colonization of Korea by Japan. (*p. 362*)

yin/yang In Chinese belief, complementary factors that help to maintain the equilibrium of the world. Yin is associated with masculine, light, and active qualities; yang with feminine, dark, and passive qualities. (*p. 63*)

Yongle Reign period of Zhu Di (1360–1424), the third emperor of the **Ming Empire** (r. 1403–1424). He sponsored the building of the **Forbidden City,** a huge encyclopedia project, the expeditions of **Zheng He,** and the reopening of China's borders to trade and travel. (*p. 355*)

Yuan Empire (1271–1368) Empire created in China and Siberia by **Khubilai Khan.** (*p. 349*)

Yuan Shikai (1859–1916) Chinese general and first president of the Chinese Republic (1912–1916). He stood in the way of the democratic movement led by **Sun Yat-sen.** (*p. 768*)

Zapata, Emiliano (1879–1919) Revolutionary and leader of peasants in the Mexican Revolution. He mobilized landless peasants in south-central Mexico in an attempt to seize and divide the lands of the wealthy landowners. Though successful for a time, he was ultimately defeated and assassinated. (*p. 819*)

Zen The Japanese word for a branch of **Mahayana Buddhism** based on highly disciplined meditation. It is known in Sanskrit as *dhyana*, in Chinese as *chan*, and in Korean as *son*. (*p. 289*)

Zheng He (1371–1433) An imperial eunuch and Muslim, entrusted by the Ming emperor **Yongle** with a series of state voyages that took his gigantic ships through the Indian Ocean, from Southeast Asia to Africa. (*pp. 355, 422*)

Zhou The people and dynasty that took over the dominant position in north China from the **Shang** and created the concept of the **Mandate of Heaven** to justify their rule. The Zhou era, particularly the vigorous early period (1027–771 B.C.E.), was remembered in Chinese tradition as a time of prosperity and benevolent rule. In the later Zhou period (771–221 B.C.E.), centralized control broke down, and warfare among many small states became frequent. (*p. 61*)

ziggurat A massive pyramidal stepped tower made of mud-bricks. It is associated with religious complexes in ancient Mesopotamian cities, but its function is unknown. (*p. 37*)

Zoroastrianism A religion originating in ancient Iran with the prophet Zoroaster. It centered on a single benevolent deity—Ahuramazda—who engaged in a twelve-thousand-year struggle with demonic forces before prevailing and restoring a pristine world. Emphasizing truth-telling, purity, and reverence for nature, the religion demanded that humans choose sides in the struggle between good and evil. Those whose good conduct indicated their support for Ahuramazda would be rewarded in the afterlife. Others would be punished. The religion of the Achaemenid and Sasanid Persians, Zoroastrianism may have spread within their realms and influenced Judaism, Christianity, and other faiths. (*p. 120*)

Zulu A people of modern South Africa whom King Shaka united beginning in 1818. (*p. 649*)

INDEX

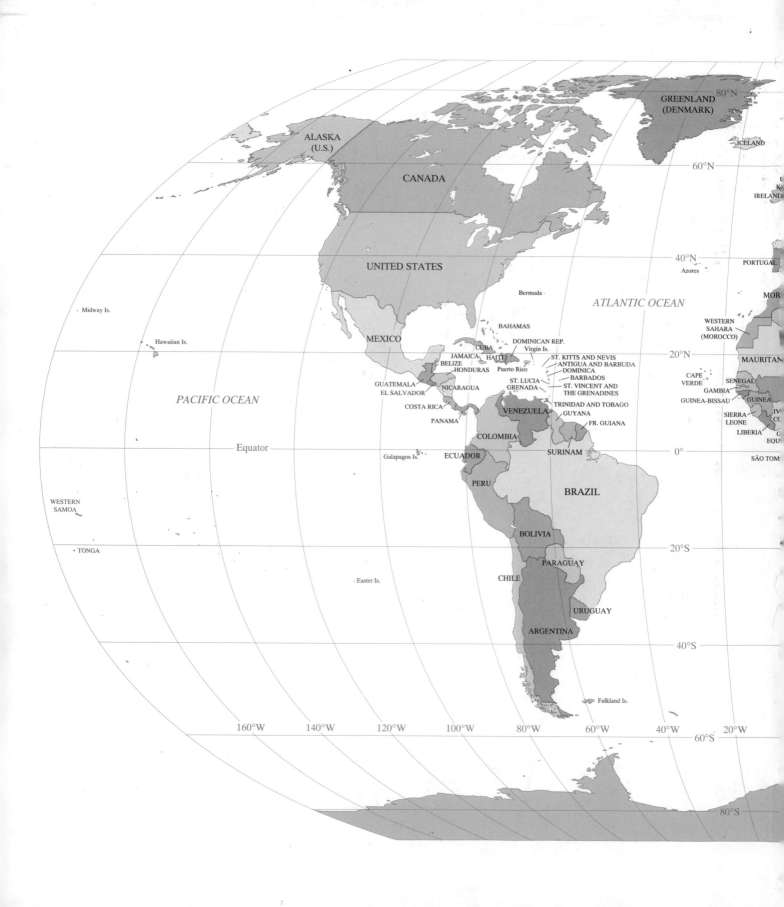